Japan

Chris Rowthorn
Ray Bartlett, Justin Ellis, Craig McLachlan, Regis St Louis,
Simon Sellars, Wendy Yanagihara

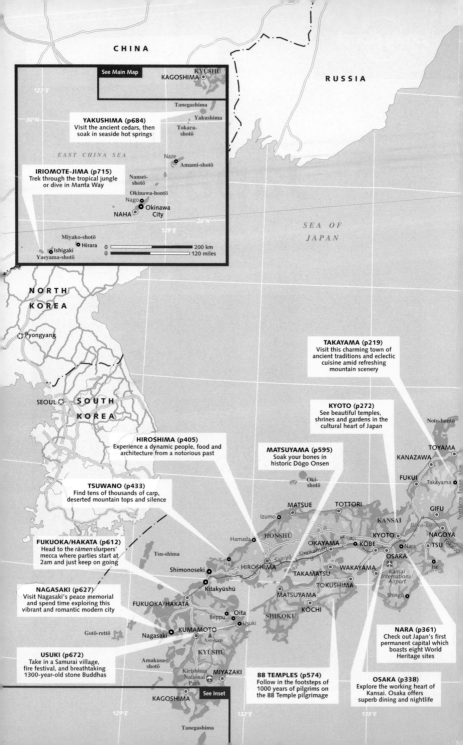

CHINA

RUSSIA

See Main Map

KYŪSHŪ
KAGOSHIMA

Tanegashima

Yakushima

YAKUSHIMA (p684)
Visit the ancient cedars, then
soak in seaside hot springs

Tokara-shotō

EAST CHINA SEA

Naze
Amami-shotō

IRIOMOTE-JIMA (p715)
Trek through the tropical jungle
or dive in Manta Way

Nansei-shotō

Okinawa-hontō
Nago
Okinawa
City

NAHA

26°N

SEA OF
JAPAN

123°E

30°N

129°E

Miyako-shotō
Hirara
Ishigaki
Yaeyama-shotō

0 ——————— 200 km
0 ——————— 120 miles

NORTH
KOREA

Pyongyang

SEOUL
SOUTH
KOREA

TAKAYAMA (p219)
Visit this charming town of
ancient traditions and eclectic
cuisine amid refreshing
mountain scenery

KYOTO (p272)
See beautiful temples,
shrines and gardens in the
cultural heart of Japan

Noto-hantō

HIROSHIMA (p405)
Experience a dynamic people, food and
architecture from a notorious past

MATSUYAMA (p595)
Soak your bones in
historic Dōgo Onsen

TOYAMA

KANAZAWA

FUKUI
Takayama

TSUWANO (p433)
Find tens of thousands of carp,
deserted mountain tops and silence

Oki-shotō

MATSUE
TOTTORI

GIFU

NAGOYA

KANSAI

Izumo

HONSHŪ

FUKUOKA/HAKATA (p612)
Head to the *rāmen* slurpers'
mecca where parties start at
2am and just keep on going

Tsu-shima

Hamada

Hagi

OKAYAMA
KOBE
KYOTO
Nara
TSU

OSAKA

Shimonoseki

HIROSHIMA

Shinkansen

WAKAYAMA

Kansai
International
Airport

Ise

NAGASAKI (p627)
Visit Nagasaki's peace memorial
and spend time exploring this
vibrant and romantic modern city

Kitakyūshū

FUKUOKA/HAKATA

TAKAMATSU

Shingū

Beppu
Oita

TOKUSHIMA

Gotō-rettō

Usuki

MATSUYAMA

NARA (p361)
Check out Japan's first
permanent capital which
boasts eight World
Heritage sites

Nagasaki
KUMAMOTO

SHIKOKU
KŌCHI

Aso-san

USUKI (p672)
Take in a Samurai village,
fire festival, and breathtaking
1300-year-old stone Buddhas

Amakusa-shotō

KYŪSHŪ

Kirishima
National
Park

MIYAZAKI

88 TEMPLES (p574)
Follow in the footsteps of
1000 years of pilgrims on
the 88 Temple pilgrimage

OSAKA (p338)
Explore the working heart of
Kansai. Osaka offers
superb dining and nightlife

KAGOSHIMA

See Inset

Tanegashima

129°E

132°E

135°E

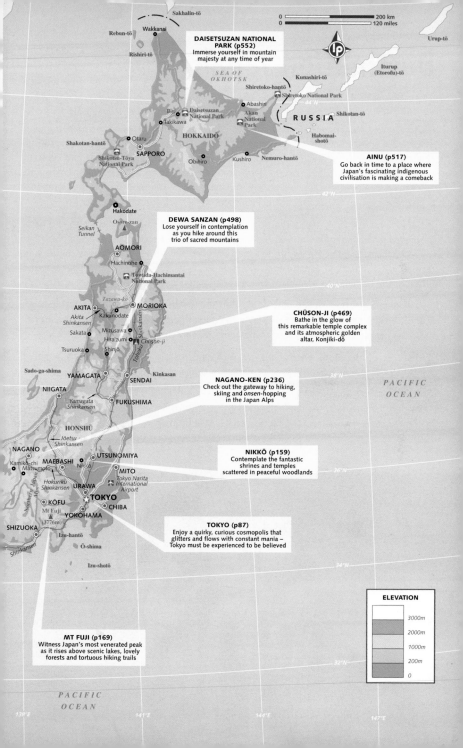

0	200 km
0	120 miles

Sakhalin-tō

Urup-tō

DAISETSUZAN NATIONAL PARK (p552)
Immerse yourself in mountain majesty at any time of year

Rebun-tō

Wakkanai

Rishiri-tō

SEA OF OKHOTSK

Kunashiri-tō

Shiretoko-hantō

Shiretoko National Park

Abashiri

Bici

Daisetsuzan National Park

Akan National Park

RUSSIA

Shikotan-tō

Takikawa

HOKKAIDŌ

Habomai-shotō

Shakotan-hantō

Otaru

SAPPORO

Obihiro

Kushiro

Nemuro-hantō

Shikotsu-Tōya National Park

AINU (p517)
Go back in time to a place where Japan's fascinating indigenous civilisation is making a comeback

Hakodate

Osore-zan

DEWA SANZAN (p498)
Lose yourself in contemplation as you hike around this trio of sacred mountains

Seikan Tunnel

AOMORI

Hachinohe

Towada-Hachimantai National Park

Tazawa-ko

AKITA

MORIOKA

Akita Shinkansen

Kakunodate

CHŪSON-JI (p469)
Bathe in the glow of this remarkable temple complex and its atmospheric golden altar, Konjiki-dō

Sakata

Mizusawa

Hiraizumi

Chūson-ji

Tsuruoka

Shinjō

Tōhoku Shinkansen

Sado-ga-shima

Kinkasan

YAMAGATA

SENDAI

NAGANO-KEN (p236)
Check out the gateway to hiking, skiing and *onsen*-hopping in the Japan Alps

NIIGATA

Yamagata Shinkansen

FUKUSHIMA

PACIFIC OCEAN

HONSHŪ

Jōetsu Shinkansen

NAGANO

Kamiko-chi

MAEBASHI

UTSUNOMIYA

Nikkō

NIKKŌ (p159)
Contemplate the fantastic shrines and temples scattered in peaceful woodlands

Matsumoto

Hokuriku Shinkansen

MITO

Tokyo Narita International Airport

URAWA

KŌFU

★ TOKYO

CHIBA

Mt Fuji (3776m)

YOKOHAMA

SHIZUOKA

Izu-hantō

TOKYO (p87)
Enjoy a quirky, curious cosmopolis that glitters and flows with constant mania – Tokyo must be experienced to be believed

Northern Japan Alps

Shinkansen

Ō-shima

Izu-shotō

MT FUJI (p169)
Witness Japan's most venerated peak as it rises above scenic lakes, lovely forests and tortuous hiking trails

ELEVATION

	3000m
	2000m
	1000m
	200m
	0

PACIFIC OCEAN

Destination Japan

Few countries make such conflicting claims on the imagination as Japan. The mere mention of the word is enough to set off a cascade of contrary images: ancient temples and futuristic cities; mist-shrouded hills and lightning-fast bullet trains; kimono-clad geisha and suit-clad businessmen; quaint thatch-roofed villages and pulsating neon urban jungles. Amazingly, all of these images are accurate. This peculiar synthesis of the modern and the traditional is one of the things that makes travel in Japan such a fascinating experience.

If traditional culture is your thing, you can spend weeks in cities such as Kyoto and Nara, gorging yourself on temples, shrines, kabuki, *nō* (stylised dance-drama), tea ceremonies and museums packed with treasures from Japan's rich artistic heritage. If modern culture and technology is your thing, Japan's cities are an absolute wonderland – an easy peek into the future of the human race, complete with trend-setting cafés and fabulous restaurants.

Outside the cities, you'll find natural wonders the length and breadth of the archipelago. From the coral reefs of Okinawa to the snow-capped peaks of the Japan Alps, Japan has more than enough natural wonders to compete with its cultural treasures.

Then there's the food: whether it's impossibly fresh sushi in Tokyo, perfectly battered tempura in Kyoto, or a hearty bowl of *rāmen* in Osaka, if you like eating you're going to love Japan.

But for many visitors, the real highlight of their visit to Japan is the gracious hospitality of the Japanese themselves. The fact is, whatever your image of Japan, it probably exists somewhere on the archipelago – and it's just waiting for you to discover it!

MARTIN MOO

Tokyo: The World's Metropolis

GREG ELMS

Watch as fish porters race through Tsukiji Fish Market (p110) for the freshest catch of the day

GREG ELMS

Check out the architectural urban landscapes of Roppongi Hills (p119)

OTHER HIGHLIGHTS

- Wander through the slightly wild ornamental garden at the Nezu Fine Art Museum (p120).
- Don't miss the chance to see up close the grace and skill of a sumō tournament (p124).
- After a day of sightseeing nothing feels better than a hot bath in an *onsen* (p122).

MICHAEL TAYLOR

Load up and join the throngs of Japanese trendy young things out to inhale fashion in the Shibuya shopping distict (p118)

Sacred Spaces

Cherry-blossom season is a delightful time
to visit Kiyomizu-dera (p296)

LIZ BARRY

FRANK CARTER

Buddhist monks kneel in ceremony for the 1250th
anniversary of Tōdai-ji (p364)

OTHER HIGHLIGHTS

- Marvel at the 850-tonne bronze
  Buddha at Kamakura (p195).
- Reward yourself with island splendour
  as you undertake the lengthy 88 Sacred
  Temples of Shikoku (p574) pilgrimage.
- Join the annual congregation of eight
  million Shintō gods at Izumo Taisha
  (p437), Japan's oldest Shintō shrine.

Check out the wooden prayer flags at the spectacular shrine and temple sites of Nikkō (p159)

JEFF CANTARUTTI

Traditional Architecture

MARTIN MOOS

The thatch-roofed *gasshō-zakuri* houses of the Shirakawa-gō region (p228) are beautiful examples of Japanese domestic architecture

FRANK CARTER

View the enchanting traditional wooden houses in Kanazawa's geisha district of Higashi (p258)

OTHER HIGHLIGHTS

- Be sure to visit the world's largest wooden building, the Daibutsu-den (p365), in Nara.
- Experience the sublime wooden palace of Katsura Rikyū (p307), built in 1624, and considered to be the pinnacle of Japanese architecture.
- Visit the hillside villa Ōkōchi sansō (p304), home of the samurai film actor Ōkōchi Denjiro.

ADINA TOVY AMSEL

Regarded as Japan's most beautiful castle, Himeji-jō (p360) is a must-see

A Walk in the Garden

MASON FLORENCE

Observe local caretakers gardening at the base of the sacred mountain Haguro-san (p498)

Many of Kyoto's numerous temples (p277) include tranquil traditional Japanese gardens

FRANK CARTER

FRANK CARTER

Reflect on carp wending trails of light through the ponds of a traditional Japanese garden

OTHER HIGHLIGHTS

- Tokyo has its fair share of great gardens, including Rikugi-en (p115), Koishikawa Kōraku-en (p394) and Hamarikyu-teien (p110).

- According to the Japanese, the nation's top three gardens are Kenroku-en (p255), Kōraku-en (p394) and Kairaku-en (p169).

Beyond the Cities

MARTIN MOOS

Absorb the evocative imagery of Rebun-dake on Rebun-tō, part of Rishiri-Regun-Sarobetsu National Park (p548)

OTHER HIGHLIGHTS

- Hidden among the towering mountain crags of the Japan Alps National Park (p231) is some of the nation's most pristine nature.
- Clamber across lava fields beneath the active volcano at Sakurajima (p661).

MASON FLORENCE

Watch the sunset through a great stone archway on Sunayama Beach (p708)

Await the new dawn atop Japan's highest peak, Mt Fuji (p169)

GRANT SOMERS

Onsen and Sentō

JOHN ASHBURNE

Serious *onsen* and *rotemburo* fans should not miss
Beppu's hidden bath at Tsuru-no-yu (p676)

OTHER HIGHLIGHTS

- Soak your bones in an open-air spring at
  Zaō Onsen Dai-rotemburo (p502), with
  sulphur-stained rocks and lush green surrounds.
- Soothe the senses with a dip in the hot springs
  of Shuzen-ji Onsen (p187).

JOHN ASHBUF

Bathe in the healing waters of the
kōshū rotemburo (p236) at
Shirahone Onsen

There are countless *onsen* (mineral hot-spring spas) found in almost every Japanese town or city

MASON FLORENCE

A Land of Culinary Delights

JOHN HAY

Get adventurous and tuck into some delicious local dried fish delicacies

JOHN HAY

Sample a traditional meal of prawn, cuttlefish and seaweed at one of Tokyo's myriad eatieries (p132)

OTHER HIGHLIGHTS

- To enjoy *soba* with terrific scenery make your way to the restaurants of Togakushi (p241).
- Fans of rich and savoury Hida beef should sit at a table in Takayama (p225).

For the impossibly refined *kaiseki ryōri* (Japanese haute cuisine) head to Kyoto (p316)

OLIVER STREWE

Matsuri: Japan Busts Loose!

FRANK CARTER

Kyoto lights up wagons with paper lanterns on the night before Gion Matsuri (p312)

OTHER HIGHLIGHTS

- Osaka's Kishiwada Danjiri Matsuri (p347) is a wild and often dangerous Japanese version of the running of the bulls, except with floats instead of bulls.

- Donning kimono, tens of thousands take part in Japan's largest *bon* dance for the Awa-odori festival (p576) in Tokushima.

SIMON CHARLES RO

A female archer awaits her turn during the Jidai Matsuri (p312), commemerating costumes between the 8th and 19th centuries

Huge flaming torches, held by men in loincloths, are paraded dramatically through Kurama's streets for Kurama no-hi Matsuri (p312)

FRANK CARTER

Contents

Regional Map Contents

HOKKAIDŌ
p514

NORTHERN
HONSHŪ p449

CENTRAL
HONSHŪ
p204

AROUND
TOKYO p158

WESTERN
HONSHŪ p391

KANSAI
p271

TOKYO
p94

SHIKOKU
p570

KYŪSHŪ
p610

OKINAWA & THE
SOUTHWEST
ISLANDS p682

The Authors

CHRIS ROWTHORN
Coordinating Author

Born in England and raised in the USA, Chris has lived in Kyoto since 1992. Soon after his arrival in Kyoto, Chris started studying the Japanese language and culture, while supporting himself by teaching English and working as an editor. In 1995 he became a regional correspondent for the *Japan Times*. He's worked on a total of 17 Lonely Planet travel guides, having written *Malaysia, Singapore & Brunei*; *Southeast Asia*; *Victoria*; *Japan*; *Hiking in Japan*; *Tokyo*; *Kyoto*; and *Read This First: Asia & India*. When he's not on the road, he spends his time seeking out Kyoto's best restaurants, temples, hiking trails and various other *anaba* (secret places known only by the locals). He also conducts walking tours of Kyoto and the rest of Japan. For more on Chris and his tours, check out his website at www.chrisrowthorn.com. For this edition Chris wrote and updated the following chapters: Destination, Getting Started, Itineraries, Snapshot, History, Environment, Food & Drink, Kansai, Directory, Transport and the Glossary.

The coordinating author's Favourite Trip

My favourite trip is a route through my 'backyard' in Kansai. It starts in Kyoto (p272), my adopted hometown. First, spend a few days in wonderful Kyoto. Then, take the Kintetsu Railway down to Nara (p328) to check out the temples and shrines there. After Nara, jump back on the Kintetsu Railway and work your way down to Ise to check out Ise-jingū (p385), Japan's most impressive Shintō shrine. From Ise, take the Japan Railway line around the horn of the Kii-hantō (Kii Peninsula) and stop in Shirahama (p381) for the night, soaking in the fabulous *onsen* (hot springs) there. From Shirahama head north and east to Wakayama (p375) to the mountain-top temple complex of Kōya-san (p377), to spend a night in a temple there. Finally, head back to Kyoto via Osaka (p338).

RAY BARTLETT
Hokkaidō; Kyūshū

Ray Bartlett published his first travel article when he was 18 and never looked back. In 1993 he moved to Japan, which is now his second home. His Japan-related interests include art, hiking, history, ceramics, and literature – which he reads and occasionally attempts to translate when he can find the time. An *onsen* aficionado, he built a *goemonburo* (bathtub) in his backyard. At home he enjoys dog walking, *sake* sipping, *onsen* soaking, forgetting foreign languages, making and collecting *yakimono* (pottery or ceramics), windsurfing and playing the clarinet so badly the dog howls. When not elsewhere, he lives on Cape Cod.

JUSTIN ELLIS
Western Honshū

Justin Ellis first came across Japan at high school in Australia. Six years of living in Kyoto has broadened his knowledge of Japan and updating the Western Honshū chapter of this book even more so. He spends his time looking for good food and ryokan and then writing about them in *Kansai Time Out* and other publications.

CRAIG McLACHLAN
Shikoku; Okinawa & the Southwest Islands

A wanderer at heart, Craig has put in a lot of footwork in Japan. He's walked from Kagoshima to Hokkaidō; climbed Japan's 100 Famous Mountains; hiked around the 88 Sacred Temples of Shikoku; walked from the Sea of Japan to the Pacific (climbing all Japan's 3000m peaks along the way); and journeyed around the 33 Temples of Kannon pilgrimage. Three of Craig's books on his adventures have been published in both English and Japanese, and he co-authored Lonely Planet's *Hiking in Japan*. A 20-year kara e practitioner, Craig has a Japan-focused MBA from the University of Hawaiʻ. When not on the road, Craig resides in Queenstown, New Zealand.

REGIS ST LOUIS
Around Tokyo; Central Honshū

After watching at least two Sho Kosugi movies as a child, Regis decided to become the world's most highly trained ninja. Although he has yet to fulfil that promise, Regis has spent a lot of time thinking about the land of the shadow warrior. Mishima, Murakami are Oe are among his great loves, and after extensive travel in Japan, he now prefers Kurosawa to Kosugi. Still pursuing the noble call, Regis has a yellow belt in both kenpo and karate, and he has mastered the short- and long-handled shoehorn. He has also written travel articles and essays for various publications. This is his sixth title for Lonely Planet.

SIMON SELLARS   Northern Honshū

Simon Sellars is a freelance writer/editor and publisher of an online cultural magazine. Simon has travelled extensively in Japan and has written a series of articles on Japanese culture, including a piece on telepaths. This is his third title for Lonely Planet.

WENDY YANAGIHARA   Tokyo

Wendy has Tokyo in her blood, and imprinted on her memory. The Japanese language was her first, and it resonates like notes on the *koto* in her ears and mind – if not so melodically on her tongue. Childhood summers spent in Japan with her mother and brother whetted her appetite for travel and *kashiwa-mochi*, and gave her an introduction at age two to the nonstop city that is Tokyo. Over the years, she has spent countless hours exploring the museums, temples and giant department stores in and around Tokyo. Years later, she returned to spend a sweltering, quaking, typhoon-lashed (and utterly sublime) season researching the capital for this book.

CONTRIBUTORS

Dr Trish Batchelor wrote the Health chapter. She is a general practitioner and travel medicine specialist who worked at the Ciwec Clinic in Kathmandu, Nepal. She is a medical advisor to the Travel Doctor New Zealand clinics. Trish teaches travel medicine through the University of Otago and is interested in underwater and high-altitude medicine, and in the impact of tourism on host countries. She has travelled extensively through Southeast and east Asia and particularly loves high-altitude trekking in the Himalayas.

Kara Knafelc wrote The Culture chapter. She's a freelance writer who has lived in both the suburbs and the centre of Tokyo. She is now based in San Francisco, where she continues to write and teach.

Getting Started

Apart from language difficulties, Japan is a very easy country in which to travel. It's safe and clean and the public transport system is excellent. Best of all, everything you need (with the possible exception of large-sized clothes) is widely available. The only consideration is the cost: Japan can be expensive. It is not nearly as expensive as many people fear, however, and there are enough cheap guesthouses and youth hostels around to bring Japan within the reach of backpackers and other budget travellers.

WHEN TO GO

Without a doubt, the best times to visit Japan are the climatically stable seasons of spring (March to May) and autumn (September to November).

Spring is the time when Japan's famous cherry trees (sakura) burst into bloom. Starting from Kyūshū sometime in March, the *sakura zensen* (cherry tree blossom line) advances northward, usually passing the main cities of Honshū in early April. Once the sakura bloom, their glory is brief, usually lasting only a week.

See Climate (p731) for more information.

Autumn is an equally good time to travel, with pleasant temperatures and soothing autumn colours; the autumn foliage pattern reverses that of the sakura, starting in the north sometime in October and peaking across most of Honshū around November.

Travelling during either winter or summer is a mixed bag – mid-winter (December to February) weather can be bitterly cold, particularly on the Sea of Japan coasts of Honshū and Hokkaidō, while the sticky summer months (June to August) can turn even the briefest excursion out of an air-conditioned environment into a steam bath. June is also the month of Japan's brief rainy season, which in some years brings daily downpours and in other years is hardly a rainy season at all.

Also keep in mind that peak holiday seasons, particularly Golden Week (late April to early May) and the mid-August O-Bon (Festival of the Dead)

DON'T LEAVE HOME WITHOUT...

What clothing you bring will depend not only on the season, but also on where you are planning to go. Japan extends a long way from north to south: the north of Hokkaidō can be under deep snow at the same time Okinawa and Nansei-shotō (the Southwest Islands) are basking in tropical sunshine. If you're going anywhere near the mountains, or are intent on climbing Mt Fuji, you'll need good cold-weather gear, even at the height of summer.

Unless you're in Japan on business, you won't need formal or even particularly dressy clothes. Men should keep in mind, however, that trousers are preferable to shorts, especially in restaurants.

You'll also need:

- Slip-on shoes – you want shoes that are not only comfortable for walking but are also easy to slip on and off for the frequent occasions where they must be removed.

- Unholy socks – your socks will be on display a lot of the time.

- Books – English-language and other foreign-language books are expensive in Japan, and they're not available outside the big cities.

- Medicine – bring any prescription medicine you'll need from home.

- Gifts – a few postcards or some distinctive trinkets from your home country will make good gifts for those you meet along the way.

are extremely popular for domestic travel and can be problematic in terms of reservations and crowds. Likewise, everything in Japan basically shuts down during Shōgatsu (New Year period).

For information on Japan's festivals and special events see p735. For information on Japan's public holidays see p736.

COSTS & MONEY

Japan is generally considered an expensive country in which to travel. Certainly, this is the case if you opt to stay in top-end hotels, take a lot of taxis and eat all your meals in fancy restaurants. But Japan does not have to be expensive, indeed it can be cheaper than travelling in places such as Europe and the USA if you are careful with your spending and, in terms of what you get for your money, Japan is good value indeed.

Food costs can be kept down by ordering set meals (setto). A fixed 'morning service' breakfast (mōningu sābisu or setto) is available in most coffee shops (kisaten) for around ¥400. At lunch time there are set meals (teishoku) for about ¥700. Cheap noodle places (often found at stations or in department stores) charge around ¥400 for a filling bowl of noodles. For an evening meal, there's the option of a set course again or a single order – ¥700 to ¥900 should cover this. Average prices at youth hostels are ¥500 for breakfast and ¥900 for dinner.

Transport is a major expense, although there are ways to limit the damage. The Japan Rail Pass and other regional rail passes are well worth the money if you intend to travel widely in a short space of time; see p764 for details. Overnight buses are cheaper than the train, and enable you to save on accommodation. Hitching is another option; see p762.

TRAVEL LITERATURE

Travel books about Japan often end up turning into extended reflections on the eccentricities or uniqueness of the Japanese. One writer who did not fall prey to this temptation was Alan Booth. *The Roads to Sata* (1985) is the best of his writings about Japan, and traces a four-month journey on foot from the northern tip of Hokkaidō to Sata, the southern tip of Kyūshū. Booth's *Looking for the Lost – Journeys Through a Vanishing Japan* (1995) was his final book, and again recounts walks in rural Japan. Booth loved Japan, warts and all, and these books reflect his passion and insight into the country.

A more recent account of a trek across the length of Japan is Craig McLachlan's enjoyable *Four Pairs of Boots* (1998). The same author's *Tales of a Summer Henro* (1997) recounts his journey around the 88 Sacred Temples of Shikoku. Both books are light, easy to read and give an excellent insight into today's Japan.

Alex Kerr's *Lost Japan* (1996) is not strictly a travel book, though he does recount some journeys in it; rather, it's a collection of essays on his long experiences in Japan. Like Booth and McLachlan, Kerr has some great insights into Japan and the Japanese, and his love for the country is only matched by his frustration at some of the things he sees going wrong there.

Donald Richie's *The Inland Sea* (1971) is a classic in this genre. It recounts the author's island-hopping journey across the Seto Inland Sea in the late 1960s. Richie's elegiac account of a vanished Japan makes the reader nostalgic for times gone by.

Pico Iyer's *The Lady and The Monk* (1991) tells of the author's year-long stay in Kyoto, studying Zen and romancing a married Japanese woman. It's a dreamy and reflective book, which gives some good insights into the country and its people.

HOW MUCH?

Business hotel accommodation (per person) ¥8000

Midrange meal ¥2500

Local bus ¥220

Temple admission ¥500

Newspaper ¥130

TOP TENS

Japan Between the Covers

The following is a very subjective list of fiction and nonfiction books about Japan, by Western and Japanese authors. For travel narratives about Japan, see p21.

- *Lost Japan* (nonfiction; 1996)
  Alex Kerr

- *Dogs and Demons* (nonfiction; 2001)
  Alex Kerr

- *The Chrysanthemum and the Sword* (nonfiction; 1989)
  Ruth Benedict

- *A Japanese Mirror* (nonfiction; 1985)
  Ian Buruma

- *Wages of Guilt* (nonfiction; 2002)
  Ian Buruma

- *Memoirs of a Geisha* (fiction; 1999)
  Arthur Golden

- *Audrey Hepburn's Neck* (fiction; 1996)
  Alan Brown

- *A Wild Sheep Chase* (fiction; 1989)
  Murakami Haruki

- *Snow Country* (fiction; 1973)
  Kawabata Yasunari

- *Nip the Buds Shoot the Kids* (fiction; 1995)
  Ōe Kenzaburō

Japan in the Movies

Japan usually fares very poorly in Western movies, which do little but trade in the worst sort of stereotypes about the country and its inhabitants. Thus, if you want to get a clear-eyed view of Japan, it makes sense to check out films mostly by Japanese directors.

- *Marusa-no-Onna* (A Taxing Woman; 1987)
  Director: Itami Juzo

- *Tampopo* (1987)
  Director: Itami Juzo

- *Ososhiki* (The Funeral; 1987)
  Director: Itami Juzo

- *Minbo-no-Onna* (The Anti-Extortion Woman; 1994)
  Director: Itami Juzo

- *Tokyo Monogatari* (Tokyo Story; 1953)
  Director: Ōzu Yasujiro

- *Maboroshi no Hikari* (Maborosi; 1995)
  Director: Koreeda Hirokazu

- *Nijushi-no-Hitomi* (Twenty Four Eyes; 1954)
  Director: Kinoshita Keisuke

- *Lost in Translation* (2003)
  Director: Sophia Coppola

- *Rashomon* (1950)
  Director: Kurosawa Akira

- *Hotaru-no-Haka* (Grave of the Fireflies; 1988)
  Director: Takahata Isao

Matsuri Magic

Witnessing a *matsuri*, a traditional festival, can be the highlight of your trip to Japan, and offers a glimpse of the Japanese at their most uninhibited. A lively *matsuri* is a world unto itself – a vision of bright colours, hypnotic chanting, beating drums and swaying crowds. For more information on Japan's festivals and special events see p735.

- Yamayaki (Grass Burning Festival), 15 January, Nara, Kansai (p367)

- Yuki Matsuri (Sapporo Snow Festival), early February, Sapporo, Hokkaidō (p524)

- Omizutori (Water-Drawing Ceremony), 1–14 March, Tōdai-ji, Nara, Kansai (p367)

- Takayama festival, 14–15 April/9–10 October, Takayama, Gifu-ken, central Honshū (p223)

- Sanja Matsuri, 3rd Friday, Saturday and Sunday of May, Sensō-ji, Tokyo (p124)

- Nachi-no-Hi Matsuri (Nachi Fire Festival), 14 July, Kumano Nachi Taisha, Wakayama-ken, Kansai (p383)

INTERNET RESOURCES

There's no better place to start your Web explorations than the Lonely Planet website (www.lonelyplanet.com). Here you'll find succinct summaries on travelling to most places on earth, postcards from other travellers and the Thorn Tree bulletin board, where you can ask questions before you go or dispense advice when you get back. You can also find travel news and updates to many of our most popular guidebooks.

Other websites with useful Japan information and links:

Japan Ministry of Foreign Affairs (MOFA; www.infojapan.org) Covers Japan's foreign policy and has useful links to embassies and consulates under 'MOFA info'.

Japan National Tourist Organization (JNTO; www.jnto.go.jp) Great information on all aspects of travel in Japan.

Japan Rail (www.japanrail.com) Information on rail travel in Japan, with details on the Japan Rail Pass.

Japan Weather Association (www.jwa.or.jp/fcst/00305e.html) Daily weather information.

Itineraries

CLASSIC ROUTES

SKYSCRAPERS TO TEMPLES

One to Two weeks/Tokyo to Kyoto

The Tokyo–Kyoto route is the classic Japan route and the best way to get a quick taste of Japan. For first-time visitors with only a week or so to look around, a few days in **Tokyo** (p87) sampling the modern Japanese experience and four or five days in the Kansai region exploring the historical sites of **Kyoto** (p272) and **Nara** (p361) is the way to go.

This allows you to take in some of Japan's most famous attractions while not attempting to cover too much ground. The journey between Tokyo and Kyoto is best done by *shinkansen* (bullet train; see p763 for more information) to save valuable time.

This route is the classic Japan route that takes in the best of modern and traditional Japan. For those with limited time who want to get a good taste of Japan, this is the logical choice.

The 550km route involves only one major train journey: the three-hour *shinkansen* trip between Tokyo and Kyoto (the Kyoto-Nara trip takes less than an hour by express train).

HOKKAIDŌ

TOKYO

KYOTO

Nara

HEADIN' SOUTH
Two weeks to One month/Tokyo to the Southwest

Travellers with more time to spend in Japan tend to head west and south before considering northern Honshū and Hokkaidō. The reason is that Kansai, western Honshū and Kyūshū are richer in sights than the northern regions of Japan.

Assuming you fly into **Tokyo** (p87), spend a few days exploring the city before heading off to the **Kansai area** (p270), notably **Kyoto** (p272) and **Nara** (p361). A good side trip en route is **Takayama** (p219), which can be reached from Nagoya.

From Kansai, many Japan Rail (JR) Pass travellers take the San-yō *shinkansen* straight down to **Fukuoka/Hakata** (p612) in Kyūshū. Some of Kyūshū's highlights include **Nagasaki** (p627), **Kumamoto** (p641), natural wonders like **Aso-san** (p646), and the hot-spring town of **Beppu** (p673).

The fastest way to return from Kyūshū to Kansai or Tokyo is by the San-yō *shinkansen* along the Inland Sea side of **western Honshū** (p390). Possible stopovers include **Hiroshima** (p405) and **Himeji** (p359), a famous castle town. From Okayama, the seldom-visited island of **Shikoku** (p569) is easily accessible. The Sea of Japan side of western Honshū is visited less frequently by tourists, and is more rural – notable attractions are the shrine at **Izumo** (p437) and the small cities of **Matsue** (p439) and **Tottori** (p445).

The Headin' South route is an extremely popular route (especially in the colder months, when heading north has obvious disadvantages).

This 2000km route involves around 25 hours of train travel and allows you to sample the metropolis of Tokyo, the cultural attractions of Kansai (Kyoto and Nara), and the varied attractions of Kyūshū and western Honshū.

NORTH BY NORTHEAST THROUGH HONSHŪ

Two weeks to One month/Tokyo/Kansai & Northern Japan

A good approach to northern Japan from either Tokyo or Kyoto is via **Matsumoto** (p245) and **Nagano** (p236), which are excellent bases for hikes in and around places like **Kamikōchi** (p232). From Nagano, you might travel up to **Niigata** (p503) and from there to the island of **Sado-ga-shima** (p507), famous for its *taiko* drummers and Earth Celebration in August. On the other side of Honshū, the city of **Sendai** (p457) provides easy access to **Matsushima** (p463), one of Japan's most celebrated scenic outlooks.

Highlights north of Sendai include peaceful **Kinkasan** (p466) and **Tazawa-ko** (p488), the deepest lake in Japan. **Morioka** (p475), **Towada-Hachimantai National Park** (p488) and **Osore-zan** (p483).

Travelling from northern Honshū to Hokkaidō by train involves a journey from Aomori through the world's longest underwater tunnel, the **Seikan Tunnel** (p518); rail travellers arriving via the Seikan Tunnel might consider a visit (including seafood meals) to the historic fishing port of **Hakodate** (p529). If you're short on time, **Sapporo** (p519) is a good base, with relatively easy access to **Otaru** (p535), **Shikotsu-Tōya National Park** (p542) and **Biei** (p553). Sapporo is particularly lively during its Yuki Matsuri (Snow Festival; see p524).

The real treasures of Hokkaidō are its national parks, which require either more time or your own transport. If you've only got three or four days in Hokkaidō, you might hit **Shiretoko National Park** (p565) and **Akan National Park** (p559). If you've got at least a week, head to **Daisetsuzan National Park** (p552). More distant but rewarding destinations include the scenic islands of **Rebun-tō** (p550) and **Rishiri-tō** (p548).

This 2600km route, which involves around 28 hours of train travel, is for those who want to combine the urban/cultural attractions of Tokyo or Kansai with a few northern Honshū attractions along the way.

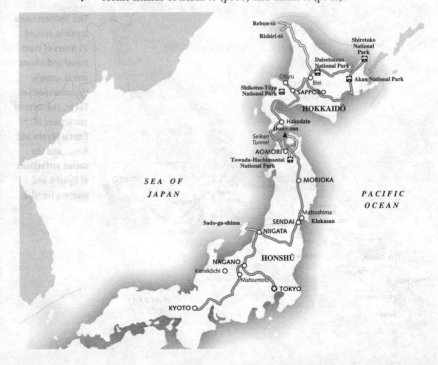

FOLK TALES & CASTLES
One to Two weeks/Northern Honshū

Take the *shinkansen* to Kōriyama, then the local line to **Aizu-Wakamatsu** (p451), a town devoted to keeping alive the tragic tale of the White Tigers (p453), a group of young samurai who committed ritual suicide during the Bōshin Civil War; the cause of their angst was the destruction of Aizu's magnificent Tsuruga-jō (since reconstructed). From Kōriyama, take the *shinkansen* to Ichinoseki, then the local line to **Hiraizumi** (p469). Once ruled by the Fujiwara clan, Hiraizumi was a political and cultural centre informed by Buddhist thought – it rivalled Kyoto until it was ruined by jealousy, betrayal and, ultimately, fratricide. Today, **Chūson-ji** (p469), a mountainside complex of temples, is among Hiraizumi's few reminders of glory, with its sumptuous, glittering Konjiki-dō, one of the country's finest shrines. From Hiraizumi, take the local train to Morioka, then a *shinkansen*/local combination to the **Tōno Valley** (p471), where you might encounter the impish *kappa* (water spirits). The region is famous for its eccentric folk tales and legends, and a number of its attractions will put you in the mood for a spot of old-time ghostbusting. From Morioka, take the *shinkansen* to **Kakunodate** (p491), a charming town that promotes itself as 'Little Kyoto'. With its impeccably maintained samurai district – a network of streets, parks and houses virtually unchanged since the 1600s – it's one of northern Honshū's most popular attractions.

The 520km route, which involves around 19 hours of train travel, takes you through the historically rich regions of northern Honshū. The highlights of this route include the temple complex of Chūson-ji and the restored samurai district in the town of Kakunodate.

ROADS LESS TRAVELLED

ISLAND-HOPPING TO OKINAWA

Three weeks to one month/Kyūshū to Okinawa

For those with the time to explore tropical laid-back Japan, this is a great option. Make full use of the one-week ferry pass (see p688) and head south from **Kagoshima** (p654) overnight to **Amami-Ōshima** (p688). **Tokunoshima** (p690) has a 600-year history of bullfighting, while **Okinoerabu-jima** (p691) is an uplifted coral reef with over 300 caves that is covered with cultivated flowers in spring. **Yoron-tō** (p692) is surrounded by coral and boasts beautiful Yurigahama, a stunning stretch of white sand inside the reef that disappears at high tide. After a week in the islands of Kagoshima-ken, you're into Okinawa and a day or two in bustling **Naha** (p695) is a must. Take time out for a day trip to nearby **Tokashiki-jima** (p706) to relax on superb Aharen beach, or for a bit of snorkelling at **Zamami-jima** (p705).

Those who are out of time can fly back to the mainland from Naha, but a great option is to keep island-hopping by ferry, visiting sugar-cane covered **Miyako-jima** (p707), on the way to **Ishigaki-jima** (p710). Ishigaki is a great base for a day trip to the 'living museum' of **Taketomi-jima** (p717). Jungle-covered **Iriomote-jima** (p715) has some brilliant hikes, while divers can swim with the rays in 'Manta Way' between Iriomote-jima and **Kohama-jima** (p718). Japan's westernmost point, and the country's top marlin fishing spot, is at **Yonaguni-jima** (p719). It's even possible to keep going by ferry from Ishigaki to Taiwan (see p700).

This 1300km route takes around 60 hours of travel time, and takes in a laid-back, tropical side of Japan that is relatively unknown outside the country. If you arrive in the dead of winter and need a break from the cold, head to the islands – you won't regret it!

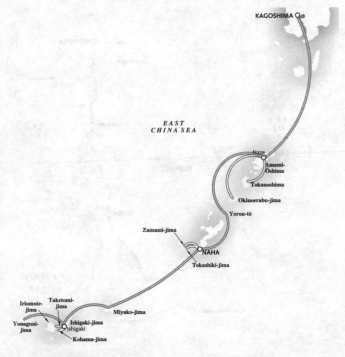

THE WILDS OF HOKKAIDŌ   Two weeks to One month/Hokkaidō

Whether you're on a JR Pass or flying directly, **Sapporo** (p519) makes a good hub for Hokkaidō excursions. A one- or two-night visit to **Hakodate** (p529) should be first on the list. Jump over to the cherry trees of **Matsumae** (p534) if you have time. Be sure to stop between Hakodate and Sapporo at **Tōya-ko** (p539), where you can soak in one of the area's many *onsen* and see Usu-zan's smoldering peak. On the route is **Shiraoi** (p517), Hokkaidō's largest Ainu living-history village. *Onsen* fans may wish to dip in the famed **Noboribetsu Onsen** (p542).

See romantic **Otaru** (p535), an easy day trip out of Sapporo, then head north to **Wakkanai** (p546). Take the ferry to **Rebun-tō** (p550) and check it out for a day, maybe two if you're planning on serious hiking. On the return see **Cape Sōya** (p547), Japan's northern-most point. Sip Otokoyama sake in **Asahikawa** (p543); from there jump to **Asahidake Onsen** (p555), hike around **Daisetsuzan National Park** (p552) for a day or two, possibly doing a day trip to the lavender fields of **Furano** (p552) or **Biei** (p553).

Head to **Abashiri** (p557). Rent a car there or in **Shari** (p564) if you're planning on going to **Shiretoko National Park** (p565). Do the entire eastern part of the island by car. Not including hiking or other stops this will take one night, two days. Check out **Nemuro** (p566), stop in **Akkeshi** (p567), and return your four-wheeled steed in **Kushiro** (p563).

Watch cranes, deer, and other wildlife in **Kushiro Shitsugen National Park** (p563), zip up to **Akan National Park** (p559) to see Mashū-ko, the most beautiful lake in Japan, and then toodle back towards Sapporo.

This 1200km route, which involves around 40 hours of travel, is popular as it allows you to do what you have time for. Use Sapporo as a hub and do day-trips or overnight trips to what's nearby, then loop out eastward, renting a car for the most remote regions.

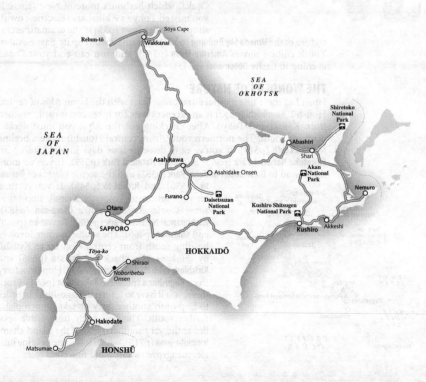

TAILORED TRIPS

NEW JAPAN

Much of what is evocative about Japan is the old: Shintō shrines, the tea ceremony in an ornamental garden, a poem brush-painted on a scroll. Yet the excitement of Japan comes from its obsession with modernisation and twists on things new.

New Japan's brightest facet is clearly Tokyo. The architectural landscape includes soaring skyscrapers like the **Shinjuku NS Building** (p116) and the microcosm that is the **Roppongi Hills** (p119) urban development. Shop for tech goodies at Ōdaiba's **Aqua City** (p120) or Ginza's **Sony Building** (p110), and the hottest *haute couture* along **Omote-sandō** (p116) or **Ginza** (p110) strips. At all hours, hip kids are out and about in **Harajuku** (p116) and **Shibuya** (p118), where you can hear the latest J-pop at HMV or Tower Records (see p152).

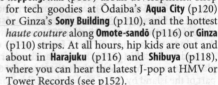

Just across Tokyo Bay, Yokohama bustles away – check out **Minato Mirai 21** (p188) for more urban futurism. Get high on **Cosmo Clock Ferris Wheel** (p188), the world's tallest, or edify at the **Yokohama Museum of Art** (p188), where contemporary art awaits. Move on to the port city of Osaka, which harbours more of New Japan. If you missed Tokyo's Akihabara (Electric Town), shop at **Den Den Town** (p351). The dramatic architecture of the **Umeda Sky Building** (p342) warrants a whirl up its glass elevator. Youth culture moves **Amerika-Mura** (p343); and you can end your Osaka evening in flashy **Dōtombori** (p343).

THE WONDERS OF NATURE

Japan has some fine natural attractions. Start with the Japan Alps of central Honshū. **Kamikōchi** (p232) is an excellent base for hikes and is easily reached from Kansai and Tokyo. After checking out the Alps, you must decide: north or south. The northern route: from central Honshū make a beeline for **Hokkaidō** (p513). If you've only three or four days in Hokkaidō, visit **Shiretoko National Park** (p565) and **Akan National Park** (p559). If you've more time, head to **Daisetsuzan National Park** (p552) and the scenic islands of **Rebun-tō** (p550) and **Rishiri-tō** (p548). If you've time

on your return to Tokyo or Kansai, stop off at some scenic attractions like **Osore-zan** (p483), **Hachimantai National Park** (p488), **Tazawa-ko** (p488) and **Kinkasan** (p466). The southern route involves heading south from central Honshū to Kyūshū by *shinkansen* to check out **Aso-san** (p646) and **Kirishima-Yaku National Park** (p652). Hop on a ferry from **Kagoshima** (p654) to **Yakushima** (p684). From there, you'll have to return to Kagoshima in order to hop onto another ferry or take an aeroplane further south. The one really unmissable spot lies at the very southern end of the island chain: **Iriomote-jima** (p715), which has some pristine jungle, mangrove swamps and fine coral reefs.

Snapshot

The winds of change are blowing across the Japanese archipelago. The old certainties that sustained the country the second half of the last century are now being called into question, and forces both inside and outside the country are tugging it in directions that make many Japanese and foreign observers uncomfortable.

Despite its small size and moribund economy, North Korea has played the role of catalyst in all of this. The issue of Japanese abductees held by North Korea dominated the Japanese news for much of 2002 and 2003. Plucked from beaches and towns along the Sea of Japan coastline in the 1970s and '80s to serve as language teachers for North Korean spies, an unknown number of Japanese nationals languished in North Korea, serving as a constant irritant in relations between the two countries.

In September 2002 Japanese Prime Minister Koizumi Junichiro made a historic trip to North Korea to negotiate their release, and later in the same year, five surviving abductees were allowed to return to Japan. Rather than satisfy the Japanese, this only inflamed them, and renewed calls were raised for the return of the returnees' kin and the remaining Japanese believed to be held in North Korea.

For its part, North Korea has done little to ease tensions between the two countries. In 1998 North Korea tested a ballistic missile by firing it directly over Japan, an incident that was understandably viewed as a threat by many Japanese. This, coupled with the suspicion that North Korea is reviving its nuclear weapons program, has had a profound effect on the Japanese. Right-wing politicians have used this provocative behaviour as an excuse to call for the scrapping of Article 9 of the Japanese constitution, the so-called 'no-war' clause, which prevents Japan from possessing armed forces (in the traditional sense of the word) and using military force as a means of settling international disputes. More extreme politicians have even begun to argue that Japan ought to develop nuclear weapons, long considered unthinkable in the world's only country to suffer an atomic attack.

In early 2004 Japan dispatched a small contingent of its Jeitai (Self-Defence Force; see p41 for more information) to Iraq to engage in humanitarian and reconstruction activities in the wake of the US invasion of Iraq. Many observers, both inside Japan and elsewhere, concluded that the Koizumi administration was compelled to offer this show of support to the Americans in hopes that America would, in turn, support Japan in the face of a possible attack by North Korea.

Thus, the actions of North Korea have pushed Japan toward a militarisation that was unthinkable only a decade ago. While some Japanese think that this is about time, others are profoundly disturbed by what they see as a return to the bad old days of pre-war Japan.

On the economic front, Japan is finally enjoying some good news. In 2003, Japan's economy grew by a healthy 3.2%, which led many observers to conclude that Japan's long recession, which started with the burst of the so-called 'Bubble Economy' in 1990, was finally over. Chinese demand for Japanese products fuelled much of this growth, and in 2003 China finally overtook the USA as Japan's biggest export market. Of course, the health of the Chinese economy also poses a threat to the Japanese, who perhaps justifiably fear that their economy will eventually be overtaken by the Chinese.

FAST FACTS

Population: 127 million people

Female life expectancy: 84.5 years

Literacy rate: 99%

GDP: US$3.5 trillion (the world's second-biggest economy)

Latitude of Tokyo: at 35.4°N, the same as Tehran, and about the same as Los Angeles (34.05°N) and Crete (35°N)

Islands in the Japanese archipelago: approximately 3900

Unesco World Heritage sites: 12 (some of these are groups of sites, like the temples of Kyoto)

World's busiest station: Tokyo's Shinjuku Station, servicing 740,000 passengers a day

Mobile phones in use: more than 86 million

Number of *rāmen* restaurants: more than 200,000

At the same time as Japan is rebounding from years of recession, it's also enjoying a new surge of international interest. The media is full of stories about the 'new Japan' and the wonders of Japanese culture. Some of this interest has been sparked by Hollywood, which produced two recent movies set in Japan: *The Last Samurai* and *Lost in Translation*. Arthur Golden's bestselling novel *Memoirs of a Geisha*, the life story of a Kyoto geisha, also generated interest. The international popularity of manga (Japanese comics) and *anime* (Japanese animation) has also undoubtedly played a role.

'Japan's birth rate is among the lowest in the world'

While Japan enjoys some long-awaited economic growth and international recognition, it still faces some problems which threaten both its economy and perhaps even its very existence. Japan's population is aging rapidly, and its birth rate is among the lowest in the world: 1.4 births per woman. This heralds a shrinking population, and some estimates have the population starting to decline as early as 2007. Unless Japan throws open its doors to immigrants, which it is loath to do for cultural and political reasons, it seems certain that the country is going to face a host of problems caused by its shrinking population.

It is certain that the 21st century will be an interesting time for Japan, faced by challenges from without and within. Whatever happens, this much is certain: as Japan responds to the various forces that shape its future, the Japanese will display their most distinctive trait – the ability to make radical changes to almost every aspect of their society while retaining something uniquely Japanese.

History

PREHISTORY

The origin of Japan's earliest inhabitants is obscure. There was certainly emigration that occurred via land bridges that once connected Japan with Siberia and Korea, but it is also thought that seafaring migrants from Polynesia may have landed on Kyūshū and Okinawa. It is likely that the Japanese people are a result of emigration from Siberia in the north, China and Korea to the west and, perhaps, Polynesian stock from the south.

The first signs of civilisation in Japan are from the Neolithic period around 10,000 BC. This is called the Jōmon (Rope Mark) period after the discovery of pottery fragments with rope marks. The people at this time lived as fishers, hunters and food-gatherers.

This period was gradually superseded by the Yayoi era, which dates from around 300 BC and is named after the site near Tokyo where pottery fragments were found. The Yayoi people are considered to have had a strong connection with Korea and their most important developments were the wet cultivation of rice and the use of bronze and iron implements.

The period following the Yayoi era has been called the Kofun (Burial Mound) period by archaeologists who discovered thousands of grave mounds concentrated mostly in central and western Japan. Judging by their size and elaborate construction, these mounds must have required immense resources of labour. It seems likely that the custom of building these tombs was brought to an end by the arrival of Buddhism, which favoured cremation.

'The first signs of civilisation in Japan are from the Neolithic period around 10,000 BC'

HISTORICAL PERIODS	
Period	Date
Jōmon	10,000–300 BC
Yayoi	300 BC–AD 300
Kofun	300–710
Nara	710–94
Heian	794–1185
Kamakura	1185–1333
Muromachi	1333–1576
Momoyama	1576–1600
Edo	1600–1868
Meiji	1868–1912
Taishō	1912–26
Shōwa	1926–89
Heisei	1989 to the present

As more and more settlements banded together to defend their land, groups became larger until, by AD 300, the Yamato clan (the forerunners of the present imperial family) had loosely unified the nation through either conquest or alliance. The Yamato leaders claimed that they were descended from the sun goddess, Amaterasu, and introduced the title of *tennō* (emperor) around the 5th century. With the ascendancy of the Yamato emperors, Japan for the first time became a true nation, stretching from the islands south of Kyūshū to the northern wilds of Honshū.

BUDDHISM & EARLY CHINESE INFLUENCE

In the mid-6th century, Buddhism was introduced from China via the Korean kingdom of Paekche. The decline of the Yamato court was halted by Prince Shōtoku (573–620), who set up a constitution and laid the

10,000 BC	300 BC
First evidence of Jōmon people in Japan (although it is thought that Japan was inhabited as early as 100,000 BC)	The Yayoi people appear in Japan (probably via Korea), practising wet rice farming and using metal tools

guidelines for a centralised state headed by a single ruler. He also instituted Buddhism as a state religion. Despite family feuds and coups d'état, subsequent rulers continued to reform the country's administration and laws.

From the earliest days of the Yamato court, it was the custom to relocate the capital following the death of an emperor (presumably to free the capital from the taint of death). However, after the shift of the capital to Nara (p361) in 710, this long-held custom was altered as the capital remained there for the next 75 years, before moving to Nagaoka-kyō in 784.

During the Nara period (710–94) there was strong promotion of Buddhism, particularly under Emperor Shōmu, who ordered the construction of Tōdai-ji and the casting of its Daibutsu (Great Buddha) as supreme guardian deity of the nation. Both the temple and Buddha image can still be seen in Nara.

The Japanese used to bury their emperors and nobles in vast earthen mounds called *kofun*, the largest of which is said to be greater in volume than the Great Pyramid of Cheops.

ESTABLISHMENT OF A NATIVE CULTURE

By the end of the 8th century, the Buddhist clergy in Nara had become so politically meddlesome that Emperor Kammu decided to relocate the capital to insulate it against their growing influence. The site eventually chosen was Heian-kyō (modern-day Kyoto; p272).

Like Nara, Heian-kyō was modelled on Chang'an (present-day Xi'an), the capital of the Tang dynasty in China, and it was to continue as the capital of Japan until 1868. The Heian period (794–1185) saw a great flourishing in the arts and important developments in religious thinking as Chinese ideas and institutions were imported and adapted to the needs of the Japanese.

Rivalry between Buddhism and Shintō, the traditional religion of Japan, was reduced by presenting Shintō deities as manifestations of Buddha. Religion was assigned a role separate from politics. Japanese monks returning from China established two new sects, Tendai and Shingon, which became the mainstays of Japanese Buddhism.

New Tales of the Taira Clan (Shin Heike Monogatari), directed by Mizoguchi Kenji – Set at the end of the 12th century, this film focuses on the power struggle between the Taira and the Minamoto clans. It is considered one of Mizoguchi's best films.

During the late Heian period, emperors began to devote more time to leisure and scholarly pursuit and less time to government. This created an opening for the Fujiwara, a noble family, to capture important court posts and become the chief power brokers, a role the clan was able to maintain for several centuries.

The Heian period is considered the apogee of Japanese courtly elegance, but out in the provinces a new power was on the rise, that of the samurai, or 'warrior class', which built up its own armed forces and readily turned to arms to defend its autonomy. Samurai families soon moved into the capital, where they muscled in on the court.

The corrupt Fujiwara were eventually eclipsed by the Taira clan, who ruled briefly before being ousted by the Minamoto family (also known as the Genji) at the battle of Dannoura (modern-day Shimonoseki) in 1185.

DOMINATION THROUGH MILITARY RULE

The Kamakura period (1185–1333) followed on from the Heian period. In 1192 Minamoto Yoritomo conquered the inhabitants of what is now Aomori-ken, thereby extending his rule to the tip of northern Honshū. For the first time in its history, all of Japan proper was now under unified rule. After assuming the title of shōgun (military leader), Minamoto set

300 AD–710 AD	Mid-6th century
The Yamato clan consolidates its power in Japan (then known as the Kingdom of Wa)	Buddhism is introduced into Japan (from Korea)

up his headquarters in Kamakura (p193), while the emperor remained the nominal ruler in Kyoto. It was the beginning of a long period of feudal rule by successive samurai families. In fact, this feudal system was to linger on, in one form or another, until imperial power was restored in 1868.

Minamoto purged members of his own family who stood in his way, but following his death in 1199 after falling from a horse, his wife's family (the Hōjō) eliminated all of Minamoto's potential successors and became the true powers behind the figureheads of shōguns and warrior lords.

During this era the popularity of Buddhism spread to all levels of society. From the late 12th century, Japanese monks returning from China introduced a new sect called Zen, the austerity of which offered a particular appeal to the samurai.

The Mongols, under their leader Kublai Khan, reached Korea in 1259 and sent envoys to Japan seeking Japanese submission. In response, the envoys were expelled. The Mongols reacted by sending an invasion fleet, which arrived in 1274 near present-day Fukuoka. This first attack was only just repulsed with a little help from a typhoon. Further envoys sent by Kublai Khan were promptly beheaded.

In 1281 the Mongols dispatched a huge army of over 100,000 soldiers to Japan to make a second attempt at invasion. After initial success, the Mongol fleet was almost completely destroyed by yet another typhoon. Ever since, this lucky typhoon has been known to the Japanese as the kamikaze (divine wind) – a name later given to the suicide pilots of WWII.

Although the Kamakura government emerged victorious in battles with the Mongols, it was unable to pay its soldiers and lost the support of the samurai class. In an attempt to take advantage of popular discontent, Emperor Go-Daigo led an unsuccessful rebellion against the government and was exiled to Oki-shotō (p444), the islands near Matsue in western Honshū, where he waited a year before trying again. The second attempt successfully toppled the government.

The Japanese Imperial Regalia (*sanshu no jingi*) – a mirror, a jewel and a sword – are considered the most sacred objects in the Shintō religion.

COUNTRY AT WAR

This heralded the start of the Muromachi period (1333–1576). Emperor Go-Daigo refused to reward his warriors, favouring the aristocracy and priesthood. This led to the revolt of Ashikaga Takauji, who'd previously changed sides to support Emperor Go-Daigo. Ashikaga defeated Go-Daigo at Kyoto, then installed a new emperor and appointed himself shōgun; the Ashikaga family later settled at Muromachi, an area of Kyoto. Go-Daigo escaped to set up a rival court at Yoshino (p374). Rivalry between the two courts continued for 60 years until the Ashikaga made a promise (which was not kept) that the imperial lines would alternate.

The Ashikaga ruled with gradually diminishing effectiveness in a land slipping steadily into civil war and chaos. Despite this, there was a flourishing of those arts now considered typically Japanese, such as landscape painting, classical *nō* (stylised dance-drama), *ikebana* (flower arranging) and *chanoyu* (tea ceremony). A number of Kyoto's famous gardens date from this period, as do such well-known monuments as Kinkaku-ji (Golden Temple; p302) and Ginkaku-ji (Silver Temple; p301). Formal trade was re-established with Ming-dynasty China, and Korea, although Japanese piracy continued to strain these relationships.

710	794
Japan's first permanent capital is established in Nara	Japan's capital is moved to Heian-kyō (present-day Kyoto)

The Ōnin War, which broke out in 1467, developed into a full-scale civil war and marked the rapid decline of the Ashikaga family. *Daimyō* (domain lords) and local leaders fought for power in bitter territorial disputes that were to last for a century. This period, from 1467 to around the start of the Momoyama period in 1567, is known as the Warring States period (Sengoku-jidai).

Politically, the Japan of the Warring States period resembled pre-Yamato Japan: the country was merely a collection of disparate groups vying for control of local areas without any centralised authority. It was up to the next generation of leaders to reverse this situation and bring the country under the control of a powerful centralised government once more.

'The arts of the Momoyama period are noted for their flamboyant use of colour and gold leaf'

RETURN TO UNITY

In 1568 Oda Nobunaga, the son of a *daimyō*, seized power from the imperial court in Kyoto and used his military genius to initiate a process of pacification and unification in central Japan. His efforts were cut short when he was betrayed by one of his own generals, Akechi Mitsuhide, in 1582. Under attack from Akechi and seeing all was lost, he disembowelled himself in Kyoto's Honnō-ji.

Oda was succeeded by his most able commander, Toyotomi Hideyoshi, who was reputedly the son of a farmer, although his origins are not clear. His diminutive size and pop-eyed features earned him the nickname of Saru-san (Mr Monkey). Toyotomi extended unification so that by 1590 the whole country was under his rule. He then became fascinated with grandiose schemes to invade China and Korea. The first invasion was repulsed in 1593 and the second was aborted on the death of Toyotomi in 1598.

The arts of the Momoyama period (1576–1600) are noted for their flamboyant use of colour and gold-leaf embellishment. There was also a vogue for building castles on an extravagant scale; the most impressive example is Osaka-jō (p342), which reputedly required three years of labour by up to 100,000 men.

THE CHRISTIAN CENTURY

In the mid-16th century, when the Europeans first made their appearance, foreign trade was little regulated by Japan's central government. The first Portuguese to be shipwrecked off southern Kyūshū in 1543 found an appreciative reception for their skills in firearm manufacture, skills which were soon adopted by the Japanese. The Jesuit missionary Francis Xavier arrived in Kagoshima in 1549 and was followed by more missionaries, who quickly converted local lords keen to profit from foreign trade and assistance with military supplies. The new religion spread rapidly, gaining several hundred thousand converts, particularly in Nagasaki (p627).

At first Oda Nobunaga saw the advantages of trading with Europeans and tolerated the arrival of Christianity as a counterbalance to Buddhism. However, once Toyotomi Hideyoshi had assumed power, this tolerance gradually gave way to a suspicion that an alien religion would subvert his rule. Edicts against Christianity were followed in 1597 by the crucifixion of 26 foreign priests and Japanese converts.

Proscription and persecution of Christianity continued under the Tokugawa government until it reached its peak in 1637, with the ferocious

1192	1281
Japan is unified under the Minamoto Yorimoto, who takes the title shōgun (military leader)	The Mongols attempt and fail to invade Japan

quelling of the Christian-led Shimabara Rebellion. This brought the Christian century to an abrupt close, although the religion continued to be practised in secret until it was officially allowed to resurface at the end of the 19th century.

PEACE & SECLUSION

The supporters of Toyotomi Hideyoshi's young heir, Toyotomi Hideyori, were defeated in 1600 by Toyotomi's former ally, Tokugawa Ieyasu, at the battle of Sekigahara. Tokugawa set up his field headquarters *(bakufu)* at Edo, now Tokyo (p87), and assumed the title of shōgun. This marked the beginning of the Edo or Tokugawa period (1600–1868). The emperor and court continued to exercise purely nominal authority in Kyoto.

A strict political regime was introduced. The Tokugawa family, besides retaining large estates, also took control of major cities, ports and mines; the remainder of the country was allocated to autonomous *daimyō*. In descending order of importance, society consisted of the nobility, who had nominal power; the *daimyō* and their samurai; the farmers; and, at the bottom of the list, artisans and merchants. To ensure political security, the *daimyō* were required to make ceremonial visits to Edo every alternate year, and their wives and children were kept in permanent residence in Edo as virtual hostages of the government. The cost of this constant movement and the family ties in Edo made it difficult for the *daimyō* to remain anything but loyal. At the lower end of society, farmers were subject to a severe system of rules that dictated in minute detail their food, clothing and housing. Social mobility from one class to another was blocked as social standing was determined by birth.

Under Tokugawa rule, Japan entered a period of *sakoku* (national seclusion). Japanese were forbidden on pain of death to travel abroad or engage in trade with foreign countries. Only the Dutch, Chinese and Koreans were allowed to remain in Japan, and they were placed under strict supervision. The Dutch were confined to the island of Dejima, near Nagasaki, and their contacts restricted to merchants and prostitutes.

The rigid emphasis of these times on submitting unquestioningly to rules of obedience and loyalty has lasted to the present day. One effect of strict rule during the Tokugawa period was the creation of an atmosphere of relative peace and security in which the arts thrived. There were great advances, for example, in haiku (17-syllable poems), *bunraku* (classical puppet theatre) and kabuki (stylised Japanese theatre). Weaving, pottery, ceramics and lacquerware became widely appreciated by the privileged classes for their refined qualities.

By the turn of the 19th century, the Tokugawa government was falling into stagnation and corruption. Famines and poverty among the peasants and samurai further weakened the system. Foreign ships started to challenge Japan's isolation with increasing insistence and the Japanese soon realised that their outmoded defences were ineffectual. Russian contacts in the north were followed by British and American visits. In 1853 Commodore Matthew Perry of the US Navy arrived with a squadron of 'black ships' to demand the opening up of Japan to trade (p182). Other countries moved in to demand the opening of treaty ports and the relaxation of restrictions on trade.

The Loyal 47 Ronin (Chushingura), directed by Mizoguchi Kenji – This film covers a well-known incident in Japanese history, the incident of the 47 rōnin, which occurred in 1701. The plot involves a group of samurai who avenge their master's death and then commit mass seppuku (hara-kiri).

1467	1590
The 10-year Ōnin War breaks out, a civil war in which Kyoto was almost completely destroyed	Toyotomi Hideyoshi fully unifies Japan, ending the chaos of the Warring States period

The arrival of foreigners proved to be the decisive blow to an already shaky Tokugawa regime. Upset by the shōgunate's handling of the foreign incursion, two large *daimyō* areas in western Japan, the Satsuma and the Chōshū, allied themselves with disenchanted samurai. They succeeded in capturing the emperor in 1868, declaring a restoration of imperial rule and an end to the power of the shōgun. A brief counterattack by Tokugawa guards in Kyoto in the same year failed. The ruling shōgun, Tokugawa Yoshinobu, resigned, and Emperor Meiji assumed control of state affairs.

Eijanaika, directed by Imamura Shohei – Set at the end of the Tokugawa period, just before the dawn of the Meiji period, this film covers a hedonistic movement among the masses that reflected the social upheaval of the times. It is a good re-creation of 19th-century Edo (present-day Tokyo).

EMERGENCE FROM ISOLATION

The initial stages of the Meiji Restoration (1868–1912) were resisted in a state of virtual civil war. The abolition of the shōgunate was followed by the surrender of the *daimyō*, whose lands were divided into the prefectures that exist today. Edo became Japan's new capital and was renamed Tokyo (Eastern Capital). The government became centralised again and Western-style ministries were appointed for specific tasks. A series of revolts by the samurai against the erosion of their status culminated in the Saigō Uprising, where the samurai were finally defeated and stripped of their power.

Despite nationalist support for the emperor under the slogan of *sonnō-jōi* (Revere the emperor; repel the barbarians), the new government soon realised it would have to meet the West on its own terms. Under the slogan *fukoku kyōhei* (rich country; strong military), the economy underwent a crash course in Westernisation and industrialisation. An influx of Western experts was encouraged and Japanese students were sent abroad to acquire expertise in modern technologies. In 1889 Japan created a Western-style constitution which, like the military revival, owed much to Prussian influences.

By the 1890s government leaders were concerned by the spread of liberal Western ideas and encouraged a swing back to nationalism and traditional values.

Meiji and His World, 1852–1912, by Donald Keene – Emperor Meiji presided over Japan during one of its most tumultuous and interesting periods – when the country went from a secluded nation to a world power. Keene traces Meiji's role in all this with a combination of exhaustive scholarship and wonderful insight.

Japan's growing confidence was demonstrated by the abolition of foreign treaty rights and by the ease with which it trounced China in the Sino-Japanese War (1894–95). The subsequent treaty recognised Korean independence and ceded Taiwan to Japan. Friction with Russia eventually led to the Russo-Japanese War (1904–05), in which the Japanese army attacked the Russians in Manchuria and Korea. The Japanese Navy stunned the Russians by inflicting a crushing defeat on their Baltic fleet at the battle of Tsu-shima. For the first time, the Japanese were able to believe that they had drawn level with the Western powers.

INDUSTRIALISATION & ASIAN DOMINANCE

On his death in 1912, Emperor Meiji was succeeded by his son, Yoshihito, who chose the name Taishō for his reign. His period of rule was named the Taishō era (1912–26). The later stages of his life were dogged by ill health that was probably attributable to meningitis.

When WWI broke out, Japan sided against Germany but did not become deeply involved in the conflict. While the Allies were occupied with war, Japan took the opportunity, through shipping and trade, to expand its economy at top speed. At the same time, Japan gained a strong foothold in China, thereby giving Japan the dominant position in Asia.

Mid-16th century	1638
The Portuguese first arrive in Japan, bringing firearms and Christianity	Japan closes itself to the outside world and remains closed until 1853, when the Americans arrive on Commodore Perry's 'black ships'

Social unrest led the government to pursue a more democratic, liberal line; the right to vote was extended, and Japan joined the League of Nations in 1920. Under the influence of the *zaibatsu* (financial cliques of industrialists and bankers), a moderate and pacific foreign policy was followed.

NATIONALISM & THE PURSUIT OF EMPIRE

The Shōwa era (1926–89) commenced when Emperor Hirohito ascended the throne in 1926. He had toured extensively in Europe, mixed with European nobility and developed quite a liking for the British lifestyle.

A rising tide of nationalism was quickened by the world economic depression that began in 1930. Popular unrest was marked by political assassinations and plots to overthrow the government. This led to a strong increase in the power of the militarists, who approved the invasion of Manchuria in 1931 and the installation there of a puppet regime controlled by the Japanese. In 1933 Japan withdrew from the League of Nations and in 1937 entered into full-scale hostilities against China.

As the leader of a new order for Asia, Japan signed a tripartite pact with Germany and Italy in 1940. The Japanese military leaders saw their main opponents to this new order for Asia, the so-called Greater East Asia Co-prosperity Sphere, in the USA.

WORLD WAR II

When diplomatic attempts to gain US neutrality failed, Japan launched itself into WWII with a surprise attack on Pearl Harbor on 7 December 1941.

At first, Japan scored rapid successes, pushing its battle fronts across to India, down to the fringes of Australia and out into the mid-Pacific. The Battle of Midway opened the US counterattack, puncturing Japanese naval superiority and turning the tide of the war against Japan. By 1945, exhausted by submarine blockades and aerial bombing, Japan had been driven back on all fronts. In August of the same year, the declaration of war by the Soviet Union and the atomic bombs dropped by the USA on Hiroshima (p409) and Nagasaki (p627) proved to be the final straw: Emperor Hirohito announced unconditional surrender.

Having surrendered, Japan was then occupied by Allied forces under the command of General Douglas MacArthur. The chief aim of the USA was a thorough reform of Japanese government through demilitarisation, the trial of war criminals and the weeding out of militarists and ultra-nationalists from the government. A new constitution was introduced that dismantled the political power of the emperor, who completely stunned his subjects by publicly renouncing any claim to divine origins. This left him a mere figurehead.

The occupation was terminated in 1952, although the island of Okinawa was only returned to Japan in 1972. Okinawa is still home to American military bases.

POSTWAR RECONSTRUCTION

At the end of the war, the Japanese economy was in ruins and inflation was rampant. A program of recovery provided loans, restricted imports and encouraged capital investment and personal saving.

Hirohito and the Making of Modern Japan, by Herbert Bix – Japan's most controversial emperor, Hirohito, ruled over Japan for an extraordinary length of time, including its tragic WWII years. Bix masterfully covers Hirohito's role in Japan's 20th-century history.

No Regrets for our Youth (Waga Seishun ni Kui Nashi), directed by Kurosawa Akira – Directed by one of Japan's master filmmakers, this film captures the atmosphere in Japan leading up to WWII, as the fascists rose to power and oppressed any who dared criticise them.

Tokyo Story (Tōkyō Monogatari), directed by Ōzu Yasujiro – Set in the period following WWII, this film explores the relationships between the younger generation and their elderly parents. It is a masterful study of changing times and attitudes in post-war Japan.

1868	1905
Japan's capital is moved to Edo (present-day Tokyo)	Japan defeats Russia in the Russo-Japanese War

By the late 1950s trade was again flourishing, and the economy continued to expand rapidly. From textiles and the manufacture of labour-intensive goods, such as cameras, the Japanese 'economic miracle' spread into virtually every sector of economic activity. Economic recession and inflation surfaced in 1974 and again in 1980, mostly as a result of steep increases in the price of imported oil, on which Japan is dependent. But despite these setbacks, Japan became the world's most successful export economy, generating massive trade surpluses and dominating such fields as electronics, robotics, computer technology, car manufacturing and banking.

Embracing Defeat: Japan in the Wake of WWII, by John Dower – Dower's volume is a fantastic study of how Japan responded to its defeat in WWII. It's a must for anyone who wants to understand modern Japan.

RECENT HISTORY

Until 1990, it looked as though the Japanese economic juggernaut was unstoppable. But there was trouble in paradise. During the 1980s, escalating property values, a bullish stock market and easy credit led to what is now known as the 'Bubble Economy'. With a seemingly endless supply of easy money on hand, developers and investors threw their money into one grand scheme after another, on the assumption that the Japanese stock prices and land values would continue rising indefinitely.

In January 1990, however, the Tokyo stock market began to slide. By October of the same year it had lost 48% of its value – the bubble was about to burst. In 1991, Japanese banks, hit by the fall in stock market values, could no longer afford to be so free with their money and raised their interest rates. In turn, land prices came crashing back to earth. The sudden economic slowdown led to the failure of many of the speculative development ventures initiated during the 1980s, leaving the country's banks with a mountain of bad loans. The repercussions were felt in every sector of the economy and the country plunged into a recession.

Partially as a result of economic turmoil, in 1993, after 38 years at the helm, the conservative Liberal Democratic Party (LDP) was swept from power by an eight-party coalition of reformers. Then, in January 1995, a massive earthquake struck Kōbe (p353); the government was confused and slow to react, and confidence in Japan's much vaunted earthquake preparedness was shattered. And to top it all off, just months later, a millennial cult with doomsday ambitions – the Aum Shinrikyō (Aum Supreme Truth Sect) – engineered a poison gas attack on the Tokyo subway system that killed 12 people and injured thousands.

Inventing Japan, by Ian Buruma – This slim volume is a brilliant synopsis of the period from 1853, when Japan was forcibly opened by Admiral Perry's 'Black Ships', to 1964, when Tokyo hosted the summer Olympics. For those who want to know how modern Japan came to be, this is just about indispensable.

In April 2001 LDP member Koizumi Junichiro assumed the role of prime minister, promising a raft of uncompromising economic reforms aimed at reviving Japan's economy. Ironically, Koizumi's major accomplishment to date has nothing to do with economic policy: in September 2002, Koizumi became the first Japanese prime minister to visit North Korea. As a result of his visit, the North Koreans admitted to having abducted 13 Japanese citizens in the 1970s and '80s in order to train North Korean spies to operate in Japan. Koizumi was able to secure the release of five of the surviving abductees, who returned to Japan amid great fanfare (and anger about those who had died while on North Korean soil).

In October 2001, partially as a result of the terrorist attacks of 11 September 2001, Japan's politicians made a seemingly innocuous change to Japan's post-war constitution (under which anything but defensive military action was proscribed): the Diet voted to allow Japan's Jieitai

1941	1964
Japan attacks Pearl Harbor, entering WWII	Tokyo hosts the summer Olympics, marking Japan's recovery from WWII and full return to the international community

(Self-Defence Force) to participate in a support capacity in military actions abroad. Critics both inside and outside Japan argued that this change opens the door for renewed Japanese militarism.

After years of turmoil and economic difficulty in the 1990s, Japan is finally enjoying a growing economy. The economy grew by 3.2% in 2003 and economic indicators remained strong in 2004. While the economy is nowhere near as strong as it was during the years of the 'Bubble Economy', it has finally emerged from its long recession and optimism can finally be felt in the land. For more information on Japan's economy see p31.

The early years of the new millennium brought another piece of good news to Japan: on 1 December 2001, Crown Princess Masako (p47) gave birth to a baby girl, whom she and Crown Prince Naruhito named Aiko. The birth of Aiko was a huge relief to the nation, since the royal couple had previously been childless, but it also rekindled an old debate as to whether a female can ascend to Japan's throne (the imperial family has been without a male child for 36 years).

> Until it was occupied by the USA following WWII, Japan had never been conquered or occupied by a foreign power.

The Culture Kara Knafelc

THE NATIONAL PSYCHE

It's true that Japanese culture can initially seem indecipherable. At first glance, you may note what appears to be a lack of individualism, a dearth of directness, and a steadfast insularism, all of which can be cause for consternation. Though these observations do have value in describing the surface of Japanese culture, there is much more here to consider, especially in the way that Japanese families, friends and workmates form deep and enduring social bonds that literally keep the society together.

These bonds are evident in the relationships and networks that constitute the core of Japanese social lives. Closeness, loyalty and respect for others are key values, while selfishness is considered one of the greatest character flaws. As you've probably heard, the group matters here – a lot – though that does not mean that the Japanese are automatons going mindlessly through the social motions, as some Western critics have erroneously suggested. Generally, people here are expected to think *of*, not *like*, the members of their circle. This can mean watching what one says, taking care to avoid uncomfortable conflicts, and apologising profusely when there's a problem, even if it is unclear who is at fault.

Interestingly, all of these rules are suspended when a group of workmates or chums goes out drinking, or more specifically, is drunk. If apologising is the great Japanese social lubricant, alcohol is the release on the pressure valve that allows people to speak their minds without fear their besotted confessions will be brought up later. Something else to think about if you're from a culture that forms fast bonds is that Japanese friendship often lasts for a lifetime, and it's not unusual for high school chums to know each other into middle or even old age. This means that if you're here for a short time, it's probably unrealistic to expect you'll have rousing tête-à-têtes with most of the people you'll meet – intimate thoughts and personal views are reserved for confidantes who are time-tested and well-trusted.

Perhaps the most important social norm in Japan is that which demands the individual carefully consider the feelings of others. And part of thinking about someone else's feelings can mean keeping yours to yourself. Thus *honne*, or personal views, are often kept private and sometimes never expressed. *Tatamae*, or the safe, conformist views one voices in order to maintain one's position within a group or company or family, are considered safe to articulate and can act as a social lubricant that helps things run smoothly. Trying to squeeze personal views out of a Japanese friend may be as uncomfortable for them as silence might be for you. There are myriad exceptions to this practice, particularly among young Japanese who seem to feel more comfortable telling you what's on their minds.

LIFESTYLE

The way most Japanese live today differs greatly from the way they lived before WWII. As the birth rate has dropped (and continues to decline) and labour demands have drawn more workers to cities, the population has become increasingly more urban (see Population, p44) and increasingly divided in its way of life.

In the City

The overwhelming majority of Japanese live in the dizzying urban environments of major cities. These urbanites live famously hectic lives

Kara Knafelc is a freelance writer who has lived in both the suburbs and the centre of Tokyo. She is now based in San Francisco, where she continues to write and teach.

dominated by often-gruelling work schedules (the Japanese work week, like the school week, usually spans from Monday to Saturday) and punctuated by lengthy commutes from city centres to more affordable outlying neighbourhoods and suburbs.

As recently as ten years ago, the nexus of all this activity was the Japanese corporation, which provided lifetime employment to the legions of blue-suited white-collar workers, almost all of them men, who lived, worked, drank, ate and slept in the service of the companies for which they toiled. Because of a 15-year recession, and because some young Japanese have been unwilling to literally work themselves to death (the Japanese word for this, death by overwork, is *karoshi*), the work world is changing, and with it, the domestic sphere.

Though the days of the family comprised of a father who is a salaryman (a white-collar worker), a mother who is a housewife, kids who study dutifully in order to earn a place at one of Japan's elite universities, and an elderly in-law who has moved in, may not be completely over, the traditional family continues to evolve with current social and economic conditions. The father, if he is lucky, still has the job he had 10 years ago, though if, like many workers, he has found himself out of a job, it is possible that his wife has found part-time work as he continues to search (the unemployment rate has hovered at around 5% for the last several years – a grim ratio by Japanese standards). The kids in the family probably still study like mad; if they are in junior high, they are working toward gaining admission to a select high school by attending a cram school, known as a *juku*; if they are already in high school, they will be working furiously toward passing university admissions exams. As for the mother- or father-in-law, who in the past would have expected eldercare from the family, she or he may have found that beliefs about filial loyalty have changed substantially since the 1980s, particularly in urban centres. This change has been brought about by shifts in governmental policy and evolving perceptions of gender roles, which have allowed women the latitude to ask that ageing relatives seek eldercare from the government or at a growing number of nursing homes.

> Who better than kids to tell you what's cool in Japan? Check out http:// web-japan.org/kids web/culture.html.

In the Country

Only one in four Japanese live in the small farming and fishing villages that dot the mountains and cling to the rugged coasts. Mass postwar emigration from these rural enclaves has doubtless changed the weave of Japanese social fabric, and the texture of its landscape, as the young continue their steady egress to the city leaving untended rice fields to slide down the hills from neglect.

Today only 15% of farming households continue to make ends meet solely through agriculture with most rural workers holding down two or three jobs. Though this lifestyle manages to make the incomes of some country dwellers higher than those of their urban counterparts, it also speaks clearly of the crisis that many rural communities are facing in their struggle to maintain their traditional way of life.

The salvation of traditional village life may well rely on the success of the 'I-turn' (moving from urban areas to rural villages) and 'U-turn' (moving from country to city, and back again) movements. Though not wildly successful, these movements have managed to attract young people who work at home, company workers who are willing to put in a number of hours on the train commuting to the nearest city, and retirees looking to spend their golden years among the thatched roofs and rice fields that symbolise a not-so-distant past.

Since 1995 the Japanese government has been promoting rural tourism, and though this practice may well infuse some villages and hamlets with much-needed cash and tempting job prospects, long-time residents have raised questions about whether hot-springs resorts and megahotels will add to their communities – or mar the landscape. Perhaps the government's ongoing plans to encourage relocation from urban centres to tiny hamlets could provide the transfusion these areas need while also helping to define much-needed boundaries for the burgeoning tourism industry. Until these boundaries are in place, please treat traditional villages and remote hamlets with special care.

For an update on the greening of Japan, check out www.greenpeace.or .jp/index_en_html, Greenpeace Japan's excellent URL.

POPULATION

Because 76% of Japan is mountainous, three quarters of its population lives in the crowded urban centres that hug its low-lying coasts. The most densely populated expanse lies along Japan's eastern seaboard and stretches south from Tokyo to Kōbe.

The other 24% of the population lives in rural hamlets and towns, many of which are traditional farming and fishing communities. Due to a rapidly declining birth rate and because young people are drawn by the charms of Japan's cities, these rural residents are part of a shrinking minority.

Though Japan is famously – and proudly – homogenous, sizable communities of ethnic Koreans and Chinese have made their home in urban centres, such as Tokyo and Yokohama. At present, more than half a million ethnic Koreans and more than 200,000 ethnic Chinese can claim, or are fighting for, Japanese citizenship. Both of these groups have paid dearly for the right to live in Japan, suffering years of discrimination and access denied to basic rights like higher education and well-paying jobs.

Facts, facts, and more facts are found at this website (www.stat.go.jp /english/index.htm) managed by the Japanese government.

The Ainu

The Ainu, of whom there are roughly 24,000 living in Japan, were the indigenous people of Hokkaidō, and some would argue, the only people who can claim to be natives of Japan. Due to ongoing intermarriage and assimilation, almost all Ainu consider themselves bi-ethnic. Today, less than 200 people in Japan can claim both parents with exclusively Ainu descent.

Burakumin

Though Japanese society does not have a codified caste system such as that which exists in India, it has maintained the Edo-era tradition of discriminating against the *burakumin* (outcasts). This minority, which is seen as a caste of untouchables, is descended from ancestors who worked in trades such as butchery and tanning. According to both Buddhist and Shintō creeds, these trades were considered filthy and degrading because of their association with the impurity of death. It is estimated today that more than three million *burakumin* live in Japan, with around one third of that population living in one of more than 4000 ancestral hamlets and the remainder living in towns and cities throughout the country. The bulk of the *burakumin* population lives in the Kansai region and continues to experience discrimination in work and family life, with many employers still unwilling to hire any member of the caste, and many parents unwilling to allow children to intermarry with a person with family ties to a *burakumin* village.

IMMIGRATION

Like many industrialised countries, Japan attracts thousands of workers hoping for high salaries and a better life. Most of this labour settles in Japan's densest urban centres and in many ways is difficult to measure because so much of it is undocumented. Most immigrants come from nearby Asian countries such as China, Korea, and the Philippines, which together supply about 75% of Japan's current immigrants; others come from South American nations like Peru and Brazil, which contribute about 20% of Japan's immigrants.

Despite the stubborn sluggishness of Japan's current economy, there are at least 1.5 million foreign residents registered with the government. In addition, it has been estimated that at least another 250,000 unregistered illegal immigrants live and work in Japan. Some 220,000 of these are estimated to have overstayed their visa, some whom have lived and worked in Japan for 10 years or more. Though unregistered immigrants have few rights, in the last several years a series of high-profile court cases involving visa overstayers has raised questions about how and if Japan should begin granting legal residence to those non-native born who have lived in Japan for years, or perhaps even decades.

Unlike countries such as Australia and Canada, which tend toward fairly open dialogues regarding immigration, Japan still seems quite closed to the idea of an influx of foreign residents. Accordingly, the government has been reluctant to grant amnesty to undocumented immigrants, though even the most isolationist citizens and policymakers have begun to acknowledge that there is a need to address hot-button issues such as healthcare and education, and how social services in Japan will inevitably be impacted by a heterogeneous population with divergent needs.

In the near future, Japan may have little choice but to embrace the idea of naturalising immigrant workers. As the population continues to shrink, it is expected that certain labour sectors – particularly those related to healthcare – will need to recruit skilled workers from outside the country, much in the same way that the USA has begun to address shortages in rural medical clinics by issuing visas to foreign-educated doctors. It remains to be seen whether the discussion will broaden and deepen, though it seems unlikely that undocumented, unskilled workers will see a boost in their rights. For now, these groups continue to face the discrimination and bureaucratic challenges their counterparts confront in most industrialised countries. And the Japanese government continues to struggle with the idea of a culture whose ethnic makeup continues to diversify, even as the recession drags on.

RELIGION
Shintō & Buddhism

Though many religions such as Christianity, Islam, Judaism, and Okinawan and Ainu animism can claim small numbers of adherents in Japan, it is Buddhism and Shintō whose influence is writ large across the culture. Most Japanese practise some rites from both religions – though these are practised without any particular religious fervour – and are likely to pay an annual visit to a shrine and a temple, particularly during important holidays like O-bon (p735) and the New Year period (Shōgatsu; p735).

Shintō, or 'the way of the gods' is widely considered to be the indigenous religion of Japan. Shintōists believe in a pantheon of gods *(kami)* who represent elements of the natural world. Consisting of thousands of deities, this pantheon includes both local spirits and global gods and goddesses. Therefore, a devout Shintōist might worship the spirit of a nearby waterfall, or that of a uniquely shaped rock while simultaneously revering the most celebrated Shintō deity, Amaterasu, the goddess of the sun to whom the royal family of Japan is said to trace its ancestry. In

Nakagami Kenji provides rare insight into the world of the *burakumin*, Japan's untouchable caste, in his book *The Cape and Other Stories from the Japanese Ghetto*. The stories are set in the slums and alleyways of the Kishu province, which is now known as the Wakayama prefecture.

addition to demonstrating a reverence for spirits representing aspects of the natural world, Shintō incorporates a form of ancestor worship that is still practised by some adherents. Today, Shintō is practised in its original form by less than 3% of the population.

Buddhism arrived from India via China and Korea sometime in the 6th century and has for the most part coexisted peacefully with Shintō. About 90 million people in Japan currently practise some form of Buddhism, though most combine their practice with the exercise of periodic Shintō rites. Like Shintōists, Buddhists practise ancestor reverence and believe in a pantheon of gods with the most commonly depicted among these being Buddha, Kannon (the goddess of mercy) and Jizō (the patron of travellers, children, and the unborn). Unlike adherents to pure Shintō, Buddhists generally believe that followers must strive to live lives of virtue and wisdom in order to find peace and enlightenment. According to the central tenets of the religion, the mundane, material world is unimportant; with this view in mind, it is not surprising that Buddhist priests often conduct funerals and the commemoration of the dead while their Shintō counterparts often preside at weddings.

Religious Tolerance

Though some 'new religions' (known as *shinkyō shukyō*) deriving their structure from Shintō, Buddhism, Neo-Confucianism or a combination of these, have inspired fervid followings and sometimes perilously rigid belief systems (the most famous among these being Aum Shinrikyō, the cult responsible for the 1995 sarin gas attacks on Tokyo's subway), religious tolerance is standard in Japan. The constitution guarantees an individual's right to worship, and though most Japanese visit shrines and temples at some point during the year, most still lead very secular lives.

WOMEN IN JAPAN

On paper, Japanese women have as many rights as Japanese men. They are able to vote, own property, obtain a first-rate education, acquire a divorce and run for elected office. In practice, however, gender discrimination is as common as prescribed gender roles are rigid, resulting in a society in which women still struggle to be recognised as equal citizens, deserving real, rather than promised, human rights.

'On paper, Japanese women have as many rights as Japanese men'

The biggest challenge that Japanese women face is in the workplace, where they are routinely harassed and passed over for promotion. Female university graduates have made some breakthroughs in acquiring competitive jobs, though as they age, they still find themselves struggling to earn a fair wage (women typically earn 20% less than their male counterparts) and to advance in companies that assume they will marry, have children and drop out of the workforce.

The Japanese government has begun to take steps to address these inequities and in 1999 passed the Basic Law for Gender Equality, which aims to create a society in which women are guaranteed the true exercise of rights that are now merely promised by constitutional law. In addition to improving work conditions and strengthening sexual harassment policies, this legislation seeks to buttress existing domestic violence laws and to increase the number of women holding office in local, prefectural and national governments.

Apparently the shift in policy has worked to improve Japanese women's lives in many respects. The number of women legislators has increased by more than 2000 at the local level in the last 10 years, and the Diet, Japan's national parliamentary body, has gained 10 women members in the same amount of time. More companies are hiring women managers; wages for the legions of female part-time workers have gone up (though the relegation of women to part-time positions is in itself a condition against which women's trade unions continue to struggle), and it has become more acceptable to file sexual harassment lawsuits.

Women's rights groups continue to work toward equality for Japanese women. Much of their energy is not surprisingly dedicated to improving labour conditions and supporting legislation that will continue to make women's domestic lives better. Some have observed that the work seems to be slow-going, so slow-going that real changes appear to be far off. But a closer look will reveal that the mountain does seem to be moving, and that Japanese women are beginning to have power outside the domestic sphere.

MEDIA

Like all democratic countries, Japan constitutionally guarantees freedom of the press. In general, journalists do have quite a bit of freedom, though both Japanese and foreign media analysts have noted that exercise of this liberty is not always easy.

For reasons that are not completely clear, many Japanese journalists practise a form of self-censorship, often taking governmental or police reports at face value rather than conducting independent investigations that might reveal what is hidden beneath the official story. Some have speculated that this practice is symptomatic of journalists working closely, perhaps too closely, with political figures and police chiefs, who tacitly encourage them to omit details that might conflict with official accounts.

Added to the problem of self-censorship is that of exclusive press clubs, also known as *kisha*. These clubs, of which there are currently more than 800 in Japan, provide a privileged few with access to the halls of government. Journalists who are not empowered by a *kisha* (and most journalists who are not Japanese have found it impossible to obtain full membership) might find themselves unable to obtain key information

OWADA MASAKO, THE RELUCTANT PRINCESS

Owada Masako's biography may be one of the most perplexing in recent memory. Born the daughter of a diplomat and raised in cosmopolitan locales around the world (she speaks several languages), she was educated at Harvard and then Oxford. In 1993 Owada took and passed the Japanese Foreign Ministry exam, and was clearly on her way to following in her father's footsteps, despite the fact that Japan's Crown Prince, Naruhito, had twice asked her to marry him.

Sometime between her second refusal and the third proposal, Owada must have changed her mind. Naruhito's third offer of marriage was accepted after he reputedly promised to protect her from the glare of imperial life, a promise he would ultimately find difficult to fulfil. Since their highly publicised marriage in 1993, Owada has been under constant pressure to produce a male heir. She gave birth to her first child, Princess Aiko, in 2001; but because of a law passed more than a century ago, Aiko cannot become heir to the throne, and pressure upon Owada to produce a male heir has only intensified.

Recently, concerned about his wife's need to be treated for anxiety and depression, Prince Naruhito has broken with imperial practice and acknowledged to the Japanese press that 'there has been a move to deny Owada's career and personality.' This denial, it seems, has created anguish, and illness, for the princess. Only time will tell if the imperial family, like the royal family in Great Britain, will be able to make some changes to its stiff structure. For now, Owada remains guarded behind thick imperial walls.

and thus are shut out of a story. Some EU reporters have argued that this constitutes a form of information monopoly and have put pressure on the Japanese government to abolish the clubs.

Despite some problems with the free flow of information, the Japanese press is considered trustworthy by most people in Japan. Newspapers enjoy wide circulation, aided perhaps by the nation's incredible 99% literacy rate, and almost all households have televisions, which broadcast news and other programs around the clock. The Internet has also made serious inroads in Japan – the cheapest broadband rates in the world have brought Internet media into 80 million households, ensuring that almost everyone is wired.

ARTS
Contemporary Visual Art

When looking at postwar Japanese art, it's impossible not to linger on Isamu Noguchi's spiny ceramic *Even the Centipede* (1952) or to come upon his bronze *Mortality* (1959–62) without pausing to think. Equally as arresting is Masami Teraoka's *AIDS Series* (1988), with its deep wood-block reds and blues and its geishas grasping packages of condoms in hopes of pre-empting the ravages of HIV. This was the generation of Japanese artists that grappled with duelling philosophies: 'Japanese spirit, Japanese knowledge' versus 'Japanese spirit, Western knowledge'. This group was known for exploring whether Western artistic media and methods could convey the space, light, substance and shadows of the Japanese spirit, or if this essence could only truly be expressed through traditional Japanese artistic genres.

Today's emerging artists and the movements they have generated have no such ambivalence. Gone is the anxiety about coopting, or being coopted by, Western philosophies and aesthetics; here is the insouciant celebration of the smooth, cool surface of the future articulated by fantastic colours and shapes. This exuberant, devil-may-care aesthetic is most notably represented by Takashi Murakami, whose work derives much of its energy from *otaku*, the geek culture that worships characters that figure prominently in *manga*, Japan's ubiquitous comic books. Murakami's exuberant, prankish images and installations have become emblematic of the Japanese aesthetic known as *poku* (a concept that combines pop art with an *otaku* sensibility), and his *Super Flat Manifesto*, which declares that 'the world of the future might be like Japan is today – super flat,' can be seen as a primer for contemporary Japanese pop aesthetics.

Beyond the pop scene, artists continue to create works whose textures, layers and topics relay a world that is broader than the frames of a comic book. Three notable artists to look for are Yoshie Sakai, whose ethereal oil paintings, replete with pastel skies and deep waters, leave the viewer unsure whether they are floating or sinking; Noriko Ambe, whose sculptural works with paper can resemble sand dunes shifting in the Sahara, or your high-school biology textbook; and the indomitable Hisashi Tenmyouya, whose work, like Masami Teraoka's, chronicles the themes of contemporary Japanese life with works that echo the flat surfaces and deep impressions of wood-block prints while singing a song of the street.

Traditional Visual Art
PAINTING

From 794–1600 Japanese painting borrowed from Chinese and Western techniques and media, ultimately transforming them toward its own aesthetic ends. By the beginning of the Edo period (1600–1868), which was marked by the enthusiastic patronage of a wide range of painting styles,

Scream Against the Sky (edited by Alexandra Monroe) provides a comprehensive look at some of the finest Japanese postwar art, photography, and sculpture. Includes wonderful glossy photos throughout.

Japanese art had come completely into its own. The Kanō school, initiated more than a century before the beginning of the Edo era, continued to be in demand for its depiction of subjects connected with Confucianism, mythical Chinese creatures or scenes from nature. The Tosa school, the members of which followed the *yamato-e* style of painting (often used on scrolls during the Heian period, 794–1185), was also kept busy with commissions from the nobility who were eager to see scenes recreated from classics of Japanese literature.

Finally, the Rimpa school (from 1600) not only absorbed the styles of painting that had preceded it, but progressed beyond well-worn conventions to produce a strikingly decorative and delicately shaded form of painting. The works of art produced by a trio of outstanding artists from this school – Tawaraya Sōtatsu, Hon'ami Kōetsu and Ogata Kōrin – rank among the finest of this period.

CALLIGRAPHY

Shodō (the way of writing) is one of Japan's most valued arts, cultivated by nobles, priests and samurai alike, and still studied by Japanese schoolchildren today as *shūji*. Like the characters of the Japanese language, the art of *shodō* was imported from China. In the Heian period (794–1185), a fluid, cursive, distinctly Japanese style of *shodō* evolved called *wayō*, though the Chinese style remained popular in Japan among Zen priests and the literati for some time later.

In both Chinese and Japanese *shodō* there are three important types. Most common is *kaisho*, or block-style script. Due to its clarity, this style is favoured in the media and in applications where readability is key. *Gyōsho*, or running hand, is semicursive, and often used in informal correspondence. *Sōsho*, or grass hand, is a truly cursive style. *Sōsho* abbreviates and links the characters together to create a flowing, graceful effect.

> '*Shodō* (the way of writing) is one of Japan's most valued arts'

UKIYO-E (WOOD-BLOCK PRINTS)

Ukiyo-e means 'pictures of the floating world' and derives from a Buddhist metaphor for the transient world of fleeting pleasures. The subjects chosen by artists for these wood-block prints were characters and scenes from the tawdry, vivacious 'floating world' of the entertainment quarters in Edo (latter-day Tokyo), Kyoto and Osaka.

The floating world, centred in pleasure districts, such as Edo's Yoshiwara, was a topsy-turvy kingdom, an inversion of the usual social hierarchies that were held in place by the power of the Tokugawa shōgunate. Here, money meant more than rank, actors and artists were the arbiters of style, and prostitutes elevated their art to such a level that their accomplishments matched those of the women of noble families.

The vivid colours, novel composition and flowing lines of *ukiyo-e* caused great excitement in the West, sparking a vogue that one French art critic dubbed 'Japonisme'. *Ukiyo-e* became a key influence on impressionists (for example, Toulouse-Lautrec, Manet and Degas) and post-Impressionists. Among the Japanese the prints were hardly given more than passing consideration – millions were produced annually in Edo. They were often thrown away or used as wrapping paper for pottery. For many years, the Japanese continued to be perplexed by the keen interest foreigners took in this art form, which they considered of ephemeral value.

CERAMICS

The ceramic arts in Japan are considered to have started around the 13th century, with the introduction of Chinese ceramic techniques and the

FAMOUS CERAMIC CENTRES

Arita-yaki porcelain is still produced in the town where the first Japanese porcelain was made – Arita (p624) in Kyūshū. In the mid-17th century, the Dutch East India Company exported these wares to Europe, where they were soon copied in ceramics factories such as those of the Germans (Meissen), the Dutch (Delft) and the English (Worcester). Arita-yaki porcelain is still produced in Arita, the town where the first Japanese porcelain was made. In the mid-17th century, it was exported to Europe by the Dutch East India Company and came to be known to Westerners as 'Imari' after the name of the port from which it was shipped. One of the most recognisable Arita-yaki styles, Kakiemon, uses designs of birds and flowers, often rendered in a vibrant red overglaze. Another popular style is executed in blue and white, and incorporates scenes from legends and daily life. In addition to Arita are some other famous ceramic centres:

- Satsuma-yaki: the most common style of this porcelain, from Kagoshima (p654) in Kyūshū, has a cloudy white, crackled glaze enamelled with gold, red, green and blue.

- Karatsu-yaki: Karatsu (p621), near Fukuoka in northern Kyūshū, produces tea-ceremony utensils that are Korean in style and have a characteristic greyish, crackled glaze.

- Hagi-yaki: the town of Hagi (p429) in Western Honshū is renowned for Hagi-yaki, a type of porcelain made with a pallid yellow or pinkish crackled glaze.

- Bizen-yaki: the ancient ceramics centre of Bizen (p397) in Okayama-ken, Honshū, is famed for its solid unglazed bowls, which turn red through oxidation. Bizen also produces roofing tiles.

- Mino-yaki: in the town of Tajimi (p214) in Gifu-ken, you'll find pieces executed in the traditional Oribe style (which is known for its deep, green glaze) as well as those created in the Shino style (which is known for its pure, white glaze and is often sought after by tea-ceremony connoisseurs). Tajimi also boasts a community of potters and ceramicists who work with more experimental forms.

- Kiyomizu-yaki: the approach-road to the temple Kiyomizu-dera (p296), in Kyoto, is lined with shops selling Kiyomizu-yaki, a style of pottery that can be enamelled, blue-painted or red-painted in appearance.

- Kutani-yaki: the porcelain from Ishikawa-ken (p258), in central Honshū, is usually green or painted.

founding of a kiln in 1242 at Seto, in central Honshū. The Japanese term for pottery and porcelain, *setomono* (literally, 'things from Seto'), clearly derives from this still-thriving ceramics centre. Today, there are over 100 pottery centres in Japan, with scores of artisans producing everything from exclusive tea utensils to souvenir folklore creatures. Department stores regularly organise exhibitions of ceramics and offer the chance to see some of this fine work up close (for more information, see below).

In this exquisite haiku travelogue, *Narrow Road to the Deep North*, Bashō Matsuo captures the wonders and contradictions of Honshu's northern region.

SHIKKI (LACQUERWARE)

The Japanese have been using lacquer to protect and enhance the beauty of wood since the Jōmon period (10,000–300 BC). In the Meiji era (1868–1912), lacquerware became very popular abroad and it remains one of Japan's best-known products. Known in Japan as *shikki* or *nurimono*, lacquerware is made using the sap from the lacquer tree *(urushi)*, a close relative of poison oak. Raw lacquer is actually toxic and causes severe skin irritation in those who have not developed immunity. Once hardened, however, it becomes inert and extraordinarily durable.

The most common colour of lacquer is an amber or brown colour, but additives have been used to produce black, violet, blue, yellow and even white lacquer. In the better pieces, multiple layers of lacquer are painstakingly applied and left to dry, and finally polished to a luxurious shine.

Contemporary Theatre & Dance

Contemporary theatre and dance are alive and well in Japan, though you'll quickly notice that most major troupes are based in Tokyo. If you're interested in taking in contemporary theatre, your best bet is to enlist the help of a translator and to hit the *shogekijō* (little theatre) scene. If contemporary dance is what you seek, check p147 for the right place to check listings.

UNDERGROUND THEATRE

Theatre the world over spent the 1960s redefining itself, and it was no different in Japan. The *shogekijō* movement, also called *angura* (underground), has given Japan many of its leading playwrights, directors and actors. It arose as a reaction to the realism and structure of *shingeki* (a 1920s movement that borrowed heavily from Western dramatic forms) and featured surrealistic plays that explored the relationship between human beings and the world. Like their counterparts in the West, these productions took place in any space available – in small theatres, tents, basements, open spaces and on street corners.

The past decade has brought a shift in the focus of *shogekijō* to more realistic and contemporary themes, such as modern Japanese history,

---

WRITTEN ON THE BODY: IREZUMI & THE DECORATED SKIN

Irezumi is widely considered the most artful tattoo form in the world. Usually completed in blue and red natural dyes, the tattoos often cover the whole body with elaborate designs featuring intricate scenes that derive from Japanese myth and folklore. The practice of creating *irezumi* was initiated in the 18th century during the Edo era, when authorities tattooed criminals in order to brand them for their crimes. When released from prison, they would seek the services of an *irezumi-shi*, who would disguise the prison marks with tigers and flowers and other patterns, thus erasing an ignominious past.

Like their clients, tattoo artists were considered criminals, and this practice continued until the Meiji era, when authorities banned tattooing in order to avoid giving visiting foreigners the impression that Japan was uncivilised or barbaric. To Japan's surprise, visiting dignitaries, including the Tsar of Russia and King George V were enamoured of the art form, so much so that the latter had

irezumi artwork

JOHN ASHBURNE

a dragon tattooed on his forearm in 1881.

Today, the art of *irezumi* is still widely practised, though it is still considered by many Japanese to be the mark of criminality or of being from a lower class. Despite these judgments, or perhaps because of them, some anti-authority outcast groups, like the biker 'speed tribes' *(bosozoku)* have begun to acquire more tattoos, though these are often of Western-style hearts or cartoon characters rather than the hand-pricked, full-body *irezumi* masterpieces.

Perhaps the best place to admire the handiwork of an *irezumi* master is in a *sentō* (public bath), where *yakuza* (Japanese mafia) bare it all, just like everybody else. You might spot a bit of ink at Shōmen-yu (p311), in Kyoto, but if you'll be staying in Tokyo, check out the baths listed on p122. (Sorry gals – this treat will only be for the gents, as women's and men's bathing is segregated.)

war, environmental degradation and social oppression. Changing cultural perceptions have propelled the movement in new directions, notably towards socially and politically critical dramas (such as those by Kaneshita Tatsuo and Sakate Yōji), psychological dramas (eg by Iwamatsu Ryō, Suzue Toshirō and Hirata Oriza) and satirical portrayals of modern society (eg by Nagai Ai and Makino Nozomi).

BUTOH

In many ways, *butoh* (contemporary dance style) is Japan's most exciting dance form. It is also its newest dance, dating only to 1959, when Hijikata Tatsumi (1928–86) performed the first *butoh* performance. *Butoh* was born out of a rejection of the excessive formalisation that characterises traditional forms of Japanese dance and of an intention to return to the ancient roots of the Japanese soul.

Butoh performances are best likened to performance art rather than traditional dance. During a performance, one or more dancers use their naked or seminaked bodies to express the most elemental and intense human emotions. Nothing is sacred in *butoh*, and performances often deal with taboo topics, such as sexuality and death. For this reason, critics often describe *butoh* as scandalous, and *butoh* dancers delight in pushing the boundaries of what can be considered tasteful in artistic performance.

'Kabuki actors are born to the art form, and training begins in childhood'

Traditional Theatre & Dance

NŌ

Nō is a hypnotic dance-drama that reflects the minimalist aesthetics of Zen. The movement is glorious, the chorus and music sonorous, the expression subtle. A sparsely furnished cedar stage directs full attention to the performers, who include a chorus, drummers and a flautist. There are two principal characters: the *shite*, who is sometimes a living person but more often a demon, or a ghost whose soul cannot rest; and the *waki*, who leads the main character towards the play's climactic moment. Each *nō* school has its own repertoire, and the art form continues to evolve and develop. One of the many new plays performed over the last 30 years is *Takahime*, based on William Butler Yeats' *At the Hawk's Well*.

KABUKI

The first performances of kabuki were staged early in the 17th century by an all-female troupe. The performances were highly erotic and attracted enthusiastic support from the merchant classes. In true bureaucratic fashion, Tokugawa officials feared for the people's morality and banned women from the stage in 1629. Since that time, kabuki has been performed exclusively by men, giving rise to the institution of *onnagata*, or *ōyama*, male actors who specialise in female roles.

Over the course of several centuries, kabuki has developed a repertoire that draws on popular themes, such as famous historical accounts and stories of love-suicide, while also borrowing copiously from *nō* (above), *kyōgen* (comic vignettes) and *bunraku* (opposite). Most kabuki plays border on melodrama, although they vary in mood.

Formalised beauty and stylisation are the central aesthetic principles of kabuki; the acting is a combination of dancing and speaking in conventionalised intonation patterns, and each actor prepares for a role by studying and emulating the style perfected by his predecessors. Kabuki actors are born to the art form, and training begins in childhood. Today they enjoy great social prestige and their activities on and off the stage attract as much interest as those of popular film and TV stars.

BUNRAKU

Japan's traditional puppet theatre developed at the same time as kabuki (opposite), when the *shamisen* (a three-stringed instrument resembling a lute or a banjo), imported from Okinawa, was combined with traditional puppetry techniques and *joruri* (narrative chanting). *Bunraku*, as it came to be known in the 19th century, addresses many of the same themes as kabuki, and in fact many of the most famous plays in the kabuki repertoire were originally written for puppet theatre. *Bunraku* involves large puppets – nearly two-thirds life-sized – manipulated by up to three black-robed puppeteers. The puppeteers do not speak; a seated narrator tells the story and provides the voices of the characters, expressing their feelings with smiles, weeping and fits of surprise and fear.

The Japan Foundation's arts website (www.jpan .org/index.html) provides sketches of numerous plays and descriptions of the contemporary performance art scene throughout Japan.

RAKUGO

A traditional Japanese style of comic monologue, *rakugo* (literally, 'dropped word') dates back to the Edo period (1600–1868). The performer, usually in kimono, sits on a square cushion on a stage. Props are limited to a fan and hand towel. The monologue begins with a *makura* (prologue), which is followed by the story itself and, finally, the *ochi* (punch line, or 'drop', which is another pronunciation of the Chinese character for *raku* in *rakugo*). Many of the monologues in the traditional *rakugo* repertoire date back to the Edo and Meiji periods, and while well known, reflect a social milieu unknown to modern listeners. Accordingly, many practitioners today also write new monologues addressing issues relevant to contemporary life.

MANZAI

Manzai is a comic dialogue, with its origins in the song-and-dance and comedy routines traditionally performed by itinerant entertainers during Shōgatsu (New Year celebrations; p735). It is a highly fluid art that continues to draw large audiences to hear snappy duos exchange clever witticisms on up-to-the-minute themes from everyday life.

A Guide to the Japanese Stage: From Traditional to Cutting Edge (by Senda Akihiko) is a helpful overview of Japan's theatre scene, past and present. Includes a theatre guide and instructions on how to get tickets.

Architecture

CONTEMPORARY ARCHITECTURE

Contemporary Japanese architecture is currently among the world's most exciting and influential. The traditional preference for simple, natural and harmonious spaces is still evident in the work of modern architects, but this style is now combined with hi-tech materials and the building techniques of the West.

Japan first opened its doors to Western architecture in 1868 during the Meiji Restoration, and its architects immediately responded to the new influence by combining traditional Japanese methods of wood construction with Western designs. Some 20 years later, a nationalistic push against the influence of the West saw a surge in the popularity of traditional Japanese building styles, and Western technique was temporarily shelved.

This resistance to Western architecture continued until after WWI, when foreign architects such as Frank Lloyd Wright came to build the Imperial Hotel in Tokyo. Wright was careful to pay homage to local sensibilities when designing the Imperial's many elegant bridges and unique guest rooms (though he famously used modern, cubic forms to ornament the interiors of the hotel). The building was demolished in 1967 to make way for the current Imperial Hotel, which shows little of Wright's touch.

By WWII many Japanese architects were using Western techniques and materials and blending old styles with the new, and by the mid-1960s had

THE ECSTASY OF KASAI AKIRA

Though it was Tatsumi Hijikata who pioneered the art of *ankoku butoh*, the 'dance of darkness,' Kasai Akira is *butoh's* most ecstatic contemporary practitioner.

Kasai began his study of *butoh* with Kazuo Ohno, one of a few *butoh* masters of the nascent art form who emerged in postwar Japan. But Kasai diverged from *butoh's* new roots combining his understanding of the performative dance form's melancholy intent with his studies of the theory of movement and the practice of other types of modern dance. The result is a form of physical expression that is expulsive, dynamic, erotic and charged. And so Kasai may appear onstage as a kabuki maiden or a solitary traveller, only to break into a hectic, passionate dance that is unchecked by expectation and by artifice. If you're interested in catching a performance, Kasai does occasionally perform in Japan (check the local English weeklies). He also performs internationally.

developed a unique style that began to attract attention on the world stage. Japan's most famous postwar architect Tange Kenzō was strongly influenced by Le Corbusier. Tange's buildings, including the Kagawa Prefectural Offices at Takamatsu (1958) and the National Gymnasium (completed 1964), fuse the sculptural influences and materials of Le Corbusier with traditional Japanese characteristics, such as post-and-beam construction and strong geometry. His Tokyo Metropolitan Government Offices (1991; see p116), located in Nishi-Shinjuku (west Shinjuku), is the tallest building in Tokyo. It may look a little sinister and has been criticised as totalitarian, but it is a remarkable achievement and pulls in around 6000 visitors daily. Those with an interest in Tange's work should also look out for the UN University, close to Omote-sando subway station in Tokyo.

In the 1960s architects such as Shinohara Kazuo, Kurokawa Kisho, Maki Fumihiko and Kikutake Kiyonori began a movement known as Metabolism, which promoted flexible spaces and functions at the expense of fixed forms in building. Shinohara finally came to design in a style he called Modern Next, incorporating both modern and postmodern design ideas combined with Japanese influences. This style can be seen in his Centennial Hall at Tokyo Institute of Technology, an elegant and uplifting synthesis of clashing forms in a shiny metal cladding. Kurokawa's architecture blends Buddhist building traditions with modern influences, while Maki, the master of minimalism, pursued design in a modernist style while still emphasising the elements of nature – like the roof of his Tokyo Metropolitan Gymnasium (near Sendagaya Station), which takes on the form of a sleek metal insect. Another Maki design, the Spiral Building, built in Aoyama in 1985, is a favourite with Tokyo residents and its interior is also a treat.

'the Edo-Tokyo Museum has been likened in form to a crouching giant'

Isozaki Arata, an architect who originally worked under Tange Kenzō, also promoted the Metabolist style before later becoming interested in geometry and postmodernism. His work includes the Cultural Centre (1990) in Mito, which contains a striking, geometrical snakelike tower clad in different metals.

A contemporary of Isozaki's, Kikutake, went on to design the Edo-Tokyo Museum (1992; see p121) in Sumida-ku, which charts the history of the Edo period, and is arguably his best-known building. It is a truly enormous structure, encompassing almost 50,000 sq metres of built space and reaching 62.2m, which was the height of Edo-jō at its peak. It has been likened in form to a crouching giant and it easily dwarfs its surroundings.

Another influential architect of this generation is Hara Hiroshi. Hara's style defies definition, but the one constant theme is nature. His Umeda Sky Building (1993; see p342), in Kita, Osaka, is a sleek, towering structure designed to resemble a garden in the sky. The Yamamoto International Building (1993) on the outskirts of Tokyo, is the headquarters of a textile factory. Both these buildings, though monumental in scale, dissolve down into many smaller units upon closer inspection – just like nature itself.

In the 1980s, a second generation of Japanese architects began to gain recognition within the international architecture scene, including Andō Tadao, Hasegawa Itsuko and Toyo Ito. This younger group has continued to explore both modernism and postmodernism, while incorporating a renewed interest in Japan's architectural heritage.

Andō's architecture in particular blends classical modern and native Japanese styles. His buildings often combine materials, such as concrete, with the strong geometric patterns that have so regularly appeared in Japan's traditional architecture. Andō's restrained and sensitive use of materials often lends itself to the design of reflective or religious spaces.

TRADITIONAL SECULAR ARCHITECTURE
Houses

With the exception of those on the northern island of Hokkaidō, traditional Japanese houses are built with the broiling heat of summer in mind. They are made of flimsy materials designed to take advantage of even the slightest breeze. Another reason behind the gossamer construction of Japanese houses is the relative frequency of earthquakes, which precludes the use of heavier building materials such as stone or brick.

Principally simple and refined, the typical house is constructed of post-and-beam timber, with sliding panels of wood or rice paper (for warmer weather) making up the exterior walls. Movable screens, or *shōji*, divide the interior of the house. There may be a separate area for the tea ceremony – the harmonious atmosphere of this space is of the utmost importance and is usually achieved through the use of natural materials and the careful arrangement of furniture and utensils.

A particularly traditional type of Japanese house is the *machiya* (townhouse) built by merchants in cities such as Kyoto and Tokyo. Until very recently, the older neighbourhoods of Kyoto and some areas of Tokyo were lined with neat, narrow rows of these houses, but most have fallen victim to the current frenzy of construction. These days, the best place to see *machiya* is in eastern Kyoto, near the temple Kiyomizu-dera (p296). Takayama (p219), like the post towns along the Kiso Valley that once offered food and rest for tired travellers, is a good spot to view traditional *machiya* architecture. The more elegant mansions of the noble classes and warriors, with their elaborate receiving rooms, sculptured gardens and teahouses, can also be viewed in places such as Kyoto (p272), Nara (p361) and Kanazawa (p254) and in former feudal cities scattered around Japan.

Farmhouses

The most distinctive type of Japanese farmhouse is the thatched-roof *gasshō-zukuri*, so named for the shape of the rafters, which resemble a pair of praying hands. While these farmhouses look cosy and romantic, bear in mind that they were often home for up to 40 people and occasionally farm animals as well. Furthermore, the black floorboards, soot-covered ceilings and lack of windows guaranteed a cavelike atmosphere. The only weapon against this darkness was a fire built in a central fireplace in the floor, known as an *irori*, which also provided warmth in the cooler months and hot coals for cooking. Multistorey farmhouses were also built to house silkworms for silk production (particularly prevalent during the Meiji era) in the airy upper gables.

Though this site (www .tokyoq.com) focuses exclusively on Tokyo, its art and architecture reviews are up to the minute and some of the best you'll find.

TEMPLE OR SHRINE?

One of the best ways to distinguish a Buddhist temple from a Shintō shrine is to examine the entrance. The main entrance of a shrine is customarily a *torii* (Shintō shrine gate), usually composed of two upright pillars, joined at the top by two horizontal cross-bars, the upper of which is normally slightly curved. *Torii* are often painted a bright vermilion, though some are left as bare wood. In contrast, the main entrance gate *(mon)* of a temple is often a much more substantial affair, constructed of several pillars or casements, joined at the top by a multitiered roof, around which there may even be walkways. Temple gates often contain guardian figures, usually *Niō* (deva kings). Keep in mind, though, that shrines and temples sometimes share the same precincts, and it is not always easy to tell where one begins and the other ends.

Castles

Japan has an abundance of castles, most of them copies of originals destroyed by fire or war or time.

The first castles were simple mountain forts that relied more on natural terrain than on structural innovations for defence, making them as frustratingly inaccessible to their defenders as they were to invading armies. The central feature of these edifices was the donjon, or a keep, which was surrounded by several smaller towers. The buildings, which sat atop stone ramparts, were mostly built of wood that was covered with plaster intended to protect against fire.

The wide-ranging wars of the 16th and 17th centuries left Japan with numerous castles, though many of these were later destroyed by the Edo and then the Meiji governments. Half a century later, the 1960s saw a boom in castle reconstructions, most built of concrete and steel, and like Hollywood movie sets – authentic-looking when viewed from a distance but distinctly modern in appearance when viewed up close.

Some of the best castles to visit today include the dramatic Himeji-jō (p360), also known as the White Egret Castle, and Edo-jō (p93), around which modern Tokyo has grown. Little of Edo-jō actually remains (the grounds are now the site of Imperial Palace), though its original gate, Ōte-mon, still marks the main entrance.

Literature

Sōseki Natsume's most known for *Kokoro*, but *I Am a Cat,* the merciless turn-of-the-20th-century narrative told from the point of view of a cat, is way more fun.

Interestingly, much of Japan's early literature was written by women. One reason for this was that men wrote in kanji (imported Chinese characters), while women wrote in hiragana (Japanese script). Thus, while the men were busy copying Chinese styles and texts, the women of the country were producing the first authentic Japanese literature. Among these early female authors is Murasaki Shikibu, who wrote Japan's first great novel, *Genji Monogatari* (The Tale of Genji). This detailed, lengthy tome documents the intrigues and romances of early Japanese court life, and although it is perhaps Japan's most important work of literature, its extreme length probably limits its appeal to all but the most ardent Japanophile or literature buff.

Most of Japan's important modern literature has been penned by authors who live in and write of cities. Though these works are sometimes celebratory, many also lament the loss of a traditional rural lifestyle that has given way to the pressures of a modern, industrialised society. *Kokoro*, the modern classic by Sōseki Natsume, outlines these rural/urban tensions as does *Snow Country*, by Nobel laureate Kawabata Yasunari. Each of these works touches upon the tensions between Japan's nostalgia for the past and its rush toward the future, between its rural heartland and its burgeoning cities.

Although Mishima Yukio is probably the most controversial of Japan's modern writers, and is considered unrepresentative of Japanese culture by many Japanese, his work still makes for very interesting reading. *The Sailor Who Fell from Grace* and *After the Banquet* are both compelling books. If you're looking for unsettling beauty, reach for the former; history buffs will want the latter tome, which was at the centre of a court case that became Japan's first privacy lawsuit.

Ōe Kenzaburo, Japan's second Nobel laureate, produced some of Japan's most disturbing, energetic and enigmatic literature. *A Personal Matter* is the work for which he is most widely known. In this troubling novel, which echoes Ōe's frustrations at having a son with autism, a 27-year-old cram school teacher's wife gives birth to a brain-damaged child. His life claustrophobic, his marriage failing, he dreams of escaping to Africa while planning the murder of his son.

Of course not all Japanese fiction can be classified as literature in high-brow terms. Murakami Ryū's *Almost Transparent Blue* is strictly sex and drugs, and his ode to the narcissistic early 1990s, *Coin Locker Babies*, recounts the toxic lives of two boys who have been left to die in coin lockers by their mothers. Like Murakami Ryū, Banana Yoshimoto is known as a smooth operator of surfaces. In her novel *Kitchen*, she relentlessly chronicles Tokyo's fast-food menus and '80s pop culture, though underlying the superficial digressions are hints of a darker and deeper world of death and loss and loneliness.

Japan's most internationally celebrated living novelist is Murakami Haruki, a former jazz club owner gone literary. His most noted work, *Norwegian Wood*, set in the late '60s against the backdrop of student protests, is both the portrait of the artist as a young man (as recounted by a reminiscent narrator) and an ode to first loves. Also an interesting read is his *A Wild Sheep Chase* in which a mutant sheep with a star on its back generates a search that takes a twenty-something ad man to the mountainous north. The hero eventually confronts the mythical beast while wrestling with his own shadows.

In April of 2004, the Akutagawa Prize, one of the nation's most prestigious, was awarded to the two youngest Japanese writers, both of them women, to have ever received it (Ōe Kenzaburo and Ishihara Shintaro were each 23 when they received the prize). Hitomi Kanehana, 19, and Risa Wataya, 20, have brought a readership back to what was a languishing fiction scene. Unfortunately, neither of these writers' work is currently available in English, though their publishing houses have been besieged by requests for translations.

Abe Kobo's beautiful novel *Woman in the Dunes* is a tale of shifting sands and wandering strangers. One of the strangest and most interesting works of Japanese fiction.

AH, THE BOREDOMS

If the USA had the Ramones, and the UK the Sex Pistols, Japan's best worst-kept secret is the Boredoms. Though they refuse to take credit for it in interviews, the Boredoms are viewed as the godfathers of the noise-music revolution in Japan. As the name implies, this genre often uses sounds that are unwanted – and strictly avoided – in most musical genres. The effect can be grating, nauseating and painful, but like Jimi Hendrix's use of reverberative feedback, can also have an organic quality that is honest, anarchic and affecting.

The Boredoms, who are currently based in Osaka, do play in Japan several times a year, though wrangling a ticket can be difficult as most are quickly snapped up by the band's loyal, longstanding cult following (they have been together since 1986). You may have a better chance of catching band member Yamatsuka Eye (also known as DJ Eye) whose solo shows are often listed in the English weeklies in major metropolitan areas.

TRADITIONAL MUSIC AND ITS INSTRUMENTS

■ Gagaku is a throwback to music of the Japanese imperial court. Today ensembles consist of 16 members and include stringed instruments, such as the *biwa* (lute) and *koto* (zither) and wind instruments such as the *hichiriki* (Japanese oboe).

■ Shamisen is a three-stringed instrument resembling a lute or banjo with an extended neck. Popular during the Edo period, particularly in the entertainment districts, it's still used as formal accompaniment in kabuki and *bunraku* (classical puppet theatre) and remains one of the essential skills of a geisha.

■ Shakuhachi is a wind instrument imported from China in the 7th century. The *shakuhachi* was popularised by wandering Komusō monks in the 16th and 17th centuries, who played it as a means to enlightenment as they walked alone through the woods.

■ Taiko refers to any of a number of large Japanese drums. Drummers who perform this athletic music often play shirtless to show the rippled movements of their backs.

Music

Japan has a huge, shape-shifting music scene supported by a local market of audiophiles who are willing to try almost anything. International artists make a point of swinging through on global tours, and the local scene surfaces every night in one of thousands of live houses. The jazz scene is enormous as are the followings for rock, house and electronica. More mainstream gleanings are the *aidoru*, idol singers whose popularity is generated largely through media appearances and is centred on a cute, girl-next-door image. Unless you're aged 15, this last option probably won't interest you.

At the moment, J-pop (Japan Pop) is being rocked by Cornelius (named after the good scientist in *Planet of the Apes*). The indie guitarist Keigo Oyamada's one-man act synthesises unlikely sounds, such as heavy metal and birds in song using a signature technique he calls 'gucha gucha,' or mixing it up. Also making the rounds, in the USA as well as in Japan, is DJ Klock, a wunderkind in a long line of experimental Tokyo turntable masters.

'Japan has a vibrant film industry and proud, critically acclaimed cinematic traditions'

Cinema

Japan has a vibrant film industry and proud, critically acclaimed cinematic traditions. Renewed international attention since the mid-1990s has reinforced interest in domestic films, which account for an estimated 40% of box-office receipts, nearly double the level in most European countries. Of course, this includes not only artistically important works, but also films in the science-fiction, horror and 'monster-stomps-Tokyo' genres for which Japan is also known.

At first, Japanese films were merely cinematic versions of traditional theatrical performances, but in the 1920s, Japanese directors starting producing films in two distinct genres: *jidaigeki* (period films) and new *gendaigeki* films, which dealt with modern themes. The more realistic storylines of the new films soon reflected back on the traditional films with the introduction of *shin jidaigeki* (new period films). During this era, samurai themes became an enduring staple of Japanese cinema.

The golden age of Japanese cinema arrived with the 1950s and began with the release in 1950 of Kurosawa Akira's *Rashōmon*, winner of the Golden Lion at the 1951 Venice International Film Festival and an Oscar for best foreign film. The increasing realism and high artistic standards of the period are evident in such landmark films as *Tokyo Story* (*Tōkyō Monogatari*, 1953), by the legendary Ōzu Yasujirō; Mizoguchi Kenji's classics *Ugetsu Monogatari* (Tales of Ugetsu, 1953), and *Saikaku Ichidai Onna* (The Life of Oharu, 1952); and Kurosawa's 1954 masterpiece *Shichinin no Samurai* (Seven Samurai). Annual attendance at the country's cinemas reached 1.1 billion in 1958, and Kyoto, with its large film studios, such as Shōchiku, Daiei and Tōei, and its more than 60 cinemas, enjoyed a heyday as Japan's own Hollywood.

As it did elsewhere in the world, TV spurred a rapid drop in the number of cinema-goers in Japan in the high-growth decades of the 1960s and '70s. But despite falling attendance, Japanese cinema remained a major artistic force. These decades gave the world such landmark works as Ichikawa Kon's *Chushingura* (47 Samurai, 1962), and Kurosawa's *Yōjimbo* (1961).

The decline in cinema-going continued through the 1980s, reinforced by the popularisation of videos, with annual attendance at cinemas bottoming out at just over 100 million. Yet Japan's cinema was far from dead: Kurosawa garnered acclaim worldwide for *Kagemusha* (1980), which shared the Palme d'Or at Cannes, and *Ran* (1985). Imamura Shōhei's heartrending *Narayama Bushiko* (The Ballad of Narayama) won the Grand Prix at Cannes in 1983. Itami Jūzō became perhaps the most widely known Japanese director outside Japan after Kurosawa, with such biting satires as *Osōshiki* (The Funeral, 1985), *Tampopo* (Dandelion, 1986) and *Marusa no Onna* (A Taxing Woman, 1988). Ōshima Nagisa, best known for controversial films such as *Ai no Corrida* (In the Realm of the Senses, 1976), scored a critical and popular success with *Senjo no Merry Christmas* (Merry Christmas, Mr Lawrence) in 1983.

In the 1990s popular interest in Japan seemed to catch up with international attention as attendance rates began to rise once again. In 1997 Japanese directors received top honours at two of the world's three most prestigious film festivals: *Unagi* (Eel), Imamura Shohei's black-humoured look at human nature's dark side won the Palme d'Or in Cannes – making him the only Japanese director to win this award twice; and 'Beat' Takeshi Kitano took the Golden Lion in Venice for *Hana-bi*, a tale of life and death, and the violence and honour that links them. The undisputed king of popular Japanese cinema, 'Beat' Takeshi Kitano is a true Renaissance man of media: he stars in and directs his films, and is a newspaper columnist, author and poet.

To carry on a proud tradition in cinema, a new generation of directors is emerging; it includes Koreeda Hirokazu, with *Maboroshi no Hikari* (Wonderful Life) and *Distance*, Kurosawa Kiyoshi, with *Cure*, and Ichikawa Jun, winner of the Best Director's prize at the Montreal Film Festival in 1997 for *Tōkyō Yakyoku* (Tokyo Drugstore).

ANIME

The term *anime*, a Japanese word derived from French and English, is used worldwide to refer to Japan's highly sophisticated animated films. Unlike its counterparts in other countries, *anime* occupies a position very near the forefront of the film industry in Japan. *Anime* films encompass all genres, from science fiction and action adventure to romance and historical drama, and while *anime* is supported by three key media – TV, original video animation and full-length feature films – it is the stunning animation of the latter that has brought *anime* critical acclaim worldwide.

Unlike its counterparts in many other countries, *anime* targets all age and social groups. *Anime* films include deep explorations of philosophical questions and social issues, humorous entertainment and bizarre fantasies.

Tokyo Story (*Tōkyō Monogatari*, 1953) is Ōzu Yasujirō's story of an older couple who come to Tokyo to visit their children only to find themselves treated with disrespect and indifference.

Distance (2001) is a subtle meditation on togetherness and loneliness. Koreeda's follow-up film to *After Life* follows four people into the woods as they seek the truth about lovers and friends who belonged to a mysterious cult.

The films offer breathtakingly realistic visuals, exquisite attention to detail, complex and expressive characters and elaborate plots. Leading directors and voice actors are accorded fame and respect, while characters become popular idols.

Japan's most famous *anime* genius is Miyazaki Hayao, creative head of Studio Ghibli since 1984. Miyazaki's films include *Kaze no Tani no Nausicaa* (Nausicaa of the Valley of the Winds, 1984), *Tonari no Totoro* (My Neighbour Totoro, 1988) and *Majō no Takkyubin* (Kiki's Delivery Service, 1989). During 1997 Miyazaki's *Mononoke-hime* (The Princess Mononoke), a fantasy about a 14th-century princess who fights the destruction of the forests, opened at 250 theatres across Japan, the largest opening in Japanese cinema history. History was made again in 1998 when *Mononoke-hime* broke the Japanese box-office record set by *ET* in 1982. In 1998 the film opened to a tremendous reception in the United States after Disney signed an agreement to release subtitled and dubbed versions of Miyazaki films. Miyazaki continued his winning streak with the fantastical *Sen to Chihiro no Kamikakushi* (Spirited Away, 2002), which has won a number of local and international awards.

FASHION

It's impossible to visit Japanese cities and not notice their incredible sense of style. From the chaotic getups worn by teenagers in Yoyogi-kōen in Tokyo to the sleek black shoes that click along the avenues in Kyoto, people here think carefully about design and trends and beauty.

In the last 20 years, the fashion scene has been loosely organised around the work of three designers – Issey Miyaki, Rei Kawakubo and Yohji Yamamoto – all of whom show in London, Paris and New York, in addition to maintaining a presence in Tokyo. Together they are revered as some of the most artistic and innovative designers in the business, though it has often been said that their pieces are simply too radical to wear.

If you'll be passing through Tokyo, you might want to stop in Harajuku to check out the many black ensembles with oddly placed armholes (p151).

SPORT
Sumō

A fascinating, highly ritualised activity steeped in Shintō beliefs, sumō is the only traditional Japanese sport that pulls big crowds and dominates primetime TV. The 2000-year-old sport, which is based on an ancient combat form called *sumai* (to struggle), attracts huge crowds on weekends. Because tournaments take place over the span of 15 days, unless you're aiming for a big match on a weekend, you should be able to secure a ticket. Sumō tournaments *(bashō)* take place in January, May and September at the Ryōgoku Kokugikan Sumō Stadium (p124), in Tokyo; in March at the Furitsu Taiiku-kan Gymnasium in Osaka; in July at the Aichi Prefectural Gymnasium (p211), in Nagoya; and in November at the Fukuoka Kokusai Centre, in Fukuoka (p612). Most popular are matches where one of the combatants is a *yokozuna* (grand champion). At the moment, sumō's hottest ticket is Asashoryu, a Mongolian-born master who swept the 2004 Spring Grand Sumō Tournament with a perfect 15-0 record.

Soccer

Japan was already soccer crazy when the World Cup came to Saitama and Yokohama in 2002. Now, it's a chronic madness, and five minutes of

Did you know that there are more than six million vending machines in Tokyo alone?

conversation with any 10-year-old about why they like David Beckham should clear up any doubts you might have to the contrary. Japan's national league, also known as J-League (www.j-league.or.jp/eng/), is in season from March until November and can be seen at stadiums around the country. Exciting international matches will likely be played at one of the excellent stadiums built for the world cup, such as those which can be found in Yokohama (p188), Sapporo (p519) and Kōbe (p353), among others.

Baseball

Baseball was introduced to Japan in 1873 and became a fixture in 1934 when the Yomiuri started its own team after Babe Ruth and Lou Gehrig had swung through town. During WWII, the game continued unabated, though players were required to wear unnumbered, khaki uniforms and to salute each other on the field. Today, baseball is still widely publicised and very popular though many fans have begun to worry about the future of the sport in Japan as some of the most talented national players, such as Hideo Nomo and Hideki Matsui, migrate to major league teams in the USA. If you're visiting Japan between April and October and are interested in catching a game, two exciting places to do so are the historic Koshien Stadium (Map p339), which is located just outside of Osaka and was built in 1924 as Japan's first stadium, and Tokyo Dome (p150), affectionately known as the 'Big Egg' and home to Japan's most popular team, the Yomiuri Giants.

'Baseball was introduced to Japan in 1873'

Environment

Stretching from the tropics to the Sea of Okhotsk, the Japanese archipelago is a fantastically varied place. With everything from coral reef islands to snow-capped mountains, few countries in the world enjoy such a richness of different climes and ecosystems. Unfortunately, this wonderful landscape is also one of the world's most crowded, and almost every inch of the Japanese landscape and coastline bears the imprint of human activity (see the boxed text, opposite).

Although Japan's environment has been manipulated and degraded by human activity over the centuries, there are still pockets of real beauty left, some quite close to heavily populated urban areas. Indeed, there is decent hiking in the mountains within two hours of Tokyo, an hour of Osaka, and a few minutes from downtown Kyoto.

Nature lovers are likely to be most troubled by the condition of Japan's rivers and coasts: almost all of Japan's rivers are dammed, forced into concrete channels, and otherwise bent to the human will, and an astonishing amount of Japan's coast is lined with 'tetrapods' (giant concrete structures in the shape of jacks used to prevent erosion).

Given the incredibly active nature of the Japanese archipelago – the country has always been plagued by volcanoes, earthquakes, typhoons, landslides and other natural disasters – it's perhaps not surprising that the Japanese are eager to tame the wild nature of their islands. Unfortunately, this means that the visitor to Japan is often forced to try to imagine what the land looked like before the industrial revolution. Fortunately, environmental consciousness is on the rise in Japan, and more effort is being put into recycling, conservation and protection of natural areas. We can only hope that some of Japan's remaining areas of beauty will be preserved for future generations.

| Japan incinerates an estimated 75% of its solid waste.

THE LAND

Japan is an island nation but it has not always been so. As recently as the end of the last ice age, around 10,000 years ago, the level of the sea rose enough to flood a land bridge which connected Japan to the Asian continent. Today, Japan consists of a chain of islands that rides the back of a 3000km-long arc of mountains along the eastern rim of the continent. It stretches from around 25°N at the southern islands of Okinawa to 45°N at the northern end of Hokkaidō. Cities at comparable latitudes are Miami and Cairo in the south and Montreal and Milan in the north. Japan's total land area is 377,435 sq km, and more than 80% of it is mountainous.

Japan consists of some 3900 small islands and four major ones: Honshū (slightly larger than Britain), Hokkaidō, Kyūshū and Shikoku. Okinawa, the largest and most significant of Japan's many smaller islands, is about halfway along an archipelago that stretches from the western tip of Honshū almost all the way to Taiwan. It is far enough from the rest of Japan to have developed a culture that differs from that of the 'mainland' in many respects.

There are several disputed islands in the Japanese archipelago. The most important of these are the Kuril Islands, north of Hokkaidō. Seized by Russia at the close of WWII, they have been a source of tension between Japan and Russia ever since. While the Japanese have made some progress toward their return in recent years, they remain, for the time being, part of Russia.

If Japanese culture has been influenced by isolation, it has equally been shaped by the country's mountainous topography. A number of the mountains are volcanic, and more than 40 of these are active, many of them on the southern island of Kyūshū. On the plus side, all this geothermal activity is responsible for Japan's fabulous abundance of hot springs *(onsen)*.

In addition to its volcanoes, Japan has the dubious distinction of being one of the most seismically active regions of the world. It has been estimated that Japan is hit by over 1000 earthquakes a year, most of which are, fortunately, too small to notice without sophisticated seismic equipment. This seismic activity is particularly concentrated in the Kantō region, in which Tokyo is situated. But earthquakes can strike just about any part of the archipelago, as the citizens of Kōbe discovered in the disastrous earthquake of January 1995, which killed more than 6000 people.

WILDLIFE

The latitudinal spread of the islands of Japan makes for a wide diversity of flora and fauna. The Nansei and Ogasawara archipelagos in the far south are subtropical, and flora and fauna in this region are related to those found

---

WHAT HAPPENED TO THE HILLS?

Visitors to Japan are often shocked at the state of the Japanese landscape. It seems that no matter where you look, the hills, rivers, coastline and fields bear the unmistakable imprint of human activity. Indeed, it is only in the highest, most remote mountains that one finds nature untouched by human hands. Why is this?

Undoubtedly, population density is the crucial factor here. With so many people packed into such a small space, it is only natural that the land should be worked to the hilt. However, it is not just simple population pressure that accounts for Japan's scarred and battered landscape: misguided land management policies and money-influenced politics also play a role.

Almost 70% of Japan's total land area is wooded. Of this area, almost 40% is planted, most of it with uniform rows of conifers, known as *sugi* (cryptomeria). Even national forests are not exempt from tree farming and these forests account for 33% of Japan's total lumber output. The end result of this widespread tree farming is a rather ugly patchwork effect over most of Japan's mountains – monotonous stands of *sugi* interspersed with occasional swaths of bare, clear-cut hillside.

To make matters worse, the planting of monoculture forests and the practice of clear cutting reduces the stability of mountain topsoil, resulting in frequent landslides. To combat this, land engineers erect unsightly concrete retaining walls over huge stretches of hillside, particularly along roadsides or near human habitations. These, combined with high-tension wire towers and the patchwork forests, result in a landscape that is quite unlike anything elsewhere in the world.

As if this weren't enough, it is estimated that only three of Japan's 30,000 rivers and streams are undammed. In addition to dams, concrete channels and embankments are built around even the most inaccessible mountain streams. Although some of this river work serves to prevent flooding downstream, much of it is clearly gratuitous and can only be understood as the unfortunate result of Japanese money-influenced politics.

In Japan, rural areas wield enormous power in national politics, as representation is determined more by area than by population. In order to ensure the support of their constituencies, rural politicians have little choice but to lobby hard for government spending on public works projects, as there is little other work available in these areas. Despite the negative effects this has on the landscape and economy, Japanese politicians seem unable to break this habit.

The upshot of all this is a landscape that looks, in many places, like a giant construction site. Perhaps the writer Alex Kerr put it best in his book *Lost Japan:* 'Japan has become a huge and terrifying machine, a Moloch tearing apart its own land with teeth of steel, and there is absolutely nothing anyone can do to stop it.' For the sake of the beauty that remains in Japan, let's hope he is wrong.

on the Malay Peninsula. Mainland Japan (Honshū, Kyūshū and Shikoku), on the other hand, shows more similarities with Korea and China, while subarctic northern and central Hokkaidō have their own distinct features.

Animals

Japan's land bridge to the Asian continent allowed the migration of animals from Korea and China. The fauna of Japan has much in common with these regions, though there are species that are unique to Japan, such as the Japanese giant salamander and the Japanese macaque. In addition, Nansei-shotō, which has been separated from the mainland for longer than the rest of Japan, has a few examples of fauna (for example the Iriomote cat) that are classified by experts as 'living fossils'.

Japan's largest carnivorous mammals are its bears. Two species are found in Japan – the *higuma* (brown bear) of Hokkaidō, and the *tsukinowaguma* (Asiatic brown bear) of Honshū, Shikoku and Kyūshū. The brown bear can grow to a height of 2m and weigh up to 400kg. The Asiatic brown bear is smaller at an average height of 1.4m and a weight of 200kg.

Japanese macaques are medium-sized monkeys that are found in Honshū, Shikoku and Kyūshū. They average around 60cm in length and have short tails. The last survey of their numbers was taken in 1962, at which time there were some 30,000. They are found in groups of 20 to 150 members.

A survey carried out in 1986 by the Japanese government's Environment Agency found that 136 species of mammals were in need of protection and that 15 species were already extinct. Endangered species include the Iriomote cat, the Tsushima cat, Blakiston's fish owl and the Japanese river otter.

Plants

The flora of Japan today is not what the Japanese saw hundreds of years ago. This is not just because a lot of Japan's natural landscape has succumbed to modern urban culture, but also because much of Japan's flora is imported. It is thought that some 200 to 500 plant species have been introduced to Japan since the Meiji period, mainly from Europe but also from North America. Japanese gardens laid out in the Edo period and earlier are good places to see native Japanese flora, even though you won't be seeing it as it might have flourished naturally.

Dogs and Demons: Tales from the Dark Side of Modern Japan – Alex Kerr's book is essential for anyone who wants to understand why Japan's environment is in such a sorry state. In particular, Kerr explores the power of the construction industry over the government.

A large portion of Japan was once heavily forested. The cool to temperate zones of central and northern Honshū and southern Hokkaidō were home to broad-leaf deciduous forests, and still are, to a certain extent. Nevertheless, large-scale deforestation is a feature of contemporary Japan. Pollution and acid rain have also taken their toll. Fortunately, the sheer inaccessibility of much of Japan's mountainous topography has preserved some areas of great natural beauty – in particular the alpine regions of central Honshū and the lovely national parks of Hokkaidō.

NATIONAL PARKS

Japan has 28 *kokuritsu kōen* (national parks) and 55 *kokutei kōen* (quasi-national parks). Ranging from the far south (Iriomote National Park) to the northern tip of Hokkaidō (Rishiri-Rebun-Sarobetsu National Park), the parks represent an effort to preserve as much as possible of Japan's natural environment. Although national and quasi-national parks account for less than 1% of Japan's total land area, it is estimated that 14% of Japan's land is protected or managed for sustainable use.

When discussing Japan's national and quasi-national parks, it must be noted that these parks are quite different from national parks in most other countries. Few of the parks have facilities that you might expect in national parks (ranger stations, camping grounds, educational facilities etc). More importantly, national park status doesn't necessarily mean that the area in question is free from residential, commercial or even urban development. Indeed, in many of these parks, you'd have no idea that you were in a national or quasi-national park unless you looked on a map.

The highest concentration of national parks and quasi-national parks is in northern Honshū (Tōhoku) and Hokkaidō, where the population density is relatively low. But there are also national parks and quasi-national parks, such as Chichibu-Tama and Nikkō, within easy striking distance of Tokyo. The largest of Japan's national parks is the Seto-Nai-Kai National Park (Inland Sea National Park; *Seto-Nai-Kai Kokuritsu-kōen*), which extends some 400km east to west, reaches a maximum width of 70km and encompasses almost 1000 islands of various sizes.

ENVIRONMENTAL ISSUES

Japan was the first Asian nation to industrialise. It has also been one of the most successful at cleaning up the resulting mess, though problems remain. In the early postwar years, when Japan was frantically rebuilding its economy, there was widespread public ignorance of the problems of pollution, and the government did little to enlighten the public.

Industrial pollution was at its worst from the mid-1960s to the mid-1970s. But public awareness of the issue had already been awakened by an outbreak in 1953 of what came to be called Minamata disease, after the town of the same name, in which up to 6000 people were affected by mercury poisoning. It was not until 1968 that the government officially acknowledged the cause of the 'disease'.

By the late 1960s public consciousness of environmental problems had reached levels that the government could not ignore. Laws were passed to curb air and water pollution. These have been reasonably successful, though critics are quick to point out that while toxic matter has been mostly removed from Japanese waters, organic pollution remains a problem. Similarly, controls on air pollution have had mixed results: photochemical smog emerged as a problem in Tokyo in the early 1970s; it remains a problem and now affects other urban centres around Japan.

In 1972 the government passed the Nature Conservation Law, which aimed to protect the natural environment and provide recreational space for the public. National parks, quasi-national parks and prefectural parks were established, and it appears that these measures have been successful in increasing wildlife numbers.

More recently, Japan has been facing a new set of problems, including dioxin given off by waste incineration plants and a series of accidents at nuclear reactors and nuclear fuel processing facilities. The only up side is that these accidents have forced the government to revise its safety guidelines for the nuclear power industry.

Of course, the news isn't all bleak. The governor of Kumamoto-ken announced in 2002 that the Arase Dam on Kuma-gawa would be removed, starting in 2010. In a country with a surplus of unnecessary dams, this is a major step in the right direction.

As a casual visitor to Japan, you may feel that you have few chances to make a positive environmental impact. There is, however, one thing you can do to cut down waste and pollution: use as little packaging as possible. One shopping trip in Japan will impress upon you just how fond the Japanese are of packaging – some would say overpackaging – purchases and gifts. The solution to this is simply to refuse excess packaging. One

Environmental Politics in Japan: Networks of Power and Protest – This book by Jeffrey Broadbent is one of the best English-language books on environmental politics and policies in Japan.

Japan Environmental Exchange (JEE; www.jca .apc.org/jee/indexE.html) With offices in Tokyo and Kyoto, the JEE is one of the best foreigner-friendly environmental groups in Japan. Visit its site to check on their upcoming environmental projects.

Friends of the Earth Japan (FoEJ; www.foe japan.org/en/) The Japan chapter of Friends of the Earth International runs weekly hikes in the Tokyo area and has a good list of environmental events on its site.

A RESORT IN PARADISE

Iriomote-jima (p715) is Okinawa's second-largest island. Over 90% of the area is covered with semitropical jungle and the coastline is fringed with lovely coral reefs. Half the island has been designated as the Iriomote National Park, and the entire island is rich in protected species, including the Iriomote cat and the crowned eagle.

Nearby Ishigaki-jima is dotted with large-scale luxury resorts, but so far Iriomote has escaped this sort of development. This is partly because the islanders have a high level of environmental awareness. Indeed, businesses on the island have always stressed the importance of protecting the environment and have been national leaders in developing ecotourism.

However, in 2003 a Tokyo company called Unimat, which makes its money in the field of consumer finance and real estate, announced plans to build a resort on Iriomote. The Iriomote city government gave their approval to the plan and construction started on the resort in 2004, despite fierce opposition from many island residents. Frustrated by their failure to stop the construction, some island residents and their mainland allies filed a suit against the company in an effort to block further construction.

The plaintiffs argue that it is important to protect the beach on which the resort is located from development. The beach, which was called Tsudumari-hama (an ancient name that made reference to the beach as a stopping place for boats) by the locals, has had its name officially changed by the developers to Tsukigahama (the beach of moon). The beach is considered a sacred place by the local people, who believe that it is a place where the gods descend and play. In addition to being a divine playground, it also offers places for green turtles, which are considered by locals to be messengers of the sea gods, to come and lay their eggs.

This suit, which raises questions of both human rights and environmental protection, is unique in Japanese history. At present, some 414 official plaintiffs and 98 lawyers are battling the developers to save one of Japan's most beautiful islands from heedless development. Not just those in Japan, but environmentalists the world over, are watching with interest.

line that will come in handy is: *'fukuro wa irimasen'* (I don't need a bag). Another is the simple *'kekkō desu'* (That's alright), which can be used to turn down offers for additional packaging.

Another way to save trees and cut down on waste is to carry your own chopsticks around with you, which you can use instead of the ubiquitous *waribashi* (disposable chopsticks) that are provided in restaurants. One simple way to acquire your own personal set of choppers is to take away the first nice pair of *waribashi* that you are given in a restaurant.

Every year, 24 billion pairs of *waribashi* (disposable chopsticks) are used in Japan.

Food & Drink

Those familiar with *nihon ryōri* (Japanese cuisine) know that eating is half the fun of travelling in Japan. Even if you've already tried some of Japan's better-known specialities in Japanese restaurants in your own country, you're likely to be surprised by how delicious the original is when served on its home turf. More importantly, the adventurous eater will be delighted to find that Japanese food is far more than just sushi, tempura or sukiyaki. Indeed, it is possible to spend a month in Japan and sample a different speciality restaurant every night.

Those in search of a truly Japanese experience will probably want to avoid Western-style fast food. Luckily this is quite easy to do, although some may baulk at charging into a restaurant where both the language and the menu are likely to be incomprehensible. The best way to get over this fear is to familiarise yourself with the main types of Japanese restaurants so that you have some idea of what's on offer and how to order it. Those timid of heart should take solace in the fact that the Japanese will go to extraordinary lengths to understand what you want and will help you to order.

With the exception of *shokudō* (all-round restaurants) and *izakaya* (pub-style restaurants), most Japanese restaurants concentrate on a speciality cuisine. This naturally makes for delicious eating, but does limit your choice. In the Restaurants & Sample Menus section of this chapter we will introduce the main types of Japanese restaurants, along with a menu sample of some of the most common dishes served (see p71).

FOOD & DRINK REGIONAL SPECIALITIES

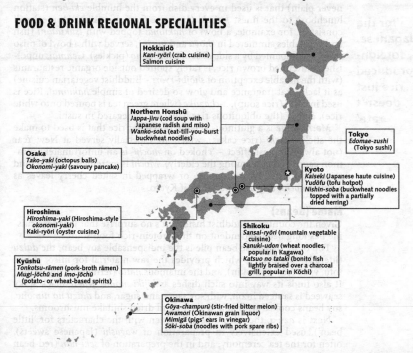

Hokkaidō
Kani-ryōri (crab cuisine)
Salmon cuisine

Northern Honshū
Jappa-jiru (cod soup with Japanese radish and miso)
Wanko-soba (eat-till-you-burst buckwheat noodles)

Tokyo
Edomae-zushi (Tokyo sushi)

Osaka
Tako-yaki (octopus balls)
Okonomi-yaki (savoury pancake)

Kyoto
Kaiseki (Japanese haute cuisine)
Yudōfu (tofu hotpot)
Nishin-soba (buckwheat noodles topped with a partially dried herring)

Hiroshima
Hiroshima-yaki (Hiroshima-style okonomi-yaki)
Kaki-ryōri (oyster cuisine)

Shikoku
Sansai-ryōri (mountain vegetable cuisine)
Sanuki-udon (wheat noodles, popular in Kagawa)
Katsuo no tataki (bonito fish lightly braised over a charcoal grill, popular in Kōchi)

Kyūshū
Tonkotsu-rāmen (pork-broth rāmen)
Mugi-jōchū and *imo-jōchū* (potato- or wheat-based spirits)

Okinawa
Gōya-champurū (stir-fried bitter melon)
Awamori (Okinawan grain liquor)
Mimigā (pigs' ears in vinegar)
Sōki-soba (noodles with pork spare ribs)

For information on how to eat in a Japanese restaurant see the boxed text, p78. For information on eating etiquette in Japan, see the tips set out in boxed text, p70.

STAPLES

Despite the mind-boggling variety of dishes throughout the island chain, the staples that make up Japanese cuisine remain the same nationwide: *shōyu* (soy sauce), miso, tofu, *mame* (beans), and above all, the divine crop, rice.

Rice (O-kome)

The Japanese don't just consume *kome* (rice) all day, every day. They venerate it. This may baffle visitors, not least the members of the US and Australian rice lobby who flock to Japan in droves to try to prise open its lucrative rice market. Yet for the Japanese, foreign-produced rice just doesn't rate. It's Japanese-produced rice or nothing.

In its uncooked form it is called *o-kome,* the *o-* denoting respect, *kome* meaning rice. Cooked Japanese style, it is called *go-han* (the *go-* prefix is the highest indicator of respect), denoting rice or meal. Truck drivers, however, may use the more informal *meshi,* something akin to 'grub'. When it is included in Western-style meals, it is termed *raisu.*

On average, Japanese consume an astonishing 70kg of *kome* per person per year. Culturally, most Japanese feel a meal is simply incomplete without the inclusion of *kome.* It is the building block on which a Japanese meal is based, the heart of the Japanese culinary DNA.

Hakumai is plain, white rice (yet no Japanese writer would ever describe it as 'plain' – lucent, perhaps? delicately scented? robust even, but never plain) that is used in every dish from the humble *eki-ben* (station lunchbox) to the finest *kaiseki* (Japanese formal cuisine). A meal will consist of, for example, a bowl of *hakumai* topped with *tsukudani* (fish and vegetables simmered in *shōyu* and *mirin*), served with a bowl of miso soup, accompanied by a side dish of *tsukemono* (pickles). *Genmai,* unpolished, unrefined brown rice, is rarely spotted outside organic restaurants (with the notable exception of *shōjin-ryōri* – Buddhist vegetarian cuisine) as it lacks that fragrance and glow so desired of simple *hakumai.* Rice is used in *zōsui* (rice soup), *o-chazuke* (where green tea is poured onto white rice), *onigiri* (the ubiquitous rice balls) and vinegared in sushi.

'for the Japanese, foreign-produced rice just doesn't rate'

Mochi-gome is a glutinous version of regular rice that is used to make the sticky *mochi* (rice cakes), which are especially served at New Year (not always to best effect – 'choked on *mochi*' is an unfortunately common cause of death among the elderly). *Mochi* is extremely popular, and is served toasted as *yaki-mochi,* or wrapped in salted cherry leaves as *sakura-mochi,* a spring speciality of Kyoto.

Mame (Beans)

Given the country's Buddhist history, it's no surprise that Japanese cuisine has long been dependent on this protein-rich food source.

Top of the Japanese bean pile is the indispensable soy bean, the *daizu* (literally, 'big bean'), which provides the raw material for miso, *shōyu*, tofu, *yuba* (soy milk skin), and the infamous *nattō* (fermented soy beans). It also finds its way into such dishes as *hijiki-mame,* where black spiky seaweed is sauteed in oil, with soy sauce and sugar, and *daizu no nimono,* soy beans cooked with *konbu* (kelp) and dried shiitake mushrooms.

Next is *azuki,* the adzuki bean (written with the characters for 'little bean'), used extensively in preparation of *wagashi* (Japanese sweets), often for the tea ceremony, and in the preparation of *seki-han* (red-bean rice), which is used at times of celebration and to commemorate a teen-age girl's first menstruation. *Kintoki* is a large red variety of *azuki*, often cooked in sugar, which is named for its resemblance to the red-faced legendary child Kintarō.

Miso

A precursor of miso arrived on the Japanese mainland from China some-time around AD 600, not long after Buddhism. Its inhabitants have been gargling it down as *misoshiru* (miso soup) ever since, at breakfast, lunch and dinner. Made by mixing steamed soy beans with *kōji* (a fermenting agent) and salt, miso is integral to any Japanese meal, where it is likely to be present as *misoshiru* or as a flavouring. It is also used in *dengaku* (fish and vegetables roasted on skewers), where it is spread on vegetables such as eggplant and *konnyaku* (devil's tongue).

There are three types of miso: the most common is *kome-miso,* made with rice; *mame-miso,* made from soy beans, most common along the Tokai coastline of Honshū; and *mugi-miso,* a barley miso popular through-out Kyūshū (except in Fukuoka, where they too make *kome-miso*).

Misoshiru is made of a mixture of *dashi* (stock), miso and shellfish such as *shijimi* (freshwater clams) or *asari* (short-necked clams); assorted vege-tables such as *daikon* (giant white radish), carrot or burdock (especially good for the digestion); pork; or simply tofu. In preparation it should never boil, and is often served with a topping of sliced spring onion or *mitsuba* (Japanese wild chervil). Good *shijimi misoshiru* combined with the aromatic pepper *sanshō* is a heavenly combination, and it's rumoured to be good for your liver after too much sake.

'miso is an essential source of protein'

When miso is not used in a soup, it is often used as dressing for *aemono* (cooked leafy vegetables, poultry or fish blended with the dressing) and *ni-mono* (simmered dishes). Combined with rice vinegar, white miso becomes *su-miso.* Both may also accompany mountain vegetables and river fish.

Miso is an essential source of protein, calorie free, Buddhist-friendly and packed with salt. It has also proven effective in treating radiation victims. One cannot help but wonder what thousands of Ukrainians thought on receiving hundreds of tons of the stuff from the Japanese government in the wake of the Chernobyl disaster.

Tofu

Tofu is oft-maligned in the West, largely as a result of the plastic-wrapped, porridge-like goo that was passed off in its name in health-food stores in the '70s. Yet tofu is one of Japan's most sublime creations. Best of all is to get up with the larks and head down to your local tofu maker for postdawn, freshly made, creamy tofu that is still warm.

Tofu is sold as the soft 'silk' *kinugoshi* and the firm *momen* (or *momen-goshi*). The former is mainly used in soups, especially *misoshiru.* The latter is eaten by itself, deep-fried in *agedashi-dōfu* or used in the Kyoto classic *yudōfu,* a hotpot dish. Both *momen* and *kinugoshi* take their names from the technique used when the hot soy milk is strained – if the material used is cotton, the resulting firm tofu is *momen;* when silk *(kinu)* is used, it's *kinugoshi.*

A classic way to eat tofu is as *hiyayakko,* cold blocks of tofu covered with soy, grated ginger and finely sliced spring onion. This is a favourite on the menus of *izakaya.*

Abura-age is thinly sliced, especially thick tofu traditionally fried in ses-ame oil (more recently, however, producers use salad oil or soy bean oil). It is a key ingredient in the celebratory *chirashi-zushi* (sushi rice topped with cooked egg and other tidbits like shrimp and ginger) and in *inari-zushi* (where vinegared rice is stuffed into a fried tofu pouch), named after the fox-deity and rice-god that protects shrines throughout the country, the most notable being Fushimi-Inari Taisha in Kyoto. Kyoto is indeed tofu heaven, with the temple areas of Nanzen-ji and Sagano particularly famous.

The monks of Kōya-san in Nara make their own distinctive greyish, thick *kōya-dōfu*, always served cold.

Yuba is a staple of *shōjin-ryōri* and a speciality of Kyoto. It is a marvellous accompaniment to sake when it is served fresh with grated wasabi and *shōyu tsuyu* (dipping sauce). Its creation is a time- and labour- intensive process in which soy milk is allowed to curdle over a low heat and then is plucked from the surface using either chopsticks or equipment especially designed for the process. Lazy types can buy it prepacked, and dried it is added to soups.

Shōyu (Soy Sauce)

Surprisingly, *shōyu* is a relatively new addition to Japanese cuisine, although a primitive form of it, *hishio*, was made in the Yayoi period by mixing salt and fish. *Shōyu* in its current form dates back to the more recent Muromachi era. It only achieved widespread popularity somewhere between 1603 and 1867 when it was first exported to Europe. Unsubstantiated rumour has it that Louis XV was one of the West's first avid *shōyu* fans.

EATING ETIQUETTE

When it comes to eating in Japan, there are quite a number of implicit rules, but they're fairly easy to remember. If you're worried about putting your foot in it, relax – the Japanese almost expect foreigners to make fools of themselves in formal situations and are unlikely to be offended as long as you follow the standard rules of politeness from your own country.

Among the more important eating 'rules' are those regarding chopsticks. Sticking them upright in your rice is considered bad form – that's how rice is offered to the dead! It's also bad form to pass food from your chopsticks to someone else's – another Buddhist funeral rite which involves passing the remains of the cremated deceased among members of the family using chopsticks.

It's worth remembering that a lot of effort has gone into the preparation of the food so don't pour soy sauce all over it (especially the rice) and don't mix it up with your chopsticks. Also, if possible, eat everything you are given. And don't forget to slurp your noodles!

When eating with other people, especially when you're a guest, it is polite to say 'Itadakimasu' (literally, 'I will receive') before digging in. This is as close as the Japanese come to saying grace. Similarly, at the end of the meal, you should thank your host by saying 'Gochisō-sama deshita' which means, 'It was a real feast'.

When drinking with Japanese remember that it is bad form to fill your own drink; fill the glass of the person next to you and wait for them to reciprocate. Filling your own glass amounts to admitting to everyone at the table that you're an alcoholic. It is polite to raise your glass a little off the table while it is being filled. Once everyone's glass has been filled, the usual starting signal is a chorus of 'kampai' which means 'cheers!'. Constant topping up means a bottomless glass – just put your hand over your glass if you've had enough.

There is also a definite etiquette to bill-paying. If someone invites you to eat or drink with them, they will be paying. Even among groups eating together it is unusual for bills to be split. The exception to this is found among young people and close friends and is called *warikan* (each person paying their own share). Generally, at the end of the meal something of a struggle will ensue to see who gets the privilege of paying the bill. If this happens, it is polite to at least make an effort to pay the bill – it is extremely unlikely that your Japanese hosts will acquiesce.

Twentieth-century mass production made a household name out of Kikkōman, but *shōyu* is still made using traditional methods at small companies throughout the country. It comes in two forms: the dark brown 'thicker taste' *koikuchi-shōyu*, and the chestnut-coloured 'thinner', much saltier *usukuchi-shōyu* (sweetened and lightened by the addition of *mirin*). *Koikuchi* is used for a variety of applications, especially in the Kantō region around Tokyo, and is perfect for teriyaki, where meat or fish is brushed with *shōyu*, *mirin* and sugar, and grilled. The aromatic *usukuchi-shōyu*, a favourite of the Kansai region, is best suited to clear soups and white fish. It is especially important in enhancing the colour of a dish's ingredients.

The importance of *shōyu* lies not merely in its use as a condiment – it is integral to many cooking and pickling processes, and to *tsuyu*, the linchpin of Japanese noodle cuisine.

RESTAURANTS & SAMPLE MENUS
Shokudō

A *shokudō* is the most common type of restaurant in Japan, and is found near train stations, tourist spots and just about any other place where people congregate. Easily distinguished by the presence of plastic food displays in the window, these inexpensive places usually serve a variety of *washoku* (Japanese dishes) and *yōshoku* (Western dishes).

At lunch, and sometimes dinner, the easiest meal to order at a *shokudō* is a *teishoku* (set-course meal), which is sometimes also called *ranchi setto* (lunch set) or *kōsu*. This usually includes a main dish of meat or fish, a bowl of rice, miso soup, shredded cabbage and some Japanese pickles (*tsukemono*). In addition, most *shokudō* serve a fairly standard selection of *donburi-mono* (rice dishes) and *menrui* (noodle dishes). When you order noodles, you can choose between *soba* and udon, both of which are served with a variety of toppings. If you're at a loss as to what to order, simply say *kyō-no-ranchi* (today's lunch), and they'll do the rest. Expect to spend from ¥800 to ¥1000 for a meal at a *shokudō*.

'A *shokudō* is the most common type of restaurant in Japan'

RICE DISHES

katsu-don	かつ丼	rice topped with a fried pork cutlet
niku-don	牛丼	rice topped with thin slices of cooked beef
oyako-don	親子丼	rice topped with egg and chicken
ten-don	天丼	rice topped with tempura shrimp and vegetables

NOODLE DISHES

soba	そば	buckwheat noodles
udon	うどん	thick, white wheat noodles
kake soba/udon	かけそば/うどん	*soba*/udon noodles in broth
kitsune soba/udon	きつねそば/うどん	*soba*/udon noodles with fried tofu
tempura soba/udon	天ぷらそば/うどん	*soba*/udon noodles with tempura shrimp
tsukimi soba/udon	月見そば/うどん	*soba*/udon noodles with raw egg on top

Izakaya

An *izakaya* is the Japanese equivalent of a pub. It's a good place to visit when you want a casual meal, a wide selection of food, a hearty atmosphere and, of course, plenty of beer and sake. When you enter an *izakaya*, you are given the choice of sitting around the counter, at a table or on a tatami floor. You usually order a bit at a time, choosing from a selection of typical Japanese foods like *yakitori*, sashimi and grilled fish, as well as Japanese interpretations of Western foods like french fries and beef stew.

Izakaya can be identified by their rustic façades and the red lanterns outside their doors bearing the kanji for *izakaya* (see p78). Since *izakaya* food is casual fare to go with drinking, it is usually fairly inexpensive. Depending on how much you drink, you can expect to get away with spending ¥2500 to ¥5000 per person. (See the following *Yakitori* section for more dishes available at *izakaya*.)

> **'yakitori is not so much a full meal as an accompaniment for beer and sake'**

agedashi-dōfu	揚げだし豆腐	deep-fried tofu in a dashi broth
jaga-batā	ジャガバター	baked potatoes with butter
niku-jaga	肉ジャガ	beef and potato stew
shio-yaki-zakana	塩焼魚	a whole fish grilled with salt
yaki-onigiri	焼きおにぎり	a triangle of grilled rice with *yakitori* sauce
poteto furai	ポテトフライ	french fries
chiizu-age	チーズ揚げ	deep-fried cheese
hiya-yakko	冷奴	a cold block of tofu with soya sauce and spring onions
tsuna sarada	ツナサラダ	tuna salad over cabbage
yaki-soba	焼きそば	fried noodles with meat and vegetables
kata yaki-soba	固焼きそば	hard fried noodles with meat and vegetables
sashimi mori-awase	刺身盛り合わせ	a selection of sliced sashimi

Yakitori

Yakitori (skewers of grilled chicken and vegetables) is a popular after-work meal. *Yakitori* is not so much a full meal as an accompaniment for beer and sake. At a *yakitori-ya* (*yakitori* restaurant) you sit around a counter with the other patrons and watch the chef grill your selections over charcoal. The best way to eat here is to order several varieties, then order seconds of the ones you really like. Ordering can be a little confusing since one serving often means two or three skewers (be careful – the price listed on the menu is usually that of a single skewer).

In summer, the beverage of choice at a *yakitori* restaurant is beer or cold sake, while in winter it's hot sake. A few drinks and enough skewers to fill you up should cost ¥3000 to ¥4000 per person. *Yakitori* restaurants are usually small places, often near train stations, and are best identified by a red lantern outside and the smell of grilling chicken.

yakitori	焼き鳥	plain, grilled white meat
hasami/negima	はさみ/ねぎま	pieces of white meat alternating with leek
sasami	ささみ	skinless chicken-breast pieces
kawa	皮	chicken skin
tsukune	つくね	chicken meat balls
gyū-niku	牛肉	pieces of beef
rebā	レバー	chicken livers
tebasaki	手羽先	chicken wings
shiitake	しいたけ	Japanese mushrooms
piiman	ピーマン	small green peppers
tama-negi	玉ねぎ	round, white onions
yaki-onigiri	焼きおにぎり	a triangle of rice grilled with *yakitori* sauce

Sushi & Sashimi

Like *yakitori*, sushi is considered an accompaniment for beer and sake. Nonetheless, both Japanese and foreigners often make a meal of it, and it's one of the healthiest meals around.

There are two main types of sushi: *nigiri-zushi* (served on a small bed of rice – the most common variety) and *maki-zushi* (served in a seaweed roll). Lesser-known varieties include *chirashi-zushi* (a layer of rice covered in egg and fish toppings), *oshi-zushi* (fish pressed in a mould over rice) and *inari-zushi* (rice in a pocket of sweet, fried tofu). Whatever kind of sushi you try, it will be served with lightly vinegared rice. Note that *nigiri-zushi* and *maki-zushi* will contain a bit of wasabi (hot green horseradish).

Sushi is not difficult to order. If you sit at the counter of a sushi restaurant you can simply point at what you want, as most of the selections are visible in a refrigerated glass case between you and the sushi chef. You can also order à la carte from the menu. When ordering, you usually order *ichi-nin mae* (one portion), which usually means two pieces of sushi. Be careful, since the price on the menu will be that of only one piece. If ordering à la carte is too daunting, you can take care of your whole order with just one or two words by ordering *mori-awase*, an assortment plate of *nigiri-zushi*. These usually come in three grades: *futsū nigiri* (regular *nigiri*), *jō nigiri* (special *nigiri*) and *toku-jō nigiri* (extra-special *nigiri*). The difference is in the type of fish used. Most *mori-awase* contain six or seven pieces of sushi.

Be warned that meals in a good sushi restaurant can cost upwards of ¥10,000, while an average establishment can run from ¥3000 to ¥5000 per person. One way to sample the joy of sushi on the cheap is to try an automatic sushi place, usually called *kaiten-zushi,* where the sushi is served on a conveyor belt that runs along a counter. Here you simply reach up and grab whatever looks good to you (which certainly takes the pain out of ordering). You are charged by the number of plates of sushi that you have eaten. Plates are colour-coded by their price and the cost is written either somewhere on the plate itself or on a sign on the wall. You can usually fill yourself up in one of these places for ¥1000 to ¥2000 per person.

Before popping the sushi into your mouth, dip it in *shōyu*, which you pour from a small decanter into a low dish specially provided for the purpose. If you're not good at using chopsticks, don't worry, sushi is one of the few foods in Japan that is perfectly acceptable to eat with your hands. Slices of *gari* (pickled ginger) will also be served to help refresh the palate. The beverage of choice with sushi is beer or sake (hot in the winter and cold in the summer), with a cup of green tea at the end of the meal.

> 'sushi is one of the few foods in Japan that is perfectly acceptable to eat with your hands'

ama-ebi	甘海老	sweet shrimp
awabi	あわび	abalone
ebi	海老	prawn or shrimp
hamachi	はまち	yellowtail
ika	いか	squid
ikura	イクラ	salmon roe
kai-bashira	貝柱	scallop
kani	かに	crab
katsuo	かつお	bonito
maguro	まぐろ	tuna
tai	鯛	sea bream
tamago	たまご	sweetened egg
toro	とろ	the choicest cut of fatty tuna belly
unagi	うなぎ	eel with a sweet sauce
uni	うに	sea urchin roe

Sukiyaki & Shabu-shabu

Restaurants usually specialise in both these dishes. Popular in the West, sukiyaki is a favourite of most foreign visitors to Japan. Sukiyaki consists of thin slices of beef cooked in a broth of *shōyu*, sugar and sake, and is accompanied by a variety of vegetables and tofu. After cooking, all the ingredients are dipped in raw egg before being eaten. When made with high-quality beef, like Kōbe beef, it is a sublime experience.

Shabu-shabu consists of thin slices of beef and vegetables cooked by swirling the ingredients in a light broth, then dipping them in a variety of special sesame seed and citrus-based sauces. Both of these dishes are prepared in a pot over a fire at your private table; don't fret about preparation – the waiter will usually help you get started, and keep a close watch as you proceed. The key is to take your time, add the ingredients a little at a time and savour the flavours as you go.

Sukiyaki and *shabu-shabu* restaurants usually have traditional Japanese décor and sometimes a picture of a cow to help you identify them. Ordering is not difficult. Simply say sukiyaki or *shabu-shabu* and indicate how many people are dining. Expect to pay from ¥3000 to ¥10,000 per person.

Tempura

Tempura consists of portions of fish, prawns and vegetables cooked in fluffy, nongreasy batter. When you sit down at a tempura restaurant, you will be given a small bowl of *ten-tsuyu* (a light brown sauce), and a plate of grated *daikon* to mix into the sauce. Dip each piece of tempura into this sauce before eating it. Tempura is best when it's hot, so don't wait too long – use the sauce to cool each piece, and dig in.

> 'Tempura is best when it's hot'

While it's possible to order à la carte, most diners choose to order *teishoku* (full set), which includes rice, *miso-shiru* and Japanese pickles. Some tempura restaurants offer tempura courses that include different numbers of tempura pieces.

Expect to pay between ¥2000 and ¥10,000 for a full tempura meal. Finding these restaurants is tricky as they have no distinctive façade or décor. If you look through the window you'll see customers around the counter watching the chefs as they work over large woks filled with oil.

tempura moriawase	天ぷら盛り合わせ	a selection of tempura
shōjin age	精進揚げ	vegetarian tempura
kaki age	かき揚げ	tempura with shredded vegetables or fish

Rāmen

The Japanese imported this dish from China and put their own spin on it to make what is one of the world's most delicious fast foods. *Rāmen* dishes are big bowls of noodles in a meat broth, served with a variety of toppings, such as sliced pork, bean sprouts and leeks. In some restaurants, particularly in Kansai, you may be asked if you'd prefer *kotteri* (thick) or *assari* (thin) soup. Other than this, ordering is simple: just sidle up to the counter and say *rāmen*, or ask for any of the other choices usually on offer (a list follows). Expect to pay between ¥500 and ¥900 for a bowl. Since *rāmen* is derived from Chinese cuisine, some *rāmen* restaurants also serve *chāhan* or *yaki-meshi* (both dishes are fried rice), *gyōza* (dumplings) and *kara-age* (deep-fried chicken pieces).

Rāmen restaurants are easily distinguished by their long counters lined with customers hunched over steaming bowls. You can sometimes hear a *rāmen* shop as you wander by – it's considered polite to slurp the noodles and aficionados claim that slurping brings out the full flavour of the broth.

rāmen	ラーメン	soup and noodles with a sprinkling of meat and vegetables
chāshū-men	チャーシュー麺	rāmen topped with slices of roasted pork
wantan-men	ワンタン麺	rāmen with meat dumplings
miso-rāmen	みそラーメン	rāmen with miso-flavoured broth
chānpon-men	ちゃんぽん麺	Nagasaki-style rāmen

Soba & Udon

Soba and udon are Japan's answer to Chinese-style *rāmen*. *Soba* are thin, brown buckwheat noodles; udon are thick, white wheat noodles. Most Japanese noodle shops serve both *soba* and udon in a variety of ways. Noodles are usually served in a bowl containing a light, bonito-flavoured broth, but you can also order them served cold and piled on a bamboo screen with a cold broth for dipping.

By far the most popular type of cold noodles is *zaru soba*, which is served with bits of *nori* (seaweed) on top. If you order these noodles, you'll receive a small plate of wasabi and sliced spring onions – put these into the cup of broth and eat the noodles by dipping them in this mixture. At the end of your meal, the waiter will give you some hot broth to mix with the leftover sauce, which you drink like a kind of tea. As with *rāmen*, you should feel free to slurp as loudly as you please.

Soba and udon places are usually quite cheap (about ¥900 a dish), but some fancy places can be significantly more expensive (the décor is a good indication of the price). See Noodles Dishes under *Shokudō*, earlier, for more *soba* and udon dishes.

| zaru soba | ざるそば | cold noodles with seaweed strips served on a bamboo tray |

Unagi

Unagi (eel) is an expensive and popular delicacy in Japan. Even if you can't stand the creature when served in your home country, you owe it to yourself to try *unagi* at least once while in Japan. It's cooked over hot coals and brushed with a rich sauce of *shōyu* and sake. Full *unagi* dinners can be expensive, but many *unagi* restaurants offer *unagi bentō* (boxed lunches) and lunch sets for around ¥1500. Most *unagi* restaurants display plastic models of their sets in their front windows, and may have barrels of live eels to entice passers-by.

unagi teishoku	うなぎ定食	full-set unagi meal with rice, grilled eel, eel-liver soup and pickles
una-don	うな丼	grilled eel over a bowl of rice
unajū	うな重	grilled eel over a flat tray of rice
kabayaki	蒲焼き	skewers of grilled eel without rice

Fugu

The deadly *fugu* (globefish or pufferfish) is eaten more for the thrill than the taste. It's actually rather bland – most people liken the taste to chicken – but is acclaimed for its fine texture. Nonetheless, if you have the money to lay out for a *fugu* dinner (around ¥10,000), it makes a good 'been there, done that' story back home (see the boxed text, p84).

Although the danger of *fugu* poisoning is negligible, some Japanese joke that you should always let your dining companion try the first piece – if they are still talking after five minutes, you can consider it safe and have

'you owe it to yourself to try *unagi* at least once while in Japan'

'*Fugu* is a seasonal delicacy best eaten in winter'

some yourself. If you need a shot of liquid courage in order to get you started, try a glass of *hirezake* (toasted *fugu* tail in hot sake) – the traditional accompaniment to a *fugu* dinner.

Fugu is a seasonal delicacy best eaten in winter. *Fugu* restaurants usually serve only *fugu*, and can be identified by a picture of a *fugu* on the sign out the front.

Fugu is the speciality of western Honshū, and Shimonoseki is a good place to give it a try. Of course, you can also find *fugu* in other parts of Japan.

fugu teishoku	ふぐ定食	a set course of *fugu* served several ways, plus rice and soup
fugu chiri	ふぐちり	a stew made from *fugu* and vegetables
fugu sashimi	ふぐ刺身	thinly sliced raw *fugu*
yaki fugu	焼きふぐ	*fugu* grilled on a hibachi at your table

Tonkatsu

Tonkatsu is a deep-fried breaded pork cutlet that is served with a special sauce, usually as part of a set meal *(tonkatsu teishoku)*. *Tonkatsu* is served both at speciality restaurants and at *shokudō*. Naturally, the best *tonkatsu* is to be found at the speciality places, where a full set will cost ¥1500 to ¥2500. When ordering *tonkatsu*, you are able to choose between *rōsu* (a fatter cut of pork) and *hire* (a leaner cut).

tonkatsu teishoku	とんかつ定食	a set meal of *tonkatsu*, rice, *miso shiru* and shredded cabbage
minchi katsu	ミンチカツ	minced pork cutlet
hire katsu	ヒレかつ	*tonkatsu* fillet
kushi katsu	串かつ	deep-fried pork and vegetables on skewers

Kushiage & Kushikatsu

This is the fried food to beat all fried foods. *Kushiage* and *kushikatsu* are deep-fried skewers of meat, seafood and vegetables eaten as an accompaniment to beer. *Kushi* means 'skewer' and if food can be fit on one, it's probably on the menu. Cabbage is often eaten with the meal.

You order *kushiage* and *kushikatsu* by the skewer (one skewer is *ippon*, but you can always use your fingers to indicate how many you want). Like *yakitori*, this food is popular with after-work salarymen and students and is therefore fairly inexpensive, though there are upmarket places. Expect to pay ¥2000 to ¥5000 for a full meal and a couple of beers. Not particularly distinctive in appearance, the best *kushiage* and *kushikatsu* places are found by asking a Japanese friend.

ebi	海老	shrimp
ika	いか	squid
renkon	れんこん	lotus root
tama-negi	玉ねぎ	white onion
gyū-niku	牛肉	beef pieces
shiitake	しいたけ	Japanese mushrooms
ginnan	銀杏	ginkgo nuts
imo	いも	potato

Okonomiyaki

The name means 'cook what you like', and an *okonomiyaki* restaurant provides you with an inexpensive opportunity to do just that. Sometimes described as Japanese pizza or pancake, the resemblance is in form only. At an *okonomiyaki* restaurant you sit around a *teppan* (iron hotplate), armed with a spatula and chopsticks to cook your choice of meat, seafood and vegetables in a cabbage and vegetable batter.

Some restaurants will do most of the cooking and bring the nearly finished product over to your hotplate for you to season with *katsuo bushi* (bonito flakes), *shōyu, ao-nori* (an ingredient similar to parsley), Japanese Worcestershire-style sauce and mayonnaise. Cheaper places, however, will simply hand you a bowl filled with the ingredients, and expect you to cook it for yourself. If this happens, don't panic. First, mix the batter and filling thoroughly, then place it on the hotplate, flattening it into a pancake shape. After five minutes or so, use the spatulas to flip it and cook for another five minutes. Then dig in.

Most *okonomiyaki* places also serve *yaki-soba* (fried noodles) and *yasai-itame* (stir-fried vegetables). All of this is washed down with mugs of draught beer.

One final word: don't worry too much about preparation of the food – as a foreigner you will be expected to be awkward, and the waiter will keep a sharp eye on you to make sure no real disasters occur.

mikkusu	ミックスお好み焼き	mixed fillings of seafood, *okonomiyaki* meat and vegetables
modan-yaki	モダン焼き	*okonomiyaki* with *yaki soba* and a fried egg
ika okonomiyaki	いかお好み焼き	squid *okonomiyaki*
gyū okonomiyaki	牛お好み焼き	beef *okonomiyaki*
negi okonomiyaki	ネギお好み焼き	thin *okonomiyaki* with spring onions

> 'kaiseki is a largely vegetarian affair'

Kaiseki

Kaiseki is the pinnacle of Japanese cuisine, where ingredients, preparation, setting and presentation come together to create a dining experience quite unlike any other. Born as an adjunct to the tea ceremony, *kaiseki* is a largely vegetarian affair (though fish is often served, meat never appears on the *kaiseki* menu). One usually eats *kaiseki* in the private room of a *ryōtei* (an especially elegant style of traditional restaurant), often overlooking a private, tranquil garden. The meal is served in several small courses, giving the diner an opportunity to admire the plates and bowls, which are carefully chosen to complement the food and season. Rice is eaten last (usually with an assortment of pickles) and the drink of choice is sake or beer.

All this comes at a steep price – a good *kaiseki* dinner costs upwards of ¥10,000 per person. A cheaper way to sample the delights of *kaiseki* is to visit a *kaiseki* restaurant for lunch. Most places offer a boxed lunch containing a sampling of their dinner fare for around ¥2500.

Unfortunately for foreigners, *kaiseki* restaurants can be intimidating places to enter. If possible, bring a Japanese friend or ask a Japanese friend to call ahead and make arrangements.

kaiseki	懐石	traditional, expensive Kyoto-style cuisine
ryōtei	料亭	a restaurant serving a variety of traditional Japanese dishes
bentō	弁当	boxed lunch
ume	梅	regular course
take	竹	special course
matsu	松	extraspecial course

Sweets

Although most restaurants don't serve dessert (plates of sliced fruit are sometimes served at the end of a meal), there is no lack of sweets in Japan. Most sweets (known generically as *wagashi*) are sold in speciality stores for you to eat at home. Many of the more delicate-looking ones are made to balance the strong, bitter taste of the special *matcha* tea served during the tea ceremony.

Some Westerners find Japanese sweets a little challenging, due to the liberal use of a sweet, red adzuki-bean paste called *anko*. This unusual filling turns up in even the most innocuous-looking pastries. But don't let anyone make up your mind for you: try a Japanese sweet for yourself.

With such a wide variety of sweets, it's impossible to list all the names. However, you'll probably find many variations on the *anko*-covered-by-*mochi* theme.

Sweet shops are easy to spot; they usually have open fronts with their wares laid out in wooden trays to entice passers-by. Buying sweets is simple – just point at what you want and indicate with your fingers how many you'd like.

wagashi	和菓子	Japanese-style sweets
anko	あんこ	sweet paste or jam made from adzuki beans
mochi	餅	pounded rice cakes made of glutinous rice
yōkan	ようかん	sweet red-bean jelly

DRINKS

Drinking plays a big role in Japanese society, and there are few social occasions where beer or sake is not served. Alcohol (in this case sake) also plays a ceremonial role in various Shintō festivals and rites, including the marriage ceremony. As a visitor to Japan, you'll probably find yourself in lots

---

EATING IN A JAPANESE RESTAURANT

When you enter a restaurant in Japan, you'll be greeted with a hearty 'Irasshaimase!' (Welcome!). In all but the most casual places the waiter will next ask you 'Nan-mei sama?' (How many people?). Answer with your fingers, which is what the Japanese do. You will then be led to a table, a place at the counter or a tatami room.

At this point you will be given an *oshibori* (a hot towel), a cup of tea and a menu. The *oshibori* is for wiping your hands and face. When you're done with it, just roll it up and leave it next to your place. Now comes the hard part: ordering. If you don't read Japanese you can use the romanised translations in this book to help you, or direct the waiter's attention to the Japanese script. If this doesn't work there are two phrases which may help: 'O-susume wa nan desu ka?' (What do you recommend?) and 'O-makase shimasu' (Please decide for me). If you're still having problems, you can try pointing at other diners' food or, if the restaurant has them, dragging the waiter outside to point at the plastic food models in the window.

When you've finished eating, you can signal for the bill by crossing one index finger over the other to form the sign of an 'x'. This is the standard sign for 'cheque please'. You can also say 'O-kanjō kudasai'. Remember there is no tipping in Japan and tea is free of charge. Usually you will be given a bill to take to the cashier at the front of the restaurant. At more upmarket places, the host of the party will discreetly excuse him- or herself to pay before the group leaves. Unlike some places in the West, one doesn't usually leave cash on the table by way of payment. Only the bigger and more international places take credit cards, so cash is always the surer option.

When leaving, it is polite to say to the restaurant staff, 'Gochisō-sama deshita' which means, 'It was a real feast'. The Useful Words & Phrases section (p85) contains more useful restaurant words and phrases.

of situations where you are invited to drink, and tipping back a few beers or glasses of sake is a great way to get to know the locals. However, if you don't drink alcohol, it's no big deal. Simply order *oolong cha* (oolong tea) in place of beer or sake. While some folks might put pressure on you to drink alcohol, you can diffuse this pressure by saying '*sake o nomimasen*' (I don't drink alcohol).

What you pay for your drink depends on where you drink and, in the case of hostess bars, with whom you drink. Hostess bars are the most expensive places to drink (up to ¥10,000 per drink), followed by upmarket traditional Japanese bars, hotel bars, beer halls and casual pubs. If you are not sure about a place, ask about prices and cover charges before sitting down. As a rule, if you are served a small snack with your first round, you'll be paying a cover charge (usually a few hundred yen, but sometimes much more).

Izakaya and *yakitori-ya* are cheap places for beer, sake and food in a casual atmosphere resembling that of a pub. All Japanese cities, whether large or small, will have a few informal bars with reasonable prices. Such places are popular with young Japanese and resident *gaijin* (foreigners), who usually refer to such places as *gaijin* bars. In summer, many department stores open up beer gardens on the roof. Many of these places offer all-you-can-eat/drink specials for around ¥3000 per person.

'rice wine has been brewed for centuries in Japan'

| izakaya | 居酒屋 | pub-style restaurant |
| yakitori-ya | 焼鳥屋 | yakitori restaurant |

Beer

Introduced at the end of the 1800s, *biiru* (beer) is now the favourite tipple of the Japanese. The quality is generally excellent and the most popular type is light lager, although recently some breweries have been experimenting with darker brews. The major breweries are Kirin, Asahi, Sapporo and Suntory. Beer is dispensed everywhere, from vending machines to beer halls, and even in some temple lodgings. A standard can of beer from a vending machine is about ¥250, although some of the gigantic cans cost over ¥1000. At bars, a beer starts at ¥500 and the price climbs upwards, depending on the establishment. *Nama biiru* (draught beer) is widely available, as are imported beers.

| biiru | ビール | beer |
| nama biiru | 生ビール | draught beer |

Sake

Rice wine has been brewed for centuries in Japan. Once restricted to imperial brewers, it was later produced at temples and shrines across the country. In recent years, consumption of beer has overtaken that of sake, but it's still a standard item in homes, restaurants and drinking places. Large casks of sake are often seen piled up as offerings outside temples and shrines, and the drink plays an important part in most celebrations and festivals.

Most Westerners come to Japan with a bad image of sake, the result of having consumed low-grade brands overseas. Although it won't appeal to all palates, some of the higher grades are actually very good, and a trip to a restaurant specialising in sake is a great way to sample some of the better brews.

There are several major types of sake, including *nigori* (cloudy), *nama* (unrefined) and regular, clear sake. Of these, clear sake is by far the most common. Clear sake is usually divided into three grades: *tokkyū* (premium), *ikkyū* (first grade) and *nikyū* (second grade). *Nikyū* is the routine choice. Sake can be further divided into *karakuchi* (dry) and *amakuchi* (sweet). As well as the national brewing giants, there are thousands of provincial brewers producing local brews called *jizake*.

Sake is served *atsukan* (warm) and *reishu* (cold), with warm sake, not surprisingly, being more popular in winter. When you order sake, it will usually be served in a small flask called *tokkuri*. These come in two sizes, so you should specify whether you want *ichigō* (small) or *nigō* (large). From these flasks you pour the sake into small ceramic cups called *o-choko* or *sakazuki*. Another way to sample sake is to drink it from a small wooden box called *masu*, with a bit of salt on the rim.

However you drink it, with a 17% alcohol content, sake (particularly the warm stuff) is likely to go right to your head. After a few bouts with sake you'll come to understand why the Japanese drink it in such small cups. Particularly memorable is a real sake hangover born of too much cheap sake. The best advice is not to indulge the day before you have to get on a plane.

sake	酒	Japanese rice wine
nigori	にごり	cloudy sake
nama	生	regular clear sake
tokkyū	特級	premium grade sake
ikkyū	一級	first-grade sake
nikkyū	二級	second-grade sake
karakuchi	辛口	dry sake
amakuchi	甘口	sweet sake
jizake	地酒	local brew
atsukan	あつかん	warm sake
reishu	冷酒	cold sake
o-choko	おちょこ	ceramic sake cup
sakazuki	杯	ceramic sake cup

'After a few bouts with sake you'll come to understand why the Japanese drink it in such small cups'

Shōchū

For those looking for a quick and cheap escape route from the sorrows of the world, *shōchū* is the answer. It's a distilled spirit made from a variety of raw materials, including potato (in which case it's called *imo-jōchū*) and barley (in which case it's called *mugi-jōchū*). It's quite strong, with an alcohol content of about 30%. In recent years it has been resurrected from its previous lowly status (it was used as a disinfectant in the Edo period) to become a trendy drink. You can drink it *oyu-wari* (with hot water) or *chūhai* (in a highball with soda and lemon). A 720mL bottle sells for about ¥600 which makes it a relatively cheap option compared to other spirits.

shōchū	焼酎	distilled grain liquor
oyu-wari	お湯割り	shōchū with hot water
chūhai	チューハイ	shōchū with soda and lemon

Wine, Imported Drinks & Whiskey

Japanese wines are available from areas such as Yamanashi, Nagano, Tōhoku and Hokkaidō. Standard wines are often blended with imports from South America or Eastern Europe. The major producers are Suntory, Mann's and Mercian. Expect to pay at least ¥1000 for a bottle of something drinkable. Imported wines are often stocked by large liquor stores or department stores in the cities. Bargains are sometimes available at ¥600, but most of the quaffable imports cost considerably more.

Prices of imported spirits have been coming down in recent years and bargain liquor stores have been popping up in bigger cities. However, if you really like imported spirits, it is probably a good idea to pick up a duty-free bottle or two on your way through the airport. Whiskey is available at most drinking establishments and is usually drunk *mizu-wari* (with water and ice) or *onzarokku* (on the rocks). Local brands, such as Suntory and Nikka, are sensibly priced, and most measure up to foreign standards. Expensive foreign labels are popular as gifts.

Most other imported spirits are available at drinking establishments in Japan. Bars with a large foreign clientele, including hotel bars, can usually mix anything you request. If not, they will certainly tailor a drink to your specifications.

whiskey	ウィスキー	whiskey
mizu-wari	水割り	whiskey, ice and water
onzarokku	オンザロック	whiskey with ice

Nonalcoholic Drinks

Most of the drinks you're used to at home will be available in Japan, with a few colourfully named additions like Pocari Sweat and Calpis Water. One convenient aspect of Japan is the presence of drink machines on virtually every street corner, and at ¥120, refreshment is rarely more than a few steps away.

COFFEE & TEA

Kōhii (coffee) served in a *kisaten* (coffee shop) tends to be expensive in Japan, costing between ¥350 and ¥500 a cup, with some places charging up to ¥1000. A cheap alternative is one of the newer coffee-restaurant chains like Doutor or Pronto, or doughnut shops like Mr Donut (which offers free refills). An even cheaper alternative is a can of coffee, hot or cold, from a vending machine. Although unpleasantly sweet, at ¥120 the price is hard to beat.

When ordering coffee at a coffee shop in Japan, you'll be asked whether you like it *hotto* (hot) or *aisu* (cold). Black tea also comes hot or cold, with *miruku* (milk) or *remon* (lemon). A good way to start a day of sightseeing in Japan is with a *mōningu setto* (morning set) of tea or coffee, toast and eggs, which costs around ¥400.

kōhii	コーヒー	regular coffee
burendo kōhii	ブレンドコーヒー	blended coffee, fairly strong
american kōhii	アメリカンコーヒー	weak coffee
kōcha	紅茶	black, British-style tea
kafe ōre	カフェオレ	café au lait, hot or cold
orenji jūsu	オレンジジュース	orange juice

JAPANESE TEA

Unlike black tea, which Westerners are familiar with, most Japanese tea is green and contains a lot of vitamin C and caffeine. The powdered form used in the tea ceremony is called *matcha* and is drunk after being whipped into a frothy consistency. The more common form, a leafy green tea, is simply called *o-cha*, and is drunk after being steeped in a pot. In addition to green tea, you'll probably drink a lot of a brownish tea called *bancha*, which restaurants serve for free. In summer, a cold beverage called *mugicha* (roasted barley tea) is served in private homes.

'most Japanese tea is green and contains a lot of vitamin C and caffeine'

o-cha	お茶	green tea
sencha	煎茶	medium-grade green tea
matcha	抹茶	powdered green tea used in the tea ceremony
bancha	番茶	ordinary-grade green tea, has a brownish colour
mugicha	麦茶	roasted barley tea

CELEBRATIONS

When the Japanese celebrate it must include food and drink, and lots of it, whether it is in a rural festival to appease the rice gods (themselves not averse to the odd glass of sake) or in the party-hard *izakaya* of the big cities. And it's fun. Everyone seems to know about the famous Japanese reserve – everyone, that is, except the Japanese themselves.

The celebratory year begins in homes and restaurants on 1 January, with the multicourse, lavish, colourful *osechi-ryōri*. Served in *jūbako* (four-layered lacquerware boxes), *osechi* originated primarily as a means of giving the overworked Japanese housewife three days' much-needed rest – its ingredients last well.

The third of February sees beans employed not as a meal ingredient, but as weapons in the fight against evil, at the Setsubun Matsuri. At shrines throughout the country, worshippers and tourists gleefully pepper costumed demons with hard soy beans, to the cry of '*oni wa soto, fuku wa uchi*' (out with the demons, in with good luck). The ceremony traditionally marks the end of winter, though this must have been calculated by an obscure ancient calendrical theorem, because it is always bloody freezing. Householders scatter soy beans through their homes for similar protection against evil, and then, for added good luck, consume the number of beans equivalent to their age. The citizens of Kyoto, a city historically beset by fires, plagues and invasions, have adopted their own unique talismanic ritual in addition to the above. They face this year's '*ehō*' (lucky direction), and consume, without talking, a double-sized roll of *maki-zushi*.

'Householders scatter soy beans through their homes for protection against evil'

Common at many celebrations, but especially at the Hina Matsuri (Girls' Day celebration; 3 March) is *seki-han*, red rice, made from glutinous and nonglutinous rice mixed with either *azuki* or black-eyed peas, which give it its sweetness and characteristic pink colour. This colour is the reason it is given to pubescent girls to commemorate their first menstruation. The Hina Matsuri sees gender-role enforcement meeting culinary custom as young girls are given Venus clams, their two identical halves representing faithfulness, their closed shell chastity. In addition to *seki-han*, diamond-shaped *hishi-mochi* rice cakes, *hina-zushi* (pink, yellow and brown sushi) and *shiro-zake* (white, cloudy sake) is commonly served.

Late March or early April sees the much-anticipated coming of the cherry blossoms. The entire nation is glued to the TV to follow the *sakura-zensen,* 'the cherry-blossom front', as it works slowly northwards from mid-Kyūshū through Shikoku and Honshū until it finally hits Hokkaidō sometime in May. Accompanying the front are *hanami,* the 'flower-viewing' parties that during the brief, glorious reign of the pink blossoms, transform every inch of open space into a riot of alcohol-drenched, raucous contemplation of the evanescence of life and beauty.

The Tango no Sekku (5 May) Boys' Festival is an altogether more muted family affair. Its culinary highlight is *ise-ebi* (a type of giant prawn or small lobster), which is cleverly carved into the shape of a samurai's traditional armour. It is then served on a bed of vinegared rice, which resembles a flowing river. At the base of the stream are small fried fish, symbolising carp swimming valiantly upstream. Around the plates are iris leaves, representing swords. The overall picture is meant to champion those good ole prefeminist boyish virtues of 'courage' and 'struggle against adversity', with a passing nod to bloodletting and armed warfare. *Mochi* is again present as *kashiwa-mochi,* pounded glutinous rice with a sweet filling, wrapped in an aromatic oak leaf.

The Japanese summer is long, hot and very humid. Its star festival is Kyoto's July Gion Matsuri, nicknamed Hamo Matsuri, the Pike-conger Festival, for the large quantities of the beast consumed during that time. Pike-conger and eel are famed for their invigorating qualities and their ability to restore flagging appetites. Both are summer favourites, especially in Kansai.

The harvest moon on 15 September is the time for *tsukimi* – 'moon-viewing' parties. This aristocratic practice is somewhat in decline, though visitors to Kyoto at this time can hop in a boat and row out to the middle of the lake within Daikaku-ji grounds to compose the odd haiku or waka or two (p304). Whichever poetic form you choose, make sure to have a handy supply of *tsukimi-dango* (rice dumplings on skewers) to fend off hunger. It is customary to offer these, or the newly in-season sweet potatoes, to the lunar object of your poetic meanderings.

> **'The harvest moon is the time for *tsukimi* – 'moon-viewing' parties'**

On 15 November, families with children aged seven, five or three take them to the local shrine for the Shichi-go-san Matsuri. Boys of five are decked out in the male kimono, while girls of seven and three wear their best kimono. It is a major source of tantrum throwing, as most kids are more used to jeans and Converse All-Stars than rope-tight silk and wooden clogs. But the general way to appease the children is with the in-season, freshly roasted chestnuts, either served hot, as-is, from miniature flat-bed trucks parked outside the shrine, or in *kuri-gohan* (chestnut rice) prepared at home.

Old Year's night finishes with the ringing, 108 times, of the *joya-no-kane* (gong), to relegate the traditional 108 Buddhist sins into a past life. The population then heads, en masse, for the country's Shintō shrines to offer prayers and alms to guide them into the new year. Inevitably, it's a freezing midwinter night, and the warm *ama-zake* (sweet sake served at winter festivals) served at the shrine helps keep out the winter chill. The first dish of the year will be *toshi-koshi soba*, long buckwheat noodles symbolising long life and wealth, as *soba* dough was once used by gold traders to collect gold dust. To cries of '*yoi o-toshi o*' (Have a Happy New Year) and, post-midnight, '*akemashite omedetō gozaimasu*' (Happy New Year), the cycle of eating and celebration continues anew...

VEGETARIANS & VEGANS

Vegetarians who eat fish should have almost no trouble dining in Japan: almost all *shokudō, izakaya* and other common restaurants offer a set meal with fish as the main dish. Vegans and vegetarians who don't eat fish will have to get their protein from tofu and other bean products. Note that most *miso-shiru* is made with *dashi* that contains fish, so if you want to avoid fish, you'll also have to avoid *miso-shiru*.

Most big cities in Japan have vegetarian and/or organic restaurants which naturally will serve a variety of choices that appeal to vegetarians and vegans. (See the Eating sections of the destination chapters for specific recommendations.) In the countryside, you'll simply have to do your best to find suitable items on the menu, or try to convey your dietary preferences to the restaurant staff. Note that many temples in Japan serve *shōjin ryōri*, Buddhist vegetarian cuisine, which is made without meat, fish or dairy products. A good place to try this is Kōya-san in Kansai (p380).

For some ways to express your dietary preferences to restaurant staff, see Useful Words & Phrases (p85).

EATING WITH KIDS

Travelling with children in Japan is easy, as long as you come with the right attitudes, equipment and the usual parental patience. There's such a variety of food on offer that even the most particular eaters can find something to their liking, and if noodles and rice begins to pale there's always McDonald's and Japanese fast-food chains in almost every city. At most budget restaurants during the day, you can find 'okosama-ranchi' (children's special), which is often Western style and actually rather good, though its minihamburgers and wiener sausages won't appeal to nonmeat eaters.

The Useful Words & Phrases section (opposite) contains a few phrases that will come in handy when dining out with children in tow.

HABITS & CUSTOMS

Japanese people generally eat breakfast at home, where a few slices of bread and a cup of coffee are quickly taking over from the traditional Japanese breakfast of rice, fish and miso soup as the breakfast of choice. If they don't eat at home, a *mōningu setto* (morning set) of toast and coffee at a coffee shop is the norm.

ARE YOU A CULINARY DAREDEVIL? *John Ashburne*

There are few cuisines that actively threaten to dispatch you into the next life. Japan's famed, poisonous *fugu*, also known as globefish, blowfish or pufferfish, is one such dish. Its ancient nickname is the *teppō*, 'the pistol', from its tendency to bump off careless eaters. Its active ingredient is tetrodoxin, a clear, tasteless, odourless poison 13 times stronger than arsenic. One species of *fugu* contains enough to kill 33 people. Specially trained chefs remove most of the poison, leaving just enough to numb your lips. Though the danger of *fugu* poisoning is negligible, no one ever pisses off *fugu* chefs.

Yet some consumers actively choose to poison themselves. How's this for bold? A good friend's grandfather, a man of somewhat decadent sensibilities, would eat *fugu* liver (a practice now outlawed) and slip into a state of semiparalysis for three days! Apparently the near-death sensation was rather agreeable, and he was always somewhat disappointed when he regained full control of his limbs. Lonely Planet Publications wishes to remind the reader: DO NOT TRY THIS AT HOME.

Fugu, life-threatening as it may be, at least has the saving grace of having shuffled off its own mortal. No such luck with 'dancing-eating' or *odorigui*, the practice of wilfully consuming live animals. It originated in Fukuoka and the chosen Fukuoka victim is usually *shirouo*, a small transparent fish, which at least wriggles to its suffocating oesophagal doom half-drunk, washed down with sake.

Really bold diners can try the same thing with an octopus. In a Gunma sushi shop I once fatally left the ordering to 'friends', who grinned malevolently and asked for the 'special'. The chef promptly lifted a poor cephalopod from a large tank on the counter, sliced up one tentacle, put it on a plate with some soy sauce, and passed the still twisting and writhing limb to yours truly. The sensation, as the suckers attach to the roof of your mouth, is impossible to convey. Equally difficult to put into words is how it feels to try to murder an octopus leg by chewing it to death.

Same sushi shop. Same evening. It got worse. Dismayed by my refusal to pass out, the said friends brought out the big guns in the shape of *shirako*. Staring at the frothy, white objects shaped like pasta-spirals but exuding an unmistakable deep-sea odour, I feebly requested a translation. Poker-faced Mr Suto offered the deadpan 'cod sperm'. I ate. I turned green. I drank large quantities of cold beer.

That was 15 years ago. Since then I have consumed many odd dishes, and survived. But it's only now that I can recognise Mr Suto's translation error. *Shirako* is not 'cod sperm' at all. It is the 'sperm-filled reproductive gland of the male cod'.

Enjoy!

Lunch is often eaten at a *shokudō* or a noodle restaurant, usually in the company of coworkers, but alone if a partner can't be found.

Evening meals are a mixed bag. Many people, of course, eat at home, but the stereotype of the salaryman heading out for drinks and dinner every evening after work with his workmates has some basis in fact.

Weekends are when almost everyone, if they can afford it, heads out for dinner with friends, and at this time, many eateries are packed with groups of people eating, drinking, conversing and generally having a ball.

Mealtimes are pretty much the same as in many parts of the West: breakfast is eaten between 6am and 8am, lunch is eaten between noon and 2pm, and dinner is eaten between 7pm and 9pm.

USEFUL WORDS & PHRASES
Eating Out

Table for (one/two/three/...), please.
(hirori/futari/san-nin/...-nin) onegai shimas[u]   (一人/二人/三人/...人)、お願いします。

I'd like to reserve a table for eight o'clock (tonight/tomorrow night).
(konban/ashita no ban)   (今晩/明日の晩)
hachi-ji ni yoyaku shitai no des[u] ga   八時に予約したいのですが。

We have a reservation.
yoyaku shimash[i]ta   予約しました。

We don't have a reservation.
yoyaku sh[i]teimasen   予約していません。

What's that?
are wa nan des[u] ka?   あれは何ですか?

What's the speciality here?
koko no tokubetsu ryōri wa nan des[u] ka?   ここの特別料理は何ですか?

What do you recommend?
o-susume wa nan des[u] ka?   おすすめは何ですか?

Do you have ...?
... ga arimas[u] ka?   ...がありますか?

Can I see the menu, please?
menyū o misete kudasai   メニューを見せてください。

Do you have a menu in English?
eigo no menyū wa arimas[u] ka?   英語のメニューはありますか?

I'd like ...	*... o kudasai*	...をください。
Please bring me ...	*... o onegai shimas[u]*	...をお願いします。
some/more bread	*pan*	パン
some pepper	*koshō*	コショウ
a plate	*sara*	皿
some salt	*shio*	塩
soy sauce	*shōyu*	醤油
a spoon	*supūn*	スプーン
some water	*mizu*	水
some wine	*wain*	ワイン

The bill/check, please.
(o-kanjō/o-aiso) o onegai shimas[u]   (お勘定/おあいそ)をお願いします。

You May Hear

May I help you?	*irasshaimase*	いらっしゃいませ。
Welcome!	*irasshai!*	いらっしゃい!
By yourself?	*o-hitori-sama des[u] ka?*	お一人さまですか?

(Two/Three/Four) persons?	*(ni/san/yon)*	(二名/三名/四名)
	-mei-sama des[u] ka?	さまですか?
This way, please.	*kochira e dōzo.*	こちらへどうぞ。
May I take your order?		
	(go-chūmon wa) o-kimari des[u] ka?	(ご注文は)お決まりですか。

Vegetarian & Special Needs

I'm a vegetarian.
watashi wa bejitarian des[u] — 私はベジタリアンです。

I'm a vegan, I don't eat meat or dairy products.
watashi wa saishoku-shugisha des[u] kara, — 私は菜食主義者ですから、
niku ya nyūseihin wa tabemasen — 肉や乳製品は食べません。

Do you have any vegetarian dishes?
bejitarian-ryōri ga arimas[u] ka? — ベジタリアン料理がありますか?

Is it cooked with pork lard or chicken stock?
kore wa rādo ka tori no dashi — これはラードか鶏の
o tsukatte imas[u] ka? — だしを使っていますか。?

I'm allergic to (peanuts).
watashi wa (pīnattsu) arerugii des[u] — 私は(ピーナッツ)アレルギーです。

I don't eat ...	*... wa tabemasen*	...は食べません
meat	*niku*	肉
pork	*buta-niku*	豚肉
seafood	*shiifūdo*	シーフード/海産物

Children

Are children allowed?
kodomo-zure demo ii des[u] ka? — 子供連れでもいいですか?

Is there a children's menu?
kodomo-yō no menyū wa arimas[u] ka? — 子供用のメニューはありますか?

Do you have a highchair for the baby?
bebii-yō no isu wa arimas[u] ka? — ベビー用の椅子はありますか?

Tokyo 東京

Sweeping swaths of skyscrapers and flashing neon blaze to the beat of live and recorded sales pitches blaring on Shinjuku streets. Dark-suited salarymen stride down the Ginza strip alongside the impeccably-clad ladies who lunch, arms crooked at the elbow to tote shopping bags from Prada and Louis Vuitton. Train cars fill and empty with surging rush-hour crowds, incense rises from small shrines, and the fish market begins its day before dawn while party people await 5am trains to roll them into bed.

Changing the face (and hair colour) of Tokyo is a younger generation of thinkers, movers and shakers who never knew life in the Bubble Economy. With alternative thinking, intercultural exchange expanding and a birth rate declining, these are fascinating times for Tokyo. Though old Edo is not much in evidence, underneath the concrete jungle and forward-thinking pumps the lifeblood of tradition. Small shops still line the streets of Tokyo's outlying neighbourhoods, and every now and then you'll find a surprising little pocket from another era.

Tokyo is a riddle of contradictions that springs from tensions between large-scale commercialisation and meticulous detail; the frantic rhythms of contemporary consumer culture and the still, quiet moments that are the legacy of other, older traditions. It is a creative behemoth, inevitably reinventing, re-creating, resolving itself… And it may well be the perfect metaphor for the globe as it spins and wobbles through the 21st century. Naturally, it's a blast.

HIGHLIGHTS

- Dodge the flying fish on the floor of **Tsukiji Fish Market** (p110) and reward yourself with early-morning sushi
- Attend the seasonal spectacle of sumō at the **Ryōgoku Kokugikan Sumō Stadium** (p124) for a day of salt-slinging, belly-slapping and solemn ritual
- Get soaked – and steamed, and slackened – with a Japanese bath experience at **Azabu-Jūban Onsen** (p122)
- Commit to film the vampy goth kids at **Jingū-bashi** (p117) who will pose and preen for your photographic pleasure
- View Buddhist artwork, and then contemplate its meaning, in the ornamental garden at **Nezu Fine Art Museum** (p120)
- Get down with your funky self, or observe the wildlife, in the mayhem of **Roppongi's** (p146) nocturnal environs
- Stop for a moment at the Hachikō statue, shop the innumerable shrines to commerce and end your sojourn with a drink in **Shibuya** (p118)

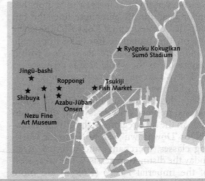

- TELEPHONE CODE: 03
- POPULATION: 12.4 MILLION

TOKYO

HISTORY

Tokyo is something of a miracle, a city that rose from the ashes of WWII to become one of the world's leading economic centres.

Tokyo was formerly known as Edo (literally 'Gate of the River'), so named for its location at the mouth of Sumida-gawa. The city first became significant in 1603, when Tokugawa Ieyasu established his shōgunate (military government) there. Edo grew into a city from which the Tokugawa clan governed the whole of Japan. By the late 18th century it had become the most populous city in the world. When the authority of the emperor was restored in 1868, the capital moved from Kyoto to Edo, and Edo was renamed Tokyo (Eastern Capital).

After 250 years of isolation, Tokyo began transforming itself into a modern metropolis. Remarkably, it has succeeded in achieving this despite two major disasters that each practically levelled the city – the Kantō Earthquake and ensuing fires of 1923, and the US air raids of 1944 and 1945.

Comparable to these geographic setbacks, Japan's economic bubble burst in 1989 and, even though the economy has not yet fully bounced back, Tokyo today is a thriving, uniquely Japanese version of a dynamic 21st-century city.

ORIENTATION

Tokyo is a vast conurbation spreading out across the Kantō Plain from Tokyo Bay (Tokyo-wan). The central metropolitan area is made up of 23 *ku* (wards), while outlying areas are divided into 27 separate *shi* (cities), a *gun* (county) and four island-districts. Nearly everything of interest to visitors lies on or near the JR Yamanote line, the rail loop that circles central Tokyo. Those areas not on the Yamanote line, like Roppongi, Tsukiji and Asakusa, are nonetheless within easy reach, as the whole area is crisscrossed by Tokyo's excellent subway system.

In Edo times, Yamanote referred to 'Uptown': the estates and residences of feudal barons, military aristocracy and other Edo elite, in the hilly regions of the city. Shitamachi, or 'Downtown', was home to the working classes, merchants and artisans. Even today the distinction persists. The areas west of the Imperial Palace (Kōkyo) are more modernised, housing the commercial and business centres of modern Tokyo; the areas

---

TOKYO IN...

One Day

Show up as early as you can to **Tsukiji Fish Market** (p110) for a look at the day's sushi catch – the brave can then breakfast on the same. Follow this with a cup of coffee and a stroll up Chūō-dōri in **Ginza** (p110), browsing the techie toys at the **Sony Building** (p110) or **Leica Gallery** (p110). Stop for a weekday lunch in the plaza of **Tokyo International Forum** (p110), wander around the **Imperial Palace East Garden** (p109), and perhaps end the day with a cocktail at the **Palace Hotel** (p126).

One Week

Jump right in with a walking tour of **East Shinjuku** (p122). Try the one-day itinerary of Ginza and Central Tokyo, above. Make sure to save Saturday night for wild Roppongi, perhaps pulling an all-nighter. Spend a sleepy Sunday afternoon meeting some of Harajuku's **goth kids** (p117), and try to squeeze in a visit in to **Yoyogi-kōen** (p117). Shopping in Shibuya is a must; explore **Loft** (p152) for toys and trinkets. Consider taking a classic tour of **Asakusa** (p113) via *jinriksha* (people-powered rickshaw), followed by a soak in an *onsen* (mineral hot-spring/spa area). Your last day? Revisit and savour your favourite neighbourhood.

---

east of the palace, like Asakusa and Ueno, retain more of the character of old Edo.

A trip around the JR Yamanote line makes a good introduction to the city. You might start at Tokyo Station, the first point of arrival for many travellers. Near to the station are the Marunouchi and Ōtemachi office districts and the high-class shopping district of Ginza. Continuing north from Tokyo Station brings you to Akihabara, the discount electronics centre of Tokyo. Further along is Ueno, home to many of the city's museums. After rounding the top of the loop you descend into Ikebukuro, a bawdy shopping and entertainment district. A few stops further on is Shinjuku, a massive shopping, entertainment and business district considered by many the heart of modern Tokyo. From there, trains continue through to the teen-oriented, fashionable shopping areas of Harajuku, Shibuya and

Ebisu. A swing through Shinagawa at the bottom of the loop then then brings you back to Tokyo Station and completes the loop.

The information in this chapter is presented in an anticlockwise direction around the Yamanote line.

Maps

We strongly recommend you pick up a copy of the free *Tourist Map of Tokyo* from one of the Tourist Information Centers (TICs – see p92). This excellent map has detailed insets of Tokyo's major neighbourhoods as well as subway and rail maps. For more in-depth exploration of the city, pick up a copy of *Tokyo City Atlas: A Bilingual Atlas* (Kodansha), which includes *banchi* (street address) numbers essential for finding addresses.

Tokyo's train and subway lines are much easier to navigate with the excellent colour-coded map that is available free at subway stations and tourist information counters around town. We've included it in the colour section of this guide.

INFORMATION
Bookshops

Tokyo's traditional bookshop area is Jimbō-chō. Mostly catering to Japanese readers, it is still a fascinating place to browse for Edo-period gardening manuals and the like. There's a startling variety of, er, adult literature, too. The annual Jimbō-chō book fair is a bibliophile paradise. It occupies the whole district on 27 to 28 October.

Aoyama Book Center (Map pp106-7; ☎ 3479-0479; 6-1-20 Roppongi, Minato-ku; ☒ 10am-5.30am, closed 2nd & 3rd Tue each month) A prime spot for night owls,

with a great international selection of magazines, right along Roppongi-dōri; take exit 1 from Roppongi Station.

Good Day Books (Map p105; ☎ 5421-0957; 3rd fl, Asahi Bldg, 1-11-2 Ebisu, Shibuya-ku; ☒ Wed-Mon) The best used English-language books are in Ebisu – everything from Hesse to Harry Potter, and a good selection of Japan-related art books at affordable prices; take the east exit from Ebisu JR Station.

Kinokuniya Shinjuku-ku (Map p101; ☎ 3354-0131; 3-17-7 Shinjuku, Shinjuku-ku; ☒ 10am-8pm); Takashimaya (Map p101; ☎ 5361-3301; 5-24-5 Sendagaya, Shibuya-ku; ☒ 10am-8pm) One of Japan's better bookshop chains, Kinokuniya's newer branch in the annex of the Takashimaya Times Square complex has one of the largest selections of English-language books in Tokyo, on the 6th floor. To get there from Shinjuku JR Station, take the south exit and walk towards Takashimaya Times Square. The older main branch is right on Shinjuku-dōri and easily reached from Shinjuku Station's east exit.

Maruzen (Map p96; ☎ 3272-7211; 2-3-10 Nihombashi, Chūō-ku; ☒ 10am-8pm Mon-Sat, 10am-7pm Sun & public holidays) In Nihombashi near Ginza, Maruzen's collection of books is almost equal to Kinokuniya's and it's always much quieter. From Nihombashi Station (exit B1), Maruzen is several metres down Chūō-dōri.

Tower Books (Map p103; ☎ 3496-3661; 7th fl, Tower Records Bldg, 1-22-14 Jinnan, Shibuya-ku; ☒ 10am-11pm) Tower carries a large selection of English-language books and a fabulous array of magazines and newspapers from around the world. Its magazines are considerably cheaper than elsewhere around town. Take the Hachikō exit from Shibuya JR Station and walk north up Jingū-dōri.

Yaesu Book Center (Map p96; ☎ 3281-1811; 2-5-1 Yaesu, Chūō-ku; ☒ 10am-9pm Mon-Sat, 10am-7pm Sun & public holidays) English and other foreign-language books are sold on the 7th floor. Head south from Tokyo Station's Yaesu south exit, and look for the streetside statue of the boy with book and bundled sticks on Sotobori-dōri.

BOOKS ON TOKYO

There are a number of publications that might supplement the one you have in your hands, particularly if you are planning to become a resident of Tokyo. For a comprehensive guide to the city, pick up Lonely Planet's *Tokyo*.

The Best of Tokyo by Don Morton and Tsunoi Naoko (Tuttle) is a light-hearted look at the city, with recommendations ranging variously from 'best traditional Japanese dolls' to 'best toilet'. *Tokyo for Free* by Susan Pompian (Kodansha) lists more than 400 things that you can do for free in a very expensive city.

Old Tokyo: Walks in the City of the Shogun by Enbutsu Sumiko (Tuttle) details walking tours in Tokyo with fascinating historical and cultural detail. *Little Adventures in Tokyo* (Kodansha) by Rick Kennedy, one of Tokyo's most famous expats, introduces some of his secret finds in and around Tokyo.

Tokyo: A Guide to Recent Architecture by Tajima Noriyuki (Elipsis Könemann) is a great guide to Tokyo's architectural masterpieces and oddities.

Conversation Lounges

Mickey House (Map pp94-5; ☎ 3209-9686; 2-14-4 Takadanobaba, Shinjuku-ku; beer & cocktails ¥500; ⏰ 6-11.30pm Mon-Sat) An 'English bar' that serves ¥350 all-you-can-drink coffee and tea as well as reasonably priced beer and food. Entry is free for English-speaking foreigners. Take the main exit at JR Takadanobaba, go east on Waseda-dōri and look for the Tōzai-line subway station entrance on your left; Mickey House is on the 4th floor of the Yashiro Building.

Courier Services

Travellers wary of hauling gigantic packs through Tokyo subways and stations should take advantage of the baggage courier services operating from Narita Airport. For about ¥2000 per large bag, a courier will deliver the goods to your hotel the next day (or pick it up the day before your flight out). At Narita, find the courier counters in each terminal hall; signs in English point the way.

ABC (☎ 0120-9191-20)

NPS Skyporter (☎ 3590-1919)

Cultural Centres

Cultural centres in Tokyo generally act as focal points of the national groups they represent, and usually have good bulletin boards, events, small libraries and language classes.

British Council (Map pp94-5; ☎ 3235-8031; enquiries@britishcouncil.or.jp; 1-2 Kagurazaka, Shinjuku-ku; ⏰ 10am-8.30pm Mon-Fri, 9.30am-5.30pm Sat) From Iidabashi Station, take exit B3 or the JR west exit and walk several blocks south along the canal on Sotobori-dōri.

Goethe Institut Tokyo Bibliotek (Map pp106-7; ☎ 3584-3201; info@tokyo.goethe.org; 7-5-56 Akasaka, Minato-ku; ⏰ 10am-1pm & 2-5pm Mon-Thu, 10am-1pm & 2-3.30pm Fri) Take exit A4 from Aoyama-itchōme Station, and walk eastward on Aoyama-dōri; turn right at Sōgetsu Kaikan and walk one more block to Goethe Institut.

Institut Franco-Japonais de Tokyo (Map pp94-5; ☎ 5261-3933; www.ifjtokyo.or.jp in Japanese & French; 15 Ichigaya Funagawara-chō, Shinjuku-ku; ⏰ noon-8pm Mon, 9.30am-8pm Tue-Fri, 9.30am-7pm Sat, noon-6pm Sun) From Iidabashi Station, take exit B3 or the JR west exit and head south about 300m along Sotobori-dōri.

Emergency

Emergency numbers are: police ☎ 110; and fire and ambulance ☎ 119. You should be able to get your point across in simple English. If you have problems communicating, ring the **Japan Helpline** (☎ 0120-461-997; ⏰ 24hr), an emergency number. See opposite for more information about dealing with a medical emergency.

Immigration Offices

The **Tokyo Regional Immigration Bureau** (Map pp94-5; ☎ 5796-7112; www.moj.go.jp; 5-5-30 Konan, Minato-ku; ⏰ 9am-noon & 1-5pm Mon-Fri) is reached via Tennōzu-Isle Station on either the Tokyo Monorail (board from Hamamatsuchō Station on the JR Yamanote line) or the Rinkai line (transfer from Shin-kiba subway station). Print a map from the web page for a clear route from Tennōzu-Isle Station.

See p734 for information on foreign embassies and consulates in Tokyo.

Internet Access

In some neighbourhoods it can be surprisingly challenging to find Internet access. Manga Kissa, the 24-hour comic reading rooms dotted around the major transport hubs, usually offer inexpensive Net access, but they're often crowded and smoky.

Some of the best Net cafés:

Café J Net New New (Map p103; ☎ 5458-5935; 7th fl, Saito Bldg, 34-5 Udagawa-chō, Shibuya-ku; per hr ¥500; ⏰ 24hr) With cheap eats and bottomless drinks, this is right off Bunkamura-dōri in Shibuya.

Kinko's Ebisu (Map p105; ☎ 5795-1485; 1st fl, Ebisu MF Bldg, 4-6-1 Ebisu, Shibuya-ku); Ikebukuro (Map p100; ☎ 5979-5171; 1st fl, Tokyu Bldg West Tower, 3-28-1 Nishi-Ikebukuro, Toshima-ku); Ueno (Map pp98-9; ☎ 5246-9811; 4-3-4 Higashi-Ueno, Taito-ku) US-based office-service company, offers 24-hour Internet access at most of its outlets throughout Tokyo.

Manga Hiroba (Map pp106-7; ☎ 3497-1751; www.mangahiroba.com/e/; 2nd fl, Shuwa Roppongi Bldg, 3-14-12 Roppongi, Minato-ku; 1st hr ¥380, 30min thereafter ¥150; ⏰ 24hr) Along Gaien-higashi-dōri in Roppongi, this one's handy for pre- or post-party surfing, but is always crowded; cheap pasta, burgers and snacks start at ¥380.

Manga@Cafe-Gera Gera (Map p101; ☎ 5285-0585; 1-23-1 Kabukichō, Shinjuku-ku; 1st hr ¥380, 10min thereafter ¥30; ⏰ 24hr) This is a late-night favourite, in front of Shinjuku Koma Theatre; take the east exit from Shinjuku Station and head for Kabukichō.

Marunouchi Café (Map p96; ☎ 3212-5025; 3-3-1 Marunouchi, Chiyoda-ku; ⏰ 8am-9pm Mon-Fri, 11am-8pm Sat, Sun & public holidays) Just a couple of blocks from either Tokyo, Yūrakuchō or Hibiya subway stations.

Sony Style (Map p108; ☎ 5531-2358; 4th fl, Aqua City, 1-7-1 Daiba, Minato-ku; ⏰ 11am-9pm) For the privilege of free Net access you might have to pretend you are going to buy that digital camera–equipped robotic dog.

TnT Internet Café (Map p100; ☎ 5950-9983; 1st fl, Liberty Ikebukuro Bldg, 2-18-1 Ikebukuro, Toshima-ku; per hr ¥1000; ☯ noon-7pm, closed Sun & 1st, 3rd & 5th Wed of the month) Accessible from the west exit of Ikebukuro JR Station, this Internet café has Internet but no café.

Internet Resources

There are thousands of websites about Tokyo. Here are four of the most useful:

Metropolis (www.metropolis.co.jp) The best all-round site for Tokyo. Lots of events and job listings.

Tokyo Journal (www.tokyo.to) Has interesting articles and interviews from time to time.

Tokyo Meltdown (www.bento.com/tleisure.html) Current and hip, with especially good record-store listings.

Tokyo Q (http://club.nokia.co.jp/tokyoq/index.html) Great all-round Tokyo site. Plenty of listings of current and upcoming events.

Laundry

Most hotels, midrange and up, have laundry services. If you are in a budget ryokan (traditional Japanese inn), ask the staff for the nearest *koin randorii* (laundrette). Costs range from ¥150 for a load of washing, and drying costs about ¥100 for 10 minutes.

Kuriningu-yasan (dry-cleaners) are in almost every neighbourhood. The standards are high and some offer rush service. It's about ¥200 for your basic business shirt.

Left Luggage

There are coin lockers in all train and bus stations in Tokyo. Smaller lockers start at ¥300 (you can leave luggage for up to three days). Otherwise, the Akaboshi (Red Cap) luggage service on the Yaesu side of Tokyo Station will store small/large bags during the day for ¥300/400 (you must pick up your luggage by the end of the day you leave it). For longer periods, there is an overnight luggage-storage service in Tokyo Station that will hold luggage for up to two weeks, with rates starting at ¥500 per bag per day. Ask at the main information counter on the Yaesu side for a map to both of these services.

Libraries

American Center (Map pp106–7; ☎ 3436-0901; 11th &12th fl, ABC Bldg, 2-6-3 Shiba-kōen, Minato-ku; ☯ noon-6pm Mon-Fri) Has a reference library relating to US culture and policies; take the Toei Mita line to Shiba-kōen Station (exit A3) and walk two blocks north along Hibiya-dōri to the ABC Building.

Bibliotheque de la Maison Franco-Japonaise (Map p105; ☎ 5421-7643; biblio@mfj.gr.jp; 3-9-25 Ebisu, Shibuya-ku; ☯ 10.30am-6pm Mon-Sat) From Ebisu JR Station, take the Skywalk to the terminus, turn left at the exit, and walk two blocks before turning left at the primary school. The library will be on your right.

British Council (see opposite) Comprehensive selection of books and magazines.

Goethe Institut Tokyo Bibliotek (see opposite; ☯ noon-6pm Mon-Thu, noon-8pm Fri) With 15,000 volumes.

Japan Foundation Library (Map pp106–7; ☎ 5562-3527; www.jpf.go.jp/e/about/library/index.html; 20th fl, ARK Mori Bldg, 1-12-32 Akasaka, Minato-ku; ☯ 10am-5pm Mon-Fri, closed last Mon each month) Has some 30,000 English-language publications and is open only to foreigners; Roppongi itchōme Station, exit 3.

National Diet Library (Map p106–7; ☎ 3581-2331; www.ndl.go.jp/en/; 1-10-1 Nagata-chō, Chiyoda-ku; ☯ 9.30am-5pm Mon-Sat) This small treasure has 1.3 million books in Western languages; take the Yūraku-chō or Hanzōmon lines to Nagata-chō Station, exit 2.

Media

There's plenty of English-language information on Tokyo, starting with the four English-language newspapers (*Japan Times, Daily Yomiuri, Mainichi Daily News, Asahi Shimbun*). The best listings of Tokyo events can be found in Saturday's *Japan Times*.

The *Tokyo Journal*'s Cityscope listings section makes it worth the purchase price, but the magazine is hobbled by its hipper-than-thou attitude.

These days, the free weekly *Metropolis* is the magazine of choice for most Tokyo residents, although its cultural listings are not as detailed as those in the *Tokyo Journal*. However, for club events and concerts, this is the best magazine.

Medical Services

All hospitals listed have English-speaking staff, and 24-hour emergency departments. Travel insurance is advisable to cover any medical treatment you may need while in Tokyo. Medical treatment is among the best in the world, but also the most expensive.

Japanese Red Cross Medical Center (Map pp106–7; Nihon Sekijūjisha Iryō Sentā; ☎ 3400 1311; 4-1-22 Hiro-o, Shibuya-ku)

St Luke's International Hospital (Map pp94–5; Seiroka Byōin; ☎ 3541 5151; 9-1 Akashicho, Chūō-ku)

Tokyo Medical & Surgical Clinic (Map pp106–7; ☎ 3436 3028; www.tmsc.jp; 2nd fl, Mori Bldg 32, 3-4-30 Shiba-kōen, Minato-ku)

Money

Banks are open from 9am to 3pm Monday to Friday. Look out for the 'Foreign Exchange' sign outside. Some post offices also offer foreign-exchange services, and almost all major branches have English-language ATMs.

Tokyo has a reasonable number of automated teller machines (ATMs) that accept foreign-issued cards. The best bet for foreign travellers is Citibank, which has 24-hour English-language ATMs, open every day. Other ATMs that accept foreign-issued cards are at Sunny's Card Plaza in the Yaesu Underground Mall beneath Tokyo Station; and on the 1st floor of the Yūraku-chō Mullion Building (Map p96).

For lost or stolen credit cards, or credit card enquiries, the main numbers to know in Tokyo:

American Express (☎ 3352-1555, 24hr hotline 0120-020-666)

MasterCard (☎ 5728-5200)

Visa (☎ 5251-0633, 24hr hotline 0120-13-3173)

Post

The Tokyo central post office is outside Tokyo Station (take the Marunouchi exit and then cross the street to the south). Call ☎ 5472-5851 for postal information in English. Poste restante mail will be held at the central post office for 30 days.

Telephone & Fax

Almost all public phones in Tokyo take prepaid phone cards. For domestic directory assistance, call ☎ 104 and ask to be transferred to an English speaker. For details on making international calls from a public phone, see p743.

You can send faxes from the front desk of many hotels (some allow nonguests to use their services for a fee), some convenience stores and from Kinko's copy stores (its basic rate to send an international fax is ¥200 plus phone charges).

Tourist Information

The Japan National Tourist Organization (JNTO) runs a **tourist information centre** (☎ 0476-34-6251; ✆ 9am-8pm) on the 1st floor of Terminal 2 of Narita Airport. Staffed by knowledgeable folks who speak English, this centre is a good place to get oriented or to make a hotel booking if you haven't yet figured out where to stay.

The JNTO operates another **TIC** (Map p96; ☎ 3216-1901; www.jnto.go.jp; 2-10-1 Yūraku-chō, Chiyoda-ku; ✆ 9am-5pm Mon-Fri, 9am-noon Sat) in the Central Tokyo area, on the 10th floor of the Kōtsū Kaikan Building in Yūraku-chō. It has by far the most comprehensive information on travel in Tokyo and Japan, and is an essential port of call. From Yūraku-chō Station, take exit A8, the Kōtsu Kaikan Building is right outside the station.

TIC offices will make accommodation reservations, but only for hotels and ryokan that are members of the **Welcome Inn group** (www.itcj.or.jp/indexwel.html). The Tokyo TIC also offers **Teletourist** (☎ 3201-2911), a round-the-clock taped information service on current events in town. It can also arrange for tours of the city with volunteer guides.

The Information Bureau of Tokyo operates an **information counter** (✆ 9am-6pm Mon-Sat) for foreign travellers; one is on the ground floor of Tokyo Station (Map p96) near the central Yaesu exit.

The **Tokyo Convention & Visitors Bureau** (TCVB; Map p96; ☎ 3287-7024; 1st fl, Tokyo Chamber of Commerce & Industry Bldg, 3-2-2 Marunouchi, Chiyoda-ku; ✆ 10am-5pm Mon-Fri, 10am-4pm Sat, Sun & public holidays) near the Imperial Palace is a good place to pick up a Grutto Pass (¥2000). The pass is a book of tickets entitling the bearer to free or discounted entrance at more than forty Tokyo museums and zoos. It's valid for two months after the first visit, and it's a fabulous deal for travellers who plan on visiting several of Tokyo's museums. The Grutto Pass is also available at most participating museums.

In Asakusa, stop by the friendly **Asakusa Tourist Information Center** (Map pp98-9; ☎ 5246-1151; 4-5-6 Higashi-Ueno, Taito-ku; ✆ 10am-5pm), where guides offer free daily tours of the area on Sundays at 1.30pm and 3pm.

Travel Agencies

In Tokyo there are a number of travel agencies where English is spoken and where discounting on flights and domestic travel is the norm. For an idea of current prices check the *Japan Times* or *Metropolis*.

Three well-established agencies where English is spoken:

Across Traveller's Bureau Ikebukuro (Map p100; ☎ 5391-3227; 3rd fl, Nippon Life Higashi-Ikebukuro Bldg, 1-11-1 Higashi-Ikebukuro, Toshima-ku); Shibuya (Map p103; ☎ 5467-0077; www.across-travel.com; 3rd fl, TK Shibuya

---

KEITAI

Japan has been seriously bitten by the *keitai denwa* (mobile phone) bug. With over 80 million in use, there's almost one *keitai denwa* for every 1.5 Japanese. When you're riding a busy train in Japan, you may feel like half of those 80 million *keitai denwa* are in use around you. When they're not talking on their *keitai*, it seems that young Japanese are busy text-messaging each other, downloading email, scrolling through their digital photos or playing games. The coolest models feature in-built digital video cameras, and of course, hand-held Internet access is *de rigueur*.

East Bldg, 1-14-14 Shibuya, Shibuya-ku; 🕙 10am-7pm Mon-Fri, 10am-5pm Sat); Shinjuku (Map p101; ☎ 3340-6745; 2nd fl, Yamate Shinjuku Bldg, 1-19-6 Nishi-Shinjuku, Shinjuku-ku)

No 1 Travel Ikebukuro (Map p100; ☎ 3986-4690; 4th fl, Daini Mikasa Bldg, 1-16-10 Nishi-Ikebukuro, Toshima-ku) Just across from the west exit of Ikebukuro JR Station, along Azalea-dōri; Shibuya (Map p103; ☎ 3770-1381; 7th fl, Shibuya Ichino Bldg, 1-11-1 Jinnan, Shibuya-ku) From Hachikō exit of Shibuya JR Station, turn right after Tower Records; Shinjuku (Map p101; ☎ 3200-8871; www.no1-travel.com; 7th fl, Don Quixote Bldg, 1-16-5 Kabuki-chō, Shinjuku-ku; 🕙 10am-6pm Mon-Fri) Take east exit of Shinjuku JR Station, cross to north side of Yasukuni-dōri.

STA Travel (Map p100; ☎ 5391-2922; www.statravel.co.jp/en/index.html; 7th fl, Nukariya Bldg, 1-16-20 Minami-Ikebukuro, Toshima-ku; 🕙 9am-5.30pm Mon-Fri, 9.30am-12.30pm Sat)

Useful Organisations & Services

There are innumerable associations for foreign residents and travellers. For the one most suited to your needs and interests, we recommend checking the listings sections of *Metropolis* and *Tokyo Journal*.

There is a lot of information and support available to foreign residents and travellers in Tokyo, including several useful telephone services. For general information try the **Foreign Residents' Advisory Center** (☎ 5320-7744; 🕙 9.30am-noon & 1-4pm Mon-Fri). **JR English Information** (☎ 3423-0111; 🕙 10am-6pm Mon-Fri) offers information on train schedules and fares. **Tokyo English Lifeline** (☎ 5774-0992; 🕙 9am-11pm) can help with information and counselling.

DANGERS & ANNOYANCES

Tokyo can be annoying at times but it is rarely dangerous. If possible, avoid the rail network during peak hours – around 8am to 9.30am and 5pm to 7pm – when the surging crowds would try anyone's patience.

Some travellers may also be disturbed by the overtly sexual nature of some of the signs and sights in Tokyo's red-light districts, like Shinjuku's Kabuki-chō and parts of Ikebukuro. Those venturing into hostess clubs should be prepared to spend liberally, and should watch their drinks carefully, as both drinks and credit cards of the unwary may be corrupted.

Earthquakes

Check the locations of emergency exits in your hotel and be aware of earthquake safety procedures (see p732). If an earthquake occurs, the Japan Broadcasting Corporation (NHK) will broadcast information and instructions in English on all its TV and radio networks. Tune to channel 1 on your TV, or to NHK (639 kHz AM), FEN (810 kHz AM) or InterFM (76.1 FM) on your radio.

SIGHTS

Hopping on and off the JR Yamanote loop and criss-crossing town on the metro lines, you can easily catch the major sights from wherever you're based in Tokyo. From Central Tokyo, where Ginza glam is just a short walk from the serene Imperial Palace, the neighbourhoods to the north harbour the big national museums in Ueno Park and Shitamachi (Old Town). Moving southeast, Shinjuku's skyscrapers are just a few stops from Harajuku and Shibuya, teeming with trendy young fashionistas. Stylish Ebisu lies farther south before the Yamanote line swoops north again. Metro lines whisk you westward towards the diplomatic district of Akasaka and the nightlife of Roppongi. You can even stroll, shop and dine along the waterfront of Tokyo Bay in Ōdaiba, with a lovely driver-less train trip over the bay.

Central Tokyo 東京中心部　　　　Map p96
IMPERIAL PALACE 皇居
The Imperial Palace, or Kōkyo, is the home of Japan's emperor and the imperial family. The palace itself is closed to the public for

(Continued on page 109)

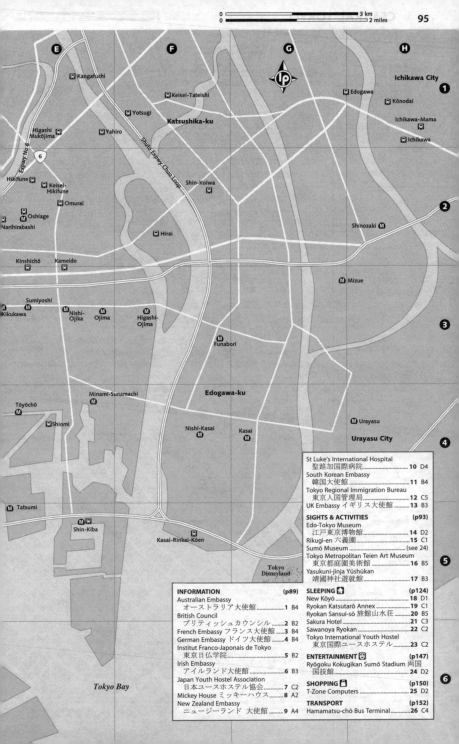

St Luke's International Hospital
聖路加国際病院.................................**10** D4
South Korean Embassy
韓国大使館......................................**11** B4
Tokyo Regional Immigration Bureau
東京入国管理局.................................**12** C5
UK Embassy イギリス大使館..............**13** B3

SIGHTS & ACTIVITIES (p93)
Edo-Tokyo Museum
江戸東京博物館.................................**14** D2
Rikugi-en 六義園............................**15** C1
Sumō Museum ....(see 24)
Tokyo Metropolitan Teien Art Museum
東京都庭園美術館.............................**16** B5
Yasukuni-jinja Yūshūkan
靖國神社遊就館.................................**17** B3

SLEEPING 🏠 (p124)
New Kōyō.....................................**18** D1
Ryokan Katsutarō Annex **19** C1
Ryokan Sansui-sō 旅館山水荘...........**20** B5
Sakura Hotel..................................**21** C3
Sawanoya Ryokan.........................**22** C2
Tokyo International Youth Hostel
東京国際ユースホステル..................**23** C2

ENTERTAINMENT 🎭 (p147)
Ryōgoku Kokugikan Sumō Stadium 両国
国技館..**24** D2

SHOPPING 🛍 (p150)
T-Zone Computers..........................**25** D2

TRANSPORT (p152)
Hamamatsu-chō Bus Terminal..........**26** C4

INFORMATION (p89)
Australian Embassy
オーストラリア大使館........................**1** B4
British Council
ブリティッシュカウンシル **2** B2
French Embassy フランス大使館.........**3** B4
German Embassy ドイツ大使館.............**4** B4
Institut Franco-Japonais de Tokyo
東京日仏学院....................................**5** B2
Irish Embassy
アイルランド大使館............................**6** B3
Japan Youth Hostel Association
日本ユースホステル協会.....................**7** C2
Mickey House ミッキーハウス.............**8** A2
New Zealand Embassy
ニュージーランド 大使館...................**9** A4

0   500 m
0   0.3 miles

A   **B**   **C**   **D**

To Kitanomaru-kōen (600m);
National Museum of Modern
Art (600m); Science Museum
(800m); Crafts Gallery (800m);
Nihon Budōkan (1km);
Yasukuni-jinja (1.5km);
Yasukuni-jinja Yūshūkan (1.5km)

Imperial Palace
East Garden

Kōkyo-Gaien

1

See Roppongi, Nishi-Azabu &
Akasaka Map (pp106–7)

Ōtemachi

Ōtemachi

Ōtemachi

Wadakura
Square

Maruzen
Building

Tokyo

Nijūbashimae

Tokyo

2

Imperial Palace
Outer Garden

Imperial Palace
Plaza

Yaesu

Kyōbashi

Nihombashi

3

Yūrakuchō Line

Hibiya Line

Hibiya

Hibiya-kōen

Marunouchi Line

Hibiya

Yūrakuchō

Takarachō

Kyōbashi

Kyōbashi

Ginza

Ginza

Kyōbashi

Hatchōbori

4

Kokkai-dōri

Chiyoda Line

Uchisaiwaichō

Ginza

Ginza

Shintomi

Shintomichō

5

Shimbashi

Uchisaiwaichō

Sotobori-dōri

Ginza Line

Shimbashi

Shimbashi

Shimbashi

Higashi-ginza

Tsukiji

Shimbashi

Shiodome

Tsukijishijō

6

To
Shinagawa
(2km)

Hamarikyū-teien
(Detached Palace
Garden)

Tsukiji
Produce
Market

Tsukiji
Fish
Market

Tsukiji

To Harumi (1.5km);
Tokyo International
Trade Center (6km)

Yanaka Cemetery

Kototoi-dōri

A

B

C

D

1

2

Yanaka

Kototoi-dōri

● 65

Uguisudani 🚉

22

3

Ueno-Sakurgai

72

To Sawanoya
Ryokan (100m)

🏛 12

🏛 13

🏛 24

34 🏨

Keisei Line

🏛 11

Ikenohata

🚇 2

🏛 23

68

38 🏨

9
🏠

Ueno

🏛 16

🏛 25

🏛 15

4

🛥 26

6
🚹

Suijōdobutsu-ike

Ueno-kōen

71

Dōbutsuen-dōri

Benten-bashi

64

Kōen
Exit

Ueno 🚉

Korin-chō
Motorcycle
Neighbourhood

30
🏨

Bōto-ike

● 66

Yamanote & Keihin-Tōhoku Lines

Takasaki & Jōetsu Lines

Tōhoku Main Line & Jōban Line

Tōhoku & Jōetsu Shinkansen

Korinchō Rd

Shinobazu-dōri

Chiyoda Line

60
●

Shinobazu-ike

Hirokō-ji
Exit
Asakusa Exit

M Ueno

5

🏛 17

Inarichō

Ikenohata

20 🏛

7
●

55 🚻

32 🏨

Shinobazu-dōri

44 🍴

Arcade

Ekimae-dōri

52 🚻

Nakamichi-dōri

45 🍴

49 🍴

57

40 🍴

Higashi-Ueno

Chūō-dōri

43 🍴

54 🚻

6

Yushima M

Kasuha-dōri

Ueno Naka-dōri

Ameyoko

Ueno Okachimachi chūō-dōri

Show-dōri

Yushima

Ueno

Ueno-okachimachi

Okachimachi 🚉

Toei Ōedo Line

Kasuga-dōri

Ueno

0 ___ 300 m
0 ___ 0.2 miles

**To New
Kōyō (500m)**

INFORMATION (p89)

Asakusa Tourist Information Center	
浅草文化観光センター	**1** H6
Police 交番	**2** A3
Police 交番	**3** G5
Post Office 郵便局	**4** F6
Sumitomo Mitsui Bank	
住友三井銀行	**5** H6
Ueno-kōen Information Centre	
上野公園 インフォメーション	
センター	**6** C4

SIGHTS & ACTIVITIES (p111)

Ameya-yokochō Arcade	
アメヤ横丁	**7** B5
Asakusa Kannon Onsen	
浅草観音温泉	**8** H4
Five-Storeyed Pagoda 五重塔	**9** B4
Five-Storeyed Pagoda 五重塔	**10** H5
Gallery of Eastern Antiquities	
東洋館	**11** C3
Gallery of Hōryūji Treasures	
法隆寺宝物館	**12** B3
Hyōkei-kan 表慶館	**13** C3
Kaminari-mon 雷門	**14** H6
National Museum of Western Art	
国立西洋美術館	**15** C4

National Science Museum
国立科学博物館 ... **16** C4
Saigō Takamori Statue
西郷隆盛像 ... **17** B5
Sensō-ji Office 浅草寺事務所 ... **18** H5
Sensō-ji 浅草寺 ... **19** H4
Shitamachi History Museum
下町風俗資料館 ... **20** B5
Sumida-gawa Cruise
隅田川水上バス ... **21** H6
Tokugawa Shōgun Cemetery ... **22** C2
Tokyo Metropolitan Museum of Art
東京都美術館 ... **23** B3
Tokyo National Museum Main Hall
東京国立博物館 ... **24** C3
Tōshō-gū 東照宮 ... **25** A4
Ueno Zoo 上野動物園 ... **26** A4

SLEEPING (p126)

Asakusa Plaza Hotel
浅草プラザホテル ... **27** H6
Asakusa View Hotel
浅草ビューホテル ... **28** G4
Capsule Hotel Riverside
カプセルホテルリバーサイド **29** H6
Hotel Green Capital
ホテルグリーンキャピタル ... **30** C4
Hotel Parkside
ホテルパークサイド ... **31** A6
Hotel Suntargas
ホテルサンターガス ... **32** C6
Kikuya Ryokan ... **33** F5
Ryokan Katsutarō 旅館勝太郎 ... **34** A3
Ryokan Mikawaya Honten
旅館三河屋本店 ... **35** H5
Ryokan Shigetsu 旅館指月 ... **36** H5
Sakura Ryokan ... **37** E3
Suigetsu Hotel Ōgaisō
水月ホテル鷗外荘 ... **38** A4
Taito Ryokan 台東旅館 ... **39** F5
Ueno Kinuya Hotel
上野きぬやホテル ... **40** C6

EATING (p134)

Asakusa Imahan 浅草今半 ... **41** G5
Daikokuya 大黒屋 ... **42** G5
Futaba ... **43** B6
Ganko Sushi がんこ寿司 ... **44** B5
Izu-ei 伊豆栄 ... **45** B6
Kamiya Bar 神谷バー ... **46** H6
Khroop Khrua クローブクルア ... **47** H5
Owariya 尾張屋 ... **48** G5
Samrat ... **49** B6
Sometaro 染太郎 ... **50** F5
Tatsumiya 辰巳屋 ... **51** F5
Ueno Yabu Soba 上野 藪蕎麦 ... **52** C6
Vin Chou 萬鳥 ... **53** F5

DRINKING (p144)

Warrior Celt ... **54** B6

SHOPPING (p150)

Marui Department Store
丸井百貨店 ... **55** C5
Matsuya Department Store
松屋百貨店 ... **56** H5

OTHER

Ameyoko Centre Building
アメ横センタービル ... **57** B6
Asakusa-jinja 浅草神社 ... **58** H4
Banryū-ji 萬隆寺 ... **59** G4
Benzaiten 弁財天 ... **60** A5
Chingo-dō 鎮護堂 ... **61** G5
Dembō-in ... **62** G5
Hōzō-mon 宝蔵門 ... **63** H5
Japan Arts Academy Hall ... **64** B5
Kanei-ji 寛永寺 ... **65** B2
Kiyomizu Kannon-dō ... **66** B5
Public Toilet 公衆便所 ... **67** F5
Rinnō-ji 輪王寺 ... **68** C3
Rox Building ... **69** G5
Sensō-ji Hospital ... **70** H4
Tokyo Metropolitan Festival Hall ... **71** B4
Tokyo National University of Fine
Arts & Music ... **72** B3

Asakusa

Kototoi-dōri

Nishi Asakusa

Dembō-in

Hanakawado

To Hotel Skycourt
Asakusa (100m)

Sumida-
kōen

Kaminarimon-dōri

Kaminarimon

Tawaramachi

Kaminarimon

Asakusa-dōri

Asakusa

Azuma-bashi

To Asahi
Flamme D'Or;
(50m); La Ranarita
Azumabashi (50m);
Sumida River
Brewing Company (50m)

Komagata-bashi

Kokobuki

0   300 m
0   0.2 miles

A   **B**   **C**   **D**

Shutō Expwy No 4

Odakyū Line

Chūō/ Sōbu Line

Sendagaya

1

13

Saikyō Line

4

Sendagaya

53

22

Yoyogi-kōen

2

12

See Shinjuku Map (p101)

26

Meiji-jingū-
naien Garden

72

See Roppongi, Nishi-Azabu & Akasaka Map (pp106-7)

Yoyogi-kōen

Harajuku

35

37

Kitte-dōri

Jingūmae

3

18

Takeshita-dōri

Jingū-bashi 11

14 61

Meiji-jingūmae 42

79

Harajuku

4

80

43

34

Yoyogi-kōen

27

60

Jinnan

45

66

Meiji-dōri

Omote-sandō

Indakira-dōri

Yamanote Line

Saikyō Line

Jingūmae

24

81

85

86

4

Jingū-dōri-kōen

Meiji-dōri

25

59

Hanzōmon Line

Kamiyamachō

50

48

36 5

44

Omote-sandō

Ginza Line

Chiyoda Line

15

20 17

16

32

Aoyama-dōri

63

57

33

65

Jingūmae

Udagawachō

58

68

Kottō-dōri
(Antique St)

51

74

67

6

5

Shōtō

2 47 77

69

64

9

To Blue Note
Tokyo (100m)

7

71

Hanzōmon Line

73

31

62

82

83

40

70

39 3

55

29

Shibuya-ku

21

1

8

Dōgenzaka

38

76

84

Shibuya Miyamasu-zaka-dōri

M Shibuya

46

19 10

Ginza Line

56 54

M Shibuya
Tōkyū Shibuya

49

Keiō Inokashira Line

Shibuya

75

Tōkyū Den-en-toshi Line

52

Tamagawa-dōri

6

41

Shuto Expwy No 3

28

78

Sakuragaokachō

30

23

Tōkyū-Tōyoko Line

Yamanote Line

Dōgen-zaka

Bunkamura-dōri

Sakae-dōri

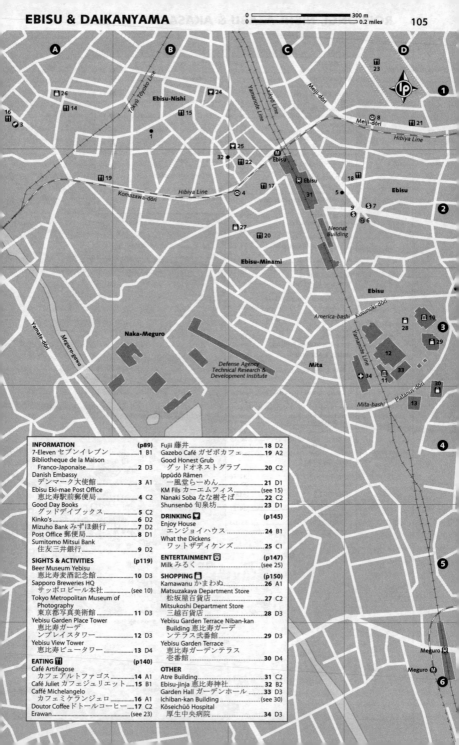

0   300 m
0   0.2 miles

INFORMATION (p89)
7-Eleven セブンイレブン 1 B1
Bibliotheque de la Maison
 Franco-Japonaise
 フランコ・ジャポネ 2 D3
Danish Embassy
 デンマーク大使館 3 A1
Ebisu Eki-mae Post Office
 恵比寿駅前郵便局 4 C2
Good Day Books
 グッドデイブックス 5 C2
Kinko's 6 D2
Mizuho Bank みずほ銀行 7 D2
Post Office 郵便局 8 D1
Sumitomo Mitsui Bank
 住友三井銀行 9 D2

SIGHTS & ACTIVITIES (p119)
Beer Museum Yebisu
 恵比寿麦酒記念館 10 D3
Sapporo Breweries HQ
 サッポロビール本社 .... (see 10)
Tokyo Metropolitan Museum of
 Photography
 東京都写真美術館 11 D3
Yebisu Garden Place Tower
 恵比寿ガーデ
 ンプレイスタワー 12 D3
Yebisu View Tower
 恵比寿ビュータワー 13 D4

EATING (p140)
Café Artifagose
 カフェアルトファゴス 14 A1
Café Juliet カフェジュリエット 15 B1
Caffé Michelangelo
 カフェミケランジェロ 16 A1
Doutor Coffee ドトールコーヒー ... 17 C2
Erawan .... (see 23)

Fujii 藤井 18 D2
Gazebo Café ガゼボカフェ 19 A2
Good Honest Grub
 グッドオネストグラブ 20 C2
Ippúdô Rämen
 一風堂らーめん 21 D1
KM Fils カーエムフィス .... (see 15)
Nanaki Soba なな樹そば 22 C2
Shunsenbô 旬泉坊 23 D1

DRINKING (p145)
Enjoy House
 エンジョイハウス 24 B1
What the Dickens
 ワットザディケンズ 25 C1

ENTERTAINMENT (p147)
Milk みるく .... (see 25)

SHOPPING (p150)
Kamawanu かまわぬ 26 A1
Matsuzakaya Department Store
 松坂屋百貨店 27 C2
Mitsukoshi Department Store
 三越百貨店 28 D3
Yebisu Garden Terrace Niban-kan
 Building 恵比寿ガーデ
 ンテラス弐番館 29 D3
Yebisu Garden Terrace
 恵比寿ガーデンテラス
 壱番館 30 D4

OTHER
Atre Building 31 C2
Ebisu-jinja 恵比寿神社 32 B2
Garden Hall ガーデンホール 33 D3
Ichiban-kan Building .... (see 30)
Köseichûô Hospital
 厚生中央病院 34 D3

INFORMATION	(p89)
Almond アーモンド	1 D5
American Center	
東京アメリカンセンター	2 G6
Aoyama Book Center	
青山ブックセンター	3 D5
ARK Mori Building ARK 森ビル	4 E4
Chinese Embassy 中国大使館	5 C6
Citibank シティバンク	6 D5
Goethe Institut Tokyo	
ゲーテインスティ	
トゥート東京	7 C2
Hobson's ホブソンズ	8 D5
International ATM	
キャッシュコーナー	9 E2
International ATM	
キャッシュコーナー	10 D4
Japan Foundation Library	(see 4)
Japanese Red Cross Medical Center	
日本赤十字社医療センター	11 A6
Manga Hiroba	(see 72)
Netherlands Embassy	
オランダ大使館	12 F5
Nishi-Azabu Post Office	
西麻布郵便局	13 B5
Police Box 交番	14 D3
Police Station 交番	15 E3
Post Office 郵便局	16 D5
Post Office 郵便局	17 D3
Sumitomo Mitsui Bank	
住友三井銀行	18 E2
Tokyo Medical & Surgical Clinic	
東京クリニック	19 F6
Tokyo Mitsubishi Bank	20 E2
US Embassy アメリカ大使館	21 F3
Visa Cash Corner	22 D5
Visa ビザ	23 A3
World Trade Center Building	(see 25)
SIGHTS & ACTIVITIES	**(p119)**
Azabu Jūban Onsen	
麻布十番温泉	24 D6
Hato Bus Tours	25 H6
Hie-jinja 日枝神社	26 E2
Koshi-No-Yu Sento 越の湯銭湯	(see 24)
Mori Art Museum 森美術館	27 C5
Mori Tower	(see 27)
Nezu Fine Art Museum	
根津美術館	28 A5
Ōkura Shūkokan	29 F4
Roppongi Hills 六本木ヒルズ	30 C5
Sōgetsu Art Museum	(see 31)
Sōgetsu School of Ikebana	31 C2
Tokyo City View	
東京シティビュー	(see 27)
Tokyo Tower 東京タワー	32 F6
Zōjō-ji	33 G6
SLEEPING	**(p131)**
Akasaka Prince Hotel	
赤坂プリンスホテル	34 E1
Akasaka Yōkō Hotel	
赤坂陽光ホテル	35 D3

ANA Hotel Tokyo	
全日空ホテル東京	36 E4
Asia Center of Japan	37 C3
Capitol Tōkyū Hotel	
キャピタル東急ホテル	38 E2
Capsule Hotel Fontaine Akasaka	
カプセルホテル	
フォンテーヌ赤坂	39 E2
Capsule Inn Akasaka	
かぷせるイン赤坂	40 D3
Grand Hyatt Tokyo	
グランドハイアット東京	41 C5
Hotel Ibis ホテルアイビス	42 D5
Hotel New Otani	
ホテルニューオータニ	43 D1
Hotel Sunroute Akasaka	
ホテルサンルート赤坂	44 E2
Hotel Ōkura ホテルオークラ	45 F4
Marroad Inn Akasaka	
マロウドイン赤坂	46 D3

TOKYO SUBWAY MAP

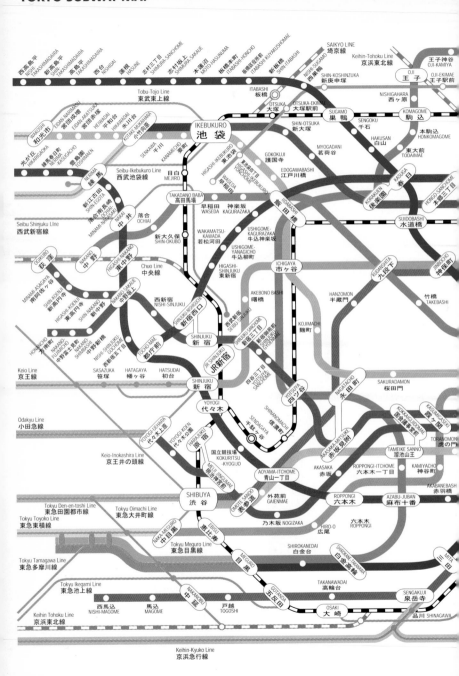

Sensō-ji (p113), Asakusa, Tokyo

GREG ELMS

Sumō wrestlers (p124), Ryōgoku
Kogugikan Sumō Stadium, Tokyo

MARTIN MOOS

Japanese girls in 'costume play' (p117), Tokyo

JOHN ASHBURNE

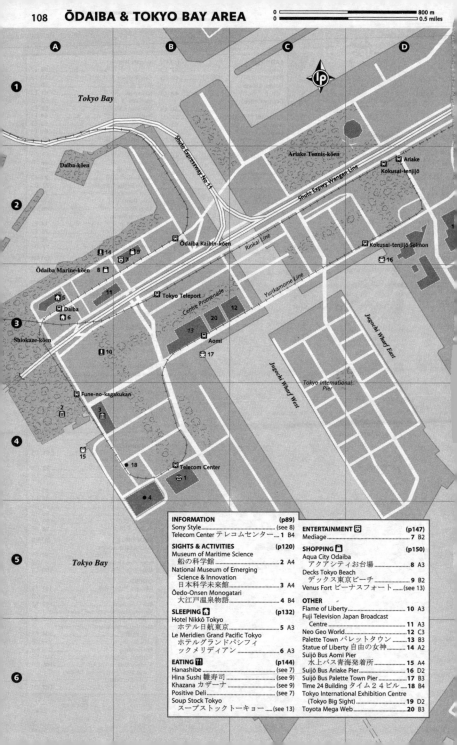

0 |————————| 800 m
0 |————————| 0.5 miles

Tokyo Bay

Shuto Expressway No 11

Daiba-kōen

Ariake Tennis-kōen

Ariake
Kokusai-tenjijō

Ōdaiba Kaihin-kōen

Rinkai Line

Shuto Expwy Wangan Line

Kokusai-tenjijō Seimon
16

14 9
Ōdaiba Marine-kōen 8

5 Daiba
6

11

Tokyo Teleport

Centre Promenade

Yurikamome Line

12

20
13
Aomi
17

Jūgochi Wharf East

3

Shiokaze-kōen

10

Jūgochi Wharf West

Tokyo International
Pier

Fune-no-kagakukan

2

3

15

18

Telecom Center
1

4

Tokyo Bay

INFORMATION	(p89)
Sony Style	(see 8)
Telecom Center テレコムセンター	1 B4

SIGHTS & ACTIVITIES	(p120)
Museum of Maritime Science 船の科学館	2 A4
National Museum of Emerging Science & Innovation 日本科学未来館	3 A4
Ōedo-Onsen Monogatari 大江戸温泉物語	4 B4

SLEEPING	(p132)
Hotel Nikkō Tokyo ホテル日航東京	5 A3
Le Meridien Grand Pacific Tokyo ホテルグランドパシフィックメリディアン	6 A3

EATING	(p144)
Hanashibe	(see 7)
Hina Sushi 雛寿司	(see 9)
Khazana カザーナ	(see 9)
Positive Deli	(see 7)
Soup Stock Tokyo スープストックトーキョー	(see 13)

ENTERTAINMENT	(p147)
Mediage	7 B2

SHOPPING	(p150)
Aqua City Odaiba アクアシティお台場	8 A3
Decks Tokyo Beach デックス東京ビーチ	9 B2
Venus Fort ビーナスフォート	(see 13)

OTHER	
Flame of Liberty	10 A3
Fuji Television Japan Broadcast Centre	11 A3
Neo Geo World	12 C3
Palette Town パレットタウン	13 B3
Statue of Liberty 自由の女神	14 A2
Suijō Bus Aomi Pier 水上バス青海発着所	15 A4
Suijō Bus Ariake Pier	16 D2
Suijō Bus Palette Town Pier	17 B3
Time 24 Building タイム24ビル	18 B4
Tokyo International Exhibition Centre (Tokyo Big Sight)	19 D2
Toyota Mega Web	20 B3

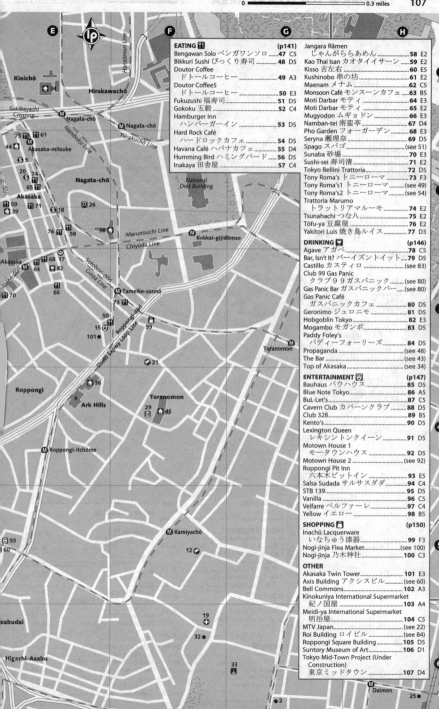

EATING (p141)

Bengawan Solo ベンガワンソロ	**47** C5
Bikkuri Sushi びっくり寿司	**48** D5
Doutor Coffee ドゥトールコーヒー	**49** A3
Doutor Coffee5 ドゥトールコーヒー	**50** E3
Fukuzushi 福寿司	**51** D5
Gokoku 五穀	**52** C4
Hamburger Inn ハンバーガーイン	**53** D5
Hard Rock Café ハードロックカフェ	**54** D5
Havana Café ハバナカフェ	**55** D5
Humming Bird ハミングバード	**56** E3
Inakaya 田舎屋	**57** C4
Jangara Rámen じゃんがららあめん	**58** E2
Kao Thai Isan カオタイイサーン	**59** E2
Kisso 吉左右	**60** E5
Kushinobo 串の坊	**61** E2
Maenam メナム	**62** C5
Monsoon Café モンスーンカフェ	**63** B5
Moti Darbar モティ	**64** E3
Moti Darbar モティ	**65** E2
Mugyodon ムギョドン	**66** E3
Namban-tei 南蛮亭	**67** D4
Pho Garden フォーガーデン	**68** E3
Seryna 瀬理奈	**69** D5
Spago スパゴ	(see 51)
Sunaba 砂場	**70** E2
Sushi-sei 寿司清	**71** E2
Tokyo Bellini Trattoria	**72** D5
Tony Roma's トニーローマ	**73** F3
Tony Roma's1 トニーローマ	(see 49)
Tony Roma's2 トニーローマ	(see 54)
Trattoria Marumo トラットリアマルーモ	**74** D5
Tsunahachi つな八	**75** E2
Tôfu-ya 豆腐屋	**76** E2
Yakitori Luis 焼き鳥ルイス	**77** D3

DRINKING (p146)

Agave アガベ	**78** D5
Bar, Isn't It? バーイズントイット	**79** D5
Castillo カスティロ	(see 83)
Club 99 Gas Panic クラブ99ガスパニック	(see 80)
Gas Panic Bar ガスパニックバー	(see 80)
Gas Panic Café ガスパニックカフェ	**80** D5
Geronimo ジェロニモ	**81** D5
Hobgoblin Tokyo	**82** E3
Mogambo モガンボ	**83** D5
Paddy Foley's パディーフォーリーズ	**84** D5
Propaganda	(see 48)
The Bar	(see 43)
Top of Akasaka	(see 34)

ENTERTAINMENT (p147)

Bauhaus バウハウス	**85** D5
Blue Note Tokyo	**86** A5
BuL-Let's	**87** C5
Cavern Club カバーンクラブ	**88** D5
Club 328	**89** B5
Kento's	**90** D5
Lexington Queen レキシントンクイーン	**91** D5
Motown House 1 モータウンハウス	**92** D5
Motown House 2	(see 92)
Roppongi Pit Inn 六本木ピットイン	**93** E5
Salsa Sudada サルサスダダ	**94** C4
STB 139	**95** C5
Vanilla	**96** C5
Velfarre ベルファーレ	**97** C4
Yellow イエロー	**98** B5

SHOPPING (p150)

Inachū Lacquerware いなちゅう漆器	**99** F3
Nogi-jinja Flea Market	(see 100)
Nogi-jinja 乃木神社	**100** C3

OTHER

Akasaka Twin Tower	**101** E3
Axis Building アクシスビル	(see 60)
Bell Commons	**102** A3
Kinokuniya International Supermarket 紀ノ国屋	**103** A4
Meidi-ya International Supermarket 明治屋	**104** C5
MTV Japan	(see 22)
Roi Building ロイビル	(see 84)
Roppongi Square Building	**105** D5
Suntory Museum of Art	**106** D1
Tokyo Mid-Town Project (Under Construction) 東京ミッドタウン	**107** D4

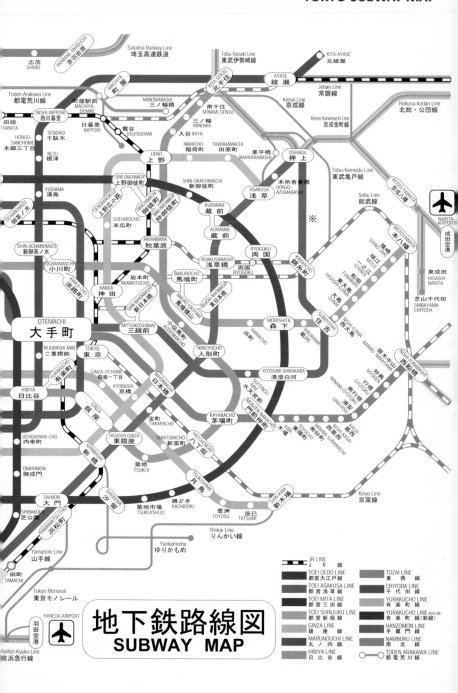

Shibuya (p118), Tokyo

Imperial Palace East Garden (p109), Tokyo

Omote-sandō (p116), Tokyo

Park Hyatt Tokyo (p130), Tokyo

(Continued from page 93)

all but two days of the year, 2 January and 23 December (the emperor's birthday). Even if you can't enter the palace itself, it is possible to wander around its outskirts and visit the gardens, where you can at least get a view of the palace with the bridge, **Nijū-bashi**, in the foreground.

The present palace was completed in 1968. It replaced the palace built in 1888 and destroyed by Allied bombing in WWII. It occupies the site of the castle, Edo-jō, from which the Tokugawa shōgunate ruled Japan. In its time the castle was the largest in the world, though apart from the massive moat and walls, little remains of it today.

It is an easy walk from Tokyo Station, or from Hibiya or Nijū-bashi-mae subway stations, to the Nijū-bashi. The walk involves crossing Babasaki Moat and the expansive Imperial Palace Plaza (Kōkyo-mae Hiroba). The vantage point, which is popular with photographers, gives you a picture-postcard view of the palace peeking over its fortifications, behind Nijū-bashi.

IMPERIAL PALACE EAST GARDEN
皇居東御苑

The **Imperial Palace East Garden** (Kōkyo Higashi-gyoen; ☎ 3213-2050; admission free; ☒ 9am-4pm Tue-Thu, Sat & Sun, last entry 3pm) is the only quarter of the palace proper that is open to the public. The main entrance is through the **Ōte-mon**, a 10-minute walk north of Nijū-bashi. This was once the principal gate of Edo-jō; the garden itself lies at what was once the heart of the old castle. You'll be given a numbered plastic token to turn in when you depart. The store inside the garden sells a good map for ¥150. The nearest subway station is Ōtemachi (C10 exit), which places you about 100m from Ōte-mon.

KITANOMARU-KŌEN 北の丸公園

This park is quite pleasant, and is a good spot for a leisurely stroll or summer picnic. You can get there from Kudanshita or Takebashi subway stations.

Kitanomaru-kōen contains the **Nihon Budō-kan** (☎ 3216-5100), where you may witness a variety of martial arts. South of the Nihon Budōkan is the **Science Museum** (☎ 3212-2440; www.jsf.or.jp/index_e.html; 2-1 Kitanomaru-kōen, Chiyoda-ku; adult/child ¥600/250; ☒ 9am-4.50pm Tue-Sun), which is a decent rainy-day stop for science buffs or

those with children in tow, particularly since most exhibits are interactive. An English booklet is included with the entry fee.

Continuing south from the Science Museum brings you to the **National Museum of Modern Art** (☎ 3214-2561; www.momat.go.jp/english/; 3-1 Kitanomaru-kōen, Chiyoda-ku; adult/18 & under/student ¥420/70/130; ☒ 10am-5pm Tue-Wed, Sat & Sun, 10am-8pm Fri). The permanent exhibition here features Japanese art from the Meiji period (1868–1912) onwards. It is worth checking in the *Tokyo Journal* or *Metropolis* to see if any special exhibitions are being held. Your ticket (hold on to the stub) gives you free admission to the nearby **Crafts Gallery** (☎ 3211-7781; 1-1 Kitanomaru-kōen, Chiyoda-ku; adult/18 & under/student ¥200/40/70; ☒ 10am-5pm Tue-Sun), which houses a good display of crafts such as ceramics, lacquerware and dolls.

YASUKUNI-JINJA 靖国神社

If you take the Tayasu-mon exit (just past the Budōkan) of Kitanomaru-kōen, across the road and to your left is **Yasukuni-jinja** (Map pp94-5; 3-1-1 Kudankita, Chiyoda-ku), the Shrine for Establishing Peace in the Empire. Dedicated to the 2.4 million Japanese war-dead since 1853, it is the most controversial shrine in all Japan.

The Japanese constitutional separation of religion and politics and the renunciation of militarism didn't stop a group of class-A war criminals being enshrined here in 1979; it also doesn't stop annual visits by politicians on the anniversary of Japan's defeat in WWII (15 August).

The loudest protests are from Japan's Asian neighbours, who suffered most from Japanese aggression. This is not to say you should boycott the shrine; it is well worth a visit. Black vans blasting right-wing propaganda (in Japanese) are often there to remind you where you are, however.

YASUKUNI-JINJA YŪSHŪKAN
靖國神社遊就館

Next to the Yasukuni-jinja is the **Yūshūkan** (☎ 3261-8326; www.yasukuni.or.jp; adult/child/student ¥800/300/500; ☒ 9am-5.30pm Mar-Oct, 9am-5pm Nov-Feb, closed 28-31 Aug & 28-31 Dec), a war memorial museum that features items commemorating Japanese war-dead. There are limited English explanations, but an English pamphlet is available. Interesting exhibits include the long torpedo in the large exhibition hall that is actually a *kaiten* (human torpedo), a submarine version of the *kamikaze* (WWII suicide pilots). There are also displays of military uniforms, samurai armour and paintings of famous battles. Perhaps most interesting of all are the excerpts from books (some in English) arguing that America forced Japan into bombing Pearl Harbor.

TOKYO INTERNATIONAL FORUM
東京国際フォーラム

The **forum** (☎ 5221-9000; www.t-i-forum.co.jp/english; 3-5-1 Marunouchi, Chiyoda-ku; ⏰ 8am-11pm), midway between Tokyo Station and Ginza, is a remarkable edifice. The prominent glass wing of this convention centre looks like a glass ship plying the urban waters of central Tokyo. In contrast, the west wing is a boxy affair of cantilevered, overhanging spaces and cavernous atria. Exit A4b from Yūraku-chō Station will put you right into the TIF plaza.

GINZA 銀座

Ginza is to Tokyo what Park Ave is to New York City. Back in the 1870s, Ginza was one of the first areas to modernise, featuring a large number of novel (for Tokyoites of that time) Western-style brick buildings. Ginza was also home to Tokyo's first department stores and other harbingers of the modern world, such as gas lamps.

Today, other shopping districts rival Ginza in opulence, vitality and popularity, but Ginza retains a distinct snob value. It is still the place to go and be seen emptying the contents of a bulging wallet. Even if you are on a tight budget, Ginza is an interesting area in which to browse – the galleries are usually free and there are lots of discount coffee shops.

On Saturday afternoons and Sundays the smaller streets are closed to vehicles, making for a nice stroll. Start your exploration at the Sukiyabashi train crossing, a 10-minute walk from the Kōkyo, directly above Ginza subway station.

Sony Building ソニービル

Perfect for a rainy day, the **Sony Building** (☎ 3573-2371; www.sonybuilding.jp; 5-3-1 Ginza, Chūō-ku; admission free; ⏰ 11am-7pm) has fascinating hands-on displays of Sony's many products, including some that have yet to be released. Although there's often a wait, kids love the free video and virtual-reality games on the 6th floor. If nothing else, you can put your feet up and relax for a while in one of the building's two Hi-Vision theatres.

Galleries

Ginza is overflowing with galleries, many of them so small that they can be viewed in two or three minutes. Others feature work by unknown artists who have hired the exhibition space themselves. Wander around a bit and you'll run into galleries displaying a kaleidoscopic variety of contemporary art – you're sure to be confronted with something intriguing to your particular sensibilities, especially if you're into graphic design. They are scattered throughout Ginza but are concentrated in the area south of Harumi-dōri, between Ginza-dōri and Chūō-dōri.

Idemitsu Art Museum (☎ 3213-9402; 9th fl, Teigeki Bldg, 3-1-1 Marunouchi, Chiyoda-ku; adult/student ¥800/500; ⏰ 10am-5pm Tue-Thu, Sat & Sun, 10am-7pm Fri) holds Japanese and Chinese art and is famous for its collection of work by the Zen monk Sengai. It's a five-minute walk from either Hibiya or Yūraku-chō Station, next door to the Imperial Theatre.

Probably the best of the photographic galleries in the area, showing outstanding work of both up-and-coming photographers and long-time professionals, is **Leica Gallery** (☎ 3567-6706; www.leica-camera.com/kultur/galerie /tokyo/index_e.html; 3rd fl, Matsushima Bldg, 3-5-6 Ginza, Chūō-ku; ⏰ 10.30am-5.30pm Tue-Sun).

Kabuki-za 歌舞伎座

Even if you don't plan to attend a kabuki performance, it's worth taking a look at the beautifully dramatic exterior of **Kabuki-za** (see above).

HAMARIKYŪ-TEIEN 浜離宮庭園

Often referred to in English as the **Detached Palace Garden** (admission ¥300; ⏰ 9am-4.30pm), a visit can be combined either with a visit to Ginza or, via the Sumida-gawa Cruise, with a visit to Asakusa (p113). The garden has walks, ponds and teahouses.

TSUKIJI FISH MARKET 築地市場

The **Tsukiji Fish Market** (☎ 3541-2640; www.tsukiji -market.or.jp; 5-2 Tsukiji, Chūō-ku; ⏰ 24hr) is where all that seafood comes after it's been fished out of the sea and before it turns up on a sashimi platter. The day begins very early, with the arrival of fish and its wholesale auctioning. The wholesale market is not open to the general public – probably a blessing, given that you'd have to be there before 7am to see the action. You are free to visit the outer market and wander around the wholesalers' and intermediaries' stalls that sell directly to restaurants, retail stores and other buyers. It is a fun place to visit, but at its best before 8am. Watch out for your shoes – there's a lot of muck and water on the floor. Be extremely wary of the motorised vegetable-delivery carts that speed around the market, especially if you're with small children. To get there, take the Hibiya line to Tsukiji Station, exit 1.

HIBIYA-KŌEN 日比谷公園

If Ginza has left you yearning for greenery, retrace your steps along Harumi-dōri, back through Sukiyabashi Crossing to Hibiya-kōen. This was Tokyo's first Western-style park, and it makes for a pleasant break, especially if you head for the benches overlooking the pond on the park's eastern side. Also on the park's eastern side, about midway down, is a small restaurant where you can pause for coffee or ice cream. Exit A10 or A14 from Hibiya Station will put you in the park.

Ueno 上野   Map pp98–9

Ueno is one of the last places in Tokyo where the old Shitamachi spirit lingers on. Like Asakusa, it is a place where you can catch a glimpse of what life was like before the economic miracle of the 1970s and '80s. The heart of Ueno is crusty old Ameya-yokochō Arcade, a bustling market that feels worlds away from the hyper-trendy shopping meccas of Shibuya and Harajuku. The best reason to visit Ueno, however, is Ueno-kōen, which has the highest concentration of museums and galleries anywhere in Japan. A trip to Ueno, perhaps paired with a jaunt to nearby Asakusa, is the perfect counterpoint to a day spent in ultra-modern Shinjuku.

UENO-KŌEN 上野公園

Ueno Hill was the site of a last-ditch defence of the Tokugawa shōgunate by about 2000 Tokugawa loyalists in 1868. They were duly dispatched by the imperial army, and the new Meiji government decreed that Ueno Hill would be transformed into Tokyo's first public park. Today, Ueno-kōen may not be the best of Tokyo's parks, but it certainly packs in more attractions than any of the others. Ueno-kōen is accessible via the Park

exit from Ueno JR Station, or exit 7 from the subway. Across the street from the Park exit is a large map showing the layout of the park and museum complex.

The park is famous as Tokyo's most popular site for *hanami* (blossom viewing) in early to mid-April. Of course, this doesn't mean that Ueno-kōen is the best place to see the blossoms (see p116 for an altogether quieter *hanami* spot). In addition to the cherry blossoms, check out the lotuses in the pond, Shinobazu-ike, at the southern end of the park. It's also worth noting that Ueno-kōen is the centre of Tokyo's surprisingly large population of homeless people; their blue tents fill almost every inch of available land in the northern reaches of the park. And in true Japanese tradition, most have shoes lined up neatly outside.

Saigō Takamori Statue 西郷隆盛像

This slightly unusual statue of a samurai walking his dog, near the southern entrance to the park, is a favourite meeting place. Saigō Takamori started out supporting the Meiji Restoration but ended up ritually disembowelling himself in defeated opposition to it. The turnabout in his loyalties occurred when the Meiji government withdrew the powers of the military class to which he belonged (see p659).

Tokyo National Museum 東京国立博物館本館

The **Tokyo National Museum** (☎ 3822-1111; www .tnm.jp; 13-9 Ueno-kōen, Taito-ku; adult/student ¥420/130; ⏰ 9.30am-5pm Tue-Thu, Sat & Sun, 9.30am-8pm Fri Apr-Sep) is the one museum in Tokyo that is worth going out of your way to visit. Not only is it Japan's largest museum, housing some 87,000 items, it also has the world's largest collection of Japanese art. Only a portion of the museum's huge collection is displayed at any one time. Entry is free on the second Saturday of each month.

The museum has four galleries, the most important of which is the **Main Hall** (Hon-kan). It's straight ahead as you enter, and houses a very impressive collection of Japanese art, from sculpture and swords to lacquerware and calligraphy. The **Gallery of Eastern Antiquities** (Tōyō-kan), to the right of the ticket booth, has a collection of art and archaeological finds from all of Asia east of Egypt. The **Hyōkei-kan**, to the left

TOKYO

of the ticket booth, has a collection of Japanese archaeological finds. There is a room devoted to artefacts once used by the Ainu, the indigenous people of Hokkaidō.

Finally, and perhaps best of all, there is the **Gallery of Hōryūji Treasures** (Hōryūji Hōmotsu-kan), which houses some of Japan's most important Buddhist artworks, all from Hōryū-ji in Nara.

A nice way to cap off a visit to the museum is with a stroll in the **Tokugawa Shōgun Cemetery**, behind the museum.

Tokyo Metropolitan Museum of Art
東京都美術館
The **Metropolitan Museum of Art** (☎ 3823-6921; www.tobikan.jp; 8-36 Ueno-kōen, Taito-ku; special exhibits ¥900-1000; ☯ 9am-5pm Tue-Sun, closed 3rd Mon each month) has several galleries that run temporary displays (admission fee varies) of contemporary Japanese art. Galleries feature both Western-style art such as oil paintings and Japanese-style art such as *sumi-e* (ink brush) and *ikebana*. Apart from the museum's main gallery, the rental galleries are not curated by the museum, so exhibitions can be of differing standards.

National Science Museum
国立科学博物館
With most of its interpretive signage in Japanese only, this **museum** (☎ 3822-0111; www .kahaku.go.jp/english/; 7-20 Ueno-kōen, Taito-ku; adult & student/18 & under ¥420/70; ☯ 9am-4.30pm Tue-Sun) is only visit-worthy for its excellent special exhibitions – usually around ¥500 extra. But it's a good place to bring the kids, especially combined with a trip to the Ueno Zoo.

National Museum of Western Art
国立西洋美術博物館
The **National Museum of Western Art** (☎ 3828-5131; www.nmwa.go.jp; 7-7 Ueno-kōen, Taito-ku; adult/student ¥420/130; ☯ 9.30am-5pm Tue-Thu, Sat & Sun, 9.30am-8pm Fri) has an impressive, though rather indifferently displayed, permanent collection. It frequently hosts special exhibits (added charge for admission) on loan from other museums of international repute.

Shitamachi History Museum
下町風俗資料館
This **museum** (☎ 3823-7451; adult/student ¥300/100; 2-1 Ueno-kōen, Taito-ku; ☯ 9.30am-4.30pm Tue-Sun) recreates life in Edo's Shitamachi, the plebeian downtown quarter of old Tokyo. Exhibits include a merchant's shop, sweet shop, the home and business of a copper-boiler maker, and a tenement house. You're free to try out the games or try on the clothes, making for a fun, hands-on visit.

Ueno Zoo 上野動物園
Established in 1882, **Ueno Zoo** (☎ 3828-5171; 9-83 Ueno-kōen, Taito-ku; adult/child/student ¥600/free/200; ☯ 9.30am-5pm Tue-Sun) was the first of its kind in Japan. It's a good outing if you have children; otherwise, it can be safely dropped from a busy itinerary. The zoo is very popular with Japanese visitors for its pandas (who are charming, but not on view on Friday).

Tōshō-gū 東照宮
Dating from 1651 this shrine, like its counterpart in Nikkō, is dedicated to Tokugawa Ieyasu, who unified Japan (For more infor-

---

HOMELESS IN TOKYO

Like in other cosmopolitan cities across the globe, some people are trampled in the stampede towards 'progress'. Tokyo is no different, although the stigma associated with being homeless (*homuresu*) is harsher than in Western countries (who harbour similar attitudes) – sadly, being homeless is associated with laziness, substance abuse and bad moral character.

Tokyo's homeless population is estimated at more than 30,000, although official figures peg it at significantly less. The most visible settlement of homeless people, though there are outposts under bridges from Nishi-Azabu to Nishi-Shinjuku, undoubtedly exists in Ueno-kōen (p111). There's a vast tent-and-box community living in the park, where daytime is inundated with tourists soaking up museum culture and street performances but night-time is ruled by this disenfranchised population.

Most of these people, neglected by the Metropolitan Government, are middle-aged men who, despite their circumstances, are still fastidious enough to hang their laundry to dry on plastic clotheslines and line up their shoes outside of their makeshift dwellings.

mation, see p37). The **shrine** (☎ 3822-3455; 9-88 Ueno-kōen, Taito-ku; admission ¥200; 🕙 9am-4.30pm Dec-Feb, 9am-5.30pm Mar-Nov) is one of the few extant early-Edo structures, having fortunately survived Tokyo's innumerable disasters.

Ameya-yokochō Arcade アメヤ横丁

Ameya-yokochō was famous as a black-market district after WWII, and is still a lively shopping area where many bargains can be found. Shopkeepers are much less restrained than elsewhere in Tokyo, attracting customers with raucous cries that rattle down the crowded alleyways like the trains overhead. Look for the big romaji (Japanese roman script) sign opposite Ueno Station's south side.

Around Ueno 上野周辺
KAPPABASHI-DŌRI かっぱ橋通り

At Tawaramachi, which is just two stops from Ueno subway station on the Ginza line, is Kappabashi-dōri. This is where you go if you're setting up a restaurant. You can get flags that advertise the food in your restaurant, personalised cushions, crockery and, most importantly, all the plastic food you'll ever need. Whether you want a plate of spaghetti bolognaise with an upright fork, a plastic steak and chips, a lurid pizza or a bowl of *rāmen* (Chinese-style noodles), it's all there. Items aren't particularly cheap, but some of them are very convincing and could make unusual Japanese mementos.

Kappabashi-dōri is a five-minute walk northwest of any of Tawaramachi subway station's exits; look for the giant chef's head atop the Niomi utensil shop.

Asakusa 浅草   Map pp98–9

Long considered the heart of old Shitamachi, Asakusa is an interesting area to explore on foot. The big attraction is the temple, Sensō-ji, also known as Asakusa Kannon-dō. In Edo times, Asakusa was a halfway stop between the city and its most infamous pleasure district, Yoshiwara. In time, however, Asakusa developed into a pleasure quarter in its own right, eventually becoming the centre for that most loved of Edo entertainments, kabuki. In the very shadow of Sensō-ji a fairground spirit prevailed and a whole range of very secular entertainments were provided, from kabuki theatres to brothels.

When Japan ended its self-imposed isolation with the commencement of the Meiji Restoration, it was in Asakusa that the first cinemas opened, in Asakusa that the first music halls appeared and in Asakusa's Teikoku Gekijō (Imperial Theatre) that Western opera was first performed before Japanese audiences. It was also in Asakusa that another Western cultural import – the striptease – was introduced. A few clubs still operate in the area.

Unfortunately, Asakusa never quite recovered from the bombing at the end of WWII. Sensō-ji was rebuilt, but other areas of Tokyo assumed Asakusa's pleasure-district role. Asakusa may be one of the few areas of Tokyo to have retained something of the spirit of Shitamachi, but the bright lights have shifted elsewhere – notably to Shinjuku.

SENSŌ-JI 浅草寺

This **temple** (☎ 3842-0181; 2-3-1 Asakusa, Taito-ku; 🕙 6am-5pm, temple grounds 24hr) enshrines a golden image of Kannon (the Buddhist Goddess of Mercy) which, according to legend, was miraculously fished out of the nearby Sumida-gawa by two fishermen in AD 628. The image has remained on the spot ever since, through successive rebuildings of the temple. The present temple dates from 1950.

If you approach Sensō-ji from Asakusa subway station, the entrance is via Kaminari-mon (Thunder Gate). The gate's protector gods are Fūjin, the god of wind, on the right; and Raijin, the god of thunder, on the left.

Near Kaminari-mon, you'll probably be wooed by *jinriksha* (people-powered rickshaw) drivers in traditional dress with gorgeous lacquer rickshaws; they can cart you around on tours (¥2000/5000/9000 for 10/30/60 minutes, per person), providing commentary in English or Japanese.

Straight ahead is Nakamise-dōri, the temple precinct's shopping street, where everything from tourist trinkets to genuine Edo-style crafts is sold. There's even a shop selling wigs to be worn with kimono. Try the *sembei* (crackers) that a few shops specialise in – you'll have to queue as they are very popular with Japanese visitors.

Nakamise-dōri leads to the main temple compound. Whether the ancient image of Kannon actually exists is a secret – it's not on public display. Not that this stops a

TOKYO

steady stream of worshippers making their way to the top of the stairs to bow and clap. In front of the temple is a large incense cauldron: the smoke is said to bestow health and you will see visitors rubbing it into their bodies through their clothes.

DEMBŌ-IN 伝法院

To the left of the temple precinct is Dembō-in (Dembō Garden). Although it is not open to the public, it is possible to obtain a pass by calling in to the **main office** (☎ 3842-0181; 2-3-1 Asakusa, Taito-ku; ☼ dawn–dusk) to the left of Sensō-ji's Five-Storeyed Pagoda. The garden is one of Tokyo's best, containing a picturesque pond and a replica of a famous Kyoto teahouse. It's closed on Sunday, public holidays and whenever a ceremony is being held in the garden. To avoid disappointment, it's best to call a few days in advance to see if it will be open when you plan to visit.

SUMIDA-GAWA CRUISE 隅田川クルーズ

This **cruise** (every 10 to 15 minutes, from 9.30am to 6pm) may not be the most scenic river cruise you've ever experienced, but the *suijō basu* (water bus) is a great way to get to or from Asakusa.

The cruise departs from next to the bridge, Azuma-bashi, in Asakusa and goes to Hamarikyū-teien (p110) and Hinode Pier (Map pp98–9). Probably the best option is to buy a ticket to Hamarikyū-teien (¥620; you'll have to pay an additional ¥300 entry fee for the garden). After looking around the garden it is possible to walk into Ginza in about 10 to 15 minutes. The fare to Hinode Pier is ¥660.

Ikebukuro 池袋   **Map p100**

Traditionally Shinjuku's poor cousin, bawdy Ikebukuro has been treated to something of a facelift in recent years. Agreed, it shouldn't be high on a busy itinerary, but it's worth noting that its attractions include two of the world's largest department stores (Seibu and Tōbu – the world's largest is Yokohama Seibu), one of the tallest buildings in Asia (the Sunshine City building), the second-busiest station in Tokyo, the world's largest automobile showroom (Toyota Amlux), and the escalator experience of a lifetime (Tokyo Metropolitan Art Space). Like Shinjuku, Ikebukuro divides into an east side and a west side.

EAST SIDE 東池袋

Billed as a 'city in a building', **Sunshine City** (☎ 3989-3319; 3-1-1 Higashi-ikebukuro, Toshima-ku) is essentially 60 floors of office space and shopping malls, with a few overpriced cultural and entertainment options thrown in. If you've got ¥620 to burn, you can take a lift (operates 10am to 8.30pm) to the lookout on the 60th floor and gaze out on Tokyo's murky skyline. Sunshine City is 300m north of Higashi-Ikebukuro Station (take exit 2).

Not in the Sunshine City building itself, but on the 7th floor of the Bunka Kaikan of Sunshine City, is the **Ancient Orient Museum** (☎ 3989-3491; 3-1-4 Higashi-ikebukuro, Toshima-ku; admission ¥500, special exhibitions ¥900; ☼ 10am-5pm). It is strictly for those with a special interest in ancient odds and ends such as coins and beads.

Also of interest to some might be the **Sunshine Planetarium** (☎ 3989-3475; 10th fl, World Import Mart Bldg, 3-1-3 Higashi-Ikebukuro, Toshima-ku; adult/child ¥1600/800; ☼ noon-5.30pm Mon-Fri, 11am-6.30pm Sat & Sun), though shows are in Japanese, and the **Sunshine International Aquarium** (☎ 3989-3466; 10th fl, World Import Mart Bldg, 3-1-3 Higashi-Ikebukuro, Toshima-ku; adult/child ¥1600/800; ☼ 10am-6pm).

Nanjatown (☎ 5950-0765; 2nd fl, World Import Mart Bldg, 3-1-3 Higashi-Ikebukuro, Toshima-ku; adult/child ¥300/200; ☼ 10am-10pm), also known as the Ikebukuro Gyōza Stadium, is a great place to pig out on the famous Chinese dumplings. It's also a spectacle in itself, with 12 shops from across the country competing for the King Gyōza title. We recommend the 'healthy' Kyūshū-based Temujin, which serves its dumplings in a Yuzu citrus, vinegar–soy sauce dip. Don't set foot near the place if you've an aversion to garlic.

Department Stores

Just why Ikebukuro should have two of the world's largest department stores is a mystery. **Tōbu** (☎ 3981-2211; 1-1-25 Nishi-Ikebukuro, Toshima-ku; ☼ 10am-9pm Mon-Sat, 10am-8pm Sun) is the bigger of the two, but **Seibu** (☎ 3981-0111; 1-16-15 Minami-ikebukuro, Toshima-ku; ☼ 10am-9pm Mon-Sat, 10am-8pm Sun), for many years the world's biggest, still feels bigger and busier. You can easily spend an entire afternoon just wandering around the basement food-floor of Seibu sampling the little tidbits on offer. The 12th floor has an art museum and the top floor is restaurant city, with something like 50 restaurants, many of them offering great lunch specials. Tōbu closes on varying days twice monthly.

Art Galleries

In the annexe of the Seibu department store is **Seibu Art Gallery**, which has changing art exhibits, usually of fairly high standard. In Tōbu's Metropolitan Plaza is **Tōbu Art Museum**, which also features changing art exhibits. Admission to both galleries varies according to the exhibit.

WEST SIDE 西池袋

There's not really a lot to see on the west side, but anyone who hasn't been to Ikebukuro for a couple of years should check out the area between Tokyo Metropolitan Art Space and the southern end of the station. **Metropolitan Plaza** (☎ 5954-1111; 1-1-1 Nishi-Ikebukuro, Toshima-ku; restaurants ☽ 11am-10.30pm) is packed with classy boutiques, restaurants (8th floor) and a massive HMV (music store, 6th floor – great browsing). Just across the road is the **Spice 2** (1-10-10 Nishi-Ikebukuro, Toshima-ku; restaurants ☽ 11am-10pm) building, which does a repeat performance of Metropolitan Plaza.

TOKYO METROPOLITAN ART SPACE
東京芸術会館

Part of the 'Tokyo Renaissance' plan launched by the Department of Education, this huge cultural bunker was plonked down just where Tokyo needed it most – on Ikebukuro's west side. Designed to host performance art, the building has four halls. Those without a ticket for anything should treat themselves to the soaring escalator ride (it's said to be the world's longest escalator) – it doesn't get much more exciting than this in Ikebukuro!

Around Ikebukuro 池袋周辺

RIKUGI-EN 六義園

Just three stops from Ikebukuro, near JR Komagome Station (Yamanote line), **Rikugien** (Map p87; ☎ 3941-2222; 6-16-3 Hon-Komagome, Bunkyō-ku; admission ¥300; ☽ 9am-5pm Tue-Sun) is one of Tokyo's better gardens. It's a 10-hectare (25-acre) Edo-style *kaiyū*, or 'many pleasure' garden, built around a tranquil, carp-filled pond. The landscaped views here are said to evoke famous scenes from Chinese and Japanese literature. The garden was established in the late 17th century by Yana-gisawa Yoshiyasu and, after falling into disuse, was restored by the founder of the Mitsubishi group, Iwasaki Yataro.

Shinjuku 新宿　　　　　　**Map p101**

If you have only a day in Tokyo and want to dive headfirst into the modern Japanese phenomenon, Shinjuku is where to go. Here, nearly everything that makes Tokyo interesting is crammed in cheek to elbow: high-class department stores, discount shopping arcades, flashing neon, buttoned-up government offices, swarming push-and-shove crowds, street-side video screens, stand-up noodle bars, hostess clubs, shyly tucked-away shrines and seamy strip bars.

Shinjuku is a sprawling business, commercial and entertainment centre that never lets up. Every day approximately two million people pass through the station alone, making it one of the busiest in the world. On the western side of the station is Tokyo's highest concentration of skyscrapers and, presiding over them, Tange Kenzō's Tokyo Metropolitan Government Offices – massive awe-inspiring structures. The eastern side of the station – the more interesting by far – is a labyrinth of department stores, restaurants, boutiques, neon and sleaze.

EAST SIDE 東新宿

Shinjuku's east side is an area good for roaming around and losing one's way rather than a place for seeking out sights.

Kabuki-chō 歌舞伎町

Tokyo's most notorious red-light district lies east of Seibu Shinjuku Station, north of Yasukuni-dōri. This is one of the world's more imaginative red-light areas, with 'soaplands' (massage parlours), love hotels, peep shows, pink cabarets ('pink' is the Japanese equivalent of 'blue' in English), porno-video booths and strip shows that involve audience participation. The streets here are all crackling neon and drunken salarymen. High-pitched female voices wail out invitations to enter their establishments through distorting sound-systems, and Japanese punks earn a few extra yen passing out advertisements for karaoke boxes.

Most of what goes on is very much off-limits to foreigners, but it's still an interesting area for a stroll. If you do want to get a peek at the action, try one of the strip bars that deploy foreign touts on the street – count on at least ¥7000 for a show and a drink or two.

Kabuki-chō is not wall-to-wall sex; there are also some very straight entertainment options, including cinemas and some good restaurants (p136).

Hanazono-jinja 花園神社

Nestled in the shadow of Kabuki-chō is this quiet, unassuming shrine, **Hanazono-jinja** (☎ 3209-5265; 5-17-3 Shinjuku, Shinjuku-ku). It only takes around 10 minutes to stroll around the grounds, but it's a fine place to sit down and take a break. You hardly know you're in Shinjuku. The shrine is particularly pleasant when it's lit up in the evening. It is 300m north of Shinjuku-sanchōme Station (take exit B2).

Shinjuku-gyoen 新宿御苑

This **park** (☎ 3350-0151; Naito-chō, Shinjuku-ku; admission ¥200; ○ 9am-4.30pm Tue-Sun) is one of The city's best escapes and top cherry blossom-viewing spots and, at 57.6 hectares (144 acres), one of the city's largest parks. It dates back to 1906 and was designed as a European-style park, though a Japanese garden is also included. Other features are a French garden, a hot-house containing tropical plants and, near the hothouse, a pond with giant carp.

WEST SIDE 西新宿

Shinjuku's west side is mainly administrative, but photography freaks, take note: the area behind the Keiō department store is home to Tokyo's largest camera stores, Yodobashi Camera and Sakuraya Camera. Yodobashi has practically everything you could possibly want that relates to photography, all at very reasonable prices. It even has a limited selection of second-hand photographic equipment.

Elsewhere, the attractions of Shinjuku's west side are mainly the interiors of buildings and the observation floors of the impressive Tokyo Metropolitan Government Offices (which might very well appeal to photographers).

Tokyo Metropolitan Government Offices 東京都庁

These **offices** (☎ 5320-7890; 2-8-1 Nishi-Shinjuku, Shinjuku-ku; admission free; North tower ○ 9.30am-10pm Tue-Sun, South tower 9.30am-5.30pm Mon, Wed-Fri,

9.30am-7pm Sat & Sun, open later during summer, closed 29 Dec-3 Jan) are also known as Tokyo Tochō. These two adjoining buildings are worth a visit for their stunning architecture and for the great views from the **twin observation floors**. On really clear days, you might even spot Mt Fuji to the west.

Despite its critics, most visitors are won over by the buildings' complex symmetry and computer-chip appearance. Particularly impressive is the spacious Citizen's Plaza in front of the No 1 building – more reminiscent of a Roman amphitheatre than anything Japanese.

To reach the No 1 building's observation floors, take one of the two 1st-floor lifts. The offices are easily accessed from the Tochōmae Station on the Toei Ōedo line.

Shinjuku NS Building 新宿 NS ビル

The interior of this building is hollow, featuring a 1600 sq metre atrium illuminated by sunlight, which comes in through the glass roof. Overhead, at 110m, is a 'sky bridge'. The atrium itself features a 29m-tall pendulum clock that is said to be the largest in the world. The 29th and 30th floors have a large number of restaurants, all of which sport excellent views over Tokyo.

Pentax Forum
ペンタックスフォーラム

On the 1st floor of the Shinjuku Mitsui Building is **Pentax Forum** (☎ 3348-2941; 2-1-1 Nishi-Shinjuku, Shinjuku-ku; admission free; ○ 10.30am-6.30pm, closed 1 Jan), a must for photography buffs. You can play with the cameras, and there's a good exhibition space. Access the forum from Tochōmae Station (exit B2).

Harajuku & Aoyama
原宿・青山   **Map p103**

Harajuku and Aoyama are where Tokyoites come to be spendy and trendy – albeit in a blasé kind of way. They're pleasant areas to stroll in and watch locals in contented consumer mode in the bountiful boutiques and bistros. **Takeshita-dōri** buzzes with bleach-headed teenagers shopping for illiterate T-shirts and fishnet stockings; **Omote-sandō**, with its alfresco cafés and boutiques, is still the closest Tokyo gets to Paris; the bistro alleys of Aoyama sport some of the best international cuisine in town; and **Meiji-jingū** is Tokyo's most splendid shrine.

For unforgettable holiday snaps, check out the Sunday madness at **Jingū-bashi** (below), right next to Harajuku JR Station.

MEIJI-JINGŪ 明治神宮

Completed in 1920, the **shrine** (www.meijijingu .or.jp; 1-1 Yoyogi Kamizono-chō, Shibuya-ku; admission free; dawn-dusk) was built in memory of Emperor Meiji and Empress Shōken, under whose rule Japan ended its long isolation from the outside world. Unfortunately, like much else in Tokyo, the shrine was destroyed in the bombing at the end of WWII. Rebuilding was completed in 1958.

Meiji-jingū might be a reconstruction of the original but, unlike so many of Japan's postwar reconstructions, it is altogether authentic. The shrine itself was built with Japanese cypress, while the cypress for the huge *torii* (gates) came from Alishan in Taiwan.

The **Meiji-jingū-neien Garden** (admission ¥500; 9am-4.30pm) offers peaceful strolls, as it is almost deserted on weekdays. It's particularly beautiful in June, when the irises are in bloom.

Meiji-jingū Treasure Museum (3379-5511; adult/student ¥500/200; 9am-4pm) is an unremarkable collection of items from the lives of the emperor and empress.

YOYOGI-KŌEN 代々木公園

Although this isn't one of Tokyo's most impressive gardens, weekends here are prime for stumbling upon the cool and unusual – *shamisen* (three-stringed lute) or punk rock practice, greased-up cats cutting a rug in full rockabilly drag, and fire-eating, for example. At 53.2 hectares (133 acres), its wooded grounds make for a relaxing walk even if there aren't any interesting goings-on. It's at its best on a sunny Sunday in spring or autumn. The park is accessible from the Harajuku JR Station, or from the Chiyoda line, which stops at Yoyogi-kōen Station.

OTA MEMORIAL ART MUSEUM 太田記念美術館

Leave your shoes in the foyer and pad in slippers through this **museum** (3403-0880; www.ukiyoe-ota-muse.jp/english.html; 1-10-10 Jingūmae, Shibuya-ku; admission ¥700; 10.30am-5.30pm Tue-Sun). About 50m from Meiji-jingūmae subway station, the Ota museum has a stellar collection of *ukiyo-e* (wood-block prints) and offers a good opportunity to see works by Japanese masters of the art, including Hiroshige. There's an extra charge for special exhibits. You'll find it up a hill on a narrow road behind Laforet.

GALLERIES

Aoyama is packed with tiny galleries, most of them free. Up Killer-dōri, in particular, look out for **Watari-um** (Watari Museum of Contemporary Art; 3402-3001; official@watarium.co.jp; 3-7-6 Jingūmae, Shibuya-ku; adult/student ¥1000/800; 11am-7pm Tue-Sun). On Sundays, the attached café and museum shop take up the basement and lobby area where exhibits are advertised. In addition to art books, it carries funky gifts and probably the best supply of postcards in Tokyo. From the Gaien-mae subway station, head towards Aoyama and then right at the Bell Commons building.

COS-PLAY-ZOKU

When Tokyo's forces of Law and Order donned their riot gear to oust the Takenokozoku – the dancers clad in bright pastel clothes, with 1950s rockabilly haircuts – from Yoyogi-kōen (above), no-one imagined that the Takenokozoku would be replaced by an even odder, younger crowd.

Enter the Cos-play-zoku, the Costume Play Gang. Mainly teenage girls from the dormitory towns and cities around Tokyo's fringe, the Cos-play-zoku assemble at Harajuku's Jingū-bashi each weekend, bedecked in goth make-up, a mixture of SM queen arch-vamp, black taffeta, blue lipstick and cartoon nurse exaggeration.

Cos-play-zoku are united in their fondness for Japanese *visual-kei* (visual type) bands, such as L'Arc En Ciel and Zard, and a sense of pride in their alienation. Many of the girls are *ijime-ko*, kids bullied in school, who find release and expression in their temporary weekend identities.

The end result is Tokyo's most fun circus, as each weekend hordes of excited photographers, bewildered tourists and plain voyeurs gather to catch the show. The girls revel, primp and pose for the cameras until dusk, when they hop back on the trains for the slow return to 'normal' life in the faceless housing blocks of Chiba and Kawasaki.

The futuristic **Spiral Building** (☎ 3498-1171; 5-6-23 Minami-Aoyama, Minato-ku; admission free; ☽ 11am-8pm) features changing exhibits, shows, dining and live music. Check out the shop on the 2nd floor for more arty books, jewellery, stationery and appealing gifts.

Kotto-dōri, or 'Antique Street' as it's called in the tourist literature, is a good place to seek out both galleries and souvenirs.

Shibuya 渋谷   Map p103
In the bustling, youth-oriented shopping district of Shibuya, it's easy to get the feeling that everyone over the age of 35 has been sent back to Ueno or Ikebukuro. Like Shinjuku, Shibuya is not exactly rich in sights but it possesses some of the best department-store browsing to be had in all Tokyo. You may want to avoid – or head for – the area on weekends, when the streets are jammed with fashionable Tokyo kids.

HACHIKŌ STATUE ハチ公像
In the 1920s, a professor who lived near Shibuya Station kept a small Akita dog, who would come to the station every day to await his master's return. The professor died in 1925, but the dog continued to show up and wait at the station until his own death 11 years later. The poor dog's faithfulness was not lost on the Japanese, and they built a statue to honour his memory.

TOBACCO & SALT MUSEUM たばこと塩の博物館
This small **museum** (☎ 3476-2041; 1-16-8 Jinnan, Shibuya-ku; adult/18 & under ¥100/50; ☽ 10am-6pm Tue-Sun, closed 1 Jan & 1st Tue of Jun) has some fairly interesting exhibits detailing the history of tobacco and the methods of salt production practised in premodern Japan (Japan has no salt mines and until recently harvested salt from the sea). As usual, there's little in the way of English explanations, but a lot of the material is self-explanatory. You can get to the museum from the Hachikō exit of Shibuya JR Station.

TEPCO ELECTRIC ENERGY MUSEUM 電力館
Folks with kids in tow and an interest in electric power might want to stop by the **Tepco Electric Energy Museum** (Denryoku-kan; ☎ 3477-1191; 1-12-10 Jinnan, Shibuya-ku; admission free; ☽ 10am-6pm Thu-Tue). It may be seven floors of

advertising for Tokyo Electric Power, but the displays are well presented and cover a lot of ground. Anything and everything associated with electricity gets the treatment. It's just north of the Marui One department store, 500m from Shibuya Station, exit 7.

LOVE HOTEL HILL
The area around the top of Dōgenzaka is probably the world capital of **love hotels**. There are love hotels to suit all tastes, from miniature Gothic castles to Middle-Eastern temples (and these are just the buildings – the rooms are even more varied). It's OK to wander in and take a look at the screen with illuminated pictures of the various rooms available.

This area is gradually being populated by other entertainment options such as alfresco cafés, restaurants, performance halls and pubs. **Dr Jeekahn's** is an upmarket video-game parlour in the neighbourhood, and the building also houses two popular nightclubs (p148). Just down the road are the trendy O-East and O-West clubs on either side of the Dōgenzaka road.

AOYAMA-DŌRI 青山通り
Aoyama-dōri runs from Akasaka to Shibuya, taking in the Akasaka Palace grounds (not a major attraction) and Harajuku. Halfway between Akasaka and Aoyama-itchōme Station, on the left-hand side, is the Sōgetsu Kaikan building, headquarters of the **Sōgetsu School of Ikebana** (☎ 3408-1151; www.sogetsu.or.jp /english/index.html; Sōgetsu Kaikan Bldg, 7-2-21 Akasaka, Minato-ku; ☽ 10am-5pm Mon-Thu & Sat, 10am-8pm Fri). If you are interested in *ikebana*, this is a fascinating place to visit. The avant-garde Sōgetsu School was founded on the idea that there are no limits to *ikebana*, nor to where or when it can be practised. There are displays of *ikebana*, and a bookshop and coffee shop. Call ahead for information about classes (¥4850, including flowers and tax).

On the 6th floor of the same building is **Sōgetsu Art Museum** (☎ 3408-9112; admission ¥500; ☽ 10am-5pm Mon-Thu & Sat, 10am-8pm Fri), notable for its highly idiosyncratic and eclectic collection of art treasures from across the centuries. Exhibits range from Indian Buddhas to works by Matisse to elaborate arrangements of Ferragamo shoes (in true Tokyo fashion).

Ebisu & Daikanyama
恵比寿・代官山　　　　　　　　**Map p105**

Ebisu and Daikanyama are pleasant alternatives to the crowds and madness of nearby Shibuya and Shinjuku. Daikanyama, in particular, is a great spot for a casual afternoon stroll, with its almost Western ambience and abundant alfresco cafés. However, most people come to Ebisu and Daikanyama at night to sample some of Tokyo's better clubs and bars. If you do come during the day, most sights worth seeing are in the new Ebisu Garden Place, easily reached from JR Ebisu Station by an aerial walkway.

YEBISU GARDEN PLACE
恵比寿ガーデンプレイス

This is a **complex** (☎ 5423-7111; 4-20-3 Ebisu, Shibuya-ku) of shops, restaurants and a 39-floor **tower**, surrounded by an open mall area – perfect for hanging out on warmer days, when you may catch live music. Garden Place also features the headquarters of Sapporo Breweries, which contains the **Beer Museum Yebisu** (☎ 5423-7255; 4-20-1 Ebisu, Shibuya-ku; admission free; ◔ 10am-6pm Tue-Sun). There are lots of good exhibits, the best of which is the 'Tasting Lounge', where you can sample Sapporo's various brews (¥200 a glass).

There are lots of outdoor cafés scattered around the complex. If you're hungry, most serve light meals as well. The restaurants on the 38th and 39th floors of **Yebisu Garden Place Tower** offer excellent views.

Japan's first large-scale museum devoted entirely to photography, **Tokyo Metropolitan Museum of Photography** (☎ 3280-0099; www.syabi .com/english/index_eng.html; 1-13-3 Mita, Meguro-ku; admission varies; ◔ 10am-6pm Tue, Wed, Sat & Sun, 10am-8pm Thu & Fri) is in new premises. The emphasis in this museum is on Japanese photography, but international work is also displayed. From JR Ebisu Station take the covered walkway to Yebisu Garden Place.

Roppongi & Akasaka
六本木・赤坂　　　　　　　**Map pp106–7**

Rife with restaurants and bars, Roppongi's nightlife rules. Though there aren't any compelling reasons to visit the neighbourhood during the daytime, the **Roppongi Hills** development is worth checking out for shopping, cinema, and art exhibitions.

Likewise, Akasaka is of interest less for its sights than for its high concentration of high-end hotels. Still, the area has a few sights worth taking in if you find yourself here.

ROPPONGI HILLS　六本木ヒルズ

This massive development was no less than 17 years in the making, conceived by developer Minoru Mori, who envisioned improving people's quality of urban life by centralising home, work and leisure into a compressed city. If a million visitors per weekend is any indication of success, this is overshadowed only by the magnitude of the place itself. The shopping/dining/entertainment/housing complex is embellished with public art and a Japanese garden and is so big as to warrant **guided tours** (☎ 6406-6677; tours from ¥2000; ◔ 10am-5pm) – book seven days in advance. To get there, take the Hibiya or Toei Ōedo subway lines to Roppongi Station and head for the Roppongi Hills exit.

Mori Art Museum　森美術館

Making its debut in 2003, this contemporary **art museum** (☎ 6406-6100; www.mori.art.museum; 52nd & 53rd fls, Roppongi Hills Mori Tower, 6-10-1 Roppongi, Minato-ku; ◔ 10am-10pm Mon, Wed & Thu, 10am-5pm Tue & 10am-midnight Fri-Sun) boasts an enviable location at the top of Mori Tower. Exhibitions tend toward the (mind-bogglingly myriad) multi-media installation variety and thus far have been of a respectably high calibre. As yet lacking a permanent collection, the museum is only open during its temporary exhibitions. Check the website for current exhibitions; admission averages ¥1500 and includes entry to Tokyo City View.

Tokyo City View　東京シティビュー

The eponymous **view** (☎ 6406-6652; adult/child ¥1500/1000; ◔ 9am-1am, last admission midnight) offers 360-degrees' worth of Tokyo from the 52nd floor of Mori Tower. If the floor-to-ceiling windows don't give you enough of an eyeful, another ¥500 gains entrée to the open-air deck. Admission to Tokyo City View includes admission to the Mori Art Museum.

HIE-JINJA　日枝神社

The **shrine** (☎ 3581-2471; 2-10-5 Nagata-chō, Chiyoda-ku), next to the Capitol Tōkyū Hotel, 250m northwest of Tameike-sannō subway station (exit 5), is not one of Tokyo's major attractions; it's modern and largely cement. However, the highlight – particularly pretty during cherry-blossom season – is the walk up to the shrine through a 'tunnel' of orange **torii** (shrine gates). Walking along Sotoburi-dōri, look for the concrete plaza–style entrance leading up to the shrine's gates.

HOTEL SIGHTS

Some of Akasaka's luxury hotels are sights in themselves. Hotel New Otani (p131), for example, has preserved part of a **400-year-old garden** that was once the property of a Tokugawa regent. The carp pond is spectacular.

The **Ōkura Shūkokan** (☎ 3583-0781; 2-10-3 Toranomon, Minato-ku; adult/student ¥700/500; ✆ 10am-4.30pm Tue-Sun) has an impressive collection of lacquer writing boxes and no less than three National Treasures. The two-storey museum is also surrounded by a small but well-populated sculpture garden. It is definitely worth a look if you're on this side of town.

For views over the area – unless you're visiting the Mori Art Museum (p119), ANA Hotel Tokyo and Akasaka Prince Hotel both offer skyline spectacles from their lofty upper reaches.

TOKYO TOWER 東京タワー

Tokyo's Eiffel Tower-lookalike, **Tokyo Tower** (☎ 3433-5111; www.tokyotower.co.jp; 4-2-8 Shiba-kōen, Minato-ku), is more impressive from a distance; up close, the 330m tower is a tourist trap. The **Grand Observation Platform** (adult/child ¥820/460; ✆ 9am-10pm) is only 150m high; if you want to peer through the smog at Tokyo's uninspiring skyline from 250m, it will cost you a further ¥600 to get to the **Special Observation Platform** (✆ 9am-10pm). The tower also features an overpriced **aquarium** (admission ¥1000; ✆ 10am-9pm), a **wax museum** (admission ¥850; ✆ 10am-9pm), the **Holographic Mystery Zone** (admission ¥400; ✆ 10am-9pm) and showrooms; the best deal if you do go: a combination ticket (¥1900).

Tokyo Tower is a fair trudge from Roppongi; instead, you could take the Hibiya subway line one stop to Kamiyachō Station.

ZŌJŌ-JI 増上寺

Behind Tokyo Tower, **Zōjō-ji** (☎ 3432-1531; 4-7-35 Shiba-kōen, Minato-ku) was the family temple of the Tokugawas. It makes a nice stroll if you're in the vicinity.

NEZU FINE ART MUSEUM 根津美術館

This **museum** (☎ 3400-2536; www.nezu-muse.or.jp/index_e.html; 6-5-1 Minami-Aoyama, Minato-ku; adult/

student ¥1000/700; ✆ 9.30am-4.30pm Tue-Sun) houses a well-known collection of Japanese art including Buddhist paintings, calligraphy and sculpture. Also on display are Chinese and Korean art exhibits, and teahouses where tea ceremonies are performed. The exhibits are well displayed and of high quality. Spend some time savouring its wonderful, slightly wild ornamental garden. It's about half a kilometre from Omote-sandō Station (exit A4 or A5).

AOYAMA REIEN 青山霊園

Better known as Aoyama Botchi, this cemetery is perfect for a stroll and provides a nice break from the crowds of Omote-sandō and nearby Roppongi. It's also a good alternative to Ueno-kōen during *hanami* season and is accessible from the Gaien-mae Station on the Ginza subway line.

Ōdaiba/Tokyo Bay

お台場・東京湾   **Map p108**

Tokyo is rediscovering the fact that it's a waterfront city, and there has been a spate of recent development in and around the Tokyo Bay area. Perhaps the most popular Tokyo Bay spot is the Ōdaiba/Ariake area.

There's tons to do here, most of it is along the lines of amusement park madness: you could spend an entire day in one of the shopping or entertainment complexes here. Check out Decks for its Hong Kong theme, the women-only shopping experience of Venus Fort (with kitschy 18th-century Italian styling!), or Aqua City for a mish-mash of consumer desirables.

The easiest way to get to Ōdaiba is on the Yurikamome line, which you can reach from Shimbashi Station. Within Shimbashi Station, signage in English tapers off the closer you get to the Yurikamome line, so look for signs featuring the line's logo.

MUSEUM OF MARITIME SCIENCE

船の科学館

This **museum** (☎ 5500-1111; 3-1 Higashi-Yashio, Shinagawa-ku; adult/child ¥700/400; ✆ 10am-5pm Mon-Fri, 10am-6pm Sat, Sun & public holidays), down in the Ōdaiba/Tokyo Bay area, is one of Tokyo's better museums. Known as Fune-no-kagakukan, it has four floors of excellent displays dealing with every aspect of ships and shipping, with loads of highly detailed models. The 4m-long version of the largest battleship ever built, the *Yamato*, is stunning in detail and craftsmanship. There are also lots of hands-on exhibits that kids will love.

To get to the museum, you should take the Yurikamome New Transit line from Shimbashi Station and get off at the Fune-no-kagakukan stop.

Elsewhere in Tokyo
PARKS & GARDENS
If you've been hitting the bitumen and haven't seen a tree for days, there are several parks and gardens to cure what ails you. (You'll find others listed earlier in this chapter.)

Koishikawa Kōraku-en (Map pp94-5; ☎ 3811-3015; 1-6-6 Kōraku, Bunkyō-ku; admission ¥300; ☷ 9am-5pm) has to be one of the least-visited (by foreigners at least) and best gardens in Tokyo. A stroll-garden with a strong Chinese influence, it was established in the mid-17th century. It is next to Kōraku-en Amusement Park (see right) and Tokyo Dome, near Kōraku-en subway station on the Marunouchi line.

MUSEUMS & GALLERIES
Museums and galleries abound in Tokyo. In many cases their exhibits are small and specialised and the admission charges prohibitively expensive for travellers with a limited budget and a tight schedule. For a more complete listing, get hold of the TIC's *Museums & Art Galleries* pamphlet. Better still, look out for *Tokyo Museums – A Complete Guide* by Thomas & Ellen Flannigan, which covers everything from the Tombstone Museum to the Button Museum.

Edo-Tokyo Museum (Map pp94-5; ☎ 3626-9974; www.edo-tokyo-museum.or.jp; 1-4-1 Yokoami, Sumida-ku; admission ¥600; ☷ 10am-6pm Tue-Sun) is the best of Tokyo's new museums. Just the building itself, which looks like it has been spirited from the set of Star Wars, is a wonder. The Nihombashi divides this vast display into re-creations of Edo-period Tokyo and Meiji-period Tokyo. It is close to Ryōgoku Station on the JR Sōbu line, and can be combined with a visit to the Sumō Museum.

Sumō Museum (Map pp94-5; ☎ 3622-0366; 1-3-28 Yokoami, Sumida-ku; admission free; ☷ 10am-4.30pm Mon-Fri), close to the main entrance of Ryōgoku Kokugikan Sumō Stadium, is quite a treat; but unfortunately there is nothing in the way of English explanations. Note that during the grand tournaments in January, May and September, the museum

is open daily, but only to those attending the tournament. It's just outside Ryōgoku Station on the JR Sōbu line.

Tokyo Metropolitan Teien Art Museum (Map pp94-5; ☎ 3443-0201; 5-21-9 Shirokanedai, Minato-ku; ☷ 10am-6pm, closed 2nd & 3rd Wed each month) lacks a permanent display of its own, but the building itself was designed by French architect Henri Rapin and it lies in pleasant gardens. Take the east exit of Meguro Station (on the Yamanote line), walk straight ahead along Meguro-dōri for around five minutes and look out for the museum on the left. The entry price varies with each exhibition.

The **National Museum of Emerging Science and Innovation** (Map p108; ☎ 3570-9150; www .miraikan.jst.go.jp; 2-41 Aomi, Kōtō-ku; adult/under 18 ¥500/200; ☷ 10am-5pm Wed-Mon), also known as the Miraikan, is undoubtedly Japan's best science museum. Its hands-on exhibits are fun, as well as genuinely educational, whether you're 'driving' a virtual horse around Ōdaiba, building your own robot, or fathoming how Medaka riverfish could copulate in zero gravity aboard the space shuttle. To get to the museum, you take the Yurikamome New Transit line to Fune-no-kagakukan; from there, it's a five-minute walk.

AMUSEMENT PARKS
The wonderland **Tokyo Disneyland** (Map pp94-5; ☎ 045-683-3777; www.tokyodisneyresort.co.jp; 1-1 Maihama, Urayasu-shi, Chiba; passport-ticket adult/child 4-11/child 12-17 ¥5500/3700/4800; ☷ 8.30am-10pm Jun-Aug, 9am-10pm Sep-Nov, 10am-6pm Dec-Feb, 9am-10pm Mar-May) is a near-perfect replica of the original in Anaheim, California. Its opening hours vary seasonally – phone ahead or check the website to be sure. It's open year-round except for about a dozen days a year (most of them in January). A variety of tickets are available, including an all-inclusive 'passport' that gives you unlimited access to all the rides. As at the original Disneyland, there are often long queues at popular rides (30 minutes to one hour is normal). Tokyo Disneyland has a **ticket office** (Map p96; ☎ 3595-1777; ☷ 10am-7pm) in Hibiya.

There is now a direct train service to Disneyland: it's best to take the Keiyō line from Tokyo Station to Maihama Station (¥210, 15 minutes).

Kōraku-en Amusement Park (Map pp94-5; ☎ 5800-9999; 1-3-61 Kōrakuen, Bunkyō-ku; adult/child ¥1200/600, most rides ¥600, unlimited rides adult/child ¥3300/2600; 10am-10pm Jun-Aug, 10am-6pm Dec-Feb, 10am-8pm Mar-May & Sep-Nov), next to Kōraku-en subway station on the Marunouchi subway line, is of the old shake-rattle-and-roll school, and is popular precisely for that reason. The Ultra Twister roller coaster takes 1st prize for most of the visitors. Geopolis is a new hi-tech addition to the amusement park, with attractions like the Geopanic indoor roller coaster and, our favourite, Zombie Zone.

ACTIVITIES
Baths & Spas
A nice hot bath or spa is a great way to relax after a day pounding the pavements of Tokyo.

The new **Ōedo-Onsen Monogatari** (Map p108; ☎ 5500-1126; info@oom.jp; 2-57 Aomi, Kōtō-ku; adult/child ¥2700/1500, 6pm-2am ¥1900/1500; 11am-9am, last entry at 2am) uses natural mineral water piped from 1400m beneath Tokyo Bay. The theme of the 'amusement park', as it bills itself, is modelled on old Edo times, and though it sounds a little hokey, the park is attractively designed, with lovely outdoor pools as well as traditional baths. Admission fees cover the rental of *yukata* and towels, and there are old-style restaurants and souvenir shops for a post-bath bite and browse. Note that there are additional charges on weekends and holidays if you arrive after 6pm and stay for more than four hours. To get to the *onsen*, take the Yurikamome line to the Telecom Center Station.

A few more *sentō* (public baths), *onsen* (mineral hot spring spa area) and spas:

Asakusa Kannon Onsen (Map pp98–9; ☎ 3844-4141; 2-7-26 Asakusa, Taito-ku; admission ¥700; 6.30am-6pm Fri-Wed) Next to Sensō-ji, the water's fine here, and a good place for a soul-soothing soak.

Azabu-Jūban Onsen & Koshi-No-Yu Sentō (Map pp106–7; ☎ 3404-2610; 1-5 Azabu-Jūban, Minato-ku; admission ¥1260; 11am-9pm Wed-Mon; Azabu-jūban Station, Namboku or Ōedo lines) You might not expect to find an *onsen* in the middle of Tokyo, but here it is. The dark, tea-coloured water here is scalding hot. Downstairs is a *sentō* (☎ 3404-2610; admission ¥400; 3-11.30pm Wed-Mon) and upstairs a plusher *onsen*. The water comes from the same source; the only difference is the price and the fact that upstairs there's a room to lounge in after your bath.

Finlando Sauna (Map p101; ☎ 3209-9196; 1-20-1 Kabuki-chō, Shinjuku-ku; admission noon-5pm ¥1900, 5pm-midnight ¥2100, midnight-noon ¥2600; 24hr) This is a huge complex of baths and steam rooms right in the middle of Shinjuku's Kabuki-chō. This is a good place – for men only – to escape the madness of the streets outside. Massages, ¥3060 for 45 minutes, come highly recommended.

Green Plaza Ladies Sauna (Map p101; ☎ 3207-5411; 1-29-2 Kabuki-chō, Shinjuku-ku; admission 6am-10pm ¥2700, 10pm-6am ¥3300; 24hr) A central bath and spa for women, this place is also in Shinjuku's Kabuki-chō. A 40-minute massage costs ¥3260.

WALKING TOUR
If you've only a day or two in Tokyo, East Shinjuku is a great place to stroll around for a taste of Tokyo's cheery sensory overload. From inside Shinjuku Station, follow the east exit or Kabuki-chō exit signs. Once

---

THE FLOWERS OF EDO

Today there is little left of Shitamachi, the old 'downtown', and the only way to get some idea of the circumstances in which the lower classes of old Edo lived is by visiting somewhere like Ueno's Shitamachi History Museum (p112) or the Edo-Tokyo Museum (p121) in Ryōgoku. Edo was a city of wood, and its natural stained-wood frontages and dark-tiled roofs gave the city an attractiveness little in evidence in modern Tokyo. Nevertheless, the poor lived in horribly crowded conditions, in flimsy wooden constructions, often with earthen floors. Huge fires regularly swept great swaths through the wooden buildings of the congested city. In a perverse attempt to make the best of misfortune, Edo-dwellers seemed almost to take pride in the fires that periodically purged the city, calling them *Edo-no-hana* (literally 'flowers of Edo').

The flowers of Edo bloomed with such frequency that it has been estimated that any Shitamachi structure could reckon on a life span of around 20 years, often less, before being destroyed by fire. Preventative measures included building houses that could be completely sealed at the approach of a fire; candles would be left burning inside, starving the houses' interior of oxygen. Private fire brigades operated with standard-bearers who would stake out their territory close to a burning building and exact payment if they managed to save it.

Modern building techniques have eliminated most of Edo's 'flowers', but you can still see the occasional wooden structure that has miraculously survived into the 21st century.

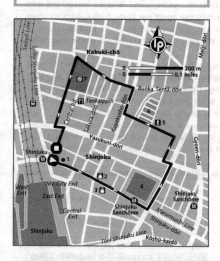

Distance: 2km
Duration: 2 hours

you've passed through the ticket gates, take the 'My City' exit. As you surface, directly ahead of you is the **Studio Alta Building (1)** and its enormous video screen.

Continue walking east down Shinjuku-dōri past the bargain men's clothing and shoe stores. A little further on is **Kinokuniya bookshop (2;** p89), with its superb collection of English books on the 7th floor. Continue walking and you pass **Mitsukoshi department store (3;** p151) on the right and on the left is the Art Deco **Isetan Building (4;** p137), which contains fashionable boutiques and the Isetan Art Gallery on the 5th floor of the building. The gallery hosts print, ceramic, and fine art exhibits by Japanese artists; hours vary; admission is free.

Turn left at Isetan and walk down to Yasukuni-dōri. A lane on the opposite side of the road leads to **Hanazono-jinja (5;** p116), which nestles so close to Tokyo's most infamous red-light district that its clientele can make for some interesting people-watching. The shrine has a reputation for bringing success to business ventures – both legitimate and otherwise.

Exit Hanazono-jinja onto **Golden Gai (6;** p145), a tiny network of alleyways devoted entirely to small, stand-up watering holes.

Traditionally the haunt of bohemian Tokyo-ites, it's a safe area to take a walk, even by night (by day it's usually deserted). If you decide to stop for a drink, keep in mind that some bars serve regulars only. It's said that the Golden Block is gradually being bought up by Seibu department store, but for the time being Golden Gai hangs on.

Continue in the same direction along the alleyways that run parallel to Yasukuni-dōri and you reach **Kabuki-chō** (p115), Tokyo's notorious red-light district. Despite its reputation, it's a relatively safe area to stroll around. Most of what goes on in these environs is pretty much off-limits to foreigners, though single men are likely to be approached by touts offering to take them to one of the 'pink cabarets'.

Kabuki-chō must be one of the more imaginative red-light areas in the world, with 'soaplands' (massage parlours), love hotels, 'no-pants' coffee shops (it's the waitresses who doff their briefs, not the customers), peep shows, porno-video booths and strip shows that involve audience participation.

Continue along the perimeter of Kabuki-chō and look for the enormous **Koma Theatre (7)**, which started off as a cinema, but quickly switched to stage shows. It still hosts performances of a more mainstream variety than those elsewhere in Kabuki-chō. The square facing the Koma is ringed by cinemas and is also a popular busking spot at night, though *yakuza* are usually quick about moving anyone too popular along. Take any of the lanes radiating off the square to see Kabuki-chō at its best.

From this point wander back to Yasukuni-dōri and take one of the lanes that connect it with Shinjuku-dōri.

TOKYO FOR CHILDREN

Tokyo is a dangerous place to take children because they'll be doted upon, find sources of stimulation from all sides, and will be accosted by a neverending parade of activities and tempting treats.

Rainy-day activities range from museum visits – try the Science Museum (p112) or the Sony Building (p110) to check out the cutting-edge tech toys on display for play (big kids will enjoy this as well). Fair-weather jaunts could include Ueno Zoo (p112), Yoyogi Park (p117), and the touchy-feely Shitamachi History Museum (p112).

TOKYO

SUMŌ

Sumō, whose origins can be traced back about 1500 years, was originally religious in nature. Together with dances and theatre, the wrestling matches that were precursors to sumō made up a part of ritual prayers for good harvests. Over the years, sumō became integrated into cultural life under the Imperial Court, evolving into the sport we know today, with its rules and rituals such as the scattering of coarse salt into the ring, the powerful foot-stomping of the colourfully be-decked *rikishi* (wrestlers) and the psychological staredown at the beginning of each match.

Travellers who visit Tokyo in January, May or September should not miss their chance to attend a Grand Tournament at Tokyo's **Ryōgoku Kokugikan Sumō Stadium** (Map pp94-5; ☎ 3623-5111; 1-3-28 Yokoami, Sumida-ku; ☻ 10am-6pm). Tickets range from ¥1000 to around ¥45,000 for box seats (seating four people each). You can also rent radios providing commentary in English (¥200 refundable deposit). It's a spectacular experience of pomp, ceremony and seriousness.

If you don't attend the tournament, you can also get a handbook at the stadium and take a self-guided walking tour of the neighbourhood, which houses several *heya* (sumō stables). You may catch a glimpse of *rikishi* dressed in *yukata* (summer kimono) and *geta* (wooden sandals), walking to the stadium.

To get there, take the JR Sōbu line to Ryōgoku Station; the green-roofed Ryōgoku Kokugikan is just outside the exit.

The most dangerous of all are Tokyo's toy stores, notably **Hakuhinkan Toy Park** (p152), **Kiddyland** (p152), and **Loft** (p152).

TOURS

One of the most reliable Tokyo-tour operators is **Hato Bus Tours** (Map pp106-7; ☎ 3435-6081; www.hatobus.co.jp/english/; World Trade Center Bldg, 2-4-1 Hamamatsu-chō, Minato-ku; ☻ 9am-7pm). Its Panoramic Tour (¥9800 including lunch) takes in most of Tokyo's major sights; tours depart from Hamamatsu-chō bus terminal. Probably the widest range of Tokyo tours is available from the **JTB's Sunrise Tours office** (☎ 5796-5454; www.jtb.co.jp/sunrisetour/index.html; ☻ 9am-6pm). Sunrise offers general sightseeing tours, such as morning tours and afternoon tours (each ¥5000). Both Hato and Sunrise offer English-speaking guides and/or taped explanations and headsets.

Night tours of the city are offered by Sunrise Tours and by **Gray Line** (☎ 3433-8388). Sunrise's Kabuki Night tour (¥9800) includes a sukiyaki and sake dinner, kabuki at Ginza's Kabuki-za Theatre and a geisha show.

All of these tours pick up guests at various major hotels around town. Sunrise and Gray Line also offer tours to sightseeing spots around Tokyo.

FESTIVALS & EVENTS

There is a festival of one sort or another every day in Tokyo. Call or visit the JNTO's TIC for up-to-date information. Some of the major celebrations:

Ganjitsu (New Year) When Tokyoites head to Meiji-jingū (p103), Sensō-ji (Map pp98–9) or Yasukuni-jinja (Map p96).

Hanami (Cherry Blossom Viewing; early to mid-April) Chaotic at Ueno-kōen (p111), peaceful at Shinjuku-gyoen (p116).

Sanja Matsuri (3rd weekend of May) A massive festival where 100 *mikoshi* (portable shrines) are paraded through Asakusa.

Samba Matsuri (late August) The same area's wild summer festival.

Bōnen-kai Season (late December) This last one isn't an official festival at all, but the period leading up to New Year, when the Japanese hold their drink-and-be-merry year-end parties.

SLEEPING

In Tokyo you can choose from the whole range of Japanese accommodation, from capsule hotels to ryokan, but budget accommodation in Tokyo is a bit pricier than elsewhere. Hotels are expensive, and to add insult to financial injury, they charge an additional 5% 'metropolitan area' tax.

Business hotels are a good compromise solution, with rates in Tokyo from ¥7000 for singles and around ¥10,000 for doubles. Most midrange hotels in Tokyo are business hotels. Since there's little to distinguish one business hotel from another, we recommend choosing one in an area convenient to the sights you'd like to see. Always check what time your hotel locks its doors before heading out at night – though some hotels stay open all night, many lock up at midnight or 1am.

Ryokan and *minshuku* (Japanese equivalent of a B&B) are better still, if you can make a few concessions to Japanese etiquette, with rates from around ¥4500 per person.

At youth hostels and so-called 'gaijin houses' (foreigner houses) you can get single rates down to ¥3500 per person (which is about as low as it gets in Tokyo). There are two caveats however: the youth hostels impose an early evening curfew; and the gaijin houses are generally way out in the boondocks and only take long-termers.

Tokyo International Youth Hostel (Map pp94-5; ☎ 3235-1107; 1-1 Kagurakashi, Shinjuku-ku; dm ¥3500) You don't have to be a member here but book ahead and provide some identification (a passport will do) when you arrive. To get there, take the west exit (when coming by JR) or the B2b exit (when coming by subway) out of Iidabashi Station. It's on the 18th floor of the Central Plaza building, one minute from the station (look for the tall, glass-fronted building). You may be charged an extra fee for air-con in summer and heating in winter, and breakfast/dinner costs ¥400/800. Check-in is 4pm to 9.30pm. The Narita airport TIC (see p92) has a step-by-step instruction sheet on the cheapest way to get to the hostel from the airport.

Yoyogi Youth Hostel (Map p103; ☎ 3467-9163; 3-1 Yoyogi Kamizono-chō, Shibuya-ku; dm members/non-members ¥3000/4000) This less-appealing choice offers no meals and no cooking facilities. However, all the rooms are singles and are clean. Check-in is from 5pm to 8pm. To get there, take the Odakyū line to Sangūbashi Station. Exit the station, turn left and walk 200m, then cross the tracks and turn right. Walk 150m and cross the pedestrian bridge. Continue on in the same direction and enter the National Olympics Memorial Youth Center compound. The guards at the gate have a map to the hostel.

The **Welcome Inn Reservation Center** (Narita Airport Terminals 1 & 2; www.itcj.or.jp/indexwel.html; ◷ 9am-7.30pm), with another location at the TIC (p92) in central Tokyo, is a free booking service that will make reservations for you at hotels and ryokan in the Japan Welcome Inn hotel group.

MISSING THE MIDNIGHT TRAIN

Cinderellas who've stayed out partying past midnight and found that their last train has turned into a *kabocha* (Japanese pumpkin) need not fret. If dancing the night away doesn't appeal, and an astronomically-priced taxi ride doesn't compute, give the capsule hotel a miss and try a manga café instead.

Curl up in a comfy recliner with a bottomless Coke and web-surf the night away (or read, watch a movie or snooze) in a manga café, where full-night rates are a bargain for any budget. You check in at a reception desk, pre-pay for your stay, and while away the wee hours in a cosy private space. Most manga cafés serve food, have libraries of DVDs and manga, and have staff making regular rounds to assure safe surfing and sleeping.

Spend the night at Manga Hiroba (p90), Café J Net New New (p90) or Manga@Cafe -Gera Gera (p90).

If it is imperative that you find inexpensive accommodation, be certain to make a booking before you arrive. Flying into Narita (particularly at night) without accommodation lined up can be nightmarish. For hotels near Narita airport, see p198.

For more detailed information on capsule hotels, gaijin houses, hostels and love hotels, see p721.

Central Tokyo 東京中心部

Along with Akasaka, Ginza is home to the thickest concentration of elite hotels anywhere in Tokyo. Prices here reflect the glamorous surroundings and proximity to Tokyo Station, great shopping, good restaurants, all manner of theatre, and the political and financial districts of the city.

BUDGET
Sakura Hotel (Map pp94-5; ☎ 3261-3939; reserve@ sakura-hotel.co.jp; 2-21-4 Kanda-Jimbōchō, Chiyoda-ku; dm/ s/d ¥3780/7140/8000; ⬛ 🖳) Though not exactly within Central Tokyo (it's only a couple of subway stops away), Sakura Hotel is a good guesthouse in Jimbōchō with private rooms as well as cosy dorm rooms. There's a small restaurant/bar on the premises with an attached outdoor terrace. To get there from Jimbōchō Station, take the A6 exit and turn right, walk two blocks and turn right

at the *kōban* (police box); the hotel is 200m on the right. Email ahead for reservations; check-in is from 1pm.

MIDRANGE

Yaesu Terminal Hotel (Map p96; ☎ 3281-3771; www .yth.jp; 1-5-14 Yaesu, Chūō-ku; s/d ¥11,340/16,590; ✗ 🖳) Between Tokyo Station and Takashimaya department store, this recently-refurbished hotel sports sleek, clean lines. Its rooms are quite small, but the prices are good for this area and it feels a touch more elegant than your typical business hotel. The in-house restaurant's wall of plate-glass windows look out on the streetside treetops. Check-in is 1pm; access it from the Yaesu north exit from Tokyo Station.

Hotel Yaesu-Ryūmeikan (Map p96; ☎ 3271-0971; www.ryumeikan.co.jp/yaesu_e.htm; 1-3-22 Yaesu, Chūō-ku; s/d ¥8600/15,400; ✗) The cheapest deal in the area and not a bad choice, this hotel has Japanese-style rooms at rates comparable to the Western-style accommodations. It's a five-minute walk from Tokyo Station's Yaesu north exit. Check-in is 2pm.

Tokyo Station Hotel (Map p96; ☎ 3231-2511; www.tshl.co.jp/main_f.html; 1-9-1 Marunouchi, Chiyoda-ku; s/d ¥11,600/26,600; ✗ ✗) This is a good place to crash if you can't face any more travel upon arriving at Tokyo Station. The rooms are pretty basic, but the hotel has a certain quaint, red-carpeted charm, and you can't beat the location. Remain stationary! Check-in is 2pm.

Ginza Nikkō Hotel (Map p96; ☎ 3571-4911; 8-4-21 Ginza, Chūō-ku; s/d/tw ¥14,000/29,000/28,000; ✗ ✗) In a prime location right on Sotobori-dōri between Ginza and Shimbashi, this is a quality place with smallish, cosy rooms. Check-in is 1pm; from Shimbashi Station, take exit 5.

Mitsui Urban Hotel Ginza (Map p96; ☎ 3572-4131; 8-6-15 Ginza, Chūō-ku; s/d ¥14,500/25,000; 🅿 ✗ ✗) Rooms here have an elegant feel and the usual amenities; this is a solid choice for comfortable accommodations in the southern end of Ginza. From Shimbashi Station, use exit 3 to access the hotel; check-in is 1pm.

Other midrange possibilities in Central Tokyo:

Ginza International Hotel (Map p96; ☎ 3574-1121; 8-7-13 Ginza, Chūō-ku; s/d/tw ¥13,000/18,000/22,000; 🅿 ✗ ✗) In a similar class to the Ginza Nikkō and located nearby; check in at 1pm, access from Shimbashi Station, exit 3.

Hotel Ginza Daiei (Map p96; ☎ 3545-1111; 3-12-1 Ginza, Chūō-ku; s/d/tw ¥11,970/16,000/21,500; ✗) North of Kabuki-za Theatre in Ginza, a slightly scruffy business hotel; check in at 2pm, arrive from Higashi-ginza Station (exit A7).

TOP END

Hotel Seiyo Ginza (Map p96; ☎ 3535-1111; www .seiyo-ginza.com; 1-11-2 Ginza, Chūō-ku; r ¥47,250-210,000; 🅿 ✗ ✗ 🖳) For an extravagant experience of over-the-top service in impossibly dignified surroundings, make a beeline for this exclusive place. On a small, intimate scale – with only 77 rooms – the Seiyo Ginza is the only hotel in Tokyo with 24-hour butler service for all guests. Make sure to book in advance. Check-in is 2pm; Ginza-itchōme Station is your nearest access.

Palace Hotel (Map p96; ☎ 3211-5211; www .palacehotel.co.jp/english/; 1-1-1 Marunouchi, Chiyoda-ku; s/d/tw ¥25,200/34,650/33,600; 🅿 ✗) Directly alongside the Kōkyo, this hotel has an old-fashioned atmosphere and arguably the best location in Tokyo. Many rooms here command impressive views over the palace. The service is wonderful and the hotel's restaurants are among the best in Tokyo. Check-in is noon; exit C13b from Ōtemachi Station.

Imperial Hotel (Map p96; ☎ 3504-1111; www .imperialhotel.co.jp; 1-1-1 Uchisaiwai-chō, Chiyoda-ku; main bldg d ¥36,750; 🅿 ✗ ✗ 🖳) One of Tokyo's grand old hotels, the Imperial is within walking distance of the sights of Ginza and Hibiya-kōen. It has all the standard amenities in a very elegant setting, and rooms are large and tastefully appointed. Check-in is noon.

Renaissance Tokyo Hotel Ginza Tōbu (Map p96; ☎ 3546-0111; www.marriott.com/tyorn; 6-14-10 Ginza, Chūō-ku; s/d ¥17,850/29,400; 🅿 ✗ ✗ 🖳) This bright, softly sparkling hotel is just south of Kabuki-za Theatre. The restaurants and bars are excellent and its rooms are spacious. Take exit A1 from Higashi-ginza Station; check-in is noon.

Ueno 上野

Ueno may be a bit of a trek from the bright lights, but it's a great sightseeing base, (especially for museum buffs) and there are several budget ryokan in the area.

The ryokan here are better value but if they're all full, the business hotels in the neighbourhood are generally cheaper than those in other areas around Tokyo.

BUDGET

Ryokan Katsutarō Annex (Map pp94-5; ☎ 3828-2500; www.katsutaro.com; 3-8-4 Yanaka, Taito-ku; s/d/tr ¥6300/10,500/14,700; ✂ 🖳) All of the bright, Japanese-style rooms at the spotless new Annex have Western-style baths attached. There's LAN access in each room, but with free Internet access *and* free coffee in the lobby, why not hang out downstairs to chat with the cheery proprietress? The easiest access is via Sendagi Station (exit 2) on the Chiyoda line; call ahead for directions in English. Credit cards are accepted here and check-in is at 3pm at both Katsutaro branches.

Ryokan Katsutarō (Map pp98-9; ☎ 3821-9808; 4-16-8 Ikenohata, Taito-ku; s/d/tr without bathroom ¥5200/8400/12,300, d/tr with bathroom ¥9600/13,200; ✂ 🖳) This tiny, quaint ryokan is run by the brother of the Annex's manager. He'll give you a code that opens the front door, so you can let yourself in after the 11pm curfew. A Western breakfast costs an extra ¥500. From Nezu Station on the Chiyoda line, take exit 2 and call for directions.

Sawanoya Ryokan (Map pp94-5; ☎ 3822-2251; 2-3-11 Yanaka, Taito-ku; s without bathroom ¥4940-5250, d/tr with bathroom ¥9870/14,175) A cosy, family-run ryokan, Sawanoya is a good choice if you're looking for that personal, homely feel. The ryokan is within walking distance of Nezu subway station on the Chiyoda line; call for walking directions from the station. If you're coming from Narita airport, it will probably be easier and just as cheap (if there are more than one of you) to catch a taxi from Ueno Station. Check-in is 2pm.

Sakura Ryokan (Map pp98-9; ☎ 3876-8118; www .sakura-ryokan.com/index-en.html; 2-6-2 Iriya, Taito-ku; s with/without bathroom ¥6600/5500, d with/without bathroom ¥11,000/10,000; ✂) One stop away from Ueno on the JR Yamanote or Hibiya subway lines, Sakura Ryokan is a good base for museum lovers, and decent value. Call from the station for directions, or better yet, print out a map and directions from their website before you get on the train. Either way, you'll want to disembark at Iriya Station, exit 1. Check-in is 3pm.

New Kōyō (Map pp94-5; ☎ 3873-0343; www .newkoyo.com; 2-26-13 Nihonzutsumi, Taito-ku; small/large s with shared bathroom ¥2500/2700, d ¥4800) This flophouse-turned-guesthouse is the cheapest place to stay in Tokyo; reserve well in advance. There are small, very basic Western/

Japanese-style singles and two doubles. It's two stops north of Ueno on the Hibiya line. Take a left out of Minowa Station's exit 3 and walk to the first set of lights. Take a left, walk past three sets of lights and take a right just before the Lawson convenience store; it's on the right in the second block. Check-in is from noon.

MIDRANGE

Suigetsu Hotel Ōgaisō (Map pp98-9; ☎ 3822-4611; www.ohgai.co.jp/index-e.html; 3-3-21 Ikenohata, Taito-ku; Western-style s ¥8000, Japanese-style d ¥16,800; ✂ ✂) On the western side of the park, those who want a change from the typical Western-style hotel may want to try this place. This hotel mostly has Japanese-style tatami (woven floor-mat) rooms, and there are several large Japanese-style baths. There's also a lovely Japanese garden in the centre of the building complex. Check-in is 3pm; though it's a long walk, easiest access is from Ueno Station.

Hotel Parkside (Map pp98-9; ☎ 3836-5711; www .parkside.co.jp; 2-11-18 Ueno, Taito-ku; s/d ¥9200/15,500, Japanese-style d ¥16,500; ✂ ✂ 🖳) Overlooking the park itself, this is another good choice, particularly if you can get a room at the front. The place is pleasant and clean, with Japanese-style rooms also available. Check-in is 2pm.

Hotel Green Capital (Map pp98-9; ☎ 3842-2411; www.thehotel.co.jp; 7-8-23 Ueno, Taito-ku; s/d ¥7875/13,125; ✂) This typical business hotel is quite close to Ueno Station and has polite staff and slightly bigger-than-average rooms to recommend it. The rooms are clean and new, and the prices competitive. Check-in is 3pm.

Ueno Kinuya Hotel (Map pp98-9; ☎ 3833-1911; 2-14-28 Higashi-Ueno, Taito-ku; s/d without bathroom from ¥5500/9300; ✂) This place has decent Japanese-style rooms if the other options are full, but women might not feel comfortable with the shared-bathroom situation. Check-in is 1pm.

Hotel Suntargas (Map pp98-9; ☎ 3833-8686; www.suntargas.co.jp; 2-19-3 Higashi-Ueno, Taito-ku; s/d ¥7350/10,500; ✂ ✂) Another business hotel not far from the station, this is slightly less appealing than the Ueno Kinuya. The weekend and holiday rates are about ¥2000 cheaper than those listed here. Check-in is 4pm. Take exit 3 from Ueno Station and cross the expressway to get to the hotel.

Asakusa 浅草   **Map pp98–9**

If you don't mind sacrificing central location for the funky Shitamachi (downtown) atmosphere, Asakusa is a fine place to stay. The area also has several reasonably priced ryokan.

BUDGET

Ryokan Shigetsu (☎ 3843-2345; www.shigetsu.com; 1-31-11 Asakusa, Taito-ku; Western-style s/d with bathroom ¥7665/14,700, Japanese-style s/d ¥9450/16,800; ✗ ❖ 🖳) This highly recommended ryokan is an immaculate, comfortable place to stay, although the service can feel a bit chilly. There's a good Japanese bath on the top floor, which overlooks Sensō-ji. It has free Net access. Check-in is 3pm.

Taito Ryokan (☎ 3843-2822; www.libertyhouse.gr .jp; 2-1-4 Nishi-Asakusa, Taito-ku; s/d with shared bathroom ¥3000/6000; ✗ ❖ 🖳) The intimate, wood-floored Taito Ryokan is great value, especially with its English-speaking managers with whom conversing is a delight. It can be noisy, and palatial it ain't, but who cares at this price. The website has a map containing detailed directions to the ryokan, which has an easy-to-miss exterior.

Ryokan Mikawaya Honten (☎ 3841-8954; 1-30-12 Asakusa, Taito-ku; Japanese-style with/without bathroom ¥6825/6300; ❖) A short walk from Asakusa Station, this is a decent option in Asakusa, with Japanese-style rooms and in the middle of Nakamise-dōri dining and shopping bustle. Check-in is 3pm.

Kikuya Ryokan (☎ 3841-4051; 2-18-9 Nishi-Asakusa, Taito-ku; s with/without bathroom ¥4500/5600, d with/without bathroom ¥7000/8400; ✗ ❖ 🖳) In Nishi Asakusa just off Kappabashi-dōri, this ryokan gets good reports as a quiet and friendly place to stay. Access it from Tawaramachi Station on the Ginza line; and check-in at 2pm.

Capsule Hotel Riverside (☎ 3844-1155; 2-20-4 Kaminarimon, Taito-ku; capsules ¥3300) Within stumbling distance from Asakusa Station, this is one capsule hotel that accepts women (the 8th floor is women-only). Capsules are a bargain at this cosy place. Look for the entrance around the back of the building. Check-in is 3pm Monday to Friday and 2pm Saturday and Sunday.

Hotel Skycourt Asakusa (☎ 3875-4411; 6-35-8 Asakusa, Taito-ku; dm members ¥5250, s/d/tw nonmembers ¥6000/10,500/13,000; ❖) This clean business hotel also functions as a youth hostel. To get there from Asakusa, walk up Edo-dōri past the Tōbu Station (keeping it on your left) to the third set of lights. Take the street just to the left of the *kōban* and walk 100m past the first set of lights.

MIDRANGE

Asakusa Plaza Hotel (☎ 3845-2621; www.asakusaplaza .jp; 1-2-1 Asakusa, Taito-ku; s/d/tw ¥6930/11,000/12,700; ❖ 🖳) This standard-issue business hotel is convenient to local sights, centrally located right on Kaminarimon-dōri. Unless you speak some Japanese, reserve a room via their website; check-in is 4pm.

Hotel Skycourt Asakusa (left) Another good option, this business hotel doubles as a youth hostel.

TOP END

Asakusa View Hotel (☎ 3847-1111; www.viewhotels .co.jp/asakusa/english/index.html; 3-17-1 Nishi-Asakusa, Taito-ku; ✗ ❖ 🖳 ⓧ ; s/d/tw ¥13,650/23,000/26,000) Just about Asakusa's only luxury hotel, this 28-storey building boasts an assortment of restaurants, one storey with Japanese-style rooms, wide garden and temple views, and a shopping area. Check-in is 1pm.

Ikebukuro 池袋   **Map p100**

BUDGET

Kimi Ryokan (☎ 3971-3766; www.kimi-ryokan.jp; 2-36-8 Ikebukuro, Toshima-ku; s/d ¥4500/6500; ✗ ❖ 🖳) Kimi Ryokan is the best budget choice in Tokyo, with clean, inexpensive Japanese-style rooms and the most convivial lounge area of Tokyo's ryokan. The Kimi is outfitted with showers and a Japanese-style bath. There's a notice board, and the owner's constantly changing *ikebana* adds cheer to the place. Be sure to book ahead; there's nearly always a waiting list. Check-in is 3pm. Print a helpful map from the website; the ryokan is easily accessible from the west exit of Ikebukuro JR Station.

House Ikebukuro (☎ 3984-3399; www.housejp .com.tw/englishindex.htm; 2-20-1 Ikebukuro, Toshima-ku; s/d/tr ¥5000/6000/8000, 'apt' r for 2/3 people ¥8500/10,500; 🅿 ❖ 🖳) Also on the west side of Ikebukuro, this has a variety of rooms, all with shared bathroom and a common kitchen. The best, however, are the apartment-like rooms in the annexe, with fridge and microwave. Check-in is 3pm. It's less than 100m from the C1 exit of Ikebukuro subway station; check the website for a detailed map.

MIDRANGE

There are innumerable business hotels, love hotels and capsule hotels in the Ikebukuro area. Be aware, however, that the capsule hotels in this neighbourhood are not nearly as accustomed to foreign guests as their cousins in Akasaka and Shinjuku.

Hotel Clarion Tokyo (☎ 5396-0111; www.clarionto kyo.com; 2-3-1 Ikebukuro, Toshima-ku; s/d ¥14,000/20,000;
P ⊠ ✷ 🖳) Rooms here are quite spacious compared with the usual standard for business hotels. The staff are helpful, high-speed Internet is available in all rooms, and major credit cards are accepted. Check-in is 2pm.

Hotel Grand City (☎ 3984-5121; info@grand-city.gr.jp; 1-30-7 Higashi-Ikebukuro, Toshima-ku; s/d ¥7665/10,000; P ⊠ ✷ 🖳) On the east side of Ikebukuro, this is a standard but friendly business hotel with relatively inexpensive rates and even a ladies-only floor. It's comfortable and bland. Check-in is 2pm.

Hotel Theatre (☎ 3988-2251; hotel@theatres.co.jp; 1-21-4 Higashi-Ikebukuro, Toshima-ku; ⊠ ✷ 🖳 ; s/d ¥9135/12,600) Also to the east of the station, this is centrally located and clean. Check-in is 2pm.

Hotel Sunroute Ikebukuro (☎ 3980-1911; www .sunroute-ikebukuro.com in Japanese; 1-39-4 Higashi-Ikebukuro, Toshima-ku; s/d/tw ¥10,395/16,380/18,060; ⊠ ✷ 🖳) Just along the street from the main Bic Camera store, this place has pleasant, clean rooms and friendly staff, some of whom speak English. Check-in is 2pm.

More of Ikebukuro's midrange options:

Ark Hotel (☎ 3590-0111; 3-5-5 Higashi-Ikebukuro, Toshima-ku; s/d/tw ¥9240/16,800/17,850; ✷) Another comfortable place with clean rooms and polite staff; check-in is 3pm.

Hotel Sun City Ikebukuro (☎ 3986-1101; www.h -suncity.com; 1-29-1 Ikebukuro; s/d ¥7800/12,600; ⊠) Basic rooms with some on-premises drinking and dining options; check-in is 3pm.

Ikebukuro Royal Hotel (☎ 5396-0333; 2-41-7 Ike-bukuro, Toshima-ku; s/tw ¥8190/12,390; P ✷) A basic business hotel with a lovely Japanese bath; enter through restaurant to reach reception; check-in is 3pm.

Shinjuku 新宿   **Map p101**

This area is a good hunting ground if you're after business hotels accustomed to foreign guests. Moreover, the intense competition in the area helps keep prices down, and it's a convenient neighbourhood in which to base yourself.

BUDGET

Green Plaza Shinjuku (☎ 3207-5411; 1-29-3 Kabuki-chō, Shinjuku-ku; capsules ¥4200) Just down the road from the Shinjuku Prince Hotel on Shinjuku's east side, you get your own personal capsule and admission to the hotel's sauna (p122). The front desk of this hotel is on the 3rd floor; check-in is 3pm.

Shinjuku-Kuyakusho-Mae Capsule Hotel (☎ 3232-1110; 1-2-5 Kabuki-chō, Shinjuku-ku; capsules ¥4200) Smack in the middle of Kabuki-chō, this conveniently located capsule hotel is strategically located for stumbling in after drunken revelry, to safely encapsulate yourself away from the sleazy Kabuki-chō action. Check-in commences at 2pm.

MIDRANGE

Shinjuku Park Hotel (☎ 3356-0241; shinjukupark hotel.com; 5-27-9 Sendagaya, Shibuya-ku; s/tw ¥7900/13,800, Japanese-style r ¥24,800; P ⊠ ✷ 🖳) Just south of the Takashimaya Times Square complex, the Shinjuku Park Hotel has larger rooms than most business hotels and its prices are competitive. Try booking a room with a view of the park. Check-in is 3pm.

Hotel Sun Lite Shinjuku (☎ 3356-0391; www .sunlite.co.jp/index-e.htm; 5-15-8 Shinjuku, Shinjuku-ku; s/d/tw ¥8715/12,075/14,175; P ✷) In east Shinjuku, this is a good choice. The staff are friendly and relaxed, and the place is clean and quiet, with small but well-maintained rooms. Check-in is 3pm; take exit C7 of Shinjuku-sanchōme Station.

Shinjuku New City Hotel (☎ 3375-6511; www .newcityhotel.co.jp/eng/index.html; 4-31-1 Nishi-Shinjuku, Shinjuku-ku; s/d/tw ¥9000/15,000/14,000) On the far side of Shinjuku's Chūō-kōen, this hotel has bigger rooms than average, by business hotel standards. Some have pretty park views, and staff here are friendly. Access it from Tochōmae Station, exit A4; check-in is 3pm.

Shinjuku Washington Hotel (☎ 3343-3111; www .wh-rsv.com/english/index.html; 3-2-9 Nishi-Shinjuku, Shinjuku-ku; s/d/tw ¥11,960/17,850/18,370; P ⊠ ✷) This efficient business hotel has lots of restaurants and amenities. Rooms and windows are small, but views from the upper floors are excellent. There's also a ladies-only floor. Check-in is 2pm. From Shinjuku Station, take the south exit to Kōshū-kaidō, turn right on Gijido-dōri and take the first left after that.

Central Hotel (☎ 3354-6611; 3-34-7 Shinjuku, Shinjuku-ku; s/d ¥11,550/17,850; ⊠ ✷) With blandly pleasant and clean rooms, this is

THE AUTHOR'S CHOICE

Park Hyatt Tokyo (Map pp101-2 ☎ 5322-1234; tokyo.park.hyatt.com; 3-7-1-2 Nishi-Shinjuku, Shinjuku-ku; s & d ¥54,600; P ✗ 🛇 💻 🗐) On the upper floors of the 53-floor Shinjuku Park Tower, you might recognise this island of luxury in the sky from the 2003 film *Lost in Translation*. The understated elegance of the spacious, stylish rooms is complemented by the rooftop pool, gym overlooking the city, and immaculate spa and sauna facility. If you're looking to splurge on accommodation in Tokyo, this is the place to do it. Even if you don't stay here, at least stop by for a drink in the New York Bar. Check-in is 1pm Monday to Friday and 3pm Saturday and Sunday.

another decent and, well, central choice in the heart of east Shinjuku. Check-in is 1pm; it's about a block east of the central east exit from Shinjuku Station.

Star Hotel Tokyo (☎ 3361-1111; 7-10-5 Nishi-Shinjuku, Shinjuku-ku; s/d ¥9450/17,850; P 🛇) In west Shinjuku, this hotel is very conveniently located, but the rooms and service are blindingly average. Check-in is 1pm. From the west exit of Shinjuku Station, cross Ōme-kaidō and turn left on Yasukuni-dōri.

TOP END

Century Hyatt Tokyo (☎ 3349-0111; tokyo.century.hyatt .com/; 2-7-2 Nishi-Shinjuku, Shinjuku-ku; s/d ¥23,000/32,000, Japanese-style ste ¥72,000; P ✗ 🛇 💻 🗐) The Century Hyatt has spacious rooms in both Western and Japanese styles. With its sumptuously shiny lobby and a 28th-floor pool, the place is popular with international businesspeople. Ask about seasonal discounts when booking ahead. Check-in is 1pm.

Keiō Plaza Hotel (☎ 3344-0111; www.keioplaza .com/index.html; 2-2-1 Nishi-Shinjuku, Shinjuku-ku; s/d ¥22,000/26,000, Japanese-style ste ¥80,000; P ✗ 🛇 💻) In west Shinjuku, the Keiō Plaza has 47 floors and a simple, refined style. Rooms provide excellent views of the area and there's a wealth of restaurants in the hotel. Check-in is 1pm.

Hotel Century Southern Tower (☎ 5354-0111; www.southerntower.co.jp; 2-2-1 Yoyogi, Shibuya-ku; s/d ¥16,000/22,000; P ✗ 🛇 💻) This towering hotel, true to its name, is in west Shinjuku on the upper floors of the Odakyū Southern Tower building. The relatively modest

rooms are blessed with soaring, spectacular city and park views. Check-in is 2pm.

Shibuya 渋谷

BUDGET

Ryokan Sansui-sō (Map pp94-5; ☎ 3441-7475, fax 3449-1944; 2-9-5 Higashi-Gotanda, Shinagawa-ku; s/tw/tr without bathroom ¥4900/8600/12,000, tw with bathroom ¥9000) Close to JR Gotanda Station on the Yamanote line, this cute ryokan is not ideally located, but it's only a few stops from Shibuya Station. To get there, take the east exit out of Gotanda Station. Turn right, take the first right after the big Tōkyū department store and then the first left. Turn left and then right, walk past the bowling centre and look for the sign on the right directing you down the side-street to the ryokan. Fax ahead to reserve a room; check-in is 2pm.

MIDRANGE

This is a pricey area to base yourself and the pickings are slim. Less-expensive business hotels in Ueno, Ikebukuro and even Shinjuku represent much better value for money.

Shibuya Tōbu Hotel (Map p103; ☎ 3476-0111; 3-1 Udagawa-chō, Shibuya-ku; s ¥11,800-13,800, d ¥20,000-26,000; ✗ 🛇 💻) Probably the nicest place to stay in Shibuya, the rooms here are stylish, clean and relatively spacious. The common areas are pleasant, there are loads of in-house restaurants and the friendly, attentive staff speak English. Check-in is 2pm. From the Hachikō exit at Shibuya JR Station, walk up Jingū-dōri, turn left after the Tower Records Building, right at Parco department store and the hotel will be on your left.

Shibuya Tōkyū Inn (Map p103; ☎ 3498-0109; 1-24-10 Shibuya, Shibuya-ku; s/d ¥13,440/21,840; ✗ 🛇 💻) At a similar standard as the Shibuya Tōbu Hotel, the vaguely retro-style nonsmoking rooms are probably the best of the bunch. There's a fee for in-room Internet access. Check-in is 3pm; the hotel is right on Meiji-dōri.

TOP END

Shibuya Excel Hotel Tōkyū (Map p103; ☎ 5457-0109; 1-12-2 Dogenzaka, Shibuya-ku; s/d/tw ¥20,790/26,565/28,875; ✗ 🛇 💻) Right next to the JR station in the Shibuya Mark City Building, the Shibuya Excel is nothing if not central. There are two ladies-only floors and the usual amenities you'd expect to find in an upscale business hotel. Check-in is 2pm.

Roppongi & Akasaka

六本木・赤坂 **Map pp106–7**

Both Roppongi and Akasaka are good areas in which to hang your hat if you want access to central Tokyo and a lively nightlife.

Akasaka has a high concentration of luxury hotels because this is a great area in which to be based: there are loads of good restaurants nearby, the political and business centres are within walking distance and Roppongi's nightlife is just down the road.

BUDGET

Capsule Hotel Fontaine Akasaka (☎ 3583-6554; 4-3-5 Akasaka, Minato-ku; capsules men/women Mon-Fri ¥4800/4500, Sat & Sun ¥4500) This upmarket capsule hotel is one of the few in Tokyo that accepts women. It also happens to be one of the more luxurious, featuring lovely bath and sauna facilities and comfortable, bright sitting areas. Check-in is 5pm to 10am; access it from Akasaka-mitsuke Station.

Capsule Inn Akasaka (☎ 3588-1811; 6-14-1 Akasaka, Minato-ku; capsules ¥3500) Fortunately, this capsule hotel is a short walk from Akasaka Station. Unfortunately, it's limited only to guests with the Y chromosome (males). Check-in is 5pm.

Asia Center of Japan (☎ 3402-6111; www.asia center.or.jp; 8-10-32 Akasaka, Minato-ku; s/d/tw ¥7500/ 9500/12,000; ❷ 🖳) Near Aoyama-itchōme subway station on the Ginza line, this is a popular option. This place attracts many long-term stayers and is often fully booked (call ahead). The station is under the easily recognisable Aoyama Twin Tower building on Aoyama-dōri. Walk past the building towards Akasaka-mitsuke, turn right on Gaien-Higashi-dōri (towards Roppongi), and the Asia Center is a short walk up the second street on the left. Rooms have pay-TV (rooms with bathrooms are more expensive). Booking over the Internet garners discounts of around 10%. Check-in is 2pm.

MIDRANGE

Hotel Sunroute Akasaka (☎ 3589-3610; www.sun route.jp; 3-21-7 Akasaka, Minato-ku; s/d/tw ¥13,125/ 15,225/18,375; ❌ ❷ 🖳) A bright, friendly spot with well-designed rooms all equipped with high-speed Internet access, this is conveniently located near the Akasaka-mitsuke subway station and is a fifteen-minute walk from Roppongi nightlife. There's no restaurant, but there is an Excelsior Café (akin to Starbucks) downstairs. Check-in is 2pm.

Akasaka Yōkō Hotel (☎ 3586-4050; 6-14-12 Akasaka, Minato-ku; s/d ¥9345/13,650; ❷ ❌ ❷ 🖳) In Akasaka, this is a reasonably priced business hotel about midway between Akasaka and Roppongi. Although it's quite simple, the modest rooms are clean and comfortable and the staff are friendly. From the Yōkō, you're close enough to walk to Roppongi for a wild night out, but far enough to retire peacefully to quieter pastures afterwards. Check-in is 3pm.

Marroad Inn Akasaka (☎ 3585-7611; www.toto -motors.co.jp/marroad/eindex.htm; 6-15-17 Akasaka, Minato-ku; s/d/tw ¥9900/10,800/15,800; ❌ ❷ 🖳) On the same street as Akasaka Yōkō Hotel, 100m closer to Roppongi, this is another standard business hotel with similar features. Check their website for Internet discounts. Check-in is 4pm.

Hotel Ibis (☎ 3403-4411; www.ibis-hotel.com; 7-14-4 Roppongi, Minato-ku; s/d/tw ¥13,382/16,285/22,145; ❷ ❌ ❷ 🖳) In Roppongi, right near the famous Roppongi Crossing, the Ibis is a clean, modern hotel with small rooms and a few restaurants and bars. This being Roppongi, you can count on the staff being used to foreign guests. Check-in is 1pm.

TOP END

Hotel Ōkura (☎ 3582-0111; www.hotelokura.co.jp; 2-10-4 Toranomon, Minato-ku; s/d ¥30,450/34,125; ❷ ❌ ❷ 🖳 ❷) Near the US embassy, this is the home of visiting dignitaries and businesspeople and has a charming, unpretentious aesthetic. The hotel is on a low-lying scale, and the best of the very spacious accommodations are first-floor, garden-view balcony rooms. The hotel grounds also house the **Ōkura Shūkokan** (p120). Check-in is noon; access it from Tameike-sannō Station, exit 13.

Hotel New Otani (☎ 3265-1111; www1.new otani.co.jp/en/tokyo/index.htm; 4-1 Kioi-chō, Chiyoda-ku; s/d ¥30,450/35,700, Japanese-style ste ¥57,750; ❷ ❌ ❷ 🖳 ❷) This hotel, 240m north of Akasaka-mitsuke subway station (exit D) and not far from the Akasaka Prince, is renowned for the Japanese garden around which it is constructed. The swish hotel is immense, with all the details you'd expect from a hotel of this class, including high-end boutiques, an art museum and a whiff of attitude. Check-in is noon.

Capitol Tōkyū Hotel (☎ 3581-4511; www.capitol tokyu.com; 2-10-3 Nagata-chō, Chiyoda-ku; s/d ¥26,000/

TOKYO

38,000; (P) (X) (X) (L) (R)) This elegant place is up on the same hill as Hie-jinja, accessible from Tameike-sannō Station. The hotel is built around a fine Japanese garden, with good restaurants and bars from which to take in the view. In warmer months, you can enjoy the outdoor swimming pool. Check-in is noon.

Akasaka Prince Hotel (☎ 3234-1111; www.prince hotels.co.jp/akasaka; 1-2 Kioi-chō, Chiyoda-ku; Western-style s/d ¥28,875/42,735, Japanese-style ste ¥92,400; (X) (R)) This skyscraper hotel is something of a landmark, with an older, '70s retro appeal. The rooms provide excellent views and plenty of space, a commodity in short supply in Tokyo. Find it most easily from Nagata-chō Station; check-in is noon.

Grand Hyatt Tokyo (☎ 4333-1234; http://tokyo .grand.hyatt.com/; Roppongi Hills, 6-10-3 Roppongi, Minato-ku; s/d ¥29,700/34,700; (P) (X) (X) (L) (R)) Suitably slick for the futuristic hot spot that is Roppongi Hills, the Grand Hyatt gleams with a polished refinement. Though the look is decidedly urban, the interior makes liberal use of natural materials, lending an earthy feel to this modern, well-outfitted hotel. Word to the wise: book the west side for views of Mt Fuji. The hotel is situated nearest Roppongi Station.

ANA Hotel Tokyo (☎ 3505-1111; www.anahotels .com/tokyo/e/index.html; 1-12-33 Akasaka, Minato-ku; s & d ¥31,185, Japanese-style ste ¥98,175; (P) (X) (X) (L) (R)) Midway between Akasaka and Roppongi in the fashionable Ark Hills area (use the Roppongi-itchōme Station), this is an excellent choice for those seeking a plush environment. The newly-refurbished 37-storey hotel has all the amenities, from fitness clubs to fancy restaurants, all wrapped in a sleek, sophisticated package. Check-in is 1pm.

Ōdaiba & Tokyo Bay
お台場・東京湾 **Map p108**

Although it isn't the most convenient neighbourhood for exploring Tokyo, you do get breathing room in Ōdaiba. If you do choose to stay out here, make sure to book a room with a view. Both hotels are short walks from Daiba Station on the Yurikamome line.

TOP END

Hotel Nikkō Tokyo (☎ 5500-5500; www.hnt.co.jp /english/index.htm; 1-9-1 Daiba, Minato-ku; s/d ¥32,340/ 38,115; (P) (X) (X) (L) (R)) The Nikkō can boast a spa (¥3000), an outdoor hot tub and a sauna. The spacious rooms are decorated in a low-key palette with elegant style. Deluxe rooms feature a bathroom with a window above the tub so you can enjoy the lights on the Rainbow Bridge as you soak.

Le Meridien Grand Pacific Tokyo (☎ 5500-6711; grandpacific.lemeridien.com; 2-6-1 Daiba, Minato-ku; s/d ¥30,030/35,805; (P) (X) (X) (L) (R)) Ornate and polished, Le Meridien is plushly outfitted with extra luxuries – including boutiques, an art gallery and a florist – in addition to amenities like a pool and gym.

EATING

No city in Asia can match Tokyo for the sheer variety and quality of its restaurants. As well as refined Japanese cuisine, Tokyo is loaded with great international restaurants – everything from Cambodian to African. One thing to keep in mind is that Japanese food tends to be cheaper than international food. For ¥750 you can get a good bowl of noodles in a *shokudō* (all-round eatery); the same money will buy you a plate of spaghetti in one of Tokyo's many cheap Italian places, but it's sure to be a disappointment. If you fancy international food, be prepared to pay a little extra for the good stuff.

Whatever you choose to eat, you rarely have to look far for a restaurant in Tokyo. Check out the basements and upper floors of the big department stores for *resutoran-gai* (restaurant streets) – these invariably have a good selection of Japanese, Chinese and Italian restaurants with inexpensive lunchtime specials. Train stations are the home of *rāmen* shops, *obentō* (boxed meal) stands and *kareraisu* (curry rice) restaurants. Big commercial districts like the east side of Shinjuku simply brim with restaurants – serving everything from *kaiten-zushi* (revolving, or 'conveyor-belt' sushi) to pizza.

During the day, the best eating areas are the big shopping districts like Shibuya, Shinjuku, Harajuku and Ginza. By night, try Aoyama and Roppongi for some of Tokyo's best international and Japanese food. For something more traditional, try an *izakaya* (Japanese pub/eatery) or Yakitori Alley in central Tokyo, or the down-at-the-heels eating arcade of Omoide-Yokochō in Shinjuku.

If you are going to be in Tokyo for some time, pick up a copy of John Kennerdell's *Tokyo Restaurant Guide* (Yohan) or Rick

Kennedy's *Good Tokyo Restaurants*. Alternatively, check out the Tokyo Food Page website (www.bento.com/tokyofood.html), or Tokyo Q's food section (http://club.nokia.co.jp/tok yoq), for some up-to-the-minute picks.

For quick, cheap eats, or a cup of coffee in an air-conditioned (albeit smoky) café, there are chain coffeeshops like Doutor Coffee, Excelsior Coffee and Starbucks. These chains are dotted all over Tokyo and usually offer sandwiches and snacks at budget prices.

Vegetarian food is less common than you might expect in Tokyo. Luckily, many places that aren't strictly vegetarian, such as Japanese noodle and *tofu* (bean curd) shops, serve a good variety of no-meat and no-fish dishes. For more information, pick up the TIC's *Vegetarian & Macrobiotic Restaurants in Tokyo* handout. This lists strictly vegetarian restaurants, wholefood shops, *shōjin-ryōri* (Buddhist-temple fare) restaurants, and Indian restaurants that offer a good selection of vegetarian dishes.

Central Tokyo 東京中心部   Map p96
JAPANESE

If all you need is a quick bite, you'll find plenty of decent places to eat in the underground mall below Tokyo Station. Outside the station, on the Yaesu side, there are some more-interesting choices.

Kyūbei (☎ 3571-6523; 8-7-6 Ginza, Chūo-ku; dinner from ¥10,000; ☯ lunch & dinner Mon-Sat) In southern Ginza near Shimbashi (take exit 3 from the Shimbashi JR Station) is this high-quality sushi place with prices to match. If you treat yourself to one high-end sushi experience, make Kyūbei the venue.

Mikuniya (☎ 3271-3928; 2-5-11 Nihombashi, Chūo-ku; meals ¥1800-3500; ☯ lunch & dinner Mon-Sat) A great place to sample *unagi* (eel) in pleasant surroundings. Its standard *unagi* set is recommended. There's no English sign, so look for what looks like polished driftwood with gold lettering above the door. Take exit B4 from Nihombashi Station.

Sushi Tetsu (☎ 3275-0717; Yaesu, Chūo-ku; lunch/dinner ¥2500/6000; ☯ lunch & dinner) Near Mikuniya, Sushi Tetsu is a serious sushi restaurant – a good alternative to the bad *kaiten-zushi* places nearby. Take the Yaesu central exit from Tokyo Station.

Jangara Rāmen (☎ 3289-2307; 1st fl, New Ginza Bldg, 7-11-10 Ginza, Chūo-ku; meals ¥1000; ☯ 11am-1.30am) Jangara is the place to head down to (from Shimbashi Station, take exit 1) for all-the-rage *rāmen*; order *zenbu iri* (all-in) *rāmen* for ¥1000.

Sakata (☎ 3563-7400; 1-5-13 Ginza, Chūo-ku; from ¥850; ☯ lunch & dinner Mon-Fri, lunch Sat) Sakata is widely recognised as Tokyo's best noodle spot, and indeed the *sanuki udon* (a thick noodle of silky texture and exceptional firmness) is divine. There's no English signage, but gracious Sakata-san will go out of his way to feed you. Peak times may mean that this spot's slim counters and several tables will be completely full.

Shin-Hi-No-Moto (☎ 3214-8021; 2-4-4 Yūraku-chō, Chiyoda-ku; meals ¥2500; ☯ 5pm-midnight) Another great spot under the tracks, this lively *izakaya* is just around the corner from both Yūraku-chō and Hibiya subway stations (exit to Yūraku-chō Denki Bldg). The Chinese and Myanmarese staff speak English.

Lion Beer Hall (☎ 3571-2590; 7-9-20 Ginza, Chūo-ku; meals ¥2500; ☯ 11.30am-11pm) Ginza is also a good place to dip into Japanese beer-hall culture – Sapporo Lion, being the neighbourhood's biggest beer hall, is a good place to start. The extensive menu includes everything from Japanese snacks to German sausages. Find it on Chūo-dōri.

New Torigin (☎ 3571-3334; 5-5-7 Ginza, Chūo-ku; meals ¥1500; ☯ 4-10pm Mon-Fri, 11.30am-9.30pm Sat & Sun) Just south of Harumi-dōri, this place is hidden away down a very narrow back-alley but signposted in English (look for the yellow sign with a chicken on it). There's an English menu too, and this authentic, very popular little place does excellent *yakitori*, and the steamed-rice dish known as *kamameshi*.

Robata (☎ 3591-1905; 1-3-8 Yūraku-chō, Chiyoda-ku; meals ¥2500; ☯ 5.30-11pm) Back near the railway tracks, this is one of Tokyo's most celebrated *izakaya*. A little Japanese ability is helpful here, but the point-and-eat method works just fine. It's hard to spot the sign, even if you can read Japanese; it's better just to look for the rustic, weathered façade. Access it from Hibiya Station, exit A4.

Chichibu Nishiki (☎ 3541-4777; 2-13-14 Ginza, Chūo-ku; meals ¥2500; ☯ 5-10.30pm Mon-Fri) Another atmospheric spot in the same price range as Robata, this is a traditional *izakaya* with good, cheap food in a very authentic setting. It's tucked away a few blocks behind Kabuki-za.

Edogin (☎ 3543-4401; 4-5-1 Tsukiji, Chūo-ku; ☯ 11am-9pm Mon-Sat) Just up the way from Tsukiji Fish

Market, this small place receives steady traffic for good reason. The *teishoku* (lunchtime set) is a steal at ¥1000. The atmosphere is all form and function, though a splash of colour is added by the fish tank, from which you're welcome to choose your lunch. Take exit 6 from Higashi-ginza Station.

Hina Sushi (☎ 5531-0017; 4-1-2 Ginza, Chūō-ku; meals ¥2500; ☯ 11.30am-2pm & 5-10.30pm Tue-Fri, 11.30am-10.30pm Sat, 11.30am-9.30pm Sun) This excellent sushi chain has a branch in Ginza, on the 2nd floor of the Nishi Ginza department store. The all-you-can-eat sushi (¥4300) is a superb deal for this quality.

Ten-ichi (☎ 3571-1949; 6-6-5 Ginza, Chūō-ku; lunch/dinner ¥3500/8000; ☯ 11.30am-9.30pm) The place for tempura, assuming you want to splash out.

Zakuro (☎ 3535-4421; 4-6-1 Ginza, Chūō-ku; dinner from ¥5000; ☯ 11am-9.30pm) Another good spot for a splurge on traditional Japanese food, Zakuro is on the B1 floor of the Ginza Saison Restaurant Plaza, behind Mitsukoshi department store. The speciality here is *shabu-shabu* (thin slices of beef and vegetables cooked in a broth at the table).

Friendly, atmospheric *yakitori* (charcoal-broiled chicken and other meats or vegetables, cooked on skewers) restaurants can be found under the railway tracks in Yūraku-chō's so-called Yakitori Alley.

Alternatively head south to Ginza, where restaurants are more plentiful. Although it's expensive in the evening, lunch deals are competitive. A few *resutoran-gai* to check:

Ginza Palmy Building The restaurants are on the basement floor, where ¥400 buys a decent bowl of *rāmen* at **Naokyū Rāmen** (☎ 3571-0957; 5-2-1 Ginza, Chūō-ku; ☯ 11am-9pm).

Matsuzakaya department store (☎ 3572-1111; 6-10-1 Ginza, Chūō-ku; ☯ 10.30am-7.30pm) Check out the B2 floor.

Restaurant City (☎ 3567-1211; 3-6-1 Ginza, Chūō-ku; ☯ 10am-8pm) On the 8th floor of the Matsuya department store.

INTERNATIONAL

On weekdays, colourful little lunch trucks set up shop in the tree-shaded plaza of the Tokyo International Forum (p110). Cheap eats of an international variety range from falafels to tacos to North Indian curry, and most meals cost less than ¥1000.

Nair's (☎ 3541-8246; 4-10-7 Ginza, Chūō-ku; lunch/dinner ¥1500/3000; ☯ 11am-8.30pm) A popular restaurant in eastern Ginza towards Tsukiji,

this always seems to have a queue at lunch. Japanese showbiz types like to drop by for some incognito Indian.

Mikuni's Café Marunouchi (☎ 5220-3921; 1st fl, Furukawa Sogo Bldg, 2-6-1 Marunouchi, Chiyoda-ku; lunch sets from ¥1260; ☯ lunch & dinner) Multi-course Italian lunch sets end with something sweet and decadent. The pastry at the circular counter here is worth a nibble; the tiny scones verge on perfection.

Maxim's de Paris (☎ 3572-3621; B3 fl, Sony Bldg, 5-3-1 Ginza, Chūō-ku; lunch/dinner with wine ¥6300/21,000; ☯ 11am-3pm & 5.30-11pm Mon-Sat) In another price range entirely, Maxim's is housed in the Sony Building. The interior and the menu are dead ringers for the original in Paris, assuring diners a memorable meal.

Sabatini di Firenze (☎ 3573-0013; 7th fl, Sony Bldg, 5-3-1 Ginza, Chūō-ku; lunch/dinner with wine ¥7000/20,000; ☯ noon-3pm & 5.30-11pm) In the same building as Maxim's de Paris, Sabatini serves over-the-top, authentic Italian fare for a special night out.

Ueno 上野   Map pp98–9
JAPANESE

The Ueno area is a happy hunting ground for cheap food. You'll find a good variety of cheap Japanese places in and around Ameyoko arcade, where you can also pick up takeaway foods like *yakitori*, rice balls and fruit from vendors.

Ueno Yabu Soba (☎ 3831-4728; 6-9-16 Ueno, Taito-ku; meals ¥1800; ☯ 11.30am-9pm Thu-Tue) Near the arcade, this is a famous *soba* (buckwheat noodles) shop. To really fill up, get the *ten-seiro* (noodles topped with shrimp and vegetable tempura) set. Look for the black granite sign in front that says 'Since 1892'. The large picture menu makes ordering a snap.

Ganko Sushi (☎ 5688-8845; 6th fl, Nagafuji Bldg, 4-9-6 Ueno, Taito-ku; meals ¥2500; ☯ 11.30am-3pm & 4.30-11pm) Try Ganko Sushi for decent sushi and *teishoku* (set-course meal) deals at lunch and dinner. It has a picture menu and seems fairly accustomed to foreign customers. Try the sushi *mori-awase* (assortment) or the tempura *bentō* for lunch or dinner.

Futaba (☎ 3835-2672; 2-8-11 Ueno, Taito-ku; meals ¥1500-3000; ☯ lunch & dinner) Though the nondescript beige exterior doesn't look like much, the proof of Futaba's long-running popularity is in its pudding – or rather, its pork cutlets. This is a great, though perhaps a bit gruff, spot in Ueno to try a traditional taste of *tonkatsu* (deep-fried breaded pork cutlets).

Izu-ei (☎ 3831-0954; 2-12-12 Ueno, Taito-ku; meals from ¥2500; ❍ 11am-9.30pm) Izu-ei is a lovely choice for authentic Japanese food – the speciality here is *unagi* and it is tasty. The Izu-ei *unagi bentō* (eel lunch box) includes tempura, which is best eaten near the window for a lovely view of the giant waterlilies on Shinobazu-ike. There's a limited picture menu.

INTERNATIONAL

Samrat (☎ 5688-3226; 2nd fl, OAK Bldg, 4-8-9 Ueno, Taito-ku; lunch set ¥935; ❍ 11am-10pm) Samrat is a reliable Tokyo chain serving up a good Indian lunch set that includes a drink.

Asakusa 浅草   Map pp98–9
JAPANESE

The area between Sensō-ji and Kaminari-mon-dōri is the best place in Asakusa to seek out Japanese food. This area is about 100m west of exits 1 and 2 of Asakusa Station.

Daikokuya (☎ 3844-1111; 1-38-10 Asakusa, Taito-ku; set meals ¥3000-4300; ❍ 11.30am-8.30pm Mon-Sat) Near Nakamise arcade, this is the place to get tempura, a speciality in Asakusa. It is authentic and the tempura is excellent. Expect to pay about ¥1800 for a meal at lunchtime.

Owariya (☎ 3841-8780; 1-7-1 Asakusa, Taito-ku; meals ¥1300; ❍ 11.30am-8.30pm) In a similar vein to Daikokuya, this serves tempura and a variety of noodle dishes – try the tempura *donburi*.

Tatsumiya (☎ 3842-7373; 1-33-5 Asakusa, Taito-ku; lunch/dinner ¥850/2500-4000; ❍ 5-10pm Tue-Sun) Tatsumiya is an old Edo-period restaurant, cluttered with curious bric-a-brac, that specialises in *nabe ryōri* (stew; literally 'pot cuisine') during the winter months.

Asakusa Imahan (☎ 3841-1114; 3-1-12 Nishi-Asakusa, Taito-ku; meals ¥7300; ❍ 11.30am-9.30pm Tue-Sun) Imahan is a superb place to try *sukiyaki* or *shabu-shabu*. The meat is high quality, the preparation excellent and the atmosphere dignified…with prices to match.

Sometaro (☎ 3844-9502; 2-2-2 Nishi-Asakusa, Taito-ku; meals ¥1000; ❍ noon-10pm) In Nishi-Asakusa, try this place for good, DIY *okonomiyaki* (meat, seafood and vegetables in a cabbage-and-vegetable batter) in really funky surroundings. You cook it yourself on a griddle built into your table. Look for the rustic, overgrown façade.

Vin Chou (☎ 3845-4430; 2-2-13 Nishi-Asakusa, Taito-ku; meals ¥3000; ❍ 5am-11pm Thu-Tue, 4-10pm Sun) This is, of all things, a French-style *yakitori* joint, offering foie gras with your *tori negi* (chicken and leek). All rather chichi, for this neck of the woods. It's opposite the Taitō Ryokan.

Khroop Khrua (☎ 3847-3461; 2nd fl, 1-33-4 Asakusa, Taito-ku; dishes ¥1000; ❍ lunch & dinner Tue-Sat, noon-9pm Sun) Serving Thai and Vietnamese dishes in a cool, 2nd-floor, wood-floored dining room, Khroop Khrua is a healthy option for those craving a little spice. There are lots of vegetarian choices, with classic dishes like papaya salad.

Kamiya Bar (☎ 3841-5400; 1-1-1 Asakusa, Taito-ku; ❍ 11.30am-10pm Wed-Mon) Kamiya is said to be the oldest bar in Japan, having opened in 1880. There's a beer hall on the ground floor, where you order and pay for beer and food as you enter. Upstairs, Western and Japanese food is served.

INTERNATIONAL

Apart from the standard fast-food offerings, the only decent international choices in Asakusa are just across Azuma-bashi in the Asahi Beer Flamme D'Or building (you can't miss it – it's got the giant 'golden turd' on top).

La Ranarita Azumabashi (☎ 5608-5277; 1-23-1 Azuma-bashi, Sumida-ku; lunch/dinner ¥2500/6000; ❍ 11.30am-2pm & 5-9pm Mon-Sat, 11.30am-3pm & 4-8pm Sun) At La Ranarita, find good Milanese cuisine on the 22nd floor of the Asahi Beer building. It has great pizza capricciosa and is an excellent date spot for nonsufferers of vertigo.

Sumida River Brewing Company (☎ 5608-3831; 1-23-1 Azumabashi, Sumida-ku; set lunch ¥700; ❍ 11.30am-1.30pm & 5-10pm Mon-Fri, 11.30am-10pm Sat & Sun) This place offers average but inexpensive pub food with *ji-biru* (local beers), which start at ¥470 for a small glass.

Ikebukuro 池袋   Map p100
JAPANESE

Though not a dining destination in itself, Ikebukuro has plenty of fine places to fill up. At lunchtime, don't forget to check out the restaurant floors in Seibu, Tōbu and Marui department stores.

On the station's eastern side, look for revolving sushi restaurants.

Akiyoshi (☎ 3982-0644; 3-30-4 Nishi-Ikebukuro, Toshima-ku; meals ¥3000; ❍ 5-11pm) Akiyoshi is the place to try for a tasty *yakitori* in approachable, laid-back surroundings. There's a large picture menu to help you order. There's no English sign, but you can easily spot the long counters and smoky grills from out on the street.

Sushi Kazu (☎ 3590-4884; 2-10-8 Ikebukuro, Toshima-ku; meals from ¥3000; 🕚 11.30am-5am Mon-Sat) This good, standard-issue sushi bar is definitely a step up from all those revolving sushi bars in the neighbourhood. Formal Japanese-style dining rooms are also available for larger groups.

Tombo (☎ 3983-1686; 3-23-5 Nishi-Ikebukuro, Toshima-ku; meals ¥1250; 🕚 11am-3pm & 5-9pm Mon-Sat) On the west side, the welcoming folks at Tombo serve good *tonkatsu* (deep-fried breaded pork cutlet), fried shrimp and related fare. There's a menu in English, and the *hire katsu teishoku* (set meal with fancier *tonkatsu*) is recommended.

Tonerian (☎ 3985-0254; 1-38-9 Nishi-Ikebukuro, Toshima-ku; meals ¥3000; 🕚 5-11.15pm) One of Ikebukuro's many *izakaya*, this is a busy place with friendly staff. Turn up here to learn about good *jizake* (regional sake) – the master, who speaks English, will be glad to make suggestions. Look for all the empty sake bottles piled up outside.

Tapa (☎ 5950-2528; 1st & 2nd fl, Otowa Bldg, 1-15-2 Higashi-Ikebukuro, Toshima-ku; meals ¥3000; 🕚 11am-11.30pm Sun-Thu, 11am-4am Fri & Sat) Somewhere between an *izakaya* and a Spanish tapas bar, Tapa is on Ikebukuro's east side, not far from Tōkyū Hands. There's another branch on the 13th floor of Tōbu department store.

Yamabuki (☎ 3971-1287; lunch/dinner ¥980/1100; 🕚 11am-8.45pm) Call on Yamabuki for that wonderful Japanese delicacy, *unagi*; it serves *unadon* (*unagi* over rice). There is a picture menu. Look for all the eel in the window.

Sasashu (☎ 3971-9363; 2-2-6 Ikebukuro, Toshima-ku; meals from ¥6000; 🕚 5-10pm Mon-Sat) Sasashu is a high-quality sake specialist and serves *kamonabe* (duck stew). A little Japanese language ability would come in handy here, for pairing top-notch sake with complementary dishes. Across the street from a liquor store, its dignified old Japanese façade stands out from the strip joints.

INTERNATIONAL

Those hungry for international fare can find lots of cheap deals in Ikebukuro, some of which are easily accessed on department-store restaurant floors. In particular, try the

11th to 17th floors of Tōbu and the 8th floor of Tōbu's Metropolitan Plaza.

Domani (☎ 5954-8114; 1-11-1 Nishi-Ikebukuro, Toshima-ku; lunch/dinner ¥1000/2500; 🕚 11am-4.30pm & 5.30-9.40pm) This Italian restaurant serves good meals on the 8th floor of Tōbu's Metropolitan Plaza.

Malaychan (☎ 5391-7638; 3-22-6 Nishi-Ikebukuro, Toshima-ku; lunch & dinner Mon-Sat, 11am-11pm Sun) On a corner across from Nishi-Ikebukuro-kōen, Malaychan is one of Tokyo's few Malaysian restaurants. The food is so-so, but it's easy to order from the big picture menu and the drinks are good. *Nasi lemak* (rice with assorted dishes) is a filling introduction to Malaysian food at ¥1070.

Myun (My Dung; ☎ 3985-8967; 2nd fl, 5-1-6 Nishi-Ikebukuro, Toshima-ku; dishes ¥500; 🕚 lunch & dinner) Although there's no atmosphere to speak of, excepting the J-pop soundtrack, Myun serves a good Vietnamese lunch set and a dinner set with seven items. The restaurant is on the second floor; look for the green sign, streetside.

Capricciosa (☎ 5396-0773; 3-30-3 Nishi-Ikebukuro, Toshima-ku; lunch/dinner ¥2000/3000; 🕚 lunch & dinner) We don't recommend Capricciosa for authentic Italian cuisine, rather as the place to head to if your appetite's bigger than your budget and pasta is what you desire.

Gara (☎ 3971-3940; 3-22-8 Nishi-Ikebukuro, Toshima-ku; mains from ¥700; 🕚 11am-midnight) Offering Indian food of a nouveau-Japanese bent, Gara is a good place for people-watching and appreciating the visual appeal of your meal.

Shinjuku 新宿 Map p101

JAPANESE

Shinjuku is a good place to hunt for bargain meals. Some of the cheaper offerings are pretty grim, including some leathery *kaiten-zushi*, but a little searching turns up some pleasant surprises.

Kurumaya (☎ 3352-5566; 3-21-1 Kabuki-chō, Shinjuku-ku; mains ¥1200; 🕚 lunch & dinner) One of the more elegant spots in east Shinjuku, Kurumaya's seafood and steak sets are excellent value. Highly recommended is the *ise ebi* (Japanese lobster). It's on the corner directly across from Kirin City beer hall.

Ibuki (☎ 3352-4787; 3-23-6 Shinjuku, Shinjuku-ku; sukiyaki course ¥2500, shabu-shabu ¥3200; 🕚 4pm-midnight) An excellent *sukiyaki* and *shabu-shabu* restaurant, Ibuki has an English menu and sign and gets a lot of foreign visitors. Ibuki offers friendly service in a traditional atmosphere, and they even accept major credit cards.

Shinjuku Negishi (☎ 3232-8020; 2-45-2 Kabuki-chō, Shinjuku-ku; lunch or dinner ¥2000; ☿ 11am-3pm & 5.30-10.30pm) Also in Kabuki-chō, this place serves beef tongue and beef stew. It's tasty stuff, and the set meal it comes with is healthy. This cosy little spot is sandwiched between Beijing Rāmen and Tainan Tamii Taiwanese restaurant (right).

Keika Kumamoto Rāmen (☎ 3354-4591; 3-7-2 Shinjuku, Shinjuku-ku; meals ¥800; ☿ 11am-10.45pm) Out towards Shinjuku-sanchōme, this is the place to try for authentic *rāmen*. The noodles are distinctively chewy and the broth is thick. Try the *chashūmen* (*rāmen* with roast pork). You order and pay as you enter.

Suehiro (☎ 3356-4656; 9th fl, Toyo Bldg, 3-36-10 Shinjuku, Shinjuku-ku; lunch or dinner ¥1000; ☿ 11am-3pm & 5-10.30pm Mon-Sat, 11am-9.30pm Sun) In a similar vein to Daikokuya, Suehiro specialises in cheap lunch and dinner sets – Japanese versions of Western favourites like steak and burgers.

Daikokuya (☎ 3202-7272; 4th fl, Naka-Dai Bldg, 1-27-5 Kabuki-chō, Shinjuku-ku; meals from ¥2000; ☿ 5-11.30pm Mon-Fri, 3pm-midnight Sat & Sun) A good place for hungry, budget-minded travellers, with its all-you-can-eat *yaki-niku* (grilled meat), *shabu-shabu* and *sukiyaki* courses. There's an all-you-can-drink option too.

For a taste of Occupation-era Tokyo – tiny restaurants packed willy-nilly into a wonderfully atmospheric old alley – try Omoide-yokochō street beside the JR tracks just northwest of Shinjuku Station. Here, local workers stop off for yakitori, *oden* (fishcakes, *tofu*, vegetables and eggs simmered for hours in a kelp-flavoured broth), noodles and beer before braving the trains back home. Most places serve similar things and few have names, so pick one that appeals to you. What they serve will be piled high on the counters; just point and eat. Expect to pay about ¥2000 per person for a memorable time.

Don't forget to check the offerings on the restaurant floors of east Shinjuku's many department stores. In particular, Isetan Building has eight floors of restaurants including a branch of **Kushinobō** (☎ 3356-3865; 8th fl, 3-15-17 Shinjuku, Shinjuku-ku; lunch/dinner ¥860/3500; ☿ 11.30am-9.30pm), a *kushi-katsu* specialist that serves good lunch sets and fancier dinner courses. **Takashimaya Times Square** (☎ 5361-3301; 5-24-2 Sendagaya, Shibuya-ku; ☿ 10am-9pm) also has

a restaurant park on its 12th to 14th floors, with 28 restaurants to choose from.

Outside of the department stores you'll also find plenty of choice. **Tsunahachi** (☎ 3352-1012; 3-31-8 Shinjuku, Shinjuku-ku; ☿ 11.30am-9pm) behind Mitsukoshi department store has excellent tempura at reasonable prices. Its ¥2500 tempura *teishoku* is highly recommended for dinner. Best of all, there's an English menu and the staff seem accustomed to foreign customers.

INTERNATIONAL

Good deals on international food are all over Shinjuku. However, there's a lot of junk mixed in with the bargains around here. Beware of all-you-can-eat specials and other such gimmicks – there's a reason why the food is so cheap. In addition to the places listed here, see Clubhouse (p145).

Beijing Rāmen (☎ 3200-3560; Kabuki-chō, Shinjuku-ku; ☿ 11am-9pm) In Kabuki-chō, the impassive cooks here dish out good Chinese-style *rāmen*. The noodles are authentic, and so are the Chinese staff. If you sit at the counter, you can peer into the open kitchen to watch them expertly pulling noodles from blobs of dough. *Rāmen* starts at ¥800 and six *gyōza* (steamed dumplings) go for ¥300.

Tainan Tamii (☎ 3464-7544; 2-41-5 Kabuki-chō, Shinjuku-ku; dishes ¥300-600; ☿ 11am-2pm & 5pm-3am Mon-Sat) Come here for great Taiwanese cuisine in a rowdy *izakaya* atmosphere. The menu comes complete with photographs of the dishes, which are, as per genre, small but tasty.

Tokyo Dai Hanten (☎ 3202-0123; 3rd fl, Oriental Wave Bldg, 5-17-13 Shinjuku, Shinjuku-ku; per person around ¥4000; ☿ 11.30am-10pm) Established in 1960, Tokyo Dai Hanten is one of the few possibilities for yum cha or dim sum. For Sunday brunch it serves dim sum à la Hong Kong, rolling it by on trolleys. Take exit B1 from Shinjuku-sanchōme Station.

Canard (☎ 3200-0706; B1 fl, 5-17-6 Shinjuku, Shinjuku-ku; lunch/dinner courses from ¥1600/2800; ☿ lunch & dinner) Tucked into a tiny alley near Hanazono-jinja, Canard serves homemade French food in cosy (read: *très petit!*) surroundings. With wine, the bill adds up, but the meal is worth every yen.

Court Lodge (☎ 3378-1066; 2-10-9 Yoyogi, Shibuya-ku; lunch sets ¥800-900; ☿ 11am-11pm) In this crammed, clean, cheerily busy restaurant, the super-friendly and efficient staff serve

---

THE AUTHOR'S CHOICE

Mominoki House (Map pp103-4 ☎ 3405-9144; 1st fl, YOU Bldg, 2-18-5 Jingūmae, Shibuya-ku; mains around ¥1500; ⏰ 11am-10.30pm Mon-Sat) Even if you're not of the vegetarian bent, you might be all *tonkatsu*-ed out. Those seeking a little relief from deep-fried delicacies can stop into Mominoki House, where the excellent macrobiotic menu covers the vegan to the vegetarian to...the chicken. Even better, your meals are served in a rambling little warren of a space whose corners are filled with jazz and happy plants.

---

tasty Sri Lankan food. You don't have to go inside if you're claustrophobic; they sell takeaway in front.

Raobian Gyozakan (☎ 3348-5810; 3rd fl, Ogawa Bldg, 1-18-1 Nishi-Shinjuku, Shinjuku-ku; courses around ¥3000; ⏰ 11.30am-11.30pm) This plush little place serves authentic thick-skinned Beijing-style *gyōza* and other Chinese fare. Though the portions are small, the *gyōza* here are so good that you don't need sauce for dipping.

New York Grill (☎ 5323-3458; meals ¥6000; ⏰ 11.30am-midnight, brunch 11.30am-2.30pm Sun) On the 52nd floor of the Park Hyatt Tower (p130) this is power dining at its best – hearty portions of steak and seafood and a drop-dead delicious view. One bargain worth mentioning is the Sunday brunch (¥5800); the price includes a glass of champagne.

Harajuku & Aoyama
原宿 • 青山 **Map p103**
JAPANESE
In trendy Harajuku and Aoyama there aren't many Japanese places; international cuisine is the rule here. However, there are a couple of spots worth recommending.

Maisen (☎ 3470-0071; 4-8-5 Jingūmae, Shibuya-ku; lunch sets ¥1500; ⏰ 11am-10pm) Maisen is a shrine dedicated to that classic Japanese dish, *tonkatsu*. Its *hire katsu teishoku* is good value, but if you don't feel like pork, there's a variety of other delish Japanese dishes. Try getting a table in the spacious dining room at the very back.

INTERNATIONAL
Harajuku and Aoyama have more bistros, cafés and trattorias than most small European cities. The heart of it all is the famous promenade of Tokyo's young and beautiful: Omote-sandō.

Tokyo Apartment Café (☎ 3401-4101; 1-11-11 Jingūmae, Shibuya-ku; meals from ¥600; ⏰ 11am-4am) A popular, inexpensive option opposite Condomania, the Apartment Café offers panzerotti, cocktails and even Fruits Conscious Frozen.

Rat Ngon Store (☎ 3478-9478; 1-16-7 Jingūmae, Shibuya-ku; meals from ¥750; ⏰ noon-3pm & 6-11pm) A friendly, rodentless spot ('*rat ngon*' means very tasty in Vietnamese), offering reasonably priced, Asian-esque sets. It's near the west end of Takeshita-dōri, behind Popland, crammed into a tiny space on the 3rd floor of an apartment building, next to a hairdresser specialising in Afros.

Vegetarians will find more to their liking in the Crayon House building, which houses two organic restaurants.

Hiroba (☎ 3406-6409; B1 fl, Crayon House, 3-8-15 Kita-Aoyama, Minato-ku; lunch buffet ¥1260; ⏰ 11am-10pm) Situated in the Crayon House Building, this bright little spot does an excellent organic lunch buffet that includes some non-vegetarian options; be sure to ask what's what.

Organic Restaurant Home (☎ 3406-6409; B1 fl, Crayon House, 3-8-15 Kita-Aoyama, Minato-ku; set lunches from ¥1800; ⏰ 11am-10pm) Also in the Crayon house basement, this is more of a sit-down-and-order spot. Both Japanese- and Western-style dishes are on offer here. It's also connected to a small organic food store, where you can grab a snack to take with you.

Fujimamas (☎ 5485-2262; www.fujimamas.com; 6-3-2 Jingūmae, Shibuya-ku; meals from ¥4000; ⏰ 11am-10pm) A very pleasant and hugely popular fusion restaurant melding European and Asian ingredients under the auspices of chef/co-owner Mark Vann. Good wines and especially nice rooms upstairs in what was once a tatami-maker's workshop. It also has a good children's menu and is in the alley directly behind the Penny Black store. Reservations are recommended.

Fonda de la Madrugada (☎ 5410-6288; B1 fl, Villa Blanca, 2-33-12 Jingūmae, Shibuya-ku; lunch/dinner from ¥3800/6000; ⏰ 5.30pm-2am Sun-Thu, 5.30pm-5am Fri & Sat) Fonda de la Madrugada serves the best Mexican food in Tokyo. Head up past the Turkish embassy to this favourite with expats and the business community. Complete with open courtyards and strolling mariachi musicians, everything from the rooftiles to the chefs has been imported from Mexico. It's not cheap, but it's worth the expenditure.

¡Hola! Refresco Café (meals from ¥250; ✪ noon-2pm & 6pm-1am Mon-Sat) Say *hola* (or hello, or hey, *konnichi-wa*) to the cheapest 'Mexican' food in Tokyo. This tiny lunch counter more or less hits the right note of saturated-colour ambience, but misses in terms of culinary authenticity. Still, the Japanese taco interpretation and taco-rice dishes make for a tasty change of pace, and the prices can't be beat.

Bamboo Café (✪ 3407-8427; 5-8-8 Jingūmae, Shibuya-ku; light meals ¥1000; ✪ 11am-10pm) This popular indoor-outdoor café-style restaurant offers fare like sandwiches made on three different types of bread, and salads to go with them. The cosy tables are perfect for whiling away an hour over cappuccino before getting lost in the alleys branching off this side of Omote-sandō.

Las Chicas (✪ 3407-6865; 5-47-6 Jingūmae, Shibuya-ku; lunch/dinner ¥1000/1500; ✪ 11am-11pm) Take a gander at expat life in Las Chicas' pleasant, expansive surroundings. This is where the cool come to pose and peer. Offering pizzas to salads to sandwiches, the upscale grub is pretty good and the wine list is solid. There's a bar to repair to after dinner, and designer boutiques to browse beforehand.

News Deli (✪ 3407-1715; 3-6-26 Kita-Aoyama, Minato-ku; lunch specials from ¥900; ✪ 9am-12.30am Sun-Thu, 9am-2am Fri & Sat) The weekday lunch specials at News Deli are a good deal and the cheery, deli-style setting is a nice backdrop for perusing a paper over a nosh. Or you can nurse a cocktail and enjoy an eclectic mix of music later in the evening.

Tony Roma's (✪ 3479-5214; Avex Bldg, 3-1-30 Minami-Aoyama, Minato-ku; lunch/dinner ¥1000/3000; ✪ noon-10.30pm) On Aoyama-dōri, Tony Roma's is cholesterol central, the place to pig out on American-style ribs and onion rings. There are also passable salads for those lacking lust for the porcine.

Shibuya 渋谷   Map p103
JAPANESE
Take the briefest of looks around Shibuya, and it will probably occur to you that there must be a lot of restaurants lurking in all those department stores – you are correct. Winners: to collect your prize, proceed to

the 7th floor of Parco Part 1 or the 8th floor of the One-Oh-Nine Building.

Hina Sushi (✪ 3462-1003; 2-21-1 Shibuya, Shibuya-ku; meals from ¥2000; ✪ lunch & dinner Tue-Fri, 11.30am-10.30pm Sat, 11.30am-9.30pm Sun) Behind the Q-Front Building in Shibuya, Hina Sushi has an all-you-can-eat special (¥4500) that's good value for sushi of this quality. There's a time limit, so come ravenous.

Akiyoshi (✪ 3464-1518; lunch from ¥900; ✪ 11am-2pm & 5-11.30pm) A good choice for *yakitori*, this is an approachable place with a large picture menu. Dinner here should cost about ¥3000, and there are a few options for vegetarians.

Kushinobō (✪ 3496-8978; lunch courses from ¥1000; ✪ noon-2pm & 5-10.30pm) This is the place to sample that great Japanese treat, *kushi-katsu* – deep-fried stuff on a stick. It's on the 5th floor of the J & R Building, across from Wendy's. Plan on ¥3000 for dinner.

Sakana-tei (✪ 3780-1313; 4th fl, Koike Bldg, 2-23-15 Dōgenzaka, Shibuya-ku; meals from ¥3500; ✪ 5.30-11pm Mon-Fri, 3.30-10.30pm Sat) This looks more like a concrete modernist bomb shelter than a good value, slightly posh *izakaya* and sake-specialist. But that's what it is, up in Dōgenzaka and handily placed for pre- or post-Love Hotel Hill trysts. Call ahead to reserve a spot.

Fujiya Honten (✪ 3461-2128; B1 fl, 1-2-3 Sakura-gaoka-chō, Shibuya-ku; meals ¥700; ✪ 5-9pm) This is for the bold budget-diner. Venture into this marvellous, legendary old *tachi-nomi* (stand-up-and-drink place) on the southwest side of Shibuya Station, and you'll find it filled with post-race punters from the nags at Ōi (Tokyo's famous horse-racing track). Wash down the *oden* with beer and sake at rock-bottom prices, and prepare to be engaged in friendly, slurred conversation. Be warned: we've never seen a woman in the place. It's down the small street between Ringer Hut and the spectacles dealer, in the basement, where else?

INTERNATIONAL
There's no shortage of international cuisine in Shibuya. The best places to look are the small streets around the station and the built-up shopping areas around the giant department stores.

Sonoma (✪ 3462-7766; 2-25-17 Dōgenzaka, Shibuya-ku; dishes ¥1100-6000; ✪ 5.30-11.30pm Sun-Thu, 5.30pm-4am Fri & Sat) Sonoma's well-balanced menu of

Californian cuisine is set off by a warm, well-lit space. Mains on offer include pork chops with brown sugar, sage and apples, and seared tuna with red onion jam. Dinner here gains you admission to the Ruby Room (p148) upstairs, a fitting place for an all-night nightcap.

Loco Moco (☎ 3477-1039; B1 fl, 1-17-5 Jinnan, Shibuya-ku; meals ¥900; 🕑 11.30am-10.30pm Mon-Fri, 11am-10.30 Sat & Sun) Lighter versions of *loco moco* – rice bowls topped with a fried egg and fish or meat with sauce – are this restaurant's bread and butter. Hawaiian embroidery accents the brick and exposed pipes of this basement eatery, and the slack-key guitar soundtrack is immeasurably soothing.

Wired Cafe (☎ 5428-2620; 6th fl, Q-Front Bldg, 21-6 Udagawa-chō, Shibuya-ku; mains around ¥1250; 🕑 10am-2am) If you happen to crave sweet stuff with a side of Internet time, turn your nose up at the Starbuck's on the 2nd fl and head for Wired Cafe for decadent French toast smothered in chocolate, bananas and berries. They also serve dishes like curry, pasta or taco salad for around ¥1250. An added bonus: the unique experience of sitting behind that gigantic electronic billboard on the front of the building.

Samrat (☎ 3770-7275; B1 fl, Kiraku Bldg, 29-2 Udagawa-chō, Shibuya-ku; lunch set ¥935; 🕑 11am-10pm) Another link in the Samrat chain; come here for the usual Indian curries and curry sets. There's usually a tout outside beckoning people into the basement. The lunch sets are good value, with all-you-can-eat nan bread and rice, and a drink.

Reikyō (☎ 3461-4220; 2-25-18 Dōgenzaka, Shibuya-ku; meals ¥3000; 🕑 noon-2pm & 5pm-1am Fri-Wed) A busy, atmospheric place that's been around for decades, Reikyō serves good, reasonably-priced Taiwanese fare. Take the Hachikō exit from the Shibuya JR station and take the left fork at the 109 Building. Turn right at the first alley, and you can't miss Reikyō's triangular red-brick building.

Kantipur (☎ 3770-5358; B1 fl, 16-6 Sakuragaoka-chō, Shibuya-ku; meals around ¥2800; 🕑 lunch & dinner) This is a Nepali restaurant that seems to borrow a lot from India, but there's a broad range of menu items – including vegetarian dishes – and the portions are large. This place is in the basement of its building, and the entrance is a little tough to spot; look for the small, brightly-coloured signs, streetside.

Ebisu & Daikanyama

恵比寿・代官山 **Map p105**

JAPANESE

Try the 6th floor of the Atre building, over Ebisu Station, for all the standard Japanese favourites, but venture forth into the neighbourhood for these worthwhile eating establishments.

Fujii (☎ 3473-0088; 1-13-6 Ebisu, Shibuya-ku; 🕑 11am-10pm Mon-Sat) This is a good place to sample fresh, handmade udon. We recommend the tempura udon for ¥1500. It's in a corner shop with an electric sign out front, with a running LED message written in Japanese.

Nanaki Soba (☎ 3496-2878; 1-13-2 Ebisu-Nishi, Shibuya-ku; meals ¥1500-3000; 🕑 11.30am-1.50pm & 5-10pm Mon-Sat) A modest little noodle shack recognisable by its traditional-looking wood exterior, Nanaki dishes out noodles with a fine texture and flavour. The atmosphere is simple and food-focused, the prices reasonable, and the menu broader than *soba*, if you're not in the mood for noodles.

Ippūdō Rāmen (☎ 5420-2225; 1-3-13 Hiro-o, Shibuya-ku; meals ¥900; 🕑 11am-4pm) This *rāmen* shop on Meiji-dōri is nationally famous for its Kyūshū-style *rāmen* into which you can grate fresh garlic cloves. You'll have to queue at peak periods, but it's worth the wait.

Shunsenbō (☎ 5469-9761; 1-1-40 Hiro-o, Shibuya-ku; lunch/dinner courses from ¥1000/3800; 🕑 11am-3pm & 5.30-10pm) This place specialises in tofu dishes and *shabu-shabu*. Courses are a real bargain considering the quality of the food and the elegant surroundings. Best of all, there's an English menu. It's in the Ebisu Prime Square Plaza complex, on the ground floor, you can get there by taking the east exit from Ebisu JR Station.

You'll find Japanese restaurants few and far between in Daikanyama, as the area has its gaze fixed firmly on the West.

INTERNATIONAL

Daikanyama rivals Harajuku and Aoyama as the centre of Tokyo café society and, as such, it's a good place to grab a cappuccino and do some people watching. You'll also find plenty of trendy foreign restaurants, some of which are good and some of which are merely fashionable.

Caffé Michelangelo (☎ 3770-9517; 29-3 Sarugaku-chō, Shibuya-ku; set lunch ¥1360; 🕑 11am-midnight) Tokyo's best impersonation of Paris, Caffé Michelangelo is a prime place to watch the beautiful people on a weekend afternoon. You'll pay for the pleasure, though – coffee starts at ¥600. Lunch sets are a much better deal, including soup, coffee and dessert.

Café Artifagose (☎ 5489-1133; 1st fl, 20-23 Daikanyama, Shibuya-ku; meals ¥900; 11am-8pm) With outdoor patio seating, superb breads and cheeses and a fine selection of drinks, Café Artifagose is easy to find by following your nose toward the heavenly, yeasty scent of fresh bread and flaky pastry.

Gazebo Café (☎ 3461-4348; 1st fl, 1-33-15 Daikanyama, Shibuya-ku; 8.30-midnight) Halfway between Ebisu and Daikanyama along Komazawa-dōri, Gazebo Café has a good selection of tea. Though the view isn't much, the sandwiches are pretty good and the pastry counter contains a few tempting treats to have with your cuppa.

KM Fils (☎ 5784-5883; lunch/dinner from ¥1000/3700; noon-3pm & 6-11pm Mon & Wed-Fri, 11.30am-2pm & 6-9pm Sat & Sun) The sophisticated, Mediterranean-flavoured menu at this chic French bistro was designed by its well-respected namesake, chef Kiyoshi Miyashiro. Jazz in the background and lovely dishes in the foreground – prices are a pleasant surprise – more than compensate for the stilted service.

Café Juliet (☎ 3770-5656; mains ¥700; 11.30am-midnight Tue-Thu, noon-4am Fri & Sat) Upstairs from KM Fils and set back from the street, Café Juliet has a pleasant outdoor eating area. Choose from pasta, sandwiches and similar light fare, but perhaps consider an alternative venue for coffee – though good, is inexplicably expensive here.

Erawan (☎ 3409-8001; 1st fl, Ebisu Prime Square Tower, 1-1-40 Hiro-o, Shibuya-ku; mains ¥1300; 11.30am-11pm) Creative, spicy twists in taste and presentation characterise the Thai fusion cuisine served at Erawan. Pair your selection with one of the reasonably-priced wines off the respectably broad drink menu and appreciate the alchemy of a Thai-French-Japanese meltdown on your palate.

Good Honest Grub (☎ 3710-0400; www.goodhonestgrub.com; 1-11-11 Ebisu-Minami, Shibuya-ku; meals ¥1500; 11.30am-10.30pm Tue-Sun) This small, vegetarian-friendly eatery is a cheery place for brunch – served weekends and holidays from 9am to 4.30pm. Smoothies, hearty wraps and sandwiches, and a weekday happy hour from 5.30pm to 7.30pm (all drinks ¥550) are all excellent reasons to turn up here.

Monsoon Café (☎ 5489-3789; 15-4 Daikanyama, Shibuya-ku; meals around ¥3000; 11.30am-5am) With an appealing mix of Southeast Asian standbys like Vietnamese spring rolls and Malaysian satay, Monsoon Café is an attractive spot for its cuisine as well as for the alfresco seating and extensive drink menu. Daikanyama Station on the Toyoko line is the nearest stop.

Roppongi 六本木 Map pp106–7
JAPANESE

As you might expect from foreigner-central, Roppongi's Japanese restaurants tend to be expensive and very accessible to gaijin. This makes it the perfect area for any long-awaited, lavish Japanese meal. There are also some cheap spots around if you just need a quick bite before hitting the bars. All of the following restaurants are accessible from Roppongi Station.

Bikkuri Sushi (☎ 3403-1489; 1st fl, Yua Roppongi Bldg, 3-14-9 Roppongi, Minato-ku; meals from ¥1000; 11am-5am) A long-time favourite for Roppongi revellers and a late-night *kaiten-zushi* place that's seen it all. *Bikkuri* means 'surprise' in Japanese, but unless you're picking up dishes blindfolded, there shouldn't be many of those.

Namban-tei (☎ 3402-0606; 4-5-6 Roppongi, Minato-ku; meals ¥6000; 5-11pm Sun-Fri) Something of a local institution, Namban-tei is known for its excellent *yakitori* in pleasant, traditional Japanese surroundings. It won't be cheap but it will be delicious. Look for its unassuming wood shopfront on the alley corner.

Inakaya (☎ 5575-1012; 4-10-11 Roppongi, Minato-ku; meals from ¥10,000; 5-11pm) Just a couple of blocks off Roppongi Crossing, Inakaya has achieved fame as a top-end *robatayaki* (rustic bar-restaurant serving food grilled over charcoal). It does raucous, bustling, don't-stand-on-ceremony *robatayaki* with gusto. It's possible to spend lots of money here *and* have fun.

Kisso (☎ 3582-4191; 5-17-1 Roppongi, Minato-ku; meals around ¥10,000; 11am-2pm & 5.30-10pm Mon-Sat) Kisso is the perfect place to sample Japan's gourmet cuisine, *kaiseki ryōri* (beautifully presented multicourse meals). It's best to order a course and put your dining fate into the hands of the chef. On the B1 floor of the Axis building, this is doubtless the most accessible *kaiseki* in all of Tokyo. Access it from Roppongi Station's exit 3.

Fukuzushi (☎ 3402-4116; 5-7-8 Roppongi, Minato-ku; meals around ¥10,000; ☯ 11.30am-1.30pm & 5.30-10pm Mon-Sat) Some of the best sushi in town is served here, in an upscale atmosphere that is decidedly more relaxed than at some of the more traditional places in Ginza and Tsukiji. The fish here is fresh, the portions are large, and there's even a cocktail bar. It lies in the alley beyond the Hard Rock Café, downstairs from Spago.

Gokoku (☎ 3796-3356; 7-4-5 Roppongi, Minato-ku; meals ¥6000; ☯ 6pm-midnight Mon-Sat) Gokoku is close to the top-end category, but if you lie low with your drink orders, you can eat for midrange prices – at least by Roppongi standards. The menu changes but it is always hearty Edo-style fare.

Seryna (☎ 3402-1051; 3-12-2 Roppongi, Minato-ku; lunch/dinner ¥6000/15,000; ☯ noon-11pm) A long-time expat favourite for entertaining important guests from abroad, Seryna houses three restaurants under its roof: Seryna Honten (*shabu-shabu* and *sukiyaki*), Mon Cher Ton Ton (Kōbe-beef steaks and *teppanyaki*, or table-top grilling), and Kani Seryna (crab dishes). It has a solid menu and a pretty rock garden but feels vaguely aged. Exit 5 from Roppongi Station will put you on the correct side of Roppongi-dōri.

INTERNATIONAL
It's only logical that there be an abundance of international restaurants in Roppongi, Tokyo's foreign nightlife playground. From cheap hamburger joints to expensive imports like Wolfgang Puck's Spago, whatever food you fancy is here. After supper, the bars and clubs of Roppongi beckon. The following eateries are accessible from Roppongi Station.

Havana Café (☎ 3423-3500; 4-12-2 Roppongi, Minato-ku; meals ¥1000; ☯ 11.30am-5am) One of the best places to start your evening, casual Havana Café serves reliable grub like burritos and sandwiches for less than ¥1000, and also has great happy-hour drink specials. The street-side seating and large-windowed dining room open onto a quiet backstreet – as you sip that first drink, it's difficult to imagine that Roppongi lurks just round the corner.

Bengawan Solo (☎ 3408-5698; 1st fl, Kaneko Bldg, 7-18-13 Roppongi, Minato-ku; meals ¥1100; ☯ 11.30am-3pm & 5-10pm Mon-Sat) On Roppongi-dōri, this Indonesian eatery offers a taste of Southeast Asian isles. It's been around for ages, and

though the indifferent interior disappoints, the food never does. The *gado gado* (salad with peanut sauce) lunch is a bargain, and the beef in coconut-cream is dreamy. Look for the food models displayed outside.

Humming Bird (☎ 3401-3337; Hanatsubaki Bldg, 3-15-23 Roppongi, Minato-ku; set dinner ¥6000; ☯ 6pm-3am Mon-Sat, 5pm-midnight Sun) Crisp white table-cloths, wood-slat design and Vietnamese birdcages adorn the interior of this posh but relaxed place. Mixing French colonial and Vietnamese mood and food, Humming Bird wings its guests to gustatory bliss. Though it's recommended that you indulge in a set dinner, there's also an à la carte *pho* (Vietnamese beef noodle soup) worth trying for ¥900.

Tokyo Bellini Trattoria (☎ 3470-5650; 3-14-12 Roppongi, Minato-ku; lunch/dinner from ¥1000/3000; ☯ 11.30am-2am Sun-Thu, 11.30am-3am Fri-Sun) Inexpensive lunch specials are a good deal at Bellini, including salad, a main like pasta or pizza (gloriously heavy on garlic), coffee and dessert. The excellent people-watching to be had along Gaien-higashi-dōri is a complimentary side dish, if you can snag a table in the front.

Monsoon Café (☎ 5467-5221; 2-10-1 Nishi-Azabu, Minato-ku; meals ¥3500; ☯ 5pm-5am Mon-Fri, 11.30am-5am Sat & Sun) Across from the Aoyama Reien along Gaien-nishi-dōri, Monsoon serves Southeast Asian classics like Vietnamese fresh spring rolls, Thai coconut and lemon-grass soup, and chicken satay. With indoor-outdoor café-style seating, big rattan chairs and attentive staff, it's a good hangout for enjoying a tropical drink.

Spago (☎ 3423-4025; 2nd fl, 5-7-8 Roppongi, Minato-ku; lunch sets ¥1500-3000, dinner from ¥7000; ☯ 11.30am-2pm & 6-10pm) You can't go wrong with Spago's creative Californian cuisine, for which it is justifiably renowned. Like its older sister in LA, Tokyo's Spago celebrates the freshest ingredients – laced with Asian influences, this semi-upscale spot is a good place to splurge if you crave architectural, innovative cuisine, or a glass of buttery Californian chardonnay. Find it in the alley beyond the Hard Rock.

Hard Rock Café (☎ 3408-7018; 5-4-20 Roppongi, Minato-ku; lunch/dinner ¥1000/2000; ☯ 11.30am-2am Mon-Thu, 11.30am-4am Fri & Sat, 11.30am-11.30pm Sun) and Tony Roma's are in the same building, accessible from exit 3 of Roppongi Station. We figure you know what to expect from the former – loud music, oversized portions of passable American food and plenty of reasonably priced beverages. Tony Roma's is another American joint that serves barbecued spare ribs with all the fixings. At either place, a good dinner is in the ¥3000 range. There's another branch of Tony Roma's in Akasaka.

Other Roppongi options:

Hamburger Inn (☎ 3405-8980; 3-15-22 Roppongi, Minato-ku; meals ¥1000; ☾ 11.30am-5am Mon-Sat) A Roppongi standby staying open all night and serving forgettable burgers for around ¥400.

Maenam (☎ 3404-4745; 1st & 2nd fl, Togensha Bldg, 3-1-20 Nishi-Azabu; meals ¥3500; ☾ 11.30am-4am) Another good Southeast Asian favourite, this tackily-decorated but competent Thai place is down towards Nishi-Azabu.

Akasaka 赤坂   Map pp106–7
JAPANESE

Akasaka is packed with excellent Japanese restaurants, though bear in mind that bargains are few and far between. For starters, take a stroll in the streets running off and parallel to Sotobori-dōri. In this neighbourhood there are branches of slightly expensive – but reliably worthwhile – restaurant chains such as the following three.

Sushi-sei (☎ 3582-9503; 3-11-4 Akasaka, Minato-ku; lunch/dinner ¥1500/4000; ☾ 11.30am-2pm & 5pm-11.30pm Mon-Sat) If you're set on sushi, this branch of the famous Tsukiji sushi chain won't disappoint. The lunch sets are priced very reasonably for the quality, and with a reputation like theirs, you can be sure you're eating some of the freshest fish around.

Kushinobō (☎ 3586-7390; 2-14-3 Nagata-chō, Minato-ku; dinner courses from ¥2500; ☾ 6-9.30pm Mon-Sat) Sometimes it's necessary to give in to those dark cravings for something deep-fried, and because these lunches are fairly inexpensive, you can at least console yourself with your budgetary virtue. Come to Kushinobō at times like these for *kushiage* (skewers of deep-fried meat, seafood and vegetables) and *kushi-katsu*, this place's speciality. It's on the 3rd floor of the Akasaka Tōkyū Hotel.

Tsunahachi (☎ 3588-5110; 3-1-6 Akasaka, Minato-ku; dinner courses from ¥2500; ☾ lunch & dinner) On the 8th floor of the Belle Vie building, this is a good tempura place with similar prices to Kushinobō. The set lunches are a good deal, with all the usual favourites on offer.

Tōfu-ya (☎ 3582-1028; 3-5-2 Akasaka, Minato-ku; lunch/dinner ¥800/4300; ☾ 11.30am-1.30pm & 5-11pm Mon-Fri) This is the perfect introduction to a largely vegetarian cuisine that many visitors miss out on; however, some Japanese-language ability will be helpful here.

Sunaba (☎ 3583-7670; 6-3-5 Akasaka, Minato-ku; meals ¥2000; ☾ 11am-7.30pm Mon-Fri, 11am-7pm Sat) Sunaba has some of the city's finest buckwheat noodles. They invented tempura *soba*, and serve it in an exquisite, dense, smoky *tsuyu* (dipping sauce) – sublime. It's next to the Kokusai Shin-Akasaka building. There's also a sister shop in Nihombashi.

Yakitori Luis (☎ 3506-2306; 5-4-14 Akasaka, Minato-ku; meals ¥1500; ☾ 5-11.15pm Mon-Sat, 5-10.30pm Sun) For *izakaya* dining close to Akasaka subway station, this is a popular *yakitori* haven. Look for signs pointing to the basement; the stairwell is set a little way back from the street.

Jangara Rāmen (☎ 3595-2130; 2-12-8 Nagata-chō, Minato-ku; meals from ¥580; ☾ 11.45am-2am Tue-Thu, 11.45am-3.30am Sat, 11.45am-1am Fri, Sun & public holidays) Near the entrance to Hie-jinja, this is a popular place worth trying for a great bowl of *rāmen*. Live a little and order the *zenbu-iri* (all-in) *rāmen*.

INTERNATIONAL

Along with nearby Roppongi, Akasaka is one of Tokyo's most cosmopolitan neighbourhoods. While most of the action is in the midrange bracket, a stroll through the narrow streets just west of Akasaka-mitsuke subway station will turn up a number of good lunch bargains.

Moti Darbar (☎ 3582-3620; 3rd fl, 3-8-8 Akasaka, Minato-ku; lunch/dinner ¥800/2000; ☾ 11.30am-11pm) Part of Tokyo's best Indian chain, there are two branches of Moti in Akasaka, each just a few minutes' walk from Akasaka or Akasaka-mitsuke subway stations. Lunch sets include curry and lassi or coffee. If you feel like ordering in, they also deliver (☎ 3479-1955).

Trattoria Marumo (☎ 3585-5371; 1st fl, Tōyama Bldg, 3-8-14 Akasaka, Minato-ku; lunch/dinner ¥1500/3000; ☾ 11.30am-midnight Mon-Sat, noon-11pm Sun) Serving respectable Italian fare, this pleasant pizzeria can quell your cravings for pasta without busting the bank. There are loads of food models in the window, but both the window and door may be difficult to spot behind the overgrown plants in front.

Pho Garden (☎ 5114-0747; 2-14-1 Akasaka, Minato-ku; mains ¥1000; ☾ 11.30am-11pm Mon-Fri, noon-11pm Sat, noon-10pm Sun) With contemporary Viet-pop on the soundtrack and authentic dishes on the menu, settle into a seat near one of the many windows and savour a taste of Vietnam. Enjoy some *goi sen* (lotus root salad) or *pho* (beef noodle soup), accompanied by a Saigon beer.

Kao Thai Isan (☎ 5114-5507; 4-3-2 Akasaka, Minato-ku; mains around ¥800; ◷ 11am-11pm Mon-Sat) A friendly spot for northeastern Thai food, this is a good place to try Isan-style barbecue and green papaya salad for a warmly-lit, low-key dinner. To soothe your throat with a Singha beer, you'll need to cough up ¥580 first. Find it on Hitotsugi-dōri, just up the street from the Capsule Hotel Fontaine.

Mugyodon (☎ 3586-6478; 2nd fl, Sangyo Bldg, 2-17-74 Akasaka, Minato-ku; dinner ¥5000; ◷ 5pm-midnight Mon-Sat) This is a popular, friendly Korean place open for dinner only. This is your chance to sample the real thing, not the usual Japanese version.

Ōdaiba お台場 Map p108

JAPANESE

There are several Japanese restaurants on this trendy island in the bay.

Hina Sushi (☎ 5531-0017; Sunset Beach Restaurant Row, 1-3-5 Daiba, Minato-ku; meals ¥4300; ◷ lunch & dinner Tue-Sun) This reliable spot offers excellent sushi on Restaurant Row (next to Decks), and a good all-you-can-eat lunch.

Hanashibe (☎ 3599-5575; Aqua City, 1-7-1 Daiba, Minato-ku; mains ¥700; ◷ 11am-11pm) For Kyoto specialities and house-brewed sake, check out Hanashibe on the 3rd floor of the Mediage entertainment complex next to Aqua City. Try three types of sake in a tasting set (¥700), which you can match with small snacks or full meals.

INTERNATIONAL

Ōdaiba is a pleasant place to sample some reasonable international fare, as most of the restaurants have good views of the bay or the beach. For fun – or for dim sum – check out the array of Hong Kong-style eateries at Daiba Little Hong Kong on the 6th and 7th floors of the Decks Tokyo Beach complex.

Positive Deli (☎ 3599-4551; Aqua City, 1-7-1 Daiba, Minato-ku; meals ¥700; ◷ 11am-11pm) The stylish and casual Positive Deli serves up meals from *donburi* to deli sandwiches, all of which you can accompany with a glass of Australian wine. You'll find it on the 3rd floor of the

Mediage entertainment complex, from where you can enjoy the big bay view.

Khazana (☎ 5500-5082; 1-6-1 Daiba, Minato-ku; lunch buffet ¥800; ◷ 11am-10pm) Up on the 5th floor of the Decks Tokyo Beach complex, this Indian restaurant serves a good all-you-can-eat buffet lunch and has a fair amount of vegetarian goodies on the menu. You'll have to come early to get one of the coveted tables out on the deck.

Soup Stock Tokyo (☎ 3599-2333; 3rd fl, Venus Fort, Aomi-itchōme, Kōtō-ku; meals from ¥580; ◷ 11am-10pm) Selling savoury, wholesome, inexpensive soup, Soup Stock has a branch in the Venus Fort shopping complex. They offer soup sets with fresh bread and a drink (¥950), and there are usually at least ten different varieties to choose from. Try the garlic soup with *onsen tamago* (hot-spring boiled eggs).

DRINKING

Bars and clubs change with the weather in Tokyo, which makes the job of coming up with specific recommendations rather difficult. The following is a rundown on bars and clubs popular at the time of writing. For up-to-the-minute information, check the websites listed on p91.

Ueno & Asakusa 上野 浅草 Map pp98–9

Yawn – definitely not the neighbourhoods for a night out in Tokyo. However, if you do find yourself up in old Shitamachi at night, try the **Warrior Celt** (☎ 3836-8588; 3rd fl, Ito Bldg, 6-9-22 Ueno, Taito-ku; ◷ 5pm-5am Tue-Sat, 5pm-midnight Sun-Mon) pub in Ueno, where drinks are only ¥500 from 5pm to 7pm. It's a friendly place with a good selection of English and Irish brews, as well as live music some nights. In Asakusa, try the beer halls in the Asahi Flamme D'Or complex. Otherwise, check out the long-standing Kamiya Bar (p135).

Ikebukuro 池袋 Map p100

There are lots of *izakaya* on both sides of the station (p135), but if you're in the mood for more of a Western pub experience, check out these pubs.

Dubliners (☎ 5951-3614; B1 fl, Sun Glow Bldg, 1-10-8 Nishi-Ikebukuro, Toshima-ku; ◷ 11am-11pm) This is worth a try if you'd prefer something Western-style. It's a faux-Irish pub offering Kilkenny and Guinness draught.

Black Sheep (☎ 3987-2289; B1 fl, 1-7-12 Higashi-Ikebukuro, Toshima-ku; ◷ 6pm-3am Mon-Thu, 6pm-5am Fri

& Sat) Behind Bic Personal Computer Store, this is in a similar vein as the Dubliners but open much later. The place is often packed on weekend nights when it features live bands.

Bobby's Bar (☎ 3980-8875; 3rd fl, Milano Bldg, 1-18-10 Nishi-Ikebukuro, Toshima-ku; ⏰ 7pm-3am) On the western side of the station is this late-night option. There's table soccer, darts and good pub grub. Early birds will enjoy the happy hour, 7pm to 9pm Monday to Thursday.

Shinjuku 新宿   Map p101

Gaudy Shinjuku is awash with nightspots of every shape and size, many of which fall into the sordid category and don't cater to foreigners. That said, there's still plenty to do here at night if you have the energy to face the madness of an evening on the streets of Shinjuku.

Golden Gai is one of the city's most interesting night zones. Even if you don't feel like a drink, take a night stroll through this maze of tightly packed little establishments, just to feel the atmosphere – the whole place seems lost in a boozy, run-down time warp.

Bon's (☎ 3209-6334; 1-1-10 Kabuki-chō, Shinjuku-ku; admission ¥900; ⏰ 7pm-5am) This is one sure-fire spot. Drinks start at ¥700. Look for it next to the police box; it's hard to miss the signage painted on its wall.

Clubhouse (☎ 3359-7785; 3rd fl, Marunaka Bldg, Shinjuku, Shinjuku-ku; pub food ¥400-1200; ⏰ 5pm-midnight Sun-Thu, 5pm-late Fri & Sat) Officially, Clubhouse is a sports bar, but in reality it's just a good, friendly place for a drink. It carries a selection of imported and domestic beer, including a few of its own custom brews. It also serves a variety of pub food for dinner, including a fair number of vegetarian options. It's most easily accessed from Shinjuku sanchōme Station, exit C3.

Rolling Stone (☎ 3354-7347; 3-2-7 Shinjuku, Shinjuku-ku; admission ¥500, beers ¥600; ⏰ 9pm-4am) Out towards Nichōme (take exit C5 from Shinjuku sanchōme Station), this grubby, low-life place has been around since the dawn of time and still manages to pull in the crowds on Friday and Saturday nights.

Garam (☎ 3205-8668; 7th fl, Dai 6 Star Bldg, 1-16-6 Kabuki-chō, Shinjuku-ku; admission ¥1500; ⏰ 8pm-5am) A club that feels like a bar, this is a small, friendly place, where the master DJ spins a range of hip-hop, dub and reggae. The cover charge includes one drink.

Harajuku & Aoyama 原宿・青山   Map p103

These adjoining areas are a good option when the Roppongi crush is too much to bear. Don't forget that Harajuku and Aoyama are all about cafés, and you can spend an evening drinking beer and wine in them just as you might in Paris.

Oh God (☎ 3406-3206; B1 fl, Jingūbashi Bldg, 6-7-18 Jingūmae, Shibuya-ku; ⏰ 6pm-6am) This place has been going for years; miraculously, it's still trucking. The format seems a little tired, but if your needs run to pool tables and movie screenings, it's just the ticket.

Mix (☎ 3797-1313; B1 fl, 3-6-19 Kita-Aoyama, Minato-ku; admission with 2 drinks ¥2500; ⏰ 10pm-late) You can usually count on this tiny, hole-in-the-wall club near the Omote-sandō crossing, even when others in the neighbourhood are flat. It's small, smoky, crowded and always friendly. Music ranges from reggae to hip-hop. It's rather hard to find; look for the stairs heading down to the basement.

Las Chicas (p139; ⏰ 6-11pm) This restaurant has a bar and a members' club, both of which are good spots for a drink. It's out towards Shibuya; take exit B2 from Omote-sandō Station.

Ebisu & Daikanyama 恵比寿・代官山   Map p105

These two neighbourhoods are excellent choices for a night out in Tokyo, striking the perfect balance between hip and casual. They're especially good if you just can't face the mayhem of Roppongi or Shinjuku.

What the Dickens (☎ 3780-2099; 4th fl, Roob 6 Bldg, 1-13-3 Ebisu-Nishi, Shibuya-ku; ⏰ 5pm-1am Tue & Wed, 5pm-2am Thu-Sat, 3pm-midnight Sun) A good British pub we like. It has the usual beers on tap, some decent pub-grub and the occasional good live music.

Enjoy House (☎ 5489-1591; 2nd fl, Kokuto Bldg, 2-9-9 Ebisu-Nishi, Shibuya-ku; ⏰ 1pm-2am Mon-Thu, 1pm-4am Fri-Sun, closed Mon & 1st Sun each month) Near What the Dickens, this is one of Tokyo's better clubs/lounges, where you can kick back and listen to a variety of music, from rock to house, in an opium-den atmosphere. Best of all, there's no cover charge.

Bon (☎ 3447-1063; 2-24-9 Ebisu, Shibuya-ku; drinks around ¥700; ⏰ 3pm-2am Tue-Thu, 3pm-4am Fri & Sat, noon-11pm Sun) Sweet treats, confectionery cocktails, luscious patrons and several comfortable floors to sprawl in make this a bon-bon

TOKYO

of a bar. Bon is a relaxed spot for a pleasing drink, with floor cushions scattered in cosy seating areas and a lounge in which to hang during your dizzyingly sweet evening.

See p141 for information on the Monsoon Café, a chill place for a drink on the outskirts of Daikanyama.

Roppongi & Akasaka
六本木・赤坂 **Map pp106–7**

Roppongi is not part of Japan – it's a multinational twilight zone that feels like Mardi Gras blew over on a hurricane from New Orleans, where gaijin get together with adventurous locals to booze and schmooze until the first trains at dawn. Because of this, many long-term locals avoid it like the plague, leaving it for punters fresh off the plane, military goons and riff-raff out trolling for local talent. That said, Roppongi still rocks, and you'll probably want to check it out at least once.

Meet up in front of that pink-painted pastry purveyor, Almond (everyone does; you can't miss it), and then jump in.

Geronimo (☎ 3478-7449; 2nd fl, Yamamuro Bldg, 7-14-10 Roppongi, Minato-ku; ⏰ 6pm-6am Mon-Fri, 7pm-6am Sat & Sun) This kooky shot bar gets packed out with all sorts of off-work expats and some of their Japanese associates. All drinks are half-price at happy hour: 6pm to 9pm weeknights, and 7pm to 9pm weekends. Beer (including Red Hook!) is ¥800 no matter what time you go. Geronimo is right on the corner at Roppongi Crossing.

Mogambo (☎ 3403-4833; 1st fl, Osawa Bldg, 6-1-7 Roppongi, Minato-ku; ⏰ 6pm-6am) If Geronimo's campy Native American theme doesn't do it for you, check out its sister club Mogambo, with a similar crowd and prices – and equally campy jungle theme. Mogambo is on the southern side of Roppongi-dōri, a block south of Geronimo.

Castillo (☎ 3475-1629; 1st fl, Dai 2 Aoi Bldg, 6-1-8 Roppongi, Minato-ku; ⏰ 7pm-6am Mon-Fri, 8pm-6am Sat & Sun) Next door to Mogambo, this small club/bar plays '70s and '80s disco and soul classics. You can dance or just kick it and relax here, but you can't enter unless you're wearing 'smart casual clothes' (what the sign says).

Agave (☎ 3497-0229; B1 fl, Clover Bldg, 7-15-10 Roppongi, Minato-ku; ⏰ 6.30pm-2am Mon-Fri, 6.30pm-4am Sat) You could probably convince yourself you're in Mexico after a few too many margaritas at Agave. Luckily, this amiable spot is more about savouring the subtleties of its 400-plus

varieties of tequila rather than tossing back shots of Cuervo. Mariachi musicians will woo you as you sip *añejo* (aged tequila).

Bar, Isn't It? (☎ 3746-1598; 3rd fl, MT Bldg, 3-8-18 Roppongi, Minato-ku; admission with 1 drink ¥1000; ⏰ 6pm-late Thu-Sat) An offshoot of the successful Osaka chain. The formula is simple: a big space, so-so bar food and all drinks for ¥500. All together, it works pretty well, and it's a good place to meet people.

Gas Panic Bar (☎ 3405-0633; www.gaspanic.co.jp; 2nd & 3rd fls, 3-15-24 Roppongi, Minato-ku; ⏰ 6pm-5am) This used to be one giant gaijin-bar. It's been split into three bars, and forms one of Roppongi's rowdier culs-de-sac. Along with the original there's Club 99 Gas Panic and Gas Panic Café. All three are cheap places to drink, especially during happy hour. On the down side, they tend to get crammed with all sorts of characters, and fights are not unknown. Roppongi Station's exit 3 will get you there.

Hobgoblin Tokyo (☎ 3568-1280; www.hobgoblin-tokyo.com; 1st fl, Aoba Roppongi Bldg, 3-16-33 Roppongi, Minato-ku; ⏰ 11am-2pm & 5pm-1am Mon-Fri, 5pm-1am Sat) Far better than your average Britpub replica, Akasaka's Hobgoblin is run by an Oxfordshire brewery. It serves good pub fare and excellent imported microbrews. Hobgoblin is in the basement of the building next to the clearly marked Marugen 23 building. From Akasaka Station, take exit 2.

Akasaka can be an expensive and staid place to drink, especially with Roppongi just a 20-minute walk away. But those in search of high-rise views to go with their cocktails can find plush bars at the top of the neighbourhood's luxury hotels. Both 40th floor bars are **Top of Akasaka** (☎ 3234-1121; drinks from ¥1500; ⏰ 11.30am-2pm & 5pm-2am Mon-Fri, noon-2am Sat, noon-11pm Sun) in the Akasaka Prince Hotel (p132), and **Bar** (☎ 3265-1111; ⏰ 5pm-midnight Mon-Fri, noon-midnight Sat & Sun) in the New Otani tower (p131).

Also check out these Roppongi bars:

Paddy Foley's (☎ 3423-2250; B1 fl, Roi Bldg, 5-5-1 Roppongi, Minato-ku; ⏰ 5pm-late) Decent Irish-style pub, popular with the expat business community – with good pints (about ¥900), convivial surroundings and some space to breathe.

Propaganda (☎ 3423-0988; 2nd fl, Yua Roppongi Bldg, 3-14-9 Roppongi, Minato-ku; ⏰ 6pm-dawn, happy hour 6-9pm & 5.30pm-11pm Mon-Sat) Above Bikkuri Sushi, an inexpensive shot bar with good happy-hour specials; also a popular pick-up joint.

ENTERTAINMENT

Tokyo is very much the centre of the Japanese world, and has the best of everything. On the nightlife front, there are those who maintain that Osaka is more cutting edge, but then Osaka offers nowhere near the diversity of entertainment options available in Tokyo – traditional entertainment such as kabuki, avant-garde theatre, countless cinemas, live houses, pubs and bars. See p51 for more information on Japanese theatre.

Cinemas

Shibuya and Shinjuku are Tokyo's cinema meccas, but you'll find cinemas near any major train station. Check the *Japan Times*, *Metropolis* or the *Tokyo Journal* to see what's on. Discounted tickets are sold in the basement of the Tokyo Kōtsū Kaikan (Map p96) building in Ginza, Shinjuku's Studio Alta building (Map p101; 5th floor), Harajuku's Laforet building (Map p103; 1st floor) and Shibuya's 109 Building (Map p103; 2nd floor).

Gay & Lesbian Venues

Tokyo's gay and lesbian enclave is Shinjuku-ni-chōme, the area east of Shinjuku san-chōme Station's C8 exit. There are lots of little bars here, and though some can be rather daunting to enter, the following two venues have been around awhile and are friendly.

Arty Farty (Map p101; ☎ 5362-9720; 2nd fl, 2-11-7 Shinjuku, Shinjuku-ku; ☺ 5pm-5am Mon-Sat, 4pm-5am Sun) Closest to Shinjuku sanchōme Station (exit C8), Arty Farty is an easy place to meet guys, with fabulous all-you-can-drink specials. It's a good place to start your evening and find out about the area's other possibilities. Women are only admitted Sunday, and usually only with gay men.

Kinswomyn (Map p101; ☎ 3354-8720; 3rd fl, Daiichi Tenka Bldg, 2-15-10 Shinjuku, Shinjuku-ku; cocktails ¥750; ☺ 7pm-4am Wed-Mon) Women are welcome Sunday and every other open night at this long-running establishment, a cosy spot for Japanese and foreign women alike.

Advocates Bar (Map p101; ☎ 3358-8638; B1 fl, 7th Tenka Bldg, 2-18-1 Shinjuku, Shinjuku-ku; ☺ 8pm-4am) Advocates Bar is just that – a bar. This place is so small that as the crowd gets bigger during the course of an evening, it becomes more like a block party and takes to the streets. Family of all genders are welcome here.

For other up-to-the-minute gay and lesbian bars and clubs, check out the *Tokyo Journal*'s Cityscope section, which sometimes has a special section called 'Tokyo Out'.

Music

Tokyo is the only city in Asia where you may have the luxury of seeing up-and-coming performers playing in intimate venues. Check the latest issue of *Metropolis* or *Tokyo Journal* or pick up some flyers at Cisco, Manhattan or Tower Records in Shibuya to see who's playing around town. Ticket prices generally range from ¥5000 to ¥8000, depending on performer and venue.

DANCE CLUBS

Find the greatest concentration and breadth of style in Roppongi, baby (Map pp106–7).

Club 328 (☎ 3401-4968; www.02.246.ne.jp/~azabu 328; B1 fl, Kotsu Anzen Center Bldg, 3-24-20 Nishi-Azabu, Minato-ku; admission ¥2000-2500; ☺ 8pm-5am) DJs at San-ni-pa (aka San-ni-hachi) spin a quality mix of sounds, from funk to reggae to R&B. With its refreshing un-Roppongi feel and a cool crowd of Japanese and gaijin, Club 328 is a good place to boogie 'til the break of dawn. Two drinks are included with the cover. Find Club 328 across the street from the Hobson's ice cream shop at the Nishi-Azabu crossing.

Salsa Sudada (☎ 5474-8806; 3rd fl, La Palette Bldg, 7-13-8 Roppongi, Minato-ku; ☺ 6pm-6am) Experienced salsa dancers should plan on kicking up their heels (and shaking that booty) for hours, while beginners can take lessons here on Sunday nights. Multinational dancers come regularly to this place, one of the most popular salsa joints in the city.

Bul-Let's (☎ 3401-4844; www.bul-lets.com; B1 fl, Kasumi Bldg, 1-7-11 Nishi-Azabu, Minato-ku; admission from ¥1500) Near Yellow, this mellow basement space plays worldwide trance and ambient sounds for barefoot patrons. Beds and sofas round out this carpeted club.

Lexington Queen (☎ 3401-1661; www.lexington queen.com; B1 fl, Gotō Bldg, 3-13-14 Roppongi, Minato-ku; ☺ 8pm-5am) The Lex was one of Roppongi's first discos and is still the place where every visiting celebrity ends up. The cover here starts around ¥2000 unless you've had your visage on the cover of *Vogue* or *Rolling Stone*. But, even non celebrities get a free drink with admission.

Vanilla (☎ 3401-6200; www.clubvanilla.com; TSK Bldg, 7-14-30 Roppongi, Minato-ku; admission from ¥1500; ⏱ 7pm-late) Aimed more towards a Japanese clientele, Vanilla harbours fewer drunken gaijin yahoos than nearby clubs. Three floors of dance space are filled with different beats and crowds of peeps. From Roppongi Station, take exit 4 heading west on Roppongi-dōri, pass Mizuho Bank and turn right down the next alley.

Motown House 1 (☎ 5474-4605; www.motownhouse.com; 2nd fl, Com Roppongi Bldg, 3-11-5 Roppongi, Minato-ku; ⏱ 6pm-5am) On the other side of Gaien-higashi-dōri, Motown House is on the first street in from the corner. Along with the standard rock and roll, this house plays soul, funk, hip-hop and pop, as the name might imply. It's also got a long bar with drinks starting at ¥800. On the next block, the second branch, **Motown House 2** (☎ 5474-2931; B1 fl, Roppongi Plaza Bldg; ⏱ 8pm-5am Sun-Thu, 8pm-8am Fri & Sat), has a similar setup as the first.

Velfarre (☎ 3402-8000; http://velfarre.avex.co.jp/; 7-14-22 Roppongi, Minato-ku; admission from ¥3000; ⏱ 7pm-midnight) On the club front, Velfarre is Roppongi's disco Hilton. Dance clubs don't get much bigger, flashier or better behaved than this place. The cover includes a drink or three. Take exit 4 from Roppongi Station, and cut down beside the Mizuho bank. Velfarre is in the basement of what looks like a car park.

A night out in youth-oriented Shibuya may make those past the ripe old age of 25 feel slightly ancient, but once you're out shaking it on the dance floor, who cares?

Ruby Room (Map p103; ☎ 3780-3022; 2F, Kasumi Bldg, 2-25-17 Dōgenzaka, Shibuya-ku; ⏱ 9pm-late) This dark, sparkly cocktail lounge is on a hill behind the 109 Building. The Ruby Room hosts both DJed and live music (the cover is around ¥1500 and includes a free drink), and is a fun place for older kids hanging in Shibuya.

Club Asia (Map p103; ☎ 5458-1996; 1-8 Maruyama-chō, Shibuya-ku; ⏱ 11pm-5am) This massive techno/soul club is worth a visit if you're a young twentysomething. Events here are usually jam-packed no matter what night it is and usually cost about ¥2500. There's also a good restaurant serving a variety of Southeast Asian food.

Harlem (Map p103; ☎ 3461-8806; 2nd & 3rd fls, Dr Jeekahn's Bldg, 2-4 Maruyama-chō, Shibuya-ku; admission ¥2000-3000; ⏱ 10pm-5am Tue-Sat) This is the

gathering place for Tokyo B-boys and B-girls. The music is soul and hip-hop spun by international DJs, and the cover includes one drink.

Womb (Map p103; ☎ 5459-0039; www.womb.co.jp; 2-16 Maruyama-chō, Shibuya-ku; admission ¥1500-4000; ⏱ 8pm-late) 'Oomu' (as it's pronounced by the Japanese) is all about house, techno and drum 'n' bass. The four floors of drinking, dancing and dining get crowded on weekends. If you bring a flyer – make the rounds of Shibuya record shops beforehand, or print one from their website – they'll knock ¥500-1000 off the cover. Picture ID required at the door.

Yellow (Map pp106-7; ☎ 3479-0690; B1 & B2 fl, Cesarus Bldg, 1-10-11 Nishi-Azabu, Minato-ku; admission ¥2000-3500) Around Tokyo, Yellow is one of the best places to head for electronica. It's an interesting, inky basement space that plays host to some of Tokyo's better club events. Look for the entrance next to a 'coin parking' lot.

LIVE MUSIC

Tokyo's home-grown live-music scene is not as vibrant as one might suspect, but it's still possible to catch some good live acts. Roppongi (Map pp106-7) is the place for 'oldies-but-goodies'.

Crocodile (Map p103; ☎ 3499-5205; B1 fl, New Sekiguchi Bldg, 6-18-8 Jingūmae, Shibuya-ku; admission from ¥2000; ⏱ 6pm-2am) In Harajuku right on Meiji-dōri, Crocodile has live music seven nights a week. It's a spacious place with room for dancing if the music moves you. Tunes cover the gamut from night to night, be it jazz, reggae or rock-and-roll. The cover includes one drink.

Milk (Map p105; ☎ 5458-2826; B1 fl, Roob 6 Bldg, 1-13-3 Ebisu-Nishi, Shibuya-ku) Down in Ebisu, beneath What the Dickens (p145), Milk has live music on Thursday and Friday nights. Check out the kitchen – there's no food but it's a great place to chat and sip on a gin and tonic between sets. There's a good mix of musical genres here, from dub and hip-hop to electronica.

La.mama (Map p103; ☎ 3464-0801; info@lamama.net; B1 fl, Primera Dogenzaka Bldg, 1-15-3 Dōgenzaka, Shibuya-ku) For a dose of current local-centric music, this is a good bet for catching live, mainstream-Japanese rockers. The room is fairly spacious, but even when the place gets crowded you'll never be far from the stage. Shows average about ¥2300 at the door.

Eggman (Map p103; ☎ 3495-1561; 1-6-8 Jinnan, Shibuya-ku; admission around ¥2500; ✹ 6.30pm-late) Follow the spiral staircase down to this underground spot. A smaller venue compared with Shibuya's giant dance clubs, Eggman features live bands – mostly local, mostly rock-and-roll.

Loft (Map p101; ☎ 5272-0382; B2F, Tatehana Bldg, 1-12-9 Kabuki-chō, Shinjuku-ku; ✹ 5pm-late) Had they been Japanese, the Rolling Stones would have played at Loft long before they cut their first single. This Shinjuku institution is smoky, loud and lots of fun on a good night.

Cavern Club (Map pp106-7; ☎ 3405-5207; 1st fl, Saito Bldg, 5-3-2 Roppongi, Minato-ku; admission ¥1300) Flawless I-wanna-hold-your-hand covers are belted out by four Japanese mop-heads.

Kento's (Map pp106-7; ☎ 3401-5755; 5-3-1 Roppongi, Minato-ku; admission ¥1300) Features 1950s standards.

Bauhaus (Map pp106-7; ☎ 3403-0092; 2nd fl, Reine Roppongi Bldg, 5-3-4 Roppongi, Minato-ku; admission ¥1800) This is where you go to forget the 1950s and forget the Beatles; it's the place for 1970s and '80s rock covers. The cover includes one drink.

At **Club Quattro** (Map p103; ☎ 3477-8750; 5th fl, Club Quattro Bldg, 32-13 Udagawa-chō, Shibuya-ku) and **O-West** (Map pp106-7; ☎ 5784-7088; 2-3 Maruyama-chō, Shibuya-ku) or **O-East** (Map p103; ☎ 5458-4681; 2-14-8 Dōgenzaka, Shibuya-ku) in Shibuya, you need to book tickets in advance, rather than just turn up in the hope of catching a good live act.

JAZZ

People take their jazz seriously in Tokyo. For listings of performances, check the latest issue of *Tokyo Journal* or *Metropolis*.

Blue Note Tokyo (Map pp106-7; ☎ 3407-5781; Raika Bldg, 6-3-16 Minami-Aoyama, Minato-ku; admission ¥6000-10,000; ✹ 5.30pm-1.30am Mon-Sat) In Aoyama, this is Tokyo's big-name jazz venue. The cover charge keeps the riff-raff away and allows aficionados within spitting distance of the greats of jazz. Take exit B3 from Omotesandō subway station and walk down Kottodōri towards Nishi Azabu; it's opposite the Idee store.

STB 139 (Sweet Basil; Map pp106-7; ☎ 5474-1395; http://stb139.co.jp; 6-7-11 Roppongi, Minato-ku; admission ¥3000-7000; ✹ 6-11pm Mon-Sat) A two-minute walk south of Roppongi Station (exit 3), this is a large, lovely space that draws similarly big-name acts. Performances are mostly jazz, covering the gamut of the genre.

Roppongi Pit Inn (Map pp106-7; ☎ 3585-1063; 3-17-7 Roppongi, Minato-ku) Fans of fusion and alternative-direction jazz should swing by Roppongi Pit Inn, a popular spot for younger jazz aficionados. Performances are of high quality and deliciously varying styles.

TECHNO EVENTS

Electronica has caught on in Tokyo in a big way. Tokyo attracts some of the best DJs and live acts and boasts an impressive line-up of superb local talent. Some of the better events take place in Nishi-Azabu's Yellow (opposite) and Shibuya's Club Asia (opposite) and Womb (opposite) for techno. Check *Metropolis* to see what's on while you're in town or stop by Cisco or Tower Records in Shibuya to pick up some flyers.

Theatre

BUNRAKU

Kokuritsu Gekijō (National Theatre; ☎ 3265-7411; 4-1 Hayabusa-chō, Chiyoda-ku; admission ¥1500-9200; ✹ performance starts 11.30am & 5pm) Performances are staged several times a year, even though Osaka is the home of *bunraku* (classical puppet theatre). The theatre is in Hayabusa-chō, near Nagata-chō Station on the Yūraku-chō subway line. Check with the TIC or the theatre for information (tickets available 10am to 6pm).

KABUKI

Kabuki-za (Map p96; ☎ 5565-6000; 4-12-5 Ginza, Chūo-ku; admission ¥2520-16,800) This is the simplest way to see kabuki in Tokyo, and directly accessible from Higashi-Ginza Station's exit 3. Performances and times vary from month to month, so you'll need to check with the TIC or with the theatre directly for programme information. Earphone guides providing 'comments and explanations' in English are available for ¥650 plus ¥1000 deposit.

Kabuki performances can be quite a marathon, lasting from four to five hours. If you're not up to it, you can get tickets for the 4th floor from ¥600 to ¥1000 and watch only part of the show (ask for *hitomakumi*) but earphone guides are not available in these seats. Fourth-floor tickets can be bought on the day of the performance. There are generally two performances, starting at around 11am and 4pm.

Kokuritsu Gekijō, (above) Japan's national theatre, also has kabuki performances, with a range of seat prices. Earphone guides are available. Check with the TIC or the theatre for performance times.

NŌ

Nō (classical Japanese dance-drama) performances are held at various locations around Tokyo. Tickets cost between ¥2100 and ¥15,000, and it's best to get them at the theatre itself. Check with the TIC or the appropriate theatre for times.

Kanze Nō-gakudō (Map p103; ☎ 3469-6421; 1-16-4 Shōtō, Shibuya-ku) One of the oldest and most highly respected schools of *nō* in Tokyo, Kanze Nō-gakudo is about a 15-minute walk west from Shibuya Station (Hachikō exit). Call ahead to the theatre to find out if performances are on while you're in town.

National Nō Theatre (Kokuritsu Nō-gakudō) (Map p103; ☎ 3423-1331; 4-18-1 Sendagaya, Shibuya-ku; admission ¥2800-5600) The National Nō Theatre stages its own productions (for which written English synopses are provided), but also hosts privately-sponsored *nō* performances. To get to the theatre, exit Sendagaya Station with Shinjuku to your left and follow the road that hugs the railway tracks. The theatre is on the left.

Tea Ceremonies

A few hotels in Tokyo hold tea ceremonies that you can see and occasionally participate in for a fee of ¥1000 to ¥1500. **Hotel New Otani** (☎ 3265-1111; ceremonies 11am & 1pm Thu-Sat) has ceremonies on its 7th floor on Thursday, Friday and Saturday at 11am and 1pm (see p131). Ring before you go to make sure the day's sitting hasn't been booked out. **Hotel Ōkura** (☎ 3582-0111; admission ¥1050; ⏰ 10am-4pm Mon-Sat), see p131, and **Imperial Hotel** (☎ 3504-1111) also hold daily tea ceremonies (see p126).

Sports
BASEBALL

Although soccer has made some headway in recent years, baseball remains Japan's most popular team sport. There are two professional leagues, the Central and the Pacific. The baseball season runs from April until the end of October. Check the *Japan Times* to see who's playing while you're in town. The cheapest unreserved outfield seats start at ¥1500. The two main places to see baseball in Tokyo are the **Tokyo Dome** (Big Egg; Map pp94-5; ☎ 5800-9999; 1-3-61 Kōraku, Bunkyō-

ku), next to Kōraku-en Amusement Park (a two-minute walk from Suidobashi Station on the JR line), and **Jingū Kyūjo** (Jingū Stadium; Map pp106-7; ☎ 3404-8999; 13 Kasumigaoka, Shinjuku-ku), close to JR Shinanomachi Station.

SUMŌ

Sumō tournaments at Tokyo's **Ryōgoku Kokugikan Stadium** (Map pp94-5; ☎ 3623-6111; 1-3-28 Yokoami, Sumida-ku; ticket office ⏰ 10am-5pm) in Ryōgoku take place in January, May and September and last for 15 days. The best seats are all bought up by those with the right connections, but if you don't mind standing, you can get in for around ¥1000. Tickets can be bought up to a month prior to the tournament, or you can simply turn up on the day (you'll have to arrive very early, say 6am, to be assured of seats during the last days of a tournament). The stadium is adjacent to Ryōgoku Station (Sōbu line), on the northern side of the railway tracks. If you can't go in person, NHK televises sumō from 3.30pm daily during each tournament.

SHOPPING

Although Tokyo is a notoriously expensive city, the determined shopper can still come up with a few bargains. Naturally, the best one-stop shopping options are the department stores, which stock virtually everything, including souvenirs. Unless a major sale is on, however, department stores are expensive places to shop. Keep in mind that department stores close at least one day each month, usually a Monday or Wednesday.

Antiques & Souvenirs

One of the best places to look for antiques and interesting souvenirs is in the basement of the **Hanae Mori building** (Map p103; 3-6-1 Kita-Aoyama, Minato-ku) in Harajuku, which has more than 30 antique shops. Not far from here, the **Oriental Bazaar** (Map p103; ☎ 3400-3933; 5-9-13 Jingūmae, Shibuya-ku; ⏰ 10am-7pm Fri-Wed) is a good one-stop shop for gifts. It has a wide range of good souvenirs – fans, folding screens, yukata and pottery – some at very affordable prices.

Those interested in handicrafts shouldn't miss the **Japan Traditional Crafts Center** (Map p100; ☎ 5954-6066; 1st & 2nd fl, Metropolitan Plaza Bldg, 1-11-1 Nishi-Ikebukuro, Toshima-ku; ⏰ 11am-7pm). Temporary shows of handmade crafts such as weavings, mosaics, bows and arrows, ceramics and *washi* are held on the 3rd floor. Other lovely examples available for purchase are on the 1st and 2nd floors. It's near the Metropolitan exit of Ikebukuro JR Station.

Inachū Lacquerware (Map pp106–7; ☎ 3582-4451; 1-5-2 Akasaka, Minato-ku; ☒ 10am–6pm Mon–Sat) Lacquerware from Wajima is famous throughout Japan for its beauty and craftsmanship; Inachu is one of the pricier shops around, but all wares are of the highest quality.

Another great selection of souvenirs can be found in Ueno at the Tokyo National Museum's gift shop (p111). In addition to art books, postcards and the like, it has woodblock prints and *komono* (small arts and crafts) and a variety of other Japanese goods at reasonable prices.

Clothes

For general off-the-rack wear, Shinjuku (Map p101) and Shibuya (Map p103) are the best areas to shop around and compare prices. The department stores are good places to look. For a great mix of youth and slightly-more-mature casual wear at reasonable prices (by Tokyo standards – an ¥8000 skirt, for example, or ¥3000 for a T-shirt), browse the following behemoths.

Isetan (Map p101; ☎ 3352-1111; 3-14-1 Shinjuku, Shinjuku-ku; ☒ 10am–7.30pm)

Laforet (Map p103; ☎ 5411-3330; 1-11-6 Jingūmae, Shibuya-ku; ☒ 11am–8pm) For those with an outrageous sartorial style, Laforet is worth a trip just to check out what the other young shoppers are wearing.

Marui One (Map p101; ☎ 3464-0101; 3-18-1 Shinjuku, Shinjuku-ku) Marui has branches in Shinjuku, Shibuya and Ikebukuro; Marui One is more hipster than teenybopper.

Matsuzakaya (Map p96; ☎ 3572-1111; 6-10-1 Ginza, Chūō-ku; ☒ 10am–8pm Mon–Sat, 10am–7.30pm Sun)

Mitsukoshi (Map p96; ☎ 3562-1111; 4-6-16 Ginza, Chūō-ku; ☒ 10am–7.30pm Mon–Sat, 10am–7pm Sun)

Parco (Map p103; ☎ 3464-5111; 15-1 Udagawa-chō, Shibuya-ku; ☒ 10am–8.30pm) There are several branches of Parco around Shibuya; this is the flagship store.

Seibu (Map p103; ☎ 3462-0111; 21-1 Udagawa-chō; ☒ 10am–8pm) This branch of Seibu is also connected via passageway to its younger-generation spinoffs, Seed and Loft.

Takashimaya (Map p96; ☎ 3211-4111; 2-4-1 Nihombashi, Chūō-ku; ☒ 10am–7.30pm) For more conservative wear from a venerable Tokyo establishment.

Venus Fort (Map p108; ☎ 3599-0700; Aomi-itchōme, Kōtō-ku; ☒ 11am–10pm) Down in Ōdaiba, besides being an attraction in itself, has a bounty of boutiques catering to women's fashion.

Areas like Harajuku (Map p103), Aoyama (Map p103) and Nishi-Azabu (Map pp106–7) are some of the best places for specialised boutiques.

Finally, if you want to see where the Tokyo girls buy their knee-high black stiletto boots and pink lace-up Uggs, look no further than Shibuya's **Frontier** (Map p103; ☎ 3464-4579) shoe shop – with a fantabulous display o' boots outside.

Computer Equipment

Akihabara (秋葉原) is Tokyo's discount electrical and electronics mecca. Nowhere in the world will you find such a range of electrical appliances. If you have a short attention span, you'll be perfectly suited to spending half a day flitting from store to noisy store. Some larger stores (Laox and Sofmap are reliable options) have tax-free sections with export models for sale – don't forget to ask for duty-free.

Although the vast majority of offerings are aimed at computers with Japanese operating systems, **T-Zone Computers** (Map pp94–5; ☎ 5209-7501; ☒ 11am–8pm Mon–Fri, 10am–8pm Sat, Sun & public holidays) is one store that stocks a small selection of computers with English operating systems, English-language software and related peripherals. It's on the eastern side of Chūō-dōri, 500m northwest of Akihabara.

While prices may be competitive with those you are used to at home, it's unusual to find prices that match those of dealers in Hong Kong or Singapore. You should be able to knock 10% off the marked prices by bargaining, though this is often not the case with the tax-free items in the bigger stores. To find the shops, take the Electric Town exit of Akihabara Station. You'll see the sign on the platform if you come in on the JR Yamanote line.

Flea Markets

Flea markets sound like promising places to shop for interesting antiques and souvenirs, but bear in mind that this is Tokyo and there are unlikely to be any real bargains. At the very least, take a look at somewhere like the Oriental Bazaar (opposite) and make a note of prices before embarking on a flea-market shopping spree. Tokyo's main flea markets take place at city shrines, including those listed on p152.

Hanazono-jinja (Map p101; 5am-4pm every Sun) Close to Isetan department store on the eastern side of Shinjuku Station.

Nogi-jinja (Map pp106–7; dawn-dusk 2nd Sun of each month) From Nogi-zaka subway station on the Chiyoda line – the shrine is on Gaien-higashi-dōri.

Tōgō-jinja (Map p103; 6am-3pm 1st, 4th & 5th Sun of each month) Take the Takeshita-dōri exit from Harajuku JR Station.

Kids' Stuff

Japanese are particularly creative when it comes to finding things to keep their kids occupied, and Tokyo has some great toy shops. Places to take kids to are **Loft** (Map p103; 3462-3807; 21-1 Udagawa-chō, Shibuya-ku; 10am-8pm Sun-Wed, 10am-9pm Thu-Sat) in Shibuya and **Kiddyland** (Map p103; 3409-3431; 6-1-9 Jingūmae, Shibuya-ku; 10am-8pm, closed 3rd Tue of each month) in Harajuku. The latter has five floors of stuff that your kids would probably be better off not knowing about. **Hakuhinkan Toy Park** (Map p96; 3571-8008; www.hakuhinkan.co.jp; 8-8-11 Ginza, Chūō-ku; 11am-8pm) in Ginza is a big toy shop that has a child-oriented theatre and restaurants on its upper floors.

Music

Shibuya (Map p103) is music central; the area northwest of Shibuya Station is home to several shops, including branches of the Recofan and Disk Union chains, which stock rare and second-hand CDs. The best of the lot is the massive Shibuya branch of **Tower Records** (Map p103; 3496-3661; 1-22-14 Jinnan, Shibuya-ku; 10am-11pm) – which has the most extensive range in Tokyo and lots of listening stations. Even if you're not a music lover, the 7th-floor bookshop is worth a look. The big three, Tower Records, Virgin and HMV, all have several branches in Tokyo.

For vinyl, try the record stores in Shibuya, most notably **Cisco Records** (Map p103; 3462-0366; 2nd fl, 11-1 Udagawa-chō; 11am-9pm) for electronica, and **Manhattan Records** (Map p103; 3477-7737; 1st fl, 10-1 Udagawa-chō, Shibuya-ku; noon-9pm) for hip-hop (the latter is worth a trip just to glimpse all the Japanese B-Boys).

Ningyō (Japanese Dolls)

Next to JR Asakusabashi Station, Edo-dōri (Map pp98–9) is the place for *ningyō*. Both sides of the road have large numbers of shops specialising in both traditional and contemporary Japanese dolls.

Photographic Equipment

Check the Shinjuku section for information on the big camera stores there. Ginza's Harumi-dōri is another place for photographic equipment – there are several good secondhand photographic shops where Japanese gear can often be bought at reasonable prices.

Other Japanese Goods

Washi (handmade paper) is one of the cheaper and more interesting souvenir possibilities. One place that stocks a good selection is **Haibara** (Map p96; 3272-3801; 2-7-6 Nihombashi, Chūō-ku; 9.30am-6.30pm Mon-Fri, 9.30am-5pm Sat) in Central Tokyo; take exit C3 from Nihombashi Station. All the major department stores have a section devoted to *washi*.

Kamawanu (Map p105; 3780-0182; 23-1 Sarugaku-chō, Shibuya-ku; 11am-7pm), in Daikanyama, is a little shop specialising in *tenugui*, those ubiquitous Japanese hand-towels that you find in *sentō* and *onsen*. It's also got a limited selection of other craft goods.

Takumi Handicrafts (Map p96; 3571-2017; 8-4-2 Ginza, Chūō-ku; 11am-7pm Mon-Sat) Has quality ceramics, textile handicrafts, folk toys and lacquerware at this two-storey shop near Shimbashi Station (exit 5).

GETTING THERE & AWAY

Air

With the exception of China Airlines, all international airlines (p749) use Narita airport rather than the more conveniently located Haneda airport.

Immigration and customs procedures are usually straightforward, but they can be time consuming for non-Japanese. Note that Japanese customs officials are probably the most scrupulous in Asia; backpackers arriving from anywhere remotely third-worldish (the Philippines, Thailand etc) can expect some questions and perhaps a thorough search.

You can change money in the customs hall after having cleared customs, and in the arrival hall. The rates are the same as those offered in town.

Narita has two terminals, Nos 1 and 2. This doesn't complicate things too much as both have train stations that are connected to JR and Keisei lines. The one you arrive at will depend on the airline you are flying with. Both terminals have clear English signposting for train and limousine bus services. The main information counter for foreign travellers is the **TIC** (☎ 0476-34-6251), on the 1st floor of Terminal 2. There's another information counter, in Terminal 1, that can handle most questions.

Be sure to check which terminal your flight leaves from, and give yourself plenty of time to get out to Narita – the train ride itself can take from 45 minutes to 1½ hours.

Boat

A ferry journey can be a great, relatively inexpensive way to get from Tokyo to other parts of the country. Prices given here are for 2nd-class travel. Though phone numbers are listed here, most lines are not staffed with English-speaking staff. It's easiest to book passage through a local travel agency or the JNTO.

From Tokyo is the long-distance **Nankai Ferry** (☎ 0120-732-156) to Kōchi (¥10,600); the **Ocean Ferry** (☎ 3567-0971) goes to Tokushima (¥8610, 18 hours) in Shikoku and to Kitakyūshū (¥12,600, 33 hours) in Northern Kyūshū; and **Oshima Transportation** (☎ 3273-8911) goes to Naha (¥22,000, 45 hours) on Okinawa. Long-distance ferry services to Hokkaidō are no longer available from Tokyo, however **Shōsen Mitsui Ferry** (☎ 5501-1855) and **Higashi Nihon Ferry** (☎ 3535-0558) has departures from Ibaragi prefecture to Tomakomai in Hokkaidō (¥6400, 20 hours).

Bus

Long-distance buses are generally little or no cheaper than trains, but are sometimes a good alternative for long-distance trips to areas serviced by expressways.

There are a number of express buses running between Tokyo, Kyoto and Osaka. Overnight buses leave at 10pm from the Yaesu side of Tokyo Station and arrive at Kyoto and Osaka between 6am and 7am the following day. They cost from ¥8000 to ¥8500 (if you're coming back, you'll save money by buying a return ticket). The buses are a JR service and can be booked at one of the green windows at a JR station.

Buses also run from Tokyo Station to Nara (¥8400, 9½ hours), Kōbe (¥8690, 9½ hours), Hiroshima (¥11,600, 12 hours), Fukui (¥8300, eight hours), Nagano (¥4000, four hours), Yamagata (¥6420, 5½ hours), Takamatsu (¥10,000, 9½ hours), Sendai (¥6210,

5½ hours), Morioka (¥7850, 7½ hours) and Aomori (¥10,000, 9½ hours).

From Shinjuku Station there are buses running to the Fuji and Hakone regions, including, for Mt Fuji climbers, direct services to the 5th station (see p172). The Shinjuku long-distance bus station is across from the west exit of Shinjuku Station.

Train

All major JR lines radiate from Tokyo Station; northbound trains stop at Ueno Station, which, like Tokyo Station, is conveniently on the JR Yamanote line. Private lines – which are often cheaper and quicker for making day trips out of Tokyo – start from various stations around Tokyo. With the exception of the Tōbu Nikkō line, which starts in Asakusa, all private lines originate somewhere on the Yamanote line.

For fares to major cities from Tokyo, see p764.

SHINKANSEN

There are three *shinkansen* (bullet train) lines that connect Tokyo with the rest of Japan: the Tōkaidō line, which passes through Central Honshū, changing its name along the way to the Sanyō line before terminating at Hakata in Northern Kyūshū; the Tōhoku line, which runs northeast via Utsunomiya and Sendai as far as Morioka, with the Yamagata branch heading from Fukushima to Yamagata and the Akita branch heading from Morioka to Akita; and the Jōetsu line, which runs north to Niigata, with the Nagano branch heading from Takasaki to Nagano-shi.

Of these lines, the one most likely to be used by visitors to Japan is the Tōkaidō line, as it passes through Kyoto and Osaka in the Kansai region. All three *shinkansen* lines start at Tokyo Station, though the Tōhoku and Jōetsu lines make a stop at Ueno Station, and the Tōkaidō line now stops at Shinagawa Station in south-central Tokyo.

PRIVATE LINES

The private lines generally service Tokyo's sprawling suburbia. The Tōkyū Tōyoko line, running between Shibuya Station and Yokohama; the Odakyū line, running from Shinjuku to Odawara and the Hakone region; the Tōbu Nikkō line, running from Asakusa to Nikkō; and the Seibu Shinjuku line from Ikebukuro to Kawagoe are the most useful.

OTHER JR LINES

The regular Tōkaidō line serves the stations that the Tōkaidō *shinkansen* line zips through without stopping. Trains start at Tokyo Station and pass through Shimbashi and Shinagawa Stations on the way out of town. There are *kyūkyō* (express) services to Yokohama and to Izu-hantō via Atami, and from there trains continue – very slowly – to Nagoya, Kyoto and Osaka.

Northbound trains start in Ueno. The Takasaki line goes to Kumagaya and, of course, Takasaki, with onward connections from Takasaki to Niigata. The Tōhoku line follows the Takasaki line as far north as Ōmiya, from where it heads to the far north of Honshū via Sendai and Aomori. Getting to Sendai without paying any express surcharges will involve changes at Utsunomiya and Fukushima. For those intent on saving the expense of a night's accommodation, there are also overnight services.

GETTING AROUND

Tokyo has an excellent public transport system. Everything of note is conveniently close to a subway or JR station. Bus services are difficult to use if you don't read *kanji* (character-script), but the average visitor to Tokyo won't need the buses anyway.

To/From Narita Airport

Narita airport is 66km from central Tokyo, and is used by almost all the international airlines but by only a small number of domestic operators. Travel to or from Tokyo takes from 50 minutes to 1½ hours or more, depending on your mode of transport and destination in town.

Depending on where you're going, it is generally cheaper and faster to travel into Tokyo by train than by limousine bus. However, rail users will probably need to change trains somewhere, and this can be confusing on a jetlagged first visit. Limousine buses provide a hassle-free direct route to a number of Tokyo's top hotels (you don't have to be staying at the hotels to use the buses).

TRAIN

There are three rail services between Tokyo and both terminals at Narita airport: the private **Keisei line** (☎ 3621-2242; www.keisei.co.jp in Japanese); the **JR Narita Express N'EX** (www.jreast .co.jp/e/index.html for information; www.world.eki-net

.com for reservations); and the JR 'Airport Narita' service. The Keisei service arrives at Nippori and Ueno, from either of which you can change to the Yamanote line for access to Ikebukuro, Shinjuku and other destinations. N'EX and the 'Airport Narita' service arrives at Tokyo Station (from where you can change to almost any line). N'EX also runs to Shinjuku, Ikebukuro and Yokohama.

The Keisei line has two services: the Keisei Skyliner, which does the trip between Narita and Ueno (¥1920, one hour), and the Keisei *tokkyū* (limited express; ¥1000, one hour and 11 minutes). Times and fares to and from Nippori are marginally less. Tokkyū services are much more frequent than the Skyliner, and what is another 11 minutes?

The N'EX services are fast, extremely comfortable and include amenities like drink-dispensing machines and telephones. They go to or from Tokyo Station (¥2940, 55 minutes); to Shinjuku Station (¥3110, 1½ hours); to or from Ikebukuro Station (¥3110, one hour and 40 minutes); and to or from Yokohama Station (¥4180, 1½ hours). N'EX services run approximately half-hourly between 7am and 10pm, but Ikebukuro services are very infrequent; in most cases you will be better off heading to Shinjuku and taking the Yamanote line from there. Seats are reserved only, but can be bought immediately before departure if they are available.

'Airport Narita' trains cost ¥1280 and take 1½ hours to or from Tokyo. Trains only run approximately once an hour.

The Keikyū rail line runs between Narita and Haneda airports (¥1560, 1¾ hours), with several direct trains a day.

LIMOUSINE BUS

Don't be misled by the name; they're just ordinary buses and take 1½ to two hours (depending on the traffic) to travel between Narita airport and a number of major hotels around Tokyo. Check departure times before buying your ticket, as services are not all that frequent. The fare to or from hotels around Asakusa, to or from Ikebukuro, Akasaka, Ginza, Shiba, Shinagawa, Shinjuku or Haneda airport it is around ¥3000. There is also a direct service between the airport and Yokohama (¥3500, two hours).

To/From Haneda Airport

Most domestic flights and China Airlines to/from Taiwan use the convenient Haneda airport.

Transport to or from Haneda Airport is a simple matter, as the **Tokyo Monorail** (www.tokyo-monorail.co.jp) runs from 5.15am to 11.15pm between the airport and Hamamatsu-chō Station on the JR Yamanote line (¥470, 22 minutes, every 10 minutes).

Taxis from the airport to places around central Tokyo cost around ¥6000. Limousine buses connect Haneda with TCAT (¥900), Tokyo Station (¥900), Ikebukuro and Shinjuku (¥1200) and several other destinations in Tokyo.

There is a direct bus service between Haneda and Narita (¥3000, two hours).

Bus

Pick up a copy of the free TOEI Bus Route Guide from the TIC. When using a bus, it pays to have the name of your destination written in Japanese so you can either show the driver or match up the kanji with the route map yourself (there's not much in the way of English signposting on buses or at bus stops). It's a flat ¥200 for city destinations.

Car

For those who enjoy a challenge. You'll need an international licence. Three companies that usually have English-speakers on hand are **Dollar Rent-a-Car** (☎ 3567-2818), **Nippon Rent-a-Car** (☎ 3485-7196) and **Toyota Rent-a-Car** (☎ 5954-8008). Typical rates for small cars are ¥8000 or ¥9000 for the first day, and ¥5500 to ¥7000 each day thereafter. On top of this there is a ¥1000-per-day insurance fee. Mileage is usually unlimited.

Train

Tokyo has a crowded but otherwise awesome rail network. Between the JR and private above-ground and subway lines, you can get to almost anywhere in town quickly and cheaply. But night owls beware: it closes from around midnight until 5am or 6am.

Avoiding Tokyo's rush hour is not often possible, though things tend to quiet down from 10am to 4pm.

JR LINES

Undoubtedly, the most useful line in Tokyo is the JR Yamanote line, which does a 35km loop around the city, taking in most of the important areas. You can do the whole circuit in an hour for the ¥130 minimum charge – a great introduction to the city. Another useful above-ground JR route is the Chūō line, which cuts across the centre of town between Shinjuku and Akihabara. Tickets are transferable on all JR lines.

The major JR stations (Tokyo, Shibuya, Shinjuku, Ikebukuro and Ueno) are massive places with thronging crowds and never enough English signposting. Just working out how to buy a ticket can drive a newcomer to the edge of madness. If it's a JR train you're taking, look for the JR sign (usually green) and the rows of vending machines. If you don't know the fare, put in the minimum ¥130 and push the top left-hand button (the one with no price on it). When you get to your destination you can pay the balance at a fare adjustment machine, found near the ticket gates. English signposting points the way to the railway platforms.

If you're going to be doing a lot of travelling on JR lines (even just the Yamanote line) we strongly suggest buying a JR 'IO' card. These work like debit cards that you can insert directly into automated ticket wickets (the correct fare will be deducted automatically). IO cards come in denominations of ¥1000, ¥3000 and ¥5000 and can be purchased from ticket machines marked with, er, a large watermelon and a penguin, or from ticket windows.

Travellers planning to spend an extended period of time in Tokyo might consider getting a Suica smart card, whose convenience factor is alluring – the Suica card can be swiped over the wicket without being removed from a wallet, and they can be recharged. They can even be used to purchase items at convenience stores in the stations. These cards require a ¥500 deposit, refundable when you return the card.

For English-language train information, you can call the **JR English Information line** (☎ 3423 0111; ◷ 10am-6pm Mon-Fri).

SUBWAY LINES

There are 12 subway lines in Tokyo (13 if you include the Yūrakuchō New Line), of which eight are TRTA lines and four are TOEI lines. This is not particularly important to remember, as the subway services are essentially the same, have good connections from one to another and can be used with the same subway pass or special transfer tickets. Train lines are colour-coded on the excellent maps that are available free at subway stations and tourist information counters around town.

Ticket prices start at ¥160 for short hops, but if your trip involves a change of train you can be sure it will cost upwards of ¥190. As with the JR system, if you are in doubt at all (there are still subway stations in Tokyo where the only pricing maps are in Japanese), buy a ticket for ¥160 and upgrade if necessary at your destination.

Unless you purchase a special ticket (and this would require Japanese-reading ability), you'll have to buy a separate ticket when you switch from TRTA and TOEI subway lines.

The subway equivalent of the JR Suica card is the SF Metro card. It comes in denominations of ¥1000, ¥3000 and ¥5000 and can be used directly in the automatic ticket gates. Best of all, it's good for travel

on both subway systems and saves you time when switching between the two systems.

DISCOUNT TICKETS & TRAIN PASSES

There are no massively discounted tickets available for travel around Tokyo. The best deal is the Tokyo Combination Ticket, which allows travel on any subway, tram, TOEI bus or JR train in the metropolitan area until the last train of the day. It costs ¥1580 and is available from subway and JR stations and even post offices.

Taxi

Taxis are so expensive that you should only use them when there is no alternative. Rates start at ¥630, which gives you 2km (1.5km after 11pm), after which the meter starts to clock an additional ¥80 for every 347m; you also click up ¥80 for every two minutes you sit idly gazing at the scenery in a typical Tokyo traffic jam.

Around Tokyo
東京近郊

Forest-covered mountains, dazzling temples and rugged coastline lie at the back door of metropolitan Tokyo. *Onsen* (hot springs) lovers, shrine-seeking pilgrims and those who simply want to bask in the beauty that inspired some of Japan's best-loved painters have much to discover in this region.

To the west looms Mt Fuji, one of Japan's most famous icons. You can climb through enchanting forests to its jagged summit – as pilgrims have done for centuries – or soak up its splendour in tranquil lakeside towns nestled at Fuji-san's base. Nikkō, another site that looms large in the cultural landscape, lies to the north of Tokyo, and its gilded shrines and exquisitely crafted temples look all the more spectacular amid the cool woodland setting. Nearby *onsen* offer warm relaxation to the weary.

Kamakura, to the south, boasts an even greater number of temples, and its sylvan hiking trails are just means of exploring its 900-year history. Nearby, Yokohama slakes more temporal appetites in its handsome Chinatown, where epicureans feast on Cantonese and Mandarin dishes, as well as other delights from the Middle Kingdom.

Southwest of the city, the Izu-hantō peninsula offers quite different temptations: you'll find charming towns near the sea, lovely windswept beaches and cliff-top *onsen* overlooking the Pacific. Those seeking an island getaway needn't even leave Tokyo prefecture. An overnight boat ride from the city (or a short flight) leads to Izu-shotō, a chain of volcanic islands fringed with white-sand beaches and set against a lush subtropical backdrop. Hiking, surfing and beach-combing are among the attractions, and some would swear that the immaculately fresh sashimi alone is worth the journey.

HIGHLIGHTS

- Climb **Mt Fuji** (p169), Japan's highest mountain, and watch the sunrise from its majestic summit

- Find your spiritual centre while exploring the dazzling temples of **Nikkō** (p159)

- Recover from the madness of the metropolis at one of Izu-hantō's idyllic **onsen** (p187)

- Hike forest trails in search of hidden shrines around **Kamakura** (p193)

- Swim the blue waters surrounding the volcanic island of **Nii-jima** (p200)

- Scramble up the jagged peaks dotting **Chichibu-Tama National Park** (p166)

AROUND TOKYO

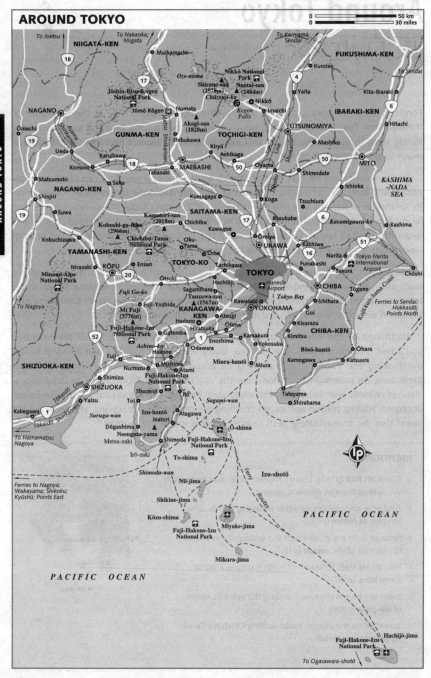

AROUND TOKYO

0 — 50 km
0 — 30 miles

To Joetsu — NIIGATA-KEN

To Nakaoka; Niigata

Muikamachi

To Koriyama; Sendai

FUKUSHIMA-KEN

Kuroiso

To Sendai

18

Oze-numa

Nikkō National Park

Shirane-san (2578m)

Nantai-san (2484m)

Yaita

Kita-Ibaraki

6

17

Jōshin-Etsu-Kōgen National Park

Jōmō Kōgen

Numata

Chūzenji-ko

Nikkō

Kegon Falls

Imaichi

IBARAKI-KEN

Hitachi

NAGANO

Akagi-san (1828m)

UTSUNOMIYA

19

Ōmachi

Shibukawa

GUNMA-KEN

TOCHIGI-KEN

Mashiko

MITO

Ueda

Karuizawa

Kiryū

Ashikaga

Oyama

50

Shimodate

Ishioka

KASHIMA -NADA SEA

NAGANO-KEN

Komoro

Saku

Takasaki

MAEBASHI

50

Koga

Tsuchiura

Matsumoto

Kumagaya

Kasukabe

Kashima

Shiojiri

SAITAMA-KEN

17

Kasumigaura-ko

19

Suwa

Kumotori-san (2018m)

Chichibu

Kawagoe

Ōmiya

Kashiwa

6

51

Kobuchizawa

Kobushi-ga-take (2966m)

Chichibu-Tama National Park

Oku-Tama

URAWA

16

Narita

Tokyo Narita International Airport

YAMANASHI-KEN

Nirasaki

KŌFU

Enzan

Ōme

Tachikawa

TOKYO

Funabashi

Sakura

Chōshi

Minami-Alps National Park

20

TOKYO-KO

Hachiōji

Haneda Airport

CHIBA

Tōgane

To Nagoya

Ōtsuki

Fuji Go-ko

Sagamihara

Tanzawa-san (1567m)

Kawasaki

Tokyo Bay

Ichihara

Kujū kuri-hama Coast

52

Mt Fuji (3776m)

Fuji-Yoshida

KANAGAWA-KEN

Hadano

Atsugi

YOKOHAMA

Goi

Kisarazu

Ferries to Sendai; Hokkaidō; Points North

Fuji-Hakone-Izu National Park

Gotemba

Ōfuna

Hiratsuka

Kamakura

Yokosuka

CHIBA-KEN

Kimitsu

SHIZUOKA-KEN

Ashino-ko

Hakone

1

Odawara

Enoshima

Bōsō-hantō

Ōhara

Fuji

Numazu

Mishima

Atami

Miura-hantō

Kamogawa

Katsuura

Shimizu

Shuzenji

Itō

Miura

Tateyama

SHIZUOKA

Yaizu

Toi

Fuji-Hakone-Izu National Park

Sagami-wan

Shirahama

Kakegawa

1

Suruga-wan

Izu-hantō inatori

Atagawa

Ō-shima

Tōkaidō Shinkansen

Dōgashima

Nesugata-yama

Metsu-zaki

Shimoda

Fuji-Hakone-Izu National Park

To Hamamatsu; Nagoya

Irō-zaki

To-shima

Shimoda-wan

Nii-jima

Izu-shotō

Ferries to Nagoya; Wakayama; Shikoku; Kyūshū; Points East

Shikine-jima

Kōzu-shima

Miyake-jima

PACIFIC OCEAN

Fuji-Hakone-Izu National Park

Mikura-jima

PACIFIC OCEAN

Hachijō-jima

Fuji-Hakone-Izu National Park

To Ogasawara-shotō

NORTH OF TOKYO

North of Tokyo are the prefectures Saitama-ken, Gunma-ken and Tochigi-ken, which include numerous places of interest, such as the Chichibu-Tama National Park, hot springs and the temple- and shrine-centre of Nikkō.

NIKKŌ 日光

☎ 0288 / pop 17,368

Scattered among hilly woodlands, Nikkō boasts a stunning array of brightly painted shrines and temples. This is one of Japan's major tourist attractions, and it's worth trying to slot a visit into even the most whirlwind tour. Note, however, that Nikkō can get extremely crowded, so it's best to visit early on a weekday to avoid the hordes (most of the attractions are open from 8am to 5pm, or until 4pm from November to March).

History

Nikkō's history as a sacred site stretches back to the middle of the 8th century, when the Buddhist priest Shōdō (735–817) established a hermitage there. For many years it was a famous training centre for Buddhist monks, before declining into obscurity. That is, until it was chosen as the site for the mausoleum of Tokugawa Ieyasu, the warlord who took control of all Japan and established the shōgunate that ruled for over 250 years until the Meiji Restoration ended the feudal era.

Tokugawa Ieyasu was laid to rest among Nikkō's towering cedars in 1617, but his grandson Tokugawa Iemitsu, in 1634, commenced work on the shrine that can be seen today. The original shrine, Tōshō-gū, was completely rebuilt using an army of some 15,000 artisans from across Japan. The work on the shrine and mausoleum took two years to complete and the results continue to receive mixed reviews.

Tōshō-gū was constructed as a memorial to a warlord who devoted his life to conquering Japan. Tokugawa Ieyasu was a man of considerable determination and was not above sacrificing a few scruples in order to achieve his aims. He is attributed with having had his wife and eldest son executed because, at a certain point, it was politically expedient for him to do so. More than anything else,

the grandeur of Nikkō is intended to inspire awe; it is a display of wealth and power by a family that for nearly three centuries was the supreme arbiter of power in Japan.

Orientation

Both the JR Nikkō Station and the nearby Tōbu Nikkō Station lie within a block of Nikkō's main road (Rte 119). From here, it's a 30-minute walk uphill to the shrine area, taking you past restaurants, hotels and the tourist information centre. From the stations to the shrine area, you can take bus No 1 or 2 to the Shin-kyō bus stop for ¥190.

The tourist office in town and the information desk in Tōbu Nikkō Station provide maps of Nikkō and the surrounding area.

Information

INTERNET ACCESS

Kyōdo Center tourist information office (☎ 53-3795; per 30 min ¥100; ☯ 8.30am-5pm) Has several computers available.

INTERNET RESOURCES

Nikko Perfect Guide (www.nikko-jp.org/english/index .html)

MEDICAL SERVICES

Kawaii-inn Clinic (☎ 54-0319) On the main road, three blocks southeast of the Kyōdo Centre tourist information office.

POST

Post office (☯ 9am-6pm Mon-Fri, 9am-5pm Sat) On the main road, three blocks northwest of the Kyōdo Center tourist information office. Has international ATM and currency exchange.

TOURIST INFORMATION

Hikers should pick up a copy of *Yumoto-Chūzenji Area Hiking Guide* which has maps and information on local flora and fauna. It costs a pittance (¥150) and is available from some of the pensions in the area, as well as at the information counters in Nikkō. The small *Guidebook for Walking Trails* (¥150) is useful for short walks.

Kyōdo Center tourist information office (☎ 53-3795; ☯ 9am-5pm) Has a wealth of useful pamphlets and maps, with a friendly English speaker always on hand. Here you can also arrange for free guided tours in English through TVIGA (adminTVIGA@hotmail.com).

Tourist information desk (☎ 53-4511; ☯ 8.30am-5pm) Tōbu Nikkō Station has a small desk where you can pick up a town map.

NIKKŌ

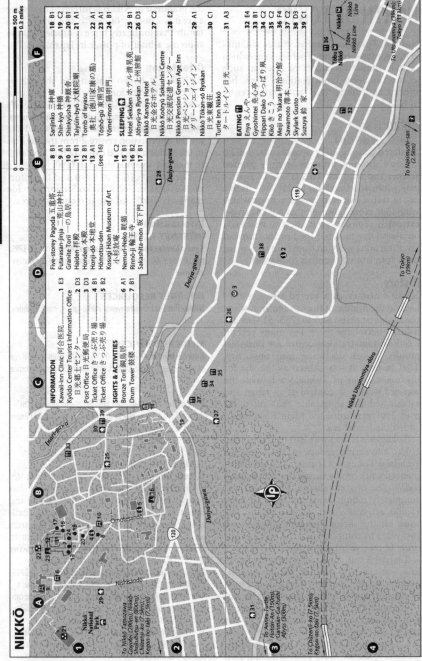

INFORMATION
Kawaii-inn Clinic 河合医院 1 E3
Kyodo Center Tourist Information Office
日光郷土センター 2 D3
Post Office 日光郵便局 3 D3
Ticket Office きっぷ売り場 4 B1
Ticket Office きっぷ売り場 5 B2

SIGHTS & ACTIVITIES
Bronze Torii 銅鳥居 6 A1
Drum Tower 鼓楼 7 B1
Five-storey Pagoda 五重塔 8 B1
Futarasan-jinja 二荒山神社 9 A1
Granite Torii 一の鳥居 10 B1
Haiden 拝殿 11 B1
Honden 本殿 12 B1
Honji-dō 本地堂 13 A1
Hōmotsu-den 宝物殿 .... (see 16)
Kosugi Hōan Museum of Art
小杉放菴 14 C2
Nemuri-Neko 眠猫 15 B2
Rinnō-ji 輪王寺 16 B2
Sakashita-mon 坂下門 17 B1
Sanjinko 三神庫 18 B1
Shin-kyō 神橋 19 C2
Shinkyūsha 神厩舎 20 B1
Taiyūin-byō 大猷院廟 21 A1
Tomb of Ieyasu
奥社（徳川家康の墓）.............. 22 A1
Tōshō-gū 東照宮 23 A1
Yōmei-mon 陽明門 24 B1

SLEEPING
Hotel Seikōen ホテル清晃苑 25 B1
Johsyū-ya Ryokan 上州旅館 26 D3
Nikkō Kanaya Hotel
日光金谷ホテル 27 C2
Nikkō Kooryū Sokushin Centre
日光交流促進センター 28 E2
Nikkō Pension Green Age Inn
日光ペンション
グリーンエイジイン 29 A1
Nikkō Tokan-sō Ryokan
日光東観荘 30 C1
Turtle Inn Nikkō
タートルイン日光 31 A3

EATING
Enya えんや 32 E4
Gyoshintei 魚心亭 33 B1
Hippari Dako ひっぱり凧 34 C2
Kikō をこう 35 C2
Meiji no Yakata 明治の館 36 F4
Sawamoto 澤本 37 C2
Skylark Gusto 38 D3
Suzuya 鈴家 39 C1

To Nikkō Tamozawa
Goyotei (200m); Nikkō-
Shizen (200m; 400m)
Chūzenji-ko (7.5km);
Kegan-no-taki (7.5km)

To Annex Turtle
Hotori-An (150m);
Ganman-Ga-Fuchi
Abyss (300m)

To Chūzenji-ko (7.5km);
Kegan-no-taki (7.5km)

To Nakimuchi-san
(2.5km)

To Utsunomiya (39km);
Tokyo (113km)

Tōbu
Nikkō Line

Nikkō
Line

To Tokyo
(39km)

Nikkō
Utsunomiya-dōri

500 m
0.3 miles

Sights

Tōshō-gū is the centrepiece of Nikkō's shrine area, with a number of impressive buildings nearby. Although you can buy separate tickets to Nikkō's attractions, it makes sense to buy a 'combination ticket' for ¥1000, valid for two days. This covers entry to the temple, Rinnō-ji, the shrines, Tōshō-gū and Futarasan-jinja, but not to the Nemuri-Neko (Sleeping Cat) in Tōshō-gū, a sight that will set you back an extra ¥520. Two booths in the shrine area sell the combination ticket – one beside Rinnō-ji, the other outside of the Omote gate fronting Tōshō-gū. Even if you do include a visit to the Nemuri-Neko, buying a combination ticket is still much cheaper than buying each of the tickets separately.

SHIN-KYŌ 神橋

This lovely red bridge over the Daiya River is a much-photographed reconstruction of the 17th century original. It is famed as the spot where Buddhist monk Shōdō Shōnin, who first established a hermitage in Nikkō in 782, was carried across the river on the backs of two huge serpents, no less.

RINNŌ-JI 輪王寺

The original Tendai-sect Rinnō-ji was founded 1200 years ago by Shōdō Shōnin. Sambutsu-dō (Three Buddha Hall) has huge gold-lacquered images, the most impressive of which is of Kannon, the goddess of mercy and compassion. The central image of the Senjū (1000-armed Kannon) is Amida Nyorai (one of the primal deities in the Mahayana Buddhist cannon), flanked by Batō (a horse-headed Kannon), whose special domain is the animal kingdom.

Hōmotsu-den (Treasure Hall; admission ¥300), also in the temple grounds, has a collection of treasures associated with the temple, but admission is not included in the combination ticket (for more information, see above).

TŌSHŌ-GŪ 東照宮

A huge stone *torii* (Shintō shrine entrance gate) marks the entrance to this shrine, while to the left is a **five-storey pagoda**, originally dating from 1650 but reconstructed in 1818. The pagoda has no foundations and is said to contain a long suspended pole that swings like a pendulum, restoring equilibrium in the event of an earthquake.

The true entrance to the shrine is through the *torii* at the gate, **Omote-mon**, protected on either side by Deva kings. Directly through the entrance are the **Sanjinko** (Three Sacred Storehouses). On the upper storey of the last storehouse are imaginative relief carvings of elephants by an artist who famously had never seen the real thing. To the left of the entrance is **Shinkyūsha** (Sacred Stable), a plain building housing a carved white horse. The stable's only adornment is an allegorical series of **relief carvings** depicting the life cycle of the monkey. They include the famous 'hear no evil, see no evil, speak no evil' threesome who has become emblematic of Nikkō.

Just beyond the stable is a granite font at which, in accordance with Shintō practice, worshippers cleanse themselves by washing their hands and rinsing their mouths. Next to the gate is a **sacred library** containing 7000 Buddhist scrolls and books; it's closed to the public.

Pass through another *torii*, climb another flight of stairs, and on the left and right are a **drum tower** and a belfry. To the left of the drum tower is **Honji-dō**, a hall with a huge ceiling painting of a dragon, known as the Roaring Dragon. A monk in attendance will bang two wooden sticks together to demonstrate the strange acoustic properties of the hall; the echo is said to sound like the roar of a dragon – something of a stretch.

Next comes **Yōmei-mon**, an elaborately decorated gate, which is crowded with detail. Among glimmering gold leaf and red lacquerwork, animals – mythical and otherwise – jostle for your attention. Intricate patterns decorate the walls with coloured relief carvings and paintings of flowers, dancing girls, mythical beasts and Chinese sages. The overall effect is more Chinese than Japanese, and it's a grand spectacle, no matter what the critics say. Worrying that its perfection might arouse envy in the gods, those responsible for its construction had the final supporting pillar on the left-hand side placed upside down as a deliberate error.

Through the Yōmei-mon and to the right is **Nemuri-Neko**. While the sleeping cat is famous throughout Japan for its lifelike appearance, you may be disappointed by this tiny wooden feline. **Sakashita-mon** here opens onto a path that climbs up through towering cedars to **Ieyasu's tomb**, a relatively simple affair. If you are using the combination ticket you will have to pay an extra ¥520 to see the cat and the tomb.

To the left of Yōmei-mon is the **Jin-yōsha**, a storage depot for Nikkō's mikoshi (portable shrines), which come into action during the May and October festivals. The **Honden** (Main Hall) and **Haiden** (Hall of Worship) can also be seen in the enclosure.

FUTARASAN-JINJA 二荒山神社

Shōdō Shōnin founded this shrine. It's dedicated to the mountain, Nantai, the mountain's consort, Nyotai, and their mountainous progeny, Tarō. It's essentially a repeat performance of Tōshō-gū on a smaller scale, but worth a visit nonetheless.

TAIYŪIN-BYŌ 大猷院廟

Taiyūin-byō enshrines Ieyasu's grandson Iemitsu (1604–51) and is very much a smaller version of Tōshō-gū. The smaller size gives it a less extravagant air, but it has been suggested that it is more aesthetically pleasing than its larger neighbour. Many of the features to be seen in the Tōshō-gū are replicated on a smaller scale: the storehouses, drum tower and Chinese gate, for example. The shrine also has a wonderful setting in a quiet grove of cryptomeria. Entry is included in the combination ticket (p161).

KOSUGI HŌAN MUSEUM OF ART 小杉放庵美術館

Back towards the river, not far from Nikkō's shrines and temples, is the **Kosugi Hōan Museum of Art** (☎ 50-1200; 2388-3 Sannai; admission ¥700; ⏰ 9.30am-5pm Tue-Sun). This modern museum holds a collection of landscape paintings by local artist Kosugi Hōan (1920–64). This is a good rainy-day option in Nikkō.

GAMMAN-GA-FUCHI ABYSS 含満ヶ淵

If the crowds of Nikkō leave you yearning for a little quiet, take the 20-minute walk to Gamman-Ga-Fuchi Abyss, a collection of *jizō* statues (the small stone statues of the Buddhist protector of travellers and children) set along a wooded path. One of the statues midway along is known as the Bake-jizō, who mocks travellers foolish enough to try to count all the *jizō* (they're said to be uncountable). To reach Gamman-Ga-Fuchi Abyss, take a left after crossing the Shin-kyō bridge and follow the river, crossing another bridge en route; it's about 800m from Shin-kyō.

NIKKŌ TAMOZAWA GOYŌTEI 日光田母沢御用邸

The **Nikkō Tamozawa Goyōtei** (☎ 53-6767; admission ¥500; ⏰ 9am-4.30pm Wed-Mon), the handsome villa and gardens where the Emperor spent WWII, has been painstakingly restored to its former glory and is well worth a visit. It's reachable by following Rte 120 about 1km west of the Shin-kyo bridge.

Festivals & Events

Tōshō-gū Autumn Festival (17 October) This one needs only the equestrian archery to be an autumnal repeat of the performance in May.

Tōshō-gū Grand Festival (17 and 18 May) This is Nikkō's most important annual festival. It features horseback archery (on the first day) and a 1000-strong costumed re-enactment of the delivery of Ieyasu's remains to Nikkō (on the second day).

Yayoi Matsuri (16 and 17 April) A festival procession of *mikoshi*, portable shrines, is held at Futarasan-jinja.

Sleeping

Nikkō's accommodation options are good value, and most places are used to foreign guests. Thus, it's a fine choice for a quick night out of Tokyo, and staying overnight makes sense if you want to combine a visit to Nikkō with the further sights of Chūzenjiko, and Yumoto Onsen (p164).

BUDGET

Nikkō Kōryū Sokushin Center (☎ 54-1013; www.city .nikko.tochigi.jp/nyh/; 2845 Tokorono; f with/without bath & toilet ¥5000/4100, breakfast/dinner ¥600/1200) This budget option has excellent facilities with Western and Japanese rooms with views. It's a 15-minute walk northwest of the stations, behind a school. Check-in is from 3pm.

Jōhsyū-ya Ryokan (☎ 54-0155; www.johsyu-ya.co .jp; 911 Nakahatsuishi; s/d/tr per person ¥4500/3500/2980) This fairly new budget inn, on the main road beside the post office, has simple but clean Japanese-style and Western rooms.

MIDRANGE

Turtle Inn Nikkō (☎ 53-3168; www.turtle-nikko.com; 2-16 Takumi-cho; s/d without bath ¥5100/9600, s/d with bath ¥5900/11,200, breakfast/dinner ¥1050/2100) This well-kept inn is one of the more popular pensions in Nikkō, with large rooms, English-speaking staff and delicious meals. From the Tōbu-Nikkō Station, take a bus to the Sōgō-kaikan-mae bus stop, backtrack 50m to the fork in the road and follow the river for five minutes. Check-in is from 3pm.

Annex Turtle Hotori-An (☎ 53-3663; www.turtle
-nikko.com; 8-28 Takumi-cho; s/d with bath ¥6800/13,000,
breakfast/dinner ¥1050/2100) Excellent tatami and
Western-style rooms lie just west of the
Turtle Inn, over the river but on the same
road. Greenery surrounds the bathhouse.
Check-in is from 2pm.

Nikkō Tōkan-sō Ryokan (☎ 54-0611; 2335 Yamachi;
r with 2 meals per person ¥7000-14,000, min 2 people) This
clean and spacious place provides a fine ryokan experience, though it's sometimes fully
booked by bus tours. North of the Kosugi-
Hōan Museum, it's reached by taking a right
after crossing the Shin-kyō bridge and the
next left after 120m. Check-in is from 3pm.

Hotel Seikōen (☎ 53-5555; www.hotel-seikoen
.com; 2350 Sannai; d per person ¥12,000-17,000) The
Seikōen has lovely rooms. Both Japanese-
and Western-style. The hotel is on the same
road as the Nikkō Tōkan-sō Ryokan, about
100m west. Check-in is from 2pm.

TOP END
Nikkō Kanaya Hotel (☎ 54-0001; www.kanayahotel
.co.jp/nkh/index-e.html; 1300 Kami-Hatsuishi-machi; d
¥10,000-40,000) Near the Shin-kyō bridge,
Nikkō's oldest and classiest hotel offers a
variety of rooms; the best have fine views,
spacious quarters and private bathrooms.
Check-in is from 3pm.

Nikkō Pension Green Age Inn (☎ 53-3636; 10-9
Nishi Sando; r per person with/without breakfast & dinner
¥9800/5800) A charming atmosphere prevails at
this large, Tudoresque inn near the temples.
Check-in is from 3pm.

Eating

Nikkō's overnight visitors often eat where
they're staying, but there are a number of
places on the main road between the stations and the shrine area; most close by 8 or
9pm. A local favourite is *yuba* – thin strips
of tofu that are a staple of *shōjin-ryōri* (Buddhist vegetarian cuisine); it's sometimes
served in soba.

Hippari Dako (☎ 53-2933; lunch ¥800; 🕑 11am-
7pm) A Nikkō institution among foreign
travellers, Hippari Dako has filling sets of
yakitori (chicken on skewers) and *yaki-
udon* (fried noodles). Hippari Dako is
on Rte 119, before crossing the Shin-kyō
bridge. English menu.

Enya (☎ 53-4862; dinner from ¥2000; 🕑 11.30am-
10pm) A few blocks west of the stations on
the main road, Enya serves *shabu-shabu*

and grilled meats, which pair nicely with
imported microbrews.

Kikō (☎ 53-3320; mains ¥700-1300; 🕑 11am-3pm
& 5pm-midnight) This welcoming homestyle
restaurant serves Korean dishes, like grilled
pork and *kimchi rāmen*. It's a few doors
down from Hippari Dako, with a sign advertising Korean cooking. On Rte 119, easily
spotted by its large sign. English menu.

Skylark Gusto (☎ 50-1232; mains ¥500-1000;
🕑 10am-2am Mon-Fri, 7am-2am Sat) Nikkō's only
late-night restaurant serves Western and
Japanese dishes at low prices. Pizzas, pasta
and *tonkatsu* (pork cutlet) are among the
offerings. English menu.

Meiji no Yakata (☎ 54-2149; pie slices ¥315-420;
🕑 10am-6pm) This charming bakery next to
Tōbu Nikkō Station has cheesecake, tarts,
cookies and the like.

Suzuya (☎ 54-0293; set lunch ¥1400; 🕑 11am-3pm)
East of the temple complex and just before
crossing the Inari-gawa bridge, you'll find
tasty bowls of soba, including lunch sets
of *yuba-ryōri*.

Gyoshintei (☎ 53-3751; dinner per person around
¥4000; 🕑 noon-8pm) Overlooking an elegant
garden, this traditional Japanese restaurant
serves exquisite Buddhist vegetarian dishes.
For a taste of authentic *shojin-ryōri*, Gyoshintei is worth the splurge. It's located
about 250m north of the Shin-kyō bridge.

Sawamoto (☎ 54-0163; meals around ¥2000;
🕑 11am-2pm & 5-7pm) A good *unagi* (eel) specialist, Sawamoto serves tasty sets. It closes
several times a month according to the
owner's whim. It is on Rte 119, about 50m
before the Shin-kyō bridge.

There are also enclosed stalls just off
Omotesandō selling *soba* noodles and the
like for around ¥800.

Getting There & Away

The best way to visit Nikkō from Tokyo is via
the Tōbu-Nikkō line from Asakusa Station.
The station is in the basement of the Tōbu
department store (it's well signposted from
the subway). All seats are reserved on *tokkyū*
(limited express) trains (¥2740, one hour 50
minutes) but you can usually get tickets just
before setting out. Trains run every 30 minutes or so from 7.30am to 10am; and hourly
after 10am. *Kaisoku* (rapid) trains (¥1320,
two hours, hourly from 6.20am to 4.30pm)
require no reservation. For either train, you
may have to change at Imaichi. Be sure to

ride in the first two cars to reach Nikkō (only the first two cars go all the way to Nikkō).

Travelling by JR is costly and time consuming – it's really only of interest to those with a Japan Rail Pass. The quickest way is to take the *shinkansen* (bullet train) from Tokyo to Utsunomiya (¥4800, 50 minutes) and change there for an ordinary train to Nikkō (¥740, 45 minutes).

NIKKŌ-KINUGAWA FREE PASS
This pass may save you money on a multi-day trip around Nikkō. It's valid for two days, costs ¥5000 and is available from Tōbu railways in Asakusa. It includes transport from Asakusa to Nikkō (but not the express surcharge) and all bus costs between Nikkō and Chūzenji, Yumoto Onsen, Kinugawa, the plateau of Kirifuri-kōgen, and Ikari-ko as well as cable-car fares around Chūzenji-ko (for more information on Chūzenji and Yumoto, see right).

TŌBU NIKKŌ BUS FREE PASS
If you're heading to Yumoto (right) or Chuzenji Onsen (right), you should consider this two-day bus pass. It allows unlimited hopping on and off buses between Nikkō and Yumoto (¥3000) or Nikkō and Chuzenji Onsen (¥2000). Buy it at Tōbu Nikkō Station.

AROUND NIKKŌ 日光周辺
☎ 0288
Nikkō is part of the Nikkō National Park, which covers 1402 sq km, sprawling over Fukushima, Tochigi, Gunma and Niigata prefectures. It is a mountainous area, complete with extinct volcanoes, lakes, waterfalls and marshlands. There are good hiking opportunities and some remote hot-spring resorts.

Yashio-no-yu Onsen やしおの湯温泉
A 5km bus ride from Nikkō, this modern *onsen* (admission ¥500; ⏰ 10am-5pm Fri-Wed) is a good place to relax after a day of exploring shrines and temples. It has several different baths, including a *rotemburo* (outdoor spa bath). Take a Chūzenji-bound bus from either train station in Nikkō and get off at the Kiyomizu Itchōme stop. The *onsen* is across the river from the bus stop; walk back toward Nikkō, under the Rte 120 bypass and across the bridge.

Chūzenji-ko 中禅寺湖
Ten kilometres west of Nikkō, this lake is chiefly a scenic attraction, and it's probably not worth cutting short your visit to Nikkō to see it. If you've time, however, then the lake and the 97m-high falls, **Kegonno-taki** (華厳滝) are definitely worth visiting. The waterfall features an elevator (¥530 return) down to a platform where you can observe the full force of the plunging water. Also worth a visit is a third **Futarasan-jinja**, complementing the *jinja* (shrine) in the Tōshō-gū area and on the mountain, Nantai-san (2484m). The shrine is about 1km west of the falls, along a path skirting the north shore of Chūzenji-ko.

For good views of the lake and Kegon-no-taki, get off the bus at the Akechi-daira bus stop (the stop before Chūzenji Onsen) and take the Akechi-daira (Akechi Plateau) cable car (one way/return ¥390/710) up to a viewing platform. From here, it's a pleasant 1.5km walk across the Chanoki-no-daira to a vantage point with great views over the lake, the falls and Nantai-san. From here you can walk down to the lake and Chūzenji Onsen.

Chūzenji-ko has the usual flotilla of cruise boats waiting by the dock. The lake, which reaches a depth of 161m, is a fabulous shade of deep blue in good weather, and this, along with the mountainous backdrop, makes for a pleasant cruise. You can also hire a rowboat for ¥1000 per hour.

See the following section for information on the **Senjōgahara Shizen-kenkyu-rō** (Senjōgahara Plain Nature Trail) from Chūzenji-ko to Yumoto.

SLEEPING
Chūzenji Pension (中禅寺ペンション; ☎ 55-0888; r per person from ¥11,000) Nikkō has the best-value accommodation, but if you prefer a bit of seclusion, you might enjoy this pleasant inn; rates include two meals. To reach the pension from the Nikkō-Chūzenji road (Rte 120), turn left at the lakeside and cross the bridge. The pension is on the left, about 100m down the road. Check-in 3pm.

GETTING THERE & AWAY
There are buses from the Nikkō Station area to Chūzenji Onsen (¥1160, 50 minutes).

Yumoto Onsen 湯元温泉
From Chūzenji-ko, you might continue on to the quieter hot-springs resort of **Yumoto**

A DAY IN THE BATH

Even the most committed urbanite needs a break from Tokyo at some point, and the perfect antidote to the stress of the metropolis is a day spent at a rural hot spring. These vary from the deluxe to the primitive, but none need break the bank; indeed, many public baths offer free entry. Holders of the Japan Rail Pass can use JR lines to hop as far afield as Niigata, Tochigi or Fukushima prefectures, utilising the *shinkansen* (bullet train) to get swiftly out of the city.

However, the star in the Kanto area hot-spring firmament is Gunma Prefecture, with water bubbling out of the ground at every turn. It is easily accessible from Ueno Station via Takasaki (*shinkansen* ¥4600, 45 minutes; *tokkyū* ¥3190, 1¼ hours; *futsū* ¥1890, 110 minutes) and Jomo-Kogen Stations (*shinkansen* ¥5550, 70 minutes) on the Jōetsu *shinkansen* line, or via Maebashi (*tokkyū* ¥3190, 100 minutes; *futsū* ¥1890, two hours) and Shibukawa (*tokkyū* ¥3570, 100 minutes; *futsū* ¥2210, 2¼ hours) on the Takasaki and Ryomo or Agatsuma lines, respectively.

The following Gunma springs are highly recommended:

Ikaho Onsen Great public bath with views over Mt Haruna. Take the Jōetsu line from Takasaki to Shibukawa Station (*tokkyū/futsū* ¥1410/400, 20/30 minutes), then local bus to the *onsen* (¥550, 20 minutes).

Kusatsu Onsen Quintessential old-time *onsen* town. Take the Agatsuma line from Takasaki to Naganohara Kusatsuguchi Station (*tokkyū/futsū* ¥2520/1110, 60/100 minutes), then local bus to the *onsen* (¥670, 30 minutes).

Minakami Onsen A thriving *onsen* town where you can white-water raft in summer. Take the Jōetsu line from Takasaki to Minakami Station (*tokkyū/futsū* ¥2360/950, 60/90 minutes), then it's a 15-minute walk.

Shiriyaki Onsen Very odd and primitive – literally, the 'arse-burning' hot spring, favourite of haemorrhoid sufferers of the Heike clan – where you simply strip and climb in the river. Bring a packed lunch as there's nothing else here, and start out early. Take the Agatsuma line from Takasaki to Naganohara-Kusatsu Station (*tokkyū/futsū* ¥2520/1110, 60/100 minutes), then local bus to Hanashiki Onsen (¥800, 30 minutes); from there it's a 10-minute walk.

Takaragawa Onsen Complete with river bathing, oft-voted the nation's best. Take the Jōetsu line from Takasaki to Minakami Station (*tokkyū/futsū* ¥2360/950, 60/90 minutes), then local bus to the *onsen* (¥1100, 40 minutes).

The beautiful **Chōjūkan inn** (☎ 0273-85-6634) at Hoshi Onsen allows bathing only. Although it's a train ride, bus ride and a hike, getting there is part of the fun. Try to arrive around noon to sample the inn's mountain-vegetable steamed rice. Women can sneak into the (far superior) men's bath here. In fact, it's almost expected.

Onsen by bus (¥840, 30 minutes). Alternatively, you can hike there in around three hours from the falls, Ryūzu-daki, on the central northern part of Chūzenji-ko (or do this in reverse).

The hike, known as **Senjōgahara Shizen-kenkyu-rō**, takes around three hours. From Chūzenji Onsen, take a Yumoto-bound bus and get off at **Ryūzu-daki** (¥410, 20 minutes), the start of the hike. The hike follows the Yu-gawa across the picturesque marshland of **Senjōgahara** to Yuno-ko (look out for the 75m-high falls, **Yu-daki**, in this area). from where it wends around the western edge of the lake to Yumoto Onsen. From Yumoto, you can catch a bus back to Nikkō (¥1650, 1½ hours).

Before heading back to Nikkō, you might stop off at **Onsen-ji**, a small temple with its own **onsen** (admission ¥500; 🕙 10am-3pm), a good spot to rest hiking-weary muscles.

OZE-GA-HARA & LAKE OZE-NUMA
尾瀬ヶ原・尾瀬沼

Oze-ga-hara, the 1400m-high marshlands around Lake Oze-numa, are the largest of their kind in Japan, covering an area of around 8 sq km. The area is noted for its birdlife and wildflowers, in particular the unfortunately monickered *mizubashō* (skunk cabbage). Even when the wildflowers aren't in bloom, the hiking is lovely, as much of it passes over wooden planks laid across the marshes.

Because Oze is one of the premier hiking destinations around Tokyo, it can be packed on summer weekends. During the summer months we strongly suggest that you go on a weekday. You can also escape the crowds by ascending the mountain, **Hiuchi-ga-take**, which offers a great view over the marshes.

During the hiking season (28 May to 10 October) direct overnight buses run from

Tokyo and Shinjuku Stations to three of the area's trailheads. There is a slight discount for return travel but basic one-way rates with **Oze Chokutsu Bus** (☎ 03862-0819) are: ¥4500 to Ōshimizu, ¥5300 to Hatomachi-tōge, and ¥6500 to Numayama-tōge. Make sure you book both ways if you want to use this service.

Otherwise, the best bet for getting into the Oze region is to start from Numata in Gunma-ken. From Ueno Station, take a Jōetsu-line *kaisoku* (rapid) train to Takasaki (1½ hours) and then take a *futsū* (local train) to Numata (45 minutes). The whole journey costs ¥2520. From Numata Station there are regular buses to the Ōshimizu trailhead (¥2200, two hours).

CHICHIBU-TAMA NATIONAL PARK
秩父多摩国立公園

While the hikes in Chichibu-Tama National Park cannot compete with those further afield, they do make a pleasant escape from the concrete jungles of Tokyo. The park is divided into the Chichibu and Oku-Tama regions. These two regions are connected by a two-day hiking trail that runs over the top of Kumotori-san (2017m), the highest point in the Tokyo metropolitan area. For those with less time, a trip to the mountaintop shrine complex of Mitake-jinja in the Oku-Tama region, perhaps paired with a hike to the summit of nearby Ōtake-san (1266m), makes a great day trip.

Chichibu Region 秩父周辺
☎ 0494

Before heading to other destinations, have a look around the small town of Chichibu. Several interesting old Japanese and Western buildings stand on the road leading to **Chichibu-jinja** from Ohanabatake Station. The shrine itself is pleasant, although most of the buildings are modern reconstructions.

Southwest of the town, near the top of Mitsumine-san (1329m), **Mitsumine-jinja** is the starting point for the two-day walk that connects Chichibu with Oku-Tama. The shrine was founded some 2000 years ago and has long been favoured as a mountain retreat by the Tendai Buddhist sect. Set in a grove of towering cryptomeria trees, the shrine is worth a visit even if you don't intend to do the hike. Although it's possible to walk up to the shrine in two hours, most people take

the Mitsumine-san cable car (one way/return ¥950/1650). The shrine festival on 2 and 3 December is a huge spectacle that attracts 170,000 visitors each year.

To get to the cable car, take the Chichibu Tetsudō line from Ohanabatake Station to Mitsumine-guchi Station (¥460, 20 minutes, every 30 minutes) then switch to a Chichibu-ko-bound bus and get off at Ōwa (¥300, 15 minutes, every 30 minutes). The cable-car station is a 15-minute walk uphill across the river from the bus stop.

Nagatoro 長瀞

From mid-March to mid-November boats leave from Oyahana-bashi, 700m from Kami-Nagatoro Station, to shoot the **Arakawa River rapids**. The trip costs ¥1550 and lasts 50 minutes. You can also take the **Hodō-san cable car** (one way/return ¥420/720) to the top of Hodō-san (497m), although it isn't as good as the trip up Mitsumine-san. The cable car is a 15-minute walk from Nagatoro Station.

SLEEPING & EATING

New Chichibu (☎ 24-4444; s/tw ¥4800/7500) This business hotel, a five-minute walk south of Chichibu Station, is the best option in Chichibu itself, with simple, decent rooms. Free breakfast included. Check-in is from 3pm.

Soba Fuku (そばふく; ☎ 23-2572; lunch/dinner ¥1200; 🕙 11.30am-2.30pm & 4.30-7pm Tue-Sun) Chichibu's speciality is *teuchi soba* (traditional handmade buckwheat noodles). Soba Fuku, across the street from Seibu Chichibu Station, has excellent soba; tempura *soba* is a favourite.

GETTING THERE & AWAY

The cheapest and quickest way of getting to the Chichibu area from Tokyo is via the Seibu Ikebukuro line (which becomes the Seibu Chichibu line) from Seibu Ikebukuro Station (*futsū* ¥750, 1¾ hours with changes en route; *tokkyū* Chichibu 17 ¥1370, 1½ hours direct). Alternatively, JR trains run from Ueno Station to Kumagaya Station on the Takasaki line (¥1110, 70 minutes) where you will have to change to the Chichibu Tetsudō line to continue to Chichibu Station (¥840, 45 minutes). All things considered, unless you're travelling on a Japan Rail Pass, it's cheaper to set off from Ikebukuro even if you're based in Ueno.

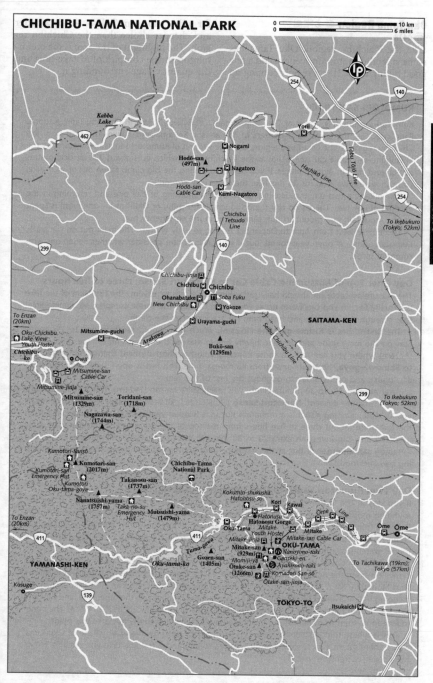

CHICHIBU-TAMA NATIONAL PARK

Oku-Tama Region 奥多摩周辺
☎ 0428

Like the Chichibu region, Oku-Tama has some splendid mountain scenery and a few good hiking trails. If you're only coming up for a day trip from Tokyo, this is a better and cheaper choice than the Chichibu region. The highlight of the area is the mountaintop shrine complex of Mitake-jinja and the quaint village surrounding it.

KUMOTORI-SAN TRACK

Kumotori-san (literally, 'Taker of Clouds Mountain'; 雲取山; 2017m), in Chichibu-Tama National Park, straddles the prefectural borders of Yamanashi, Saitama and Tokyo. The hike from the Chichibu region to the Oku-Tama region, over the summit of Kumotori-san, is made easier by the Mitsumine-san cable car (see p166) at the Chichibu end, which cuts about 730 vertical metres out of your hike in eight minutes. If you object to having the big climb taken out of your hike, you can always walk up (or do this hike the other way around!).

This hike is a two-day trip, leaving Tokyo on the morning of day one and returning in the evening of day two. There's no real reason to stay in Chichibu or Oku-Tama – one night is spent on the mountain in a mountain hut, camping or in the emergency hut.

This hike is best from April to December (spring to early winter). The main hut on the track, Kumotori Sansō, is open year round, but if you go in winter consider weather conditions with common sense.

Day One: Top of Mitsumine Cable Car to Kumotori Sansō; three to five hours

The Mitsumine cable car should have just whipped you up to 1090m. The first 2km of the hike is virtually flat, so you can warm up as you amble through the shrine complex, Mitsumine-jinja. Pass through the complex and head onto the track to start the climb.

The first target is **Kirimo-ga-mine** (1523m), which you should reach in one to 1½ hours. Stay on the main ridge and descend briefly before making the long climb to Mae-shiraiwa-san (1776m) where you can rest on some benches. Another short descent then climb brings you to **Shiraiwa-goya**, 1½ hours or so from Kirimo-ga-mine. This hut is open daily from 20 July to 31 August, and on Saturday throughout the rest of the year.

After another 20- to 30-minute climb, you reach Shiraiwa-san (1921m). This is followed by a 30- to 45-minute descent. **Kumotori-Sansō** (雲取山荘; ☎ 0494-23-3338; with/without meals ¥6000/3500, camping ¥300) is a mountain hut that is open year round. It's a short climb from the low point (about three to five hours from the top of the cable car). If you are adequately prepared and can invest an extra 20 to 30 minutes in climbing, you can stay for free in the Kumotori-san **emergency hut** at the summit. There are no facilities there: you'll need a sleeping bag and food.

Day Two: Kumotori Sansō to Oku-Tama; five to seven hours

If you stay at the hut or camp, you'll start day two by climbing to the peak. Views of the surrounding mountains from the bald, rocky top are stunning. This is the highest point in Tokyo! Descend from the peak to the south, go right at all trail junctions, and after 45 minutes you'll come to **Kumotori Oku-tama-goya**, a hut open year round. Camping here is permitted, and there's water available.

The track continues along the ridge to Nanatsuishi-yama (Seven Stone Mountain; 1757m) then carries on along the right side of the main ridge to the **emergency hut** on Takanosu-san (Hawk's Nest Mountain; 鷹ノ巣山; 1737m). At the intersection thereafter, you can either climb the peak by going left, or avoid it by going right. The tracks meet up again on the other side, and descend to a spot just to the north of Mutsuishi-yama (Six Stone Mountain; 六ツ石山; 1479m). The none-too-steep descent from Kumotori-san should have taken three to 4½ hours to this point.

This is where things steepen. It's a 1½- to two-hour drop to the small village of Oku-Tama, where there's a visitors centre, countless places to eat, and a train to take you back to Tokyo. See above for transport details.

MITAKE-SAN 御岳山

Buses run from Mitake Station to the Mitake-san cable-car terminus (¥270, 10 minutes) where a cable car takes you near the summit (one way/return ¥570/1090, ¥50 less each way with an Okutama Furii Kippu – Okutama Free Pass). About 20 minutes on foot from the top of the cable car is **Mitake-jinja**, said to date back some 1200 years. The area around the shrine has great views of the surrounding mountains and the Kantō Plain.

If you plan to hike around Mitake-san (926m) pick up the excellent *Okutama Nature Map* from the **Mitake Visitors Center** (☎ 78-8836; ⏰ 8am-4.30pm Tue-Sun), which is 250m beyond the top of the cable car, near the start of the village.

ŌTAKE-SAN HIKE 大岳山

If you've got the time, the five-hour round-trip hike from Mitake-jinja to the summit of Ōtake-san (大岳山; 1266m) is highly recommended. Although there's some climbing involved, it's a fairly easy hike and the views from the summit are excellent – Mt Fuji is visible to the south on clear days. On the way, take the detour down to **Nanoyono-taki** (waterfalls set amid lush forest), **Ganseki-en rock garden** (a beautiful path that crosses back and forth across a gurgling stream) and **Ayahirono-taki** (another waterfall). All that greenery and silence may come as a shock after a few days cooped up in Tokyo.

SLEEPING & EATING

Mitake Youth Hostel (御嶽ユースホステル; ☎ 78-8501; www.jyh.or.jp; dm ¥2750) Up on Mitake-san, this comfortable hostel has fine tatami rooms inside a handsome old building. It's midway between the top of the cable car and Mitake-jinja. Check-in is from 3pm.

Komadori San-sō (駒鳥山荘; ☎ 78-8472; r per person ¥5100-5700) Further on, just below the shrine, this *minshuku* (Japanese-style B&B) is a friendly place at ease with foreigners. Meals cost extra. Check-in is from 3pm.

Momiji-ya (紅葉屋; ☎ 78-8475; mains ¥800-1100; ⏰ noon-5pm) On Mitake-san, this quaint *soba* shop serves tasty *soba* dishes with nice views. Among the favourites is *kamonanban* (duck) *soba*. It's on the main street to the shrine.

GETTING THERE & AWAY

To reach Oku-Tama take the JR Chūō line from Shinjuku Station to Tachikawa Station (¥450, 26 minutes) and change to the JR Ōme line to Oku-Tama Station (¥620, 1¼ hours); if heading to Mitake-san disembark at Mitake (¥440, 45 minutes). Unless you've got a Japan Rail Pass, if you visit on weekends or a national holiday, we highly recommend the Oku-tama Free Pass (¥2040), available at JR ticket windows, which covers return travel between Oku-tama and Tokyo and unlimited use of JR trains in the Oku-tama region.

MITO 水戸

☎ 0292 / pop 234,000

This former castle town is notable for its garden, **Kairaku-en** (admission garden/pavilion free/¥180), one of Japan's three most celebrated landscape gardens (the other two are Kenroku-en in Kanazawa and Kōraku-en in Okayama). The 18-acre gardens date back to 1842 and are popular for their *ume* (plum blossoms), which bloom in late February or early March.

There's an entry charge for the pavilion **Kobun-tei**, a tasteful reproduction of a Mito clan-lord's villa. To reach the garden take a bus from Mito Station to Kairakuen-mae bus stop (20 minutes). From Ueno Station take the JR Jōban line to Mito (*tokkyū*, 1¼ hours). Ordinary services from Ueno take just under two hours and stop at Kairaku-en Station (one stop before Mito).

WEST OF TOKYO

Many of the destinations popular with Tokyo residents lie to the west of the city, including the scenic Fuji Go-ko region, Mt Fuji itself, the tourist mecca of Hakone, and the *onsen* and beach resorts of the Izu-hantō.

MT FUJI AREA 富士山周辺

☎ 0555

Mt Fuji, Japan's most familiar symbol, dominates the region southwest of Tokyo. Although Hakone is probably the most famous spot for Fuji-viewing, those with an aversion to crowds will prefer the scenic Fuji Go-ko region.

Mt Fuji 富士山

Japan's highest mountain stands 3776m high. When it's capped with snow in late autumn, winter and spring, it's a picture-postcard perfect volcanic cone. Fuji-san, as it's known in

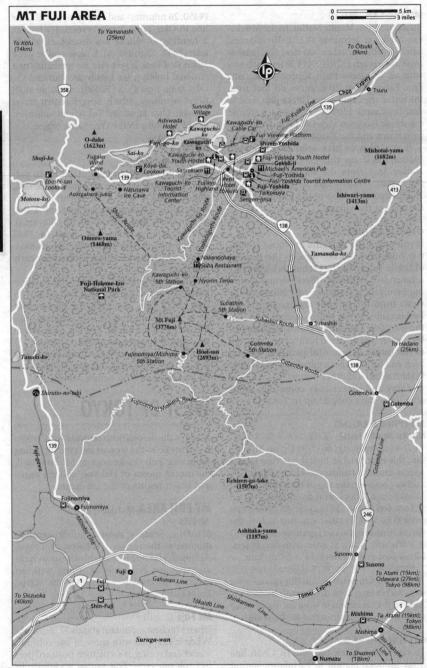

MT FUJI AREA

0 ___ 5 km
0 ___ 3 miles

To Kōfu (14km)

To Yamanashi (25km)

To Ōtsuki (9km)

358

Chūō Expwy

Tsuru

Fuji Kyūkō Line

139

Sunnide Village

Ashiwada Hotel

Kawaguchi-ko Cable Car

Kawaguchi-ko

Fuji Viewing Platform

O-dake (1623m)

Fuji-go-ko

Kawaguchi-ko

Shimo-Yoshida

Mishotai-yama (1682m)

Shoji-ko

Sai-ko

Fugaku Wind Cave

Kōyō-dai Lookout

Kawaguchi-ko Youth Hostel

Fuji-Yoshida Youth Hostel

Gekkō-ji

Michael's American Pub

Fuji-Yoshida

Eboshi-san Lookout

139

Sanrokuen

Fuji-Yoshida Tourist Information Centre

Fuji-Yoshida

Motosu-ko

Narusawa Ice Cave

Kawaguchi-ko Tourist Information Center

Fujikyu Highland

Petit Hotel Ebisuya

Taikokuya

Sengen-jinja

413

Ishiwari-yama (1413m)

Aokigahara-jukai

138

Omuro-yama (1468m)

Yamanaka-ko

Fuji-Hakone-Izu National Park

Nakanochaya

Soba Restaurant

Kawaguchi-ko 5th Station

Nyonin Tenjo

Subashiri 5th Station

Subashiri Route

Subashiri

To Hadano (25km)

Tanuki-ko

Mt Fuji (3776m)

Hōei-san (2693m)

Gotemba 5th Station

Gotemba Route

138

Shiraito-no-taki

Fujinomiya/Mishima 5th Station

Fujinomiya/Mishima Route

Gotemba Line

Gotemba

Gotemba

139

Fuji-gawa

Echizen-ga-take (1507m)

246

Fujinomiya

Minobu Line

Fujinomiya

Ashitaka-yama (1187m)

Susono

Susono

To Atami (15km); Odawara (27km); Tokyo (98km)

To Shizuoka (40km)

1

Fuji

Fuji

Gakunan Line

Shinkansen Line

Tōmei Expwy

Shin-Fuji

Tōkaidō Line

Mishima

To Atami (15km); Tokyo (98km)

1

Mishima

Izu-Hakone Line

Suruga-wan

Numazu

To Shuzenji (18km)

Japanese, last blew its top in 1707, covering the streets of Tokyo with volcanic ash. On an exceptionally clear day you can see Mt Fuji from Tokyo, 100km away, but for much of the year you'd be hard pressed to see it from 100m away. Your best chance of spying the notoriously shy mountain is in late autumn, winter and early spring when the air is fairly clear. Even during these times, the mountain may be visible only in the morning before it retreats behind a curtain of clouds.

INFORMATION

Climbing Mt Fuji, Mt Fuji Climber's Guide-book and *Mt Fuji & Fuji Five Lakes* brochures are available from the Tokyo **Tourist Information Center** (TIC; ☎ 3201-3331) and provide exhaustive detail on transport to the mountain and how to climb it, complete with climbing schedules worked out to the minute.

The best tourist information centres at the base of the mountain are the **Fuji-Yoshida Information Center** (☎ 22-7000; ⏰ 9am-5.30pm), to the left as you exit the Fuji-Yoshida train station, and the **Kawaguchi-ko Tourist Information Center** (☎ 72-6700; ⏰ 8.30am-5pm Sun-Fri, 8.30am-6.30pm Sat & holidays), to the left of the Kawaguchi-ko train station. Both have friendly, English-speaking staff and plenty of maps and brochures of the area. During the climbing season (1 July to 31 August), there is also climbing information provided by staff in **English** (☎ 24-1236; 9.30am-5.30pm Mon-Fri).

MT FUJI VIEWS

You can get a classic view of Mt Fuji from the *shinkansen* as it passes the city of Fuji (sit on the northern side of the train). There are also good views from the Hakone area, Nagao-tōge Pass on the road from Hakone to Gotemba, and the northwest coast of the Izu-hantō. But the best and closest views are from the Fuji Go-ko region where, on a clear day, the looming mountain seems to fill the sky.

CLIMBING MT FUJI

Officially, the climbing season on Mt Fuji is from 1 July to 31 August, and the Japanese, who love to do things 'right', pack in during those busy months. You can actually climb Mt Fuji at any time of year, and it may be preferable to do so just outside the official season to avoid the crowds, but keep in mind that transport services may be less frequent and some of the huts may be closed. Of course, any time there's snow on the mountain you'll need the proper equipment and experience to climb Mt Fuji, and a midwinter ascent is strictly for expert mountaineers.

Be warned that no free water is available on the mountain. Either bring your own or shell out ¥500 for a half-litre bottle.

Although children and grandparents regularly reach the summit, this is a serious mountain and not to be trifled with. It's high enough for altitude sickness and, as on any mountain, the weather can be volatile. On the summit it can go from sunny and warm to wet, windy and cold in remarkably little time. Even if conditions are fine, you can count on it being close to freezing in the mornings in high season, and much colder in low season. Whatever you do, don't climb Mt Fuji without clothing appropriate for cold and wet weather.

The mountain is divided into 10 'stations' from base to summit, but these days most climbers start from one of the four '5th Stations', which you can reach by road. From the end of the road, it takes about 4½ hours to reach the top and about three hours to descend. On the peak, it takes about an hour to make a circuit of the crater. The Mt Fuji Weather Station, on the southwestern edge of the crater, is on the actual summit of the mountain.

Ideally, dawn is the best time to reach the summit – both to see *goraiko* (sunrise) and because early morning is the time when the mountain is least likely to be shrouded in cloud. Sometimes it takes an hour or two to burn the morning mist off, however. To time your arrival for dawn you can either start up in the afternoon, stay overnight in a mountain hut and continue early in the morning, or climb the whole way at night. You do not want to arrive on the top too long before dawn, as it's likely to be very cold and windy.

Although nearly all climbers start from the 5th Stations, it is possible to climb all the way up from a lower level. The low-level trails are now used mainly as short hiking routes around the base of the mountain, but those who have time should consider the challenging but rewarding hike from base to summit on either the Yoshidaguchi Route (see p172) from Fuji-Yoshida or on the Shoji Route from near Shoji-ko. There are alternative sand trails on the Kawaguchi-ko, Subashiri and Gotemba Routes, which you can descend rapidly by running and sliding, pausing from time to time to get the sand out of your shoes.

5th Stations

There are four 5th Stations around Mt Fuji and it's quite feasible to climb from one and descend to another. On the northern side of Fuji is the Kawaguchi-ko 5th Station

(2305m), which you can reach from the town of Kawaguchi-ko. This station is particularly popular with climbers starting from Tokyo. The Yoshidaguchi Route (which starts much lower down) is the same as the Kawaguchi-ko Route for much of the way.

The route from the **Subashiri 5th Station** (1980m) meets the Yoshidaguchi Route just after the 8th Station. The **Gotemba 5th Station** is reached from the town of Gotemba and, at 1440m, is much lower than the other 5th Stations. From Gotemba station it takes seven to

---

THE YOSHIDAGUCHI TRAIL UP MT FUJI

Before the construction of the road to the 5th Station, Fuji climbers began at the Sengen-jinja near present-day Fuji-Yoshida. Here, pilgrims walked through towering cryptomeria trees past old stone lanterns, paid their homage to the gods at the shrine, and then began their 19km ascent up Japan's most sacred mountain.

Today, this path offers climbers a chance to participate in this centuries-old tradition and experience the volcano in all its beauty. Purists feel this is the best way to climb, and in truth, scaling just the summit of Mt Fuji is a little like beginning a marathon at mile 15. If you start from the 5th Station you'll miss the most beautiful part of the climb, which passes through lush forests along a path that you'll have almost entirely to yourself. You'll also have a much fuller experience of Fuji-san: you'll see the sunset, the sunrise, sleep in a mountain hut, miss the crowds and perhaps get a sense of that elusive spirit so deeply sought by pilgrims in the past.

One of three routes up Mt Fuji, the Yoshidaguchi trail is the oldest path up the mountain. To reach the trail from the shrine, veer to the right before the main building, and turn left onto the main road. This is paved, and you'll soon see a walking path alongside the road. When this roadside trail ends, take the first turn to the right to meet up with the woodland path.

After about 1¼ hours of walking you'll reach **Nakanochaya**, an ancient site marked by carved stones left by previous climbers. You'll also find a quaint **tea and soba restaurant** here (the last place to refuel before the 5th Station). From here you enter Fuji's lush forests.

Around 90 minutes later you'll reach Umagaeshi, which once housed the old stables where horses were left before entering the sacred area of the mountain. As you approach, you'll see a big yellow sign to your left, marking the path. Follow this through the *torii* with monkeys on either side, as it continues uphill. Another 20 minutes and you'll pass the 1st Station.

Between the 2nd and the 3rd Stations, just a bit of navigation is required. The Fuji path meets up with the **Nyonin Tenjo** (Women's Holy Ground), which until 1832 was as far up as women were allowed to go. All that remains is an altar, hidden in the forest. Just before entering you'll cross through a set of posts. Take a right, walk for 150m and look for the posts on the left, which mark the continuation of the path. Around an hour later, the path meets up with the 5th Station road. You'll find the Fuji path 150m on, cutting up to the right. You can stay at one of the 5th Stations in the vicinity or if you still have energy, continue up another two hours to one of the 7th Station huts.

It takes about five hours to reach the 5th Station from the Sengen-jinja. The next day, you'll have a much harder 4 ½-hour ascent up the scarred, barren mountain. Many rise at midnight and climb in darkness, but you can let the crowds go, get up at 4.30am and complete the ascent as the sun peeks through the clouds. On the descent, you can catch a bus at the Kawaguchi-ko 5th Station, which will take you to Kawaguchi-ko station.

Pick up maps and get the latest climbing information from the Fuji-Yoshida Information Center (p171). The *Climbing Mt Fuji* brochure is invaluable.

For more information and details on climbing Mt Fuji you should visit the excellent website at www.city.fujiyoshida.yamanashi.jp.

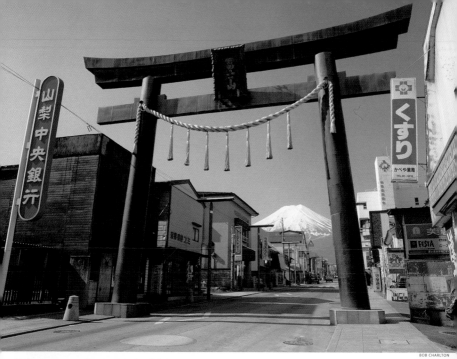

Torii entrance to Sengen-jinja (p173), Mt Fuji area

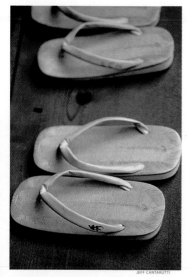

Monks' sandals, Nikkō (p161)

Detail of carving of three wise monkeys,
Tōshō-gū (p161), Nikkō

JAMES MARSHALL

Chinatown (p190), Yokohama

Girls dressed in kimono, Kamakura (p196)

JEFF CANTARUTTI

Hase-dera (p195), Kamakura

DAVIE

eight hours to reach the top of Mt Fuji, as opposed to 4½ to five hours on the other routes. The **Fujinomiya (Mishima) 5th Station** (2380m) is convenient for climbers coming from Nagoya, Kyoto, Osaka and western Japan. It meets the Gotemba Rte right at the top.

Equipment
Make sure you have plenty of clothing suitable for cold and wet weather, including a hat and gloves. Bring drinking water and snack food. If you're climbing at night, bring a torch (flashlight) or headlamp, and spare batteries.

Mountain Huts
From the 5th to the 8th Station are about a dozen lodges scattered along the trails. Accommodation here is pretty basic: most charge around ¥5000 for a mattress or a sleeping bag on the floor squeezed between other climbers. The huts also prepare simple meals for guests and passing climbers, and you're welcome to rest inside as long as you order something. If you don't feel like eating, a one-hour rest costs ¥500. Camping on the mountain is not permitted.

GETTING THERE & AWAY
See the following Fuji Go-ko section for details on transport to Kawaguchi-ko, the most popular arrival point for Tokyo Fuji-climbers. Travellers intending to head west from the Fuji area towards Nagoya, Osaka and Kyoto can take a bus from Kawaguchi-ko or Gotemba to Mishima Station on the *shinkansen* line.

From Kawaguchi-ko, there are bus services up to Kawaguchi-ko 5th Station (¥1700, 55 minutes) from April to mid-November. The schedule varies considerably during that period – call **Fuji Kyūkō bus** (☎ 72-2911) for details. At the height of the climbing season, there are buses until quite late in the evening – ideal for climbers intending to make an overnight ascent.

Taxis operate from the train station to the Kawaguchi-ko 5th Station for around ¥8000, plus tolls, which is not much more than the bus fare when divided among four people.

There are also daily direct buses (¥2600, 2½ hours) from the Shinjuku bus terminal to the Kawaguchi-ko 5th Station. For details call ☎ 03-5376-2222. This is by far the fastest and cheapest way of getting from Tokyo

to the 5th Station. If you take two trains and a bus, the same trip can cost nearly ¥6000.

From Subashiri, buses to the Subashiri 5th Station cost ¥1220 and take 55 minutes. From Gotemba station they cost ¥1500.

From Gotemba, buses to the Gotemba 5th Station (¥1080, 45 minutes) operate four to six times daily, but only during the climbing season.

The southern route up the mountain is most popular with climbers from western Japan approaching the mountain by *shinkansen*. Bus services run from Shin-Fuji (¥2400) and Mishima (¥2390) train stations to Fujinomiya (Mishima) 5th Station in just over two hours. There are **reservation centres** in Tokyo and Fuji (Tokyo ☎ 03-5376-2222; Fuji ☎ 72-5111).

Fuji Go-ko 富士五湖
The Fuji Go-ko (Fuji Five Lakes), scattered around the northern side of Mt Fuji, are the perfect reflecting pools for the mountain's majesty. Particularly pleasant during the autumn *kūyū* (maple) season, the lakes make a good overnight trip out of Tokyo. Most visitors to the region do little more than stroll around, enjoying the views, but those with energy can hike in the mountains above the lakes. Hiking maps are available from the information centres in Kawaguchi-ko and Fuji-Yoshida (p171).

SIGHTS & ACTIVITIES
On the lake of the same name, **Kawaguchi-ko** is the best place from which to explore the Fuji Go-ko area. It's also a popular departure point for climbing Mt Fuji. Around 600m north of the Kawaguchi-ko Station, on the lower eastern edge of the lake, is the **Kawaguchi-ko cable car** (one way/return ¥400/700) to the **Fuji Viewing Platform** (1104m). You can walk to the cable car from Kawaguchi-ko Station; ask at the Kawaguchi-ko Tourist Information Center (p171) for a map.

At Fuji-Yoshida, a 15-minute walk from the station, is the atmospheric **Sengen-jinja**, which dates from 1615 (although this area is thought to have been the site of a shrine as early as 788). In the days when climbing Mt Fuji was a pilgrimage and not an annual tourist event, a visit to this shrine was a necessary preliminary to the ascent. The entrance street to the shrine still has some Edo-era pilgrims' inns. From Fuji-Yoshida Station you can walk (15 minutes) or take a bus to Sengen-jinja-mae bus stop (¥150, five minutes).

Another site that's not so sacred, but popular nonetheless, is **Fujikyu Highland** (☎ 23-2111; h 9am-5pm Mon-Fri, 9am-7pm Sat, 9am-6pm Sun & holidays; admission only ¥1000, one-day pass incl amusements ¥4300), an amusement park one stop west of Fuji-Yoshida Station.

Yamanaka-ko is the largest of the lakes, but it doesn't offer much in the way of attractions – unless you count an enormous swan-shaped hovercraft that does 35-minute circuits of the lake for ¥900.

The area around the smaller **Sai-ko** is less developed than the areas around the larger lakes. There are good views of Mt Fuji from the western end of the lake and from the **Kōyō-dai lookout**, near the main road. Close to the road are the **Narusawa Ice Cave** and the **Fugaku Wind Cave**, both formed by lava flows from a prehistoric eruption of Mt Fuji. There's a bus stop at each of the caves, or you can walk from one to the other in about 20 minutes.

The views of Mt Fuji from further west are not so impressive, but tiny **Shoji-ko** is said to be the prettiest of the Fuji Go-ko. Continue to Eboshi-san, a one- to 1½-hour climb from the road, to a lookout over the **Aokigahara-jukai** (Sea of Trees) to Mt Fuji. The last lake along is **Motosu-ko**, the deepest and least visited of the lakes.

FESTIVALS & EVENTS
The **Yoshida no Hi Matsuri** (Fire Festival; 26–27 August) is an annual festival held to mark the end of the climbing season and to offer thanks for the safety of the year's climbers. The first day involves a mikoshi (portable shrine) procession and the lighting of bonfires on the town's main street. On the second day, festivals are held at the town's Sengen-jinja.

SLEEPING
Lodging options are plentiful around the Fuji Go-ko, though most travellers base themselves at Fuji-Yoshida or Kawaguchi-ko. The **tourist information offices** (Kawaguchi-ko ☎ 72-6700; Fuji-yoshida ☎ 22-7000) can make reservations for you. Fuji climbers should consider overnighting in one of the mountain huts.

Fuji-Yoshida Youth Hostel (富士吉田 ユース ホステル; ☎ 22-0533; www.jyh.or.jp; dm ¥2835) Of the two hostels in the area, this is the better option, with friendly staff and nice rooms,

both Western- and Japanese-style. The hostel is around 600m south of Shimo-Yoshida Station; exit the station, walk down the main street, heading south, keeping Lawson's on the left. Go through three sets of lights, and turn down the small alley on the right. Check-in 4pm.

Taikokuya (大国屋; ☎ 22-3778; Hanchō-dōri; d per person ¥6600) This old pilgrim's inn in Fuji-Yoshida has elegant tatami rooms in a traditional setting. A handsome private garden fronts the ryokan. It's on the main road heading toward Mt Fuji, a 10-minute walk from Fuji-Yoshida Station.

Hotel Sunnide Village (ホテルサニーデビレ ッジ; ☎ 76-6004; info@sunnide.com; backpacker plan rate ¥4000, r per person with bath ¥6000) This lovely lodge commands a great view over Kawaguchi-ko towards Mt Fuji (you can enjoy this view from its outdoor bath). If you go through the Kawaguchi-ko Tourist Information Center you can qualify for its 'backpacker plan' rate. Note that no advance reservations are accepted for this rate; you just have to turn up and hope for the best. Free pick-up from the station. Check-in is from 3pm.

Ashiwada Hotel (足和田ホテル; ☎ 82-2587; s/d with bath ¥6000/12,000) This friendly hotel on the edge of the lake boasts impressive views of Mt Fuji. It's at the western end of Kawaguchi-ko (take bus No 6 from Kawaguchi-ko to the Nagahama stop, then walk five minutes, ¥270). Pick-up service at Kawaguchi Station available. Check-in is from 2pm.

Petit Hotel Ebisuya (プチホテルエビスヤ; ☎ 72-0165; r per person ¥5250) One of several business hotels around Kawaguchi-ko Station, Ebisuya offers comfortable Western- and Japanese-style rooms in a Tudoresque building. Indoor bath has fine views of Mt. Fuji. Check-in is from 3pm.

Kawaguchi-ko Youth Hostel (河口湖ユース ホステル; ☎ 72-1431; dm ¥3045; h mid-Mar–early Nov) This rather regimented hostel is about 500m southwest of Kawaguchi Station; turn left as you come out of the tourist information centre, left after the 7-Eleven, right at the first set of lights and, finally, left in front of the power station. Bike rental (per day ¥800). Check-in is from 4pm.

EATING
Fuji-Yoshida has the best selection of restaurants, though Kawaguchi-ko also has its gems. Many people eat where they're staying

but there are other options. Fuji-Yoshida is particularly known for its *teuchi udon* (homemade, white wheat noodles). Among the varieties are noodles with tempura, *kitsune* (fried tofu) and *niku* (beef). Stop by the **Fuji-Yoshida Tourist Information Center** (☎ 22-7000) for a map and list of spots to sample the noodles (around ¥500) in private homes. You'll also find a restaurant floor on the basement level of Fuji-Yoshida Station with snack options including *takoyaki* and *okonomiyaki*.

Sanrokuen (山麓園; ☎ 73-1000; meals per person ¥2100-4200; ☺ 11am-8pm Fri-Wed) This charming *irori* (fireplace) restaurant in Kawaguchi-ko allows diners to grill their own meals around charcoal pits set in the floor. Skewers of fish, chicken, tofu, quail, steak and veggies are available, and it's an enjoyable place to have a long meal. From Kawaguchi-ko Station, take a left, turn left again after the 7-Eleven, and after 600m, you'll see it on the right. Look for the thatched roof.

M2 (☎ 23-9309; mains ¥800-1300; ☺ 11am-10pm) One block away from the Fuji-Yoshida Youth Hostel, this quaint restaurant serves Western and Japanese dishes at good prices. Risotto, pork cutlet, pasta and sandwiches are among the offerings. The miniature toys and kitschy artwork adds to the charm.

Michael's American Pub (☎ 24-3917; ☺ 8pm-2am, Fri-Wed) For a slice of traditional Americana – burgers, pizzas and brew – drop by this expat and local favourite. From Fuji-Yoshida Station, walk north to the main road (Akafuji-dōri) and take a right. After crossing the river, take the third left.

GETTING THERE & AWAY
Kawaguchi-ko and Fuji-Yoshida are the two main travel centres in the Fuji Go-ko area. Buses (¥1700, 1¾ hours) operate directly to Kawaguchi-ko from the Shinjuku long-distance bus station, outside the western exit of Shinjuku station in Tokyo. There are departures up to 16 times daily at the height of the Fuji climbing season. Some buses continue on to Yamanaka-ko and Motosu-ko. In Tokyo, call **Keiō Kōsoku Bus** (☎ 03-5376-2222) for reservations and schedule information. In Kawaguchi-ko, reservations can be made through **Toumei Highway Bus** (☎ 72-2922).

You can also get to the lakes by train, although it takes longer and costs more. JR Chūō-line trains go from Shinjuku to Ōtsuki (*tokkyū* ¥2230, one hour; *futsū* ¥1280, one

hour and 50 minutes). At Ōtsuki, cross the platform to the Fuji Kyūkō line, which runs to Kawaguchi-ko (*futsū* ¥1110, one hour). The train actually goes to Fuji-Yoshida first (¥990, 50 minutes) then reverses the short distance to Kawaguchi-ko. On Sundays and holidays from March to November there is a direct local train from Shinjuku and Tokyo Stations (¥2370 from Shinjuku, ¥2530 from Tokyo, both two hours).

From Fuji-Yoshida and Kawaguchi-ko, buses run north to Kōfu, from where you can continue northwest to Matsumoto.

GETTING AROUND
There's a comprehensive bus network in the area, including regular buses from Fuji-Yoshida Station that pass by the four smaller lakes and around the mountain to Fujinomiya (¥2150, 1½ hours) on the southwestern side. From Kawaguchi-ko, there are nine to 11 buses daily to Mishima (¥2130, two hours) on the *shinkansen* line.

HAKONE 箱根
☎ 0460 / pop 15,227
Hakone is the Japanese tourist mecca par excellence. If the weather cooperates and Mt Fuji is clearly visible, the Hakone region can make a fun trip from Tokyo. You can enjoy cable-car rides, visit an open-air museum, poke around smelly volcanic hot springs and cruise Ashino-ko. You can also soak in the region's *onsen* or stay overnight in a traditional ryokan. Unfortunately, at times – particularly during the height of summer – the Hakone experience can have a highly packaged feel.

An interesting loop through the region takes you from Tokyo by train and toy (tiny, local) train to Gōra, passing Miyanoshita and Chōkoku-no-Mori en route; then by funicular and cable car up the 1153m-high mountain, Sōun-zan, to almost the top, and back down to Ashino-ko; by boat around the lake to Moto-Hakone, where you can walk a short stretch of the Edo-era Old Tōkaidō highway; and from there by bus back to Odawara, where you catch the train to Tokyo. (The energetic can also walk 3½ hours along the lovely old highway back to Hakone-Yumoto, where trains depart for Tokyo.)

On weekends, this region is almost always busy. To beat the crowds, plan your trip during the week. For online info, visit www.kankou.hakone.kanagawa.jp.

AROUND TOKYO

HAKONE

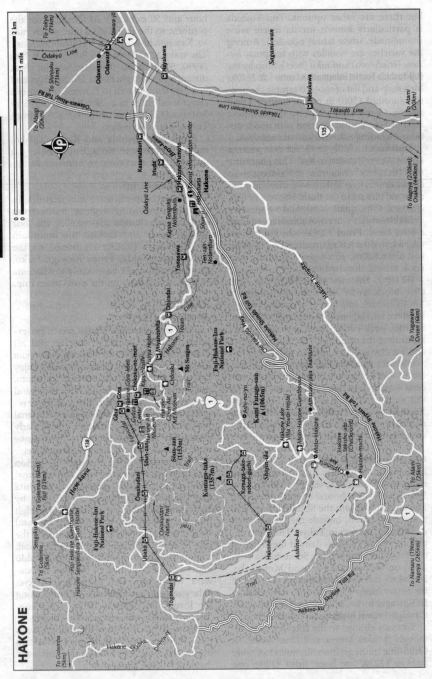

FESTIVALS & EVENTS

Ashino-ko Kosui Matsuri (31 July) At Hakone-jinja near Moto-Hakone, this festival features firework displays over Ashino-ko.

Hakone Daimonji-yaki Matsuri (6 August) During this summer festival, the torches are lit on Myojoga-take so that they form the shape of the Chinese character for 'big' or 'great'.

Hakone Daimyō Gyoretsu parade (3 November) This parade is a re-enactment by 400 costumed locals of a feudal lord's procession.

SLEEPING

In addition to places listed beneath individual destinations, there are several other decent choices in the Hakone area.

Fuji Hakone Guest House (富士箱根ゲストハウス; ☎ 4-6577; www.fujihakone.com; r per person ¥5250-6300) Run by a welcoming, English-speaking family, the guesthouse has handsome tatami rooms and a cozy *onsen* bath. It's a popular spot with foreign travellers. Take a No 4 bus from Odawara Station to Senkyōrō-mae bus stop (50 minutes). There's an English sign close by. Check-in is from 3pm.

Hakone Sengokuhara Youth Hostel (箱根仙石原; ☎ 4-8966; www.jyh.or.jp; dm/r per person ¥2900/5250) Run by the same family, this pleasant hostel is directly behind the Fuji Hakone guesthouse. It has Japanese-style dorms and private rooms. Check-in is 4pm to 6pm.

GETTING THERE & AWAY

There are three ways of getting to the Hakone region from Tokyo: by the Odakyū express bus service, which leaves from the western side of Shinjuku Station; by JR from Tokyo Station; and by the private Odakyū line from Shinjuku Station.

Bus

The Odakyū express bus service has the advantage of running directly into the Hakone region, to Ashino-ko and to Hakone-machi (¥1950, two hours). The disadvantage is that the bus trip is much less interesting than the combination of Romance Car, toy train (Hakone-Tō-zan line), funicular, cable car and ferry. Buses run from the western exit of Shinjuku Station 11 times daily.

Train

JR trains run on the Tōkaidō line between Tokyo Station and Odawara (*futsū* ¥1450, 1½ hours; *tokkyū* ¥2880, 70 minutes; Kodama *shinkansen* ¥3130, 35 minutes).

The private Odakyū line (www.odakyu-group.co.jp/english/index.htm) runs into Hakone from Shinjuku Station. Quickest and most comfortable is the Romance Car to Odawara (¥1720, 1¼ hours) or to Hakone-Yumoto (¥2020, one hour and 25 minutes). There is also a *kyūkō* (regular express) service (¥1150, 1½ hours) to Hakone-Yumoto.

At Odawara, it's possible to change to the narrow gauge, or toy train, on the Hakone-Tōzan line, which takes you to Gōra (¥650, 50 minutes). Catch this on platform No 4. Alternatively, if you are already on the Odakyū line, you can continue on to Hakone-Yumoto and change to the Hakone-Tōzan line (¥390 to Gōra, 35 minutes) by walking across the platform.

GETTING AROUND

Boat

Ferry services crisscross Ashino-ko, running between Tōgendai, Hakone-machi and Moto-Hakone every 30 minutes. From Tōgendai, the fare is ¥970 to Moto-Hakone or Hakone-machi; between Moto-Hakone and Hakone-machi it's ¥250. The 'Pirate Ship' has to be seen to be believed – it's tourist kitsch at its worst, but fun all the same.

Bus

The Hakone-Tōzan and Izu Hakone bus companies service the Hakone area and between them they manage to link up most of the sights. If you finish up in Hakone-machi, Hakone-Tōzan buses run between here and Odawara for ¥1150. Hakone-en to Odawara costs ¥1270. Buses run from Moto-Hakone to Yumoto for ¥900 every 30 minutes from 10am to 3pm.

Train

The Odakyū line offers a Hakone Furii Pasu (Free Pass) costing ¥5500 in Shinjuku or ¥4170 in Odawara (the place to buy it if you are travelling on a Japan Rail Pass) and allows you to use any mode of transport within the Hakone region for four days. The fare between Shinjuku and Hakone-Yumoto is included in the pass. It's a good deal for a Hakone circuit, as the pass will save at least ¥1000 even on a one-day visit to the region.

Odawara 小田原

Odawara is famous for its **castle** (admission ¥400; ◷ 9am-5pm, closed 29 Dec-1 Jan), which is an uninspired reconstruction of the original. It's worth visiting during the cherry-blossom season – there are some 1000 sakura (cherry) trees planted on the grounds. The castle and surrounding park area is a 10-minute walk southeast of Odawara Station. There is little else of interest in Odawara, which is principally a transit point for Hakone.

Hakone-Yumoto Onsen 箱根湯元温泉

A pleasant town nestled at the foot of the mountains, Yumoto is Hakone's most popular hot-springs resort. It's possible to stop off between Odawara and Gōra, and spend the day soaking in the baths here if the weather looks dodgy. You can also approach the town on foot from Moto-Hakone via the Old Tōkaidō Highway (see p180).

Pick up a town map and get the latest info at the excellent **Tourist Information Center** (☎ 5-8911; ☒ 9.30am-5.30pm), a five-minute walk from the train station on the main road. There's always an English-speaker on hand.

Onsen are the main attraction of Hakone-Yumoto. **Kappa Tengoku Notemburo** (かっぱ天国; ☎ 5-6121; admission ¥750; ☒ 10am-10pm), behind the station, is a popular outdoor bath, worth a dip if the crowds aren't too bad. More upmarket are the fantastic *onsen* of **Ten-zan Notemburo** (天山野天風呂; ☎ 6-4126; admission ¥1200; ☒ 9am-11pm), which has a larger selection of indoor and outdoor baths. To get there, take the free shuttle bus from the bridge outside the station.

SLEEPING & EATING

Hotel Okada (ホテルおかだ; ☎ 5-6000; r per person from ¥11,800) Most travellers prefer staying further up the mountain, but for a bit of pampering, try this large hotel on the edge of the Sukumo-gawa. It has excellent Japanese- and Western-style rooms, a large bath complex (8th floor) and a swimming pool. Take bus A from the train station (¥100, 10 minutes).

Yumoto Onsen's good restaurants make it a fine place to stop for lunch.

Hatsuhana (はつはな; ☎ 5-8287; mains ¥750-1100; ☒ 10am-7pm) For tasty soba dishes, head to this pleasant spot on the Hayakawa. After passing the tourist information centre, take a left at the next main street. It's just over the bridge on the left.

The **Ten-zan Notemburo** complex also has several good restaurants inside, including a fine *shabu-shabu* (sautéed beef) spot.

Miyanoshita

If you take the Hakone-Tōzan railway toward Gōra, the first worthwhile stop is the village of Miyanoshita. Here you'll find a handful of antique shops along the main road, some splendid ryokan, and a pleasant hiking trail skirting up the 800m Mt Sengen. The entrance to the trail is 20m from the station, up the steps.

Miyanoshita also has one of Hakone's finest hotels. Opened in 1878, the **Fujiya Hotel** (富士屋ホテル; ☎ 2-2211; www.fujiyahotel.co.jp; d from ¥19,000) is one of Japan's earliest Western-style hotels and is highly rated on all fronts, featuring handsome guest rooms with hot spring water piped into each one. Foreign travellers should inquire about the weekday special of US$125 for double rooms (you can pay the equivalent sum in yen). The hotel is around 250m west of the station. Check-in is from 2pm.

Chōkoku-no-Mori

Two stops beyond Miyanoshita, you'll reach Chōkoku-no-Mori, where you'll find the excellent **Hakone Open-Air Art Museum** (彫刻の森美術館; ☎ 2-1161; www.hakone-oam.or.jp; admission ¥1600; ☒ 9am-5pm Apr-Nov, 9am-4.30pm Dec-Mar). Although tickets are pricey, there's an impressive selection of 19th- and 20th-century Japanese and Western works in a beautiful setting. Outdoors, you'll find sculptures by Henry Moore, Rodin, Maillol and Miro, while interior galleries contain works by Giacometti and Calder; there's also a Picasso pavilion (with some 300 pieces) and paintings by Kotaro Takamura, Yuzo Fujikawa and other Japanese artists. Several decent restaurants and a teahouse are inside. The Hakone Free Pass (see p177) does not gain you free admission, though it will earn you a discount.

A charming ryokan lies 300m uphill from the museum on the left. **Chōraku** (長楽; ☎ 2-2192; r per person with/without meals ¥8800/5150) has simple but nicely maintained tatami rooms with kitchenettes. There's an *onsen* on the 1st floor. Check-in is from 3pm.

For exquisite sushi, don't miss **Kappei-zushi** (かつ平寿し; ☎ 2-3278; mixed sushi ¥1500; ☒ 9am-8pm), a nondescript spot that delivers fresh, tender slices of sashimi. Picture menu available. It's a few metres downhill from the museum on the same side of the street.

Gōra 強羅

Gōra is the terminus of the Hakone-Tōzan line and the starting point for the funicular and cable-car trip to Tōgendai on Ashino-ko. The town also has a couple of its own attractions that may be of minor interest to travellers. **Gyōza Center** (set meals ¥1000-14,000; ⏰ 11.30am-3pm & 5-8pm), is a two-storey shop famous for its *gyōza* (dumplings), available a dozen different ways. Basic sets include rice and miso (soya-bean paste) soup. The restaurant is 200m downhill from the Gōra Station.

HAKONE GŌRA-KŌEN 箱根強羅公園

Just a short walk beside the funicular tracks up Sōun-zan is the park, **Hakone Gōra-kōen** (☎ 2-2825; admission ¥500; ⏰ 9am-5pm Sep-Jun, 9am-9pm Jul-Aug). Hakone Gōra-kōen has a rock garden, alpine and seasonal plants, a fountain and several greenhouses with tropical flowers.

Sōun-zan & Ōwakudani 早雲山・大桶谷

From Gōra, continue to near the 1153m-high summit of Sōun-zan by funicular (¥410, 10 minutes). If you don't have a Hakone Free Pass (see p177), tickets are sold at the booth to the right of the platform exit.

Sōun-zan is the starting point for what the Japanese refer to as a ropeway, a 30-minute, 4km cable-car ride to Tōgendai (one way/return ¥1330/2340). On the way, the gondolas stop at Ōwakudani, where you can take a look around the volcanic hot springs before continuing. In fine weather Mt Fuji looks fabulous from here.

From Sōn-zan, there are also several hiking trails: one to Mount Kami (1¾ hours); the other up to Owakudani (1¼ hours), which is sometimes closed owing to the mountain's toxic gases.

Ōwakudani is a volcanic cauldron of steam, bubbling mud and mysterious smells. The 25-minute **Ōwakudani Nature Trail** leads through the charred, somewhat apocalyptic landscape to some of the boiling pits. Here you can buy black boiled eggs, cooked in the dark mud. Numerous signs warn travellers not to linger too long, as the gases are indeed poisonous.

Next to the cable-car stop, there's also a building with restaurants and souvenir shops.

Ashino-ko 芦ノ湖

Ashino-ko is touted as the primary attraction of the Hakone region; but it's Mt Fuji, with its snow-clad slopes glimmering in reflection on the water, that lends the lake its poetry. Unfortunately, the venerable mountain is frequently hidden behind a dirty-grey bank of clouds. If this is the case when you visit, you have the consolation of a ferry trip across the lake; you can always buy a postcard of the view. See p177 for details about lake transport.

Komaga-take 駒ヶ岳

The mountain Komaga-take (1357m) is a good place from which to get a view of the lake and Mt Fuji. From Tōgendai, boats run to Hakone-en, where a cable car (one way/return ¥620/1050) goes to the top. You can leave the mountain by the same route or by a five-minute funicular descent (¥370/630) to Komaga-take-nobori-guchi. Buses run from here to Hakone-machi (¥300), Hakone-Yumoto (¥820) and to Odawara (¥1050). Note that this region is not covered by the Hakone Free Pass.

ROCK CARVINGS

Not far from Komaga-take-nobori-guchi is **Moto-Hakone Jizō**, a group of Buddhas and other figures carved in relief on rocks that lie between Komaga-take and Kami Futago-san (1065m). Although they date from the Kamakura era (1192–1333), most are still fairly well preserved. To get there from the funicular, turn right and follow the road down until you reach a T-junction. Turn left here and then left again; the carvings are around 400m up the road.

Moto-Hakone 元箱根

Moto-Hakone is a pleasant spot on the lake with a few interesting sights within easy walking distance of the jetty. Although it's a bit touristy, you'll find some decent lodging options here.

SIGHTS & ACTIVITIES

It is impossible to miss **Hakone-jinja** (☎ 3-7213; treasure hall ¥300; ⏰ 9am-4pm) with its red *torii* rising from the lake. A pleasant stroll around the lake to the *torii* leads along a path lined with huge cedars. A wooded grove surrounds the shrine, and there is a treasure hall in the grounds.

Another pleasant place to walk is **Cryptomeria Avenue**, more properly known as Suginamiki, a 2km path between Moto-Hakone and Hakone-machi. The path is lined with cryptomeria trees that were planted more than 360 years ago. It runs behind the busy lakeside road.

Those looking for a bit more exercise can head back to Hakone-Yumoto along the **Old Tōkaidō Highway**. Up the hill from the lakeside Moto-Hakone bus stop, this road once linked the ancient capital, Kyoto, with Edo (now known as Tokyo). A 3½-hour walk along the old road leads to Hakone-Yumoto Station. Along the way, you'll pass the **Amazake-jaya Teahouse** (甘酒茶屋) where you can enjoy a refreshing cup of *amazake* (a warm sake) in the centuries-old setting. You can also stop in the small village of Hatajuku, and end your walk at the historic temple of **Sōun-ji** near Hakone Yumoto Station.

SLEEPING

Hakone Lake Villa Youth Hostel (箱根レイクヴィラユースホステル; ☎ 3-1610; dm ¥2900) Hidden in a wooded spot over the lake, this hostel offers Japanese- and Western-style dorm rooms, a large outdoor deck, *onsen* and tasty meals. From Odawara Station, take a bus from the No 3 stand and get off at the Futako Jaya bus stop (50 minutes). From the stop, head downhill 50m, continue along the dirt road and you'll see it on the right.

Moto Hakone Guesthouse (元箱根ゲストハウス; ☎ 3-7880; www.fujihakone.com; r per person ¥5250) A popular spot with foreign tourists, this guesthouse offers simple but pleasant Japanese-style rooms. From Odawara Station, take a bus from the No 3 stand and get off at the Ashino-ko-en-mae stop (55 minutes). Walk downhill 25m and turn left. You can also walk (12 minutes uphill) or bus it from Moto Hakone. Check-in is from 3pm.

Hakone-machi 箱根町

Hakone-machi lies further around the lake, beyond Moto-Hakone. The town's main attraction is the **Hakone Sekisho-ato** (Hakone Checkpoint), which was operated by the Tokugawa shōgunate from 1619 to 1869 as a customs post between Edo and the rest of Japan. The present-day checkpoint is a recent reproduction of the original.

IZU-HANTŌ 伊豆半島

About 100km southwest of Tokyo, the peninsula, Izu-hantō, with its abundant *onsen* and rugged coastline, is one of Japan's most popular resort destinations. Things can get crowded on the peninsula on weekends and holidays, particularly in summer. Luckily, once you get past the touristy resort of Atami, the crowds usually thin out. And over on the west coast, where transport is by bus only, things are always much quieter.

A suggested two- or three-day itinerary involves heading straight down the east coast to Shimoda. After exploring the town, neighbouring Rendai-ji Onsen and perhaps the rugged headlands of the cape, Irō-zaki, catch a bus for the scenic ride to Dōgashima on the west coast. Here, you can bathe in a cliffside *onsen*, swim in the Pacific in warmer months and enjoy stunning views up and down the coast. From Dōgashima, you can catch another bus to the *onsen* village of Shuzen-ji. After sampling the excellent baths there, you can take the Izu-Hakone Tetsudō line to Mishima and from there switch to the JR Tōkaidō line for the trip back to Tokyo.

Atami 熱海

☎ 0557 / pop 42,664

Atami is an overdeveloped hot-springs resort with little, aside from its museum, to detain foreign travellers. Overlooking the coastline, the sleek **MOA Museum of Art** (☎ 84-2511; www.moaart.or.jp; admission ¥1600; ◷ 9.30am-4.30pm Fri-Wed; closed 6-10 Jan & 25-31 Dec) has a decent collection of Japanese and Chinese art, spanning over 1000 years it includes paintings, ceramics, calligraphy and sculpture. One of the most striking expositions is the full-size replica of a golden tearoom. Take the bus from stop No 4 outside Atami Station to the last stop, MOA Bijitsukan (¥160, eight minutes).

Discount tickets to the museum (¥1300) and town information are available at the **tourist office** (☎ 81-2033; ◷ 9.30am-5.30pm), inside the station building.

Because of Atami's popularity with domestic tourists, rooms are overpriced; head down to Itō or Shimoda to find more reasonable lodgings.

GETTING THERE & AWAY

JR trains run from Tokyo Station to Atami on the Tōkaidō line (*futsū* ¥1890, two hours; Kodama *shinkansen* ¥3570, 55 minutes;

IZU-HANTŌ

To Shimizu (45km);
Shizuoka (59km)

To Tokyo
(104km)

Numazu

Mishima

To Hakone

Atami

Mishima

Numazu

Kannami

Atami

Nirayama

Sagami-wan

Ōhito

Naga-hama

Ōse-zaki

Mito-hama

Shuzen-ji Youth Hostel

Itō-hama

Shuzen-ji Onsen

Shuzen-ji

Itō
Tourist
Information
Center

Heda

Shuzen-ji

Nishi-Izu
Skyline

▲ Daruma-yama
(982m)

136

Kawana

Jogasaki
Coast

Suruga-wan

Ippeki-ko

135

Jogasaki-kaigan

Kadowakizaki Point

Tōi-hama

Tōi

Amagi-san
(1406m)

Izu-Kōgen

Amagi Tunnel

Atagawa

Atagawa

Ferry to
Ō-shima
(40km)

136

Information Office

Dōgashima

Inatori

Sawada-kōen
Rotemburo Onsen

Sanyo-sō Youth Hostel

414

Higashiizu

Matsu-zaki

Matsu-zaki

Kawazu

Ferry to
Ō-shima
(32km)

Rendai-ji

Rendai-ji

Shira-hama

Kanaya Ryokan/Onsen

Hagachi-zaki

Gensu Youth Hostel

Shimoda

Shimoda

Sotoura-kaigan

Minamiizu

Kisami

Lighthouse

Ō-hama

Ferry to Nii-jima (48km);
Shikine-jima (54km);
Kozu-shima (55km)

Yumiga-hama

Irō-zaki

AROUND TOKYO

---

tokkyū Odoriko ¥4070, 1¼ hours). It's also possible to approach Atami via Shinjuku by taking the Odakyū line to Odawara (¥850, 70 minutes) and then connecting with the Tōkaidō line to Atami (¥400, 29 minutes).

Itō 伊東
☎ 0557

Itō is another hot-springs resort and is famous as the place where Anjin-san (William Adams), the hero of James Clavell's book *Shogun*, built a ship for the Tokugawa shōgunate. Itō Station has a beachfront **Tourist Information Center** (☎ 37-6105; ☺ 9am-5pm), beside the bay cruises dock.

Near Itō is the striking **Jogasaki coast** of windswept cliffs formed by lava. A harrow-

ing 48m-long suspension bridge leads over Kadowakizaki Point, with waves crashing 23m below. Close by is a hiking trail skirting along the cliffs. To reach the coast, take the No 3 Kaiyō Kōen-Iki bus (¥700 per 30 minutes).

Yamaki (山喜旅館; ☎ 37-4123; r per person ¥5250) is a traditional ryokan set in an old wooden building surrounded by gardens. Its trim rooms and *onsen* are good value. Check-in is from 3pm.

GETTING THERE & AWAY

Itō is connected to Atami by the JR Itō line (¥320, 25 minutes). The JR limited express Odoriko service also runs from Tokyo Station to Itō (¥4090, 45 minutes).

ONSEN MANIA! *John Ashburne*

In his quintessential tome *Things Japanese* (1890), humorist and Japan-expert Basil Hall Chamberlain wryly observed 'Cleanliness is one of the few original items of Japanese civilisation'. Chamberlain was impressed by the Japanese mania for *onsen* (mineral hot-spring spas), not least by the pool in rural Gunma-ken where 'the bathers stay in the water for a month on end, with a stone on their lap to prevent them from floating in their sleep'.

A century later, *onsen* addicts may not be weighing themselves down with boulders, but the fascination with hot springs remains as strong as ever, and the activity has developed into a fine art with its own rules of etiquette. Baths are found just about everywhere due to plenty of underground thermal activity – poke a stick in the ground and out comes *o-yu* (literally, 'honourable hot water'). *Onsen* range from pristine mountain retreats to workaday bath houses and kitschy, overdeveloped spa towns.

Getting naked with total strangers is not, for most of us, the cultural norm, but shy gaijin (foreigners) should know that the Japanese perceive bathing as a great social leveller; company presidents rub naked shoulders with truck drivers, priests with publicans – and all revel in the anonymity that nudity allows. Only the *yakuza* (Japanese mafia) stand out with their magnificent *irezumi* (tattoos) or, in yakuza parlance, *iremono*. They are often happy if you show an interest in checking out their tattoos.

The baths themselves come in as many different shapes and sizes as the customers. Essentially, you will either visit solely for an *o-furo* (literally, 'the honourable bath'), or you will stay at an *onsen ryokan* (traditional hot-spring inn) to enjoy good food, copious amounts of alcohol, karaoke and a soak in the establishment's private baths, either indoors or out. Ryokan will often allow you to have a soak even if you aren't staying there (ask for *ofuro-nomi*). This is an excellent and affordable way to experience some beautiful, traditional baths. Unfortunately, bathing is also big business and rampant commercialism has marred many once-lovely *onsen*.

While famed commercial resorts, such as Dōgo Onsen in Shikoku and Beppu in Kyūshū, provide a good introduction to *onsen*, the effort it takes to seek out less touristed springs is worthwhile. If you find a rare, unvisited bath, the effect is scintillating. A few special *onsen* well worth visiting include Ibusuki (p664) and Kurokawa (p650) in Kyūshū, Yunomine (p384) in Kansai and Bessho Onsen (p244) in central Honshū.

There are two excellent books devoted to hot springs: *A Guide to Japanese Hot Springs* and *Japan's Hidden Hot Springs*. Both are worth seeking out for anyone looking to *onsen*-hop their way through Japan.

So, whether it's being buried up to the neck in a thermally heated sand bath, soaking in a pool in a remote forest or luxuriating in a glitzy resort, the *onsen* experience is one of Japan's greatest treasures. Where else can you safely get naked with a mobster?

Shimoda 下田

☎ 0558 / pop 27,722

If you have time for just one town on the peninsula, make it Shimoda, the most pleasant of the peninsula's *onsen* towns. Shimoda is famous as the residence of the American Townsend Harris, the first Western diplomat to live in Japan. The Treaty of Kanagawa, which resulted from Commodore Perry's visit (see p37), ended Japan's centuries of self-imposed isolation by opening the ports of Shimoda and Hakodate to US ships and establishing a consulate in Shimoda in 1856.

The southern end of town around Perry Rd is perfect for strolling and has a few temples scattered about.

INFORMATION

Main Post Office (☎ 22-1531; ⏰ 10am-5pm) The main post office has an international ATM; it's a few blocks from Perry Rd.

Shimoda Tourist Association (☎ 22-1531; ⏰ 10am-5pm) This office can help you book accommodation. Take a left out of the station, walk to the first intersection, and you'll see it on the southwest corner.

Volunteer English Guide Association (☎ 23-5151; maimai-h@i-younet.ne.jp; ⏰ 8.30am-5.15pm Tue-Sun) Offers free guided tours.

SIGHTS & ACTIVITIES

Ryōsen-ji & Chōraku-ji 了仙寺 長楽寺

A 25-minute walk south of Shimoda Station is Ryōsen-ji, famous as the site of another

Onsen Etiquette

The Japanese hot-spring *o-furo* is blissfully free of the rules and regulations that make life a minefield of potential societal gaffes for the average Japanese citizen. No doubt this liberation from the strictures of polite society is what makes *onsen* so popular. The first-time-naked gaijin (foreigner) needn't be intimidated – once the basics have been mastered.

Soap is a commodity kept as far from the bath water as possible. Have a rinse in the adjacent shower. If there's no shower, squat on one of the Lilliputian stools provided and ladle hot water over your body, using one of the available buckets. Then gracefully ease yourself into the water. Incidentally, stealing someone else's bucket or stool while they are soaking is officially frowned upon but, in fact, seems to be an undeclared national pastime.

One should endeavour to slip into the water with the minimum of disturbance, not unlike a cherry blossom petal delicately slipping into a moonlit Kyoto temple pond. In the event that the water is hot enough to strip the skin off a rhino, it is perfectly acceptable to do a reverse long-jump action, although if you can slowly ease yourself into the superheated water, grimacing is positively encouraged.

An essential piece of *onsen* equipment is a 'modesty' towel to delicately cover your most private bits and pieces. Once they are safely underwater, this useful item can be dipped in the water, rinsed out (outside the bath) and placed on your head, à la Northern England male beachgoer, c 1958. This is rumoured to prevent you from passing out (another minor social infringement). In the more rural, single-sex baths, however, no one bothers with a modesty towel – bathers wibble and wobble around, starkers as the day they were born.

It's that simple. And if you do commit a faux pas, most people are too busy forgetting work and looking forward to a night of karaoke to care.

Onsen Lingo

dansei-no-yu	男性の湯	male bath
otoko-yu	男湯	male bath
josei-no-yu	女性の湯	female bath
onna-yu	女湯	female bath
konyoku	混浴	mixed bath
kazoku-no-yu	家族の湯	family bath
rotemburo	露天風呂	outdoor bath
kawa-no-yu	川の湯	river bath
dōukutsuburo/anaburo	洞窟風呂/穴風呂	cave bath
sunaburo	砂風呂	sand bath

treaty, supplementary to the Treaty of Kanagawa, signed by Commodore Perry and representatives of the Tokugawa shōgunate.

Next to the temple is a small **museum** (☎ 22-0657; admission ¥500; ⏰ 8.30am-5pm, closed 1-3 Aug & 24-26 Dec) with exhibits relating to the arrival of Westerners in Japan. These include pictures depicting the tragic life of Okichi-san, a courtesan who was forced to give up the man she loved in order to attend to the needs of the barbarian Harris. When Harris left Japan five years later, Okichi was stigmatised for having had a relationship with a foreigner and was eventually driven to drink and suicide. Downstairs, there's an important collection of erotic Buddhist artwork.

Nearby Ryōsen-ji is Chōraku-ji, another pleasant little temple that's worth a quick look.

Hōfuku-ji 宝福寺

In the centre of town is Hōfuku-ji, which has a **museum** (☎ 22-0960; admission ¥300; ⏰ 8am-5pm) that memorialises the life of Okichi-san and includes scenes from the various movie adaptations of her life.

Shimoda Kōen & Wakanoura Promenade
下田公園 ベイサイドプロムナード
If you keep walking east from Perry Rd, you'll reach the pleasant hillside park of **Shimoda Kōen** overlooking the bay. It's loveliest

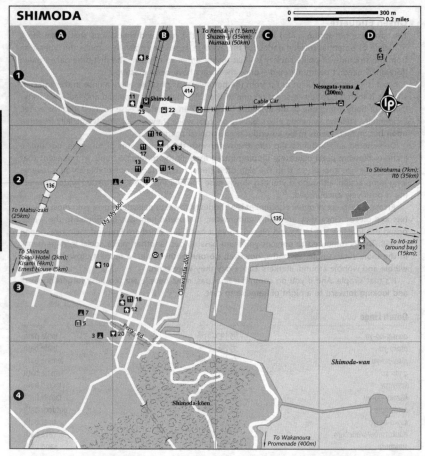

SHIMODA

in June, when the hydrangeas are in bloom. Before entering the park, the coastal road is also a fine place to walk. If you have an hour or so, keep following it around the bay, passing an overpriced aquarium, and eventually you'll meet up with the 2km-long **Wakanoura Promenade**, a stone path along a peaceful stretch of beach. Turn right when you meet up with the road to return to Perry Rd.

Nesugata-yama 寝姿山

About 200m east of Shimoda Station is the cable-car station to Nesugata-yama (Mt Nesugata; 200m). Cable cars run every 10 minutes to a **park** (⏰ 9am-5pm) that has a photography museum, a small temple, good views of Shimoda and the bay, Shimoda-

wan, and a reasonably priced restaurant. A return cable-car trip, including admission to the park, costs ¥1200.

Beaches

There are good beaches around Shimoda, particularly around Kisami, south of town. You can take an Irō-zaki-bound bus (No 3 or No 4; ¥360); ask to be dropped at Ōhama Iriguchi and walk 10 minutes towards the coast. North of Shimoda is the lovely white-sand beach of Shirahama (bus No 7; ¥320), which can get packed in July and August.

Bay Cruises

Several cruises depart from the Shimoda harbour area. Most popular with Japanese tourists is a 'Black Ship' cruise around the bay (¥920, 20 minutes), which departs every 30 minutes (approximately) from 9.10am to 3.30pm.

Three boats a day (9.40am, 11.20am and 2pm) leave on a course for Irō-zaki. You can leave the boat at Irō-zaki (¥1530, 40 minutes) and travel on by bus northwards up the peninsula, or stay on the boat to return to Shimoda.

FESTIVALS & EVENTS

Kuro-fune Matsuri (Black Ship Festival; 3rd Friday, Saturday and Sunday in May) Held in Shimoda, it commemorates the first landing of Commodore Perry with parades by the US Navy Marine band and firework displays. It's most interesting to see how the Japanese have made a virtue out of this potentially bitter historical event.

Shimoda Taiko Matsuri (Drum Festival; 14–15 August) Features a spectacular parade of *dashi* floats, and some serious Japanese-style drumming. The climax comes on the 15th.

SLEEPING

There are lots of *minshuku* around and the **Shimoda Tourist Association** (☎ 22-1531; ⏰ 10am-5pm) can help with reservations.

Ōizu Ryokan (☎ 22-0123; 3-3-25 Shimoda-shi; r per person ¥3500) Popular with international travellers for its excellent prices, Ōizu has plain but comfy Japanese-style rooms, all with air-con and TV, and a two-seater hot-spring bath. It's

in the south end of town, two blocks north of Perry Road. Check-in is from 3pm.

Shimoda-ya (☎ 22-0446; 2-13-31 Shimoda-shi; r per person with/without meals ¥8500/5500) This *minshuku* offers pleasant Japanese rooms with a rate that includes two meals. It's a few blocks past Hofuku-ji on the left-hand side. Check-in is from 2.30pm.

Kokumin-shukusha New Shimoda (☎ 23-0222; 1-4-13 Nishi-Hongo; r per person with/without meals ¥4855/7480) This drab but friendly inn offers decent tatami rooms and a large *onsen*. Take a right out of the station, another right at the first light, walk 2½ blocks and it's on your right.

Station Hotel Shimoda (☎ 22-8885; 1-1-3 Nishi-Hongo; s/d ¥5800/9800) Right next to the station, this unassuming business hotel has small but clean rooms. Check-in is from 4pm.

Uraga Hotel (☎ 23-6600; 3-3-10 Shimoda-shi; s/d ¥7000/9800) This business hotel has clean, new, comfortable rooms. It's a 20-minute walk from the station, on the same road as the post office. Check-in is from 3pm.

Shimoda Tokyu Hotel (下田東急ホテル; ☎ 22-2411; www.tokyuhotels.co.jp; 5-12-1 Shimoda-shi; s/d from ¥14,000/16,000) Perched on a cliff overlooking the Pacific, this resort south of town offers spacious rooms, indoor and outdoor *onsen* and a swimming pool. Rate includes two meals and free shuttle to and from the station. Check-in is from 2pm.

Ernest House (☎ 22-5880; www.artfarm.co.jp/ernesthouse/index_e.html; r per person ¥5250-8400) Two minutes' walk from the beach in Shirahama, this delightful hotel has bright, attractive rooms, and guests can order picnic breakfasts (¥1050), best enjoyed on the beach. Reservations are recommended for rooms. From Shimoda Station, take an Irō-zaki bound bus (No 3 or No 4; ¥360); ask to be dropped off at the Kisami stop, from which it's a 15-minute walk to Ernest House, in the direction of the coast. Check-in is from 3pm.

EATING

Seafood is the speciality in Shimoda and there are lots of good places around to try it.

Isoka-tei (☎ 23-1200; lunch/dinner from ¥1000/2500; ⏰ 11.30am-3pm & 5.30-10pm) This friendly spot serves hearty seafood sets which you can choose from a picture menu. From the Tourist Association, head three blocks down My My-dōri, take a left, and it'll be on the next corner.

Matsu Sushi (☎ 22-1309; sets from ¥1500; ☻ 11am-8pm Thu-Tue) For mouth-watering sashimi, don't miss this good-value sushi bar near the station.

Musashi (☎ 22-0934; mains from ¥800; ☻ 11am-2pm & 5.30-7.30pm Wed-Mon) This casual spot serves tasty Japanese *shokudō* (cafeteria) favourites, including tempura *soba*, and *rāmen* with grilled pork. Take a left out of the station, turn right down the narrow lane and take the first left.

Gorosaya (☎ 23-5638; lunch/dinner ¥1575/3150; ☻ 11.30am-2pm & 5-9pm Fri-Wed) For elegant but understated ambience and fantastic seafood, head to Gorosaya. From the Tourist Association, head two blocks down My My-dōri, take a left, and it'll be on your left. Look for the wooden fish decorating the entrance. English menu.

Porto Caro (3-3-7 Shimoda-shi; mains ¥1200-1800; ☻ 11.30am-2pm & 6-10pm) This stylish Italian bistro serves tasty pastas, pizzas and other Italian fare. It's two blocks north of Perry Rd, on the same road as the post office.

Fresh Bakery Kongarian (☎ 27-1611; pastries ¥100-200; ☻ 7am-6pm) This small bakery has donuts, breads and other snack fare. It's 2½ blocks south of the tourism office on the right.

DRINKING

Ja Jah (☎ 27-1611; ☻ 7pm-1am Tue-Sun) This cosy bar is a good place to kick back with some good tunes and friendly people. DJs sometimes spin (R&B, soul, hip-hop) on weekends.

Cheshire Cat Jazz House (☎ 23-3239; ☻ 11am-1am Thu-Sun) For live jazz, visit this low-key spot on My My-dōri. It's easily spotted by its English sign.

GETTING THERE & AWAY

Shimoda is as far as you can go by train on the Izu-hantō. You can take the Odoriko *tokkyū* from Tokyo Station (¥6160, 2¾ hours) or an Izu Kyūkō line train from Itō Station (¥1570, one hour). Trains also run from Atami (¥1890, 1½ hours).

Bus platform No 5 in front of the station is for buses going to Dōgashima (¥1360, one hour), while platform No 7 is for those bound for Shuzen-ji (¥2180, two hours).

Car rental is available at **Nippon Rent-a-Car** (☎ 22-5711) just outside the train station on the right.

Rendai-ji & Kanaya Onsen
蓮台寺・金谷温泉

A stop north of Shimoda on the Izu Kyūkō line is Rendai-ji (¥160, five minutes), home to one of the best *onsen* on the peninsula, **Kanaya Onsen** (admission ¥1000; ☻ 9am-10pm). Housed in atmospheric **Kanaya Ryokan** (金谷旅館; ☎ 22-0325; r per person with/without meals ¥15,000/7000), this traditional bath is well worth a side trip from Shimoda. The highlight is the enormous bath on the men's side, inside a weathered wooden hall. Women who want to check out this bath are welcome, but bathing suits are not permitted (towels are). The women's bath is nothing to sneeze at, and both sides have private outdoor baths.

From Rendai-ji Station, go straight across the river and main road to the T-junction and turn left; the *onsen* is 50m on the right.

Irō-zaki 石廊崎

Irō-zaki, the southernmost point of the peninsula, is noted for its cliffs and lighthouse. It also has a jungle park, a tropical garden and some fairly good beaches. You can get to the cape from Shimoda by boat (see p184) or by bus (¥930, 45 minutes) from the No 4 bus platform.

Matsu-zaki 松崎
☎ 0558

The sleepy village of Matsu-zaki is known for its collection of some 200 **traditional houses** with *namako-kabe* walls – diamond-shaped tiles set in plaster. They're concentrated in the south of town, on the far side of the river.

Three kilometres to the east of town is the **Sanyo-sō Youth Hostel** (三余荘ユースホステル; ☎ 42-0408; dm ¥2900), a traditional old building with fine (shared) tatami rooms. From Shimoda take a Dogashima-bound bus from the No 5 platform and get off at the Yūsu-hosteru-mae bus stop (50 minutes). Rental bikes are available for exploring the countryside. Check-in is between 4pm and 6.30pm.

Buses from Shimoda to Dōgashima pass through Matsu-zaki. The fare from Shimoda is ¥1230; from Dōgashima ¥520.

Dōgashima 堂ヶ島

From Shimoda, it's a picturesque bus journey to Dōgashima, on the western side of the peninsula. There are no breathtaking views, but the hilly countryside and the narrow road that winds its way past fields and through small rural townships make for an interesting trip.

For help booking accommodation and info on onward transportation, stop by the **information office** (☎ 52-1268; ☼ 8.30am-5pm) in front of the bus stop and above the tourist jetty. They'll also loan you a bicycle for free.

The main attractions at Dōgashima are the dramatic **rock formations** that line the seashore. The park just across the street from the bus stop has some of the best views. It's also possible to take a return boat trip (¥1880/920, 50/20 minutes) from the nearby jetty to visit the town's famous shoreline **cave**. The cave has a natural window in the roof that allows light to pour in. You can look down into the cave from paths in the aforementioned park.

About 700m south of the bus stop, you'll find the stunning **Sawada-kōen Rotemburo onsen** (沢田公園露天風呂温泉; admission ¥500; ☼ 7am-7pm Wed-Mon Sep-Jul, 6am-8pm Wed-Mon Aug) perched high on a cliff overlooking the Pacific. Go early in the day if possible; around sunset it's standing room only. Males and females bathe separately.

GETTING THERE & AWAY
Buses to Dōgashima (¥1360, one hour) leave from platform No 5 in front of Shimoda Station. From Dōgashima you can catch a bus onward to Shuzen-ji (¥1970, 1½ hours), a journey that affords fantastic views over Suruga-wan north to Mt Fuji. Indeed, when the air is clear and the mountain is blanketed by snow, it's worth the bus fare for the view alone – you'll swear you're looking at a Hokusai print. The best views are to be had a few kilometres south of Toi.

Shuzen-ji Onsen 修善寺
☎ 0558
A tiny *onsen* town set in a lush valley, Shuzen-ji is one of the peninsula's most charming. There are some fine places to stroll, and at dusk the town bells play 'Moon River'. Shuzen-ji Onsen is connected to the Tōkaidō line by the Izu-Hakone Tetsudō line, making it, along with Atami, one of the two main entry points to the peninsula. Everything of interest to travellers is in Shuzen-ji Onsen, a bus ride (¥210, 10 minutes) west of Shuzen-ji Station.

SIGHTS & ACTIVITIES
In the middle of Shuzen-ji Onsen, you'll find **Shuzen-ji**, an attractive and tranquil temple that dates back to 807. It's said to have been founded by Kōbō Daishi, who established the Shingon sect, one of Japan's major schools of Buddhism, which arose during the Heian Period (8th to the 12th centuries). The present structure dates from 1489.

Of course, the real reason to visit Shuzen-ji is to take a dip in one of its famous *onsen*. Right in the middle of the village you'll find the mineral hot spring **Tokko-no-yu** (admission free; ☼ 24hr) with mixed bathing, on a rocky promontory over the Katsura-gawa. Given the bath's central location and lack of proper walls, it's hardly surprising that naked foreigners become instant tourist attractions.

For a little privacy, head to the wonderful baths at **Kikuya Ryokan** (菊屋旅館; admission ¥1050) opposite the bus stop. Nonguests are welcome from 11.30am to 2.30pm. This is one of the few places in Japan where the women's baths are better than the men's.

If the baths at Kikuya are out of your price range, try the nameless local *sentō* (public bath) which uses hot-spring water, opposite Kikuya, past the bus stop, 50m up a narrow lane on the left. There's no one on duty – just put your ¥300 in the box when you enter.

SLEEPING & EATING
Shuzen-ji Youth Hostel (修善寺ユースホステル; ☎ 72-1222; dm ¥3045, breakfast/dinner ¥630/1050; ☼ closed 18-22 Jan & 30 May-9 Jun) In the hills west of town, this hostel is a good choice, featuring tasty meals, decent rooms and a peaceful setting. It's a 15-minute bus ride from Shuzen-ji Station; take a bus from the No 6 platform at Shuzen-ji Station to the New Town-guchi stop (last bus 5.30pm). It's a five-minute walk from the bus stop. Check-in is from 3.30pm.

Kikuya Ryokan (☎ 72-2000; r per person ¥20,000) This is an elegant place, connected to the baths mentioned earlier, with rates that include two extravagant meals Check-in 3pm.

Fukui (民宿福井; ☎ 72-3434; r per person ¥4875) This friendly *minshuku* is a popular choice for foreign guests. It has decent tatami rooms and a small gardenside *rotemburo* (outdoor bath). To reach Fukui, take a right when you get off the bus and head 350m up the road. Take a right at the sign (Japanese) and follow the narrow path uphill to the second set of stairs. Check-in is from 3pm.

Okura (おくら; ☎ 72-0007; meals around ¥900-1600; ⏰ 11.30am-2pm & 5.30-10pm) This casual spot is a local favourite for its good *soba*, tempura and *tonkatsu*. It's about 75m east (to the left) of the bus station.

GETTING THERE & AWAY
From Tokyo, access to Shuzen-ji is via Mishima on the Tōkaidō line. Izu-Hakone Tetsudō trains between Mishima and Shuzen-ji (¥500) take around 30 minutes. Buses run between Shuzen-ji and Shimoda (¥2180, two hours) and Shuzen-ji and Dōgashima (¥1970, 1½ hours).

SOUTH OF TOKYO

Just a short train ride from Tokyo, Yokohama is a vibrant but less chaotic metropolis than its big sister to the north. Further south lies the fascinating old capital of Kamakura, a mecca for shrine lovers.

YOKOHAMA 横浜
☎ 045 / pop 3,555,000
Japan's second-largest city may tread on Tokyo's coat-tails, but this former maritime centre buzzes with an energy of its own, and makes a pleasant sidetrip from the capital. The streets of its renowned Chinatown draw a diverse mix of visitors, as do the centres of Kannai and Sakuragi-chō, and the new seaside development of Minato Mirai 21. At night the city offers plenty of urbane attractions, when the restaurants, clubs and bars spring into life. By day, check out the harbour and the peaceful greenery of Sankei-en.

Orientation
Most sights are quite a way from Yokohama Station and it makes more sense to go to Sakuragi-chō or Kannai Station. Even more convenient is the brand-new Minato Mirai subway line (which connects to Yokohama Station). This line has stations at the Minato Mirai 21 complex, a 12-minute walk to Shinko Pier, and at the edge of Chinatown (Chūkagai) near Yamashita-kōen, the Foreigners' Cemetery and Harbour View Park.

Information
On the 1st floor of the Landmark Tower in the Minato Mirai 21 complex, there are a dozen computers with free Internet access.

Animi (☎ 222-3316; 4-2-7 Minato Mirai; per hr ¥100; ⏰ 10am-8pm) Internet access. Walk 15 minutes northwest of Minato Mirai 21 Station.

Chinatown 80 Information Center (☎ 662-1252; Honcho-dōri; ⏰ 10am-10pm) For the latest goings-on in Chinatown, stop by the centre, a few blocks from the Motomachi subway station.

Citibank (⏰ 24hr) An international ATM is outside the western exit of Yokohama Station on the 2nd floor of the First Building; look for it on the southwestern side of the Yokohama Bay Sheraton. An ATM is also available at the Sakuragi-chō post office.

Minato Mirai 21 Information Center (☎ 211-0111; 1-1-62 Sakuragichō; ⏰ 9am-6pm) There are English speakers here who can provide a wealth of information, including the free Yokohama City Guide with detailed maps of Yokohama's most important neighbourhoods. It's directly outside the northern exit of Sakuragi-chō Station.

Post office A block east of the Sakuragi-chō Station.

Sights & Activities
MINATO MIRAI 21 みなとみらい 21
This new development (the '21' stands for '21st century') just north of Sakuragi-chō Station is another Japanese excursion into the metropolis-of-the-future theme. One of the highlights is the new **Landmark Tower**, which not only is the tallest building in Japan, but also has the world's fastest lift (45km/h). The **Landmark Tower Sky Garden** (admission ¥1000; ⏰ 10am-9pm Sep-Jun, 10am-10pm Jul & Aug) observatory is on the 69th floor.

Across from Landmark Tower you'll find the interesting **Yokohama Maritime Museum** and the **Nippon Maru sailing ship** (☎ 221-0280; 2-1-1 Minato Mirai; admission to both ¥600; ⏰ 10am-6.30pm Tue-Sun Jul-Aug, 10am-4.30pm Tue-Sun Sep-Jun). Beyond the Maritime Museum is **Cosmo World** (☎ 641-6591; 2-8-1 Shinkō; ⏰ 11am-9pm Mon-Fri, 11am-10pm Sat & Sun) amusement park, where the price varies according to the ride. The best part of Cosmo World is the **Cosmo Clock Ferris Wheel** (admission ¥700; ⏰ 11am-9pm Mon-Fri, 11am-10pm Sat & Sun), the world's highest at 105m. Northeast of Landmark Tower, and next along from Queen's Square, is the dramatic, sail-shaped **Pacifico Yokohama** complex, housing the National Convention Hall of Yokohama and the Yokohama Grand Intercontinental Hotel.

Behind Landmark Tower, you'll find the **Yokohama Museum of Art** (☎ 221-0306; 3-4-1 Minato Mirai; admission ¥500; ⏰ 10am-6pm Fri-Wed), which has a decent collection of modern art. Perhaps more exciting than the art on display

AROUND TOKYO

YOKOHAMA

0 _____ 500 m
0 _____ 0.3 miles

INFORMATION	
Aními アニミ	1 A1
Chinatown 80 Information Center	
横浜中華街80	2 D4
Minato Mirai 21 Information Center	
みなとみらい21	3 B2
Post Office 郵便局	4 B2

SIGHTS & ACTIVITIES	
Cosmo World	
横浜コスモワールド	5 B1
Kantei-byō 関帝廟	6 D4
Landmark Tower	
ランドマークタワー	7 B1
Marine Tower マリンタワー	8 E4
Minato Mirai 21 みなとみらい21	9 B1
Mitsubishi Minato Mirai Industrial Museum	
三菱みなとみらい技術館	10 A1
Nippon Maru Sailing Ship 日本丸	11 B1
Pacífico Yokohama	
パシフィコ横浜	12 B1
Silk Museum シルク博物館	13 D3
Yokohama Archives of History	
横浜開港資料館	14 C3
Yokohama Customs House	
横浜税関	15 C3
Yokohama Daisekai 横浜大世界	16 D4

SLEEPING 🏠	
Hotel New Grand	
ホテルニューグランド	19 D3
Kanagawa Youth Hostel	
神奈川ユースホステル	20 A2
Pan Pacific Hotel Yokohama	
パンパシフィック ホテル横浜..	21 B1
San-ai Yokohama Hotel	
三愛ヨコハマホテル	22 A2
Star Hotel Yokohama	
スターホテル横浜	23 D4
Toyoko Inn Sutajum-mae Honkan	
東横インスタジアム前本館	24 C4
Yokohama Isezakichō Washington Hotel	
横浜伊勢佐木町	
ワシントンホテル	25 B4
Yokohama Royal Park Hotel Nikkō	
横浜ロイヤルパーク	26 B1

Yokohama Maritime Museum	
横浜マリタイム ミュージアム..	17 B2
Yokohama Museum of Art	
横浜美術館	18 A1

EATING 🍴	
Baikotei 梅香亭	27 C3
Heichinrō Honten 聘珍楼本店	28 D4
Manchinrō Honten 萬珍楼本店	29 D4
Su-Rosaikan 四五六菜館	30 C4

DRINKING 🍸	
Gaspanic Yokohama	31 A1
Peace	32 C4
Rockwells	33 C4
Sirius ホテルニッコン	(see 26)
Windjammer ウインドジャマー	34 C4

SHOPPING 🛍	
Queen's Square Yokohama	
クイーンズ スクエア	(see 21)
Yokohama World Porters 横浜ワールド	
ポーターズ (みなとみらい)	35 C2

To Tokyo (30km)
To Yokohama Station (450m)
Shin-Yokohama Station (4km)
Shin-Yokohama Ramen
Hakubutsukan (4.5km)

To Yokohama Station

To Yokohama
Heli Cruising (200m)

Sea Bass

To Daikoku Pier (3.7km)

To Yokohama Bay Bridge (3km)

To Yokosuka (18km)

To Sankei-en (3km)

Sakuragi-chō
Takashima-chō
Minato Mirai
Bashamichi
Kannai
Isezakichōjamachi
Hinodechō
Nihon Ōdori
Yokohama-kōen
Motomachi-Chūkagai
Chinatown
Yokohama Stadium

Tokyo-wan

Gambandari Pier (South Pier)

Nippon-Maru Memorial Park

Hikawa Maru

Yamashita Pier

Harbour View Park

Foreigners' Cemetery

To Chōja-machi (500m)
To Yamate Jūban-kan (100m)

is the Tange Kenzō–designed building, particularly the dramatic main hall. Nearby, the **Mitsubishi Minato Mirai Industrial Museum** (☎ 224-9031; 3-3-1 Minato Mirai; adult/child ¥500/200; ☺ 10am-5.30pm Tue-Sun) is one of Japan's better science and technology museums, with a wildly enjoyable helicopter simulator, along with lots of other good hands-on exhibits.

For a less-simulated airborne adventure, take a helicopter tour of Yokohama. **Yokohama Heli Cruising** (横浜ヘリクルージング; ☎ 223-1155; 5-min/10-min flight ¥4000/12,500; ☺ Fri-Sun) offers short but exhilarating flights from their heliport in Rinko Park, a seven-minute walk northeast of Queen's Square. Flights depart around sunset.

YAMASHITA-KŌEN AREA 山下公園周辺
This area, east of Kannai Station, is traditionally Yokohama's sightseeing district. At the heart of it all is the seafront Yamashita-kōen. Moored alongside the park you'll find the **Hikawa Maru** (☎ 641-4362; adult/child ¥800/400; ☺ 9.30am-7pm winter, 9.30am-8pm rest of year), a retired luxury passenger liner that's a lot of fun for the kids.

Across the street is the **Silk Museum** (☎ 641-0841; 1 Yamashita-kōen-dōri; admission ¥300; ☺ 9am-4.30pm Tue-Sun), which covers all aspects of silk and silk production and has some lovely kimono and obi (sashes) on display. Well worth visiting is the nearby **Yokohama Archives of History** (☎ 201-2100; 3 Nihon-Ō-dōri; admission ¥200; ☺ 9.30am-5pm Tue-Sun), with displays (in English) that chronicle Yokohama's history, from the opening of Japan (via Yokohama) in the 1850s to the mid-20th century.

Back in a southeasterly direction, you'll find the **Marine Tower** (☎ 641-7838; 15 Yamashita-kōen-dōri; admission ¥700; ☺ 10am-7pm winter, 10am-9pm rest of year) offering a diminutive (106m) view over the harbour. **Bike rental** (☎ 641-7838; per 2hr ¥300) is available in front. Other attractions relatively nearby include **Harbour View Park** and the **Foreigners' Cemetery**, the final resting place of 4000 foreign residents and visitors to Yokohama – a look at some of the headstones reveals some fascinating inscriptions.

CHINATOWN 中華街
Not far from the harbour area is Chinatown (known as 'Chūkagai' in Japanese). This is one of Yokohama's greatest tourist attractions and the narrow streets are often packed with visitors who come to ogle the over-the-top Chinese façades of the neighbourhood's stores and restaurants. Needless to say, food is the main attraction here, but be warned that prices are high.

The eight-storey **Yokohama Daisekai** (☎ 681-5588; 3 Minami-mon; admission ¥500; ☺ 10am-8pm) is something of a Chinese theme park, modelling itself on the gilded age of Shanghai of the '20s and '30s. In addition to displays of Chinese silks, carved boxes and other crafts, attractions include 10-minute theatre shows, three floors of restaurants and several souvenir shops. To beat the crowds, avoid coming on weekends. Chinese opera, jazz and other performances are held here throughout the year. Stop in to see what's on.

A few blocks away stands **Kantei-byō**, a Chinese temple in the heart of the district.

SANKEI-EN 三渓園
Opened to the public in 1906, the beautifully landscaped gardens of **Sankei-en** (☎ 621-0634; www.sankeien.or.jp; 58-1 Honmoku-sannotani; admission ¥500; ☺ 9am-5pm, closed 29-31 Dec) feature walking paths among ponds, 17th-century buildings, several fine tea-ceremony houses and a 500-year-old, three-storey pagoda. The inner garden is a fine example of traditional Japanese garden landscaping. From Yokohama or Sakuragi-chō Station, take the No 8 bus to Honmoku Sankei-en-mae bus stop (10 minutes). Alternatively, take a JR Negishi-line train from Sakuragi-chō to Negishi Station and change to a city bus at Bus Stop No 1 (take bus No 58, 99, 101, 108 or 126). Get off at the Honmoku stop (35 minutes), from which it's an easy seven-minute walk to the southern entrance of the park.

SHIN-YOKOHAMA STATION AREA
新横浜駅周辺
Near Shin-Yokohama Station, this noodle-lover's paradise, **Shin-Yokohama Rāmen Hakubutsukan** (☎ 471-0503; www.raumen.co.jp/English; 2-14-21 Shinyokohama; admission/meals ¥300/900; ☺ 11am-11pm), is a kind of *rāmen* theme park that tells the history of the cuisine – and *rāmen* houses – in a replica of a 1958 Shitamachi (downtown district). Most enjoyable of all are the nine regional *rāmen* shops, where you can sample some excellent bowls. *Sumire* is the long-standing favourite. It's a five-minute walk east from Shin-Yokohama Station; turn left after the co-op, and right at the Family Mart convenience store. It is clearly signposted in

English and Chinese. Expect long lines if arriving on public holidays.

Sleeping

With a few exceptions, prices are generally high in Yokohama. The city's top hotels lie in the Minato Mirai 21 area.

Echigoya Ryokan (☎ 641-4700; 1-14 Ishikawa-chō; s/d from ¥5500/9000) In the heart of the stylish Motomachi shopping district, Echigoya is one of Yokohama's most charming digs. Tatami rooms are spacious and comfortable if a bit elderly. From the Ishikawa-cho Station's south exit walk to the right down Motomachi-dōri. Go two blocks and Echigoya will be on your right on the 2nd floor. Reserve well in advance.

Toyoko Inn Sutajium-mae Honkan (☎ 664-1045; www.toyoko-inn.com/eng; Osanbashi-dōri; s/d ¥7140/9240) This simple but nicely outfitted business hotel has small, comfortable rooms with decent lighting. From JR Kannai Station's south exit, walk along the main road towards the stadium, and take the first left after passing the stadium. It's two blocks further.

San-ai Yokohama Hotel (☎ 242-4411; 3-95 Hanasaki-cho; s/d from ¥7875/12,600) San-ai has small, comfortable rooms set on a quiet street. Bigger discounts often given on weekdays. From the west side of Sakuragi-chō JR Station, cross the busy road heading southeast, go three short blocks and take a right. After 80m, turn to the left and you'll see the hotel.

Yokohama Isezakichō Washington Hotel (☎ 243-7111; www.wh-rsv.com; 5-33 Choja-machi; s/d/tw from ¥9200/16,300/18,700) You'll find clean, comfortable rooms at this hotel facing Isezakichōjamachi metro station. A lounge and a restaurant with fine views are on hand.

Star Hotel Yokohama (☎ 651-3111; 11 Yamashita-kōen-dōri; d from ¥15,750) The least expensive of the harbourfront hotels facing Yamashita-kōen has excellent rooms; most are spacious with great views. Rooftop bar opens in the summer.

Hotel New Grand (☎ 681-1841; 10 Yamashita-kōen-dōri; s/tw Mon-Fri from ¥12,000/20,000, Sat & Sun from ¥20,000/29,000) This 260-room hotel has a prime waterfront location, and was once a favourite of visiting foreign dignitaries. Now it is simply a classy, upmarket option with some old-world charm, despite its 1992 modernisation. From Motomachi Station, walk two blocks northwest along Honcho-dōri, take a right, go two blocks and you'll see it on the right.

Yokohama Royal Park Hotel Nikkō (☎ 221-1111; www.yrph.com; 2-2-1-3 Minato Mirai; s/tw/d from ¥29,000/34,000/34,000) This hotel has the best location, on the upper floors of Landmark Tower. Watch out for their frequent cut-price deals for women travellers.

Pan Pacific Hotel Yokohama (☎ 682-2222; www.panpacific.com; 2-3-7 Minato Mirai; d from ¥30,000) In the Queen's Square Yokohama complex, this stylish hotel boasts superbly furnished rooms, all with balconies and excellent views. Several good but pricey restaurants inside. Check the website for discounted rates.

Kanagawa Youth Hostel (☎ 241-6503; 1 Momijigaoka; dm Sep-May ¥2800, Jun-Aug ¥2980) This well-worn hostel has an institutional feel and grumpy management. It is the cheapest place in town, however. From the west side of Sakuragi-chō JR station, take a right, walk back along the tracks (and graffiti-covered wall), take the first left, go over the bridge and you'll see it further on the right. Check-in is from 5pm; curfew 11pm.

Eating

In Yokohama, the done thing is to have a bang-up dinner in Chinatown. Plan on spending about ¥5000 per head for a good dinner and perhaps half that for lunch. Most places offer set courses. For an eclectic mix of cuisines visit the restaurant floors of Landmark Plaza and Queen's Square.

Yokohama Daisekai (☎ 681-5588; 3 Minami-mon; mains from ¥900; ⏰ 10am-10pm) On the 2nd, 3rd and 4th floors of the Yokohama Daisekai, you'll find nearly a dozen speciality Chinese restaurants allowing visitors to try many tasty regional dishes.

Manchinrō Honten (☎ 681-4004; 153 Yamashita-chō; dinner for 2 ¥8400; ⏰ 11am-10pm Tue-Sun) One of Chinatown's oldest and most popular Cantonese restaurants, Manchinrō serves delicacies prepared by a respected Hong Kong chef.

Heichinrō Honten (☎ 681-3001; 149 Yamashita-chō; lunch/dinner course ¥3000/5000; ⏰ 11am-10.15pm) Neck and neck with Manchinrō, the equally elegant Heichinrō is another Cantonese favourite, serving excellent fare with a wide variety of dim sum. Large picture menu.

Su-Rosaikan (☎ 641-4569; 202 Yamashita-chō; mains from ¥1000; ⏰ 11.30am-10pm Mon-Thu, 11am-11pm Fri-Sun) This low-key Chinese restaurant serves up delicious bowls of *rāmen*, dim sum and noodle dishes. Picture menu.

Baikōtei (☎ 681-4870; 1-1 Aioicho; mains around ¥1000; ☯ 11am-9pm Mon-Sat) This weathered classic is famed for its Hayashi rice, and serves a mean *katsu-don* as well. Look out for the sign that announces Baikō Emmies: English Spoken. It is very near Yokohama-kōen.

Yamate Jūban-kan (☎ 621-4466; 247 Yamatechō; mains from ¥2000; ☯ 11am-9pm) Overlooking the Foreigners' Cemetery on the hill above Motomachi-Chūkagai Station, this French restaurant serves consistently good cuisine. A casual café occupies the 1st floor, while upstairs is the classic restaurant, dishing out longstanding favourites – like the Kaika steak set. Reservations recommended.

Drinking & Entertainment

There is plenty to do in Yokohama in the evening. Many of the city's bars are on the outskirts of Chinatown.

Peace (☎ 650-2200; Osanbashi-dōri; mains around ¥1000; ☯ 11am-2am Sun-Thu, 11am-4am Fri & Sat) This stylish bistro and lounge attracts a young, attractive crowd. Peace has an extensive cocktail menu and decent food, with live music some nights. It's facing the Yokohama stadium.

Windjammer (☎ 662-3966; 215 Yamashitachō; live music cover ¥300-500, drinks from ¥900; ☯ 6pm-1.30am) This nautically inspired bar serves up potent cocktails and occasional live jazz.

Rockwells (☎ 641-6950; 2-14 Minami Saiwai-chō; beers from ¥800, pub food ¥1200; ☯ 6pm-1am) One of several British-style pubs in the area, Rockwells has the usual beers on tap and a good selection of pub food.

Gaspanic Yokohama (☎ 680-0291; 4-8-1 Minato Mirai; ☯ 6pm-midnight Sun-Wed, 6pm-5am Thu-Sat) A branch of the Roppongi cheap-booze, cheap-thrills emporium, this place peddles it: gas and panic in Minato Mirai. Drinks are ¥300 until 9.30pm every day, and on Thursday, all night. The results are not hard to imagine.

Sirius (2-2-1-3 Minato Mirai; drinks from ¥1000; ☯ 5pm-1am) This bar, on the 70th floor of Landmark Tower, is an elegant cocktail lounge in the Yokohama Royal Park Hotel Nikkō. The place to go for drinks with a view.

Shopping

Near Cosmo World, **Yokohama World Porters** is a huge shopping complex with lots of restaurants on the ground floor. Northeast of Landmark Tower is **Queen's Square Yokohama**, yet another shopping and dining complex.

You can sometimes catch street performances out the front. Other good places to lighten your wallet include the shopping strips of Moto-machi and Isezaki-cho.

Getting There & Away

There are numerous trains from Tokyo – the cheapest being the Tōkyū Tōyoko line from Shibuya Station to Sakuragi-chō Station (*futsū/kyūkō* ¥290, 44/37 minutes). Trains stop at Yokohama Station on the way to Sakuragi-chō Station.

The Keihin Tōhoku line goes through Yokohama Station (¥450, 40 minutes) to Kannai Station (¥480, 47 minutes) from Tokyo and Shinagawa Stations. The Tōkaidō line from Tokyo or Shinagawa Stations also runs to Yokohama Station (¥450, 25 minutes).

To Kamakura, you take the Yokosuka line from Yokohama Station (¥380, 25 minutes). The Tōkaidō *shinkansen* stops at Shin-Yokohama Station, a fair way to the northwest of town, on its way between Tokyo and the Kansai region. Shin-Yokohama Station is connected to Yokohama, Sakuragi-chō and Kannai Stations by the Yokohama line and by a less convenient subway line.

Getting Around

TO/FROM THE AIRPORT

Trains and buses connect Narita to Yokohama; take the train to be sure of arriving at a particular time. Trains run from Yokohama Station. You can choose Narita Express (N'EX) services (¥4180, 1½ hours) or JR Airport Narita services (¥1890, two hours). Limousine buses travel frequently between the Yokohama City Air Terminal (YCAT, in the Sky Building east of Yokohama Station, next to Sogō department store) and Narita (¥3500, about two hours).

BOAT

The **Sea Bass ferry** (☎ 661-0347) connects Yokohama Station, the Minato Mirai 21 complex and Yamashita-kōen. Boats run between 10am and 7.30pm. The full fare from Yokohama Station to Yamashita-kōen is ¥600; the trip takes 20 minutes.

BUS

Although trains are more convenient for getting around town, Yokohama does have an extensive bus network. To travel within the city, you pay a flat fee of ¥210.

KAMAKURA 鎌倉
☎ 0467

The capital of Japan from 1185 to 1333, Kamakura rivals Nikkō as the most culturally rewarding day trip from Tokyo and has a huge number of Buddhist temples and the occasional shrine dotted around the surrounding countryside. If you start early you can cover a lot of ground in a day, but two days will also allow you to visit the temples of East Kamakura and take some nice walks. The town itself is small and pleasant and makes a fine base. Although Kamakura gets packed on weekends and in holiday periods, midweek can be very peaceful in the outlying temples.

History

In the 10th century, the power of the emperor in Kyoto was largely ceremonial; real power had for some time rested in the hands of the Fujiwara clan. As the power of the Fujiwara declined, the Taira clan, led by Taira Kiyomori, and the Minamoto clan, led by Minamoto Yoshitomo, began an all-out struggle for supreme power. In 1159 the Taira routed the Minamoto forces.

Although many executions followed, by chance Yoshitomo's third son's life was spared and the boy was sent to live in an Izu-hantō temple. As soon as the boy, Minamoto Yoritomo, was old enough, he began to gather support for a counterattack on his clan's old rivals. In 1180 he set up his base at Kamakura, far away from the debilitating influences of Kyoto court life, close to other clans loyal to the Minamoto and, having the sea on one side and densely wooded hills on the others, easy to defend.

With a series of victories over the Taira behind him, Minamoto Yoritomo was appointed shōgun in 1192; he governed Japan from Kamakura. When he died without an heir power passed to the Hōjō, the family of Yoritomo's wife.

The Hōjō clan ruled Japan from Kamakura for more than a century until, in 1333, weakened by the cost of maintaining defences against threats of attack from Kublai Khan in China, the Hōjō clan was defeated by Emperor Go-Daigo. Kyoto once again became the capital.

Orientation

Kamakura's main attractions can be covered on foot, augmented by the occasional bus ride. Cycling is also practical (p197). Most temples are signposted in English and Japanese. You can start at Kamakura Station and travel around the area in a circle, or start north of Kamakura at Kita-Kamakura Station and visit the temples between there and Kamakura on foot. The itinerary in this section follows the latter route.

Information

Kamakura Tourist Information Center (☎ 22-3350; ◷ 9am-5.30pm) Just outside Kamakura Station's east exit, this helpful office distributes maps and brochures, and can book accommodation.
Post Office (1-10-3 Komachi; ◷ 9am-7pm Mon-Fri, 9am-3pm Sat) With ATMs.

Sights & Activities

ENGAKU-JI 円覚寺
Engaku-ji (☎ 22-0487; admission ¥200; ◷ 8am-5pm Apr-Sep, 8am-4pm Oct-Mar) is on the left as you exit Kita-Kamakura Station. It is one of the five main Rinzai Zen temples in Kamakura. Engaku-ji was founded in 1282, allegedly as a place where Zen monks might pray for soldiers who lost their lives defending Japan against the second of Kublai Khan's invasion attempts. Today the only real reminder of the temple's former magnificence and antiquity is **San-mon**, a 1780 reconstruction. At the top of the long flight of stairs through the gate is the **Engaku-ji bell**, which was cast in 1301 and is the largest bell in Kamakura. The **Hondō** (Main Hall) inside San-mon is a recent reconstruction, dating from the mid-1960s.

TŌKEI-JI 東慶寺
Tōkei-ji (admission ¥100; ◷ 8.30am-5pm Mar-Oct, 8.30am-4pm Nov-Feb), across the railway tracks from Engaku-ji, is notable for its lush grounds as much as for the temple itself. On weekdays, when visitors are few, it can be a pleasantly relaxing place.

Historically, the temple is famed as having served as a women's refuge. A woman could be officially recognised as divorced after three years as a nun in the temple precincts. Today there are no nuns; the grave of the last abbess can be found in the cemetery, shrouded by cypress trees.

JŌCHI-JI 浄智寺
A couple of minutes further on from Tōkei-ji is **Jōchi-ji** (admission ¥150; ◷ 9am-4.30pm), another temple with pleasant grounds. Founded in

1283, this is considered one of Kamakura's five great Zen temples.

DAIBUTSU HIKING COURSE

If time permits, consider taking the Daibutsu Hiking Course, which begins at the steps just up the lane from Jōchi-ji and follows a woodland path for 3km to the Daibutsu. Along the course you'll pass the small **shrine of Kuzuharaoka-jinja**, from which you'll see signs to the landscaped park of **Genjiyama-kōen**. From here, head down the stairs, keep

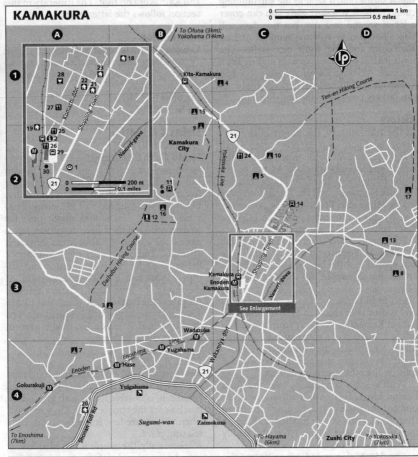

KAMAKURA

To Ōfuna (3km); Yokohama (14km)

Kita-Kamakura

Kamakura City

Ten-en Hiking Course

Daibutsu Hiking Course

Kamakura Enoden Kamakura

See Enlargement

Wadazuka

Yugahama

Hase

Gokurakuji

Yuigahama

Sugami-wan

Zaimokuza

To Enoshima (7km)

To Hayama (6km)　Zushi City　To Yokosuka (7km)

going down the hill and take a right to reach **Zeniarai Benten**, one of Kamakura's more unusual shrines. A cavelike entrance leads to a shrine where visitors come to bathe their money in the natural spring with the hope of bringing good fortune. You can either return back up the steps to the path or continue down the paved road, turning right at the first intersection, walking along a path lined with cryptomeria and ascending up through the shrine of **Sasuke-inari jinja** before meeting up with the Daibutsu path once again. In total it takes about 90 minutes to complete the hike.

KENCHO-JI & TEN-EN HIKING COURSE

Continuing towards Kamakura along the main road from Jōchi-ji, on the left you'll pass the turn-off to **Kenchō-ji** (建長寺; admission ¥300; 🕒 8.30am-4.30pm), the first-ranked of the five great Zen temples. Founded in 1253, Kenchō-ji once comprised seven buildings and 49 subtemples, most of which were destroyed in the fires of the 14th and 15th centuries. However the 17th and 18th centuries saw its restoration, and you can still get a sense of its splendour. Today, Kencho-ji functions as a working monastery. Among the highlights are the **Butsuden** (Buddha hall), brought piece by piece from Kyoto; the painstakingly landscaped Zen garden, shaped like the kanji for 'mind'; and the juniper grove, believed to have sprouted from seeds brought from China by Kencho-ji's founder some seven centuries ago.

Another excellent walk through the countryside begins by walking around the **Hojo** (main hall) and up the steps to the entrance of the **Ten-en Hiking Course**. From here it's a two-hour walk to Zuisen-ji, along one of the most scenic spots in Kanagawa; those with less time can take a shorter (80-minute) trail to Kamakura-gū.

ENNŌ-JI 円応寺

Across the road from Kenchō-ji is **Ennō-ji** (admission ¥200; 🕒 9am-3.30pm Nov-Mar, 9am-4pm Apr-Oct), which is distinguished primarily by its collection of statues depicting the judges of hell. Presiding over them is Emma, an ancient Hindu deity known in Sanskrit as Yama. The ideas of hell and judgement became important Buddhist concepts with the rise of the Jōdo (Pure Land) school (see p45).

TSURUGAOKA HACHIMAN-GŪ 鶴岡八幡宮

Further down the road, where it turns towards Kamakura Station, is **Tsurugaoka Hachiman-gū** (admission free; 🕒 9am-4pm), the main shrine of Kamakura. It was founded by Minamoto Yoriyoshi, of the same Minamoto clan that ruled Japan from Kamakura (see p34). There is some debate as to whether Hachiman, the deity to which the shrine is dedicated, has always been regarded as the god of war; the construction of this shrine may simply be a reflection of the fact that Hachiman is also the guardian deity of the Minamoto clan. Whatever the case, this Shintō shrine presents the visitor with an atmosphere drastically different to the repose of the Zen temples clustered around Kita-Kamakura Station.

DAIBUTSU 大仏

The Kamakura **Daibutsu** (Great Buddha; admission ¥200; 🕒 7am-6pm Mar-Nov, 7am-5pm Dec-Feb) was completed in 1252 and is Kamakura's most famous sight. Once housed in a huge hall, today the statue sits in the open, its home having been washed away by a tsunami in 1495. Cast in bronze and weighing close to 850 tonnes, the statue is 11.4m tall. Its construction is said to have been inspired by Yoritomo's visit to Nara (where there is another, even bigger, *daibutsu*) after the Minamoto clan's victory over the rival Taira clan. Even though Kamakura's Daibutsu doesn't quite match Nara's in stature, it is commonly agreed that it is artistically superior.

The Buddha itself is the Amida Buddha (*amitābha* in Sanskrit), worshipped by the followers of the Jōdo school as a figure of salvation.

Buses from stop No 2, 7 or 10 in front of Kamakura Station run to the Daibutsu-mae stop. Alternatively, take the Enoden Enoshima line to Hase Station and walk north for 10 minutes. Better yet, take the Daibutsu hiking course.

HASE-DERA 長谷寺

Not far from the Daibutsu-mae bus stop is the temple, **Hase-dera** (admission ¥300; 🕒 8am-5.30pm Mar-Sep, 8am-4.30pm Oct-Feb), also known as Hase Kannon-ji. The grounds have a garden and an interesting collection of statues of Jizō, the patron saint of travellers and the souls of departed children.

Ranked like a small army of urchins, the statues are clothed to keep them warm, by women who have lost children through abortion or miscarriage. The main point of interest in the grounds, however, is the Kannon statue.

Kannon (*avalokiteshvara* in Sanskrit), the goddess of mercy, is the Bodhisattva of infinite compassion and, along with Jizō, is one of Japan's most popular Buddhist deities. This 9m-high carved wooden *jūichimen* (11-faced Kannon) is believed to date from the 8th century. The 11 faces are actually one primary face and 10 secondary faces, the latter representing the 10 stages of enlightenment. It is said that the 11 faces allow Kannon, ever vigilant for those in need of her assistance, to cast an eye in every direction.

OTHER SHRINES & TEMPLES

If you're still in the mood for temples, there are plenty more in and around Kamakura, which has somewhere in the vicinity of 70 temples and shrines.

From the Daibutsu it is best to return to Kita-Kamakura Station by bus and take another bus out to the temples in the eastern part of town. These have the advantage of being even less popular with tourists than the temples in Kita-Kamakura; they may lack the grandeur of some of Kamakura's more famous temples, but they more than make up for this with their charm. There is also a delightfully restful villagelike atmosphere in the town's outer fringes.

The grounds of this secluded Zen temple, **Zuisen-ji** (☎ 22-1191; admission ¥100; 9am-5pm) make for a pleasant stroll and include Zen gardens laid out by Kokushi Musō, the temple's founder. It is possible to get there from the Egara Ten-jin shrine on foot in about 10 to 15 minutes; turn right where the bus turns left in front of the shrine, take the next left and keep following the road. From Zuisen-ji you can access the Ten-en Hiking Course.

This interesting little temple, **Sugimoto-dera** (☎ 22-3463; admission ¥200; 8am-4.30pm) founded in 734, is reputed to be the oldest in Kamakura. Its ferocious-looking guardian deities and a statue of Kannon are its main draw. Take a bus from stop No 5 in front of Kamakura Station to the Sugimoto Kannon bus stop.

Down the road (away from Kamakura Station) from Sugimoto-dera, on the right-hand side, **Hōkoku-ji** (☎ 22-0762; admission ¥200; 9am-4pm) is a Rinzai Zen temple with quiet, landscaped gardens where you can relax under a red parasol with a cup of Japanese tea. This is also one of the more active Zen temples in Kamakura, regularly holding *zazen* (Soto-school meditation) classes for beginners. Take bus No 23, 24 or 36 from Kamakura Station (¥190, five minutes).

Festivals & Events

Bonbori Matsuri (7–9 August) During this festival, hundreds of lanterns are strung up around Tsurugaoka Hachiman-gū.

Hachiman-gū Matsuri (14–16 September) Festivities include a procession of mikoshi (portable shrines) and, on the last day, a display of horseback archery.

Kamakura Matsuri A week of celebrations held from the second Sunday to the third Sunday in April. It includes a wide range of activities, most of which are centred on Tsurugaoka Hachiman-gū.

Sleeping

Hotel New Kamakura (☎ 22-2230; s/d from ¥7000/ 10,000) This friendly new hotel near the station has cheery rooms with large windows, dark wood floors and comfortable furnishings. Western- and Japanese-style rooms available. From Kamakura Station, take the west exit, and a sharp right down the alley. Turn left at the 'Motor Pool' sign and inquire of the parking attendant about rooms. Reservations recommended.

Komachi-sō (☎ 23-2151; s/tw ¥5000/9000) This pleasant and affordable *minshuku* offers decent rooms and a good breakfast at ¥1000. It's located on a narrow lane parallel to Wakamiya-dōri, just behind the back entrance to the Kamakura Marriage Avenue Hotel. Check-in is from 4pm.

Kamakura Marriage Avenue (☎ 25-6363; s/d ¥8400/15,750) Also known by its old moniker Tsurugaoka Kaikan, this recently renovated hotel boasts some fine rooms – Western- and Japanese-style – as well as a lobby aglow with early '80s glam. Check-in is from 2.30pm.

Ajisai (☎ 22-3492; r per person from ¥6830) Ajisai is an affordable option with decent Western-style rooms. For views of the shrine, book a room on the 4th floor. Located on Wakamiya-dōri, 50m the from entrance to Tsurugaoka-Hachiman-gū. Check-in is from 3pm.

Shangri La Tsurugaoka (☎ 25-6363; s/tw ¥6825/13,650) Shangri La it ain't – just a handily placed business hotel. Check-in is from 3pm.

Kamakura Kagetsuen Youth Hostel (☎ 25-1238; dm/s/d ¥3308/7300/10,400) Set right on the beach, this hostel boasts good ocean views from its Western- and Japanese-style rooms. From Kamakura Station take an Enoden Enoshima train to Hase Station. Turn left out of the station, walk down to the seafront road and take a right, heading west for about 10 minutes. The hostel is inside the Kagestuen Hotel. Check-in is from 4pm.

Eating & Drinking

Komachi-dōri shopping street is lined with restaurants, and the main road to Tsurugaoka Hachiman-gū is another fine culinary haunt. Both streets run northeast from the station.

Komachi-Ichiba (☎ 24-7921; lunch/dinner from ¥980/1700; ⏲ 11.30am-2.30pm & 4pm-10.30pm) Offering tasty, fresh seafood sets, Komachi-Ichiba is excellent value. It is on the 2nd floor of the station building, above the information centre. Its sister operation, a tempura shop next door, shares the same kitchen and same hours.

Kawagoe-ya (☎ 24-2580; meals around ¥1200; ⏲ 11am-8pm Fri-Wed) Specialising in Kyoto-style *soba*, this stylish place is to the left of Kamakura Station's east exit, in the basement below McDonald's.

T-Side (☎ 24-9572; sets from ¥2100; ⏲ 11am-9.30pm) For a taste of India, head to this Bollywoodesque restaurant two blocks from the station. A wide-ranging menu includes steamed dumplings, tandoori chicken and other Indian specialities. It's on the 2nd floor of a building on Komachi-dōri, with an English sign out the front.

Chaya Kado (☎ 23-1673; mains from ¥800; ⏲ 10am-5pm) Up in Kita-Kamakura, this *soba* shop serves tasty sets like tempura and *oden gozen*, which contains various morsels simmered in a rich broth. It's off the main road; when heading north, take a left after passing Kencho-ji.

Milk Hall (☎ 22-1179; ⏲ 11am-10.30pm) This quaint café/bar/antique store makes a fine setting for coffee or a cocktail, featuring live jazz some nights. From Kamakura Station's east exit, head two blocks down Komachi-dōri, take a left, and then another left down the first alley.

Getting There & Away

Yokosuka line trains run to Kamakura from Tokyo (¥890, 56 minutes), Shimbashi and Shinagawa Stations. It's also possible to catch a train from Yokohama (¥330, 27 minutes) on the Yokosuka line. If you're planning to get off at Kita-Kamakura Station, it's the stop after Ōfuna.

It's possible to continue on to Enoshima from Kamakura, either via the Enoden Enoshima line from Kamakura Station (¥250, 25 minutes) or by bus from stop No 9 in front of Kamakura Station (¥300, 35 minutes).

The **JR Kamakura-Enoshima Free Pass**, valid for two days, covers the trip to and from Tokyo, and allows unlimited use of JR trains around Kamakura, the Shōnan monorail between Ōfuna and Enoshima, and the Enoden Enoshima line between Fujisawa and Enoshima. From Tokyo Station the pass costs ¥1970; from Yokohama Station ¥1130.

Getting Around

You can walk to most temples from Kamakura or Kita-Kamakura Station. Sites in the west, like the Daibutsu, can be reached via the Enoden Enoshima line from Kamakura Station. Alternatively, you can take buses from Kamakura Station. Bus trips around the area cost either ¥170 or ¥190. Another good option is renting a bicycle; **Rental Cycles** (☎ 24-2319; per hr/day ¥500/1500; ⏲ 8.30am-5pm) is outside the east exit of Kamakura Station, and right up the incline.

EAST OF TOKYO

Much of Chiba-ken, to the east and southeast of Tokyo, is suburbia. There are few compelling reasons to visit the area. However, most visitors to Japan arrive or depart from Narita airport, and the town is a fine prelude to Japan.

NARITA 成田

☎ 0476 / pop 97,421

Narita is a pleasant town, with a traditional atmosphere among its quiet streets. At the centre of town is a lovely temple, with lush gardens adjoining it – perfect for unwinding before or after a long flight.

You can pick up a copy of the Narita map/pamphlet at the **Narita Tourist Information Center** (☎ 24-3198; ⏲ 8.30am-5.15pm) just outside the eastern exit of JR Narita Station. You might also stop by the **Narita Tourist Pavilion** (☎ 24-3232; Omotesandō; ⊙ 10am-5pm Tue-Sun) to see its exhibits on Narita's history. Either office can book accommodation.

Both the Keisei Narita and the JR Narita Stations are within a block of Omotesandō, a pleasant street lined with restaurants and shops that leads directly to Narita-san-kōen and Shinshōji.

Sights & Activities

The town's centrepiece is the impressive **Narita-san Shinshō-ji** (成田山新勝寺) and its attractive grounds, **Narita-san-kōen** (成田山公園). While the temple was founded some 1000 years ago, the main hall is a 1968 reconstruction. The temple itself remains an important centre of the Shingon sect of Buddhism and attracts as many as 10 million visitors a year. Entrance is allowed until 3.30pm.

In Narita-san-kōen, you'll find the **Narita-san Calligraphy Museum** (☎ 24-0774; admission ¥500; ⊙ 9am-4pm Tue-Sun), which has a good collection of *shodō* (calligraphy) for real aficionados. The **Reikōkan Historical Material Museum** (☎ 22-0234; admission ¥300; ⊙ 9am-4pm Tue-Sun), under the temple's upper pagoda, and its nearby annex house a collection of artefacts from 18th-century Japanese life and various temple treasures – again, probably of interest only to real aficionados. Even if you skip both of these attractions, be sure to stroll along the ponds at the eastern edge of the park.

Festivals & Events

Gion Festival (held for three days at the beginning of July) Narita's most spectacular festival is the 300-year-old Gion, featuring colourful floats and costumed processions.
Setsubun (last day of winter in the Japanese lunar calendar) Another notable festival in Narita-san Shinshō-ji, which falls on 3 or 4 February.
Hatsumōde (First Shrine Visit; 1 January) Things get hectic at the temple on Hatsumōde and Setsubun, so a high level of crowd-tolerance is a must.

Sleeping

Narita is a pleasant place to stay and a good choice for those with early flights or for arriving visitors seeking a gentler transition to Japan than the Tokyo experience.

Ohgiya Ryokan (扇屋旅館; ☎ 22-1161; www .naritakanko.jp/ohgiya; s/d without bath ¥6300/10,500, s/d with bath ¥7350/13,650) This friendly Japanese inn has comfortable rooms, seven of which open onto the lovely garden. It's a 10-minute walk from JR Narita or Keisei Narita Stations, up Omotesandō towards the temple, but forking to the left just before the tourist pavilion. It's 200m further on the left. Check-in is from 3pm.

Kirinoya Ryokan (桐の屋旅館; ☎ 22-0724; www.root.or.jp/kirinoya; s/d ¥5000/9000) Near Narita-san-kōen, this friendly place bills itself as a 'ryokan museum': it's filled with armour, swords and other historical bric-a-brac. It's on Higashi-sando, reachable by taking the first left after passing the entrance to Narita-san-kōen, and following the road for the next 400m. It's on the left. Meals available. Check-in is available between 1pm and 11pm.

Being so close to the airport, Narita has a representative selection of Western-style hotels. The following three hotels operate regular shuttle buses to and from the airport; ask at the hotel reservation counter in the arrivals hall for the correct boarding stand. Coming from Tokyo, it's best to go to the airport and then take the shuttle bus to your hotel.

ANA Hotel Narita (☎ 33-1311; www.anahotel-narita .com/english; s/d from ¥18,480/23,100) If you don't mind paying a little more, the ANA is the pick of the bunch.
Narita Excel Hotel Tokyū (☎ 33-0109; http://narita .panpacific.com; s/d from ¥8000/11,000)
Narita Kikusai Hotel (☎ 23-2300; s/d from ¥5400/9800) Cheaper but decent.

Eating & Drinking

Omotesandō is packed with good places to eat or drink.

Edokkozushi (江戸っ子寿司; ☎ 22-0530; 736 Hanazaki-cho; from ¥2000; ⊙ 11am-2.30pm & 5-10pm) Dine on excellent sushi and sashimi at this fine spot on Omotesandō, a three-minute walk from either station, next to Chiba Bank on the right.

Kikuya (菊屋; ☎ 22-0236; 385 Nakamachi; sets from ¥1500; ⊙ 10am-8.30pm) A simple but stylish place serving tasty lunch and dinner sets, including sashimi, tempura and other Japanese fare. Look for the English sign reading 'Chrysanthemum Housu' (sic) across from the Tourist Pavilion.

The Barge Inn (☎ 23-2546; Omotesandō; meals from ¥950; ⊙ 4pm-2am, lunch buffet 11.30am-2.30pm Sat & Sun only) A popular gathering spot for expats, this nicely aged pub features good food, with evenings dedicated to jazz, DJs or quiz nights. English spoken.

Getting There & Away

From Tokyo Narita international airport you can take either the Keisei line (*futsū/kyūkō* but not the Skyliner, ¥250, five minutes) or JR (*futsū/yūkō* – the N'EX usually doesn't stop – ¥190/230 from Terminal 2/1, five minutes). From Tokyo, the easiest way to get to Narita is via the Keisei line from Ueno (*kyūkō* ¥810, 85 minutes) or the JR Airport Narita from Tokyo Station (¥1110, 1¼ hours). For information on using these services, see p154.

IZU-SHOTŌ 伊豆諸島

The semitropical Izu-shotō, known in English as Izu Seven Islands, are peaks of a submerged volcanic chain that projects far down into the Pacific from the Izu-hantō. Until the beginning of the 20th century the island chain was a place of exile; now it's a popular holiday destination for Tokyo residents. Activities on the islands include swimming, snorkelling, diving, fishing, dolphin watching, bicycling, hiking and relaxing in outdoor *onsen*.

Although it's relatively expensive to reach the islands, free campsites are available on most of them and you can take your food over on the ferry. To escape the crowds avoid holiday periods and head for the more remote islands, such as the fascinating Hachijō-jima, hands-down the pick of the bunch.

Getting There & Away

Ferries to the islands leave from Tokyo's Takeshiba Pier (near Hamamatsu-chō Station). Most ferries from Tokyo depart at 10pm and arrive at the islands early the next morning. Some of the islands are also serviced by ferries from Atami and Itō. Call **Tōkai Kisen ferry service** (☎ 5472-9009) for departure times and reservations (in Japanese). Ō-shima, Miyake-jima and Hachijō-jima, have airports and can be reached by plane from Tokyo's Haneda airport.

Getting Around

Island-hopping is possible but requires some serious planning, as services vary seasonally and departures can be quite infrequent. If you do intend to island-hop, consult with the **Tokyo TIC** (☎ 3201-3331; ⏰ 9am-5pm Mon-Fri, 9am-12pm Sat) to choose the best route and schedule. If you have money to burn, you can also travel from

island to island by helicopter. Rates average ¥10,000 per flight and there is usually one flight per day to and from each island. Call **Tokyo Island Shuttle** (☎ 2-5222) for details.

Ō-SHIMA 大島
☎ 04992

Due to its proximity to the mainland, Ō-shima is the most popular island in the group. It's also the largest at 91 sq km. Be warned that Ō-shima is overrun with young Tokyoites on weekends and holidays.

Information

Pick up the TIC's informative Ōshima Island pamphlet or call the **Izu Seven Islands Tourist Federation** (☎ 3436-6955) in Tokyo for more information before setting out. Once on the island, stop by the helpful **Ōshima Tourist Association** (☎ 2-2177). It's right at the pier, visible as soon as you get off the ferry. While you're there, pick up some half-price *onsen* tickets.

Sights & Activities

The main attraction of Ō-shima is the active volcano **Mihara-yama**, which last erupted in November 1986 forcing the evacuation of island residents to Tokyo. Buses run near the summit from Motomachi port (¥860, 25 minutes, six daily); from there you can hike to the observatory of the volcanic crater (one hour), and then circle the crater (45 minutes) or hike to Ōshima-Kōen.

Onsen are the island's other main attraction. **Hama-no-yu** (admission ¥400; ⏰ 1-7pm), 10 minutes' walk north of the port, has good ocean views but gets packed on weekends. It's mixed bathing; swimsuits are required. A quieter place is **Ōshima Onsen Hotel** (admission ¥800; ⏰ 1-9pm), an outdoor *onsen* with a good view of Mihara-yama. Take a bus from Motomachi port and get off at Mihara-yama *onsen* stop.

Sleeping & Eating

Umi-no-furusato-mura (☎ 4-1137; camp site with/without own tent ¥2000/4000, plus per person ¥200/300) This camping ground is the cheapest place to stay, with prepitched tents for six people. It's on the opposite side of the island and not serviced by any bus – hitching is one option for getting there.

Tachibana-sō (☎ 2-2075; r per person with/without 2 meals ¥6300/4200) This atmospheric old *minshuku* has decent rooms and is conveniently

located on the main road, five minutes'
walk straight in from the pier. Check-in is
from 11am.

Izu Ōshima Kokumin-shukusha (☎ 2-1285; r per
person ¥8000) Not far from the pier, this is an
institutional place where rates include two
meals. Check-in is from 4pm.

Kāchan (☎ 2-1127; meals from ¥1100; ☉ 11am-
3pm & 5-9pm Wed-Mon) This cosy *izakaya* is on
the seaside road less than five minutes north
of the pier. They are particularly proud of
their 'Iso udon' – a rice bowl topped with a
variety of sashimi and *bekkō-zushi*, literally
'tortoise-shell sushi'. Look for the wooden
front decorated with glass net-floats.

Getting There & Away

There are three flights per day from Tokyo
(Haneda) to Ō-shima with Air Nippon Koku
(¥10,500, 40 minutes).

Ferry services run daily to Ō-shima from
Tokyo (2nd class, ¥3810, 7½ hours). From
Atami there are two express ferries daily (2nd
class, ¥4500, one hour). There's also a daily
ferry from Itō (2nd class, ¥3500, 1½ hours).

TO-SHIMA 利島
☎ 04992

To-shima, 27km southwest of Ō-shima, is
the smallest island in the Izu-shotō, with a
circumference of only 8km. The island is
mountainous, although its volcano is now
dormant, and there are no swimming beaches.
Much of the island is used for the cultivation
of camellias, which makes it a picturesque
place to visit between December and February, when the flowers are in bloom.

The island has six *minshuku* with prices
of ¥6000 to ¥6800 with two meals. For information contact the **Izu Seven Islands Tourist
Federation** (☎ 03-3436-6955; ☉ 9am-10pm).

There's a daily ferry from Tokyo to To-
shima (2nd class, ¥4240, 9½ hours).

NII-JIMA 新島
☎ 04992

Nii-jima has an area of 23 sq km and its
beaches have made it so popular that there
are now over 200 *minshuku* on the island.
Even with this abundance of accommodation
it's a good idea to ring the **Nii-jima Tourist Association** (☎ 5-0048) for help with reservations
if you're visiting during a holiday period.

From Nii-jima port, a five-minute walk
north leads to the striking white-sand beach

Maehama, which stretches for 4km. Several
hot springs lie a short walk south of the
port. The Parthenon-inspired **Yunohama Hot
Springs** (☉ 24hr), near the Tourist Association, boasts spectacular views of the Pacific;
bathing suit required. On the island's east
side, the 6.5km white-sand beach of Ha-
bushiura – and more importantly its big
waves – attracts flocks of surfers in the
summer.

Other attractions of Nii-jima include the
Glass Art Center (☎ 5-5140; www.niijimaglass.com),
1km south of the port, where you can see
some fine work made from the island's naturally magnetic Koga stone (which is found
only in Nii-jima and in Sicily). You can often
see the glassblowers in action.

In addition to *minshuku*, Nii-jima has one
camp ground, **Wadahama**, open year-round.

There's a daily ferry from Tokyo to Nii-
jima (2nd-class, ¥5120, 10 hours).

SHIKINE-JIMA 式根島
☎ 04992

Six kilometres south of Nii-jima is tiny
Shikine-jima, with an area of only 3.8 sq km.
The island has swimming beaches, *onsen*
and plenty of accommodation.

Ferries to Shikine-jima depart from Tokyo
once daily (2nd class, ¥5120, 10 hours). Six
ferries a week leave from Shimoda on the
Izu-hantō (2nd class, ¥3600, 3½ hours).

MIYAKE-JIMA 三宅島
☎ 04994

Miyake-jima is 180km south of Tokyo. It
is the third-largest island in the Izu group,
with a circumference of 36km. The island's
volcano, **Osu-yama**, said to erupt every 20
years, last did so in 2002. Residents, all of
whom were evacuated, were still retuning
to the island at press time; but all tourist facilities are closed, and there were no
scheduled boat departures. Check with the
Miyake-jima Tourist Association (☎ 6-1144) for
the latest information.

HACHIJŌ-JIMA 八丈島
☎ 04996

Hachijō-jima (68 sq km) is 290km south of
Tokyo. It is the southernmost and second-
largest island in the Izu-shotō. Its distance
from Tokyo keeps it relatively free of the
crowds that descend on the more northerly
islands of the Izu group. It also attracts an

interesting mix of surfers, stoners, ecologists and refugees from the big-city rat race.

Information

Before leaving Tokyo, pick up the TIC's informative Hachijo-jima & Aogashima Islands pamphlet.

Hachijō-jima Tourist Organisation (☎ 2-1377) Can answer questions in Japanese.

Tourist Information Office (☎ 2-1121) After arrival, you can get information at this office in the town hall, in the centre of the island on the main road.

Sights & Activities

The address is Tokyo prefecture, but the vibe is Okinawa. Hiking, climbing, watersports and seeking out glow-in-the-dark mushrooms are all favourite activities.

The island is dominated by two dormant volcanoes, **Hachijō-Fuji** and **Mihara-yama**, whose slopes are covered with lush semitropical vegetation.

Hachijō-jima's highlights include good beaches, a botanical garden, and two historical sights, the shrine of **Tametomo-jinja** and **Sofuku-ji** temple. There are also some great *onsen* in which to soak after a day of sightseeing.

Urami-ga-taki Onsen (admission free; ⏱ 10am-9pm) is not to be missed. It's tucked into a thick forest overlooking a waterfall. It has mixed bathing. Take a Sueyoshi-bound bus from the port (you may have to change at Kashitate Onsen Mae) to Nakata-Shōten Mae and walk for 20 minutes towards the ocean. Another good choice is **Sueyoshi Onsen Miharashi-no-yu** (admission ¥500; ⏱ 10.30am-9.30pm Wed-Mon) with separate bathing for men and women. There are great views over the Pacific – try going at sunset. Take the same bus that goes to Urami-ga-taki Onsen and get off at Sueyoshi.

History buffs will be interested in the **Tama-ishi-gaki walls** that the exiled population on the island built to prevent landslides and to protect themselves from typhoons. The walls are made from the uncannily round volcanic rocks that the exiles carried by hand up from the shoreline. These can be seen in the Ōsato-chiku area on the southwest coast of the island.

Project WAVE (☎ 2-5407; wave@isis.ocn.ne.jp) offers a variety of ecotourism options, including hiking, bird-watching, sea kayaking and scuba diving. Its owner, Iwasaki-san, speaks English.

Sleeping & Eating

Ashitaba-sō (☎ 7-0434; r per person ¥6500) This is a good *minshuku* that includes two meals in the rates. The owner is a friendly, chatty fellow who serves heaped portions of locally caught seafood. Reservations 24 hours in advance (in Japanese) are required Check-in is from 11am.

Hachijō-jima Kokusai Kankō Hotel (☎ 2-0671; r per person ¥7000) A newish place with comfortable rooms – in summer it becomes a bonkfest for holidaying university students from around the Kansai region. Expect dodgy chat-up lines, Hawaiian shirts and an excess of blonde hair-dye. Actually it's fun if you're in the mood, and there's a great communal bath.

Sokodo Camp-jō (☎ 2-1121) This camping ground is next to the Sokodo port and is free. Toilets, cold showers and cooking facilities are available. You must reserve (in Japanese only) a spot at the ward office.

Getting There & Away

In the summer season, ferries depart Tokyo daily at 10.30pm and travel via Miyake-jima (2nd class, ¥7180, 11 hours). Departures are less frequent outside the summer (June to August) season. Alternatively, there is a more frequent air service between Haneda airport and the island with Air Nippon (¥13,400 if booked a day in advance, one hour, five flights a day). Air Nippon's toll-free information line is ☎ 0120-029-222.

Getting Around

You can negotiate most of the island by bicycle and there are rental places along the main street. The airport has a scooter rental place that offers good deals. Otherwise, the Chō-ei bus covers the island's most important destinations.

OGASAWARA-SHOTŌ
小笠原諸島

Although technically part of the prefecture Tokyo-tō, these islands are far to the south of the Izu-shotō. They have a climate similar to that of the Nansei-shotō (Southwest Islands, often referred to as Okinawa) and, like those islands, remained occupied by US forces until 1968, long after the occupation of the mainland islands had ended.

The main group of islands includes **Chichijima** (Father Island), **Haha-jima** (Mother Island) and **Ani-jima**, on which you will find a number of *minshuku* and where **scuba diving** is popular. Further south are the Kazan-shotō (Volcano Islands) which include **Iwo-jima**, one of the most famous battle sites of WWII. The island is still off limits to visitors because of the live ammunition there.

Boats to Chichi-jima leave approximately once a week from Tokyo (2nd class, ¥22,570, 25 to 30 hours). For more information call **Ogasawara Kaiun** (☎ 3451-5171). Boats between Chichi-jima and Haha-jima leave daily (2nd class, ¥3780, two hours).

Central Honshū
本州中部

Central Japan, 'Chūbu' in Japanese, stretches between Tokyo and Kyoto, the Pacific and the Sea of Japan. Sprinkled with traditional towns, a rugged northern coastline and the massive Japan Alps, Chūbu's attractions are as diverse as its landscape. Visitors can trek along hiking trails through valleys and over summits scattered along the Japan Alps National Park. Nearby *onsen* (mineral hot-spring bath) towns offer welcome recovery for the weary and are enjoyed equally by wintertime skiers, who are drawn to the many slopes around Nagano.

Takayama, gateway to the Hida district, is admired for its traditional houses along the banks of the Miya-gawa. Friendly locals, delicious Hida cuisine and the verdant countryside are hallmarks of this lovely city. Nearby, the Unesco World Heritage sites of Shirakawa-gō provide another opportunity to view Hida's rich architectural tradition. Over the rugged banks of the Kiso-gawa stands Inuyama-jō, Japan's oldest castle. Matsumoto-jō, a black-and-white castle from the 16th century, offers an even more striking image, framed by the mountains; while its nearby Nakamachi district is a charming place to stroll.

Cliff-top hiking trails, beachside festivals and incredibly fresh seafood await visitors in Noto-hantō, the jagged peninsula stretching into the Sea of Japan. South of there lies Kanazawa, a historic city whose handsome streets once housed thriving samurai and geisha districts. Those seeking a taste of urban life on a smaller scale than Tokyo or Osaka often find Nagoya a surprisingly pleasant option. It's one of the country's most modern urban centres and it doesn't renege on the stylish futurism that dominates so many of Japan's cityscapes.

HIGHLIGHTS

- Stroll the handsome streets of **Takayama** (p219), a city known for its traditional architecture and skilled woodworkers
- Reconnect with the past at **Inuyama-jō** (p216) and **Matsumoto-jō** (p245), which are two of Japan's finest – and oldest – castles
- Discover the rugged beauty of **Noto-hantō** (p262), a windswept peninsula where small fishing villages set the stage for seafood feasts
- Commune with snow monkeys at **Jigokudani Yaen-kōen** (p242), followed by hiking or skiing in the mountains near Nagano
- Revel in the stunning mountain scenery of the **Japan Alps National Park** (p231)
- Find your centre in **Kenroku-en** (p255), an exquisite garden in the vibrant city of Kanazawa
- Train with Zen Buddhist monks in the 13th-century **Eihei-ji temple** (p268)
- Sleep in a thatched *gasshō-zukuri* house in the **Shōkawa Valley** (p227)

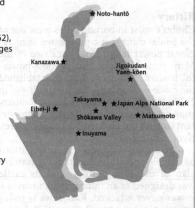

★ Noto-hantō

Kanazawa ★

★ Jigokudani Yaen-kōen

Takayama ★ ★ Japan Alps National Park

Eihei-ji ★ ★ ★ Matsumoto
Shōkawa Valley

★ Inuyama

CENTRAL HONSHŪ

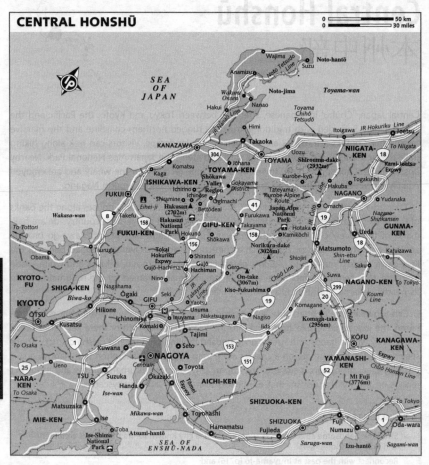

CENTRAL HONSHŪ

History

Chūbu's most important cities grew out of the feudal clans that consolidated their regional power long before the dawn of the Meiji period. One of Japan's most powerful leaders, Tokugawa Ieyasu, established the castle of Nagoya-jō for his ninth son in 1612. Around this castle, trade and industry soon arose and the town became an important stop on the Tōkaidō post road between Kyoto and Edo (Tokyo).

Matsumoto followed a similar pattern of development under the Ogasawara clan of the 15th century; and its castle was designed as an impregnable fortress – it was never attacked. Kanazawa is today an artistic centre and owes this legacy to the powerful Maeda clan. After their overthrowing the autonomous Buddhist government of the 16th century, bountiful rice production soon made them prosperous and the Kaga region became one of Japan's wealthiest. The wealthy Maeda family became a great patron of the arts and the city remains a culturally rich by-product of this history.

Religion also left its mark on Chūbu. The founding of Nagano's Zenkōji temple dates from the 7th century, when its construction was ordered to house the sacred Ikkō Sanzon, a golden statue said to have been made by the Buddha himself in the 6th century BC. It arrived in Japan in 552, allegedly the first Buddha image in the country. After the

Geta (traditional wooden sandals)

DAVID RYAN

Paper lanterns at Fukashi-jinja for
Tenjin Matsuri (p247), Matsumoto

JOHN ASHBURNE

Torii to a Shintō shrine, Nagano (p236), Nagano-ken

ANTONY GIBLIN

FRANK CARTER

Gasshō-zakuri architecture, Gokayama
(p229), Shokawa Valley

Japanese 'snow monkeys' (macaques), Jigokudani
Yaen-kōen (p242), Nagano-ken

ANTONY GIBLIN

Kenroku-en (p255), Kanazawa, Ishikawa-ken

JOHN ASHE

temple's completion, Nagano became an immensely important pilgrimage site and today it continues to attract some four million pilgrims a year.

Climate

Owing to its geographic diversity, Central Honshū has a climate that varies considerably. In the Japan Alps, winters are cold and long with abundant snowfall, beginning in November and continuing through February, with the highest peaks covered through June. Those who prefer hiking in the mountains to skiing them should come in July and August, when the snows are generally melted and temperatures are warmest. In the lowlands, the best time to visit is in the autumn (late September to early November) or in the spring (April and May), when temperatures are mild and clear sunny skies are the norm. During the summer, lowland destinations like Nagoya often become oppressively hot and humid. Rainfall is also most considerable in the summer and summer is followed by typhoon season, which usually peaks in September.

National Parks

The **Japan Alps National Park** (p231), accessible via Matsumoto or Takayama, is dotted with spectacular peaks and features *onsen* towns, ski slopes and some excellent hiking trails. A few hours west, **Hakusan National Park** (p266), is another fine place to enjoy the mountains, attracting skiers in the winter, hikers in the summer and *onsen*-lovers year-round.

Getting There & Away

Nagoya is the gateway to Central Honshū and its new international airport provides easy access for those planning to explore the region. The city is one of Japan's major transport hubs, with *shinkansen* lines to Tokyo, Osaka, Kyoto and Hiroshima.

Those wishing to enter Central Honshū by sea can do so from Russia. Ferries operated by **FKK Air Service** (☎ 0766-22-2212; http://fkk-air.toyama-net.com in Japanese only) travel between Fushiki in Toyama-ken and Vladivostok. Boats depart Vladivostok on Monday at 6pm and arrive 36 hours later in Fushiki. From Japan ferries leave on Friday at 6pm, arriving in Russia on Sunday morning. One-way fares start at ¥26,000.

Getting Around

Nagoya is the transport hub of southern Chūbu. The mountainous inland area is served by the JR Takayama and Chūō lines, which run roughly parallel from north to south with hubs in Takayama and Matsumoto, respectively. In the northern area, the JR Hokuriku line follows the coast along the Sea of Japan, linking Fukui, Kanazawa and Toyama.

Bus is the main form of transport in the mountainous midsection, but schedules can be inconvenient or, between November and May, stop entirely (except for ski resorts). For some destinations, renting a car can be the most affordable, time-efficient and pleasant option – particularly when visiting the Noto-hantō peninsula and Hakusan National Park.

NAGOYA 名古屋

☎ 052 / pop 2.2 million

Japan's fourth-largest city, Nagoya is a major industrial centre; it's also the birthplace of *pachinko* (Japanese pinball). Neither of these attributes marks Nagoya as a standout tourist destination, but the city does have some decent attractions and plenty of urban amusement, on a far more relaxed scale than Tokyo.

During WWII Nagoya was practically levelled by Allied bombardment. Since then it has rebuilt itself into a modern city with wide boulevards, gleaming skyscrapers and an excellent transport system. Despite its size Nagoya has a small-town feel to it, and locals and expats alike take pride in this friendly, often overlooked city.

In addition to its castle, museums and gardens, Nagoya has a plethora of dining and shopping possibilities, both at more affordable prices than elsewhere in Japan. Nagoya is also a convenient hub for day trips to southern Gifu-ken and Ise-jingū (p385).

ORIENTATION

Nagoya is built on a grid with wide avenues. On the western edge of the city centre, Nagoya Station (known locally as Meieki) is a city in itself with shops, restaurants, hotels and observation decks in two looming 50-plus-storey towers, the city's most useful landmarks. Several train lines converge here.

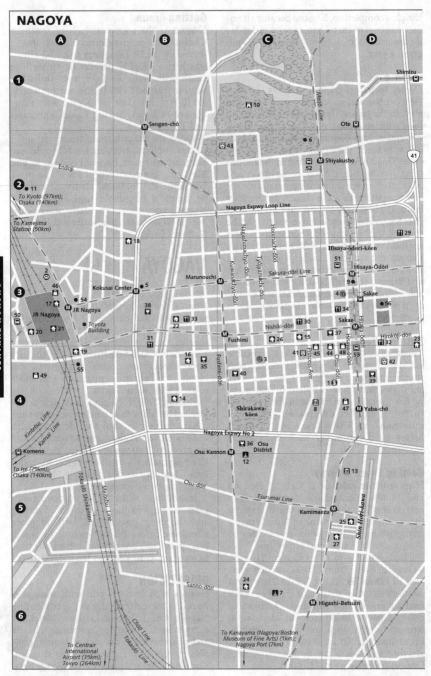

NAGOYA

CENTRAL HONSHŪ

Shimizu

Sengen-chō

10

43

Ote

6

Shiyakusho
52

Endoji

To Kyoto (97km);
Osaka (140km)

11

To Kamejima
Station (50km)

Nagoya Expwy Loop Line

18

Hisaya-ōdōri-kōen

51

Hisaya-Ōdōri

Nagahamachyo-dōri

Honmachi-dōri

Tyōyamachi-dōri

Kuwanachyo-dōri

Sakura-dōri Line

Marunouchi

Kokusai Center

5

29

9

Sakae

4

56

54

17

JR Nagoya

46

2

34

Sakae

JR Nagoya

Toyota
Building

38

33

22

Nishiki-dōri

30

Hirokōji-dōri

32

23

50

20

21

31

Fushimi

26

15

37

Hisaya-ōdōri

53

19

55

16

35

Fushimi-dōri

@ 3

41

45

44

Osu-dōri

48

42

39

49

40

1

14

8

47

Yaba-chō

Shirakawa-
kōen

13

Nagoya Expwy No 2

Kintetsu Line

Kansai Line

36

Osu
District

Komeno

Osu Kannon

12

To Ise (79km);
Osaka (140km)

Meitetsu Line

Tokaidō Shinkansen

Osu-dōri

Tsurumai Line

Shin Hori-kawa

Kamimaezu

25

27

Sanno-dōri

24

7

Chūō Line

Tokaidō Line

Higashi-Betsuin

To Centrair
International
Airport (35km);
Tokyo (264km)

To Kanayama (Nagoya/Boston
Museum of Fine Arts) (1km);
Nagoya Port (7km)

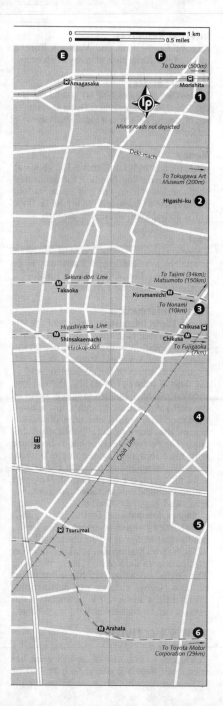

shinkansen platforms are on the west side of the station, while on the east side you'll find the private Meitetsu and Kintetsu lines as well as the subway and bus stations.

From the east exit, Sakura-dōri runs towards the massive TV tower, in the centre of the narrow park-like Central Park (Hisaya-ōdōri-kōen). South of the TV tower is the Sakae district, which is packed with restaurants, bars, cafés and shops. The castle, Nagoya-jō, is just north of the city centre.

English-language signs make navigating the city easier.

Maps

At the tourist office, be sure to pick up the *Live Map Nagoya*, a foldout city map; and *Access*, a publication that includes a subway map and more detailed street maps for around Sakae, Nagoya and Kanayama Stations.

INFORMATION
Bookshops

Nagoya's best selection of English-language books is in Sakae.

Kinokuniya Books (Map pp206-7; ☎ 265-2621; 3-18-1 Sakae; ⊙ 10am-8pm) Sixth floor of the Nadya Park building, two blocks west of the Yaba-chō Station.

Maruzen (Map pp206-7; ☎ 261-2251; 3-2-7 Sakae; ⊙ 10am-8pm) On busy Hirokoji-dōri, three blocks west of the Sakae Station.

Emergency

Kyukyuiryō Jōhō Sentā (Emergency Medical Information Centre; ☎ 263-1133) Advice (in Japanese only) on where to receive weekend and holiday emergency treatment.

Nagoya International Centre (☎ 581-0100; 1-47-1 Nagono; ⊙ 9am-8.30pm Tue-Sat, 9am-5pm Sun & holidays) Provides emergency advice; the best place to call (English is spoken).

Internet Access

Chikōraku (Map pp206-7; ☎ 587-2528; 1-25-2 Meieki; 1st hr ¥490; ⊙ 24hr) In the basement of the Meitetsu Lejac building, near Nagoya Station.

Kinko's (Map pp206-7; ☎ 231-9211; 2-3-31 Sakae; 1st 10min ¥100, 1st hr ¥1100; ⊙ 24hr) Two blocks east and two blocks south of Fushimi Station.

Media Cafe Popeye (Map pp206-7; ☎ 955-0059; 3-6-15 Nishiki; per hr ¥400; ⊙ 24hr). One block south of Hisaya-Ōdōri Station, on the 3rd floor of the Tatenomachi building facing the TV tower.

Nagoya International Centre (Map pp206-7; ☎ 581-0100; 1-47-1 Nagono; per hr ¥500; ⊙ 9am-8.30pm Tue-Sat, 9am-5pm Sun & holidays)

Internet Resources

Nagoya Convention and Visitor's Bureau has useful information at www.ncvb.or.jp.

Medical Services

Tachino Clinic (Map pp206-7; ☎ 541-9130; Dai-Nagoya Bldg, 3-28-12 Meieki) Opposite the east exit of Nagoya Station, this clinic has staff who speak English, French, German and Spanish.

Money

Citibank has 24-hour Cirrus ATM access at its branch in the Sugi building, three minutes' walk southwest from exit 7 of Sakae Station. There is also a Citibank ATM on the 1st floor of the arrival lobby at Nagoya airport.

Post

There's a small post office with an ATM inside Nagoya Station and a seriously large one, Eki-mae Post Office (Map pp206–7), north of the station's east exit.

Tourist Information

Nagoya Tourist Information (Map pp206-7; ☎ 541-4301; ⊙ 9am-7pm) is in the central concourse of Nagoya Station, with smaller offices at the north exit of **Kanayama Station** (☎ 323-0161; ⊙ 9am-7pm), south of the city centre, and in the **Oasis 21 building** (☎ 963-5252; ⊙ 10am-8pm) in Sakae. All have English-language maps of the city, information on sights and accommodation, and at least one English speaker behind the counter. Useful publications include *The Best of Nagoya*, a handy brochure with most tourist information you'll need, the advertising-sponsored *Info Guide* and a public transport map. English-language listings publications include *Japanzine*, *Avenues* and *Nagoya Calendar*.

Nagoya International Centre (Map pp206-7; ☎ 581-0100; 1-47-1 Nagono; ⊙ 9am-8.30pm Tue-Sat, 8am-5pm Sun & holidays) is a 10-minute walk east of the Nagoya Station along Sakura-dōri, on the 3rd floor of the Kokusai Centre building. The English-speaking staff has information on both Nagoya and regional destinations. You'll find a library, TV newscasts from overseas and a bulletin board for postings.

SIGHTS & ACTIVITIES
Nagoya-jō 名古屋城

Tokugawa Ieyasu, one of Japan's great heroes, built **Nagoya-jō** (Map pp206-7; ☎ 231-1700; 1-1 Hommaru; admission ¥500; ⊙ 9am-4.30pm) for his

AROUND NAGOYA

ninth son on the site of an older castle, from 1610 to 1614. Although it was destroyed in WWII and replaced in 1959 with a ferroconcrete replica, it is nonetheless worth a visit: there's a decent museum inside featuring armour, treasures and histories of the Oda, Toyotomi and Tokugawa families. A lift will save you climbing stairs. Note the 3m-long replicas of the famous *shachi-hoko*, gilded dolphin-like sea creatures at either end of the roof (and in every souvenir shop).

Within the castle grounds, the garden, **Ninomaru-en**, has a teahouse in an attractive setting. It's particularly lovely during the cherry blossom season. Just southwest of the castle grounds is the elegant **Nagoya Nō Theatre** (Map pp206-7; ☎ 231-0088; 1-1-1 San-no-

maru; admission free; ☽ 9am-5pm), which features a small museum.

The castle is a five-minute walk from Shiyakusho Station on the Meijō subway line.

Atsuta-jingū 熱田神宮
Hidden among 1000-year-old cypress trees, the 3rd-century **Atsuta-jingū** (Map p209; ☎ 671-4151; 1-1-1 Atsuta-Jingū; admission free; ☽ 24hr) is one of the most sacred Shintō shrines. It is said to house the *kusanagi-no-tsurugi* (sacred sword – literally, the 'grass-cutting sword'), one of the *sanshu no jingi* – three regalia – that were, according to legend, handed down to the imperial family by the goddess Amaterasu Ōmikami. (The other two are the curved jewels at the imperial palace

in Tokyo and the sacred mirror housed at Ise Jingū.) You won't be able to view the regalia but don't feel left out; no one but the emperor and a few selected Shintō priests ever get to see them.

There is a small **museum** (☎ 671-0852; admission ¥300; ⏰ 9am-4.30pm, closed last Wed & Thu of each month), housing Tokugawa-era swords, masks and paintings, including some important cultural properties.

The shrine is about five minutes' walk from exit 2 of Jingū-nishi Station on the Meijō subway line. Or, take the Meitetsu Nagoya Honsen line to Jingū-mae and then walk west for five minutes.

Tokugawa Art Museum 徳川美術館

Boasting over 10,000 pieces, this worthwhile **museum** (Map pp206-7; ☎ 935-6262; www.cjn.or.jp/tokugawa; 1017 Tokugawa-chō; admission ¥1200; ⏰ 10am-5pm Tue-Sun) contains furnishings, armour, calligraphy, painted scrolls, lacquerware and ceramics that previously belonged to the Tokugawa family. A priceless 12th-century scroll depicting *The Tale of Genji* is locked away except for a short stint in late November; the rest of the year, visitors must remain content with a video.

The museum is three minutes' walk from the Shindeki bus stop, east of Nagoya-jō. Take a bus from Shiyakusho subway station (near Nagoya-jō) or from stop 4 at the Meitetsu Shin-Nagoya Station.

Noritake Garden ノリタケの森

On the lush grounds of one of Japan's best-known **porcelain makers** (Map pp206-7; ☎ 561-7290; 3-1-36 Noritake-shinmachi; admission ¥500; ⏰ 10am-5pm Tue-Sun), a craft centre here offers a peek at the production process and a porcelain museum, plus a chance to glaze your own dish (¥1500). Signage is in English throughout the grounds. Naturally, there are ample shopping opportunities – the 'Box' outlet store offers a 40% discount on discontinued items. Admission to the grounds and shops is free. It's a five-minute walk north of Kamejima Station, or 15 minutes from Nagoya Station.

Ran no Yakata Orchid Gardens ランの館

These **gardens** (Map pp206-7; ☎ 243-0511; 4-4-1 Osu; admission ¥700; ⏰ 10am-8pm Thu-Tue) contain over 250 species of orchid, presented inside a greenhouse and a walled garden, with a path leading through the flowering plants. There are indoor and outdoor cafés. It's two blocks south of Yaba-chō Station.

Nadya Park ナディヤパーク

A futuristic skyscraper museum/shopping complex in Sakae, Nadya Park houses the tiny but fascinating **International Design Centre Nagoya** (Map pp206-7; ☎ 265-2106; 3-18-1 Sakae; admission ¥300; ⏰ 11am-8pm Wed-Mon) on the 4th floor, a secular shrine to the deities of conceptualisation, form and function. Exhibits (with signage in English) trace the history of design from Art Deco to the present.

Also in Nadya Park is the Loft department store, which shopping buffs will find equally alluring.

Nadya Park is five minutes' walk northwest of Yaba-chō Station on the Meijō line, or eight minutes' walk southwest of Sakae Station on the Higashiyama and Meijō lines.

Nagoya/Boston Museum of Fine Arts 名古屋ボストン美術館

This excellent **museum** (Map p209; ☎ 684-0101; www.Nagoya-boston.or.jp; 1-1-1 Kanayama-chō; admission special & long-term exhibitions ¥1200, long-term exhibitions only ¥400; ⏰ 10am-7pm Tue-Fri, 10am-5pm Sat & Sun) is a collaborative effort between Japanese backers and the Museum of Fine Arts, Boston. Rotating exhibits showcase both Japanese and non-Japanese masterpieces, with good English signage.

The museum is to the right of the south exit of Kanayama Station.

Nagoya Port Area 名古屋港

Redeveloped to attract tourists, the cargo port now boasts several mildly interesting attractions. The hi-tech **Port of Nagoya Public Aquarium** (Map p209; ☎ 654-7000; www.nagoyaaqua.jp/english/index.html; 1-3 Minatomachi; adult/child ¥2000/1000; ⏰ 9.30am-8pm Tue-Sun 21 Jul-31 Aug, 9.30am-5pm rest of year) is one of Japan's largest and it's generally a hit with kids (particularly the penguin tank). The **Port Tower** (Map p209; ☎ 652-1111; 1-3 Minatomachi; admission ¥300; museum ⏰ 9.30am-5pm Tue-Sun) offers good views of the harbour and also contains the **Maritime Museum** and the **Fuji Antarctic Exploration Ship**. All of them can be visited with a combination ticket for ¥2400/1200 (adult/child), which must be purchased before 1pm. Attractions are signposted in English. Take the Meijō subway line to Nagoya-kō Station.

FESTIVALS & EVENTS

The festival **Atsuta Matsuri**, held in early June at Atsuta-jingū, features displays of martial arts, sumō matches and fireworks. Street vendors peddle their wares by the light of thousands of lanterns.

On the first Saturday and Sunday of June, the **Tennō Matsuri** takes place in Higashi-ku on Deki-machi street, near the Tokugawa Art Museum. Large *karakuri* (mechanical puppets) are paraded on floats in the precincts of the shrine, Susano-o-jinja.

The Nagoya Basho **sumō tournament** takes place at the **Aichi Prefectural Gymnasium** (Map pp206-7; ☎ 962-9300; 1-1 Hommaru) from the first to the third Sunday of July. Non-reserved seats (from ¥2800) are available from the box office on the day of the bout from 8.30am. Arrive early in the afternoon and you can walk unchallenged to the very front of the arena to watch the lower-ranked wrestlers up close. It's also a great photo opportunity. The gymnasium is in the grounds of Nagoya-jō.

The **Minato Matsuri**, held around 20 July at Nagoya port, features a street parade with more than 1500 dancers, as well as a water-logging contest that dates back to the Edo period (1600–1867).

Nagoya Matsuri, held in mid-October in Hisaya-ōdōri-kōen (aka Central Park, north of the TV Tower), is the big event of the year. It includes costume parades, processions of floats with *karakuri* puppets, folk dancing, music and a parade of decorated cars.

In late October to late November, the **Kiku-no-hana Taikai** (Chrysanthemum Exhibition) sets the grounds of Nagoya-jō awash in colour; a separate *ningyō* (doll) exhibit incorporates the flowers into scenes from Japanese history and legend.

Nagoya hosted the first **World Expo 2005** (www-1.expo2005.or.jp/en) of the 21st century, which focussed on sustainable development. To find out if the pavilions (east of downtown in Aichi-ken) are still open when you're in town, visit the website.

SLEEPING

Accommodation in Nagoya is clustered around Nagoya Station and Sakae. Most of the business hotels in the Nagoya Station area are fairly pricey; the cheapest are around the less-used west exit.

Budget

Aichi-ken Seinen-kaikan Youth Hostel (Map pp206-7; ☎ 221-6001; 1-18-8 Sakae; dm ¥2850) This decent, central hostel is usually the first budget place to be booked out. Private single rooms and Japanese-style family rooms are also available. From Fushimi Station, exit 7, walk three blocks west and take a left after the Hilton, from where it's two blocks further south. Check-in is 3pm to 8pm, curfew 11pm.

Sauna and Capsule Well Be (Map pp206-7; ☎ 586-2641; 1-25-2 Meieki; capsule ¥4100) This capsule hotel has a large sauna and is close to Nagoya Station. It's on the fourth floor of the Meitetsu Lejac Building, one block south of the station. Check-in is from 4pm; check-out noon.

Fuji Sauna and Capsule (Map pp206-7; ☎ 962-5711; 3-22-31 Nishiki; capsule ¥4000) Nagoya's largest capsule hotel has an extensive sauna and relaxation area. Check-in 4pm. From Sakae Station, exit 8, walk west along Nishiki-dōri, go three blocks and turn left. It's on your left.

Nagoya Youth Hostel (Map p209; ☎ 781-9845; fax 781-9023; 1-50 Tashiro-chō; dm ¥2200) Five kilometres east of the city centre, near the park Higashi-yama-kōen, this hostel has decent rooms. From Nagoya Station, take the Higashiyama subway line to Higashiyama-kōen Station. From exit 3 walk along the park then follow the signs right, past the zoo entrance. Check-in is 3pm to 9pm.

Midrange

Kimiya Ryokan (Map pp206-7; ☎ 551-0498; hott@hotmail.com; Ushijima-chō; r per person ¥4500) This friendly, family-style ryokan is good value for its tatami rooms. The best ones overlook the garden. English spoken. From Kokusai Centre Station exit 1, walk north for seven minutes. It's on the left.

Nagoya Rolen Hotel (Map pp206-7; ☎ 211-4581; www.rolenhotel.co.jp; 1-8-40 Sakae; s/d from ¥4200/8400) This tidy business hotel has small, basic rooms (the cheapest with shared bath) and a decent location. From Fushimi Station exit 10, take a left at the nearer corner, go three blocks and it's on your right.

Ryokan Meiryū (Map pp206-7; ☎ 331-8686; 2-4-21 Kamimaezu; www.japan-net.ne.jp/~meiryu; s/d ¥5250/8400) This well-run ryokan has English-speaking staff, as well as a coin laundry, a nice communal bath and a men's steam room. From Kamimaezu subway station exit 3, walk along the street and take the first left. It's 1½ blocks down, on the left.

Yamazen Ryokan (Map pp206-7; ☎ 321-1792; fax 321-3076; Kamimaezu; r per person with/without breakfast ¥5700/5000) Although staff don't speak much English, Yamazen has a kindly, welcoming atmosphere and a 40-plus-year history. From Kamimaezu subway station exit 3, walk along the street and take the third left. It's 20m down on the right.

Ryokan Marutame (Map pp206-7; ☎ 321-7130; www .jin.ne.jp/marutame; 2-6-17 Tachibana; s/d from ¥5000/9600) This modern ryokan has clean but basic rooms, English-speaking staff and coin-operated laundry. From Higashi Betsuin Station, exit 4, cross the street, walk past the Higashi Betsuin temple and turn right. It's on the left.

Petit Ryokan Ichifuji (Map p209; ☎ 914-2867; www .jin.ne.jp/ichifuji; 1-7 Saikōbashi-dōri; s/d from ¥4800/8400) About 30 minutes' subway ride from Nagoya Station, this friendly spot has clean, comfortable rooms and a communal *hinokiburo* (cypress wood bath). Take the Meijō subway line to Heiandōri Station, turn right out of exit 2 and walk south for three minutes. The ryokan is signposted in English.

Nagoya Flower Hotel (Map pp206-7; ☎ 451-2222; fax 451-3462; 15-4 Meieki; s/d from ¥6400/10,600) Conveniently located just outside Nagoya Station's west exit, Nagoya Flower Hotel has clean, basic rooms. Upper-storey rooms are in better condition but cost more.

Silk Tree Hotel Nagoya (Map pp206-7; ☎ 222-1113; fax 222-1141; 2-20-5 Sakae; s/d/tw from ¥6000/9000/12,000) This fairly new business hotel has decent rooms and it's close to the Sakae action. From Fushimi Station, exit 1, turn left on Nishiki-dōri. It's 3½ blocks down on the right. Check-in is from 3pm.

Top End

Hotel Associa Nagoya Terminal (Map pp206-7; ☎ 561-3751, 0120-489-174; www.associa.com/nth; 1-1-4 Meieki; s/d from ¥11,434/17,325) This handsome hotel attached to the station boasts a variety of Western- and Japanese-style rooms, all comfortably outfitted and most with excellent views. Discounts are available for Japan Rail Pass holders. Check-in is from 1pm.

Meitetsu Grand Hotel (Map pp206-7; ☎ 582-2233; www.meitetsu-gh.co.jp; 1-2-4 Meieki; s/tw/d from ¥9,500/19,000/20,000) Towering above Meitetsu & Kintetsu, to the right of Nagoya Station (Sakura-dōri exit), this rather dapper hotel has decent-sized doubles and twins with good lighting. Of less value are the cheaper, windowless singles. Check-in from noon.

Nagoya Tōkyū Hotel (Map pp206-7; ☎ 251-2411; www.nagoyatokyu.com; 3-1-8 Sakae; s/d from ¥17,325/19,635) One of Sakae's best hotels, the Tōkyū has earned fans for its large, nicely furnished rooms and doting staff. From Sakae exit 12, walk four blocks east along Hirokoji-dōri. It's on the right. Check-in from 1pm.

Nagoya Marriott Associa Hotel (Map pp206-7; ☎ 584-1111; www.associa.com/english/nma; 1-1-2 Meieki; s/d from ¥20,000/28,000) Spacious rooms and deluxe, well, everything. It's literally Nagoya's uppermost lodging, in the south tower above Nagoya Station. Check-in from 2pm.

EATING

Nagoya's most famous regional dish is *kishimen* (flat, handmade noodles, served either cold or in hot broth). Other culinary stars include *kōchin* (free-range chicken) and *hitsumabushi* (*unagi* [eel] sets), but there's a decent range of international fare as well. The city's greatest concentration of restaurants is in Sakae.

Ebisuya (Map pp206-7; ☎ 961-3412; 3-20-7 Sakae; dishes from ¥680; ☯ lunch & dinner) One of the city's best-known *kishimen* chains, Ebisuya has a laid-back atmosphere and tasty, inexpensive bowls of noodles.

Torigin Honten (Map pp206-7; ☎ 973-3000; 3-14-22 Nishiki; meals from ¥1600; ☯ dinner) For top *kōchin*, Torigin has been going strong for 30 years. Chicken is served in many forms, including *kushiyaki* (skewered), *kara-age* (deep-fried chicken pieces), *zōsui* (mild rice hot-pot) and sashimi (what you think it is). Some may find the individual dishes a little dainty for the price, but *teishoku* (set menus) are available from ¥2900.

Nanaya Colonial (Map pp206-7; ☎ 587-5778; 5-25-1 Sakae; mains from ¥900; ☯ 5pm-midnight) This stylish restaurant overlooking the Horikawa River serves beautifully- presented Pan-Asian dishes. Among the eclectic choices: Chinese yam with scallops, rare tuna steak and grilled eel with rice. English menu available.

Casablanca (Map pp206-7; ☎ 264-7188; 1-9-14 Izumi; dishes from ¥480-3200; ☯ lunch & dinner) For authentic Moroccan cuisine, head to this cosy restaurant northeast of the TV tower, where you can enjoy North African delights like hummus, tabouli, lemon chicken tajine and kebabs. For an aperitif don't neglect the *boukha* (fig brandy). Belly dancing on the second and fourth Saturday of each month (¥1000 surcharge).

Tiger Café (Map pp206-7; ☎ 220-0031; 1-8-26 Nishiki; sandwiches/lunch specials from ¥500/800; ☼ 11am-3am Mon-Sat, 11am-midnight Sun) This bistro does an admirable Parisian imitation, with tiled floors, sidewalk seating and Deco details. Smoked salmon sandwich and the *croque monsieur* are favourites, as are the good-value lunch specials.

Acme Night Rush Dining (Map pp206-7; ☎ 242-7070; 1-47-12 Shinsakae; mains ¥800-1300) A bit out of the way, this large, open restaurant has a clubby feel to it – enhanced by the DJs spinning world music to manga backdrops most nights. Fusion fare ranges from swordfish to herb-roasted salmon to thin-crust pizzas. From Yaba-chō Station, exit 3, take a left at the first intersection, walk six blocks and take a left. You'll see it on the left.

Nova Urbana (Map pp206-7; ☎ 263-0354; 4-2-7 Sakae; meals ¥1800-2800; ☼ 5.30pm-4am Tue-Sat, 5pm-1am Sun) Celebrate Japan's Brazilian ties with an all-you-can-eat dinner buffet (men ¥2580, women ¥1980), including *churrasco* grills. After dinner it doubles as a samba club.

DRINKING

Heaven's Door (Map pp206-7; ☎ 971-7080; 3-23-10 Nishiki; ☼ 6pm-4am Tue-Sun) Probably Nagoya's best bar, Heaven's Door follows a simple recipe – cosy ambience, friendly staff and simply fantastic music (all vinyl, no less). Rolling Stones fans should visit just to see the loo. From Sakae Station, exit 8, walk one block west down Nishiki-dōri and take a left. It'll be on your right, down the stairs.

Eric Life (Map pp206-7; ☎ 222-1555; 2-11-18 Osu; ☼ noon-midnight Thu-Tue) This *über*-stylish café in the funky Osu district is a youthful place for coffee, a light meal or a cocktail in the evening.

Other Side (Map pp206-7; ☎ 566-2323; 5-4-14 Meieki; ☼ 5pm-1am) At this small, friendly bar near the International Centre, you can mingle with a mix of gaijin and Japanese over the rock-infused juke box.

Shooters (Map pp206-7; ☎ 202-7077; 2-9-26 Sakae; ☼ 5pm-3am Mon-Fri; 11.30am-3am Sat & Sun) This US-style sports bar attracts a mostly gaijin, mostly raucous crowd. Japanese and foreign staff pours daily drink specials, and the menu includes burgers, pasta and Tex-Mex. It's near exit 5 of Fushimi subway station.

Elephant's Nest (Map pp206-7; ☎ 232-4360; 1-4-3 Sakae; ☼ 5.30pm-1am Sun-Thu, 5.30am-2am Fri & Sat) Near the Hilton, Elephant's Nest is another favourite expat haunt, with a welcoming vibe, darts and traditional English fare. It's on the second floor.

Red Rock Bar & Grill (Map pp206-7; ☎ 262-7893; 4-14-6 Sakae; ☼ 5.30pm until late Tue-Sun) In Sakae, the Aussie-owned Red Rock has a warm ambience and plenty of tasty pub food.

ENTERTAINMENT

Nagoya's nightlife might not match Tokyo's or Osaka's, but what it lacks in scale it makes up for in ebullience. For the latest party listings, visit www.mangafrog.com. Among the more popular dance clubs is **Lush-Underground** (Map pp206-7; ☎ 242-1388; 4-3-15 Sakae; admission ¥1500; ☼ 10pm until late), which attracts fine DJs (and serious crowds) most weekends. Another long-running favourite is **iD Cafe** (Map pp206-7; ☎ 251-0382; 3-1-15 Sakae; ☼ 7pm until late), with five floors – each with different music – and a young-ish Japanese crowd. **Plastic Factory** (Map p209; ☎ 0723-9971; 32-13 Kanda-chō) is actually in a former plastic factory east of the city center. From exit 2 of the Imaike subway station, walk north along the road for five minutes; turn right at the street before the Mini Stop convenience store, and you'll see the club down the road on the left.

Nagoya also offers live jazz, rock and classical music, including some well-known Japanese and international artists. Check English-language listings magazines for dates and times.

SHOPPING

Nagoya and the surrounding area are known for arts and crafts, including *arimatsu-narumi shibori* (elegant tie-dying), *cloisonné* (enamelling on silver and copper), ceramics and *Seki* blades (swords, knives, scissors etc).

One of the most enjoyable places to browse is the Osu district, in the streets around the Osu Kannon temple. Here you'll find vintage clothing shops, a record shop, cafés and a hodge-podge of old and new. The Ōsu Kannon temple (Map pp206–7) also hosts a colourful antique market on the 18th and 28th of each month.

The major shopping centres are in Sakae and around Nagoya Station. For souvenir items (such as handmade paper, pottery and tie-dyed fabric), browse in the giant department stores, such as Matsuzakaya, Maruei and Mitsukoshi in Sakae, or Takashimaya or Meitetsu & Kintetsu, near Nagoya Station.

CENTRAL HONSHŪ

For more shopping possibilities, see Noritake Garden (p210).

GETTING THERE & AWAY
Air
The new **Central Japan International Airport** (Centrair; Map p209; ☎ 0569-38-1195; www.centrair.jp /en/), opened in February 2005, is the new international gateway to the city and handles most of Nagoya's domestic flights. It is built on a man-made island in Ise-wan (Ise Bay), 35km south of the city. Coming from Tokyo, the *shinkansen* is generally quicker (two hours) than the hassle of flying.

Boat
The **Taiheiyo ferry** (☎ 582-8611) runs between Nagoya and Tomakomai (Hokkaidō, ¥8700, 38 hours) via Sendai (¥7400, 21 hours) every second evening at 8pm. Take the Meijō subway south to its terminus at Nagoya-kō Station and head for Nagoya ferry port.

Bus
JR and **Meitetsu Highway buses** (☎ 563-0489) operate services between Nagoya and Kanazawa (¥4060, four hours, 10 daily), Kyoto (¥2500, 2¾ hours, 19 daily), Osaka (¥2900, 3¼ hours, six daily) and Tokyo (¥6420, six hours, 13 daily). They also run overnight buses to Hiroshima (¥8400, nine hours), Kōchi (¥9070, 9¾ hours), Fukuoka (¥10,500, 11 hours) and Nagasaki (¥12,230, 12 hours).

Train
Nagoya is a major *shinkansen* stop. Fares and times from Tokyo are as follows: Hikari (¥10,580, two hours), Osaka (¥6380, one hour), Kyoto (¥5440, 44 minutes) and Hiroshima (¥13,430, three hours). The Kintetsu line also has indirect services to Nara (*tokkyū*, ¥3750, 2½ hours).

To the Japan Alps, you can take the JR Chūō line to Nagano (Shinano *tokkyū*, ¥6620, three hours) via Matsumoto (¥5360, two hours). A separate train serves Takayama (Hida *tokkyū*, ¥5870, 2½ hours).

Gifu connects with Nagoya Station on the JR Tōkaidō line (¥450, 18 minutes), and the Meitetsu Nagoya line (¥540, 25 minutes).

Direct trains serve Inuyama from Nagoya via the Meitetsu Inuyama line (*kyūkō* [ordinary express train], ¥540, 30 minutes). JR travellers can connect via Gifu to Unuma and walk across the river from Inuyama.

GETTING AROUND
To/From the Airport
The new Central Japan International Airport (Centrair) is accessible from Nagoya Station by taking the Meitetsu Tokoname line to the last stop. Express trains take 35 minutes to reach the airport (¥870).

Bus
There is an extensive city bus system (¥200 per ride), although the subway is easier for those with a limited grasp of Japanese. The city bus centre is on the 2nd floor of Matsuzakaya department store, just northeast of Nagoya Station; some buses, like those to the Tokugawa Art Museum, operate from the Meitetsu Shin-Nagoya Station.

Subway
Nagoya has an excellent subway system with four lines, all clearly signposted in English and Japanese. The most useful lines for visitors are the Meijō (purple), Higashiyama (yellow) and Sakura-dōri (red) lines. The last two run via Nagoya Station. Fares cost ¥200 to ¥320. If you plan to do a lot of travel by bus and subway, you can save money with a one-day pass (¥850), available at subway stations. The one-day 'Ikomai Pass' (¥1300) includes all transport plus free or discounted admission to selected attractions.

SOUTHERN GIFU-KEN
岐阜県南

The main destinations in this area, consisting of outlying Aichi-ken and southern Gifuken, are Inuyama, Gifu (easy day trips from Nagoya) and Gujō-Hachiman (an hour's bus ride north from Gifu). Inuyama has a noteworthy castle and some worthwhile side trips, both Inuyama and Gifu are famed for *ukai* (cormorant fishing), and Gujō-Hachiman is an attractive town surrounded by mountains and crisscrossed by rivers. Ceramic art enthusiasts will want to visit Tajimi, famed for Mino pottery, east of Nagoya.

TAJIMI 多治見
☎ 0572 / pop 94,000
The Mino district has an almost 1800-year history as a centre for pottery, and Tajimi, which is at Mino's heart, regards itself the

nation's ceramics capital. *Mino-yaki* (Mino ware) gained fame, particularly during the Momoyama period, for distinctive traits including the milky *yuzu-hada* (citron skin) glaze of the Shino style and the irregular shapes of the Oribe style.

The **tourist information office** (☎ 24-6460; ⏰ 9.30am-4pm Thu-Tue), above the police box to the right from the Tajimi station's south exit, can provide the latest information and a simple Japanese map of the town.

In the hills east of town, the **Gifu-ken Tōji Shiryōkan** (Prefectural Ceramic Museum; ☎ 23-1191; 1-9-4 Higashi-machi; admission ¥300; ⏰ 9.30am-4.30pm Tue-Sun) is in an understated modern building. There's little English signage, but you can ask for an English leaflet or just let the works (both ancient and *very* contemporary) speak for themselves. Next door, **Tōji no Sato** (☎ 25-2233; 1-9-17 Higashi-machi; prices from ¥1000; ⏰ 9.30am-4.30pm Tue-Sun, reservation required) is a workshop where you can create your own ceramic masterpiece (eg, cup or dish), which staff will later fire and/or glaze and then ship for you. Depending on the technique you choose, firing can take up to five days! Both locations are five minutes' walk from Higashi-machi bus stop (¥250 from Tajimi Station, six buses most days). A taxi from Tajimi Station costs about ¥1350.

Down the road, a large ceramic park hosts the **Gendai Tōgei Bijutsu-kan** (Museum of Modern Ceramic Art; 岐阜県現代陶芸美術館; ☎ 28-3100; www.cpm-gifu.jp/museum/english; 4-2-5 Higashi-machi; admission ¥320 ⏰ 10am-6pm Tue-Sun), one of Gifu's newest additions. The museum, which opened in 2002, has an astounding collection of modern pieces from around the world. Art and sculpture lovers shouldn't miss this place. Special exhibitions cost more (around ¥800).

Local producers gather to display their creations, and bargains are to be found, at the twice-annual **Tajimi Chawan Matsuri** (Teacup Festival) during mid-April and mid-October. The rest of the year, the Mino-yaki Danchi (Mino-ware Village) has many dealers; it's reachable by bus from north of Tajimi Station (¥300, 10 minutes, several daily).

Tajimi is easily reached from Nagoya on the JR Chūō line (*kaisoku* [rapid train], ¥650, 25 minutes).

INUYAMA 犬山

☎ 0568 / pop 69,000

Dubbed the 'Japan Rhine' by a 19th-century geologist, Inuyama's Kiso river makes a picturesque scene beneath the town's striking castle. At night, the setting becomes all the more cinematic as fishermen come to practice *ukai*. By day, Inuyama's quaint streets, its manicured Uraku-en garden and 17th century teahouse make for a daytrip from Nagoya after exploring its castle. Other attractions include the architecture of Meiji-mura Museum, shooting the rapids down the Kiso-gawa and some rather racy shrines.

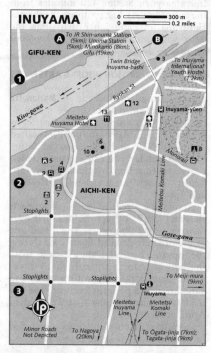

Orientation & Information

The castle and *ukai* area are within easy walking distance of Inuyama-yūen Station on the Meitetsu Komaki line. However, the **tourist information office** (☎ 61-6000; www .city.inuyama.aichi.jp/e_index.html; ☿ 9am-5pm) is in Inuyama Station, one stop south, where the Meitetsu Komaki line meets up with the Meitetsu Inuyama line; the office has useful English-language pamphlets and maps, and can book accommodation.

Sights & Activities

INUYAMA-JŌ 犬山城

A national treasure, Japan's oldest **castle** (☎ 61-1711; 65-2 Aza Kitakoken; admission ¥500; ☿ 9am-5pm) is said to have originated with a fort in 1440; the current *donjon* (main keep) dates from 1537 and has withstood war, earthquake and restoration to remain an excellent example of Momoyama-period architecture. Stone walls reach 5m high, and inside are narrow, steep staircases and military displays. There's a fine view of mountains and plains from the top storey.

The castle is a 15-minute walk west of Inuyama-yūen Station (20 minutes from Inuyama Station). Just south are the shrines Haritsuna Jinja and Sankō-Inari Jinja, the latter with interesting statues of *komainu* (protective dogs).

KARAKURI EXHIBITION ROOM & ARTEFACTS MUSEUM

One block south of the castle, the **Marionette (Karakuri) Exhibition Room** (からくり展示館; ☎ 61-3932; 8 Aza Kitakoken; ☿ 9am-5pm), contains a small display of the puppets crafted during the Edo and Meiji era. On Saturday and Sunday you can see the wooden characters in action, manipulated by puppeteer Shobei Tamaya (held at 10.30am and 2pm).

Across the street is the small **Artefacts Museum** (犬山市文化資料館; ☎ 65-1728; 8 Aza Kitakoken; ☿ 9am-5pm), where you'll find one of the ornately detailed floats used during the Inuyama Festival. Dating back to 1650, the festival features a parade of 13 three-tiered floats decked out with lanterns and *karakuri*, which perform to music. The festival takes place on the first weekend in April, at Haritsuna Jinja.

Admission to both museums is included in the cost of the ticket to Inuyama-jō.

URAKU-EN & JO-AN TEAHOUSE

有楽園・茶室如安

The strolling garden **Uraku-en** (☎ 61-4608; 1 Mikadosaki; admission ¥1000; ☿ 9am-5pm Mar-Nov, 9am-4pm Dec-Feb) is 300m east of Inuyama-jō, in a corner of the grounds of the Meitetsu Inuyama Hotel. Rated as one of the finest teahouses in Japan, **Jo-an** was constructed in 1618 in Kyoto by Oda Urakusai, a younger brother of Oda Nobunaga, and it spent time in Tokyo and Kanagawa prefecture before its relocation here in 1972.

Urakusai was a renowned tea master who founded his own tea ceremony school. He was also a closet Christian whose adopted name (the Portuguese 'João') was bestowed on the teahouse. Visitors may peek into the teahouse but are not allowed inside, except for four days each in March and November.

You must swap your shoes for open-toed sandals before entering the gravel-path garden.

CORMORANT FISHING

Ukai takes place close to Inuyama-yūen Station, by Twin-Bridge Inuyama-bashi. Book your ticket at the Inuyama tourist office in the morning or reserve at the **dock office** (☎ 61-0057; Jul & Aug ¥2800, Jun & Sep ¥2500), near the cormorant fishing pier.

Boats depart nightly from 5.30pm June to August, with the show starting around 7.45pm. In September boats depart at 5pm, with things kicking off at 7.15pm.

KISO-GAWA RAPIDS TRIP

Flat-bottomed wooden boats shoot the rapids on a 13km section of the Kiso-gawa. The ride takes an hour and costs ¥3400/1700 for adults/children; it entails little risk, except for a soaking. Contact **Nihon Rhein Kankō** (☎ 0574-28-2727; ☿ mid-Mar-late Nov). There is a free shuttle bus from Inuyama-yūen Station.

Festivals & Events

In addition to the colourful parade of floats during the **Inuyama Festival** (first weekend in April), the city also hosts the summer **Nihon Rhine Festival**, held on 10 August on the banks of the river and culminating in fireworks.

Sleeping & Eating

Inuyama International Youth Hostel (犬山国際 ユースホステル; ☎ 61-1111; fax 61-2770; 162- 1 Tsugaohimuro; tatami r s/d ¥3700/5800, Western-style

CENTRAL HONSHŪ

tw ¥6400) Inuyama's cheapest option (25-minute walk northeast of Inuyama-yūen Station) has comfortable rooms, friendly staff and a stone bath. Reservations recommended. Meals available by advance notice – and recommended (no restaurants nearby).

Minshuku Yayoi (民宿三月; ☎ /fax 61-0751; r per person with 2 meals from ¥6000) Across from Inuyama-yūen Station, this friendly inn has simple but comfy tatami rooms and shared bathrooms. This place prides itself on its home cooking.

Rinkō-kan (臨江館; ☎ 61-0977; rinkokan@triton .ocn.ne.jp; 8-1 Aza Nishi-Daimonsaki; r per person with/without 2 meals from ¥10,650/4620) Overlooking the river, this cheery hot-spring hotel has handsome Japanese rooms that are popular with the cormorant fishing crowd. It is known for its *rotemburo* (open-air baths), Jacuzzi and local cuisine.

Bistro (☎ 61-0534; 22-3 Aza Nishi-Daimonsaki; ☻ 11am-2.30pm & 6-10pm Thu-Tue) Near the river, this low-key restaurant serves tasty Italian fare in a charming but simple setting.

Getting There & Away

Inuyama is connected with Nagoya (¥540, 30 minutes) and Shin-Gifu Station in Gifu city (¥440, 35 minutes) via the Meitetsu Inuyama line. Alternatively, from JR Unuma Station on the JR Takayama line, a short walk across the river, there are frequent trains to JR Gifu Station (¥320, 30 minutes).

AROUND INUYAMA 犬山近辺
Meiji-mura Museum 明治村

Few Meiji period buildings have survived war, earthquake or rabid development, but this open-air **museum** (☎ 67-0314; www.meiji mura.com; 1 Uchiyama; admission ¥1600; ☻ 9.30am-5pm Mar-Oct, 9.30am-4pm Nov-Feb, closed Mon Dec-Feb) has brought together more than 65 of them from all over Japan. There are public offices, private homes and banks, as well as some trains and buses. Among them is the entryway designed by Frank Lloyd Wright for Tokyo's Imperial Hotel – that building has since been replaced by a more generic version. The clash of Western and Japanese architectural styles provides a sense of that period's cultural schizophrenia. Allow at least half a day to enjoy the place at an easy pace.

A bus to Meiji-mura (¥410, 20 minutes) departs every 30 minutes from Inuyama Station.

Ōgata-jinja 大縣神社

This 2000-year-old **shrine** (☎ 67-1017) is dedicated to the female Shintō deity Izanami and draws women devotees seeking marriage or fertility. The precincts of the shrine contain rocks and other items resembling female genitals.

The popular **Hime-no-Miya Grand Festival** takes place here on the Sunday before 15 March (or on 15 March if it's a Sunday). Locals pray for good harvests and prosperity by parading through the streets bearing a *mikoshi* (portable shrine) with replicas of female genitals.

Ōgata-jinja is a 30-minute walk southeast of Gakuden Station on the Meitetsu Komaki line.

Tagata-jinja 田県神社

Izanagi, the male counterpart of Izanami, is commemorated at this **shrine** (☎ 76-2906). The main hall has a side building containing a collection of phalluses, left as offerings by grateful worshippers.

The **Tagata Hōnen Sai Festival** takes place on 15 March at the Tagata-jinja when the highly photogenic, 2m-long, 60kg 'sacred object' is paraded, amid much mirth, around the neighbourhood. Arrive well before the procession starts at 2pm.

Tagata-jinja is five minutes' walk west of Tagata-jinja-mae Station, one stop south of Gakuden Station on the Meitetsu Komaki line.

YAOTSU 八百津
☎ 0574 / pop 13,950

This town has become a pilgrimage site as the birthplace of Sugihara Chiune, Japan's consul in Lithuania during early WWII. Sugihara saved some 6000 Jews from Nazi extermination by issuing transit visas against Japanese government orders; the 'Sugihara survivors' escaped to Kōbe and Japanese-controlled Shanghai and, later, to other countries. The story is the subject of the 1997 Academy Award–winning short film *Visas and Virtue*.

On Yaotsu's Jindō-no-oka (Hill of Humanity) is a **museum** (admission ¥300; ☻ 9.30am-5pm Tue-Sun) with photos of this inspiring story. Further information can be found at www.town.yaotsu.gifu.jp, or contact the **city office** (☎ 43-2111, ext 252, English speaker available).

Yaotsu is most easily reached by car, but from Nagoya you can take the Meitetsu

Hiromi line to Akechi (¥900, one hour), then transfer to the Yao bus (¥400, 25 minutes) to Yaotsu; it's a short taxi ride to the museum. The city office may be able to help with logistics if you phone at least a day in advance.

GIFU 岐阜
☎ 058 / pop 400,500

In 1891 Gifu was hit by a colossal earthquake and later given a thorough drubbing in WWII, so the city centre is not much to look at. That said, visitors come for *ukai* and handicrafts, as well as a reasonably colourful district in the side streets north of the station and a post-war reconstruction of the castle Gifu-jō atop the nearby mountain, Kinka-zan.

Orientation & Information
JR Gifu Station and Meitetsu Shin-Gifu Station are separated by several minutes' walk in the southern part of the city centre.

The **tourist information office** (☎ 262-4415; ⏰ 9am-7pm Mar-Dec, to 6pm Jan-Feb) on the 2nd floor of the JR Gifu station provides English-language city maps and accommodation lists.

Sights & Activities
CORMORANT FISHING
The *ukai* season in Gifu (where Charlie Chaplin fished) lasts from 11 May to 15 October. Boats depart every evening, except after heavy rainfall or on the night of a full moon.

Tickets are sold at hotels or, after 6pm, at the **booking office** (☎ 262-0104 for advance reservations; adult/child ¥3300/2900) just below the bridge, Nagara-bashi, and reservations are advised. Food and drink are not provided on the boats, so bring your own for the two-hour boat ride. Cheaper boats cost ¥3000/2600 per adult/child, but you can't take food aboard.

Fishing takes place around Nagara-bashi, which can be reached by bus 11 from JR Gifu Station. You can also get a good view of the action by walking along the river east of the bridge.

GIFU-KŌEN 岐阜公園
A few of the attractions of this lush, hillside park are the **Gifu City History Museum** (☎ 265-0010; 2-18-1 Ōmiya-chō; admission ¥300; ⏰ 9am-5pm Tue-Sun) and the **Mt Kinka Ropeway** (☎ 262-6784;

¥1050 return; ⏰ 9am-5pm mid-Oct–mid-Mar, to 10.30pm late Jul–Aug, to 6pm mid-Mar–late Jul, Sep–mid-Oct) up to the summit of Kinka-zan. From here you can check out **Gifu-jō** (☎ 263-4853; admission ¥200; closes 30min before ropeway), a small but picturesque modern reconstruction of the original castle. Those who'd rather huff it can hike to the castle (one hour). To reach the park take bus 11 from Gifu Station to Gifu-kōen mae (¥200, 20 minutes).

SHŌHŌ-JI 正法寺
The main attraction of this orange-and-white **temple** (☎ 264-2760; admission ¥150; ⏰ 9am-5pm) is the papier-mache *daibutsu* (Great Buddha), which is nearly 14m tall and was created from about a tonne of paper sutras. Completed in 1832, the *daibutsu* took 38 years to make. The temple is a short walk southwest of Gifu-kōen.

Sleeping
Gifu has plenty of accommodation, and the tourist information office at the station can provide a list and a helpful map. Most options are north of the station.

Weekly Shō (☎ 272-9730, toll free 0120-626-540; 1-14 Kinen-chō; s/tw from ¥3200/5400) Bargain-priced, basic Western-style rooms and, despite its name, nightly rates; you can clean your room yourself with a vacuum provided, or pay extra to have it serviced. From JR Gifu Station, north exit, walk down Nagarabashi street, take a right at the third light and it's two blocks further on the right.

Yamaguchiya Honkan (旅館山口屋本館; ☎ 262-4650; 2-9 Tamamiya-machi; r per person ¥4500) A bit closer to the station, this cosy ryokan gets many repeat customers for its handsome tatami rooms and friendly service. From JR Gifu Station, north exit, walk down Nagarabashi street, take a left at the first light, then turn down the second alley on your right.

Shopping
Gifu is famous for its *kasa* (oiled paper parasols/umbrellas) and *chōchin* (paper lanterns), which are stocked in all the souvenir shops. The tourist information office has a map to speciality stores.

Sakaida Eikichi Honten (坂井田永吉本店; ☎ 271-6958; 27 Kanōnaka; ⏰ 9am-5pm Mon-Fri) both makes and sells *kasa*. It often closes at lunchtime. It's a 12-minute walk southeast of JR Gifu Station.

Getting There & Away

The JR Tōkaidō line will get you here from Nagoya (*tokkyū* ¥1180, 20 minutes; *futsū* ¥450, 30 minutes). Meitetsu line trains from Shin-Gifu serve Inuyama (¥440, 35 minutes) and Shin-Nagoya Station (¥540, 35 minutes).

GUJŌ HACHIMAN 郡上八幡

☎ 0575 / pop 16,800

Nestled in the mountains at the confluence of several rivers, Gujō Hachiman is a small, pleasant town famed for its **Gujō Odori Matsuri**, Japan's third-largest dance festival. Following a tradition dating to the 1590s, townsfolk let down their hair with frenzied folk dancing on 31 nights between early July and early September. Visitor participation is encouraged and during the four main days of the festival (13–16 August) the dancing goes all night. Other times of year, the town's sparkling rivers, narrow lanes and stone bridges make a fine setting for a stopover.

The **tourist office** (☎ 67-0002; ⏰ 8.30am-5pm) is by the bridge Shin-bashi in the centre of town, about five minutes' walk from the Jōka-machi Plaza bus terminal.

The tiny hilltop castle **Gujō Hachiman-jō** (☎ 65-5839; admission ¥300; ⏰ 8am-6pm Jun-Aug, 9am-5pm Sep-May), had been a humble fortress dating back to about 1600; the current, grander building dates from only 1933. It contains weapons, armour and the like, and offers fine views. From the bus terminal it's about a 20-minute walk.

The famous spring, **Sōgi-sui**, near the centre of town, is something of a pilgrimage site, named for a Momoyama-era poet. People who rank such things place Sōgi-sui at the top of the list for clarity.

Gujō Tōsenji Youth Hostel (ユースホステル郡上洞泉寺; ☎ 67-0290; fax 67-0291; 417 Ozaki-chō; dm per person ¥3200, closed 11-16 Aug) This attractively refurbished hostel is pleasantly situated on the grounds of a temple, though there are only Japanese-style loos and no bath on the premises (there's a *sentō* nearby).

Satō Minshuku (里民宿; ☎ 65-2316; r per person with 2 meals from ¥7500) Practically across from the bus terminal, this welcoming, old-style place has decent rooms, some decorated with antiques.

Bizenya Ryokan (備前屋旅館; ☎ 65-2068; fax 67-0007; r per person with 2 meals ¥10,000) Boasting large rooms with shared facilities and a handsome garden, this ryokan provides a relaxing overnight experience. It's between the bus terminal and the tourist office.

The most convenient access to Gujō Hachiman is via bus from Gifu (¥1560, one hour, four daily). From Nagoya Station, the easiest way is also by bus (2 hours). The town centre is easily walkable, but the tourist office hires out bicycles (¥300/1500 per hour/day).

HIDA DISTRICT 飛騨地域

The centrepiece of this ancient, mountainous region is the handsome town of Takayama, where the legacy of a strong craft tradition lives on in its merchant houses, temples and shrines. Hida is known for *gasshō-zukuri* (hands-in-prayer) architecture, which you'll spot in the Unesco World Heritage sites of Shirakawa-gō and nearby Gokayama, though the latter is not part of Hida. Hida's culinary fame rests in its Hida beef and to a lesser extent in its *soba* (buckwheat noodles).

TAKAYAMA 高山

☎ 0577 / pop 67,700

With its old inns, shops and sake breweries, Takayama is a rarity – a city (admittedly a small one) that has managed to retain its traditional charm. Vibrant morning markets, hillside shrines and a laid-back populace add to the town's allure, and it should be a high priority on any visit to central Honshū. Give yourself two days to enjoy the place; it's easily tackled on foot or bicycle.

Takayama was established in the late 16th century as the castle town of the Kanamori family, although in 1692 it was placed under direct control of the *bakufu* (shōgunate) in Edo. The present layout dates from the Kanamori period, and sights include more than a dozen museums, galleries and exhibitions covering lacquer and lion masks, folk craft and architecture.

Takayama remains the region's administrative and transport hub, and it makes a good base for trips around Hida and Japan Alps National Park (p231).

The Takayama Matsuri (April and October; see p223) is rated as one of Japan's three great festivals and attracts over half a million spectators. If you plan to attend, book your accommodation well in advance, or visit as a day trip from a nearby town.

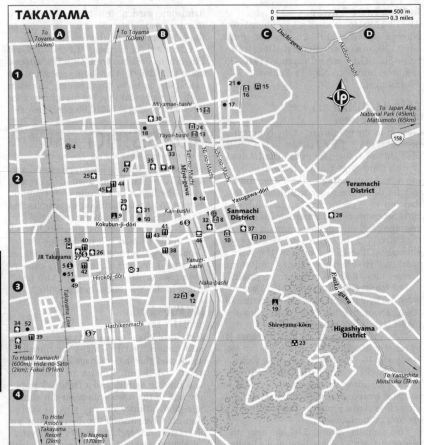

Orientation

All the main sights except Hida-no-Sato (Hida Folk Village) are in the centre of town, a short walk east from the station. Streets are arranged in a grid pattern. From the station, Kokubun-ji-dōri, the main street, heads east, across the river Miya-gawa (about 10 minutes' walk), where it becomes Yasugawa-dōri. South of Yasugawa-dōri is the historic Sanmachi district of immaculately preserved old homes.

Hida-no-Sato is a 10-minute bus ride west of the station.

Information

The town's **tourist information office** (☎ 32-5328; ⊗ 8.30am-5pm Nov-Mar, 8.30am-6.30pm Apr-Oct), di-

rectly in front of JR Takayama Station, has English-speaking staff, as well as English-language maps and information on sights and accommodation. It can also provide info on Takayama's festivals, as well as bus schedules between Takayama and Japan Alps National Park and the Shōkawa Valley. On the Web, visit www.hida.jp/e-taka.htm.

To arrange a home visit, homestay or volunteer interpreter for non-Japanese languages (including sign language), contact the city's **International Affairs Office** (☎ 32-3333, ext 2407; 2-18 Hanaoka), located inside the Takayama Municipal Building, one month in advance.

Postal ATMs are at the main post office on Hirokōji-dōri, a few blocks east of the station. Ōgaki Kyōritsu Bank also has foreign-card ATMs southeast of the station and near the Miya-gawa Morning Market. Jōroku Bank, one block east of the station, can change cash or travellers' cheques.

Internet access is available free of charge at the tourist office (one computer); at the **Takayama Municipal Office** (2-18 Hanaoka; 9am-5pm Mon-Fri) with two computers, seven minutes' walk north of the station; and at a **pre-school** (Yasugawa-dōri; per 30 min ¥100; 10am-5pm) in the Sanmachi district.

Sights & Activities

TAKAYAMA-JINYA 高山陣屋

Originally built in 1615 as the administrative centre for the Kanamori clan, **Takayama-jinya** (Historical Government House; 32-0643; 1-5 Hachiken-machi; admission ¥420; 8.45am-5pm Mar-Oct, 8.45am-4.30pm Nov-Feb) is now the only remaining prefectural office of the Tokugawa shōgunate; the main gate was once reserved for high officials. The present main building dates from 1816 and it was used as a local government office until 1969.

As well as government offices, a rice granary and a garden, there's a torture chamber with explanatory detail. Free guided tours in English are available upon request. Takayama-jinya is a 15-minute walk east of the train station.

SANMACHI 三町

The centre of the old town, this district of three main streets (Ichi-no-Machi, Ni-no-

Machi and San-no-Machi) is lined with traditional shops, restaurants, museums and private homes. Sake breweries are easily recognised by the round baskets of cedar fronds hanging above their entrance, though most of the year they just sell their wares (see p223).

Fujii Folkcraft Art Gallery (35-3778; 21 San-no-machi; admission ¥700; 9am-5pm) This private collection contains folk craft and ceramics from Japan (particularly from the Muromachi and Edo periods), China and Korea. It's in an old merchant's house.

Hirata Folk Art Museum (Hirata Kinen-kan; 33-1354; 39 Ni-no-machi; admission ¥300; 9am-5pm) This merchant's house, dating from the turn of the 20th century, displays items from everyday rural Japanese life.

Takayama Museum of Local History (32-1205; 75 Ichi-no-machi; admission ¥300; 8.30am-5pm Mar-Nov, 9am-4.30pm Dec-Feb, closed Mon Nov-Mar) Devoted to the crafts and traditions of the region, this museum houses images carved by Enkū, a woodcarving priest who wandered the region in the 17th century. There are also several small but nicely maintained gardens.

MERCHANT HOUSES 吉島家日下部民芸館

North of Sanmachi are two excellent examples of Edo period merchants' homes, with the living quarters in one section and the warehouse in another. Design buffs shouldn't miss **Yoshijima-ke** (Yoshijima house; 32-0038; Ichi-no-machi; admission ¥500; 9am-5pm Mar-Nov, 9am-4.30pm

Wed-Sun Dec-Feb), well covered in architectural publications. Its lack of ornamentation allows you to focus on the lovely, spare lines, soaring roof and skylight. Down the block, **Kusakabe Mingeikan** (Kusakabe Folk Art Museum; ☎ 32-0072; 1-52 Ōshinmachi; admission ¥500; ☺ 8.30am-5pm Mar-Nov, 8.30am-4.30pm Dec-Feb), built in the 1890s, showcases the striking craftsmanship of traditional Takayama carpenters' skills. Inside is a collection of folk art.

INRŌ BIJUTSUKAN 印籠美術館

Traditional kimono do not have pockets, so fashionable Japanese used to carry *inrō* (medicine boxes) on strings held in place by *netsuke* (toggles). Both are elaborately designed and carved creations in wood, bone, stone and ivory, and are among Japan's most celebrated works of art. This **museum** (☎ 32-8500; Ichi-no-machi; admission ¥500; ☺ 9am-5pm Wed-Mon Apr-Nov) displays some 300 rare and historic examples.

TAKAYAMA YATAI KAIKAN 高山屋台会館

The **Takayama Yatai Kaikan** (Festival Floats Exhibition Hall; ☎ 32-5100; 178 Sakura-machi; admission ¥820; ☺ 8.30am-5pm Mar-Nov, 9am-4.30pm Dec-Feb) features a rotating selection of four of the 23 multi-tiered *yatai* (floats) used in the Takayama Matsuri. These spectacular creations, some dating from the 17th century, are prized for their flamboyant carvings, metalwork and lacquerwork. A famous feature of some floats is *karakuri*, marionettes that perform amazing tricks and acrobatics courtesy of eight accomplished puppeteers using 36 strings. A video gives a sense of the festival.

English-speakers will be offered free use of a tape recorder, further explaining details of the floats.

Your ticket also admits you to the **Sakurayama Nikkō-kan** next door, with intricate models of the famous shrines at Nikkō, which you can witness at dawn and dusk, courtesy of an imaginative lighting simulation. You can also visit the shrine **Sakurayama Hachiman-gū**, where the festival is based.

You may pass some unusual slender garages around town with three-storey doors; these house the *yatai* that are not in the museum.

SHISHI KAIKAN 獅子会館

Just south of the Yatai Kaikan is the **Shishi Kaikan** (Lion Mask Exhibition Hall; ☎ 32-0881; 53-1 Sakura-machi; admission ¥600; ☺ 8.30am-5.30pm late Apr-late Oct, 9am-5pm late Oct-late Apr). It has a display of over 800 lion masks and musical instruments connected with the lion dances that are commonly performed at festivals in central and northern Japan. Admission includes twice-hourly demonstrations of *karakuri* – a good opportunity for a close-up view of these marvellous puppets in action.

SHUNKEI KAIKAN 春慶会館

West of the Festival Floats Exhibition Hall on the other side of the river, this **exhibition hall** (☎ 32-3373; 1 Kando-chō; admission ¥300; ☺ 8am-5.30pm Apr-Oct, 9am-5pm Nov-Mar) displays Takayama's fine lacquerware, with more than 1000 Shunkei pieces, and an exhibit showing production techniques. Unlike many other Japanese lacquer styles, Takayama's Shunkei lacquerware is designed to show off the wood grain.

HIDA KOKUBUN-JI 飛騨国分寺

Takayama's oldest **temple** (☎ 32-1295; Kokubun-ji-dōri; admission ¥300; ☺ 9am-4pm) was originally built in the 8th century; fires later ravaged the shrine, and the oldest of the present buildings dates from the 16th century. The temple's treasure hall houses some Important Cultural Properties, and the courtyard boasts a three-storey pagoda and an impressively gnarled gingko tree, which is in remarkably good shape considering it's believed to be 1200 years old. The temple is a five-minute walk northeast of the station, off Kokubun-ji-dōri.

TERAMACHI & SHIROYAMA-KŌEN
寺町・城山公園

These hilly districts in the east side of town are linked by a walking trail, particularly enjoyable in the early morning or late afternoon. Teramachi has over a dozen temples (one houses the youth hostel) and shrines that you can wander around before taking in the lush greenery of the park. Various trails lead through the park and up the mountainside to the ruins of the castle, **Takayama-jō**. As you descend, you can take a look at the temple, **Shōren-ji**, which was transferred to this site from the Shōkawa Valley when a dam was built there in 1960.

The walk takes a leisurely two hours and from the temple it's a 10-minute walk back to the centre of town.

HIDA-NO-SATO 飛騨の里

This large open-air **museum** (☎ 34-4711; 1-590 Okatmoto-chō; admission ¥700; ☉ 8.30am-5pm) is highly recommended for dozens of traditional houses, dismantled at their original sites throughout the region and rebuilt here. During clear weather, there are good views across the town to the peaks of the Japan Alps.

Hido-no-Sato is in two sections. The western section features 12 old houses and a complex of five traditional buildings with artisans (see p229). Displays are well presented and offer an excellent chance to see what rural life was like in previous centuries.

The eastern section of the village, which is a pleasant walk away, is centred around the Omoide Taikenkan, where you can try making candles, *sembei* (rice crackers) etc. Other buildings include the Go-kura Storehouse (used for storage of rice as payment of taxes) and the Museum of Mountain Life. Allow at least three hours to explore the whole place on foot.

Hida-no-Sato is a 30-minute walk from Takayama Station, but the route through urban sprawl is not enjoyable. Either hire a bicycle in town (p226), or take the Hida-no-Sato bus (¥250, 10 minutes) from stop 2 at the bus station. A discount ticket 'Hida-no-Sato setto ken' is available, combining the return fare and admission to the park for ¥900. Be sure to check return times for the bus.

MAHIKARI-KYŌ MAIN WORLD SHRINE 真光教

Dominating Takayama's western skyline is the golden roof of the **Main World Shrine** (☎ 34-7008; admission free; ☉ 8.30am-4.30pm, closed for monthly religious holidays) of the new religion Mahikari-kyō, which is said to combine Buddhism and Shintō. Opinion is divided on whether its believers are harmless loop-the-loops or anti-Semitic doomsday cultists. A guided tour might allow you to decide for yourself (call in advance for an English-speaking guide; an English pamphlet is available).

MORNING MARKETS

Asa-ichi (morning markets) take place every morning from 7am to noon, starting an hour earlier from April to October. The **Jinya-mae Market** (陣屋前朝市) is in front of Takayama-jinya; the **Miya-gawa Market** (宮川朝市) is larger, along the east bank of the Miya-gawa, between Kaji-bashi and Yayoi-bashi. The markets provide a pleasant way to start the day, with a stroll past gnarled farmers at their vegetable stands and stalls selling crafts, pickles, souvenirs and that all-important steaming cuppa joe.

Festivals & Events

Takayama's famed festival is in two parts. **Sannō Matsuri** takes place on 14 and 15 April; a dozen *yatai*, decorated with carvings, dolls, colourful curtains and blinds, are paraded through the town. In the evening the floats are decked out with lanterns and the procession is accompanied by sacred music. **Hachiman Matsuri**, on 9 and 10 October, is a slightly smaller version starting at Sakurayama Hachiman-gū (opposite).

If you plan to visit Takayama during either of these times, you must book accommodation months in advance and expect to pay a 20% premium. You could also stay elsewhere in the region and commute to Takayama.

In January and February several of the sake breweries in Sanmachi, many dating back to the Edo period, arrange tours and tastings.

CENTRAL HONSHŪ

HIDA'S TAKUMI WOODWORKERS

Some 1300 years ago there lived a carpenter named Takumi, said to be so skilled that word of his work spread as far as the capital, Heian-kyō (now Kyoto).

At that time, the Japanese regions had to pay taxes in rice, which posed a problem for Hida, with little farmland but many forested mountains. So in the year 718, in lieu of taxes, Hida was permitted to send Takumi – and a cadre of carpenters and carvers – to construct the legendary shrines and temples of Kyoto and Nara.

Today, 'Takumi' has become a general term for woodworkers of great skill and precision. Takumi work appears in homes, furniture and statues, and *karakuri* puppets for Hida's famed *yatai*, festival floats that are storeys tall.

Takumi's name has been adopted by woodworking shops throughout Hida and you can learn more about Takumi-style woodworking at the Takumi-kan (p226) in Furukawa.

Sleeping

The tourist information office (p220) assists with reservations.

BUDGET

Hida Takayama Tenshō-ji Youth Hostel (☎ 32-6345; fax 32-6392; 83 Tensho-ji-machi; dm ¥2940) In an attractive temple in Teramachi, this hostel is a peaceful place, though some guests gripe about its lights-out and wake-up schedule. The hostel is a 25-minute walk across town from the train station, or board the bus for Shin-Hotaka, get off at the Betsuin-mae stop and walk east about five minutes.

Hotel Yamaichi (☎ 34-6200; www.kbnet.jp.org /11pm/kamaya/hyoshi.html; 181-2 Ishiura-chō; Japanese/ Western r per person from ¥3800/4800; 🖳) In an old building 10 minutes by bus south of town, this inn has simple, decent rooms (Western rooms have private bathrooms) and free Internet access for guests. The friendly English-speaking owners often pick up guests from the station; if they can't they'll pay half the taxi fare. Check in from 3pm.

MIDRANGE

Rickshaw Inn (☎ 32-2890; www.rickshawinn.com; 54 Suehiro-chō; s/tw with bath ¥6500/11,600, without bath 4900/9800; 🖳) A travellers' favourite, this good-value inn has pleasant Japanese and Western-style rooms, a small kitchen and cosy lounge. The friendly English-speaking owners have excellent information about Takayama. Reserve well in advance.

Murasaki Ryokan (☎ 32-1724; fax 33-7512; 1-56 Nanoka-machi; r per person with/without 2 meals from ¥7500/4000) This nicely-aged ryokan features Japanese-style rooms and a splendid wall of flowers along the building's front, the product of decades of work.

Ō-Machi (☎ 32-3251; 38 Ichi-no-machi; r per person ¥4000) Four blocks east of the river near the Takayama Museum of Local History, Ō-Machi offers small but clean tatami rooms. Owner speaks some English and guests can use the kitchen.

Minshuku Kuwataniya (☎ 32-5021; www.kuwa taniya.com; 1-50-30 Sowa-machi; r per person with/without bath ¥6450/4350) Close to the train station, this is Takayama's longest-running *minshuku* (since the 1920s), with both Japanese- and Western-style rooms, hot-spring bath and free bicycle use. Dinner (available for ¥2310) always features Hida's famed beef. It's half a block north of Hida Kokubun-ji temple.

Sōsuke (☎ 32-0818; www.irori-sosuke.com; 1-64 Okamoto-machi; r per person ¥5040) West of the train station, across from Takayama Green Hotel, Sōsuke has pleasant tatami rooms and the English-speaking staff prepares excellent dinners (¥2100) – including meals for vegetarians. The handsomely renovated building dates from the 1800s and retains a traditional style, including an *irori* (hearth), though it is on a busy road.

Yamashita (☎ 33-0686; fax 32-8513; 4377 Onako-machi; r per person with 2 meals ¥8500) This farmhouse-style *minshuku* in Enakochō has decent tatami rooms and lies about 10 minutes by car south of the city centre; pick-up from the train station is available. Dinner is served around the *irori*. It's a good option if you don't mind staying in the outskirts of town.

Country Hotel Takayama (☎ 35-3900; fax 35-3910; 6-38 Hanasato-machi; s/tw from ¥5900/7800) Conveniently located across from the station, the 11-storey Country Hotel has small, well-maintained Western-style rooms. Entrance is behind the Family Mart.

Takayama City Hotel Four Seasons (☎ 36-0088; fax 36-0080; 1-1 Kanda-machi; s/tw from ¥6900/13,100) Featuring nicer-than-average business hotel rooms (some with hardwood floors), the Four Seasons is popular among Japanese travellers. It also has a communal *onsen*. It's a 15-minute walk from the station, two blocks west of the river.

Best Western Hotel (☎ 37-2000; fax 37-2005; 6-6 Hanasato-machi; s/d/tw from ¥9240/12,600/14,700) One block from the station, this fairly new hotel offers spacious, comfortably furnished rooms. Lounge and restaurant on-site.

TOP END

Asunaro Ryokan (☎ 33-5551; www.yado-asunaro.com; 2-96 Hatuda-machi; r per person with/without bath from ¥15,750/13,650; 🖳) This excellent ryokan has handsome tatami rooms, a spacious *onsen* bath and decadent dinners and breakfasts (included in the price). At night, guests can warm themselves by the *irori*. Staff speak some English. Free Internet.

Sumiyoshi Ryokan (☎ 32-0228; fax 33-8916; 4-21 Hon-machi; r per person with 2 meals from ¥10,000) This delightfully traditional inn is set in an old merchant's house; some rooms have river views. No English spoken.

Ryokan Gōto (☎ /fax 33-0870; San-no-machi; r per person with breakfast from ¥9000) Another of this city's lovely traditional inns, Gōto lies in the heart of Sanmachi, with eclectic touches scattered about the ryokan. No English spoken.

Takayama Green Hotel (☎ 33-5500; www.takayama-gh.com; 2-180 Nishinoishiki-chō; r per person with 2 meals from ¥15,000) This beautifully outfitted *onsen* hotel has Japanese, Western and combination rooms, in a tower southwest of the station. Nicely landscaped *rotemburo* is a nice feature.

Eating

Takayama's specialities include *soba*, *hoba-miso* (sweet miso paste cooked on a *hoba* [magnolia] leaf) and *sansai* (mountain vegetables). Street-foods include *mitarashi-dango* (skewers of grilled riceballs seasoned with soya sauce), *shio-sembei* (salty rice crackers) and skewers of grilled Hida beef (among the finest grades of meat in Japan, though relatively new on the scene).

Myogaya (☎ 32-0426; 5-15 Hanasato-chō; mains around ¥1000; ☼ 8-10.30am, 11.30am-3pm & 5-7pm Wed-Mon) A block east of the train station, this tiny restaurant and food shop prepares tasty vegetarian curry with brown rice, samosas, fruit juices and even dandelion tea. English menu.

Suzuya (☎ 32-2484; 24 Hanakawa-chō; sets ¥1200-3000; ☼ 11am-3pm & 5-8pm Wed-Mon) In the centre of town, Suzuya is one of Takayama's long-standing favourites, and it's highly recommended (though packed at lunch) for local specialities like Hida beef, *hoba-miso* and various stews. English menu.

Yamatake-Shōten (☎ 32-0571; meals per person from around ¥4000; ☼ 11am-2pm & 4.30-9pm Tue-Sun, closed 3rd Tue of each month) An excellent place to sample savoury Hida beef, this informal restaurant allows customers to choose their own cuts, which are then brought to the table for cooking over the inset charcoal grill.

Chapala (☎ 33-7777; mains from ¥600; ☼ 11.30am-1pm & 6-11pm Mon-Sat, closed 1st Mon of each month) Two blocks west of the river, this cosy restaurant serves tasty chilli con carne, burritos, quesadillas, guacamole and chips, and other Tex-Mex favourites. Margaritas and Coronas accompany the proceedings nicely.

Murasaki (☎ 32-0571; small plates from ¥400; ☼ 5pm-1am Mon-Sat, 5pm-midnight Sun, closed 3rd Tue of each month) This popular *izakaya* (Japanese-style pub) has a big picture-menu of tasty bites, potent *chuhi* cocktails and the cheapest beer in town – the sum total of which attracts a rather lively crowd. Two blocks west of the river, Murasaki is easily identified by the gigantic red paper lantern out front.

La Viennoiserie de Nicolas (☎ 36-0054; 6-28 Hanasato-machi; pastries from ¥320; ☼ 10am-4pm) A block from the train station, this tiny pastry shop serves some decadent treats – *pain au chocolat*, cheesecake, rhubarb pie – all lovingly prepared by the French owner.

Jingoro Rāmen (☎ 33-7563; mains from ¥550; ☼ 11am-1.30pm Mon-Sun & 6pm-2am Mon-Sat) Takayama's most venerable *rāmen* restaurant is a simple affair: broth, noodles and pork (or not) – but the savoury results are extremely satisfying. English menu.

Drinking

Red Hill Pub (☎ 33-8139; ☼ 7pm-midnight Tue-Sun). A mix of locals and expats gather at this charming and welcoming bar. You'll find an excellent selection of domestic and imported brews and an eclectic mix of tunes.

Bagus (☎ 36-4341; ☼ 7pm-1am Mon-Sat) This friendly reggae bar has a youthful energy. A 10-minute walk from the train station, good music and potent drinks await. It's on the 2nd floor.

Tonio (☎ 34-341; ☼ 6pm-midnight Mon-Sat) This English-style pub lies closer to the river, with Guinness on tap and a startling variety of imported whiskies.

Café Doppio (☎ 32-3638; coffee from ¥300; ☼ 9am-6pm) For a pick-me-up, stop by this pleasant café on the edge of the river. Cappuccinos, espressos, macchiatos and waffles.

Shopping

Takayama is renowned for crafts. *Ichii itto-bori* (woodcarvings) are fashioned from yew and can be seen as intricate components of the *yatai* floats or for sale as figurines. Woodworking expertise also extends to furniture (see Hida's Takumi Woodworkers, p223).

Shunkei lacquerware was introduced from Kyoto several centuries ago and is used to produce boxes, trays and flower containers. The city-run exhibition hall, **Shunkei Kaikan**, has adjacent shops with outstanding lacquerware and porcelain, and, occasionally, good deals.

Local pottery styles range from the rustic *Yamada-yaki* to the decorative *Shibukusa-yaki* styles.

Around town, good places to find handicrafts are Sanmachi, the morning markets, and the section of Kokubun-ji-dōri between the Miya-gawa and the train station. Probably the most common souvenirs are *sarubobo* (monkey babies), dolls of red cloth dressed in blue fabric, with pointy limbs and featureless faces.

Getting There & Away

The bus station is on your left outside the train station. Many roads in this region close in the winter, so bus schedules vary seasonally and don't run at all in winter on some routes. For exact dates check with the tourist offices.

Keiō Highway buses (☎ 32-1688) connect Takayama and Shinjuku (¥6500, 5½ hours, several daily, reservations required).

For getting around in Japan Alps (Chūbu-Sangaku National Park) see p232.

Takayama is connected with Nagoya on the JR Takayama line (Hida *tokkyū*, ¥5870, 2¼ hours, 10 daily). Some of these continue to Toyama (¥3280, 1½ hours).

Express trains run from Osaka (¥8070, five hours) and Kyoto (¥7440, 4½ hours), although it's usually faster to take the *shinkansen* and change in Nagoya.

At the train station you'll find **Eki Rent-a-Car System** (☎ 33-3522) and there's a branch of **Nippon Rent-a-Car** (☎ 34-5121) southwest of the train station, near Sōsuke *minshuku*.

Getting Around

Most sights in Takayama can be covered easily on foot. You can amble from the train station across to Teramachi in 25 minutes.

The only place you'll really need to take the bus is to Hida-no-Sato (¥220, 10 minutes, half-hourly).

Takayama is a good place to explore by bicycle. Some lodgings rent or loan cycles, or rent from **Himawari** (34-1183; ⏰ 8am-5pm; per hr/day ¥200/1200), right next to the train station; or **Hara Cycle** (☎ 32-1657; per hr/day ¥300/1300) on Kokubun-ji-dōri.

FURUKAWA 古川

☎ 0577 / pop 18,000

Home of the somewhat mystifying *Hadaka Matsuri* (Naked Festival), Furukawa is a pleasant riverside town with lovely streetscapes, peaceful temples and some interesting museums, all framed against the mountains surrounding it. Just 15 minutes from Takayama, Furukawa makes a nice

day trip and, if you are in the region on 19 or 20 April, don't miss the festival.

Orientation & Information

Hida-Furukawa train and bus stations adjoin each other east of the town centre, and the sights are within 10 minutes' walk. There's an **information office** (☎ 73-3180; ⏰ 8.30am-5.30pm) at the bus station, which offers an English pamphlet and Japanese maps, but if you don't speak Japanese you'll be better off getting information in Takayama (p220); staff in either city can book accommodation in Furukawa.

Sights

Heading out of the train station, walk two blocks to the right (north) and take a left. This leads to the historic district of **Setakawa to Shirakabe-dozo**, where you'll find handsome riverside streets filled with white- and darkwood-walled shops, storehouses and private homes. Before strolling along the carp-filled canal (fish food available for ¥50), take in the two museums in the square.

If you're not in town for the festival, the **Matsuri Kaikan** (Festival Museum; ☎ 73-3511; admission ¥800; ⏰ 9am-5pm Apr-Nov, 9am-4.30pm Dec-Mar) shows it in all its glory. You can don 3-D glasses to watch a video of the festivities, see some of the *yatai* that are paraded through the streets, try manipulating *karakuri* like those used on the *yatai*, and watch craftsmen demonstrating *kirie* (paper cut-outs) or *ittobori* (wood carving).

Across the square, **Takumi-kan** (Takumi Craft Museum; ☎ 73-3321; admission ¥200; ⏰ 9am-5pm Mar-Nov, 9am-4.30pm Dec-Feb) is a must for woodworkers, craftspeople and design fans. There's a hands-on room where you can try assembling blocks of wood cut into different joint patterns – not as easy as it sounds.

Follow the canal street west for three blocks and take a right to reach the riverside **Honkō-ji**, an intricately carved temple showcasing Furukawa's fine craftsmanship. From the temple, instead of retracing your steps, walk back along Ichi-no-machi, a street sprinkled with craft shops, sake breweries (marked by the large cedar balls hanging above the entrance) and traditional storehouses. Among them is **Mishima-ya** (☎ 73-4109; ⏰ 9am-6pm Thu-Tue), a shop that has made candles for over two centuries; traditional shapes are concave or tapered with the wide end at the top.

Festivals & Events

The **Furukawa Matsuri**, as the Hadaka Matsuri is formally known, takes place every 19 and 20 April. The highlight is the Okoshi Daiko, when squads of boisterous young men dressed in loincloths parade through town at midnight, competing to place small drums atop a stage bearing a giant drum. OK, it's not *naked*-naked, but we didn't make up the name.

During the **Kitsune-bi Matsuri** (Fox Fire Festival) on 16 October, locals make up as foxes, parade through the town by lanternlight and enact a wedding at the shrine, Okura Inari-jinja. The ceremony, deemed to bring good fortune, climaxes with a bonfire at the shrine.

Sleeping & Eating

Hida Furukawa Youth Hostel (飛騨古川ユースホテル; ☎/fax 75-2979; hidafyh@d2.dion.ne.jp; 180 Shimpo; dm with/without 2 meals ¥4900/3300; ☻ closed 30 Mar-10 Apr) This friendly and attractive hostel sits amid farmland about 6 km from the town centre, or 1.2km west of Hida-Hosoe Station (two stops north of Hida-Furukawa). Pick-up from station available after 6pm by advance notice. The park, Shinrin-kōen, is across the street. Japanese- and Western-style rooms available.

Ryokan Tanbo-no-Yu (旅館たんぼの湯; ☎ 73-2014; fax 73-6454; r per person with 2 meals ¥7000) In the town centre, this charming ryokan has spacious Japanese rooms with shared bathrooms, plus a bath with red-brown waters said to be good for cuts, bruises and rheumatism. Visitors can bathe for ¥500. No English is spoken.

Kitchen Kyabingu (キッチン きゃびんぐ; ☎ 73-4706; dishes ¥350-2400; ☻ 11am-2pm & 5-9pm Tue-Sun) This cosy lunch spot in the historic district serves delicious *Hida-gyu* (Hida beef). Most people order the beef curry with rice (¥800) or the *teishoku*, starring sizzling steak on a hot iron plate (¥2400).

Getting There & Around

There are some 20 daily connections each way between Takayama and Furukawa. Hida-Furukawa train station is three stops north of Takayama (*futsū*, ¥230, 15 minutes), or you can bus it (¥360, 30 minutes). Central Furukawa is an easy stroll, or you can rent bikes at the taxi office **Miyagawa** (☎ 73-2321; per hr ¥200), a left out of the station and 50m on.

SHŌKAWA VALLEY REGION 庄川

This remote, dramatically mountainous district between Takayama and Kanazawa is best known for farmhouses in the thatched, A-frame style called *gasshō-zukuri* ('hands-in-prayer'; see boxed text, p229). They're rustic and lovely, particularly in clear weather or in the snow, and they hold a special place in the Japanese heart. The valley's main centres are Shirakawa-gō to the south and Gokayama about 30 minutes' drive to the north (technically not in Hida but in Toyama-ken). Rte 156 connects the two.

In the 12th century, the region's remoteness and inaccessibility are said to have attracted stragglers from the Taira clan, which had been virtually wiped out by the Genji clan in a brutal battle in 1185. During feudal times Shirakawa-gō, like the rest of Hida, was under direct control of the shōgun, while Gokayama was a centre for the production of gunpowder for the Kaga region.

Fast-forward to the 1960s: when construction of the gigantic Miboro Dam was about to submerge some local villages, many *gasshō* houses were moved to their current sites for safekeeping. Although much of what you'll find has been specially preserved for, and supported by, tourism, it still presents a view of rural life found in few other parts of Japan.

Most of Shirakawa-gō's sights are in the heavily visited community of Ogimachi. In Gokayama, the community of Ainokura has the greatest concentration, although other sights are spread throughout hamlets over several kilometres along Rte 156. Ogimachi and Ainokura are Unesco World Heritage sites (along with the Gokayama settlement of Suganuma), and can get swamped by tour buses, quickly destroying these towns' magic. Avoid coming on weekends and holidays.

One of the region's biggest draws is the chance to stay overnight in a *gasshō-zukuri* house that's been turned into an inn. You'll also experience the region's idyllic charm after the tour buses have left. Advance reservations are highly recommended; the Shirakawa-gō tourist office can help with local bookings (in Japanese). Takayama's tourist office can help if you don't speak Japanese. Don't expect rooms with private facilities, but some inns have *irori* for guests to eat around.

Bus services to and around the region are infrequent and vary seasonally, so it's

CENTRAL HONSHŪ

important to check schedules. For maximum flexibility (and perhaps even a cost saving) you may prefer to rent a car. Either way, traffic can be severe on weekends and throughout the peak tourist times of May, August and October. Expect snow, and lots of it, between late December and late March.

Shirakawa-gō 白川郷
☎ 05769

The region's central settlement, **Ogimachi**, has over 110 *gasshō-zukuri* buildings and is the most convenient place to orient yourself for tourist information and transport.

Ogimachi's main **tourist office** (☎ 6-1013; www.shirakawa-go.org; ⏰ 9am-5pm) is in the centre of town near the Gasshō-shuraku bus stop. The office has a Japanese map of Shirakawa-gō, including a detailed map of Ogimachi. No English is spoken. There's a smaller tourist office near the Deai bridge. Either office can reserve lodging for you.

SIGHTS

On the site of the former castle, **Shiroyama Tenbōdai** provides a lovely overlook of the valley. It's a 15-minute walk via the road behind the east side of town, or you can climb the path (five minutes) from near the intersection of Rtes 156 and 360.

This well-presented group, **Gasshō-zukuri Minka-en** (合掌造り民家園; ☎ 6-1231; admission ¥500; ⏰ 8am-5.30pm Fri-Wed Aug, 8.40am-5pm Fri-Wed Apr-Jul, Sep-Nov, 9am-4pm Fri-Wed Dec-Mar), features over a dozen *gasshō-zukuri* buildings, collected from the surrounding region and reconstructed in this open-air museum amid seasonal flowers. Several of the houses are used for demonstrating regional crafts, such as woodwork, straw handicrafts and ceramics; many items are for sale.

You can wander away from the houses for a pleasant stroll through the trees further up the mountain. Feel free to take a picnic, but Shirakawa-gō has a rule that you must carry your trash out of town.

The largest *gasshō* house in Shirakawa-gō, **Wada-ke** (和田家; ☎ 6-1058; admission ¥300; ⏰ 9am-5pm, closed occasionally) once belonged to a wealthy silk-trading family and dates back to the mid-Edo period. Appropriately, you'll find silk-harvesting equipment upstairs, as well as a valuable lacquerware collection.

Next door to Ogimachi's small temple, **Myōzen-ji Folk Museum** (明善寺; ☎ 6-1009; admis-

sion ¥300; ⏰ 8.30am-5pm Apr-Nov, 9am-4pm Dec-Mar) displays the traditional paraphernalia of daily rural life.

Doburoku Matsuri Exhibition Hall (どぶろく祭りの館; ☎ 6-1655; admission ¥300; ⏰ 9am-4pm Apr-Nov) Shirakawa-gō's big festival is held in mid-October at the shrine Shirakawa-Hachiman-jinja, and features coordinated dancing groups of locals, including the lion dance and much *niwaka* (improvised buffoonery). But the real star is *doboroku*, a very potent unrefined sake. Perhaps the most illustrative part of this exhibition hall is the video of the festival (in Japanese).

In Hirase Onsen, about 13km south of Ogimachi on Rte 156, the elderly **Kyōdō Yokujō** (public bath; 平瀬温泉; ☎ 6-1311; admission ¥330; ⏰ 10am-10pm Fri-Wed Apr-Nov, 11am-9pm Fri-Wed Feb & Mar) is a good place to soak up the local atmosphere; its waters are said to be beneficial for the skin and fertility. About another 15km up the Ōshirakawa river (via a mountain road full of blind curves), **Ōshirakawa Rotemburo** (大白川露天風呂; ☎ 090-2770-2893; admission ¥200; ⏰ 8.30am-5pm Oct-Jun, to 6pm Jul & Aug) is much admired for

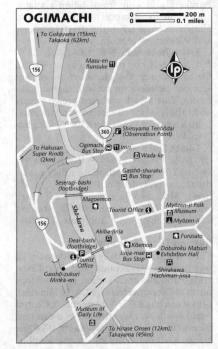

OGIMACHI
0 ——— 200 m
0 ——— 0.1 miles

To Gokayama (15km);
Takaoka (62km)

156

Masu-en
Bunsuke

360
Shiroyama Tenbōdai
(Observation Point)

To Hakusan
Super Rindō
(2km)

Ogimachi ⊡ Irori
Bus Stop
⊞ Wada-ke

Gasshō-shuraku
Bus Stop

Seseragi-bashi
(footbridge)

Magoemon

Myōzen-ji Folk
Museum
⊞ Myōzen-ji

156

Tourist Office

Akiba-jinja

Deai-bashi
(footbridge)

⊡ Furusato

Kōemon
Jinja-mae
Bus Stop

Doburoku Matsuri
Exhibition Hall

Tourist
Office

Gasshō-zukuri
Minka-en

Shirakawa
Hachiman-jinja

Museum of
Daily Life

To Hirase Onsen (12km);
Takayama (45km)

its views of an emerald-green lake set amid the mountains.

SLEEPING & EATING

Some Japanese is helpful in making reservations at one of Ogimachi's many *gasshō-zukuri* inns.

Kōemon (幸エ門; ☎ 6-1446; fax 6-1748; r per person ¥8000) In the town centre, Kōemon has handsome rooms with heated floors, darkwood panelling and shared bathrooms. The friendly fifth-generation owner speaks English and his love of Shirakawa-gō is infectious. Try to book the room facing the pond.

Magoemon (孫右エ門; ☎ 6-1167; fax 6-1851; r per person ¥8500) Another friendly place, Magoemon has slightly larger rooms, some with river views. All prices include two meals – served around the handsome *irori* – but not the nightly heating surcharge (¥300) during cold weather.

Furusato (ふるさと; ☎ 6-1033; r per person ¥8000) This much-photographed place near Myōzen-ji is run by a kindly older innkeeper and has quaint touches among the decent-sized tatami rooms.

The town centre has a few casual restaurants (look for *soba* or *hoba miso*); most open only for lunch.

Irori (いろり; ☎ 6-1737; mains ¥700-1200; ☒ 11am-5pm) On the main road near Wada-ke, Irori serves regional specialities like *hoba miso* and *yakidofu* (fried tofu), as well as sansai (mountain vegetable) or *tempura soba* to patrons who gather around the warm hearths inside.

Masu-en Bunsuke (ます園文助; ☎ 6-1268; dishes ¥300-500, teishoku ¥1500-4000; ☒ 9am-9pm) Uphill from the town centre, this attractive restaurant specialises in fresh trout, which are raised in ponds near the restaurant.

Gokayama District 五箇山
☎ 0763
Gokayama is so isolated that road links and electricity didn't arrive until 1925.

Communities with varying numbers of *gasshō-zukuri* buildings are scattered over many kilometres along Rte 156. The following briefly describes the communities and sights you'll come across as you travel north from Shirakawa-gō or the Gokayama exit from the Tōkai–Hokuriku Expressway; if your time is limited, head straight for Ainokura.

SUGANUMA 菅沼
This World Heritage site, 10km north of Ogimachi and down a steep hill, features an attractive group of *gasshō-zukuri* houses worth a stroll. The **Minzoku-kan** (Folklore Museum; 民族館; ☎ 67-3652; admission ¥300; ☒ 9am-4pm May-Nov) consists of two houses, with items from traditional life, and exhibits on traditional gunpowder production.

GASSHŌ-ZUKURI ARCHITECTURE

Winter in the Hida region can be fierce, and inhabitants faced snow and cold long before the advent of propane heaters and 4WD vehicles. One of the most visible symbols of that adaptability is *gasshō-zukuri* architecture, seen in the steeply slanted straw-roofed homes that still dot the landscape around the region.

The sharply angled roofs were designed to prevent heavy snow accumulation, a serious concern in a region where nearly all mountain roads close from December to April. The name *gasshō* comes from the Japanese word for 'praying', because the shape of the roofs was thought to resemble two hands clasped in prayer. *Gasshō* buildings often featured pillars crafted from stout cedar trees to lend extra support. The attic areas were ideal for silk cultivation.

Larger *gasshō* buildings were inhabited by wealthy families, up to 30 people under one roof. Peasant families lived in huts of the size that are now used as tool sheds.

The *gasshō-zukuri* building has become an endangered species, with most examples having been gathered together and preserved in folk villages, including Hida-no-Sato in Takayama (p223) and in the Shōkawa Valley (p227). This sometimes means that two homes that are now neighbours were once separated by several days or weeks of travel on foot or sled. But local authorities have worked hard to recreate their natural surroundings, making it possible to imagine what life in the Hida hills might have looked like hundreds of years ago.

About 1km further up Rte 156, **Kuroba Onsen** (くろば温泉; ☎ 67-3741; admission ¥600; ⓨ 11am-9pm Wed-Mon Apr-Oct, 11am-8pm Nov-Mar) is a complex of baths overlooking the river, with fine mountain views to boot.

KAMINASHI 上梨

About 4km beyond Suganuma is Kaminashi. The house museum **Murakami-ke** (村上家; ☎ 66-2711; admission ¥300; ⓨ 8.30am-5pm Apr-Nov, 9am-4pm Dec-Mar, closed 2nd & 4th Wed of each month) dates from 1578, making it one of the oldest in the region. The proud owner shows visitors around and then sits them beside the *irori* and sings local folk songs. There's a detailed English-language leaflet.

Also close by is the shrine **Hakusan-gū**. The main hall dates from 1502 and has been designated an Important Cultural Property. Its **Kokiriko Festival** on 25 and 26 September is a two-day festival featuring costumed dancers performing with rattles that move like snakes. On the second day everyone joins in.

AINOKURA 相倉

This World Heritage site is the most impressive of Gokayama's villages, with over 20 *gasshō* buildings in an agricultural valley amid splendid mountain views. It's a pleasant place just to stroll, and the **Ainokura Museum of Life** (相倉民族館; ☎ 66-2732; admission ¥200; ⓨ 8.30am-5pm) displays local crafts and paper. By the central car park there's an **information office** (☎ 66-2123), which distributes an English pamphlet.

Just before Ainokura, buses leave Rte 156 for Rte 304 towards Kanazawa. From the Ainokura-guchi bus stop it's about 400m to Ainokura.

Continue along Rte 156 for several kilometres until **Gokayama-Washi-no-Sato** (Gokayama Japanese Paper Village; 五箇山和紙の里; ☎ 66-2223; admission ¥200; ⓨ 8.30am-5pm), where you will find exhibits of *washi* (Japanese handmade paper) art and a chance to make your own (reservation required).

SLEEPING

Ainokura is a great place for a *gasshō-zukuri* farmhouse stay, as you'll have the place to yourself after the tour buses leave. Try the welcoming **Yomoshiro** (与茂四郎; ☎ 66-2377; fax 66-2387); **Goyomon** (五ヨ門; ☎ 66-2154; fax 66-2227), with excellent views from the 2nd storey; or **Chōyomon** (長ヨ門民宿; ☎ 66-2755;

fax 66-2765), with its atmospheric, darkwood sliding doors. All cost around ¥8000 per person, including two meals. Ainokura also has a **camping ground** (☎ 66-2123; per person ¥500; ⓨ mid-Apr–late Oct, unless there's snow).

Getting There & Away

BUS

Between April and late November, five buses a day operated by **Nōhi Bus Company** (☎ 0577-32-1688) link Shirakawa-gō with Takayama (¥2400, 1¾ hours), passing through Hirase Onsen (¥2100, 80 minutes). Nōhi has two buses a day connecting Kanazawa with Shirakawa-gō (¥2700, 3½ hours). Schedule varies from December through March and depends largely on the weather.

Between Ogimachi and Gokayama, **Kaetsuno Bus** (☎ 0766-22-4888) operates four buses a day, stopping at all the major sights and continuing to Takaoka on the JR Hokuriku Line (1 hour). If you wish to get off somewhere other than an official stop (eg at Kuroba Onsen), let the driver know.

CAR

From Takayama (the most popular starting point) the trip takes about two hours, with interchanges at Gokayama and Shōkawa. From Hakusan, the scenic toll road Hakusan Super-Rindō ends near Ogimachi (cars ¥3150). During colder months, be sure to check first with regional tourist offices on road conditions.

People do hitch, although one should take the usual precautions.

GERO 下呂

☎ 0576 / pop 15,178

Framed against a mountainous backdrop with a rushing river coursing through town, Gero is a favourite among Japanese tourists for its numerous *onsen*, even if the town is an unfortunate homonym for 'vomit'. The town's sprawl of concrete buildings dampens its appeal, but the waters, reputedly beneficial for rheumatism, athletic injuries and complexion, are excellent.

Gero is fairly compact; you can walk nearly anywhere from the train station within 20 minutes. Day-use bathing prices hover around ¥1000 per visit, but the ¥1200 'Yumeguri Tegata' is a wooden plaque on a rope (and a nice souvenir) that allows one-time access to three among a selection of *onsen*. It's available at the **tourist information office** (☎ 25-4711; ◷ 8.30am-5.30pm), outside the train station, where you can also make lodging reservations and pick up an English-language map.

Gero boasts its own hot-spring temple – **Onsen-ji** – overlooking the town, while on the edge of the centre is **Gero Onsen Gasshō Village** (下呂温泉合掌村; ☎ 25-2239; admission ¥800; ◷ 8.15am-5pm), the most polished of its ilk with 10 buildings from the Shirakawa-gō area; there's a museum of *komainu*, stone dog sculptures often seen in pairs guarding Shintō shrines and said to have roots back to the Egyptian sphinx. One train station (3.2km) away, **Gero Furusato** (下呂ふるさと; ☎ 25-4174; admission free; ◷ 9am-5pm Tue-Sun) offers clues to this ancient era via stone and earthenware.

The **Gero Onsen Matsuri** (Hot Spring Festival), from 1 to 3 August, is a lively one. On 1 August, men clad in *fundoshi* (loincloths) and toting fireworks perform a dance to Ryūjin, the Dragon God. The following day sees a parade of women dressed as geisha and the local Gero Odori folk dance.

Sleeping

Most lodgings are across the river from the train station and even the simplest have *onsen*-fed baths.

Minshuku Katsuragawa (民宿桂川; ☎ 25-2615; s/tw ¥4000/7000) Facing the river, about 12 minutes' walk from the station, this *minshuku* attracts a few budget travellers, though the rooms are small and no meals are served.

Miyanoya Minshuku (みやのや民宿; ☎ 25-2399; fax 25-3367; r per person with 2 meals from ¥6800) A few minutes further on Onsen-gai (Onsen St), this ageing but friendly *minshuku* has simple but nicely maintained rooms and a games room.

Ogawaya (小川屋; ☎ 25-3121; yado@gero-ogawaya.net; r per person with 2 meals ¥19,000) This large, elegant Japanese-style resort has comfortable tatami rooms and excellent baths including a *rotemburo* and a 25m indoor pool. Most rooms face the river.

Getting There & Away

Tokkyū trains serve Gero from Gifu (¥3280, 67 minutes), Nagoya (¥4300, 1½ hours) and Takayama (¥1990, 40 minutes). If you're heading to the Kiso Valley (p250), two buses a day to Nakatsugawa (¥1700, 50 minutes) will save you hours, yen and hardship over the train.

JAPAN ALPS NATIONAL PARK 中部山岳国立公園

Boasting some of Japan's most dramatic scenery, this mountain-studded park – also called Chūbu-Sangaku National Park – has long been a favourite of alp-lovers. The park's highlights include hiking the valleys and peaks of Kamikōchi, skiing at Norikura and soaking up the splendour of Shirahone Onsen, a gem of a hot-spring resort. The northern part of the park extends to the Tateyama–Kurobe Alpine Route (p252).

Orientation & Information

The park straddles the border between Gifu-ken and Nagano-ken, with the Gifu-ken (western) side also known as Oku-Hida Onsen, while the Nagano-ken (eastern) side is Azumi-mura. Several maps and pamphlets are published by the Japan National Tourist Organization (JNTO) and by local tourist authorities in English (particularly the one put out by Azumi-mura), with more detailed hiking maps in Japanese.

Getting There & Around

The main gateway cities are Takayama (p219) to the west and Matsumoto (p245) to the east. Service from Takayama is by bus, while most travellers from Matsumoto catch the private Matsumoto Dentetsu train to Shim-Shimashima Station (¥680, 30 minutes) to transfer to buses. Within the park, the main transit hubs are Hirayu Onsen and Kamikōchi.

Bus schedules are known to change annually, and the schedules short-change visits to some areas and *long*-change others. Before setting out it is essential that you check the schedules. Note that some communities within the park cover a lot of ground, so if you're arriving by bus make sure to ask which stop to get off. You may also consider the three-day 'Free Coupon' (¥6400) for unlimited transport within the park, and connections to Matsumoto and Takayama. See Sample Bus Routes: Japan Alps National Park (p232), for fares and travel times.

SAMPLE BUS ROUTES: JAPAN ALPS NATIONAL PARK

Within the park, bus fares and schedules change seasonally and annually; however, the following are fares and travel times on common bus routes in and around the area. Discounted return fares are listed where available. Depending on your intended route, the Free Coupon (¥6400), valid for three days, may be the most economical option. You can find current fare and schedule information at tourist offices in Matsumoto and Takayama, or at www.alpico.co.jp /access/route_k/honsen/info_e.html or www.alpico.co.jp/access/express/kamikochi_takayama /info_e.html.

Bus Fares

from	to	fare (¥; one way or one way/return)	duration (mins; one way)
Takayama	Hirayu Onsen	1530	55
	Kamikōchi	2000	80
Matsumoto	Shin-Shimajima	680 (train)	30
		750 (bus)	
	Kamikōchi	2500/4600	100
	Shin-Hotaka	2800/5000	120
Shin-Shimajima	Naka-no-yu	1650	50
	Kamikōchi	2050/3500	70
	Shirahone Onsen	1400/2300	75
	Norikura Tatami-daira	3150	105
Kamikōchi	Naka-no-yu	680	20
	Hirayu Onsen	1050/1800	30
	Shirahone Onsen	1500	40
Hirayu Onsen	Naka-no-yu	540	10
	Shin-Hotaka	870	35
	Norikura Tatami-daira	1050	45

Renting a car may save money, time and nerves. However, some popular routes, particularly the Norikura Skyline Rd (linking Hirayu Onsen and Norikura), and the road between Naka-no-yu and Kamikōchi, are open only to buses and taxis.

KAMIKŌCHI 上高地
☎ 0263

The park's biggest drawcard, Kamikōchi has some of the most spectacular scenery in Japan and a variety of hiking trails from which to see it. In the late 19th century, foreigners 'discovered' this mountainous region and coined the term 'Japan Alps'. A British missionary, Reverend Walter Weston, toiled from peak to peak and sparked Japanese interest in mountaineering as a sport. He is now honoured with his own annual festival (first Sunday in June, the official opening of the hiking season), and Kamikōchi has become a base for strollers, hikers and climbers.

Kamikōchi is closed mid-November to late April, and in peak times (late July to late August, and during the foliage season in October), it is busier than Shinjuku Station. Between June and mid-July is the rainy season, which makes outdoor pursuits depressingly soggy. It's perfectly feasible to visit Kamikōchi as a day trip, but you'll miss out on the pleasures of staying in the mountains and taking early-morning or late-evening walks when the crowds aren't around.

Orientation

Private cars are prohibited between Naka-no-yu and Kamikōchi; access is only by bus or taxi, and then only as far as the Kamikōchi bus station. (Those with private cars can park them in a car park in Naka-no-yu for ¥500 per day.) A short distance on foot from the bus station, the Azusa-gawa is spanned by Kappa-bashi (named for a water sprite of Japanese legend), from where a variety of trails snake into the mountains.

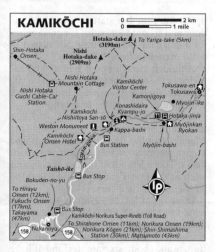

KAMIKŌCHI

There are dozens of long-distance options for hikers and climbers, varying in duration from a couple of days to a week. *Hiking in Japan* by Paul Hunt, Mason Florence et al provides practical advice. Large Japanese-language maps of the area show routes and average hiking times between huts, major peaks and landmarks. Favourite trails and climbs (which can mean human traffic jams on trails during peak seasons) include Yariga-take (3180m) and Hotaka-dake (3190m) – also known as Oku-Hotaka-dake. Other more distant destinations include Nakabusa Onsen and Murodō, which is on the Tateyama–Kurobe Alpine Route (p252). For long-distance hikes there are mountain huts available; inquire at the tourist office for details.

If you want to hike between Kamikōchi and Shin-Hotaka Onsen (p235), there's a steep trail that crosses the ridge below NishiHotaka-dake (2909m) at Nishi Hotaka San-sō (Nishi Hotaka Mountain Cottage) and continues to Nishi Hotaka-guchi, the top station of the cable car for Shin-Hotaka Onsen. The hike takes nearly four hours (because of a steep ascent). Softies might prefer to save an hour of sweat and do the hike in the opposite direction.

Those heading off on long hikes or climbs should be well prepared. Even in summer, temperatures can plummet, or the whole area can be covered in sleeting rain or blinding fog. On the other hand, in clear weather it's possible to see all the way to Mt Fuji.

CENTRAL HONSHŪ

Information

The **information office** (☎ 95-2405; ◷ 9am-5pm late Apr–mid-Nov) at the bus station distributes the useful *Kamikōchi Pocket Guide* with a map of the main trails. The office is geared mostly to booking accommodation, though non-Japanese speakers may want to book through the tourist information office in Takayama or Matsumoto, both of which have English-speaking staff.

The **Kamikōchi Visitor Centre** (☎ 95-2606; ◷ 8am-5pm late Apr–mid-Nov) has exhibits on the flora and fauna of Kamikōchi, and explanations of its geological history. It's a 10-minute walk from the bus station along the main trail.

Sights & Activities

The river valley offers basically level, short-distance walks. A three-hour round trip starts east of Kappa-bashi along the right-hand side of the river past Myōjin-bashi (45 minutes) to Tokusawa (45 minutes) before returning. By Myōjin-bashi is the idyllic pond **Myōjin-ike** (admission ¥250), which marks the innermost shrine of the **Hotaka-jinja**. There's also a trail on the other side of the river but it's partly a service road.

West of Kappa-bashi, you can amble along the right-hand side of the river to **Weston Monument** (15 minutes) or keep to the left-hand side of the river and walk to the pond **Taishō-ike** (20 minutes). There's also a pleasant, clearly signposted 3km hike uphill from the Taishō-ike bus stop.

ONSEN

On cold or drizzly days, the hot baths at **Kamikōchi Onsen Hotel** (上高地温泉ホテル; ☎ 95-2311; admission ¥600) are a refreshing respite from the weather.

The area's best-kept secret is at Naka-no-yu, just before the bus-only tunnel branches up to Kamikōchi proper. Go in the small store next to the Naka-no-yu bus stop, pay ¥500, get the key and cross the road bridge where you'll find a door set in the mountainside. Open this and inside is **Bokuden-no-yu** (ト伝の湯), a tiny gem of a hot-spring cave bath dripping with minerals. It is yours privately until you return the key.

Sleeping & Eating

Accommodation in Kamikōchi is pricey and advance reservations are essential.

Kamikōchi Konashidaira Kyampu-jō (上高地小梨平キャンプ場; ☎ 95-2321; camp sites per person from ¥700, tents/bungalows from ¥2000/6000) About 15 minutes' walk from the bus station, this camping ground can get packed with tents. Rental tents and bungalows available.

Among the hotels, all rates quoted here include two meals, and some lodgings shut down their electricity generators in the middle of the night (emergency lighting stays on).

Kamikōchi Nishiitoya San-sō (上高地西糸屋山荘; ☎ 95-2206; www.nishiitoya.com; bunk beds ¥7700, d per person ¥10,550) Dating from the early 20th century, this friendly lodge offers decent rooms, a cosy lounge and a large *onsen* facing the Hotake mountains. It's just west of the Kappa-bashi bridge. Some English spoken.

Myōjinkan Ryokan (明神館; ☎ 95-2036; www.myojinkan.co.jp/index3.html; dm ¥8400, r per person from ¥10,500) Up along the river near Myōjin-ike, this pleasant ryokan has simple tatami rooms with good lighting. The peak of Myōjin-dake looms directly behind.

Tokusawa-en (徳沢園; ☎ 95-2508; camp sites per person ¥500, Japanese dm per person ¥9000, private r per person from ¥13,000) A marvellously secluded place, about 3km northeast of Kappa-bashi; rooms do not have private facilities.

Dotted along the trails and around the mountains are dozens of spartan *yama-goya* (mountain huts), which provide two meals and a futon from around ¥8000 per person; some also serve simple lunches. Aside from pricey hotel restaurants, the restaurant **Kamonjigoya** (嘉門次小屋; ☎ 95-2418; lunch set ¥1500; ⏰ 8.30am-4pm) is worth seeking. It's famed for its *iwana*, which are grilled on skewers over an *irori*. It's near Myojin-bashi bridge, just outside the entrance to Myojin-ike pond.

HIRAYU ONSEN 平湯温泉
☎ 0578

This hot-spring resort is a busy hub for bus transport on the Gifu-ken side of the park. It has a cluster of *onsen* lodgings and an excellent modern hot-spring complex, and even the bus terminal has a **rotemburo** (admission ¥600; ⏰ 8am-5pm). The **information office** (☎ 9-3030; ⏰ 9am-5pm), opposite the bus station, has leaflets and maps and can book accommodation. No English is spoken.

The hot-spring complex **Hirayu-no-mori** (ひらゆの森; ☎ 9-3338; admission ¥500; ⏰ 10am-9pm),

uphill from the bus station, boasts one indoor and six outdoor baths. It's great either for a quick dip between buses, or as part of a day excursion from Takayama.

Although Hirayu is not remote and relaxing in the way other Chūbu-Sangaku villages are, there are some nice inns within a few minutes' walk of the bus station.

Ryosō Tsuyukusa (旅荘つゆくさ; ☎ 9-2620; fax 9-3581; r per person with 2 meals ¥7400) This friendly spot has decent tatami rooms and a cosy wooden *rotemburo* with mountain views. Take a left out of the bus station and a left at the first T-junction. It'll be on the left before the road curves.

Eitarō (栄太郎; ☎ 9-2540; fax 9-3526; r per person with 2 meals ¥10,500) This ryokan offers more nicely outfitted rooms and a pleasant *rotemburo*. Take a left out of the bus station, walk about six minutes and it'll be on the left.

Hirayu-kan (平湯館; ☎ 9-3111; fax 9-3113; r per person with 2 meals from ¥13,000) This elegant inn has both Japanese- and Western-style rooms, a splendid garden, and indoor and outdoor baths. From the bus station, take a left, stay on the main road, go through one T-junction and it will soon be on your right.

Hirayu Camping Ground (平湯キャンプ場; ☎ 9-2610; fax 9-2130; camp sites per person ¥600, parking ¥1500) To reach this small camping ground, take a right out of the station, go about 700m and it's on the left-hand side.

For drivers, the 4km-plus Abō tunnel from Hirayu Onsen eastward into the park costs ¥600 each way.

FUKUCHI ONSEN 福地温泉
☎ 0578

This relatively untouristed hot spring, a short ride north of Hirayu Onsen, has rural charm, a morning market and two outstanding baths.

One of central Honshū's finest *onsen* ryokan, **Yumoto Chōza** (湯元長座; ☎ 9-2146; fax 9-2010; r per person with 2 meals from ¥18,000) has exquisite mountain cuisine served at *irori*, elegant traditional architecture, and five indoor and two outdoor pools. Half of the rooms have en-suite *irori*. Reservations are essential. By bus, get off at Fukuchi-onsen-shita.

This restaurant-cum-hot-spring, **Mukashibanashi-no-sato** (昔ばなしの里; ☎ 9-2793; bath ¥500; ⏰ 8am-5pm) is housed in a traditional farmhouse with fine indoor and outdoor baths, free on the 26th of each month. Out the front, there's an **asa-ichi** (morning market; ☻ 6am-10pm Apr-late Nov). By bus, get off at Fukuchi-onsen-ue bus stop.

SHIN-HOTAKA ONSEN 新穂高温泉
☎ 0578

This hot-spring resort, north of Fukuchi Onsen, is home to the Shin-Hotaka cable car, reportedly the longest of its kind in Asia, whisking you up close to the peak of Nishi Hotaka-dake (2909m) for a superb mountain panorama. The **cable car** (☎ 9-2252; one way/return ¥1500/2800; ☻ 6am-4.15pm late Jul-late Aug, 8.30am-3.45pm late Aug-late Jul) is near the Shin-Hotaka Onsen bus station.

If you are fit, properly equipped and have ample time, there are a variety of hiking options from Nishi Hotaka-guchi (the top cable-car station). In a little under three hours you can hike over to **Kamikōchi** (p232).

Information is available at the **Oku-Hida Spa Tourist Information Centre** (☎ 9-2458; ☻ 9am-4pm) near the bus station. Also near the bus station is a rather spartan **public onsen** (☎ 9-2548; admission free; ☻ 8am-9pm). During summer it gets crowded with tourists, but in the off-season your only company is likely to be a few weary shift workers from the electric plant across the river.

Sleeping
This far up into the mountains, most options charge ¥12,000 to ¥16,000 per night. Accommodation is clustered around the Shin-Hotaka Onsen-guchi and Shin-Hotaka Onsen bus stops (a few kilometres apart).

Shin-Hotaka Camping ground (新穂高キャンプ場; ☎ 9-2513; camp sites ¥600; ☻ Jul & Aug) Near the Shin-Hotaka Onsen bus stop.

Yamanoyado (民宿山の宿; ☎ 9-2733, 9-3215; r per person with 2 meals ¥8000) Near Shin-Hotaka Onsen-guchi, this functional *minshuku* has basic rooms.

Mahoroba (民宿まほろば; ☎ 9-2382, 9-3077; r per person with 2 meals ¥8000) A bit less convenient but better value is this friendly place with a very nice *rotemburo* (mostly *konyoku* [mixed bathing] except for women-only hours). It's near Naka-o Onsen bus stop, two stops past Shin-Hotaka Onsen-guchi. Upon request (in Japanese), someone will pick you up at the bus stop. Otherwise you'll have to walk uphill for about 1km.

NORIKURA-KŌGEN & NORIKURA ONSEN 乗鞍高原・乗鞍温泉
☎ 0263

Below 3026m-high Norikura-dake, the alpine plateau of Norikura-kōgen is blissfully free of Kamikōchi crowds and offers cycling, hiking and skiing. It's famous for the Norikura Skyline Rd (closed November to May; closed to private vehicles all year), a scenic route leading to the Norikura Tatami-daira bus stop at the foot of the mountain. From there, a trail (40 minutes) leads to the peak. You might glimpse a *raichō* (ptarmigan), the prefectural symbol; or if you're really fortunate, the magnificent *inuwashi* (dog eagle).

Norikura Onsen is a collection of hot-spring accommodation on the plateau. You'll find the **tourist office** (☎ 93-2147; ☻ 9am-5pm Mar-Oct, 9am-4.30pm Nov-Feb) at Kankō Centre. Its main bus stops are Kankō Centre, Suzuran and Ski-jō-mae, near the bulk of the accommodation.

Norikura Onsen is surrounded by well-marked **trails**, one of the best being the 40-minute woodland walk from the Suzuran bus stop to the beautiful waterfall, **Zengoro-no-taki**.

Sleeping
Norikura Tatami-daira is not an ideal place to stay, but there are several dozen lodgings in Norikura Onsen.

Norikura Kōgen Onsen Youth Hostel (乗鞍高原温泉ユースホステル; ☎ 93-2748; www.jyh .or.jp; Japanese dm ¥3360) The cheapest option in the area, this friendly youth hostel can rent ski gear (¥3000) and has a wealth of info on nearby hiking trails. The wooden *onsen* makes for a splendid soak after a day's activity. It's at the end of the road, a 10-minute trek from the Ski-jō-mae bus stop.

Also near this bus stop are **Ryokan Mitake-sō** (旅館みたけ荘; ☎ 93-2016; r per person with 2 meals ¥8000-10,000), an unassuming place with a *rotemburo*, and the fine, Western-style **Pension Chimney** (☎ 93-2902; r per person with 2 meals ¥8500).

SHIRAHONE ONSEN 白骨温泉
☎ 0263

Intimate and dramatic, this hot-spring resort straddles a deep gorge and features some traditional inns with open-air baths. It could easily be visited as part of a trip to Kamikōchi or Norikura (an 8km hike away).

It is said that bathing here for three days ensures three years without a cold, and the milky-blue hydrogen sulphide waters have a wonderful silky feel. The riverside **kōshū rotemburo** (public outdoor bath; admission ¥500; ☺ 9.30am-5pm) is in the village centre. Diagonally opposite, the **tourist information office** (☎ 93-3251; ☺ 9am-5pm) maintains a list of inns that have opened their baths to the public that day (admission from ¥600). **Awanoyu** (☎ 92-2101), furthest up the hill, allows *kon-yoku* (mixed bathing).

Budget travellers may wish to dip and move on; nightly rates start at ¥9000 with two meals, and advance reservations are highly recommended. **Tsuruya Ryokan** (☎ 93-2331; fax 93-2029; r per person with 2 meals ¥10,000) has both contemporary and traditional touches, great indoor and outdoor baths, and fine views of the gorge.

NAGANO-KEN 長野県

Nagano-ken is one of the most enjoyable regions to visit in Japan, not only for the beauty of its mountainous terrain (it claims to be 'the Roof of Japan'), but also for the traditional architecture and rich culture that lives on in many parts of the prefecture.

Apart from the sections of the prefecture in Chūbu-Sangaku National Park, there are several quasi-national parks that attract large numbers of campers, hikers, mountaineers and hot-spring aficionados. Skiers can choose from dozens of resorts; the ski season lasts from late December to late March.

NAGANO 長野
☎ 026 / pop 360,000

The prefectural capital Nagano has been around since the Kamakura period, when it was a temple town centred around the magnificent Zenkōji. The temple is still Nagano's main attraction, drawing more than four million visitors every year.

After a brief flirtation with international fame while hosting the 1998 Winter Olympics, Nagano has reverted to its friendly small-town self, though it's just a bit more worldly. Nagano is also an important transport hub and, not surprisingly, the mountains surrounding the city offer superb recreational opportunities: skiing, hiking, soaking in *onsen* and exploring the region's many mountain shrines.

Orientation

As a temple city, Nagano is on a grid with Zenkōji occupying a prominent position, overlooking the city centre from the north. Chūō-dōri leads south from the temple, doing a quick dogleg before hitting JR Nagano Station, 1.8km away; it is said that street-planners considered Zenkōji so holy that it should not be approached directly. Bus stops and the private Nagano Dentetsu train line are just outside JR Nagoya Station's Zenkōji exit.

Information
BOOKSHOP

Heiandō bookshop (☎ 224-4545; West Plaza Nagano; ☺ 10am-10pm) Facing the station, Nagano's largest bookshop carries English-language books and magazines (4th floor).

INTERNET ACCESS
Boo Foo Woo (☎ 226-0850; 2nd fl, Daita Bldg, Chūō-dōri; per hr ¥390; ☺ 24hr) This popular Internet café is a six-minute walk from the station, just off Chūō-dōri.

INTERNET RESOURCES
The prefectural website www.city.nagano.nagano.jp has limited information, but does list all of Nagano's annual festivals.

MONEY & POST
There's a post office and an international ATM in the West Plaza Nagano building opposite the station's Zenkōji exit.

TOURIST INFORMATION
ANPIE (Association of Nagano Prefecture for Promoting International Exchange; ☎ 235-7186; 692-2 Habashimo; ☺ 8.30am-5.15pm Mon-Fri) On the 2nd floor of the Kenchō (prefectural office), this association can help English-speaking visitors and has an international lounge. It's on Shōwa-dōri, a 25-minute walk from the station. Bus Nos 31 and 18 go there from bus stop 4 in front of the station.
International Relations Section (☎ 224-5447; 1613 Midori-chō; ☺ 8.30am-5.15pm Mon-Fri) Inside Nagano City Hall, this office has English (and Chinese) speakers available. Take a right out of the station, walk for 10 minutes, and take a right on busy Shōwa-dōri. It's three blocks further, on the right.
Tourist Information Centre (☎ 226-5626; ☺ 9.30am-6pm) Inside JR Nagano Station, this friendly outfit has good English-language colour maps and guides to both Nagano and the surrounding areas. Staff can also book accommodation in the city centre.

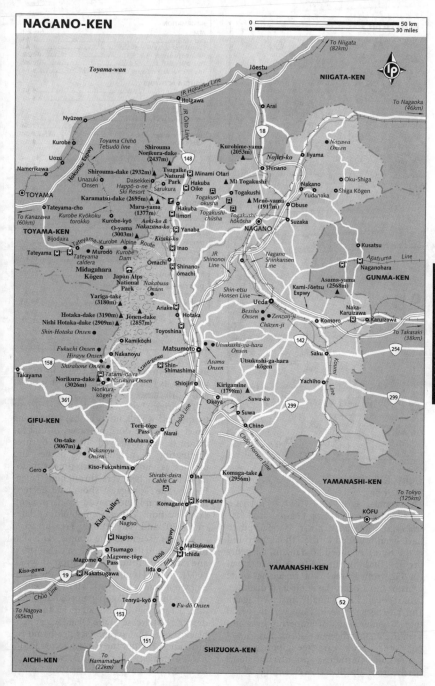

NAGANO-KEN

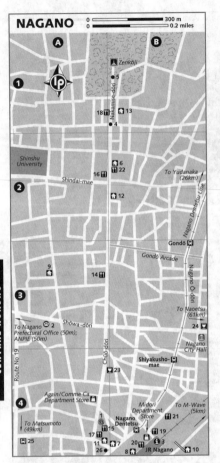

NAGANO

0 — 300 m
0 — 0.2 miles

Sights & Activities

ZENKŌJI 善光寺

This **temple** (☎ 186-026-234-3591; 491 Motoyoshi-chō; admission free; ⏱ 4.30am-4.30pm summer, 6am-4pm winter, sliding hr rest of year) is believed to have been founded in the 7th century and is the home of the Ikkō-Sanzon, allegedly the first Buddhist image to arrive in Japan (in 552, from Korea). The image has quite a history; it's been the subject of disputes, lost, recovered and, finally, installed again. Don't expect to see it, however; it is said that 37 generations of emperors have not seen the image, though visitors may view a copy every seven years (see opposite).

Zenkōji's immense popularity stems partly from its liberal welcoming of be-

lievers from all Buddhist sects, including women; its chief officiants are both a priest and a priestess.

The original site was south of the current temple, off what's now the busy shopping street Nakamise-dōri; however, in that location it was destroyed 11 times by fires originating in neighbouring homes and businesses – and rebuilt each time with donations from believers throughout Japan. Finally, the Tokugawa shōgunate decreed that the temple be moved to its present, safer location. The current building dates from 1707 and is a National Treasure.

Visitors ascend to the temple via Nakamise-dōri and the impressive gates Niō-mon and Sanmon (under restoration through 2007). In the Hondō (main hall), the Ikkō-Sanzon image is in an ark left of the central altar, behind a dragon-embroidered curtain. To the right of the altar, visitors may descend a staircase to the Okaidan, a pitch-black tunnel that symbolises death and rebirth and provides the closest access to the hidden image; taller visitors: watch your head! As you navigate the twisting tunnel,

---

ZENKŌJI LEGENDS

Few Japanese temples have the fascination of Zenkōji, thanks in part to the legends related to it. Among these legends:

■ **Ikkō-Sanzon** This image, containing three statues of the Amida Buddha, was brought to Japan from Korea in the 6th century and remains the temple's *raison-d'être*. It's wrapped like a mummy and kept in an ark behind the main altar, and it's generally said that nobody has seen it for 1000 years. However, in 1702, in response to rumours that the ark was empty, the shōgunate ordered a priest to confirm its existence and take measurements – that priest remains the last confirmed person to have viewed it.

■ **Following an Ox to Zenkōji** Long ago, an impious old woman was washing her kimono when an ox appeared, caught a piece of the cloth on his horn and ran away with it. The woman was as stingy as she was impious, and she gave chase for hours. Finally, the ox led her to Zenkōji, and she fell asleep under its eaves. The ox came to her in a dream, revealed himself to be the image of the Amida Buddha and disappeared. The woman saw this as a miracle and became a pious believer. Today, people in Kantō say, 'I followed an ox to Zenkōji' to mean that something good happened unexpectedly.

■ **The Doves of Sanmon** Zenkōji's pigeon population is renowned, making the rattan *hatto-guruma* (wheeled pigeon) a favourite Nagano souvenir. Natives claim the birds forecast bad weather by roosting on the Sanmon gate, but many visitors also claim to see five white doves in the plaque above the central portal. They're talking about the short strokes on the three characters that make up 'Zenkōji'. In the upper character (善, 'zen') they're the two upper-most strokes; in the middle character (光, 'kō') they're the strokes on either side of the top; and in the 'ji' (寺) it's the short stroke on the bottom left.

■ **Binzuru** A follower of Buddha, Binzuru trained in healing. He was due to become a Bosatsu (Bodhisattva, or enlightened one) and go to the land of the immortals, but the Buddha instructed him to remain on earth and continue to do good works. At most temples with images of Binzuru, he's outside the main hall, but at Zenkōji you'll find his statue just inside. His body is worn from all the visitors who have touched it to help heal ailments of the corresponding parts of their own bodies; you can see the lines where the face was once replaced.

---

dangle your arm along the right-hand wall until you feel something heavy, moveable and metallic – said to be the key to salvation (a bargain for the ¥500 admission).

It's worth getting to the temple shortly after it opens to witness the morning service and the *ojuzu chodai*, in which the priest or priestess touches the Buddhist holy beads to the heads of all who line up and kneel. Check with the tourist information centre or the Zenkōji office for the times of the service.

Any bus from bus stop 1 in front of Nagano Station will get you to Zenkōji (¥100).

M-WAVE SKATING ARENA

One of the star attractions during the 1998 Olympics, the state-of-the-art **speed-skating arena** (☎ 222-3300; www.nagano-mwave.co.jp; ☻ 10am-4pm Wed-Mon museum, skating hr vary) today houses an Olympic memorial museum with exhibits relating to the games. Photos, medals, the original torch and uniforms are on display. Visitors can also watch footage from other Olympics and ride a rather amusing bobsled simulator. Skating, while pricey, is perhaps the best way to experience **M-Wave** (admission ¥1500, skate rental ¥600). Buses leave from the east exit of Nagano Station. Take a Yashima-bound bus from stop 1 and exit at M-Wave (¥260).

Festivals & Events

Gokaichō Matsuri is held at Zenkōji once every seven years from early April to mid-May, when five million pilgrims come to view a copy of Zenkōji's sacred image of Buddha – the only time it can be seen. Unfortunately, the next festival isn't until 2010.

Sleeping

Shukubō (temple lodgings) are available at Zenkōji's subtemples. Contact the tourist office or **Zenkōji** (☎ 186-026-234-3591); if it's the latter be sure to dial all the digits to permit caller ID, without which staff might not pick up the phone. Rooms with two meals generally cost ¥7000 to ¥10,000 per person.

There are a number of fairly uninspiring business hotels around the train station. For a more traditional experience, book a room at one of the ryokan around Zenkō-ji.

Zenkō-ji Kyōju-in Youth Hostel (☎ 232-2768; fax 232-2767; 479 Motoyoshi-chō; dm ¥3360) This atmospheric hostel is housed in a handsome, 100-plus year-old subtemple of Zenkōji. Be sure to reserve. No meals are served.

Shimizuya Ryokan (☎ 232-2580; fax 234-5911; 49 Daimon-chō; r per person from ¥4500) A few blocks south of Zenkōji, this friendly, family-run ryokan offers good value, with a smokey darkwood interior, spotless tatami rooms and an old dog that slumbers in the entryway.

Hotel Metropolitan Nagano (☎ 291-7000; www .metro-n.co.jp; 1346 Minami-Ishido-chō; s/d/tw from ¥9240/19,635/18,480) The modern and elegant Metropolitan features airy, comfortable rooms, with an on-site café, restaurant and top-floor lounge. Japan Rail Pass holders get a 20% discount. It's just outside the west exit of the station and to the left.

Hotel Sunroute Nagano-Higashi-guchi (☎ 264-7700; fax 264-6611; 1-28-3 Minami-Chitose; s/tw/d from ¥8085/15,435/14,385) This relatively new business hotel has clean, modern rooms with nice wood touches. It's outside the station's east exit, over the pedestrian bridge and to the left.

Nagano Station Hotel (☎ 228-5111; 1359 Suehiro-chō; s/d/tw from ¥6000/10,000/12,000) This decent business hotel is a popular option for its clean, decent-sized rooms with big windows. Exit the west side of the station, cross the street and you'll see it just past the Mister Donut on the right.

Gohonjin Fujiya (☎ 232-1241; fuziya@avis.ne.jp; 80 Daimon-chō; r per person with 2 meals from ¥9000) Nagano's most famous and venerable hotel has been in business for 17 generations. The current building (c 1923) is rather Western-looking but functions as a traditional Japanese inn. Fujiya has friendly English-speaking staff and beautiful rooms: the best overlook a tranquil garden in back.

Hotel Saihokukan (☎ 235-3333; www.saihokukan .com; 528-1 Minami Kenchō; s/d/tw from ¥6825/14,700/ 15,750) Dating from 1890, this handsome Western hotel has lots of elegant flourishes among its fine rooms, and stylish in-house restaurants and bars. Rooms on the low

end can be a bit small, though the suites are favoured by the Imperial family. From the station's west exit, walk straight out and take the third right; it's eight minutes further on the left.

Hotel Ikemon (☎ 227-2122; fax 227-6600; 1362 Suehiro-chō; s from ¥4500) One of the cheapest Western hotels in town, Ikemon is nothing special, with cramped rooms and dim hallways, though the price is right.

Eating & Drinking

Nagano is famed for *soba*, and many restaurants around Zenkōji serve it. The station area is the best culinary hunting ground.

La Tavola nel Bosco (☎ 264-6270; 1358 Suehiro-chō; mains ¥800-1400; ☽ 11.30am-2pm & 6-9pm) This upstairs trattoria serves tasty thin-crust pizzas, hearty pastas and other Italian fare to a mix of locals and expats. No English menu. It's on Chūō-dōri, one block from the station.

Rakucha Rengakan (☎ 231-6001; 67-1 Daimon-chō; mains from ¥1200, shōjin-ryōri set ¥3150; ☽ 11.30am-2pm & 5.30-9pm Tue-Sun) In a brick building, a few blocks south of Zenkō-ji on Chūō-dōri, you'll find fresh, traditional cuisine with eclectic accents. Curry rice, grilled salmon and the more exquisite *shōjin-ryōri* (traditional Buddhist vegetarian) sets are among the offerings. English menu.

Gomeikan (☎ 232-1221; 515 Daimon-chō; mains from ¥1200; ☽ 11am-8pm Thu-Tue) This long-time Nagano favourite serves delicious *tonkatsu* (deep-fried breaded pork cutlet), vegetarian Indian curry and other traditional bites in an old, renovated building three blocks south of Zenkō-ji on Chūō-dōri. English menu.

Bakery's Street Café (☎ 232-0269; 1283 Toigosho; mains from ¥480; ☽ 7.30am-7pm) Blessed with the scent of freshly baked bread, this inviting café makes a pleasant stop on your stroll to Zenkō-ji. Pastries, croissants and cinnamon rolls, as well as satisfying deli sandwiches (caprese, pastrami, BLT), are among the temptations. It's on Chūō-dōri, a 12-minute walk from the station.

Paskaru (☎ 224-1000; 1-16-1 Minami-Chitose; meals from ¥1800; ☽ 6-11.30pm) Near Nagano Station, this hidden gem serves incredibly fresh sashimi. From the west exit, head down the narrow alley to the right of the station, go one block, cross the street and it's in the building on the right, on the third floor. You've arrived when you reach the door painted with the image of the Beatles members. Beatles fans will undoubtedly enjoy the music selections inside.

Munch (☎ 228-7080; 1-16-1 Minami-Chitose; small dishes from ¥300; ⏰ 11.30am-2pm & 6.30pm-midnight) A youthful energy pervades this tiny spot near the train station. *Kim-chi* and small dishes are the speciality here. Try the *tako wasabi* (octopus), *goya champu* (egg and peppers), or let the chef (the one in braids and the trucker hat) surprise you. It's to the right of the station's west exit.

Chō Bali Bali (☎ 243-2891; 1366 Suehiro-chō; mains from ¥600; ⏰ noon-2.30pm & 6pm-midnight Tue-Sun) This stylish space gathers a festive crowd most nights and serves eclectic Asian dishes. Highly recommended. English menu.

Marusei (☎ 232-5776; 486 Motoyoshi-chō; dishes ¥600-1300; ⏰ 11am-4pm Thu-Tue) A stone's throw from the temple on Nakamise-dōri, tiny unassuming Marusei serves *soba* and their well-liked *tonkatsu* (deep-fried breaded pork cutlet); the Marusei *bentō* (¥1300) lets you try both.

Oyaki Kōbō (☎ 223-4537; oyaki around ¥140 each; ⏰ 8.30am-7.30pm) Good for quick bites; this *oyaki* shop, outside the station's west exit, has tasty flavours like pumpkin, mushroom and eggplant.

Groovy (☎ 227-0480; 1398 Kita-ishidō-machi; http: //nagano.cool.ne.jp/jazzgroovy; cover ¥1000-3500) This music spot is popular with local jazz lovers for its live shows. It's on Chūō-dōri, a six-minute walk from the train station.

Liberty (☎ 235-2870; 1602 Midori-chō; ⏰ 11.30am-2pm & 6pm-1am) Nagano's most popular gaijin pub has Guinness on tap, decent pub food and a friendly crowd. From the west exit of JR Nagano, take a right on busy Nagano-Odōri and another right (at the second stoplight) on Showa-dōri.

Getting There & Away

Nagano *shinkansen* trains run twice hourly from Tokyo Station (Asama, ¥7970, 1¾ hours). The JR Shinonoi line connects Nagano with Matsumoto (*tokkyū*, ¥2770, one hour) and Nagoya (*tokkyū*, ¥6930, three hours).

TOGAKUSHI 戸隠

☎ 026 / pop 5200

This mountainous, forested region is northwest of Nagano and makes a splendid day trip from there. Hikers enjoy the refreshing alpine scenery from late spring to autumn, while winter belongs to the skiers. Togakushi's elevation makes it unsuitable for rice-growing, but it has been famed for *soba* for centuries.

Three subshrines (Hōkōsha, Chūsha and Okusha), each separated by several kilometres, make up the Togakushi Shrine. One bus line serves all three, but the greatest concentration of sights and accommodation is in the community of Chūsha, near the Chūsha-Miyamae bus stop. Here you'll find the historic, wooded Chūsha shrine; one tree here is said to be 800 years old, and Chūsha is a good skiing base in the winter. You can hike a meandering 90-minute trail to Okusha, at the foot of Mt Togakushi, passing by Kagami-ike Pond and the Togakushi Botanic Garden. At the edge of the botanic garden you'll meet up with the long, cedar-lined path to Okusha. Pick up maps from the tourist office in Nagano.

From Okusha avid alpinists can make the strenuous climb to the top of 1911m-high Mt Togakushi. In winter, Okusha is inaccessible except for hearty snowshoers.

Across from the turn-off to Okusha is **Togakushi Minzoku-kan** (戸隠民俗館; ☎ 254-2395; admission ¥500; ⏰ 9am-5pm), a collection of buildings that attest to the ninja-training school that was once here. A museum displays photos, clothing and weaponry employed by the ninja there. Next door, you can bungle your way through the Ninja House, which is full of trick doors, false staircases and curious mazes.

Near Chūsha, the slopes of **Togakushi Snow World** (☎ 254-2106; one-day pass ¥4000; ⏰ 13 Dec-4 Apr) has decent runs (the longest is 3000m) and fewer crowds than the resorts around Hakuba.

In Chūsha, **Togakushi Kōgen Yokokura Youth Hostel** (戸隠高原横倉ユースホステル; ☎ 254-2030; dm with/without 2 meals ¥4750/3000) is in an early Meiji-era building (Japanese toilets only), near the entrance to the ski area. Ryokan-quality private rooms are available from ¥7000 per person, with two meals. Prices at other ryokan start at around ¥8000 per person. To savour local *soba*, grab lunch at well-known **Uzuraya Soba** (うずら家そば; ☎ 254-2219; dishes ¥800-1700; ⏰ lunch), which serves hand-made *soba* noodles until they run out. It's also in Chūsha, directly across from the steps to the shrine.

Closer to Okusha (400m before the shrine), **Soba Nomi** (そばの実; ☎ 254-2102; dishes from ¥840;

10.30am-4.30pm) is another fine choice, with delicious *soba* and large windows overlooking the forest.

Buses via the scenic Togakushi Birdline Highway depart from Nagano approximately once an hour between 6.55am and 6.45pm and arrive at Chūsha-Miyamae bus stop in about an hour (¥1160) – do not get off at Chūsha bus stop, which is basically a bus transit point. To Okusha the fare is ¥1360. If you plan to take many buses look into the Togakushi Kōgen Free Kippu pass (¥2500), which is available from JR Nagano Station and is valid on area buses for three days.

OBUSE 小布施
☎ 026 / pop 12,000

This little town northeast of Nagano occupies a big place in Japanese art history. The famed *ukiyo-e* (woodblock print) artist Hokusai (1760–1849) worked here during his last years, making it a pilgrimage site for his legions of fans. The town is also noted for its *kuri* (chestnuts), which you can sample steamed with rice or in ice cream or sweets. Pick up a map of the town from the Nagano tourist office (p236) before setting out.

The first stop should be the excellent museum **Hokusai-kan** (北斎館; ☎ 247-5206; admission ¥500; 9am-5pm), which displays some 30 of his inspiring prints at any one time as well as several colourful floats, which are decorated with Hokusai's imaginative ceiling panels. From the train station, cross the street and walk down the road perpendicular to the station; take the second right then keep an eye out for the signs to the museum. It's a 10-minute walk from the station.

A block away, Hokusai's patron, Takai Kōzan, is commemorated in the **Takai Kōzan Kinenkan** (高井鴻山記念館; ☎ 249-4049; admission ¥200; 9am-5pm). This businessman was also an accomplished artist, albeit of more classical forms than Hokusai's.

A few blocks east stands the **Taikan Bonsai Museum** (大観盆栽館; ☎ 247-7000; admission ¥500; 9am-5pm), containing displays of rare species and a lovely ornamental garden. A good restaurant sits on the grounds.

Obuse also has nine other **museums**, showcasing everything from Japanese lamps to antique pottery.

Obuse also boasts the nearest *rotemburo* to Nagano, **Anakannon-no-yu** (穴観音の湯; ☎ 247-2525; admission ¥500; 10am-10pm May-Sep,

10am-9pm Oct-Apr); bring a towel. It's about 30 minutes' walk from the train station; occasional buses are available.

To reach Obuse, take the Nagano Dentetsu line from Nagano (*tokkyū*, ¥750, 22 minutes; *futsū*, ¥650, 30 minutes). You can obtain maps, info and rent bikes (¥400 per hour) at the **Obuse Guide Centre** (おぶせガイドセンター; ☎ 247-5050; 9am-6pm), which you'll pass on the way to the museum coming from the station.

YUDANAKA & SHIGA KŌGEN
湯田中 志賀高原
☎ 0269 / pop 18,000

This region of hot springs and winter Olympic sites is perhaps best known for **Jigokudani Onsen** (Hell Valley Hot Springs; 地獄谷温泉) and the monkeys who soak in its waters. There are also hiking and winter sports activities.

Jigokudani Yaen-kōen (Wild Monkey Park; 地獄谷野猿公苑; ☎ 33-4379; www.jigokudani-yaenkoen.co.jp; admission ¥500; 8.30am-5pm Apr-Oct, 9am-4pm Nov-Mar) One of the best places to observe wild monkeys in the country, Jigokudani has been the gathering spot of some 200 animated simians since the 1960s. Today the monkeys have their own *onsen*, and there's always a few monkeys enjoying the hot springs or splashing about in the river below.

Shiga Kōgen (志賀高原; ☎ 34-2404; 1-/2-day ticket ¥4500/8500; 9am-9pm Dec-Apr) The site of various events in the 1998 Olympics, Shiga Kōgen has some excellent runs. It consists of 21 linked resorts, 80km of slopes in all (the longest is 6km). One lift ticket gives access to most of the mountains. The **Shiga Kōgen Tourist Office** (☎ 34-2404; 9am-5pm) has English speakers who can help navigate the slopes and can book accommodation. During the rest of the year, the mountains' lakes, ponds and overlooks make an excellent destination for hikers.

Kōraku-kan (後楽館; ☎ 33-4376; r per person with 2 meals from ¥10,545) Across the river from Jigokudani, this simple *onsen* hotel is where monkeys get to commune with bathing humans. Accommodation at this ryokan here is basic, with small but clean-swept tatami rooms. Aside from the tasty mountain vegetable tempura, the highlight is the *onsen*. Several pleasant indoor and concrete riverside outdoor *onsen* are available 24 hours for guests. For day visitors (8am to 10am and noon to 3pm) entry costs ¥400. Outdoor *onsen* users are warned that uninvited guests – of the decidedly hairy variety – may join them in the baths from time to time.

Uotoshi Ryokan (魚歳旅館; ☎ 33-1215; fax 33-0074; www.avis.ne.jp/~miyasaka/; r per person with/without two meals from ¥7300/3800) In the peaceful little town of Yudanaka, Uotoshi is nothing fancy but its host is commendably hospitable. The English-speaking owner may demonstrate *kyūdō* (Japanese archery) on request. You can arrange to be picked up at Yudanaka Station, or walk from there to the ryokan (seven minutes). Take a left out of the station, follow the road over the river; when the road ends take a right. It's 20m further on.

Yuyado Sekiya (湯宿せきや; ☎ 33-2268; fax 33-5885; r per person with 2 meals from ¥12,000) For more spacious rooms with a bit more ambience, head to this ryokan by the Kanbayashi Onsen bus stop. It's surrounded by woodlands, and has lovely indoor and outdoor baths.

Pâtisserie Bonne Bouche (パティスリーボンブーシュ; ☎ 33-8639; ☺ 9am-6pm Thu-Tue) A few minutes' walk past Kanbayashi Onsen bus stop on the way to Jigokudani, this tidy café serves fresh baked goods, deli sandwiches and a variety of soups and rice curries.

From Nagano, take the Nagano Dentetsu line to the terminal at Yudanaka (*tokkyū*, ¥1230, hourly), where a small **information office** (☎ 33-2138; ☺ 9am-5pm) distributes maps. From Yudanaka, take the bus for Kanbayashi Onsen Guchi and get off at Kanbayashi Onsen (¥220, 15 minutes, 8 daily). From here walk uphill along the road about 400m. If you're headed to Jigokudani, you'll see a sign at the trailhead that reads 'Monkey Park'; follow the trail for a tree-lined 1.6km to the ryokan and Yaen-kōen. Note that some trains do not go all the way to Yudanaka.

To reach Shiga Kōgen, you can continue from the Yudanaka bus stop along the highway via an Oku-Shiga–bound bus (¥1050, 30min); during ski season direct buses run from Nagano Station (¥2100, two hours).

HAKUBA & AROUND 白馬
☎ 0261

Skiing in winter, and hiking and mountaineering in summer attract large numbers of visitors to this quite pleasant town surrounded by mountains in northern Chūbu-Sangaku National Park. Hiking trails tend to be less clogged during September and October, but even in midsummer you should be prepared for hiking over snow-covered terrain on the highest peaks.

For information, maps and lodging assistance, visit the **Hakuba Shukuhaku Joho Centre** (☎ 72-6900; 6900@hakuba1.com), to the right of the Hakuba train/bus station. Check out www.vill.hakuba.nagano.jp/e/index.htm, a useful website.

Inside the Mominoki Hotel in Happō-o-ne (p244), **Evergreen Outdoor Centre** (☎ 72-5150; www.evergreen-outdoors.com) offers an array of half-day adventures, including rafting (¥8000), paragliding (¥5000), canoeing (¥5000) and mountain biking (¥5000), as well as snowshoeing and backcountry treks in the winter. English-speaking guides are available.

Sights & Activities
SHIROUMA-DAKE 白馬岳
The four-hour ascent of this mountain (2932m) is a popular hike and on clear days the views from the summit are spectacular. You should be properly prepared before heading out. Mountain huts provide meals and basic accommodation, about one hour out from and near the summit (around ¥9000 per person with two meals).

Buses leave Hakuba Station for the trailhead at Sarukura (¥980, 30 minutes, late May to September). From here, you can hike west to the peak in about six hours. A more leisurely option is a return trip via the same trail as far as Daisekkei (Great Snowy Gorge), about 1¾ hours away.

The trail southwest of Sarukura leads uphill for three hours to **Yari Onsen** (鑓温泉; ☎ 72-2002; onsen ¥300; r per person with 2 meals ¥8500) and its open-air hot spring with breathtaking mountain views. It's Japan's highest *rotemburo*, at 2100m. There's also a mountain hut if you wish to stay.

TSUGAIKE NATURAL PARK 栂池自然園
This **park** (Tsugaike Shizen-en; admission ¥300) lies north of Shirouma Norikura-dake in an alpine marshland. A three-hour hiking trail covers most of the park, which is renowned for its alpine flora.

During summer there are one to two buses an hour (¥540, 30 minutes) from Hakuba to Tsugaike-kōgen; from there you'll find a gondola and ropeway into the park (¥3300 round-trip, including park admission). Discount tickets are available at the Hakuba Shukuhaku Joho Centre. From the park to Shirouma, allow seven hours' hike.

HAPPŌ-O-NE SKI RESORT
八方尾根スキーリゾート

This is a busy **ski resort** (☎ 72-3066; 1-day lift ticket ¥4600; ⊙ Dec-Apr) in the winter and a popular hiking area in the summer. From Hakuba Station, a five-minute bus ride takes you to Happō; from here it's a 10-minute walk to the gondola (open 8am to 5pm) base station. From the top station of the cable car you can use two more chairlifts (open 8am to 4.30pm), and then hike along a trail for an hour or so to the pond Happō-ike on a ridge below Karamatsu-dake. From here you can follow a trail for an hour up to Maru-yama, continue for 1½ hours to the Karamatsu-dake San-sō (mountain hut) and then climb to the peak of **Karamatsu-dake** (2695m) in about 30 minutes. The return fare is ¥2260 if purchased at the Hakuba tourist office, ¥2600 otherwise.

NISHINA SAN-KO 仁科三湖

While travelling south from Hakuba, Nishina San-ko (Nishina Three Lakes) provide some short walks. Nakazuna-ko and Aoki-ko are close to Yanaba Station, and Kizaki-ko is next to Inao Station.

Sleeping & Eating

There are over 800 lodgings around Hakuba. The Hakuba Shukuhaku Joho Centre (p243) helps arrange rooms starting at about ¥7000 per person with two meals. Staff speak English.

Lodge Hakuba (ロッジはくば; ☎ 72-3095; www.avis.ne.jp/~l-hakuba; r per person weekday/weekend from ¥6500/8000) Near the cable car base lodge at Happō-o-ne offers both Western- and Japanese-style rooms. Some English spoken.

Wade Ryokan (上手旅館; ☎ 72-2435; fax 72-2363; r per person with 2 meals ¥7500) Nearby, this is a *kokumin-shukusha* (people's lodge), popular with travellers.

Hayaokidori (早起き鳥; ☎ 75-2142; www.haku bajapan.com; s/d with 2 meals ¥11,025/18,270) This friendly family-run lodge has earned many fans for the excellent home-cooking, tranquil setting and hospitable hosts. English spoken. It's a five-minute walk from Kamishiro Station, two stops south of Hakuba Station.

Gravity Worx (☎ 72-5434; dishes ¥580-940; ⊙ noon-10pm Wed-Mon low season, Mon-Sun rest of year) This friendly snowboard shop/café serves homemade pizza, pasta and cakes. It's a popular hangout for gaijin (English is spoken). Take a right out of Hakuba Station; it's on the main road on the right (one minute's walk).

Getting There & Away

Hakuba is connected with Matsumoto by the JR Ōito line (*tokkyū*, ¥2770, one hour; *futsū*, ¥1110, 1¾ hours). Continuing north, you can change trains at Minami Otari to meet the JR Hokuriku Honsen line at Itoigawa, with connections towards Niigata, Toyama and Kanazawa. From Nagano, buses leave from in front of Nagano Station (¥1400, one hour).

BESSHO ONSEN 別所温泉
☎ 0268 / pop 1600

If you're visiting just one central Honshū hot-spring town, Bessho is a good choice; it's almost as convenient from Tokyo as from Nagano, and retains much old-world charm. Bessho's excellent waters, reputed to cure diabetes and constipation while beautifying your complexion, bring in tourists aplenty, but overall it feels undeveloped.

Bessho is mentioned in *The Pillow Book* by the Heian era poetess Sei Shōnagon; it flourished as an administrative centre during the Kamakura period (1185–1333). The town is still referred to as 'Little Kamakura' for dramatic temples constructed at that time.

The national treasure **Anraku-ji** (☎ 38-2062; admission ¥100; ⊙ sunrise-sunset), renowned for its octagonal pagoda, is 10 minutes on foot from Bessho Onsen Station, while **Chūzen-ji** (☎ 38-4538; admission ¥100; ⊙ 9am-4pm) and **Zen-zan-ji** (☎ 38-2855; admission ¥100; ⊙ 9am-5pm) are both a very enjoyable 5km hike away.

There are three central **public baths** (admission ¥150; ⊙ 6am-10pm). Ō-yu has a small *rotemburo*, Ishi-yu is famed for its stone bath and Daishi-yu, most frequented by the locals, is known for being relatively cool.

Bessho Onsen Ryokan Association (☎ 38-2020; fax 38-8887) can help with hotel bookings. **Ueda Mahoroba Youth Hostel** (上田まほろばユースホステル; ☎ 38-5229; fax 38-1714; dm with/without 2 meals ¥4720/3040) is comfortable and secluded, surrounded by lush scenery. It's eight minutes' walk south from the train station (no *onsen*).

Ryokan Katsura-sō (旅館桂荘; ☎ 38-2047; katsuraso@po7.ueda.ne.jp; r per person with 2 meals ¥10,500) This 2-storey ryokan has nice tatami rooms, friendly staff and excellent sansai cuisine. The rooms on upper floors have valley views.

Ryokan Hanaya (旅館花屋; ☎ 38-3131; fax 38-7923; r per person with 2 meals from ¥20,000) This traditional ryokan consists of 10 splendid buildings surrounded by lovely, manicured gardens. Spacious tatami rooms open onto the scenery outside. Some rooms have private hot springs baths attached; guests without remain content with handsome indoor and outdoor baths. Reserve far in advance.

To reach Bessho Onsen, take the JR Nagano *shinkansen* to Ueda (from Tokyo, ¥6490, 1½ hours; from Nagano, ¥1410, 13 minutes) then change to the private Ueda Kōtsū line to Bessho Onsen (¥570, 27 minutes, about hourly).

MATSUMOTO 松本
☎ 0263 / pop 211,000

From the moment you step off the train and hear the piped-in voice singing 'Ma-*tsumotoooh*', you sense you're somewhere different. Matsumoto has a superb castle, some pretty streets, and an atmosphere that's both laid-back and surprisingly cosmopolitan.

The city has been around since at least the 8th century. Formerly known as Fukashi, it was the castle town of the Ogasawara clan during the 14th and 15th centuries, and it continued to prosper through the Edo period. Today, Matsumoto's street aesthetic combines the black-and-white of its castle with *namako* (lattice-patterned) *kura* (storehouses) and 21st-century Japanese architecture; plus, views of the Japan Alps are never much further than around the corner. Parts of the city centre were recently given a contemporary makeover, and the area by the Metoba-gawa and the Nakamachi district boasts smart galleries, comfortable cafés and reasonably priced, high-quality accommodation.

Asama Onsen and Utsukushi-ga-hara are day trips, while Hotaka can be either a day trip or the start of a hiking route. Matsumoto is also a regional transit hub to the Japan Alps National Park, among other destinations.

Orientation & Information

For a castle town, Matsumoto is relatively easy to get around. Although small streets radiate somewhat confusingly from the train station, soon you're on a grid. Any place on our Matsumoto map is within 20 minutes' walk of the train station.

The **tourist information office** (☎ 32-2814; 1-1-1 Fukashi; ◯ 9.30am-6pm Apr-Oct, 9.30am-5.30pm Nov-Mar) is at street level outside Matsumoto Station's eastern exit. English-speaking staff have English-language pamphlets and maps, and can book accommodation.

Fureai International Information Centre (☎ 48-7000; 4010-27 Isemachi-dōri; ◯ 8.30am-9pm Mon-Fri, 10am-5pm Sat) Free Internet use, a lending library and a lounge with news broadcasts in English. It's in the M-Wing building, the entrance marked by a multi-coloured sphere.

The main post office is located on Hon-machi-dōri. The bar **People's** (☎ 37-5011; 1-4-11 Fukashi; per hr ¥200; ◯ 6pm-1am) also has Internet access. For information on the city, visit www.city.matsumoto.nagano.jp.

Sights & Activities
MATSUMOTO-JŌ 松本城

Even if you spend only a couple of hours in Matsumoto, make sure you visit this **castle** (☎ 32-2902; 4-1 Marunōchi; admission ¥600; ◯ 8.30am-6pm late Jul-Aug, 8.30am-5pm rest of year), one of four castles declared National Treasures (the others are Hikone, Himeji and Inuyama).

The magnificent three-turreted donjon was built c 1595, in contrasting black-and-white, leading to the nickname Karasu-jō (Crow Castle). Steep steps lead up six storeys, with impressive views from each level. Lower floors display guns, bombs and gadgets with which to storm castles, and a delightful *tsukimi yagura* (moon-viewing pavilion). It has a tranquil moat full of carp, with the occasional swan gliding beneath the handsome red bridges. The basics are explained over loudspeakers in English and Japanese. You can also ask at the entrance about a free tour in English; or call the **Goodwill Guide Group** (☎ 32-7140; ◯ 8am-noon), which give free one-hour tours by advance notice.

The castle grounds (and your admission ticket) also include the **Matsumoto City Museum/Japan Folklore Museum** (☎ 32-0133; 4-1 Marunōchi; ◯ 8.30am-4.30pm), with small exhibits relating to the region's history and folklore, including a collection of *tanabata* dolls (p248) as well as the wooden phalluses which play a prominent role in the September Dōsojin festival (opposite).

NAKAMACHI 中町
The narrow streets of this former merchant district make a fine setting for a stroll, as most of its storehouses have been transformed into galleries, craft shops and cafés. **Nakamachi Kura Shikku-Kan** (☎ 36-3053; 2-9-15 Chūō; 🕐 9am-10pm) showcases locally produced arts and crafts, and there's a relaxing coffee house next door.

MATSUMOTO CITY MUSEUM OF ART 松本美術館
New in 2002, this sleek **museum** (☎ 39-7400; 4-2-22 Chūō; admission ¥800; 🕐 9am-5pm Tue-Sun) has a good collection of Japanese artists, many who hail from Matsumoto or depict scenes of the surrounding countryside. Highlights include the striking avant-garde works of Yayoi Kusama, the finely crafted landscapes of Kazuo Tamura and the calligraphy of Shinzan Kamijo. The museum also attracts good temporary exhibitions.

JAPAN UKIYO-E MUSEUM 日本浮世絵美術館
This **museum** (☎ 47-4440; 2206-1 Shimadachi; admission ¥1000; 🕐 10am-5pm Tue-Sun) is a must for *ukiyo-e* (woodblock print) lovers. Several generations of the Sakai family have collected over 100,000 prints, paintings, screens and old books – the largest private collection in the world. English signage is minimal, but an explanatory leaflet in English is provided.

The museum is about 3km from Matsumoto Station or 15 minutes' walk from Ōniwa Station on the Matsumoto Dentetsu line (¥170, seven minutes) or about ¥2000 by taxi.

ASAMA ONSEN 浅間温泉
This hot-spring resort northeast of town isn't rustic, but its history is said to reach back to the 10th century and include writers and poets. The waters are also said to be good for gastrointestinal and skin troubles,

and women's disorders. Among dozens of baths and inns (and the youth hostel), **Hot Plaza Asama** (☎ 46-6278; admission ¥840; ⏱ 10am-8pm Wed-Mon) has many pools in a traditional building. Buses from Matsumoto Station take about 20 minutes.

UTSUKUSHI-GA-HARA-KŌGEN 美ヶ原高原
From April to mid-November, this alpine plateau is a popular excursion from Matsumoto. There are pleasant walks and the opportunity to see cows in pasture (a constant source of fascination to the Japanese).

Utsukushi-ga-hara Kōgen Bijutsukan (Utsukushi-ga-hara Open-Air Museum; 美ヶ原高原美術館; ☎ 0268-86-2331; admission ¥1000; ⏱ 9am-5pm late Apr-late Nov) is in the same vein (with the same owner) as the Hakone Open-Air Museum (p175), a large sculpture garden (some 450 pieces) with fine views of the surrounding mountains.

Most Japanese visitors reach the museum by car. Buses (¥1300, 80 minutes) run several times daily in midsummer with spotty-to-nonexistent service the rest of the season; check before you go. Taxis to the museum start at a cool ¥10,700 (yes, one way). See p249 for information on car rental.

Festivals & Events
Tenjin Matsuri (23–24 July) The festival at Fukashi-jinja features elaborately decorated *dashi* and a fireworks display. The second day is livelier.

Takigi Nō Matsuri (during August) The atmospheric festival features nō (classical Japanese dance-drama) by torchlight, performed outdoors on a stage in the park below the castle.

Dōsojin Matsuri (Fourth Saturday in September) Phallic merriment is to be had at the festival held in honour of *dōsojin* (roadside guardians) at Utsukushi-ga-hara Onsen.

Yohashira Jinja Matsuri (aka Shintōsai, around the beginning of October) Features displays of fireworks and large dolls.

Asama Hi-Matsuri (around the beginning of October) Asama Onsen celebrates the spectacular fire festival with torch-lit parades that are accompanied by drumming.

Oshiro Matsuri (Castle Festival, around 3 November) A cultural jamboree including costume parades, puppet displays and flower shows.

Sleeping
In the station area, you'll mostly find cramped, charmless business hotels; more atmospheric ryokan are in the Nakamachi district.

BUDGET
Nishiya (☎ /fax 33-4332; 2-4-12 Ōtemachi; r per person ¥3600) In a quiet neighbourhood on the way to the castle, this ryokan is showing its age, but remains popular for its low-priced tatami rooms and friendly owner. Take a left out of the station, cross the bridge and take the third right. It will be on your right.

Asama Onsen Youth Hostel (浅間温泉ユースホステル; ☎ 46-1335; 1-7-15 Asama Onsen; dm ¥3200; ⏱ closed 28 Dec-3 Jan) Although rather unsightly from the outside, this hostel offers quick access to nearby *onsen* and significant discounts to Hot Plaza Asama. Doors close at 9pm. From Matsumoto bus station, take bus No 6 to Shita-Asama (¥300) or bus No 7 to Dai-Ichi Kōkō-mae (¥240). Either bus takes 20 minutes, and the hostel is then five minutes on foot heading south.

Nunoya (☎ /fax 32-0545; 3-5-7 Nakamachi; r per person ¥5250) Another charmer in Nakamachi, this classic wooden inn offers good-quality tatami rooms with shared bathrooms. Breakfast costs an additional ¥525.

MIDRANGE
Marumo (☎ 32-0115; fax 35-2251; 3-3-10 Chūō; r per person with breakfast ¥6300) In the Nakamachi district, this beautiful ryokan dates from 1868 and has lots of traditional charm, including its own bamboo garden and a lovely coffee shop. Although rooms aren't huge, it's quite popular, so book ahead. It's on a side street between Nakamachi -dōri and the rushing Metoba-gawa.

Enjyoh Bekkan (☎ 33-7233; www.mcci.or.jp/www /enjyoh; 110-1 Satoyamabe; s/d from ¥5565/10,290) Outside town, at Utsukushi-ga-hara Onsen, Bekkan has large pleasant rooms, a nice garden and indoor hot-spring baths available 24 hours. From Matsumoto, take the bus to Utsukushi-ga-hara Onsen (¥330, 20 minutes); it's 300m to the ryokan.

Ace Inn (☎ 35-1188; http://ace.alpico.co.jp; 1-1-3 Fukashi; s from ¥6700) About the nicest option near the station, the Ace Inn has small rooms (singles only), but rates include a simple breakfast and free Internet access in the lobby. It's to the right as you exit the station.

Hotel Kagetsu (☎ 32-0114; www.mcci.or.jp/www /kagetsu; 4-8-9 Ōtemachi; r per person from ¥6825) A pleasant alternative near the castle, Kagetsu has nice-sized Japanese- or Western-style rooms with full facilities, plus generous communal baths. Rooms in the newer building

CENTRAL HONSHŪ

cost a little more but are smarter. Look for Internet specials.

Roynet Hotel (☎ 37-5000; www.roynet.co.jp; 1-10-7 Chūō; s/d ¥7200/9800) In the town centre, Roynet offers decent-sized rooms. Above rates are for Roynet/Royal Hotels *kai-in* (members). To become a *kai-in*, fill out a form and pay a one-time ¥500 charge when you check in.

TOP END

Ichiyama (☎ 32-0122; fax 32-2968; 2-1-17 Chūō; s/d with breakfast Apr-Nov ¥10,500/16,800, Dec-Mar ¥9500/15,800) In a replica of a Meiji-era *kura* (storehouse), this handsome and welcoming inn has wood-beamed ceilings, whitewashed walls and lots of elegant touches among its Japanese- and Western-style rooms. Take a left out of the station and a right on Kōen-dōri. It's just past the Parco department store.

Hotel Buena Vista (☎ 37-0111; www.buena-vista .co.jp; 1-2-1 Honjo; s/tw from ¥11,550/16,170) Matsumoto's nicest Western hotel has several restaurants, a café and the 14th-floor Sky Lounge. Rooms are comfortably furnished (if not huge) with fine amenities, and the upper floors boast views of the mountains.

Eating & Drinking

Matsumoto is renowned for *shinshū-soba*, eaten either hot (*kake-soba*; in broth) or cold (*zaru-soba*; with wasabi and soya-based sauce). Other regional specialities include *basashi* (raw horsemeat), *hachinoko* (bee larvae) and *inago* (crickets). Tamer are *oyaki*, little wheat buns filled with various vegetables.

Nomugi (☎ 36-3753; 2-9-11 Chūō; soba ¥1000; ☯ lunch, closed Tue & sometimes Wed) In Nakamachi, this is one of central Japan's finest *soba* shops. Its owner used to run a French restaurant in Tokyo before returning to his hometown. There's one dish: *zaru-soba* in a handcrafted wicker basket; in colder seasons there's also hot *kake-soba* (¥1200).

Kura (☎ 33-6444; 2-2-15 Chūō; dishes from ¥300, teishoku ¥900-2000; ☯ 11.30am-2pm & 5.30-10pm Thu-Tue) Located near Nakamachi, Kura serves nicely prepared Japanese dishes for lunch and dinner in a stylish former warehouse like its namesake. The tempura is exceptional, as is the sashimi and *soba*. For the daring: top-notch *basashi*. English menu.

Bistro La Provence (☎ 33-8689; 3-3-5 Ōtemachi; mains from ¥1200; ☯ 10am-9pm) Two blocks north

of the river, this bistro delivers on its authentic Provençal cuisine, courtesy of the talented French chef. Roasted *confit* of duck with cooked vegetables and salmon with ratatouille are among the changing selections. Small but decent wine selection.

Robata Shōya (☎ 37-1000; 11-1 Chūō; dishes ¥300-980; ☯ 5pm-midnight) This lively *yakitori-ya* is a fun corner place with a large selection of grills, seasonal specials and a (sort of) English menu.

Vamonos (☎ 36-4878; 1-4-13 Chūō; mains from ¥800; ☯ 11am-3pm & 6pm-10pm) Two blocks east of the train station near Kōen-dōri, this second-floor Mexican restaurant still remains fairly undiscovered despite its decent enchiladas, burritos, nachos and other Tex-Mex selections. Look for the Spanish sign.

Sweet (☎ 32-5300; 4-8-9 Ōtemachi; pastries from ¥170; ☯ 7am-7pm) On the north side of the river, this charming café serves coffee, cappuccino and baked goods.

Ajisai (☎ 35-5533; 3-8-11 Ōtemachi; pastries from ¥170; ☯ 7am-7pm Mon & Wed-Fri, 9am-6pm Sat & Sun) For creamy gelato, cappuccinos and light snacks, head to this café near the castle.

Old Rock (☎ 38-0069; 2-30-20 Chūō; mains from ¥600; ☯ noon-3pm & 5pm-midnight) A block south of the river, this popular gaijin pub attracts a lively crowd on weekend nights. Good lunch specials and a wide selection of beers.

Coat (☎ 34-7133; 2-3-24 Chūō; ☯ 11am-4pm & 5pm-midnight) Run by a dexterous bartender, Coat proffers cocktails of a certain sophisticated but intoxicating quality. In fact, Hayashi-san's inventive 'otomenadeshiko' cocktail won first prize at the Japan Bartenders Association competition a few years back.

Shopping

Matsumoto is synonymous with *temari* (balls embroidered in geometric patterns) and doll-making. You can find both at **Berami** (Belle Amie; ☎ 33-1314; 3-7-23 Chūō; ☯ 10am-5pm Thu-Tue) on Ōhashi-dōri. Doll styles include *Tanabata* (flat wood or cardboard cut-outs dressed in paper) and *Oshie-bina* (dressed in fine cloth). Takasago street, one block south of Nakamachi, also has several doll shops.

Collectors of old books will be agog at the selection (and seeming disorganisation) at **Seikandō** (☎ 32-2333; 3-5-13 Ōtemachi; ☯ 9am-6pm) near the castle. And Nawate-dōri north of the river is a colourful place for souvenirs and cafés.

CENTRAL HONSHŪ

Getting There & Away

For information about reaching Japan Alps National Park, see p231.

AIR

Matsumoto airport has flights to Fukuoka, Osaka and Sapporo.

BUS

The company **Alpico/Matsumoto Dentetsu** (☎ 32-0910) runs buses between Matsumoto and Shinjuku in Tokyo (¥3400, 3¼ hours, 18 daily), Osaka (¥5710, 5¼ hours, two daily), Nagoya (¥3460, 3½ hours, four daily) and Takayama (¥3100, 2½ hours, four daily). All departures are from Matsumoto bus station, in the basement of the Espa building across from the train station (reservations advised).

CAR

Renting a car often turns out to be the best way to do side trips. **Nippon Rent-A-Car** (☎ 33-1324; 1-1 Fukashi) has the best deals (from about ¥5000 a day), just outside the train station. **Eki Rent-a-Car** (☎ 32-4690; 1-1 Fukashi) is a few doors down.

TRAIN

Matsumoto is connected with Tokyo's Shinjuku Station (*Super Azusa, Azusa,* ¥6510, 2½ hours, hourly), Nagoya (Shinano *tokkyū,* ¥5670, two hours) and Nagano (Shinano *tokkyū,* ¥2570, 50 minutes; *futsū,* ¥1110, 70 minutes). On the JR Ōito Line, trains serve Hotaka (¥320, 30 minutes) and Hakuba (*Azusa tokkyū,* ¥2570, 55 minutes; *futsū,* ¥1110, 1½ hours).

Getting Around

The castle and the city centre are easily covered on foot. Bicycle is also an excellent way to zip around town. The desk at the Matsumoto City Museum/Japan Folklore Museum (p245) beside the castle loans them out, free of charge. The 'town sneaker' bus loops through the centre for ¥100 (9am to 6pm).

An airport shuttle bus connects Matsumoto airport with the city centre (¥540, 25 minutes). Buses are timed to flights. A taxi costs around ¥4500.

HOTAKA 穂高
☎ 0263 / pop 32,880
Not to be confused with Shin-Hotaka in Japan Alps National Park, Hotaka is home

to Japan's largest wasabi (Japanese horse-radish) farm. It is an easy day trip from Matsumoto and a popular starting point for mountain hikes.

The **tourist office** (☎ 82-9363; ☽ 9am-5pm Jun-Oct, 9am-4pm Nov-May) and **bicycle rental** (per hr ¥300), the recommended way to get around, are outside the Hotaka Station exit. Both have basic maps, which, while in Japanese, are sufficient for navigation.

Sights & Activities
DAI-Ō WASABI-NŌJO 大王わさび農場
A visit to the **Dai-ō Wasabi Farm** (☎ 82-2118; admission free; ☽ 8.30am-5.30pm Jul & Aug, shorter hr rest of year) is *de rigueur* for wasabi lovers, and even wasabi haters may have fun. An English map guides you among wasabi plants (wasabi is grown in flooded fields), restaurants, shops and workspaces, all set amid rolling hills. There are lots of free sampling opportunities; wasabi finds its way into everything from wine to rice crackers, ice cream to chocolate. 'Wasabi juice' (¥400) is a kind of milk shake.

The farm is about 15 minutes' bike ride from Hotaka Station. There are also some calmer municipal wasabi fields.

ROKUZAN BIJUTSUKAN 碌山美術館
Ten minutes' walk from the station, the **Rokuzan Art Museum** (☎ 82-2094; admission ¥700; ☽ 9am-5.10pm Apr-Oct, to 4.10pm Nov-Mar, closed Mon Nov-Apr) showcases the work of Meiji-era sculptor Rokuzan Ogiwara (whom the Japanese have labelled the 'Rodin of the Orient') and his Japanese contemporaries. Strolling through the four buildings and garden, you may be struck by how much cross-cultural flow there was between East and West.

NAKABUSA ONSEN 中房温泉
Seasonal buses from Hotaka Station serve these remote **hot springs** (admission per 50min ¥1610; ☽ mid-Jul–mid-Aug, Sat & Sun late May–early Nov). A taxi costs ¥7000. From here, there are several trails for extended mountain hikes, and *onsen* accommodation (p250).

JŌNEN-DAKE 常念岳
From Hotaka Station, it takes about 30 minutes by taxi to reach Ichi-no-sawa, a trailhead for experienced hikers to climb Jōnen-dake (2857m) – the ascent takes about 5½ hours. There are many options

for mountain hikes extending over several days in the region, but you must be properly prepared. Hiking maps and information are available at regional tourist offices, although the more detailed maps are in Japanese.

Sleeping

Most people visit Hotaka as a day trip from Matsumoto, but some accommodation is available.

Azumino Pastoral Youth Hostel (安曇野パストラルユースホステル; ☎ 83-6170; dm ¥3100; ⏰ 8 Feb-16 Jan) Amid farmland, four kilometres west of Hotaka Station (a one-hour walk), this pleasant hostel has plenty of rustic charm.

Nestled up near Nakabusa Onsen are two inns where you can soak up the nourishing minerals of the local hot springs.

Nakabusa Onsen Ryokan (中房温泉旅館; ☎ 090-8771-4000; r with 2 meals from ¥8000) This place can accommodate up to 250 people (usually in shared rooms) and has several bathing pools.

Ariake-so Kokuminshukusha (有明荘国民宿舎; ☎ 090-2321-9991; r per person with 2 meals from ¥9500) This is a smaller lodge with equally basic rooms and refreshing hot springs on site.

Getting There & Away

Hotaka is about 30 minutes (¥320) from Matsumoto on the JR Ōito line.

KISO VALLEY REGION 木曽

☎ 0264

Thickly forested and Alpine, southwest Nagano-ken is traversed by the twisting, craggy former post road, the Nakasendō. Like the more famous Tōkaidō, the Nakasendō connected Edo (present-day Tokyo) with Kyoto, enriching the towns along the way. Today, several small towns feature carefully preserved architecture of those days, making this a highly recommended visit.

It was not always so. *Kiso hinoki* (Japanese cypress) was so highly prized that it was used in the construction of the Edo and Nagoya castles; it is still used for the reconstruction of Ise Jingū, Shintō's holiest shrine, every 20 years. To protect this asset, the region was placed under control of the Tokugawa shōgunate, and locals could be put to death for cutting down even their own trees; restrictions remained in effect well after the

Meiji Restoration. The resulting lack of maintenance left many local buildings beyond repair or unreconstructed after fires. Further economic decline came with the introduction of new roads and commercial centres to the north, and the later construction of the Chūō train line effectively cut the region off.

However, with the 1960s came a move to preserve the architecture of the post towns, and tourism has become a major source of income. Even if most of the remaining buildings are technically Meiji- and Taishō-era reconstructions, the streetscapes are pure Edo and the effect is dramatic.

Tsumago & Magome 妻籠 馬籠

These are two of the most attractive towns on the Nakasendō. Both close their main streets to vehicular traffic and they're connected by an agreeable hike.

Tsumago feels like an open-air museum. Designated by the government as a protected area for the preservation of traditional buildings, no modern developments such as TV aerials or telephone poles are allowed to mar the scene; it's particularly beautiful in early morning mist. The **Tsumago tourist information office** (観光案内館; ☎ 57-3123; fax 57-4036; ⏰ 8.30am-5pm) is in the centre of town, which is about 15 minutes' walk from end to end. Some English is spoken and there's English-language literature.

Down the street and across, **Waki-honjin** (脇本陣; ☎ 57-3322; admission ¥600; ⏰ 9am-5pm) is a former rest stop for retainers of *daimyō* (regional lords under the shōguns) on the Nakasendō. Reconstructed in 1877 under special dispensation from the emperor Meiji, it contains a lovely moss garden and a special toilet built in case Meiji happened to show up (apparently he never did). If some elements remind you of Japanese castles, that's because the Waki-honjin was built by a former castle builder, out of work due to Meiji's antifeudal policies. The property also contains the **Shiryōkan** (local history museum), housing elegant exhibits on Kiso and the Nakasendō, with some English signage.

Across from the Shiryōkan, **Tsumago Honjin** (妻籠本陣; ☎ 57-3322; admission ¥300; ⏰ 9am-5pm) is where the *daimyō* themselves spent the night, though this building is more noteworthy for its architecture than its exhibits. A combined ticket (¥700) admits you to all these buildings.

The tourist facility **Kisoji-kan** (木曽路館; ☎ 58-2046; baths ¥800; ✆ 10am-8pm), a few hilly kilometres above Tsumago, has a *rotemburo* with panoramic mountain vistas. Some Tsumago lodgings offer discount tickets, and there's a free shuttle bus to/from town (10 minutes, at least hourly).

On 23 November, the **Fuzoku Emaki Parade** is held along the Nakasendō in Tsumago, featuring townsfolk in Edo-period costume.

Magome, meanwhile, is more developed, with houses, restaurants, inns (and souvenir shops) lining a steep pedestrian road. It also has better access to transport, with bus stops at the bottom of the hill. Some structures are Edo style, some are not; still, Magome is undeniably pretty and has nice views. Magome's **tourist information office** (観光案内館; ☎ 59-2336; fax 59-2653; ✆ 8.30am-5pm) is about halfway up the road on the right. Here you can pick up maps of the area and staff will gladly book accommodation for you.

Magome was the birthplace of the author Shimazaki Tōson (1872–1943). His master-piece, *Ie* (The Family), published in English in 1976, records the decline of two pro-vincial Kiso families. A **museum** (藤村記念館; ☎ 59-2047; admission ¥500; ✆ 8.30am-5pm Apr-Oct, 8.30am-4.15pm Nov-Mar, closed 2nd Tue, Wed & Thu Dec) is devoted to his life and times, though it's pretty impenetrable for non-Japanese speakers.

The 7.8km **hike** connecting Tsumago (elevation 420m) and Magome (elevation 600m) peaks at the top of the steep pass, Magome-tōge (elevation 801m). From there, the trail to/from Tsumago passes forest and farmland, while the Magome approach is largely on paved road. It takes around 2½ hours to hike between these towns. There are English signs along the way and you'll have the opportunity to stop off at several small waterfalls en route. The Magome–Tsumago bus (¥640, 30 minutes, at least four daily in each direction) also stops at the pass.

BAGGAGE FORWARDING

If you're hiking between Magome and Tsumago, you can use a handy **baggage-for-warding service** (¥500 per bag; available Mon-Sun late Jul–Aug, Sat, Sun & holidays late March–late Nov) from either tourist office to the other. Deposit your bags between 8.30am and 11.30am for delivery by 1pm.

SLEEPING

It's worth a stay in these towns, particularly Tsumago, to have them to yourself once the day-trippers clear out. Both tourist informa-tion offices can help book accommodation at numerous ryokan (from around ¥9000 per person) and *minshuku* (from around ¥7000); prices include two meals.

Minshuku Daikichi (大吉旅館; ☎ 57-2595; fax 57-2203; r per person ¥8400) In Tsumago, this *min-shuku* feels very traditional – with handsome tatami rooms and fine wood features, despite its 1970s construction. Every room boasts a view. It's at the edge of town (take the right-hand fork uphill from the centre).

Matsushiro-ya (松代屋旅館; ☎ 57-3022; fax 57-3386; r per person ¥10,500; ✆ Thu-Tue) One of Tsumago's standout lodgings, this hand-some inn sits on the village's most pictur-esque street and offers large tatami rooms. Parts of the inn date back to 1804.

Fujioto (藤乙; ☎ 57-3009; fax 57-2239; r per person ¥10,000) Another much-photographed and excellent ryokan, Fujioto has impressive rooms, a graceful garden and English-speaking staff. You will find it near Tsuma-go's Waki-Honjin.

Magome-Chaya (馬籠茶屋; ☎ 59-2038; www .magomechaya.com; r per person with/without 2 meals from ¥7850/4700) This friendly, well-kept place is in the centre of Magome, near the water wheel. Meals are served across the street in its restaurant.

If you don't plan on dining in, bring your own food; restaurants and food shops close by 5pm. A popular street food in both towns is *gohei-mochi*, skewered rice dumplings that are coated with sesame-walnut sauce.

GETTING THERE & AWAY

Nakatsugawa and Nagiso Stations on the JR Chūō line provide access to Magome and Tsumago, respectively, though both are still at some distance. Nakatsugawa is connected with Nagoya (Shinano *tokkyū*, ¥2740, 47 minutes) and Matsumoto (Shinano *tokkyū*, ¥3980, 70 minutes). A few *tokkyū* daily stop in Nagiso; otherwise it's about 20 minutes from Nakatsugawa by occasional *futsū* (¥320).

Highway buses operate between Ma-gome and Nagoya's Meitetsu Bus Centre (¥1810, 1½ hours), as well as Tokyo's Shin-juku Station (¥4500, 4½ hours). If you're heading to/from the Hida district, two daily buses each way between Nakatsugawa and Gero (¥1700, 50 minutes) will save loads of money, time and grief.

Buses leave hourly from outside Nakatsugawa Station for Magome (¥540, 30 minutes). There's also infrequent bus service between Magome and Tsumago (¥640, 30 minutes).

From Tsumago, you can catch the bus to Nagiso Station (¥270, 10 minutes) or, if you're still in the mood to hike, walk there in one hour. To/from Kisoji-kan, the shuttle bus serves Nagiso Station.

TOYAMA-KEN 富山県

TOYAMA 富山
☎ 076 / pop 325,000

The heavily industrialised city of Toyama has few tourist attractions, but you may pass through en route to the northern Japan Alps or the Japan Sea coast.

If you have time, **Chokei-ji** (長慶寺; ☎ 441-5451; Kuresan Kōen; admission free; ⏰ 24hr) is known for 500 statues of *rakan* (Buddha's disciples); and the **Toyama Folkcraft Village** (富山市民俗民芸村; ☎ 433-8270; 1118-1 Anyōbo; admission ¥630; ⏰ 9am-4.30pm Tue-Sun) exhibits a range of traditional crafts – folk art, ceramics, a tea ceremony house.

Information

The **information office** (☎ 432-9751; 1-1-1 Sakuramachi; ⏰ 8.30am-8pm), outside Toyama Station's south exit, has useful maps and pamphlets on the Tateyama–Kurobe Alpine Route (right), Unazuki Onsen (opposite) and Gokayama (p227), and staff speak English. JNTO issues a leaflet entitled *Tateyama, Kurobe & Toyama*, which has details on transport links and accommodation.

Sleeping & Eating

There are many lodgings within a few minutes' walk of the train station's south exit.

Toyama Excel Hotel Tōkyū (富山エクセルホテル東急; ☎ 441-0109; www.tokyuhotels.co.jp; 1-2-3 Sakuramachi; s/d from ¥9817/17,325) Featuring large, comfortable rooms, the Toyama Excel is conveniently located in a tower above the CIC shopping centre, facing the train station. The hotel also contains two of Toyama's best restaurants on the 15th floor.

Relax Inn (☎ 444-1010; www.relax-inn.co.jp; 1-7-22 Sakuramachi; s/d from ¥4800/8800) This fairly new

business hotel offers small but nicely maintained rooms. Go straight out of the station and up Ichiban-machi, keeping CIC on your right. It's two blocks up on the left.

You'll find a good selection of restaurants on the 6th floor of the Marier building to the left of the train station.

Hong Hu (☎ 445-1655; ⏰ 11am-10pm) This restaurant serves good Chinese dishes, with nice views over the city. Chicken dumplings and yam soup or sautéed shrimp with tomato chilli sauce are among the selections. English menu.

Yakuto (☎ 425-1871; courses from ¥2000; ⏰ noon-7pm) One of Toyama's unique offerings, Yakuto serves *yakuzen-ryōri*, a local speciality made with medicinal herbs; it's by the Nishi-chō tram stop, 10 minutes' ride from the station (¥200).

For a quick bite inside Toyama Station, try fresh *oshi-zushi* (fish that's been pressed down onto rice, from ¥130) from *bentō* merchants, or irresistible cinnamon cream puffs at **Maple House** (☎ 441-1193; ¥130 each; ⏰ 10am-8pm).

Getting There & Away

AIR
Daily flights operate between Toyama and major Japanese cities. There are less-frequent flights to Seoul and Vladivostok.

TRAIN
The JR Takayama line links Toyama with Takayama (*tokkyū* ¥3080, 1½ hours; *futsū* ¥1620, 2¼ hours). The Toyama Chiho Tetsudō (aka Chitetsu) line links Toyama with Tateyama, the starting (or finishing) point for those travelling the Tateyama–Kurobe Alpine Route. Chitetsu also links Toyama with Unazuki Onsen, the starting point for a trip up Kurobe-kyō.

The JR Hokuriku line runs west to Kanazawa (*tokkyū* ¥2410, 35 minutes; *futsū* ¥950, one hour), Kyoto (Rai-chō *tokkyū* ¥7560, three hours) and Osaka (¥8290, 3½ hours). The same line runs northeast via Naoetsu (¥3980, 1¼ hours) to the ferry terminal for Sado-ga-shima and Niigata (¥7130, three hours), and Aomori at the very tip of northern Honshū.

TATEYAMA–KUROBE ALPINE ROUTE
立山黒部アルペンルート

JNTO publishes a leaflet entitled *Tateyama, Kurobe & Toyama* with details on this route, which extends between Toyama and Shinano-ōmachi. The route is divided in nine sections using various modes of transport. The best place to take a break, if only to escape the Mickey Mouse commentaries and enjoy the tremendous scenery, is Murodō. Transport buffs will want to do the lot, but some visitors find that a trip from Toyama as far as Murodō is sufficient, thereby skipping the expense of the rest. Transport costs for the 90km trip from Toyama to Shinano-ōmachi (between Hotaka and Hakuba) add up to ¥10,320 for adults.

Peak season is between August and late October, and transport and accommodation reservations are strongly advised for travel in these months. Better yet, avoid this period.

The route is closed from late November to late April. For the precise dates, which vary each year, check with a tourist office.

Although the route will take you from Toyama to Shinano-ōmachi, travel is possible in either direction. From Toyama Station, take the chug-a-lug Toyama Tateyama line (¥1170, 50 minutes) through rural scenery to Tateyama (475m). If you are making an early start or a late finish on the route, there are plenty of ryokan in Tateyama.

From Tateyama, take the cable car (¥700, seven minutes) to **Bijodaira** and then the bus (¥1660, 50 minutes) via the spectacular alpine plateau of Midagahara Kōgen to **Murodō** (altitude 2450m). You can break the trip at Midagahara and do the 15-minute walk to see **Tateyama caldera** – the largest non-active crater in Japan. The upper part of the plateau is often covered with deep snow until late into the summer – the road is kept clear by piling up the snow to form a virtual tunnel.

At Murodō, the natural beauty of the surroundings has been somewhat spoilt by a monstrous bus station to service the annual flood of visitors. From here, there are various options for short hikes. To the north, just 10 minutes away on foot, is the pond, **Mikuri-ga-ike**. Twenty minutes further on is **Jigokudani Onsen** (Hell Valley Hot Springs): no bathing here, unless you don't mind boiling bath water. To the east, you can hike for about two hours – including a very steep final section – to the peak of **O-yama** (3003m) for an astounding panorama. For the keen long-distance hiker who has several days or even a week to spare, there are fine routes south to Kamikōchi or north to Keyaki-daira in the Kurobe-kyō.

Continuing on the route from Murodō, there's a bus ride (¥2100, 10 minutes) to Daikanbō, via a tunnel dug through Tateyama. By our calculations this is roughly 3½ times the per-minute cost of a Tokyo to Kyoto *shinkansen*.

At **Daikanbō** you can pause to admire the view before taking the cable car (¥1260, seven minutes) to Kurobe-daira, where another cable car whisks you down (¥840, five minutes) to Kurobeko beside the vast **Kurobe Dam**.

There's a 15-minute walk from Kurobeko to the dam, where you can descend to the water for a cruise, or climb up to a lookout point, before taking the trolley bus to **Ogisawa** (¥1260, 16 minutes). From here, a bus ride (¥1330, 40 minutes) takes you down to Shinano-ōmachi Station – at an altitude of 712m. From here there are frequent trains to Matsumoto (one hour), from where you can connect with trains for Tokyo, Nagoya and Nagano.

There's no denying that it's a unique way to travel, but not everyone will agree it's worth the cost.

KUROBE-KYŌ & UNAZUKI ONSEN
黒部峡・宇奈月温泉
☎ 0765
From Unazuki Onsen, the Kurobe Kyōkoku mountain train (aka *torokko*) provides a scenic Alpine run through Kurobe-kyō, Japan's deepest gorge. The train runs from late April through November. Train buffs especially love this service, with open carriages used on most runs (surcharge for enclosed carriages). A museum across from the *torokko* station details the mountain train's *raison-d'être*, the Kurobe dam (Technological marvel or environmental desecration? You decide.). From the other end, Keyaki-daira, you can hike to an observation point for a panorama of the northern Japan Alps. Keyaki-daira is also linked with Hakuba and Murodō by trails suitable for well-prepared, seasoned hikers with several days to spare.

Sleeping
There is no shortage of large luxury hotels in Unazuki Onsen, starting from ¥15,000 during *torokko* season and ¥10,000 other times;

however, some lovely corporate guesthouses welcome non employees at more reasonable rates. The **Unazuki Ryokan Association** (宇奈月温泉旅館協同組合; ☎ 62-1021; fax 62-1025, in Japanese only) can help with lodgings.

Etsuzan-so (越山荘; ☎ 62-1016; fax 62-1017; r per person with 2 meals from ¥7700) NTT-owned, this comfortable inn has large rooms and indoor *onsen* overlooking the gorge.

Kurobe-so (黒部荘; ☎ 62-1149; fax 62-1856; r per person with 2 meals from ¥9130) A spacious affair close to the train stations, Kurobe-so has nicely maintained rooms and a rooftop bath with sweeping views.

Kuronagi Onsen Ryokan (黒薙温泉旅館; ☎ /fax 62-1820; r per person with 2 meals ¥9000) If you take the *torokko* to Kuronagi Station (¥480, 25 minutes) and hike about 20 minutes through the woods, you'll reach this ryokan. This informal place looks like it may have been built for dam workers, but has a riverside *kon-yoku* (mixed bathing) *rotemburo* as well as a separate women's bath. Be mindful of the *torokko* schedules – if you miss the train, you won't make it here.

Getting There & Away

Take the Toyama Chihō Tetsudō line (next to JR Toyama Station) to Unazuki Onsen (¥1790, 1½ hours, hourly). If you're arriving on the JR Hokuriku line from the north, change to the Toyama Chihō Tetsudō line at Uozu (¥900, 40 minutes).

From Unazuki Onsen Station, it's a five-minute walk to the Kurobe Kyōkoku Tetsudō (*torokko*). The fare from Unazuki Onsen to the terminus at Keyaki-daira is ¥1440 (80 minutes).

ISHIKAWA-KEN 石川県

This prefecture, made up of the former Kaga and Noto fiefs, offers visitors a nice blend of cultural and historical sights and natural beauty. Kanazawa, the Kaga capital and power base of the feudal Maeda clan, boasts traditional architecture and one of Japan's most famous gardens. To the north, the peninsula, Noto-hantō, has beautiful seascapes, rolling hills and quiet fishing villages. Hakusan National Park, near the southern tip of the prefecture, offers some great hiking, though it can be tough to reach even during peak season.

KANAZAWA 金沢

☎ 076 / pop 458,000

Blessed with a number of cultural attractions, the city of Kanazawa is most famed for Kenroku-en, its fine garden that dates from the 17th century. The city also has the handsome streetscapes of the former geisha and samurai districts, a smattering of attractive shrines and some worthwhile museums – including one of Japan's newest galleries, which is dedicated to 21st-century art.

Kanazawa (the capital of Ishikawa-ken) is also a vibrant and rather modern city, with more than its fair share of functional urban architecture.

The city's main sights can be seen hurriedly in a day or so, and side trips to Noto-hantō and Eihei-ji in Fukui-ken are highly recommended.

History

During the 15th century, Kanazawa came under the control of an autonomous Buddhist government, which was ousted in 1583 by Maeda Toshiie, head of the powerful Maeda clan.

Then the fun started.

Three centuries of bountiful rice production made the Kaga region Japan's wealthiest; it was known as Kaga-Hyaku-Man-Goku for the one million *koku* (about five million bushels) of rice produced annually. Wealth allowed the Maedas to patronise cultural and artistic pursuits (see Get Lacquered, Go To Pot, Dye And Be Gilded, p258), and today Kanazawa remains one of Japan's key cultural centres. During WWII, the absence of military targets spared Kanazawa from destruction, thus preserving its historical and cultural sites.

Orientation

Kanazawa is a sprawling city with a labyrinthine layout befitting its castle-town past, but bus service makes it easy to get from the train station to the main sightseeing districts, which can then be covered on foot.

The Katamachi district is the commercial and business hub; its busiest intersection is known as the Katamachi Scramble. Another useful orientation point is the Kōrinbo 109 department store; from here it's a short walk east to Kenroku-en and its surrounding attractions. The samurai houses in the Nagamachi district are a short walk west from Kōrinbo 109. Northeast of Katamachi, across the Asano-gawa, is the picturesque Higashi geisha district; the hills of Higashiyama to its east are popular for walks and city views. Just south of Katamachi, across the Sai-gawa, is the Teramachi temple district.

Information
BOOKSHOPS
Libro Books (☎ 232-62502; 1-5-3 Honmachi; ✆ 10am-8pm) English-language books and magazines; it's in the Rifare building.

Kikuya bookshop (☎ 220-5055; 2-1 Kōrinbō; ✆ 10am-10pm) Small selection of English-language titles; beneath Kōrinbo 109.

INTERNET ACCESS
In addition to free Internet access at the Ishikawa Foundation for International Exchange (below), free access is also available at **t1's Labo** (☎ 232-2886; 8 Tatemachi; ✆ 11am-7pm Thu-Tue) on the busy shopping street.

INTERNET RESOURCES
For information about the city with useful links, visit www.city.kanazawa.ishikawa.jp.

LAUNDRY
There are several coin-operated laundries: one in Higashi Geisha and another in Katamachi.

TOURIST INFORMATION
Ishikawa Foundation for International Exchange (☎ 262-5931; www.ifie.or.jp; 1-5-3 Honmachi; ✆ 9am-6pm Mon-Sat, 9am-5pm Sun) This organisation has reams of information, foreign periodicals and satellite TV news, as well as free Internet access. It's on the 3rd floor of the Rifare building, a few minutes' walk southeast of the train station.

Kanazawa Tourist Information Office (☎ 232-3933; 1 Hiro-oka-machi; ✆ 9am-7pm) Inside Kanazawa Station, this friendly office provides the excellent bilingual map *Kanazawa Japan* (with details on sights, crafts and local specialities) and can help with hotel bookings. Some staff speak English. You can also arrange free guided tours around Kanazawa's cultural sites through the Goodwill Guides based here.

MONEY & POST
The most convenient post office is in Katamachi, close to Kōrinbō 109 department store. There's also a branch inside Kanazawa Station. Both have international ATMs.

Sights & Activities
This list is arranged in geographical order, to be used as a walking tour. For just the highlights with a balance of history, culture and local colour, try Kenroku-en, Ishikawa Prefectural Museum for Traditional Products & Crafts, the Honda Museum, the Nagamachi and Higashi Geisha districts, Ōhi Pottery Museum and Ōmichō Market.

NAGAMACHI DISTRICT 長町
Once inhabited by samurai, this attractive, well-preserved district framed by two canals features winding streets lined with tile-roofed mud walls. **Nomura Samurai House** (☎ 221-3553; 1-3-32 Nagamachi; admission ¥500; ✆ 8.30am-5.30pm Apr-Sep, to 4.30pm Oct-Mar), though partly transplanted from outside Kanazawa, is worth a visit for its decorative garden.

In another former samurai house is **Saihitsu-an** (Yūzen Silk Centre; 1-3-16 Nagamachi; ☎ 264-2811; admission ¥500; ✆ 9am-noon & 1-4.30pm Fri-Wed), where you can watch the process of *Kaga yūzen* kimono-dyeing (see Get Lacquered, Go To Pot, Dye And Be Gilded, p258).

Towards the Sai-gawa, **Shinise Kinenkan** (☎ 220-2524; 2-2-45 Nagamachi; admission free; ✆ 9am-5pm) offers a peek at a former pharmacy and, upstairs, a moderate assortment of local traditional products. If the flowering tree made entirely of candy gives you a sweet tooth, slake it at **Murakami** (☎ 223-2800), a handsome *wagashi* (Japanese candy) shop next to the Nomura samurai house.

21ST CENTURY MUSEUM OF CONTEMPORARY ART
金沢 21 世紀 美術館
Designed by the critically acclaimed Tokyo architecture firm SANAA, this stunning ultra-modern **museum** (☎ 220-2800; www.kanazawa21.jp; 1-2-1 Hirosaka; admission ¥900; ✆ 10am-6pm Tue-Thu & Sun, 10am-8pm Fri & Sat) opened in late 2004 to showcase some of Japan's – and the world's – leading contemporary artists. Music and dance performances are also staged here. Check the website for upcoming events.

KENROKU-EN 兼六園
Kanazawa's star attraction, **Kenroku-en** (☎ 234-3800; 1-1 Marunouchi; admission ¥300; ✆ 7am-6pm Mar-15 Oct, 8am-4.30pm 16 Oct-Feb) is ranked by Japanese as one of their nation's three top gardens (the other two are Kairaku-en in Mito and Kōraku-en in Okayama).

CENTRAL HONSHŪ

The name (*kenroku* means 'combined six') refers to a renowned garden from Sung-dynasty China that required six attributes for perfection: seclusion, spaciousness, artificiality, antiquity, abundant water and broad views (on clear days to the Sea of Japan). Originally, Kenroku-en formed the outer garden of Kanazawa-jō, but from the 17th century it was enlarged, reaching completion in the early 19th century; the garden opened to the public 1871. In winter, the branches of Kenroku-en's trees are famously suspended with rope via a post at each tree's centre, forming elegant conical shapes that protect the trees from breaking under Kanazawa's heavy snows. In spring, irises turn Kenroku-en's waterways into rivers of purple.

Kenroku-en is certainly attractive, but enormous crowds can diminish the intimacy of the garden. Visit at opening time and you'll have the place to yourself.

ISHIKAWA-MON & KANAZAWA-JŌ
石川門　金沢城跡

Originally built in 1580, **Kanazawa-jō** (☎ 234-3800; 1-1 Marunouchi; grounds admission free, castle admission ¥300; ◷ grounds 7am-6pm Mar-15 Oct, 8am-4.30pm 16 Oct-Feb; castle 9am-4.30pm) housed the Maeda clan for 14 generations. Unfortunately, nothing remains of its original incarnation, although the elegant gate **Ishikawa-mon**, rebuilt in 1788, still provides a dramatic entry to the castle grounds via the moat facing Kenroku-en. The castle itself was reconstructed in 2001

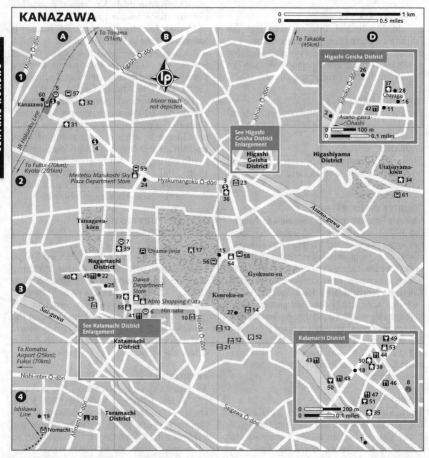

and offers a glimpse of its unique wood-frame construction.

SEISON-KAKU VILLA

A Maeda lord built this stylish retirement **villa** (☎ 221-0580; 2-1 Dewa-machi; admission ¥600; ⏱ 8.30am-4.30pm Thu-Tue), on the southeastern edge of Kenroku-en, for his mother in 1863. It's worth a visit for the elegant chambers and furnishings. A detailed English-language pamphlet is provided.

ISHIKAWA PREFECTURAL MUSEUM FOR TRADITIONAL PRODUCTS & CRAFTS
石川県立伝統産業工芸館

Behind Seison-kaku, this **museum** (☎ 262-2020; 2-1 Dewa-machi; admission ¥250; ⏱ 9am-5pm; closed every 3rd Thu Apr-Nov, every Thu Dec-Mar) is not flashy but offers fine displays of over 20 regional crafts. Be sure to pick up the free English-language headphone guide. If you come across a must-buy, the museum has an English-language map to shops on nearby Hirosaka street (p261).

ISHIKAWA PREFECTURAL ART MUSEUM
石川県立美術館

This **museum** (☎ 231-7580; 2-1 Dewa-machi; admission ¥350; ⏱ 9.30am-5pm) specialises in antique exhibits of traditional arts, with special em-phasis on colourful Kutani-yaki porcelain, Japanese painting, and *Kaga yūzen* (silk-dyed) fabrics and costumes. Admission costs more (¥1200) for special exhibitions.

NAKAMURA MEMORIAL MUSEUM
中村記念美術館

This **museum** (☎ 221-0751; 3-2-29 Honda-machi; admission ¥300; ⏱ 9.30am-5pm) is reached via a narrow flight of steps below the Ishikawa Prefectural Art Museum. Rotating exhib-its usually include *chanoyu* (tea ceremony) utensils, calligraphy and traditional crafts from the collection of a wealthy sake brewer Nakamura Eishun.

HONDA MUSEUM 本多　品館
Members of the Honda family were chief retainers to the Maeda clan, and this **mu-seum** (☎ 261-0500; 3-1 Dewa-machi; admission ¥500; ⏱ 9am-5pm Mon-Sun Mar-Dec, Tue-Thu Nov-Feb) exhibits the family collection of armour, household utensils and works of art. The bullet-proof coat and the family vase are particularly interesting, and there's a de-tailed catalogue in English.

GYOKUSEN-EN 玉泉園
For more intimacy and fewer crowds than Kenroku-en, this Edo-period **garden**

GET LACQUERED, GO TO POT, DYE AND BE GILDED

Much as the Medici family was the patron of some of the great artists of the Italian Renaissance, during the Edo Period, Kanazawa's ruling Maeda family fuelled the growth of important crafts. Many of these crafts are still practised today.

Kanazawa & Wajima Lacquerware

This luminous black lacquerware starts with hard, durable wood, such as zelkova, or Japanese chestnut, finely carved with any defects removed or filled. Many layers of undercoating and middle coating are applied, each rubbed down with washi (Japanese paper) before the next application. Before the final topcoat, decoration is applied through maki-e (painting) or gilding. With the last coat of lacquer, artists must take great care that dust does not settle on the final product.

Ōhi Pottery

A central aesthetic to tea ceremony is wabi-sabi: introspective, humble and understated, yet profound and prepared with great thought. Ōhi pottery seems its ceramic equivalent, with deliberately simple, almost primitive designs, rough surfaces, irregular shapes and monochromatic glazes, typically in black or amber. Little surprise, then, that Ōhi ware has long been used by tea practitioners; the same family, with the professional name Chōzaemon, have been keepers of the Ōhi tradition since the early Edo period.

Kutani Porcelain

Known for elegant shapes and bold hues of red, blue, yellow, purple and green, Kutani ware could hardly be more different from Ōhi pottery. Kutani ware is said to date back to the early Edo period, and it shares design characteristics with Chinese porcelain and Japanese Imari ware. Typical motifs include birds, flowers, trees and landscapes.

Kaga Yūzen Silk Dyeing

This kimono-dyeing technique is characterised by sharp colours (red, ochre, green, indigo and purple) and realistic depictions of nature, such as flower petals that have begun to brown around the edges.

It's highly specialised, labour-intensive work. A pattern is drawn on the fabric with grey-blue ink from spiderwort flowers, and the lines are traced over with rice paste using a cone like a fine pastry tube; this keeps the dyes from running as they are painted onto the silk. The colours are filled in and coated with more rice paste, and then the entire sheet of silk is dyed with the kimono's background colour.

Only then is the fabric rinsed clean (traditionally in a river) and steamed to fix the colours. White lines between the elements, where the initial spiderwort ink has washed away, are a characteristic of Kaga yūzen. To dye one kimono takes about three months.

Gold Leaf

It starts with a lump of pure gold the size of a ¥10 coin, which is rolled to the size of a tatami mat, as little as .0001mm thick. The gold leaf is cut into squares of 10.9cm – the size used for mounting on walls, murals or paintings – or then cut for gilding on lacquerware or pottery. Tiny particles find their way into tea, sweets and hand lotion. Kanazawa makes over 98% of Japan's gold leaf.

(☎ 221-0181; 1-1 Marunouchi; admission ¥500; ☿ 9am-4pm Mar-early Dec) rises up a steep slope. Enjoy a cup of tea here while contemplating the tranquil setting for an additional ¥500.

ŌHI POTTERY MUSEUM 大樋美術館

This museum (☎ 221-2397; Hashiba-cho; admission ¥700; ☿ 9am-5pm Tue-Sun) was established by the Chōzaemon family, now in its 10th gen-

eration. The first Chōzaemon developed this brooding style in nearby Ōhi village, using special, slow-fired amber glaze, specifically for use in chanoyu.

HIGASHI GEISHA DISTRICT ひがし茶屋街

North of the Ōhi Pottery Museum and across Asano-gawa, this enclave of narrow streets was established early in the 19th century as a centre for geisha to entertain wealthy patrons. **Higashi Chayagai** (east tea house street) is romantically preserved with the slatted, wooden façades of geisha houses.

One famous, traditional former geisha house is **Shima** (☎ 252-5675; 1-13-21 Higashiyama; admission ¥400; ☻ 9am-6pm); note the case of elaborate combs and *shamisen* picks. Across the street, **Kaikarō** (☎ 253-0591; 1-14-8 Higashiyama; admission ¥700; ☻ 9am-5pm) is an early–19th-century geisha house refinished with contemporary fittings and art; the red lacquered staircase near the entryway is a bold introduction.

The **Sakuda Gold Leaf Company** (☎ 251-6777; 1-3-27 Higashiyama; admission free; ☻ 9am-6pm) is a good place to observe the *kinpaku* (gold leaf) process and pick up gilded souvenirs (including pottery, lacquerware and, er, golf balls). You'll be offered a free cup of tea containing flecks of gold leaf, meant to be good for rheumatism. Even the walls of the loos are lined with gold and platinum.

On most nights you can visit the local *sentō* (public bath), **Higashi-yu** (1-13-2 Higashiyama; admission ¥350).

TERAMACHI DISTRICT 寺町
Beside Sai-gawa, southwest of the centre, this old neighbourhood was established as a first line of defence and still contains dozens of temples and narrow backstreets – a good place for a peaceful stroll. The temple **Myōryū-ji** (☎ 241-0888; 1-2-12 No-machi; admission ¥800; ☻ 9am-4.30pm Mar-Nov, 9am-4pm Dec-Feb, reservations required), better known as **Ninja-dera**, is a five-minute walk from the river. Completed in 1643, it was designed as a hideout in case of attack, and contains hidden stairways, escape routes, secret chambers, concealed tunnels and trick doors. The popular name refers to the temple's connection with ninjutsu (the art of stealth) and the ninja (practitioners of ninjutsu). Admission is by tour only (in Japanese). To reach the temple, take Minami Ō-dōri across the river, take a left at the first major intersection, then the first right.

The nearby **Kutani Kosen Gama Kiln** (☎ 241-0902; 5-3-3 No-machi; admission free; ☻ 9am-4.30pm) is a must for pottery lovers. Short tours give visitors a glimpse of the process and history of this fine craft.

ŌMICHŌ MARKET 近江町市場
A warren of several hundred shops, many of which specialise in seafood, this **market**

(35 Ōmichō; ☻ 9am-5pm) is a great place to break from sightseeing and watch daily life. It's between Katamachi district and Kanazawa Station; the most convenient bus stop is Musashi-ga-tsuji.

Courses
Japanese-language classes are offered through the **Ishikawa Foundation for International Exchange** (☎ 262-5931; 1-5-3 Honmachi).

Festivals & Events
Kagatobi Dezomeshiki (Early January) Scantily clad firemen brave the cold, imbibe sake and demonstrate ancient fire-fighting skills on ladders.

Asano-gawa Enyūkai (Second weekend of April) Performances of traditional Japanese dance and music are held on the banks of Asano-gawa.

Hyakumangoku Matsuri (Second Saturday in June) This is the main annual festival in Kanazawa, commemorating the first time the region's rice production hit 1,000,000 *koku* (around 150,000 tonnes), under the leadership of the first Lord Maeda. The highlight is a huge parade of townsfolk dressed in costumes from the 16th century. Other events include *takigi nō* (torch-lit performances of nō drama), *tōrō nagashi* (lanterns floated down the river at dusk) and a special *chanoyu* at Kenroku-en.

Sleeping
The Kanazawa Tourist Information Office (p255) can help with reservations; the main concentration of lodgings is in Katamachi and the Kanazawa Station area, while Nagamachi and Higashiyama retain a more traditional atmosphere.

BUDGET
Matsui Youth Hostel (☎ 221-0275; 1-9-3 Katamachi; dm ¥3100) Tucked away in Katamachi, this small and relaxed hostel has a folksy air about it. From the Katamachi Scramble, walk east along Saigawa Ō-dōri and take the third right. It's 75m down on the right. Doors close at 10pm.

Kanazawa Youth Hostel (☎ 252-3414; kanazawa@jyh.gr.jp; 37 Suehiro-chō; dm ¥2900; ☻ closed early–mid-Feb) Commanding a superb position in the hills to the east of the city, this strict hostel has Japanese- and Western-style rooms, with some private rooms available (extra charge). Unfortunately, bus services are infrequent. From the station, take bus No 90 for Utatsuyama-kōen and get off after about 25 minutes at the Yūsu-Hosteru-mae bus stop.

MIDRANGE

Murataya Ryokan (☎ 263-0455; muratRya@spacelan
.ne.jp; 1-5-2 Katamachi; r per person ¥4700) Well-kept
rooms with friendly hosts await at this travellers' favourite in Katamachi. It's a convenient
base for exploring the area's restaurants and
nightlife, and there's an English- language
map of local establishments.

Yamadaya (☎ /fax 261-0065; 2-3-28 Nagamachi;
r per person without meals/with breakfast/with 2 meals
¥4000/4500/6000; 🖳) This friendly place offers
decent tatami rooms in a former samurai
house in Nagamachi. Free Internet access
for guests. No English spoken. It's on a side
street just west of the Nomura Samurai
House.

Minshuku Yōgetsu (☎ 252-0497; 1-13-22 Higashiyama; r per person with/without breakfast ¥5000/4500) A
stay at this historic, humble place, a former
geisha house next door to Shima, allows
you to have the Higashi geisha district practically to yourself at night. Small rooms, but
friendly host.

Hotel Econo Eki-mae (☎ 223-2131; 8-8 Konohana-
machi; s/d ¥5250/9450) One of the more-afford-
able options near the station, this basic
business hotel has clean, simple rooms.

Garden Hotel Kanazawa (☎ 263-3333; www.gar
denhotel-kanazawa.co.jp; 2-16-16 Honmachi; s/d/tw from
¥7276/11,550/13,860) Also near the station, this
business hotel has comfortable rooms with
big windows. Twins and doubles are room-
ier than singles.

APA Hotel Kanazawa Chūō (☎ 235-2111; www
.apahotel.com; 1-5-24 Katamachi; s/d/tw from ¥8085/
12,705/15,015) In the heart of Katamachi's
nightlife, this well-located business hotel
opened in 2003 and offers nicely appointed
rooms (though singles are cramped). Guests
also have use of indoor and outdoor baths
on the 14th floor.

New Grand Hotel (☎ 233-1311; www.new-grand
.co.jp; 1-50 Takaoka-machi; s/d or tw from ¥9817/18,480)
Near the Nagamachi district, this business
hotel has handsome, nice-sized rooms spread
among its two buildings. Several restaurants
and a 12th-floor bar with views on site.

TOP END

Kanazawa Excel Hotel (☎ 231-2411; www.tokyuhotels
.co.jp; 2-1-1 Kōrinbo; s/d/tw from ¥14,437/19,635/17,902)
The city's most upmarket hotel, Kanazawa
Excel has sleek and stylish rooms with
plenty of amenities. It's adjacent to the
Kōrinbō 109 department store.

Matsumoto (☎ 221-0302; fax 221-0303; 1-7-2 Owari-
chō; r per person with breakfast ¥15,000) This charming ryokan has huge rooms with private
bath. Its restaurant is also excellent; dinner
costs an extra ¥10,000. It's on the little street
west of Ishikawa Bank. No English spoken.

Eating

Kanazawa's *Kaga ryōri* (Kaga cuisine) is
characterised by seafood; even the most
humble *bentō* (box lunches) at the train station nearly all feature some type of fish. *Oshi-
zushi*, which is a thin layer of fish pressed
atop vinegared rice and cut into pieces, is
said by some to be the precursor to modern
sushi. Another favourite is *jibuni*, which is
duck or chicken coated with flour and boiled
with shiitake mushrooms and green vegetables. Packed with restaurants, Katamachi
is the best place to browse for a meal.

For delicious and relatively cheap sushi,
try one of the tiny restaurants that line the
walkways of **Ōmichō Market**. Not many have
English menus, but you should be able to
make yourself understood. A lot of places
here also serve seafood *donburi* (seafood
served atop a deep bowl of rice). *Teishoku*
(daily specials) cost ¥800 to ¥1200. Ōmichō's
restaurants close around 7pm or 8pm.

Janome-sushi (☎ 231-0093; 1-1-12 Kōrinbō; sets
from ¥2500; ⏰ 11am-2pm & 5-10pm Mon-Sat) Near
Kōrinbō 109, this highly regarded sushi restaurant serves plenty of fresh sashimi and
Kaga cuisine.

Tamazushi (☎ 221-2644; 2-14-9 Katamachi; sets
¥1000-3000) Down near Sai-gawa in Katamachi, this minimalist restaurant is one of
Kanazawa's best sushi spots. Sushi *teishoku*
are displayed in the front window.

Monja tei (☎ 260-6868; 1-4-8 Katamachi; dishes
¥800-2000; ⏰ lunch & dinner) This tiny gem is a
great place to sample *okonomiyaki*; in the
summer the sides open up for Katamachi
people-watching.

Jiyūken (☎ 252-1996; 1-6-6 Higashiyama; most
mains ¥700-2850; ⏰ 11.30am-2.45pm & 4.30-9.45pm)
In the Higashi geisha district, this simple
but welcoming spot has been serving *yōshoku* (Japanese takes on Western cuisine:
beef stew, grilled chicken, omelettes etc)
since 1909. The *teishoku* is a steal at ¥880.

Legian (☎ 262-6510; 2-31-30 Katamachi; most dishes
¥600-1000) For popular, authentic Indonesian
cuisine head to this quaint spot by the river.
Good lunch specials; English menu.

Père Noël (☎ 233-0300; 1-11-2 Katamachi; dishes ¥950-1400; 🕑 5.30pm-midnight Mon-Sat) This cosy French restaurant serves excellent dishes at reasonable prices. Among the selections: pork medallions, *confit de canard*, quiche and soups. English menu.

Pilsen (☎ 221-0688; 1-9-20 Katamachi; dishes ¥600-1800) Two blocks from the Katamachi Scramble, this German-style beer hall boasts a fascinating hybridised menu: where else can you get a sausage plate *and* warm tofu-mushroom salad at the same meal?

Drinking

Most of Kanazawa's bars and clubs are holes-in-the-wall, jam-packed into high rises in Katamachi. Some are straightforward bars; others are barely disguised girlie clubs.

Polé Polé (☎ 260-1138; 2-31-30 Katamachi; 🕑 8pm-5am Mon-Sat) In the same building (and sharing the same owners) as Legian restaurant (p260), this dark and grungy bar draws an interesting mix of gaijin and locals. The narrow floor is littered with peanut shells, and the music (reggae) is loud.

Apre (☎ 221-0090; 1-6-12 Kōrinbō; 🕑 6pm-1am) A mix of locals and gaijin fill this large two-storey bar near Kōrinbo 109. There's free Internet upstairs, a pool table, plenty of food and beer selections and a lively crowd (at least on weekends).

I no Ichiban (☎ 261-0001; 1-9-20 Katamachi; 🕑 6pm-3am Mon-Sat, 6pm-midnight Sun) A slender *izakaya* that serves plenty of cocktails, I no Ichiban has ambience in spades – so much so that it's almost unrecognisable from the street; look for the wood-panel screen and tiny stand of bamboo.

CJ's Cantina (☎ 231-3447; 2-22-16 Katamachi; dishes ¥900-1600; 🕑 6pm-1am) Feast on hearty Tex-Mex fare at this bar/restaurant in Katamachi. Burritos, enchiladas, and taco salad pair nicely with the decent beer and cocktail selection. English menu.

Entertainment

Nō theatre is alive and well in Kanazawa, and performances are held once a week during summer at **Ishikawa Prefectural Nō Theatre** (☎ 264-2598; 3-1 Dewa-machi).

Shopping

For a quick view or purchase of Kanazawa crafts, you can visit **Kankō Bussankan** (Ishikawa Local Products Shop; ☎ 222-7788). The Hirosaka district, between Kōrinbo 109 and Kenroku-en, has some nice shops on its south side; most locals recommend that you shop for local crafts in department stores. At the other end of the spectrum, the **100 Yen Shop** (Tatemachi) has an amazing assortment, from house wares to toys, in the middle of the trendy Tatemachi pedestrian street in Katamachi.

Getting There & Away

AIR

Komatsu airport has air connections with Tokyo, Sendai, Fukuoka and Sapporo. There's also an international connection with Seoul.

BUS

There are regular expressway bus services from the Hokutetsu Kankō Bus Company bus station in front of Kanazawa Station's east exit, to Tokyo (Ikebukuro, ¥7840, 7½ hours), Yokohama (¥8250, 7½ hours), Kyoto (¥4060, four hours) and Nagoya (¥4060, four hours). See p262 for bus services to Noto-hantō. Some buses also stop at Kenroku-en-shita bus stop.

TRAIN

Kanazawa is linked to southwestern destinations by the JR Hokuriku line: Fukui (*tokkyū*, ¥2950, 50 minutes), Kyoto (*tokkyū*, ¥6710, 2¼ hours) and Osaka (*tokkyū*, ¥7440, 2¾ hours). The same line runs northeast to Toyama (*tokkyū*, ¥2610, 35 minutes) and further north up the coast. To travel to Takayama (*tokkyū*, ¥5840, 2¼ hours) you need to change at Toyama. The quickest way to travel between Tokyo and Kanazawa is via the Jōetsu *shinkansen* at Echigo-Yuzawa (¥13,200, 3¾ hours); see p511.

The JR Nanao line connects Kanazawa with Wakura Onsen on Noto-hantō (*tokkyū*, ¥2220, one hour).

Getting Around

TO/FROM THE AIRPORT

Buses connect Komatsu airport with Kanazawa Station (¥1100, 40 minutes, timed to aeroplane departures and arrivals). Buses leave from the Hokutetsu bus station and also stop at Kōrinbo 109 department store.

BICYCLE

Rental is available at **Nippon Rent-a-Car** (☎ 263-0919; per 4hr/day ¥630/1050), left of the station's west exit.

BUS

The bus network is extensive, and any bus from station stop 6, 7 or 8 will take you to the city centre (fares from ¥200, day pass ¥900). The Hokutetsu Kankō bus company also operates the 'Kanazawa Loop Bus', circling all the major tourist attractions in 45 minutes. Buses leave approximately every 15 minutes from 8.30am to 6pm (day pass ¥500).

CAR

Car rental is available at **Nippon Rent-a-Car** (☎ 263-0919), left of the station's west exit.

NOTO-HANTŌ 能登半島

For an enjoyable combination of rugged seascapes, traditional rural life and a light diet of cultural sights, this peninsula atop Ishikawa-ken is highly recommended.

Although day trips from Kanazawa are offered, they don't do the peninsula justice; buzzing through the sights leaves little time to savour the pace of rural life as the locals do. Unless you're under your own power, a speedy trip may not be an option anyway: train service has been scaled back and bus service is infrequent. With your own car, the Noto Toll Rd offers a quick, not-too-outrageously expensive compromise.

Orientation & Information

Noto juts out from Honshū like a boomerang, with few sights dotting its flat west coast; the town of Wajima is the hub of the rugged north, known as Oku-Noto.

Kanazawa **tourist information office** (☎ 076-232-6200) can handle most queries regarding Noto-hantō. The office stocks the *Easy Living Map* of Ishikawa-ken, including the peninsula. JNTO's leaflet *Noto Peninsula* also has concise information.

On the peninsula, the best tourist office is at Wajima on the north coast. Telephone information about Noto can be obtained through the **Noto tourist office** (☎ 0767-53-7767, in Japanese) in the city of Nanao.

Festivals & Events

Noto-hantō has dozens of festivals throughout the year. On 31 July, the small community of Kōda on Noto-jima (off the peninsula's east coast) hosts a spectacular **fire festival**.

Gojinjō Daikō Nabune Matsuri, held in Wajima between 31 July and 1 August, features wild drumming performed by drummers wearing demon masks and seaweed headgear. The **Wajima Taisai** (late August) features the towering, illuminated *kiriko* festival floats for which the region is famous.

Sleeping

The peninsula has plenty of accommodation, though reservations are advised during the peak months of July and August. A night or two in a Japanese inn will also net you healthy portions of delicious sashimi, grilled fish and shellfish.

There are camping grounds tucked away in a few pockets of the peninsula, although most are difficult to reach using public transport. Call ahead to reserve sites, especially in summer.

Shopping

Particularly in Oku-Noto, you won't have to look far before you see shops groaning with the main regional craft – lacquerware. A large proportion of Wajima's townsfolk are engaged in producing *Wajima-nuri*, renowned for its durability and rich colours.

Getting There & Around

AIR

In the Centre of Oku-Noto, the **Noto airport** (NTQ; ☎ 0768-26-2100) connects the peninsula with Tokyo's Haneda airport. ANA (☎ 0120-029-222) offers two direct flights daily. Buses (coordinated with flight arrivals and departures) connect the airport to Anamizu (¥330, 22 minutes), the nearest town.

BICYCLE

A stay along the coasts should appeal to cyclists as the coastal terrain is mostly flat. However, some inland roads are quite steep and have blind curves; this is also true along the Noto-kongō coast. The tourist information offices have a very good map (in Japanese) called *Noto Hantō Rōdo Mappu* (能登半島ロードマップ), which covers the area on a scale of 1:160,000.

BUS

Hokutetsu Kankō bus company's Oku-noto express buses run between Kanazawa and Wajima (¥2200, two hours, 11 daily), with a few continuing to Sosogi. Buses leave from stop 1 outside Kanazawa Station. There are five buses daily between Wakura Onsen and Wajima (¥1200, one hour).

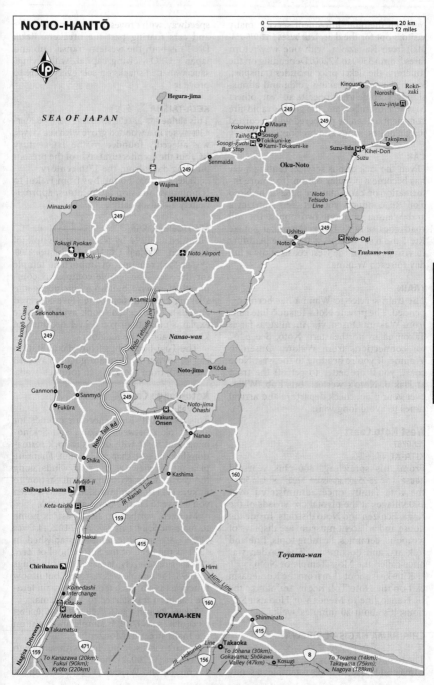

NOTO-HANTŌ

Sea of Japan

Hegura-jima

Kinoura
Noroshi
Rokō-
zaki
Suzu-jinja

249

249

Yokoiwaya   Maura
Taihō   Sosogi
Sosogi-guchi   Tokikuni-ke
Bus Stop   Kami-Tokikuni-ke

Takojima

Suzu-Iida   Kihei-Don
Suzu

Senmaida

Oku-Noto

Wajima

ISHIKAWA-KEN

Kami-ōzawa

Minazuki

249

Noto
Tetsudo
Line

Tokugi Ryokan
Monzen   Sōji-ji

1   Noto Airport

Ushitsu

249

Noto-Ogi

Noto

Tsukumo-wan

Noto-kongō Coast

Sekinohana

Anamizu

Nanao-wan

Togi

Noto-jima   Kōda

Ganmon   Sanmyō

249

Noto-jima
Ōhashi

Fukūra

Wakura
Onsen

Nanao

Shika

Myōjō-ji

Kashima

160

Shibagaki-hama

JR Nanao Line

Keta-taisha

159

Hakui

415

Chirihama

Himi

Toyama-wan

Himi Line

Komedashi
Interchange
Kita-ke
Menden

Shinminato

160

415

Takamatsu

471

TOYAMA-KEN

Takaoka

8

Nagisa Driveway

159

To Kanazawa (20km);
Fukui (90km);
Kyōto (220km)

156

JR Hokuriku Line

To Jōhana (30km);
Gokayama; Shōkawa
Valley (47km)   Kosugi

To Toyama (14km);
Takayama (75km);
Nagoya (188km)

0   20 km
0   12 miles

CENTRAL HONSHŪ

Given the quite infrequent service, many visitors opt for the daily **tour buses** (☎ 076-234-0123) from Kanazawa, with one way/return fares from ¥3500 to ¥7200. Depending on the itinerary, the ticket price includes transport, lunch, Japanese-speaking guide and admission fees. Some tours operate all year, others May to November, and the guide's rapid-fire commentary can be peppered with recorded jungle noises, songs and breaking waves.

CAR

Given the lack of bus service, renting a car has become a popular option (for more information on car rental, see p262). The Noto Toll Rd conducts you between Kanazawa and Wajima in about two hours; the toll road goes only as far as Anamizu – take Rte 1 the rest of the way. If you're planning to visit sights on the west coast, allow a full day to reach Wajima.

TRAIN

The train service to Wajima has been suspended. The private Noto Tetsudō line runs from Wakura Onsen, via Anamizu as far as Takojima in northeastern Noto. See p262 for connections from Wakura Onsen to Wajima. If you're heading to the west Noto coast, you'll do better to get off the train at Hakui, Noto's western bus hub. Whatever your plan, check departure and arrival times to avoid long waits.

West Noto Coast
☎ 0767
KITA-KE 喜多家
From this sprawling, 300-plus year-old **house** (☎ 28-2546; admission ¥700; ☽ 8am-5pm), the Kita family once administered over 100 villages at the pivotal crossroads of the Kaga, Echizen and Noto districts. Inside the house and adjacent museum are displays of weapons, ceramics, farming tools, fine and folk art, and documents. The garden was once called the Moss Temple of Noto.

Kita-ke is about 1km from the Komedashi exit on the Noto Toll Rd; by train, take the JR Nanao line to Menden or Hōdatsu Stations; it's about 20 minutes' walk.

CHIRIHAMA NAGISA DRIVEWAY 千里浜なぎさドライブウエイ
The 8km beach, linking the towns of Chirihama and Hakui, at times resembles a sandy

speedway, with droves of buses, motorcycles and cars roaring past the breakers. **Hakui** (羽咋) is both the western transit hub and Japan's UFO-viewing capital, with flying-saucer-shaped snacks on sale everywhere to prove it.

KETA-TAISHA 気多大社
This **shrine** (☎ 22-0602; admission ¥100; ☽ 8.30am-4.30pm), set in a wooded grove with sea views, was allegedly founded in the 1st century BC, but the architectural style of the present building dates from the 17th century.

Take the Togi-bound bus from Hakui to Ichinomiya bus stop (10 minutes, approximately 10 buses daily).

MYŌJŌ-JI 妙成寺
Founded in 1294 by Nichijō, a disciple of Nichiren, **Myōjō-ji** (☎ 27-1226; admission ¥500; ☽ 8am-5pm) remains an important temple for the sect. The temple complex is composed of several buildings, including the strikingly elegant **Gojū-no-tō** (Five-Storeyed Pagoda). An excellent book available here explains more than you'd ever dreamed of knowing about the religion.

The Togi-bound bus from Hakui Station can drop you at Takidani-guchi (¥390, 18 minutes); from there, it's 15 minutes' walk.

Noto-kongō Coast 能登金剛
☎ 0768
This rocky, cliff-lined shoreline extends for about 16km between Fukūra and Sekinohana, and is set with dramatic rock formations like the gate-shaped Ganmon. There are pleasant sea views as the road winds along the coast. Buses go from Hakui Station to Fukūra (¥1110, 70 minutes, four daily); often you'll have to change buses at Sanmyō.

Monzen, further up the coast, is home to majestic **Sōji-ji** (総持寺; ☎ 42-0005; admission ¥400; ☽ 8am-5pm), the temple established in 1321 as the head of the Sōtō school of Zen. After a fire severely damaged the buildings in 1898, the temple was restored, but it now functions as a branch temple; the main temple has been transferred to Yokohama.

Tokugi Ryokan (德木旅館; ☎ 42-0010; r per person with 2 meals ¥7000) is simple and right on the main street in Monzen.

Monzen is also a bus hub with service to Kanazawa (¥2200, 2½ hours), Hakui (¥1510, 1½ hours) and Wajima (¥740, 35 minutes).

CENTRAL HONSHŪ

Wajima 輪島

☎ 0768 / pop 27,300

This fishing port, the largest town in Oku-Noto, is a historic centre for the production of lacquerware and has become a significant, if understated, centre for tourism. The town centre is nicely refurbished, and the morning market is fun.

The **tourist information office** (☎ 22-1503; ☺ 7am-10pm) at Wajima Station provides English leaflets and maps, and the staff can book accommodation (from 9am to 6pm, in person only). Note that although trains no longer run to the station, it is still a bus hub.

For more info, visit the city's website: www.wajima-city.or.jp.

WAJIMA SHIKKI SHIRYŌKAN/SHIKKI KAIKAN 輪島漆器会館

The lacquerware hall and museum is in the centre of town next to the Shin-bashi. The 2nd-floor **museum** (☎ 22-2155; admission ¥200; ☺ 8.30am-5pm) displays lacquerware production techniques and some impressive old pieces, including bowls that were being swilled out of when Hideyoshi was struggling to unify Japan 500 years ago. There's a **shop** (admission free) downstairs where you can purchase contemporary works. None is cheap but they are undeniably beautiful.

ISHIKAWA WAJIMA URUSHI ART MUSEUM 石川輪島漆芸美術館

In the southwest corner of the town centre, this stately contemporary museum (☎ 22-9788; admission ¥600; ☺ 9am-5pm, closed when changing exhibits) has a large, rotating collection of lacquerware in galleries on two floors; works are both Japanese and foreign, ancient and contemporary. It's about 15 minutes' walk west of the train station.

KIRIKO KAIKAN キリコ会館

A selection of the impressive, illuminated lacquered floats used in the Wajima Taisai and other regional festivals is on display in this **hall** (☎ 22-7100; admission ¥500; ☺ 8am-6pm mid-Jul–Aug, 8am-5pm Sep–mid-Jul). Some of the floats are up to 15m tall. From the train station, it is 20 minutes on foot or you can take the bus to Tsukada bus stop (six minutes).

HEGURA-JIMA 舶倉島

For a nice day trip, take the ferry to Hegura-jima, which boasts a lighthouse, several shrines and no traffic. Bird-watchers flock to the island in spring and autumn for the astounding array of birds that are seen during the migratory season. If you want to extend your island stay, there are plenty of *minshuku*.

Weather permitting, there are two daily **ferries** (☎ 22-4381) each way from late July to late August (¥1900 each way), with one each way daily the rest of the year.

SLEEPING & EATING

Wajima has dozens of *minshuku*, where meals include copious and delicious seafood; the tourist information office (☎ 22-1503) can book accommodation from 9am to 6pm (in person only).

Asunaro (あすなろ; ☎ /fax 22-0652; r per person with/without 2 meals ¥7350/4800) About 15 minutes on foot from the station, this is hardly fancy but kindly and home style, with an *onsen* and an *irori*.

Fukasan (深三; ☎ 22-9933; fax 22-9934; r per person with 2 meals ¥7000) By the harbour, this is a contemporary *minshuku* with rustic elegance, an *onsen* and waves crashing outside your window.

Sodegahama Camping Ground (☎ 22-2211; fax 22-9920; camp sites ¥600; ☺ late Jul & Aug; office 4pm-9am) About 10 minutes by bus west of town. Take a Monzen-bound bus to Sodegahama or hike for 20 minutes.

If you're not eating at your inn, there are some lovely restaurants by the harbour, though some close by early evening.

Madara-kan (まだら館; ☎ 22-3453; sets ¥800-3000) This restaurant serves local specialities, including *zosui* (rice hot-pot), *yaki-zakana* (grilled fish) and seasonal seafood; there are pictures in the window.

Yabu Honten (やぶ本店; ☎ 22-2266; dishes ¥450-1300) A tidy noodle shop on the main pedestrian street.

SHOPPING

The **asa-ichi** (morning market; ☺ 8am-noon, closed 10th & 25th each month) is highly entertaining, though undeniably touristed. Fishwives ply their wares with plenty of sass and humour that cuts across the language barrier. To find the market, walk north along the river from the Wajima Shikki Shiryōkan and turn right just before Iroha-bashi. The **yu-ichi** (evening market; ☺ 3.30pm-dusk) is lower-key, across the river on the grounds of Sumiyoshi-jinja.

CENTRAL HONSHŪ

GETTING THERE & AWAY
See p262 for information on reaching Wajima. From Wajima, buses bound for Ushitsu stop in Sosogi (¥740, 40 minutes). Buses to Monzen (¥740, 35 minutes) leave every one to two hours.

Sosogi & Northeast Soto Coast 曽々木
☎ 0768
Heading east from Wajima you'll pass the famous, slivered *dandan-batake* (rice terraces) at Senmaida before arriving in the village of Sosogi. After the Taira were defeated in 1185, one of the few survivors, Taira Tokitada, was exiled to this region. The Tokikuni family, which claims descent from Tokitada, eventually divided into two parts and established separate family residences here.

The first residence, **Tokikuni-ke** (Tokikuni Residence; 時国家; ☎ 32-0075; admission ¥500; ☼ 8.30am-5pm Apr-Nov, 9am-4.30pm Dec-Mar), built in 1590 in the style of the Kamakura period, is a designated National Important Cultural Property and has a *meishō tei-en* (famous garden).

A few minutes' walk away, **Kami Tokikuni-ke** (Upper Tokikuni Residence; ☎ 32-0171; admission ¥420; ☼ 8.30am-6pm Apr-Sep, 8.30am-5pm Oct-Mar), with its impressive thatched roof and elegant interior, was constructed early in the 19th century. Entry to either home includes an English leaflet. From Wajima Station, the bus ride takes about 40 minutes.

If you visit the Sosogi coast in winter, look for *nami-no-hana* (flowers of the waves), masses of foam that form when waves gnash the rocky shore.

The road northeast from Sosogi village passes the remote cape Rokō-zaki and rounds the tip of the peninsula to less dramatic scenery on the eastern coast. At the cape, you can amble up to **Noroshi lighthouse**; a nearby signpost marks the distances to faraway cities. A coastal **hiking trail** runs west along the cape. The scenery is nice, and during the week when the tourist buses run less frequently, the town of Noroshi reverts to its true role as a sleepy fishing village.

SLEEPING
Sosogi village is an agreeable choice for an overnight; there are many options.

Yokoiwaya (横岩屋; ☎ 32-0603; fax 32-0663; r per person from ¥7000) About six minutes' walk from the bus stop, with comfortable rooms and outstanding seafood dinners – in most Japanese cities the dinner alone would easily cost this price.

Taihō (大峰; ☎ 32-0546; r per person with 2 meals ¥6500) Three minutes' walk from the Sosogi-guchi bus stop, facing the ocean, Taihō offers simple tatami rooms and good seafood meals.

Both of the above places are within a short distance of the rock formation *madoiwa* (window rock); several hiking trails are nearby.

Garō Minshuku Terai (Terai's Art Gallery Minshuku; てらい; ☎ 86-2038; r per person with 2 meals ¥6500) In Noroshi, this is one of the more unusual places to stay, with artwork adorning the walls and shelves. Pleasant tatami rooms.

Rokō-zaki Lighthouse Pension (禄剛崎; ☎ /fax 86-2030; r per person with 2 meals ¥8800) In Suzu, this charming inn feels rather youthful and has both Japanese- and Western-style rooms with sink and toilet (some with private bath).

HAKUSAN NATIONAL PARK
白山国立公園
☎ 0761
Travellers with a thirst for exercise (and time on their hands) may want to venture into this national park, in the southeast corner of Ishikawa-ken and spilling over into neighbouring Fukui, Toyama and Gifu prefectures. The park has several peaks above 2500m; the tallest is Hakusan (2702m), a sacred mountain that, along with Mt Fuji, has been worshipped since ancient times. In summer, hiking and scrambling uphill to catch mountain sunrises are the main activities, while in winter, skiing and *onsen* bathing take over.

For information, you can phone the **Hakusan Visitor Centre** (白山室堂; ☎ 93-1001), which also handles reservations for the Murodō Centre (opposite), or the **Shiramine Town Hall** (☎ 98-2011). Japanese skills are helpful at both places.

The alpine section of the park is crisscrossed with trails, offering hikes of up to 25km. For hikers who are well equipped and in no hurry, there is a 26km trek to Ogimachi (p228) in Shōkawa Valley. However, camping is prohibited in the park except at designated camping grounds, meaning you'll have to either hike very fast or break the rules.

Those looking to hike on and around the peaks are required to stay overnight at either Murodō Centre (opposite) or Nanryū

CENTRAL HONSHŪ

Mountain Lodge (below). Getting to either of these requires a hike of 3½ to five hours. That doesn't stop the park from swarming with visitors, however.

The surrounding area of the park is dotted with little villages offering *onsen*, *minshuku* and ryokan accommodation and camping grounds.

Sleeping

Murodō Centre (室堂; ☎ 93-1001; r per person with 2 meals ¥7700; ☼ 1 May-15 Oct) and **Nanryū Mountain Lodge** (南竜; ☎ 98-2022; camp site per person ¥300; r per person with 2 meals ¥7300; ☼ Jul-Sep) are your two choices in the alpine area of the park. Both are rather cramped; when the lodges are full, each person gets about one tatami mat's worth of sleeping space. Murodō can hold up to 750 people in its four lodges, while Nanryū is smaller (holding 150 people) but has private cabins for up to five people for ¥12,000 (meals available for extra). There is also a **camping ground** (tent rental ¥2200) at Nanryū, which is the only place in the alpine area where camping is permitted. During the July to August peak season, reservations must be made at least one week in advance for both Murodō and Nanryū.

The closest access point is Bettōde-ai. From here it's 6km to Murodō (about 4½ hours' walk) and 5km to Nanryū (3½ hours). You can also access the lodges from trailheads at Ichirino and Chūgū Onsen, but these involve hikes of around 20km.

Ichirino, Chūgū Onsen, Shiramine and Ichinose all have *minshuku* and **ryokan**. Per-person rates with two meals start at ¥7000.

There are several camping grounds in the area. **Ichinose Yaeijō** (☎ 98-2121; camp sites per person ¥300) has 20 camp sites near Ichinose, which is in turn close to the trailhead at Bettōde-ai. **Midori no Mura Campground** (☎ 98-2716; camp sites per person ¥400, bungalows ¥6000), near Shiramine, has tents and bungalows for rent. There is also a **camping ground** near Chūgū Onsen. Most of the camping grounds open only from June to October, with the exception of the one at Nanryū Sansō Mountain Lodge, which operates year-round.

Getting There & Away

This is not easily done, even during the peak summer period. The main mode of transport is the Hokuriku Tetsudō (aka Hokutetsu) Kankō bus from Kanazawa Sta-

tion to Bettōde-ai. From late June to mid-October, up to three buses operate daily (¥2000, two hours).

Hokutetsu also has daily departures for Ichirino and Chūgū Onsen. Check with the Kanazawa **tourist information office** (☎ 232-6200; ☼ 9am-7pm) or the Hokutetsu bus station by Kanazawa Station for the latest schedule.

If you're driving from the Shōkawa Valley, you can take the spectacular toll road, Hakusan Super-Rindō (cars ¥3150).

FUKUI-KEN 福井県

FUKUI 福井

☎ 0776 / pop 252,000

Fukui, the prefectural capital, was given quite a drubbing in 1945 during the Allied bombing, and what was left largely succumbed to a massive earthquake in 1948. It was totally rebuilt and is now a major textile centre. There's no real reason to linger here, but Fukui makes a useful sightseeing base. Between 19 and 21 May, Fukui celebrates the **Mikuni Matsuri** with a parade of giant warrior dolls.

Fukui City Sightseer Information (☎ 20-5348; 1-1-1 Chūō; ☼ 8.30am-5pm) is inside Fukui Station, and can provide pamphlets in English (no English spoken). Northwest of the station are the central business district and the walls of what was once Fukui castle. On the other side of the castle grounds, **Fukui International Activities Plaza** (福井県国際交流会館; ☎ 28-8800; 3-1-1 Hoei; ☼ 9am-6pm Tue-Sun, to 8pm Thu) has lots of English-language information and free Internet access.

Hotel Riverge Akebono (ホテルリバージュアケボノ; ☎ 22-1000, 0120-291-489; fax 22-8023; 3-10-12 Chūō; s/d ¥6200/11,000) On the bank of the Asuwa-gawa, 10 minutes' walk from the station, Akebono has nice rooms with private facilities and common baths on the top floor 'observation deck' (bathers observe the city, not the other way around). From the main street perpendicular to the station, turn left after Tsuchiya furniture store.

A delicious regional speciality is *oroshi soba* (*soba* noodles topped with grated *daikon* and shaved bonito flakes).

Ori-Ori-ya (織々屋; ☎ 27-4004, 3-4-14 Chūō; skewers ¥100-300), close to Hotel Riverge Akebono, is an ingenious *izakaya* where you

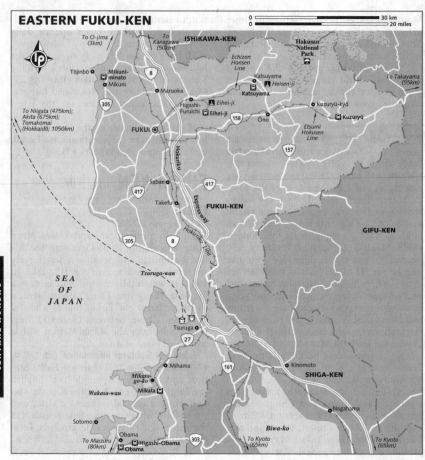

EASTERN FUKUI-KEN

select your own ingredients and grill them yourself at the table.

Fukui is connected by the JR Hokuriku line with Kanazawa (¥2430, 50 minutes) and Tsuruga (¥2100, 40 minutes); there's also convenient access to Nagoya (¥5040, 2½ hours), Kyoto (¥4300, 1½ hours) and Osaka (¥5340, two hours).

EIHEI-JI 永平寺
☎ 0776

Founded in 1244 by Dōgen, Eihei-ji is now one of the two head temples of the Sōtō sect of Zen Buddhism and is ranked among the most influential Zen centres in the world. It is a palpably spiritual place – amid mountains, mosses and ancient cedars. At most

times some 150 priests and disciples are in residence, and serious students of Zen should consider a retreat here.

The **temple** (☎ 63-3102; admission ¥400; 🕐 5am-5pm) is geared to huge numbers of visitors who come either as sightseers or for the rigorous Zen training. Among the approximately 70 buildings, the standard circuit concentrates on seven major ones: *tosu* (toilet), San-mon (main gate), *yokushitsu* (bath), *daikuin* (kitchen), *Butsuden* (Buddha Hall), *Hattō* (Dharma Hall) and *Sō-dō* (Priests' Hall). You walk among the buildings on wooden walkways in your stockinged feet. A new **Shōbōkaku** exhibits many Eihei-ji treasures.

The temple is regularly closed for periods varying from a week to 10 days. Before you visit, be sure to check ahead with the temple, a nearby tourist office or **Japan Travel-Phone** (☎ 0088-22-4800).

You can attend the temple's three-day, two-night *sanzensha* (religious trainee program), which follows the monks' training schedule, complete with 3am prayers, cleaning, *zazen* (sitting meditation) and ritual meals in which not a grain of rice may be left behind. It costs ¥9000, and reservations must be made at least a fortnight in advance. Call ☎ 63-3640 or fax 63-3631 for bookings. Japanese ability is not necessary, but it helps to be able to sit in the half-lotus position. Everyone who has completed this course agrees it is a remarkable experience. A single night's stay, *sanrōsha*, is also possible for ¥8000 (with two meals; reserve at least one month in advance). If you'd like to eat a special vegan lunch (¥3000) you must confirm this before your arrival.

Sleeping

There's a somewhat off-putting tourist village beneath the temple.

Eihei-ji Monzen Yamaguchi-sō (永平寺門前 山口荘; ☎/fax 63-3122; 22-3 Shihi-ji; dm ¥2900) On the tourist village's edge, this secluded youth hostel has large shared tatami rooms and Japanese-style toilets only. It's five minutes on foot from Eihei-ji.

Green Lodge (グリーンロッジ; ☎/fax 63-3126; 6-3 Shihi-ji; r per person with 2 meals ¥7300) Close to Eihei-ji, this two-storey inn offers basic accommodation.

Getting There & Away

From Fukui, take the Keifuku bus (¥720, 35min, four daily) from stop 5, a couple of blocks from Fukui Station.

TŌJINBŌ 東尋坊

On the coast about 25km northwest of Fukui are the towering rock columns and cliffs at Tōjinbō, a too-popular tourist destination that's also a place of legend: one says that Tōjinbō was an evil Buddhist priest who was cast off the cliff by angry villagers in 1182. It is said that the sea surged for 49 days thereafter, a demonstration of the priest's fury from beyond his watery grave.

Visitors can take a boat trip (¥1010, 30 minutes) to view the **rock formations** or travel further up the coast to **O-jima**, a small island with a shrine that is joined to the mainland by a bridge.

At least three buses serve Tōjinbō daily (¥1110, one hour) from bus stop No 7 near Fukui Station.

TSURUGA 敦賀

Tsuruga, south of Fukui and north of Biwa-ko, is a thriving port and major train junction. The **Shin Nihonkai ferry company** (☎ 0770-23-2222; www.snf.co.jp in Japanese) operates 11 sailings a week to Tomakomai, Hokkaidō (2nd class from ¥6700, 19 hours nonstop); of these, four stop en route at Niigata (¥4100, 9½ hours) and Akita (¥5600, 18¾ hours). Buses timed to ferry departures serve Tsuruga-kō port from Tsuruga Station (¥340, 20 minutes).

Kansai 関西

For fans of traditional Japanese culture, Kansai is an unmissable destination. Nowhere else in the country can you find so much of historical interest in such a compact area. And, since plenty of international carriers now fly into Kansai International Airport, it is perfectly possible to make Kansai your first port of call in Japan.

Kansai's major drawcards are Kyoto and Nara. Kyoto was the imperial capital between 794 and 1868, and is still considered by most Japanese to be the cultural heart of Japan. Nara predates Kyoto as an imperial capital and also has an impressive array of temples, burial mounds and relics. Both cities should feature prominently in even the busiest travel itinerary.

Osaka is a great place to sample Japanese city life in all its mind-boggling intensity, while Kōbe is one of Japan's most cosmopolitan and attractive cities. Himeji, west of Kōbe, has the best of Japan's many feudal castles. Kyoto is the logical base for an exploration of Kansai, but you could also base yourself in Osaka or Nara. The former allows you to enjoy Japanese modern city life and excellent transport connections, the latter is much quieter and is a good place to relax. You will almost certainly find that Kansai is the perfect place to sample both modern and traditional Japan without having to spend too much time moving from place to place.

The main attractions of the prefecture Mie-ken, are Ise-jingū, Japan's most sacred Shintō shrine, and the seascapes around the peninsula, Shima-hantō. Wakayama-ken offers *onsen* (hot-spring spas), a rugged coast and the temple complex of Kōya-san, Japan's most important Buddhist centre. Finally, the northern coast of Kansai, known as the San-in Coast, has some fabulous scenery, a number of good beaches and the lovely Tango-hantō (Tango Peninsula).

HIGHLIGHTS

- Visit **Kyoto** (p272), Japan's cultural capital, with more than 2000 temples and shrines
- Sample the bustling nightlife of **Osaka** (p338), Japan's most down-to-earth city
- Uncover the roots of Japanese culture in **Nara** (p361), the country's ancient capital
- Soak in open-air hot springs in mountainous **Kii-hantō** (p375)
- Spend a quiet night in atmospheric temple lodgings atop sacred **Kōya-san** (p377)
- Explore the fabulous coastline and rolling hills of the **Tango-hantō** (Tango Peninsula, p336) in northern Kyoto-fu

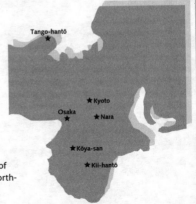

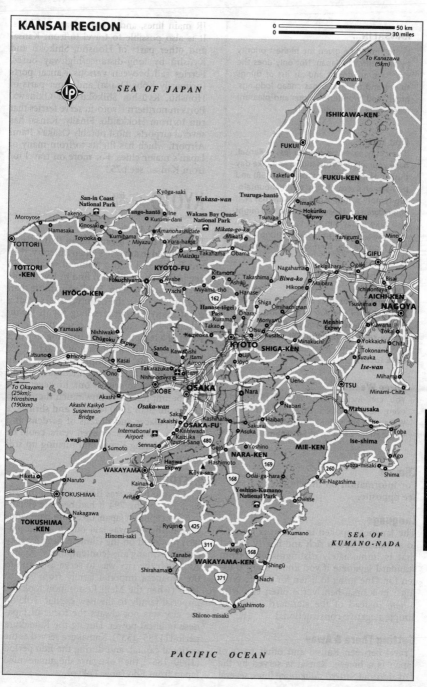

KANSAI REGION

0 — 50 km
0 — 30 miles

SEA OF JAPAN

ISHIKAWA-KEN

To Kanazawa (5km)

Komatsu

FUKUI

FUKUI-KEN

Takefu

Tsuruga-hantō

Imajō

Hokuriku Expwy

GIFU-KEN

Mino

Taniguni

Kyōga-saki

San-in Coast National Park

Wakasa-wan

Tango-hantō Ine
Kurumi-dani

Wakasa Bay Quasi-National Park

Mikata-go-ko

Tsuruga

GIFU

Moroyose Takeno
Hamasaka Kinosaki

Kumihama
Miyazu

Amanohashidate
Yura-hama

Mikata

Obama

Takahama

Nagahama
Sekigahara Ogaki

Bisai

Toyooka

Maizuru

Ichinomiya

AICHI-KEN

TOTTORI

KYOTO-FU

Takashima

Biwa-ko

Tsushima

NAGOYA

TOTTORI -KEN

HYŌGO-KEN

Fukuchiyama Ayabe
Wachi

Kitamura

Ashiū

Hikone

Maibara

Yamasaki

Miyama-chō Hanase

Shiga

Omihachiman

Kuwana Tokai

Yokkaichi Chita

Nishiwaki
Chūgoku Expwy

162

Hanase-tōge Pass
Kurama

Ohara

Takao

Moriyama

Minakuchi

Tokoname
Suzuka

Tatsuno

Himeji

Kasai

Sanda Kawachi

Kameoka

Ujī

KYOTO

Otsu

Kusatsu

SHIGA-KEN

Ueno

Mihama

Ōno

Takarazuka
Nishinomiya

Itami Airport

Iyō

TSU

Minami-Chita

To Okayama (25km); Hiroshima (190km)

Akashi Kaikyō Suspension Bridge

Akashi

KŌBE

OSAKA

Nara

Nabari

Matsusaka

Ise-wan

Awaji-shima

Osaka-wan

Sakai

Takaishi

OSAKA-FU

Kashihara

Haibari

Ise

Toba

Sumoto

Kishiwada

Kaizuka

480

Asuka

MIE-KEN

Ise-shima

Ago

Kansai International Airport

Izumi-Sano

Yoshino

Goza-misaki

Shima

Hiketa

Naruto

WAKAYAMA

Sennan

Hanwa Expwy

Gojō

NARA-KEN

169

260

Kii-Nagashima

TOKUSHIMA

Nakagawa

Kainan

Hashimoto

Kōya-san

Odai-ga-hara

168

Owase

Arita

Yoshino-Kumano National Park

TOKUSHIMA -KEN

Yuki

Hinomi-saki

Ryūjin

425

Kumano

SEA OF KUMANO-NADA

311

Hongū

168

Tanabe

WAKAYAMA-KEN

Shingū

Shirahama

371

Nachi

Kushimoto

Shiono-misaki

PACIFIC OCEAN

KANSAI

KANSAI IN...

Kyoto should be given the highest priority by any visitor to Japan. Not only does the city have an almost endless list of things to see and do, it also has cheap lodgings, great food, wonderful shops and pleasant hikes in its surrounding hills.

One Week

If you only have one week or less in Kansai, base yourself in **Kyoto** (right) and take day trips to **Nara** (p361) and **Osaka** (p338) and perhaps an overnight trip to the mountain-top temple complex of **Kōya-san** (p377). If you're keen on Japanese castles, you might also take a day trip out to Himeji to see the castle, **Himeji-jō** (p360), visiting **Kōbe** (p353) on the way there or back if you have the time.

Two Weeks

You can travel to some of Kansai's more distant sights. In addition to the Kyoto-based itinerary listed earlier, you could head down to Mie-ken's **Ise-jingū** (p385), and perhaps hit some of the attractions in **southern Nara** (p372).

Three Weeks

You can include destinations that are even more remote, such as the **onsen** in Wakayama-ken's Hongū (p384) region and the seaside spa town of **Shirahama** (p381).

Climate

For information on the climate of Kansai, see opposite.

Language

The Japanese spoken in Kansai is referred to as Kansai-ben, a rich and hearty dialect that is immediately distinguishable from standard Japanese if you know what to listen for. One thing to listen for is verb endings: in Kansai-ben, verbs often end with '~*hen*' instead of the standard '~*nai*' (in simple negative constructions).

Getting There & Away

Travel between Kansai and other parts of Japan is a breeze. Kansai is served by the Tōkaidō and San-yō *shinkansen* lines, several JR main lines, and a few private rail lines. It is also possible to travel to/from Kansai and other parts of Honshū, Shikoku and Kyūshū by long-distance/highway buses. Ferries sail between various Kansai ports (primarily Kōbe/Osaka) and other parts of Honshū, Kyūshū, Shikoku and Okinawa. Ports in northern Kyoto-fu serve ferries that run to/from Hokkaidō. Finally, Kansai has several airports, most notably Osaka's Itami Airport, which has flights to/from many of Japan's major cities. For more on travel to/from Kansai, see p753.

KYOTO 京都

☎ 075 pop / 1.4 million

If there are two cities in Japan that have to be included in anyone's Japan itinerary, they are Tokyo and Kyoto. Some of what you'll see in Tokyo, you'll also find in Kyoto: lots of concrete and neon. But Kyoto, more than any other city in the country, offers what a great many Westerners long for in Japan: raked pebble gardens, the sensuous contours of a temple roof, the tripping step of a latter-day geisha in pursuit of a taxi.

Despite this, first impressions are likely to be something of an anticlimax. If you take the time to seek it out, however, you will be impressed by how much there is to see: more than 2000 temples and shrines, a trio of palaces and dozens of gardens and museums. Months, or even years, could be spent exploring Kyoto and turning up still more surprises.

HISTORY

The Kyoto basin was first settled in the 7th century, and by 794 it had become Heian-kyō, the capital of Japan. Like Nara, a previous capital, the city was laid out in a grid pattern modelled on the Chinese Tang dynasty capital, Chang'an (contemporary Xi'an). Although the city was to serve as home to the Japanese imperial family from 794 to 1868 (when the Meiji Restoration took the imperial family to the new capital, Tokyo), the city was not always the focus of Japanese political power. During the Kamakura period (1185–1333), Kamakura served as the national capital, and during the Edo period (1600–1867), the Tokugawa shōgunate ruled Japan from Edo (now Tokyo).

SPECIAL TICKET DEALS

The **Kansai Thru Pass** is an excellent way to get around Kansai on the cheap. This pass, available at the travel counter in the arrivals hall of Kansai International Airport and at the main bus information centre in front of Kyoto Station, allows unlimited travel on all bus and train lines in Kansai except the Japan Railways (JR) line (the pass covers travel on the Nankai line, which serves Kansai International Airport). It also qualifies you for discounts at several attractions around Kansai.

When you buy the pass, be sure to pick up the handy companion English guide-map, which shows all the bus and train lines available.

Two-day passes cost ¥3800 and three-day passes cost ¥5000. It's possible to purchase multiple passes for longer explorations of Kansai. Like the Japan Rail Pass, however, these passes are only available to travellers on temporary visitor visas (you'll have to show your passport). For more on the pass, visit the **Kansai Thru Pass website** (www.surutto.com/conts/ticket/3dayeng/).

The problem was that from the 9th century, the imperial family was increasingly isolated from the mechanics of political power, and the country was ruled primarily by military families, or shōgunates. While Kyoto still remained capital in name and was the cultural focus of the nation, imperial power was, for the most part, symbolic and the business of running state affairs was often carried out elsewhere.

Just as imperial fortunes have waxed and waned, the fortunes of the city itself have fluctuated dramatically. During the Ōnin War (1466–67), which marked the close of the Muromachi period, the Kyoto Gosho (Imperial Palace) and most of the city

KYOTO UNESCO WORLD HERITAGE SITES

In 1994, 13 of Kyoto's Buddhist temples, three Shintō shrines and one castle met the criteria to be designated World Heritage Sites by the UN. Each of the 17 sites has buildings or gardens of immeasurable historical value and all are open for public viewing.

- **Castle** Nijō-jō (p299)
- **Shrines** Kamigamo-jinja (p303), Shimogamo-jinja (p312), Ujigami-jinja in Uji (p309)
- **Temples** Byōdō-in (p309), Daigo-ji (p308), Enryaku-ji (p305), Ginkaku-ji (p301), Kinkaku-ji (p302), Kiyomizu-dera (p296), Kōzan-ji (p307), Ninna-ji (p306), Nishi Hongan-ji (p276), Ryōan-ji (p306), Saihō-ji (p307), Tenryū-ji (p303), Tō-ji (p300)

were destroyed. Much of what can be seen in Kyoto today dates from the Edo period (1600–1867). Although political power resided in Edo, Kyoto was rebuilt and flourished as a cultural, religious and economic centre. Fortunately Kyoto was spared the aerial bombing that razed other Japanese urban centres in the closing months of WWII.

Today, even though it has seen rapid industrialisation, Kyoto remains an important cultural and educational centre. It has some 20% of Japan's National Treasures and 15% of Japan's Important Cultural Properties. Perhaps more impressive, Kyoto is home to a total of 17 Unesco World Heritage sites (see the boxed text, left). In addition, there are 24 museums and 37 universities and colleges scattered throughout the city. Even though the city centre looks remarkably like the centre of a dozen other large Japanese cities, a little exploration will turn up countless reminders of Kyoto's long history.

CLIMATE

Without a doubt, the best times to visit Kyoto are the climatically stable seasons of spring (March to May) and autumn (late September to November).

The highlight of spring is the cherry blossom season, which usually arrives in Kyoto in early April. Bear in mind, though, that the blossoms are notoriously fickle, blooming any time from late March to mid-April.

Autumn is an equally good time to travel, with pleasant temperatures and soothing autumn colours. The shrines and temples of Kyoto look stunning against a backdrop of blazing leaves, which usually peak between late October and mid-November.

KANSAI

KYOTO IN...

Kyoto is worth considering as a base for travel in Japan, especially as it is within easy reach of Osaka Itami and Kansai International Airports. And Kyoto is by far the best choice as a base for travel in Kansai because it has a wealth of accommodation and is close to Nara, Osaka, Kōbe, Mie-ken and Wakayama-ken.

It is difficult to suggest a minimum itinerary for Kyoto – you should certainly consider it a city you must see while you are in Japan and allocate as much time as possible. The absolute minimum amount of time you should spend in Kyoto is two days, during which you could just about scratch the surface by visiting the **Higashiyama area** (p294) in eastern Kyoto. Five days would give you time to include **Arashiyama** (p303), **northwestern Kyoto** (p302) and **southwest Kyoto** (p299). Ten days would allow you to cover these areas and also **northern** (p305 and p306) and **southeastern Kyoto** (p308), while leaving a day or so for places further afield or for in-depth exploration of museums, shops and culture.

Kyoto is also an excellent place to indulge specific cultural interests, whether they be in the arts, Buddhism or crafts. The best place to find information on these subjects is the Tourist Information Center (TIC, p276).

A final word of advice is that it's easy to overdose on temples in Kyoto. If you don't find temples to your liking, there are plenty of other options. Instead, go for a hike in the mountains, browse in the shops around **Shijō-dōri** (p326), do some people-watching on Kiyamachi-dōri in **downtown Kyoto** (p277) or, best of all, find a good restaurant and sample some of the **finest food** (p316) in all of Japan.

Japanese people are well aware that Kyoto is most beautiful at these times and the main attractions can be packed with local tourists. Likewise, accommodation can be hard to find; if you do come at these times, be sure to book well in advance.

Travelling in either winter or summer is a mixed bag. Mid-winter (December to February) weather can be quite cold (but not prohibitively so), while the extremely sticky summer months (June to August) can turn even the briefest excursion out of the air-conditioning into a soup bath.

June is the month of Japan's brief rainy season, which varies in intensity from year to year; some years there's no rainy season, other years it rains virtually every day.

ORIENTATION

Kyoto is a fairly easy city to find your way around. Kyoto Station (which serves Japan and Kintetsu Railways) is in the south, and from there Karasuma-dōri runs north past Higashi Hongan-ji to the commercial centre of town. The commercial and nightlife centres are between Shijō-dōri and Sanjō-dōri (to the south and north, respectively) and between Kawaramachi-dōri and Karasuma-dōri (to the east and west, respectively).

Although some of Kyoto's major sights are in the city centre, most of Kyoto's best sightseeing is on the outskirts of the city, in the eastern and western parts of town. These areas are most conveniently reached by bus or bicycle. Outside the city itself, the mountain villages of Ōhara, Kurama and Takao make wonderful day trips and are easily accessible by public transport.

Kyoto has retained a grid system based on the classical Chinese concept. This system of numbered streets running east to west and avenues running north to south makes it relatively easy to move around with the help of a map from the TIC.

Maps

Available at the TIC, the *Tourist Map of Kyoto-Nara* fulfils most map needs and includes a simplified map of the subway and bus systems. You might also want to pick up a copy of the Japanese city bus map at any major bus stop; even if you don't read Japanese, the detailed route maps are useful. The TIC also has a leaflet called *Walking Tour Courses in Kyoto* which has detailed walking maps for major sightseeing areas in and around Kyoto (Higashiyama, Arashiyama, Northwestern Kyoto and Ōhara).

INFORMATION
Bookshops

Green E Books (Map pp286–7; ☎ 751-5033; Kawabata-dōri-Marutamachi; ⏰ 1-10pm Mon-Fri, 11am-10pm Sat, 11am-9pm Sun) This small bookshop is Kyoto's only used

English-language bookshop. The selection is small but well chosen, and there are lots of books on India and Japan. It's up a flight of stairs.

Maruzen (Map p289; ☎ 241-2161; Kawaramachi-dōri-Takoyakushi; ☽ 10am-9pm) Kyoto's best bookshop is between Sanjō-dōri and Shijō-dōri. It has a large selection of English-language books, magazines and maps as well as a limited number of French-, German- and Spanish-language books. It also carries a full range of Lonely Planet guides.

Emergency

Although most emergency line operators do not speak fluent English, if you speak very slowly and have your address handy, you should be able to get your point across.

Ambulance (☎ 119)
Fire (☎ 119)
Police (☎ 110)

Internet Access

C Coquet (Map pp280-1; ☎ 212-0882; Marutamachi-dōri-Teramachi; Internet free with drink/food order; ☽ 9am-10pm Fri-Wed) This new restaurant/café is a great place to log on, and you can do it with your own machine if you don't want to use the machines provided.

Kyoto International Community House (KICH; Map pp286-7; ☎ 752-3010; 2-1 Torii-chō, Awataguchi; per 30min ¥200; ☽ 9am-9pm Tue-Sun) The machines here have Japanese keyboards and you are limited in the sites you can visit, but it's a fairly cheap place to log on.

Kyoto Prefectural International Centre (Map p291; ☎ 342-5000; 9F Kyoto Eki Bldg, Karasuma-dōri-Shiokōji kudaru; per 30min ¥250; ☽ 10am-6pm, closed 2nd & 4th Tue each month) One of the cheaper places in town. In addition to using the machines provided, you can also log on with your own machine here.

Internet Resources

Japan National Tourist Organization (JNTO) www.jnto.go.jp
JNTO Sightseeing Maps of Kyoto www.jnto.go.jp/eng/spn/kyoto/sightseeing/index.html
JR East Rail Information www.jreast.co.jp/e/index.html
Kansai Time Out www.kto.co.jp
Kyoto Shimbun News www.kyoto-np.co.jp/kp/english/index.html
Kyoto Temple Admission Fees www.templefees.com
Kyoto Visitor's Guide Kyoto www.kyotoguide.com

Media

The free *Kyoto Visitor's Guide* is the best source of information on upcoming events in Kyoto. It has restaurant reviews, day walks, detailed maps of the city, useful information sections and feature articles about various aspects of the city. Try to pick up a copy as soon as you arrive in Kyoto. It's available at the TIC, Maruzen bookshop, Kyoto International Community House and most major hotels.

Another excellent source of information about Kyoto and the rest of the Kansai area is *Kansai Time Out*, a monthly English-language listings magazine. Apart from lively articles, it has a large section of ads for employment, travel agencies, meetings, lonely hearts etc. It's available at Maruzen bookshop and at the TIC.

Medical Services

Kyoto Holiday Emergency Clinic (☎ 811-5072; Shichihonmatsu-Marutamachi agaru west) Spread over three different hospitals according to the type of complaint. If you require urgent attention, contact the clinic and they will direct you to the appropriate hospital.

Japan Baptist Hospital (Map pp282-3; ☎ 781-5191; 47 Yamanomoto-chō Kitashirakawa; ☽ 8.30-11am & 1-3.45pm, closed Sat afternoon, Sun & holidays) Usually has some English-speaking doctors on staff; you can visit without an appointment. It's in northeastern Kyoto; to get there, take bus 3 from the intersection of Shijō and Kawaramachi streets, and get off at the Shibuse-chō (last) stop (30 minutes). It's a short walk up the hill.

Money

Most of the major banks are near the Shijō-Karasuma intersection, two stops north of Kyoto Station on the Karasuma line subway. International transactions (like wire transfers) can be made at **Tokyo Mitsubishi Bank** (Map p289; ☎ 221-7161; ☽ 9am-3pm Mon-Fri), which is one block southwest of this intersection. Other international transactions can be made at **Citibank** (Map pp284-5; ☎ 212-5387, office ☽ 9am-3pm Mon-Fri, ATM 24hr), just west of this intersection. Finally, you can change travellers cheques at most post offices around town, including the Kyoto Central Post Office (p276) next to Kyoto Station.

INTERNATIONAL ATMS

There's an **international ATM** (Map p291; ☽ 10am-9pm) on the B1 floor of the Kyoto Tower Hotel, very close to the TIC and Kyoto Station. In the middle of town, you'll find another **international ATM** (Map p289; ☽ 7am-11pm) in the Zest underground mall, 200m west of the Kawaramachi-Oike intersection, near exit 7. Citibank (above) has a 24-hour ATM that accepts most foreign-issued cards. Lastly,

KANSAI

note that all the post offices in Kyoto have ATMs that accept most international bank cards. These ATMs are open the same hours as the post office in question (usually 9am to 5pm Monday to Friday, sometimes Saturday morning from 9am to noon).

Post

Kyoto Central Post Office (Map p291; ☎ 365-2414; Higashishiokōji-chō; ☺ 9am-7pm Mon-Fri, 9am-5pm Sat, 9am-12.30pm Sun & holidays) Conveniently located next to Kyoto Station (take the Karasuma exit, as the post office is on the northwestern side of the station). There's an after-hours service counter on the southern side of the post office, which is open 24 hours a day, 365 days a year.

Telephone

There are pay phones all over town. However, international pay phones are becoming increasingly hard to find. Your best bet is the lobby of any major hotel.

Tourist Information

Kyoto City Tourist Information Center (Map p291; ☎ 343-6656; ☺ 8.30am-7pm) Inside the new Kyoto Station building, on the 2nd floor just across from Café du Monde. Though it's geared towards Japanese visitors, English-speaking staff are usually on hand and can be of assistance when the TIC is closed.

Kyoto Tourist Information Center (TIC; Map p291; ☎ 344-3300; ☺ 10am-6pm, closed 2nd & 4th Tue of each month & 29 Dec-3 Jan) The best source of information on Kyoto, this is located on the 9th floor of the Kyoto Station building. To get there from the main concourse of the station, take the west escalator to the 2nd floor, enter Isetan Department Store and take an immediate left and look for the elevator on your left and take it to the 9th floor. It's right outside the elevator, inside the Kyoto Prefectural International Center (Map p291). There is a Welcome Inn Reservation counter at the TIC which can help with accommodation bookings.

Travel Agencies

Kyoto has several good central travel agents who can arrange discount air fares, visas, car rental, accommodation and other services.

No 1 Travel (Map p289; ☎ 251-6970; Shinkyōgoku-dōri-Shijō agaru, 3F Kyōgoku Tōhō Bldg; ☺ 10am-6.30pm Mon-Fri, 11am-5pm Sat, closed Sun & holidays)

Useful Organisations

The Kyoto International Community House (above) is an essential stop for those planning a long-term stay in Kyoto, but it can also be quite useful for short-term visitors.

Here you can rent typewriters, send and receive faxes, and use the Internet (¥200 for 30 minutes). It has a library with maps, books, newspapers and magazines from around the world, and a notice board displaying messages regarding work, accommodation, rummage sales etc.

You can also make arrangements through KICH to meet a Japanese family at home. Let staff know at least one day – preferably two days – in advance.

KICH is in eastern Kyoto, about 500m west of Nanzen-ji. You can walk from Keihan Sanjō Station in about 30 minutes (1.5km). Alternatively, take the Tōzai line subway from central Kyoto and get off at Keage Station, from which it's a 350m (five-minute) walk downhill.

SIGHTS
Kyoto Station Area
Map p291

Although most of Kyoto's attractions are further north, there are a few attractions within walking distance of the station. And now that it's been redone, the station itself is something of an attraction.

HIGASHI HONGAN-JI 東本願寺

When Tokugawa Ieyasu engineered the rift in the Jōdo Shin-shū school of Buddhism, he founded this **temple** (☎ 371-9181; Karasuma-dōri-Shichijō; admission free; ☺ 5.50am-5.30pm, to 4.30pm in winter) as competition for Nishi Hongan-ji (below). Rebuilt in 1895 after a fire, it's certainly monumental in its proportions, but it's less impressive artistically than its counterpart. A curious item on display is a length of rope made from hair donated by female believers, which was used to haul the timber for the reconstruction. The temple, which is a five-minute walk north of Kyoto Station, is now the headquarters of the Ōtani branch of the Jōdo Shin-shū school of Buddhism.

NISHI HONGAN-JI 西本願寺

In 1591 Toyotomi Hideyoshi built this **temple** (☎ 371-5181; Horikawa-dōri-Hanaya-chō; admission free; ☺ 5.30am-5.30pm, closes later in summer), known as Hongan-ji, as the new headquarters for the Jōdo Shin-shū (True Pure Land) school of Buddhism, which had accumulated immense power. Later, Tokugawa Ieyasu saw this power as a threat and sought to weaken it by encouraging a breakaway faction of this school to found Higashi Hongan-ji (*higashi* means 'east') in 1602. The original Hongan-ji then became known as Nishi Hongan-ji (*nishi* means 'west'). It now functions as the headquarters of the Hongan-ji branch of the Jōdo Shin-shū school, with over 10,000 temples and 12 million followers worldwide.

The temple contains five buildings, featuring some of the finest examples of architecture and artistic achievement from the Azuchi-Momoyama period (1568–1600). Unfortunately, the **Goe-dō** (Main Hall) is presently being restored and will be 'under wraps' until 2010. Nonetheless, it's worth a visit to see the **Daisho-in Hall**, which has sumptuous paintings, carvings and metal ornamentation. A small garden and two *nō* (classical Japanese dance-drama) stages are connected with the hall. The dazzling **Kara-mon** has intricate ornamental carvings. Both the Daisho-in Hall and the Kara-mon were transported here from Fushimi-jō.

If you'd like a guided tour of the temple (in Japanese only), reservations (preferably several days in advance) can be made either at the **temple office** (☎ 371-5181) or through the TIC. The temple is a 12-minute walk northwest of Kyoto Station.

KYOTO STATION 京都駅

Kyoto's **station building** (Karasuma-dōri-Shiokōji) is a striking steel and glass structure – a futuristic cathedral for the transportation age. Unveiled in September 1997, the building met with some decidedly mixed reviews. Some critics assailed it as out of keeping with the traditional architecture of Kyoto; others loved its wide-open spaces and dramatic lines.

Whatever the critics' views, you'll be impressed by the huge atrium that soars over the main concourse. Take some time to explore the many levels of the station, all the way up to the 15th-floor observation level. If you don't suffer from fear of heights, try riding the escalator from the 7th floor on the eastern side of the building up to the 11th-floor aerial skywalk, high over the main concourse.

In the station building you'll find several **food courts** (see p316), the **Kyoto Prefectural International Centre** (see p275), a performance space and **Isetan department store**.

SHŌSEI-EN 渉成園

About five minutes' walk east of Higashi Hongan-ji, the garden **Shōsei-en** (☎ 371-9181; Karasuma-dōri-Kamijuzuyachō; admission free; ⏰ 9am-3.30pm) is worth a look. The lovely grounds, incorporating the Kikoku-tei villa, were completed in 1657. Bring a picnic (and some bread to feed the carp) or just stroll around the beautiful Ingetsu-ike pond. Just when you're caught up in the 'old-Kyoto' moment, note the two love hotels looming in the background outside the wall (modern 'borrowed scenery').

PERIOD COSTUME MUSEUM 風俗博物館

This **museum** (Fūzoku Hakubutsukan; ☎ 342-5345; www .iz2.or.jp/english/index.htm; 5F Izutsu Bldg Shinhanayachō-dōri-Horikawa higashi iru; admission ¥400; ⏰ 9am-5pm Mon-Sat) displays wax figures wearing costumes representative of different periods in Japanese history; these include samurai warriors, merchants and fire fighters – not a must-see but worth a peek on a rainy day. From the northeast corner of Nishi Hongan-ji, it's just across Horikawa-dōri.

Downtown Kyoto   Map p289

Downtown Kyoto looks much like any other Japanese city, but there are some attractions like Nishiki Market, the Museum of Kyoto and Ponto-chō (a quaint traditional street). If you'd like a break from temples and shrines, then downtown Kyoto can be a welcome break. It's also good on a rainy day, because of the number of covered arcades and indoor attractions.

NISHIKI MARKET 錦市場

If you are interested in seeing all the really weird and wonderful foods that are required for cooking in Kyoto, wander through **Nishiki Market** (☎ 211-3882; Nishikikōji-dōri btwn Teramachi & Takakura; ⏰ 9am-5pm, varies for individual stalls), Kyoto's best full-time market. It's in the centre of town, one block north of (and parallel to) Shijō-dōri. This market is a great place to visit on a rainy day or if you need a break from temple hopping. The variety of foods on display is staggering, and the frequent cries of Irasshaimase! (Welcome!) are heart-warming.

MUSEUM OF KYOTO 京都文化博物館

Housed in and behind the former Bank of Japan, a classic brick Meiji-period building, this **museum** (☎ 222-0888; Sanjō-dōri-Takakura;

(Continued on page 294)

KANSAI

To Ohara (5km);
Obama (80km)

See Northeast Kyoto Map (pp282-3)

To Hiei-zan
(6.5km)

Yaseyūen

Iwakura

Hachiman-
Mae

Takanga-ike

Kokusaikaikan

Shugakuin

Sakyō-ku

Ichijōji

Kyoto-
Seikadai-mae

Kino

Takaragaike
Myō. Takara-ga-ike-kōen
(Daimonji Okuribi
Fire Festival Characters)

Takara-ga-ike-kōen

H6

(Daimonji Okuribi
Fire Festival Characters)
法

Chayama

Mototanaka

Okazaki-
kōen

Higashiyama-ku

Biwa-ko Sosui
Canal

Subway Line

Keage

To Kurama (4km);
Kibune (4.5km);
Hanase-tōge (14km);
Ashiyū (49km)

Kyoto Sangyō
University

Kurama-gawa

Kyoto
Institute of
Technology

Matsugasaki

Kitayama-dōri

Kamigamo-jinja

Shirakawa-dōri

Kitayama

Kyoto
Botanical
Gardens

Kyoto
Municipal
Zoo

Keihan

Sanjō Keihan

Higashiyama

Keage

Kamo-gawa

Ōtani
University

Kitaōji-dōri

Dōshisha
University

Kitaōji

Kurumaguchi

Imadegawa

Imadegawa-dōri

Kyoto Imperial
Palace Park

Karasuma-dōri

Marutamachi-dōri

Marutamachi

Karasuma
Oike

Sanjō-dōri

Kyōto-Shiyakusho-mae

Karasuma

Kawaramachi

Shijō

See Downtown Kyoto Map (p289)

See Northwest Kyoto Map (pp280-1)

Shōden-ji

Kita-ku

Kamigyō-ku

Honkawa-dōri

Nijō-mae

Nijō-jō

Nijō

Nakagyō-ku

Omiya

Nakagyō-ku

Senbon-dōri

Funaokayama-kōen

Kitano
Temman-gū

Kitano
Hakubaichō

Honkawa-dōri

Sanjō Guchi

Hidari Daimonji
(Daimonji Okuribi
Fire Festival Character)

Kitano

Shinmachi-dōri

Ritsumeikan
University

Tōjin

Myōshinji

Hanazono

Ukyō-ku

Ryōanjimichi

Onuma

Uzumasa Line

Izumiya

Kakonoyashiro

Kyoto University of
Foreign Studies

Takagachi

Narutaki

Tokiwa

Uzumasa

Katabiranotsuji

Katsura-gawa

Keifuku
Arashiyama
Line

Yamanouchi

Hirosawa-no-ike

Kisunazaki

Arisugawa

Katsura-gawa

To Takao, Kōzan-ji;
Saimyō-ji (1km);
Jingo-ji (1.5km)

To Takao, Kōzan-ji;
Saimyō-ji (1km);
Jingo-ji (1.5km)

Funa-gata
(Daimonji Okuribi
Fire Festival Character)

164

See Arashiyama &

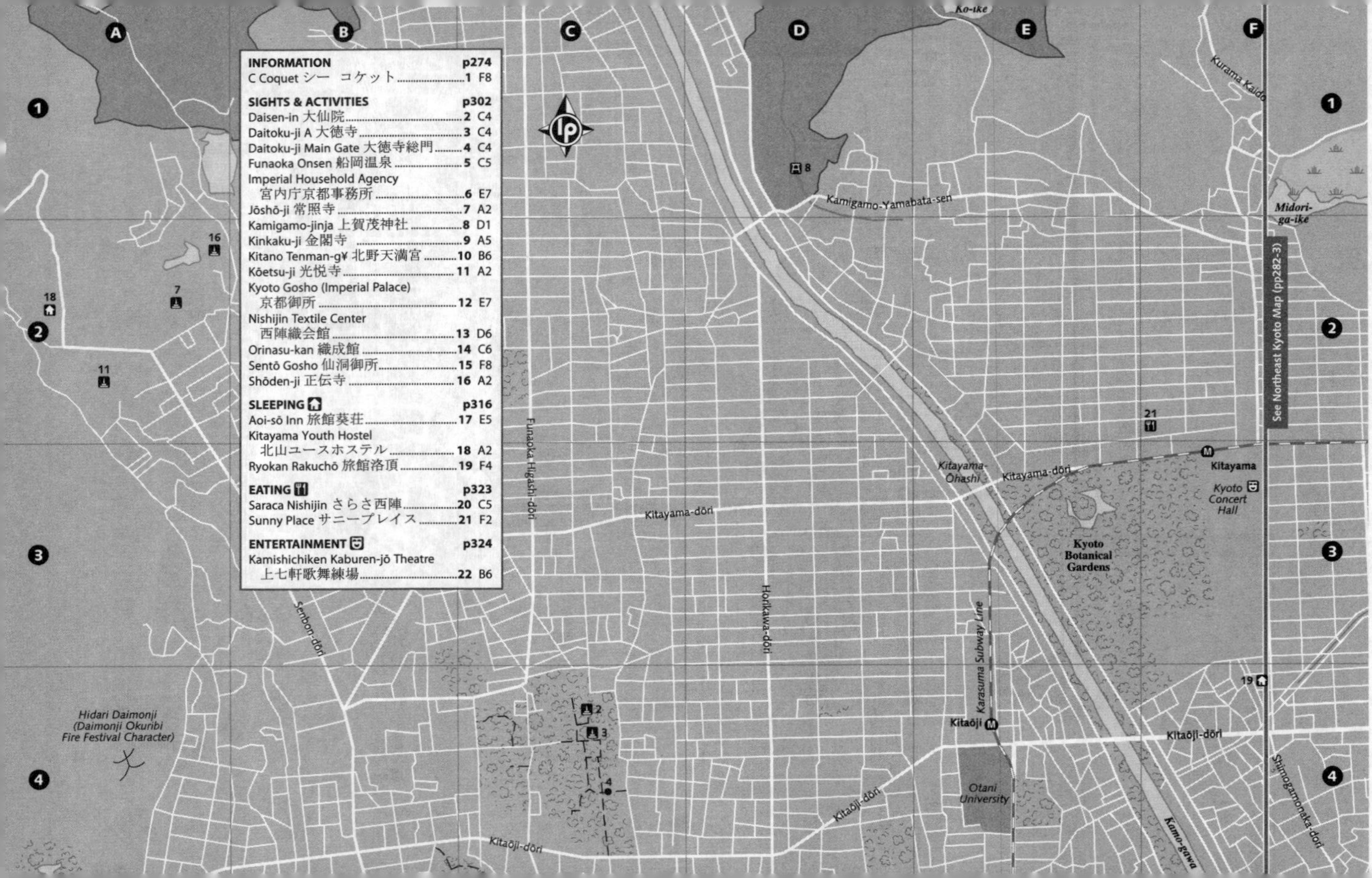

Ko-ike
Kurama Kaido
Midori-ga-ike
Kamigamo-Yamabata-sen
See Northeast Kyoto Map (pp282-3)
Funaoka Higashi-dōri
Kitayama-dōri
Kitayama-Ōhashi
Kitayama
Kyoto Concert Hall
Kyoto Botanical Gardens
Horikawa-dōri
Senbon-dōri
Karasuma Subway Line
Kitaōji
Kitaōji-dōri
Otani University
Kamo-gawa
Shimogamonaka-dōri
Hidari Daimonji (Daimonji Okuribi Fire Festival Character)

INFORMATION p274
C Coquet シー コケット 1 F8

SIGHTS & ACTIVITIES p302
Daisen-in 大仙院 2 C4
Daitoku-ji A 大徳寺 3 C4
Daitoku-ji Main Gate 大徳寺総門 4 C4
Funaoka Onsen 船岡温泉 5 C5
Imperial Household Agency 宮内庁京都事務所 6 E7
Jōshō-ji 常照寺 7 A2
Kamigamo-jinja 上賀茂神社 8 D1
Kinkaku-ji 金閣寺 9 A5
Kitano Tenman-g¥ 北野天満宮 10 B6
Kōetsu-ji 光悦寺 11 A2
Kyoto Gosho (Imperial Palace) 京都御所 12 E7
Nishijin Textile Center 西陣織会館 13 D6
Orinasu-kan 織成館 14 C6
Sentō Gosho 仙洞御所 15 F8
Shōden-ji 正伝寺 16 A2

SLEEPING p316
Aoi-sō Inn 旅館葵荘 17 E5
Kitayama Youth Hostel 北山ユースホステル 18 A2
Ryokan Rakuchō 旅館洛頂 19 F4

EATING p323
Saraca Nishijin さらさ西陣 20 C5
Sunny Place サニープレイス 21 F2

ENTERTAINMENT p324
Kamishichiken Kaburen-jō Theatre 上七軒歌舞練場 22 B6

0   400 m
0   0.2 miles

Shimogamonichi-dōri
Kamo-kaidō
Aoi-bashi

Izumoji-bashi

Kuramaguchi

Kuramaguchi-dōri

17

Shimei-dōri

Kuramagochi-dōri

Kamigoryōmae-dōri

Horikawa-dōri

Kamigyō-ku

Kamitachiuri-dōri

Mushakoji-dōri

Imadegawa-dōri

Dōshisha Women's
College, High School
& Junior High School

Dōshisha
University

Karasuma-dōri

Imadegawa

Mushakōji-dōri

Kyoto Imperial Palace Park

6

12

15

Kawaramachi-dōri

Teramachi-dōri

Kojinguchi-dōri

ALTI (Kyoto Fumin Hall)

Karasuma Subway Line

Shimmachi-dōri

Nakatachiuri-dōri

Nakachōjamachi-dōri

Horikawa-dōri

Inokuma-dōri

Marutamachi

Marutamachi-dōri

Kuramaguchi-higashi-dōri

20

Kenkun-dōri

Kuramaguchi-higashi-dōri

5

Teranouchi-dōri

Motoseiganji-dōri

13

Yokoshimme-dōri

Omiya-dōri

Ichijo-dōri

Kamigyō-ku

Imadegawa-dōri

Nakasuji-dōri

Sasayachō-dōri

14

Kamichōjamachi-dōri

Chiokōin-dōri

Uranomon-dōri

Jōrukuji-dōri

Senbon-dōri

Shimotachiuri-dōri

Sawaragichō-dōri

Nishiki-dōri

22

4
10
**Kitano
Temman-gū**

Demizu-dōri

Shimmarutamachi-dōri

Keifuku
Kitano Line

**Kitano
Hakubaichō**

See Southwest Kyoto Map (pp284–5)

0 | 400 m
0 | 0.2 miles

SLEEPING 🏠 p315
Casa Carinho B&B
　カーサ カリーニョ B&B.. **10** C6
Holiday Inn Kyoto
　ホリデーイン京都 **11** B4
ISE Dorm
　アイエスイードーム **12** C8
Kaguraya B&B................... **13** C7
Three Sisters Inn Main Building
　スリーシスターズイン
　洛東荘本館 **14** C8
Yonbanchi 番地 **15** C8

EATING 🍴 p321
Bon Bon Café
　ボンボンカフェ **16** A6

Buttercups
　バターカップス **17** D7
Café Carinho /Asian Diner
　カフェ カリーニョ
　アジアン ダイナー **18** C6
Café Peace カフェ ピース .. **19** B6
Didi ディディ **20** B5
Eating House Hi-Lite
　和洋食堂ハイライト **21** B6
Falafel Garden **22** B6
Ginsen **23** C6
Hiragana-kan
　ひらがな館 **24** C6
Kuishinbō-no-Mise
　くいしん坊の店.............. **25** D6
Kushi Hachi 串八 **26** D6

Omen おめん..................... **27** D7
Prinz プリンツ **28** C5
Shinshindō Notre Pain Quotidien
　新進堂 **29** C6
Tenka-ippin Honten
　天下一品本店 **30** D5
Tranq Room
　トランクルーム............... **31** D8
Womb **32** D5
Yatai 屋台 **33** C6

SHOPPING 🛍 p326
Qanat Rakuhoku
　カナート洛北................... **34** B4

TRANSPORT p327
Ei Rin 栄輪....................... **35** B6

See Northwest Map (pp280–1)

See Downtown Kyoto Map (p289)

Shimogamohon-dōri

Teramachi-dōri

Kawaramachi-dōri

Shinkyōgoku
Covered Arcade

Teramachi Covered Arcade

Kyoto-Shiyakusho-mae

Nijo-dōri-Fuyachō

Sakaimachi-dōri

Ainomachi-dōri

Karasuma-Oike

Oike-dōri

Sanjo-dōri

Rokkaku-dōri

Nishiki-kōji
(Nishiki Market)

Sakaimachi-dōri

Ayakōji-dōri

Bukkōji-dōri

Takatsuji-dōri

Matsubara-dōri

Gokomachi-dōri

Tominokōji-dōri

Fuyachō-dōri

Yanaginobamba-dōri

Sakaimachi-dōri

Takakura-dōri

Kawaramachi-dōri

Takase-gawa

Kamo-gawa

Gojo Ohashi

Gojo

Karasuma-dōri

Maruyamachi

Marutamachi-dōri

Ryōgaemachi-dōri

Muromachi-dōri

Koromonotana-dōri

Ebisugawa-dōri

Takeyamachi-dōri

Abura no kōji-dōri

Oshikōji-dōri

Ogawa-dōri

Horikawa-dōri

Kamaza-dōri

Tōzai Subway Line

Karasuma Subway Line

Karasuma

Shijo

Bukkōji-dōri

Nishinotōin-dōri

Takoyakushi-dōri

Nishikikōji-dōri

Shijo-dōri

Horikawa-dōri

Nijōjō-mae

Nijōjō-ku

Aneyakōji-dōri

Sanjo-dōri

Rokkaku-dōri

Ōmiya

Shijo-Ōmiya

Ōmiya-dōri

Kuromon-dōri

Keifuku Arashiyama Line

Nakagyō-ku

Mibu-dōri

Takatsuji-dōri

Gojo-dōri

Tanbaguchi

Hankyū Kyoto Line

Hijiashi-dōri

Sagano Line
(Sanin Main Line)

Nijō

Sanjo-dōri

Nishiōji-dōri

Sanjo Guchi

Keifuku Arashiyama Line

Sai

Saiin

Manjūji-dōri

Karasuma-Gojo Crossing

Yobai-dōri

See Kyoto Station Area Map (p291)

Keihan Main Line
Kawabata-dōri
Shichijō
Shichijō-Ōhashi
Shiokōji-bashi
Tōkaidō Main Line (Biwako Line) & Kōsei Line
Nara Line
Tōkaidō Shinkansen Line
Higashiyama-bashi
Tōfukuji
Tobakaidō
Kawaramachi-dōri
Kujō-dōri
Takeda Kaidō
Kamujuzayachō-dōri
Shimojuzayachō-dōri
Shōsei-en
Higashinotōin-dōri
Karasuma-dōri
Kyoto
Kyoto
Karasuma Subway Line
Kujō
Minami-ku
Rokujō-dōri
Hanayachō-dōri
Matobakōji
Shichijō-dōri
Nishinotōin-dōri
Shiokōji-dōri
Hachijō-dōri
Horikawa-dōri
Aburakōji-dōri
Kintetsu Kyoto Line
Tōji
Tōji-dōri
Kyoto Minami Kaikan
Shimogyō-ku
Shimabara
Umekōji-kōen
Hachijō-dōri
Tōkaidō Main Line (Kyoto Line)
Minami-ku
Kujō-dōri
Ōmiya-dōri
Shiokōji-dōri
Sagano Line (San-in Main Line)
Tōkaidō Main Line (Kyoto Line)
Tōkaidō Shinkansen Line
Kujō-dōri

See Northeast Map (pp282-3)

Tetsugaku-no-Michi

Higashiyama-ku

Biwa-ko Sosui Canal

Tōzai Subway Line

Higashiyama Driveway

Keage

Pedestrian Tunnel

Sanjō-dōri

Shirakawa-dōri

Shirakawa

Marutamachi-dōri

Okazaki-jinja

Nijō-dōri

Kyoto Municipal Zoo

Okazaki-kōen

Budō Centre

Higashiyama-dōri

Nishiōji-dōri

Marutamachi Crossing

Higashiyama Marutamachi Crossing

Higashitakeyachō-dōri

Reisen-dōri

Nijō-dōri

Higashiyama-Sanjō Crossing

Sanjō-dōri

Higashiyama

Maruyama-kōen

Higashiyama-ku

Ninen-zaka

Yasaka Pagoda

Kiyomizu

Ishibeikōji

Higashiōji-dōri

Yasaka-jinja

Ninen-zaka

Kawabata-Marutamachi Crossing

Shimogamo-dōri

Keihan Main Line

Kawabata-Marutamachi Crossing

Mandokoro-bashi

Nijō-Ōhashi

Tōzai Subway Line

Kyoto-Shiyakusho-mae

See Downtown Kyoto Map (p289)

Keihan Sanjō

Sanjō

Hanami-kōji

Furumonzen-dōri

Shinbashi

Shimonzen-dōri

Shinbashi-dōri

Gion

Nawate-dōri

Shijō

Teramachi-dōri

Kawaramachi-Oike Crossing

Teramachi Covered Arcade

Shinkyōgoku Covered Arcade

Sanjō Covered Arcade

Pontocho

Kawaramachi-dōri

Kawaramachi

Shijō-dōri

Kawabata-dōri

Kamo-gawa

Takase-gawa

Yamatōoji-dōri

Ebisu-jinja

Miyagawachō-dōri

0 _____ 400 m
0 _____ 0.2 miles

Higashiyama Driveway

Shioikan-dōri

Gojō-dōri

Tōkaidō Main Line (Biwako Line) & Kosei Line

Tōkaidō Shinkansen Line

Chishaku-in XU+667 AXU+7A4D\U+9662

Higashioji-dōri

Chawan-zaka

Gojō-zaka

Sannen-zaka

8

7

1

Higashioji-dōri

Yamatooji-dōri

Shichijō-dōri

12

20

See Kyoto Station
Area Map (p291)

See Southwest Kyoto Map (pp284-5)

Gojō-dōri

Gojō

Gojō Ohashi

Kawabata-dōri

Shichijō Ohashi

Shichijō

Shiokōji-bashi

Nara Line

Tōfukuji

Higashiyama-bashi

Keihan Main
Line

Tobakaidō

5
6
7
8

DOWNTOWN KYOTO

0 200 m
0 0.1 miles

A **B** **C** **D** **E** **F**

Gion

Shinbashi

Ponto-chō

Nakagyō-ku

Kamo-gawa

Kyoto
City Hall

To Tokyo Mitsubishi
Bank (150m)

Karasuma-Oike Crossing
Karasuma-Oike
Kawaramachi-Oike Crossing
Sanjō Keihan
Sanjō-Kawaramachi Crossing
Shijō-Kawaramachi Crossing

Tōzai Subway Line
Hankyū Kyoto Line

Oike-dōri
Karasuma-dōri
Takakura-dōri
Sanjō-dōri
Tominokoji-dōri
Fuyachō-dōri
Rokkaku-dōri
Takoyakushi-dōri
Nishikikōji-dōri
Shijō-dōri
Aneyakōji-dōri
Yanaginobanba-dōri
Kawaramachi-dōri
Kiyamachi-dōri
Kawabata-dōri
Nawate-dōri
Furumonzen-dōri
Hanami-kōji
Shinkawa • Minami-dōri
Kiri-dōshi
Magohashi-dōri
Sanjō-dōri
Shinkyōgoku Covered Arcade
Teramachi Covered Arcade
Sanjō Covered Arcade

Oike-Ohashi
Sanjō-Ohashi
Sanjō-Kawaramachi Crossing
Shijō-Ohashi

Kyoto-Shiyakusho-mae
Sanjō

Shijō

Karasuma

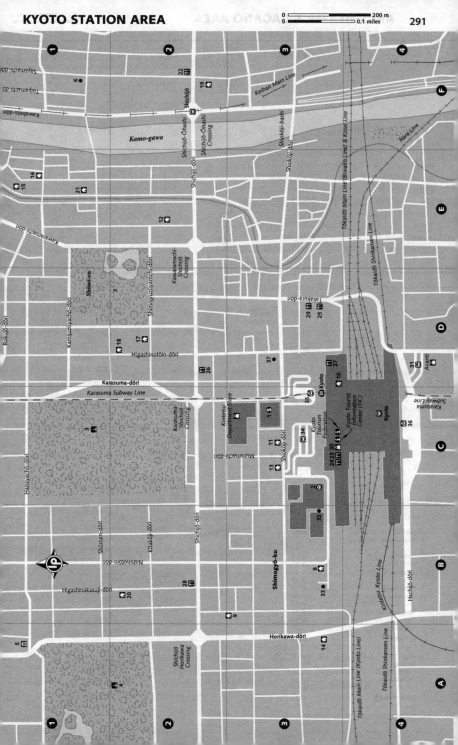

| 0 | | 200 m |
| 0 | | 0.1 miles |

Torii-gata
(Daimonji Okuribi
Fire Festival Character)

Osawa-no-ike

Ukyō-ku

Shin-marutamachi-dōri

Sagano Line (San-in Main Line)

Sagano Kankō Line

Saga Arashiyama

Torokko Saga

Oi-gawa

Okura-ike

Torokko Arashiyama

Keifuku Arashiyama Line

Rokuō

Sagaekimae

Kameyama-kōen

Keifuku Arashiyama

Nishikyō-ku

Convenience Store

Sanjō-dōri

Hozu-gawa

Katsura-gawa

Nakanoshima-kōen

Arashiyama

Iwatayama
Monkey Park

ŌHARA

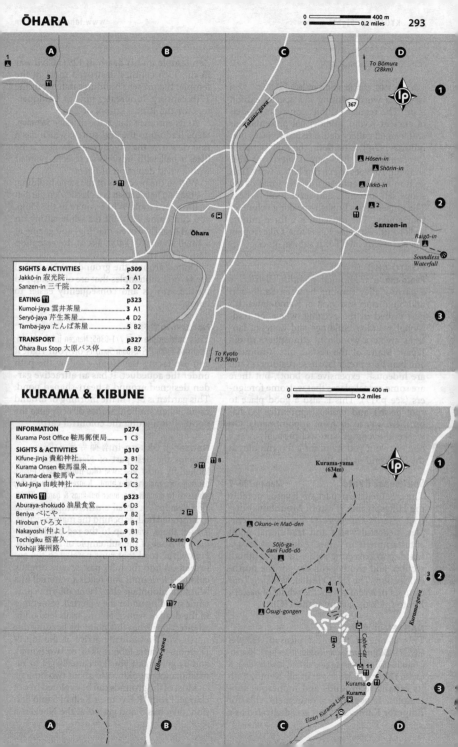

293

To Bōmura
(28km)

367

Takano-gawa

Hōsen-in
Shōrin-in
Jakkō-in

Ōhara

Sanzen-in

Raigō-in

Soundless
Waterfall

To Kyoto
(13.5km)

SIGHTS & ACTIVITIES	p309
Jakkō-in 寂光院	1 A1
Sanzen-in 三千院	2 D2

EATING 🍴	p323
Kumoi-jaya 雲井茶屋	3 A1
Seryō-jaya 芹生茶屋	4 D2
Tamba-jaya たんば茶屋	5 B2

TRANSPORT	p327
Ōhara Bus Stop 大原バス停	6 B2

KURAMA & KIBUNE

INFORMATION	p274
Kurama Post Office 鞍馬郵便局	1 C3

SIGHTS & ACTIVITIES	p310
Kifune-jinja 貴船神社	2 B1
Kurama Onsen 鞍馬温泉	3 D2
Kurama-dera 鞍馬寺	4 C2
Yuki-jinja 由岐神社	5 C3

EATING 🍴	p323
Aburaya-shokudō 油屋食堂	6 D3
Beniya べにや	7 B2
Hirobun ひろ文	8 B1
Nakayoshi 仲よし	9 B1
Tochigiku 栃喜久	10 B2
Yōshūji 雍州路	11 D3

Kurama-yama
(634m)

Okuno-in Maō-den

Kibune

Sōjō-ga-
dani Fudō-dō

Kurama-gawa

Ōsugi-gongen

Cable-car

Kurama

Kibune-gawa

Eizan Kurama Line

(Continued from page 277)

admission ¥500, extra for special exhibits; ⊙ 10am-7.30pm Tue-Sun) is worth visiting if a special exhibit is on. The regular exhibits consist of models of ancient Kyoto, audiovisual presentations and a small gallery dedicated to Kyoto's film industry. On the 1st floor, the Roji Tempō is a reconstructed Edo-period merchant area showing 10 types of exterior lattice work (this section can be entered for free; some of the shops sell souvenirs and serve local dishes). The museum has English-speaking volunteer tour guides. The museum is a three-minute walk southeast of the Karasuma-Oike stop on the Karasuma and Tōzai subway lines.

PONTO-CHŌ 先斗町
Ponto-chō, a traditional nightlife district, is a narrow alley running between Sanjō-dōri and Shijō-dōri just west of Kamo-gawa. It's best visited in the evening, when the traditional wooden buildings and hanging lanterns create a wonderful atmosphere of old Japan. Many of the restaurants, teahouses and bars here prefer Japanese customers (and are hideously expensive to boot), but there are some casual places that welcome foreigners (see p317). This is also a good place to spot geisha and *maiko* (apprentice geisha) on their way to or from appointments. On weekend evenings, you will probably notice one or two if you stand for a few minutes at the Shijō end of the alley.

Southeast Kyoto   Map pp286–7
The southeastern part of Kyoto, notably the Higashiyama (Eastern Mountains) district, merits top priority for its fine temples, peaceful walks and traditional night entertainment in Gion. Allocate at least a full day to cover the sights in the southern section, and another full day for the northern section. The JNTO leaflet, *Walking Tour Courses in Kyoto* covers the whole of eastern Kyoto (pick up a copy at the TIC).

NANZEN-JI 南禅寺
This is one of the most pleasant **temples** (☎ 771-0365; nanzenji.com/english/index.html; Nanzen-ji Fukuchi-chō; admission to grounds free, inner buildings & garden ¥1000; ⊙ 8.40am-5pm) in all Kyoto, with its expansive grounds and numerous subtemples. It began as a retirement villa for Emperor Kameyama but was dedicated as a

Zen temple on his death in 1291. Civil war in the 15th century destroyed most of the temple; the present buildings date from the 17th century. It operates now as headquarters for the Rinzai school of Zen.

At its entrance stands the massive **San-mon**. Steps lead up to the 2nd storey, which has a fine view over the city. Beyond the gate is the **Hōjō**, a hall with impressive screens painted with a vivid depiction of tigers.

Within the precincts of the same building, the **Leaping Tiger Garden** is a classic Zen garden well worth a look. While you're in the Hōjō, you can enjoy a cup of tea while sitting on tatami (tightly woven matting) and gazing at a small waterfall (¥400, ask at the reception desk of the Hōjō).

Dotted around the grounds of Nanzen-ji are several subtemples that are often skipped by the crowds and consequently easier to enjoy.

Nanzen-in 南禅院
This **subtemple** (☎ 771-0365; Nanzen-ji Fukuchi-chō; admission ¥300; ⊙ 8.40am-5pm) is on your right if you are facing the Hōjō – follow the path under the aqueduct. It has an attractive garden designed around a heart-shaped pond. This garden is best in the morning or around noon, when sunlight shines directly into the pond, illuminating the colourful carp.

Nanzen-ji Oku-no-in 南禅寺奥の院
Perhaps the best part of Nanzen-ji is overlooked by most visitors: **Oku-no-in** (☎ 771-0365; nanzenji.com/english/index.html; Nanzen-ji Fukuchi-chō; admission to grounds free, inner buildings & garden ¥1000; ⊙ 8.40am-5pm), a small shrine/temple hidden in a forested hollow behind the main precinct. To get there, walk up to the red brick aqueduct in front of the subtemple of Nanzen-in. Follow the road that runs parallel to the aqueduct up into the hills, past several brightly coloured *torii* until you reach a waterfall in a beautiful mountain glen. Here, pilgrims pray while standing under the waterfall, sometimes in the dead of winter. Hiking trails lead off in all directions from this point; by heading due north, you'll eventually arrive at the top of Daimon-ji-yama (about 7km, or two hours), and by going east you'll eventually get to Yamashina (about 5km, also about two hours).

Most of the grounds can be explored free of charge. From JR Kyoto or Keihan Sanjō Station, take bus 5 and get off at the Nanzen-ji

KANSAI

Eikan-dō-michi stop. You can also take the Tōzai line subway from the city centre to Keage and walk for five minutes downhill.

Tenju-an 天授庵

This **temple** (☎ 771-0365; Nanzen-ji Fukuchi-chō; admission ¥300; ⏰ 8.40am-5pm) stands at the side of the San-mon, a four-minute walk west of Nanzen-in. Constructed in 1337, the temple has a splendid garden and a great collection of carp in its pond.

Konchi-in 金地院

When leaving Tenju-an, turn left and continue for 100m – **Konchi-in** (admission ¥400; ⏰ 8.30am-5pm) is down a small side street on the left. The stylish gardens fashioned by the master landscape designer Kobori Enshū are the main attraction.

CHION-IN 知恩院

In 1234 **Chion-in** (☎ 531-2111; Shinbashi-dōri-Yamatoōji Higashi iru; admission to grounds free, admission to inner buildings & garden ¥400; ⏰ 9am-4pm Mar-Nov, 9am-3.40pm Dec-Feb) was built on the site where a famous priest by the name of Hōnen had taught and eventually fasted to death. Today it is still the headquarters of the Jōdo school of Buddhism, which was founded by Hōnen, and a hive of activity. For visitors with a taste for the grand, this temple is sure to satisfy.

The oldest of the present buildings date back to the 17th century. The two-storey **San-mon**, a Buddhist temple gate at the main entrance, is the largest temple gate in Japan and prepares you for the massive scale of the temple. The immense main hall contains an image of Hōnen. It's connected to another hall, the Dai Hōjō, by a 'nightingale' floor. The massive scale of the buildings reflects the popularity of the Jōdo school, which holds that earnest faith in the Buddha is all you need to achieve salvation.

After visiting the main hall, with its gold altar, you can walk around the back of the same building to see the temple's gardens. On the way, you pass a darkened hall with a small statue of Amida Buddha on display, glowing in the darkness. It makes a nice contrast to the splendour of the main hall.

The giant **bell**, cast in 1633 and weighing 74 tonnes, is the largest in Japan. The combined muscle-power of 17 monks is needed to make the bell ring for the famous ceremony that heralds the new year.

The temple is close to the northeastern corner of Maruyama-kōen. From Kyoto Station take bus 206 and get off at the Chion-in-mae stop or walk up (east) from the Keihan Sanjō or Shijō Station.

EIKAN-DŌ 永観堂

Also known as Zenrin-ji, **Eikan-dō** (☎ 761-0007; www.eikando.or.jp/English/index_eng.htm; Sakyo-ku Eikandō; admission ¥600 ⏰ 9am-5pm) is made interesting by its varied architecture, gardens and works of art. It was founded in 855 by the priest Shinshō, but the name was changed to Eikan-dō in the 11th century to honour the philanthropic priest Eikan.

The best way to appreciate this temple is to follow the arrows and wander slowly along the covered walkways connecting the halls and gardens.

In the Amida-dō Hall, at the southern end of the complex, is the statue of Mikaeri Amida (Buddha Glancing Backwards).

From the Amida-dō Hall, head north to the end of the covered walkway. Change into the sandals provided, then climb the steep steps up the mountainside to the **Taho-tō** (Taho Pagoda), where there's a fine view across the city.

SHŌREN-IN 青蓮院

This **temple** (☎ 561-2345; Higashiyama-ku Sanjō-Awataguchi; admission ¥500; ⏰ 9am-5pm) is hard to miss, with the giant camphor trees growing just outside its walls. Shōren-in was originally the residence of the chief abbot of the Tendai school of Buddhism. The present building dates from 1895, but the main hall has sliding screens with paintings from the 16th and 17th centuries. Often overlooked by the crowds that descend on other Higashiyama temples, this is a pleasant place to sit and think while gazing out over the beautiful gardens.

The temple is a five-minute walk north of Chion-in (left).

TŌFUKU-JI 東福寺

Founded in 1236 by the priest Enni, **Tōfuku-ji** (☎ 561-0087; www.tofukuji.jp/index2.html; Higashiyama-ku Honmachi; admission to grounds free, main temple ¥400, each subtemple ¥400; ⏰ 9am-4pm Dec-Oct, 8.30am-4.30pm Nov) now belongs to the Rinzai sect of Zen Buddhism. As this temple was intended to compare with Tōdai-ji and Kōfuku-ji in Nara, it was given a name combining characters from the names of each of these temples.

KANSAI

Despite the destruction of many of the buildings by fire, this is still considered one of the five main Zen temples in Kyoto. The huge **San-mon** is the oldest Zen main gate in Japan. The *tosu* (lavatory) and *yokushitsu* (bathroom) date from the 14th century. The present temple complex includes 24 subtemples; at one time there were 53.

The **Hōjō** was reconstructed in 1890. The gardens, laid out in 1938, are worth a visit. As you approach the northern gardens, you cross a stream over Tsūten-kyō (Bridge to Heaven), which is a pleasant leafy spot – the foliage is renowned for its autumn colour. The northern garden has stones and moss neatly arranged in a chequerboard pattern.

The nearby **Reiun-in** subtemple receives few visitors to its attractive garden.

Tōfuku-ji is a 20-minute walk (2km) southeast of Kyoto Station. You can also take a local train on the JR Nara line and get off at Tōfukuji Station, from which it's a 10-minute walk southeast.

MARUYAMA-KŌEN 円山公園

This **park** (Maruyama-chō Higashiyama-ku) is a great place to escape the bustle of the city centre and amble around gardens, ponds, souvenir shops and restaurants. Peaceful paths meander through the trees and carp glide through the waters of a small pond in the centre of the park.

For two weeks in early April, when the park's many cherry trees come into bloom, the calm atmosphere of the park is shattered by hordes of revellers enjoying *hanami* (blossom viewing). The centrepiece is a massive *shidarezakura,* a weeping cherry tree – truly one of the most beautiful sights in Kyoto, particularly when lit from below at night. For those who don't mind crowds, this is a good place to observe the Japanese at their most uninhibited. It is best to arrive early and claim a good spot high on the eastern side of the park, from which point you can safely peer down on the mayhem below.

The park is a five-minute walk east of the Shijō-Higashiōji intersection. To get there from Kyoto Station, take bus No 206 and get off at the Gion stop.

TETSUGAKU-NO-MICHI (PATH OF PHILOSOPHY) 哲学の道

The **Tetsugaku-no-Michi** (Sakyō-ku Ginkaku-ji) has long been a favourite with contemplative strollers who follow the traffic-free route beside a canal lined with cherry trees that are spectacular when in bloom. It only takes 30 minutes to complete the walk, which starts just north of Eikan-dō and ends at Ginkaku-ji. During the day, be prepared for crowds of tourists; a night stroll will definitely be quieter.

A map of the walk is part of the *Walking Tour Courses in Kyoto* leaflet, available at the TIC.

KIYOMIZU-DERA 清水寺

This ancient **temple** (☎ 551-1234; Higashiyama-ku Kiyomizu; admission ¥300; ◷ 6am-6pm), was first built in 798, but the present buildings are reconstructions dating from 1633. As an affiliate of the Hossō school of Buddhism, which originated in Nara, it has successfully survived the many intrigues of local Kyoto schools of Buddhism through the centuries and is now one of the most famous landmarks of the city. This, unfortunately, makes it a prime target for busloads of Japanese tourists, particularly during cherry-blossom season. Some travellers are also put off by the rather mercantile air of the temple – endless stalls sell good-luck charms, fortunes and all manner of souvenirs.

The main hall has a huge veranda that is supported by hundreds of pillars and juts out over the hillside. Just below this hall is the waterfall, **Otowa-no-taki**, where visitors drink sacred waters believed to have therapeutic properties. Dotted around the precincts are other halls and shrines. At Jishu-jinja, the shrine on the grounds, visitors try to ensure success in love by closing their eyes and walking about 18m between a pair of stones – if you miss the stone, your desire for love won't be fulfilled!

The steep approach to the temple is known as Chawan-zaka (Teapot Lane) and is lined with shops selling Kyoto handicrafts, local snacks and souvenirs.

To get there from Kyoto Station take bus 206 and get off at either the Kiyōmizu-michi or Gojō-zaka stop and plod up the hill for 10 minutes.

HEIAN-JINGŪ 平安神宮

This impressive shrine complex, **Heian-jingū** (☎ 761-0221; Okazaki Nishitennō-chō; admission to shrine precincts free, garden ¥600; ◷ 6am-6pm mid-Mar–mid-Aug, 6am-4.30pm Sep–mid-Mar), was built in 1895 to commemorate the 1100th anniversary of the founding of Kyoto. The buildings are colourful replicas, reduced to two-thirds of the size of the Kyoto Gosho of the Heian period.

The spacious garden, with its large pond and Chinese-inspired bridge, is also meant to represent the kind of garden that was popular in the Heian period. About 500m in front of the shrine there is a massive steel *torii* (Shintō shrine entrance gate). Although it appears to be entirely separate from the shrine, this is actually considered the main entrance to the shrine itself.

Two major events are held here: Jidai Matsuri (Festival of the Ages; p312), on 22 October, and Takigi Nō (see p367), from 1 to 2 June.

Take bus No 5 from Kyoto Station or Keihan Sanjō Station and get off at the Kyoto Kaikan Bijutsu-kan-mae stop and walk north, or walk up from Keihan Sanjō Station (15 minutes).

FUREAI-KAN KYOTO MUSEUM OF TRADITIONAL CRAFTS
京都伝統産業ふれあい館

This **museum** (☎ 762-2670; Okazaki Seishoji-chō; admission free; ⏰ 9am-5pm) in the Heian-jingū area (opposite) is a great spot to check out some interesting displays of traditional Kyoto crafts. Exhibits include woodblock prints, lacquerware, bamboo goods and gold-leaf work.

SANJŪSANGEN-DŌ 三十三間堂

The original **Sanjūsangen-dō** (☎ 525-0033; Higashiyama-ku Chaya-machi; admission ¥600; ⏰ 8am-5pm Apr–mid-Nov, 9am-4pm mid-Nov–Mar) was built in 1164 at the request of the retired emperor Go-shirakawa. The temple burnt to the ground in 1249 but a faithful copy was constructed in 1266.

The temple's name refers to the 33 (*sanjūsan*) bays between the pillars of this long, narrow building that houses 1001 statues of the 1000-armed Kannon (the Buddhist goddess of mercy). The largest Kannon is flanked on either side by 500 smaller Kannon images, neatly lined up in rows.

There are an awful lot of arms, but if you're picky and think the 1000-armed statues don't have the required number of limbs, then you should remember to calculate according to the nifty Buddhist mathematical formula that holds that 40 arms are the equivalent of 1000 arms, because each saves 25 worlds.

Visitors also seem keen to spot resemblances between friends or family members and any of the hundreds of images.

At the back of the hall are 28 guardian statues in a great variety of expressive poses. The gallery on the western side of the hall is famous for the annual **Tōshi-ya Matsuri**, held on 15 January, during which archers shoot arrows the length of the hall. The ceremony dates back to the Edo period, when an annual contest was held to see how many arrows could be shot from the southern end to the northern end in 24 hours. The all-time record was set in 1686, when an archer successfully landed over 8000 arrows at the northern end.

The temple is a 1.5km walk east of Kyoto Station; alternatively, take bus 206 or 208 and get off at the Sanjūsangen-dō-mae stop. It's also very close to Keihan Shichijō Station. From the station, walk north on Karasuma-dōri, then turn right onto Shichijō-dōri and walk east; the temple is on the right.

YASAKA-JINJA 八坂神社

This colourful **shrine** (☎ 561-6155; Higashiyama-ku Gion; admission free; ⏰ 24hr) is just down the hill from Maruyama-kōen. It's considered the guardian shrine of neighbouring Gion and is sometimes endearingly referred to as 'Gionsan'. This shrine is particularly popular as a spot for *hatsu-mōde* (the first shrine visit of the new year). If you don't mind a stampede, come here around midnight on New Year's Eve or over the next few days. Surviving the crush is proof that you're blessed by the gods! Yasaka-jinja also sponsors Kyoto's biggest festival, Gion Matsuri (p312).

KŌDAI-JI 高台寺

This **temple** (☎ 561-9966; Higashiyama-ku Kōdai-ji; admission ¥500; ⏰ 9am-5pm) was founded in 1605 by Kita-no-Mandokoro in memory of her late husband, Toyotomi Hideyoshi. The extensive grounds include gardens designed by the famed landscape architect Kobori Enshū, and teahouses designed by the renowned master of the tea ceremony Sen-no-Rikyū.

The temple is a 10-minute walk north of Kiyomizu-dera (opposite). Check at the TIC for the scheduling of summer and autumn night-time illuminations of the temple (when the gardens are lit by multicoloured spotlights).

KANSAI

GION 祇園周辺

Gion, one minute walk from Keihan Shijō Station, is a famous entertainment and geisha district on the eastern bank of Kamo-gawa. Modern architecture, congested traffic and contemporary nightlife establishments rob the area of some of its historical beauty, but there are still some lovely places left for a stroll. Gion falls roughly between Sanjō-dōri and Gojō-dōri (north and south, respectively) and Higashiyama-dōri and Kawabata-dōri (east and west, respectively).

Hanami-kōji is a street running north to south that bisects Shijō-dōri. The southern section is lined with 17th-century traditional restaurants and teahouses, many of which are exclusive establishments for geisha entertainment. If you wander around here in the late afternoon or early evening, you can often glimpse geisha or *maiko* on their way to or from appointments.

If you walk north from Shijō-dōri along Hanami-kōji, the fourth intersection you will come to is **Shinmonzen-dōri**. Wander in either direction along this street, which is packed with old houses, art galleries and shops specialising in antiques. Don't expect flea-market prices.

For more historic buildings in a waterside setting, wander down **Shirakawa Minami-dōri**, which is parallel with, and a block south of, the western section of Shinmonzen-dōri. This is one of Kyoto's most beautiful streets, especially in the evening.

KAWAI KANJIRŌ MEMORIAL HALL 河井寛次郎博物館

This **museum** (☎ 561-3585; Higashiyama-Gojō-zaka; admission ¥900; ⏰ 10am-4.30pm Tue-Sun, closed 10-20 Aug & 24 Dec-7 Jan) was once the home and workshop of one of Japan's most famous potters, Kawai Kanjirō. The house is built in rural style and contains examples of his work, his collection of folk art and ceramics, and his kiln.

The hall is a 10-minute walk north of the Kyoto National Museum. Alternatively, take bus 206 or 207 from Kyoto Station and get off at the Umamachi stop.

THE LIVING ART OF THE GEISHA

Behind the closed doors of the exclusive teahouses and restaurants that dot the back streets of Kyoto, women of exquisite grace and refinement entertain gentlemen of considerable means. Patrons may pay more than $3000 to spend an evening in the company of two or three geisha – kimono-clad women versed in an array of visual and performing arts, including playing the three-stringed *shamisen*, singing old teahouse ballads and dancing.

An evening in a Gion teahouse begins with an exquisite *kaiseki* (Japanese cuisine which obeys very strict rules of etiquette for every detail of the meal, including the setting) meal. While their customers eat, the geisha or *maiko* (apprentice geisha) enter the room and introduce themselves in Kyoto dialect.

A *shamisen* performance, followed by a traditional fan dance, is often given, and all the while the geisha and *maiko* pour drinks, light cigarettes and engage in charming banter.

It is virtually impossible to enter a Gion teahouse and witness a geisha performance without the introduction of an established patron. With the exception of public performances at annual festivals or dance presentations, they perform only for select customers. While geisha are not prostitutes, those who decide to open their own teahouses once they retire at 50 or so may receive financial backing from well-to-do clients.

Knowledgeable sources estimate that there are perhaps 80 *maiko* and just over 100 geisha in Kyoto. Although their numbers are ever-decreasing, geisha (geiko in the Kyoto dialect) and *maiko* can still be seen in some parts of Kyoto, especially after dusk in the back streets between Kamo-gawa and Yasaka-jinja and along the narrow Ponto-chō alley. Geisha and *maiko* can also be found in other parts of the country, most notably Tokyo. However, it is thought that there are less than 1000 geisha and *maiko* remaining in all Japan.

The best way to get a feel for the world of geiko and *maiko* is to take a walking lecture with **Peter MacIntosh** (☎ 090-5169-1654, www.kyotosightsandnights.com). Morning and evening tours (¥4000 and ¥3000, respectively) take in the major Kyoto geisha district and chances of spotting geisha are high. Peter can also arrange an evening with a geisha for those interested.

KYOTO MUNICIPAL MUSEUM OF ART
京都市美術館

The **Kyoto Municipal Museum of Art** (☎ 771-4107; Okazaki Enshōji-chō; admission varies by exhibition; ☯ 9am-4.30pm Tue-Sun) organises several major exhibitions a year. These exhibitions are drawn from its vast collection of post-Meiji-era art works. Kyoto-related works form a significant portion of this near-modern and modern collection.

MIYAKO MESSE みやこめっせ

The **Miyako Messe** (☎ 762-2670; Okazaki Seishōji-chō; admission free; ☯ 9am-5pm) has exhibits covering things like woodblock prints, lacquerware, bamboo goods and gold-leaf work. It's in the basement of the Miyako Messe (Kyoto International Exhibition Hall).

NATIONAL MUSEUM OF MODERN ART
京都国立近代美術館

This **museum** (☎ 761-4111; Okazaki Enshōji-chō; www.momak.go.jp/menu_e.html; admission ¥400; ☯ 9.30am-5pm Tue-Sun) is renowned for its collection of contemporary Japanese ceramics and paintings. Exhibits are changed on a regular basis (check with the TIC or *Kansai Time Out* for details).

NOMURA MUSEUM 野村美術館

The **Nomura Museum** (☎ 751-0374; Nanzen-ji Shimoka-wahara; admission ¥700; ☯ 10am-4.30pm Tue-Sun) is a 10-minute walk north of Nanzen-ji. Exhibits include scrolls, paintings, tea-ceremony implements and ceramics that were bequeathed by the wealthy business magnate Tokushiki Nomura.

KYOTO NATIONAL MUSEUM
京都国立博物館

The **Kyoto National Museum** (☎ 531-7509; www.kyohaku.go.jp/eng/index_top.html; Higashiyama-ku Chaya-machi; admission ¥420, extra for special exhibitions; ☯ 9.30am-5pm Tue-Sun) is housed in two buildings opposite Sanjūsangen-dō. There are excellent displays of fine arts, historical artefacts and handicrafts. The fine arts collection is especially highly regarded, containing some 230 items that have been classified as National Treasures or Important Cultural Properties.

Southwest Kyoto   Map pp284–5

Southwest Kyoto is not the most prepossessing part of the city, but there are a few major sights in the area, such as Nijō-jō, Tō-ji and the Umekōji Steam Locomotive Museum.

NIJŌ-JŌ 二条城

This **castle** (☎ 841-0096; Nijo-dōri-Horikawa; admission ¥600; ☯ 8.45am-4pm, gates close 5pm, closed Tue in Dec, Jan, Jul & Aug) was built in 1603 as the official Kyoto residence of the first Tokugawa shōgun, Ieyasu. The ostentatious style of construction was intended as a demonstration of Ieyasu's prestige and to signal the demise of the emperor's power. As a safeguard against treachery, Ieyasu had the interior fitted with 'nightingale' floors (floors that sing and squeak at every move, making it difficult for intruders to move about quietly) and concealed chambers where bodyguards could keep watch.

After passing through the grand **Kara-mon** gate, you enter **Ninomaru Palace** (admission palace & garden ¥600; ☯ 8.45am-4pm, closed 26 Dec-4 Jan), which is divided into five buildings with numerous chambers. The Ohiroma Yon-no-Ma (Fourth Chamber) has spectacular screen paintings. Don't miss the excellent **Ninomaru Palace Garden**, which was designed by the tea master and landscape architect Kobori Enshū.

The neighbouring **Honmaru Palace** dates from the middle of the 19th century and is only open for special viewing in the autumn.

To reach the castle, take bus 9 from Kyoto Station to the Nijō-jō-mae stop. Alternatively, take the Tōzai line subway to the Nijō-jō-mae Station.

NIJŌ JINYA 二条陣屋

A few minutes' walk south of Nijō-jō, **Nijō Jinya** (☎ 841-0972; Ōmiya-dōri-Oike; admission ¥1000; reservations necessary in Japanese; ☯ 10am, 11am, 2pm, 3pm Thu-Tue) is one of Kyoto's hidden gems. Seldom seen by short-term visitors, it was built as a merchant's home in the mid-1600s and served as an inn for provincial feudal lords visiting the capital. What appears to be an average Edo-period mansion, however, is no ordinary dwelling.

The house contains fire-resistant earthen walls and a warren of 24 rooms that were ingeniously designed to protect the *daimyō* (domain lords) against possible surprise attacks. Here you'll find hidden staircases, secret passageways and a whole array of

KANSAI

counter-espionage devices. The ceiling skylight of the main room is fitted with a trap door through which samurai could pounce on intruders, and sliding doors feature alternating panels of translucent paper to expose the shadows of eavesdroppers.

One-hour tours are conducted several times a day in Japanese and advance reservations must be made. Those who don't speak Japanese are asked to bring a Japanese-speaking guide.

SHINSEN-EN 神泉苑

While you're in the neighbourhood of Nijō-jō (p299), you might want to take a look at the garden, **Shinsen-en** (☎ 821-1466; Oike-dōri, Shinsen-en-chō; admission free), just south of the castle (it's outside the walls and therefore free). This forlorn garden, with its small shrines and pond, is all that remains of the original imperial palace, abandoned in 1227.

TŌ-JI 東寺

This **temple** (☎ 691-3325; Minami-ku Kujō; admission to grounds free, Kondō & Treasure Hall ¥500; ⏰ 9am-4.30pm) was established in 794 by imperial decree to protect the city. In 818, the emperor handed the temple over to Kūkai, the founder of the Shingon school of Buddhism. Many of the buildings were destroyed by fire or fighting during the 15th century; most of those that remain date from the 17th century.

The **Kōdō** (Lecture Hall) contains 21 images representing a Mikkyō (Esoteric Buddhism) mandala. The **Kondō** (Main Hall) contains statues depicting the Yakushi (Healing Buddha) trinity. In the southern part of the garden stands the five-storey pagoda, which burnt down five times, was rebuilt in 1643 and is now the highest pagoda in Japan, standing 57m high.

The **Kōbō-san market/fair** is held here on the 21st of each month. The fairs held in December and January are particularly lively.

Tō-ji is a 15-minute walk southwest of Kyoto Station.

UMEKŌJI STEAM LOCOMOTIVE MUSEUM 梅小路蒸気機関車館

A hit with steam-train buffs and kids, this **museum** (☎ 314-2996; Shimogyō-ku Kannon-ji-chō; admission adult/child ¥400/100, train ride adult/child ¥200/100; ⏰ 9.30am-5pm Tue-Sun) features 18 vintage steam locomotives (dating from

1914 to 1948) and related displays. It's in the former Nijō station building, which was recently relocated here and carefully reconstructed. For an extra ¥200 (¥100 for children), you can take a 10-minute ride on one of the fabulous old trains (departures at 11am, 1.30pm and 3.30pm). From Kyoto Station, take bus No 33, 205 or 208 to the Umekō-ji Kōen-mae stop (make sure you take a west-bound bus).

SUMIYA PLEASURE HOUSE 角屋もてなしの文化美術館

This **house** (☎ 351-0024; Nishishinyashikiageya-chō; Japanese-language tours available; admission ¥1000; ⏰ 10am-4pm Tue-Sun) is one of the last remaining *ageya* found in Shimabara. This district northwest of Kyoto Station was Kyoto's original pleasure quarters. At its peak during the Edo period (1600–1867) the area flourished, with over 20 enormous *ageya* – magnificent banquet halls where artists, writers and statesmen gathered in a 'floating world' ambience of conversation, art and fornication. Geisha were often sent from their quarters (*okiya*) to entertain patrons at these restaurant-cum-brothels. By the start of the Meiji period, however, such activities had drifted north to the Gion district and Shimabara had lost its prominence.

Though the traditional air of the district has dissipated, a few old structures remain. The tremendous **Shimabara-no-ō-mon** gate, which marked the passage into the quarter, still stands, as does the Sumiya Pleasure House (the last remaining *ageya*), now designated a National Cultural Asset. Built in 1641, this stately two-storey, 20-room structure allows a rare glimpse into Edo-era nirvana. With a delicate lattice-work exterior, Sumiya has a huge open kitchen and an extensive series of rooms (including one extravagantly decorated with mother-of-pearl inlay).

Special tours (requiring advance reservations) allow access to the 2nd storey and are conducted daily. An English pamphlet is provided, but you might consider arranging a volunteer guide through the TIC.

MIBU-DERA 壬生寺

Founded in 991, **Mibu-dera** (☎ 841-3381; Bōjō-Bukkō-ji; admission free; ⏰ 8.30am-5.30pm) belongs to the Risshū school. In the late Edo period, it became a training centre for samurai. Mibu-dera houses tombs of pro-shōgunate

KYOTO RAIL MAP

Legend

- Eizan Line
- Hankyū Line
- Sagano Line (San-in Main Line)
- Tōkaidō Main Line
- Karasuma Subway Line
- Keifuku Line
- Keifuku Cable Line
- Keihan Line
- Keihan Keishin Line
- Kintetsu Line
- Kosei Line
- Nara Line
- Tōkaidō Shinkansen Line
- Tōzai Subway Line

To Kurama/Kibune

Kyoto Seikadimae 京都精華大前
Kino 木野　Iwakura 岩倉
Hachiman-mae 八幡前　Miyakehachiman 三宅八幡
Yaseyūen 八瀬遊園　Cable Yaseyūen ケーブル八瀬遊園
Cable Hiei ケーブル比叡　Ropeway Hiei ロープウェイ比叡
Sanchō (Summit) ロープウェイ比叡山頂
Takagara-ike 宝ヶ池
Kokusaikaikan 国際会館
Matsugasaki 松ヶ崎
Shūgakuin 修学院
Kitayama 北山
Kitaōji 北大路
Ichijōji 一乗寺
Kuramaguchi 鞍馬口
Chayama 茶山
Imadegawa 今出川
Mototanaka 元田中
Demachiyanagi (Eizan) 出町柳
Demachiyanagi (Keihan) 出町柳
Maratumachi 丸太町
Marutamachi 丸太町
Karasuma-Oike 烏丸御池
Nijō 二条　Nijōjō-mae 二条城前
Kyoto-Shiyakusho-mae 京都市役所前
Sanjō-Keihan 三条京阪
Yamanouchi 山ノ内
Sanjō Guchi 三条口
Higashiyama 東山
Nijō 二条
Karasuma 烏丸
Sanjō 三条
Keage 蹴上
Omiya 大宮
Saiin 西院
Shijō 四条
To Shiga
Sai 西院
Shijō-Omiya 四条大宮
Shijō 四条
Kawaramachi 河原町
Misasagi 御陵
To Ishiyama
Tanbaguchi 丹波口
Gojō 五条
Gojō 五条
KYOTO STATION 京都
Shichijō 七条
Yamashina 山科
Shinomiya 四宮
To Nagoya; Tokyo
Tōji 東寺　Kujō 九条
Tōfukuji 東福寺
Higashino 東野
Jūjō 十条　Jūjō 十条
Tobakaidō 鳥羽街道
Nagitsuji 椥辻
Kamitobaguchi 上鳥羽口
Kuinabashi くいな橋
Fushimi-Inari 伏見稲荷　Inari 稲荷
Ono 小野
Takeda 竹田
Fukakusa 深草
Daigo 醍醐
Fujinomori 藤森
JR Fujinomori JR藤森
Fushimi 伏見
Sumizome 墨染
Ishida 石田
Fushimi-Momoyama 伏見桃山
Tanbabashi 丹波橋
Momoyama 桃山
Chūshojima 中書島
Momoyama-Goryōmae 桃山御陵前
Momoyama-Minamiguchi 桃山南口
Rokujizō 六地蔵
Kohata 木幡
Kangetsu-kyō 観月橋
Kohata 木幡
Yodo 淀
Mukaijima 向島
Obaku 黄檗
Obaku 黄檗
To Osaka (Yodoyabashi)
To Nara
To Uji

Kitano-Hakubaichō 北野白梅町
Hamazono 花園
Saga Arashiyama 嵯峨嵐山
Uzumasa 太秦
To Hozukyō; Kameoka
Arashiyama 嵐山
Rokuoin 鹿王院
Katabira-no-Tsuji 帷子ノ辻
Kaikonoyashiro 蚕ノ社
Sagaekimae 嵯峨駅前
Kurumazaki 車折
Arisugawa 有栖川
Uzumasa 太秦
Matsuo 松尾
Nishikyōgoku 西京極
Nishiōji 西大路
Kamikatsura 上桂
Mukomachi 向日町
To Osaka (Umeda)
Katsura 桂
Higashi Muko 東向日
Nishi Muko 西向日
Nagaokakyo 長岡京
To Osaka
Kamitobaguchi 上鳥羽口

OSAKA SUBWAY & TRAM MAP

OSAKA SUBWAY & TRAM MAP

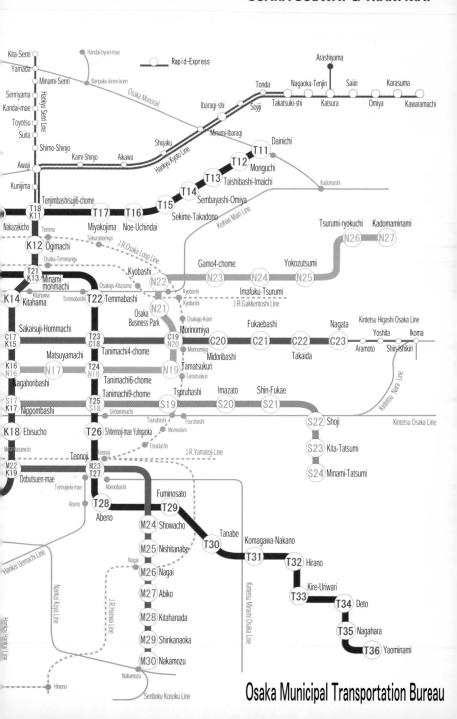

Osaka Municipal Transportation Bureau

Geisha, Kyoto

FRANK CARTER

Fushimi-Inari Taisha (p308), Kyoto

PHIL WEYMOUTH

Kōya-san (p377), Kii-hantō

CHRISTOPHER GROENH

Shinsen-gumi members, who fought bloody street battles resisting the forces that succeeded in restoring the emperor in 1868. Except for an unusual stupa covered in Jizō statues, the temple is of limited interest. It is, however, definitely worth visiting during Mibu kyōgen performances (late April), or the Setsubun celebrations (early February).

Northeast Kyoto
Map pp282–3

This is one of the city's richest areas for sightseeing. It includes such first-rate attractions as Ginkaku-ji, Honen-in, Shūgaku-in Rikyū, Shisen-dō and Manshu-in.

GINKAKU-JI 銀閣寺
Definitely worth a visit is **Ginkaku-ji** (☎ 771-5725; Sakyo-ku Ginkaku-ji; adult ¥500; ⏰ 8.30am-5pm), but be warned that bus loads of visitors often jam the narrow pathways.

In 1482 Shōgun Ashikaga Yoshimasa constructed a villa here as a genteel retreat from the turmoil of civil war. The villa's name translates as 'Silver Pavilion', but the shōgun's ambition to cover the building with silver was never realised. After Yoshimasa's death, the villa was converted into a temple.

You approach the main gate between tall hedges, before turning sharply into the extensive grounds. Walkways lead through the gardens, which include meticulously raked cones of white sand (probably symbolic of a mountain and a lake), tall pines and a pond in front of the temple. A path also leads up the mountainside through the trees.

From JR Kyoto or Keihan Sanjō Station, take bus 5 and get off at the Ginkaku-ji-michi stop. From Demachiyanagi Station or Shijō Station, take bus 203 to the same stop.

HŌNEN-IN 法然院
This fine **temple** (☎ 771-2400; Sakyō-ku Shishigatani; admission free; ⏰ 6am-4pm) was established in 1680 to honour Hōnen, the charismatic founder of the Jōdo school. This is a lovely, secluded temple with carefully raked gardens set back in the woods. Be sure to visit in early April for the cherry blossoms and early November for the maple leaves, when the main hall is opened for a special viewing.

The temple is a 12-minute walk from Ginkaku-ji (above), on a side street east of Tetsugaku-no-Michi. Look for the sign, then cross the bridge over the canal and follow the road uphill through the bamboo groves.

SHŪGAKU-IN RIKYŪ 修学院離宮
This imperial **villa** (☎ 211-1215; Sakyō-ku Shūgakuin; admission free), or detached palace, was begun in the 1650s by the abdicated emperor Go-Mizunoo, and work was continued after his death in 1680 by his daughter Akenomiya.

Designed as an imperial retreat, the villa grounds are divided into three large garden areas on a hillside: lower, middle and upper. The gardens' reputation rests on their ponds, pathways and impressive use of 'borrowed scenery' in the form of the surrounding hills; the view from the Rinun-tei Teahouse in the upper garden is particularly impressive.

Tours, in Japanese, start at 9am, 10am, 11am, 1.30pm and 3pm (50 minutes). Admission is free, but you must make advance reservations through the Imperial Household Agency (see p302 for details).

From Kyoto Station, take bus 5 and get off at the Shūgaku-in Rikyū-michi stop. The trip takes about an hour. From the bus stop it's a 15-minute walk (about 1km) to the villa. You can also take the Eiden Eizan line from Demachiyanagi Station to the Shūgaku-in stop and walk east about 25 minutes (about 1.5km) towards the mountains.

MANSHU-IN 曼殊院
This **temple** (☎ 781-5010; Ichijō-ji Takenouchi-chō; admission ¥500; ⏰ 9am-5pm) was originally founded by Saichō on Hiei-zan, but was relocated here at the beginning of the Edo period. The architecture, works of art and garden are impressive. The temple is about 30 minutes' walk (about 3km) north of Shisen-dō.

SHISEN-DŌ 詩仙堂
This **temple** (☎ 781-2954; Ichijō-ji Monkuchi-chō; admission ¥500; ⏰ 9am-5pm) was built in 1641 by Jōzan, a scholar of Chinese classics and a landscape architect, who wanted a place to retire to at the end of his life. The garden is a fine place to relax, with only the rhythmic 'thwack' of a bamboo *sōzu* (animal scarer) to interrupt your snooze.

The temple is a five-minute walk from the Ichijōji-sagarimatsu-mae bus stop on the No 5 route.

KYOTO INTERNATIONAL CONFERENCE HALL
国立京都国際会館

This **centre** (☎ 705-1234; www.kich.or.jp/en/index.html; Takaragaike Sakyō-ku) is an unfortunate attempt at replicating Japan's traditional thatched roof *gasshō-zukuri* style in concrete. Behind the conference hall, the Hosho-an Teahouse (designed by Soshitsu Sen, Grand Tea Master XV of the Urasenke school) is worth a look.

Northwest Kyoto   Map pp280-1

Northwest Kyoto has many excellent sights spread over a large swath of Kyoto. Highlights include the Kyoto Gosho, Kinkaku-ji and Daitoku-ji.

KINKAKU-JI 金閣寺

The famed **Golden Temple** (Kinkaku-ji; ☎ 461-0013; Kita-ku Kinkaku-ji-chō; admission ¥400; ◷ 9am-5pm) is one of Japan's best-known sights. The original building was constructed in 1397 as a retirement villa for Shōgun Ashikaga Yoshimitsu. His son converted it into a temple. In 1950 a young monk consummated his obsession with the temple by burning it to the ground. The monk's story was fictionalised in Mishima Yukio's *The Golden Pavilion*.

In 1955 a full reconstruction was completed that exactly followed the original design, but the gold-foil covering was extended to the lower floors.

To get to the temple from Kyoto Station, take bus 205 and get off at the Kinkaku-ji-michi stop. From Keihan Sanjō, take bus 59 and get off at the Kinkaku-ji-mae stop.

KYOTO GOSHO 京都御所

The original **imperial palace** was built in 794 and was replaced numerous times after destruction by fire. The present building, on a different site and smaller than the original, was constructed in 1855. Enthronement of a new emperor and other state ceremonies are still held there.

The Gosho does not rate highly in comparison with other attractions in Kyoto and you must apply for permission to visit (see below). However, you shouldn't miss the park surrounding the Gosho (see right).

To get there, take the Karasuma line subway to Imadegawa or a bus to the Karasuma-Imadegawa stop and walk 600m southeast.

Reservation & Admission

Permission to visit the Gosho is granted by the Kunaichō, the **Imperial Household Agency** (☎ 211-1215; ◷ 8.45am-noon & 1-4pm Mon-Fri, closed holidays), which is inside the walled park sur-

rounding the palace, a short walk from Imadegawa Station on the Karasuma line. You have to fill out an application form and show your passport. Children can visit if accompanied by adults over 20 years of age (but are forbidden entry to the other three imperial properties of Katsura Rikyū, Sentō Gosho and Shūgaku-in Rikyu). Permission to tour the palace is usually granted the same day (try to arrive at the office at least 30 minutes before the start of the tour you'd like to join). Guided tours, sometimes in English, are given at 10am and 2pm from Monday to Friday. The tour lasts about 50 minutes.

The Imperial Household Agency is also the place to make advance reservations to see the Sentō Gosho, Katsura Rikyū and Shūgaku-in Rikyu. Application forms are also available from JNTO offices outside the country and JNTO-run TICs inside Japan.

SENTŌ GOSHO PALACE 仙洞御所

The **palace** (☎ 211-1215; Kamigyō-ku Kyoto goen) is a few hundred metres southeast of the main Kyoto Gosho. Visitors must obtain advance permission from the Imperial Household Agency and be over 20 years old (see left). Tours (in Japanese) start at 11am and 1.30pm. The gardens, which were laid out in 1630 by Kobori Enshū, are the main attraction.

KYOTO IMPERIAL PALACE PARK 京都御苑

The Kyoto Gosho is surrounded by the spacious **Kyoto Imperial Palace Park** (Kamigyō-ku Kyoto goen; admission free; ◷ dawn-dusk), which is planted with a huge variety of flowering trees and open fields. It's perfect for picnics, strolls and just about any sport you can think of. Take some time to visit the pond at the park's southern end, which contains gorgeous carp. The park is most beautiful in the plum- and cherry-blossom seasons (March and April respectively). It is between Teramachi-dōri and Karasuma-dōri (to the east and west) and Imadegawa-dōri and Marutamachi-dōri (to the north and south).

DAITOKU-JI 大徳寺

The precincts of this temple, which belongs to the Rinzai school of Zen, contain an extensive complex of 24 subtemples, of which two are mentioned in following sections; eight are open to the public. If you want to examine Zen culture intensively, this is the place to visit.

Daitoku-ji (☎ 491-0019; Kita-ku Murasakino Daitokuji-chō; admission free; ☽ dawn-dusk) itself is on the eastern side of the grounds. It was founded in 1319, burnt down in the next century and rebuilt in the 16th century. The **San-mon** contains an image of the famous tea master, Sen-no-Rikyū, on the 2nd storey.

According to some historical sources, Toyotomi Hideyoshi was so enraged when he discovered he had been demeaning himself by walking under Rikyū that he forced the master to commit *seppuku* (ritual suicide by disembowelment) in 1591.

Around Daitoku-ji, two subtemples particularly worth a visit are **Daisen-in** (☎ 491-8346; Kita-ku Murasakino Daitokuji-chō; admission free; ☽ 9am-4.30pm), for its two famous (if small) gardens, and **Kōtō-in** (☎ 492-0068; Kita-ku Murasakino Daitokuji-chō; admission ¥400; ☽ 9am-4.30pm) for its lovely maples in autumn.

Admission charges to the various subtemples vary but are usually around ¥400. Those temples that accept visitors are usually open from 9am to 4.30pm.

The temple bus stop is Daitoku-ji-mae and convenient buses from Kyoto Station are Nos 205 and 206. Daitoku-ji is also a short walk west of Kitaō-ji subway station on the Karasuma line.

KITANO-TENMAN-GŪ 北野天満宮
This **shrine** (☎ 461-0005; www.kitanotenmangu.or.jp /eigo/index.html; Kamigyo-ku Bakuro-chō; admission free; ☽ 5am-dusk) is of moderate interest. However, if you're in town on the 25th of any month, be sure to catch the **Tenjin-san market/fair** held here. This is one of Kyoto's two biggest markets and is a great place to pick up some interesting souvenirs. The markets held in December and January are particularly colourful.

From Kyoto Station, take bus 50 and get off at the Kitano-Tenmangū-mae stop. From Keihan Sanjō Station, take bus No 10 to the same stop.

KAMIGAMO-JINJA 上賀茂神社
This **shrine** (☎ 781-0011; Kamigamo Motoyama; admission free; ☽ 8am-5.30pm) is one of Japan's oldest shrines and predates the founding of Kyoto. Established in 679, it is dedicated to Raijin, the god of thunder, and is one of Kyoto's 17 Unesco World Heritage sites. The present buildings (over 40 in all), including the impressive Haiden hall, are exact reproduc-

tions of the originals, dating from the 17th to 19th century. The shrine is entered from a long approach through two *torii*. The two large conical white-sand mounds in front of Hosodono hall are said to represent mountains sculpted for gods to descend upon.

NISHIJIN TEXTILE CENTER 西陣織会館
In the heart of the Nishijin textile district, this **centre** (☎ 451-9231; Horikawa-dōri-Imadegawa; admission free; ☽ 9am-5pm) is a good place to observe the weaving of fabrics used in kimono and their ornamental belts (*obi*). There are also displays of completed fabrics and kimono. It's on the southwest corner of the Horikawa-dōri and Imadegawa-dōri intersection.

ORINASU-KAN 織成館
This **museum** (☎ 431-0020; Kamigyo-ku, Daikoku-chō; admission ¥500; ☽ 10am-4pm Tue-Sun) is housed in a Nishijin weaving factory. It has impressive exhibits of Nishijin textiles. The Susamei-sha building next door is also open to the public and worth a look. With advance reservations, traditional weaving workshops can be attended.

Arashiyama & Sagano Area   Map p292
Arashiyama and Sagano are two districts well worth a visit in this area if you feel like strolling in pleasant natural surroundings and visiting temples tucked into bamboo groves. The JNTO leaflet *Walking Tour Courses in Kyoto* has a good map of the area, and you should make an effort to pick up a copy before heading out. Note that Arashiyama is wildly popular with Japanese tourists and can be packed, particularly in the cherry-blossom and maple-leaf seasons.

Bus 28 links Kyoto Station with Arashiyama. Bus 11 connects Keihan Sanjō Station with Arashiyama. The most convenient rail connection is the ride from Shijō-ōmiya Station on the Keifuku-Arashiyama line to Arashiyama Station. You can also take the JR San-in line from Kyoto Station or Nijō Station and get off at Saga Arashiyama Station (be careful to take only the local train, as the express does not stop in Arashiyama).

TENRYŪ-JI 天龍寺
One of the major temples of the Rinzai school of Zen, **Tenryū-ji** (☎ 881-1235; Saga Tenryū-ji; admission ¥600; ☽ 8.30am-5.30pm Mar-Oct, to 5pm Nov-Feb) was built in 1339 on the former site

of Emperor Go-Daigo's villa after a priest had dreamt of a dragon rising from the nearby river. The dream was interpreted as a sign that the emperor's spirit was uneasy and the temple was constructed as appeasement – hence the name *tenryū* (heavenly dragon). The present buildings date from 1900, but the main attraction is the 14th-century Zen garden.

ŌKŌCHI SANSŌ 大河内山荘

This **villa** (☎ 872-2233; Saga Ogura-yama; admission ¥1000; ⏰ 9am-5pm) is the home of Ōkōchi Denjiro, an actor in samurai films. The gardens allow fine views over the city and are open to visitors. The admission fee is hefty but includes tea and a cake. The villa is a 10-minute walk through bamboo groves north of Tenryū-ji.

GIŌ-JI 祇王寺

This quiet **temple** (☎ 861-3574; Saga Nisonin Monzen-chō; admission ¥300; ⏰ 9am-5pm) was named for the Heian-era *shirabyōshi* (traditional dancer) Giō. Giō, aged 21, committed herself here as a nun after her romance with Taira-no-Kiyomori, the mighty commander of the Heike clan. She was usurped by a fellow entertainer Hotoke Gozen (who later deserted Kiyomori to join Giō at the temple). Enshrined in the main hall are five wooden statues: these are Giō, Hotoke Gozen, Kiyomori, and Giō's mother and sister (who were also nuns at the temple).

ADASHINO NEMBUTSU-JI 化野念仏寺

This rather unusual **temple** (☎ 861-2221; Sagatorii Moto Adashino-chō; admission ¥500; ⏰ 9am-4.30pm) is where the abandoned bones of paupers and destitutes without next of kin were gathered. Thousands of stone images are crammed into the temple grounds, and these abandoned souls are remembered each year with candles here in the **Sentō Kuyō ceremony** held on the evenings of 23 and 24 August.

DAIKAKU-JI 大覚寺

This **temple** (☎ 871-0071; Saga Osawa-chō; admission ¥500; ⏰ 9am-4.30pm) is a 25-minute walk (about 2km) northeast of Nison-in, 100m north of Daikaku-ji bus stop on the Nos 28 and 91 bus routes. It was built in the 9th century as a palace for Emperor Saga, who converted it into a temple. The present buildings date from the 16th century but

are still palatial in style, with some impressive paintings. The large pond, **Osawa-no-ike**, was once used by the emperor for boating. Close to the temple entrance, there are separate terminals for Kyoto city buses (bus No 28 connects with Kyoto Station) and Kyoto buses (No 71 connects with Kyoto Station and No 61 with Keihan Sanjō Station).

TAKIGUCHI-DERA 滝口寺

The history of this temple reads like a Romeo and Juliet romance. **Takiguchi-dera** (☎ 871-3929; Saga Kameyama-chō; admission ¥300; ⏰ 9am-5pm) was founded by Heian-era nobleman Takiguchi Nyūdō, who entered the priesthood after being forbidden by his father to marry his peasant consort Yokobue. One day Yokobue came to the temple with her flute to serenade Takiguchi, but was again refused by him; she wrote a farewell love sonnet on a stone (in her own blood) before throwing herself into the river to perish. The stone remains at the temple.

NISON-IN 二尊院

Near Jōjakko-ji, **Nison-in** (☎ 861-0687; Saga Nison-in Monzen-chō; admission ¥500; ⏰ 9am-4.30pm) is in an attractive setting up the wooded hillside. The long approach to the temple, which is lined with lovely maple trees, is the biggest drawcard. Still, if you only have limited time, we recommend nearby Giō-ji.

JŌJAKKŌ-JI 常寂光寺

If you continue north of Ōkōchi Sansō (left), the narrow road soon passes stone steps on your left which lead up to the pleasant grounds of **Jōjakkō-ji** (☎ 861-0435; Saga Ogurayama; admission ¥300; ⏰ 9am-5pm). The temple is famous for its maple leaves and the Tahōtō pagoda. The upper area of the temple precincts afford good views east over Kyoto.

KAMEYAMA-KŌEN 亀山公園

Behind Tenryū-ji, this **park** is a nice place to escape the crowds of Arashiyama. It's laced with trails, the best of which leads to a lookout over Katsura-gawa and up into the Arashiyama mountains. Keep an eye out for the monkeys; and keep children well away from the occasionally nasty critters.

RAKUSHISHA 落柿舎

This **hut** (☎ 881-1953; Saga Ogura yama; admission ¥150; ⏰ 9am-5pm) belonged to Mukai Kyorai, the best-known disciple of illustrious haiku poet Bashō. Literally, 'House of the Fallen Persimmons'; legend holds that Kyorai dubbed the house Rakushisha after waking one morning after a storm to find the persimmons he had planned to sell from the garden's trees scattered on the ground.

HOZU-GAWA TRIP 保津川下り

The **Hozu-gawa river trip** (☎ 0771-22-5586; Hozu-cho Kameoka-shi; admission ¥3900; ◷ 9am-3.30pm, closed 29 Dec-4 Jan) is a great way to enjoy the beauty of Kyoto's western mountains without any strain on the legs. The river winds through steep, forested mountain canyons before it arrives at its destination, Arashiyama. Between 10 March and 30 November, there are seven trips (from 9am to 3.30pm) per day. During the winter, the number of trips is reduced to four per day and the boats are heated.

The ride lasts two hours and covers 16km between Kameoka and Arashiyama through occasional sections of white water – a scenic jaunt with minimal danger. The boats depart from a dock that is eight minutes on foot from Kameoka Station. Kameoka is accessible by rail from Kyoto Station or Nijō Station on the JR San-in (Sagano) main line. The Kyoto TIC provides a leaflet in English and a photocopied timetable sheet for rail connections. The train fare from Kyoto to Kameoka is ¥400 one way by regular train (don't spend the extra for the express as it makes little difference in time).

KYOTO OUTSKIRTS

Some of Kyoto's most interesting attractions lie outside the immediate city centre. For those with sufficient time to spend in Kyoto, a half-day or full-day trip to some of these attractions is well worth the effort.

Northeast Outskirts

HIEI-ZAN & ENRYAKU-JI 比叡山・延暦寺

A visit to 848m-high Hiei-zan and the vast **Enryaku-ji complex** (Map p332; ☎ 077-578-0001; Sakamoto Honmachi Ōtsu city; admission ¥550; ◷ 8.30am-4.30pm, closes earlier in winter) is a good way to spend half a day hiking, poking around temples and enjoying the atmosphere of a key site in Japanese history. Enryaku-ji was founded in 788 by Saichō, also known as Dengyō-daishi, the priest who established the Tendai school. From the 8th century the temple grew

in power; at its height it possessed some 3000 buildings and an army of thousands of *sōhei*, or warrior monks. In 1571 Oda Nobunaga saw the temple's power as a threat to his aims of unifying the nation and he destroyed most of the buildings, along with the monks inside. This school did not receive imperial recognition until 1823. Today only three pagodas and 120 minor temples remain.

The entire complex is divided into three sections – Tōtō, Saitō and Yokawa. The **Tōtō** (eastern pagoda section) contains the Kompon Chū-dō (primary central hall), which is the most important building in the complex. The flames on the three Dharma (the law, in Sanskrit) lamps in front of the altar have been kept lit for over 1200 years. The Daikō-dō (great lecture hall) displays life-size wooden statues of the founders of various Buddhist schools. This part of the temple is heavily geared to group access, with large expanses of asphalt for parking.

The **Saitō** (western pagoda section) contains the Shaka-dō, which dates from 1595 and houses a rare Buddha sculpture of the Shaka Nyorai (Historical Buddha). The Saitō, with its stone paths winding through forests of tall trees, temples shrouded in mist and the sound of distant gongs, is the most atmospheric part of the temple. Hold onto your ticket from the Tōtō section, as you may need to show it here.

The **Yokawa** is of minimal interest and a 4km bus ride away from the Saitō area. The Chū-dō (central hall) here was originally built in 848. It was destroyed by fire several times and has undergone repeated reconstructions (most recently in 1971). If you plan to visit here, as well as Tōtō and Saitō, allow a full day for in-depth exploration.

Getting There & Away

You can reach Hiei-zan and Enryaku-ji by either train or bus. The most interesting way is the train/cable car/ropeway route. If you're in a hurry or would like to save money, the best way is a direct bus from Sanjō Keihan or Kyoto Stations.

By train, take the Keihan line north to the last stop, Demachiyanagi, and change to the Yase-yūen/Hiei-bound Eizan Dentetsu Eizan-line train (be careful not to board the Kurama-bound train which sometimes leaves from the same platform). At the last stop, Yase-yūen (¥260), board the cable car

(¥530, nine minutes) and then the ropeway (¥310, three minutes) to the peak, from which you can walk down to the temples.

By bus, take Kyoto bus (not Kyoto city bus) No 17 or 18, which run from Kyoto Station to the Yase-yūen stop (¥390, about 50 minutes). From there it's a short walk to the cable car station.

Alternately, if you want to save money (by avoiding the cable car and ropeway) there are direct Kyoto buses from Kyoto and Keihan Sanjō Stations to Enryaku-ji, which take about 70 and 50 minutes respectively (both cost ¥800).

Northwest Outskirts

RYŌAN-JI 龍安寺

This **temple** (Map pp278-9; ☎ 463-2216; Ukyō-ku Ryōan-ji; admission ¥400; ⊙ 8am-5pm Mar-Nov, 8.30am-4.30pm Dec-Feb) belongs to the Rinzai school of Zen and was founded in 1450. The main attraction is the garden arranged in the *kare-sansui* (dry-landscape) style. An austere collection of 15 rocks, apparently adrift in a sea of sand, is enclosed by an earthen wall. The designer, who remains unknown, provided no explanation.

The viewing platform for the garden can be packed solid but the other parts of the temple grounds are also interesting and less of a target for the crowds. Among these, Kyoyo-chi pond is perhaps the most beautiful, particularly in autumn. Probably the best advice for Ryōan-ji is to come as early in the day as possible.

From Keihan Sanjō Station, take bus No 59 to the Ryōan-ji-mae stop.

NINNA-JI 仁和寺

This **temple** (Map pp278-9; ☎ 461-1155; web.kyoto-inet.or.jp/org/ninnaji/eigo.htm; Ukyō-ku, Omuroōuchi; admission ¥500; ⊙ 9.30am-4.30pm) was built in 842 and is the head temple of the Omura branch of the Shingon school of Buddhism. The present temple buildings, including a five-storey pagoda, are from the 17th century. The extensive grounds are full of cherry trees that bloom in early April.

Admission to most of the grounds is free, but separate admission fees are charged for some of the temple's buildings, many of which are closed most of the year. To get there, take bus No 59 from Keihan Sanjō Station and get off at the Omuro Ninna-ji stop. From Kyoto Station take bus No 26.

MYŌSHIN-JI 妙心寺

The vast temple complex **Myōshin-ji** (Map pp278-9; ☎ 461-5226; Ukyō-ku Hanazono Myoshin-ji-chō; admission ¥400; ⊙ 9.10am-3.40pm, closed 1hr at lunch) dates back to the 14th century, and belongs to the Rinzai school of Zen. There are over 40 temples, but only four are open to the public.

From the northern gate, follow the broad stone avenue flanked by rows of temples to the southern part of the complex.

The real highlight here is the wonderful garden of **Taizō-in** (Map pp278-9; admission ¥400; ⊙ 9am-5pm), a temple in the southwestern corner of the grounds.

The northern gate of Myōshin-ji is an easy 10-minute walk south of Ninna-ji; or take bus No 10 from Keihan Sanjō Station to the Myōshin-ji Kita-mon-mae stop.

TŌEI UZUMASA MOVIE VILLAGE
東映太秦映画村

In the Uzumasa area, **Tōei Uzumasa Movie Village** (Tōei Uzumasa Eiga Mura; Map pp278-9; ☎ 864-7716; Ukyo-ku, Uzumasa Higashi Hachioka-chō; admission adult/child under 6/child 6-18 ¥2200/1100/1300; ⊙ 9am-5pm Mar-Nov, 9.30am-4pm Dec-Feb) is one of Kyoto's most notorious tourist traps. However, it does have some recreations of Edo-period street scenes that give a decent idea of what Kyoto must have looked like before the advent of concrete.

The main conceit of the park is that real movies are actually filmed here. While this may occasionally be the case, more often than not this entails a bunch of bored flunkies being ordered around by an ersatz movie 'director' complete with megaphone and a vintage 1930s-era movie camera. This seems to delight some tourists but left us a little less than convinced.

Aside from this, there are displays relating to various aspects of Japanese movies and regular performances involving Japanese TV and movie characters like the Power Rangers. This should entertain the kids – adults will probably be a little bored.

KŌRYŪ-JI 広隆寺

One of the oldest temples in Japan, **Kōryū-ji** (Map pp278-9; ☎ 861-1461; Ukyō-ku Uzumasa Hachioka-chō; admission ¥700; ⊙ 9am-5pm Mar-Nov, 9am-4.30pm Dec-Feb) was founded in 622 to honour Prince Shōtoku, an enthusiastic promoter of Buddhism.

The Hattō (Lecture Hall), to the right of the main gate, houses a magnificent trio of 9th-century statues: Buddha flanked by manifestations of Kannon.

The Reihōkan (Treasure House) contains numerous fine Buddhist statues, including the Naki Miroku (Crying Miroku) and the world-renowned Miroku Bosatsu, which is extraordinarily expressive. A national upset occurred in 1960 when an enraptured (at least that's what he said) student clasped the statue and snapped off its little finger.

Take bus 11 from Keihan Sanjō Station, get off at the Ukyō-ku Sogo-chosha-mae stop and walk north. The temple is also close to Uzumasa Station on the Keifuku Arashiyama line.

Takao District 高雄エリア

Takao (Map pp278–9) is a secluded district tucked far away in the northwestern part of Kyoto. It is famed for autumn foliage and the temples of Jingo-ji, Saimyō-ji and Kōzan-ji.

Jingo-ji (神護寺; Map pp278-9; ☎ 861-1769; Ukyō-ku Takao-chō; admission ¥400; ⌚ 9am-4pm) is the best of the three temples in the Takao District. This mountain temple sits at the top of a long flight of stairs that stretch up from Kiyotaki-gawa to the temple's main gate. The Kondō (Gold Hall) is the most impressive of the temple's structures; it's roughly in the middle of the grounds; at the top of another flight of stairs.

After visiting the Kondō, head in the opposite direction along a wooded path to an open area overlooking the valley. Don't be surprised if you see people tossing small disks over the railing into the chasm below. These are *kawarakenage* – light clay disks that people throw to rid themselves of their bad karma. Be careful: it's addictive, and at ¥100 for two, it can become expensive. You can buy the disks at a nearby stall. The trick is to flick the disks very gently, convex side up, like a Frisbee. When you get it right, they sail all the way down the valley, taking all that bad karma away with them.

The other two temples are within easy walking distance of Jingo-ji; **Saimyō-ji** (西明寺; Map pp278-9; ☎ 861-1770; Umegahata Toganoo-chō Ukyō-ku; admission free; ⌚ 9am-5pm) is the better of the two. It's about five minutes' walk north of the base of the steps that lead up to Jingo-ji (follow the river upstream). To get to **Kōzan-ji** (高山寺; Map pp278-9; ☎ 861-4204; Umegahata Toganoo-chō Ukyō-ku; admission ¥600; ⌚ 8.30am-5pm) you must walk back up to the main road and follow it north for about 10 minutes.

There are two options for buses to Takao: an hourly JR bus from Kyoto Station which takes about an hour to reach the Takao stop (get off at the Yamashiro-Takao stop); and Kyoto city bus No 8 from Shijō-Karasuma (get off at the Takao stop). To get to Jingo-ji from these bus stops, walk down to the river then look for the steps on the other side.

Southwest Outskirts

KATSURA RIKYŪ 桂離宮

This **palace** (Katsura Detached Palace; Map pp278-9; ☎ 211-1215; Nishikyō-ku Katsura misono; admission free) is considered to be one of the finest examples of Japanese architecture. It was built in 1624 for the emperor's brother, Prince Toshihito. Every conceivable detail of the villa, the tea-houses, the large pond with islets and the surrounding garden has been given meticulous attention.

Tours (around 40 minutes), in Japanese, commence at 10am, 11am, 2pm and 3pm. You should be there 20 minutes beforehand. An explanatory video is shown in the waiting room and a leaflet is provided in English. You must make advance reservations with the Imperial Household Agency (p302). Visitors must be over 20 years of age.

To get to the villa from Kyoto Station, take bus No 33 and get off at the Katsura Rikyū-mae stop, which is a five-minute walk from the villa. The easiest access from the city centre is to take a Hankyū line train from Hankyū Kawaramachi Station to Hankyū Katsura Station, which is a 15-minute walk from the villa. Don't take a *tokkyū* (express) train as they don't stop in Katsura.

SAIHŌ-JI 西芳寺 (苔寺)

The main attraction at this **temple** (Map pp278-9; ☎ 391-3631; Nishikyō-ku Matsuo Jingatani-chō; admission ¥300, entry as part of tour only, must reserve in advance) is the heart-shaped garden, designed in 1339 by Musō Kokushi. The garden is famous for its luxuriant mossy growth, hence the temple's other name, Koke-dera (Moss Temple). Visiting the temple is recommended only if you have the time and patience to follow the reservation rules. If you don't, visit nearby Jizō-in (p308) to get a sense of the atmosphere of Saihō-ji without the expense or fuss.

KANSAI

Take bus No 28 from Kyoto Station to the Matsuo-taisha-mae stop and walk 15 minutes southwest. From Keihan Sanjō Station, take Kyoto bus No 63 to Koke-dera, the last stop, and walk for two minutes.

Reservations

To visit Saihō-ji, you must make a reservation. Send a postcard at least one week before the date you wish to visit and include details of your name, number of visitors, address in Japan, occupation, age (you must be over 18) and desired date (choice of alternative dates preferred). The address is Saihō-ji, 56 Kamigaya-chō, Matsuo, Nishikyō-ku, Kyoto-shi 615-8286. Enclose a stamped self-addressed postcard for a reply to your Japanese address. You might find it convenient to buy an Ōfuku-hagaki (send and return postcard set) at a Japanese post office.

You should arrive at the time and on the date indicated by the temple office. After paying your ¥3000 'donation', you must spend up to 90 minutes copying or chanting sutras (collection of dialogues and discourses) or doing Zen meditation before finally being guided around the garden for 90 minutes.

JIZŌ-IN 地蔵院

This delightful little **temple** (Map pp278-9; ☎ 381-3417; Nishikyō-ku Yamadakitano-chō; admission ¥500; ◑ 9am-4.30pm) could be called the 'poor man's Saihō-ji'. It's only a few minutes' walk south of Saihō-ji, in the same atmospheric bamboo groves. While the temple does not boast any spectacular buildings or treasures, it has a nice moss garden and is almost completely ignored by tourists, making it a great place to sit and think. For directions, see Saihō-ji p307.

Southeast Outskirts

FUSHIMI-INARI TAISHA 伏見稲荷大社

This intriguing **shrine** (Map pp278-9; ☎ 641-7331; Fushimi-ku Fukakusa Yabunouchi-chō; admission free; ◑ dawn-dusk) was dedicated to the gods of rice and sake by the Hata family in the 8th century. As the role of agriculture diminished, deities were enrolled to ensure prosperity in business. Nowadays, the shrine is one of Japan's most popular, and is the head shrine for some 30,000 Inari shrines scattered the length and breadth of Japan.

The entire complex, consisting of five shrines, sprawls across the wooded slopes

of Inari-yama. A pathway wanders 4km up the mountain and is lined with hundreds of red *torii*. There are also dozens of stone foxes. The fox is considered the messenger of Inari, the god of cereal grains. The Japanese traditionally see the fox as a sacred, somewhat mysterious figure capable of 'possessing' humans – the favoured point of entry is under the fingernails. The key often seen in the fox's mouth is for the rice granary.

The walk around the upper precincts of the shrine is a pleasant day hike. It also makes for a very eerie stroll in the late afternoon and early evening, when the various graveyards and miniature shrines along the path take on a mysterious air.

To get to the shrine from Kyoto Station, take a JR Nara line train to Inari Station. From Keihan Sanjō Station take the Keihan line to Fushimi-Inari Station. There is no admission charge for the shrine. The shrine is just east of both of these stations.

DAIGO-JI 醍醐寺

Daigo-ji (☎ 571-0002; Fushimi-ku Daigo Garan-chō; admission to grounds free, during cherry blossom & autumn foliage seasons ¥600; ◑ 9am-5pm) was founded in 874 by the priest Shobo, who gave it the name of Daigo. This refers to the five periods of Buddha's teaching, which were often compared to the five forms of milk prepared in India, the highest form of which is called *daigo* (ultimate essence of milk).

The temple was expanded into a vast complex of buildings on two levels – Shimo Daigo (Lower Daigo) and Kami Daigo (Upper Daigo). During the 15th century, the lower level buildings were destroyed, with the sole exception of the five-storey pagoda. Built in 951, this pagoda still stands and is lovingly noted as the oldest of its kind in Japan and the oldest existing building in Kyoto.

In the late 16th century, Hideyoshi took a fancy to Daigo-ji and ordered extensive rebuilding. It is now one of the main temples of the Shingon school of Buddhism. To explore Daigo-ji thoroughly and leisurely, mixing hiking with temple viewing, you will need at least half a day.

To get to Daigo-ji, take the Tōzai line subway from central Kyoto to the last stop, Daigo, and walk east (towards the mountains) for about 10 minutes. Make sure that the train you board is bound for Daigo, as some head to Hama-Ōtsu instead.

Sampo-in

Sampo-in (☎ 571-0002; Fushimi-ku Daigo Higashioji-chō; admission ¥600; ⏰ 9am-5pm) was founded as a sub-temple (of Daigo-ji; see opposite) in 1115, but received a total revamp under Hideyoshi's orders in 1598. It is now a fine example of the amazing opulence of that period. The Kanō paintings and the garden are special features.

The garden is jam-packed with about 800 stones – the Japanese mania for stones goes back a long way. The most famous stone here is Fujito-no-ishi, which is linked to deception, death and a fabulous price that was spurned; it's even the subject of a *nō* play, *Fujito*.

Climb to Daigo-yama

From Sampō-in, walk up the large avenue of cherry trees, through Niō-mon gate and past the pagoda. From there you can continue for a steep climb through the upper part of Daigo-yama, browsing through temples and shrines on the way. Allow at least 50 minutes to reach the top.

UJI 宇治

Uji is a small city to the south of Kyoto. Its main claims to fame are Byōdō-in and tea cultivation. The stone bridge at Uji – the oldest of its kind in Japan – has been the scene of many bitter clashes in previous centuries.

Uji can be reached by rail in about 40 minutes from Kyoto on the Keihan Uji line or JR Nara line.

When arriving in Uji by Keihan train, leave the station, cross the river via the first bridge on the right, and then turn left to find Byōdō-in. When coming by JR, the temple is about 10 minutes' walk east (towards the river) of Uji Station.

Byōdō-in 平等院

This **Buddhist temple** (Map pp278-9; ☎ 0774-21-2861; Uji-shi Uji renge; admission ¥600; ⏰ 8.30am-5.30pm Mar-Nov, 9am-4pm Dec-Feb) was converted from a Fujiwara villa in 1052. The Hōō-dō (Phoenix Hall), more properly known as the Amida-dō, was built in 1053 and is the only original remaining building. The phoenix was a popular mythical bird in China and was revered by the Japanese as a protector of Buddha. The architecture of the building resembles the shape of the bird, and there are two bronze phoenixes perched opposite each other on the roof. The building

was originally intended to represent Amida's heavenly palace in the Pure Land. This building is one of the few extant examples of Heian-period architecture, and its graceful lines make one wish that far more of its type had survived Kyoto's past.

Inside the hall is the famous statue of Amida and 52 Bosatsu (Bodhisattvas) dating from the 11th century and attributed to the priest-sculptor Jōchō.

The temple, complete with its reflection in a pond, is one of Japan's top attractions and draws huge crowds. For a preview without the masses, take a look at the ¥10 coin.

Far Northern Outskirts

ŌHARA 大原

Since ancient times Ōhara, a quiet farming town about 10km north of Kyoto, has been regarded as a holy site by followers of the Jōdo school. The region provides a charming glimpse of rural Japan, along with the picturesque Sanzen-in, Jakkō-in and several other fine temples. It's most popular in autumn, when the maple leaves change colour and the mountain views are spectacular. During the peak foliage season (late October to mid-November) avoid this area on weekends as it will be packed.

Sanzen-in 三千院

Founded in 784 by the priest Saicho, **Sanzen-in** (Map p293; ☎ 744-2531; Ōhara Raikōin-chō; admission ¥600; ⏰ 8.30am-4.30pm Feb-Dec, 8.30am-4pm Jan) belongs to the Tendai sect of Buddhism. Saicho, considered one of the great patriarchs of Buddhism in Japan, also founded Enraku-ji on nearby Hiei-zan. The temple's Yusei-en is one of the most photographed gardens in Japan, and rightly so. Take some time to sit on the steps of the Shin-den Hall and admire its beauty.

After seeing Yusei-en, head off to the Ojo-gokuraku Hall (Temple of Rebirth in Paradise) to see the impressive Amitabha trinity, a large Amida image flanked by attendants Kannon and Seishi, gods of mercy and wisdom, respectively. After this, walk up to the hydrangea garden at the back of the temple, where, in late spring and summer, you can walk among hectares of blooming hydrangeas.

If you feel like a short hike after leaving the temple, head up the hill around the right side of the temple to the **Soundless**

KANSAI

Waterfall (you'll note that it sounds pretty much like any other waterfall). The sound of this waterfall is said to have inspired Shomyo Buddhist chanting.

To get to Sanzen-in, follow the signs from Ōhara's main bus stop up the hill past a long arcade of souvenir stalls. The entrance is on your left as you crest the hill.

Jakkō-in寂光院

The history of **Jakkō-in** (Map p293; ☎ 744-2545; Ōhara Kusao-chō; admission ¥500; ⏰ 9am-5pm) is exceedingly tragic. The actual founding date of the temple is subject to some debate (somewhere between the 6th and 11th centuries), but it acquired fame as the temple which harboured Kenrei Mon-in, a lady of the Taira clan. In 1185 the Taira were soundly defeated in a sea battle with the Minamoto clan at Dan-no-ura. With the entire Taira clan slaughtered or drowned, Kenrei Mon-in threw herself into the waves with her son Antoku, the infant emperor; she was fished out – the only member of the clan to survive.

She was returned to Kyoto, where she became a nun living in a bare hut until it collapsed during an earthquake. Kenrei Mon-in was accepted into Jakkō-in and stayed there, immersed in prayer and sorrowful memories, until her death 27 years later. Her tomb is located high on the hill behind the temple.

Unfortunately the main building of the temple burned down in May 2000 and the newly reconstructed main hall is lacking some of the charm of the original. Nonetheless, it's a nice spot.

Jakkō-in lies to the west of Ōhara. Walk out of the bus station up the road to the traffic lights, then follow the small road to the left. Since it's easy to get lost on the way, we recommend familiarising yourself with the kanji for Jakkō-in (see above) and following the Japanese signs.

KURAMA & KIBUNE 鞍馬・貴船

Only 30 minutes north of Kyoto on the Eiden Eizan main line, Kurama and Kibune are a pair of tranquil valleys long favoured by Kyoto-ites as places to escape the crowds and stresses of the city below. Kurama's main attractions are its mountain temple and its *onsen* (hot spring bath). Kibune, over the ridge, is a cluster of ryokan overlooking a mountain stream, which is best

enjoyed in the summer, when the ryokan serve dinner on platforms built over the rushing waters of Kibune-gawa, providing welcome relief from the summer heat.

The two valleys lend themselves to being explored together. In the winter, one can start from Kibune, walk for an hour or so over the ridge, visit Kurama-dera and then soak in the *onsen* before heading back to Kyoto. In the summer, the reverse is best; start from Kurama, walk up to the temple, then down the other side to Kibune to enjoy a meal suspended above the cool river.

If you happen to be in Kyoto on the night of 22 October, be sure not to miss the Kurama-no-hi Matsuri (Kurama Fire Festival; p312), one of the most exciting festivals in the Kyoto area.

To get to Kurama and Kibune, take the Eiden Eizan line from Kyoto's Demachi-yanagi Station. For Kibune, get off at the second-to-last stop, Kibune Guchi, take a right out of the station and walk about 20 minutes up the hill. For Kurama, go to the last stop, Kurama, and walk straight out of the station. Both destinations are ¥410 and take about 30 minutes to reach.

Kurama-dera鞍馬寺

This **temple** (Map p293; ☎ 741-2003; Sakyō-ku Kurama Honmachi; admission ¥200; ⏰ 9am-4.30pm) was established in 770 by the monk Gantei from Nara's Tōshōdai-ji. After seeing a vision of the deity Bishamon-ten, guardian of the northern quarter of the Buddhist heaven, he established Kurama-dera in its present location, just below the peak of Kurama-yama. Originally belonging to the Tendai sect, Kurama has been independent since 1949, describing its own brand of Buddhism as Kurama Kyō.

The entrance to the temple is just up the hill from the Eiden Eizan main line's Kurama Station. A tram goes to the top for ¥100; alternatively, hike up by following the main path past the tram station. The trail is worth taking if it's not too hot, as it winds through a forest of towering old-growth *sugi* (cryptomeria) trees. At the top, there is a courtyard dominated by the Honden (Main Hall). Behind the Honden, a trail leads off to the mountain's peak.

At the top, those who want to continue to Kibune can take the trail down the other side. It's a 45-minute hike from the Honden of Kurama-dera to the valley floor of Kibune. On the way down there are two pleasant mountain shrines.

Kurama Onsen 鞍馬温泉
One of the few *onsen* within easy reach of Kyoto, **Kurama Onsen** (Map p293; ☎ 741-2131; Sakyō-ku Kurama Honmachi; admission ¥1100; ☉ 10am-9pm) is a great place to relax after a hike. The outdoor bath, with a fine view of Kurama-yama, costs ¥1100. The inside bath costs ¥2300, but even with the use of sauna and locker thrown in, it's difficult to imagine why one would opt for the indoor bath. For both baths, buy a ticket from the machine outside the door of the main building (instructions are in Japanese and English).

To get to Kurama Onsen, walk straight out of Kurama Station, turn left up the main road and follow it for about 10 minutes. You'll see the baths down on your right. There's also a free shuttle bus that runs between the station and the *onsen*, leaving approximately every 30 minutes.

Kibune-jinja 貴船神社
This **shrine** (Map p293; ☎ 741-2016; Kibune-chō Kurama; admission free; ☉ dawn-dusk), halfway up the valley, is worth a quick look, particularly if you can ignore the unfortunate plastic horse statue at its entrance. Admission is free. From Kibune you can hike over the mountain to Kurama-dera, along a trail that starts halfway up the village on the eastern side (or vice versa – see opposite).

ACTIVITIES
Baths
FUNAOKA ONSEN 船岡温泉
This old **bath** (Map pp280-1; ☎ 441-3735; 82-1 Minami-Funaoka-chō-Murasakino Kita-ku; admission ¥350; ☉ 3pm-1am Mon-Sat, 8am-1am Sun & holidays) on Kuramaguchi-dōri is the best in all of Kyoto. Funaoka Onsen boasts an outdoor bath, a sauna, a cypress-wood tub, an electric bath, a herbal bath and a few more for good measure. Be sure to check out the *ranma* (carved wooden panels) in the changing room. Carved during Japan's invasion of Manchuria, the panels offer insight into the prevailing mindset of that era (frankly, we're surprised that they haven't been taken down, due to their violent content, which would be sure to upset Chinese visitors to the bath).

To find it, head west about 400m on Kuramaguchi-dōri from the Kuramaguchi-Horiikawa intersection. It's on the left not far past Lawson convenience store. Look for the large rocks out the front.

GOKŌ-YU 五香湯
This popular **bath** (Map pp284-5; ☎ 841-7321; 590-1 Kakinomoto-chō-Gojō agaru Kuromon-dōri; admission ¥350; ☉ 2.30pm-12.30am Mon-Sat, 7am-midnight Sun, 11am-midnight holidays, closed Mon & 3rd Tue of each month) is another great spot to sample the joys of the *sentō* (public bathhouse). It's a large two-storey bath with a wide variety of tubs. There's also a giant sauna with two rooms; one is merely hot, the other is incendiary! We also like the TV–fish tank in the entrance (you'll see what we mean). Note that Gokoyu is a little hard to find – turn north of Gojō-dōri at a store that sells charcoal and gas burners.

SHŌMEN-YU 正面湯
Perhaps the mother of all *sentō*, **Shōmen-yu** (Map p291; ☎ 561-3232; 310 Shōmen-chō-Shōmen agaru Sayamachi-dōri-Higashiyama-ku; admission ¥350; ☉ 1pm-1am Mon, Wed-Sat, 9am-1am Sun) is three storeys high, with an outdoor bath on the roof. This is your chance to try riding an elevator naked (if you haven't already had the pleasure). Everything is on a grand scale here, including the sauna, which boasts a TV and room for 20. Men, don't be surprised if you spot some *yakuza* (gangsters) among the bathers (recognisable by their tattoos). It's a five-minute walk from Keihan Shichijō Station.

FESTIVALS & EVENTS
There are hundreds of festivals in Kyoto throughout the year. Listings can be found in *Kyoto Visitor's Guide*, *Kansai Time Out* or weekend editions of the *Japan Times* and the *Yomiuri Daily*. The following are some of the major or most spectacular festivals. These attract hordes of spectators from out of town, so book accommodation well in advance.

February
Setsubun Matsuri at Yoshida-jinja (3 or 4 February; check with the TIC) This festival is held on the day of *setsubun*, which marks the last day of winter in the Japanese lunar calendar. In this festival, people climb up to Yoshida-jinja in the northern Higashiyama area to watch a huge bonfire. It's one of Kyoto's more dramatic festivals. The action starts at dusk.

PRIVATE TOURS OF KYOTO

A private tour is a great way to see the sights and learn about the city without having to worry about transport and logistics. There are a variety of private tours on offer in Kyoto.

All Japan Private Tours & Speciality Services (www.kyotoguide.com/yjpt) This company offers exclusive unique tours of Kyoto, Nara and Tokyo as well as business coordination and related services.

Chris Rowthorn's Walks and Tours of Kyoto and Japan (www.chrisrowthorn.com) Lonely Planet *Kyoto* and *Japan* author Chris Rowthorn offers private tours of Kyoto, Nara, Osaka and other parts of Japan.

Johnnie's Kyoto Walking (http://web.kyoto-inet.or.jp/people/h-s-love/) Hirooka Hajime, aka Johnnie Hillwalker, offers an interesting guided walking tour of the area around Kyoto Station and the Higashiyama area.

Naoki Doi (☎ 090 9596 5546; www3.ocn.ne.jp/~doitaxi/) This English-speaking taxi driver offers private taxi tours of Kyoto and Nara.

Peter MacIntosh (☎ 090-5169-1654; www.kyotosightsandnights.com) Canadian Peter MacIntosh offers guided walks through Kyoto's geisha districts. He can also arrange geisha entertainment in Kyoto teahouses and restaurants.

May

Aoi Matsuri (Hollyhock Festival; 15 May) This festival dates back to the 6th century and commemorates the successful prayers of the people for the gods to stop calamitous weather. Today, the procession involves imperial messengers in ox carts and a retinue of 600 people dressed in traditional costume; hollyhock leaves are carried or used as decoration. The procession leaves at around 10am from the Kyosho Gosho and heads for Shimogamo-jinja, where ceremonies take place. It sets out from here again at 2pm and arrives at Kamigamo-jinja at 3.30pm.

July

Gion Matsuri (17 July) Perhaps the most renowned of all Japanese festivals, this one reaches a climax on the 17th with a parade of over 30 floats depicting ancient themes and decked out in incredible finery. On the three evenings preceding the main day, people gather on Shijō-dōri, many dressed in beautiful *yukata* (light summer kimono), to look at the floats and carouse from one street stall to the next.

August

Daimon-ji Gozan Okuribi (16 August) This festival, commonly known as Daimon-ji Yaki, is performed to bid farewell to the souls of ancestors. Enormous fires are lit on five mountains in the form of Chinese characters or other shapes. The fires are lit at 8pm and it is best to watch from the banks of Kamo-gawa or pay for a rooftop view from a hotel. Better yet, head up to Hirosawano-ike in northwestern Kyoto, rent a rowing boat and watch *torii-gata* (the character for 'gate') burn over the pond. Here, in addition to the burning figure, people float hundreds of lanterns with burning candles inside them on the surface of the pond – the effect is magical.

October

Kurama-no-hi Matsuri (Kurama Fire Festival; 22 October) In perhaps Kyoto's most dramatic festival, huge flaming torches are carried through the streets by men in loincloths. The festival climaxes around 10pm at Yuki-jinja

(Map p293) in the village of Kurama, which is 30 minutes by train from Kyoto Station on the Eiden Eizan Line. The train leaves from Demachiyanagi Station.

Jidai Matsuri (Festival of the Ages; 22 October) This festival is of recent origin, only dating back to 1895. More than 2000 people, dressed in costumes ranging from the 8th century to the 19th century, parade from Kyoto Gosho to Heian-jingū.

SLEEPING

Kyoto has the widest range of foreigner-friendly accommodation in all Japan, with a variety of options in every budget range. Choices range from the country's finest and most expensive ryokan to youth hostels and funky old guesthouses. Kyoto is a good place in which to sample the ryokan experience, and there are dozens of inexpensive ryokan in the city that specialise in serving foreign guests.

Keep in mind that the most convenient areas in which to be based, in terms of easy access to shopping, dining and most of the major attractions, are eastern and southwestern Kyoto.

Transport information is from Kyoto Station unless otherwise noted.

For details on hotels near Itami airport see p348, near Kansai airport see p349.

Kyoto Station Area   Map p291
BUDGET

Tour Club (☎ 353-6968; www.kyotojp.com; Higashinakasuji, Shōmen agaru; dm ¥2415, d ¥6980-7770, tr ¥8880-9345) Run by a charming and informative young couple, this clean, well-maintained guesthouse is a favourite of many foreign visitors. Facilities include Internet access, bicycle rentals, laundry, money exchange and free tea and coffee. All private rooms have a private bath and toilet, and there is a spacious quad room for families. This is probably the best choice in this price bracket. It's a 10-minute walk from Kyoto Station; turn north off of Shichijō-dōri at the Second House coffee shop (looks like a bank) and keep an eye out for the Japanese flag.

Budget Inn (☎ 344-1510; www.budgetinnjp.com; Aburanokōji-Shichijō sagaru; dm/tr/q ¥2500/9900/11,990) This new guesthouse is an excellent choice. It's got two dorm rooms and six private rooms, all of which are clean and well maintained. All rooms have their own bath and toilet, and there is a spacious quad room which is good for families. The staff here is very helpful and friendly and Internet access, laundry and bicycle rental are available. All in all, this is a great choice in this price range. It's a seven-minute walk from Kyoto Station; from the station, walk west on Shiokōji-dōri and turn north at the Esso Station (one street before Horikawa) and look for the English-language sign out front.

Riverside Takase (☎ 351-7925; www.upwell.jp /kyoto/takase.html; Kiyamachi-dōri-Kaminokuchi agaru; s/d/tr ¥3300/6400/9600) With five decent rooms, this place is a 15-minute walk from Kyoto Station or take bus No 17 or 205 from Kyoto Station (stand A2, 10 minutes). Get off when at the Kawaramachi-Shōmen stop.

Ryokan Hiraiwa (☎ 351-6748; fax 351-6969; www2 .odn.ne.jp/hiraiwa/Index_e.htm; Kaminokuchi agaru-Ninomiyacho-dōri; r per person ¥4240-5250) This ryokan is used to foreigners and offers basic tatami rooms. It is close to both central and eastern Kyoto.

Ryokan Murakamiya (☎ 371-1260; www2.odn .ne.jp/ryokanmurakamiya/etop.html; Shichijō-agaru-Higashinotōin-dōri; r per person ¥4700) This homely little ryokan is conveniently located close to the station. Like other ryokan in this class, it's simple and clean.

Ryokan Kyōka (☎ 371-2709; web.kyoto-inet.or.jp /people/kyoka/kyoka.html; Shimojyuzuyamachi-dōri-Higashinotōin; r per person without bath ¥4200) Getting a little long in the tooth, this ryokan has 10 fairly spacious rooms. It's fairly close to Kyoto Station and also within walking distance of downtown.

Ryokan Ōtō (☎ 541-7803; fax 541-7804; Shichijō-dōri-Kamogawa higashi; s/d/tr from ¥4000/7600/11,000) A member of the Japanese Inn Group, the Ōtō is a decent choice but lacks the atmosphere of some of Kyoto's other ryokan. The location is pretty good for exploring the southern Higashiyama area.

K's House Kyoto (☎ 342-2444; kshouse.jp/index .html; Shichijō agaru-Dotemachi-dōri; dm ¥2500, s/d/tw per person from ¥3500/2900/2900) K's House is a large new guesthouse with both private and dorm rooms. The rooms are simple but adequate and there are spacious common areas. It's about a 10-minute walk from Kyoto Station.

Yuhara Ryokan (☎ 371-9583; fax 371-9583; Shōmen agaru-Kiyamachi-dōri; r per person ¥4200) With a riverside location and a family atmosphere, Yuhara is popular with foreigners. It's a short walk from the attractions on downtown and eastern Kyoto.

MIDRANGE

Hotel Granvia Kyoto (☎ 344-8888; www.granvia -kyoto.co.jp/e/; Shiokōji sagaru-Karasuma-dōri; s/d/tw ¥14,000/18,000/20,000) Built into the station building right over Kyoto Station, this hotel is gleaming and new and takes the prize in terms of convenient location. It has an extensive variety of restaurants and bars on its premises, and spacious and modern rooms.

Kyoto New Hankyū Hotel (☎ 343-5300; hotel. newhankyu.co.jp/kyoto-e/index.html; Shiokōji-dōri; s/d/ tw from ¥13,860/27,720/25,410) Across the street from Kyoto Station, this hotel has clean but rather drab rooms.

APA Hotel (☎ 365-4111, fax 365-8720; ahkyoto@apa .co.jp; Nishinotōin-Shiokōji kudaru; s/tw from ¥8000/15,000) This new business hotel has competitive rates. It's only five minutes on foot from Kyoto Station, making it a good choice for those with early morning departures.

Hotel Hokke Club Kyoto (☎ 361-1251; Karasuma-Central gate, Kyoto Station; s/tw from ¥8400/13,650) Directly opposite the northern side of Kyoto Station. It sometimes offers special rates on double and twin rooms – ask when reserving or checking in.

TOP END

Rihga Royal Hotel Kyoto (☎ 341-1121; www.rihga .com/kyoto/; Horikawa-Shiokōji; s¥13,000-20,000, d¥21,000-30,000, tw ¥16,000-27,000) A large hotel with a swimming pool and several good restaurants on the premises. It's a 10-minute walk from Kyoto Station.

Downtown Kyoto   Map p289
MIDRANGE

Hotel Gimmond (☎ 221-4111; www.gimmond.co.jp /kyoto/khome-e.htm; Takakura-dōri-Oike-dōri; s/d/tw from

¥9586/16,170/16,747) Centrally located and clean, this is justifiably popular with foreign visitors. It's very close to Oike Station on the Karasuma line subway.

Sun Hotel Kyoto (☎ 241-3351; Kawaramachi-dōri-Sanjō kudaru; s/d/tw ¥8505/12,810/12,810) Our favourite business hotel in Kyoto has small but clean rooms. It's right in the heart of Kyoto's nightlife district. From Kyoto Station take bus 5 (stand A1, 20 minutes) to the Kawaramachi-Sanjō stop, then backtrack for 100m.

TOP END

Hiiragiya Ryokan (☎ 221-1136; www.hiiragiya.co.jp /en/; Fuyachō-Aneyakōji-agaru; r per person ¥30,000-60,000 with 2 meals) Impossibly elegant, this place is favoured by celebrities from around the world. From the art displayed in the rooms, to the service, to the food, everything at the Hiiragiya is the best available.

Tawaraya Ryokan (☎ 211-5566; fax 221-2204; Fuyachō-Oike kudaru; r per person ¥35,000-75,000) Tawaraya has been operating for over three centuries and is classed as one of the finest places to stay in the world. Guests at this ryokan have included the imperial family and overseas royalty. It is a classic in every sense. Reservations are essential, preferably many months ahead.

Kyoto Hotel Ōkura (☎ 211-5111; www.kyotohotel .co.jp/oike/index_e.html; Kawaramachi-Oike; s/d/tw from ¥16,000/28,000/22,000) An enormous new place right in the centre of town at the Oike-Kawaramachi intersection and commanding an impressive view of the Higashiyama mountains. Rooms here are spacious and well maintained.

Kinmata Ryokan (☎ 221-1039; fax 231-7632; Shijō agaru-Gokōmachi-dōri; r per person ¥40,000-50,000 with 2 meals) Kinmata commenced operations early in the 19th century and this is reflected in the original décor, interior gardens and *hinoki* (cypress) bathroom. The exquisite *kaiseki* meals alone are a good reason to stay here. It's in the centre of town, close to Nishiki Market.

Southeast Kyoto   Map pp286–7

BUDGET

Higashiyama Youth Hostel (☎ 761-8135; Sanjō-dōri-Shirakawabashi; dm ¥2650) This is close to the sights of Higashiyama. It's very regimented, but if you're the kind of person who likes being in bed by 9.30pm, this might suit. To get there,

take bus No 5 from Kyoto Station (stand A1, 30 minutes) to the Higashiyama-Sanjō stop.

MIDRANGE

Ryokan Uemura (☎ /fax 561-0377; Ishibe-kōji-Shimogawara; r per person ¥9000 with breakfast) This beautiful little ryokan is at ease with foreign guests. It's on a quaint cobblestone alley, just down the hill from Kōdai-ji. Rates include breakfast, and there is a 10pm curfew. Book well in advance, as there are only three rooms. Note that the manager prefers bookings by fax and asks that cancellations also be made by fax (with so few rooms, it can be costly when bookings are broken without notice). Take bus No 206 from Kyoto Station (stand D2, 15 minutes) and get off at Yasui bus stop, then walk in the direction of Kōdai-ji.

Hotel Fujita Kyoto (☎ 222-1511; information@fujita -kyoto.com; Kamogawa Nijō-Ōhashi Hotori; s/d/tw from ¥10,395/26,565/18,480) In the middle of town, this has good rooms. It is convenient to the nightlife areas and many sightseeing spots.

Hotel Heian No Mori Kyoto (☎ 761-9111; fax 761-1333; Okazaki Higashitenno-chō; d/tw from ¥9900/12,100) This large, pleasant hotel is located close to the Higashiyama mountains. It's close to Ginkaku-ji, Nanzen-ji and the Tetsugaku-no-michi (Path of Philosophy). The rooftop beer garden is perfect for summer drinking.

Kyoto Traveller's Inn (☎ 771-0225; traveler@mbox .kyoto-inet.or.jp; Heianjingū Torii-mae; s/tw ¥6825/12,600) This business hotel is very close to Heian-jingū, offering Western- and Japanese-style rooms. The restaurant on the 1st floor is open till 10pm. It's good value for the price.

Gion Fukuzumi (☎ 541-5181; www.gion-fukuzumi .com/eng/index.html; Shinbashi-nishiiru-Higashiōji; r per person from ¥8000) The Gion Fukuzumi is a group tour–oriented ryokan housed in a Western-style building. It has clean, new rooms and is in a good Gion location.

Three Sisters Inn Annex (Rakutō-so Bekkan; ☎ 761-6333; Irie-chō-Okazaki; s/d without bathroom ¥5635/11,270, s/d with bathroom ¥10,810/18,170, tr with bathroom ¥23,805) In the same neighbourhood, this is run by another one of the three eponymous sisters, and is an excellent choice. Close to Heian-jingū, this pleasant little inn is popular with foreign guests. The features are similar to the main building (p316), but it's somewhat more intimate and the garden walkway adds to the atmosphere. Take bus No 5 from Kyoto Station (stand A1, 30 minutes), get off at Dōbutsuen-mae stop and walk for five minutes.

TOP END

Westin Miyako Hotel (☎ 771-7111; www.westinmiyako -kyoto.com; Sanjō-dōri-Keage; s/d/tw from ¥23,000/25,000/ 23,000, Japanese-style r from ¥35,000) Perched on the mountains, this is a graceful hotel and a choice for visiting foreign dignitaries. The surroundings stretch over 6.4 hectares of hillside and gardens. Prices increase weekends.

Yachiyo Ryokan (☎ 771-4148; fax 771-4140; Fukuchi-chō; r per person from ¥18,000 with 2 meals) Located just down the street from Nanzen-ji temple, this large ryokan is at home with foreign guests. Rooms are spacious and clean, and some look out over private gardens. English-speaking staff are available.

Southwest Kyoto
Map pp284–5

BUDGET
Crossroads Inn (www.rose.sannet.ne.jp/c-inn/; Ebisu Banba-chō- Shimogyō-ku; r per peson from ¥4000) Crossroads Inn is a charming little guesthouse with clean, well-maintained rooms and a friendly owner. It's good value but a little hard to find: turn north off Shichijō-dōri just west of the Umekōji-kōen-mae bus stop across from the Daily Yamazaki convenience store. Reservations are by email only.

Ryokan Hinomoto (☎ 351-4563; http://members .aol.com/innmember3/inn3/11hinomo.html; Matsubara agaru-Kawaramachi-dōri; s/d from ¥4000/7500) This is most convenient to the nightlife action and has a nice wooden bathtub. Take bus No 17 or 205 from Kyoto Station (stand A2, 1pp282–3, 5 minutes) and get off at the Kawaramachi-matsubara stop.

J Hoppers Kyoto (☎ /fax 681-2282; www.j-hoppers .com/index.htm; Nakagoryo-chō-Higashi kujō; dm ¥2500, r ¥3000-3500) Located on the south side of Kyoto Station, J Hoppers is a popular guesthouse with a variety of private rooms and dorms. It's quite close to some southern attractions like Tōfuku-ji and Fushimi.

Uno House (☎ 231-7763; Shinkarasuma-dōri; dm ¥1650, s from ¥2250, r ¥7500) This is a long-time fixture of the Kyoto guesthouse scene and has a convenient central location and casual atmosphere. Sure, it's a little noisy and run down, but you can't beat the price. Take the Karasuma line subway from Kyoto Station, get off at the Marutamachi stop (seven minutes) and walk east for 10 minutes.

MIDRANGE
Kyoto ANA Hotel (☎ 231-1155; www.anahotels.com /eng/hotels/uky/index.html; Nijō-jō-mae-Horikawa-dōri; s/

d/tw from ¥13,000/19,000/16,000) A good choice in terms of on-site facilities (pool, restaurants, shopping). It's just opposite Nijō-jō.

International Hotel Kyoto (☎ 222-1111; information@kyoto-kokusai.com; Nijōjō-mae-Horikawa-dōri; s/d from ¥8085/18,480 tw ¥16,170-31,185) Directly across from Nijō-jō, this is a slightly less appealing choice than the nearby Kyoto ANA Hotel. It's a large facility that is used to foreign guests.

Karasuma Kyoto Hotel (☎ 371-0111; www.kyoto hotel.co.jp/karasuma/index_e.html; Karasuma-dōri-Aneyakōji; s/d/tw ¥8800/20,000/16,000) A good midtown choice, with clean, fairly new rooms. It's a five-minute walk from Shijō Station on the Karasuma line subway.

Hirota Guest House (☎ 221-2474; h-hirota@msi.biglo be.ne.jp; Tominokōji-nishi-Nijō-dōri; r per person from ¥5500, ste per person ¥7000, private cottage per person ¥9000) Unassuming from the outside, the popular Hirota is a pleasant Japanese-style inn in an old sake brewery. Its cheerful English-speaking owner, Hirota-san, is a former tour guide and a valuable source of information.

TOP END
Hiiragiya Ryokan Annex (☎ 231-0151; Gokōmachi-dōri-Nijō kudaru; r per person from ¥15,000 with 2 meals) Not far from the Hiiragiya main building, the Hiiragiya Ryokan Annex offers top-notch ryokan service (with two meals) and surroundings, but at slightly more affordable rates.

Kyoto Tōkyū Hotel (☎ 341-2411; www.tokyuhotels .co.jp/en/index.html; Horikawa-dōri-Gojō kudaru; s/d/tw from ¥18,480/28,875/30,030) This is a big, modern hotel with large rooms and good facilities. It's on the south side of town, but within walking distance of Kyoto Station.

Northeast Kyoto
Map pp282–3

BUDGET
Yonbanchi (yonbanchi@mac.com; 4, Shinnyo-chō; r per person ¥5000) This charming B&B has an excellent location for sightseeing in the Ginkaku-ji/Yoshida-yama area. One of the two guest rooms, which sleeps up to three people, looks out over a small Japanese garden. The house is a late–Edo-period samurai house located just outside the main gate of Shinnyo-dō, a temple famed for its maple leaves and cherry blossoms. There is a private entrance and no curfew. Reservation is via email only.

Casa Carinho B&B (www.gotokandk.com; Jōdo-ji-Nish-ida-chō; r per person ¥5000) Located close to Ginkaku-ji, this cosy guesthouse has two Japanese-style

KANSAI

rooms, and is run by a charming couple with a wealth of inside information on Kyoto. Reservation is via email only.

Kaguraya B&B (kaguraya@mac.com; Sakyō-ku-Kaguraoka-chō 8; d per person ¥5000, s per person ¥7500) Kaguraya is 100-year-old traditional Japanese house, with a garden and panoramic views of the eastern hills of Kyoto. Two large rooms are available. A Western breakfast is provided and bicycle hire available. Reservation is via email only.

ISE Dorm (771-0566; Higashi-Fukunokawa-chō; r per day ¥2800, per month ¥20,000-56,000) Basic short- and long-term accommodation. Facilities on offer include phone, fridge, aircon, shower and washing machine. On the negative side, the place can be noisy. Take bus 206 from Kyoto Station (stand D2, 30 minutes) to the Kumano-jinja-mae stop.

MIDRANGE

Holiday Inn Kyoto (721-3131; onetoone@hi-kyoto.co.jp; Nishibiraki-chō-Takano; s/d/tw ¥9,000/12,000/17,000) Up in the north end of town, near Takano, this hotel has good facilities but is a bit of a hike to the major attractions.

Three Sisters Inn Main Building (Rakutō-sō Honkan; 761-6336; Kasugakita-dōri-Okazaki; s/d/tr ¥8900/13,000/19,500) This is a good choice with comfortable rooms. It is well situated in Okazaki for exploration of the Higashiyama area. Take bus 5 from Kyoto Station (stand A1, 30 minutes), get off at Dōbutsuen-mae stop and walk for five minutes.

Northwest Kyoto
BUDGET

Utano Youth Hostel (Map pp278-9; 462-2288; web.kyoto-inet.or.jp/org/utano-yh/; Nakayama-chō; dm ¥2800) This is the best youth hostel in Kyoto. Bear in mind, though, that while it is conveniently located for touring sights in northwest Kyoto, it's something of a hike to those in other areas of the city. From Keihan Sanjō Station, take bus No 10 or 59 (from stands 3 or 2, respectively, 40 minutes) to the Yuusu-hosteru-mae stop. The hostel is only a one-minute walk up the hill from the stop.

Ryokan Rakuchō (Map pp280-1; 721-2174; www003.upp.so-net.ne.jp/rakucho-ryokan/indx.html; Higashi hangi chō-Shimogamo; s/tw/tr ¥5300/8400/12,600) This is a friendly little ryokan in the northern part of the city.

Kitayama Youth Hostel (Map pp280-1; /fax 492-5345; Kōetsuji-hotori; dm ¥2940) This hostel is a

superb place from which to visit the rural Takagamine area with its fine, secluded temples such as Kōetsu-ji, Jōshō-ji and Shōden-ji. To get here from the bus stop, walk west past a school, turn right and continue up the hill to the hostel (five minutes' walk).

Aoi-sō Inn (Map pp280-1; 431-0788; www5.ocn.ne.jp/~aoisoinn/; Karasuma-Shimei-dōri; r per person from ¥2800) This is a tightly-packed warren of rooms built around a small garden. It's cheap and decent value for the price. The inn is a five-minute walk northwest of Kuramaguchi Station (exit No 2).

EATING

Kyoto has great restaurants in every price bracket and it's one of the best places in Japan to make a thorough exploration of Japanese cuisine. And if you get tired of Japanese food, there are heaps of great foreign restaurants about town.

Kyoto Station Area   Map p291

The new Kyoto station building is chock-a-block with restaurants, and if you find yourself anywhere near the station around meal time, this is probably your best bet in terms of variety and price.

For a quick cuppa while waiting for a train try Café du Monde on the 2nd floor overlooking the central atrium. Or you might want to snag a few pieces of sushi off the conveyor belt at Kaiten-zushi Iwamaru, on the ground floor at the east end of the station building.

For more substantial meals there are several food courts scattered about. The best of these can be found on the 11th floor on the west side of the building: the Cube food court and Isetan department store's Eat Paradise food court.

Other options in the station include Kyoto Rāmen Koji, a collection of seven rāmen restaurants on the 10th floor (underneath the Cube), and Italia Ichiba Bar, a casual Italian place with excellent views north over Kyoto, which is also on the 10th floor (take the escalators, exit to the right and walk past NOVA English school).

Outside the station building, there are lots of good places to eat.

JAPANESE

Iimura (351-8023; Shichijō-dōri-Higashinotōin; set lunch ¥650; 11.30am-2pm) About 10 minutes' walk north of the station, this is a classic little restaurant that's popular with locals who come for its ever-changing set Japanese lunch. Just say *kyō no ranchi* (today's lunch) and you should be fine. It's in a traditional Japanese house, set back a bit from the street.

Amazon (☎ 561-8875; Shichijō-dōri-Kawabata; coffee from ¥400; ⏰ 7.30am-6pm Thu-Tue) A typical Japanese coffee shop that turns out some surprisingly tasty sandwiches. It's good for a bite or a cuppa while heading to/from Sanjūsangen-dō.

Dai Ichi Asahi Rāmen (☎ 351-6321; Takakura-dōri-Shiokōji; small rāmen from ¥500; ⏰ 5am-2am Fri-Wed) An unprepossessing noodle joint that brings to mind the film *Tampopo*.

Shinpuku Saikan Honten (☎ 371-7648; Takakura-dōri-Shiokōji; rāmen from ¥600; ⏰ 7.30am-11pm; ⏰ Thu-Tue) Another classic *rāmen* joint famous for its chicken-flavoured broth.

INTERNATIONAL

Second House (☎ 342-2555; Shichijō-dōri-Nishinotōin; coffee from ¥400; ⏰ 10am-11pm) A good spot for a cuppa or light lunch when you're near Nishi Hongan-ji. It's in an old bank building.

Downtown Kyoto
Map p289
JAPANESE

Kane-yo (☎ 221-0669; Shinkyōgoku-dōri-Rokkaku; unagi over rice from ¥890; ⏰ 11.30am-9pm) This is a good place to try *unagi* (eel). You can sit downstairs with a nice view of the waterfall or upstairs on the tatami. The *kane-yo donburi* set (¥850) is great value; it's served until 3pm. Look for the barrels of live eels outside and the wooden façade.

Biotei (☎ 255-0086; Sanjō-dōri-Higashinotōin; lunch ¥840; ⏰ 11.30am-2pm & 5-8.30pm Tue-Sat, closed Sun, Mon, holidays, Thu dinner & Sat lunch) Located diagonally across from the Nakagyō post office, this is a favourite of Kyoto vegetarians. Best for lunch, it serves a daily set of Japanese vegetarian food (the occasional bit of meat is offered as an option, but you'll be asked your preference).

Tōsai (☎ 213-2900; Takoyakushi-dōri-Sakaimachi East; ⏰ 5-10pm, closed Mon & 1st Sun of each month) A great place to try a range of healthy and well-prepared Japanese dishes, there are plenty of choices here for vegetarians (the name of the place means 'Bean/Vegetable'). It's just east of a corner, next to a tiny parking lot – look for the traditional Japanese exterior.

Ōzawa (☎ 561-2052; Gion-Shirakawa Nawate Higashi iru South; lunch ¥2500, dinner from ¥3800; ⏰ 11.30am-10pm, last order 9pm, Fri-Wed) Located on one of the most beautiful streets in Gion, this charming little restaurant offers excellent tempura in refined Japanese surroundings. Unless you choose a private tatami room, you'll sit at the counter and watch as the chef prepares each piece of tempura individually right before your eyes. Considering the location and the quality of the food, this place is a great value.

Tomi-zushi (☎ 231-3628; Shinkyōgoku-dōri-Shijō; dinner ¥3000; ⏰ 5pm-midnight Fri-Wed) This is one of our favourites for good sushi in lively surroundings. Here, you rub elbows with your neighbour, sit at a long marble counter and watch as some of the fastest sushi chefs in the land do their thing. Go early or wait in line. It's near the Shijō-Kawaramachi crossing. Look for the lantern and the black and white signs.

Gonbei (☎ 561-3350; Higashiyama-Gion-chō; soba from ¥630; ⏰ noon-9.30pm Fri-Wed) This is a quaint little Gion noodle house with an English menu.

A-Bar (☎ 213-2129; Nishikiyamachi-dōri; dishes from ¥500; ⏰ 5pm-midnight) This student *izakaya* (Japanese pub-style venue) with a log-cabin interior is popular with expats and Japanese students for a raucous night out. The food is fairly typical *izakaya* fare, with plenty of fried items and some decent salads. It's a little tough to find – look for the small black and white sign at the top of a flight of steps near a place called Reims.

Kagizen Yoshifusa (☎ 525-0011; Higashiyama-ku Gion-chō; tea from ¥400; ⏰ 9.30am-6pm Tue-Sun) One of Kyoto's oldest and best-known *okashi-ya* (sweet shops) sells a variety of traditional sweets and has a cosy tearoom upstairs where you can sample cold *kuzukiri* (transparent arrowroot noodles), served with a *kuromitsu* (sweet black sugar) dipping sauce. It's in a traditional *machiya* (traditional Japanese townhouse) up a flight of stone steps.

Kōsendō-sumi (☎ 241-7377; Aneyakōji-dōri-Sakaimachi; lunch from ¥870; ⏰ 11am-4pm Mon-Sat, closed Sun & holidays) A good pick for a pleasant lunch while in the city centre. Kōsendō-sumi in an old Japanese house and serves a daily set lunch of simple Japanese fare. It's near the Museum of Kyoto.

Ponto-chō Uan (☎ 221-2358; Ponto-chō-Sanjō kudaru; dinner from ¥5000; ⏰ 5pm-10pm Thu-Tue) An elegant Ponto-chō *kaiseki* restaurant with a great platform for riverside dining in the summer. It's best to have a Japanese speaker call and reserve for you here.

Mishima-tei (☎ 221-0003; Teramachi-dōri-Sanjō kudaru; sukiyaki sets from ¥4400; ⏰ 11.30am-10pm Thu-Tue) In the Sanjō covered arcade, this is an inexpensive place to sample sukiyaki. There is an English menu and a discount for foreign travellers.

Misoka-an Kawamichi-ya (☎ 221-2525; Fuyachō-dōri-Sanjō; dishes ¥700-3800; ⏰ 11am-8pm Fri-Wed) This is the place to head for a taste of some of Kyoto's best *soba* noodles in traditional surroundings. They've been hand-making noodles here for 300 years. Try a simple bowl of *nishin soba* (*soba* noodles topped with fish), or the more elaborate *nabe* dishes (cooked in a special cast-iron pot). Look for the *noren* (Japanese curtains) and the traditional Japanese exterior.

Yoshikawa (☎ 221-5544; Tominokoji-dōri-Oike kudaru; lunch ¥2000-6000, dinner ¥6000-12,000; ⏰ 11am-2pm & 5-8pm Mon-Sat) This is the place to go for delectable tempura. It offers table seating, but it's much more interesting to sit and eat around the small counter and observe the chefs at work. It's near Oike-dōri.

Morita-ya (☎ 231-5118; Kiyamachi-dōri-Sanjō agaru; meals from ¥3800; ⏰ noon-11pm) Kyoto's most famous beef restaurant serves excellent sukiyaki and *shabu-shabu* in traditional tatami rooms, some overlooking the Kamo-gawa. It's on Kiyamachi-dōri, down a narrow alley paved with stones.

844 Store Café (☎ 241-2120; Nishikiyamachi-dōri; dishes from ¥700; ⏰ 5.30-11pm Wed-Mon) Another favourite of Kyoto vegetarians, this offbeat little café serves things like vegie gyōza (Chinese dumplings) and assorted rice and tofu dishes. It's a colourful place down a tiny alley.

Yagura (☎ 561-1035; Shijō-dōri-Kawabata; ⏰ 11am-9.30pm Fri-Wed) A classic little noodle house where the house speciality, nishin soba, goes for ¥1000. We love the funky wooden interior of this place. It's between a *rāmen* joint and a Japanese gift shop – look for the bowls of noodles in the window.

Uontana (☎ 221-2579; Rokkaku-dōri-Shinkyōgoku; dinner from ¥3000; ⏰ noon-3pm & 5-10pm Thu-Tue) At this slick upscale *izakaya* you can try a range of sake and elegantly presented Japanese fare. There is an English menu.

Tagoto Honten (☎ 221-3030; Sanjō-dōri-Teramachi; noodle dishes from ¥997; ⏰ 11am-9pm) One of Kyo-to's oldest and most revered soba restaurants makes a good break for those who have overdosed on *rāmen*. It's in the Sanjō covered arcade. There is an English menu.

Umezono (☎ 221-5017; Kawaramachi-dōri-Rokkaku; mitarashi dangō set ¥500; ⏰ 10.30am-7.30pm) Locals line up at this Kyoto institution for *mitarashi dangō* (sweet rice gluten balls), a peculiarly Japanese sweet.

Santōka (☎ 532-1335; Sanjō-dōri-Kawabata; rāmen from ¥750; ⏰ 11am-2am) The young chefs at this sleek new restaurant dish out some seriously good Hokkaidō-style *rāmen*. You'll be given a choice of three kinds of soup when you order: *shio* (salt), *shōyu* (soy sauce) and miso – we highly recommend the miso soup. For something totally decadent, try the *tokusen toroniku rāmen*, which is made from pork cheeks, of which only 200 grams can be obtained from one animal (this will come on a separate plate from the *rāmen* – just shovel it all into your bowl). It's on the east side/ground floor of the new Kyōen restaurant/shopping complex.

Ganko Zushi (☎ 255-1128; Sanjō-dōri-Kawaramachi; lunch ¥1000, dinner ¥3000; ⏰ 11.30am-10.30pm) Near Sanjō-ōhashi bridge, this is a good place for sushi or just about anything else. Look for the large display of plastic food models in the window.

Shirukō (☎ 221-3250; Nishikiyamachi-dōri-Shijō; lunch or dinner from ¥2600; ⏰ 11.30am-9pm Thu-Tue) This is a good spot to try Kyoto *obanzai-ryōri* (home-style cooking). The restaurant features more than 10 varieties of miso soup, and the *rikyū bentō* (¥2600) is a bona fide work of art. It's down a pedestrian street near Shijō-Kawaramachi crossing. Look for the *noren* and the rustic façade.

Musashi Sushi (☎ 222-0634; Kawaramachi-dōri-Sanjō; all plates ¥100; ⏰ 11am-10pm) This is the place to go to try *kaiten-zushi* (conveyor-belt sushi). Sure, it's not the best sushi in the world, but it's cheap, easy and fun. Look for the mini-sushi conveyor belt in the window. It's just outside the entrance to the Sanjō covered arcade.

Ichi-ban (☎ 751-1459; Sanjō Ōhashi East; dinner from ¥3000; ⏰ 5.30pm-midnight Mon-Sat, closed Sun & holidays) This popular little *yakitori* (skewered meats or vegetables) joint on Sanjō-dōri has an English menu and a friendly young owner to help with ordering. Best of all, it has that classic old *yakitori-ya* (yakitori restaurant) ambience – smoking charcoal grills, old beer posters on the wall and *oden* (winter stew) bubbling away on the counter. Look for the yellow and red sign and the big lantern.

Oharameya (☎ 561-1905; Higashiyama-ku Gion-chō-Kitagawa; drinks/sweets from ¥500/800, sweet set ¥1800 & ¥2500; ☯ 11am-7.30pm) This is the place to get a thorough education in Japanese sweets. To do so, ask for the full course *amato kaiseki* (sweet set). It's got food models in a glass case out the front.

Zu Zu (☎ 231-0736; Ponto-chō-Takoyakushi; dinner from ¥3000; ☯ 6pm-2am) This is a fun little Ponto-chō *izakaya*. There is no English menu here so your best bet is to ask the waiter for a recommendation or point at what other diners are eating. The fare is sort of nouveau-Japanese – things like shrimp and tofu or chicken and plum sauce. Look for the white stucco exterior and black bars on the windows.

Inoda Coffee (☎ 221-0507; Sakaimachi-dōri-Sanjō; coffee from ¥500; ☯ 7am-8pm) This is a Kyoto coffee institution with branches throughout the city centre. Though slightly overrated for the price, the old-Japan atmosphere at its main shop on Sakaimachi-dōri, south of Sanjō-dōri, is worth a try. It's in a converted *machiya*.

Issen Yōshoku (☎ 533-0001; Nawate-dōri-Shijō; okonomiyaki ¥630; ☯ 11am-3am Mon-Sat, 10.30am-10pm Sun & holidays) Heaped with bright red ginger and green scallions, the *okonomiyaki* at this Gion institution is a garish snack – which somehow seems fitting considering the surrounding neighbourhood.

Katsu Kura (☎ 212-3581; Teramachi-dōri-Sanjō; tonkatsu from ¥819; ☯ 11am-9.30pm) This restaurant in the Sanjō covered arcade is a good place to sample *tonkatsu* (deep-fried breaded pork cutlet). It's not the best in Kyoto, but it's relatively cheap and casual.

INTERNATIONAL

Merry Island Café (☎ 213-0214; Kiyamachi-dōri-Oike; lunch ¥800; ☯ 11.30am-11pm Tue-Sun) Behind the Kyoto Hotel, this is a good place for coffee or a light lunch. In warm weather the front doors are opened and the place takes on the air of a sidewalk café.

Yak & Yeti (☎ 213-7919; Gokōmachi-dōri-Nishikikōji; curry lunch sets from ¥600; ☯ 11.30am-4.30pm, 5-9.30pm Tue-Sun) This is a little Nepalese place that serves reliably good curry sets for lunch and tasty à la carte dinners. One visit and

you'll see why many Kyotoites make this a regular pit stop.

Daniel's (☎ 212-3268; Nishikikoji-dōri-Takakura; mains from ¥750; ☯ 11.30am-3pm, 5.30-11pm) Behind Daimaru department store, this is a cramped Italian restaurant that does good work with pasta and fish dishes. It's on the 2nd floor.

Ask A Giraffe (☎ 257-8028; Karasuma-dōri-Aneyakōji, 1F Shin-Puh-Kan; coffee from ¥400, cakes from ¥430, daily lunch set ¥900; ☯ 11am-11pm, closed irregularly) This casual café is our favourite of the six restaurants in the new Shin-Puh-Kan shopping complex. They offer light meals (sandwiches, pastas, salads) and all the standard coffee and drinks, which make a nice pick-me-up while shopping here. Like you, we're totally puzzled by the name.

Saracca (☎ 231-8797; Tominokoji-dōri-Sanjō; coffee from ¥400, light meals from ¥700; ☯ noon-10pm Thu-Tue) You'll have to look long and hard to find a coffee shop more relaxing than this one. They serve a variety of international food, some of it vegetarian. It's above a bike shop.

Kerala (☎ 251-0141; Kawaramachi-dōri-Sanjō; lunch from ¥850, dinner from ¥3000; ☯ 11.30am-2pm, 5-9pm) This is where we go for reliable Indian lunch sets. The dinners, however, are a little overpriced. It's on the 2nd floor; look for the display of food in the glass case on street level.

Kōbeya Dining (☎ 253-3751; Kawaramachi-dōri-Shijō; lunch/dinner from ¥700; ☯ 10am-9.30pm, café closes 9pm) This casual bakery café makes the perfect refreshment stop while shopping in the Shijō-Kawaramachi area – it's very easy to enter and ordering is a breeze since most items are laid out for your perusal. You'll find the usual coffee/tea suspects and some decent salads and sandwiches are also available.

Hati Hati (☎ 212-2228; Nishikiyamachi-dōri-Takoyakushi, B1 Kyoto Kankō Bldg; dishes from ¥600; ☯ 6pm-2am Sun-Thu, 6pm-3am Fri & Sat) This is our pick for the best Indonesian restaurant in Kyoto. Run by an Indonesian expat, the food is authentic and the atmosphere is cool. It's sometimes closed for private functions. It's downstairs in the Kankō building – look for the white, brick building and the green entry to the stairs.

Capricciosa (☎ 221-7496; Kawaramachi-dōri-Sanjō kudaru; dinner from ¥1500; ☯ 11.30am-11pm) For heaping portions of pasta at rock-bottom prices you won't do much better than this long-time student favourite. It's near the Sanjō-Kawaramachi crossing.

Doutor Coffee (☎ 213-4041; Shijō-dōri-Fuya-chō Nishi iru; coffee ¥180; ☯ 7.30am-10pm Mon-Fri, 7.30am-10pm Sat, 8am-10pm Sun & holidays) For a cheap coffee fix you can't beat Doutor Coffee. There are branches all over Kyoto, including this one on Shijō-dōri.

Southeast Kyoto   Map pp286–7
JAPANESE
Asuka (☎ 751-9809; Sanjō-dōri-Higashiyama Nishi iru; meals from ¥1000; ☯ 11am-11pm) With an English menu, and a staff of old Kyoto *mama-sans* at home with foreign customers this is a great place for a cheap lunch or dinner while sightseeing in the Higashiyama area. The tempura *moriawase* (assorted tempura set) is a big pile of tempura for only ¥1000. Look for the red lantern.

Aunbo (☎ 525-2900; Higashiyama-Yasaka Torii mae; lunch ¥2500, dinner ¥6000-10,000; ☯ noon-2pm, 5.30-10pm Thu-Tue) Aunbo serves elegant, creative Japanese cooking in traditional Gion surroundings – the last time we were here we started with sublime sashimi, went on to fried *yuba* (tofu skimming) pockets and went from there. We recommend asking for the set and leaving the difficult decisions to the master. Aunbo takes reservations in the evening. There is no English sign; look for the traditional Japanese façade.

Earth Kitchen Company (☎ 771-1897; Marutamachi-dōri-Kawabata; lunch ¥700; ☯ 10.30am-6.30pm Mon-Fri, 10.30am-3.30pm Sat, closed Sun & holidays) Located on Marutamachi-dōri near the Kamo-gawa, this is a tiny spot that seats just two people but does a bustling business serving tasty takeaway lunch *bentō*. If you fancy a picnic lunch for your temple-hopping, this is the place.

Hinode Udon (☎ 751-9251; Nanzenji-Kitanobō-chō; noodle dishes from ¥400; ☯ 11am-6pm Mon-Sat) Filling noodle and rice dishes are served at this pleasant little shop with an English menu. Plain udon (thick, white noodles) here is only ¥400, but we recommend you spring for the *nabeyaki udon* (pot-baked udon in broth) for ¥800. This is a good spot for lunch when temple-hopping near Ginkaku-ji or Nanzen-ji.

Gion Koishi (☎ 531-0301; Higashiyama Gion North; tea from ¥500; ☯ 11am-7pm, closed 2nd & 4th Wed of each month) This is where we go when we want to cool down on a hot summer day in Gion. The speciality here is *uji kintoki*

(¥700), a mountain of shaved ice flavoured with green tea, sweetened milk and sweet beans (it tastes a lot better than it sounds, trust us). This is only available in the summer months. Look for the models of the sweets and tea out front.

Karako (☎ 752-8234; Okazaki-Tokusei-chō; rāmen from ¥650; ☯ 11.30am-3pm, 6pm-midnight Wed-Mon) This is our favourite *rāmen* restaurant in Kyoto. While it's not much on atmosphere, Karako has excellent *rāmen* – the soup is thick and rich and the *chāshū* (pork slices) melt in your mouth. We recommend that you ask for the *kotteri* (thick soup) *rāmen*. Look for the lantern outside.

Okariba (☎ 751-7790; Okazaki-Higashitenno-chō; dinner ¥4000; ☯ 5-10.30pm Mon-Sat) For an experience you won't soon forget, try Okariba, near Hotel Heian no Mori. If it crawls, walks or swims, it's probably on the menu. The *inoshishi* (wild boar) barbecue is a good start. Non–red-meat eaters can try the fresh *ayu* (Japanese trout).

Okutan (☎ 771-8709; Nanzen-ji; set meals ¥3000; ☯ 10.30am-5pm Fri-Wed) Just outside the grounds of Nanzen-ji, this is a fine restaurant located inside the garden of Chōshō-in. Try a course of *yudōfu* (tofu cooked in a pot) together with vegetable side dishes.

Senmonten (☎ 531-2733; Hanamikōji-dōri-Shinbashi; 10 dumplings ¥460; ☯ 6pm-2am Mon-Sat, closed Sun & holidays) Senmonten serves only one thing: crisp fried gyōza – they're the best in town. Look for the metal and glass front door.

Daikichi (☎ 771-3126; Sanjō Ōhashi East; dinner about ¥3000; ☯ 5pm-1am) This is a good *yakitori* joint with a friendly owner. It's on Sanjō-dōri; look for the red lanterns outside.

Kanō Shōju-an (☎ 751-1077; Sakyo-ku-Nyakuoji-chō; matcha & sweet ¥1050; ☯ 10am-4.30pm Thu-Tue) Delightful tea house off the Tetsugaku-no-Michi where you can enjoy Japanese tea and a sweet (¥1050, ask for *tenzen*).

Mikō-an (☎ 751-5045; Kawabata-dōri-Ebisugawa; lunch/dinner ¥800/1000; ☯ 11am-11pm) This is a great choice for a vegetarian lunch or dinner. Just ask for the *setto* (set meal). It's on Kawabata-dōri north of Nijō-dōri. Look for the white front and the small sign with the name written in English on street level.

INTERNATIONAL
Zac Baran (☎ 751-9748; Higashiōji-dōri-Marutamachi; dishes from ¥500; ☯ noon-3am) Near the Kyoto Handicraft Centre, this is a good spot for

a light meal or a drink. It serves a variety of spaghetti dishes, as well as a good lunch special. Look for the picture of the Freak Brothers near the downstairs entrance. If you fancy dessert when you're done, step upstairs to the Second House Cake Works.

Southwest Kyoto
Map pp284–5

JAPANESE

Den Shichi (☎ 463-9991; Nishioji-dōri-Imadegawa; sushi dinners from ¥3000; ☯ 11.30am-2pm, 5pm-10.30pm Tue-Sun) Like its sister restaurant in Saiin, this Kitano Hakubaichō restaurant is a good-value sushi restaurant which also offers incredibly cheap lunch specials, including *tekkadon* (raw tuna over rice) for ¥480. In terms of price and quality, Den Shichi is always a good bet. Look for the black and white sign and the pictures of the lunch specials in the window.

Mukade-ya (☎ 256-7039; Shinmachi-dōri-Nishikikōji; meals from ¥3000; ☯ 11am-2pm & 5-9pm Thu-Tue) An atmospheric restaurant located in an exquisite *machiya* west of Karasuma-dōri. For lunch try the *bentō*: two rounds (five small dishes each) of delectable *obanzai* fare (¥3000). *Kaiseki* courses start at ¥5000.

Shin-shin-tei (☎ 221-6202; Nijo-dōri-Fuyachō; rāmen from ¥600; ☯ 10.30am-4pm Tue-Sat, closed Sun, Mon & holidays) This place is famous for its *shiro miso rāmen* (white miso *rāmen*). The place may not look like much, but the *rāmen* here is excellent. Look for the yellow and black sign.

Shizenha Restaurant Obanzai (☎ 223-6623; Koromonotana-dōri-Oike; lunch/dinner ¥840/2100; ☯ 11am-9pm, closed Wed dinner) A little out of the way, but good value, Obanzai serves a good buffet-style lunch/dinner of mostly organic food. It's northwest of the Karasuma-Oike crossing, set back from the street a bit.

INTERNATIONAL

Le Bouchon (☎ 211-5220; Nijo-dōri-Teramachi; ☯ 11.30am-2.30pm, 5.30-9.30pm Fri-Wed) This reliable little French place usually has a cheap lunch set on offer (around ¥900). À la carte dinners will run closer to ¥2500. We imagine the French menu may be a relief after fighting your way through all those Japanese menus.

Bistro de Paris (☎ 256-1825; Shinmachi-dōri-Shijō; lunch from ¥1600, dinner from ¥2500; ☯ 11.30am-1.30pm, 5.30-9.30pm Tue-Sun) This is our choice for tasty French cuisine – nothing too fancy, just good. It's near the Shijō-Karasuma crossing.

Café Bibliotic HELLO! (☎ 231-8625; Nijo-dōri-Yanaginobanba higashi iru; food from ¥700, coffee ¥400; ☯ noon-11pm, closed irregularly) Like its name suggests, books line the walls of this cool café located in a converted *machiya*. You can get the usual range of coffee and tea drinks here, as well as light café lunches. It's popular with young ladies who work nearby and it's a great place to relax with a book or magazine. Look for the plants out front.

Northeast Kyoto
Map pp282–3

JAPANESE

Omen (☎ 771-8994; Shirakawa-dōri-Imadegawa; noodles ¥1000; ☯ 11am-10pm Fri-Wed) This noodle shop is named after the thick, white noodles served in a hot broth with a selection of seven fresh vegetables. Just say *omen* and you'll be given your choice of hot or cold noodles, a bowl of soup to dip them in and a plate of vegetables (you put these into the soup along with some sesame seeds). It's a great bowl of noodles but that's not the end of the story: everything in the frequently changing menu is delicious. Best of all, there's a menu in English. It's about five minutes' walk from Ginkaku-ji in a traditional Japanese house with a lantern outside.

Kushi Hachi (☎ 751-6789; Shirakawa-dōri-Imadegawa; dinner from ¥2000; ☯ 5pm-11.30pm Tue-Sun) Kushi Hachi, part of a popular Kyoto chain, is a fun spot to sample *kushi katsu*, a fried dish that is well suited to Western palates. We like to sit at the counter and watch as the frenetic chefs work the grills and deep-fryers. With a picture menu, ordering is a snap.

Café Peace (☎ 707-6856; Higashiōji-dōri-Imadegawa; drinks from ¥550, food from ¥600; ☯ 11.30am-10.30pm Mon-Sat, 11.30am-9.30pm Sun & holidays) This is a pleasant spot for a cuppa or a light meal. It's on the 3rd floor but there's a small sign on street level.

Eating House Hi-Lite (☎ 721-1997; Sakyō-ku-Hyakumanben; set meals from ¥540; ☯ 11am-11pm, closed Sun, 2nd Sat each month & holidays) This is where Kyoto University students go for cheap, filling meals. Try the *cheezu chicken katsu teishoku* (fried chicken with cheese set meal) for ¥540; it's a little greasy but how can you complain at these prices? The name is written in English on the sign.

Hiragana-kan (☎ 701-4164; Higashiōji-dōri-Mikage; lunch/dinner from ¥800; ☯ 11.30am-4pm,

6pm-10pm Wed-Mon) This place, popular with Kyoto University students, dishes up creative variations on chicken, fish and meat. Most entrees come with rice, salad and miso soup for around ¥800. The menu is only in Japanese, but if you're at a loss for what to order try the tasty roll chicken katsu, a delectable and filling creation of chicken and vegetables. Look for the words 'Casual Restaurant' on the white awning.

Kuishinbō-no-Mise (☎ 712-0656; Kitashirakawa-Kubota-chō-Hyakumanben East; set meals from ¥500; 11.30am-2pm & 6-11pm Thu-Tue) Similar to Hi-Lite, the lunch/dinner specials are great value (at dinner ask for the *sabisu-teishoku* – daily set meal). Look for the photos of dishes displayed at the front of the restaurant.

Yatai (Imadegawa-dōri; dishes from ¥300; dusk-midnight) This little tent (*yatai*) pops up along Imadegawa-dōri every evening and serves a variety of foods to go, along with beer and sake. It's fun but don't expect any English to be spoken (though pointing at what you want is easy at a *yatai*).

Tenka-ippin Honten (☎ 722-0955; Shirakawa-dōri-Kitaōji; rāmen from ¥600; 11am-3pm Fri-Wed) This is the original store of Kyoto's most famous *rāmen* chain. We love the thick soup *kotteri rāmen* they serve here (but we didn't say it was healthy).

INTERNATIONAL

Café Carinho/Asian Diner (☎ 752-3636; Imadegawa-dōri-Shirakawa; coffee from ¥400, lunch from ¥750; 11am-10pm Tue-Thu, 11am-11pm Fri-Sun) Located near Ginkaku-ji, this is a cosy little café. It serves good, strong Brazilian coffee, tasty cakes and some excellent sandwiches. The friendly owner speaks English.

Didi (☎ 791 8226; Higashiōji-dōri-Tanaka-Okubo-chō; lunch from ¥750, dinner from ¥900; 11am-9.30pm Thu-Tue) On Higashiōji-dōri, north of Mikage-dōri, you'll find this friendly little smoke-free restaurant serving passable Indian lunch/dinner sets. There are plenty of vegetarian choices on the menu.

Prinz (☎ 712-3900; Higashikurama-dōri-Shirakawa; coffees from ¥300, lunch set from ¥1200; 8am-2am, last order at 11.30pm) Behind the blank white façade of Prinz, you'll find a café/restaurant, gallery, book shop, garden and library – a chic island of coolness in an otherwise bland residential neighbourhood. You can sit at the counter and request music from the CDs that line the walls of the place. The lunch

set usually includes a light assortment of Western and Japanese dishes, usually on the healthy side of things. All in all, this is a very interesting stop while you're in the northeast part of town.

Bon Bon Café (☎ 213-8686; Imadegawa-dōri higashi iru-Kawaramachi; drinks from ¥300, sandwiches from ¥500; 10am-midnight) If you find yourself in need of a light meal or drink while you're in the Demachiyanagi area, this casual open café is an excellent choice. There are a variety of cakes and light meals on offer. While there is no English menu, much of the ordering can be done by pointing and the young staff can help you figure out what's not on display. It's on the west bank of the Kamo-gawa and outdoor seats here are very pleasant on warm evenings.

Buttercups (☎ 751-7837; 103 Shimobanba-chō-Jōdo-ji Sakyō-ku; coffee from ¥230, meals from ¥580; noon-10pm Wed-Mon) This is a favourite of the local expat community and a great place for lunch, dinner or a cup of coffee. There is an international menu and this is one of the only places in town where you can get a proper salad.

Falafel Garden (☎ 712-1856; Yanagi-chō; falafel from ¥400; 11am-11pm Fri-Wed) This new little falafel restaurant is an excellent place for a healthy meal in the Demachiyanagi area. There is a picture menu and a variety of set meals are available.

Shinshindō Notre Pain Quotidien (☎ 701-4121; Sakyō-ku-Hyakumanben; coffee from ¥340; 8am-6pm Wed-Mon) This atmospheric old Kyoto coffee shop is a favourite of Kyoto University students for its curry and bread lunch set (¥780) – it's kind of an acquired taste. It's near Kyoto University.

Tranq Room (☎ 762-4888; Shirakawa-dōri-Jyōdoji Shinnyo-chō; coffees from ¥400, meals from ¥600; noon-2am Mon-Fri, noon-midnight Sat, Sun & holidays) Tranq Room (which gets its name from the word 'tranquil') is a mod little café/bar/restaurant that is popular with many of the expats who live nearby. It has a very open feeling and is a good place to hang in the evening. It's on the west side of the street, just north of a pedestrian overpass.

Womb (☎ 721-1357; Ichijoji-Hinokuchi-chō; drinks from ¥400, lunch set from ¥1300; 11.30am-11pm, last order at 10pm, closed Wed & 3-6pm weekdays) Womb appears to be an experiment in stark Spartan design – it's all open spaces, blank walls and simple furniture. Following with the

Spartan ethic, the menu is limited to only a few decent dishes like creative sushi and healthy noodle dishes. This place often holds art events in the evening.

Northwest Kyoto   Map pp280–1
Saraca Nishijin (☎ 432-5075; Kuramaguchi-dōri-Ōmiya; coffee from ¥400, lunch from ¥900; ♥ noon-10pm Thu-Tue) This is one of Kyoto's most interesting cafés – it's built inside an old *sentō* and the original tiles have been preserved. Light meals and the usual coffee drinks are the staples here. It's near Funaoka Onsen.

Arashiyama & Sagano Area   Map p292
JAPANESE
Yoshida-ya (☎ 861-0213; Saga-Tenryū-ji Tsukurimichi chō; lunch from ¥800; ♥ 10am-6pm Wed-Mon) This quaint and friendly little *teishoku-ya* (set meal restaurant) is the perfect place to grab a simple lunch while in Arashiyama. All the standard *teishoku* favourites are on offer, including things like *oyakodon* (egg and chicken over a bowl of rice) for ¥1000. You can also cool off here with a refreshing *uji kintoki* (sweet *matcha* over shaved ice, sweetened milk and sweet beans) for ¥600. Prices are a little higher here than at similar restaurants downtown, but you're paying for the location. There is no English sign; it's the first place south of the station and it's got a rustic front.

Shigetsu (☎ 882-9725; Saga-Tenryū-ji; lunch from ¥3000; ♥ 11am-2pm) To sample *shōjin ryōri* try Shigetsu in the precinct of Tenryū-ji. It has beautiful garden views.

Yudōfu Sagano (☎ 871-6946; Sagano-Tenryū-ji; lunch/dinner course from ¥3800; ♥ 11am-7pm) This is a good place to try that classic Arashiyama dish: *yudōfu*. Lunch and dinner courses go for ¥3800 (simply ask for the *yudōfu cosu*). Look for the wagon wheels outside.

Togetsu-tei (☎ 871-1310; Arashiyama-Togetsukyō South; lunch from ¥5250; ♥ 11am-7pm, closed irregularly) On the south side of Togetsu-kyō Bridge, this place has great riverside views and tatami-mat seating. Try the tofu *ryōri hana setto* (tofu full course, ¥3500). It's on the island just across the bridge from central Arashiyama.

Gyātei (☎ 862-2411; Saga-Tenryū-ji; lunch ¥1580, dinner ¥3000; ♥ 11am-2.30pm, 5-9.50pm Tue-Sun) Just beside the station, there's an all-you-can-eat lunch buffet of Japanese fare (includes over 30 dishes). Gyātei is not the pinnacle

of Japanese cuisine, but if volume is what you're after, this is the place. Look for the ochre building.

INTERNATIONAL
Sunday's Sun (☎ 861-8836; Saga-Tenryū-ji; lunch from ¥900; ♥ 7am-2am) If you fancy some Western food, then head into this casual 'family restaurant' for things like steak and chicken.

Far Northern Outskirts
ŌHARA 大原   Map p293
Kumoi-jaya (☎ 744-2240; Ōhara Sanzenin hotori; meals from ¥800; ♥ 9am-5pm) Near Jakkō-in, Kumoi-jaya serves a delectable miso-based *nabe* (chicken stew, ¥2000) and has cheaper udon noodles (¥800). It's just off the main road in a new white building.

Seryō-jaya (☎ 744-2301; Ōhara Sanzenin hotori; lunch sets from ¥2756; ♥ 11am-5pm) Just by the entry gate to Sanzen-in, Seryō-jaya serves wholesome sansai *ryōri* (mountain vegetable cooking), fresh river fish and soba noodles topped with grated yam. There is outdoor seating in warmer months. It's across from the entrance to Sanzen-in; look for the food models.

Tamba-jaya (☎ 744-2527; Ōhara Sanzenin hotori; lunch from ¥1000; ♥ 9am-5pm) Also near Jakkō-in, this place dishes up great home-made udon – you can fill up on the *inaka-teishoku* (country cooking set, ¥1000).

KURAMA 鞍馬   Map p293
Aburaya-shokudō (☎ 741-2009; Kurama-honmachi; meals from ¥800; ♥ 9.30am-5.30pm, closed the end of each month) Just down the steps from the main gate of Kurama-dera, this classic old-style *shokudō* reminds us of what Japan was like before it got rich. The sansai *teishoku* (¥1700) is a delightful selection of vegetables, rice and soba topped with grated yam.

Yōshūji (☎ 741-2848; Kurama-honmachi; meals from ¥1050; ♥ 10am-6pm Wed-Mon) Yōshūji serves superb *shōjin ryōri* in a delightful old Japanese farmhouse with an *irori* (open hearth). The house special, a sumptuous selection of vegetarian dishes served in red lacquered bowls, is called *kurama-yama shōjin zen* (¥2500). Or if you just feel like a quick bite, try the *uzu-soba* (soba topped with mountain vegetables, ¥1050). It's half way up the steps leading to the main gate of Kurama-dera; look for the orange lanterns out front.

KANSAI

KIBUNE貴船   **Map p293**

Visitors to Kibune from June to September should not miss the chance to cool down by dining at one of the picturesque restaurants beside the Kibune-gawa. Known as kawa-doko, meals are served on platforms suspended over the river as cool water flows just underneath. Most of the restaurants offer some kind of lunch special for around ¥3000. For a full *kaiseki* spread (¥5000 to ¥10,000) have a Japanese person call to reserve in advance. In the cold months you can dine indoors overlooking the river.

Beniya (☎ 741-2041; Kurama-Kibune-chō; meals from ¥3000; ☒ 11.30am-7.30pm) This elegant riverside restaurant serves *kaiseki* sets for ¥6000/8000/10,000, depending on size. There is a wooden sign with white lettering.

Hirobun (☎ 741-2147; Kurama-Kibune-chō; noodles ¥1200, kaiseki courses from ¥7000; ☒ 11am-10pm) If you don't feel like breaking the bank on a snazzy course lunch, head for this place where you can sample *nagashi-somen* (¥1200), thin white noodles that flow to you in globs down a split bamboo gutter; just pluck them out and slurp away (*nagashi-somen* is served until 5pm). Look for the black and white sign and the lantern.

Nakayoshi (☎ 741-2000; Kurama-Kibune-chō; lunch from ¥3500, dinner from ¥8500; ☒ 11am-7pm) One of the more reasonably priced restaurants is Nakayoshi, which serves a lunch *bentō* for ¥3500. *Kaiseki* dinners cost ¥8500.

Tochigiku (☎ 741-5555; Kurama-Kibune-chō; sukiyaki from ¥8000; ☒ 11.30am-9pm, closed irregularly) Try this lovely riverside restaurant for sukiyaki and *kaiseki* sets. There is a small English sign.

ENTERTAINMENT

Most of Kyoto's cultural entertainment is of an occasional nature, and you'll need to check with the TIC or a magazine like *Kansai Time Out* to find out whether anything interesting coincides with your visit. Regular cultural events are generally geared at the tourist market and tend to be expensive and, naturally, somewhat touristy.

In addition to cultural entertainment, Kyoto has a great variety of bars, clubs and discos, all of which are good places to meet Japanese folks. And if you happen to be in Kyoto in the summer, many hotels and department stores operate rooftop beer gardens with all-you-can-eat-and-drink deals

and good views of the city. Check the *Kyoto Visitor's Guide* for details.

Bars

Kyoto is loaded with great bars and clubs – if you've got the energy left over after sightseeing, Kyoto is a great place to party!

Ing (Map p289; ☎ 255-5087; Nishikiyamachi-dōri-Takoyakushi; meals ¥250-700, drinks from ¥580; ☒ 6pm-2am Mon-Thu, 6pm-5am Fri & Sat) Another one of our favourite spots, this little joint is the place for cheap bar snacks and drinks, good music and friendly company. It's on the 2nd floor of the Royal building; you'll know you're getting close when you see all the hostesses out trawling for customers on the streets nearby.

Tadg's Irish Pub (Map p289; ☎ 525-0680; Yamatōji-dōri-Shijō agaru; drinks from ¥600; ☒ 5pm-midnight Mon-Fri, later Sat & Sun) Tadg's is one of our favourite bars in Kyoto. It's a delightfully convivial spot which plays host to a good crowd of expats and Japanese every night of the week. This is an easy spot for solo travellers to enter – you'll soon be drawn into the conversation. Tadg serves a variety of pub favourites, including a tasty fish and chips and Irish stew. Some evenings there are open-mike nights and live Irish music. Tadg's serves a roast dinner every Sunday and Christmas and Thanksgiving dinners. It's on the 2nd floor of the Kamo Higashi building; take the steps on your right just after you enter.

Pig & Whistle (Map p289; ☎ 761-6022; Kawabata-dōri-Sajō; drinks from ¥500; ☒ 5pm-midnight Sun-Thu, 5pm-1am Fri & Sat) British-style pub with darts, pint glasses and, of course, fish and chips, this is one of Kyoto's most popular gaijin bars. It's a good place to meet Japanese folks and local expats.

Ace Café (Map p289; ☎ 241-0009; Kiyamachi-Sanjo agaru 10th fl Empire Bldg; drinks from ¥600; ☒ noon-3am) Hip café/bar where you can enjoy a light lunch during the day, or a few drinks in the evening, all while enjoying a first-class view over eastern Kyoto and the Higashiyama mountains.

Zappa (Map p289; ☎ 255-4437; Takoyakushi-dōri-Kawaramachi; dishes from ¥850; ☒ 6pm-midnight Mon-Sat) Unbeatable if you're looking for a more intimate venue. It's a cosy, little place that once played host to David Bowie (he's said to have discovered the place by chance and decided to drop in for a drink). They serve savoury

Southeast Asian fare and a few Japanese tidbits for good measure. It's down a narrow alley; turn south at the wooden *torii*.

Boogie Lounge (Map p289; ☎ 212-2200; Kawaramachi-dōri-Sanjō kudaru; drinks from ¥700; ☼ 7pm-5am, closed irregularly) This place brings back the '70s in a big way, complete with a disco ball and a groovy funk/soul soundtrack. There are plush seats scattered about, but unless you're early, you'll have no choice but to stand and/or dance. We feel strangely at home here, but maybe that's because the owner seems to have stolen our record collection.

Rub-a-Dub (Map p289; ☎ 256-3122; Kiyamachi-dōri-Sanjō; meals from ¥500, drinks from ¥600; ☼ 7pm-2am Sun-Thu, 7pm-4am Fri & Sat) At the northern end of Kiyamachi-dōri, Rub-a-Dub is a funky little reggae bar with a shabby tropical look. It's a good place for a quiet drink on weekdays, but on Friday and Saturday nights you'll have no choice but to bop along with the crowd. Look for the stairs heading down to the basement beside the popular (and delightfully 'fragrant') Nagahama Rāmen shop.

Hub (Map p289; ☎ 212-9026; Kawaramachi-dōri-Sanjō kudaru; drinks ¥350-1000; ☼ 5pm-midnight Sun-Thu, 5pm-3am Fri & Sat, happy hr 5-7pm) We think of this place as the Kyoto English teachers' lounge – it's the main watering hole of expats teaching in area *eikaiwa* (private English schools). It's a spacious, two-level bar with plenty of room to spread out and relax. If you're after info about teaching English in Kyoto, this is an obvious choice.

Hill of Tara (Map p289; ☎ 213-3330; Oike-dōri-Kawaramachi; meals from ¥1000, drinks from ¥500; ☼ 5pm-midnight Sun-Thu, 5pm-1am Fri & Sat) Near the Oike-Kawaramachi intersection, this is one of our favourite places for a drink in Kyoto. It's a convivial Irish-style pub with Guinness on tap and occasional live Irish music. They also serve a variety of Irish pub food.

Teddy's (Map p289; ☎ 255-7717; Kiyamachi-Sanjō agaru; ☼ 6pm-2am) Part club and part bar, this place really gets going late in the evening when the tables are cleared away and the dancing starts (usually to dancehall reggae). On weekend nights there's a cover charge of ¥500. It's on the 7th floor of the Empire building.

MataMata (former Dua Orang; Map p289; ☎ 211-1349; 272-1 Kitakurumaya-chō; ☼ 6pm-3am) A cool bar with an Indonesian theme (it also serves good Indonesian food). The interior is pleasantly bohemian and you might easily forget you're in Kyoto while drinking here. It's on the 5th floor of the Royal building (same building as Ing – see opposite).

Clubs

Metro (Map pp286-7; ☎ 752-4765; Kawabata-dōri-Marutamachi kudaru; admission free Wed & Thu, ¥2000 Fri-Sun; ☼ 10pm-3am) This is one of the most popular clubs in town. It's part disco, part live house and even hosts the occasional art exhibition. Every night is a different theme; check the *Kansai Time Out* for forthcoming events. On weekends there's usually an admission charge of between ¥1500 and ¥2000 (with one drink), while Wednesday and Thursday are usually free. It's inside the exit 2 of the Keihan Marutamachi Station.

Geisha Dances

Annually in autumn and spring, geisha and their *maiko* apprentices from Kyoto's five schools dress elaborately to perform traditional dances in praise of the seasons. The cheapest tickets cost about ¥1650 (unreserved on tatami mats), better seats cost ¥3000 to ¥3800, and spending an extra ¥500 includes participation in a quick tea ceremony. The dances are similar from place to place and are repeated several times a day. Dates and times vary, so check with the TIC.

Gion Odori (祇園をどり; ☎ 561-0160; Higashiyama-ku-Gion; ¥3300, ¥3800 with tea; ☼ 1.30pm & 3.30pm) Gion Kaikan Theatre (Map pp286-7) Near Yasaka-jinja; 1 to 10 November.

Kamogawa Odori (鴨川をどり; ☎ 221-2025; Ponto-chō-Sanjō kudaru; ¥2000; ☼ 12.30pm, 2.20pm & 4.10pm) Ponto-chō Kaburen-jō Theatre (Map p289), Ponto-chō; 1 to 24 May.

Kitano Odori (北野をどり; ☎ 461-0148; Imadegawa-dōri-Nishihonmatsu nishi iru; ¥3800, ¥4300 with tea; ☼ 1pm & 3pm) Kamishichiken Kaburen-jō Theatre (Map pp280-1), east of Kitano-Tenman-gū; 15 to 25 April.

Kyō Odori (京をどり; ☎ 561-1151; Kawabata-dōri-Shijō kudaru; ¥3800, ¥4300 with tea; ☼ 12.30pm, 2.30pm & 4.30pm) Miyagawa-chō Kaburen-jō Theatre (Map pp286-7), east of the Kamo-gawa between Shijō-dōri and Gojō-dōri; from the first to the third Sunday in April.

Miyako Odori (都をどり; ☎ 561-1115; Higashiyama-ku-Gion-chō South; ¥1900 (non reserved seat), ¥3800 (reserved seat), ¥4300 (reserved seat with tea); ☼ 12.30pm, 2pm, 3.30pm & 4.50pm) Gion Kōbu Kaburen-jō Theatre (Map pp286-7), near Gion Corner; throughout April.

Kabuki

Minami-za Theatre (Map p289; ☎ 561-0160; Shijō-Ōhashi; ¥4200-12,600; ☺ irregular) In Gion, this is the oldest kabuki theatre in Japan. The major event of the year is the Kao-mise Festival (1–26 December), which features Japan's finest kabuki actors. Other performances take place on an irregular basis. Those interested should check with the TIC. The most likely months for performances are May, June and September.

Musical Performances

Musical performances featuring the koto, *shamisen* and *shakuhachi* are held in Kyoto on an irregular basis. Performances of *bugaku* (court music and dance) are often held at Kyoto shrines during festival periods. Occasionally contemporary *butō* dance is also performed in Kyoto. Check with the TIC to see if any performances are scheduled to be held while you are in town.

Nō

Kanze Kaikan Nō Theatre (Map pp286-7; ☎ 771-6114; Sakyō-ku-Okazaki; admission free-¥8000; ☺ 9am-5pm Tue-Sun) This is the main theatre for performances of *nō*. *Takigi-Nō* is a picturesque form of *nō* performed in the light of blazing fires. In Kyoto, this takes place in the evenings of 1 and 2 June at Heian-jingū – tickets cost ¥2000 if you pay in advance (ask at the TIC for the location of ticket agencies) or you can pay ¥3300 at the entrance gate.

Traditional Dance, Theatre & Music

Gion Corner (Map pp286-7; ☎ 561-1119; Gion-Hanamikōji-dōri; admission ¥2800; ☺ performances nightly at 7.40pm & 8.40pm 1 Mar-29 Nov, closed 16 Aug) The shows presented here are a sort of crash course in Japanese traditional arts. You get a chance to see snippets of the tea ceremony, Koto music, *ikebana* (flower arrangement), *gagaku* (court music), *kyōgen* (ancient comic plays), *Kyōmai* (Kyoto-style dance) and *bunraku* (puppet plays). However, these are rather touristy affairs and may not satisfy those in search of more authentic experiences. On top of this, 50 minutes of entertainment for ¥2800 is a little steep by anyone's standards.

SHOPPING

The heart of Kyoto's shopping district is around the intersection of Shijō-dōri and Kawaramachi-dōri. The blocks to the north

and west of here are packed with stores selling both traditional and modern goods. Kyoto's largest department stores (Hankyū, Takashimaya, Daimaru and Fujii Daimaru) are grouped together in this area.

Antiques

The place to look for antiques in Kyoto is Shinmonzen-dōri, in Gion. The street is lined with great old shops, many of them specialising in one thing or another (furniture, pottery, scrolls, prints etc). You can easily spend an afternoon strolling from shop to shop here, but be warned: if something strikes your fancy you're going to have to break out the credit card – prices here are steep!

Cameras & Electronics

Camera No Naniwa (Map p289; ☎ 222-0728; Shijō-dōri-Fuya-chō; ☺ 10am-8pm) This vast camera/film/electronics emporium is part of a huge low-cost Osaka chain. You can find some great bargains here, but don't expect much in terms of personal service.

Camping & Outdoor Equipment

Kōjitsu (Map p289; ☎ 257-7050; Kawaramachi-dōri-Sanjō agaru; ☺ 10am-8pm) If you plan to do some hiking or camping while in Japan, you can stock up on equipment at this excellent little shop on Kawaramachi. You'll find that Japanese outdoor sporting equipment is very high quality (with prices to match).

Food & Kitchen Utensils

Nishiki-kōji (Map pp288–9), in the centre of town, is Kyoto's most fascinating food market (see p277). If you do choose to visit, be sure to stop into the knife shop **Aritsugu** (Map p289; ☎ 221-1091; Nishikikōji-dōri-Gokōmachi nishi iru; ☺ 9am-5.30pm) near the eastern end of the market. Here, you can find some of the best kitchen knives available in the world, as well as a variety of other kitchenware.

For an even more impressive display of food, check the basements of any of the big department stores on Shijō-dōri (perhaps Daimaru has the largest selection). It's difficult to believe the variety of food on display, or some of the prices (check out the ¥10,000 melons or the Kōbe beef, for example).

Japanese Arts & Crafts

The paved streets of Ninnen-zaka and of Sannen-zaka (close to Kiyomizu-dera), in eastern Kyoto, are renowned for their crafts and antiques. You'll also find lots of pottery shops along Gojō-dōri, between Kawabata-dōri and Higashiōji-dōri.

North of city hall, Teramachi-dōri, between Oike-dōri and Marutamachi-dōri, there are a number of classic old Kyoto shops and it is pleasant for strolling around and window-shopping.

Kakimoto Washi (Map pp284-5; ☎ 211-3481; Teramachi-dōri-Nijō agaru; ☽ 9am-6pm Mon-Sat, closed Sun & holidays) This place sells a good selection of *washi* (Japanese paper). It's not as good as Morita Washi (see following), but it's great for things like *washi* computer paper.

Morita Washi (Map pp284-5; ☎ 341-1419; Higashinotōin-dōri-Bukkōji agaru; ☽ 9.30am-5.30pm, to 4.30pm Sat) Not far from Shijo-Karasuma it sells a fabulous variety of handmade *washi* for reasonable prices.

Kyūkyo-dō (Map p289; ☎ 231-0510; Teramachi-Aneyakōji agaru; ☽ 10am-6pm Mon-Sat, closed Sun & 1-3 Jan) This old shop in the Teramachi covered arcade sells a selection of incense, *shodō* (calligraphy) goods, tea-ceremony supplies and *washi*. Prices are on the high side but the quality is good.

Benri-dō (Map p289; ☎ 231-4351; Tominokōji-dōri-Sanjō; ☽ 10.30am-7.30pm, closed 1st & 3rd Wed each month) We love this new postcard shop inside a converted *machiya*. They have postcards of the most famous pieces from art museums across Japan. This is a great shop for unique postcards to send or bring home.

Ippo-dō (Map pp284-5; ☎ 211-3421; Teramachi-dōri-Nijō; ☽ 9am-7pm Mon-Sat) This is an old-fash-ioned tea shop selling all sorts of Japanese tea. You can ask to sample the tea before buying.

Kyoto Handicraft Center (Map pp286-7; ☎ 761-5080; Marutamachi-dōri-Kumano jinja east; ☽ 10am-6pm, closed 1-3 Jan) Just north of the Heian-jingū, this is a huge cooperative that sells, demonstrates and exhibits crafts (wood-block prints and *yukata* are a good buy here). It's the best spot in town for buying Japanese souvenirs and is highly recommended.

Kyoto Craft Center (Map pp286-7; ☎ 561-9660; Gion-chō-Kitagawa; ☽ 11am-7pm Thu-Tue) Near Maruyama-kōen, this centre also exhibits and sells a wide range of handicrafts and souvenirs.

GETTING THERE & AWAY
Air
Kyoto is served by Osaka Itami airport, which handles mostly domestic traffic, and the new Kansai International Airport (KIX), which handles most international flights. There are frequent flights between Tokyo and Itami (¥18,800, 70 minutes) but unless you're very lucky with airport connections you'll probably find it as quick and more convenient to take the *shinkansen* (bullet trains). There are ample connections to/from both airports, though the trip to/from Kansai International Airport can be both expensive and time consuming.

Bus
The overnight bus (JR Dream Kyoto Go) runs between Tokyo Station (Yaesu-guchi long-distance bus stop) and Kyoto Station Bus Terminal (Map p291).

KANSAI

MARKETS & MALLS

If you're in town when one of the following markets is on, by all means go! Markets are the best places to find antiques and bric-a-brac at reasonable prices and are the only places in Japan where you can actually bargain for a better price.

On the 21st of each month, **Kōbō-san Market** is held at Tō-ji to commemorate the death of Kōbō Daishi (Kūkai), who in 823 was appointed abbot of the temple.

Another major market, **Tenjin-san Market**, is held on the 25th of each month at Kitano Tenman-gū, marking the day of the birth (and, coincidentally, the death) of the Heian-era statesman Sugawara Michizane (845–903).

If you aren't in Kyoto on the 21st, there's also a regular antiques fair at Tō-ji on the first Sunday of each month. In addition, the **Antique Grand Fair** is a major event, with over 100 dealers selling a wide range of Japanese and foreign curios. It is held thrice-yearly at Pulse Plaza (Map pp278–9) in Fushimi (southern Kyoto). Ask at the TIC for more details as times vary each year.

Qanat Rakuhoku (Map pp282-3; ☎ 707-0700; Takano Nishibiraki-chō; ☽ 10am-9pm) This huge new complex in Takano (northern Kyoto) has stores selling just about everything as well as a big food court with a Starbucks and a place that sells decent pizza (something of a rarity here).

The trip takes about eight hours and there are usually two departures nightly in either direction, at 10pm and 11pm. The fare is ¥8180/14,480 one way/return. You should be able to grab some sleep in the reclining seats. There is a similar service to/from Shinjuku Station's Shin-minami-guchi in Tokyo.

Other JR bus transport possibilities include (the following fares are given as one way/return) Kanazawa (¥4060/7310), Tottori (¥3870/6970), Hiroshima (¥6620/11,720), Nagasaki (¥11,310/20,380) and Kumamoto (¥10,800/19,440).

Hitching

Although we never recommend it, for long-distance hitching head for the Kyoto-Minami Interchange of the Meishin Expressway, about 4km south of Kyoto Station. Take the No 19 bus from Kyoto Station and get off when you reach the Meishin Expressway signs. From here you can hitch east towards Tokyo or west to southern Japan.

Train
SHINKANSEN (TOKYO, OSAKA, NAGOYA & HAKATA)

Kyoto is on the Tōkaidō–San-yō Hikari *shinkansen* line to/from Tokyo (¥13,220, two hours 50 minutes); to/from Nagoya (¥5340, 44 minutes); to/from Osaka (¥1380, 15 minutes); to/from Hakata (¥15,210, three hours 40 minutes). Other stops on this line include Hiroshima, Okayama, Kōbe and Yokohama.

OSAKA

The fastest train other than the *shinkansen* between Kyoto Station and Osaka is the JR *shinkaisoku* (special rapid train), which takes 29 minutes (¥540). In Osaka, the train stops at both Shin-Osaka and Osaka Stations.

There is also the cheaper private Hankyū line, which runs between Hankyū Kawaramachi, Karasuma and Ōmiya Stations in Kyoto and Hankyū Umeda Station in Osaka (*tokkyū* or limited express Umeda–Kawaramachi, ¥390, 40 minutes).

Alternatively, you can take the Keihan main line between Demachiyanagi, Sanjō, Shijō or Shichijō Stations in Kyoto and Keihan Yodoyabashi Station in Osaka (*tokkyū* to/from Sanjō ¥400, 45 minutes). Yodoyabashi is on the Midō-suji subway line.

NARA

Unless you have a Japan Rail Pass, the best option is the Kintetsu line (sometimes written in English as the Kinki Nippon railway) linking Kyoto (Kintetsu Kyoto Station, on the south side of the main Kyoto station building) and Nara (Kintetsu Nara Station). There are direct limited-express trains (¥1110, 33 minutes) and ordinary express trains (¥610, 45 minutes), which may require a change at Saidai-ji.

The JR Nara line connects Kyoto Station with JR Nara Station (*shinkaisoku* ¥690, 46 minutes) but departures are often few and far between.

TOKYO

The *shinkansen* line has the fastest and most frequent rail links. The journey can also be undertaken by a series of regular JR express trains, but keep in mind that it takes around eight hours and involves at least two (often three or four) changes along the way. The fare is ¥7980. Get the staff at the ticket counter to write down the exact details of each transfer for you when you buy your ticket.

GETTING AROUND
To/From the Airport

OSAKA ITAMI AIRPORT 大阪伊丹空港

There are frequent limousine buses between Osaka Itami airport (Map p271) and Kyoto Station (the Kyoto Station airport bus stop is opposite the south side of the station, in front of Avanti department store). Buses also run between the airport and various hotels around town, but on a less regular basis (check with your hotel). The journey should take around 55 minutes and the cost is ¥1370. Be sure to allow extra time in case of traffic.

At Itami, the stand for these buses is outside the arrivals hall; buy your tickets from the machines and ask one of the attendants which stand is for Kyoto.

MK Taxi Sky Gate Shuttle limousine van service (☎ 721-2237) also offers limousine van service to/from the airport for ¥2000 (call at least two days in advance to reserve) or ask at the information counter in the arrivals hall on arrival in Osaka.

KANSAI INTERNATIONAL AIRPORT (KIX)
関西国際空港

The fastest, most convenient way to travel between KIX (Map p271) and Kyoto is on the special Haruka airport express, which makes the trip in about 75 minutes. Most seats are reserved (¥3490) but there are usually two cars on each train with unreserved seats (¥2980). Open seats are almost always available, so you don't have to purchase tickets in advance. First and last departures from Kyoto to KIX are 5.45am and 8.16pm; first and last departures from KIX to Kyoto are 6.29am and 10.18pm.

If you have time to spare, you can save some money by taking the *kanku kaisoku* (Kansai airport express) between the airport and Osaka Station and taking a regular *shinkaisoku* to/from Kyoto. The total journey by this method takes about 90 minutes with good connections and costs ¥1800, making it the cheapest option.

It's also possible to go by limousine bus between Kyoto and KIX (¥2300, about two hours). In Kyoto, the bus departs from the same place as the Itami-bound bus (see opposite).

A final option is the **MK Taxi Sky Gate Shuttle limousine van service** (☎ 721-2237), which will pick you up anywhere in Kyoto city and deliver you to KIX for ¥3000. Call at least two days in advance to reserve. The advantage of this method is that you are delivered from door to door and you don't have to lug your baggage through the train station. MK has a counter in the arrivals hall of KIX, and if there's room they'll put you on the next van to Kyoto. A similar service is offered by **Yasaka Taxi** (☎ 803-4800).

Bicycle

Kyoto is a great city to explore on a bicycle; with the exception of outlying areas it's mostly flat and there is a new bike path running the length of the Kamo-gawa.

Unfortunately, Kyoto must rank near the top in having the world's worst public facilities for bike parking and the city regularly impounds bikes parked outside of regulation bike-parking areas. If your bike does disappear, check for a poster in the vicinity (in both Japanese and English) indicating the time of seizure and the inconvenient place you'll have to go to pay a ¥2000 fine and retrieve your bike.

BICYCLE RENTAL

Tour Club (see p312) rents large-frame and regular bicycles for ¥800, with a ¥3000 deposit. Bicycles can be picked up between 8am and 9.30pm. They offer a similar deal at their sister inn, Budget Inn (p313).

Another great place to rent a bike is **Kyoto Cycling Tour Project** (KCTP; Map p291; ☎ 467-5175; www.kctp.net). These folks rent mountain bikes (¥1500 per day) which are perfect for getting around the city. Bicycles can be delivered upon request (¥500) or you can pick them up at their shop. KCTP also conducts a variety of bicycle tours of Kyoto, which are an excellent way to see the city (check the website for details).

Near Sanjō Station on the Keihan line, **Kitazawa Bicycle Shop** (Map p289; ☎ 771-2272; Kawabata-dōri; 🕔 8am-5pm) rents out bicycles for ¥200 per hour and ¥1000 per day. It's a 200m walk north of the station next to the river on the east side.

Nearby on Kawabata-dōri, north of Sanjō-dōri, **Rental Cycle Yasumoto** (Map p289; ☎ 751-0595; Kawabata-dōri; 🕔 9am-5pm) also offers a similar deal.

Most rental outfits require you to leave ID such as a passport or driver's licence.

BICYCLE PURCHASE

If you plan on spending more than a week or so exploring Kyoto by bicycle, it might make sense to purchase a used bicycle. A simple *mama chari* (shopping bike) can be had for as little as ¥3000. Try the used cycle shop **Ei Rin** (Map pp282-3; ☎ 752-0292; Imadegawa-dōri) near Kyoto University. Otherwise, you'll find a good selection of used bikes advertised for sale on the message board of the Kyoto International Community House.

Bus

Kyoto has an intricate bus network that is an efficient way to get around at moderate cost. Many of the bus routes used by foreign visitors have announcements in English. The core timetable for buses is between 7am and 9pm, though a few run earlier or later.

The bus terminal at Kyoto Station is on the northern side of the station and has three main departure bays (departure points are indicated by the letter of the bay and number of the bus stand within that bay).

The TIC's Kyoto Transportation Guide is a good map of the city's main bus lines, with a detailed explanation of the routes and a Japanese/English communication guide on the reverse side.

KANSAI

Bus stops throughout the city usually display a map of bus stops in the vicinity on the top section. On the bottom section there's a timetable for the buses serving that stop. Unfortunately, most of this information is written in Japanese, and those who don't read the language will simply have to ask locals waiting at the stop for help.

Entry to the bus is usually through the back door and exit is via the front door. Inner city buses charge a flat fare (¥220), which you drop into the clear plastic receptacle on top of the machine next to the driver. The machine gives change for ¥100 and ¥500 coins or ¥1000 notes, or you can ask the driver.

On buses serving the outer areas, you take a *seiri-ken* (numbered ticket) when entering. When you leave, an electronic board above the driver displays the fare corresponding to your ticket number.

To save time and money, you can buy a *kaisū-ken* (book of five tickets) for ¥1000. There's also a one-day card (*shi-basu senyō ichinichi jōshaken kaado*) valid for unlimited travel on city buses and subways that costs ¥500. A similar pass (Kyoto *kankō ichinichi jōsha-ken kaado*) that allows unlimited use of the bus and subway costs ¥1200. A two-day bus/subway pass (*futsuka jōsha-ken*) costs ¥2000. *Kaisū-ken* can be purchased directly from bus drivers. The other passes and cards can be purchased at major bus terminals and at the main bus information centre.

The main bus information centre is located in front of Kyoto Station. Here, you can pick up bus maps, purchase bus tickets and passes (on all lines, including highway buses), and get additional information. Nearby, there's an English/Japanese bus information computer terminal; just enter your intended destination and it will tell you the correct bus and bus stop.

When heading for locations outside the city centre, be careful which bus you board. Kyoto city buses are green, Kyoto buses are tan and Keihan buses are red and white.

Subway

The quickest way to travel between the north and the south of the city is to take the Karasuma line subway, which operates from 5.30am to 11.30pm. The minimum fare is ¥200.

There's also the new Tōzai line subway, which runs east–west across the city, from Daigo Station in the east to Nijō Station in the west, stopping at Sanjō-Keihan en route.

Taxi

Kyoto taxi fares start at ¥630 for the first 2km. The exception is **MK Taxis** (☎ 721-2237), which start at ¥580.

MK Taxis also provide tours of the city with English-speaking drivers. For a group of up to four people, prices start at ¥12,620 for a three-hour tour. Another company offering a similar service is **Kyōren Taxi Service** (☎ 672-5111).

KITAYAMA AREA
北山周辺

Starting on the north side of Kyoto city and stretching almost all the way to the Sea of Japan, the Kitayama mountains (literally 'Northern Mountains') are a natural escape prized by Kyoto city dwellers. Located directly north of Kurama, over the Hanase-tōgei pass, is the quiet rural valley of Hanase, which is home to farmers, artists and nature lovers. Further north, at the end of a Kyoto bus line, is Hirogawara, a small village that even has a small single-lift ski area that is open from January to March. Hirogawara is also the departure point for hikes entering the famous Ashiū virgin forest. The entire Kitayama area is a delight for cyclists, hikers, cross-country skiers and photographers.

Sleeping

There is good camping in the area. Otherwise, a good place to stay is **Hanase Suisen-Kyō** (水仙郷; fax 075-712-7023; www.suisenkyo.com; Kyoto-fu, Sakyō-ku, Hanase Harachi-chō; r ¥3200 per person; bookings by email/fax only), which is located between the small towns of Obuse and Hirogawara. It's a secluded riverside getaway that must be reached via footbridge (200m across the river from the bus stop). Facilities include three guest rooms, bicycles, a picnic table, and traditional living areas. Personalised tours of the area and prepared meals are available. To get there, take the bus described following and get off at Naka-no-cho (¥930, one hour 20 minutes from Kyoto).

KANSAI

Getting There & Away

Kyoto bus 32 (not Kyoto city bus) runs five times daily (four in winter) from Demachiyanagi (buses depart from the stand outside the Eizan-densha train station). It costs ¥1050 and takes one hour and 40 minutes to the end of the line in Hirogawara. Check the local bus times and incorporate a visit to Kurama to double your sightseeing pleasure.

SHIGA-KEN 滋賀県

Just across the Higashiyama mountains from Kyoto is Shiga-ken, a small prefecture dominated by Biwa-ko, Japan's largest lake. The prefecture has a variety of attractions that are easily visited as day trips from Kyoto. Ōtsu and Hikone are the major sightseeing centres. See Hiei-zan (p305) and Enryaku-ji (p305). JNTO publishes a leaflet entitled *Lake Biwa, Ōtsu & Hikone*, with useful maps and concise information. It's available at any JNTO-operated TIC, including the Kyoto TIC.

ŌTSU 大津
☎ 077 / pop 286,000

Ōtsu has developed from a 7th-century imperial residence (the city was capital of Japan for just five years) into a lake port and major post station on the Tōkaidō highway between eastern and western Japan. It is now the capital of Shiga-ken.

The **information office** (☎ 522-3830; ☯ 8.45am-5.25pm) is at JR Ōtsu Station. Some English is spoken here, and it has an excellent free map of the area entitled the *Biwako Ōtsu Guide Map*.

Mii-dera 三井寺
Mii-dera (☎ 522-2238; 246 Onjōji-chō; admission ¥500; ☯ 8am-5pm), formally known as Onjō-ji, is a short walk northwest from Keihan Hama-Ōtsu Station. The temple, founded in the late 7th century, is the head branch of the Jimon branch of the Tendai school of Buddhism. It started its days as a branch of Enryaku-ji on Hiei-zan, but later the two fell into conflict, and Mii-dera was repeatedly razed by Enryaku-ji's warrior monks.

Festival & Events

The **Ōtsu Matsuri** takes place on 7 and 8 October at Tenson-jinja, close to JR Ōtsu Station.

Ornate floats are displayed on the first day and paraded around the town on the second day. If you're in town on 8 August, be sure to catch the **Ōtsu Dai Hanabi Taikai** (Ōtsu Grand Fireworks Festival), which starts at dusk. The best spots to watch are along the waterfront near Keihan Hama-Ōtsu Station. Be warned that trains to and from Kyoto are packed for hours before and after the event.

Getting There & Away

From Kyoto you can either take the JR Tōkaidō line from JR Kyoto Station to Keihan Hama-Ōtsu Station (¥190, 10 minutes), or travel on the Kyoto Tōzai subway line from Sanjō Keihan Station to Hama-Ōtsu Station (¥390, 25 minutes).

SAKAMOTO 坂本

Sakamoto Station is the main station for access from Shiga-ken to Enryaku-ji.

Hiyoshi-taisha 日吉大社

If you fancy a detour on your visit to Hiei-zan, **Hiyoshi-taisha** (Hie-taisha; ☎ 578-0009; 5-1-1 Sakamoto; admission ¥300; ☯ 9am-4.30pm) is a 15-minute walk from Sakamoto Station. Dedicated to the deity of Hiei-zan, the shrine is closely connected with Enryaku-ji.

Getting There & Away

Sakamoto is best reached by taking the Kyoto Tōzai line subway from Sanjō-Keihan Station in Kyoto to Keihan Hama-Ōtsu Station; change there to a Keihan-line Sakamoto-bound *futsū*. The total fare is ¥590, and with good connections the trip takes about 40 minutes. You can also take the JR line to the Hiei-zan Sakamoto Station – be careful to take the Kosei (West Lake) line (¥320, 20 minutes).

HIRA-SAN 比良山

Hira-san is the high mountain range that rises to the west of Biwa-ko. It is a great hiking destination and there are many excellent hiking courses crisscrossing the peaks. It is best accessed by the JR Kosei line, which leaves from Kyoto Station (but be careful to board a Kosei-line train, as most trains on that track head to the other side of the lake).

A good base for hiking in the area is the **Maiko Hut** (舞子ハット; ☎ 077-596-8190; www .trekstation.co.jp/index5.html; dm ¥3500, r per person from ¥4000). The folks here will happily pick you

KANSAI

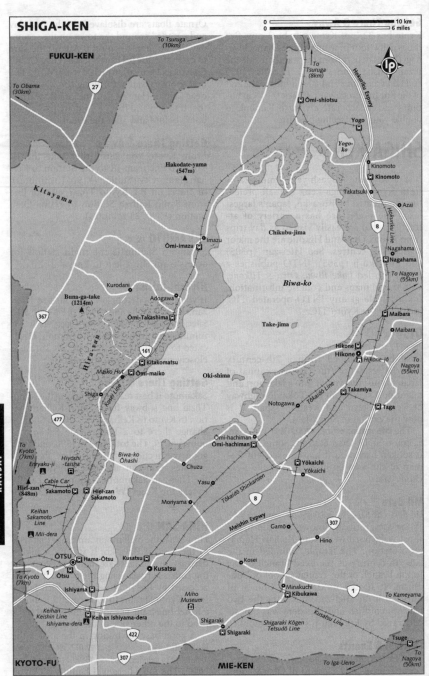

SHIGA-KEN

0 ——————— 10 km
0 ——————— 6 miles

FUKUI-KEN

To Tsuruga
(10km)

To Obama
(30km)

27

To Tsuruga
(8km)

Hokuriku Expwy

Ōmi-shiotsu

Yogo

Yogo-ko

Kinomoto
Kinomoto

Kitayama

Takatsuki

Azai

Hakodate-yama
(547m)

Hokuriku Line

8

Ōmi-imazu   Imazu

Chikubu-jima

Nagahama
Nagahama

To Nagoya
(55km)

Kurodani

Biwa-ko

Buna-ga-take
(1214m)

Adogawa

Ōmi-Takashima

Take-jima

Maibara
Maibara

Hira-san

161

Kitakomatsu

Kosei Line

Maiko Hut   Ōmi-maiko

Oki-shima

Hikone
Hikone   Hikone-jō

To
Nagoya
(55km)

Shiga

Takamiya

367

477

Notogawa

Tōkaidō Line

Taga

Ōmi-hachiman
Ōmi-hachiman

To Kyoto
(7km)

Hiyoshi
-taisha

Biwa-ko
Ōhashi

Chuzu

Yōkaichi
Yōkaichi

Enryaku-ji

Cable Car

Yasu

Tōkaidō Shinkansen

Hiei-zan
(848m)

Sakamoto   Hiei-zan
Sakamoto

Moriyama

8

Keihan
Sakamoto
Line

Meishin Expwy

Gamō

307

Mii-dera

Hino

ŌTSU   Hama-Ōtsu

Kusatsu

Kosei

To Kyoto
(7km)

1   Ōtsu

Kusatsu

To Kameyama

Ishiyama

Minakuchi
Kibukawa

1

Keihan
Keishin Line
Ishiyama-dera   Keihan Ishiyama-dera

Miho
Museum

Kusatsu Line

422

Shigaraki

Shigaraki Kōgen
Tetsudō Line

Tsuge

307

Shigaraki

To
Nagoya
(50km)

KYOTO-FU

MIE-KEN

To Iga-Ueno

KANSAI

up at Ōmi-maiko station (about 30 minutes from Kyoto) on the Kosei line if you call ahead to make arrangements. They can also arrange guided walks in the Hira-san range in English.

Several good hikes in the Hira-san range are described in Lonely Planet's *Hiking in Japan*, including the superb Yatsubuchi-no-taki hike, which we reckon is the best one-day hike near Kyoto.

ISHIYAMA-DERA 石山寺

This **temple** (☎ 537-0013; 1-1-1 Ishiyama-dera; admission ¥500; ☉ 8am-4.30pm), founded in the 8th century, now belongs to the Shingon sect. The room next to the Hondō (Main Hall) is famed as the place where Lady Murasaki wrote *The Tale of the Genji*. The temple precincts are in a lovely forest with lots of good trails to explore, including the one that leads up to Tsukimitei hall, from which there are great views over Biwa-ko.

The temple is a 10-minute walk south from Keihan Ishiyama-dera Station (continue along the road in the direction that the train was travelling). Take the Kyoto Tōzai line subway from Sanjō-Keihan Station in Kyoto to Keihan Hama-Ōtsu and change there to a Keihan-line Ishiyama-dera-bound *futsū* (¥520, 16 minutes). Alternatively, take the JR Tōkaidō line from JR Kyoto Station to JR Ishiyama-dera Station. *Kaisoku* (rapid) and *futsū* trains run this route (¥230, 10 minutes). Switch at JR Ishiyama Station to the Keihan line for the short journey to Keihan Ishiyama-dera Station (¥160, three minutes).

MIHO MUSEUM

The **museum** (☎ 0748-82-3411; www.miho.or.jp; 300, Momodani, Shigaraki; admission adult/child ¥1000/300; ☉ 10am-5pm Tue-Fri & Sun, 10am-7pm Sat, Tue-Sun mid-Mar–mid Jun, Jul–mid-Dec) is visually stunning, located in the countryside of Shiga-ken near the village of Shigaraki. The IM Pei-designed museum houses the Shumei Family art collection, which includes examples of Japanese, Middle Eastern, Chinese and South Asian art.

A visit to the museum is something like a visit to the secret hideout of an arch-villain in a James Bond film and there is no doubt that the facility is at least as impressive as the collection. Since a trip to the museum from Kyoto or Osaka can take the better

part of a day, we highly recommend calling the museum to check what's on before making the trip.

To get there, take the JR Tōkaidō line from Kyoto or Osaka to Ishiyama Station, and change to a Teisan bus bound for the museum.

HIKONE 彦根

☎ 0749 / pop 106,000

Hikone is the second-largest city in the prefecture and of special interest to visitors for its lovely castle, which dominates the town.

Orientation & Information

There is a good **tourist information office** (☎ 22-2954; ☉ 9am-5pm), on your left as you leave the station, with helpful maps and literature. The *Street Map & Guide to Hikone* has a map on one side and a suggested one-day bicycle tour of Hikone's sights on the back.

The castle is straight up the street from the station – about a 10-minute walk away.

Hikone-jō 彦根城

This **castle** (☎ 22-2742; 1-1 Konki-chō; admission ¥500; ☉ 8.30am-5pm) was completed in 1622 by the Ii family, who ruled as *daimyō* (feudal lords) over Hikone. It is rightly considered one of the finest remaining castles in Japan. Much of it is original, and you can get a great view across the lake from the upper storeys. The castle is surrounded by more than 1000 cherry trees, making it a popular spot for spring-time *hanami* activities.

After visiting the castle, don't miss nearby **Genkyū-en** (admission included in castle ticket; ☉ 8.30am-5pm), a lovely Chinese-influenced garden that was completed in 1677. Ask someone at the castle to point you in the right direction. There's a teahouse in the garden where ¥500 gets you a cup of *matcha* (powdered green tea) and a sweet to enjoy as you gaze over the scenery.

Festivals & Events

The **Hikone-jō Matsuri** takes place at the castle during the first three days in November. At this time children dress up in the costume of feudal lords and parade around the area.

Perhaps more interesting, however, is the **Birdman Contest**, held on the last Friday and Saturday of August at Matsubara Beach in Hikone. Here you will find contestants launching themselves over Lake Biwa in all manner of flimsy human-powered flying machines. It's really a whole lot of fun to watch.

Getting There & Away

Hikone is less than an hour in travelling time (*shinkaisoku*, ¥1110) from Kyoto on the JR Tōkaidō line. If you take the *shinkansen*, it is best to ride from Kyoto to Maibara (¥3330, 25 minutes) and then backtrack from there on the JR Tōkaidō line to Hikone (¥180, five minutes). Maibara is a major rail junction, the meeting place of the JR Tōkaidō, Hokuriku and Tōkaidō *shinkansen* lines. By *shinkaisoku*, Maibara is 52 minutes from Kyoto on the JR Tōkaidō line (¥1110).

NAGAHAMA 長浜

☎ 0749 / pop 61,063

Nagahama is interesting for its old *machiya* and kura (storehouses), which can be found in the streets east of the station. Some of the old buildings have been converted into atmospheric shops and are worth popping into as you explore the area. The speciality of the area is glass, and Nagahama's artisans produce a variety of high-quality and interesting work – souvenir hunters take note! Several of the buildings have also been converted into restaurants.

There is a **tourist information office** (☎ 63-7055; ☯ 10am-5pm) just outside the station, where you can pick up a detailed Japanese-language map of the area.

If you're in the area from 14 to 16 April, check out the **Nagahama Hikiyama Matsuri**, in which costumed children perform Hikiyama *kyōgen* (comic drama) on top of a dozen festival floats decked out with elaborate ornamentation.

Sleeping & Eating

Kokumin-shukusha Hōkō-sō (国民宿舎豊公荘; ☎ 62-0144; 10-1 Kōen-chō; r per person from ¥7000) This place is five minutes' walk west of the station in Hōkōen Park (*kokumin-shukusha* are people's lodges – cheap accommodation).

There are two classic old *shokudō* (simple, all-round Japanese eateries) in town on the right side of Ekimae-dōri, about a block east of the station. **Tora-ya Shokudō** (とらや 食堂; ☎ /fax 65-1455; Nagahama-chō; ☯ Fri-Wed) is the best place for cheap eats in town, with

such things as *kitsune donburi* (rice with pieces of fried tofu) for only ¥350 (look for the dilapidated old house on the corner). **Nakajimaya Shokudō** (中島屋食堂; ☎ 62-0205; Nagahama-chō; ☯ Tue-Sun) is a step up in price and comfort (look for the wooden front and the food models). Both of these places are time machines back to a forgotten Japan and are well worth stopping for.

For something more upscale, along with a tasty brew to wash it down with, try the **Beer Restaurant Nagahama Roman Beer** (ビア レストラン 長浜浪漫ビール; ☎ 63-4300; 14-1 Asahi-chō; per 330ml beer ¥498; ☯ 11.30am-10pm Wed-Mon), a microbrewery and restaurant about five minutes' walk from JR Nagahama Station, to the south (ask the folks at the tourist information office to point it out on a map).

Getting There & Away

Nagahama is a 10-minute ride north of Maibara on the JR Hokuriku line (*shinkaisoku*, ¥190, 10 minutes). See left for transport details to Maibara.

NORTHERN KANSAI & THE SAN-IN COAST
関西北部・山陰海岸

The spectacular coastline east from Tottori all the way to the Tango-hantō (Tango peninsula) in Kyoto-fu is known as the San-in Kaigan Kokuritsu Kōen – the San-in Coast National Park. There are sandy beaches, rugged headlands, rocky islets and a cruisy atmosphere.

There are train lines the length of the area, but they spend a fair bit of time inland and in tunnels. The best way to see the coastline is on wheels, whether it be a rental car, a motorbike, a bicycle or by thumb. If you stick to the trains, make the effort to get off every now and then.

The text in this section moves from west to east, starting at the Tottori-ken/Hyōgo-ken border. It is a continuation of the route along the San-in Coast described in the Western Honshū chapter. If you're heading east to west, read this section backwards. See San-In Coast National Park (p447) for more details on this area.

MOROYOSE 諸寄

If you want to check out life in a small Sea of Japan fishing village, Moroyose, in Hyōgo-ken near the border with Tottori-ken, provides a great chance. There is the convenient Moroyose Station on the JR San-in line, a sandy beach, an *asa-ichi* (morning fish market) at 9am Sunday to Friday at the port, and the **Youth Hostel Moroyose-sō** (諸寄荘ユースホ ステル; ☎ 0796-82-3614; 461 Moroyose; r per person ¥2625-2835, breakfast/dinner ¥525/945), just a short stroll from it all.

Just over the hill to the east is **Hamasaka**, which has cruises (from ¥1000), an *onsen* and a beach backed by a huge stand of pine trees among which you can camp.

TAKENO 竹野

Takeno is a gem of a fishing village/summer resort that is full of accommodation and eateries. It is extremely popular in summer. There is an **information office** (☎ 0796-47-1080; ⏲ 8.30am-5pm) on the main beachfront, a couple of kilometres north of Takeno Station on the JR San-in line. There is good summer swimming, and **Bentenhama camping area** (弁天浜キャンプ場; ☎ 0796-47-0888; camp sites adult/child ¥800/400) is a short walk away among pine trees that are bent at awkward angles by the winter winds. **Kitamaekan** (北 前館; ☎ 0796-47-2020; adult/child ¥400/250; ⏲ 9am-9pm Fri-Wed) is an *onsen* complex where the baths are on the 2nd floor with a great view of the beach and sea. **Hamaya Ryokan** (はま や旅館; ☎ 0796-47-0028; Takenohama; r per person ¥10,500 with 2 meals) is right on the beachfront next to the information office, but if it's full there are plenty of other options.

KINOSAKI 城崎

☎ 0796 / pop 4300

Inland off the coast, on the Maruyama-gawa, is the lovely little *onsen* town of Ki-nosaki, which makes a pleasant overnight excursion from Kyoto, Osaka or Kōbe. It is a laid-back place to roam around and soak in hot springs.

Information

Opposite the station is the **information office** (☎ 32-4141; ⏲ 9am-6pm) where the staff are extremely enthusiastic. They can provide an English brochure/map, suggest accommodation and make bookings. A smattering of English is spoken. The same office

has rental bicycles available for ¥400 for two hours or ¥800 a day. If you're just passing through, you could leave your bags in a coin locker, pick up a bicycle, go for a ride, have a bath or just soak your feet, and then carry on.

Sights & Activities

Kinosaki's biggest attraction is its **onsen** (admission ¥500; ⏲ Mon-Sun), of which there are six open to the public. Guests staying in town stroll the canal from bath to bath wearing *yukata* and *geta* (wooden sandals). Most of the ryokan and hotels in town have their own *uchi-yu* (private baths), but also provide their guests with free tickets to the ones outside (*soto-yu*).

Our favourite *onsen* in town is **Kounoyu** (鴻の湯; admission ¥500; ⏲ 7am-11pm), which has a nice *rotemburo* (outdoor bath). It's at the far end of town – get a map from the information office.

The town also has a **cable car** up to **Onsenji**, a temple built to commemorate the founding of the *onsen* in 738. The temple is halfway up, but if you go to the top, there are some fine views out to the coast.

Savoury crab from the Sea of Japan is a speciality in Kinosaki during the winter months.

On 14 and 15 October the **Danjiri Matsuri** sees teams of *mikoshi* (portable shrine) bearers clashing for pole position to get to the local shrine.

Sleeping

If you don't mind paying a bit of money, Kinosaki is a great place to experience a night in a traditional Japanese inn.

Nishimuraya Honkan (西村屋本館; ☎ 32-2211; honkan@nishimuraya.ne.jp; 469 Yushima, Kinosaki-chō; f per person from ¥27,450) This is a classic and the ultimate of inns here. If you would like to try the high-class ryokan experience, this is a good place. However, you'll have to book well in advance, as it's popular.

Tsuruya Ryokan (つるや旅館; ☎ 32-2924; 606 Yushima, Kinosaki-chō; r per person ¥6300 with breakfast) Far more affordable and still of a high standard, this is where Mr Tamura, who speaks English, will attend to your needs. Tsuruya is near the base of the ropeway, a ten-minute walk from the station.

Other options are **Tsutaya Ryokan** (つたや 旅館; ☎ 32-2511; 485 Yushima, Kinosaki-chō) along the canal, as well as **Mikuniya** (三国屋; ☎ 32-2414; www2.nkansai.ne.jp/hotel/mikuniya/english/index .htm; 221 Yushima, Kinosaki-chō), in front of the JR Kinosaki Station. Both have per person rates with two meals starting at ¥15,750.

Finally, if you don't mind staying a bit away from the centre of town, **Suishōen** (水翔苑; 32-4571; www.suisyou.com in Japanese; Kinosaki-chō; r per person from ¥7000) is a new large ryokan with a London taxi that will whisk you straight to the *onsen* of your choice and pick you up when you're done. It's a strangely pleasant feeling to ride in the back wearing nothing but a *yukata*!

Getting There & Away

Kinosaki is on the JR San-in line, 10 minutes north of Toyooka, 2½ hours from Osaka, and three hours from Kyoto. There are occasional *tokkyū* trains from Osaka and Kyoto.

EAST INTO KYOTO-FU

If you're using the JR San-in line, unfortunately it disappears inland and there isn't another JR line on the coast until the JR Obama line at Nishi-Maizuru, some 60km to the east. There's some great stuff coming up though, including Amanohashidate, and fortunately the Kita-Kinki Tango Miyazu-sen, a private line, picks up the link. It's quite a scenic ride which takes you through a lovely bit of rural Japan. If you're on a JR pass, this section will cost you extra. From Kinosaki, take the JR San-in line into Toyooka, a largish town that serves as a train junction, change to the Kita-Kinki Tango Miyazu-sen, and carry on east.

If you're heading westwards along the coast and want to visit Amanohashidate, you'll have to change to the Kita-Kinki Tango Miyazu-sen at Nishi-Maizuru.

KUMIHAMA 久美浜

The second station out from Toyooka is Kumihama, which is in Kyoto-fu. The large seawater bay named **Kumihama-wan** is connected to the Sea of Japan through a narrow gap at its northern end that has a bridge across it. There are free bicycles for use (¥1000 deposit) at the station, where there is an **information office** (☎ 0772-82-1781; ⏰ 9am-5pm). It's 16km for the full loop around the bay and a great bike ride if the weather is halfway decent. There's a good swimming beach out on the Sea of Japan coast. If you want to stay out there, try the **Ryokan Hamanoji Rinkō-an** (旅

館 浜の路 臨江庵; ☎ 0772-83-1096; 1795 Minatomiya, Kumihama-chō; r per person from ¥15,000, dinner from ¥7500), which has a pick-up service available from the JR Tangokanno Station.

TANGO-HANTŌ 丹後半島

At the eastern end of the San-in Coast National Park is the Tango-hantō, which juts north into the Sea of Japan. The train line cuts across its base to Amanohashidate, so if you want to check out the peninsula, you'll have to take to the road. A bus runs around the peninsula, passing a number of small scenic fishing ports. At the end of the peninsula, a large car park and restaurant mark the start of the 40-minute round-trip walk (about 3km) to the **Kyōga-misaki Lighthouse** (経ヶ岬灯台).

The village of **Ine** (伊根), on a perfect little bay on the eastern side of the Tango-hantō, is particularly interesting. There are *funaya* houses that are built right out over the water, under which boats are drawn in, as if in a carport. The best way to check it out is by boat, and **Ine-wan Meguri** tour boats putter around the bay (¥650, 30 minutes) from March to December. Buses (¥1100) reach Ine in half an hour from Amanohashidate.

Sleeping

One of the best ways to see the Tango-hantō is with **Two to Tango** (http://homepage.mac.com /divyam/; lodging & 3-day all-inclusive tour per person ¥100,000). This is an exclusive tour of the Tango Peninsula offered by a French longtime resident who's lived in Kyoto-fu for more than 20 years. You stay in a secluded farmhouse in Kurumi-dani (in the heart of the Tango-hantō) and make trips over scenic roads to excellent *onsen*, restaurants and lovely beaches. Everything is taken care of, including the driving. The tour gives you an intimate look at a side of Japan rarely glimpsed by foreign travellers and it's perfect for a gentle entry into the country or to wind down after a hectic trip.

There are several fine *minshuku* (B&B-style accommodation) in the town of Ine including **Yoza-sō** (与謝荘; ☎ 0772-32-0278; 507 Hirata; per person from ¥9000 with two meals).

WAKASA-WAN 若狭湾

The area east of Tango-hantō is known as the **Wakasa-wan Kokutei Kōen** (Wakasa Bay Quasi-National Park), and includes parts of northern Kyoto-fu and western Fukui-ken.

It is fairly easily accessed from the cities of Kansai and has beaches that are very popular in summer.

Amanohashidate 天橋立

☎ 0772 / pop 22,532

Amanohashidate (Bridge to Heaven) is rated as one of Japan's 'three great views', along with Miyajima (p412) and the islands of Matsushima-wan (p463). The 'bridge' is really a long, narrow tree-covered (8000 pine trees!) sand-spit, 3.5km in length. Just a couple of narrow channels prevent it from cutting off the top of the bay, Miyazu-wan, as a separate lake. The sand-spit itself is pleasant, and someone with a good deal of foresight has done a great job keeping the construction and concrete boys away. There is good swimming, as well as beach showers, toilet facilities and covered rest areas the length of the spit. It is worth noting, of course, that this area is something of a tourist circus, and it's not particularly scenic, despite it's top-three-views rating.

The town of Amanohashidate consists of two separate parts, one at each end of the spit. At the southern end there are a number of hotels, ryokan, restaurants, a popular temple and JR Amanohashidate Station. There's an **information counter** (☎ 22-8030; ☉ 10am-6pm), stocking an English brochure, at the train station.

At the other end, a funicular railway (¥640 return) and a chairlift run up the hillside to the Kasamatsu-kōen vantage point, which affords a brilliant view of the sand-spit.

From here, incidentally, you're supposed to view the sand-spit by turning your back to it, bending over and observing it framed between your legs! (It supposedly makes the Amanohashidate look like it is 'floating'.)

SLEEPING

Amanohashidate Youth Hostel (天橋立ユースホステル; ☎ 27-0121; 905 Nakano, Miyazu-shi; per person with/without 2 meals ¥4250/2950) At the northern end of the 'bridge', this modern-thinking YH even has beer on tap in its dining room. To get there take a bus from JR Amanohashidate Station and get off at the Jinja-mae bus stop (20 minutes), from where it's a 1km walk (with signs from the bus stop). If you've got plenty of time, allow an hour to walk along the spit to get there.

There are a number of ryokan and hotels near the station at the southern end of the 'bridge', though they're generally fairly expensive. Best deals:

Minshuku Maruyasu (民宿まるやす; ☎ 22-2310; toy63@par.odn.ne.jp; Miyazu-shi, in front of Amanohashidate Station; r per person with/without meals ¥7560/5145)

Young Inn Amanohashidate (ヤングイン天橋立; ☎ 22-0650; 310 Monju; s/tw per person ¥4725/3675)

Toriki Ryokan (鳥喜旅館; ☎ 22-0010; 463-5 Monju; r with 2 meals ¥15,750)

EATING

There are several decent but slightly overpriced shokudō at the southern end of the 'bridge', including **Resutoran Monju** (レストラン文珠) which has asari udon (udon noodles with clams), a local speciality, for ¥1000. Look for the red and white sign as you approach Chion-ji (the temple at the southern end of the 'bridge').

GETTING THERE & AWAY

The Kita-kinki Tango Tetsudō line runs between JR Stations at Toyooka to the west and NishiMaizuru to the east. Amanohashidate Station is on this line, 1¼ hours from Toyooka (futsū ¥1160) and 40 minutes from Nishi-Maizuru (futsū ¥620). There are several direct trains from Kyoto daily, but JR pass holders will have to fork out for the Kita-kinki Tango Tetsudō part of the route.

GETTING AROUND

You can cross the 'bridge to heaven' on foot, bicycle or on a motorcycle of less than 125cc capacity. Bicycles can be hired at a number of places for ¥400 for two hours or ¥1600 a day. Tour boats (¥520) also operate across Miyazu-wan.

MAIZURU 舞鶴

There's nothing overly appealing about the two ports of Nishi-Maizuru and Higashi-Maizuru, but they play important parts in the area's transportation networks. If you've come from the west on the Kita-Kinki Tango Tetsudo trains, **Nishi-Maizuru** is the end of the line and where the JR Obama line comes out to meet the coast. If you're on your way to Amanohashidate, this is where you'll have to change to the private line.

There are regular ferry services to Otaru in Hokkaidō from Higashi-Maizuru (and also from Tsuruga at the eastern end of the

Wakasa-wan – see p269). This is a cheap and interesting way of getting to Hokkaidō. The cheapest tickets are ¥8200 for the 20-hour journey. Call **Shin-Nihonkai Ferry** (☎ 06-6345-2921) for details.

OSAKA 大阪

☎ 06 / pop 2.48 million

Osaka is the working heart of Kansai. Famous for its down-to-earth citizens and hearty cuisine, Osaka combines a few historical and cultural attractions with all the delights of a modern Japanese city. Indeed, Osaka is surpassed only by Tokyo as a showcase of the Japanese urban phenomenon.

This isn't to say that Osaka is an attractive city; almost bombed flat in WWII, it appears an endless expanse of concrete boxes punctuated by *pachinko* parlours and elevated highways. But the city somehow manages to rise above this and exert a peculiar charm. At night, the city really comes into its own; this is when all those drab streets and alleys come alive with flashing neon, beckoning residents and travellers alike with promises of tasty food and good times.

Osaka's highlights include Osaka-jō and its surrounding park, Osaka Aquarium with its enormous whale shark, the Blade Runner nightscapes of the Dōtombori area and the wonderful Open Air Museum of Old Japanese Farmhouses. But Osaka has more to offer than its specific sights; like Tokyo, Osaka is a city to be experienced in its totality, and casual strolls are likely to be just as rewarding as structured sightseeing tours.

HISTORY

Osaka has been a major port and mercantile centre from the beginning of Japan's recorded history. It was also briefly the first capital of Japan (before the establishment of a permanent capital at Nara). During its early days, Osaka was Japan's centre for trade with Korea and China, a role which it shares today with Kōbe and Yokohama.

In the late 16th century, Osaka rose to prominence when Toyotomi Hideyoshi, having unified all of Japan, chose Osaka as the site for his castle. Merchants set up around the castle and the city grew into a busy economic centre. This development was further encouraged by the Tokugawa shōgunate, which adopted a hands-off approach to the city, allowing merchants to prosper unhindered by government interference.

In the modern period, Tokyo has usurped Osaka's position as economic centre of Japan, and most of the companies formerly headquartered in Osaka have moved east. Nonetheless, Osaka remains an economic powerhouse and the prefecture has recorded a GDP bigger than the individual GDPs of all but eight countries in the world in the past several years. However, the city has been hard hit by Japan's ongoing recession and many businesses have closed, particularly those that used to cater to businessmen out entertaining clients.

ORIENTATION

Osaka is usually divided into two areas: Kita and Minami. Kita (Japanese for 'north') is the city's main business and administrative centre and contains two of its biggest train stations, JR Osaka and Hankyū Umeda Stations.

Minami (Japanese for 'south') is the city's entertainment district and contains the bustling shopping and nightlife zones of Namba and Shinsaibashi. It's also home to two major train stations, JR Namba and Nankai Namba Stations.

The dividing line between Kita and Minami is formed by two rivers, the Dōjima-gawa and the Tosabori-gawa, between which you'll find Nakano-shima, a peaceful green island that is home to the Museum of Oriental Ceramics. About 1km southeast of Nakano-shima you'll find Osaka-jō and its surrounding park, Osaka-jō-kōen.

To the south of the Minami area you'll find another group of sights clustered around Tennō-ji Station. These include Shitennō-ji, Tennō-ji-kōen, Den-Den Town (the electronics neighbourhood) and the retro entertainment district of Shin-Sekai.

The bay area, to the west of the city centre, is home to another set of attractions including the excellent Osaka Aquarium and Universal Studios Japan theme park.

Keep in mind that, while JR Osaka Station is centrally located in the Kita area, if you're coming from Tokyo by *shinkansen* you will arrive at Shin-Osaka Station, which is three stops (about five minutes) north of Osaka Station on the Midō-suji subway line.

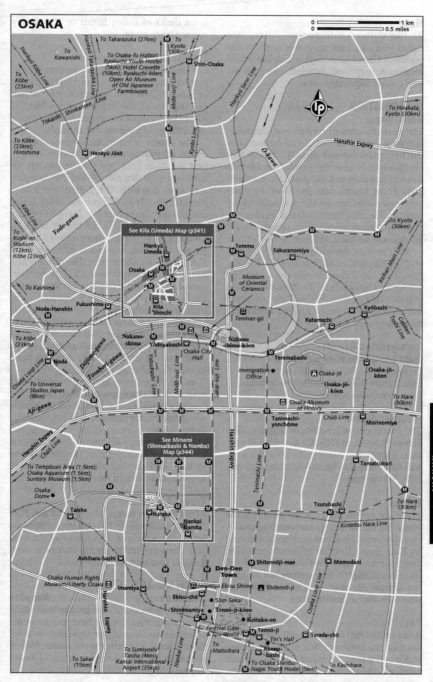

OSAKA

0 ———— 1 km
0 ———— 0.5 miles

To Takarazuka (27km)
To Kyoto (30km)
To Osaka-fu Hattori Ryokuchi Youth Hostel (5km); Hotel Crevette (10km); Ryokuchi-kōen; Open Air Museum of Old Japanese Farmhouses
Shin-Osaka

To Kawanishi

To Kōbe (23km)

To Kōbe (23km); Hiroshima

Hankyū Jūsō

Tōkaidō Shinkansen Line

Midō-suji Line

Hankyū Sentri Line

Kyoto Line

Ō-gawa

Hanshin Expwy

To Hirakata; Kyoto (30km)

Kōbe Line

Yodo-gawa

See Kita (Umeda) Map (p341)

Hankyū Umeda

Osaka

Kita Shinchi

Temma

Sakuranomiya

To Kyoto (30km)

To Kōshi-en Stadium (12km); Kōbe (23km)

To Kashima

Fukushima

Noda-Hanshin

Museum of Oriental Ceramics

Keihan Main Line

Gakken Toshi Line

Kyōbashi

Katamachi

To Kōbe (23km)

Osaka Loop Line

Noda

To Universal Studios Japan (8km)

Aji-gawa

Dōjima-gawa

Tosabori-gawa

Nakano-shima

Yodoyabashi

Osaka City Hall

Yotsubashi Line

Midō-suji Line

Sakai-suji Line

Tenman-gū

Nakano-shima-kōen

Temmabashi

Immigration Office

Osaka-jō

Osaka-jō-kōen

Osaka-jō-kōen

To Nara (30km)

Hanshin Expwy

Chūō Line

Osaka Museum of History

Tanimachi-yonchōme

Chūō Line

Morinomiya

See Minami (Shinsaibashi & Namba) Map (p344)

Tanimachi Line

Hanshin Expwy

Tamatsukuri

To Tempōzan Area (1.5km); Osaka Aquarium (1.5km); Suntory Museum (1.5km)

Osaka Dome

Taisho

Namba

Nankai Namba

Tsuruhashi

To Nara (30km)

Kintetsu Nara Line

Ashihara-bashi

Osaka Human Rights Museum/Liberty Osaka

Imamiya

Hanshin Expwy

Den-Den Town

Shitennōji-mae

Momodani

Osaka Loop Line

Imamiya Ebisu Shrine

Ebisu-chō

Shinimamiya

Shin-Sekai

Tennō-ji-kōen

Shitennō-ji

Keitaku-en

Nankai Line

Festival Gate & Spa World

Tennō-ji

Tin's Hall

Terada-chō

To Sumiyoshi Taisha (4km); Kansai International Airport (35km)

To Matsubara

Abeno-bashi

To Osaka Shiritsu Nagai Youth Hostel (5km)

To Sakai (15km)

To Kashihara

KANSAI

Maps

At the visitors' information offices (see right) you can pick up a free copy of the excellent *Osaka City Map*, which has a subway/train map and detailed insets of the city's most important areas.

INFORMATION
Bookshops

The best selection of foreign and Japanese-language books in Osaka can be found at the huge new **Junkudō** (Map p341; ☎ 4799-1090; 10am-9pm) bookstore, inside the Dōjima Avanza Building in Kita, about ten minutes' walk from Osaka Station. Most English-language books are on the 3rd floor, along with a café, and English travel guides, including a good selection of Lonely Planet guides, are on the 2nd floor.

Also in Kita, **Kinokuniya** (Map p341; ☎ 6372-5821; 10am-9pm) inside Hankyū Umeda Station, also has a decent selection of foreign books and magazines. In Minami, **Athens** (Map p344; ☎ 6253-0185; 10am-10pm) bookshop has a good selection of English books and magazines on its 4th floor.

Immigration Offices

Osaka immigration office (Map p339; ☎ 6941-0771; 9am-5pm Mon-Fri) The main office for the Kansai region is a three-minute walk from exit 3 of Temmabashi Station on the Keihan main line.

Internet Access

The tourist offices have lists of Internet cafés. **Kinko's** (Map p344; ☎ 6245-1922; Minami; per 10 min ¥200; 24hr) **Web House** (Map p341; ☎ 6367-9555; Kita; per 30 min ¥600; 11am-8pm)

Money

There are several banks in the underground malls and on the streets surrounding Osaka, Hankyū Umeda and Nankai Namba Stations. In Kita, you'll find an international ATM down the street from the Osaka Hilton Hotel. In Minami, there's an international ATM at the **Citibank** (Map p344; ☎ 6213-2731; 9am-3pm Mon-Fri, ATM 24hr) in Shinsaibashi.

Post

Osaka Central Post Office (Map p341; ☎ 6347-8034) Outside the southern side of Osaka Station in Kita. The post office has a useful 24-hour service window. For fax services, try the front desks of major hotels or almost any convenience store.

Tourist Information

For up-to-date information on events happening while you're in town, pick up a copy of *Kansai Time Out* magazine. Also worth picking up at the information offices is *Meet Osaka*, a pocket-sized reference guide to forthcoming events and festivals.

The Osaka Tourist Association operates **visitors information offices** (8am-8pm, closed 31 Dec-3 Jan); Namba Station (Map p344; ☎ 6643-2125; Minami); Osaka Station (Map p341; ☎ 6345-2189; Kita); Shin-Osaka Station (Map p339; ☎ 6305-3311); Tennō-ji Station (Map p339; ☎ 6774-3077), the main office being the one in Osaka Station. Many travellers have problems finding the tourist office in Osaka Station. To get there from JR trains, go out the Midō-suji ticket gate/exit, turn right, and walk about 50m. The office is just outside the station, beneath a pedestrian overpass, beside the city bus terminal. From the subway, go out exit No 9, and look for it outside the station, beside the bus terminal.

Osaka and Kansai International Airports also have information counters. All the offices can help book accommodation, but to avail yourself of this service you will have to visit the office in person.

In addition to the previously mentioned map, the information offices stock the incredibly useful *Osaka Tourist Guide*, which will handily supplement the information in this book.

There are many discount ticket shops on the B1 floor of the Ekimae Daisan building in Kita, and another one nearby on street level in Kita-Shinchi (see Map p341).

Travel Agencies

A'cross Travellers Bureau (Map p341; ☎ 6345-0150; 1-4-10 Sonezakishinchi; 10am-7pm Mon-Fri, 10am-5pm Sat) In the Kita area, this is one of the best and cheapest travel agents in town, with English speakers always on hand.

SIGHTS & ACTIVITIES
Kita Area キタ Map p341

By day, Osaka's centre of gravity is the Kita area. While Kita doesn't have any great attractions to detain the traveller, it does have a few good department stores, lots of places to eat and the eye-catching Umeda Sky building.

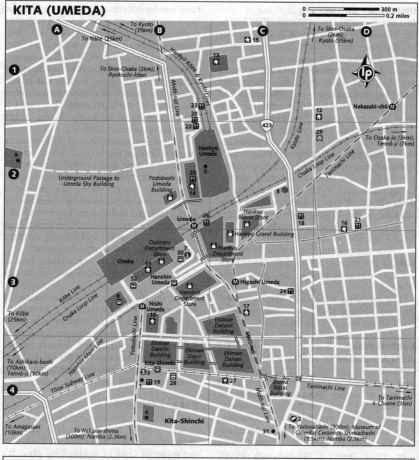

KITA (UMEDA)

KANSAI

UMEDA SKY BUILDING 梅田スカイビル

Just northwest of Osaka Station, the Umeda Sky building is Osaka's most dramatic piece of modern architecture. The twin-tower complex looks like a space-age version of Paris's Arc De Triomphe. Residents of Osaka are sharply divided about its appearance: some love its futuristic look while others find it an eyesore. What is certain is that the view from the top on a clear day is impressive.

There are two observation galleries: an outdoor one on the roof and an indoor one on the floor below. Getting to the top is only half the fun as you take a glassed-in escalator for the final five storeys (definitely not for vertigo sufferers). Tickets for the **observation decks** (☎ 6440-3855; 1-1-88 Ōyodonaka Kita-ku; admission ¥700; ⏰ 10am-10.30pm) include the white-knuckled escalator ride and can be purchased on the 3rd floor of the east tower.

Below the towers, you'll find **Takimi-koji Alley**, a re-creation of an early Showa-era market street crammed with restaurants and *izakaya*.

The building is reached via an underground passage that starts just north of both Osaka and Umeda Stations.

Central Osaka   Map p339
OSAKA MUSEUM OF HISTORY 大阪歴史博物館

Just southwest of Osaka-jō, the new **Osaka Museum of History** (Osaka Rekishi Hakubutsukan; ☎ 6946-5728; 4-1-32 Ōtemae, Chūō-ku; admission ¥600; ⏰ 9.30am-5pm Mon, Wed, Thu, Sat & Sun, 9.30am-8pm Fri) is housed in a fantastic new building adjoining the Osaka NHK Broadcast Center. The display floors of the museum occupy the 7th to the 10th floors of the new sail-shaped building.

The displays are broken into four sections by floor; you start at the top and work your way down, passing in time from the past to the present. The displays are very well done and there are plenty of English explanations; taped tours are available.

The museum is a two-minute walk northeast of Tanimachi-yonchōme Station.

OSAKA-JŌ 大阪城

This **castle** (Osaka Castle; ☎ 6941-3044; 1-1 Osaka-jō Chūō-ku; admission to grounds free, to castle keep ¥600; ⏰ 9am-5pm Sep-May, 9am-8pm Jun-Aug) was built as a display of power by Toyotomi Hideyoshi after he achieved his goal of unifying Japan.

One hundred thousand workers toiled for three years to construct an 'impregnable' granite castle, finishing the job in 1583. However, it was destroyed just 32 years later, in 1615, by the armies of Tokugawa Ieyasu.

Within 10 years the castle had been rebuilt by the Tokugawa forces, but it was to suffer a further calamity when another generation of the Tokugawa clan razed it rather than let it fall to the forces of the Meiji Restoration in 1868.

The present structure is a 1931 concrete reconstruction of the original, which was refurbished at great cost in 1997 (serious fans of Japanese castles should head west to see the castle at Himeji, p360). The interior of the castle houses an excellent collection of displays relating to the castle, Toyotomi Hideyoshi and the city of Osaka. On the 8th floor there is an observation deck offering excellent views of Osaka and surrounding areas.

The castle and park are at their best in the spring cherry-blossom and fall-foliage seasons.

The Ōte-mon gate, which serves as the main entrance to the park, is a 10-minute walk northeast of Tanimachi-yonchōme Station (sometimes written as Tanimachi 4-chome) on the Chūō and Tanimachi subway lines. You can also take the Osaka Loop line, get off at Osaka-jō-kōen Station and enter through the back of the castle.

Nakano-shima 中之島

Sandwiched between Dōjima-gawa and Tosabori-gawa, this island is a pleasant oasis of trees and riverside walkways in the midst of Osaka's unrelenting grey. It's also home to **Osaka City Hall**, the Museum of Oriental Ceramics (below) and **Nakano-shima-kōen**. The latter, on the eastern end of the island, is a good place for an afternoon stroll or picnic lunch.

MUSEUM OF ORIENTAL CERAMICS 東洋陶磁美術館

With more than 2700 pieces in its permanent collection, this **museum** (☎ 6223-0055; 1-1-26 Nakanoshima, Kita-ku; admission ¥500; ⏰ 9.30am-5pm Tue-Sun) has one of the finest collections of Chinese and Korean ceramics in the world. At any one time, about 300 of the pieces from the permanent collection are on display, and there are often special exhibits (which cost extra).

To get to the museum, go to Yodoya-bashi Station on either the Midō-suji line or the Keihan line (different stations). Walk north to the river and cross to Nakanoshima. Turn right, pass the city hall on your left, bear left with the road, and look for the squat brown brick building.

Minami Area ミナミ   Map p344

A few stops south of Osaka Station on the Midō-suji subway line (get off at either Shinsaibashi or Namba Stations), the Minami area is the place to spend the evening in Osaka. Its highlights include the Dōtombori Arcade, the National Bunraku Theatre, Dōgusuji-ya Arcade and Amerika-Mura.

DŌTOMBORI 道頓堀

Dōtombori is Osaka's liveliest nightlife area. It's centred around **Dōtombori-gawa** and **Dōtombori Arcade**, a strip of restaurants and theatres where a peculiar type of Darwinism is the rule for both people and shops: survival of the flashiest. In the evening, head to **Ebisubashi** bridge to sample the glittering nightscape, which brings to mind a scene from the science-fiction movie *Blade Runner*.

Only a short walk south of Dōtombori Arcade you'll find **Hōzen-ji**, a tiny temple hidden down a narrow alley. The temple is built around a moss-covered **Fudō-myōō statue**. This statue is a favourite of people employed in *mizu shobai* (water trade) who pause before work to throw some water on the moss-covered statue. Nearby, you'll find **Hōzen-ji Yokochō**, a tiny alley filled with traditional restaurants and bars.

Next to Hōzen-ji, the small **Kamigata Ukiyo-e Museum** (☎ 6211-0303; 1-6-4 Nanba, Chūo-ku; admission ¥500; ◷ 11am-6pm Tue-Sun) houses a small collection of *ukiyo-e* (wood block prints of the so-called 'floating world') prints in the Nishiki-e style. While the collection is poorly displayed and dimly lit, it does offer a chance to see some original *ukiyo-e* prints. Oddly, the 3rd floor of the museum is devoted to displays on rice and rice growing, making this museum a rival of Tokyo's Tobacco and Salt Museum in terms of bizarre museum collections. The odd pairing celebrates the fact that profits from Osaka's rice trade were used to support the work of Osaka's *ukiyo-e* artists.

To the south of Dōtombori, in the direction of Nankai Namba Station, you'll find a maze of colourful arcades with more restaurants, *pachinko* parlours, strip clubs, cinemas and who knows what else. To the north of Dōtombori, between Midō-suji and Sakai-suji, the narrow streets are crowded with hostess bars, discos and pubs.

DŌGUYA-SUJI ARCADE 道具屋筋

If you desperately need a *tako-yaki* (octopus ball) fryer, a red lantern to hang outside your shop or plastic food-models to lure the customers in, this shopping arcade is the place to go. You'll also find endless knives, pots, pans and just about anything else that's even remotely related to the preparation and consumption of food.

AMERIKA-MURA アメリカ村

Amerika-Mura (which means 'America Village') is a compact enclave of trendy shops and restaurants, with a few discreet love hotels thrown in for good measure. The best reason to come is to check out the hordes of colourful Japanese teens living out the myth of America.

In the middle of it all is Amerika-Mura Triangle Park, an all-concrete park with benches where you can sit and watch the parade of fashion victims. Amerika-Mura is one or two blocks west of Midō-suji, bounded on the north by Suomachi-suji and on the south by Dōtombori-gawa.

NATIONAL BUNRAKU THEATRE
国立文楽劇場

Although *bunraku*, or puppet theatre, did not originate in Osaka, the art form was popularised at this **theatre** (☎ 6212 2531; 1-12-10 Nihonbashi Chūo-ku) . The most famous *bunraku* playwright, Chikametsu Monzaemon (1653–1724), wrote plays set in Osaka concerning the classes that traditionally had no place in Japanese art: merchants and the denizens of the pleasure quarters. Not surprisingly, *bunraku* found an appreciative audience among these people, and a theatre was established to put on the plays of Chikametsu in Dōtombori. Today's theatre is an attempt to revive the fortunes of *bunraku*.

Performances are only held at certain times of the year: check with the tourist information offices. Tickets normally start at around ¥2300; earphones and program guides in English are available.

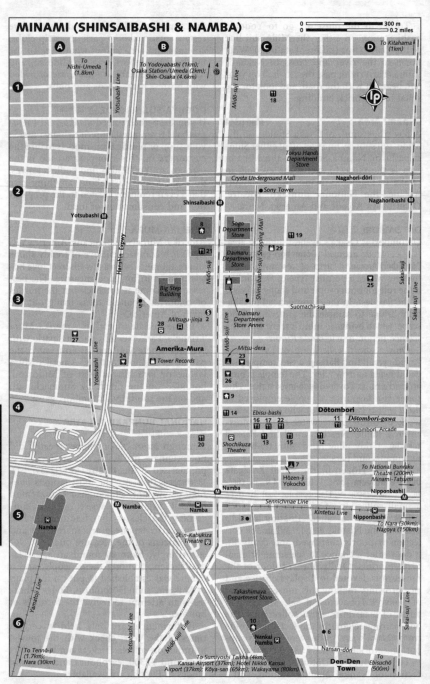

MINAMI (SHINSAIBASHI & NAMBA)

0 _____ 300 m
0 _____ 0.2 miles

To Kitahama (1km)

To Nishi-Umeda (1.8km)

To Yodoyabashi (1km); Osaka Station/Umeda (2km); Shin-Osaka (4.6km)

Yotsubashi Line

Midō-suji Line

18

Tokyu Hands Department Store

Crysta Underground Mall

Nagahori-dōri

Shinsaibashi

Sony Tower

Nagahoribashi

Yotsubashi

Sogo Department Store

8

21

19

29

Daimaru Department Store

Hanshin Expwy

Midō-suji

Shinsaibashi-suji Shopping Mall

Big Step Building

5

25

1

Suomachi-suji

Sakai-suji Line

28

Mitsugu-jinja

2

Daimaru Department Store Annex

27

Yotsubashi Line

24

Amerika-Mura

Tower Records

Mitsu-dera

23

26

9

Sakai-suji

14

Ebisu-bashi

Dōtombori

11

Dōtombori-gawa

20

16 17 22

Dōtombori Arcade

Shochikuza Theatre

13 15 12

To National Bunraku Theatre (200m); Minami-Tatsumi

7

Hōzen-ji Yokochō

Namba

Sennichmae Line

Nipponbashi

Namba

Namba

Kintetsu Line

Nipponbashi

3

Shin-Kabukiza Theatre

To Nara (30km); Nagoya (150km)

Namba

Yamatoji Line

Takashimaya Department Store

Midō-suji Line

10

Nankai Namba

6

Nansan-dōri

Sakai-suji Line

To Tennō-ji (1.7km); Nara (30km)

To Sumiyoshi Taisha (4km); Kansai Airport (37km); Hotel Nikkō Kansai Airport (37km); Kōya-san (65km); Wakayama (80km)

Den-Den Town

To Ebisuchō (500m)

KANSAI

INFORMATION			
Athens アテネ書店	1 C3	
Citibank (International ATM)		
シティバンク	2 B3	
Discount Ticket Shop		
格安チケット売り場	3 C5	
International ATM 国際ATM	(see 14)	
Kinko's キンコーズ	4 C1	

SIGHTS & ACTIVITIES	
Amerika-Mura Triangle Park	
アメリカ村三角公園	5 B3
Dōguya-suji Arcade 道具筋屋	6 D6
Hōzen-ji 法善寺	7 C5
Kamigata Ukiyo-e Museum	(see 7)

SLEEPING	
Hotel Nikkō Osaka ホテル日航大阪	8 B2

Hotel Riva Nankai	
ホテルリーバ南海	9 C4
Swissotel Nankai Osaka	
スイスホテル南海大阪	10 C6

EATING	
Chibō 千房	11 D4
Dōtombori Rāmen Daishokudō	
道頓堀ラーメン大食堂	12 D4
Ganko Zushi がんこ寿司	13 C4
Gin Sen 銀扇	14 C4
Imai Honten 今井本店	15 C4
Kani Dōraku Honten かに道楽本店	16 C4
Krungtep クンテープ	17 C4
Namaste ナマステ	18 C1
Nishiya にし家	19 C2
Santana サンタナ	20 B4

Ume no Hana 梅の花	21 B3
Zuboraya づぼらや	22 C4

DRINKING	
American Beauty	
アメリカンビューティー	23 C4
Arc en Ciel アークアンシェル	(see 10)
Cellar ザ セラー	24 B4
Murphy's マーフィーズ	25 D3
Pig & Whistle	
ビッグ ＆ ホイッスル	26 C4
SoulFuckTry ソウルファクトリー	27 A3

ENTERTAINMENT	
Grand Café グランドカフェ	28 B3

SHOPPING	
Naniwa Camera カメラのナニワ	29 C3

Tennō-ji & Around
天王寺公園　　　　　　　　　**Map p339**

FESTIVAL GATE フェスティバルゲート

South of Shin-Sekai and west of Tennō-ji-kōen you'll find the new entertainment complex of **Festival Gate** (☎ 6635-1000; 3-4-36 Ebisu higashi, Naniwa-ku; admission free; ◷ 10am-10pm), which is really an amusement park surrounded by a huge shopping/dining complex. The rides are in the open atrium of the complex and the roller coaster snakes its way over and around the walls of the places, offering tantalising glimpses of the city and the nearby Spa World bathing complex. It's a good spot to bring the kids, but you'll really have to shell out the yen to enjoy yourself here.

SHIN-SEKAI 新世界

For something completely different, take a walk through this retro entertainment district just west of Tennō-ji-kōen. At the heart of it all you'll find crusty old Tsūten-kaku tower, a 103m-high structure that dates back to 1912 (the present tower was rebuilt in 1969). When the tower first went up it symbolised everything new and exciting about this once-happening neighbourhood (shin-sekai is Japanese for 'New World').

Now, Shin-Sekai is a world that time forgot. You'll find ancient pachinko parlours, run-down theatres, dirt-cheap restaurants and all manner of raffish and suspicious characters.

SHITENNŌ-JI 四天王寺

Founded in 593, **Shitennō-ji** (☎ 6771-0066; 1-11-18 Shitennō-ji, Tennōji-ku; admission free; ◷ 9am-5pm, closed 28 Dec-1 Jan) has the distinction of being one of the oldest Buddhist temples in Japan, although none of the present buildings are originals; most are the usual concrete re-productions, with the exception of the big stone torii (Shintō entrance gate). The torii dates back to 1294, making it the oldest of its kind in Japan. Apart from the torii, there is little of real historical significance, and the absence of greenery in the raked-gravel grounds makes for a rather desolate atmosphere. The adjoining **museum** (admission ¥200) is of limited interest.

The temple is most easily reached from Shitennōji-mae Station on the Tanimachi subway line. Take the southern exit, cross to the left side of the road and take the small road that goes off at an angle away from the subway station. The entrance to the temple is on the left.

SPA WORLD スパワールド

Next door to Festival Gate is the super-spa known as **Spa World** (☎ 6631-0001; 3-4-24 Ebisu higashi, Naniwa-ku; per hr/day Mon-Fri ¥2400/2700, Sat, Sun & holidays ¥2700/3000; ◷ 10am-9am the following day). Billed as the world's largest spa, it consists of two floors of baths, one Asian themed and one European themed, and a rooftop waterworld with pools and waterslides, along with restaurants and relaxation areas.

The Asian and European bath floors are sex segregated; one month the ladies get the Asian bath floor and the men the European bath floor, and then it switches to the opposite, so you'll have to visit twice to sample all the baths (they're fairly similar, so you're not missing much if you don't). We particularly like the rotemburo (outdoor bath) on the roof, where you can show off your tan to folks whizzing by on the Festival Gate roller coaster (and from which you can see Tsūten-kaku tower rising like a retro space ship to the north). Be sure to bring a bathing suit if you want to visit the waterworld (or you can rent one for ¥300).

KANSAI

TENNŌ-JI-KŌEN 天王寺公園

A visit to this park (☎ 6771-8401; 1-108 Chausu-yama-chō, Tennōji-ku; admission ¥150; ⏰ 9.30am-5am Tue-Sun) can easily be combined with a visit to Shitennō-ji and Shin-Sekai.

The park has a botanical garden, a zoo and a circular garden known as **Keitaku-en**. However, the best reason to visit the park is for the Sunday karaoke songfests held on the road that runs through the middle of the park. Here, enterprising members of Tennō-ji's sizable homeless population rig up generators and karaoke machines and charge passers by ¥50 or ¥100 to belt out classic *enka* (folk ballads) numbers.

The park is above Tennō-ji Station, which is on the Midō-suji subway line and the Osaka Loop line.

OPEN AIR MUSEUM OF OLD JAPANESE FARMHOUSES 日本民家集落博物館

In Ryokuchi-kōen this fine open-air **museum** (☎ 6862-3137; 1-2 Hattori Ryokuchi, Toyonaka-shi; admission ¥500; ⏰ 10am-5pm Apr-Oct, 10am-4pm Nov-Mar Tue-Sun) features 11 traditional Japanese country houses and other structures brought here from all over Japan. All have been painstakingly reconstructed and filled with period-era tools and other displays. Most impressive is the giant *gasshō-zukuri* (thatch-roofed) farmhouse from Gifu-ken.

The parklike setting, with plenty of trees and bamboo, gives the whole museum a pleasantly rustic air – and the whole place comes alive with fiery red maple leaves during the November foliage season. For anyone even remotely interested in traditional Japanese architecture, we highly recommend this excellent attraction. An English-language pamphlet is available.

To get there, take the Midō-suji subway line to Ryokuchi-kōen and walk northwest into the park.

OSAKA HUMAN RIGHTS MUSEUM/LIBERTY OSAKA 大阪人権博物館／リバティ大阪

This **museum** (☎ 6561-5891; 3-6-36 Naniwa nishi, Naniwa-ku; admission ¥250; ⏰ 10am-5pm Tue-Sun), which goes by two names, is dedicated to the suffering of Japan's Burakumin people and other oppressed groups, including Koreans, the handicapped, the Ainu and women. The most fascinating exhibits deal with the Burakumin, outcasts in Japan's four-tiered caste system that was officially outlawed in 1879 under the Emancipation Edict issued by the Meiji government.

An English-language leaflet is available, and you can borrow a tape recorder and English tape for free. Take the JR Osaka Loop line to Ashihara-bashi Station, exit via the southern exit, walk south down the main street for five minutes and the museum is on the right of the pedestrian crossing.

SUMIYOSHI TAISHA 住吉大社

This **shrine** (☎ 6672-0753; 2-9-89 Sumiyoshi; admission free; ⏰ dawn-dusk) is dedicated to Shintō deities associated with the sea and sea travel, in commemoration of a safe passage to Korea by a 3rd-century empress.

Having survived the bombing in WWII, Sumiyoshi Taisha actually has a couple of buildings that date back to 1810. The shrine was founded in the early 3rd century and the buildings that can be seen today are faithful replicas of the originals. They offer a rare opportunity to see a Shintō shrine that predates the influence of Chinese Buddhist architectural styles.

The main buildings are roofed with a kind of thatch rather than the tiles used on most later shrines. Other interesting features are a collection of more than 700 stone lanterns donated by seafarers and business people, a stone stage for performances of *bugaku* and court dancing and the attractive Taiko-bashi, an arched bridge set in a park.

It's next to both Sumiyoshi-taisha Station on the Nankai main line and Sumiyoshi-tori-mae Station on the Hankai line (the tram line that leaves from Tennō-ji Station).

UNIVERSAL STUDIOS JAPAN ユニバーサルスタジオジャパン

Universal Studios Japan (☎ 4790-7000; Universal City; adult/child ¥5500/3700; ⏰ 9am-7pm Mon-Fri, 9am-9pm Sat, Sun & holidays) is Osaka's answer to Tokyo Disneyland. Closely based on its two sister parks in the United States, the park features a wide variety of rides, shows, restaurants and other attractions.

To get there, take the JR Loop Line to Nishi-kujō Station, switch to one of the distinctively painted Universal Studio shuttle trains and get off at Universal City Station. From Osaka Station the trip costs ¥170 and takes about 20 minutes. There are also some direct trains from Osaka Station (ask at the tourist office for times; the price is the same).

Tempozan Area 天保山エリア

Trudging through the streets of Kita or Minami, you could easily be forgiven for forgetting that Osaka is actually a port city. A good remedy for this is a trip down to Tempozan, the best of Osaka's burgeoning seaside developments. On an island amid the busy container ports of Osaka Bay, Tempozan has several attractions to lure the travellers, especially those with children in tow.

Before hitting the main attractions, you might want to get some perspective on it all by taking a whirl on the **Giant Ferris Wheel** (大観覧車; Daikanransha; ☎ 6576-6222; 1-1-10 Kaigan-dōri, Minato-ku; admission ¥700; ☷ 10am-10pm). Said to be the largest ferris wheel in the world, the 112m-high wheel offers unbeatable views of Osaka, Osaka Bay and Kōbe. Give it a whirl at night to enjoy the vast carpet of lights formed by the Osaka/Kōbe conurbation.

Next to the ferris wheel, you'll find **Tempozan Marketplace** (天保山マーケットプレース; ☎ 6576-5501; 1-1-10 Kaigan-dōri, Minato-ku; admission free; ☷ shops 10am-8pm, restaurants 11am-10pm), a shopping and dining arcade that includes the **Naniwa Kuishinbō Yokochō** (なにわ食いしんぼ横丁; ☎ 6576-5501; 1-1-10 Kaigan-dōri, Minato-ku; admission free; ☷ 10am-8pm), a faux-Edo-period food court where you can sample all of Osaka's culinary specialities.

OSAKA AQUARIUM 海遊館

Although it's fairly expensive, **Osaka Aquarium** (☎ 6576-5501; 1-1-10 Kaigan-dōri, Minato-ku; adult/child ¥2000/900; ☷ 10am-8pm) is well worth a visit. It's centred around the world's largest aquarium tank, which is home to the aquarium's star attraction, a whale shark, which shares its quarters with an astonishing variety of lesser sharks, rays, tuna and other fish.

A walkway winds its way around the main tank and past displays of life found on eight different ocean levels. The giant spider crabs in the Japan Ocean Deeps section look like alien invaders from another planet. Presentations have both Japanese and English captions and an environmentally friendly slant to them.

Take the Chūō subway line to the Osaka-kō, from where it's about a five-minute walk to the aquarium. Get there for opening time if you want to beat the crowds – on weekends and holidays long queues are the norm.

SUNTORY MUSEUM
サントリーミュージアム

On the southern side of Osaka Aquarium is the **Suntory Museum complex** (☎ 6577-0001; www.suntory.com/culture-sports/smt; 1-5-10 Kaigan-dōri, Minato-ku; admission ¥1000; ☷ 10.30am-7.30pm), which holds an IMAX 3-D theatre and an art gallery with a collection of modern art posters and glass artwork. The building itself, designed by Andō Tadao, is at least as impressive as any of the displays. The **IMAX theatre** (☎ 6577-0001; www.suntory.com/culture-sports/smt; 1-5-10 Kaigan-dōri, Minato-ku; admission ¥1000; ☷ 11am-9.20pm Tue-Sun) usually has screenings on the hour; check the *Meet Osaka* guide to see what's showing.

FESTIVALS & EVENTS
January

Toka Ebisu (9–11 January) Huge crowds of more than a million people flock to the Imamiya Ebisu Shrine to receive bamboo branches hung with auspicious tokens. The shrine is near Imamiya Ebisu Station on the Nankai line.

Doya Doya (14 January) Billed as a 'huge naked festival', this event involves a competition between young men, clad in little more than headbands and loincloths, to obtain the 'amulet of the cow god'. This talisman is said to bring a good harvest to farmers. The festival takes place from 2pm at Shitennō-ji (Map p339).

April

Shōryō-e (22 April) Shitennō-ji (Map p339) holds afternoon performances of *bugaku*. Performances are usually held from 1pm to 5pm.

June

Otaue Shinji (14 June) Women and girls dressed in traditional costume commemorate the establishment of the imperial rice fields. The festival is held at Sumiyoshi Taisha.

July

Tenjin Matsuri (24–25 July) This is one of Japan's three biggest festivals. Try to make the second day, when processions of *mikoshi* and people in traditional attire start at Temman-gū and end up in O-kawa (in boats). As night falls, the festival is marked with a huge fireworks display.

September

Kishiwada Danjiri Matsuri (14 to 15 September) Osaka's wildest festival, a kind of running of the bulls except with *danjiri* (festival floats), many weighing over 3000kg. The *danjiri* are hauled through the streets by hundreds of people using ropes, and in all the excitement there have been a couple of deaths – take care and stand back. Most of the action takes place on the second day.

KANSAI

The best place to see it is west of Kishiwada Station on the Nankai Honsen line (from Nankai Station).

SLEEPING

There are plenty of places to stay in and around the two centres of Kita and Minami. It's possible to base yourself in Kyoto when exploring Osaka, and you'll find more budget accommodation in the old capital, which is about 40 minutes away by train. If you plan to sample some of Osaka's nightlife, it's probably best to stay in Osaka – unless you're one of those rare folks who actually enjoys riding the first train at dawn with a hangover.

Budget

New Japan Sauna & Capsule Hotel (Map p341; ☎ 6312-2100; 9-5 Dōyama-chō Kita-ku; capsules ¥2500 for men only, sauna from ¥525) Located in one of Kita's busiest entertainment districts, this is the place to stay if you miss the last train. It's also the place to give the capsule hotel experience a try.

Osaka Shiritsu Nagai Youth Hostel (大阪市 立長居ユースホステル; ☎ 6699-5631; www.oct .zaq.ne.jp/nagai-yh/english/index.html; 1-1 Nagai-kōen, Higashisumiyoshi-ku; dm YHA members/nonmembers ¥2500/2700, tw ¥3450, r/f per person ¥3000/3500) This is the nearest youth hostel to the centre of Osaka. Bed price varies, depending upon the season. There are also private rooms and a family room for up to four people. Take the Midō-suji subway line south from the centre of town to Nagai Station, go out exit No 1 and walk for 10 minutes towards the stadium. The hostel is at the back of the stadium. Or (for Japan Rail Pass holders), take the JR Hanwa line to Tsurugaoka Station and walk southeast for five minutes.

Osaka-fu Hattori Ryokuchi Youth Hostel (大阪府服部緑地ユースホステル; ☎ 6862- 0600; 1-3 Hattori Ryokuchi, Toyonaka-shi; dm ¥2500) No membership is necessary at this hostel, about 15 minutes from Kita or 30 minutes from Minami. Take the Midō-suji line to Ryokuchi-kōen Station, take the western exit, enter the park and follow the path past a fountain and around to the right alongside the pond.

Midrange

KITA AREA キタ **Map p341**

There are a few business hotels scattered around Hankyū Umeda and Osaka Stations.

Umeda OS Hotel (☎ 6312-1271; www.oshotel.com /e/index.html; 2-11-5 Sonezaki Kita-ku; s/d/tw ¥8300/ 11,800/11,800) A step up in quality, this clean, modern hotel is about five minutes south of Osaka Station.

Hotel Sunroute Umeda (☎ 6373-1111; 3-9-1 Toyosaki Kita-ku; s/d/tw from ¥8820/12,600/15,750) A reasonable business hotel, and perhaps the best value, just north of Hankyū Umeda.

Hotel Green Plaza Osaka (☎ 6374-1515; 2-5-12 Nakazaki nishi Kita-ku; s/d/tw from ¥7900/17,400/11,400) Not far from the Osaka Nōgaku Hall, this is drab but economical.

MINAMI AREA ミナミ **P344**

Considering the wealth of dining and entertainment options in the area, the Minami area is probably the best place in Osaka to be based.

Hotel Riva Nankai (☎ 6213 8281; fax 6213 8640; yoyaku@hotel-riva.com; 2-5-15 Shinsaibashisuji Chūō-ku; s/d/deluxe from ¥11,550/15,750/17,850) Located just a short walk from the Dōtombori area, this is the most reasonably priced hotel (as opposed to business hotel) in Minami.

ITAMI AIRPORT

Hotel Crevette (ホテル くれべ; ☎ 6843-7201; 1-9-6 Kūkō, Ikeda-shi; s/d/tw from ¥6500/13,860/13,860) This is the best deal near Itami. Prices are discounted if you make reservations at the main tourist information counter at the airport. The folks at the information counter can also arrange for the hotel's shuttle bus to pick you up. They also have a regular shuttle bus to the airport for departures.

Top End

KITA AREA キタ **Map p341**

The Kita area is brimming with top-end accommodation options.

Hotel Hankyū International (☎ 6377 2100; www .hhi.co.jp; 19-19 Chayamachi Kita-ku; s/d/tw ¥34,650/ 46,200/48,510) North of Hankyū Umeda Station, this is the most luxurious hotel in town.

Hotel Granvia Osaka (☎ 6344 1235; fax 6344 1130; 3-1-1 Umeda Kita-ku; s/d/tw ¥15,592/24,832/24,832) This hotel can't be beaten for convenience: it's located directly over Osaka Station. Rooms and facilities are of a high standard.

Hilton Osaka (☎ 6347-7111; fax 6347 7001; 1-8-8 Umeda, Kita-ku; s ¥17,400-27,800 d ¥29,000-31,300 tw ¥29,000-31,300) Just outside JR Osaka Station, this is one of the city's more luxurious hotels.

Hotel New Hankyū (☎ 6372 5101; fax 6374 6885; 1-1-35 Shibata Kita-ku; s ¥15,592, d ¥28,875-33,495, tw 22,522-39,270) Next to Hankyū Umeda Station, this is a reasonable choice with decent rooms.

MINAMI AREA ミナミ　　　Map p344
While most of Osaka's luxury hotels are in Kita, you'll find a few top-end choices in Minami as well.

Hotel Nikkō Osaka (☎ 6244-1111; fax 6245 2432; 1-3-3 Nishishinsaibashi Chūō-ku; s/d/tw ¥18,500/ 28,5000/28,500) In Shinsaibashi, this is a good choice, with excellent facilities and a convenient location.

Swissotel Nankai Osaka (☎ 6646-1111; 5-1-60 Namba Chūō-ku; s/d/tw ¥25,000/28,000/28,000) This is the most impressive hotel in the area and is directly above Nankai Namba Station. Rooms are clean and well appointed. The views from the rooms are great and the facilities are excellent.

KANSAI INTERNATIONAL AIRPORT
Hotel Nikkō Kansai Airport (☎ 0724-55-1111; www .nikkokix.com; 1 Senshū Kūkō kita, Izumisano-shi; s ¥11,550-21,945 d ¥17,325-32,340 tw ¥16,170-32,340) Expensive, but the only hotel at the airport, with clean new rooms. You should definitely ask for a discount or promotional rate outside peak travel times.

EATING
What Osaka offers is a chance to enjoy what ordinary Japanese enjoy – good food and drink in a rowdy atmosphere. The Osakans call it 'kuidaore', which means 'eat until you drop'. Osaka presents ample opportunities to do just that, with thousands of restaurants lining its cramped streets.

Kita キタ　　　Map p341
JAPANESE
Isaribi (☎ 6373-2969; 1-5-12 Shibata; dinner from ¥2300; ☯ 11am-2pm, 5-11.15pm Mon-Fri, 4.30-11.15pm Sat, Sun & holidays) This is a great *robatayaki* place, down a flight of stairs outside Hankyū Umeda Station. It's a little tricky to spot – look for an English sign reading 'Karaoka Snack Garo'.

Umeda Hagakure (☎ 6341-1409; 1-1-3 Umeda; noodles from ¥600; ☯ 11am-2.45pm, 5-7.45pm Mon-Sat) Locals line up outside this place for their fantastic udon noodles. It's on the B2 floor of the Ekimae Daisan building. There are many pictures outside to help with ordering.

Ganko Umeda Honten (☎ 6376 2001; 1-5-11 Shibata) This giant dining hall serves all the usual Japanese favourites, including sushi.

Nawa Zushi Shiten (☎ 6312 9892; 14-1 Sonezaki-chō) This is one of the area's most popular sushi restaurants. It's in an olive brick building in a somewhat racy entertainment district.

A great place for a cheap lunch or dinner while in Kita is the **Shin-Umeda Shokudō-Gai** which is located across the street from the Umeda Visitors Information Office under the JR tracks. There are heaps of good restaurants here that vie for the lunch/dinner custom with cheap set meals, many of which are displayed outside, making ordering easier. Two that we really like are **Kiji Honten** (☎ 6361-5804; 9-20 Kakuda-chō, Shin Umeda Shokudōgai; ☯ noon-10.15pm Mon-Sat), a good *okonomiyaki* place (try the mixed *okonomiyaki* for around ¥800); and an *oden* and fish specialist called **Maru** (☎ 6361- 4552; 9-26 Kakuda-chō, Shin Umeda Shokudōgai; ☯ noon-10.15pm Mon-Sat), where the lunchtime sashimi set meal costs about ¥800. Check the Kita map for the kanji and look for it on the sign (there's usually a young lady outside beckoning customers).

Another good food court in Kita is the **Kappa Yokochō Arcade** (marked 'Kappa Plaza' in English), just north of Hankyū Umeda Station. Here, you'll find **Gataro** (☎ 6373-1484; 1-7-2 Shibata; dinner around ¥3000; ☯ 11am-11pm), a cosy little spot that does creative twists on standard *izakaya* themes. Look for the glass front on the left as you head north in the arcade.

There are also many good spots to eat outside the above-mentioned arcades, including. **Oshi Dori** (☎ 6375 5818; Hankyū Sanbangai) This is a reliable *yakitori* specialist not far from Kinokuniya books. To get there from Kinokuniya, start facing the book store, walk around the store to the left and look for the sign that reads 'Jizo Yokocho' in English, after which it's on the right.

INTERNATIONAL
There are several cafés and bakeries in Osaka Station itself. Otherwise, you might try the offerings in the nearby Osaka Hilton, which has a wide variety of restaurants on its two basement floors. You could also try some of the following spots.

Osteria Gaudente (☎ 6344-8685; 1-11-4 Umeda, Kita-ku; lunch from ¥945; ☯ 11.30am-3pm, 5.30-10.30pm) This reliable Italian specialist packs

KANSAI

'em in at lunchtime and also does a good dinner service.

Pina Khana (☎ 6375-5828; 1-7-2 Shibata Kita-ku; lunch/dinner from ¥850/3000; ☉ 11am-3pm, 5-10pm) A crowded spot in the Kappa Yokochō Arcade, this is our favourite Indian restaurant in Kita.

Herradura (☎ 6361-1011; 10-7 Dōyama-chō Kita-ku; dinner ¥2000-5000; ☉ 5pm-3am Mon-Sat) An intimate spot for Mexican food, including taco platters and frozen margaritas.

Café Org (☎ 6312-0529; 7-7 Doyama-chō, Kita-ku; drinks from ¥250, meals ¥900-2500; ☉ 11am-11pm) At this open-plan, casual café you can grab a light meal or a quick pick-me-up while exploring Kita. Decent sandwiches start at ¥300 here.

Court Lodge (☎ 6342-5253; 1-4-7 Sonezakishinchi; curry sets from ¥800; ☉ 11am-9.30pm Mon-Sat) This tiny hole-in-the-wall spot serves filling sets of Sri Lankan food. Look for the beer signs in the window.

Minami ミナミ

Map p344

JAPANESE

Ume no Hana (☎ 6258 3766; OPA Bldg, 11th fl, 1-4-3 Nishi Shinsaibashi, Chūō-ku; dinner ¥5000) This is part of an upscale chain that serves a variety of tofu-based dishes. Take the elevators from Midōsuji and look for the restaurant posted only in Japanese (the other one on the 11th floor is posted in English).

Nishiya (☎ 6241-9221; 1-18-18 Higashi Shinsaibashi Chūō-ku; noodle dishes from ¥800, dinner average ¥4000; ☉ 11am-10pm) An Osaka landmark that serves udon noodles and a variety of hearty *nabe* (iron pot) dishes for reasonable prices. Look for the semi-rustic façade and the food models.

Gin Sen (☎ 6213-2898; 2-4-2 Shinsaibashi-suji Chūō-ku; all-you-can-eat kushi-katsu lunch/dinner ¥1980/2980; ☉ 11.30am-11pm) This place serves delicious *kushi katsu*, a greasy but tasty treat. It's on the 2nd floor of the Gurukas building.

Dōtombori is crammed with restaurants, most of which are bad. They cater to the hoards of Japanese tourists who descend on the area. If you must eat here, the best of a bad lot are the following places: **Kani Dōraku Honten** (☎ 6211 8975; 1-6-18 Dōtombori Chūō-ku; lunch/dinner from ¥1600/3000; ☉ 11am-11pm), a crab specialist; **Ganko Zushi** (☎ 6212-1705; 1-8-24 Dōtombori Chūō-ku; set meals from ¥1000; ☉ 11.30am-11pm), a sushi specialist; **Zuboraya** (☎ 6211-0181; 1-6-10 Dōtombori Chūō-ku; fugu sashimi ¥1800, full dinners

from ¥3000; ☉ 11am-12.30am), a *fugu* (Japanese puffer fish) specialist; **Chibō** (☎ 6212-2211; 1-5-5 Dōtombori Chūō-ku; okonomiyaki from ¥800; ☉ 11am-2am), a good place to try one of Osaka's most popular dishes: *okonomiyaki*; **Dōtombori Rāmen Daishokudō** (☎ 6213 1014; 1-4-20 Dōtombori Chūō-ku; rāmen ¥650-900), an arcade that consists of nothing but *rāmen* restaurants; and **Imai Honten** (☎ 6211 0319; 1-7-22 Dōtombori Chūō-ku; Kake-udon ¥550, Kitsune-udon ¥735), one of the areas oldest and most revered udon specialists. We recommend eating at one of the many restaurants off the main Dōtombori strip.

INTERNATIONAL

Krungtep (☎ 4708-0088; 1-6-14 Dōtombori Chūō-ku; lunch buffet/dinner ¥980/2000; ☉ 11.30am-3pm, 5-11pm Mon-Fri, 11.30am-11pm Sat & Sun) Dōtombori's most popular Thai place serves fairly authentic versions of the standard favourites like green curry and fried noodles. Look for the small English sign – it's on the B1 floor.

Namaste (☎ 6241-6515; 3-7-28 Minamisemba Chūō-ku; lunch sets/dinner from ¥750/2000; ☉ 11.30am-2.30pm, 5.30-10.30pm) Up in the Shinsaibashi area, this is a friendly Indian restaurant that serves filling set meals at reasonable prices. Look for the Indian flag.

Santana (☎ 6211-5181; 2-2-17 Dōtombori Chūō-ku; lunch/dinner sets from ¥1000/2000; ☉ noon-3pm, 5-11pm Tue-Sun) Our favourite Indian place in Minami has lots of vegie choices and delicious samosas.

DRINKING

Osaka is a hard working city, but when quitting time rolls around, Osakans know how to party. Take a stroll through Minami on a Friday night and you'd be excused for thinking that there is one bar for every resident of the city. Whatever your taste, you're sure to find something to your liking among this vast array of bars and clubs.

Kita キタ

Map p341

Although Minami is Osaka's real nightlife district, there are plenty of bars, clubs and *izakaya* in the neighbourhoods to the south and east of Osaka Station (but be warned that most of the places in Kita-Shinchi cater only to Japanese salarymen on expense accounts).

Canopy (☎ 6341-0339; 1-11-20 Sonezakishinchi Kita-ku; ☉ 5pm-6am Mon-Sat, 5pm-midnight Sun) Café-style bar that pulls in a crowd of local expats for after-work snacks and drinks. The happy hour special here is a good and popular deal.

Windows on the World (☎ 6347-7111; 1-8-8 Umeda Kita-ku; ⏰ 11.30am-midnight, cocktail hr 5pm-midnight) An unbeatable spot for drinks with a view – it's on the 35th floor of the Osaka Hilton. Be warned that there's a ¥2500 per person table charge and drinks average ¥1000.

Minami ミナミ

Map p344

This is the place for a wild night out in Osaka. You simply won't believe the number of bars, clubs and restaurants they've packed into the narrow streets and alleys of Dōtombori, Shinsaibashi, Namba and Amerika-Mura. Go on a weekend night and you'll be part of a colourful human parade of Osaka characters – this is one of Japan's best spots for people-watching.

Pig & Whistle (☎ 6213-6911; meals from ¥1100, drinks from ¥720) Like its sister branch in Kyoto, this is a good place to go for a pint and a plate of fish and chips.

Murphy's (☎ 6282-0677; 1-6-31 Higashishinsaibashi Chūō-ku; cost average ¥1000 per person; ⏰ 2pm-1am Sun-Thu, 2pm-3am Fri & Sat) This is one of the oldest Irish-style pubs in Japan, and a good place to rub shoulders with local expats and Japanese. It's on the 6th floor of the Reed Plaza Shinsaibashi building.

Tin's Hall (Map p339; ☎ 6773-5955; 10-3 Minamikawahori-machi; ⏰ 6pm-2am Mon-Fri, 6pm-5am Sat) The best bar down south in the Tennō-ji area. It's a casual spot with good burgers and a great happy hour special: beers are only ¥300 from 6pm to 9pm. To get there, leave Tennō-ji Station by the north exit, go right and walk along the main road, turn right one block beyond the Tōei Hotel and look for it on the right.

SoulFuckTry (☎ 6539 1032; 1-9-14 Minami Horie, Nishi-ku; drinks from ¥700) This interestingly-named bar/club describes itself as a soul disco and that's pretty much what it is.

Cellar (☎ 6212 6437; B1 Shin-sumiya Bldg, 2-17-13 Nishishinsaibashi, Chuo-ku) Live music is often the draw here at this popular basement bar on the west side of Nishishinsaibashi.

Arc en Ciel (☎ 6646-5125; 5-1-60 Namba Chūō-ku; ⏰ 11.30am-2.30pm, 5.30pm-11pm Mon-Fri, 5.30pm-midnight Sat & Sun) This is where we go when we want something a little swanky. It's on the 36th floor of the Nankai South Tower Hotel. The view is fantastic and the prices

are too: there's a ¥1500 per person table charge and drinks average ¥1200.

American Beauty (☎ 6484-2299; 2-7-10 Shinsaibashi-suji, Chūō-ku; ⏰ 7.30pm-late) A cosy little downstairs bar where the music runs to rock and roll and the crowd includes both foreigners and Japanese. Bonus points for guessing the origin of the name (hint: it's the name of one of their best albums).

ENTERTAINMENT

For up-to-date listings of forthcoming club events, check *Kansai Time Out*.

Clubs

Karma (Map p341; ☎ 6344-6181; 1-5-18 Sonezakishinchi Kita-ku) A very long-standing club in Kita that is popular with Japanese and foreigners alike. On weekends they usually host techno events with cover charges averaging ¥2500.

Grand Café (Map p344; ☎ 6213-8637; 2-10-21 Nishishinsaibashi, Chūō-ku) This hip underground club hosts a variety of electronica/DJ events. There's a comfy seating area and several dance floors. Look for the blue sign at street level.

Traditional Japanese Entertainment

National Bunraku Theatre (Map p344; ☎ 6212-2531; 1-12-10 Nihonbashi, Chūō-ku) This is Osaka's main *bunraku* (Japanese puppet) theatre. It's probably the best place in Japan to see *bunraku*. Just be warned that performances sell out quickly, so plan ahead.

Osaka Nōgaku Hall (Map p341; ☎ 6373-1726; 2-3-17 Nakasakinishi Kita-ku) A five-minute walk east of Osaka Station, this hall holds *nō* shows about twice a month, most of which cost ¥4000.

Unfortunately, neither place has regularly scheduled shows. The best thing is to check with the tourist information offices about current shows, check the listings in the *Meet Osaka* guide or look in *Kansai Time Out*.

SHOPPING

Osaka has almost as many shops as it has restaurants. Look for department stores in the area around JR Osaka and Umeda Stations. Most of the major department stores are represented here.

Osaka's speciality is electronics, and **Den Den Town** (Map p344) is Osaka's Tokyo's Akihabara. Taking its name from the Japanese

KANSAI

word for electricity, *denki,* Den Den Town is an area of shops almost exclusively devoted to electronic goods. To avoid sales tax, check if the store has a 'Tax Free' sign outside and bring your passport. Most stores are closed on Wednesday. Take the Sakaisuji subway line to Ebisu-cho Station and exit at No 1 or No 2 exit. Alternatively, it's a 15-minute walk south of Nankai Namba Station.

For anything related to cooking and eating, head to the **Dōguya-suji Arcade** in Minami (p343). Also in Minami, you'll find **Naniwa Camera** (Map p344; ☎ 6281-4100; 🕑 10am-8pm), which has the lowest prices on cameras, equipment and film in town. For used camera equipment, try the many shops on the ground floors of the Ekimae Dai buildings (there are four of them) south of Osaka Station.

GETTING THERE & AWAY

Air

Osaka is served by two airports: the old Itami airport, which now handles only domestic traffic, and the new Kansai International Airport (KIX), which handles all international and some domestic flights.

Boat

The **Japan China International Ferry Company** (in Japan ☎ 06-6536-6541; www.fune.co.jp/chinjif/index.html in Japanese) connects Shanghai and Osaka/Kōbe. A 2nd-class ticket costs around US$200. The journey takes around 48 hours. A similar service is provided by the **Shanghai Ferry Company** (in Japan ☎ 06-6243-6345, in China ☎ 021-6537-7999; www.shanghai-ferry.co.jp). The ferries leave from the Osaka Nankō international ferry terminal, which can be reached by taking the New Tram service from Suminoe-kōen Station to Nankoguchi Station. The Osaka tourist information offices are a good source of information on schedules and bookings.

Ferries also depart from Nankō ferry terminal and Kanome-futō and Benten-futō piers for various destinations around Honshū, Kyūshū and Shikoku. Kyūshū destinations include Beppu (¥7900, 13 hours) and Miyazaki (¥8380). Other possibilities in Kyūshū are Shinmoji in the north of the island near Shimonoseki and Shibushi in the south of the island. Possibilities in Shikoku are Kōchi (¥4500, nine hours), Matsuyama (¥5500, eight hours) and Takamatsu (hydrofoil, ¥6100). Note that prices listed here are for a 2nd-class ticket, which, on overnight ferries, usually means a place on a tatami floor in a large, open room.

For detailed information about sailing schedules and bookings contact the tourist information offices.

Bus

There is a long-distance highway bus service between Osaka and cities all across Honshū, Shikoku and some cities in Kyushū. Destinations include Tokyo (¥8610, eight hours), Nagasaki (¥11,000, 10 hours) and Kagoshima (¥12,000, 12 hours). Buses usually depart from either Osaka, Hankyū Umeda or Namba Stations; check with the tourist information offices for more details.

Train

KŌBE

The fastest way between Kōbe and Osaka is the JR *shinkaisoku* that runs between Osaka Station and Kōbe's Sannomiya and Kōbe Stations (¥390, 21 minutes).

There is also the private Hankyū line, which takes a little more time but is cheaper. It runs from Osaka's Hankyū Umeda Station to Kōbe's Sannomiya Station (*tokkyū* ¥310, 27 minutes).

KYOTO

The fastest way to travel by train between Kyoto and Osaka, other than *shinkansen,* is to catch the JR *shinkaisoku* (¥540, 29 minutes).

Another choice is the cheaper private Hankyū line that runs between Hankyū Umeda Station in Osaka and Hankyū Kawaramachi, Karasuma and Ōmiya Stations in Kyoto (*tokkyū* to Kawaramachi ¥390, 42 minutes).

Alternatively, you can take the Keihan main line between Sanjō, Shijō or Shichijō Stations in Kyoto and Keihan Yodoyabashi Station in Osaka (*tokkyū* to Sanjō ¥400, 48 minutes). Yodoyabashi is on the Midō-suji subway line.

NARA

The JR Kansai line links Osaka (Namba and Tennō-ji Stations) and Nara (JR Nara Station) via Hōryū-ji (*kaisoku* ¥540, 35 minutes).

The private Kintetsu Nara line also connects Osaka (Kintetsu Namba Station) with

Nara (Kintetsu Nara Station). *Kyūkō* (express) and *futsū* services take about 35 minutes and cost ¥540. *Tokkyū* trains do the journey in five minutes' less time but at almost double the cost, making them a poor option.

SHINKANSEN

Osaka is on the Tōkaidō/San-yō *shinkansen* line that runs between Tokyo and Hakata in Kyūshū, Hikari *shinkansen* to/from Tokyo (¥13,750, three hours) and Hikari *shinkansen* to Hakata (¥14,590, 2¾ hours). Other cities on this line include Hiroshima, Kyoto, Kōbe and Okayama.

GETTING AROUND
To/From the Airport
ITAMI AIRPORT

There are frequent limousine buses running between the airport and various parts of Osaka. Buses run to/from Shin-Osaka Station every 15 minutes from about 6.30am to 7.30pm (¥490, 25 minutes). Buses run at about the same frequency to/from Osaka and Namba Stations (¥620, 30 minutes). At Itami, buy your tickets from the machine outside the arrivals hall.

There are also direct airport buses to/from Kyoto (¥1370, 50 minutes) and Kōbe (¥1020, 40 minutes).

KANSAI INTERNATIONAL AIRPORT

There are a variety of routes between KIX and Osaka. Limousine buses travel to/from Shin-Osaka, Osaka Umeda, Kyobashi, Tenmabashi, Osaka City Air Terminal (OCAT) Namba, Uehonmachi, Tennō-ji and Nanko (Cosmo Square) Stations. The fare is ¥1300 for most routes and the journeys take an average of 50 minutes, depending on traffic conditions. OCAT, in JR Namba Station, allows passengers on Japanese and some other airlines to check in and deposit baggage before boarding trains to the airport. Check with your airline for details.

The fastest way by train to/from the airport is the private Nankai express Rapit, which departs from Nankai Namba Station on the Midō-suji subway line (¥1400, 30 minutes). The JR Haruka limited airport express operates between the airport and Tennō-ji Station (¥2270, 31 minutes) and Shin-Osaka (¥2980, 48 minutes).

Regular JR express trains called *kanku kaisoku* also operate between the airport and

Osaka Station (¥1160, 66 minutes), Kyōbashi Station (¥1160, 70 minutes), Tennō-ji Station (¥1030, 50 minutes) and JR Namba Station (¥1030, 61 minutes).

Bus

Osaka does have a bus system, but it is nowhere near as easy to use as the rail network. Japanese-language bus maps are available from the tourist offices.

Train & Subway

Osaka has a good subway network and, like Tokyo, a JR loop line (known in Japanese as the JR Kanjō-sen) that circles the city area. In fact, there should be no need to use any other form of transport while you are in Osaka unless you stay out late and miss the last train.

There are seven subway lines, but the one that most short-term visitors are likely to find most useful is the Midō-suji line, which runs north to south stopping at Shin-Osaka, Umeda (next to Osaka Station), Shinsaibashi, Namba and Tennō-ji Stations. Most rides cost between ¥200 and ¥300.

If you're going to be using the rail system a lot on any day, it might be worth considering a 'one-day free ticket'. For ¥850 (¥650 on Fridays and the 20th of every month) you get unlimited travel on any subway, the New Tram line and all city buses (but not the JR line). Note, however, that you would really have to be moving around a lot to save any money with this ticket. These tickets can be purchased from some of the ticket machines in most subway stations; push the button for 'one-day free ticket' then press the illuminated button reading '¥850'.

KŌBE 神戸

☎ 078 / pop 1.42 million

Perched on a hillside overlooking Osaka-wan, Kōbe is one of Japan's most attractive cities. It's also one of the country's most famous, largely as a result of the tragic earthquake of 17 January 1995, which levelled whole neighbourhoods and killed more than 6000 people. Fortunately, the city has risen, Phoenix-like, from the ashes and is now more vibrant than ever.

One of Kōbe's best features is its relatively small size – most of the sights can be reached on foot from the main train stations. Of

KANSAI

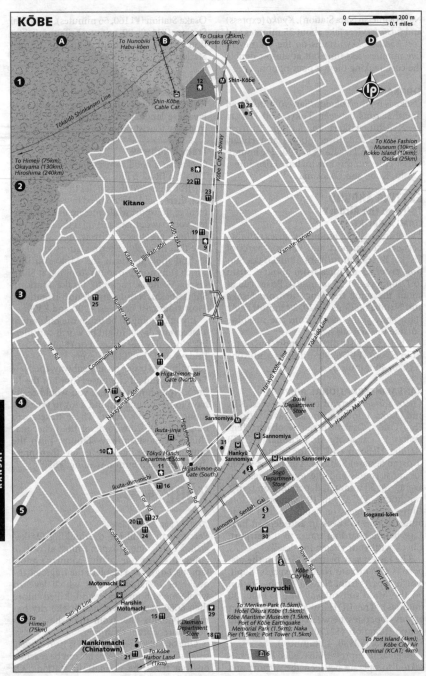

KŌBE

KANSAI

To Osaka (25km);
Kyoto (60km)

0 ——— 200 m
0 ——— 0.1 miles

To Nunobiki
Habu-kōen

Shin-Kōbe
Cable Car

Tōkaidō Shinkansen Line

Shin-Kōbe

12

28
5

To Himeji (75km);
Okayama (130km);
Hiroshima (240km)

Kitano

Kōbe City Subway

8
22
23

To Kōbe Fashion
Museum (10km);
Rokko Island (10km);
Osaka (25km)

19
9

Jiinkan-dōri

Kitano-zaka

26

Fudō-zaka

Yamate-kansen

Hunter-zaka

25

13

Tor Rd

Community Rd

14

Higashimon-gai
Gate (North)

Nakayamate-dōri

17 3

Ikuta-jinja

Higashimon-gai
Gate (South)

Hanshin Kōbe Line

Tōkaidō Line

Daiei
Department
Store

Hanshin Main Line

Sannomiya

Sannomiya

10

Tōkyū Hands
Department Store

11

Ikuta-shin-michi

16

31

Hankyū
Sannomiya

4

Hankyū Kōbe Line

Hanshin Sannomiya

Sogō
Department
Store

Isogami-kōen

Tor Rd

Ikuta Rd

Kokawa-suji

20 27

24

Sannomiya Sentā-Gai

2

30

Flower Rd

Kōbe
City Hall

Port Line

To Port Island (4km);
Kōbe City Air
Terminal (KCAT; 4km)

Motomachi

San-yō Line

Hanshin
Motomachi

15

Kyukyoryuchi

To Meriken Park (1.5km);
Hotel Ōkura Kōbe (1.5km);
Kōbe Maritime Museum (1.5km);
Port of Kōbe Earthquake
Memorial Park (1.5km); Naka
Pier (1.5km); Port Tower (1.5km)

29

To
Himeji
(75km)

Nankinmachi
(Chinatown)

7

21

To Kōbe Harbor Land
(1km)

Daimaru
Department
Store

18

6

course, it must be noted that none of these
sights are attractions you really must see:
Kōbe is likely to appeal more to residents
than to travellers. However, it does have
some good restaurants, cafés and bars and
is a good place for a night out in Kansai if
you just can't face the mayhem of Osaka.

ORIENTATION

Kōbe's two main entry points are Sannomiya and Shin-Kōbe Stations. Shin-Kōbe
Station, in the northeast of town, is where
the *shinkansen* stops. A subway (¥200, one
minute) runs from here to the busier Sannomiya Station, which has frequent rail connections with Osaka and Kyoto. It's possible
to walk between the two stations in around
20 minutes. Sannomiya Station marks the
city centre, although a spate of development
in Kōbe Harbor Land is starting to swing the
city's centre of gravity to the southwest. Before starting your exploration of Kōbe, pick
up a copy of the *Kōbe City Map* at one of the
two information offices (see right).

INFORMATION
Bookshops

For second-hand books, try **Wantage Books**
(☎ 232-4517; ☑ 9.30am-5.30pm Mon-Fri), up near
Shin-Kōbe Station. It has a great selection
and low prices, and all proceeds go to char-
ity. In the same building is the office of
Kansai Time Out, Kansai's best 'what's on'
magazine.

Money

There's an international ATM in the Sannomiya Sentah Gai shopping arcade. Behind
Kōbe city hall there's a **Citibank** (☎ 392-4122;
☑ 9am-3pm Mon-Fri, ATM 24hr) with machines
that also accept a variety of cards.

Tourist Information

The city's main **tourist information office**
(☎ 322-0220; ☑ 9am-7pm) is on the ground
floor on the south side of JR Sannomiya
Station's west gate (follow the signs for San-
tica, a shopping mall). There's a smaller
information counter on the 2nd floor of
Shin-Kōbe Station. Both information centres carry the useful *Kōbe City Map* and the
Kōbe Guide Map, both free.

SIGHTS
Kitano 北野

Twenty minutes' walk north of Sannomiya
is the pleasant hillside neighbourhood of
Kitano, where local tourists come to enjoy
the feeling of foreign travel without leaving
Japanese soil. A European/American atmosphere is created by the winding streets
and *ijinkan* (literally 'foreigners' houses')
that housed some of Kōbe's early Western
residents. Admission to some is free, to others ¥300 to ¥700, and most are open from
9am to 5pm daily. Although these brick and
weatherboard dwellings may not hold the
same fascination for Western travellers that
they hold for local tourists, the area itself is
pleasant to stroll around and is dotted with
good cafés and restaurants.

Shin-kōbe Cable Car & Nunobiki Habu-kōen
新神戸ロープウェイ・布引ハーブ公園

The **Shin-Kōbe cable car** (ropeway; one way/return
¥550/1000; ☑ 9.30am-5pm Dec-Feb, 9.30am-8pm Mar-May,
Sep-Nov, 9.30am-9pm Jun-Aug) leaves from behind
the OPA shopping centre near Shin-Kōbe
Station and ascends to a mountain ridge
400m above the city. The views from the top
over Kōbe and the bay are particularly pretty
after sunset. There's a complex of gardens,

KANSAI

restaurants and shops below the top station known as the **Nunobiki Habu-kōen** (Nunobiki Herb Garden; admission ¥200). Note that you can easily walk down to the bottom station from the Herb Garden in about 30 minutes.

Kōbe City Museum 神戸市立博物館

This **museum** (Kōbe Shiritsu Hakubutsukan; ☎ 391-0035; 24 Kyō machi, Chūō-ku; admission ¥200; ☉ 10am-4.30pm Tue-Sun) has a collection of so-called Namban (literally 'southern barbarian') art and occasional special exhibits. Namban art is a school of painting that developed under the influence of early Jesuit missionaries in Japan, many of whom taught Western painting techniques to Japanese students.

Nankinmachi (Chinatown) 南京町

Nankinmachi, Kōbe's Chinatown, is not on a par with Chinatowns elsewhere in the world, but it is a good place for a stroll. It's particularly attractive in the evening, when the lights of the area illuminate the gaudily painted façades of the shops. Unfortunately most of the restaurants in the area are overpriced and somewhat disappointing (we list a good exception, Motomachi Gyōza-en, opposite). The best idea is to grab a takeaway snack here and eat elsewhere.

Kōbe Harbor Land & Meriken Park
神戸ハーバーランド

Five minutes' walk southeast of Kōbe Station, Kōbe Harbor Land is awash with new megamall shopping and dining developments. This may not appeal to foreign travellers the way it does to the local youth, but it's still a nice place for a stroll in the afternoon. For a good view of the area, take the free glass lift to the 18th floor of the **Ecoll Marine building**.

A five-minute walk to the east of Harbor Land you'll find Meriken Park, on a spit of reclaimed land jutting out into the bay. The main attraction here is the **Kōbe Maritime Museum** (Kōbe Kaiyō Hakubutsukan; ☎ 327-8983; 2-2 Hatoba-chō, Chūō-ku; admission ¥600; ☉ 10am-4.30pm Tue-Sun). The museum has a small collection of ship models and displays, with some English explanations.

Just east of the Maritime Museum, the **Port of Kōbe Earthquake Memorial Park** (☉ 24hr) preserves part of a concrete pier that was destroyed in the 1995 earthquake. The extent of the damage should give you a good idea just how strong the earthquake was.

Rokko Island 六甲アイランド

An artificial island, the main attraction here is the **Kōbe Fashion Museum** (Kōbe Fashion Bijutsukan; ☎ 858-0050; 2-9-1 Kōyōchōnaka, Higashinada-ku; admission ¥500; ☉ 11am-5.30pm Sat-Tue & Thu, 11am-7.30pm Fri). The museum's collection of mostly foreign fashion is not quite up to the dramatic building in which it's housed but it's worth a look if you're interested in fashion. To reach the museum, take the Rokko Liner monorail (¥240) from JR Sumiyoshi (four stops east of Sannomiya) and get off at the Island Centre stop.

FESTIVALS & EVENTS

Luminarie, Kōbe's biggest yearly event, is held every evening from around 12 to 25 December to celebrate the city's miraculous recovery from the 1995 earthquake (check with the Kōbe tourist information office to be sure of the dates as they change slightly every year). The streets southwest of Kōbe City Hall are decorated with countless illuminated metal archways, which when viewed from within look like the interior of some otherworldly cathedral.

SLEEPING

Hotel Ōkura Kōbe (ホテルオークラ神戸; ☎ 333-0111; www.kobe.hotelokura.co.jp; 2-1 Hatoba-chō Chūō-ku; s/d ¥19,635/31,185) On the waterfront behind Meriken Park, this is the most elegant hotel in town and has fine rooms.

Shin-Kōbe Oriental Hotel (☎ 291-1121; www.orientalhotel.co.jp/e/index.htm; 1 Kitano-chō, Chūō-ku; s/d ¥13,000/23,000) Towering above Shin-Kōbe Station, this hotel claims the best views of any hotel in town. While the rooms may be smallish, the location more than makes up for it. There are several good dining options on site and in the mall below the hotel.

Green Hill Hotel Kōbe (☎ 222-0909; fax 222 1139; 2-8-3 Kanō-chō Chūō-ku; s/tw ¥8925/15,330) Close to Shin-Kōbe, this business hotel is conveniently located near Kitano and Sannomiya. The rooms are clean and pleasant enough, considering the price. There are several good on-site restaurants and the standards of food and service are high.

Green Hill Hotel Urban (☎ 222-1221; www.ghu.jp/index_e.html; 2-5-16 Kanō-chō Chūō-ku; s/d ¥4500/9000) This good value place has a convenient location not far from Shin-Kōbe Station. The rooms are standard business hotel–style but well kept. Rates include breakfast.

Hotel Tor Road (☎ 391-6691; htorroad@oak.ocn.ne .jp; 3-1-19 Nakayamate-dōri, Chūō-ku; s/d ¥8662/15,592) On the hill leading up to Kitano, this is a pleasant little hotel with fairly large rooms. This hotel is conveniently located for exploration of both the Motomachi area and Sannomiya.

Kōbe Washington Hotel Plaza (☎ 331-6111; fax 331 6651; 2-11-5 Shimoyamate-dōri, Chūō-ku; s/d ¥8100/17,500) Close to Sannomiya Station, this hotel has small but clean rooms. While the common areas and building may be fairly drab, the service is quite good here.

EATING
Japanese

Although Kōbe is more famous for its international cuisine, there are plenty of good Japanese restaurants to be found.

Kintoki (☎ 331-1037; 1-7-2 Motomachi-dōri, Chūō-ku; lunch/dinner from ¥500; ⏰ 10.30am-9pm Mon-Sat, 10.30am-7pm Sun, closed holidays) This is a good place to go for a taste of what Japan was like before it got rich. It's an atmospheric old *shokudō* that serves the cheapest food in the city. You can order standard noodle and rice dishes from the menu (plain soba or udon noodles are ¥250 and a small rice is ¥160) or choose from a variety of dishes laid out on the counter. Look for the blue and white awning.

Kōbe A-1 (☎ 331 8676; 2-2-9 Shimoyamate-dōri, Chūō-ku; Kōbe beef course from ¥6500) This downtown steak specialist is a good spot to try Kōbe beef.

Mikami (☎ 242-5200; 2-5-9 Kitano-chō; lunch/dinner from ¥400; ⏰ 11.30am-10pm Mon-Sat, closed Sun & holidays) This is a friendly spot for good-value lunch and dinner sets of standard Japanese fare. Noodle dishes are available from ¥400 and *teishoku* (set meals) from ¥600. There is also an English menu. Look for the large doghouse outside.

Native (☎ 242-7677; 2-9-1 Kanō-chō, Chūō-ku; lunch/dinner around ¥1000/3000; ⏰ 11.30am-2am Mon-Thu, 11.30am-4am Fri-Sun) This small, modern café/restaurant serves light and healthy Japanese fare. There's an English sign and a glass front.

Tada (☎ 222-1715; 2-9-15 Yamamoto-dōri, Chūō-ku; lunch/dinner from ¥650; ⏰ 11am-9pm Tue-Sun) This casual *okonomiyaki* place in Kitano has counter seating. It also serves *teppanyaki* (grilled meat) beef from ¥1100 for a set. Look for the white brick façade.

Yoshinoya (☎ 265-6269; 1-1-12 Ikuta-chō, Chūō-ku; buta-don (pork over rice) from ¥320; ⏰ 24hr) Close to Shin-Kōbe Station, this is a fast-food *gyū-don* (beef over rice) specialist that is good for a quick, light meal (to order a regular-sized bowl of beef over rice just say 'gyū-don nami').

Wakoku (☎ 262 2838; 1-1 Kitano-chō Chūō-ku; 3F Shin Kōbe Oriental Ave; lunch/dinner from ¥2500/6800) This is our top choice for Kōbe beef. It's an elegant place that serves absolutely top-quality beef.

International

Kōbe has loads of international cuisine, including good Indian, Chinese and Italian restaurants. There are also lots of trendy café-style spots in Kōbe, including a clutch of restaurants just north of Motomachi Station in the fashionable Tor Rd area.

Court Lodge (☎ 222-5504; 1-23-16 Nakayamate-dōri Chūō-ku; lunch/dinner average ¥1000-2000; ⏰ 11am-10.30pm), right in the heart of Kitano, this Sri Lankan place serves tasty set meals and delicious Ceylon tea.

Gaylord (☎ 251-4359; 1-26-1 Nakayamate-dōri Chūō-ku; lunch/dinner from ¥900/3000; ⏰ 11.30am-2.30pm, 5.30-9.30pm) Large Indian eatery where you have to pay a little more to enjoy excellent set meals and delicious curries. Look for the Indian sign.

Kōkaen (☎ 231-7079; 2-21-12 Nakayamate-dōri Chūō-ku; lunch/dinner ¥1000/4000; ⏰ 11.30am-1.30pm, 5-9pm Wed-Mon) This is a favourite of local cognoscenti for authentic Chinese and Vietnamese food.

Lois Café (☎ 322 0904; 45 Harima-chō Chūō-ku; dinner from ¥2500) This hip pan-Asian place draws Kōbe's chic young crowd for light meals and conversation.

Modernark Pharm (☎ 391-3060; 3-11-15 Kitanagasa-dōri Chūō-ku; lunch/dinner from ¥900/1500; ⏰ 11.30am-11pm Mon-Sat, 11.30am-10pm Sun) This interesting little restaurant serves tasty sets of Japanese and Western dishes, including burritos and rice dishes. Look for the plants.

Motomachi Gyōza-en (☎ 331-4096; 2-8-11 Sakaemachi-dōri Chūō-ku; 6 dumplings ¥380; ⏰ 11.45am-2pm, 5-8pm Tue-Sun) The best spot in Nankin-machi for Chinese dumplings (that's about all this place serves). Try its wonderful fried dumplings (yaki gyōza) at lunch or dinner. At dinner they also make steamed gyōza (sui gyōza). Use the vinegar, soy sauce and miso on the table to make a dipping sauce.

It's next to a small parking lot – look for the red and white awning.

Nailey's Café (☎ 231-2008; 2-8-12 Kanō-chō Chūō-ku; coffee from ¥400, lunch/dinner from ¥900/1200; ☽ 11.30am-midnight) Hip little café that serves espresso, light lunches and dinners. This is also a good spot for an evening drink.

Patisserie Tooth Tooth (☎ 334-1350; 3-2-17 Kitanagasa-dōri, Chūō-ku; cakes from ¥380, light meal from ¥900; ☽ 11am-9pm, closed irregularly) Near Motomachi Station, this is a fashionable European-style café-restaurant that serves light meals. Look for the red awning.

Upwards (☎ 230-8551; 1-7-16 Yamamoto-dōri, Chūō-ku; lunch/dinner from ¥1000; ☽ 11.30am-midnight Tue-Sun) This fashionable eatery in Kitano serves light Italian fare in an airy, open space. It's another good spot for a drink in the evening. There's an English sign.

Weekend (☎ 332 3131; 3-12-3 Kitanagasa-dōri, Chūō-ku; lunch from ¥800) Weekend is typical of the cool cafés that are popping up all over Kōbe. It's a good spot for a sandwich, a drink or a full meal. There's an English sign.

DRINKING & ENTERTAINMENT

Kōbe has a large foreign community and a number of bars that see mixed Japanese and foreign crowds. For Japanese-style drinking establishments, try the *izakaya* in the neighbourhood between the JR tracks and Ikuta-jinja. Also bear in mind that a lot of Kōbe's nightlife is centred around the city's many cafés, most of which transform into bars come evening (see p357).

Munchen Club (☎ 335 0170; 47 Akashi-chō Chūō-ku) A decent German-style pub that draws its share of foreign residents. It's close to Daimaru department store, on the basement floor.

Polo Dog (☎ 331 3944) A short walk from Sannomiya Station, this is a small casual bar at home with foreign customers. There's a sign on ground level; it's above a game parlour.

GETTING THERE & AWAY
Boat

The **China Express Line** (in Japan ☎ 078-321-5791, in China ☎ 022-2420-5777; www.celkobe.co.jp, in Japanese) operates a ferry between Kōbe and Tientsin. A 1st-/2nd-class ticket costs ¥26,000/23,000. The journey takes around 48 hours.

There are regular ferries between Kōbe and Shikoku (Imabari and Matsuyama) and Kyūshū (Ōita). Most ferries depart from Rokko Island and are operated by **Diamond Ferry Company** (☎ 857-9525, in Japanese). The cheapest fares are as follows: Imabari ¥4300, Matsuyama ¥5200 and Ōita ¥7400.

Train

JR Sannomiya Station is on the JR Tōkaidō line as well as the private Hankyū and Hanshin lines (both of which run to/from Osaka). The fastest way between Kōbe and Kyoto or Osaka is on the JR *shinkaisoku*, going to/from Kyoto (¥1050, 54 minutes) and to/from Osaka Station (¥390, 21 minutes).

The Hankyū line is the more convenient of the two private lines, the limited express to/from Osaka's Hankyū Umeda Station (¥310, 27 minutes) and the *tokkyū* to/from Kyoto, changing at Osaka's Jūsō Station (¥600, one hour).

Shin-Kōbe Station is on the Tōkaidō/San-yō *shinkansen* line, the Hikari *shinkansen* goes to/from Fukuoka (¥14,270, two hours 43 minutes) and to/from Tokyo (¥14,270, three hours nine minutes).

Note that there are several **discount ticket shops** near Hankyū Sannomiya Station.

GETTING AROUND
To/From the Airport
ITAMI OSAKA AIRPORT

It's possible to take a bus directly to/from Osaka's Itami airport (¥1020, 40 minutes). In Kōbe, the buses stop on the southwestern side of Sannomiya Station.

KANSAI INTERNATIONAL AIRPORT

There are a number of routes between Kōbe and KIX. By train, the fastest way is the JR *shinkaisoku* to/from Osaka Station, and the JR *kanku kaisoku* between Osaka Station and the airport (total cost ¥1660, total time 90 minutes with good connections). There is also a direct limousine bus to/from the airport (¥1800, 70 minutes). The Kōbe airport bus stop is on the southwestern side of Sannomiya Station.

Public Transport

Kōbe is small enough to travel around on foot. JR, Hankyū and Hanshin railway lines run east to west across Kōbe, providing access to most of Kōbe's more distant sights. A subway line also connects Shin-Kōbe Station with Sannomiya Station (¥200, one minute). There is also a city loop bus service which makes a grand circle tour of most of the city's sightseeing spots (¥250 per ride, ¥650 for an all-day pass). The bus stops at both Sannomiya and Shin-Kōbe Stations; look for the retro-style green buses.

HIMEJI 姫路

☎ 0792 / pop 479,000

If you see no other castles in Japan you should at least make an effort to visit Himeji-jō, unanimously acclaimed as the most splendid Japanese castle still standing. It's also known as Shirasagi, the 'White Egret', a title that derives from the castle's stately white form. The surrounding town itself is pretty drab, but the nearby Hyōgo Prefectural Museum of History and Kōko-en are worth a visit.

Himeji can easily be visited as a day trip from Kyoto, Osaka or Kōbe. On the way to Himeji, take a look out the train window at the new Akashi Kaikyō Suspension Bridge. Its 3910m span links the island of Honshū with Awaji-shima, making it the longest suspension bridge in the world. It comes into view on the southern side of the train about 10km west of Kōbe.

ORIENTATION & INFORMATION

There's a **tourist information counter** (☎ 85-3792) at the station; it's on the ground floor to the right as you come off the escalator. Between 10am and 3pm, English-speaking

INFORMATION	
Himeji Post Office 姫路郵便局	1 B3

SIGHTS & ACTIVITIES	
Castle Ticket Office 姫路城切符売り場	2 A2
Himeji-jō 姫路城	3 A2
Hyōgo Prefectural Museum of History 兵庫県立歴史博物館	4 B1

SLEEPING	
Himeji Washington Hotel Plaza 姫路ワシントンホテルプラザ	5 B5
Hotel Himeji Plaza ホテル姫路プラザ	6 B6
Hotel Sun Garden Himeji ホテルサンガーデン姫路 ...	7 A6
Tōyoko Inn 東横イン	8 B6

EATING	
Bistro Angelot ビストロ アンジェロ	9 A5
Fukutei ふく亭	10 B5
Morijū 森重	11 A4
Sekishin 赤心	12 B5
Tonkatsu Musashi とんかつ むさし	13 A4

TRANSPORT	
City Bus Terminal 市バスターミナル	14 A5
City South Bus Terminal 市バス南ターミナル	15 A6
Himeji North Exit 北口	16 A5
Himeji South Exit 南口	17 A6
Shinki Bus Terminal 神姫バスターミナル	18 A5

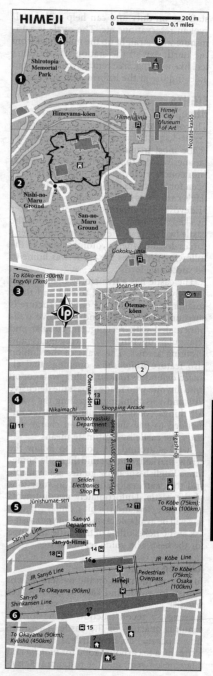

HIMEJI

KANSAI

staff are on duty and can help with hotel/ ryokan reservations etc. The castle is a 15-minute walk straight up the main road from the north exit of the station. If you don't feel like walking, free rental cycles are available; inquire at the information counter.

SIGHTS
Himeji-jō 姫路城
This **castle** (☎ 85-1146; 68 Honmachi; admission ¥600; ☻ 9am-5pm, last admission 4pm, an hr later in summer) is the most magnificent of the handful of Japanese castles that survive in their original (nonconcrete) form. Although there have been fortifications in Himeji since 1333, today's castle was built in 1580 by Toyotomi Hideyoshi and enlarged some 30 years later by Ikeda Terumasa. Ikeda was awarded the castle by Tokugawa Ieyasu when the latter's forces defeated the Toyotomi armies. In the following centuries the castle was home to 48 successive lords.

The castle has a five-storey main *donjon* (heavily fortified central tower) and three smaller *donjons*, and the entire structure is surrounded by moats and defensive walls punctuated with rectangular, circular and triangular openings for firing guns and shooting arrows. The walls of the donjon also feature *ishiotoshi* – openings that allowed defenders to pour boiling water or oil onto anyone who made it past the defensive slits and was thinking of scaling the walls. All things considered, visitors are recommended to pay the admission charge and enter the castle by legitimate means.

It takes around 1½ hours to follow the arrow-marked route around the castle. Sometimes English-speaking guides are available and they can really add a lot to your tour of the castle. Unfortunately appointments aren't accepted and it's hit or miss whether any will be available on the day of your visit – ask at the ticket office of the castle and hope for the best. The guide service is free.

Kōko-en 好古園
Just across the moat on the western side of Himeji-jō, you'll find **Kōko-en** (☎ 89-4120; 68 Honmachi; admission ¥300; ☻ 9am-4.30pm, an hr later in summer), a reconstruction of the former samurai quarters of the castle. There are nine separate Edo-style gardens, two ponds, a stream, a tea arbour (¥500 for *matcha* and a Japanese sweet) and the restaurant **Kassui-ken**, where you can enjoy lunch while gazing over the gardens. While the garden doesn't have the subtle beauty of some of Japan's older gardens, it is well done and especially lovely in the autumn foliage season.

Note that a joint ticket to both the Kōko-en and Himeji-jō costs only ¥720, a saving of ¥180. These can be purchased at the entrance to Kōko-en.

Hyōgo Prefectural Museum of History
兵庫県立博物館
This **museum** (Hyōgo Kenritsu Rekishi Hakubutsukan; ☎ 88 9011; 68 Honmachi; admission ¥200; ☻ 10am-5pm Tue-Sun, closed the day after holidays) has good displays on Himeji-jō and other castles around Japan. In addition to the displays on castles, the museum covers the main periods of Japanese history with some English explanations. At 11am, 2pm and 3.30pm you can even try on a suit of samurai armour or a kimono (ask at the front desk).

The museum is a five-minute walk north of the castle.

Engyōji 円教寺
Around 8km northeast of Himeji Station, this mountaintop **temple complex** (☎ 66-3327; 2968 Shosha, Himeji-shi; admission ¥300; ☻ 8.30am-5pm) is well worth a visit if you've got time after visiting the castle. The temple and surrounding area is most beautiful in the April cherry-blossom season or November *momiji* (maple-leaf) season. Eight of the temple buildings and seven Buddha images have been designated Important Cultural Properties.

From the top cable car station, it's about a 25-minute walk (about 2km) to the Maniden, one of the main structures of the complex, which is dedicated to Kannon (the Goddess of Mercy). Five minutes further on brings you to the Daikō-dō, a lovely wooden auditorium where parts of *The Last Samurai* were filmed. The path to both of these buildings is lined with Senjū-Kannon (Thousand-Armed Kannon) figures.

To get there, take bus 6 or 8 from Himeji Station (boarding position No 2, ¥260, 25 minutes). Get off at Shosha, and board the cable car (¥500/900 one way/return).

FESTIVALS & EVENTS
The **Nada-no-Kenka Matsuri**, held on 14 and 15 October, involves a conflict between three

mikoshi that are battered against each other until one smashes. Try to go on the second day, when the festival reaches its peak (around noon). The festival is held five minutes' walk from Shirahamanomiya Station (10 minutes from Himeji Station on the Sanyō-Dentetsu line); follow the crowds.

SLEEPING

Himeji is best visited as a day trip from other parts of Kansai. If you'd like to stay, however, there are plenty of choices.

Hotel Sun Garden Himeji (☎ 22-2231; fax 24-3731; 100 Minamiekimae-chō; s/d ¥9500/17,900) A stone's throw from the station, this hotel has clean and fairly spacious rooms and is the best choice for those who want something nicer than a business hotel.

Tōyoko Inn (☎ 84-1045; 97 Minamiekimae-chō; s/d ¥5980/8190) This new business hotel is a good choice if you want to be close to the station.

Himeji Washington Hotel Plaza (☎ 25-0111; fax 25-0133; 98 Higashiekimae-chō; s/d ¥6754/13,508) This is the best midrange choice in town. It's within easy walking distance of the castle and lots of restaurants.

Hotel Himeji Plaza (☎ 81-9000; 158 Toyozawa-chō; s/tw from ¥6000/13,800) On the other side of the station, this hotel is similar in quality but is a bit of a hike to the castle and restaurants.

EATING

The food court in the underground mall at JR Himeji Station has all the usual Western and Japanese dishes. It's just to the right as you exit the north ticket gate of the station.

Bistro Angelot (☎ 26-1113; 23 Tatemachi; lunch from ¥1000; ☯ 11.30am-3pm, 5-10pm Wed-Mon) This casual French/Italian place serves reasonable lunch courses. Look for the green awning.

Fukutei (☎ 23-0981; 75 Kamei-chō; lunch/dinner ¥1400/5000; ☯ 11am-2.30pm, 4.30-9pm Fri-Wed) Good spot for a nice lunch of simple *kaiseki* fare. From 11am to 2.30pm, try its mini-*kaiseki* course (¥1400). Look for the glass door and menu in the window.

Morijū (☎ 23-2517; 126 Uomachi; meals from ¥2500; ☯ 11.30am-1.30pm, 4.30-8.30pm Mon-Sat, closed Sun & holidays) This is another good spot for an elegant dinner of things like *unagi mamushi* (eel over rice, ¥2800) and *kaki nabe* (oyster cooked in a stew pot, ¥2500 per person). Some Japanese ability would be helpful here. Look for the black-and-white sign; it's next to a two-car garage.

Sekishin (☎ 22-3842; 301 Ekimae-chō; tonkatsu ¥550, rice ¥200; ☯ 11am-5pm, closed Tue & Thu) This tiny hole-in-the-wall joint serves tasty *tonkatsu*. You might also try its special *tonjiru* (miso soup with bits of fatty pork). Look for the white curtains with red kanji.

Tonkatsu Musashi (☎ 82-6257; 62 Nikaimachi; meals from ¥700) This is a very casual *tonkatsu* specialist that's on the way to the castle.

GETTING THERE & AWAY

The best way to Himeji from Kyoto, Osaka or Kōbe is a *shinkaisoku* on the JR Tōkaidō line going to/from Kyoto (¥2210, 1½ hours); to/from Osaka (¥1450, one hour); to/from Kōbe (¥950, 40 minutes). From Okayama, to the west, a *tokkyū* JR train on the San-yō line takes 1½ hours and costs ¥1450. You can also reach Himeji from these cities via the Tōkaidō/San-yō *shinkansen* line, and this is a good option for Japan Rail Pass holders.

NARA 奈良

☎ 0742 / pop 363,000

Japan's first real capital, Nara, is the number-two tourist attraction in Kansai after Kyoto. Like Kyoto, Nara is uninspiring at first glance, but careful inspection will reveal the rich history and hidden beauty of the city. Indeed, with eight Unesco World Heritage sites, Nara is second only to Kyoto as a repository of Japan's cultural legacy. Whatever

---

NARA UNESCO WORLD HERITAGE SITES

In 1998, eight sites in Nara met the criteria to be designated World Heritage sites by the UN. They are the Buddhist temples of Tōdai-ji, Kōfuku-ji, Gango-ji, Yakushi-ji and Tōshōdai-ji; the shrine, Kasuga Taisha; Kasuga-yama Primeval Forest; and the remains of Heijō-kyō Palace.

Each of these sites is considered to be of immeasurable historical value. All are open for public viewing. Five are covered in detail in the text; of the remaining three, Kasuga-yama Primeval Forest is directly behind Kasuga Taisha, Gango-ji is in Naramachi, and the Heijō-kyō Palace Ruins are 10 minutes' walk east of Saidai-ji Station on the Kintetsu line.

KANSAI

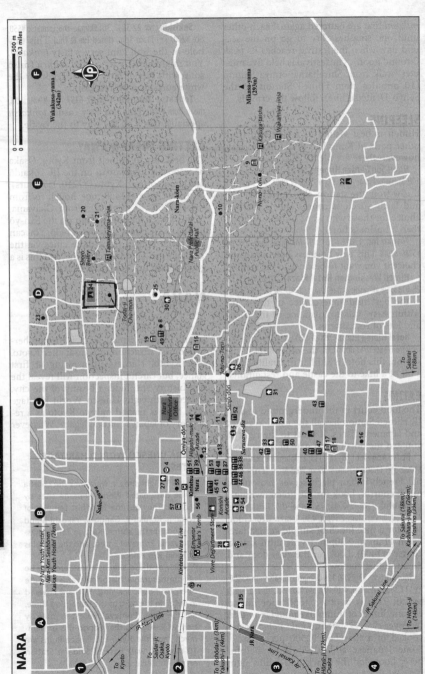

NARA

Wakakusa-yama ▲ (342m)

Mikasa-yama (293m) ▲

0 500 m
0 0.3 miles

Saho-gawa

To Nara Youth Hostel;
Nara-Ken Seishonen
Kaikan Youth Hostel (2km)

To Kyoto

JR Nara Line

To Saidai-ji;
Osaka;
Kyoto

Kintetsu Nara Line

To Toshodai-ji (3km);
Yakushi-ji (4km)

Emperor
Kaika's Tomb

Vivre Department Store

Nara Prefectural
Office

Omiya-dori

Higashi-muki
Arcade

Kintetsu
Nara

Konishi
Arcade

Nara-koen

Shoro
Belfry

Tamukeyama-jinja

Nigatsu-do

Kasuga-taisha

Wakamiya-jinja

Todai-ji
Chu-mon

Nara Prefectural
Public Hall

Ichi-no-Torii

Sanjo-dori

Sarusawa-ike

Naramachi

JR Sakurai Line

To Hōryū-ji (12km);
Osaka

JR Nara

To Kansai Line

To Sakurai (18km)

To Sakurai (18km);
Kashihara-jingu (26km);
Yoshino (35km)

To Hōryū-ji (14km)

you do, try to go to Nara on a fine day, as visiting the sites requires a lot of walking, and it's no fun at all in bad weather.

Nara is so small that it's quite possible to pack the most worthwhile sights into one full day. It's preferable to spend at least two days here, but this will depend on how much time you have for the Kansai region. Those with time to spare should allow a day for Nara-kōen and another day for the sights in western and southwestern Nara. If you only have one day in Nara, spend it walking around Nara-kōen; you would only exhaust yourself if you tried to fit in some of the more distant sights as well.

HISTORY

Nara is at the northern end of the Yamato Plain, where members of the Yamato clan rose to power as the original emperors of Japan. The remains of these early emperors are contained in *kofun* (burial mounds), some of which date back to the 3rd century AD.

Until the 7th century, however, Japan had no permanent capital, as native Shintō taboos concerning death stipulated that the capital be moved with the passing of each emperor. This practice died out under the influence of Buddhism and with the Taika reforms of 646, when the entire country came under imperial control.

At this time it was decreed that a permanent capital be built. Two locations were tried before a permanent capital was finally established at Nara (which was then known as Heijōkyō) in 710. Permanent status, however, lasted a mere 75 years. When a priest by the name of Dōkyō managed to seduce an empress and nearly usurp the throne, it was decided to move the court to a new location, out of reach of Nara's increasingly powerful clergy. This led to the new capital being established at Kyoto, where it remained until 1868.

Although brief, the Nara period was extraordinarily vigorous in its absorption of influences from China, a process that laid the foundations of Japanese culture and civilisation. The adoption of Buddhism as a national religion made a lasting impact on government, arts, literature and architecture. With the exception of an assault on the area by the Taira clan in the 12th century, Nara was subsequently spared the periodic bouts of destruction wreaked upon Kyoto, and a number of magnificent buildings have survived.

ORIENTATION

Nara retains the grid pattern of streets laid out in Chinese style during the 8th century. The two main train stations, JR Nara Station and Kintetsu Nara Station, are roughly in the middle of the city, and Nara-kōen, which contains most of the important sights, is on the eastern side, against the bare flank of Wakakusa-yama. Most of the other sights are southwest of the city and are best reached by

KANSAI

buses that leave from both train stations (or by train in the case of Hōryū-ji). It's easy to cover the city centre and the major attractions in nearby Nara-kōen on foot, though some may prefer to rent a bicycle (see p369).

Maps

Nara tourist information offices have two very useful maps: the *Welcome to Nara Sightseeing Map*, which is best for sightseeing within the city limits, and the *Japan: Nara Prefecture* map, which is best for outlying areas. In addition, their handout titled *Nara* has a basic map and useful transport information.

INFORMATION
Internet Access

Suien Tea Lounge (☎ 22-2577; 1-58 Aburasaka-cho, Nara-shi, inside Hotal Asyl Nar; 2hr Internet free with purchase of ¥525 drink; ☺ 7.30am-11pm).

Money

There is an ATM that accepts international cards on the ground floor of the building opposite Kintetsu Nara Station.

Telephone

Outside the NTT telephone company office on Sanjō-dōri there is an IC Card international phone.

Tourist Information

Nara City Tourist Center (☎ 22-3900; 23-4 Kamisanjō-chō; ☺ 9am-9pm) In Nara, the best source of information is a short walk from JR Nara or Kintetsu Nara Station.

The tourist centre can put you in touch with volunteer guides who speak English and other foreign languages, but you must book at least one day in advance. Two of these services are the **YMCA Goodwill Guides** (☎ 45-5920; 4-11 Saidaiji, Minamimachi) and **Nara Student Guides** (☎ 26-4753; www.narastudentguide.jpn.org; ☺ 9am-5pm). These services are a pleasant way to meet the Japanese – the guides are often students keen to practise their foreign languages. Remember that the guides are volunteers, so you should offer to cover their day's expenses; however, most temple and museum admission fees are waived for registered guides, so you needn't worry about those.

There are three more tourist information offices in Nara that stock maps and have

staff who can answer basic questions in English: the **JR Nara Station office** (☎ 22-9821; ☺ 9am-5pm), the **Kintetsu Nara Station office** (☎ 24-4858; ☺ 9am-5pm) and the **Sarusawa Tourist Information Office** (☎ 26-1991; ☺ 9am-5pm). All three are open from 9am to 5pm. The JR Nara Station office may be able to help with ryokan and *minshuku* reservations.

The Nara City Tourist Center office also has comprehensive listings of places to stay, information on bus tours, hiking maps and the like.

SIGHTS
Nara-kōen Area 奈良公園

The park was created from wasteland in 1880 and covers a large area at the foot of Wakakusa-yama. The JNTO's leaflet entitled *Walking Tour Courses in Nara* includes a map for this area. This walking tour is probably the best way to get the most out of a day in Nara and is highly recommended.

The park is home to about 1200 deer, which in pre-Buddhist times were considered messengers of the gods and today enjoy the status of National Treasures. They roam the park and surrounding areas in search of hand-outs from tourists, often descending on petrified children who have the misfortune to be carrying food. You can buy *shika-sembei* (deer biscuits) from vendors for ¥150 to feed to the deer. Note: don't eat them yourself, as we saw one misguided foreign tourist doing.

TŌDAI-JI 東大寺

This **temple** (☎ 22-5511; 406-1 Zōshi-chō; Daibutsu-den ¥500, Kaidan-in ¥500; ☺ 8am-4.30pm Nov-Feb, 8am-5pm Mar, 7.30am-5.30pm Apr-Sep, 7.30am-5pm Oct) with its vast Daibutsu-den Hall and enormous bronze Buddha image, is Nara's star attraction. For this reason, it is often packed with groups of school children being herded around by microphone-wielding tour guides. Nonetheless, it is an awe-inspiring sight and should be high on any sightseeing itinerary.

On your way to the temple you'll pass through **Nandai-mon**, an enormous gate containing two fierce-looking **Niō guardians**. These recently restored wooden images, carved in the 13th century by the sculptor Unkei, are some of the finest wooden statues in all of Japan, if not the world. They are truly dramatic works of art and seem ready to spring to life at any moment.

Daibutsu-den Hall 大仏殿

Tōdai-ji **Daibutsu-den** (Hall of the Great Buddha; ☎ 22 5511; 406-1 Zōshi-chō; admission ¥500; ⊙ 8am-4.30pm Nov-Feb, 8am-5pm Mar, 7.30am-5.30pm Apr-Sep, 7.30am-5pm Oct) is the largest wooden building in the world. Unbelievably the present structure, rebuilt in 1709, is a mere two-thirds of the size of the original! The Daibutsu (Great Buddha) contained within is one of the largest bronze figures in the world and was originally cast in 746. The present statue, recast in the Edo period, stands just over 16m high and consists of 437 tonnes of bronze and 130kg of gold. The Daibutsu is an image of Dainichi Buddha, the cosmic Buddha believed to precede all worlds and their respective historical Buddhas. Historians believe that Emperor Shōmu ordered the building of the Buddha as a charm against smallpox, which ravaged Japan in preceding years. Over the centuries the statue took quite a beating from earthquakes and fires, losing its head a couple of times (note the slight difference in colour between the head and the body).

As you circle the statue towards the back, you'll see a wooden column with a hole through its base. Popular belief maintains that those who can squeeze through the hole, which is exactly the same size as one of the Great Buddha's nostrils, are ensured of enlightenment. It's great fun to watch the kids wiggle through nimbly and the adults get wedged in like champagne corks – you wonder how often they have to call the fire department to extricate trapped visitors. A hint for determined adults: it's a lot easier to go through with both arms held above your head.

Nigatsu-dō & Sangatsu-dō 二月堂・三月堂

These two halls are an easy walk east of the Daibutsu-den; follow the path that winds uphill starting from the southeast corner of the Daibutsu-den.

Nigatsu-dō (☎ 22-5511; 406-1 Zōshi-chō; admission free) is famed for its Omizutori Matsuri (see p367) and a splendid view across Nara, which makes the climb up the hill worthwhile – particularly at dusk. Opening hours here are the same as those of the Daibutsu-den.

A short walk south of Nigatsu-dō is **Sangatsu-dō** (admission ¥400), which is the oldest building in the Tōdai-ji complex. This hall contains a small collection of fine statues

from the Nara period. It's open the same hours as the Daibutsu-den.

Kasuga Taisha 春日大社

This **shrine** (☎ 22-7788; 160 Kasugano-chō; admission free; ⊙ 6am-6pm) was founded in the 8th century by the Fujiwara family and completely rebuilt every 20 years according to Shintō tradition, until the end of the 19th century. It lies at the foot of the hill in a pleasant, wooded setting with herds of sacred deer awaiting hand-outs.

The approaches to the shrine are lined with hundreds of lanterns, and there are many hundreds more in the shrine itself. The **lantern festivals** held twice a year at the shrine are a major attraction (for details see Mantōrō p367).

The **Hōmotsu-den** (Treasure Hall; admission ¥420; ⊙ 9am-4.30pm) is just north of the entrance *torii* for the shrine. The hall displays Shintō ceremonial regalia and equipment used in *bugaku*, *nō* and *gagaku* performances.

Shōsō-in Treasure Repository 正倉院

The **Shōsō-in Treasure Repository** (☎ 26-2811; 129 Zōshi-chō; admission free; ⊙ grounds 10am-3pm Mon-Fri, closed Sat, Sun & holidays, bldg open only during special exhibitions) is a short walk north of Daibutsu-den. The building was used to house fabulous imperial treasures and its wooden construction allowed precise regulation of humidity through natural expansion and contraction. The treasures have been removed and are shown twice a year, in spring and autumn, at the Nara National Museum (below). The Shōsō-in building is open to the public at the same time.

SHIN-YAKUSHI-JI 新薬師寺

This **temple** (☎ 22-3736; 1352 Takabatake-cho; admission ¥500; ⊙ 9am-5pm), a pleasant 15-minute walk from Kasuga Taisha, was founded by Empress Kōmyō in 747 in thanks for her husband's recovery from an eye disease. Most of the buildings were destroyed or have been reconstructed, but the present main hall dates from the 8th century. The hall contains sculptures of Yakushi Nyorai (Healing Buddha) and a set of 12 divine generals.

NARA NATIONAL MUSEUM 奈良国立博物館

The **Nara National Museum** (Nara Koku-ritsu Hakubut-sukan; ☎ 22-7771; 50 Noborioji-chō; admission ¥420, special exhibitions ¥830; 9am-4.30pm) is devoted to Buddhist art and is divided into two wings. The western gallery has a fine collection of *butsu-zō* (statues of the Buddha), while the new eastern gallery displays sculptures, paintings and calligraphy.

A special exhibition featuring the treasures of the Shōsō-in Hall, which holds the treasures of Tōdai-ji, are displayed here in May, as well as from 21 October to 8 November (call the Nara City Tourist Center to check, as these dates vary slightly each year). The exhibits include priceless items from the cultures along the Silk Road. If you are in Nara during these periods and are a fan of Japanese antiquities, you should make a point of visiting the museum, but be prepared for crowds – these exhibits get packed!

KŌFUKU-JI 興福寺

This temple was transferred here from Kyoto in 710 as the main temple for the Fujiwara family. Although the original temple complex had 175 buildings, fires and destruction as a result of power struggles have left only a dozen still standing. There are two pagodas – a three-storey one and a five-storey one – dating from 1143 and 1426 respectively. The taller of the two pagodas is the second tallest in Japan, outclassed by the one at Kyoto's Tō-ji by only a few centimetres.

The **Kōfuku-ji National Treasure Hall** (22-7755; 48 Noborioji-chō; Kokuhō-kan; admission ¥500; 9am-4.30pm) contains a variety of statues and art objects salvaged from previous structures.

ISUI-EN & NEIRAKU ART MUSEUM 依水園・寧楽美術館

This **garden** (22-2173; 74 Suimon-chō; admission museum & garden ¥600; 9.30am-4pm Wed-Mon), dating from the Meiji era, is beautifully laid out and features abundant greenery and a pond filled with ornamental carp. It's without a doubt the best garden in the city and well worth a visit. For ¥450 you can enjoy a cup of tea on tatami mats overlooking the garden or you can have lunch in the nearby Sanshū restaurant, which also shares the view.

The adjoining art museum (Neiraku Bijutsukan), which displays Chinese and Korean ceramics and bronzes, is something of an anticlimax after the garden.

Naramachi ならまち

South of Sanjō-dōri and Sarusawa-ike pond you will find Naramachi, with many well-preserved *machiya* and kura. It's a nice place for a stroll before or after hitting the big sights of Nara-kōen, and there are several good restaurants in the area to entice hungry travellers (see p368).

Highlights of Naramachi include the **Naramachi Shiryō-kan Museum** (22-5509; 14 Nishishinya-chō; admission free; 10am-4pm Tue-Sun), which has a decent collection of bric-a-brac from the area, including a display of old Japanese coins and bills.

Naramachi Koushi-no-le (23-4820; 44 Gangōji-chō; admission free; 9am-5pm Tue-Sun) is a traditional Japanese house which, unfortunately, has been a little too thoroughly restored.

While you're in the neighbourhood, check out the **Naramachi Monogatari-kan** (26-3476; 2-1 Nakanoshinya-cho; admission free; 11am-4.30pm), an interesting little gallery that holds some worthwhile exhibitions.

Lastly, Naramachi is also home to **Gangō-ji** (23 1378; 11 Chūin-cho; admission ¥400; 9.30am-5pm, closed 28 Dec-4 Jan), a small temple that is listd as one of Nara's Unesco World Heritage sites. Despite it's World Heritage listing, it's not particularly interesting and probably only merits a quick glance from outside.

TOURS

Nara Kōtsū (22-5263) runs daily bus tours on a variety of routes, two of which include Nara city sights only and two of which include more distant sights like Hōryū-ji and the burial mounds around Asuka (see p373). An explanation tape in English is available for all but the Asuka route. Prices for the all-day trips average ¥7000 for adults (which includes all temple fees and tape-recorder rental). Lunch at a Japanese restaurant on the route is optional (reserve when buying your ticket). Nara Kōtsū has offices in JR Nara Station and across the street from Kintetsu Nara Station.

FESTIVALS & EVENTS

Nara has plenty of festivals throughout the year. The following is a brief list of the more interesting ones. Because the dates for some of these festivals vary, it's best to check with the Nara or Kyoto tourist information offices.

KANSAI

January

Yamayaki (Grass Burning Festival) Early January (the day before Seijin-no-hi). This festival commemorates a feud many centuries ago between the monks of Tōdai-ji and Kōfuku-ji: Wakakusa-yama is set alight at 6pm, with an accompanying display of fireworks. Arrive earlier to bag a good viewing position in Nara-kōen.

February

Mantōrō (Lantern Festival) Early February. Held at Kasuga Taisha at 6pm, this is a festival renowned for its illumination, with 3000 stone and bronze lanterns; a *bugaku* dance also takes place in the Apple Garden on the last day. Also held around 14 August in O-bon.

March

Omizutori (Water-Drawing Ceremony) 12 to 13 March. The monks of Tōdai-ji enter a special period of initiation during these days. On the evening of 12 March, they parade huge flaming torches around the balcony of Nigatsu-dō (in the temple grounds) and rain down embers on the spectators to purify them. The water-drawing ceremony is performed after midnight.

May

Takigi Nō (Firelight *nō* performances) 11 to 12 May. Open-air performances of *nō* held after dark by the light of blazing torches at Kōfuku-ji and Kasuga Taisha.

October

Shika-no-Tsunokiri (Deer Antler Cutting) Sundays & holidays in October. Those pesky deer in Nara-kōen are pursued in a type of elegant rodeo into the Roku-en (deer enclosure) close to Kasuga Taisha. They are then wrestled to the ground and their antlers sawn off. Tourist brochures hint that this is to avoid personal harm, though it's not clear whether they are referring to the deer fighting each other or the deer mugging the tourists.

SLEEPING

Although Nara is favoured as a day trip from Kyoto, accommodation can still be packed out for festivals and holidays and at weekends, so make reservations in advance if you plan to visit at these times. The Nara City Tourist Center has extensive lists of hotels, *minshuku*, pensions and ryokan. The JR Nara Station tourist office may be able to help with *minshuku* and ryokan reservations.

Budget

Ryokan Seikan-sō (☎ /fax 22-2670; 29 Higashikitsuji-chō; r per person without bathroom from ¥4000) This friendly place with wooden architecture and

a pleasant garden is probably the best-value ryokan in Nara.

Ryokan Matsumae (☎ 22-3686; 28-1 Higashiterabayashi-chō; r per person without bathroom from ¥5000) It lacks the atmosphere of the Seikan-sō but has a very convenient location.

Nara Youth Hostel (奈良ユースホステル; ☎ 22-1334; www.jyh.gr.jp/nara/english/neweng.html; 1716 Hōren-chō; dm per person ¥3150, breakfast/dinner ¥630/1050) This is a nicer hostel. From either JR or Kintetsu Nara Station, take bus 108, 109, 111, 113 or 115 and get off at the Shieikyūjō-mae bus stop, from where it's a one-minute walk.

Nara-ken Seishōnen Kaikan Youth Hostel (奈良県青少年会館ユースホステル; ☎ /fax 22 5540; naseikan@galaxy.ocn.ne.jp; 72-7 Handahiraki-chō; dm per person ¥2783, breakfast/dinner ¥347/945) This nondescript, concrete place has friendly staff. From JR Nara Station or Kintetsu Nara Station, take bus 12, 13, 131 or 140 and get off at the Ikuei-gakuen bus stop, from where it's a five-minute walk.

Midrange
HOTELS

Hotel Fujita Nara (☎ 23-8111; www.fujita-nara.com; 16-1 Higashimukikita-machi; s/tw ¥7200/12,200) A clean, new hotel with a convenient location. During off-peak times, you might get a reduced rate if you reserve through the Kintetsu Nara tourist information office.

Green Hotel Ashibi (☎ 26-7815; fax 24-2465; s/d/ tw ¥6400/11,000/12,000) Close to Kintetsu Nara Station, this is a small business hotel with some of the cheapest rooms in this range.

Super Hotel (☎ 20-9000; 500-1 Sanjō-chō; s/d ¥4980/6980) The cheapest hotel in town is this no-frills place across from JR Nara Station. It only opens for check-in after 3pm.

RYOKAN

Ryokan Hakuhō (☎ 26-7891; www2.ocn.ne.jp /~hakuhou/index.html; 4-1 Kamisanjō-chō; r per person without bathroom ¥6000) In the centre of town, five minutes walk from JR Nara Station, this place is starting to show its age and has less atmosphere than the Seikan-sō.

Top End
HOTELS

Nara Hotel (☎ 26-3300; narah268@gold.ocn.ne.jp; 1096 Takabatake-chō; s/d ¥16,170/26,565, tw from ¥26,565) Built near the turn of the century, this still ranks as one of the city's premier hotels.

Rooms in the old wing have much more character than those in the new wing.

Hotel Sunroute Nara (☎ 22-5151; fax 27-3759; 1110 Takabatake-chō; s/tw ¥9240/17,850) Basic business hotel near the southwest corner of Nara-kōen.

RYOKAN

Edo-san (☎ 26 2662; Takabatake-chō; r per person with 2 meals ¥18,900) Edo-san offers private Japanese-style cottages on the edge of Nara-kōen.

Kankasō (☎ 26 1128; 10 Kasugano-chō; r with dinner & breakfast ¥18,900) Kankasō is an elegant ryokan right next to Tōdai-ji.

EATING & DRINKING

Nara is full of good restaurants, most of which are in the vicinity of Kintetsu Nara Station or in Naramachi.

Tempura Asuka (☎ 26-4308; 11 Shōnami-chō; lunch/dinner from ¥1575/3675; ☽ 11.30am-2.30pm, 5pm-9.30pm Tue-Sun) Attractive tempura and sashimi sets are served in a relatively casual atmosphere. At lunchtime try its nicely presented *yumei-dono bentō* (a lunch box filled with a variety of tasty Japanese foods) for ¥1500. There is an English sign.

Beni-e (☎ 22-9493; 1-4 Higashimukiminami-machi; lunch/dinner from ¥1500/2000; ☽ 11.30am-2.30pm, 5-8pm Tue-Sun) This is one of our favourites in Nara. It serves good tempura sets for ¥1500/2000/2500 (*hana, tsuki* and *yuki* sets respectively). It's located a little back from Higashi-muki arcade, behind a shoe store.

Ayura Café (☎ 26 5339; 28 Hashimoto-chō; lunch set ¥800) We highly recommend this tiny café for it's wonderful (mostly vegie) set lunch or just a quick cuppa. It's on the 2nd floor and there's a small English sign.

Kosode (☎ 27-2582; 14 Kunōdō-chō; green tea with Japanese sweet from ¥400; ☽ 11am-6pm Tue-Sun) This charming little tea room-cum-gallery in Naramachi is highly recommended for a break when strolling the area. In addition to the pottery on display, it offers a kimono-fitting service (¥5000 for men and women).

Miyoshino (☎ 22-5239; 27 Hashimoto-chō; meals ¥650; ☽ 11am-8.30pm Thu-Tue) Miyono does good-value sets of typical Japanese fare. Stop by and check the daily lunch specials on display outside.

Ohka Café (☎ 22-1139; 13 Nakashiya-chō; coffee ¥470; ☽ 11am-5pm Tue-Sun) With indoor and outdoor garden seating, this café is a pleasant spot for a drink or a light meal when in Naramachi.

Harishin (☎ 22-2669; 15 Nakanoshinya-chō; ☽ 11.30am-2.30pm, 6-8pm Tue-Sun) This is an elegant *kaiseki* place for a special lunch or dinner in Nara. Offerings include the *kamitsumichi bentō* for ¥2625 or the mini *kaiseki* course for ¥3500.

Fluke Café (☎ 23 8981; 10 Higashimukinaka-machi; drinks from ¥400) This is one of Nara's newest and hippest cafés. It's opposite Mister Donut.

Mellow Café (☎ 27 9099; 1-8 Konishi-chō; lunch from ¥700) Located down a narrow alley, this open-plan café usually displays its daily lunch special for all to see.

Okaru (☎ 24-3686; 13-2 Higashimukiminami-machi; okonomiyaki from ¥680; ☽ 11am-10pm Thu-Tue) Homely spot in the Higashi-muki arcade for simple *okonomiyaki* – look for the food models in the window.

Tsukihi-tei (☎ 23-5470; 6 Higashimukiminami-machi; lunch/dinner from ¥1000/1500; ☽ 11am-10pm) On the 2nd floor at the north end of the Higashi-muki arcade, this place serves simple *kaiseki* sets at reasonable prices. The *tenshin bentō*, a good bet at ¥1500, includes sashimi, rice, vegetables and other tidbits.

Sanshū-tei (☎ 22-2173; 74 Suimon-chō; lunch from ¥1200; ☽ 11.30am-2pm Wed-Mon) Located beside Isui-en, one of Nara's finest gardens, this is one of the city's most interesting places to eat. Guests sit on tatami mats and enjoy the food while gazing out over the garden. Unfortunately, the main dish is enough to challenge even the most adventurous of eaters: *tororo*, a gooey dish made from grated yam, barley and rice. There are only two choices: *mugimeshitororo* (*tororo* without eel, ¥1200) or *unatoro gozen* (*tororo* with eel, ¥2400).

Drink Drank (☎ 27-6206; 8 Hashimoto-chō; smoothies ¥400, lunch sets ¥850; ☽ 10.30am-7.45pm Thu-Tue) A new shop that serves a variety of fresh fruit drinks and light lunches including sandwiches and soup.

Za Don (☎ 27-5314; 13-2 Higashimukiminami-machi; donburi from ¥400; ☽ 11am-8pm) In the Higashi-muki arcade, Za Don serves the eponymous *donburi* (rice bowl with various toppings) for absurdly low prices. It's healthy Japanese fast food and there's a picture menu to make ordering easier. It's opposite McDonald's.

Yanagi Chaya (☎ 22-7460; 49 Noborioji-chō; lunch from ¥4000; ☽ lunch & dinner Tue-Sun) With indoor and outdoor garden seating, this café is a pleasant spot for a drink or a light meal when in Naramachi.

Hiranoya (☎ 26-3918; 1-6 Konishi-chō; okonomiyaki from ¥680; ☺ 11.30am-9pm, closed Sun & 3rd Mon) A good spot for some *okonomiyaki* and similar dishes, this place has photos of *okonomiyaki* outside.

Hirasō (☎ 22-0866; 30-1 Imamikado-chō; meals per person ¥3000-4000; ☺ 10am-8pm Tue-Sun) This place in Naramachi does set meals, including local specialities like *kaki-no-ha* sushi (persimmon leaf sushi). The sign is black, white and red.

Rumours (☎ 26-4327; 9 Tsunofuri-chō, 3F Patel Bldg; meals/drinks from ¥600/500; ☺ dusk-late, closed irregularly) This English-style pub is a decent spot for a few evening drinks and a good spot to meet local residents and other travellers.

Kyōshō-An (☎ 27-7715; 26-3 Hashimoto-chō; green tea/sweets from ¥400/650; ☺ 11am-7.30pm Tue-Sun) Simple little Japanese tea shop where you can sample green tea and traditional Japanese sweets. It's on the 2nd floor – look for the pictures on the sign outside. We recommend this spot for a cool drink or sweet on a hot day. It's up a flight of white brick stairs.

GETTING THERE & AWAY
Bus
There is an overnight bus service between Tokyo's Shinjuku (highway bus terminal) and Nara (¥8400/15,120 one way/return). The bus leaves Nara at 10.30pm and reaches Tokyo the next day at 6.15am. The bus from Tokyo leaves at 11.15pm and arrives in Nara the next day at 6.50am. In Nara, call ☎ 22-5110 or check with the Nara City Tourist Center for more details. In Tokyo, call ☎ 03-3928-6011.

Train
KYOTO
Unless you have a Japan Rail Pass, the best option is the Kintetsu line, which runs between Kintetsu Kyoto Station (in Kyoto Station) and Kintetsu Nara Station. There are direct *tokkyū* trains (¥1110, 33 minutes) and *kyūkō* trains (¥610, around 45 minutes) that may require a change at Saidai-ji.

The JR Nara line connects JR Kyoto Station with JR Nara Station (*kaisoku*, ¥690, 46 minutes) but departures are not frequent.

OSAKA
The Kintetsu Nara line connects Osaka (Kintetsu Namba Station) with Nara (Kintetsu Nara Station). *Kaisoku* and *futsū* services

take about 35 minutes and cost ¥540. *Tokkyū* services do the journey in five minutes less but cost almost double, making them a poor option.

The JR Kansai line links Osaka (Namba and Tennō-ji Stations) and Nara (JR Nara Station). A *kaisoku* connects Namba and JR Nara Station (¥540, 46 minutes) and Tennō-ji and JR Nara Station (¥450, 31 minutes).

GETTING AROUND
To/From the Airport
Nara is served by Kansai International Airport. There is a **limousine bus service** (☎ 22-5110) between Nara and the airport with departures roughly every hour in both directions (¥1800, 1½ hours). At Kansai International Airport ask at the information counter, and in Nara visit the ticket office in the building across from Kintetsu Nara Station. Reservations are a good idea.

For domestic flights, there are limousine buses to/from Osaka's Itami airport (¥1440, 80 minutes).

Bicycle
Nara is a convenient size for getting around on a bicycle. **Kintetsu Sunflower Rent-a-Cycle** (☎ 24-3528) is close to the Nara City Tourist Center. Weekday rates are ¥300 per hour and ¥900 per day on weekdays and ¥350 and ¥1000 on weekends. It's just off Konishi Arcade, down a small street, the entrance to which is opposite a supermarket.

Bus
Most of the area around Nara-kōen is covered by two circular bus routes. Bus No 1 runs anticlockwise and bus No 2 runs clockwise. There's a ¥180 flat fare. You can easily see the main sights in the park on foot and use the bus as an option if you are pushed for time or get tired of walking.

The most useful buses for western and southwestern Nara (Tōshōdai-ji, Yakushi-ji and Hōryū-ji) are Nos 52, 97 and 98, which link all three destinations with the Kintetsu and JR Stations. Buses run about every 30 minutes between 8am and 5pm, but are much less frequent outside these times.

Taxi
Taxis are plentiful but expensive. A taxi ride from JR Nara Station to either of the youth hostels costs about ¥1000.

KANSAI

AROUND NARA 奈良周辺

Southern Nara-ken was the birthplace of imperial rule and is rich in historical sites that are easily accessible as day trips from Osaka, Kyoto or Nara, provided that you make an early start. Of particular historical interest are the *kofun* that mark the graves of Japan's first emperors; these are concentrated around Asuka and Sakurai. There are also several isolated temples where you can escape the crowds that plague Nara's city centre. Further afield, the mountaintop town of Yoshino is one of Japan's cherry-blossom meccas.

Easily reached by rail, Yamato-Yagi and Sakurai serve as useful transport hubs for the region. Keep in mind that the Kintetsu line is far more convenient than JR for most of the destinations in this section.

If you're starting from Nara, you may want to pick up a copy of the detailed *Japan: Nara Prefecture* map at any of the tourist information offices in Nara city before starting out.

TEMPLES SOUTHWEST OF NARA

The most important temples southwest of Nara are Hōryū-ji, Yakushi-ji and Tōshōdai-ji. These three can be visited in one afternoon. The best way to do this is to head straight to Hōryū-ji (the most distant from the centre of Nara) and then continue by bus 52, 97 or 98 (¥560, 40 minutes) up to Yakushi-ji and Tōshōdai-ji, which are a 10-minute walk apart (for more on getting to/from these temples, see the respective entries).

Hōryū-ji 法隆寺

This **temple** (☎ 75-2555; 1-1 Hōryūji-sannai, Ikaruga-chō; admission ¥1000; ◷ 8am-4.30pm 22 Feb-3 Nov, 8am-4pm 4 Nov-21 Feb) was founded in 607 by Prince Shōtoku, considered by many to be the patron saint of Japanese Buddhism. Legend has it that Shōtoku, moments after birth, stood up and started praying. A statue in the treasure museum depicts this auspicious event. Hōryū-ji is renowned not only as the oldest temple in Japan but also as a repository for some of the country's rarest treasures. Several of the temple's wooden buildings have survived earthquakes and fires to become the oldest of their kind in the world. The temple is divided into two parts, **Sai-in** (West Temple) and **Tō-in** (East Temple).

The entrance ticket allows admission to Sai-in, Tō-in and the Great Treasure Hall. A detailed map is provided and a guidebook is available in English and several other languages. The JNTO leaflet called *Walking Tour Courses in Nara* includes a basic map for the area around Hōryū-ji.

The main approach to the temple proceeds from the south along a tree-lined avenue and continues through Nandai-mon and Chū-mon before entering the Sai-in precinct. As you enter this precinct, you'll see the **Kondō** (Main Hall) on your right and a pagoda on your left.

The Kondō houses several treasures, including the triad of the **Buddha Sakyamuni**, with two attendant Bodhisattvas. Though it is one of Japan's great Buddhist treasures, it is dimly lit and barely visible (you may want to bring a flashlight). Likewise, the pagoda contains clay images depicting scenes from the life of Buddha that are barely visible without a flashlight.

On the eastern side of Sai-in are the two concrete buildings of the **Daihōzō-den** (Great Treasure Hall), containing numerous treasures from Hōryū-ji's long history. Renowned Buddhist artefacts in this hall include the Kudara Kannon and two miniature shrines: the Tamamushi Shrine and the Shrine of Lady Tachibana.

The **Tamamushi Shrine** is named for the insect tamamushi, or jewel beetle, the wings of which were used to decorate it. The colour in the original has faded, but an example of fresh *tamamushi* wings is on display and one can only imagine how the shrine must have looked when it was entirely covered with shimmering blue-green wings.

GETTING THERE & AWAY

To get to Hōryū-ji, take the JR Kansai line from JR Nara Station to Hōryū-ji Station (¥210, 10 minutes). From there, bus No 72 shuttles the short distance between the station and Hōryū-ji (¥170, eight minutes), or you can walk it in 20 minutes. Alternatively, take bus No 52, 60, 97 or 98 from either JR Nara Station or Kintetsu Nara Station and get off at the Hōryū-ji mae stop (¥760, 40 minutes by bus No 60, 60 minutes by others).

Yakushi-ji 薬師寺

This **temple** (☎ 33-6001; 457 Nishinokyō-chō; admission ¥500; ◷ 8.30am-5pm) was established by

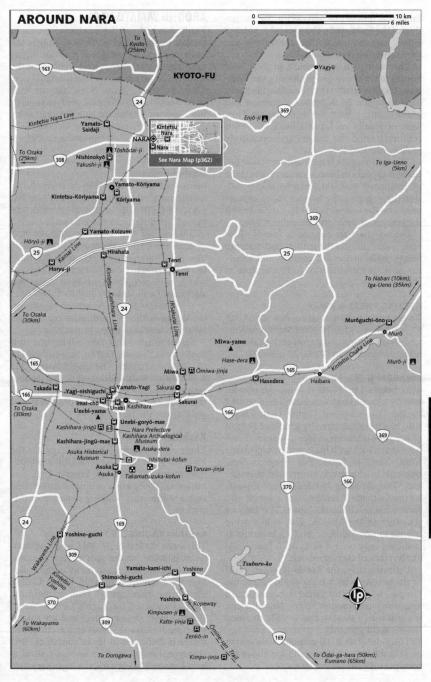

AROUND NARA

0 — 10 km
0 — 6 miles

To Kyoto (25km)

163

KYOTO-FU

Yagyū

24

Kintetsu Nara Line

Yamato-Saidaiji

NARA

Nara

Kintetsu Nara

See Nara Map (p362)

Enjō-ji

369

369

To Iga-Ueno (5km)

Nishinokyō
Tōshōdai-ji
Yakushi-ji

To Osaka (25km)

308

Yamato-Kōriyama

Kintetsu-Kōriyama
Kōriyama

Hōryū-ji

25

Kansai Line

Yamato-Koizumi

Horyu-ji

Hirahata

Kashihara Line

Tenri
Tenri

25

To Osaka (30km)

24

JR Sakurai Line

To Nabari (10km);
Iga-Ueno (35km)

Muroguchi-ōno
Murō

165

Miwa-yama

Hase-dera

Kintetsu Osaka Line

Murō-ji

Takada

166

To Osaka (30km)

Miwa
Ōmiwa-jinja

Miwa

165

Hasedera

Haibara

Yagi-nishiguchi
Yamato-Yagi
Sakurai

Imai-chō
Unebi-yama
Unebi
Kashihara

Sakurai

166

369

Kashihara-jingū
Nara Prefecture
Kashihara Archaelogical
Museum

Unebi-goryō-mae

Kashihara-jingū-mae

Asuka-dera

Asuka Historical
Museum

Ishibutai-kofun

Tanzan-jinja

Asuka
Asuka

Takamatsuzuka-kofun

370

166

24

169

Yoshino-guchi

KANSAI

309

Wakayama Line

Kintetsu Yoshino Line

Yamato-kami-ichi
Yoshino

Tsuburo-ko

Shimoichi-guchi

370

Yoshino

309

To Wakayama (60km)

Kimpusen-ji
Katte-jinja

Ropeway

Zenkō-in

Ōmine-san Trail

169

Kimpu-jinja

To Dorogawa

To Ōdai-ga-hara (50km);
Kumano (65km)

Emperor Temmu in 680. With the exception of the **East Pagoda**, the present buildings either date from the 13th century or are very recent reconstructions.

The main hall was rebuilt in 1976 and houses several images, including the famous **Yakushi Triad** (the Buddha Yakushi flanked by the Bodhisattvas of the sun and moon), dating from the 8th century. They were originally gold, but a fire in the 16th century turned the images an appealingly mellow black.

The East Pagoda is a unique structure because it appears to have six storeys, but three of them are *mokoshi* (lean-to additions), which give a pleasing balance to its appearance. It is the only structure to have survived the ravages of time, and dates from 730.

Behind the East Pagoda is **Tōin-dō** (East Hall), which houses the famous Shō-Kannon image, built in the 7th century and showing obvious influences of Indian sculptural styles.

GETTING THERE & AWAY

To get to Yakushi-ji, take bus No 52, 63, 70, 97 or 98 from either JR Nara Station or Kintetsu Nara Station and get off at the Yakushi-ji Higashiguchi stop (¥240, 20 minutes).

Tōshōdai-ji 唐招提寺

This **temple** (☎ 33-7900; 13-46 Gojō-chō; admission ¥600; ⌚ 8.30am-4.30pm) was established in 759 by the Chinese priest Ganjin (Jian Zhen), who had been recruited by Emperor Shōmu to reform Buddhism in Japan. Ganjin didn't have much luck with his travel arrangements from China to Japan: five attempts were thwarted by shipwreck, storms and bureaucracy. Despite being blinded by eye disease, he finally made it on the sixth attempt and spread his teachings to Japan. The lacquer sculpture in the Miei-dō Hall is a moving tribute to Ganjin: blind and rock steady. It is shown only once a year, on 6 June – the anniversary of Ganjin's death.

Unfortunately, the **Kon-do** (Golden Hall) of the temple, which is the main hall of the temple, is presently under reconstruction and won't reopen until 2009. Nonetheless, it's still worth visiting this temple to enjoy the peaceful grounds.

Tōshōdai-ji is a 10-minute walk north of Yakushi-ji's northern gate; see above for transport details from Nara.

AROUND YAMATO-YAGI 大和八木周辺

Easily reached on the Kintetsu line from Osaka, Kyoto or Nara, Yamato-Yagi is the most convenient transport hub for sights in southern Nara-ken. From Kyoto take the Kintetsu Nara/Kashihara line direct (*kyūkō*, ¥860, one hour). From Nara take the Kintetsu Nara line to Saidaiji and change to the Kintetsu Kashihara line (*kyūkō*, ¥430, 30 minutes). From Osaka's Uehonmachi Station, take the Kintetsu Osaka line direct (*kyūkō*, ¥540, 35 minutes).

Imai-chō 今井町

Southwest of Yamato-Yagi is Imai-chō, a neighbourhood with several classic *machiya* preserved virtually intact from the Edo period. It's a pleasant place to walk around and seven of the **buildings** (admission ¥170; ⌚ 10am-noon & 1-5pm) are open to the public. The most interesting of these is the huge **Imanishike Jyūtaku** (今西家; Imanishi House), which was completed in 1650. The **Imai Machinami Koryū Sentā** (今井まちなみ交流セン ター; ☎ 0744-24-8710; ⌚ 9am-5pm Tue-Sun), on the neighbourhood's southeast corner, has Japanese-language maps of the area.

To get to Imai-chō, take a train one stop south from Yamato-Yagi to Yagi-nishiguchi (¥150, one minute). The neighbourhood is a 10-minute walk southwest of the station; take the western exit out of the station, go right across the bridge over the canal and walk under the JR tracks.

Kashihara 橿原

Three stops south of Yamato-Yagi, on the Kintetsu Kashihara line, is Kashiharajingū-mae Station (¥200 from Yamato-Yagi, five minutes). There are a couple of interesting sights within easy walking distance of this station.

KASHIHARA-JINGŪ 橿原神宮

This **shrine** (☎ 0744-22-3271; 943 Kume-chō, Kashihara-shi; admission free), at the foot of Unebi-yama, dates back to 1889, when many of the buildings were moved here from Kyoto Gosho. The shrine buildings are built in the same style as those of Ise-jingū's Grand Shrine (Japan's most sacred shrine) and are a good example of classical Shintō architecture. The shrine is dedicated to Japan's mythical first emperor, Jimmu, and an annual festival is held here on 11 February, the legendary date of Jimmu's enthronement. The vast, park-like grounds are pleasant to stroll around. The shrine is five minutes' walk from Kashi-hara-jingū-mae Station; take the central exit out of the station and follow the main street in the direction of the mountain.

NARA PREFECTURE KASHIHARA ARCHAEOLOGICAL MUSEUM
奈良県橿原考古学研究所付属博物館

This **museum** (Nara Ken-ritsu Kashihara Kōkogaku Kenkyūjo Fuzoku Hakubutsukan; ☎ 0744-24-1101; 50-2 Unebi-chō; admission ¥400; ☽ 9am-5pm Tue-Sun) is highly recommended for those with an interest in the history of the Japanese people. The objects on display come from various archaeological sites in the area, including several *kofun*. Although most of the explanations are in Japanese, there's enough English to give you an idea of what's going on.

To get there from Kashihara-jingū, walk out the northern gate of the shrine (to your left when you stand with your back to the main hall), follow the wooded avenue for five minutes, cross the main road and continue on in the same direction for 100m before turning left. It's on the left soon after this turn.

ASUKA 飛鳥
☎ 0744 / pop 6,700

Five stops south of Yamato-Yagi (change at Kashihara-jingū-mae) and two stops south of Kashihara-jingū-mae on the Kintetsu Yoshino line is Asuka Station (¥220 from Yamato-Yagi, 20 minutes). There's a **tourist information office** (☎ 54-3624; ☽ 8.30am-5pm) at the station where you can get maps of the area's temples, palace remains, tombs and strange stones.

The best way to explore the area is by bicycle, and bicycles are available for rent at **Manyō Rent-a-Cycle** (☎ 54-3500) for ¥300 per hour or ¥900 per day. Manyō is across the street from the station – it's the second shop on your right.

Two tombs worth seeing are **Takamatsu-zuka-kofun** (高松塚古墳) and **Ishibutai-kofun** (石舞台古墳; admission ¥250; ☽ 8.30am-4.45pm). The former, which was excavated in 1972, is closed to the public but has a **museum** (飛鳥博物館; admission ¥250; ☽ 9am-4.30pm) displaying a copy of the frescoes inside the tomb. The Ishibutai-kofun is open to the public but has no frescoes. It is said to have

housed the remains of Soga no Umako but is now completely empty.

The best museum in the area is **Asuka Historical Museum** (飛鳥資料館; ☎ 54-3561; 617 Okuyama, Asukamura, Takaichi-gun; admission ¥260; ☽ 9am-4pm), which has exhibits from regional digs. It's across the street (take the underpass) from Takamatsuzuka-kofun.

If you have time left after visiting the earlier sights, take a look at **Asuka-dera** (飛鳥寺; ☎ 54-2126; 682 Okuyama, Asukamura, Takaichi-gun; admission ¥300; ☽ 9am-5.15pm), which dates from 596 and is considered the first true temple in all of Japan. Housed within is the oldest remaining image of Buddha in Japan – after more than 1300 years of venerable existence, you'll have to excuse its decidedly tatty appearance. You can just glimpse the Buddha image through the open doorway.

Lastly, if you'd like a bite to eat while in Asuka, try **Ashibi-no-sato** (あしびの郷; ☎ 0742-26-6662; 29 Wakido-chō, Nara-shi; ☽ 10am-6pm), which serves simple meals from ¥700. To get there, exit the station and follow the canal to the right for about 150m.

AROUND SAKURAI 桜井周辺

There are a few interesting places to visit close to the town of Sakurai that can be reached directly from Nara on the JR Sakurai line (*futsū*, ¥320, 30 minutes). To reach Sakurai via Yamato-Yagi (when coming from Kyoto or Osaka), take the Kintetsu Osaka line from Yamato-Yagi (*kyūkō*, ¥200, five minutes).

Tanzan-jinja 談山神社

This **shrine** (☎ 49-0001; 319 Tōnomine, Sakurai-shi; admission ¥500; ☽ 8.30am-4.30pm) lies south of Sakurai and can be reached by bus 14 from stand No 1 outside the southern exit of Sakurai Station (¥460, 25 minutes). It's tucked away in the forests of Tōnomine-san, famous for their autumn colours. Enshrined here is Nakatomi no Kamatari, patriarch of the Fujiwara line, which effectively ruled Japan for nearly 500 years. Legend has it that Nakatomi met here secretly with prince Naka no Ōe over games of kickball to discuss the overthrow of the ruling Soga clan. This event is commemorated on the second Sunday in November by priests playing a game of kickball – call it divine hackey sack.

The central structure of the shrine is an attractive 13-storey pagoda best viewed against

KANSAI

a backdrop of maple trees ablaze with autumn colours.

Hase-dera 長谷寺

Two stops east of Sakurai on the Kintetsu Osaka line is Hasedera Station. From the station, it's a 20-minute walk to lovely **Hase-dera** (☎ 47-7001; 731-1 Hase, Sakurai-shi; admission ¥500; ☽ 9am-4.30pm). After a long climb up seemingly endless steps, you enter the main hall and are rewarded with a splendid view from the gallery, which juts out on stilts over the mountainside. Inside the top hall, the huge Kannon image is well worth a look. The best times to visit this temple are in the spring, when the way is lined with blooming peonies, and in autumn, when the temple's maple trees turn a vivid red. From the station, walk down through the archway, cross the river and turn right onto the main street that leads to the temple.

Murō-ji 室生寺

This **temple** (☎ 0745-93-2003; Murō-mura, Murō, Uda-gun; admission ¥500; ☽ 8am-5pm) was founded in the 9th century and has strong connections with Esoteric Buddhism (the Shingon sect). Women were never excluded from Murō-ji as they were from other Shingon temples, and it is for this reason that it came to be known as 'the Woman's Koya'. Unfortunately the temple's lovely five-storey pagoda, which dates from the 8th or 9th century, was severely damaged in a typhoon in the summer of 1999. The newly rebuilt pagoda lacks some of the rustic charm of the old one. Nonetheless Murō-ji is a secluded place in thick forest and is well worth a visit.

Murōguchi-Ōno Station on the Kintetsu Osaka line is two stops east of Hasedera Station. It's a 15-minute bus ride from Murōguchi-Ōno Station to Murō-ji on bus 43, 44, 45 or 46 (¥400).

YOSHINO 吉野
☎ 07463 / pop 11,216

Yoshino is Japan's top cherry-blossom destination, and for a few weeks in early to mid-April, the blossoms of thousands of cherry trees form a floral carpet gradually ascending the mountainsides. It's definitely a sight worth seeing, but the narrow streets of the village become jammed tight with thousands of visitors at this time, and you'll have to be content with a day trip unless you've booked

accommodation long in advance. Once the *sakura* (cherry-blossom) petals fall, the crowds depart and Yoshino reverts back to a sleepy village with a handful of shrines and a couple of temples to entertain day-trippers.

Information

The village's main **tourist information office** is about 400m up the main street from the top cable-car station, on your right just after Kimpusen-ji. The staff don't speak much English but are quite helpful and have a specially prepared English-Japanese phrase-book to help foreign travellers. They can help with *minshuku* bookings if necessary.

Sights

As you walk up the main street, you pass through two *torii* before coming to the stone steps leading to the Ni-ō-mon of **Kimpusen-ji** (金峯山寺; ☎ 2-8371; Yoshinoyama, Yoshino-chō; admission ¥400; ☽ 8am-4.30pm). Check out the fearsome **Kongō Rikishi** (guardian figure statues) in the gate and then continue on to the massive **Zaō-dō Hall** of the temple. Said to be the second-largest wooden building in Japan, the hall is most interesting for its unfinished wooden columns. For many centuries Kimpusen-ji has been one of the major centres for Shugendō, and pilgrims have often stopped here to pray for good fortune on the journey to Ōmine-san.

About 500m further up the street, where the road forks, is **Katte-jinja** (勝手神社). Take the left fork and then the next right up the hill. You soon pass **Kizō-in** on your left and **Chikurin-in** on your right (see below). A few minutes' walk further on there is another fork, where you'll find some steps leading up to a wooden *torii*. Take the left fork and the next right up the hill for the 3km hike to **Kimpu-jinja**, a small shrine in a pleasantly wooded mountain setting. If you don't fancy this somewhat strenuous uphill hike, there are plenty of smaller shrines on the streets and alleys off Yoshino's main street.

Sleeping & Eating

Chikurin-in Gumpo en (竹林院群芳園; ☎ 2-8081; www.chikurin.co.jp/e/home.htm; Yoshinoyama, Yoshino-chō; r per person from ¥13,650) Not far past Kizō-in, on the opposite side of the street, this is an exquisite temple that now operates primarily as a ryokan. Both present and previous emperors have stayed here, and a look at the view afforded by some of the rooms explains why. Rates include two meals. Reservations are essential for the cherry-blossom season, and a good idea at all other times. Even if you don't plan to stay at the temple, you should at least visit its splendid **garden** (admission ¥300), said to have been designed by the famous tea master Sen no Rikyū.

Yoshino-yama Kizō-in (吉野山喜蔵院; ☎ 2-3014; Yoshinoyama, Yoshino-chō; dm per person with 2 meals ¥6000) This is a temple that doubles as the local youth hostel and is the cheapest option in town. It's a pleasant place to stay, and several of the hostel's rooms look out across the valley. See the earlier Sights section for directions to the temple.

The speciality of Yoshino is *kaki-no-ha* sushi (persimmon leaf sushi). Almost every store and restaurant in town sells it and you can buy two pieces to take away for ¥250. For proper meals try **Yakko Zushi** (やっこずし), opposite the tourist information office. It has the usual *shokudō* favourites. **Hatsune** (初音) restaurant, closer to the top cable-car station, is in an atmospheric old wooden building, and serves tempura *donburi* for ¥1300.

Finally, if you'd just like a cup of Japanese tea to pick you up, try the atmospheric **Hōkon-an** (芳魂庵; ☎ 2-8207; 550 Yoshinoyama; ⊙ 9am-5pm, closed irregularly) teahouse, where you can sip your tea while enjoying a lovely view over the valley. The *matcha* (powdered green tea; ¥600) comes with a Japanese sweet. Look for the rustic wooden façade on the left, just past the post office as you walk away from the cable car.

Getting There & Away

The village of Yoshino is on a shoulder of Yoshino-yama, at the bottom of which is Yoshino Station. From Yoshino Station, you can take the cable car to the village (¥350/600 one way/return) or walk up in 15 minutes on the path that leaves from beside the cable-car station. Note that the cable car stops running at 5pm – plan your day accordingly or you'll have to walk down to the station (30 minutes).

To get to Yoshino Station from Kyoto or Nara, take the Kintetsu Nara/Kashihara line (it changes name halfway) to Kashihara-jingū-mae (*kyūkō* from Kyoto, ¥860, 70 minutes; *kyūkō* from Nara, ¥480, 40 minutes) and change to the Kintetsu Yoshino line (*kyūkō*, ¥460, 52 minutes).

You can take a direct train on the Kintetsu Minami-Osaka/Yoshino lines from Osaka (Abenobashi Station, close to Tennō-ji Station) to Yoshino (*kyūkō*, ¥950, 1½ hours).

The closest JR Station to Yoshino is Yoshino-guchi, where you can transfer to trains to/from Nara, Osaka and Wakayama.

KII-HANTŌ 紀伊半島

The remote and mountainous Kii-hantō (Kii Peninsula) is a far cry from central Kansai's bustling urban sprawl. Most of the peninsula's attractions are found in Wakayama-ken, including the mountaintop temple complex of Kōya-san, one of Japan's most important Buddhist centres. Other Wakayama-ken attractions include the *onsen* clustered around the village of Hongū, the beachside hot spring resort of Shirahama, and the rugged coastline of Shiono-misaki and Kii-Ōshima.

The JR Kii main line (Kinokuni line) runs around the coast of the Kii-hantō, linking Shin-Osaka and Nagoya Stations (some trains originate/terminate at Kyoto Station). Special Kuroshio and Nankii *tokkyū* trains can get you around the peninsula fairly quickly, but once you step off these express trains, you're at the mercy of slow local trains and buses, so plan accordingly. We present the information in this section anticlockwise, working from Wakayama-shi around the horn to Mie-ken, but it's perfectly possible to do this the other way round (perhaps starting in Ise).

JNTO publishes a leaflet *Shirahama & Wakayama Prefecture*, providing concise details about sights and transport in the area.

WAKAYAMA 和歌山

☎ 073 / pop 387,000

Wakayama, the prefectural capital, is a pleasant little city useful as a transport hub for travellers heading to other parts of the prefecture. The city's main attraction is **Wakayama-jō** (和歌山城; ☎ 435-1044; 3 Ichiban-chō; admission to grounds free, castle keep ¥350; ⊙ 9am-4.30pm), a 20-minute walk (about 2km) from JR Wakayama Station. The original castle was built in 1585 by Toyotomi Hideyoshi and destroyed by bombing in WWII. The present structure is a concrete post-war reconstruction; it's picturesque from afar and unprepossessing up close. However, the gardens surrounding the castle are well worth a stroll if you're in the area.

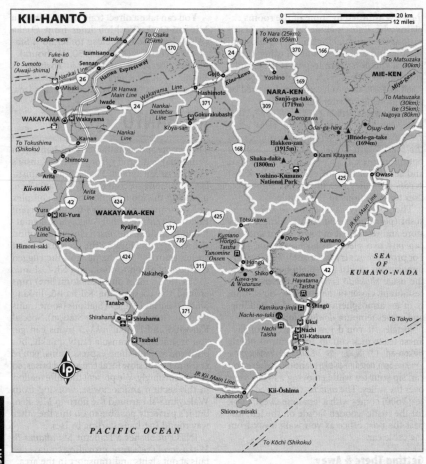

KII-HANTŌ

KANSAI

There is a useful **tourist information counter** (☎ 422-5831; 🕗 8.30am-5.15pm) inside JR Wakayama Station, which stocks copies of the excellent *Wakayama City Guide* map.

Sleeping & Eating

The most relaxing place to stay in Wakayama is the Shinwaka Ura area, a pleasant collection of *minshuku* and ryokan on a point southwest of the city.

Hotel Granvia Wakayama (ホテルグランヴィア和歌山; ☎ 425-3333; hotel@granvia-wakayama .co.jp; 5-18 Tomoda-chō; s/d/tw ¥8800/15,500/17,000) This place is right outside the station and offers new, clean rooms.

Kokumin-shukusha Shinwaka Lodge (国民宿舎 新和歌ロッジ; ☎ 444-9000; 2-3 Shinwakaura;

r per person with/without 2 meals ¥6500/4500) This is the most reasonable place in the area. Take bus 24 from the No 2 stop in front of JR Wakayama Station to the last stop, Shinwaka Ura (¥380, 40 minutes). Continue on in the same direction along the main road, go through the tunnel and look for it on your left.

For a bite to eat, head to the restaurant arcade on the basement floor beneath JR Wakayama Station. Among the choices here, you'll find **Mendori-tei** (めんどり亭; ☎ 422-3355; 478 Yoshida; 🕗 8am-11pm), which serves excellent *kushi-age* (deep-fried seafood on skewers) and *kushi-katsu* dishes (try their *kushi-age teishoku* for ¥800). Look for the brown curtains and the all-counter seating. Otherwise, a short walk from JR Wakayama Station, you'll find **Ide Shouten** (井出商店; ☎ 436-2941; 4-84 Tanakamachi; ☽ noon-midnight Fri-Wed), where you can sample the local speciality, *shoyū rāmen* (soy sauce *rāmen*) for ¥500. But call it *chuka soba* (Chinese noodles) or you'll get funny looks from the staff! To get there from the station, walk straight out of the station and turn left on the main street – it's six short blocks south on the right, just past a parking lot.

Getting There & Away

Wakayama is serviced by JR *tokkyū* trains from Shin-Osaka and Kyoto, but unless you've got a Japan Rail Pass it's cheaper to take a local train on the JR Hanwa line from Osaka's Tennō-ji Station (*futsū*, ¥830, one hour). From Osaka's Namba Station you can also take the private Nankai line to Wakayama-shi Station (*kyūkō*, ¥1400, one hour), which is linked to JR Wakayama Station by the JR Kisei main line (*futsū*, ¥180, six minutes).

Wakayama is a convenient starting point for the trip to Kōya-san (see p381 for transport details).

From Wakayama-kō port, there's a ferry service to Tokushima on **Shikoku** (☎ 431-4431); a 2nd-class ticket is ¥1730. From Fuke-kō port, just north of Wakayama, **Awaji-shima** (☎ 0724-69-3821) ferries go to Sumoto; the trip takes 30 minutes and a 2nd-class ticket is ¥1980. Ask at the tourist office in JR Wakayama Station for details on getting to the respective piers.

KŌYA-SAN 高野山
☎ 0736 / pop 7000

Kōya-san is a raised tableland in northern Wakayama-ken covered with thick forests and surrounded by eight peaks. The major attraction on this tableland is the monastic complex, also known as Kōya-san, which is the headquarters of the Shingon school of Esoteric Buddhism. Though not quite the Shangri-la it's occasionally described to be, it is one of the most rewarding places to visit in Kansai, not just for the natural setting of the area but also as an opportunity to stay in temples and get a glimpse of long-held traditions of Japanese religious life.

More than a million visitors come here annually so you should be prepared for congestion during peak holiday periods and

festivals. Summer is a popular time to visit and escape from the lowland heat. You can miss large crowds by getting up really early for a stroll around the area before returning to take part in the morning religious service usually held around 6am. Late-night strolls are peaceful and quiet, and spring and autumn foliage are especially attractive. Some hardy visitors even enjoy wandering round Kōya-san in the snow.

Although you could visit Kōya-san as a day trip from Nara, Kyoto or Osaka, it's much better to reduce the travel stress and stay overnight in one of the town's excellent *shukubō* (temple lodgings). Be sure to bring some warm clothes when you go, as up on the mountain it tends to be around 5°C colder than down on the plains.

Whenever you go, you'll find that getting there is half the fun – the train winds through a series of tight valleys with mountains soaring on all sides, and the final vertiginous cable car leg is not for the faint of heart.

History

The founder of the Shingon school of Esoteric Buddhism, Kūkai (known after his death as Kōbō Daishi), established a religious community here in 816. Kōbō Daishi travelled as a young priest to China and returned after two years to found the school. He is one of Japan's most famous religious figures and is revered as a Bodhisattva, scholar, inventor of the Japanese kana syllabary and as a calligrapher. He is believed to be simply resting in his tomb, not dead but meditating, awaiting the arrival of Miroku (Maitreya, the future Buddha).

Over the centuries, the temple complex grew in size and attracted many followers of the Jōdo (Pure Land) school of Buddhism. During the 11th century, it became popular with both nobles and commoners to leave hair or ashes from deceased relatives close to Kōbō Daishi's tomb, handy for his re-awakening. This practice continues to be very popular today and accounts for the thousands of tombs around Okuno-in.

In the 16th century, Oda Nobunaga asserted his power by slaughtering large numbers of monks at Kōya-san. The community subsequently suffered confiscation of lands and narrowly escaped invasion by Toyotomi Hideyoshi. At one stage, Kōya-san numbered about 1500 monasteries and

KANSAI

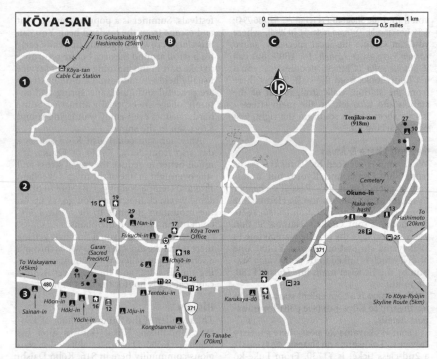

KŌYA-SAN

many thousands of monks. The members of the community were divided into *gakuryō* (clergy), *gyōnin* (lay priests) and *hijiri* (followers of Pure Land Buddhism).

In the 17th century, the Tokugawa shōgunate smashed the economic power of the lay priests, who managed considerable estates in the region. Their temples were destroyed, their leaders banished and the followers of Pure Land Buddhism were bluntly pressed into the Shingon school. During the Edo period, the government favoured the practice of Shintō and confiscated the lands that

supported Kōya-san's monastic community. Women were barred from entry to Kōya-san until 1872.

Kōya-san is now a thriving centre for Japanese Buddhism, with more than 110 temples remaining and a population of 7000. It is the headquarters of the Shingon school, which numbers 10 million members and presides over nearly 4000 temples all over Japan.

Orientation & Information

There's a small information office at the top cable-car station. However, the main office of the **Kōya-san Tourist Association** (☎ 56-2616; fax 56-2889; ☯ 8.30am-5.30pm Jul & Aug, 8.30am-4.30pm Sep-Jun) is in the centre of town in front of the Senjūin-bashi-mae bus stop. Staff speak some English, and brochures and maps are available. For a better map of the area, pick up a copy of the Japanese map from the bus office outside the top cable-car station.

The precincts of Kōya-san are divided into the Garan (Sacred Precinct) in the west and Okuno-in, with its vast cemetery, in the east.

Note that there is a joint ticket (shodō-kyōtsu-naihaiken; ¥1500) that covers entry to Kongōbu-ji, the Kondō, Dai-tō, Treasure Museum and the **Tokugawa Mausoleum** (Tokugawa-ke Reidai; admission without joint ticket ¥200). It can be purchased at the information office.

The Wakayama Interpreter Volunteer Club offers free guided **tours** (per person ¥500; ☯ 9am & 1.30pm Wed, Apr-Nov) of Kōya-san. For meetings points and details, ask at the main Kōya Tourist Association office (see above).

Sights

OKUNO-IN 奥の院

Any Buddhist worth their salt in Japan has had their remains, or just a lock or two of hair, interred in this **cemetery/temple** (☎ 56-2214; Kōyasan, Kōya-chō) to ensure pole position when the future Buddha and Kūkai return to the world.

The best way to approach Okuno-in is to walk or take the bus east to Ichi-no-hashi-mae bus stop. From here you cross the bridge, **Ichi-no-hashi**, and enter the cemetery grounds along a winding, cobbled path lined with tall cypress trees and thousands of tombs. As the trees close in and the mist swirls, the atmosphere can be quite ghostly, especially as night falls. Among the interesting graves and monuments to look out for are the **North Borneo War Victim Memorial**, which commemorates Japanese, Malay and Australian soldiers killed in North Borneo in WWII (look for the flags), and the **White Ant Memorial**, built by a pesticide company to expiate its guilt for the murder of legions of the little critters.

The **Tōrō-dō** (Lantern Hall), the main building of the complex, is at the northernmost end of the graveyard. It houses hundreds of lamps, including two believed to have been burning for more than 900 years.

Behind the hall you can see the closed doors of the Gobyō, Kūkai mausoleum.

On the way to the Lantern Hall is the bridge **Mimyo-no-hashi**. Worshippers ladle water from the river and pour it over the nearby Jizō statues as an offering for the dead. The inscribed wooden plaques in the river are in memory of aborted babies and those who died by drowning.

Between the bridge and the Tōrō-dō is a small wooden building the size of a large phone booth which contains the **Miroku-ishi**. Pilgrims reach through the holes in the wall to try to lift a large, smooth boulder onto a shelf. The interesting thing is that the stone is supposed to weigh more or less according to the weight of sin of the pilgrim. We can only report that the thing is damn heavy!

Buses return to the centre of town from the terminus just across from the concrete shopping complex.

KONGŌBU-JI 金剛峯寺

This is the headquarters of the Shingon school and the residence of Kōya-san's abbot. The present **structure** (Kōyasan, Kōya-chō; admission ¥500; ☯ 8.30am-4pm) dates from the 19th century and is definitely worth a visit.

The main hall's Ohiro-ma room has ornate screens painted by Kanō Tanyu in the 16th century. The Yanagi-no-ma (Willow Room) has equally pretty screen paintings of willows but the rather grisly distinction of being the place where Toyotomi Hidetsugu committed seppuku.

The rock garden is interesting for the sheer number of rocks used in its composition, giving the effect of a throng of petrified worshippers eagerly listening to a monk's sermon. Admission includes tea and rice cakes served beside the stone garden.

GARAN 伽藍

This is a **temple complex** (☎ 56-3215; Kōyasan, Kōya-chō; admission to each bldg ¥200; ☯ 8.30am-4.30pm) of several halls and pagodas. The most important buildings are the **Dai-tō** (Great Pagoda) and **Kondō** (Main Hall). The Dai-tō, rebuilt in 1934 after a fire, is said to be the centre of the lotus flower mandala formed by the eight mountains around Kōya-san. The nearby **Sai-tō** (Western Pagoda) was most recently rebuilt in 1834 and is more subdued. It's well worth going into the Dai-tō to see the

KANSAI

Dainichi-nyōrai (Cosmic Buddha) and his four attendant Buddhas.

TREASURE MUSEUM 霊宝館
The **Treasure Museum** (Reihōkan; Kōyasan, Kōya-chō; admission ¥600; 🕑 8.30am-4.30pm) has a compact display of Buddhist works of art, all collected in Kōya-san. There are some very fine statues, painted scrolls and mandalas.

Festivals & Events
Aoba Matsuri (15 June) Held to celebrate the birth of Kōbō Daishi. Various traditional ceremonies are performed at the temples around town.

Rōsoku Matsuri (Candle Festival, 13 August) This more interesting festival is held in remembrance of dead relatives. Thousands of mourners light candles along the approaches to Okuno-in.

Sleeping
There are more than 50 temples in Kōya-san offering *shukubō*. It's worth staying the night at a temple here, especially to try *shōjin-ryōri* (vegetarian food – no meat, fish, onions or garlic). Because *shukubō* is intended for religious pilgrims, in the morning you'll be asked to participate in *o-inori* (Buddhist prayer services) or *o-tsutome* (work). While participation is not mandatory, taking part in these practices would enable you to appreciate the daily workings of a Japanese temple.

Kōya-san's temples have recently formed a group to fix prices and now most lodgings start at ¥9500 per person including two meals. **Haryō-in** (🕾 56-2702; 702 Kōyasan, Kōya-chō; r per person ¥6500) is an exception and functions as a *kokumin-shukusha* and has rates that include two meals.

During the high season and holidays you should make advance reservations by fax through the Kōya-san Tourist Association or directly with the temples. If you arrive in Kōya-san after hours or you want to do things yourself, the following *shukubō* have English-speaking staff and are at the lower to middle end of the price spectrum.

Eikō-in (🕾 56-2514; ekoin@mbox.co.jp; 497 Kōyasan, Kōya-chō; r per person with 2 meals ¥10,000) One of the nicer temples in town, it's run by a friendly bunch of young monks and the rooms look onto beautiful gardens. Rates here are an exception to the ¥9000 set price at most other temples. This is also one of the two temples in town (the other is Kongōbu-ji) where you

can study *zazen* (sitting Zen meditation). Call ahead to make arrangements.

Henjōson-in (🕾 56-2434; 303 Kōyasan, Kōya-chō; r per person with 2 meals ¥10,000) This is another good choice. Here you get a pleasant room with a garden view, tatami furnishings, an excellent vegetarian dinner served in your room and the use of terrific wooden bathtubs. There's even a temple bar!

Kōya-san Youth Hostel (🕾 56-3889; 628 Kōyasan, Kōya-chō; dm per person ¥3360) Friendly and comfortable budget choice if the prices at the temples are out of your range. It's closed for parts of December and January. Call ahead for reservations.

Other good choices:
Muryōkō-in (🕾 56-2104; 611 Kōyasan, Kōya-chō; r per person with 2 meals ¥9,500) A down-to-earth place to stay.
Rengejō-in (🕾 56-2233; 700 Kōyasan, Kōya-chō; r per person with 2 meals ¥6,700) An elegant establishment.
Shojōshin-in (🕾 56-2006; Kōyasan, Kōya-chō; r per person with 2 meals ¥9,500) Friendly spot.

Eating
The culinary speciality of Kōya-san is *shōjin ryōri*, which you can sample at your temple lodgings. Two tasty tofu specialities are *goma-tōfu* (sesame tofu) and *kōya-tōfu* (local tofu). If you're just in town for the day, you can try *shōjin ryōri* at any of the temples that offer *shukubō*. Ask at the Kōya-san Tourist Association office and staff will call ahead to make reservations. Prices are fixed at ¥2500, ¥3500 and ¥5000, depending on how many courses you have.

There are various coffee shops dotted around town where you can have breakfast. Maruman is worth a try at lunch. All the standard lunch items are represented by plastic food models in the window. *Katsu-don* (pork cutlet over rice) is ¥810 and noodle dishes start at ¥520. It's just west of the tourist office on the main street – look for the food models in the window and the phone out front (there's no English sign).

Hanabishi Honten (🕾 56-2236; 769 Kōyasan; lunch ¥2000-6000, dinner ¥2000-16,000; 🕑 11am-7pm, reservation required after 7pm) For something nicer, you can get well-prepared sets of standard Japanese dishes here for around ¥2000. Look for the gray façade and the food models in the window (which will also help ordering, if necessary).

Getting There & Away

All rail connections to and from Kōya-san run via Gokurakubashi, which is at the base of the mountain. A cable car runs frequently from the base to the top of the mountain (five minutes, price included in most train tickets). From the cable-car station, you must take a bus into the centre of town, as walking is prohibited on the connecting road.

From Osaka (Namba Station) you can travel directly on the Nankai– Dentetsu line (by *kyūkō*) to Gokurakubashi Station (¥1230 including cable-car ticket, 1½ hours). For the slightly faster *tokkyū* service with reserved seats you pay a supplement (¥760).

From Wakayama you can go by rail on the JR Wakayama line to Hashimoto (¥820, one hour) and then continue on the Nankai-Dentetsu line to Gokurakubashi Station (¥810 including cable-car ticket, 45 minutes).

From Kyoto it's probably best to go via Namba in Osaka. From Nara, you can take the JR line to Hashimoto, changing at Sakurai and Takadate en route.

Getting Around

Buses run on three routes from the top cable-car station via the centre of town to Ichi-no-hashi and Okuno-in. The fare to the tourist office in the centre of town at Senjūin-bashi is ¥280. The fare to the final stop, Okuno-in, is ¥400. An all-day bus pass (*ichi-nichi furee kippu*; ¥800) is available from the bus office outside the top cable-car station, but once you get into the centre of town you can reach most destinations quite easily on foot (including Okuno-in, which takes about 30 minutes). Note that buses run infrequently, so you should make a note of the schedule before setting out to see the sights.

If you don't feel like walking, bicycles can be rented for ¥400 an hour or ¥1200 for the day at the Kōya-san Tourist Association Office (p379).

SHIRAHAMA 白浜

☎ 0739 / pop 20,000

Shirahama, on the southwest coast of the Kii-hantō, is Kansai's leading beach/*onsen* resort and has all the trappings of a major Japanese tourist attraction – huge resort hotels, aquariums, amusement parks, the lot. However, because the Japanese like to do things according to the rules – and the rules

say the only time you can swim in the ocean is from late July to the end of August – the place is almost deserted outside the season and you'll have the place to yourself.

There are several good *onsen* in town; there is a great white-sand beach, and the rugged sea coast south of the town is stunning. This is a great place to visit in, say, June or September, and we've swum in the sea here as late as mid-October (just keep in mind that jellyfish can be found in the ocean here in late July and August).

There's a **tourist information office** (☎ 42-2240; ⊙ 9.15am-5pm) in the station, where you can pick up a map to the main sights and accommodation. Since the station is a fair distance from the main sights, you'll need to take a bus (¥330, 20 minutes to the beach, ¥980 for an all-day pass) or rent a bicycle if you arrive by rail. The JR office at the station rents bicycles (¥500 per day).

Sights & Activities
ONSEN

In addition to its great beach, Shirahama has some of Japan's oldest developed *onsen* (they're even mentioned in the Nihon Shoki, one of Japan's earliest literary texts).

The **Sakino-yu Onsen** (崎の湯温泉; ☎ 42-3016; 1688 Shirahama-cho, Nishimuro-gun; admission ¥300 ⊙ 8am-6.30pm Thu-Tue Jun-Aug, 8am-5pm Thu-Tue Sep-May) is sensational. It's built on a rocky point with great views of the Pacific Ocean (and you can climb down the rocks to cool off if the waves aren't too big). Come early in the day to beat the crowds. It's 1km south of the main beach; walk along the seafront road and look for the point below the big Hotel Seymor. The baths are segregated by sex.

Other baths include **Shirara-yu** (白良湯; ☎ 43-2614; 3313-1 Shirahama-cho, Nishimuro-gun; admission ¥300; ⊙ 7am-10.30pm Wed-Mon, noon-10.30pm Tue), a pleasant bath right on the north end of Shirara-hama (the main beach), and **Murono-yu** (牟婁の湯; ☎ 42-0686; 1665 Shirahama-cho, Nishimuro-gun; admission ¥300; ⊙ 7am-10.30pm Fri-Wed, noon-10.30pm Thu), a simple *onsen* not far from Sakino-yu, in front of Shirahama post office.

SENJŌ-JIKI, SANDAN-HEKI & ISOGI-KŌEN
千畳敷・三段壁・いそぎ公園

Just around the point south of the Sakino-yu Onsen are two of Shirahama's natural

KANSAI

wonders: **Senjō-jiki** and Sandan-heki. Senjō-jiki (Thousand Tatami Mat Point) is a wildly eroded point with stratified layers that actually resemble the thousand tatami mats it is named for.

More impressive is the 50m cliff face of **Sandan-heki** (Three-Step Cliff), which drops away vertiginously into the sea (there are signs in Japanese warning off suicidal jumpers). While you can pay ¥1200 to take a lift down to a cave at the base of the cliff, it's better simply to clamber along the rocks to the north of the cliff – it's stunning, particularly when the big rollers are pounding in from the Pacific.

If you'd like to enjoy more rugged coastal scenery, walk south along the coast another 1km from Sandan-heki to Isogi-kōen, where the crowds are likely to be thinner and the scenery just as impressive.

These attractions can be reached on foot or bicycle from the main beach in around 30 minutes, or you can take a bus from the station (¥430, 25 minutes to Senjō-jiki, from which you can walk to the others).

SHIRARA-HAMA BEACH 白良浜

Shirara-hama, the town's main beach, is famous for its white sand. If it reminds you of Australia don't be surprised – the town had to import sand from down under after the original stuff washed away. This place is packed during July and August. In the off-peak season, it can actually be quite pleasant. The beach is hard to miss, as it dominates the western side of town. **Shirasuna-yu** (しらすな湯; ☎ 43-1126; 864 Shirahama-cho, Nishimuro-gun; ☯ 10am-7pm Tue-Sun) is a free open-air *onsen* off the boardwalk in the middle of the beach. You can soak here and then dash into the ocean to cool off – not a bad way to spend an afternoon.

The only drawback to this excellent beach is the loud music which is broadcast from loudspeakers during the summer months. The music is uniquely horrible and the only thing you can do to save yourself is to set up shop as far from the speakers as possible.

Sleeping & Eating

In Shirahama itself, there are several *min-shuku* and *kokumin-shukusha*.

Minshuku Katsuya (民宿かつ屋; ☎ 42-3814; 3118-5 Shirahama-cho, Nishimuro-gun; r per person with 2 meals ¥7000-8500, without meals ¥4000-4500) Katsuya

is the best-value *minshuku* in town and it's very central, only two minutes' walk from the main beach. It's built around a small Japanese garden and has its own natural hot-spring bath.

Kokumin-shukusha Hotel Shirahama (国民宿舍ホテル白浜; ☎ 42-3039; 5933 Shirahama-cho, Shirahama; r per person with 2 meals ¥6870) This is a good bet if Katsuya is full, and offers similar rates. The tourist information office at the station has maps to both places.

Ohgigahama Youth Hostel (扇ケ浜ユースホステル; ☎ 22-3433; http://ohgigahama.web.infoseek.co.jp/; 35-1 Shinyashiki-cho; dm ¥2625, no meals available) This is a friendly, comfortable and cheap option if you don't mind staying outside the town of Shirahama. The hostel is 10 minutes on foot from Kii-Tanabe Station, which is three stops north of Shirahama Station on the JR Kisei line.

There are many restaurants in the streets around these accommodations. **Kiraku** (喜楽; ☎ 42-3916; 890-48 Shirahama-cho, Nishimuro-gun; ☯ 11am-2pm & 4-9pm Wed-Mon) serves standard *teishoku* for around ¥800. **Ginchiro** (銀ちろ; ☎ 42-2514; Ginza-dōri, Shirahama-cho, Nishimuro-gun; set meals from ¥900; ☯ 11am-2pm & 4-9pm Thu-Tue) is more upmarket, serving tempura and *unagi* set meals (there's a picture menu). The tourist information office at the station can provide a map to both places. Alternatively, ask directions at your accommodations.

If you're on a tight budget, you can save money by self-catering; there are plenty of convenience stores in town and **Sakae Supermarket** is five minutes' walk from the main beach.

Getting There & Away

Shirahama is on the JR Kii main line. There is a *tokkyū* train from Shin-Osaka Station (¥5250, 2¼ hours). The same line also connects Shirahama to other cities on Kii-hantō such as Kushimoto, Nachi, Shingū and Wakayama City. A cheaper alternative is offered by **Meikō Bus** (☎ 0739-42-2112), which runs buses between JR Osaka Station and Shirahama (¥2700/5000 one-way/return, about three hours).

KUSHIMOTO, CAPE SHIONO-MISAKI & KII-ŌSHIMA 串本・潮岬・紀伊大島
☎ 0735

The southern tip of Kii-hantō has some stunning coastal scenery. Shiono-misaki, connected to the mainland by a narrow isthmus, has some fine rocky vistas, but the real action is over on Kii-Ōshima, a rocky island accessible by a newly completed bridge.

The main attraction on Kii-Ōshima is the coastal cliffs at the eastern end of the island, which can be viewed from the park around **Kashino-zaki Lighthouse** (樫野崎灯台). Just before the park, you'll find the **Toruko-Kinenkan Museum** (トルコ記念館; ☎ 65-0628; 1025-26 Kashino, Kushimoto-chō, Nishimuro-gun; admission ¥250; ☯ 9am-5pm), which commemorates the sinking of the Turkish ship Ertugrul in 1890. Backtracking about 1km towards the bridge, there are small English signs to the **Japan-US Memorial Museum** (日米修交記念館; ☎ 65-0099; 1033 Kashino, Kushimoto-chō, Nishimuro-gun; admission ¥250; ☯ 9am-5pm Tue-Sun), which commemorates the visit of the United States' ship *Lady Washington* in 1791, a full 62 years before Commodore Perry's much more famous landing in Yokohama in 1853. There is a lookout just beyond the museum from which you can see the magnificent **Umi-kongō** (海金剛) formations along the eastern point of the island.

If you're without your own transport, the best way to explore Kii-Ōshima is by renting a cycle at Kushimoto Station (¥600/1000 per four hours/day, discount for JR ticket holders), but be warned that there are a few big hills en route and these bikes are not performance vehicles. Otherwise, there are buses from the station, but take note of schedules as departures are few and far between.

Kushimoto itself is renowned for the Hashi-kui-iwa, a line of pillar-like rocks that have been imaginatively compared to a line of hooded monks heading towards Kii-Ōshima. To see the rocks, take a Shingū-bound bus from Kushimoto Station, and get off five minutes later at the Hashi-kui-iwa stop (¥130).

Misaki Lodge Youth Hostel (みさきロッジユースホステル; ☎ 62-1474; 2864-1 Shionomisaki, Kushimoto-chō; dm from ¥2650, lunch/dinner ¥600/1000) is the best place to stay in the area. It's in a good position, on the southern side of the cape overlooking the Pacific. It's also a *minshuku*, offering large rooms and including two meals in the rates (¥3615 per person). Take a Shiono-misaki–bound bus from Kushimoto Station (20 minutes) and get off at the last stop, Sugu-mae.

Kushimoto is one hour from Shirahama by JR *tokkyū*, and three hours (¥6080) from

Shin-Osaka. *Futsū* services are significantly cheaper but take almost twice as long.

NACHI & KII-KATSUURA
那智・紀伊勝浦

The Nachi and Kii-Katsuura area has several sights grouped around the sacred **Nachi-no-taki** (那智の滝), Japan's highest waterfall (133m). **Nachi Taisha** (那智大社), near the waterfall, was built in homage to the waterfall's *kami* (Shintō spirit god). Although it is one of the three great shrines of Kii-hantō, it is gaudy and a long climb from the waterfall car park. If you do decide to visit this shrine, you can take a trail from there to two hidden waterfalls above the main falls: these are seldom visited by tourists and are worth seeing. You can also pay ¥200 at the base of the falls to hike up to a lookout that affords a better view of the falls.

The **Nachi-no-Hi Matsuri** (Fire Festival) takes place at the falls on 14 July. During this lively event *mikoshi* are brought down from the mountain and met by groups bearing flaming torches.

Buses to the waterfall go from Nachi Station (¥470, 20 minutes) and from Kii-Katsuura Station (¥600, 30 minutes).

Getting There & Away

Kii-Katsuura can be reached by JR Kii main line trains from Shin-Osaka Station (*tokkyū*, ¥6500, four hours) and from Nagoya Station (*tokkyū*, ¥7310, 3½ hours). *Futsū* are significantly cheaper but take almost twice as long.

SHINGŪ 新宮
☎ 0735 / pop 33,000

This town is nothing exceptional to look at but functions as a useful transport hub for access to the three major Shintō shrines of the area, known as the **Kumano Sanzan** (Kumano Hayatama Taisha, Kumano Hongū Taisha and Nachi Taisha). There's a helpful **information office** (☎ 22-2840) at the station.

Sights & Activities

If you're killing time between trains or buses, you could visit the colourful **Kumano Hayatama Taisha**, a 15-minute walk northwest of Shingū Station. The shrine's **Boat Race Festival** takes place on 16 October. Another shrine worth looking at is **Kamikura-jinja**, which is famous for its **Otō Matsuri** (6 February), during which

KANSAI

more than 1000 people carrying torches ascend the slope to the shrine. The shrine is a 15-minute walk west of the station.

Sleeping & Eating

Hase Ryokan (長谷旅館; ☎ 22-2185; 2-1-7 Isada-chō; r per person with 2 meals ¥7000-8000) A two-minute walk north of the station, this ryokan is comfortable and reasonable choice for those who prefer Japanese-style accommodation. Call from the station and someone will collect you or ask at the information office for a map.

Station Hotel Shingū (ステーションホテル 新宮; ☎ 21-2200; station@rifnet.or.jp; 7031-1 Ekimae, Shingū-shi; s/d ¥4900/5900) If you'd prefer a hotel, this one is a short walk south of the station and has reasonable rooms.

There are several places to eat in the area around the station. If you're up for something a little more special, get the folks at the information office to draw you a map to **Ajino-sankin** (味のさんきん; ☎ 22-2373; 2-3-17 Midorigaoka, Shingū-shi; ❍ lunch/dinner 11am-9.30pm), which offers excellent sets of locally caught sashimi for around ¥1500. It's about a 20-minute walk (approximately 2km) from the station.

Getting There & Away

The JR Kii main line connects Shingū with Nagoya Station (*tokkyū*, ¥6990, three hours) and Shin-Osaka Station (*tokkyū*, ¥6810, four hours).

There are buses between Shingū and Hongū, about half of which make a loop of the three surrounding *onsen* (Watarase, Yunomine and Kawa-yu). See under Hongū below for details.

HONGŪ 本宮

Hongū itself isn't particularly interesting but it makes a good starting point for the *onsen* villages nearby. Hongū is also home to **Kumano Hongū Taisha** (熊野本宮大社), one of the three famous shrines of the Kumano Sanzan. The shrine is close to the Ōmiya Taisha-mae bus stop (the buses listed in this section stop here).

Nara Kōtsū and JR buses leave for Hongū from Gojō in the north (¥3250, four hours), Kii-Tanabe in the west (¥2000, two hours) and Shingū in the southeast (¥1500, 1½ hours). Shingū is the most convenient of these three access points (departures are

most frequent from there). Most Hongū buses also stop at Kawa-yu, Watarase and Yunomine *onsen* (in that order), but be sure to ask before boarding. Keep in mind that departures are few in any direction, so jot down the times and plan accordingly.

YUNOMINE, WATARASE & KAWA-YU ONSEN

☎ 0735

These three *onsen* are among the best in all of Kansai. Because each has its own distinct character, it's worth doing a circuit of all three. There are several ryokan and *minshuku* in the area, but if you are on a tight budget, it's possible to camp on the riverbanks above and below Kumano Hongū Taisha. See under Hongū (left) for transport details.

Yunomine Onsen 湯峰温泉

The town of Yunomine is nestled around a narrow river in a wooded valley. Most of the town's *onsen* are contained inside ryokan or *minshuku* but charming little **Tsubo-yu Onsen** (つぼ湯温泉; Yunomine, Hongū-chō, Higashimuro-gun; admission ¥260; ❍ 6am-9.30pm Thu-Tue, 8am-9.30pm Wed) is open to all. It's right in the middle of town, inside a tiny wooden shack built on an island in the river. Buy a ticket at the *sentō* next to **Tōkō-ji** (東光寺; ☎ 42-0256; 112 Yunomine, Hongū-chō, Higashimuro-gun; admission free), the town's main temple. The *sentō* itself is open the same hours as the *onsen* and entry is ¥300; of the two baths at the *sentō*, we suggest the *kusuri-yu* (medicine water), which is 100% pure hot-spring water.

While you're at Yunomine, try your hand at cooking some *onsen tamago* – eggs boiled in the hot water of an *onsen*. There is a pool of hot-spring water just downstream from Tsubo-yu for cooking. The shop across from the temple sells bags of five eggs for ¥200. Put them in the water before you enter the bath and they should be cooked by the time you get out.

Yunomine has plenty of *minshuku* and ryokan for you to choose from. **Minshuku Yunotanisō** (民宿湯の谷荘; ☎ 42-1620; Yunomine, Hongū-chō, Higashimuro-gun; r per person with 2 meals ¥7500) is at the upper end of the village and has pleasant tatami rooms. There's also an excellent *rotemburo* (open-air or outdoor bath) on the premises. **Ryokan Yoshino-ya** (旅館よしのや; ☎ 42-0101; 359 Yunomine, Hongū-chō,

Higashimuro-gun; r per person with 2 meals ¥8550) is a slightly more upscale place with a lovely *rotemburo*. It's near Tsubo-yu.

Kawa-yu Onsen 川湯温泉

Kawa-yu Onsen is a natural wonder, where geothermally heated water percolates up through the gravel banks of the river that runs through the middle of the town. You can make your own private bath here by digging out some of the stones and letting the hole fill with hot water; you can then spend the rest of the day jumping back and forth between the bath and the cool waters of the river. Admission is free and the best spots along the river are in front of Fujiya ryokan. We suggest bringing a bathing suit unless you fancy putting on a 'naked gaijin' show for the whole town. In the winter, from 1 December to 28 February, bulldozers are used to turn the river into a giant 1000-person *rotemburo*.

If you don't fancy splashing about in the river, try the **Kawa-yu Kōshū Yokujō** (川湯公衆浴場; ☎ 42-1777; Kawayu, Watarase, Hongū-chō, Higashimuro-gun; ¥200; ⏰ 8am-9pm, closed 1st & 3rd Wed each month), a public bath that uses natural hot-spring water. The bath is near the town's footbridge.

SLEEPING
Minshuku Kajika-sō (民宿かじか荘; ☎ 42-0518; kajikaso@shi.cypress.ne.jp; 1408 Kawayu, Hongū-chō, Higashimuro-gun; hostel/minshuku beds per person with 2 meals ¥8550) The cheapest place in Kawa-yu, this is a combination youth hostel/*minshuku*.

Hotels in Kawa-yu, as in other Japanese *onsen* towns, tend to be expensive.

Fujiya (冨士屋; ☎ 42-0007; www.fuziya.co.jp/english/index.html; Kawayu, Hongū-chō, Higashimuro-gun; r per person with 2 meals ¥14,700) Next door, this is a more upmarket ryokan with tasteful rooms. Rates at both include two meals.

Pension Ashita-no-Mori (ペンションあしたの森; ☎ 42-1525; ashitanomori-kawayu@za.ztv.ne.jp; Kawayu, Hongū-chō, Higashimuro-gun; r per person with 2 meals ¥10,000) This is in a pleasant wooden building with a good riverside location.

Watarase Onsen 渡瀬温泉

This **onsen** (admission ¥700; ⏰ 6am-9.30pm) is built around a bend in the river directly between Yunomine Onsen and Kawa-yu Onsen. It's not as interesting as its neighbours, but it does boast the largest *rotemburo* in Kansai.

ISE-SHIMA 伊勢志摩

The Ise-Shima region, on Mie-ken's Shima-hantō, is most famous for Ise-jingū, Japan's most sacred Shintō shrine. It also encompasses the tourist mecca of Toba and some pleasant coastal scenery around Kashiko-jima and Goza. Ise-Shima is easily reached from Nagoya, Kyoto or Osaka and makes a good two-day trip.

JNTO publishes *Ise-Shima*, a leaflet providing basic mapping and concise travel information for the area.

ISE 伊勢
☎ 0596 / pop 99,000
Although the town of Ise is rather drab, it's worth making the trip here to visit the spectacular Ise-jingū. This is arguably Japan's most impressive shrine; its only rival to this claim is Nikkō's Tōshō-gū, which is as gaudy as Ise-jingū is austere.

If you have some time to kill in town after visiting the shrines, take a stroll down atmospheric **Kawasaki Kaiwai** (河崎界隈), a street lined with traditional Japanese houses. It's a little tricky to find; the best way is to head to Hoshide-kan (see p387), take a right and walk towards the canal. Kawasaki-kaiwai is the street just before the canal.

Ise-jingū 伊勢神宮
Dating back to the 3rd century, Ise-jingū is the most venerated Shintō **shrine** (admission free; ⏰ sunrise-sunset) in Japan. Shintō tradition has dictated for centuries that the shrine buildings (about 200 of them) be replaced every 20 years with exact imitations built on adjacent sites according to ancient techniques – no nails, only wooden dowels and interlocking joints. Upon completion of the new buildings, the god of the shrine is ritually transferred to its new home in the Sengū No Gi ceremony, first witnessed by Western eyes in 1953. The wood from the old shrine is then used to reconstruct the *torii* at the shrine's entrance or is sent to shrines around Japan for use in rebuilding their structures. The present buildings were rebuilt in 1993 (for the 61st time) at a cost exceeding ¥5 billion.

The reason for this expensive periodic rebuilding is not clear. The official version holds that rebuilding the shrine every 20 years keeps alive traditional carpentry

KANSAI

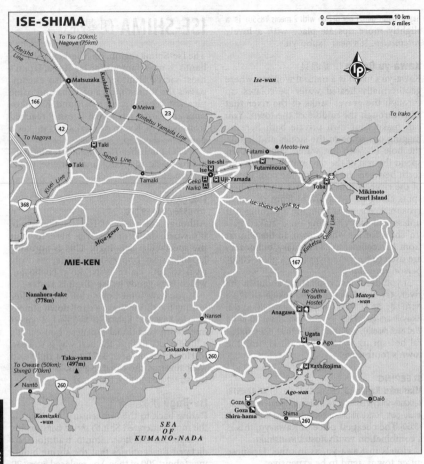

ISE-SHIMA

techniques. Perhaps the real reason goes back to pre-Buddhist Japanese taboos concerning death. Before the establishment of a permanent capital at Nara it was thought that the emperor's residence was defiled by death. This meant that the entire capital had to be razed and rebuilt with the passing of each emperor. This thinking may have carried over to the dwellings of Shintō gods resulting in the periodic reconstruction of the shrines, which continues to this day.

Visitors to the shrine are often shocked to discover that the main shrine buildings are almost completely hidden from view. Only members of the imperial family and certain shrine priests are allowed to enter the sacred inner sanctum. This is unfortu-nate, as the buildings are stunning examples of pre-Buddhist Japanese architecture. Don't despair, though, as determined neck-craning over fences allows a decent view of the upper parts of the buildings. You can also get a good idea of the shrine's architecture by looking at any of the lesser shrines nearby which are exact replicas built on a smaller scale.

There are two parts to the shrine, **Gekū** (Outer Shrine) and **Naikū** (Inner Shrine). The former is an easy 12-minute walk from Ise-shi Station; the latter is accessible by bus from the station or from outside Gekū (see opposite). If you only have time to visit one of the shrines, Naikū is by far the more impressive of the two.

Smoking is prohibited throughout the grounds of both shrines and photography is forbidden around the main halls of both shrines.

GEKŪ 外宮

The Outer Shrine dates from the 5th century and enshrines the god of food, clothing and housing, Toyouke-no-Ōkami. Daily offerings of rice are made by shrine priests to the goddess, who is charged with providing food to Amaterasu-Ōmikami, the goddess enshrined in the Naikū.

A stall at the entrance to the shrine provides a leaflet in English with a map. The main hall is approached along an avenue of tall trees and surrounded by closely fitted wooden fences that hide most of the buildings from sight. As with Naikū, determined craning of the neck and leaping around will afford some view of the buildings. Otherwise, check out the smaller shrine buildings.

To the left of the main hall is an empty plot of land on which will be built the main hall when the shrine is next rebuilt in 2013.

From Ise-shi Station or Uji-Yamada Station it's a 12-minute walk down the main street to the shrine entrance.

NAIKŪ 内宮

The Inner Shrine is thought to date from the 3rd century and enshrines the sun goddess, Amaterasu-Ōmikami, who is considered the ancestral goddess of the imperial family and the guardian deity of the Japanese nation. Naikū is held in even higher reverence than Gekū because it houses the sacred mirror of the emperor, one of the three imperial regalia (the other two are the sacred beads and the sacred sword).

A stall just before the entrance to the shrine provides the same English leaflet given out at Gekū. Next to this stall is the Uji-bashi, which leads over the crystal-clear Isuzu-gawa into the shrine. One path leads to the right and passes Mitarashi, a place for pilgrims to purify themselves in the river before entering the shrine. This isn't easy, as the river is teeming with gargantuan carp awaiting hand-outs.

The path continues along an avenue lined with towering cryptomeria trees to the main hall. Photos are only allowed from the foot of the stone steps. Here too, you can only catch a glimpse of the structure, as four

rows of wooden fences obstruct the view. If you're tempted to jump the fence when nobody's around, think again – they're watching you on closed-circuit TV cameras not so cleverly disguised as trees!

A better view of the shrine can be had by walking along its front (western) side towards the separate Aramatsurinomiya shrine. Here, you can see a large section of the shrine, and on sunny days the cypress wood of the shrine gleams almost as brightly as the gold tips of its roof beams.

To get to Naiku, take bus 51 or 55 from bus stop No 11 outside Ise-shi Station or the stop on the main road in front of Gekū (¥410, 30 minutes). Note that bus stop No 11 is about 100m past the main bus stop outside Ise-shi Station. Get off at the Naikū-mae stop. From Naikū there are buses back to Ise-shi Station via Gekū (¥410, 30 minutes from bus stop No 2). Alternatively, a taxi from Ise-shi Station to Naiku costs ¥630.

Festivals & Events

Since Ise-jingu is Japan's most sacred shrine, it's not surprising that it's also a favourite destination for *hatsu-mōde*. Most of the action takes place in the first three days of the year, when millions of worshippers pack the area and accommodation is booked out for months in advance.

The **Kagurai-sai Matsuri**, celebrated on 5 and 6 April, is a good chance to see performances of *kagura* (sacred dance), *bugaku* (ancient dance music), *nō* and Shintō music.

Sleeping

There are plenty of places to stay in Ise itself, but you'll also find lots of *minshuku* and ryokan in Futami, Kashikojima or Goza. Be aware that prices for all ryokan and *minshuku* go up on weekends and holidays.

Hoshide-kan (星出館; ☎ 28-2377; www.hoshide kan.jp/indexE.htm; 2-15-2 Kawasaki; r per person with/ without 2 meals ¥6000/4000) In Ise itself, this is a quaint wooden ryokan with some nice traditional touches. To get there from Ise-shi Station, take a left (east) outside the station, walk past a JTB travel agency, take a left at the first traffic light, take a left when you cross the tracks, go straight past Ise City Hotel, and it will be on your right (there is a small English sign). It's about 700m from the rail tracks.

Ise City Hotel (伊勢シティホテル; ☎ 28-2111; 1-11-31 Fukiage; s/tw ¥5859/12,285) On the same road as Hoshide-kan but closer to Ise-shi Station, this is a good business hotel with small but adequate rooms.

Ise-Shima Youth Hostel (伊勢志摩ユースホステル; ☎ 0599-55-0226; ise@jyh.gr.jp; 1219-82 Anagawa, Isobe-chō; r per person with breakfast ¥5040) An excellent place built on a hill overlooking an attractive bay. It's close to Anagawa Station on the Kintetsu line south of Ise-shi (only *futsū* trains stop). Walk east out of the station along the waterfront road; it's uphill on the right.

Eating

There are lots of places to eat around Ise-shi Station. If you walk straight out of the station and take your second right (at a mini clock tower), you'll find a couple of cheap *shokudō*.

For more upscale fare, head to the atmospheric Kawasaki-Kawai street.

Ajikko (あじっこ; ☎ 25-9696; 2-13-16 Kawasaki; ☯ noon-2pm & 6-11pm Fri-Wed) At this pleasant little *robatayaki* restaurant you'll probably need a Japanese speaker in your group to handle the ordering. To get there, start at Hoshide-kan (see p387), turn off the main road and walk west. Take a left on Kawasaki Kaiwai and it will be on the right – look for the *noren* (doorway curtain).

Chakura (茶くら; Kawasaki Shōnin-kan-nai; ☯ 11am-5pm, closed Tue) An atmospheric Chinese tea shop/souvenir store also on Kawasaki Kaiwai street. It's about 200m north of Ajikko on the right – cross the main street and keep walking.

Near Naikū, try the shopping arcade just outside the shrine compound. **Nikōdōshiten** (二光堂支店) is a good place to try some of the local specialities in a rough, roadhouse atmosphere. A light lunch of Ise-udon is ¥400. *Ōasari* (large steamed clams) or *sazae* (another type of shellfish) are also tasty and cost ¥400. The restaurant is about 100m north of the entrance to the arcade. **Akafuku Honten** (赤福本店; ☎ 22-2154; ☯ 5am-5pm) is about 200m further on – follow your nose to get there. Here *akafuku mochi*, a kind of Japanese sweet, is served with tea for ¥340. Look for the large, steaming cauldrons and the queue out the front.

Getting There & Away

Ise is well endowed with direct rail connections for Nagoya, Osaka and Kyoto. For those without a Japan Rail Pass, the Kintetsu line is by far the most convenient way to go. Note that there are two stations in Ise – Ise-shi Station and Uji-Yamada Station – which are only a few hundred metres apart; most trains stop at both.

From Nagoya, the *tokkyū* service on the Kintetsu line takes one hour and 20 minutes to reach Ise-shi Station (¥2690) and another 30 minutes to reach its terminus at Kashikojima (¥3480). A JR *kaisoku* from Nagoya takes up to two hours (¥2250).

From Osaka (Uehonmachi or Namba Stations), the Kintetsu limited express takes about two hours to Ise-shi Station and costs ¥3030. The same train continues on to Kashikojima (¥3810, 30 minutes).

From Kyoto, the Kintetsu *tokkyū* takes two hours and 10 minutes to Ise-shi Station (¥3520) and continues for another 30 minutes to its terminus in Kashikojima (¥4320).

If you're only going from Ise-shi to Kashikojima, take a Kintetsu *futsū* (¥670, 55 minutes). JR doesn't serve Kashikojima.

If you're taking JR from Kyoto or Osaka to Ise-shi you'll have to change up to four times and pay ¥2210 from Kyoto and ¥3260 from Osaka. Inquire at the station office for transfer details.

FUTAMI 二見

The big attractions here are Futami Okitama-jinja and the Meoto-iwa (Wedded Rocks). These two rocks are considered to be male and female and have been joined in matrimony by *shimenawa* (sacred ropes), which are renewed each year in a special festival on 5 January. The rocks are a 20-minute walk (about 1.5km) from the station. The shrine is on the shore opposite the rocks. Futami can be reached from Ise by JR (*futsū* ¥200, 10 minutes). Get off at Futaminoura Station.

TOBA 鳥羽

Unless you want a real tourist circus, you can safely give this place a miss. The JR line runs from Ise-shi Station via Futami to Toba and then on to Kashikojima. **Ise-wan Ferry Corporation** (☎ 0559-25-2880) has ferry connections from Toba-ko port to Irako on Atsumi-hantō in Aichi-ken (¥1050, 55 minutes). Boats leave from Ise-wan ferry terminal. Toba can be reached from Ise in 20 minutes by both the Kintetsu line (*kyūkō*, ¥320) or the JR line (*futsū* ¥230).

Toba Aquarium 鳥羽水族館

This rather expensive **aquarium** (☎ 0599-25-2555; 3-3-6 Toba; admission ¥2400; ۞ 8.30am-5pm 21 Mar-30 Nov, 9am-5pm 1 Dec-20 Mar) has some interesting fish and marine mammal displays and some good shows. It would make a good destination for those with children or if the rain puts a damper on outdoor activities.

AGO-WAN, KASHIKOJIMA & GOZA
英虞湾・賢島・御座

Ago-wan is a pleasant stretch of coastline, with sheltered inlets and small islands. Kashikojima, an island in the bay, is the terminus of the Kintetsu line, only 40 minutes from Ise-shi to Kashikojima (¥670, about one hour), and a good base for exploration of Ago-wan. The island itself is probably of little interest to foreign travellers as it is dominated by large resort hotels.

Those in search of peace and quiet might want to take a ferry to Goza on the other side of the bay (¥600, 25 minutes). The ferry terminal is right outside Kashikojima Station (buy your tickets from the Kinki Kankōsen office near the terminal). The ride is a good way to see the sights in the bay. There are also sightseeing boats that do a loop around the bay for ¥1500.

Goza is a sleepy fishing community where the main attractions are the fish market and Goza Shira-hama, a long white-sand beach on the southern side of town. There are small signs in English from the ferry pier to the beach; just follow the main road over the hill and across the peninsula. The beach is mobbed in late July and early August but is quite nice at other times. After the beginning of August, there may be some *kurage* (jellyfish) in the water, so ask the locals about conditions.

If you'd like to stay in Goza, there are tons of *minshuku*, some of which close down outside of summer. **Shiojisō** (潮路荘; ☎ 0599-88-3232; Goza Shirahama Kaigan; r per person ¥7500), just off the beach (look for the sign reading 'Marine Lodge Shiojisō' in English), is one of the better *minshuku*. Rates include two meals.

SOUTH OF KASHIKOJIMA 賢島以南

If you want to continue down Kii-hantō but avoid the tortuous coastal road, backtrack to Ise and then take a train on the JR Kisei main line. This line crosses from Mie-ken into Wakayama-ken and continues down to Shingū on its way round Kii-hantō, finally ending up in Osaka's Tennō-ji Station.

KANSAI

Western Honshū
本州西部

Western Honshū is a blend of urban dynamism and rural charm. The broad Chūgoku mountain range divides the region into two very distinct areas. On the southern San-yō coast (literally, 'on the sunny side of the mountains'), the mild weather of the Inland Sea (Seto-nai-kai) nurtures populous, vibrant cities; to the north, the San-in coast (literally, 'in the shade of the mountains') is on the cooler Sea of Japan, where nature takes priority.

Basking in the rays of San-yō, Okayama and Hiroshima prefectures enjoy a well-deserved reputation for generous hospitality, good food and an ambitious mercantile spirit. The post-war reconstruction of Hiroshima is undoubtedly a potent symbol of the area's outward-looking attitude and independence. From the canal-side charm of Kurashiki to pottery making in Bizen and Chinese liquor tasting in Tomo-no-ura, an enthusiastic confidence typifies the San-yō coast.

By contrast, the San-in prefectures of Tottori and Shimane are havens of peace, quiet and rugged coastal scenery. With an original castle in Matsue, serene mountains in Tsuwano and sand dunes in Tottori, the San-in coast has simply been left to its own devices. Izumo Taisha, one of the oldest and most important shrines in Japan, is the essence of the San-in coast.

Yamaguchi prefecture straddles both coasts, and continues to be a trade hub for Kyūshū, Shikoku and the Korean Peninsula. Shimonoseki, home to the potentially fatal *fugu* (blowfish), is so close to Kyūshū that you can walk there through a tunnel. The Inland Sea is a microcosm that's still a pace apart from frenetic Honshū. Anyone with time to spare should indulge in its simplicity and beauty.

HIGHLIGHTS

- Ponder the significance of **Hiroshima's** (p405) past and capture its cosmopolitan present
- Clamber up the crumbling volcano of **Daisen** (p444) from the ancient temple Daisen-ji
- Gobble up the intriguing marine life from **Karato Ichiba** (p425) in Shimonoseki and watch the sun rise over the Kanmon Strait
- Seek out hidden-away rural health spa **Tawarayama Onsen** (p428) and its curious phallic temple dedicated to the Goddess of Mercy
- Contemplate **Izumo Taisha** (p437), where the Shintō gods go on holiday, and taste the local drop at the **Shimane Winery** (p439)
- Potter through the well-preserved warehouses and museums along the canal in **Kurashiki** (p398)
- Relax on the beach while staying at the **Okayama-ken International Villa** (p397) on Shiraishi-jima in the Inland Sea
- Have a mountaintop to yourself and your own castle ruins in **Tsuwano** (p434)
- Stay in a Mongolian *pao* (circular tent) and explore contemporary Japanese and international art by the sea in **Nao-shima** (p417)

WESTERN HONSHŪ

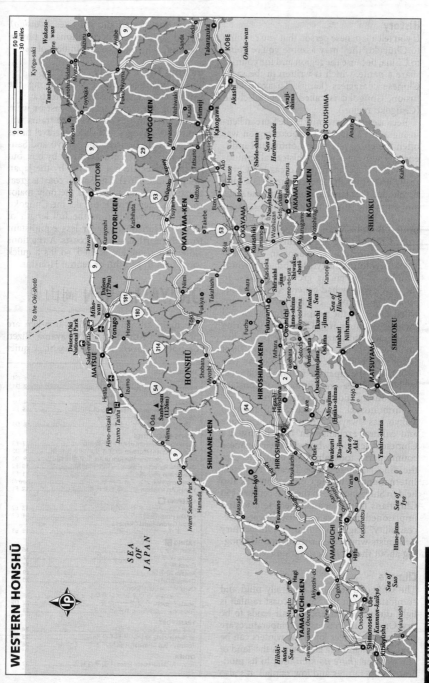

WESTERN HONSHŪ

History

If you tell a Japanese person that you're going to Chūgoku they may assume you're going to China, because the region and the country share a name, which is written in the same Chinese characters (kanji). To avoid confusion, Chūgoku is called Chūgoku-chiho (Chūgoku region).

Because of its proximity to the Korean Peninsula and China, the Chūgoku region was often the entry point for Continental influences. There are countless historical reminders of how close Japan, the Koreas and China really are. From the 2nd century AD China demanded that Japan become a tribute state, and from the 4th century AD it was common for Japanese emperors to take Korean brides. Buddhism and kanji came through from China in the 6th century. During his Korean Peninsula campaigns in 1592 and 1598 Toyotomi Hideyoshi abducted whole families of potters as growing interest in the tea ceremony had generated a desire for *punch'ŏng* ceramics. The Korean campaigns failed to secure the peninsula for Japan and the elusive entrée into China, but the firing techniques and glazes from the period live on in Japanese ceramics today. Up to 10% of Hiroshima bomb victims were Korean (see p408), and the Japanese nationals abducted by North Korea are the focus of constant public outcry and media attention.

Shimonoseki, closer to Seoul than to Tokyo, has always played a vital role in trade and cultural exchange. In 1895 it hosted a Chinese delegation who, with their Japanese counterparts, took almost a month to sign the Sino-Japanese Peace Treaty. The 2002 International Whaling Convention was also held in Shimonoseki. In the 19th century 150 Christians from Nagasaki were sent to and imprisoned in Tsuwano, chosen for its inaccessibility. Hagi was home to 19th-century reformists who were instrumental in bringing about the Meiji Restoration (p38).

Climate

The Chūgoku region is generally mild and comfortable. On the San-yō coast rainfall is light during winter and the air tends to be dry. On the San-in coast the temperatures are a couple of degrees lower, so winters can be cold. The Inland Sea is known as the 'land of fair weather' *(hare no kuni)* due to its moderate temperatures and low rainfall. It's also known for its periodic red tides *(akashio)*, caused by dense concentrations of phytoplankton, which kill large numbers of fish.

Getting There & Away

The *shinkansen* (bullet train) along the San-yō coast is the fastest way to travel in the Chūgoku region from the east or west. Along the San-in coast, express trains will limit train changes and shorten travel times by up to half. Between the San-yō and San-in coasts it's often quicker to go by bus, but most services are not covered by the Japan rail pass (see p764). The San-in coast is great to explore by car – Rte 9 is the only major road. An alternative is to take the Chūgoku Expressway, which runs the full length of western Honshū more or less equidistant from the north and south coasts. Attractions along this route are limited, so it's a quick way to get to Kyūshū or central Honshū.

OKAYAMA-KEN 岡山県

The main attractions of Okayama-ken are the cities of Kurashiki and Okayama, Bizen for pottery lovers and Takahashi, a quiet

WESTERN HONSHŪ

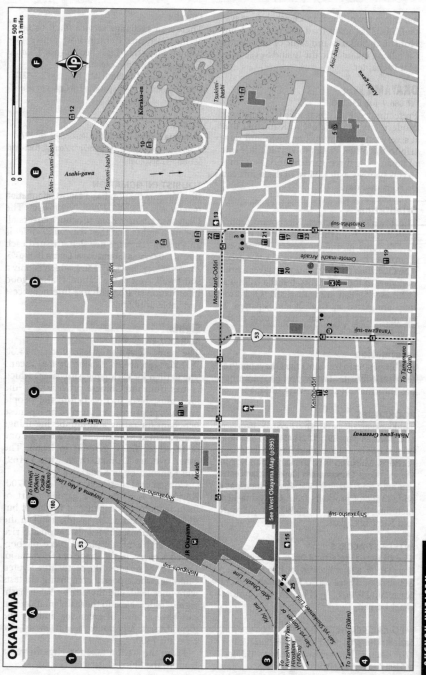

OKAYAMA

See West Okayama Map (p395)

mountain town. The Seto-Ōhashi bridge system forms the main road and rail link from Honshū to Shikoku and some of Okayama's islands are included in the Inland Sea section of this chapter.

OKAYAMA 岡山

☎ 086 / pop 630,000

Prefectural capital Okayama is a bustling, modern city. It's so close to Kurashiki that it's very easy to stay in one town and daytrip to the other. Places to visit include one of Japan's 'big three' gardens and Okayama-jō (Okayama Castle). Most of the sights can be seen in a day.

Orientation

The town's main street, Momotarō-Ōdōri, leads directly from the station to near the castle, Okayama-jō, and the garden, Kōraku-en. Tramlines run down the middle of the street. The *Okayama Culture Zone* map gives a brief overview of the city sights, but the trilingual (Chinese/Korean and English) Okayama map annotated in English and Japanese is far more useful as it also has a map of the Kibi Plain bicycle route.

Information

For longer-term residents the Okayama Prefectural website (www.pref.okayama.jp/) has information about living in Japan.

BOOKSHOPS

The **Kinokuniya** (Map p393; ☎ 212-2551; ☿ 10am-8pm) and **Maruzen** (Map p393; ☎ 233-4640; ☿ 10am-8pm) bookshops both have good English-language sections. Maruzen is in the same building as the excellent **Okayama-ken Kanko Bussan Centre** (Map p393; ☎ 234-2270; ☿ 10am-8pm), which has a wide range of products from Okayama-ken, including Bizen-yaki (see p397), lacquerware and Kurashiki glass.

INTERNET ACCESS

The **Okayama Prefectural Office** (Okayama Kenchō; Map p393; ☿ 8.30am-5pm Mon-Fri) has free Internet access. There's also **Megalo** (Map p393; per 30min/3hr ¥241/1029; ☿ 24 hr), in the Omotemachi arcade.

MEDICAL SERVICES

Saiseikai Hospital (Map p395; ☎ 086-252-2211; 1-17-18 Ifuku-chō; ☿ general consultation 8am-11.30am, accident & emergency 24hr)

MONEY

There's an exchange service (9am to 6pm) at the Okayama Central Post Office (see below), where travellers cheques (not Thomas Cook) and cash are exchanged.

Bank of Tokyo-Mitsubishi (Map p395; ☎ 223-9211; 6-36 Honmachi; ☿ 9am-3pm Mon-Fri) Cashes travellers cheques.

POST

Okayama Central Post Office (Map p395; ☎ 227-2730; 2-1-1 Naka Sange; ☿ 8am-7pm Mon-Fri, 8am-5pm Sat, 8am-12.30pm Sun)

TOURIST INFORMATION

JR Okayama Station has a **tourist information counter** (Map p395; ☎ 222-2912; ☿ 9am-6pm). The *Okayama Culture Zone* brochure covers all the main sights, and the *Okayama Insider* is an English-language newsletter issued each month. **Okayama International Centre** (Map p395; ☎ 256-2000; ☿ 9am-9pm Tue-Sun), which is only a short walk west of the station, is also a good information source with free Internet access (available until 5pm).

Sights

KŌRAKU-EN 後楽園

The name **Kōraku-en** (Map p393; admission ¥350; ☿ 7.30am-6pm Apr-Sep, 8am-5pm Oct-Mar) means 'the garden for taking pleasure later', which comes from the Chinese proverb that 'the lord must bear sorrow before the people and take pleasure after them'. The Japanese penchant for rating and numbering things is apparent at Kōraku-en; it's said to be one of the three finest gardens in Japan. The other two are Kairaku-en in Mito (p169) and Kenroku-en in Kanazawa (p255).

Constructed between 1687 and 1700, Kōraku-en is a 'strolling garden'. Part of its attraction is its expanse of flat lawn, but there are also attractive ponds; a hill in the centre; a curious, tiny tea plantation and rice paddy; and a neatly placed piece of 'borrowed scenery' in the shape of Okayama-jō. Look for the *nō* stage, the pretty little Ryuten Building, where poetry composing contests were once held, and the nearby Yatsu-hashi zigzag bridge. Next to the tea plantation you can have a bowl of green tea and try the local dessert, *kibi-dango*, a soft, sweet rice cake, for ¥300.

From the station take the Higashi-yama tram to the Shiro-shita stop (¥100).

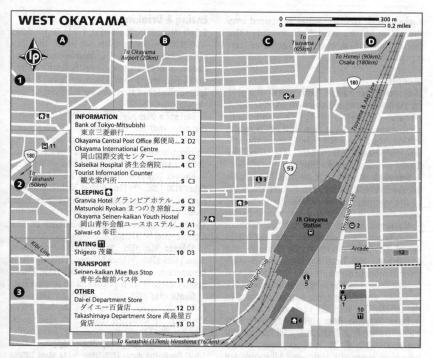

WEST OKAYAMA

INFORMATION	
Bank of Tokyo-Mitsubishi	
東京三菱銀行	1 D3
Okayama Central Post Office 郵便局	2 D2
Okayama International Centre	
岡山国際交流センター	3 C2
Saiseikai Hospital 済生会病院	4 C1
Tourist Information Counter	
観光案内所	5 C3

SLEEPING	
Granvia Hotel グランビアホテル	6 C3
Matsunoki Ryokan まつのき旅館	7 B2
Okayama Seinen-kaikan Youth Hostel	
岡山青年会館ユースホステル	8 A1
Saiwai-sō 幸荘	9 C2

EATING	
Shigezo 茂蔵	10 D3

TRANSPORT	
Seinen-kaikan Mae Bus Stop	
青年会館前バス停	11 A2

OTHER	
Dai-ei Department Store	
ダイエー百貨店	12 D3
Takashimaya Department Store 高島屋百	
貨店	13 D3

OKAYAMA-JŌ 岡山城

Known to locals as U-jō, the striking black U-jo or **Crow Castle** (Map p393; admission ¥300; 9am-5pm) as the locals call it, built in 1597, was said to be a *daimyō*'s (domain lord's) jest at Himeji's pristine White Egret Castle. Like many other great castles in Japan, U-jō was destroyed in WWII, and only the small *tsukima-yagura* (moon-viewing turret) survives. The modern reinforced-concrete castle was built in 1966 and has an interesting display inside, much of it labelled in English.

MUSEUMS

There are a number of museums and galleries in the Okayama Culture Zone. Close to the castle's back entrance, near the corner of the moat, the **Hayashibara Museum of Art** (Map p393; admission ¥300; 9am-5pm) houses a private collection of Japanese and Chinese artefacts. Opposite the main entrance to Kōraku-en is the **Okayama Prefectural Museum** (Map p393; admission ¥200; 9am-6pm Tue-Sun Apr-Sep, 9.30am-5pm Oct-Mar), which has displays about local history. Just north of Kōraku-en is the **Yumeji Art Museum** (Map p393; admission ¥700; 9am-5pm

Tue-Sun), displaying work by famed local artist Yumeji Takehisa (1884–1934).

Just north of the end of Momotarō-Ōdōri, where the tramline turns south, is the excellent **Okayama Orient Museum** (Map p393; admission ¥300; 9am-5pm Tue-Sun), which houses around 3000 artefacts from the prehistoric to the Islamic Age. Behind it is the **Okayama Prefectural Museum of Art** (Map p393; admission ¥300; 9am-5pm Tue-Sun), which has a collection of works by locally born artists, including the famous *nihonga* (Japanese-style painting) painter, Sesshū.

OTHER SIGHTS

The canal-like **Nishi-gawa Greenway Canal** (Map p393), not far east of the station, is flanked by gardens and sculptures and makes for a pleasant stroll.

Festivals & Events

The **Saidai-ji Eyō** (Naked Festival) takes place from midnight on the third Saturday in February at the Kannon-in temple in the Saidai-ji area. A large crowd of near-naked men fight for two sacred *shingi* (wooden sticks), while freezing water is poured over them. Despite the masochistic nature of this purification ritual, everyone seems to have a good time.

Sleeping

Okayama Seinen-kaikan Youth Hostel (Map p395; ☎ 252-0651; www.itcj.or.jp/facility/6/facil/633012.html; 1-7-6 Tsukura-chō; dm ¥2940; P ⊠) This hostel is in a suburban area about 1km west of Okayama station. Catch bus No 5 or 15 from the station to Seinen-kaikan Mae bus stop. The hostel manager speaks English.

Saiwai-sō (Map p395; ☎ 254-0020; 24-8 Ekimoto-chō; s/tw from ¥4200/7600; ⊠) In a quiet area west of the station, this place has Western- and Japanese-style rooms and communal baths.

Matsunoki Ryokan (Map p395; ☎ 253-411; www.matsunoki.com; 19-1 Ekimoto-chō; s/tw ¥5000/8000; P ⊠ 🖳) Also west of the station, the Matsunoki has bright, clean rooms with en-suite bathrooms in the Western and Japanese style. There are public laundry facilities, and there's free Internet access in the lobby. The staff are very attentive.

Excel Okayama (Map p393; ☎ 224-0505; www.excel-okayama.com in Japanese; 5-1 Sekikan-chō; s/tw from ¥6300/10,080; P ⊠ ✕) East-facing rooms here have views of Kōraku-en. All rooms are Western style, and the hotel is within walking distance of the town's main sights. An Italian and a Chinese restaurant are on site.

Mitsui Garden Hotel Okayama (Map p393; ☎ 235-1131; www.gardenhotels.co.jp in Japanese; 1-7 Ekimoto-chō; s/tw from ¥6900/15,200; P ⊠ ✕) Single rooms here are small and simply decorated. There's a sunny dining room on the 1st floor.

Kōraku Hotel (Map p393; ☎ 221-7111; www.hotel.kooraku.co.jp in Japanese; 5-1 Heiwa-chō; s/tw from 7500/13,800; P ⊠ ✕) Close to Nishi-gawa river, the Kōraku has spacious rooms and friendly staff. Laptop computers are available for ¥1050 a night, and the Japanese restaurant on the premises serves Okayama barazushi (a kind of chirashi-zushi served in a large bowl topped with fresh seafood, mainly Spanish mackerel and vegetables).

Granvia Hotel (Map p395; ☎ 233-3131; www.hotels.westjr.co.jp/okayama in Japanese; 1-5 Ekimoto-chō; s/tw from ¥9350/18,700; P ⊠ ✕) Near the station, the Granvia has large, opulent rooms, a plush lobby and English-speaking staff. The hotel also has a swimming pool and gym (¥1200 for one day only), and an 18-room section for women only.

Eating & Drinking

5 Deli (Map p393; ☎ 235-3532; 1-1-11 Ta-chō; dishes ¥250-1000; ☀ 7am-11pm Mon-Sat) Start the day with a café matcha – a double shot of espresso and green tea – in this funky coffee and juice bar. From 11am to 7pm, 5 Deli has sandwiches that can be adapted to suit vegetarians.

Tori-soba (Map p393; ☎ 236-0310; 1-7-24 Omote-chō; dishes ¥600-1000; ☀ 11am-7pm) This place's name is also its speciality: tori-soba means chicken noodles. If one bowl isn't enough, order a small serving of sushi to go with it.

Konaya (Map p393; ☎ 223-3023; 2-6-59 Omote-chō; dishes ¥100-1200; ☀ 11am-8.30pm Wed-Mon) Frenzied at lunch times, this place has rice balls from ¥100 and a bowl of udon noodles for ¥500. Order from a photo menu in the Omote-machi arcade.

Shigezo (Map p395; ☎ 226-3232; 6-20 Honmachi; dishes ¥1200-3500; ☀ lunch & dinner) This modern Japanese restaurant has cosy lighting. There are set menus with photos, and a wine list.

Gonta (Map p393; ☎ 233-4430; 1-2-1 Nodaya-chō; dishes ¥500-10,000; ☀ 11am-11pm Thu-Tue) Here there are 38 kinds of sushi to choose from. Ask for the Okayama speciality, barazushi.

Quiet Village Curry Shop (Map p393; ☎ 231-4100; 1-6-43 Omote-chō; dishes ¥780-1000; ☀ 11.30am-8.30pm Tue-Sun) This place is a serious curry house with good service. The chicken curry and dhal are good lunch-time options.

Okabe (Map p393; ☎ 222-1404; 1-10-1 Omote-chō; dishes ¥700-750; ☀ lunch) Order the Okabe teishoku (set menu) and be surprised by how filling tofu can be.

MOMOTARŌ, THE PEACH BOY

Okayama-ken and neighbouring Kagawa-ken, on the island of Shikoku, are linked by the legend of Momotarō, the tiny Peach Boy who emerged from the stone of a peach and, backed up by a monkey, a pheasant and a dog, defeated a three-eyed, three-toed people-eating demon. There are statues of Momotarō at JR Okayama Station, and the main road of Okayama is named after him. The island of Megi-jima, off Takamatsu in Shikoku, is said to be the site of the clash with the demon.

Momotarō may actually have been a Yamato prince who was deified as Kibitsuhiko. His shrine, Kibitsu-jinja, lies along the route of the Kibi Plain bicycle ride (p400).

Sauda-jinayoru (Map p393; ☎ 234-5306; Tenjin-chō; dishes ¥650-1000; ◷ 2pm-2am Wed-Mon, 8pm-2am Tue) Enjoy fantastic views of the symphony hall from this 2nd-floor lounge bar. There are drink and cake set menus until 8pm, after which time the bar takes priority. DJs occasionally play and the desserts are generous.

Gigina (Map p393; ☎ 224-3676; 1st fl, Uoda Bldg, 1-7-1 Omote-chō; meals ¥1300-2000; ◷ lunch & dinner Wed-Mon) Popular with the office crowd at lunch time, Gigina has Italian food and funky décor.

Getting There & Away

Okayama airport is 20km northwest of the station. There are flights to Japan's major cities and some international ones. A bus runs to/from the airport (¥680, 40 minutes). The bus leaves from Okayama station and makes stops at Saiseikai Hospital, the Okayama Sports Centre and Okayama University before arriving at Okayama airport. Buses connect with flights and there is about one bus per hour. The first bus leaves at 6.15am, the last at 6.30pm from in front of Okayama station.

Okayama is connected by the San-yō Hikari *shinkansen* to Hakata (Fukuoka; ¥12,060, two hours) to the west; and to Osaka (¥5860, 45 minutes); Kyoto (¥7330, 80 minutes, 16 daily); and Tokyo (¥16,360, four hours, 14 daily). The JR Hakubi line runs between Okayama and Yonago (¥4620, two hours), in Tottori-ken on the San-in coast.

When travelling west to Kurashiki, it's quicker to transfer from the *shinkansen* at Okayama than at Shin-Kurashiki. You also change trains at Okayama if you're heading to Shikoku across the Seto-Ōhashi.

Getting Around

Getting around Okayama is a breeze, since the Higashi-yama tram route will take you to all the main attractions. Trams charge a standard ¥140 to anywhere in town.

JR Rent-a-cycle (Map p393; ◷ 7am-10pm) hires out bikes for ¥300 per day. **Eki Rent-a-Car** (Map p393; ☎ 224-1363; 1-1 Ekimoto-chō; ◷ 8am-8pm) is next door.

AROUND OKAYAMA

To attract foreign visitors to the less frequently visited areas of the region, the Okayama Prefectural Government established five International Villas around the prefecture in 1988. Rates are ¥2500 per night for members and

there's a ¥500 joining fee. The villas are well equipped with cooking facilities, and have instructions in English on where to shop locally and where to find local restaurants and bicycles for visitors' use. The villas provide an ideal opportunity to get away from city life and see a side to Japan that not many foreigners see. They are highly recommended but are showing signs of wear and tear.

The villa at Fukiya, in the mountains in the west of the prefecture, is modelled after the traditional *shoyu-gura* (soya sauce storehouse) that once stood on the site. Fukiya is an old copper-mining town.

In central Okayama, the Takebe villa is beside the Asahi River. Next door to the modern building is Yahata Onsen, with a variety of hot baths. At the time of publication this villa was quite run down.

Hattoji, high up on a plateau in the east of the prefecture, is home to a villa in a thatched-roof farmhouse.

The Ushimado villa, on the Inland Sea coast east of Okayama, is a modern glass-enclosed structure perched high above the old village. The views are stunning, and there is a variety of activities in the area.

On the island of Shiraishi-jima in the Inland Sea, in the west of the prefecture, is a modern villa with great views and easy access to the island's main beach and hiking trails (p418).

For reservations or more information, contact the **Okayama International Villa Group** (☎ 256-2535; www.harenet.ne.jp/villa) at the Okayama International Centre. Staff speak English, and English-language brochures for each villa are available.

BIZEN 備前

☎ 0869 / pop 29,000

East of Okayama city on the JR Akō line is the 700-year-old pottery region of Bizen, renowned for its unglazed Bizen-yaki pottery. Much prized by tea-ceremony connoisseurs, Bizen ceramics are earthy and dramatic. They're often referred to as 'expensive accidents', as the firing process can have such mixed results. A morning or afternoon is enough time to enjoy Bizen.

At Imbe station, the drop-off point to explore the area, there's a **tourist information counter** (☎ 64-1100; ◷ 9am-6pm), with useful English-language pamphlets on the history of Bizen-yaki.

Sights

On the 2nd floor of the station is the **Bizen Ceramic Crafts Museum** (備前陶友会; admission free; 🕙 9.30am-5.30pm Wed-Mon), and on the north side of the station are the **Okayama Prefectural Bizen Ceramics Art Museum** (岡山県備前陶芸美術館; admission ¥500; 🕙 9.30am-4.30pm Tue-Sun) and the **Bizen Ceramics Centre** (備前焼センター; ☎ 64-2453; admission free; 🕙 10am-4.30pm Tue-Sun), all of which display the pottery of the area. Of all the galleries in Bizen's main street, **Kibi-dō** (桃蹊堂; ☎ 64-4467; 🕙 9am-6pm Mon, Tue, Thu & Sat, 9am-5pm Wed & Fri, 1-6pm Sun) is the oldest and most interesting.

There are several kilns in the area that offer a chance to try your hand at making Bizen-yaki. The cost is around ¥3000; reservations are necessary. Try **Bishū Gama** (備州窯; ☎ 64-1160; 302-2 Imbe Bizen-shi; 🕙 9am-3pm), where some English is spoken. In about two hours you can sculpt a masterpiece, but you'll need to arrange to have your creation shipped to you after it's been fired. **Bizen-yaki Traditional Pottery Centre** (備前焼伝統産業会館; ☎ 64-1001; 1657-7 Imbe Bizen-shi; 🕙 9.30-5.30 Wed-Mon), on the 3rd floor of Imbe station, holds workshops (¥3000) on weekends and holidays from April to November.

Eating

Shikisai (四季彩; ☎ 63-0088; dishes ¥500-3000; 🕙 lunch & dinner) This station eatery serves everything from simple Japanese dishes to mini-*kaiseki* (Japanese formal cuisine) course meals.

Getting There & Away

Only the first three cars of the Imbe train go to Imbe. If you have come from Himeji or points east, you'll need to change to the JR Akō line at Aioi and get off at Imbe station, possibly after changing trains at Banshū-Akō. You can carry on along the JR Akō line to get to Okayama.

KURASHIKI 倉敷

☎ 086 / pop 450,000

Kurashiki's claim to fame is a small quarter of picturesque buildings around a stretch of moat. A number of old black-tiled warehouses have been converted into an eclectic collection of museums. Bridges arch over, willows dip into the water, carp cruise the canal and the whole effect is quite delightful – it's hardly surprising that the town is a favourite with tourists, or that Kurashiki means 'warehouse village'.

In the feudal era the warehouses were used to store rice brought by boat from the surrounding rich farmlands. As this phase of Kurashiki's history faded, the town's importance as a textile centre increased and the Kurabō Textile Company expanded. Ōhara Keisaburō, the owner of the company, gathered together a collection of European art, and opened the Ōhara Museum in the 1920s. It was the first of a series of museums that have become the town's principal attraction, and it's still the finest.

Note that many of Kurashiki's prime attractions, and most of the eateries, close on Monday.

Orientation

It's about 1km from the station to the old Bikan area and, if you walk, the typical urban Japanese scenery will make you wonder whether you are in the right town. But when you turn into the canal area everything changes: Ivy Square is just beyond the canal. A number of shops along the main street, Kurashiki Chūō-dōri, sell Bizen-yaki.

Information

At the station's **tourist information counter** (☎ 426-8681; 🕙 9am-6pm) the English-speaking staff will make accommodation bookings. There are also a tourist information office and travellers' rest area called **Kurashikikan** (☎ 422-0542; 🕙 9am-6pm Apr-Oct, 9am-5pm Nov-Mar) near the bend in the canal. The Tōkyū Inn Hotel has Internet access for paying guests.

Sights

Ōhara Museum of Art (admission ¥1000; 🕙 9am-5pm Tue-Sun, Oct-Nov) is undoubtedly Kurashiki's premier museum and houses the predominantly European art collection of textile magnate Ōhara Keisaburō (1880–1943). Rodin, Matisse, Picasso, Pissarro, Monet, Cézanne, Renoir, El Greco, Toulouse-Lautrec, Gauguin, Degas and Munch are all represented here. The museum's neoclassical façade is Kurashiki's best-known landmark.

Your ticket also takes you to the museum's folk-art and Chinese-art collections, and to the contemporary-art collection housed in an **annexe** behind the main building. You have to exit the old building and walk down the street to enter the new gallery.

KURASHIKI

0 ____ 400 m
0 ____ 0.2 miles

INFORMATION
Kurashikikan Tourist Information
倉敷館観光案内所 1 C3
Tourist Information Counter
観光案内所 2 B2
Travellers' Rest Area 倉敷民芸館
倉敷館観光案内所 .... (see 1)
Tōkyū Inn Hotel 東急インホテル 3 B2

SIGHTS & ACTIVITIES
Achi-jinja 阿智神社 4 D3
Honei-ji 本栄寺 5 C3
Ivy Square アイビースクエア 6 D4

Japan Rural Toy Museum
日本郷土玩具館 7 C4
Kanryū-ji 観龍寺 8 C3
Kurashiki City Art Museum
市立美術館 9 C4
Kurashiki Museum of Folkcrafts
倉敷民芸館 10 C3
Museum of Natural History
自然史博物館 11 B3
Orient Museum
児島虎次郎記念館 .... (see 13)
Seigan-ji 誓願寺 12 C3
Torajirō Kojima Museum 13 C3

Ōhara Museum Annexe
大原美術館分館 14 C3
Ōhara Museum of Art 大原美術館 ... 15 C3
Ōhashi-ke 大橋家 16 B3

SLEEPING
Kamoi Minshuku カモイ民宿 17 D3
Kurashiki Kokusai Hotel
倉敷国際ホテル 18 C3
Kurashiki Sakura Stay
倉敷サクラステイ 19 C4
Kurashiki Youth Hostel
倉敷ユースホステル 20 D4
Ryokan Kurashiki 旅館くらしき 21 C3
Ryokan Tsurugata 22 C3
Tokusan Kan 特産館 23 C4
Young Inn Kurashiki
ヤングイン倉敷 24 B2

To Okayama
(17km)

JR Kurashiki

To Shin-Kurashiki
Station (10km);
Hiroshima (150km)

Ebisu Arcade

Kurashiki Chūō-dōri

Tsurugata-yama
kōen

EATING
Kamoi Restaurant カモ井 25 C3
Kana Izumi かないずみ 26 C3
Kiyū-tei 亀遊亭 27 C3
Mamakari-tei ままかり亭 28 C3
Restaurant & Café 旅館鶴形イン..(see 22)
Tsuneya つね家 29 C3

DRINKING
Coffee-Kan 珈琲館 30 C3
El Greco 31 C3
SWLABR 32 B3

OTHER
Mitsukoshi Department Store
三越百貨店 33 B2
Tenmaya Department Store
天満屋百貨店 34 B2

To Fukuyama
(80km);
Hiroshima
(150km)

Shirakabe-dōri

Kurashiki-gawa

To Shikoku
(50km)

The impressive collection at the **Kurashiki Museum of Folkcrafts** (admission ¥700; 🕙 9am-5pm Tue-Sun Mar-Nov, 9am-4.15pm Dec-Feb) is mainly Japanese but also includes furniture and items from other countries. The work is housed in a rustic complex of linked *kura* (warehouses).

The **Japan Rural Toy Museum** (admission ¥500; 🕙 9am-5pm) displays folkcraft toys from Japan and around the world. Japanese rural toys are also on sale.

There are also the **Museum of Natural History** (admission ¥100; 🕙 9am-5pm Tue-Sun) and the **Kurashiki City Art Museum** (admission ¥200; 🕙 9am-5pm Tue-Sun). The restored **Ōhashi-ke** (Ōhashi House; admission ¥500; 🕙 9am-5pm Tue-Sun) is a reasonable example of a late–18th-century merchant's house.

IVY SQUARE アイビースクエア
The Kurabō textile factories have moved to more modern premises, and the fine Meiji-era factory buildings (dating from 1889 and remodelled in 1974) now house a hotel, restaurants, shops and yet more museums. Ivy Square, with its ivy-covered walls and open-air café, is the centre of the complex.

The **Torajirō Kojima Museum** (admission ¥350; 🕙 9am-5pm Tue-Sun) displays work by the local artist who helped Ōhara establish his European collection. Pieces from the Middle East are housed in the associated **Orient Museum**.

SHRINES & TEMPLES
The shrine **Achi-jinja** tops the **Tsurugata-yama-kōen** park, which overlooks the old area of

KIBI PLAIN BICYCLE ROUTE

To access this excellent cycling course, take a local JR Kibi line train from Okayama for three stops to Bizen Ichinomiya. You can ride the 15km route to Sōja, drop off your bike and take a JR Hakubi line train back through Kurashiki to Okayama. Most of the course is on a cycling road that cars are not allowed to use.

Uedo Rental Bicycles (☎ 0862-84-2311; ⏱ 9am-6pm) is just outside JR Bizen Ichinomiya Station. Pick up your bike (¥200/1000 per hour/day) and free Japanese-language route map here. You'll use this map in conjunction with the one here as it is of a larger scale. Turn right and then right again to cross the railway line, and in just 300m you'll reach **Kibitsuhiko-jinja**, a shrine that fronts a large pond. From here you'll soon pick up the bicycle path, which follows a canal through the fields until it rejoins the road just before the temple Fudenkai-ji. Just 200m further on is **Kibitsu-jinja**, where a wide flight of steps leads up to an attractive hilltop setting. The shrine, built in 1425, is unusual in that it has the oratory and main sanctum topped by a single roof. The legendary Peach Boy, Momotarō (p396), is connected with the shrine.

Pedalling on, you'll pass **Koikui-jinja**, which is connected with the legendary figure of Kibitsuhiko, to reach the huge 5th-century **Tsukuriyama-kofun Burial Mound**, which rises like a gentle hill from the surrounding plain. Ideally, you need to be in a hot-air balloon or helicopter to appreciate that it's a 350m-long keyhole-shaped mound, not a natural hill. Just north of here is the birthplace of famous artist **Sesshū** (1420–1506). He was once a novice monk at **Hōfuku-ji**, which is 3km northwest of JR Sōja Station.

Finally, there are the foundation stones of the **Bitchū Kokubun-niji Convent**, the nearby **Kibiji Archaeological Museum** (⏱ 9am-4.30 Tue-Sun; admission ¥150), the excavated **Kōmorizuka Burial Mound**, and **Bitchū Kokobun-ji** with its picturesque five-storey pagoda. From here it's a few more kilometres into Sōja.

It's worth taking your own water, but occasionally the bicycle path passes close enough to a main road to divert for food. On arrival at Sōja station, return your bicycle to **Araki Rental Bicycles** (☎ 0866-92-0233; ⏱ 9am-6pm). If this ride appeals to you, you can easily plot others on the network of tracks that cover the area.

town. The **Honei-ji**, **Kanryū-ji** and **Seigan-ji** temples are also in the park.

Sleeping

Kurashiki is a great town if you're keen to stay in a traditional Japanese inn. It has an ample selection of *minshuku* (Japanese equivalent of a B&B) and ryokan.

BUDGET

Kurashiki Youth Hostel (☎ 422-7355; 1537 Mukoyama; dm ¥2940; P ✗ ✗) South of the canal area and a 15-minute climb from Ivy Square, this hostel's hilltop location overlooks the Bikan area. Meals are available.

Young Inn Kurashiki (☎ 425-3411; info@kurashiki .jp; 1-14-8 Achi; s/tw with shared bathroom ¥4200/7350; P ✗ ✗ ▣) The Young Inn has bunk-bed rooms, a large dining area and free Internet access. The hallways are a little tatty, but the rooms are clean.

MIDRANGE

Tokusan Kan (☎ 425-3056; www.tokusankan.com in Japanese; 6-21 Honmachi; s/tw with 2 meals & shared bathroom

¥7000/14,000; P ✗) This place is convenient for all the sights, but the rooms are small.

Kamoi Minshuku (☎ 422-4898; www.kamoi-jp.biz/ in Japanese; 1-24 Honmachi; s/tw with 2 meals & shared bathroom ¥6300/12,600; P ✗) Easy to find at the bottom of the steps to Achi-jinja, this place is very quiet and well managed.

Kurashiki Sakura Stay (☎ 435-7001; www.sakura stay.jp; 1-9-4 Chūō; s/tw ¥6300/10500; P ✗) This very white hotel, five minutes west of the canal, doubles as a wedding centre. The rooms are all Western style and have a minimal but clean feel. This is a good alternative to a business hotel in this range.

Kurashiki Kokusai Hotel (☎ 422-5141; www .kurashiki-kokusai-hotel.co.jp; 1-44-1 Chūō; s/tw from ¥9450/14700; P ✗ ✗) The original woodwork, tiles and murals of this spacious hotel will delight '60s design buffs. East-facing rooms have fine views of the Ōhara Museum and its gardens.

TOP END

Ryokan Kurashiki (☎ 422-0730; www.ryokan-kurashiki .jp; 4-1 Honmachi; s/tw with 2 meals from ¥20,000/40,000;

WESTERN HONSHŪ

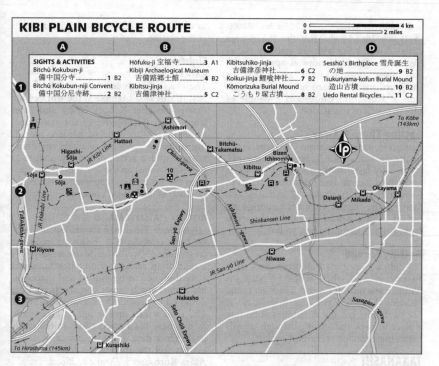

KIBI PLAIN BICYCLE ROUTE

SIGHTS & ACTIVITIES	Hôfuku-ji 宝福寺..............**3** A1
Bitchū Kokubun-ji	Kibiji Archaelogical Museum
備中国分寺............**1** B2	吉備路郷土館............**4** B2
Bitchū Kokubun-niji Convent	Kibitsu-jinja
備中国分尼寺跡....**2** B2	吉備津神社............**5** C2

Kibitsuhiko-jinja	Sesshū's Birthplace 雪舟誕生
吉備津彦神社............**6** C2	の地............**9** B2
Koikui-jinja 鯉喰神社....**7** B2	Tsukuriyama-kofun Burial Mound
Kōmorizuka Burial Mound	造山古墳............**10** B2
こうもり塚古墳............**8** B2	Uedo Rental Bicycles....**11** C2

P **X**) With views overlooking the canal, professional service and vast rooms, this is the best ryokan in Kurashiki. Some rooms have their own bathroom. The Terrance de Ryokan Kurashiki serves delicious green tea and local sweets in a room overlooking a garden.

Ryokan Tsurugata (☎ 424-1635; www.mmd.co.jp/tsurugata in Japanese; 1-3-15 Chūō; s/tw from ¥15,000/30,000; **P** **X**) Also by the canal, the Tsurugata (built in 1744) loses some of its charm in weekend wedding crowds. Still, the building and garden are impressive. The ryokan's restaurant serves nonguests, mainly at lunch time, and there's also a café.

Eating

Kamoi Restaurant (☎ 422-0606; 1-3-17 Chūō; dishes ¥500-2000; ☽ 10am-6pm Thu-Tue) The canalside Kamoi serves Japanese noodle dishes from a photo menu. Service is efficient.

Kana Izumi (☎ 421-7254; 8-33 Honmachi; dishes ¥500-2000; ☽ 11am-7.30pm Tue-Sun) Freshly made udon noodles are served in this modern restaurant just back from the canal. Meals are displayed in the window.

Tsuneya (☎ 427-7111; 3-12 Honmachi; dishes ¥600-3000; ☽ lunch & dinner Thu-Tue) This is a welcoming place specialising in *sumibiyaki* (charcoal-grilled dishes). It has a photo menu.

Mamakari-tei (☎ 427-7112; 3-12 Honmachi; dishes ¥600-3500; ☽ lunch & dinner Tue-Sun) Not far from the Ryokan Kurashiki, this is a cosy, traditional spot named after and famed for the local sardine-like fish it serves up daily (both raw and cooked). If you're not a sardine lover, try the *tōfu manjū* (fried tofu patties).

Kiyu-tei (☎ 422-5140; 1-2-20 Chūō; dishes ¥800-4000; ☽ 11.30am-8.30pm Tue-Sun) This is an old-world steakhouse in a traditional Japanese house at the north end of the canal.

Drinking

El Greco (☎ 422-0297; 1-1-11 Chūō; coffees ¥450; ☽ 10am-5pm Tue-Sun) By the canal near the Ōhara Museum (you can't miss its ivy-clad walls), El Greco is a fashionable place for coffee and cakes. It has an English-language menu.

Coffee-Kan (☎ 424-5516; 4-1 Honmachi; drinks ¥500-1000; ☽ 10am-5pm Tue-Sun) This cavernous tavern beside the Ryokan Kurashiki is another great coffee spot.

WESTERN HONSHŪ

SWLABR (☎ 434-3099; 2-18-2 Achi; dishes ¥680-900; ☺ 11.30am-2am Fri-Wed) After the Bikan area closes down, relax with the good music at SWLABR. The food stops at 8pm, but the bar-lounge continues until 2am or 3am. It's the green weatherboard house on the east side of Kurashiki Chūō-dōri a couple of blocks south of the station.

Getting There & Away
Kurashiki, only 17km from Okayama, is not on the *shinkansen* line. Travelling westwards, it's usually faster to disembark at Okayama and take a San-yō line *futsū* (local train) to Kurashiki. The trip takes 17 minutes, and *futsū* run frequently. If you're heading east, get off at Shin-Kurashiki station, two stops from Kurashiki on the San-yō line.

Getting Around
It's only a 15-minute walk from the station to the canal area, where almost everything is within a few minutes' stroll. There are rental bicycles (¥350/650 per four hours/day) at the JR station, but the difficulties of finding a place to park and cycling through crowds mean that walking is the best option.

TAKAHASHI 高梁
☎ 0866 / pop 38,000
Built along the banks of the Takahashi-gawa river, this pleasant small town, midway between Kurashiki and the central Chūgoku Expressway, gets few Western visitors, even though it has a temple with a very beautiful Zen garden and is overlooked by an atmospheric old castle. It is a comfortable day trip from Okayama.

Orientation & Information
Bitchū-Takahashi is Takahashi's train station. The **tourist information counter** (☎ 22-6789; ☺ 8am-6pm Mon-Fri, 8.30am-5pm Sat, closed public holidays), in the bus terminal beside the train station, has some information in English as well as maps in Japanese. The Raikyū-ji temple is about 1km to the north of the station, on the east side of the tracks, though to get there you'll need to walk north on the west side and then cross over. Bitchū-Matsuyama-jō castle is about 5km north of the station, up a steep hillside. If you're not up to walking or cycling there, a taxi should cost about ¥1500. There are bicycles for hire, but opening times can be erratic,

so it's best to ask at tourist information or at the station.

Sights
RAIKYŪ-JI 頼久寺
The classic **Zen garden** (admission ¥300; ☺ 9am-5pm) in this small temple is the work of the master designer Kobori Enshū and dates from 1604. It contains all the traditional elements of this style of garden, including stones in the form of turtle and crane islands, and a series of topiary hedges to represent waves on the sea. It even incorporates the mountain Atago-san in the background, as 'borrowed scenery'.

BITCHŪ-MATSUYAMA-JŌ 備中松山城
High above Takahashi stands Japan's loftiest **castle** (admission ¥300; ☺ 9am-5pm Apr-Sep 4pm Oct-Mar), the 430m Bitchū-Matsuyama-jō. It's a relic of an earlier period when fortresses were designed to be hidden and inaccessible. Later, much larger constructions were designed to protect the surrounding lands. The road winds up the hill to a car park, from where it's a steep climb to the castle itself. On a dark and overcast day you can almost feel the inspiration for a film like Akira Kurosawa's *Throne of Blood*.

The castle was originally established in 1240 and in the following centuries was enlarged until it finally covered the whole mountaintop. It fell into disrepair after the Meiji Restoration, but the townspeople took over its maintenance from 1929. It was completely restored in the 1950s, and has recently undergone further repairs and additions.

OTHER SIGHTS
Takahashi has some picturesque old samurai streets with traditional walls and gates, mainly in the area around Raikyū-ji. Around 500m to the north of Raikyū-ji is the **Takahashi Bukeyashiki-kan** (高梁武家屋敷館; admission ¥300; ☺ 9am-5pm), a well-preserved samurai (warrior class) residence dating from the 1830s. If you walk up to Raikyū-ji, you'll pass the **Local History Museum** (郷土資料館; admission ¥300; ☺ 9am-5pm), which is a fine wooden Meiji structure dating from 1904. It has displays of items associated with the area's mercantile and agricultural past. **Ikegami Mansion** (池上邸; admission ¥300; ☺ 9am-5pm) was the house of a soya-sauce merchant who also had a love

of music. The house is full of his records as well as soya-sauce paraphernalia, and there's a small café where you can have tea and snacks. A combined ticket for all three sights is ¥700.

Sleeping & Eating

Takahashi-shi Cycling Terminal (高梁市サイクリングターミナル; ☎ 22-0135; 2281-3 Kobara Matsubara-chō; s/tw with 2 meals ¥6090/12,180; P ☒) This friendly place is a 20-minute bus trip from the JR station.

Midori Ryokan (みどり旅館; ☎ 22-2537; Sakae-machi 1337; s with/without meals ¥8400/4200, tw/16,800/8400; ☒) West of the station, this building has original features and large rooms with shared bathroom.

Takahashi Kokusai Hotel (高梁国際ホテル; ☎ 21-0080; www.tkh.co.jp/; 2033 Masamune-chō; s/tw ¥7350/14,700; P ☒) The Takahashi Kokusai is a bright, modern hotel with good-sized rooms and mountain views.

Getting There & Away

Although Takahashi is not on any of the regular tourist routes through western Honshū, it wouldn't take a great effort to include it in an itinerary. The town is about 50km north of Okayama and 60km from Fukuyama. It's on the JR Hakubi line from Okayama (¥820, 50 minutes), so a stop could be made when travelling between Okayama on the San-yō coast and Yonago (near Matsue) on the San-in coast.

HIROSHIMA-KEN 広島県

In addition to Hiroshima city's atomic bomb–related attractions, Hiroshima-ken prefecture has a number of other places of interest, including nearby Miyajima and its famed Itsukushima-jinja shrine, the quaint fishing village of Tomo-no-ura, and the natural setting of the Sandan-kyō gorge in the north of the prefecture.

SOUTHERN HIROSHIMA-KEN
広島県南部
Fukuyama 福山
☎ 0849 / pop 407,000
Fukuyama is a modern industrial city, and its convenient location on the Osaka–Hakata *shinkansen* route makes it a good jumping-off point for the pretty fishing port of Tomo-

no-Ura or for Onomichi, which in turn is a jumping-off point for the Inland Sea.

If you have a few hours to spend in Fukuyama, you can visit the art gallery and museum and the reconstructed castle. There's a **tourist information office** (☎ 22-2869; ☽ 8.30am-7pm) in the station.

Tomo-no-ura 鞆の浦
☎ 0849
The delightful fishing port of Tomo-no-ura, with its numerous interesting temples and shrines, is just half an hour south of Fukuyama by bus. Due to its central location on the Inland Sea, in feudal days the port played an important role as host to fishing boats that would wait in the harbour to determine the next shift in the tides and winds before heading back out to sea.

Pick up an English-language brochure at JR Fukuyama Station information desk before you go. The brochure details Tomo-no-ura's sights and contains a map; an extremely enjoyable few hours can be had on foot or by bicycle exploring the village. Rental bikes are available (¥100 for two hours) next to the ferry building. To get your bearings, climb up to the ruins of Taigashima-jō castle.

If you set aside a day to travel from Kurashiki to Hiroshima you can spend a pleasant morning exploring Tomo-no-ura, get back to Fukuyama for lunch, and visit Onomichi in the afternoon before heading to Hiroshima.

SIGHTS

Up on the hill behind the ferry terminal, the **Taichōrō** (対潮楼; admission ¥150; ☽ 9am-5pm Tue-Sun) temple hall was built at the end of the 17th century to house a Korean delegation that would sometimes pay its respects. The view is quite lovely, and the resident attendant will happily show you the memorabilia on display.

A fascinating snack-food factory, **Uonosato** (うをの里; admission free; ☽ 9am-5pm Tue-Sun) processes most of the locally caught fish. You can watch the workers making prawn *sembei* (rice crackers) and *chikuwa* (ground-fish snacks), and you can even have a go at it yourself. You have to pay for what you make, but it's well worth it and great for children. There's a restaurant where you can sample the local noodles, *Onomichi ramen*. Tomo-no-ura is also famed for *houmei-shu*, a sweet

Chinese herb liquor. There are several places where you can sample it in the cluster of houses and museums a couple of blocks back from the waterfront.

SLEEPING & EATING

Kokuminshukusha Sensui-jima (国民宿舎仙酔島; ☎ 70-5050; 3373-2 Ushirogi Tomo-chō; s/tw with 2 meals & shared bathroom from ¥7665/15,330; P ✗), Right in front of the beach and boasting sea views, this is the most reasonable accommodation on nearby Sensui-jima island. There are Japanese- and Western-style rooms.

Tomo Seaside Hotel (鞆シーサイドホテル; ☎ 83-5111; 555 Tomo Tomo-chō; s/tw with 2 meals from ¥7350/14,700; P ✗) Close to the sights on the mainland and with great views, this hotel is a little run down but reasonable value. All rooms are Japanese style with their own bathroom, and the hotel also has a rooftop bath.

Keishokan Sazanamitei (景勝館三連亭; ☎ 982-2121; www.tomo-skole.co.jp/keisho in Japanese; 421 Tomo Tomo-chō; s/tw with 2 meals ¥16,000/32,000; P ✗) This is a deluxe ryokan with beautifully presented food. Japanese-style rooms, some with their own outdoor bath on the balcony, are all simply decorated. The cheapest rooms don't have sea views.

Sensui-jima island has a camping are and some quiet walking trails. Regular ferries to the island run from the harbour area (¥240 return, five minutes).

Chitose (千とせ; ☎ 982-3165; 552-7 Tomo Tomo-chō; meals ¥1000-3500; ✓ lunch & dinner Tue-Sun) This Japanese restaurant behind the car park next to the Seaside Hotel is popular at weekends.

Sensuian (仙酔庵; ☎ 982-2565; 555 Tomo Tomo-chō; dishes ¥580; ✓ 10am-6pm) Next door to Chitose is this tea shop, established in an old house. Sip some green tea and enjoy a sweet while looking out to sea.

GETTING THERE & AWAY

It's only 14km from Fukuyama to Tomo-no-Ura; buses run every 15 minutes from bus stop No 11 outside JR Fukuyama Station (¥530, 30 minutes).

Onomichi 尾道

☎ 0848 / pop 93,000

Onomichi is an undistinguished industrial town at first glance, hemmed in by the sea against a backdrop of hills, but it's in the hills that you'll find most of the sights. The

tourist information office (☎ 20-0005; ✓ 9am-6pm) is to the right of Onomichi station in the Teatro Shell-rune building.

SIGHTS

The Onomichi **Historical Temple Walk** takes in 21 important temples of the original 81. The tourist information office has a very detailed brochure in English about the temple walk and Onomichi. You can catch the **ropeway** (cable car; one way/return ¥280/440) up to **Senkō-ji-kōen**, which is covered with cherry and azalea blossoms in spring. Follow the paths on the way back down and take in the **Path of Literature** on the way. Many writers have visited and stayed in Onomichi, and there are stone memorials to some of them. Once you're back at the ropeway, cross the street and head for the sea to reach the road that snakes around the waterfront. Down here is an old storehouse that's now home to the **Onomichi Motion Picture Museum** (おのみち映画資料館; admission ¥500; ✓ 9am-6pm Wed-Mon). It has an evocative collection of old movie posters, magazines and memorabilia from films made in Onomichi and overseas. *Tokyo Story* (1953) is the most famous movie filmed in Onomichi, and five-minute segments of the film are on show. It's intriguing to see what Onomichi (and Tokyo) looked like in the 1950s.

SLEEPING & EATING

Onomichi Royal Hotel (尾道ロイヤルホテル; ☎ 23-2111; www.kokusai-hotel.com in Japanese; 2-9-27 Tsuchido-chō; s/tw ¥5300/10,500; P ✗) The Royal Hotel is on the waterfront and has simple business-hotel décor and good views.

Hotel Alpha 1 Onomichi (ホテルアルファ1尾道; ☎ 25-5600; 1-1 Nishi-gosho-chō; s/tw from ¥5400/10,000; P ✗ ✗). In a quiet area close to the station, this hotel's rooms are a little dark, but the staff are pleasant.

Nishiyama Ryokan (西山旅館; ☎ 37-3145; 3-27 Toyohimoto-machi; s/tw incl 2 meals ¥15,000/30,000; ✗) A block before the waterfront, the Nishiyama features traditional interiors and gardens.

Uonobu Ryokan (魚信旅館; ☎ 37-4175; www.uonobu.jp in Japanese; 2-27-6 Kubo; s/tw from ¥15,000/30,000; ✗) Right on the waterfront, this grand, elegantly furnished place is renowned for its innovative and delicious food.

Gangiya (Gangi屋; ☎ 25-4255; 2nd fl, 1-13-3 Tsuchido; dishes ¥500-2000; ✓ 5pm-midnight Tue-Sun) With views of Onomichi's floodlit waterside cranes, this is the spot for a noisy drink and a Japanese snack. It's on the second floor above Café de Plage.

Yamaneko (やまねこ; ☎ 21-5355; 2-9-33 Tsuch-ido-chō; dishes ¥700-1000; ⏰ 11.30am-10pm Tue-Thu, 11.30am-midnight Fri & Sat) On the waterfront next to a lurid junk shop, this corner café serves modern Japanese food, pizza, pasta and a wide range of drinks. There's good music and sofas.

Casalinga (☎ 722-0035; 1st fl, 1-9-10 Tsuchido; dishes ¥1000-3000; ⏰ lunch & dinner Wed-Tue, closed every 3rd Wed of the month; ✗) For groovy Italian food, look for this place between the shopping arcade and the waterfront about four blocks east of the station.

GETTING THERE & AWAY

Onomichi is at the Honshū end of the island-hopping Shimanami-kaidō bridge system to Shikoku. As such it's a gateway to Inno-shima (p419), Ikuchi-jima (p419) and Ōmi-shima (p419).

The tourist information office can supply its curiously named *Setouchi Shimanami University Campus Map*, which is an English-language brochure and map of the islands and the bridge links to Imabari on Shikoku; it details Shimanami's '100 Places of Scenic Beauty'. The islands can be reached by bus or ferry from Onomichi.

The Shin-Onomichi *shinkansen* station is 3km north of the JR San-yō line station. Buses connect the two stations, but it's easier to reach Onomichi on the JR San-yō line and change to the *shinkansen* line either at Fuku-yama (to the east) or Mihara (to the west).

Mihara 三原
☎ 0848 / pop 81,000

Mihara is on the San-yō *shinkansen* line and on the JR San-yō line. It's a convenient ferry departure and arrival point for Setoda on Ikuchi-jima, for other islands of the Inland Sea and for Shikoku. The harbour is directly south of the station. There's a **tourist information office** (☎ 67-5877; ⏰ 8am-7pm Mon-Fri, 10am-6pm Sat & Sun) in the modern JR station.

NORTHERN HIROSHIMA-KEN
広島県北部
Sandan-kyō 三段峡

The Sandan-kyō gorge, about 60km north-west of Hiroshima, is an area that you could get lost in for a few days. A mostly paved

trail follows Shiki-gawa through an 11km gorge, providing visitors to Hiroshima with accessible, beautiful Japanese nature. The hike is very popular in autumn when the leaves change colour. Pick up a copy of Lonely Planet's *Hiking in Japan* for details.

Buses run from the Hiroshima bus centre to Sandan-kyō station (¥1400, two hours), at the southern end of the gorge. Trains also go to JR Sandan-kyō Station (¥1100, two hours), which is the terminus of the JR Kabe line.

HIROSHIMA 広島
☎ 082 pop / 1,144,000

A busy, prosperous and attractive city, Hiroshima will forever be remembered for that terrible instant on 6 August 1945 when it became the world's first atomic-bomb target. Hiroshima's Peace Memorial Park is a constant reminder of that tragic day and it attracts visitors from all over the world. Yet Hiroshima is a far from depressing place; on the contrary, its citizens have recovered from nuclear holocaust to build a thriving and internationally minded community.

The city dates back to 1589, when feudal lord Mōri Terumoto named the town and established a castle.

Orientation

Hiroshima (meaning 'broad island') is built on a series of sandy islands on the delta of Ōta-gawa. JR Hiroshima Station is east of the city centre and, although there are a number of hotels around the station, the central area, with its very lively entertainment district, is much more interesting.

Peace Memorial Park and most of the atomic-bomb reminders are at the northern end of the island, immediately west of the city centre.

Hiroshima's main east–west avenue is Heiwa-Ōdōri (Peace Blvd), but the busiest road (with the main tramlines from the station) is Aioi-dōri, which runs parallel to Heiwa-Ōdōri. Just south of Aioi-dōri, and again parallel to it, is the busy Hon-dōri shopping arcade.

Information
BOOKSHOPS

Book Nook (☎ 244-8145; ⏰ 1-9pm Mon-Fri, noon-6pm Sat; 🖳) This place has second-hand Western book bargains, a handy notice board, free

WESTERN HONSHŪ

HIROSHIMA

400 m
0.2 miles

JR Hiroshima

Sanyō Shinkansen Line

To Tokuyama (90km);
Kyūshū (200km)

To Mazda
Museum (4km);
Hiroshima

To Okayama
(160km)

Enko-gawa

To Ujina
Port (4km);
Hiroshima
Nishi Airport (4km)

Kyobashi-gawa

Kyobashi-gawa

Shukkei-en

World Peace
Memorial
Cathedral

Ebisu-dōri

Hijiyama-kōen

Shintenchi
Entertainment
District

Nagarekawa
Entertainment
District

Moat

Chūō-kōen

Moat

Jonan-dōri

Rijo-dōri

Aioi-dōri

Hon-dōri Arcade

Chuo-dōri

Fukurō-machi
kōen

Hiroshima Carp
Baseball Stadium

Heiwa-Ōdori (Peace Blvd)

To Central
Post Office (100m);
Ujina Port (4km)

To Hiroshima Youth
Hostel (2km)

Motoyasu-gawa

Aioi-bashi

Motoyasu-
bashi

Peace Memorial
Park (Heiwa-kōen)

Motoyasu-gawa

To Yokogawa
Terminus

Tenma-gawa

To Myajima
(20km);
Iwakuni (40km)

To World
Friendship
Centre (1km)

Ōta-gawa

It's behind Iyo Bank and the Yamaha music store near the Hiroshima Kokusai Hotel.

INTERNET ACCESS

I Love You (⊙ 24hr) This place is on the 6th floor of the building with a yellow sign down its side that's immediately to the east of JR Hiroshima Station, and in a second location near the Peace Memorial Park end of Hondōri Arcade. It provides Internet access, and free soft drinks, coffee and tea are available. The **International Exchange Lounge** (☎ 247-9715; ⊙ 9am-7pm May-Nov, 10am-6pm Dec-Apr) has free Internet access, and there are two (expensive) Kinko's branches in town.

MONEY

International cards are accepted on the 1st floor of the **Sumitomo Mitsui Bank** (Rijo-dōri), two blocks south of Aioi-Dōri. The central post office (right) changes money during the week, and at weekends the major international hotels have exchange services. The Hiroshima Rest House (see p408) has an extensive list of post offices that change

travellers cheques, banks that do cash advances and international ATMs.

POST

Central post office (⊙ 9am-7pm Mon-Fri, 9am-5pm Sat, 9am-12.30pm Sun) Near the Shiyakusho-mae tram stop. You can change money here between 9am and 4pm, Monday to Friday.

Higashi Post Office (⊙ 9am-7pm Mon-Fri, 9am-5pm Sat, 9am-12.30pm Sun) Near the south exit of the station, is more convenient.

Naka Post Office (⊙ 9am-7pm Mon-Fri, 9am-3pm Sat) Next to the Sogō department store.

TOURIST INFORMATION

There are two excellent websites about Hiroshima. The Hiroshima Convention & Visitors Bureau website, www.hiroshima-navi .or.jp, has extensive information on sightseeing, accommodation, and access to/from the city. Check out www.gethiroshima.com for good food and nightlife recommendations, and insights into the local culture not covered by the tourist brochures.

There are two **tourist information offices** (☎ 261-1877; ⊙ 9am-5.30pm) in JR Hiroshima

Station, one at the north exit and the other at the south. The English-speaking staff can make accommodation bookings. For the benefit of those arriving by sea, Hiroshima's port, Ujina, also has an information counter with basic information.

The most comprehensive information about the city and the island of Miyajima can be found at **Hiroshima Rest House** (☎ 247-6738; ⊙ 9.30am-6pm Apr-Sep, 8.30am-5pm Oct-Mar) in Peace Memorial Park, next to Motoyasu-bashi; pick up a Seto Inland Sea Welcome Card, which can get you discounts on all sorts of things in Hiroshima, Yamaguchi and Ehime prefectures.

The **International Exchange Lounge** (☎ 247-9715; ⊙ 9am-7pm May-Nov, 10am-6pm Dec-Apr; 🖳) also in the Peace Memorial Park, has information in English, newspapers and magazines, a library and a study room. The lounge is geared towards foreigners living in Japan.

Sights

A-BOMB DOME 原爆ドーム

The symbol of the destruction visited upon Hiroshima is the **A-Bomb Dome** (Gembaku Dōmu), across the river from Peace Memorial Park. Declared a Unesco World Heritage site in December 1996, the building was the Industrial Promotion Hall until the bomb exploded almost directly above it. Its propped-up ruins, floodlit at night, have been left as an eternal reminder of the tragedy.

PEACE MEMORIAL PARK 平和記念公園

From the A-Bomb Dome cross over into **Peace Memorial Park** (Heiwa-kōen), which is dotted with memorials, including the **cenotaph** that contains the names of all the known victims of the bomb. The cenotaph frames the **Flame of Peace**, which will only be extinguished once the last nuclear weapon on earth has been destroyed, and the A-Bomb Dome across the river.

Just north of the road crossing through the park is, for many, the most poignant memorial in the park – the **Children's Peace Memorial**, inspired by leukaemia victim Sadako. When Sadako developed leukaemia at 10 years of age she decided to fold 1000 paper cranes – an ancient Japanese custom through which it is believed that a person's wishes will come true. The crane is the symbol of longevity and happiness in Japan and she was convinced that if she could achieve that target she would

recover. She died before reaching her goal, but her classmates folded the rest. The story inspired a nationwide bout of paper-crane folding, which continues to this day. Strings of paper cranes from all over Japan are kept on display around the memorial.

Nearby is the recently relocated **Korean A-Bomb Memorial**. Great numbers of Koreans were shipped from their homeland to work as slave labourers in Japanese factories during WWII, and more than one in 10 of those killed by the atomic bomb were Korean.

PEACE MEMORIAL MUSEUM
平和記念資料館

The **A-bomb museum** (admission ¥50; ⊙ 9am-6pm Apr-Jul, 8.30am-5pm 1 Aug-15 Aug, 8.30am-6pm 16 Aug-Nov, 9am-5pm Dec-Mar), as the Peace Memorial Museum is commonly known, narrates the events preceding, during and after the atomic bombing of Hiroshima on 6 August 1945. For many it is an overwhelming experience and a potent symbol of the idiocy of war.

HIROSHIMA NATIONAL PEACE MEMORIAL HALL FOR THE ATOMIC BOMB VICTIMS
国立広島原爆死没者追悼平和祈念館

Opened in August 2002, **Peace Memorial Hall** (admission free; ⊙ 9am-6pm Apr-Jul, 8.30am-5pm 1 Aug-15 Aug, 8.30am-6pm 16 Aug-Nov, 9am-5pm Dec-Mar) is a contemplative hall of remembrance and a register where the names and photographs of atomic-bomb victims are kept, along with their memoirs. It was designed by architect Tange Kenzo, who also designed the museum, cenotaph and eternal flame. The A-bomb museum reflects on the impact of the bomb and the ensuing suffering. These memoirs vividly evoke the chaos that Japan was in at this time and the inhumanity perpetrated by Japanese military personnel against civilians. It's worth taking time here to get first-hand accounts of the aftereffects of the bomb.

HIROSHIMA-JŌ 広島城

Also known as Carp Castle, **Hiroshima-jō** (admission ¥320; ⊙ 9am-4.30pm Oct-Mar, 9am-5.30pm Apr-Sep) was originally constructed in 1589, but much of it was dismantled following the Meiji Restoration, leaving only the donjon (central tower), main gates and turrets. The remainder was totally destroyed by the bomb and rebuilt in modern reinforced concrete in 1958.

HIROSHIMA

'Nothing will grow for 75 years' went the rumours after the *Enola Gay* unleashed the atomic bomb on Hiroshima on 6 August 1945. For many around the world, the bombing is still a potent symbol of people's inhumanity, and even more so for the remaining 125,000 Hiroshima *hibakusha* (atomic-bomb survivors).

The youngest *hibakusha* is 59, in the womb when the bomb was dropped. About 5000 have died every year over the past 10 years. Looking at Hiroshima in 2005, on the 60th anniversary of the bombing, it's easy to forget that it ever happened. Who will tell the *hibakusha* story when the last of their number dies? School children are visiting the Peace Museum in Hiroshima in declining numbers. The Children's Peace Memorial, where thousands of paper cranes are sent annually in memory of leukaemia victim Sadako, has been set alight by vandals. Even though they were protected by a glass enclosure and were under surveillance, the cranes were set alight by a university student from Kōbe a few days before 6 August 2003. The student wished to express frustration over 'grim employment opportunities for university graduates'.

Economic realities and political ambitions are reshaping this most peaceful of nations. Until 2004 the Japanese prime minister would meet with *hibakusha* after the 6 August memorial service. This doesn't happen any longer, as many within the opposition and the dominant Liberal Democratic Party deepen and strengthen their arguments for the development of nuclear weapons in Japan.

As the voices of the *hibakusha* grow fewer, Dr Tanaka Yuki of the Hiroshima Peace Institute, a Hiroshima City Government think-tank, believes that the tragedy of Hiroshima is being discussed less and less, as it is thought of primarily as a nuclear tragedy. He says, 'All warfare is a crime against humanity. Hiroshima, apart from being nuclear, was also an air raid. Sixty-four cities, including Tokyo, were bombed during the Second World War in Japan, and bombing has been used in all modern warfare to some degree – from WWI to Iraq.' Dr Tanaka would like to see Hiroshima reinterpreted for future generations and put into a broader world context, so that it isn't relegated to the historical dustbin once all the *hibakusha* have died.

In a further effort to reinvigorate the antinuclear argument, there are plans for a People's Tribunal on the bombing of Hiroshima and Nagasaki (for details on that atomic explosion see p630), based on crimes-against-humanity trials in places such as Bosnia. As media saturation of modern warfare desensitises people to the realities of war, Dr Tanaka's concern and vision are timely – lest we forget.

SHUKKEI-EN 縮景園

Modelled after Xi Hu (West Lake) in Hangzhou, China, **Shukkei-en** (admission ¥250; 🕙 9am-6pm Apr-Sep, 9am-5pm Oct-Mar) dates from 1620 but it was severely damaged by the bomb. The garden's name literally means 'shrunk' or 'contracted view', and it attempts to re-create grand vistas in miniature. It may not be one of Japan's celebrated classic gardens, but it makes for a pleasant stroll. It's west of the station.

Next to the garden is the splendid **Hiroshima Prefectural Art Museum** (admission ¥500, combined ticket with museum ¥600; 🕙 9am-5pm Tue-Sun, 9am-7pm Sat), featuring Salvador Dali's *Dream of Venus* and the artwork of Hirayama Ikuo, who was in the city during the bombing. Enter the garden through the museum.

OTHER SIGHTS

Hijiyama-kōen, noted for its cherry blossoms in spring, lies directly south of JR Hiroshima Station and is home to two worthy attractions. The **Hiroshima City Museum of Contemporary Art** (admission ¥320; 🕙 10am-5pm Tue-Sun) has excellent displays by modern Japanese and international artists, while the **Hiroshima City Manga Library** (admission free; 🕙 10am-5pm Tue-Sun) is a small comic-book museum.

The **Hiroshima Museum of Art** (admission ¥1000; 🕙 9am-5pm) is in an interesting 1970s building built by the Hiroshima Bank, and the **Hiroshima Children's Museum** (Planetarium; museum free, planetarium ¥440; 🕙 9am-5pm) is good fun for adults and kids. Both are in Chūō-kōen (Central Park), just southwest of the castle. The **Mazda Museum** (www.mazda.com/museum;

WESTERN HONSHŪ

⊗ 8.30-11am & 1-3.30pm Mon-Fri) is quite popular, as you get to see the 7km assembly line – the world's longest. If you feel auto-inclined, check out the details on the English-language website. Reservations are required; there is one tour in English daily at 1pm.

Activities

A love of **baseball** is not a prerequisite for having a great time at a Hiroshima Carp game. It's just as much fun watching the rowdy, organised enthusiasm of the crowd, especially when the Tokyo Giants come to town. The stadium is just north of the Peace Park, and outfield tickets start at ¥1500.

Miyajima (p412), 25km west of the city, can easily be visited as a **day trip** from Hiroshima. The tram company has a special one-day passport that includes a return tram trip to Miyajima-guchi, a return ferry to Miyajima and unlimited daily tram transport for just ¥840. You can buy the ticket at various big hotels, tram stops and at the Hiroshima Rest House information office (p408).

A variety of lunch and dinner **cruises** run from Hiroshima to Miyajima and back. On weekdays from March to September day cruises operate through the Inland Sea.

Festivals & Events

On 6 August, the anniversary of the atomic bombing, a **memorial service** is held in Peace Memorial Park and thousands of paper lanterns for the souls of the dead are floated down the Ōta-gawa from in front of the A-Bomb Dome.

Sleeping

BUDGET

Hiroshima Youth Hostel (広島ユースホステル; ☎ 221-5343; www.ttec.co.jp/~hyh; 1-13-6 Ushita Shinmachi Higashi-ku; dm ¥2440; P ⊗) This place is very out of the way and basic, but meals are available. Save the bus fare, though, and stay at the Aster Plaza (right).

Minshuku Ikedaya (☎ 231-3329; k.ikeda@ccv.ne.jp; 6-36 Dobashi-chō, Naka-ku; s/tw with shared bathroom ¥4200/8400) Convenient, quiet and set up to cater to foreigners, this place has Japanese- or Western-style rooms, and bathrooms are in the annexe across the street. There are no meals, but there are toast-, tea- and coffee-making facilities.

World Friendship Center (☎ 503-3191; www.wfc hiroshima.net; 8-10 Higashi Kannon-machi Nishi-ku; s/tw with breakfast & shared bathroom ¥3620/7000; P ⊗ ⊗) Run by an antinuclear nonprofit organisation, the World Friendship Center has three bright Japanese-style rooms, a TV lounge area and the *International Herald Tribune*. The tourist information offices (p407) can supply a brochure and instructions on how to get there.

Aster Plaza International Youth House (☎ 247-8700; 4-17 Kako-machi Naka-ku; s/tw ¥3620/6260; P ⊗) This municipal cultural centre, a block south of the Peace Park, is the best value in Hiroshima. The mainly Western-style rooms have en-suite bathrooms. There's a midnight curfew.

MIDRANGE

Hotel Yamato (☎ 263-6222; 10-11 Matsubara-chō Minami-ku; s/tw from ¥5300/9600; ⊗) Overlooking the Enkō-gawa, the Yamato has simple, dark rooms.

Hotel Sun Palace (☎ 264-6111; fax 082-261-3000; 10-12 Matsubara-chō Minami-ku; s/tw from ¥4900/8000; ⊗) Right next door to the Yamato, this hotel is in a similar range.

Hiroshima Ekimae Green Hotel (☎ 264-3939; www.ekimae-green.com in Japanese; 10-27 Matsubara-chō Minami-ku; s/tw ¥5980/11,340; P ⊗). This is the most welcoming of the station hotels. A mini-business centre, including a laundry, a photocopier and a fax, is on the premises.

Hotel Hokke Club Hiroshima (☎ 248-3371; www.hokke.co.jp in Japanese; 7-7 Naka-machi Naka-ku; s/tw ¥7140/12,600; P ⊗) Two blocks east of the Motoyasu-gawa and five minutes' walk from the Peace Park, this modern hotel has two restaurants and cheerful staff.

Hotel Sunroute Hiroshima (☎ 249-3600; www .sunroute-hiroshima.com in Japanese; 3-3-1 Otemachi Naka-ku; s/tw from ¥8925/15,750; ⌨) Quiet west-facing rooms here have views of the Peace Park. There's a laptop computer with free Internet access in the spacious lobby.

Hotel Century 21 Hiroshima (☎ 263-3111; www .century21.gr.jp; 1-1-25 Matoba-chō Minami-ku; s/tw ¥9240/15,015; P ⊗) The Century 21 boasts large rooms; those at the back facing southeast are quieter. The Japanese restaurant on the 1st floor is open all day.

TOP END

Sera Bekkan (☎ 248-2251; www.yado.to in Japanese; 4-20 Mikawa-chō Naka-ku; s/tw ¥7350/14,700, with 2 meals ¥10,500/21,000; P ⊗) A popular traditional ryokan near Fukurō-machi-kōen, the friendly Sera Bekkan has rooms with en-suite bathrooms and a Japanese restaurant on the 1st floor.

ANA Hotel Hiroshima (☎ 241-1111; www.anah -hiroshima.co.jp in Japanese; 7-20 Naka-machi Naka-ku; s/tw ¥10,395/20,213) Rooms are wide but plain, and the café downstairs is a mellow place to start the day over a buffet breakfast.

Rihga Royal Hotel Hiroshima (☎ 228-5401; www.rihga-hiroshima.co.jp; 6-78 Moto-machi; s/tw ¥13,860/16,350; P ✿ ✕) There are professional service, spacious rooms and great night-time views at Hiroshima's tallest hotel, southwest of Hiroshima-jō. Ask for a view of the castle.

Eating

Hiroshima is noted for its seafood (particularly oysters), as well as *hiroshima-yaki*, a local version of *okonomiyaki* (egg-based savoury pancakes), made with *soba* (thin buckwheat noodles) and fried egg.

Okonomi-mura (☎ 241-2210; 5-13 Shintenchi Naka-ku; dishes ¥700-1200; ✿ 11am-2am) This is an amazing grouping of some 30 ministaurants on the 2nd, 3rd and 4th floors of the Shintenchi Plaza Building behind the Parco Department Store. All specialise in *hiroshima-yaki*, and the boisterous atmosphere alone is worth the visit. A few places have English menus and display photos of meals.

Kinchai-ya (☎ 247-6448; 2nd fl, Clover Bldg, 8-21 Nakashima-machi Naka-ku; meals ¥800-1000; ✿ lunch & dinner Tue-Sun) Organic buffet lunches in a sunny converted warehouse two blocks directly south of the Peace Park draw the crowds.

Suishin (☎ 247-4411; 6-7 Tate-machi Naka-ku; dishes ¥750-1500; ✿ 11am-9pm Thu-Tue) A great place to try *kamameishi* (rice mixed with oysters, prawns or eel) or *umezosui* (plum rice casserole).

Moon (☎ 241-7444; 2-6-26 Otemachi Naka-ku; dishes ¥500-1500; ✿ dinner) Japanese minimalism prevails in this softly lit old house. There's a broad bar downstairs and two other floors of intimate dining areas. If ordering proves too complicated, settle for a pre-dinner drink.

Tosho (☎ 506-1028; 6-24 Hijiyama-chō Minami-ku; meals ¥1260-6300; ✿ lunch & dinner) In a quiet wooden building overlooking a carp pond, Tosho has set menus of traditional Japanese food with complimentary coffee. The walls near the cashier area are covered with signatures from Hiroshima Carp baseball players. Follow the green-and-white signs from Danbara 1 chōme tram stop.

The Pacela building, next to the Sogō Department Store, has all sorts of eateries. Restaurants occupy the 7th to 10th floors; most have plastic replicas to help you choose.

Tandoor (☎ 502-3371; 7th fl, Pacela Bldg, 6-78 Moto-machi Naka-ku; meals ¥700-1500; ✿ lunch & dinner Mon-Fri, 11am-9.30pm Sat & Sun) This traditional Indian restaurant has bargain lunch set menus during the week. It's à la carte only on the weekends, from a picture menu.

Hiroshima Andersen (☎ 247-2403; 7-1 Honōri Naka-ku; dishes ¥500-2000; ✿ bakery 10am-8pm, restaurants 11am-9.30pm) This place is famed for its 1st-floor bakery and 2nd-floor restaurants, which have a broad range of Italian, Chinese, Indian and many other cuisines.

Ristorante Mario (☎ 248-4956; 4-11 Nakajima-chō Naka-ku; dishes from ¥1000; ✿ lunch & dinner) Good, simple pastas and pizzas, quick service, a long wine list, and an English menu make Ristorante Mario a rather relaxing option.

La Liberte et la Paix (☎ 247-6747; 1-5-19 Otemachi Naka-ku; meals ¥1500-5000; ✿ 11.30am-10.30pm Tue-Sun) This is a very popular French restaurant in a convenient spot to have lunch before or after visiting the Peace Park. The lunchtime set menus are good value and there's a menu in English.

Drinking

Hiroshima has about 4000 bars. Shintenchi and Nagarekawa are the city's entertainment districts.

Mac (☎ 243-0343; 6-18 Nagarekawa-chō Naka-ku; drinks ¥500-700; ✿ 6pm-morning Mon-Sat) Much loved by resident gaijin, Mac has a wall of music that's testament to its dedication to variety.

Bar Alcoholiday (☎ 090-4659-9072; 3rd fl, Casablanca Bldg, 5-19 Nagarekawa-chō Naka-ku; drinks ¥500; ✿ 9pm-5am Tue-Sun) You can hear the karaoke wails as you approach this place, in a building crammed full of bars. Chie will be happy to serve you, particularly between 9pm and 10pm, when drinks are ¥100 off.

Opium (☎ 504-0255; 3rd fl, Namiki Curl Bldg, 3-12 Mikawa-chō; dishes from ¥500; ✿ 6pm-4am Mon-Thu, 6pm-5am Fri-Sun) Sip high-calibre drinks and people-watch in this cool bar. There's an English menu, and snacks, pizza and pasta dishes are available.

Getting There & Away

Hiroshima's main airport is 40km east of the city, with bus connections to/from Hiroshima station (¥1300). There are flights to/from all of Japan's major cities and some international flights. Hiroshima Nishi airport is 4km southwest of the city centre on the coast. It handles more regional services, and there are buses to/from the city centre (¥240).

Hiroshima is an important stop on the Tokyo–Osaka–Hakata *shinkansen* route. The trip from Hiroshima to Hakata (Fukuoka) takes 1¼ hours and costs ¥8700; to Osaka it's 1½ hours (¥9950), and to Tokyo 4¼ hours (¥18,050).

The JR San-yō line passes through Hiroshima onwards to Shimonoseki, hugging the coastline much of the way. The ordinary local services move along fairly quickly and are the best way to visit the nearby attractions of Miyajima and Iwakuni. Long-distance buses connect Hiroshima with all the major cities.

Hiroshima is an important port with ferry connections to other cities. The Hiroshima to Matsuyama ferry (¥2500, 2¾ hours, 10 daily) and hydrofoil (¥5800, 1¼ hours, 10 daily) services are a popular way of getting to/from Shikoku. Ferries also operate from Ujina port to Imabari on Shikoku.

Getting Around

Hiroshima has an extensive streetcar service that will get you almost anywhere you want to go for a flat fare of ¥150 (¥100 on the short No 9 route). There's even a tram that runs all the way to Miyajima port (¥270). If you have to change trams to get to your destination, you should ask for a *norikae-ken* (transfer) ticket. Pay when you get off.

Six rental bicycles are available at **Nippon Rent-a-car** (☎ 264-0919; 3-14 Kojin-machi; ☉ 24hr), four blocks southeast of the station. Bike hire costs ¥263/735 per two hours/day.

MIYAJIMA 宮島
☎ 0829 / pop 2,191

Correctly known as Itsuku-shima, Miyajima is easily reached from Hiroshima. The famous 'floating' *torii* (Shintō shrine gate) of Itsukushima-jinja is one of the most photographed tourist attractions in Japan – it's classified as one of Japan's three best views (the other two are the sand spit at Amanohashidate (p337), on the northern coast of Kyoto prefecture, and the islands of Matsushima (p463) near Sendai, in northern Honshū. Apart from the shrine, the island

has other temples, good walks and remarkably tame deer that wander the streets – watch for signs warning of the dangers of fraternising with horned species.

Information

There's a **tourist information counter** (☎ 44-2011; ☉ 9am-6pm) in the ferry terminal. Turn right as you emerge from the building and follow the waterfront to get to the shrine and the centre of the island's small town. The shopping street, packed with souvenir outlets and restaurants, is a block back from the waterfront.

Sights
ITSUKUSHIMA-JINJA 厳島神社

The **shrine** (admission ¥300; ☉ 6.30am-6pm Mar–mid-Oct, 6.30am-5.30pm mid-Oct–Nov, Jan & Feb, 6.30am-5pm Dec) that gives the island its real name dates from the 6th century (its present form dates from 1168). Its pier-like construction is a result of the island's holy status: commoners were not allowed to set foot on the island and had to approach the shrine by boat, entering through the **floating torii** out in the bay. Much of the time, however, the shrine and *torii* are surrounded not by water but by mud. The view of the *torii* that is immortalised in thousands of travel brochures requires a high tide.

On one side of the floating shrine is a **floating nō stage** built by a Mōri lord. The orange *torii*, dating from 1875 in its present form, is often floodlit at night.

The **Treasure House** (admission ¥300; 8.30am-5pm) has a collection of painted sutra (Buddhist scriptures regarded as oral teachings of Gautama Buddha) scrolls dating from the 12th century that is only rarely on display. The exhibits are perhaps of greatest interest to the scholarly.

TEMPLES & HISTORICAL BUILDINGS

Topping the hill that is immediately north of Itsukushima-jinja is **Senjō-kaku** (Pavilion of 1000 Mats; admission ¥100; 8.30am-4.30pm), built in 1587 by Toyotomi Hideyoshi. This huge and atmospheric hall is constructed with massive timber pillars and beams, and the ceiling is hung with paintings. It looks out to a colourful five-storey pagoda dating from 1407. Senjō-kaku should have been painted to match but was left unfinished when Toyotomi died (1598).

Miyajima has numerous other temples, including the 1201 **Daigan-ji**, just south of the shrine, which is dedicated to the god of music. The colourful and glossy **Daishō-in**, just behind the town, can be visited on the way down to Misen (see p414). This is a temple with everything: statues, gates, pools, carp – you name it. The rituals performed at the main Itsukushima-jinja are also administered by Daigan-ji. South of Itsukushima-jinja is the picturesque pagoda **Tahō-tō**.

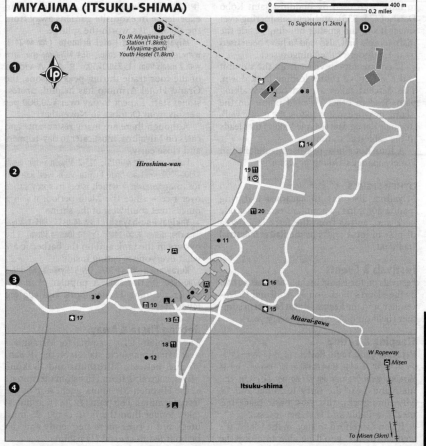

MIYAJIMA (ITSUKU-SHIMA)

MIYAJIMA HISTORY & FOLKLORE MUSEUM
歴史民俗資料館

Set in a fine garden, this **museum** (admission ¥300; 8.30am-5pm Tue-Sun) combines a 19th-century merchant's home with exhibits on trade in the Edo period, as well as displays connected with the island. There's an excellent brochure in English.

MISEN 弥山

The ascent of Misen (530m) is the island's finest walk, although the uphill part of the trip can be avoided by taking the two-stage ropeway, or cable car (one way/return ¥1000/1800). The cable car leaves you about a 20-minute walk from the top. There are monkeys and deer around the cable-car station. On the way up look for the **giant pot** said to have been used by Buddhist saint Kōbō Daishi (774–835), and kept simmering ever since! It's in the smaller building beside the main temple hall, also said to have been used by the founder of the Shingon sect.

There are superb views from the summit and a variety of routes leading back down. The descent takes a good hour. Walking paths lead to other elevated points on the island, or you can just follow the gentle walk through **Momiji-dani** (Maple Valley) that leads to the cable-car station.

A four-hour hike of Misen is detailed in Lonely Planet's *Hiking in Japan*.

OTHER SIGHTS

Miyajima also has an **aquarium** featuring 'panda dolphins', a popular beach, a seaside park and, across from the ferry landing, a display of local crafts in the **Hall of Industrial Traditions**.

Festivals & Events

Festivals on the island include **fire-walking rites** by the island's monks on 15 April and 15 November, and the **Kangensai Boat Festival** in summer (held on different dates every year).

Sleeping & Eating

Miyajima-guchi Youth Hostel (宮島口ユースホステル 56-1444; ww4.et.tiki.ne.jp/~miyayh/; 1-4-14 Miyajima-guchi Ono-chō; dm ¥2730;) On the mainland near the ferry terminal and JR Miyajima-guchi, this very basic place has meals available and Internet access.

If you can afford to stay on the island, it's well worth it – you'll be able to enjoy the island in the evening after the day worshippers have left.

Guest House Kikugawa (44-0039; www.kikugawa.ne.jp/; 796 Miyajima-chō; s/tw from ¥7140/12,600;) This charming inn is comfortable and tastefully decorated. There are eight Japanese-style rooms, and meals are available. The service is personal, and the manager speaks English. Note that weekend prices are around ¥1000 more per person.

Miyajima Mori no Yado (44-0430; Omoto Kōen Miyajima-chō; s/tw ¥5040/10,080;) Southwest of the shrine, this well-managed place has Japanese- and Western-style rooms. Dine in, as there are almost no restaurants on this side of the island.

Iwasō Ryokan (44-2233; www.iwaso.com/; Momijidani Miyajima-chō; s/tw with 2 meals ¥22,050/44,100;) The Iwasō offers a grand ryokan experience in exquisite gardens away from the throng. It's worth the splurge.

Miyajima Grand Hotel Arimoto (44-2411; www.miyajima-arimoto.co.jp/; 364 Miyajima-chō; s/tw with 2 meals from ¥15,750/31,500;) A victim of the tour trade during peak seasons, the Grand Hotel Arimoto has helpful, professional staff. Expect to pay over ¥20,000 per person from October to November.

Although there are many restaurants and cafés on Miyajima, most cater to day-trippers and close early.

Fujita-ya (44-0151; 125-2 Miyajima-chō; meals ¥2300-7000; 11am-5pm) Fujita-ya is well known for *anagomeishi* – which is eel in spicy sauce over rice – since the Meiji period; it's in a quiet street southwest of the shrine.

Yakigaki-no-hayashi (44-0335; 505-1 Miyajima-chō; dishes ¥700-1400; 10.30am-4.30pm) The oysters in the tank and on the barbecue are what everyone is eating inside.

Kurawanka (44-2077; 589-5 Miyajima-chō; dishes ¥700-1000; 11am-6pm) A popular *okonomiyaki* restaurant. Oyster, pork and egg are favourites.

Getting There & Away

The mainland ferry terminal for Miyajima is near Miyajima-guchi station on the JR San-yō line, between Hiroshima and Iwakuni. Miyajima trams from Hiroshima terminate at the Hiroden-Miyajima-guchi stop by the ferry terminal. The tram (¥270, 70 minutes) takes longer than the *futsū* (¥400, 25 minutes), but it runs more frequently and can be boarded in central Hiroshima.

From the terminal, ferries shuttle to Miya-jima (¥170, 10 minutes). One of the ferries is operated by JR, so JR passholders should use this one. High-speed ferries (¥1460, 20 minutes, eight daily) operate direct to Miyajima from Hiroshima's Ujina port.

Miyajima can be easily visited as a day trip from Hiroshima. See p410 for details of the Hiroshima tram company's good-value one-day passport.

Getting Around

Bicycles can be rented from the JR office in the ferry building, but walking around is quite easy. A free bus goes from Iwasō Ryokan to the Misen cable-car station.

THE INLAND SEA
瀬戸内海

The Inland Sea (Seto-nai-kai) is bound by the major islands of Honshū, Kyūshū and Shikoku. Four narrow channels connect it with the ocean. To the west the Kanmon-kaikyō strait separates Honshū from Kyūshū and leads to the Sea of Japan; to the south, leading to the Pacific, the Hoya-kaikyō separates Kyūshū from Shikoku; at the other end of Shikoku, the Naruto-kaikyō and Kitan-kaikyō straits flow each side of Awaji-shima.

The most interesting area of the Inland Sea is the island-crowded stretch from Takamatsu (Shikoku) and Okayama west to Hiroshima. There are said to be more than 3000 islands and islets, and there seem to be as many ferry services linking them.

There are a number of ways to visit the Inland Sea. One is to simply travel through it on the numerous ferries crisscrossing it or even running its full length. Alternatively, visit individual islands for a first-hand experience of a part of Japan which, though rapidly changing, is still much slower-paced than the fast-moving metropolitan centres.

It's possible to visit some islands by bus. There are now three bridge systems linking Honshū with Shikoku; the westernmost, known as Setonai Shimanami Kaidō, crosses 10 bridges and nine islands.

Information

Brochures, maps and general tourist information are readily available, but Donald Richie's *The Inland Sea*, originally published in 1971, makes an excellent introduction to the region. Although much of the Inland Sea's slow-moving and easy-going atmosphere has disappeared since this book was published (and indeed Richie emphasised its rapidly changing nature even at that time), it still provides some fascinating insights.

The Inland Sea section of this guidebook starts with its largest island, Awaji-shima, in the east, and then works its way westwards. Islands that are close to and associated with particular places on Honshū or Shikoku are included in those sections. For instance, Miyajima is included in the Hiroshima section and Megi-jima in the Kagawa section of the Shikoku chapter.

Getting Around

Besides the regular ferry services between Honshū, Shikoku and the various islands, **SKK** (Seto Naikai-kisen; ☎ 082-253-1212; office ⏰ 7am-9pm) offers day cruises on the Inland Sea from Hiroshima. The trips are seasonal, and lunch/dinner starts from ¥5000/7500 with cruise.

The Japan Travel Bureau (JTB) and other tour operators also run seasonal overnight cruises in the Inland Sea.

It's possible to take a ferry through the Inland Sea from Kansai to Kyūshū. Unless you check the times carefully, though, you may end up going through the Inland Sea at night, and if you just travel through you won't get a chance to taste the lifestyle on any of the islands. **Ferry Sunflower** (☎ 06-6572-5181; www.kanki.co.jp in Japanese; ⏰ ticket office 9am-5pm) has two daily Osaka–Beppu ferries, and **Diamond Ferry** (☎ 078-857-9525) has two ferries a day between Kōbe and Oita on Kyūshū.

AWAJI-SHIMA 淡路島
☎ 0799 / pop 161,000

Awaji-shima, the Inland Sea's largest island, forms the region's eastern boundary and connects with Honshū via **Akashi Kaikyō-Ōhashi** – at 3.91km, the longest suspension bridge in the world. Life on the island has changed considerably since the bridge opened, and Awaji-shima is now part of a road link from Kansai to Shikoku. At the southern end of the island, **Naruto-Ōhashi** spans the Naruto-kaikyō (Naruto Channel) across the well-known **Naruto Whirlpools** (see p578) to connect Shikoku with Awaji-shima.

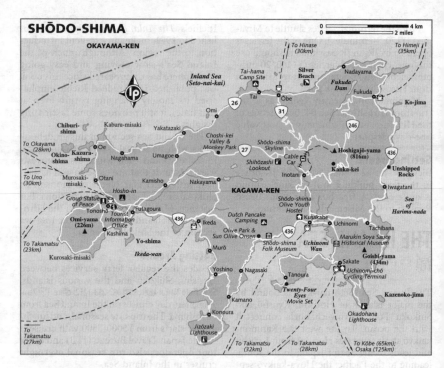

The northern part of the island will be long remembered as the epicentre of the massive 1995 earthquake that claimed over 6000 lives, mostly in and around Kōbe. The island also provided most of the material used to build the island in Osaka Bay on which Kansai's international airport sits.

The island is relatively flat and has some good beaches. It was the original home of *ningyō jōruri* **puppet theatre**, which preceded the development of *bunraku* (classic puppet theatre using huge puppets). Short performances are given several times daily in the small puppet theatre in Fukura, at the southern end of the island. Near the Kōshien ferry terminal, at **Onokoro Ai-rando-kōen** (おのころアイランド公園; admission ¥1200; ⏰ 9.30am-5.30pm Thu-Tue), there's a bizarre grouping of international sightseeing attractions constructed at ¹⁄₂₅ their original size. They include the Taj Mahal, the Parthenon, Pisa's leaning tower and other international favourites.

Sandy Ōhama beach, about halfway down the east coast, attracts crowds in summer; Goshiki beach, about halfway down the west coast, is better for swimming and known for its spectacular sunsets.

SHŌDO-SHIMA 小豆島
☎ 0879 / pop 35,000
Famed for its vast olive groves and as the location for the Japanese film classic *Twenty-Four Eyes*, Shōdo-shima translates literally as 'island of small beans'. A very mountainous island, it offers a number of interesting places to visit and makes an enjoyable escape from big-city Japan. The second-largest island in the Inland Sea, Shōdo-shima even has a miniature version of neighbouring Shikoku's 88 Temple Circuit. Administratively, Shōdo-shima is part of Shikoku's Kagawa-ken.

Orientation & Information
Tonoshō, at the western end of the island, is the usual arrival point from Takamatsu, Uno or Okayama and makes a good base from which to explore the island, although there are six ports with ferry connections to destinations here and there. At Tonoshō you'll find a **tourist information office** (☎ 62-5300; ⏰ 8.30-5.15pm) just inside the ferry build-

ing, with a very good English brochure on everything the island has to offer.

Coastal Area

Moving around the island anticlockwise, Shōdo-shima's olive-growing activities are commemorated at **Olive Park** (admission free; 🕙 8.30am-5pm) on the south coast, where there are fake Grecian ruins and olive chocolate for sale. **Shōdo-shima Folk Museum** (admission ¥310; 🕙 9am-5pm Tue-Sun, closed 20 Mar–5 May, 20 Jul–20 Aug & 20 Oct–23 Nov) is right there, as is the brand-new **Sun Olive Onsen** (admission ¥700; 🕙 noon-9pm Thu-Tue), featuring stunning views from a variety of baths, a restaurant and a training room. Shōdo-shima is serious about olives – it even has Milos in Greece as a sister island.

Cool off with a soya sauce–flavoured ice cream at the **Marukin Soya Sauce Historical Museum** (admission ¥210; 🕙 9am-4pm), between Kusakabe and Sakate.

Just north of Sakate is the turn-off to the small village of **Tanoura**, the site of the village school in the novel *Twenty-Four Eyes* and the later film of the same name. The real school and its movie-set version are both open for **visits** (combined ticket ¥750; 🕙 9am-5pm). A statue of the film's teacher and her pupils, known as the *Group Statue of Peace*, stands outside the Tonoshō ferry terminal.

South of Fukuda, on the eastern side of the island, huge rocks cut for Osaka-jō now lie jumbled down a cliff-side at **Iwagatani**. The unused rocks are classified as *zanseki* (rocks left over) or *zannen ishi* (rocks that were sorry not to be in time for shipment) and each bears the seal of the general responsible for their quarrying and dispatch. The northeastern corner of the island is still one big quarry. More unshipped castle rocks can be seen on the northern coast at **Omi**, along with the site of a shipyard used by Toyotomi Hideyoshi.

There are a number of swimming beaches around the island.

Central Mountains

The **Kanka-kei cable car** (one way/return ¥700/1250; 🕙 8.30am-5pm Nov-Feb) is the main attraction in the central mountains, making a spectacular trip up through Kanka-kei gorge. An alternative for keen walkers is a 3½-hour return trip climbing up the Omote 12 Views track and down the Ura Eight Views trail. From the cable car's arrival point at the top of the gorge, you can hike to the island's highest peak, Hoshigajō-yama (816m), in an hour.

As you descend on the road from the top towards Tonoshō, you pass **Choshi-kei Valley & Monkey Park** (admission ¥370; 🕙 8.10am-4.50pm), where monkeys from around the world are

---

NAO-SHIMA 直島

Nao-shima is a must see. The island is home to the **Benesse Island Nao-shima Cultural Village** (www.naoshima-is.co.jp/english), which features stunning art in beautiful buildings in a gorgeous natural setting. The project was started by the Fukutake Shoten publishing company to display its collection of contemporary art. Fukutake Shoten became the Benesse Corporation, and award-winning architect Andō Tadao designed its **Nao-Shima Contemporary Art Museum** (☎ 087-892-2030; Gotanji Nao-shima-chō Kagawa 761-3110; admission ¥1000; 🕙 8am-9pm). There are works here by Andy Warhol, David Hockney and Jasper Johns among others.

The opportunity to stay in an encampment of Mongolian *pao* by the sea at the **Nao-shima International Camp Site** (☎ 087-892-2030; s/tw ¥7350/14,700; 🅿 🐾) makes Nao-shima a rare experience. Meals are available at the camp site. There's also Benesse House and its annexe for upmarket accommodation – check out rates on the village website and preview each room and its own commissioned piece of art. The museum also restores and preserves old sites on the island; contemporary artists turn the sites into works of art that are then exhibited permanently. Three such sites have been completed for viewing. The **Chichu Art Museum** (admission ¥2000; 🕙 10am-6pm Mar-Sep, 10am-5pm Wed-Sun Oct-Feb) is another part of the complex. It houses some Monet waterlilies and some huge sculptures by Walter de Maria. Minibuses connect the sights, or you can hire bicycles and enjoy the scenery around the island.

Although it's much closer to Honshū, Nao-shima is officially part of Shikoku's Kagawa-ken. It can be reached from Takamatsu in Kagawa by ferry (¥510, one hour), or from Uno in Okayama-ken (¥280, 20 minutes). Uno is at the end of the JR Uno line from Okayama. Travelling via Nao-shima is a good way to get from Honshū to Shikoku, or vice versa.

WESTERN HONSHŪ

kept in cages. Wild monkeys come for a daily feed – they're used to people and will come right up to you.

Between Tonoshō and Otani is the temple **Hosho-in**, famed for its huge juniper tree, which is said to have been planted by Emperor Ojin 1500 years ago. The circumference of the trunk is 17m.

Shōdo-shima Pilgrimage

Shōdo-shima's 88 sacred places are known to Buddhist pilgrims as a miniature version of the Shikoku pilgrimage (p574). The pilgrimage covers 150km and takes about a week to complete on foot. Many of the sacred places are in secluded mountain settings that keen hikers will enjoy getting to. If you're interested you can call the **Shōdo-shima Pilgrim Association** (☎ 62-0227; ⏲ 8am-5pm in Japanese only).

Festivals & Events

The village of Shikoku-mura, in Yashima, just outside Takamatsu on Shikoku, has a village kabuki theatre that comes from Shōdo-shima. **Farmers' kabuki performances** are still held on the island on 3 May at Tonoshō and on Sports Day (around 10 October) in other centres.

Sleeping & Eating

There are a number of camping grounds around the island.

Dutch Pancake Camping (☎ 82-4616; ww8.tiki .ne.jp/~dpc-/Engframe.htm; 1869 Nishimura Otsu Uchinomi-chō; Ⓟ) This place is run by a Dutchman and his Japanese wife who are planning to build a pancake café on site behind the Sun Olive Onsen (p417). Prices and programmes are listed on the website.

Shōdo-shima Olive Youth Hostel (☎ 82-6161; www4.ocn.ne.jp/~olive-yh/index-e.html; Tonoshō-chō; dm ¥3700; Ⓟ ⊠ ✕) On the south coast, this hostel has meals available. It also hires out bicycles (four hours' hire is ¥500).

Uchinomi-chō Cycling Terminal (☎ 82-1099; 1834-15 Ko Sakate Uchinomi-chō; s with/without meals ¥5000/2700) At the Sakate ferry terminal, this place also hires out bikes – four hours' hire is ¥500, and it's ¥50 for each extra hour.

Tonoshō has a variety of hotels, ryokan and *minshuku*, particularly along the road running straight back from the waterfront.

Maruse Minshuku (☎ 62-2385; 5978 Ko Tonoshō-chō; s with 2 meals ¥5750; Ⓟ) This neat place next to the post office is easy to find.

Resort Hotel Olivean (☎ 65-2311; Yū-higaoka; s/tw with 2 meals from ¥18,900/33,600; Ⓟ ⊠ ✕). If you want something more upmarket, this place has it all and is a good place to watch the sunrise and sunset.

Getting There & Away

There are ferry services from Honshū and Shikoku to various ports on the island.

TAKING IT EASY IN THE INLAND SEA

If you want to experience the Inland Sea on smaller islands unconnected to the mainland by bridges, consider Shiraishi-jima and Manabe-jima (administratively, the islands are part of Kasaoka city). The starting point is Kasaoka, about 40 minutes west of Okayama on the JR San-yō line. It's only a five-minute stroll from Kasaoka station down to the rickety ferry terminal.

From there take a ferry to Shiraishi-jima (¥500, 35 minutes or ¥900, 20 minutes, nine daily), where the Okayama International Villa Group has one of its villas. The modern building is in an idyllic location with great views, and it has access to the beach, rocky coastline and hiking trails. The cost is ¥3000 per person per night for nonmembers. You can get more information and make bookings by contacting the organisation directly (see p397).

Next up is the ferry to Manabe-jima (¥450, 35 minutes), where the beachside **Santora Youth Hostel** (三虎ユースホステル; ☎ 0865-68-3515; www.oka.urban.ne.jp/home/suntora in Japanese; dm ¥2045) is set to take care of your every need. Meals are available at the hostel. Manabe-jima residents call their island *hana-no-shima* (flower island); due to its mild, frost-free climate a large variety of flowers are cultivated.

When you've had enough of island life, head back to Kasaoka or carry on to Tadotsu in Kagawa-ken on Shikoku by ferry. At the time of research, the only connections to Tadotsu were on Tuesday, Thursday and Saturday. The ferry company is **San-yō Kisen** (☎ 0865-69-7080). Should you be in need of accommodation in Kasaoka, **Kasaoka-ya Youth Hostel** (笠岡屋ユースホステル; ☎ 0865-63-4188; dm ¥3045) is an eight-minute walk from JR Kasaoka Station. Meals are available at the hostel.

Popular jumping-off points include Uno on Honshū (trains go to Uno from Okayama) and Takamatsu on Shikoku. There are high-speed ferries (¥1020, 35 minutes, 17 daily) and regular ferries (¥510, around an hour, 15 daily) from Takamatsu to Tonoshō.

Getting Around

If you've got plenty of time, cycling is a very enjoyable way to see Shōdo-shima. **Ryobi Rent-a-cycle** (☎ 62-5001; ◷ 7am-midnight) is inside the Ōkido Hotel on the right as you leave the ferry terminal; ask at reception. Bike hire is ¥1050 per day.

There are also bus services around the island and two daily bus tours from Tonohsō (¥3280/3980, departing 10.40am/9.40am) and one from Sakate (departing 1.20pm, ¥2500). If having your own car appeals, **Nippon Car Rental** (☎ 62-0680; ◷ 8.30am-6pm) is on the left as you leave the ferry terminal. Rates are ¥5500 for six hours.

INNO-SHIMA 因島

☎ 084 / pop 28,000

Inno-shima and the islands Ikuchi-jima and Ōmi-shima are now linked with Honshū and Shikoku; they're three of the nine islands crossed as part of the Setonai Shimanami Kaidō system. Famed for its flowers and abundance of fruit, Inno-shima is connected by bridge to Mukai-shima and on to Onomichi. The island has a moderately interesting **pirate castle** (水軍城; admission ¥310; ◷ 9am-5pm Fri-Wed) and, atop Shirataki-yama, there are 500 statues of *rakan*, the disciples of Buddha. On the first Saturday and Sunday in September there's the lively **Suigun Furusato Matsuri**, with boat races and *jindaiko* drumming.

IKUCHI-JIMA 生口島

☎ 08452 / pop 9,600

Ikuchi-jima is known for its citrus groves and beaches, including the artificial Sunset Beach on its west coast. It may not rival Hawaii's Sunset Beach for waves, but it definitely tops it in terms of summer swimmers.

Setoda, the main town on the island, is noted for the temple **Kōsan-ji** (耕三寺; combined ticket ¥1200; ◷ 9am-5pm), a wonderful exercise in kitsch. Starting in 1935, local steel-tube magnate Kanemoto Kōzō devoted a large slab of his considerable fortune to recreating numerous important temples and shrines, all in this one spot and all in grateful homage to

his mother. If you haven't got time to visit the originals, this is an interesting substitute.

Admission to Kōsan-ji includes the **Art Museum**, **1000 Buddhas Cave**, **Treasure House** and **Kōzō's mother's quarters**. The extraordinary 1000 Buddhas Cave includes an introductory 'hell', as well as winding tunnels and spiral stairs lined with 1000 Buddhas.

To get to the temple, turn right as you leave the boat landing then left up the shop-lined 600m-long street. The **Setoda History & Folklore Museum** (瀬戸田歴史資料館; admission free; ◷ 10am-4.30pm Sat, Sun & national holidays) is at the start of this street. Halfway up the same street you can turn left towards a temple on the hillside; around the back of this temple and much further up the hill is **Kōjō-ji**, dating from 1403, with a three-storey pagoda and fine views over the island. You can also get there by turning left from the pier (towards the bridge) and heading straight up the hill.

Sleeping

Setoda Shimanami Youth Hostel (瀬戸田しまなみユースホステル; ☎ 7-3137; 58 Tarumi Setoda-chō; dm ¥2700; P ⊠ ⊠) This is one of the island's two youth hostels.

Setoda Youth Hostel (瀬戸田ユースホステル; ☎ 7-0224; 668-1 Setoda-chō; dm with 2 meals ¥3885; P ⊠ ⊠) A short walk from the dock, this is easy to spot as it has a huge rainbow painted on one side.

Getting There & Away

On Honshū, ferries from Onomichi leave every 1½ hours (¥760, 35 minutes) and from Mihara every 30 minutes (¥750, 25 minutes). Other services are available. It seems a bit of a shame to do so, but yes, you can get to Setoda by bus from Onomichi.

ŌMI-SHIMA 大三島

☎ 0897 / pop 4,000

This hilly island boasts the mountain god's treasure house, **Ōyamatsumi-jinja** (大山祇神社; admission incl Kaiji Museum ¥1000; ◷ 8.30am-5pm), which commanded much respect from the Inland Sea's pirates between the 12th and 16th centuries. In fact, the pirates were more like a local navy than real pirates but, until Toyotomi Hideyoshi brought them to heel, they wielded real power in these parts. Along the way, what is reputedly Japan's largest collection of armour was built up in the shrine's treasure house. Around 80% of the armour and helmets designated as National Treasures are held there, but despite the importance of the collection, it's probably of more interest to those with a specific interest in Japanese military accoutrements than to the average visitor.

In an adjacent building known as the **Kaiji Museum** (海事博物館; admission ¥1000; 8.30am-5pm), there's a boat that was used by Emperor Hirohito in his marine-science investigations, together with a natural-history exhibit. The shrine is one of the most ancient in Japan, ranking with the shrines at Ise and Izumo.

Miyaura port is a 15-minute walk from the shrine.

Getting There & Away

You can get to Ōmi-shima by high-speed ferry service from Mihara (¥1150, 40 minutes) or from Tadonumi in Hiroshima-ken (¥290, 20 minutes). A highway bus links Ōmi-shima with Onomichi (¥1500, one hour) and Fukuyama (¥1700, one hour). The bus station is on the eastern side of the island below Tatara Ōhashi, the bridge that links Ōmi-shima with Ikuchi-jima.

YAMAGUCHI-KEN 山口県

Yamaguchi, at the western end of Honshū, straddles both the southern San-yō coast and the northern San-in coast. The great Kintai-kyō bridge at Iwakuni is a southern highlight, while Shimonoseki acts as the gateway to Kyūshū and Korea. The northern stretch includes the historically important town of Hagi and, in the central mountains, the vast cave at Akiyoshi-dai. Pick up a Seto Inland Sea Welcome Card at one of the information offices for discounts in Yamaguchi, Hiroshima and Ehime prefectures.

IWAKUNI 岩国
☎ 0827 / pop 110,000

The five-arched Kintai-kyō bridge is Iwakuni's major attraction, although the town also has a US military base (an 'unattraction' perhaps?) and a number of points of interest in the Kikko-kōen area, near the bridge. The main sights can be seen in a couple of hours.

Orientation & Information

Iwakuni has three widely separated areas. To the far west of the town centre is the Shin-Iwakuni *shinkansen* station, which is totally separate from the rest of town. Its **tourist information office** (☎ 46-0656; 10.30am-4pm Thu-Tue) is very helpful. In the central area is the old part of town with the bridge, the samurai quarter and the castle. There's a **Tourist Information Center** (9.35am-5pm) near the bridge. To the east, in the modern part of town, the JR Iwakuni Station has a helpful **Tourist Information Center** (☎ 21-6050; 9.30am-5pm Tue-Sun), as well as hotels, restaurants, bars and other conveniences.

At the bridge, the cable car can be seen climbing the mountains on the far side. The castle overlooks the town from the right of the cable car.

Sights
KINTAI-KYŌ 錦帯橋
Kintai-kyō, or the **Brocade Sash Bridge**, was built in 1673 and washed away by a flood in 1950. It was authentically rebuilt in 1953, with some cunningly concealed steel reinforcements, and rebuilt again in 2003–04. The bridge is immediately recognisable by its five steep arches. In the feudal era only samurai could use the bridge, which connected their side of the river with the rest of the town; commoners had to cross by boat. Today visitors pay ¥300 to walk across and back. The ticket office at the entrance to the bridge also sells an all-inclusive setto-ken ticket (¥930) covering the bridge (normally ¥300 on its own), the return cable-car trip (normally ¥540), and entry to Iwakuni-jō (normally ¥260) – a saving of ¥170 for all three. The bridge and castle are floodlit nightly.

SAMURAI QUARTER
Some traces remain of the old samurai quarter on the far side of the bridge. Beside the bottom of the cable-car route is the **Iwakuni Art Museum** (岩国美術館; admission ¥800; 9am-5pm Fri-Wed) with its extensive collection of samurai armour and equipment. It's said to be one of the best collections in Japan but is unlikely to impress those already suffering from artefact overload.

The old samurai quarter is now part of **Kikko-kōen** and includes picturesque moats and remnants of feudal buildings.

IWAKUNI-JŌ 岩国城
The original **castle** was built on the mountain between 1603 and 1608, but seven years

later the *daimyō* was forced to dismantle it and move down to the riverside. The castle was rebuilt in 1960 as part of Japan's great castle-reconstruction movement, but modern Japanese castles were built for tourism, not warfare, so it now stands photogenically high on the hill, in front of its initial hidden location. The well beside the path indicates where it was originally built.

You can get to the castle by cable car (one way/return ¥320/540), or road (for walking only) from beside the youth hostel. See opposite for details of all-inclusive tickets.

OTHER SIGHTS

Iwakuni is famed for its albino snakes, said to embody the spirit of Benzaiten, the goddess of good fortune. Visitors come here to pray for good luck in business. On the far side of the bridge, the **Imazu White Snake Viewing Facility** (今津白蛇弁財天; admission ¥100; 9am-5pm) has four of these strange-looking creatures.

Ukai (fishing using trained cormorants) takes place at Kintai-kyō every night from June to August, except when rain makes the water muddy or on full-moon nights. For ¥3500 you can watch this colourful and exciting method of fishing.

Sleeping & Eating

Iwakuni has places to stay on both sides of the river.

Iwakuni Youth Hostel (岩国ユースホステル; ☎ 43-1092; 1-10-46 Yokoyama; dm ¥2835) Close to most of the attractions on the west side of the Kintai-kyō bridge, this very basic hostel is in a beautiful, quiet area. Meals are available.

Hangetsu-an (半月庵; ☎ 41-221; 1-17-27 Iwakuni; s/tw with shared bathroom from ¥5500/11,000; P ☒). This clean, friendly place is on the east bank down the street continuing from the bridge; you'll see the traditional entrance a few blocks along on the left. There are also more expensive rooms with bathrooms. Meals available.

Iwakuni Kokusai Hotel (岩国国際ホテル; ☎ 41-1000; 1-1-7 Iwakuni; s/tw with 2 meals 15,750/31,500; P ☒) A homage to the '80s with a glass atrium, mirrors and ruched curtains, the Kokusai Hotel is on the east side of the river and has good views.

Shiratame Ryokan (白為旅館; ☎ 41-0074; www .gambo-ad.com/iwakuni/hotel/shiratame/info.htm in Japanese; 1-5-16 Iwakuni; s/tw with 2 meals ¥18,112/36,224; P ☒) Just in front of the east side of the

bridge, this ryokan has river views and well-presented local seafood.

There are no restaurants on the west side of the river, though you can have tea and snacks. On the east side there are a few places selling takeaway and Japanese food close to the bridge.

Midori-no-sato (緑の里; ☎ 41-1370; 1-4-10 Iwakuni; meals ¥730-980; 10am-6pm) Away from the crowds, a couple of blocks down the street continuing on from the bridge on the right-hand side, Midori-no-sato has set menus including *iwakuni-yaki*.

Getting There & Away

Iwakuni is only 44km from Hiroshima. Shin-Iwakuni station is on the *shinkansen* line, while JR Iwakuni Station is on the JR San-yō line. Kintai-kyō is about 5km from either. Buses shuttle back and forth between JR Iwakuni Station and the bridge (¥240), and between Shin-Iwakuni station and the bridge (¥280).

YAMAGUCHI 山口
☎ 083 / pop 140,000

During the Sengoku-jidai, or Warring States period (1467–1573), Yamaguchi prospered as an alternative capital to chaotic Kyoto. In 1550 the Jesuit missionary Francis Xavier paused for two months in Yamaguchi on his way to the imperial capital, but quickly returned to the safety of this provincial centre when he was unable even to find the emperor in Kyoto! In the following centuries Yamaguchi took turns with Hagi as the provincial capital and, like Hagi, Yamaguchi played an important part in the Meiji Restoration. Today it's a pleasantly peaceful town with a number of interesting attractions.

Orientation & Information

Ekimae-dōri is the main shopping street, running straight up from the station and crossing the main shopping arcade before reaching Rte 9. A very helpful **tourist information office** (☎ 933-0090; 9am-6pm) is on the 2nd floor of the train station, with English-language brochures and free Internet access.

Sights

XAVIER MEMORIAL CHAPEL
ザビエル記念聖堂

The **chapel** overlooks the town centre from a hilltop in Kameyama-kōen. Built in 1952

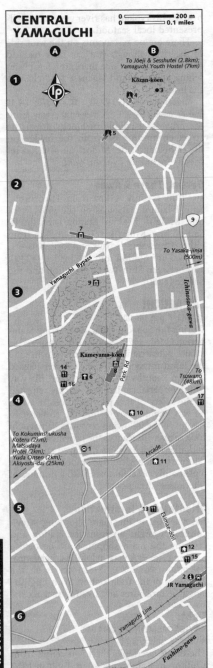

CENTRAL YAMAGUCHI

to commemorate the 400th anniversary of Francis Xavier's visit to the city, it burned down under mysterious circumstances in 1991 and was rebuilt in 1998.

ART GALLERY & MUSEUMS

At the foot of the hill stands the **Yamaguchi Prefectural Art Museum** (admission ¥190; ⌚ 9am-5pm Tue-Sun), where frequent special exhibitions are held. Just north of it is the **Yamaguchi Prefectural Museum** (admission ¥130; ⌚ 9am-4.30pm Tue-Sun). The **Yamaguchi History Museum** (admission ¥100; ⌚ 9am-5pm Tue-Sun) is just off Rte 9.

KŌZAN-KŌEN & RURIKŌ-JI
香山公園 瑠璃光寺

Further north again from the town centre is **Kōzan-kōen**, where the **five-storey pagoda** of Rurikō-ji, dating from 1404, is picturesquely sited beside a small lake. A small museum, **Rurikō-ji Shiriyokan** (admission ¥300; ⌚ 9am-5pm), has photos and details of all 40 Japanese five-storey pagodas, and a map indicating where they're located. It's illuminated at night. The temple **Rurikō-ji**, with which the pagoda is associated, is also in the park and was moved here from a small village.

The park's teahouse was also moved here; the Yamaguchi *daimyō* held secret talks in the house under the pretext of a tea ceremony. The park is also the site of the **Tōshun-ji** temple and the graves of the Mōri lords.

JŌEI-JI 常栄寺

About 3km northeast of the JR station, **Jōei-ji** was originally built as a house and is notable

WESTERN HONSHŪ

for its Zen garden, **Sesshutei** (admission ¥300; ⊙ 8am-5pm), designed by the painter Sesshū. Visitors bring *bentō* (boxed lunches) and sit on the veranda to eat, admiring the garden.

OTHER SIGHTS

Just west of the city is the hot-spring resort of **Yuda Onsen**; an eclectic mix of the traditional and the modern, it seems geared to the older tour-group 'onsen (hot springs)' set'. You can use the baths at **Ryokan Kamefuku** (旅館かめ福; admission ¥750); **Kokuminshukusha Koteru** (国民宿舎小てる; admission ¥350); and, for a taste of luxury, at the traditional ryokan **Umenoya** (梅の屋; admission ¥800). The town also has two *ashi no yu* (foot baths), where you can sit and bathe your feet for free. Buses run regularly from Yamaguchi station (¥190, 10 minutes).

North of Rte 9, the **Ichinosaka-gawa** river has a particularly pretty stretch lined with cherry trees. Naturally, they're at their best during the spring blossoming time, but they're also lovely on summer evenings, when large fireflies flit through the branches.

Festivals & Events

During **Gion Matsuri**, which takes place from 20 to 27 July, the Sagi-mai (Egret Dance) is held at Yasaka-jinja. From 6 to 7 August, during **Chōchin Tanabata Matsuri**, 10,000 decorated lanterns illuminate the city.

Sleeping

Yamaguchi Youth Hostel (山口ユースホステル; ☎ 928-0057; 801 Miyanoue; dm ¥2730) This place is about 4km from Miyano station (two stops east of Yamaguchi). Meals are available. There's free use of bicycles available and you can get a bicycle tour map at the hostel.

Sun Route Kokusai Hotel Yamaguchi (☎ 923-3610; www.hsy.co.jp; 1-1 Nakagawara-chō; s/tw ¥5193/10,395) Central to the sights in the middle of town, the Sun Route Kokusai has pleasant staff and simple rooms.

Yamaguchi Kankō Hotel (☎ 922-0356; 2-4-20 Eki-dōri; s/tw ¥4500/9000) Close to the station, the Kankō Hotel has a '70s feel completed by a photo mural. The Japanese-style rooms have shared bathrooms.

Taiyō-dō Ryokan (☎ 922-0897; 2-3 Komeya-chō; s/tw incl 2 meals ¥6000/12,000) On the shopping arcade just off Ekimae-dōri, the Taiyō-dō has wide rooms, and original '60s and '70s woodwork and furniture.

Matsudaya Hotel (松田屋; ☎ 922-0125; www.matsudayahotel.co.jp/in Japanese; 3-6-7 Yuda Onsen; s/tw with 2 meals ¥22,000/44,000; P ✗). Ichirō, the famed baseball player, stayed here when he was in town. The rooms and gardens are gorgeous, with service to match, and there's a great selection of dolls and ceramics for sale.

Kokuminshukusha Koteru (国民宿舎小てる; ☎ 922-3240; 4-3-15 Yuda Onsen; s/tw ¥5400/10,800; P ✗) Two blocks north of the main street, this is a good-value family-run place with Japanese-style rooms.

Eating

Yamabuki (☎ 922-0243; 7-24 Nakaichi-chō; dishes ¥500-1000; ⊙ lunch Mon-Fri) A few streets northeast of the arcade, near the crossing with Rte 204, is this pleasant *soba* shop where you can eat well for ¥500.

Shiva (☎ 932-4800; 2-6-26 Eki-dōri; meals ¥800; ⊙ lunch & dinner) This Indian eatery has lunch specials and a fully illustrated menu.

Frank (☎ 932-4836; Dojyomonzen; meals ¥700-900; ⊙ noon-midnight) About two blocks southwest of the arcade, this spacious café has sofas, drinks and good set lunches. Look for the red F.

Xavier Campana (☎ 923-6222; 5-2 Kameyama; dishes from ¥200; ⊙ bakery 9am-7pm, restaurant lunch & dinner) Great bread and European-style dishes make this a local favourite. It's below Xavier Chapel.

La Francesca (☎ 934-1888; 7-1 Kameyama; meals ¥1500-4200; ⊙ lunch & dinner) An Italian villa with a terrace, La Francesca has good food and professional service.

Getting There & Away

The Yamaguchi *futsū* service connects the city with Shin-Yamaguchi (¥230, 15 minutes). Shin-Yamaguchi is 10km southwest of Yamaguchi at the junction of the San-yō Osaka–Hakata *shinkansen* line and the JR Yamaguchi line, which passes through Yamaguchi and continues on to Tsuwano and Masuda on the San-in coast.

JR and Bōchō Kōtsū buses run to/from Yamaguchi to Hagi (¥1680, 70 minutes) and Akiyoshi-dai (¥1130, one hour).

Getting Around

Bicycles can be hired from the train station – a good idea, since the town's attractions are somewhat scattered (it's 8km up to Jōei-ji and back) and the footpaths are wide. The first two hours cost ¥310, or it's ¥820 daily.

AKIYOSHI-DAI 秋吉台
☎ 0837

The rolling Akiyoshi-dai tablelands are about halfway between Yamaguchi and Hagi on the northern San-in coast. The green fields are dotted with curious rock spires, and beneath this picturesque plateau are hundreds of limestone caverns, the largest of which, **Akiyoshi-dō** (admission ¥1200; ⏰ 8.30am-4.30pm), is open to the public.

Akiyoshi-dō is of interest principally for its size (the stalagmites and stalactites are not particularly noteworthy). In all, the cave extends about 10km, with a river flowing through it and a pathway that runs for about 1km. At the midpoint of the cave trail you can take a lift (elevator) up to the surface, where there is a lookout over the surrounding country. There are entrances to the cave at both ends of the pathway as well as at the lift. Buses run between the two ends if you don't want to retrace your steps.

The cave and tablelands are both pretty interesting, but they become less so if shared with busloads of visitors. If you're feeling

claustrophobic in the cave, go for a wander along the plentiful hiking trails on Japan's largest karst plateau.

Sleeping
There's a variety of accommodation around the cave area, but you'd probably be better off staying in Hagi or Yamaguchi and visiting Akiyoshi-dai as a day trip.

Akiyoshi-dai Youth Hostel (☎ 62-0341; www.jyh .or.jp/; 4236-1 Akiyoshi Shūho-chō; dm ¥2730; Ⓟ ✺) This is a large and somewhat institutional hostel. Meals are available.

Kokuminshukusha Wakatake Sansō (☎ 62-0126; Akiyoshidai Shūho-chō; s/tw with 2 meals ¥6720/13,440; Ⓟ ✺) This is a good-value place – take the meal option as, once the day-trippers have left, open restaurants are hard to find.

Getting There & Away
It takes around an hour by bus to reach the cave from Yamaguchi (¥1130; JR pass holders should take this bus) or Higashi-Hagi (¥1620, four daily). Buses also run to the cave from Shin-Yamaguchi (¥1070, 1¼ hours) and Shimonoseki (¥1730, two hours). If you've got a JR pass, take the JR bus from Yamaguchi.

SHIMONOSEKI 下関
☎ 0832 / pop 260,000

Shimonoseki is an important crossroads for travellers. At the extreme western tip of Honshū, it's separated from the island of Kyūshū by only a narrow strait. The expressway crosses the Kanmon-kaikyō strait on the Kanmon-bashi bridge; while another road, the *shinkansen* railway line and the JR railway line all tunnel underneath. If you really want to, you can even walk to Kyūshū through a tunnel under the strait! Shimonoseki is also an important connecting point to South Korea, with a daily ferry service to/from Pusan. The town has a number of points of interest and some excellent, if potentially deadly, cuisine.

Orientation
Beside JR Shimonoseki Station is the large Sea Mall Shimonoseki shopping centre, and just east is the Kaikyō Yume Tower, which looks like a midget skyscraper topped by a futuristic billiard ball. A ¥600 ticket to the tower gets you to the **observatory** (30th fl; ⏰ 9.30am-9.30pm), for a very impressive 360-degree view of the surrounding scenery.

AKIYOSHI-DAI

0 ▬▬▬▬ 400 m
0 ▬▬▬▬ 0.2 miles

Kokuminshukusha
Wakatake San-sō

Akiyoshi-dai
Youth Hostel

Lift

Outline
of Cave

To Hagi
(40km)

Entrance to
Akiyoshi-dō

Bus
Stop

Akiyoshi-dō
Tourist Centre

To
Yamaguchi
(25km)

WESTERN HONSHŪ

Information

There's a **tourist information office** (☎ 32-8383; ⏱ 9am-7pm) in JR Shimonoseki Station and another **tourist office** (☎ 56-3422; ⏱ 9am-7pm) in the Shin-Shimonoseki *shinkansen* station, two stops north of the JR station on the JR San-yō line.

Internet access and a small library are available at the **International Exchange Room 'Global Salon'** (⏱ 10am-8pm Tue-Sun; Internet access per 30 mins ¥100), on the 4th floor of the International Trade Building. (Shimonoseki was the venue for the 2002 International Whaling Convention – an interesting choice considering the city's history as a whaling port – and meetings took place in the conference rooms on the top floors.) There's an **Internet café** (per 30min ¥400) on the 1st floor of Hotel 38 Shimonoseki, which is about a two-minute walk from the station.

If you're arriving from Korea, note that there are no currency-exchange counters in the ferry terminal. The information office in the station can give you a list of international ATMs and places where you can change money.

Sights & Activities

KARATO ICHIBA 唐戸市場

A highlight of any trip to Shimonoseki is an early rise and a visit to the Karato Ichiba **fish markets**, although it's not recommended for squeamish types. The interesting stuff is on show from 4am to 8am, so if you like to sleep in, forget it. The markets kick off at 2am for those in the industry, but the public is welcome from 4am – the earlier you get there the better. It's a great opportunity to try sashimi for breakfast (in the restaurant on the 2nd floor), and the fish doesn't get any fresher – a fair bit will still be moving. People-watching is almost as much fun as goggling at the many different sea creatures.

The market is in Karato, halfway between central Shimonoseki and Hino-yama. The first bus leaves from outside the station at 5.55am (6.14am on Sunday) – it costs ¥190 and takes seven minutes. Organise a taxi if you want to go earlier. The markets are closed two Wednesdays a month.

Also in Karato, the **Kaikyō-kan aquarium** (admission ¥1800; ⏱ 9.30am-5.30pm) has stacks of impressive fish, shows, displays, a huge blue-whale skeleton and a special tank of *fugu* (see p427).

The Meiji-era former **British Consulate building** (admission free; ⏱ 9am-5pm Tue-Sun) of 1906 is close at hand. It has an interesting façade, and there's a small museum inside.

AKAMA-JINGŪ 赤間神宮

Bright vermilion, this **shrine** is dedicated to the child emperor Antoku, who died in 1185 in the naval battle of Dan-no-ura. In the Hōichi Hall stands a statue of the splendidly monikered Earless Hōichi, the hero of a traditional ghost story retold by Japanophile Lafcadio Hearn (otherwise known by his adopted Japanese name, Koizumi Yakumo; see p439). The shrine is between Karato and Hino-yama. Get off the bus (¥230, 10 minutes) at the Akama-jingū-mae bus stop.

HINO-YAMA 火の山

About 5km northeast of JR Shimonoseki Station there are superb views over the Kanmon-kaikyō from the top of 268m-high **Hino-yama**. Walk or drive to the top, as at the time of writing the ropeway was closed for repairs. Take a Ropeway-mae bus (¥360) to the Mimosusōgawa bus stop and walk up to the ropeway station, or take a Kokuminshukusha-mae bus straight to the bottom of the ropeway. By the Mimosusōgawa-kōen bus stop are lifts to take you down to the tunnel for your free 1km walk to Kyūshū. The **walkers' tunnel** is also the vehicle tunnel: walkers use the bottom third of the circular tunnel, while vehicles race along above. Bicycles and scooters use the same section as the walkers. It's a nice stroll around the seaside promenade on the Kyūshū side.

Over the road from the same bus stop is the Dan-no-ura Memorial, marking the spot where the decisive clash between the Minamoto and Taira clans took place in 1185. This is where one of the ladies of the House of Taira plunged into the sea with the infant emperor in her arms instead of surrendering to the enemy.

CHŌFU 長府

Chōfu is the old castle town area and, while little remains of the coastal castle itself, there are earth walls and samurai gates, along with a museum and some important temples and shrines. **Kōzan-ji** has a Zen-style hall dating from 1327, and the **Chōfu Museum** (長府博物館; admission ¥200; ⏱ 9.30am-5pm Tue-Sun) is also in the temple grounds.

Shimonoseki City Art Museum (下関市立美術館; admission ¥200; ⏰ 9am-5pm Tue-Sun) features contemporary Japanese artists.

Sleeping
BUDGET

Hinoyama Youth Hostel (☎ 22-3753; www.e-yh.net /shimonoseki in Japanese; 3-47 Mimosusogawa-chō; dm ¥2900; Ⓟ Ⓧ Ⓧ Ⓛ) Amazing views of the straits and relaxed service make this the best youth hostel in Chūgoku. You can take a Hino-yama bus from the station.

Kaikyō View Shimonoseki (☎ 23-0117; www.kv -shimonoseki.com in Japanese; 3-58 Mimosusogawa-chō; s/tw incl 2 meals ¥10,500/19,950; Ⓟ Ⓧ) Also at Hino-yama, Kaikyō View has great views and professional service. There are Japanese- and Western-style rooms, but the Japanese rooms have no bathrooms.

MIDRANGE

Shimonoseki Tōkyū Inn (☎ 33-0109; www.tokyu hotels.co.jp; 4-4-1 Takezaki-chō; s/tw ¥6825/12,075; Ⓟ Ⓧ Ⓧ) Beside the station, this inn has well-outfitted rooms with extras such as trouser stretchers for business travellers.

Shimonoseki Eki-Nishi Washington Hotel (☎ 61-0410; 1-4-1 Yamato-chō s/tw ¥5800/14,000; Ⓟ Ⓧ Ⓧ) This place is on the west side of the station with some good restaurants. Rooms are clean, but the singles are pokey.

TOP END

Shimonoseki Grand Hotel (☎ 31-5000; www.sgh .co.jp in Japanese; 31-2 Nabe-chō; s/tw ¥9240/16,170; Ⓟ Ⓧ) With a spacious lobby and good-sized singles, this place is close to the action of the Karato fish markets.

Eating

Head down to the combined Daimaru and Daiei department-store basements at the station as well as the Sea Mall Market in the huge Sea Mall complex, and check out the goodies and eateries.

The best spot for a raw-fish breakfast is the 2nd floor of the Karato Ichiba market. There are stalls in the markets at lunch time too, serving sushi and delicious deep-fried *fugu* for ¥500 a plate. Next door is the Kamon Wharf complex, which has more than 40 shops, the majority of them eateries.

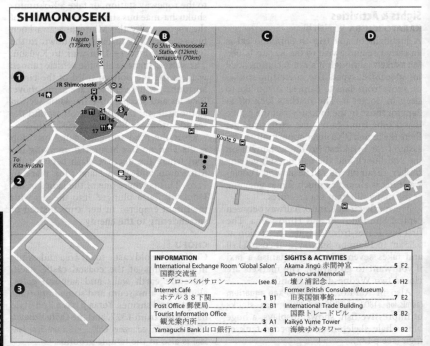

SHIMONOSEKI

DARE TO FUGU?

Fugu are known in English as globefish or blowfish, and you won't have to go to Karato Ichiba (p425) to see your first in Shimonoseki. The city revels in its reputation as the *fugu* capital of Japan, and paintings and sculptures of the fish are everywhere.

Eating raw *fugu* is considered somewhat adventurous, since the fish's liver and other organs contain tetrodotoxin, a poison that makes cyanide look like chicken feed. During the Tokugawa shōgunate and the Meiji Restoration eating *fugu* was banned in certain districts, and since 1958 only specialist chefs have been allowed to prepare and sell the potentially deadly fare. Only 30% of apprentice chefs who train for three years pass the test to get a license. Despite the precautions, every now and then people die – Kabuki actor Bandō Mitsugoro VIII, considered a national treasure, keeled over after a *fugu* party in 1975, but he had eaten four servings of *fugu* liver.

Fugu used to be a winter dish, eaten mainly between October and March, but it's now available year-round, thanks to *fugu* farms off Kyūshū.

Yabure-Kabure (☎ 34-3711; 2-2-5 Budendan; meals ¥800-10,000; ☽ lunch & dinner) Not far from the station, this is a relaxed place to try *fugu* with a range of set menus.

Kappo Nakao (☎ 31-4129; 4-6 Akamachō; meals ¥3800-26,250; ☽ lunch & dinner) In Karato, this is a sophisticated *fugu* restaurant with graceful service. The presentation and relaxed atmosphere are worth it even if you don't try the *fugu*. The set lunches are good value.

Getting There & Away

Shinkansen trains stop at Shin-Shimonoseki station, two stops from JR Shimonoseki Station. From Shimonoseki the bridge and tunnels connect roads and rail lines in Honshū with Kyūshū. Eastbound road users can take Rte 191 along the northern San-in coast, Rte 2 along the southern San-yō coast or the Chūgoku Expressway through central Honshū.

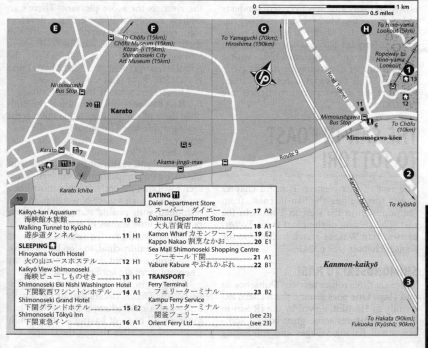

EATING 🍴	
Daiei Department Store	
スーパー ダイエー	**17** A2
Daimaru Department Store	
大丸百貨店	**18** A1
Kamon Wharf カモンワーフ	**19** E2
Kappo Nakao 割烹なかお	**20** E1
Sea Mall Shimonoseki Shopping Centre	
シーモール下関	**21** A1
Yabure Kabure やぶれかぶれ	**22** B1

TRANSPORT	
Ferry Terminal	
フェリーターミナル	**23** B2
Kampu Ferry Service	
フェリーターミナル	
関釜フェリー	(see 23)
Orient Ferry Ltd	(see 23)

SLEEPING 🛏	
Hinoyama Youth Hostel	
火の山ユースホステル	**12** H1
Kaikyō View Shimonoseki	
海峡ビューしものせき	**13** H1
Shimonoseki Eki Nishi Washington Hotel	
下関駅西ワシントンホテル	**14** A1
Shimonoseki Grand Hotel	
下関グランドホテル	**15** E2
Shimonoseki Tōkyū Inn	
下関東急イン	**16** A1

Kaikyō-kan Aquarium
海峡館水族館 **10** E2
Walking Tunnel to Kyūshū
遊歩道トンネル **11** H1

WESTERN HONSHŪ

Ferries run regularly from early morning to late at night from the Karato area of Shimonoseki to Moji-ko in Kyūshū (¥350, five minutes). From Shin-moji in Kita-Kyūshū there are ferries to Kōbe, Osaka and Tokyo in Honshū and to Matsuyama in Shikoku.

FERRIES TO KOREA & CHINA

The **Kampu Ferry Service** (☎ 24-3000) operates the Shimonoseki–Pusan ferry from the Shimonoseki International Ferry Terminal (Shimonoseki-kō Kokusai Taminaru), a short walk from the station. Head up to the **2nd floor** (⏰ 10.30am-5.30pm) for bookings. There are daily departures at 7pm from Shimonoseki, arriving in Pusan at 8.30am the following morning. Boarding time is between 6pm and 6.20pm, and one-way fares start at ¥6800 for students (¥8500 for an open tatami area), continuing upwards for cabins; there's a 10% discount on return fares. Return ferries from Pusan run to the same time schedule, leaving Pusan at 7pm and arriving in Shimonoseki at 8.30am.

If you need a visa for South Korea, arrange it before coming to Shimonoseki. There's a Korean Consulate in Hiroshima. This route is used by many long-term Western residents in Japan, so expect to have your passport rigorously inspected when you return to Japan.

Orient Ferry Ltd (☎ 32-6615) runs between Shimonoseki and Qingdao, China, with a set schedule of departures (generally twice a week). Call for exact dates and times; the cheapest one-way/return tickets are ¥18,000/34,200.

THE SAN-IN COAST TO TOTTORI

The rest of this western Honshū chapter covers travel along the San-in coast, from Shimonoseki in the west to Tottori in the east. The section of the coast from Tottori eastwards to Wakasa-wan is included in the Kansai chapter (see p334).

SHIMONOSEKI TO HAGI

There are three routes between Shimonoseki and Hagi. One goes around the western extremity of Honshū, served by the JR San-in line, and features some great coastal scenery, small fishing villages and interesting

countryside. **Ōmi-shima**, with its scenic, rocky coast, is immediately north of **Nagato** and connected to the mainland by a bridge. The island is part of the Kita Nagato Coastal Park, which extends eastwards beyond Hagi. **Ōmi-shima Kanko-kisen** (☎ 0837-26-0834) runs 1½-hour cruises (¥2200) around the island.

An alternative is to travel via the Akiyoshi cave and tablelands area (see p424).

The third option is to take the JR Mine line from Asa, east of Shimonoseki, to Nagato, and then take the JR San-in line to Hagi.

Tawarayama Onsen 俵山温泉
☎ 0837

This is a gem of an *onsen*, a fascinating backwater (literally) given over to *toji* (curative bathing). It's well off the beaten track, and very serious about its purpose: there are no karaoke bars, no *pachinko* (vertical pinball games) halls, no neon and no restaurants. Bathers come here for their health, staying for weeks at a time in the 40-odd ryokan. They bathe mainly in the two public baths, **Machi-no-yu** (町の湯; admission ¥340; ⏰ 6am-10.30pm) and **Kawa-no-yu** (川の湯; admission ¥340; ⏰ 6am-11pm). The latter, overlooking the river, is the more pleasant. There's an endless supply of lifelong *onsen* devotees wandering down the narrow main street in their *yukata* (summer kimonos). If you're looking for a place to stay while in town, the popular **Izumiya** (泉屋; ☎ 29-0231; s/tw incl 2 meals ¥8400/16,800; Ⓟ 🍴) has a huge garden.

About 2km west of the *onsen* village is the **Mara Kannon** temple. Kannon is the Buddhist deity of compassion, while *mara* is the most graphic word imaginable for the male procreative organ, somewhere off the vulgar scale beyond 'knob end'. Put the two together, and you've this astonishing little temple asking for compassion for knob ends that aren't working properly. It looks more like a garden shed than a place of worship, and it's festooned with phallic statuary. Worshippers bring little statues of erect penises and write their wishes on the sides of them – to produce a healthy child, to stop bed wetting, to undergo a desired size change and so on. These missives are left before Kannon.

The guy in the souvenir shop in Tawarayama Onsen swears that he personally knows of a case where a couple who had given up all hope of having a baby rapidly produced one after visiting the temple.

There are so many little phallic statues at the temple that they have a separate little building out the back to house the overflow. On 1 May it's the scene of a highly photographic fertility rite, the **Mara Kannon Matsuri**. Call the ryokan and check the date – sometimes it's on the 3rd.

Take the JR Mine line from Asa to the south, or Nagato to the north, to Nagato-Yumoto. Buses run from there up to Tawarayama Onsen (¥550, 20 minutes). There's also a direct bus from Shimonoseki (¥1610, two hours).

HAGI 萩
☎ 0838 / pop 45,000

Hagi has an interesting combination of temples and shrines, a fascinating old samurai quarter, some picturesque castle ruins and fine coastal views. The town also has important historical connections with the events of the Meiji Restoration. It's ironic that Hagi's claim to fame is its role in propelling Japan directly from the feudal to the modern era, while its attractions are principally its feudal past. Hagi is also noted for its fine ceramics.

History

Hagi in Honshū and Kagoshima in Kyūshū were the two centres of unrest that played major parts in the events leading up to the Meiji Restoration. Japan's long period of isolation from the outside world under the Tokugawa rule had, by about the mid-19th century, created tensions approaching breaking point. The rigid stratification of society had resulted in an oppressed peasantry, while the progressive elements of the nobility realised that Japan had slipped far behind the rapidly industrialising European nations and the USA. The arrival of Commodore Perry brought matters to a humiliating head, as the 'barbarians' simply dictated their terms to the helpless Japanese.

Japan could not stand up against the West if it did not adopt Western technology, and this essential modernisation could not take place under the feudal shōgunate. Restoring the emperor to power, even if only as a figurehead, was the route the progressive samurai chose, and Yoshida Shōin of Hagi was one of the leaders in this movement. On the surface he was also a complete failure. In 1854, in order to study first hand the ways of the West, he attempted to leave

Japan on Perry's ship, only to be handed over to the authorities and imprisoned in Edo (Tokyo).

When he returned to Hagi he hatched a plot to kill a shōgunate official, but he talked about it so much that word leaked out to his enemies. He was arrested again and, in 1859, at the age of 29, he was executed. Fortunately, while Yoshida was a failure when it came to action, he was a complete success when it came to inspiration, and in 1865 his followers led a militia of peasants and samurai that overturned the Chōshū government of Hagi. The Western powers supported the new blood in Hagi and Kagoshima, and when the shōgunate army moved against the new government in Hagi, it was defeated. That the downfall of the shōgunate came at the hands of an army of not just samurai but also peasants was further proof of the changes taking place.

In late 1867 the forces of Kagoshima and Hagi routed the shōgunate, and the emperor was restored to nominal power. In early 1868 the capital was shifted from Kyoto to Tokyo, as Edo soon became known. To this day Hagi remains an important site for visitors interested in the history of modern Japan, and Yoshida Shōin lives on at the Shōin-jinja (p432).

Orientation & Information

Hagi consists of three parts. Western and central Hagi are effectively an island created by the Hashimoto-gawa and Matsumoto-gawa rivers; eastern Hagi (with the major JR station Higashi-Hagi) lies on the eastern bank of the Matsumoto-gawa. Get off at JR Higashi-Hagi for the main sights of the city.

The main road through central Hagi starts from JR Hagi Station and runs north, past the bus station in the centre of town. There's a wide variety of shops along Tamachi arcade, close to the bus station. West of this central area is the old samurai quarter of Jōkamachi, with its picturesque streets and interesting old buildings. More such buildings can be found in Horiuchi to the northwest and Teramachi to the northeast of Jōkamachi.

Hagi's **tourist information office** (☎ 25-3145; ⏱ 9am-5pm, closed 12-1pm) is just beside the Higashi-Hagi station. Pick up the concise but informative English-language *Hagi Sightseeing Guide* (¥200).

HAGI

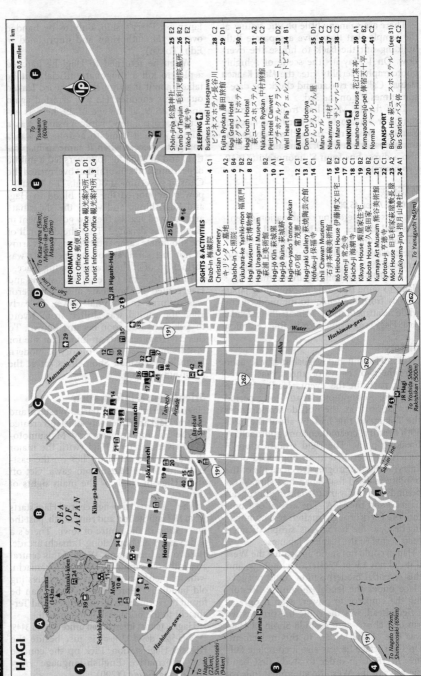

INFORMATION	
Post Office 郵便局	1 D1
Tourist Information Office 観光案内所	2 D1
Tourist Information Office 観光案内所	3 C4

SIGHTS & ACTIVITIES	
Baizō-in 梅蔵院	4 C1
Christian Cemetery キリシタン墓地	5 A2
Daishō-in 大照院	6 B4
Fukuhara-ke Yashiki-mon 福原門	7 B2
Hagi Museum 萩博物館	8 B2
Hagi Uragami Museum 萩浦上美術館	9 B2
Hagi-jō Kiln 萩城窯	10 A1
Hagi-jō Ruins 萩城跡	11 A1
Hagi-no-yado Tomoe Ryokan 萩の宿 常茂恵	12 C1
Hōfuku-ji 保福寺	13 A1
Ishii Chawan Museum 石井茶碗美術館	14 A1
Itō Hirobumi House 伊藤博文旧宅	15 B2
Jōnen-ji 常念寺	16 E2
Kaichō-ji 海潮寺	17 C1
Kikuya House 菊屋家住宅	18 C1
Kubota House 久保田家	19 C1
Kumaya Art Museum 熊谷美術館	20 B2
Kyōtoku-ji 享徳寺	21 C1
Mōri House 旧毛利家萩邸長屋	22 C1
Shizukiyama-jinja 指月山神社	23 A2
	24 A1

SLEEPING	
Business Hotel Hasegawa ビジネスホテル長谷川	25 E2
Tomb of Tenjuin 毛利天樹院墓所	26 E2
Tōkō-ji 東光寺	27 E2
Fujita Ryokan 藤田旅館	28 C2
Hagi Grand Hotel 萩グランドホテル	29 D1
Hagi Youth Hostel 萩ユースホステル	30 C1
Nakamura Ryokan 中村旅館	31 A2
Petit Hotel Clanvert プチホテルクランベール	32 C2
Well Heart Pia ウェルハートピア	33 D2
	34 B1

EATING	
Don Don Udonya どんどんうどん屋	35 D1
Maru マル	36 C2
Nakamura 中村	37 C2
San Marco サンマルコ	38 B2

DRINKING	
Hanano-e Tea House 花江茶亭	39 A1
Kumayadotenjō-pei 俥宿天十平	40 B2
Normal ノーマル	41 C2

TRANSPORT	
Bicycle Hire 萩ニュースホステル	(see 31)
Bus Station バス停	42 C2

Sights
HAGI POTTERY & KILNS
Connoisseurs of Japanese pottery rank *hagi-yaki*, the pottery of Hagi, second only to Kyoto's *raku-yaki*. As in other Japanese pottery centres, the craft came from Korea when Korean potters were abducted during Toyotomi Hideyoshi's unsuccessful invasion in the late 1500s. There are a number of shops and kilns where you can see the pottery being made and browse through the finished products. *Hagi-yaki* is noted for its fine glazes and delicate pastel colours. The small notch in the base of each piece is also a reminder of the pottery's long history. In the feudal era only samurai were permitted to use the pottery, but by cutting a tiny notch in some pieces the potters 'spoilt' their work so that it could be used by common folk.

The **Hagi-jō Kiln** (☎ 22-5226; Ni-ku 5 Horiuchi Hagi; ⏰ 8am-5pm; closed irregularly for firing) in Horiuchi has particularly fine pieces. The western end of Hagi has several interesting pottery kilns near the park, Shizuki-kōen. *Hagi-yaki* pottery can also be inspected at the **Hagi-yaki Gallery** (Hagi-yaki Kaikan; ☎ 25-9545; 3155 Higashi-ku Shinkawa Tsubaki Higashi ⏰ 8am-5.30pm; pottery making ¥1680) near the park; there's a big souvenir area downstairs.

Swede **Bertil Persson** (☎ 25-2693), who has lived in Hagi for over 30 years, has his own kiln and is happy to meet anyone seriously interested in ceramics.

During the first week of May the **Hagi-yaki Matsuri** takes place at the city gymnasium, with works from 51 local kilns on sale.

If the idea of making your own piece of *hagi-yaki* appeals, there are six operations in town providing the opportunity. The information office has a hand-out on where, when and how much.

HAGI-JŌ RUINS & SHIZUKI-KŌEN
萩城跡指月公園
There's not much of the old Hagi-jō to see, apart from the typically imposing outer walls and the surrounding moat. The **castle** (admission with Mōri House ¥210; ⏰ 8am-6.30pm Apr-Oct, 8.30am-4.30pm Nov-Feb, 8.30am-6pm Mar) was built in 1604. It was dismantled in 1874 during the Meiji Restoration – since Hagi played a leading part in the end of the feudal era and the downfall of the shōgunate, it was appropriate that the town also led the way in the removal of feudal symbols.

Now the grounds are a pleasant park, with the **Shizukiyama-jinja**, the **Hanano-e Tea House** (Hanano-e Satei) and other buildings. From the castle ruins you can climb the hillside to the 143m peak of Shizuki-yama.

SEKICHŌ-KŌEN 石彫公園
About a five-minute walk to the west of Shizuki-kōen is the new **Sekichō-kōen** (Sculpture Park), with its collection of sculptural works from around the world. Admission is free.

MŌRI HOUSE 旧毛利家萩屋敷長屋
South of the park is **Mōri House** (admission with Hagi-jō ¥210; ⏰ 8am-6.30pm Apr-Aug, 8.30am-4.30pm Nov-Feb, 8.30am-6pm Mar), a terrace house where samurai soldiers were once barracked. There's an interesting **Christian cemetery** to the south of the samurai house.

JŌKAMACHI, HORIUCHI & TERAMACHI AREAS 城下町・堀内・寺町
Between the modern town centre and the moat that separates western Hagi from central Hagi is the old samurai residential area, with many streets lined by whitewashed walls. This area is fascinating to wander around, and there are a number of interesting houses, particularly in the area known as Jōkamachi. Teramachi is noted particularly for its many fine old temples.

The Kikuya family were merchants rather than samurai, but their wealth and special connections allowed them to build a house well above their station. **Kikuya House** (admission ¥500; ⏰ 9am-5pm) dates from 1604, and has a fine gate, attractive gardens and numerous examples of construction details and materials that would normally have been forbidden to the merchant class. Across the street is **Kubota House** (combined ticket admission ¥500; ⏰ 9am-5pm), another renovated residence, which has exhibitions in conjunction with the **Hagi-no-yado Tomoe Ryokan** in eastern Hagi. At the southern perimeter of the Jōkamachi district, before you reach the little canal, is the green-tea-coloured **Ishii Chawan Museum** (admission ¥500; ⏰ 9am-4.45pm Tue-Sun, closed Jan, Jun & Dec), which has an extensive collection of tea-ceremony bowls and utensils. From the museum, go east, cross the canal and turn south to reach the **Hagi Uragami Museum** (admission from ¥800; ⏰ 9am-5pm Tue-Sun). This private collection of oriental ceramics and about 5000 woodblock prints is superb. The woodblock prints are not always on display, but catalogues and beautiful postcards are available. There are fine works by Katsushika Hokusai and Utamaro Kitagawa. Note that admission prices vary according to the temporary exhibitions. At the main entrance to the Horiuchi district is the **Hagi Museum** (admission ¥500; 9am-5pm), which has exhibitions about Hagi history, art and religion.

Kumaya Art Museum (admission ¥700; 9am-5pm Tue-Sun), in Jōkamachi, has a small collection including tea bowls, screens and other items, displayed in a series of small warehouses dating from 1768. The Kumaya family handled the trading and commercial operations of Hagi's ruling Mōri family.

The Horiuchi and Teramachi areas are dotted with temples and shrines. **Fukuhara-ke Yashiki-mon** is one of the finest of the samurai gates in Horiuchi. Nearby is the **Tomb of Tenjuin**, dedicated to Mōri Terumoto, the founder of the Mōri dynasty. There are numerous old temples in the Teramachi area, including the two-storey **Kaichō-ji**, **Hōfuku-ji**, with its statues of Jizō (the Buddha for travellers and the souls of departed children); **Jōnen-ji**, with its carved gate; and **Baizō-in**. Large **Kyūtoku-ji** has a fine garden.

TŌKŌ-JI 東光寺
East of the river stands this pretty **temple** (admission ¥300; 8.30am-5pm), home to the tombs of five Mōri lords. The odd-numbered lords (apart from No 1) were buried here; the even-numbered ones were buried at the **Daishō-in** temple. The stone walkways on the hillside behind the temple are flanked by almost 500 stone lanterns, erected by the lords' servants.

SHŌIN-JINJA 松陰神社
This Meiji-era shrine is dedicated to Yoshida Shōin. His life is illustrated in the nearby **Yoshida Shōin Rekishikan** (吉田松陰誕生地; Yoshida Shōin Historical Museum; admission ¥650; 9am-5pm). South of the shrine, **Itō Hirobumi House** is the early home of the four-term prime minister who was a follower of Yoshida Shōin, and who later drafted the Meiji Constitution. Yoshida Shōin's tomb is near Tōkō-ji.

DAISHŌ-IN 大照院
South of the centre, near JR Hagi Station, this **funerary temple** (admission ¥200; 8am-5pm) was the resting place for the first two Mōri

generations and then, after that, all even-numbered generations of the Mōri lords. Like the better-known and more frequently visited Tōkō-ji, it has pathways lined by stone lanterns that were erected by the Mōri lords' faithful retainers. The original Mōri lord's grave is accompanied by the graves of seven of his principal retainers, all of whom committed *seppuku* (ritual suicide) after their lord died. An eighth grave is that of a retainer to one of the retainers who also joined in the festivities. The shōgunate quickly banned similar excessive displays of samurai loyalty.

MYŌJIN-IKE & KASA-YAMA 明神池・笠山
About 5km east of the town is the 112m **dormant volcano Kasa-yama**. It's hardly a whopper, but there are some great things to do here. The pond at the mountain's base, **Myōjin-ike**, is connected to the sea and shelters a variety of saltwater fish.

Further up the mountain is **Hagi Glass Associates** (萩ガラス工房; 26-2555; 9am-6pm, demonstrations 4.30pm), where quartz basalt from the volcano is used to make extremely tough Hagi glassware. There are a showroom and a shop, and visitors can make their own piece of glassware. Next door is Hagi's own beer factory, where you can check out how the beer is made and taste the brew.

The road continues to the top of Kasa-yama, from where there are fine views along the coast and an intriguingly tiny 30m deep crater. Kasa-yama is close enough to make a good bicycle ride from Hagi.

Sleeping
Hagi Youth Hostel (22-0733; 109-22 Horiuchi; dm ¥2940; closed mid-Jan–mid-Feb; P) Close to the castle at the western end of the town, the hostel is a 15-minute walk from JR Tamae Station. Most of the kilns and *hagi-yaki* shops are in this quiet area.

Fujita Ryokan (22-0603; 3091 Shinkawa-chō Nishi-ku; s/tw with shared bathroom ¥3675/7350; P) On the east side of the city in a quiet area, this ryokan's Japanese-style rooms have views of Mastumoto-gawa.

Nakamura Ryokan (22-0303; 56 Kohagimachi; s/tw ¥4000/7000; P) Large tatami rooms and a traditional entrance addd character.

Well Heart Pia (22-0025; 485-2 Horiuchi; s/tw ¥5700/8500; P) A five-minute walk east of Hagi castle, this modern ryokan has rooms with great views facing Kiku-ga-hama beach. The Japanese- and Western-style rooms have their own bathroom, and meals are available.

Business Hotel Hasegawa (☎ 22-0450; 17 Karanimachi; s/tw ¥5775/10,500; P ✖) Between the station and the sights near Hagi castle, the Business Hotel has sunny Western- and Japanese-style rooms with bathrooms.

Petit Hotel Clanvert (☎ 25-8711; 370-9 Hijiwara; s/tw ¥6600/11,600; P ✖) Just across the bridge on the western side of the river from Higashi-Hagi station, this very quiet place has comfortable rooms and pleasant staff.

Hagi Grand Hotel (☎ 25-1211; 25 Kohagimachi; s/tw per person ¥8400/12,600; P ✖) Here there are large rooms and a huge *onsen* complex out the back. The foyer is a good place to sample local sweets.

Eating

Maru (☎ 26-5050; 78 Yoshida-chō; dishes ¥500-1500; ✖ dinner Tue-Sun) Maru is a fashionable *izakaya* (Japanese-style pub) with an inventive menu. Sushi, tofu and other Japanese food with a modern twist are on offer.

Nakamura (☎ 22-6619; 394 Hijiwara; meals ¥1500-2900; ✖ lunch & dinner) *Unidon* (sea urchin on rice) is the house speciality in the traditional surroundings here.

Don Don Udonya (☎ 22-7537; 377 San-ku Hishihara; dishes ¥400; ✖ 9.30am-9pm) This place has excellent udon noodles and set meals.

San Marco (☎ 25-4677; 18 Higashita-machi; meals ¥700; ✖ 11am-9pm) Hagi pizza and very simple Italian lunch and dinner set menus are on offer at this family restaurant.

Drinking

Normal (☎ 26-5088; 77 Yoshida-chō; drinks ¥500; ✖ 9pm-2am Tue-Sun) This place with a dark wooden interior is perhaps the only late-night bar in Hagi. People roll in here after dinner at Maru next door.

Kumayadotenjū-pei (☎ 26-6474; 33-5 Kohagi-chō; tea & scones ¥700; ✖ 9am-6pm) This gallery and tea room is in a late–Edo period house with a large garden.

Getting There & Away

The JR San-in line runs along the north coast through Tottori, Matsue, Masuda and Hagi to Shimonoseki.

JR buses connect Hagi with Shin-Yamaguchi (via Akiyoshi-dai), which is south of Hagi on the Tokyo–Osaka–Hakata *shinkansen* line. There are buses from Yamaguchi, and buses also go to Tsuwano (¥2080, two hours) to the east in Shimane-ken.

Hagi is served by Iwami airport, an hour to the northeast near Masuda in Shimane-ken. There are daily flights to/from Tokyo and Osaka. A bus (¥1560, 70 minutes) from in front of Higashi-Hagi station or the Hagi bus centre connects Hagi with all flights.

Getting Around

Hagi is a good place to explore by bicycle and there are plenty of rental places, including one at the youth hostel and several around the castle and JR Higashi-Hagi Station. The best rent-a-cycle place is **Smile** (☎ 22-2914; 3000 Shinkawa Minami; ✖ 8am-sunset), to the right as you leave the station.

A bus system takes in Hagi's main attractions. One trip costs ¥100, and one-/two-day passes cost ¥500/700.

From Hagi, the JR San-in line and Rte 191, the main road, pretty much hug each other and the coastline up to the prefectural border with Shimane-ken. If you're going to Tsuwano there's a direct bus from Hagi, but if you've got a JR pass you'll want to go by train up the coast to Masuda, then change to the JR Yamaguchi line for Tsuwano.

SHIMANE-KEN 島根県

Along the northern San-in coastline on the Sea of Japan, Shimane-ken is well worth making the effort to get to. Cities are few and far between, and the pace of life is decidedly slower than on the San-yō coast. Highlights include Tsuwano, a quiet, unspoilt mountain town; the great shrine at Izumo; and Matsue, where the writer and Japanophile Lafcadio Hearn lived and produced some of his best-known works.

TSUWANO 津和野
☎ 0856 / pop 5,900

In the far western reaches of Shimane-ken, about 40km east of Hagi, is Tsuwano, a pleasant and relaxing mountain town with some fine castle ruins, interesting old buildings and a wonderful collection of carp swimming in the roadside water channels – the 65,000 or so of these colourful fish outnumber the local population ten-fold!

TSUWANO

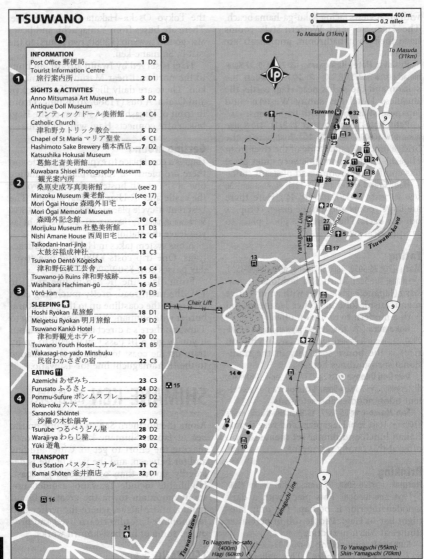

To Masuda (31km)
To Masuda (31km)
To Nagomi-no-sato (400km)
Hagi (60km)
To Yamaguchi (55km); Shin-Yamaguchi (70km)
Tsuwano
Tsuwano-kawa
Yamaguchi Line
Tonomachi
Chair Lift

Orientation & Information

Tsuwano is a long, narrow town wedged into a deep north–south valley. Tsuwano-kawa, the JR Yamaguchi line and main road all run down the middle of the valley. Pick up the bilingual booklet *Yū ni shin sai Tsuwano* (¥200) at the **Tourist Information Center** (☎ 72-1771; ⏰ 9am-5pm), just south of the train

station. The title translates as 'make yourself at home in Tsuwano' in the local dialect.

Sights & Activities

TSUWANO-JO 津和野城

The ruins of Tsuwano-jō seem to brood over the valley, with the broken stone walls draping along the ridge. The **castle** was originally constructed in 1295 and remained in use until the Meiji Restoration. An old single-seater chairlift takes you up (and down) the hillside for ¥450, and there's a further 15-minute walk to the castle ruins. At the top is a splendid view over the town and surrounding mountains. If you've got the energy and time, it's possible to follow a trail on foot all the way up from Taikodani-Inari-jinja.

TAIKODANI-INARI-JINJA 太鼓谷稲成神社
Just above the castle chairlift station, this brightly painted **shrine** is one of the largest Inari shrines in Japan. You can walk up to it from the main road through a tunnel created by more than 1100 red *torii*. Festivals are held here on 15 May and 15 November. The **Sagi Mai Matsuri** (Heron Dance Festival), which includes a procession of dancers dressed as herons, is performed on 20 and 27 July at Yasaka-jinja, near the start of the *torii* tunnel.

TONOMACHI DISTRICT 殿町
Only the walls and some fine old gates from the former **samurai quarter** of Tonomachi remain. 'Ditches' (the word used in the local tourist brochure) is too plain a word to apply to the water channels that run alongside the picturesque Tonomachi road: the crystal-clear water in the channels is home to tens of thousands of large and healthy carp. It's said that these fish were bred to provide a potential source of food should the town ever be besieged. (The feared attack never came, and the fish have thrived.)

The **Catholic church** is a reminder that Nagasaki Christians were once exiled here, while just north of the river is the **Yōrō-kan**, a school for young samurai in the late Edo period. The building now houses the **Minzoku Museum** (admission ¥200; ☉ 8.30am-5pm), an interesting little folk-art museum with all sorts of farming and cooking equipment.

Near the post office, the **Katsushika Hokusai Museum** (admission ¥500; ☉ 9.30am-5pm) features a small collection by the master Edo-period painter Hokusai and his disciples, and interestingly shows the woodblock process plate by plate.

CHAPEL OF ST MARIA マリア聖堂
The tiny **Chapel of St Maria** dates from 1951, when a German priest built it as a memorial to the exiled Catholics who died in the final period of Christian persecution before the anti-Christian laws were repealed in 1872.

OTHER SIGHTS
The beautiful **former residences** of Nishi Amane, who played an important part in the Meiji Restoration government, and Mori Ōgai, a highly regarded novelist, are in the south of the town. At the rear of the latter is the **Mori Ōgai Memorial Museum** (museum ¥500; residence grounds ¥100; ☉ 9am-5pm Tue-Sun), a modern building housing many of the writer's personal effects. The residence grounds are even more interesting than the museum.

The **Antique Doll Museum** (admission ¥800; ☉ 9.30am-5.30pm Fri-Wed) houses an astounding collection of fine European antique dolls. Perhaps more interesting (and still with a bit of European flavour) is the **Morijuku Museum** (admission ¥500; ☉ 9am-5pm), an old farmhouse with a room of etchings by Goya and paintings by local artists. Make sure you see the pinhole camera feature on the 2nd floor (the proprietor will gladly show you). **Tsuwano Dentō Kōgeisha** (admission free; ☉ 9am-5pm) has paper-making displays and a good range of paper products for sale.

Kuwabara Shisei Photography Museum (admission ¥200; ☉ 9am-4.45pm) has a small but excellent collection dedicated to contemporary photojournalism. The permanent collection features work by Tsuwano-born Kuwabara Shisei, mostly shot in Vietnam, South Korea and Minamata. It's in the same building as the information office, next to the station. Across the street is the **Anno Mitsumasa Art Museum** (admission ¥600; ☉ 9am-5pm), showing works by local artist Anno Mitsumasa. It has a good gift shop.

There are a number of sake breweries in town, some of which have tastings. Try **Hashimoto**, where Toba-san, one of the resident staff, can answer your questions in English while you sample the local brew.

South of the town is the shrine **Washibara Hachiman-gū**, about 4km from the station, where **archery contests** on horseback are held on 2 April.

If you feel like a long soak in a bath, head down to **Nagomi-no-sato** (なごみの里; admission ¥500; ☉ 10am-10pm, closed 2nd & 4th Tue of month), the Tsuwano *onsen* complex south of town. There's a restaurant, local produce for sale, and mask painting and bamboo weaving at the weekends.

WESTERN HONSHŪ

Sleeping

Tsuwano Youth Hostel (☎ 72-0373; 819 Washibara Tsuwano-chō; dm ¥3360; P ✗) About 2km south of the station in a leafy area, this hostel is beside a small temple. Meals are available.

Wakasagi-no-yado Minshuku (☎ 72-1146; Mori; s/tw with 2 meals ¥7000/14,000; P ✗) This is a pleasant, friendly and frequently recommended place; staff will even pick you up at the station.

Hoshi Ryokan (☎ 72-0136; Ekimae; s/tw with 2 meals ¥6500/13,000; ✗) Here there are huge rooms with mountain views and a very relaxed atmosphere. Rooms are Japanese style with communal bathroom.

Meigetsu Ryokan (☎ 72-0685; Uocho; s/tw with 2 meals ¥10,500/21,000; P ✗) This is a traditional ryokan where you can ask to try Tsuwano's famine food: carp!

Tsuwano Kankō Hotel (☎ 72-0333; www.tsuwano .jp in Japanese; Takaokadōri; s/tw with 2 meals ¥12,600/ 25,200; P ✗) The Kankō is a modern, sophisticated *onsen* complex with Western- and Japanese-style rooms. You can have your own outdoor bath with mountain views if you want to splash out.

Eating

Most visitors to Tsuwano usually dine in their *minshuku* or ryokan, so many restaurants are open only during the day.

Azemichi (☎ 72-1884; Takaokadō-ri; dishes ¥300; ✗ 9.30am-5pm Wed-Mon) Azemichi boasts *chōgekikara rāmen*, which are spicy hot Chinese noodles.

Tsurube (☎ 72-2098; Takaokadōri; dishes ¥800; ✗ 11am-7pm) Here the house speciality is udon noodles handmade on the premises.

Waraji-ya (☎ 72-3221; Takaokadōri; dishes ¥1000; ✗ 11am-8pm Tue-Sun) Rustic and traditional, Waraji-ya serves noodles and is well known for *tendon* (tempura-and-rice dishes). It also has an *irori* (open fireplace).

Furusato (☎ 72-0403; Gion-chō; meals ¥1200; ✗ lunch Thu-Tue) Across from the post office, Furusato serves the local speciality, *uzume-meshi* (rice served in a soup with tofu, mushrooms and mountain vegetables).

Roku-roku (☎ 72-0443; Shin-chō; dishes ¥500; ✗ 6pm-12.30am Tue-Sun) A short walk southwest of the post office, this *izakaya* is the best bet in the evening, as it's inexpensive, friendly and a good place for meeting partying locals. The *kabuto-ebi shio-yaki* (grilled and salted minilobster, ¥500) is highly recommended.

Ponmu Sufure (☎ 72-2778; 284 Gotaguchi Tsuwano-chō; meals ¥1500-3000; ✗ 10am-9pm Fri-Wed, to midnight Fri & Sat) There's good pizza and bread at the only Italian restaurant in town.

Yūki (☎ 72-0162; 271-4 Gotaguchi Tsuwano-chō; meals from ¥2000; ✗ 10.30am-7pm Fri-Wed) Yūki's *Tsuwano teishoku* (a sampler of local dishes) is recommended.

Saranoki Shōintei (☎ 72-1661; 70 Gotaguchi Tsuwano-chō; meals from ¥2625; ✗ 10am-4pm) Here you can enjoy delicious Japanese food while overlooking a traditional garden.

Getting There & Away

The JR Yamaguchi line runs from Shin-Yamaguchi on the south coast through Yamaguchi to Tsuwano and on to Masuda on the north coast. There are connections from Tsuwano to Shin-Yamaguchi (1¼ hours) and Masuda (40 minutes). A bus runs between Tsuwano and Hagi (¥2080, two hours).

During the Golden Week holiday (late April to early May), and from 20 July to 31 August, as well as sometimes on Sunday and national holidays, there is a popular steam-locomotive service from Shin-Yamaguchi to Tsuwano. SL *Yamaguchi-gō* is a restored 1937 locomotive pulling antique carriages that travels from Shin-Yamaguchi to Tsuwano in the morning, then waits for three hours, before making the return journey. The train trip costs ¥1620 and takes two hours each way. Ask for up-to-date details and book well ahead of your intended dates at JR and tourist information offices.

Getting Around

Tsuwano has several bicycle-hire places; rates are ¥500/800 per two hours/day. **Kamai-shōten** (✗ 8am-7pm) is in front of the station.

MASUDA 益田

☎ 0856 / pop 54,000

This is a modern industrial town with two temples of interest, **Mampuku-ji** (萬福寺; admission ¥300; ✗ 7am-6pm) and **Iko-ji** (医光侍; admission ¥300; ✗ 9am-5pm). Both have notable gardens said to have been designed by the famed painter Sesshū. The temples are about 10 minutes by bus from the JR station.

Masuda is the junction for the JR Yamaguchi line, which runs between Shin-Yamaguchi, Yamaguchi, Tsuwano and Masuda, and the JR San-in line, which runs from Shimonoseki through Hagi and Masuda and then up the coast. *Futsū* trains run from Masuda to Tsuwano (¥570, 40 minutes), Higashi-Hagi (¥950, 70 minutes) and Izumo (¥2210, two hours 40 minutes).

Iwami Seaside Park 岩見海浜公園

About 5km northeast of Hamada is **Iwami Seaside Park** (☎ 0855-28-2231), which is great for camping, swimming and playing on the white, sandy beach. There are plenty of options, including auto-camping (camping beside your car), free tent sites, and cabins that sleep six/four/three people for ¥5760/3760/3190. Facilities include flood-lit tennis courts, a sports ground, a coin laundry, coin showers and even Frisbee golf. You can rent just about everything you need on the spot. It's an ideal place for a reasonably priced family holiday. The park is open year-round; reservations are advised.

Just up the road is the enormous **Aquas Shimane Aquarium** (島根海洋館アクアス; ☎ 0855-28-3900; adult ¥1500; ☯ 9am-5pm Wed-Mon), which is like a theme park full of fish. It's great stuff for the family, with a touching pool (where kids can touch the fish), white dolphins, sharks, seals and even Shimane-ken's official fish, the *ago* (flying fish).

Nima 仁摩

Nima is home to the **Nima Sand Museum** (仁摩サンドミュージアム; admission ¥700; ☯ 9am-5pm, closed 1st Wed of each month), which houses the world's biggest hourglass – this monster is turned over at midnight on 31 December each year, and has exactly the right number of grains of sand to last through to the same time the next year. The 5m-long timer is suspended high in one of the museum's glass pyramids and contains about a tonne of sand.

Youth Hostel Jofuku-ji (ユースホステル城福寺; ☎ 0854-88-2233; 1114 Nima-chō Nima; dm ¥2730) If you haven't had the chance to stay at a Buddhist temple, this is a great place to start. The priest and his wife are very friendly, there's a splendid view out over the coast, and the 20-minute walk from Nima station through the paddy fields and up to the temple is quite enjoyable. Take your shoes in overnight or they might be 'done away with' by the local badger.

Sanbe-san 三瓶山

About 20km inland from Ōda is Sanbe-san, which reaches 1126m and has four separate peaks known as the Father, the Mother, the Child and the Grandchild. It takes about an hour to climb from **Sanbe Onsen**, where there's a dip in the *onsen* awaiting you on your return. The area is also a popular ski centre in winter. Buses run between Ōda and Sanbe Onsen (¥830, 40 minutes).

IZUMO 出雲

☎ 0853 / pop 85,000

Only 33km west of Matsue, Izumo has one major attraction – the great Izumo Taisha shrine. It's also home to the Shimane Winery, which is bound to be a major attraction for some.

Orientation & Information

Izumo Taisha is several kilometres northwest of central Izumo. The shrine area, basically one main street running straight up to the shrine, has a train station and a range of accommodation and restaurants. The friendly **tourist information office** (☎ 53-2298; ☯ 9am-5.30pm) in the train station has information in English. Izumo Taisha can easily be visited as a day trip from Matsue.

Sights

IZUMO TAISHA 出雲大社

This is the oldest Shintō shrine in Japan and is second in importance only to the shrines of Ise. Although it's only a shadow of its former self – the buildings once towered to a colossal 48m, today they're a modest 24m – this is still an enormously significant structure, both architecturally and spiritually.

A shrine has existed on the site for the last 1500 years. The current main shrine was last rebuilt in 1744, its 25th incarnation, whereas the surrounding buildings date back to 1874. All are constructed in the Taisha-zukuri style, considered Japan's oldest form of shrine architecture. The wooded grounds are pleasant to wander through, and the shrine itself enjoys the borrowed scenery of Yakumo Hill as a backdrop.

The shrine is dedicated to Okuninushi, the *kami* (Shintō spirit god) of marriage, among other things. Hence visitors to the shrine summon the deity by clapping four times rather than the normal two – twice for themselves and twice for their partner or partners to be.

The **Haiden** (Hall of Worship) is the first building inside the entrance *torii*; huge *shimenawa* (twisted straw ropes) hang over the

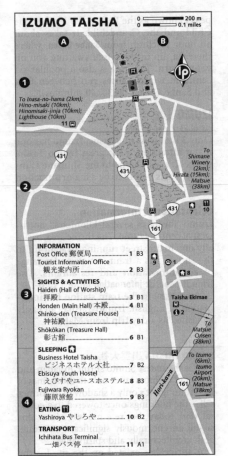

IZUMO TAISHA

INFORMATION
Post Office 郵便局 1 B3
Tourist Information Office
観光案内所 2 B3

SIGHTS & ACTIVITIES
Haiden (Hall of Worship)
拝殿 3 B1
Honden (Main Hall) 本殿 4 B1
Shinko-den (Treasure House)
神祐殿 5 B1
Shōkōkan (Treasure Hall)
彰古館 6 B1

SLEEPING
Business Hotel Taisha
ビジネスホテル大社 7 B2
Ebisuya Youth Hostel
えびすやユースホステル ... 8 B3
Fujiwara Ryokan
藤原旅館 9 B3

EATING
Yashiroya やしろや 10 B2

TRANSPORT
Ichihata Bus Terminal
一畑バス停 11 A1

entry. The main building is the largest shrine in Japan, but the **Honden** (Main Hall) cannot be entered. The shrine compound is flanked by *jūku-sha*, long shelters where Japan's eight million Shintō spirit gods stay when they turn up for their annual shindig (see right).

On the southeastern side of the compound is the **Shinko-den** (Treasure House; admission ¥150; 8.30am-4.30pm), with a collection of shrine paraphernalia. Behind the main shrine building, in the northwestern corner, is the former **Shōkōkan** (Treasure Hall; admission ¥50; 8.30am-4.30pm), which boasts a large collection of images of Okuninushi in the form of Daikoku, a cheerful chubby character standing on two or three rice bales with a sack over his shoulder and a mallet in his hand. Usually you will see

his equally happy son Ebisu standing beside him with a fish tucked under his arm.

HINO-MISAKI 日御碕
It's less than 10km from Izumo Taisha to **Hino-misaki** cape, where you'll find a picturesque lighthouse, some fine views and an ancient shrine. On the way you'll pass the pleasant **Inasa-no-hama**, a good swimming beach just 2km from Taisha Ekimae station. Buses run regularly from the station to the cape via the beach (¥840, 35 minutes). **Hino-misaki-jinja** is near the cape's bus terminus. Coastal paths lead north and south from the car park, offering fine views, particularly from the top of the **lighthouse** (日御碕灯台; admission ¥150; 9am-4.30pm).

Festivals & Events
The lunar calendar month corresponding to October is known throughout Japan as Kan-nazuki (Month without Gods). In Izumo, however, it is known as Kan-arizuki (Month with Gods), for this is the month when all the Shintō gods congregate for an annual get-together at Izumo Taisha.

In accordance with the ancient calendar, the **Kamiari-sai Matsuri** (*kamiari-sai* means 'the gods are here!') takes place from 11 to 17 October.

Sleeping & Eating
It's easy to day-trip to Izumo from Matsue or simply pause there while travelling along the coast. If you do want to stop, there's a host of places along the main street of Izumo Taisha, which runs down from the shrine to the train station.

Ebisuya Youth Hostel (53-2157; Shinmondōri Taishamachi Hikawa-gun; dm ¥3050;) Just off the main street, near the station, this hostel has meals available.

Business Hotel Taisha (53-2194; 382 Kizuki Higashi Taishamachi Hikawa-gun; s/tw with breakfast ¥5000/8000;) Five minutes' east of the entrance to the shrine, the Business Hotel has clean rooms. It faces what will be the new Izumo municipal centre.

Fujiwara Ryokan (53-2009; Seinmonmae; s/tw with 2 meals ¥10,500/21,000;) Full-sized baths and a small internal garden lend charm to this family-run business.

Izumo's *soba* gets high praise, particularly the dish known as *warigo*, where broth is poured over the noodles.

WESTERN HONSHŪ

Yashiroya (☎ 53-2596; 72-5 Kizuki-higashi; meals ¥700; ⏰ 10am-6pm Wed-Mon) A local favourite, Yashiroya is down the hill and off to the right from the shrine entrance.

Getting There & Away

The private Ichihata line starts from Matsue Shinjiko-onsen station in Matsue and runs on the northern side of Shinji-ko lake to Taisha Ekimae station (¥790, 55 minutes). The JR line runs from JR Matsue Station to JR Izumo-shi Station (¥740, one hour), where you can transfer to an Ichihata-line train to Izumo Taisha. The first option is easier and more frequent, with more than 20 services a day. If you're coming from the west, change at JR Izumo-shi Station.

The one-day L&R Free Kippu ticket (¥1500) allows unlimited travel on Ichihata trains and Shinji-ko lakeside buses, which stop at the Ichihata bus terminal.

Izumo has an airport with flights to/from most of Japan's major cities.

MATSUE 松江

☎ 0852 / pop 150,000

Matsue straddles the Ōhashi-gawa river, which connects Shinji-ko to Nakanoumi-ko and then the sea. There's a compact area in the north with almost all of Matsue's interesting sites: an original castle, a fine samurai residence, the former home of writer Lafcadio Hearn, and a delightful teahouse and garden. It's worth spending a night here to enjoy the leisurely pace.

Information

The **tourist information office** (☎ 21-4034; ⏰ 9am-6pm) in front of JR Matsue Station can arrange a free English-language tour – the Matsue Goodwill Guide – if you call a few days in advance.

There is some information, a small library and free Internet access at the **Shimane International Centre** (☎ 31-5056; 2nd fl, Kunibiki Messe Bldg; ⏰ 9am-7pm Mon-Fri, 9am-5pm Sat), about a 10-minute walk from the station.

Sights

MATSUE-JŌ 松江城

The **castle** (admission ¥550; ⏰ 8.30am-6.30pm Apr-Sep, 8.30am-5pm Oct-Mar) in Matsue is not huge or imposing but it is original, dating from 1611. Modern Japan has so many rebuilt castles, externally authentic-looking but in-

---

DRINK WITH THE GODS

There aren't many wineries in the world where they put out huge punchbowls of their product along with ladles and plastic cups and invite you to do as much 'tasting' as you like. But at the **Shimane Winery** (☎ 53-5577; ⏰ 9.30am-4.30pm) it's basically no holds barred, although it would be a shame to go overboard at the punchbowls and make an idiot of yourself.

Besides tasting, you can view the winery in action, buy a few bottles, enjoy a meal in the barbecue restaurant or sober up in the coffee shop. The winery is 2km east of Izumo Taisha on Rte 431. You can't miss the massive Spanish-looking complex, with its white walls and orange-tiled roof

---

ternally totally modern, that it can almost be a shock to step inside one where the construction is wood, not concrete. With a Universal Pass (¥920), which includes entry to the castle, Buke Yashiki Samurai Residence and the Koizumi Yakumo (Lafcadio Hearn) Memorial Museum, you can save 20%.

The regional **Matsue Cultural Museum** (admission free; ⏰ 8.30am-5pm) is inside the castle precincts. The road alongside the moat on the northeastern side of the castle is known as Shiomi Nawate and was once a narrow lane through the old samurai quarter. The high tile-topped walls survive from that era, and there are a number of places of interest.

Fun **Horikawa Pleasure Boat tours** (admission ¥1200; ⏰ 9am-5pm Mar-Jun & Sep–20 Oct, 9am-6pm Jul-Aug, 9am-4pm 21 Oct–21 Nov, 10am-3pm 12 Jan–Feb) circumnavigate the castle moat and then zip you around some of the city's canals.

KOIZUMI YAKUMO (LAFCADIO HEARN) RESIDENCE 小泉八雲旧宅

Hearn was a Greco-Irish writer born in Greece in 1850 and educated in France and the UK. He lived in the USA from 1869, came to Japan in 1890 and remained there for the rest of his life. Hearn's adopted Japanese name was Koizumi Yakumo, and his first book on Japan, *Glimpses of Unfamiliar Japan*, is a classic, providing an insight into the country at that time. The Japanese have a great interest in the outsider's view of their country, so Hearn's pretty little house is an important attraction, despite the fact that he only lived in Matsue for just over a year. While

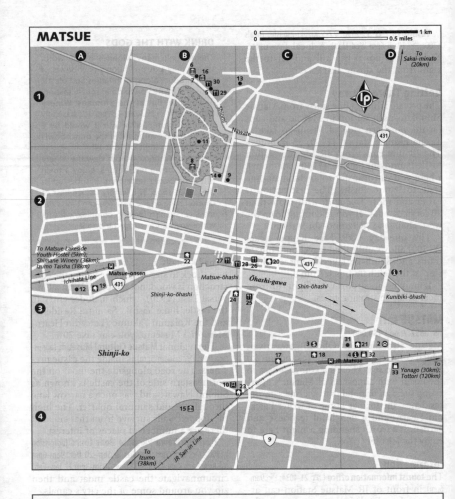

MATSUE

you're admiring the garden you can read his essay *In a Japanese Garden*, which describes how it looked a century ago. Hearn's former **residence** (admission ¥250; 🕑 9am-4.30pm) is at the northern end of Shiomi Nawate.

KOIZUMI YAKUMO (LAFCADIO HEARN) MEMORIAL MUSEUM 小泉八雲記念館
Next door to Hearn's home is this **memorial museum** (admission ¥300; 🕑 8.30am-6.30pm Apr-Sep, 8.30am-5pm Oct-Mar) with displays about Hearn's life, writing and Matsue residence. There's a stack of Japanese newspapers on which Hearn had written simple words and phrases to teach English to his son. A brochure and map in English are available, showing points of interest around the town that are mentioned in Hearn's writings.

TANABE ART MUSEUM 田部美術館
The **Tanabe Art Museum** (admission ¥600; 🕑 9am-5pm Tue-Sun) displays family items from generations of the region's Tanabe clan, including tea bowls and other tea-ceremony utensils.

BUKE YASHIKI SAMURAI RESIDENCE 武家屋敷
The well-preserved **Buke Yashiki** (admission ¥300; 🕑 8.30am-6.30pm Apr-Sep, 8.30am-5pm Oct-Mar) is a middle Edo–period samurai residence from 1730. There's a useful leaflet in English that describes the various rooms and their uses. The large, spartan residence was not the home of a wealthy samurai.

MEIMEI-AN TEAHOUSE 明々庵
A little further south is the turn-off to the delightful **Meimei-an teahouse** (admission ¥300, matcha ¥400; 🕑 9am-5pm) with its well-kept gardens and fine views of Matsue-jō. Built in 1779, the teahouse was moved to its present site in 1966. Look for the steep steps up from the road to the thatched-roof building.

SHIMANE PREFECTURAL ART MUSEUM 島根県立博物館
This impressive futuristic-looking **museum** (admission ¥300; 🕑 10am-6.30pm Tue-Sun) displays work by Monet, Rodin and current Japanese artists. It's in a fabulous location overlooking the lake, and on a sunny day it's fun to wander round the outdoor sculptures. You can also watch the sunset from the 2nd-floor viewing platform. The museum is a 15-minute walk west of the station.

EXOTIC DISHES FROM THE LAKE
Matsue's *kyodo ryōri*, or regional cuisine, includes 'seven exotic dishes from Shinji-ko'.\

- *suzuki* or *hōsho yaki* – steam-baked and paper-wrapped bass
- *shirauo* – whitebait tempura or sashimi
- *amasagi* – sweet tempura or teriyaki
- *shijimi* – tiny shellfish in miso soup
- *moroge ebi* – steamed shrimp
- *koi* – baked carp
- *unagi* – grilled freshwater eel

The seven exotic dishes are seasonal, so you can sample up to six of the wonders at any time of year. For a little indulgence, make a lunch-time reservation at **Minami-kan** (p442), an old ryokan. Have a tatami room to yourself overlooking a garden and Shinji-ko. If you order the *omakase* (chef's suggestion), the dishes just keep on coming. The *suzuki-yaki* is particularly good here. For a more laid-back experience, get yourself a counter seat at **Kawa-kyō** (p442) in the evening. At this very popular local drinking spot the company is as agreeable as the food, and someone will be on hand to translate, suggest sake and make the whole experience a night to remember. Try the trademark dish, tenderised eel with garlic and *tomburi* (plant caviar).

OTHER SIGHTS
Matsue has its own *onsen* area, just north of the lake near Matsue-onsen station on the Ichihata line. There are a number of hotels and ryokan in the area, as well as *O-yu-kake Jizō*, a *jigoku* (hell) – very hot springs that are definitely not for bathing.

The fine sunset views over the lake **Shinji-ko** are best appreciated from the Matsue-Ōhashi bridge. The **Matsue Prefectural Product & Craft Centre** (admission free; 🕑 9.30am-6pm), just southeast of the castle in the town centre, is a great place to sample local sweets, pickles and snacks. It's opposite the Horikawa Pleasure Boat tour ticket office.

Sleeping
BUDGET
Terazuya (🕿 21-3480; fax 21-3422; Tenjin-machi; s with/without 2 meals ¥7000/4000; 🅿 🕱) This clean, friendly, family-run ryokan near the Matsue Tenmangū shrine is the best budget option.

Some English is spoken here, and there's free Internet access. If you ask nicely, the father will sing traditional songs for you, the mother will perform the tea ceremony and the son will show you his calligraphy expertise. (The singing is quite enthralling.) Fax reservations are preferred.

Matsue Lakeside Youth Hostel (松江レークサイドユースホステル; ☎ 36-8620; www .shimane-yh.jp/matsue/matsue_e.html; ¥2800; P ⊠) This hostel is 30 minutes by bus from the city, so it's a good idea if you want to get away from it all. Meals are available.

Young Inn Matsue (☎ 22-2000; 5 Uomachi; s/tw ¥2100/4200; ⊠) Close to the lake, this small hotel has clean rooms with shared bathroom. There's a café on the 1st floor.

Business Ishida Hotel (☎ 21-5931; 205-11 Teramachi; s/tw ¥4000/8000; ⊠) This simple Japanese-style hotel has cute furniture and has a homely atmosphere.

Hotel 123 Matsue (☎ 27-3000; www.hotel1-2-3 .com/; 493-1 Asahi-chō; s/tw ¥4900/5950; P ⊠) Next to the station, this hotel's rooms are clean, quiet and simple. Rates include toast and coffee for breakfast.

MIDRANGE
New Urban Hotel (☎ 23-0003; www.matsue-urban.co .jp in Japanese; 590-3 Asahi-chō; s/tw ¥7140/12,600; P ⊠) At the New Urban some rooms have views of the lake and all have bathrooms.

Matsue Tōkyū Inn (☎ 27-0109; www.tokyu.co.jp /inn/in Japanese; 590 Asahimachi; s/tw ¥7875/14,910; P ⊠ ⊗) There are large, quiet rooms at this friendly place opposite the station.

Hotel Route Inn Matsue (☎ 20-6211; www.route-inn .co.jp in Japanese; 2-22 Higashi Honmachi s/tw ¥4800/11,500; P ⊠ 🖳) Across the river from JR Matsue Station, the Hotel Route Inn has views, free Internet access and a buffet breakfast.

Hotel Ichibata (☎ 22-0188; www.ichibata.co.jp/hotel in Japanese; 30 Chidōri-chō; s/tw ¥9390/16,470; P ⊠ ⊗) On the lake, the Hotel Ichibata has great views. Japanese-style rooms face the lake; the cheaper Western-style ones face inland.

Eating
Yakumo-an (☎ 25-0587; Bukeyashiki-nai 308 Kita Horiuchi; dishes ¥750-880; ⏲ 9am-4.30pm) This is a good spot to pause for lunch if you're wandering along Shiomi Nawate. The local speciality is *warigo*-style noodles, but the most popular dish is *kamo nanban* (noodles with slices of duck in broth).

Yakumo-an Bekkan (☎ 22-2400; Bukeyashiki-nai Kitahori-chō; dishes ¥550; ⏲ 10am-4pm Wed-Mon) This pleasant teahouse annexe to Yakumo-an is just on the other side of Buke Yashiki, with a large garden. *Matcha jelly* (green-tea jelly) is the trademark sweet here.

Kawa-kyō (☎ 22-1312; 65 Suetsugu Honmachi; meals ¥1500-4000; ⏲ 6-10.30pm) Near the Hotel Route Inn north of the river, Kawa-kyō offers the seven local 'exotic dishes from the lake' (see p441). There's an English menu.

Naniwa Hotori (☎ 21-2835; 21 Suetsugu Honmachi; meals ¥1970-4000; ⏲ lunch & dinner) Right on the river, this is a very bright and airy modern Japanese restaurant. You can try eel and rice with tea and 'exotic dishes of the lake' with a reservation.

Minamikan (☎ 21-5131; 14 Suetsugu Honmachi; meals ¥3000-10,000; ⏲ lunch & dinner) Enjoy haute cuisine by the river while overlooking a traditional garden. Reservations are essential.

Filaments (☎ 24-8984; 5 Hakkenya-chō; drinks ¥500-700; ⏲ 7.30pm-late) Owner Sam has thousands of CDs and likes to chat into the early hours.

Getting There & Away
Matsue is on the JR San-in line, which runs along the San-in coast. You can head down to Okayama (on the south coast) via Yonago on the JR Hakubi line. It's ¥480 to Yonago (35 minutes), then ¥5360 to Okayama (two hours).

Matsue is serviced by both Izumo and Yonago airports, and between them they have flights to all the major cities.

Highway buses also operate to/from all of Japan's major cities.

Getting Around
Matsue has an efficient Lake line bus, which runs a set route around the city's major attractions, departing every 20 minutes from 8.40am to 5.40pm. There are about 30 stops, and the full route takes 70 minutes. The system is set up for visitors: one ride costs ¥200, but a day ticket is only ¥500 and brings discounts on many of the attractions.

If you're planning to visit Izumo Taisha, make sure you invest in the one-day L&R Free Kippu ticket (¥1500), which allows unlimited travel on Ichihata trains and Shinjiko lakeside buses.

Matsue is a good place to explore by bicycle; these can be hired opposite Matsue station at **Nippon Rent-a-car** (☎ 21-7518; 589-1 Asahimachi; ☷ 8am-8pm). Rates are ¥525 for two hours or ¥1155 per day.

AROUND MATSUE & IZUMO
Shinji-ko 宍道湖
Sunset over the Yomega-shima islet in Shinji-ko is a photographer's favourite. The lake also provides the region's seven favourite local delicacies. At the western end of the lake, the garden in Gakuen-ji in Hirata is noted for its autumn colours.

At the southwestern corner of the lake, the town of Shinji has one of the finest ryokan in Japan, **Yakumo Honjin** (八雲本陣; ☎ 66-0136; Shindi-chō, Shindi Yatsuka-gun; r per person ¥15,000; Ⓟ ✖). Parts of the inn are 250 years old; ask for the old wing or you'll end up in the modern air-conditioned one. Casual visitors can have a look around for ¥300.

Shimane-hantō 島根半島
North of Matsue, the coastline of the Shimane-hantō peninsula has some spectacular scenery, particularly around Kaga; you can enter the **Kaga-no-Kukedo cave** by boat.

Fūdoki-no-Oka & Shrine 風土記の丘
About 5km south of Matsue, around the village of Yakumo-mura, there are interesting shrines and important archaeological finds. The Fūdoki-no-Oka hill is a 1st-century archaeological site, its finds displayed in the **Fūdoki-no-Oka Archaeological Museum** (風土記 の丘資料館; admission ¥200; ☷ 9am-5pm Tue-Sun). Take the Ichibata bus (¥300, 20 minutes, every 30 minutes) from Matsue station and get off at Fūdoki-no-Oka.

Nearby is **Okadayama Kofun**, an ancient burial mound. *Haniwa* pottery figures were found here, similar to those of Miyazaki on Kyūshū.

West of Fūdoki-no-Oka is the ancient **Kamosu-jinja** shrine, dedicated to Izanami, the mother of the Japanese archipelago. The shrine's Honden (Main Hall) dates from 1346.

A little further west is **Yaegaki-jinja**, dedicated to the gods of marriage and commemorating a princess's rescue from an eight-headed serpent. The events are illustrated in fine 12th-century **wall paintings**. Just for good measure, there are a number of

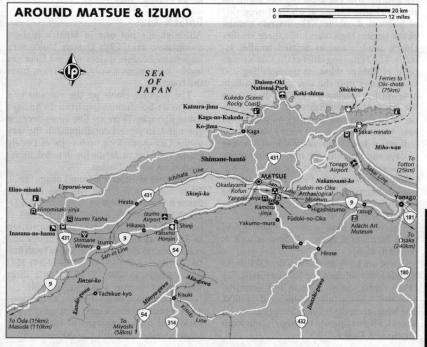

AROUND MATSUE & IZUMO

0   20 km
0   12 miles

SEA OF JAPAN

Daisen-Oki National Park
Kukedo (Scenic Rocky Coast)
Kaki-shima
Shichirui
Ferries to Oki-shotō (75km)
Katsura-jima
Kaga-no-Kukedo
Ko-jima
Kaga
Sakai-minato
Miho-wan
To Tottori (25km)
Shimane-hantō
431
Yonago Airport
Nakanoumi-ko
Ichihata Line
MATSUE
San-in Line
Fūdoki-no-Oka Archaeological Museum
Yonago
Hino-misaki
Uppurui-wan
Okadayama Kofun
Yaegaki-jinja
Kamosu-jinja
9
181
Hinomisaki-jinja
Hirata
431
Izumo Airport
Shinji-ko
Higashiizumo
Yasugi
To Osaka (240km)
Izumo Taisha
Hikawa
Shinji
Yakumo-mura
Fūdoki-no-Oka
Adachi Art Museum
Inasana-no-hama
431
Shimane Winery
Izumo
9
San-in Line
Yakumo Honjin
54
Bessho
Hirose
180
Jinzai-ko
Aka-gawa
Kisuki
432
9
Kandō-gawa
Tachikue-kyō
Miuoya-gawa
54
Kisuki Line
Jinachi-gawa
To Ōda (15km); Masuda (110km)
To Miyoshi (58km)
314

WESTERN HONSHŪ

phallic statues around, including one strategically placed in a hole in a tree trunk that apparently represents a vagina.

Adachi Art Museum 足立美術館

East of Matsue in Yasugi is the **Adachi Art Museum** (admission ¥2200; ⏰ 9am-5.30pm Apr-Sep, 9am-5pm Oct-Mar). It's set in exquisite gardens (all 43,000 sq metres of them), and features wonderful artworks by the likes of painter Yokoyama Taikan, *mingei* (folk craft) potter Kawai Kanjiro and, best of all, firebrand ceramicist Kitaoji Rosanjin. It's worth getting out there early in the day just to slowly lap up the art. A beautifully illustrated English pamphlet is available. Take the JR line to Yasugi, where there's a free connecting shuttle bus to the museum.

OKI-SHOTŌ 隠岐諸島
☎ 08512

Directly north of Matsue are the islands of the Oki-shotō, with spectacular scenery and steep cliffs. They are strictly for those who want to get away from it all. The islands were once used to exile political prisoners and *daimyō* (and, on one occasion, an emperor) who came out on the losing side of political squabbles. The islands consist of the larger Dōgo island, the three smaller Dōzen islands and associated smaller islands. The 7km-long cliffs of the Oki Kuniga coast of **Nishi-no-shima**, at times falling 250 sheer metres into the sea, are particularly noteworthy. **Kokobun-ji** on Dōgo dates from the 8th century. **Bullfights** are an attraction on Dōgo during the summer months – not man versus bull, but bull versus bull.

If you're keen to go, allow at least a couple of days and pop into the information office at Matsue station to sort out a few things before you head off. Pick up the simple English-language brochure and map of the islands called *Oki National Park*. There's also the Japanese-only website www.e-oki.net.

The islands have some *minshuku* and other forms of accommodation, as well as places to camp.

There are ferry services to the Oki-shotō islands from Shichirui or Sakai-minato. For Dōgo-shima, from Matsue bus terminal take the 7.55am bus to Shichirui (¥1000, one hour) then the 9.20am ferry (¥2530, 2½ hours). Flights operate to Dōgo island from Izumo and Osaka.

TOTTORI-KEN 鳥取県

If you like spectacular coastal scenery, sand dunes, *onsen* and volcanoes then Tottori-ken is a great place to visit, especially in summer.

YONAGO 米子
☎ 0859 / pop 140,000

Yonago is a sizable city and an important railway junction – here the JR San-in line, which runs along the Sea of Japan coast, is met by the JR Hakubi line coming up from Okayama on the San-yō side of the mountains.

There's a **tourist information office** (☎ 22-6317; ⏰ 9am-6pm) in JR Yonago Station, and things to do include a visit to the **Yonago Water Bird Park** (米子水鳥公園; admission ¥210; ⏰ 9am-5.30pm Wed-Mon), which boasts over 50 kinds of birds, including the whistling swan.

Kaike Onsen is on the coast, north of the station, and is the largest *onsen* area in the San-in region. It boasts endless hot water, plenty of accommodation, a sandy swimming beach and pine trees.

Yonago's airport has daily flights to/from Japan's major cities.

DAISEN 大山

Although it's not one of Japan's highest mountains, at 1729m Daisen looks very impressive because it rises straight from sea level – its summit is only about 10km from the coast.

The popular climb up the volcano is a five- to six-hour return trip from the ancient **Daisen-ji** temple. There are fine views over the coast and, in perfect conditions, all the way to the Oki-shotō. Pick up a copy of Lonely Planet's *Hiking in Japan* for detailed information on hiking Daisen.

Buses run to the temple from Yonago (¥800, 50 minutes), where you will also find the **Daisen-ji Tourist Information Center** (☎ 0859-52-2502; 8.30am-5pm Mon-Fri, 8.30am-6.30pm Sat & Sun). It has brochures, maps and hiking information in English as well as updated warnings and conditions on the mountain. **Daisen Youth Hostel** (大山ユースホステル; ☎ 0859-52-2501; 36-32 Daisen-chō Daisen; dm ¥2888; P ♿ ✕) is a short walk from Daisen-ji. Meals are available.

The mountain snags the northwest monsoon winds in the winter, bringing deep snow and tons of enjoyment for skiers at what is western Japan's top ski area.

Nishiki Market (p277), Kyoto

Osaka-jō (p342), Osaka

Kinkaku-ji (p302), Kyoto

Detail of curtain with geisha design

STAEVEN

Floating *torii* (p412), Miyajima

ANTONY GIBLIN

A-Bomb Dome (p408), Hiroshima

Peace Memorial Park (p408), Hiroshima

JOHN ASH

ALONG THE COAST TO TOTTORI

Tottori is known for its nashi pears, and those with a penchant for them may wish to visit the **Tottori Nijisseiki Pear Museum** (鳥取二十世紀梨記念館; admission ¥500; 9am-5pm, closed 3rd Mon of each month) in Kurayoshi.

Just north of Kurayoshi is **Lake Tōgo**, which has **Hawai Onsen** on its western side and **Tōgo Onsen** on its eastern side. There's a ton of accommodation around, including **Koho-ji Youth Hostel** (香宝寺ユースホステル; ☎ 0858-35-2054; Hawai-chō Shimoasazu Touhaku-gun; dm ¥2850, onsen ¥100), which is attached to a Buddhist temple on the western side. Meals are available at the hostel.

North of the lake is the **Lake Tōgo Hawai Seaside Park**, which has a swimming beach. The likeness of the town's name to the popular Pacific islands is not lost on the people of Hawaii, but although there's a nice beach, it's not Waimea Bay. It does have a sister city in Hawaii, though.

Travelling eastwards there's a succession of impressive **swimming beaches** split by rocky headlands all the way to Tottori city, notably Ishiwaki, Ide-ga-hama, Aoya, Hamamura Onsen and the extremely popular Hakuto. It's packed with surfers on weekends in summer. If you're on the train you'll miss a lot of it, as the line runs a fair way inland, so it's worth considering using a car to explore this area.

TOTTORI 鳥取

☎ 0857 / pop 150,000

Tottori is a large, busy town that's some distance back from the coast. The main coast road passes through Tottori's northern fringe in a blizzard of car dealers, *pachinko* parlours and fast-food outlets. The town's main attraction is its famous sand dunes. There is a helpful **tourist information booth** (☎ 22-3318; 9.30am-6.30pm) inside the station, with English-language pamphlets and maps.

Sights

Most of Tottori's attractions are concentrated in a compact little group about 1.5km northeast of the station.

Tottori-jō once overlooked the town from the hillside, but now only the castle's foundations remain. Below is the European-style **Jinpū-kaku Villa** (admission ¥150; 9am-5pm Tue-Sun), dating from 1906 and now used as a museum. Across from this building is the modern **Tottori Prefectural Museum** (admission ¥180; 9am-5pm Tue-Sun).

Tottori also has an interesting little **Folk-craft Museum** (admission ¥400; 10am-5pm Thu-Tue) near the JR station, with items from Japan, Korea, China and Europe. East of the station is the 17th-century garden **Kannon-in** (admission incl matcha service ¥600; 8am-5pm).

Ekimae Ichiba (4am-6pm Thu-Tue) is a fascinating fish market near the station. The city also has a number of *onsen* in hotels and ryokan available for public bathing.

TOTTORI-SAKYŪ (THE DUNES)
鳥取砂丘

Used as the film location for Teshigahara Hiroshi's classic 1964 film *Woman in the Dunes*, the Tottori sand dunes are on the coast about 5km from the city. There's a viewing point on a hillside overlooking the dunes, along with a huge car park and the usual assortment of tourist amenities. The dunes stretch for over 10km along the coast and, at some points, can be about 2km wide. The section where the dunes are highest is popular with parapenters, who fly off on the incoming sea breezes. You can even get a *Lawrence of Arabia* photo of yourself wearing Arabian headgear and accompanied by a camel if you choose. It's quite easy to get away from it all out on the sand, which has tracks all over the place.

You can stay at the **Tottori Cycling Terminal** (☎ 29-0800; 1157-115 Hamasaki; r per person with 2 meals ¥4800), but it's a bit isolated; there's a camping area next door. The Cycling Terminal also hires out bicycles; rates are ¥310 for four hours.

Use the Loop Bus (see Getting Around, p447) to get out to Tottori-sakyū. The bus stop for the dunes is Sakyū-Sentā (Dunes Centre); get off at the Kodomo-no-kuni iriguchi (Children's World entrance) for the Cycling Terminal.

Sleeping & Eating

Matsuya-sō (☎ 22-4891; 3-814 Yoshikata Onsen; s/tw ¥3500/6000; P) About a 10-minute walk from the station, this place is pleasant and comfortable.

Tottori Green Hotel Morris (☎ 22-2331; 2-107 Imamachi; s/tw ¥5250/9240) Here you can choose from nine different kinds of healing pillows to sleep on. The sign in English outside says 'Hotel Morris'.

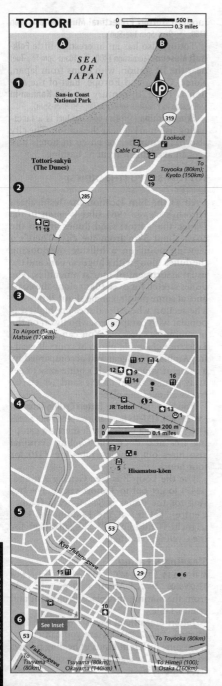

Hotel Taihei (☎ 29-1111; 752 Sakae-machi; s/tw ¥5300/9000; P ✕) Its red-brick façade makes this place easy to find.

Tottori Washington Hotel (☎ 27-8111; 102 Higashi Honji-chō; s/tw ¥7900/16,000; P ✕ ✕) Standard rooms are on offer from this national chain. In an effort to reduce waste, they no longer provide disposable razors or toothbrushes.

Daizen (☎ 27-6574; 715 Sakae-machi; meals ¥500-800; ✆ 11am-12am) For quantity and quality at a reasonable price, try the *teishoku* here. It's on the right as you enter the arcade. The *irrashais* (welcome) and *arigato gozaimashi-tas* (thank you very much) are deafening.

Flags (☎ 24-9580; 206 Sakae-machi; meals ¥620-920; ✆ 7am-10pm) A few streets north of the station, on the left, is a good little pizzeria with its own coffee shop next door.

Takumi Kappo (☎ 26-6355; 653 Sakae-machi; meals ¥800-9000; ✆ 11.30am-10pm) The lunch set meals are good value at this traditional Japanese eatery.

Jujuan (☎ 21-1919; 751 Suehiro Onsen-chō; set meals ¥800-3500; ✆ lunch & dinner). A *yakiniku* restaurant with lots of meat on skewers sizzling away.

Getting There & Away

The coastal JR San-in line runs through Tottori from Matsue (¥2210, 2¼ hours) and on to Toyooka (*futsū*, ¥1450, two hours) and Kyoto. The JR Inbi line goes to Tsuyama and on to Okayama (¥4880, two hours) on the San-yō coast.

Tottori airport is just west of town, with flights to/from Tokyo.

CAN YOU EAT NATTO?

Sooner or later, should you spend any length of time eating with Japanese acquaintances, you'll see your hitherto gracious hosts – amid much winking and elbow nudging – suddenly perform a culinary Jekyll and Hyde, in the game of 'Let's Gross Out the Gaijin'.

The rules, unstated but recognised intuitively by all, are simple: produce the weirdest food you can, and present it to the foreign guest in a situation so laced with *giri* (social obligation) that they are forced to eat it. Watch as they turn the same colour as freshly salted squid intestines. Suggested weapons in this game of gastronomic sabotage are *natto* (fermented soy beans, best topped off with a raw quail egg); *inago* (locusts), good and crunchy; and *uni* (sea urchin), orangey-yellow with the consistency and shape of wet brains.

If that fails to work, bring out the heavy guns. *Odori-dako* – octopus chopped up but very much alive, wriggling and adhering itself to the roof of one's mouth – should do the trick, but if all else fails there's one infallible weapon: *shira-ko* (raw cod sperm).

However, gaijin visitors are not without their own culinary arsenal. If you want to be on equal terms, stuff your backpack with liquorice bootlaces, steak and kidney pie, Vegemite or, horror of horrors, rice pudding. If you can get your hosts into a French restaurant, order snails and see who consumes them!

Getting Around

Tottori's efficient Loop Bus runs 8.40am to 4.30pm. On weekdays it runs every 30 minutes, and on weekends once an hour; there are irregular rest days. You can get a map and timetable from the information office.

The bus connects all of the major attractions, including the sand dunes, and costs ¥200/600 per ride/day pass. Rental bikes are available near the station.

SAN-IN COAST NATIONAL PARK
山陰海岸国立公園

The spectacular coastline east from the Tottori dunes all the way to the Tango-hantō peninsula in Kyoto-fu is known as the San-in Kaigan Kokuritsu Kōen – the San-in Coast National Park. There are sandy beaches, rugged headlands and a cruisey atmosphere.

Train lines run the length of the area, but they spend a fair bit of time inland and in tunnels. The best way to see the coastline is on wheels, whether it be by rental car, motorbike or bicycle.

Uradome Kaigan 浦富海岸

The first place of interest is Uradome Kaigan (a coastal part of the San-in Coast National Park, known for its bluffs and craggy outcrops). Forty-minute **cruises** (☎ 0857-73-1212; ¥1200; ☺ Mar-Nov) go from Ōtani-sanbashi,

which is about 35 minutes east of Tottori by bus from JR Tottori Station. The same bus travels via the dunes, so it's possible to visit the dunes and do the cruise as a day trip from Tottori. Boat is the only way to see the islets and craggy cliffs, with pines clinging precariously to their sides.

Uradome and **Makidani**, two very popular beaches, are a few kilometres east. The closest station is Iwami on the JR San-in line, 2km from the coast, where there's a **tourist information office** (☎ 0857-72-3481; ☺ 9am-6pm Tue-Sun). You can rent bicycles at the north exit of the station or arrange accommodation at the office here. **Seaside Uradome** (シーサイド浦富; ☎ 0857-73-1555; 2457-18 Uradome Iwamichō Iwami-gun; s/tw ¥4200/84000; ℗ ♨) is a 3.5km-long esplanade in Iwami that has views of Senkanmatsu and Natame Islands; it is also a lodging facility. It's on the sandy beachfront, and there's camping at Makidani beach.

Higashi-hama 東浜

The next train station heading eastwards is Higashi-hama; if you're riding the train, this is one to hop off at. It's all of 100m from the station to a long sandy beach where you can take a stroll or a dip and contemplate the fact that Japan is not all urban sprawl after all.

The Tottori-ken–Hyōgo-ken border is on the next headland.

Northern Honshū
本州の北部

> As we turn the corners of the narrow road to the deep north, we may soar with exhilaration, or we may fall flat on our faces...
>
> *Matsuo Bashō, 1644–94*

Northern Honshū is charming and atmospheric – if a bit misunderstood. It's been described as the Japanese 'deep south' (even though it's up north), a less developed agricultural region habitually treated with suspicion by city slickers.

But that's an injustice: northern Honshū has natural beauty in abundance and a gripping, well-preserved feudal past. Towns like Aizu-Wakamatsu, Tōno, Hiraizumi and Kakunodate – apparently innocuous – shield potent rituals and traditions, and unearthing them is one of the joys of travelling through here.

Northern Honshū comprises Fukushima-ken, Miyagi-ken, Iwate-ken, Aomori-ken, Akita-ken and Yamagata-ken (collectively known as Tōhoku), as well as Niigata-ken and the island Sado-ga-shima. Tōhoku was once called Michinoku, meaning 'back roads', and that sense of isolation provides fertile ground for many of Japan's most enduring myths and legends. The region also offers superb opportunities for hiking along spectacular coastlines and around spectral mountain ranges. You might encounter volcanic regions peppered with *rotemburo* (open-air hot springs), an experience too sublime to pass up. Northern Honshū is also home to some scrumptious regional cuisine and a startling array of eclectic festivals celebrating Old Japan.

English isn't widely spoken in Tōhoku's northernmost parts (actually, some of the dialects are impenetrable to southern Japanese), but it's really not that difficult to get around for non-native speakers. You'll find no shortage of friendly locals who'll help to keep you on track, delighted to share the fruits of the land they love.

HIGHLIGHTS

- Learn about bloody feudal history and the tragic White Tiger samurais at **Aizu-Wakamatsu** (p451)
- Go *kappa*-hunting at **Tōno** (p471), where these little goblins dwell
- Sample a small but remarkable taste of Hiraizumi's former glory at the **Chūson-ji** complex (p469)
- Hike around one of Northern Honshū's most sacred spots, the trio of mountains known as **Dewa Sanzan** (p498)
- Get away from the mainland crush on **Sado-ga-shima** (p507), a former island of exile with a rich, quirky history
- See if the bay of **Matsushima** (p463) can render you speechless, as it did Bashō

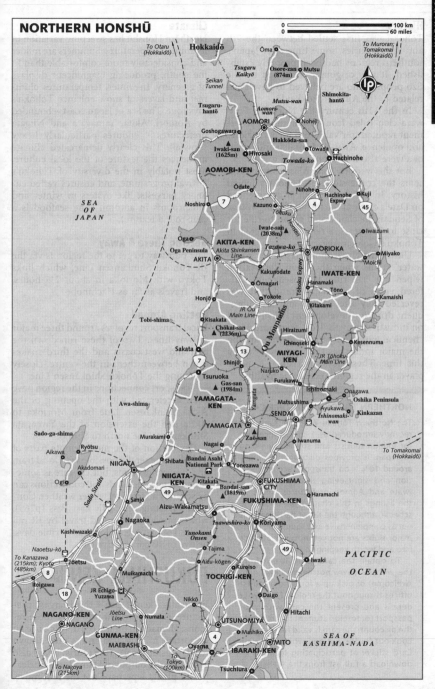

NORTHERN HONSHŪ

0 — 100 km
0 — 60 miles

To Otaru
(Hokkaidō)

Hokkaidō

Ōma

To Muroran;
Tomakomai
(Hokkaidō)

Tsugaru
Kaikyō

Osore-zan
(874m) Mutsu

Seikan
Tunnel

Mutsu-wan

Shimokita-
hantō

Tsugaru-
hantō

*Aomori-
wan*

AOMORI

Nohéji

Goshogawara

Hakkōda-san

Towada

Hachinohe

Iwaki-san
(1625m) Hirosaki

Towada-ko

AOMORI-KEN

Ōdate

Ninohe

Hachinohe
Expwy

Kuji

Tōhoku
Hansen

Kazuno

Noshiro

7

4

45

SEA
OF
JAPAN

Iwaizumi

Oga

Iwate-san
(2038m)

Akita Shinkansen
Line

MORIOKA

AKITA-KEN

Miyako

Tazawa-ko

Oga Peninsula

AKITA

Kakunodate

IWATE-KEN

Moichi

Kamaishi

Hanamaki

Tōno

Omagari

Yokote

Kitakami

Honjō

Tobi-shima

Kisakata

Chōkai-san
(2236m)

JR Ōu
Main Line

Hiraizumi

Ichinoseki

Kesennuma

Sakata

13

Shinjō

JR Tōhoku
Main Line

7

Tsuruoka

Gas-san
(1984m)

Naruko

**MIYAGI-
KEN**

Furukawa

Ishinomaki

Ōnagawa

Oshika Peninsula

Awa-shima

**YAMAGATA-
KEN**

Matsushima

Ayukawa

Kinkazan

Ishinomaki-
wan

Sado-ga-shima

YAMAGATA

SENDAI

Aikawa

Ryōtsu

Murakami

Zaō-san

Akadomari

Nagai

Iwanuma

To Tomakomai
(Hokkaidō)

Ogi

NIIGATA

Shibata

**NIIGATA-
KEN**

Bandai Asahi
National Park

Yonezawa

FUKUSHIMA
CITY

Sanjō

49

Kitakata

Bandai-san
(1819m)

FUKUSHIMA-KEN

Haramachi

Kashiwazaki

Nagaoka

Aizu-Wakamatsu

Inawashiro-ko

Kōriyama

Naoetsu-kō
To Kanazawa
(215km); Kyoto
(485km)

8

Jōetsu

Muikamachi

Yunokami
Onsen

Tajima

Aizu-kōgen

Kuroiso

Iwaki

PACIFIC

OCEAN

Itoigawa

18

JR Echigo-
Yuzawa

49

Daigo

NAGANO-KEN

NAGANO

Jōetsu
Line

Numata

TOCHIGI-KEN

Nikkō

Hitachi

UTSUNOMIYA

GUNMA-KEN

MAEBASHI

Mashiko

MITO

SEA OF
KASHIMA-NADA

Oyama

IBARAKI-KEN

To Nagoya
(215km)

To
Tokyo
(100km)

4

Tsuchiura

Ou Mountains

Sado Straits

Hiraizumi

Yamagata

History

Tōhoku was first settled between the 7th and 9th centuries, some time after Japan's southern regions had been properly established. It was originally inhabited by the Ezo people, who are believed to have been related to the Ainu of Hokkaidō.

In the 11th century the Northern Fujiwara clan ruled from Hiraizumi, a settlement reputed to rival Kyoto for its majesty and opulence. Aizu-Wakamatsu and Morioka were also important feudal towns.

But the warlord Date Masamune represents the cornerstone of Tōhoku's feudal history. In 1601 construction commenced on Date's castle at the former fishing village of Sendai; the clan would go on to rule for close to 300 years, a reign that ushered in Tōhoku's Golden Age.

Unfortunately, Tōhoku regained 'backwater' status when the Meiji Restoration wiped out clan rule. It subsequently suffered years of neglect, a trend that was reversed only after WWII and the subsequent drive for development heavily based on industrial growth. Iron, transport, steel, chemical, pulp and petroleum were among the major industries that sprouted during this time. These days, tourism is a major player in the region's economic health.

NORTHERN TŌHOKU WELCOME CARD

The Northern Tōhoku Welcome Card was recently introduced as a special incentive for foreign tourists and students residing in Japan. It provides discounts – usually around 10% – on transport, accommodation and sightseeing throughout Akita, Iwate and Aomori prefectures. Some of the listings in this chapter fall under the scheme, although the list of participants is not as comprehensive as it should be; many major sights are not yet included. Still, it's free and worth keeping to hand.

To obtain the card, print it out from the website (www.northern-tohoku.gr.jp /welcome) or pick up a form from tourist offices throughout the region. Fill in your details and present the card with your passport (or foreign student ID) to obtain the discount; the card is valid for one year. Look out for the red-and-white Welcome Card sticker at participating facilities or download a full list from the website.

Climate

Northern Honshū has sweeping variation in its annual temperatures. Summers are milder and considerably more comfortable than in the south, producing magnificent displays of greenery. In winter, temperatures plummet and layers of snow enhance Tōhoku's mystique. The Sea of Japan coast – bounded by Aomori, Akita, Yamagata and Niigata prefectures – endures particularly heavy snowfall. This clearly demarcated climate influences the texture of the local culture, most notably in the diversity of Tōhoku's festival programme, and ensures varied culinary harvests, like oysters in winter and mushrooms in autumn (fine seafood is a year-round feature).

Getting There & Away

The best way to get to the region is via the JR Tōhoku Shinkansen Line, which links Tokyo with Morioka in about 2½ hours, and travels as far as Hachinohe.

Getting Around

Local transport revolves around three major railway lines. Two of these run down the east and west coasts and the third snakes down between them in the centre, closely following the Tōhoku Shinkansen Line.

Transport connections in the region have been accelerated with the opening of the Akita Shinkansen Line from Morioka to Akita and the extension of the Yamagata Shinkansen Line north to Shinjō.

Exploration of the more remote parts of Tōhoku is generally possible with local train and bus connections, but car hire is sometimes preferable. Roads and connections can be severely affected by winter weather. Consider investing in the JR East Pass (p765), which provides unlimited travel by JR rail in the Tōhoku region for four flexible days, or five or 10 consecutive days.

FUKUSHIMA-KEN 福島県

Fukushima-ken, Japan's third-largest prefecture, can be divided into three loose regions. Hamadori, on the coast, was once an important mining area and is now known for its seaside resorts (the tourist board also promotes the output of Hamadori's nuclear power plants – perhaps not the best move,

MATSUO BASHŌ: POET OR NINJA?

Regarded as Japan's master of haiku, Matsuo Bashō (1644–94) is credited with elevating its status from comic relief to Zen-infused enlightenment. Bashō was born into a samurai family and in his late teenage years served the feudal lord Yoshitada. When Yoshitada died, his wandering spirit began to direct Bashō's life. Moving to Kyoto and then to Edo, Bashō found success as a published poet, but ultimately found the acclaim to be spiritually unsettling. He turned to Zen and the philosophy had a deep impact on his work: many comparisons have been made between his haiku and Zen *kōan* (short riddles), intended to bring about a sudden flash of insight in the listener. Bashō was also influenced by the natural philosophy of the Chinese Taoist sage, Chuangzi, and began to examine nature uncritically. Later, he developed his own poetic principle by drawing on the concept of *sabi*, a kind of spare, lonely beauty.

When he reached his 40s, Bashō decided to give his career away in favour of travelling throughout Japan, seeking to build friendships and commune with nature as he went. He published evocative accounts of his travels, including *The Records of a Weather-Beaten Skeleton* and *The Records of a Travel-Worn Satchel*, but his collection *The Narrow Road to the Deep North*, detailing his journey throughout Tōhoku in 1689, is perhaps the most famous. Like many Japanese, Bashō had initial misgivings ('I may as well be travelling to the ends of the earth', he lamented), but the north's special charms eventually rendered him lost for words, most famously on his encounter with Matsushima Bay – 'Matsushima, ah! Matsushima! Matsushima!' Bashō famously wrote (although recent evidence suggests that anecdote to be apocryphal).

The Narrow Road, a mixture of prose and haiku called *haibun*, uses Tōhoku – with its country traditions, natural beauty and way of life – as a metaphor for attaining an egoless state, a true communion with nature whereby the universe always remains. Nowhere is this more dramatically illustrated than in Bashō's visit to Hiraizumi, once a mighty feudal town that rivalled Kyoto, but which was destroyed virtually in a single stroke. Bashō wrote: 'Countries may fall, but their rivers and mountains remain. When spring comes to the ruined castle, the grass is green again.'

Some people, though, have tried to read even more into Bashō's life and work. In recent times, a bizarre theory has spread. It claims that Bashō was actually a ninja spy for the shōgunate, sent to Tohokū to report on any unrest that might be fermenting in the provinces; accordingly, his haikus are supposed to be coded missives. There's no real evidence for this, but some of the arguments are intriguing. The conspiracy theorists point out that Bashō covered 2500km on foot in 150 days (sometimes 50km a day) at the ripe old age of 46; only certain ninja, they say, were able to accomplish this, using methods of running and walking that used minute amounts of energy. He was also able to gain access to high-level feudal territory, a feat apparently impossible for ordinary people. Adding fuel to the rumours is the undeniable fact of the poet's early employment history (many ninja were also samurai), as well as the nature of his birthplace, in the Iga province – home of the famous Iga Ninja school.

Readers are advised to search on the Internet: some sites offer *The Narrow Road to the Deep North* as a downloadable text file, translated into English, along with reams of scholarship.

given Japan's recent safety record). Nakadori, the inland region, is the administrative hub and contains the capital, Fukushima City, and most of the population. Aizu, to the prefecture's west, was at the centre of the feudal war. Fukushima-ken is known for its hot springs and claims 200 of them.

AIZU-WAKAMATSU 会津若松

☎ 0242 / pop 120,000

This friendly town, in the middle of Fukushima prefecture, makes a relaxed base for exploring the Bandai Asahi National Park (p454). But Aizu-Wakamatsu has an intrigue all of its own, with a proud – if bloody and frequently tragic – samurai history. During the Edo period it was the capital of the Aizu clan, a reign that came to an end in the Bōshin Civil War in 1868, when Tsuruga castle fell after the clan sided with the Tokugawa Shōgunate against the imperial faction. This dynamic warrior past is still the glue that binds the community, with the reconstructed castle the centrepiece of a series of attractions detailing the Aizu legend.

Information

There's a **sightseeing information desk** (☎ 32-0688; ☷ 10am-6pm Mon-Sat, 10am-5pm Sun & holidays) inside Aizu-Wakamatsu Station and another at **Tsuruga-jō** (☎ 29-1511; ☷ 8.30am-5.30pm, closed 1st Mon-1st Thu Jul & 1st Tue-1st Thu Dec). The willing staff at both can supply you with English-language maps, brochures and thorough directions.

The **main post office** (cnr Chūō-dōri & Nanokomachi-dōri) is on the main street, and has an international ATM. There's a **police box** (☎ 22-5454) right next to the train station.

There's free Internet (30 minutes) at the Tsuruga-jō information desk. Pay for the net at **ePalette** (eパレット神明通店; ☎ 38-0211; basement of Tsutaya, Chūō-dōri; per hr ¥580), 10 minutes south of the main post office.

Sights

The following, arranged in a ring around the fringes of the city centre, are clearly signposted in English. It's possible to do the lot on foot in a day, but a tourist bus does the loop if you need it.

Iimori-yama (飯盛山) is the mountain where a group of 'White Tiger' samurai killed themselves during the Bōshin Civil War (opposite). At the foot of the mountain, the **Byakkotai Memorial Hall** (白虎隊記念館; Iimori-yama, Ikki-machi; admission ¥400; ☷ 8am-5pm Apr-Nov, 8.30am-4.30pm Dec-Mar) explains the story, while **Sazae-dō** (さざえ堂; ☎ 22-3163; Iimori-yama, Ikki-machi; admission ¥400; ☷ 8.15am-sunset Apr-Oct, 9.30am-4.30pm Nov-Mar), an 18th-century hexagonal hall, contains 33 statues of Kannon (the Buddhist goddess of mercy). It also has a fabulous spiral staircase that, Escher-like, allows you to walk up and down without retracing your steps.

Saigō Tanomo was the Aizu clan's chief retainer and **Aizu Bukeyashiki** (会津武家屋敷; Innai Higashiyama-machi; admission ¥850; ☷ 8.30am-5pm Apr-Oct, 9am-4.30pm Nov-Mar) is a superbly realised reconstruction of his *yashiki* (villa). Suitably opulent, there are 38 rooms, including a guest room for the Aizu lord, a tea-ceremony house, quarters for the clan's judge and a rice-cleaning mill presented here in full, noisy working order. You'll also find the room where Tanomo's wife and children committed suicide, fearing he wouldn't return from combat in the Bōshin War – although the utter impassivity of the wax models re-enacting the scene comically undercuts the drama. Another quirky

detail is the samurai lavatory: underneath is a sandbox on wheels, an 'early warning system' that could be removed so staff could monitor the health of the warriors. There's also a target range where you can try your hand at archery for ¥200.

Oyaku-en (御薬園; ☎ 27-2472; Hanaharu-machi; admission ¥310; ☷ 8.30am-5pm) is a meditative garden complex with a large, central carp pond. Originally a holiday retreat for the Aizu clan, it features a section devoted to the cultivation of medicinal herbs (available for purchase) – a practice encouraged by the lords.

Tsuruga-jō (鶴ヶ城; ☎ 27-4005; Oute-machi; admission ¥400; ☷ 8.30am-4.30pm, closed 4 days from 1st Mon in Jul, 3 days from 1st Tue in Dec), otherwise known as Crane Castle, was the headquarters of the Aizu clan. Although the present building is a 1965 reconstruction, parts of the daunting walls remain, as does the castle's moat. Inside, there's a museum with historical artefacts from battle and daily life. Displays are a bit sketchy, although the frequent martial-arts demonstrations, carried out by adepts in full warrior regalia, are engaging. The 5th storey affords a terrific view of the surrounding town and valley, including Iimori-yama.

On the castle grounds, **Rinkaku** (茶室麟閣; ☎ 27-4005; admission ¥200, combined castle ticket ¥500; ☷ 8.30am-4.30pm, closed 4 days from 1st Mon in Jul, 3 days from 1st Tue in Dec) is an evocative, 400-year-old teahouse that was rescued from the castle's destruction by a local family and returned here in 1990.

For nonfeudal glimpses into Aizu-Wakamatsu's history, try the **Fukushima Prefectural Museum** (福島県立博物館; ☎ 28-6000; 1-25 Jyoto-machi; admission ¥260; ☷ 9.30am-4.30pm, closed Mon & day after public holidays except Sat & Sun), with 400 displays ranging from prehistoric times to recent history.

The **Aizu Sake Brewing Museum** (会津酒造歴史館; ☎ 26-0031; 8-18 Higashisakae-machi; admission ¥300; ☷ 8.30am-5pm, 9.30am-4.30pm Dec-Mar) details the history of rice-wine brewing in the area. Naturally, you can sample the famous tipple for the price of admission.

Festivals & Events

Aizu-Wakamatsu holds four main festivals, coordinated according to season. The most prominent is the three-day **Autumn Festival** (22–24 September), an extravagant procession that threads through the city to Tsu-

THE WHITE TIGERS

In 1868 a group of 20 teenage samurai, known as the Byakkotai (White Tigers), looked down upon Tsuruga-jō, saw it shrouded in smoke, and concluded that imperial forces had captured the castle. Rather than surrender, they committed *seppuku* (ritual suicide by disembowelment). In reality it was the surrounding area that was ablaze and it would be weeks before the Aizu clan would fall; one lad survived and devoted the rest of his life to passing on the story. This strange tale greatly tickles Japanese sensibilities, with its tragicomic blend of blind loyalty tempered by utter futility and a ruthless universe. To the outsider, there's a dark side: Mussolini was so taken with the Byakkotai he donated a grandiose monument to commemorate the event. Topped by an eagle, it surveys the horizon from the top of Iimori-yama, surrounded by Byakkotai graves and the steady stream of Japanese tourists scanning the horizon to see what the White Tigers couldn't: a fully intact castle.

ruga-jō, accompanied by a drum-and-fife band, a children's parade and an evening lantern parade. There's also the **Higanjishi** in spring, the **Summer Festival** and winter's **Sainokami**. The city holds its **Rice Planting Festival** on 12 July.

Sleeping

Aizu-no-sato Youth Hostel (会津の里ユースホステル; ☎ 27-2054; 36 Kofune-hatakata, Aizu-Shiokawa-chō; dm from ¥2100) Set among lovely old grounds with well-worn but comfortable Japanese-style rooms, this hostel is worth leaving the city centre for. Presided over by a gregarious host who's somewhat of a Byakkotai buff, it's a 15-minute walk from Shiokawa Station on the JR Banetsu-saisen Line. From the station turn right, then take the first left and follow the red lights along the road, finally turning left at Rte 121. Ask the friendly locals for help.

Aizuno Youth Hostel (会津野ユースホステル; ☎ 55-1020; www.aizuno.com/e_index.html; 88 Kakiyashiki, Terasaki Aizu-Takada-chō; dm/private r from ¥2800/4200) Again away from Aizu's centre, although the pleasing rural setting sweetens the deal. It's a 20-minute walk west from

Aizu-Takada Station along the Tadami Line from Aizu-Wakamatsu (¥230, 20 minutes). Note: seven trains run daily, but only one in the afternoon. Find out your train's arrival time in advance and give the hostel notice – the manager will pick you up from the station (he also escorts guests to a hot spring at 6pm daily). Free bike rental and breakfast.

Minshuku Takaku (民宿多賀来; ☎ 26-6299; 104 Innai Higashiyama-machi; r with/without 2 meals from ¥6000/4500) This cosy place, with well-kept Japanese-style rooms, is five minutes east of the Aizu Bukeyashiki bus stop.

There's a slew of business hotels clustered around or near the train station, all at about the same level of cleanliness and comfort, with TVs and phones in the rooms.

Fuji Grand Hotel (フジグランドホテル; ☎ 28-3111; 5-25 Ekimae-machi; s/d from ¥4900/9900) Rates depend on views – if that's a consideration, pay more to ensure your room doesn't face the sheer concrete wall next door. It's next to the station, to the right as you exit.

Green Hotel Aizu (グリーンホテル会津; ☎ 24-5181; 3-7-23 Chūō; s/d ¥5600/9500) Five minutes southeast of the station. Western-style or tatami rooms.

Hotel Alpha One (ホテルアルファーワン; ☎ 32-6868; 5-8 Ekimae-machi; s/d from ¥5200/9500) Next door to (and virtually identical to) the Fuji Grand.

Washington Hotel (ワシントンホテル; ☎ 22-6111; 201 Byakko-machi; s/d from ¥7770/13,650) Near the Green Hotel. Roomy, with brand-new facilities.

Eating

Wappa meshi is a local dish consisting of steamed fish over rice. It's prepared in a round container made from tree bark, which imparts a woody fragrance to the meal.

Takino (田季野; ☎ 25-0808; 5-31 Sakae-chō; wappa meshi from ¥1350; ☉ 11am-10pm) An atmospheric, split-level restaurant where *wappa meshi* is served in sublime, subtly balanced combinations. Try the finely shredded crab or salmon versions. From the main post office, facing south, turn left onto Nanokomachi-dōri, then take the first right; it's down a side street about 15 minutes' walk on your left. Ask the obliging staff at the information desk to mark up a map with the exact location.

Mitsutaya (満田屋; ☎ 27-1345; 8-49 Sakae-machi; skewers from ¥180; ☉ 10am-5pm, closed 1st & 3rd Wed of each month & every Wed Jan-Mar) At this former bean-paste mill, dating from 1869, the speciality is eight varieties of *dengaku*; these are bamboo skewers with deep-fried tofu and vegetables such as taro basted in sweet miso paste and baked over charcoal. Facing west from the main post office, walk down Nanokomachi-dōri, then take the second left; it's just near the intersection with Nanokomachi-dōri.

Aizu Kaiseki Fukuman (ふくまん; ☎ 24-6377; 1-1-25 Omachi; set meals ¥3500; 11am-2pm & 5-9pm Thu-Tue) Given the area's history, it's fitting that Aizu has a restaurant devoted to *buke ryōri* (samurai cuisine). At Fukuman, try the *buke honzen*, a reproduction of a typical dinner course enjoyed by Edo warriors. You'll need to book ahead.

Getting There & Around

From Tokyo, take the JR Tōhoku *shinkansen* to Kōriyama (¥7970, 1¼ hours), then change to an hourly *kaisoku* train on the JR Banetsu-saisen Line for Aizu-Wakamatsu (¥1110, 1¼ hours). There are two daily *kaisoku* trains between Aizu-Wakamatsu and Niigata (¥2210, 2½ hours). Express buses to Niigata run four times daily (¥2000, 1¾ hours).

The **Aizu Town Bus** (まちなか周遊バス ハイカラさん; single/day pass ¥200/500) does a loop of the sights, while **Takahashi** (8am-5pm; rental per day ¥1000), near the Washington Hotel, rents bicycles.

KITAKATA 喜多方

☎ 0241 / pop 40,000

Kitakata was once the commercial shadow to the warrior-driven dynamo that was Aizu-Wakamatsu. An old Kitakata saying reflects that singular drive to production: 'A man is not a man unless he has built at least one kura [a mud-walled storehouse]'. These days, the town's 2600 coloured kura – now functioning as living quarters, sake breweries and workshops – are a perennial tourist attraction, as are its 120 *rāmen* (soup noodles) shops.

Staff at the small **tourist information kiosk** (☎ 24-2633; 8.30am-5.15pm), left of the station exit, have copies of a small English-language map.

Sample the excellent local sake at **Yamatogawa Sake Brewing Museum** (大和川酒造北方風土館; ☎ 22-2233; 4761 Teramachi; admission free; 9am-4.30pm), 15 minutes north of the station.

The **Kitakata Hotel** (キタカタホテル; ☎ 22-0139; 8269-2 Machida; s ¥5250), just across from the

station, is your standard business deal, while **Sasaya Ryokan** (笹屋旅館; ☎ 22-0008; Chūō-dōri; r per person with 2 meals/no meals from ¥8800/5500) is traditional accommodation 1km north of the station.

Genraiken (源来軒; ☎ 22-0091; 7745 Kitakata City; sets from ¥800; 10am-8pm Wed-Mon) is Kitakata's best-known *rāmen* shop, with a 70-year history and a devoted lunchtime crowd. Head south on Chūō-dōri and look for the red façade.

Getting There & Around

Kitakata is a relatively easy trip from Aizu-Wakamatsu, accessible by train along the JR Banetsu-saisen Line (¥320, 15 minutes). **Bicycle rental** (2hr/daily ¥500/1500) is available outside Kitakata Station, while a **horse-drawn carriage** (☎ 24-4111; ¥1300), shaped like a *kura*, departs from the train station for a tour of the more interesting storehouses.

BANDAI PLATEAU 磐梯高原

☎ 0241 / pop 4000

On 15 July 1888 **Bandai-san** (磐梯山; 1819m), a once-dormant volcano, suddenly erupted, spewing forth a tremendous amount of debris that's said to have lowered the mountain's height by 600m, while destroying dozens of villages and killing over 400 people. The aftershock completely rearranged the landscape, creating the plateau, Bandai-kōgen, and damming local rivers, which then formed numerous water bodies. Now Japan's second-largest national park, it's hemmed in by the Fukushima, Niigata and Yamagata prefectural boundaries, and offers stirring scenery and stellar opportunities for hiking and skiing. The most popular walk follows a 3.7km nature trail around **Goshiki-numa** (五色沼), an area of around 11 lakes and ponds known as Five Colours Lakes, after mineral deposits from the eruption imparted various hues to the waters – emerald green, cobalt blue and so on – that change with the weather. There are trailheads at the Goshiki-numa Iriguchi and Bandai-kōgen bus stops, the main transport hubs on the edge of Hibara-ko. Bandai-san itself can be climbed in a day with an early start; the most popular route starts from the Bandai-kōgen bus stop and climbs up through the skiing ground to the summit.

There's a **visitors centre** (☎ 32-2850; 8.30am-4pm) not far from the Goshiki-numa Iriguchi

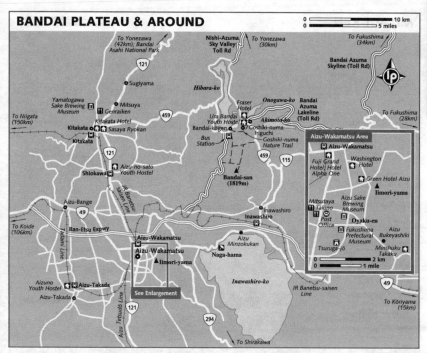

BANDAI PLATEAU & AROUND

0   10 km
0   5 miles

To Yonezawa (42km); Bandai Asahi National Park

Nishi-Azuma Sky Valley Toll Rd

To Yonezawa (30km)

To Fukushima (34km)

Bandai Azuma Skyline (Toll Rd)

Sugiyama

Hibara-ko

Yamatogawa Sake Brewing Museum

Mitsuya

Genraiken

Fraser Hotel

Onogawa-ko

Bandai Azuma Lakeline (Toll Rd)

To Fukushima (28km)

To Niigata (150km)

Kitakata Hotel

Ura Bandai Youth Hostel

Akimoto-ko

Kitakata

Sasaya Ryokan

Bandai-kogen

Goshiki-numa Iriguchi

Kitakata

Bus Station

Goshiki-numa Nature Trail

Aizu-Wakamatsu Area

Aizu-Wakamatsu

Aizu-no-sato Youth Hostel

Shiokawa

Bandai-san (1819m)

Fuji Grand Hotel Hotel Alpha One

Washington Hotel

Green Hotel Aizu

Aizu-Bange

Inawashiro

Iimori-yama

To Koide (106km)

Ban-Etsu Expwy

Inawashiro

Mitsutaya Takino

Aizu Sake Brewing Museum

Fukushima Post Office

Oyaku-en

Aizu Bukeyashiki

Aizu-Wakamatsu

Aizu Minzokukan

Fukushima Prefectural Museum

Minshuku Takaku

Aizu-Wakamatsu

Tsuruga-jō

Naga-hama

Iimori-yama

0   2 km
0   1 mile

Aizuno Youth Hostel

Aizu-Takada

Inawashiro-ko

JR Banetsu-saisen Line

Aizu-Takada

See Enlargement

To Kōriyama (15km)

To Shirakawa

---

trailhead and a **tourist information office** (☎ 62-2048; ✆ 8.30am-5pm) to the left outside JR Ina-washiro Station.

Sleeping & Eating

Several *minshuku* (Japanese B&B) cater to hikers and skiers, and cost from ¥6500 per person. For more details and other information call the **Goshiki-numa Minshuku Information Center** (☎ 32-2902).

Ura Bandai Youth Hostel (裏磐梯ユースホステル; ☎ 32-2811; urabandai-YH@nifty.com; dm from ¥2940; ✆ late Apr-Nov) This friendly old hostel has a super location, next to one of the Goshiki-numa trailheads. There's an 11pm curfew and bicycles for hire (¥1000 per day). It's a seven-minute walk from the Goshiki-numa Iriguchi bus stop, sign-posted right from the car park. The adjoin-ing camping ground has ¥1000 tents and ¥5000 cabins.

Fraser Hotel (☎ 32-3470; r per person with 2 meals from ¥14,000) This upmarket option is 100m northeast of the Goshiki-numa Iriguchi bus stop, along the highway and next to a con-venience store.

Getting There & Away

The JR Banetsu-saisen Line (*kaisoku* ¥480, 35 minutes) connects Aizu-Wakamatsu with the town of Inawashiro (猪苗代湖). From outside Inawashiro Station, frequent buses depart from stop 3 and pass by the Goshiki-numa Iriguchi stop (¥750, 25 min-utes), heading onto the Bandai-kōgen stop (¥870, 30 minutes). Hourly buses also run between Aizu-Wakamatsu Station and Ina-washiro Station (¥1140, 45 minutes).

MIYAGI-KEN 宮城県

Miyagi-ken is Tōhoku's economic and cul-tural core; its capital, Sendai, is Tohokū's most cosmopolitan city. This dual status de-rives from the reign of Date Masamune, who developed Sendai into a major culture and trade centre in the 1600s. Miyagi-ken has sev-eral attractions including Zaō Onsen, loved by skiers and *onsen* (mineral hot springs) enthusiasts, and Matsushima, a bay studded with pine-covered islands, immortalised by Bashō and popular with Japanese sightseers.

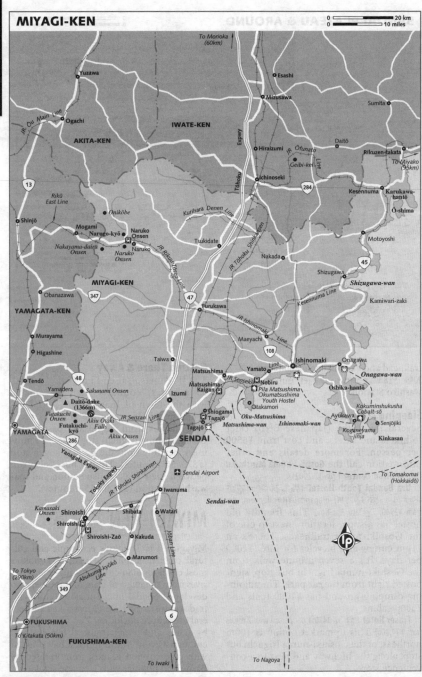

MIYAGI-KEN

0 — 20 km
0 — 10 miles

To Morioka (60km)

Yuzawa

Esashi

Mizusawa

Sumita

Ogachi

JR Ōu Main Line

IWATE-KEN

AKITA-KEN

Hiraizumi

Ōfunato

Daitō

Rikuzen-takata

13

Rikū East Line

Onikōbe

Ichinoseki

284

To Miyako (95km)

Kesennuma

Karukawa-hantō

Shinjō

Mogami

Naruko-kyō

Naruko Onsen

Kurihara Denen Line

Ō-shima

Nakayama-daira Onsen

Naruko

Naruko Onsen

Tsukidate

Motoyoshi

JR Rikū Tōsen Line

Obanazawa

347

MIYAGI-KEN

47

Nakada

Shizugawa

45

Shizugawa-wan

Kamiwari-zaki

YAMAGATA-KEN

Furukawa

JR Ishinomaki Line

Kesennuma Line

Murayama

Maeyachi

108

Higashine

Taiwa

Yamato

Ishinomaki

Onagawa

Onagawa-wan

Tendō

48

Yamadera

Sakunami Onsen

Matsushima

JR Senseki Line

Nobiru

Oshika-hantō

Daitō-dake (1366m)

Izumi

Matsushima-Kaigan

Pila Matsushima Okumatsushima Youth Hostel

Ōtakamori

Kokuminshukusha Cobalt-sō

Futakuchi Onsen

Akiu Ōtaki Falls

JR Senzan Line

Shiogama

Tagajō

Oku-Matsushima

Ayukawa

Senjōjiki

Futakuchi-kyō

Akiu Onsen

Tagajō

Matsushima-wan

Ishinomaki-wan

Koganeyama-jinja

Kinkasan

YAMAGATA

286

SENDAI

4

Yamagata Expwy

Tōhoku Expwy

JR Tōhoku Shinkansen

Sendai Airport

To Tomakomai (Hokkaidō)

Iwanuma

Sendai-wan

Kamasaki Onsen

Shiroishi

Shibata

Watari

Shiroishi

Shiroishi-Zaō

Kakuda

Marumori

To Tokyo (290km)

349

Abukuma Kyūkō Line

Jōban Line

6

FUKUSHIMA

To Kitakata (50km)

FUKUSHIMA-KEN

To Iwaki

To Nagoya

Geibi-kei

Tōhoku Expwy

JR Ōfunato Line

JR Tōhoku Shinkansen

SENDAI 仙台

☎ 022 / pop 1,008,000

Sendai, although northern Honshū's largest city, gets some unflattering press, particularly when compared to Tokyo or Osaka – as though it's the naive country cousin to those seething metropolises. It's true that Sendai is nowhere near as big as Tokyo, but everyone knows that size isn't everything. During WWII, Sendai was demolished by Allied bombing and was later rebuilt with wide streets and boulevards; you won't find the likes of Sendai's airy, tree-lined streets in the country's capital.

The people are expansive, too, with the malls frequently packed with a mad array of buskers. This party-hearty mood culminates in Sendai's propulsive Jōzenji Jazz Festival, a two-day, open-air extravaganza; the Tanabata Matsuri tops that, though, with two million visitors each year.

The city also has a compelling history as the stomping ground of the remarkable feudal lord, Date Masamune (1567–1636), known as the One-Eyed Dragon. A number of intriguing sites around town pay tribute to his overarching presence, as does the name 'Sendai' – it means '1000 generations', apparently an indication of how long Masamune felt his clan would rule.

Finally, Sendai is an ideal base to arrange tickets, exchange your rail pass, sort out post, check email and see some bright lights before heading to nearby rural *onsen* or along the coast.

Orientation

From Sendai Station, the broad sweep of Aoba-dōri, lined with many of the major department stores, banks and hotels, leads west to a park, Aoba-yama. The main shopping areas are the series of arcades along Chūō-dōri (also known as CLIS Rd) and Ichibanchō-dōri, which intersect just east of Kokubunchō-dōri, the main drag of Tōhoku's largest entertainment district. To the north is Jozenji-dōri, a delightful street lined with lush trees.

Information
BOOKSHOPS

Maruzen (Map p460; ☎ 264-0151; 1-3-1 Chūō, Aoba-ku; ◷ 10am-8pm) English-language magazines and books on the AER building's 1st floor.

THE ONE-EYED DRAGON

Date Masamune is the most famous figure in Miyagi's feudal history. Nicknamed Dokuganryū (One-Eyed Dragon), after he caught smallpox as a child and went blind in his right eye, he combined military nous with commercial instinct, ranking among the most important lords in feudal Japan. He was also an aesthete with finely developed tastes in *nō* theatre (stylised Japanese dance/drama performed on a bare stage) and calligraphy, and transformed Sendai into a major cultural centre.

Masamune became head of the Date clan at the age of 17 and quickly increased his territory through ferocious skill on the battleground. When Japan was wracked by civil war in 1598, Masamune sided with Tokugawa Ieyasu's victorious faction. For his efforts Masamune was granted control over the Sendai domain, and soon after moved his base of operations to the village of Sendai in order to gain access to the port.

He constructed Aoba Castle in 1601 and then proceeded to build Sendai as a major focus of trade, constructing a salt works and ensuring the region supplied a considerable quantity of the country's grain. He also oversaw the construction of a series of temples, shrines and other sites of spiritual significance. But Date's rule was also remarkable for his developing interest in Christianity. This culminated in his dispatch of Japan's first diplomatic envoy, seeking trade with Mexico and Europe as well as an audience with Pope Paul V.

Many predicted Masamune would soon rise to the shōgunate and control the whole of Japan, but he was never fully trusted by his superiors, due to his unorthodox manner and singular leadership; it was suspected, for example, that Masamune's European envoy was designed to drum up European support for an overthrow of the incumbent shōgun.

But the people of Sendai always remained loyal to Masamune's vision, even today, as illustrated by the recently built Miyagi Stadium: the roof of its west stand is modelled after the unique crescent symbol the warlord wore on his helmet.

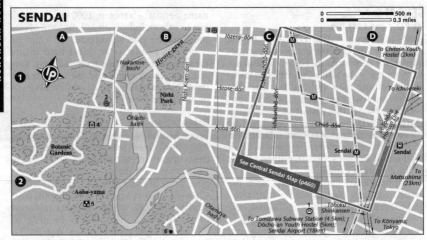

EMERGENCY

Main police station (Map p460; ☎ 222-7171; 4-1-25 4 Ichibanchō, Aoba-ku)

INTERNET ACCESS

Media & Information Center (Map p460; ☎ 724-1200; per 30min free; ☯ 10am-8pm) On the AER building's 5th floor.

Popeye Media Cafe (Map p460; ☎ 726-7890; 2-6-4 Chūō-dōri; per hr ¥500; ☯ 24hr)

Sendai International Centre (Map p458; 仙台国際 センター; ☎ 265-2471; www.sira.or.jp/english /e_top.html; ☯ 9am-8pm; per 30min free)

Sendai Mediatheque (Map p458; せんだいメディアテーク; www.smt.city.sendai.jp/en; per 30min free; ☯ 9am-8pm, library 10am-8pm Tue-Sun) From Sendai Station, take the Loople bus to stop 9.

MEDICAL SERVICES

Sendai City Hospital (☎ 263-9900; 3-1 Shimizu-koji, Wakabayashi-ku; ☯ 24hr)

POST

Central Post Office (Map p458; ☎ 267-8077; 1-7 Kitame-machi, Aoba-ku) Offers international ATM service; (☯ ATM Service 8am-11pm Mon-Fri, 9am-9pm Sat, 9am-7pm Sun) and cash advances on foreign-issued credit cards.

There is also a branch on the 1st floor of Sendai Station with international ATM.

TOURIST INFORMATION

Sendai International Centre (Map p458; 仙台国際 センター; ☎ 265-2471; www.sira.or.jp/english/e_top .html; ☯ 9am-8pm) Features an information desk with English-speaking staff, international newspaper library, bulletin board, CNN broadcasts, free Internet access and a Visa ATM.

Tourist Information Office (Map p460; ☎ 222-4069; ☯ 8.30am-8pm) Inside the station's west exit, it has possibly Tōhoku's most efficient staff, as well as the travellers' best friend: a map of Sendai that pinpoints every convenience store in town, an extraordinarily handy navigational tool in a country with a *konbini* on every street corner.

Sights & Activities

You can do Sendai on foot – it's a great way to get a feel for the city, as it morphs from concrete and streets into hills, greenery and woodland. It would take you a full day, though. The Loople tourist bus includes the following sights during its circuit.

Masamune Date's mausoleum, **Zuihō-den** (Map p458; 瑞鳳殿; ☎ 262-6250; admission ¥550; ☯ 9am-4.30pm, 9am-4pm Dec & Jan; Loople stop 4), is at the summit of a tree-covered hill by the Hirose-gawa. It was originally built in 1637, destroyed by Allied bombing during WWII and reconstructed in 1979. The present building is an exact replica of the original, faithful to the ornate and sumptuous Momoyama style: a complex, interlocking architecture, characterised by multicoloured woodcarvings.

Also atop the hill are the mausoleums of Masamune's second and third successors, Date Tadamune and Date Tsunamune. When the reconstruction commenced, the remains of the three lords, as well as personal possessions and items of armour, were excavated. These are now displayed in a museum at the site, as are likenesses of the three, accompanied by a rather finicky comparison of the lengths of their noses and the shapes of their foreheads.

Sendai-jō (Map p458; 仙台城跡; Loople stop 6) was built on Aoba-yama in 1602 by Date Masamune. It was commonly known as Aoba-jō (Green Leaves Castle), after a nearby spring that flowed even during times of drought. The castle's partial destruction during the Meiji era was completed by WWII bombing – nothing remains today, save for sections of the imposing walls and a restored *sumiyagura* (turret). Still, the park does have sweeping views over the city, a stirring statue of Masamune on horseback, and even an amusingly touristed area filled with shops and restaurants. The whole experience is an instructive guide on how to make a little from a lot; for the Japanese, it's the spirit that counts, and armed with a little knowledge of the Masamune legend, it's rather easy for the outsider to get caught up in it.

If you don't have that kind of knowledge when you climb the hill, you can get it at the **Aoba Castle Exhibition Hall** (Map p458; 青葉城資料展示館; ☎ 222-0218; admission ¥700; ☼ 9am-5pm Apr-Oct, 9am-4pm Nov-Mar). A computer-generated film depicts the castle's former glory. You can get English-language headsets.

At **Sendai City Museum** (Map p458; 仙台市博物館; San-nomaru-ato, Kawauchi, Aoba-ku; admission ¥400; ☼ 9am-4.45pm Tue-Sun; Loople stop 5) there's a scale model of Sendai castle, along with an exhaustive account of the Masamune era. Among some 13,000 artefacts loaned from the Date family is his distinctive armour.

Festivals & Events

Tanabata Matsuri (Star Festival; 6–8 August), which is Sendai's major event, celebrates a Chinese legend about the stars Vega and Altair. Vega was the daughter of a king, who fell in love with and married Altair, a common herder. The king disapproved, so he formed the Milky Way between them. Once a year, magpies are supposed to spread their wings across the universe so that the lovers can meet – traditionally on 7 July. Sendai seems to have stretched the dates a bit, but celebrates in grand style by decorating the main streets with bamboo poles festooned with multicoloured streamers and holding afternoon parades on Jōzenji-dōri. A couple of million visitors ensure that accommodation is booked solid at this time of year.

Other major festivals include the highly infectious **Jōzenji Street Jazz Festival** (second weekend of September), when 600 buskers from across Japan perform in Sendai's streets and arcades. The **Pageant of Starlight** (12–31 December) illuminates Aoba-dōri and Jōzenji-dōri with festive lights. The Ōsaki Hachiman-gū shrine plays host to **Dontosai** (14 January), when men brave subzero weather conditions to hop around almost naked in an apparent show of collective madness, but which is really a ritual supposed to bring good fortune for the new year.

Sleeping
BUDGET

Dōchū-an Youth Hostel (Map p458; 道中庵ユースホステル; ☎ 247-0511; 1 Kita-yashiki, Onoda, Taihaku-ku; dm from ¥3150) This evocative former farmhouse features genial management, bike hire, free Internet, home cooking and a fantastic old cedar bath to soak in. It's away from the city centre, if that matters, 5km south of Sendai at the end of the subway line in Tomizawa (¥290, 12 minutes), then a further 15-minute walk. The station has a sketch map to help you negotiate your way through the side streets.

Chitose Youth Hostel (Map p458; 仙台千登勢ユースホステル; ☎ 222-6329; 6-3-8 Odawara, Aoba-ku; dm from ¥3150) Closer to the city, this snug hostel, with Japanese-style rooms, is a 20-minute walk from Sendai Station's west exit. Take any bus going via Miyamachi from stop 17 at the west bus pool and get off at Miyamachi-ni-chōme; the hostel is tucked down a small side street three blocks east of the bus stop.

Takenaka Ryokan (Map p460; ☎ 225-6771; 2-9-23 Chūō, Aoba-ku; s/d ¥4200/6000) Next to Hirose-dōri Subway Station, this is a popular place with well-kept rooms.

MIDRANGE

Sendai has a preponderance of business hotels, all offering pretty much the same thing: TVs in the rooms and slightly cramped quarters. Except at the top end, of course.

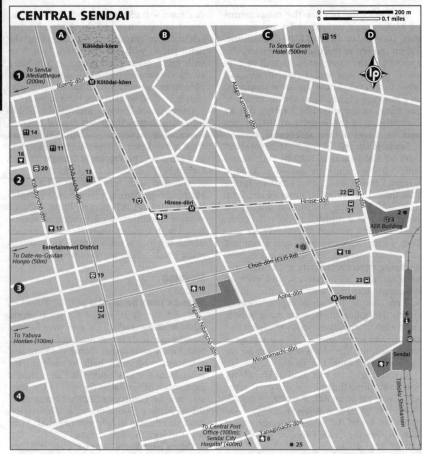

CENTRAL SENDAI

Sendai Green Hotel (Map p460; 仙台グリーン ホテル; ☎ 221-7070; 2-5-6 Nishiki-chō, Aoba-ku; s/d from ¥4100/8200) Basic, sparse rooms, although the views over the city are good. There's a spacious lounge area and accommodating staff. North of Jozenji-dōri, straight ahead from Ekimae-dōri.

Tokyo Dai-Ichi Hotel Sendai (Map p460; ☎ 262-1355; 2-3-18 Chūō, Aoba-ku; s/tw from ¥5600/12,600) A central hotel with a functional restaurant and smallish rooms.

TOP END

Hotel Metropolitan Sendai (Map p460; ☎ 268-2525; 1-1-1 Chūō, Aoba-ku; s/tw ¥11,550/24,255) The Metropolitan's rooms are comfortable enough, but its facilities go the whole hog. It features

Japanese and Chinese restaurants, a Sky Lounge, a gym, an indoor pool and even a wedding chapel, presumably for those who strike it lucky during their stay.

Sendai Kokusai Hotel (Map p460; ☎ 268-1112; 4-6-1 Chūō, Aoba-ku; s/d from ¥13,282/20,790) The Kokusai is a classy option, with a sumptuous baroque dining area, and large rooms done up in brown and cream tones.

Eating
JAPANESE

The Sendai culinary scene is known for *gyūtan* (cow tongue), which is much loved by locals. Apparently the tradition derived from hard times (as so many Tōhoku traditions do) – in the immediate postwar years, meat was scarce, so cow tongue was served instead of being thrown out. Expect deep queues at the following first three restaurants.

Umami Tasuke (Map p460; ☎ 262-2539; 1st fl Senmatsushima Bldg, 2-11-11 Kokubunchō, Aoba-ku; gyūtan from ¥750; ☣ lunch & dinner Tue-Sun) Serves excellent *gyūtan* in boiled, salted and fatty variants.

Aji-Tasuke (Map p460; ☎ 225-4641; 4-4-13 Ichibanchō, Aoba-ku; gyūtan from ¥900, sets from ¥1350; ☣ lunch & dinner Wed-Mon) Try *gyūtan* cooked over charcoal, or the set menu featuring the famous dish accompanied by oxtail soup and rice with boiled barley.

Date-no-Gyutan Honpo (伊達の牛たん本舗; ☎ 263-7710; 1-8-13 Kokubunchō, Aoba-ku; sets from ¥1600; ☣ lunch & dinner Wed-Mon) A classy *gyūtan* choice, brought into sharp focus by its telltale motto: 'Serving thick, tender and savoury meat'.

Yabuya Honten (やぶや 本店; ☎ 222-5002; 2-2-24 Omachi, Aoba-ku; mains from ¥900; ☣ lunch & dinner) A much-loved *soba* (buckwheat noodles) specialist, Yabuya Honten has been around since 1847 – more than enough time to perfect its craft. The *kamo-zaru soba* variation, served with duck, is terrific.

Sushikan (Map p460; ☎ 268-1822; 4-5-6 Ichibanchō; sets from ¥2200; ☣ lunch & dinner) This popular *kaiten-sushi* (sushi train) restaurant is known for the freshness of its dishes.

INTERNATIONAL

Namaskar (Map p460; ☎ 222-7701; basement TK Bldg, 2-2-11 Ichiban-chō, Aoba-ku; mains from ¥1300; ☣ dinner) The menu, with its spice-level warnings, comes on like Indian Cooking's Greatest Hits: tandoori chicken, chicken tikka, tandoori king prawns, prawn masala. It's all good stuff, though, and the serves are generous. Beware: the large video screen showing continuous, loud music videos is highly distracting.

Wabi Ichi (Map p460; ☎ 222-9775; 2-1-10 Kakyōuin, Aoba-ku; plates of meat from ¥4000; ☣ lunch & dinner) This is one of those grill-your-own meat ex-

travaganzas that have taken Japan by storm. The ambience here, though, has a touch of class – dine in intimate, enclosed, Japanese-style rooms with windows facing onto well-manicured rock gardens.

There's a clutch of restaurants, covering the gamut of price ranges, at the top of SS30, Sendai's second-tallest building (with 30 stories, as opposed to AER's 31). **Bansankan** (Map p460; ☎ 267-8866; pizzas from ¥1200; ☣ lunch & dinner) is on SS30's top floor and offers tasty pizzas, a mellow jazz-fusion soundtrack and heart-in-mouth views.

Drinking

The Kokubunchō area is Northern Tohoku's largest entertainment district, as noisy and as bright as you might expect, with endless rabbit warrens jammed with hole-in-the-wall bars and clubs.

Simon's Bar (Map p460; ☎ 223-8840; 1st fl Daishin Bldg, 2-9-1 Kokubunchō) This cosy little 'stand up' bar, with its talismanic name, has a lively crowd of Japanese, the occasional foreigner, and a good selection of beers and cocktails. Take the first left after Club Shaft, heading towards Jōzenji-dōri.

Vilevan (Map p460; ☎ 225-2222; 3rd fl Sunsquare-Shōji Bldg, 1-8-22 Chūō, Aoba-ku; ☣ 11am-midnight) A mellow jazz bar, well versed in the history of the genre: it was originally called the Village Vanguard, until the famous New York bar of that name 'suggested' they reconsider. There's live music on Saturday nights and decent vegetarian food.

Trad Bar Esprit (Map p460; ☎ 214-3880; ☣ 5pm-midnight Mon-Thu, 5pm-1am Fri & Sat, 5pm-11.30pm Sun) A popular trend in Japan is the 'olde tyme bar', with loads of wood panelling, photos of leathery jazz men on the walls, and bar staff done up like characters from The Sting. Esprit is one such place, and its *faux* nostalgia is an easy respite from Kokubunchō madness.

Entertainment

Club Shaft (Map p460; ☎ 722-5651; www.clubshaft .com; 4th fl, Yoshiokaya Dai 3 Bldg, Kokubunchō, Aoba-ku) This one's a sports bar during the week, with a high-fibre diet of European soccer and American baseball. On the weekends it's a dance club with a good reputation for house, breaks and hip-hop, as well as 'waving-your-arms-in-the-air-like-you-just-don't-care' retro Manchester nights.

Bar Isn't It? (Map p460; ☎ 262-0901; 3rd fl, Date One Bldg, 3-9-13 Ichiban-chō; cover charge ¥2000) The Sendai branch of the popular chain has regular promotional and club nights and late-night closing. It's a barn, really, and the music favours techno-cheese. It has a motto: 'Cheap and more fun'. Mmm.

Getting There & Away

AIR

From Sendai airport, 18km south of the city centre, there are international flights to Seoul (¥63,940, 2¾ hours), Beijing (¥111,400, six hours), Dailan (¥94,100, 3¼ hours), Guam (¥75,700, 3¾ hours), Hong Kong (¥111,500, five hours), Shanghai (¥87,500, 3¼ hours) and Honolulu (¥159,220, 7¼ hours).

Domestic destinations include Sapporo (¥24,300, 1¼ hours), Nagoya (¥24,300, 1¼ hours) and Hiroshima (¥33,400, 1½ hours). From Tokyo, the *shinkansen* is so fast that it's not worth flying.

BOAT

Sendai-kō is a major port with ferries once daily to Tomakomai on Hokkaidō (¥7600, 14¾ hours); ferries depart at noon every second day for Nagoya (¥5200, 21 hours). To get to Sendai-kō, take a *futsū* (local) train on the JR Senseki Line to Tagajō Station (¥230); it's then a 10-minute taxi ride. There are also five direct buses from stop 34 at Sendai Station, but only until 6pm (¥490, 40 minutes).

BUS

From stop 42 outside the station's east exit, there are five buses daily to Shinjuku (¥6210, 5½ hours) and Niigata (¥4500, four hours).

From stop 41, north of the station, buses run daily to Tokyo (¥6210, 7½ hours) at 11am, 10.40pm and 12.10am. From stop 40 across the street, night buses to Kyoto and Osaka depart at 7.30pm (¥12,230, 12½ hours) as well as day buses to Morioka (¥2850, 2¾

hours), Akita (¥4000, 3¾ hours) and Aomori (¥5700, five hours).

TRAIN

From Sendai, the JR Tōhoku Shinkansen Line runs south to Tokyo (¥10,080, two hours) and north to Morioka (¥5780, 50 minutes) for transfers to the Akita Shinkansen Line. Sendai is connected by the JR Senzan Line to Yamagata (*kaisoku*, ¥1110, one hour) and by the JR Senseki Line to Matsushima-kaigan (*kaisoku*, ¥400, 25 minutes).

Getting Around

Airport limousines (single/return ¥910/ 1640, 40 minutes) from stop 15.2 at the station's west bus pool depart frequently for the airport between 6.45am and 6.15pm.

The Loople tourist bus leaves from the west bus pool's stop 15.3 every 30 minutes from 9am to 4pm, making a useful sightseeing loop around the city (¥250 per ride) in a clockwise direction. A one-day pass costs ¥600 and comes with an English-language booklet detailing the bus route and sightseeing discounts for pass holders. Passes can be purchased from the bus ticket office by stop 15.3.

Sendai's single subway line runs from Izumi-Chūō in the north to Tomizawa in the south but doesn't cover any tourist attractions; single tickets cost ¥200 to ¥290.

AKIU ONSEN 秋保温泉
☎ 022 / pop 4800

Akiu Onsen was the Date clan's favourite, with a saltwater spring that's said to be a curative for back pain and arthritis. Akiu Onsen also illustrates how the Japanese are enamoured of triplicates. Akiu Onsen is considered one of the three most famous hot springs in Japan, plus it's also a good base for side trips into the mountains to see **Akiu Ōtaki** (秋保大滝), a 6m-wide, 55m-high waterfall, which is itself designated as one of Japan's three most famous waterfalls. Akiu Onsen is also handy for access to the gorge, **Futakuchi-kyō** (二口渓), with its *banji-iwa* (rock columns). There are hiking trails along the river valley and a trail from Futakuchi Onsen to the summit of **Daitō-dake** (1366m) that takes about three hours.

Hiking maps are available at Akiu Onsen's **tourist information office** (☎ 398-2323; ⏰ 9.30am-6pm). The staff can also advise on the numerous hotels, *minshuku* and camping grounds scattered throughout the area.

Getting There & Away

Buses leave frequently from stop 8 at Sendai Station's west bus pool for Akiu Onsen (¥780, 50 minutes), but only a few continue to Akiu Ōtaki (¥1070, 1½ hours).

MATSUSHIMA & OKU-MATSUSHIMA

松島奥松島

☎ 022 / pop 17,500

Matsushima Bay features around 250 islands covered in pines that have been moulded by wind and rock formations that have been misshapen by the ceaseless slapping of waves, resulting in uncanny monuments to natural forces. This conglomeration is one of Japan's Nihon Sankei (Three Great Sights) – the other two are the floating *torii* (gates) of Miyajima island and the sand-spit at Amanohashidate. As a result of that distinguished reputation, it's heavily touristed, but undeniably picturesque with peculiar charm. But really, no Miyagi sight is complete without a Masamune anecdote, so here is Matsushima's: Date was so smitten with one of the rock formations he offered a reward, half-seriously, to anyone who could deliver it to castle headquarters. No-one could.

Weekends can be trying in Matsushima, when packed crowds undercut the reflective serenity that so entranced Bashō. On the eastern curve of the bay, Oku-Matsushima is less touristed and offers several trails for exploration by bicycle or on foot.

Orientation & Information

There's a Matsushima Station, but Matsushima-kaigan is the one you want – it's closer to the main sights. Outside, the **tourist information office** (☎ 354-2263; ☼ 10am-5pm) provides maps. Luggage storage is available next door for ¥200 per day. Inside Oku-Matsushima's Nobiru Station, the **tourist information office** (☎ 88-2611; ☼ 8.30am-5.30pm) has a few bicycles for rent. From Nobiru you can cycle the 5km to Otakamori, where a 20-minute climb up the hill is rewarded with a fine panorama of the bay.

Sights

MATSUSHIMA

Zuigan-ji (admission ¥700; ☼ 8am-5pm Apr-Sep, 8am-3.30pm Oct-Mar), one of Tōhoku's finest Zen

MATSUSHIMA

INFORMATION		
Tourist Information Office		
松島観光案内所	1	A4
SIGHTS & ACTIVITIES		
Godai-dō 五大堂	2	A3
Kanran-tei 観らん亭	3	A3
Zuigan-ji 瑞巌寺	4	A3
SLEEPING		
Matsushima Century Hotel		
松島センチュリーホテル	5	B3
Sakuragawa Ryokan		
桜川旅館	6	B2
EATING		
Gozabune	7	A4
TRANSPORT		
Cruise Boats		
島観光船	8	A3

temples, was founded in 828. The present buildings were constructed in 1606 by Date Masamune to serve as a family temple. Look out for the painted screens and interior carvings of the main hall, in the Momoyama style, and the **Seiryū-den** (Treasure Hall) displaying works of art associated with the Date family. The temple is accessed via an avenue lined with tall cedars, with weathered Buddhas and altars to the sides – a frequently spooky, deeply contemplative approach.

The interior of **Godai-dō**, a small wooden temple, opens to the public just once every 33 years. If you miss the next viewing in 2006, make do with the sea view and the 12 animals of the Chinese zodiac carved in to the eaves.

The **Kanran-tei** (admission ¥200; ⏰ 8.30am-5pm Apr-Oct, 8.30am-4.30pm Nov-Mar) pavilion was presented to the Date family by Toyotomi Hideyoshi in the late 16th century. It served as a genteel venue for tea ceremonies and moon viewing – the name means 'a place to view ripples on the water'. Today, matcha (powdered green tea) is served here, and the garden includes the **Matsushima Hakubut-sukan**, a small museum housing a collection of relics from the Date family.

Fukuura-jima (福浦島; admission ¥200; ⏰ 8am-5pm Mar-Jun, 8am-6pm Jul & Aug), an island connected to the mainland by a 252m-long, red wooden bridge, makes for a leisurely half-hour walk around its botanic gardens.

Ōshima (雄島) is also connected by bridge to the mainland. It was once a monks' retreat and is renowned for its Buddhist rock carvings, statues, meditation caves and relics.

OKU-MATSUSHIMA

Natural beauty is the order of the day here. **Sagakei** is a 40m-high scenic canyon overhanging the Pacific Ocean, notable for its crashing waves; **Otakamori** (大高森) is a small hill in the middle of Miyato Island offering a terrific panorama, including Mt Zaō and Kinkasan; and **Nobiru Beach** (野蒜海岸) is a swimming beach popular with day-trippers from Sendai.

Festivals & Events

Bivalve aficionados will appreciate the **Matsushima Kaki Matsuri** (Matsushima Oyster Festival), held on the first weekend in February, where you can purchase oysters and cook them on a 100m-long grill. On 15 August, **Tōrō Nagashi Hanabi Taikai** honours the souls of the departed with the O-Bon (Festival of the Dead) ritual, when lighted lanterns are floated out to sea accompanied by an extensive fireworks display.

The approach to Zuigan-ji is enhanced from 6–8 August, when candlesticks are lit along the path for the event **Zuigan-ji Tojo**.

Sleeping

MATSUSHIMA

Sakuragawa Ryokan (☎ 354-2513; 12-1 Aza-Moto-kamaya, Takagi; r per person with 2 meals from ¥8000) This traditional accommodation option, with its well-furnished rooms, is two minutes from Takagimachi Station, one stop past Matsushima-kaigan.

Matsushima Century Hotel (☎ 354-4111; 8 Aza-Sen-zui; s/tw from ¥6800/13,450) This is near the sights and has swish interiors, a pool and sauna. It has Western- and Japanese-style rooms, and rates depend on whether you take a room with a view of the car park or the sea.

OKU-MATSUSHIMA

Pila Matsushima Okumatsushima Youth Hostel (Map p456; パイラ松島・奥松島ユースホステル; ☎ 88-2220; 89-48 Minami-Akazaki, Nobiru, Naruse-chō, Monou-gun; dm from ¥3360) This spruce hostel is in a lovely pine-clad location, just near the beach at Oku-Matsushima. There's bike hire (¥800 per day) and the staff can advise on the best way to tackle hiking trails. To get to the hostel from Nobiru Station, walk across the bridge and towards the ocean for about 15 minutes until you reach an intersection with a blue youth-hostel sign pointing down the road to the right. From there it's about 800m. Staff at the tourist information office can give you a map with directions.

Eating

Matsushima has an unimpeachable reputation among oyster-lovers.

Gozabune (御座船; ☎ 354-3709; set menus from ¥2000; ⏰ 10.30am-7pm) Try this place for a Japanese-style bivalve menu, including oysters served with tempura or *kaki*-style (with *soba* noodles).

Bistro Abalon (びすとろアバロン; ☎ 354-5777; 6-21 Sanjugari, Matsushima Aza; dishes from ¥900; ⏰ lunch & dinner Thu-Tue) Concentrates on French-style dishes, like oyster *gratin*.

Getting There & Around

The most convenient route to Matsushima-kaigan is from Sendai via the JR Senseki Line (*kaisoku* ¥400, 30 minutes). Alternatively, boat trips (¥1420, 50 minutes) to Matsushima, along the celebrated coastline, depart from Shiogama Pier every 30 minutes between 9am and 4pm from April to November, and hourly the rest of the year. Get off the train two stops before Matsushima Kaigan at Hon-Shiogama (¥320, 20 minutes). The harbour is 10 minutes on foot from Hon-Shiogama Station – turn right as you exit.

Otherwise, there are loop cruises from Matsushima through the pine-covered islets (¥1400, 45 minutes) between 8.30am and 4.30pm, but these can be overrun with sightseers.

To reach Oku-Matsushima from Matsu-shima-kaigan Station, take the JR Senseki Line six stations east (two stops by *kaisoku*) to Nobiru (¥230).

The sights are eminently walkable. Bike hire is available at the tourist information office inside Oku-Matsushima's Nobiru Station, but the crowds and narrow side-walks make cycling laborious.

ISHINOMAKI 石巻

☎ 0225 / pop 119,000

Ishinomaki, an unpretentious port city ringed by scenic mountains, sits at the mouth of the Kitakami, northern Honshū's largest river. This location has ensured its status as a major northeastern channel of commerce since the Edo era. For the trav-eller, Ishinomaki is a handy launching pad for Kinkasan. For lovers of popular cul-ture, it's also worth a visit for its colourful 'mangaland policy', a welcome respite from Tohokū's high-fibre diet of feudal nostalgia. Ishinomaki is littered with tributes to car-toonist, Shotaro Ishinomori, a local hero who created some of Japan's best-loved manga characters (see below).

Information

Main post office Behind the station, two blocks northwest.

Tourist information office (☎ 93-6448; ◷ 8.30am-5pm) Outside the station; it has combined bus-and-ferry timetables for Kinkasan-bound travellers and useful information about Ishinomaki (some in English), including a manga-themed map.

Sights

From Ishinomaki Station, walk southward onto Ekimae-ō-dōri; the third street down, bisecting it, is the main shopping strip, Tachimachi-dōri. Take a left and follow this to the water's edge; to the right is a bridge leading to a small islet (dubbed 'Mangat-tan' after Manhattan Island), where you'll find the spaceship-style **Manga Museum** (石の森萬画館; ☎ 96-5055; 2-7 Nakase; admission ¥600; ◷ 9.30am-6pm). Mostly devoted to Shotaro's work, it's a wee bit kiddie- orientated, al-though the strength of his work does shine through. There's a fascinating collection of original Shotaro sketches, *anime* screenings, including an animated history of Ishinomaki, and life-sized animatronic statues of Shotaro characters.

MANGALAND

Japan's famous manga comic books and *anime* cartoons are highly popular, with their influence spreading far beyond Japan's shores to Hollywood and beyond. A few years back, local govern-ments in Japan began to focus on this rich culture as a means to attract tourists. The town of Kawakami opened a manga museum in 1994, featuring rare editions of such manga classics as *Astro Boy* and *Gigantor*. *Astro Boy's* creator, Tezuka Osamu (1926–89), is honoured in his birthplace of Takarazuka, which opened a museum focusing on his work. In Sakai Minato, bronze statues from famous *anime* line the streets. Ishinomaki is the latest town to initiate a manga policy, re-cently constructing a museum and various monuments devoted to the work of manga pioneer, Shotaro Ishinomori (1938–98).

The artist was born as Shotaro Ishimori, but later took the name of his hometown, Ishinomori (not to be confused with Ishinomaki, although both are in Miyagi-ken). When he graduated, he moved to Tokyo to work with Tezaku Osamu, whose style Ishinomori's resembles, with its rounded, stylised lines. Perhaps Ishinomori's most famous creation is *Cyborg 009*, which started life as a manga in 1963 and was turned into an animated series in the 1970s. Shotaro's work for *Cyborg 009* was characterised by innate humanity and pleas for racial tolerance and harmony; his cyborgs (part-human, part-machine) are a clear metaphor for people of mixed race and the prejudices they tend to labour under in a 'monoculture' like Japan.

Shotaro's work is still fresh today. He initiated many new techniques and adapted the work of US science fiction writers, including Ray Bradbury, thereby introducing them to Japanese audiences. He also led the way in 'manga information' – study aids for children in the form of cartoons – which helped to popularise manga and enable it to gain mass acceptance.

Besides the museum, there are various statues and monuments to *Cyborg 009* littered about Ishinomaki, brightening up this port town.

On the way to the Manga Museum, look out for the statues and wall-length graffiti murals dedicated to Shotaro scattered along the main shopping strip and in a few side streets; the tourist office has a map with their locations. Shotaro's best-known characters, Cyborg 009 and Kamen Rider, are heavily featured, along with a supporting cast of kooky robots and animals.

Further along the islet is the **Old Ishinomaki Orthodox Church** (旧石巻ハリストス正教会教会堂; ☎ 95-1111; 3-18 Nakase; admission free; ⏰ 9am-6pm Mar-Nov, 9am-5pm Dec-Feb), Japan's oldest wooden church (dating from 1880, but no longer in use). It's a tale of two floors: downstairs is minimal, with tatami mats and thin walls; upstairs is ornate, with a Greek Orthodox altar featuring Jesus on high.

Near the Fisherman's Wholesale Market, is an impressive replica of the galleon, **San Juan Bautista** (宮城県慶長使節船ミュージアム; ☎ 24-2210; 30-2 Oomori Watanoha; admission free; ⏰ 9.30am-4.30pm). The San Juan is a monument to Date Masamune's forward-thinking rule; with an envoy of 20, it sailed to Rome as Japan's first diplomatic mission (see p457). The replica features interactive displays and dioramas of the journey.

Sleeping & Eating

There's no compelling reason to sleep in Ishinomaki, although it could be an option if you're visiting Kinkasan on a day trip or if accommodation is unavailable in Kinkasan.

Grand Hotel (グランドホテル; ☎ 93-8111; 2-10 Sengoku-chō; r per person from ¥6900) Two blocks left of the station exit, facing south, the Grand is spacious and plush, featuring comfortable Western-style or tatami rooms and five restaurants.

Nakamuraya Ryokan (中村屋旅館; ☎ 93-6633; r with 2 meals from ¥4000) Ancient and humble, with atmospheric beams made from gnarled 100-year-old cherry trees.

Moriya (もりや; ☎ 22-1660; 2-1-13 Chūō-ku; dishes from ¥1000; ⏰ 11am-6pm Thu-Tue) For noodle-lovers, Moriya has the skills to pay the bills, as the tasty tempura *soba* demonstrates.

Getting There & Away

From Sendai, the JR Senseki Line runs to Ishinomaki (*kaisoku* ¥950, one hour) via Matsushima-kaigan and Nobiru. Ishinomaki can also be reached from Ichinoseki (¥1450, 1½ hours) on the Tōhoku Main Line.

From bus stop 2 outside Ishinomaki Station, seven buses run daily to Ayukawa between 7am and 6pm (¥1460, 1½ hours). It's a wonderfully scenic trip.

KINKASAN 金華山

☎ 0225 / pop 32

Also known as Golden Mountain, Kinkasan is considered one of the three holiest places in Tōhoku, along with Dewa Sanzan (p498) and Osore-san (p483). Its spiritual significance, and the fact that it used to be a site for gold prospecting, ensures a steady stream of visitors eager for some good fortune to rub off. It's said that if you pay a visit three years running to Kinkasan's impressive shrine, you can kiss your money worries goodbye for the rest of your life. Women were banned on Kinkasan until the late 19th century, but today, for both sexes, an overnight stay is ideal for those seeking tranquillity.

Along with its shrine, the island features the pyramid-shaped Mt Kinka (445m), a handful of houses around the dock, cheeky deer and monkeys, mostly untended trails, a few leeches and the odd snake. Most visitors to Kinkasan seem to be day-trippers, which means the island is delightfully deserted in the early morning and late afternoon.

Information

There's no tourist information, no Internet and no convenience store on Kinkasan. Before you leave, check in at the Ishinomaki tourist information office, which has Kinkasan information plus timetables for getting to Ayukawa and on to Kinkasan. There's also a small **Ayukawa tourist information office** (☎ 0225-45-3456; ⏰ 8am-5pm).

Sights

Before setting out on foot, take heed: locals advise that it's no longer possible to hike around Kinkasan's northern side because of a landslip; only the southern side is considered safe. If you get lost, head south and downhill towards the sea. The dirt trail that once circled the entire island (24km) along the shore is no longer safe at the northern edge.

Turning left from the boat dock, it's a steep 20-minute walk uphill to **Koganeyama-jinja** (小金山神社), built in 794 by Emperor Shōmu as thanks for finding the gold used to finish the Great Buddha at Nara's Tōdai-ji.

From Koganeyama-jinja, it's a 50-minute hike downhill to **Senjōjiki** (千畳敷; 1000 Tatami Mats Rock), a large formation of white rock on the eastern shore of the island, and a further hour to the lighthouse propping up the southeast corner. It takes roughly 1½ hours to follow the dirt trail along the shore and cross back over the summit to the dock area.

Festivals & Events

On the first and second Sunday in October, there's an **antler-cutting ceremony** to stop the deer from injuring each other during mating season. On the last weekend in July, the **Ryūjin Matsuri** (Dragon Festival) features giant dragon floats supported by up to 50 dancers.

Sleeping & Eating

Koganeyama-jinja (☎ 45-2264; kinkasan@cocoa.ocn .ne.jp; r per person ¥9000) On the shrine grounds, this offers basic temple lodgings with two meals. If you're awake before 6am, you can attend morning prayers. Advance reservations by phone or email are mandatory.

Minshuku Shiokaze (☎ 45-2666/2244 day/evening; r per person ¥6000) This friendly *minshuku* is 500m south along the headland from the pier. Expect simple but airy rooms, great food and panoramic views out to sea. The owners can also advise on the safest hiking routes. You must book well in advance though, as the owners actually live in Ayukawa and only come out to Kinkasan if there are customers.

Another option is to stay overnight in Ishinomaki or Ayukawa. **Minami-sō** (☎ 0225-45-2501; r per person with/without 2 meals from ¥6000/4200), behind the Ayukawa Bus Station, is a friendly *minshuku*.

Getting There & Away

From Ishinomaki, seven buses run daily to Ayukawa.

During summer ferries leave from Ayukawa pier – opposite the bus station – for Kinkasan almost hourly between 8.30am and 3.40pm (one way ¥900, 30 minutes); the last return ferry is at 4pm. Service is greatly reduced the rest of the year. Reservations (☎ 53-3121) are required at peak times.

There are three high-speed catamarans daily between Kinkasan and Onagawa, the eastern gateway to the peninsula, from April to early November (one way ¥1600, 30 minutes). The last departure from Onagawa is at 1.20pm. Some of the boats have open-air fantail decks, which make for a pleasant ride. Onagawa is also the terminus for the JR Ishinomaki Line, 30 minutes from JR Ishinomaki Station (¥320). From Onagawa Station, walk straight to the waterfront, turn right and walk about 200m to the pier. The ferry ticket office is down a side street opposite the pier, little more than a hole in the wall on the right-hand side.

NARUKO ONSEN 鳴子温泉

☎ 0229 / pop 9000

Naruko is a hot-spring spa resort in the northwestern corner of Miyagi-ken with good hiking and bathing options. It's famous for its distinctive style of lacquerware and *kokeshi* (wooden dolls with brightly painted floral designs). Like all *onsen*, its waters are said to possess distinct healing qualities. Naruko has a high sulphur count, as well as sodium chloride and sodium bicarbonate, thought to be a relief for the symptoms of high blood pressure and hardened arteries.

The helpful **tourist information office** (☎ 83-3441; ◷ 8.30am-6pm), inside JR Naruko Onsen Station, has useful English-language maps and brochures and can also help book your accommodation.

Naruko-kyō (鳴子郷), a scenic, 100m-deep gorge, can be reached in 20 minutes on foot from Naruko Onsen Station. Alternatively, buses (¥200, seven minutes) run from 8.50am to 4pm. From the gorge entrance, a pleasant 4km trail leads along the river valley to Nakayama-daira. If you turn right just after the bridge, but before reaching the gorge, you'll find Shitomae checkpoint, the start of a quiet 5km country path along the route Bashō once walked. The last bus back to the station leaves at 4.29pm.

Taki-no-yu (滝の湯; admission ¥150; ◷ 7.30am-10pm) is a sheer delight – a fabulously atmospheric wooden bathhouse that's hardly changed in 150 years.

The **Japan Kokeshi Museum** (日本こけし館; ☎ 83-3600; admission ¥320; ◷ 8.30am-5pm Mar-Dec) features around 5000 *kokeshi* dolls from around the country. During the Meiji era, the Tōhoku region was almost totally neglected, with the result that a flood of men and women moved south to find work. Some say that *kokeshi* dolls were symbolic representations of those lost girls, who were often snatched away at a young age.

Ryokan Sumei-sō (☎ 83-2114; r for up to 2 people with 2 meals ¥8000, each additional person ¥1000) has clean rooms. Walking northwest from the station, it's five minutes down the main street on the left before the railway tracks. **Ryokan Okasa-kiso** (ファミリーじすい岡崎荘; ☎ 83-4050; 51 Shinyashiki; r per person ¥3220) is nearby and a little dilapidated. The functional **Ryokan Takishima** (ホテル瀧嶋; ☎ 83-3054; 2801 Shinyashiki; r for 1-2 people with 2 meals ¥6550-13,300) is across the train tracks, 10 minutes from the station.

Getting There & Away

From JR Sendai Station, take the JR Tōhoku *shinkansen* to Furakawa (¥1580, 15 minutes)

then transfer to the JR Rikuu-tōsen Line for Naruko Onsen (¥650, 45 minutes). Naruko Onsen has infrequent connections to Shinjō (¥950, one hour) for transfers to the Yamagata Shinkansen Line or local trains west to Sakata (¥950, one hour) and Tsuruoka (¥1110, one hour).

IWATE-KEN 岩手県

The area now known as Iwate-ken was once rife with feudalism. The region was separated into north, controlled by the Nambu clan, and south, under the rule of the Date clan. Later, breakaway clans – Hachinohe (from Nambu) and Ichinohe (from Date) – divided

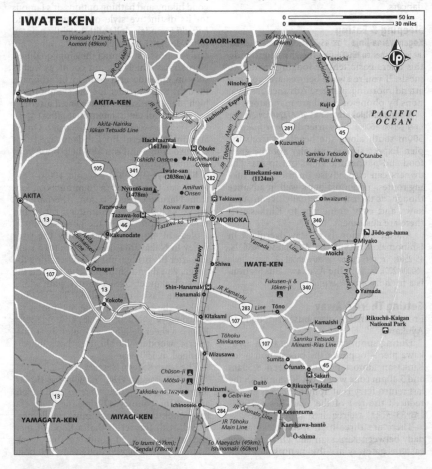

HIRAIZUMI: A 'BRIEF REMEMBERED DREAM' (BASHŌ)

The dashing warrior Minamoto Yoshitsune grew up with, and trained under, the Fujiwara clan but left Hiraizumi to fight with his half-brother Minamoto Yoritomo, the great warlord who founded the shōgunate, Japan's system of feudal government. Yoritomo was troubled by the Fujiwaras' growing power, but he was also jealous of Yoshitsune's battle skills and popularity, and suspicious of his sibling's alliance with the clan; this caused him to order his brother's death. Yoshitsune and his loyal retainer, the giant Benkei, disguised themselves as *yamabushi* (mountain priests) and returned to Hiraizumi, where they were taken in by the Fujiwaras, only to be betrayed by Fujiwara Hidehira's son. Seeing no escape, Yoshitsune set his castle on fire, killed his family and then committed *seppuku* (ritual suicide by disembowelment). Benkei, so the story goes, defended his master to the very end, even as his body was 'porcupined' with many arrows, an iconic image that will be familiar to anyone who's seen Akira Kurosawa's samurai films. Yoritomo then ordered the Fujiwara clan to be wiped out and the temples of Hiraizumi to be destroyed – a tragic end to one of the most remarkable periods of the feudal era. But there's a twist in the tale: according to local legend, the bodies of Benkei and Yoshitsune were actually those of their doubles. The real duo are said to have fled to Mongolia, where Yoshitsune became...Ghengis Khan.

Iwate further. During WWII, the prefecture was devastated and immediately embarked on a rehabilitation process marked by heavy industrial growth. Iwate-ken is the country's second-largest prefecture.

HIRAIZUMI 平泉

☎ 0191 / pop 9000

The saga of Hiraizumi is one of the most bittersweet aspects of Tōhoku's history. From 1089 to 1189, three generations of the Fujiwara family, headed by Fujiwara Kiyohira, created a political and cultural centre in Hiraizumi. With a population of around 100,000, it approached Kyoto's grandeur and sophistication. Kiyohira had made his fortune from local gold mines and, at the behest of Kyoto priests, he used his wealth and power to commence work on the creation of a 'paradise on earth', devoted to the principles of Buddhist thought as a reaction against the feudal wars that were plaguing the land. His son and grandson continued along this path, only for Kiyohira's great-grandson to bring this short century of fame and prosperity to a crashing end (see the boxed text, above). Today, only a few sights bear testament to Hiraizumi's glory, but they represent a singular experience and are well worth your time.

Information

Turning right outside Hiraizumi Station, the **tourist information office** (☎ 46-2110; ☯ 8.30am-5pm Apr-Oct, 8.30am-4.30pm Nov-Mar) has English-language pamphlets. The **post office**, with an international ATM, is 400m northwest of the station heading towards Mōtsū-ji. Free Internet access is available at the **public library** (☯ 8.30am-5pm Tue-Sun), 1500m southwest of the station.

Sights & Activities

CHŪSON-JI 中尊寺

This **temple complex** (☎ 46-2211; admission including Konjiki-dō, Sankōzō & Kyōzō ¥800; ☯ 8am-5pm Apr-Mar, 8.30am-4.30pm Nov-Mar) was established in 850 by the priest Ennin, who was responsible for many of Tōhoku's most famous temples. However, it was Fujiwara Kiyohira who decided in the early 12th century to expand the complex into a site with around 300 buildings, including 40 temples. Ironically, in the face of the grand scheme to build a Buddhist utopia, Hiraizumi was never far from tragedy and a massive fire here in 1337 destroyed most of the buildings, although two of the original constructions remain alongside the newer temples. The site is accessed via a steep approach along a tree-lined avenue. Take your time: the views over the valley, intermingled with Jizō monuments scattered among the greenery, make this an absorbing route.

The approach snakes past the **Hon-dō** (Main Hall) to an enclosed area featuring the splendid **Konjiki-dō** (Golden Hall; ☯ 8am-4.30pm Apr-Oct, 8.30am-4pm Nov-Mar). Built in 1124, Konjiki-dō is quite a sight, packed with gold detailing, black lacquerwork and inlaid

HIRAIZUMI

0 ——— 1 km
0 ——— 0.5 miles

INFORMATION
Post Office 郵便局 1 B4
Public Library 2 B4
Tourist Information Office
松島観光案内所 3 B4

SIGHTS & ACTIVITIES
Chūson-ji 中尊寺 4 A3
Hon-dō 本堂 5 A3
Konjiki-dō 金色堂 6 A3
Kyōzō 経蔵 7 A3
Mōtsū-ji 毛越寺 8 B4
Sankōzō 9 A3
Takadachi Gikei-dō
高館義経堂 10 B3

SLEEPING
Minshuku Yoshitsune-sō
民宿義経荘 11 B3
Mōtsū-ji Youth Hostel
毛越寺ユースホステル 12 B4
Shirayama Ryokan 志羅山旅館 13 B4

TRANSPORT
Bicycle Hire 旅行案内所 .... (see 3)

To Kitakami (36km);
Morioka (84km)

To Geibi-kei
Gorge (6km)

To Takkoku-no-Iwaya
Bishamon-dō (3km)

To Ichinoseki
(35km)

To Sendai
(150km)

mother-of-pearl (the region was known for its gold and lacquer resources). The centrepiece of the hall is the fabulously ornate statue of the Amida Buddha, along with attendants. Beneath the three side altars are the mummified remains of three generations of the Fujiwara family.

Beside the Konjiki-dō, the temple treasury, **Sankōzō**, contains the coffins and funeral finery of the Fujiwara clan – scrolls, swords and images transferred from long-vanished halls and temples. The sutra treasury **Kyōzō**, built in 1108, is the oldest structure in the complex. The original collection of more than 5000 sutras was damaged by fire and the remains have been transferred to the Sankōzō.

MŌTSŪ-JI 毛越寺

Dating from 850, **Mōtsū-ji** (☎ 46-2331; admission ¥500; 8.30am-5pm Apr-Oct, 8.30am-4.30pm Nov-Mar) once surpassed Chūson-ji as Tōhoku's largest temple complex; it, too, was established by Ennin. Now the temples are long gone and only the garden remains, a so-called Pure Land garden from the Heian era, designed with the Buddhist notion of preserving 'paradise' in mind – it's as peaceful as that implies. The perimeter of the large pond is a popular walk, and along with the rambling greenery may very well make you pause for reflection in the face of Hiraizumi's history.

TAKKOKU-NO-IWAYA BISHAMON-DŌ
達谷窟毘沙門堂
Five kilometres southwest of Mōtsū-ji, **Takkoku-no-Iwaya Bishamon-dō** (☎ 46-4931; admission ¥300; 9am-4.30pm) is a cave temple, dedicated to the deity Bishamon (the Buddhist guardian of warriors) by the famous general Sakanoue no Tamuramaro. It was built in 801 after Sakanoue's victory against the Ezo, the original inhabitants of northern Honshū; the present structure is a 1961 replica. You can cycle to the cave along a paved path from Mōtsū-ji in about 25 minutes.

Takadachi Gikei-dō 高館義経堂
A small memorial honouring Minamoto Yoshitsune, **Takadachi Gikei-dō** (admission ¥200; 8.30am-5pm Apr-Oct, 8.30am-4.30pm Nov-Mar) includes a monument inscribed with Bashō's 'summer grass' lament (see p451). The hall is at the top of a small hill with fine views of the Kitakami-gawa. It's 700m from the entrance to Chūson-ji.

GEIBI-KEI 猊鼻渓
A huge natural gorge, **Geibi-kei** features sheer 100m-high cliffs. Singing boatmen on flat-bottomed **boats** (per 90min ¥1500; 8.30am-4.30pm Apr-Oct, 9am-3pm Nov-Mar) regale passengers with local folk songs that echo along the cliffs. Take the bus from stop 7 outside Ichinoseki Station (¥620, 40 minutes, hourly) or the train from Ichinoseki to Geibi-kei Station on the JR Ōfunato Line (*kaisoku* ¥480, 25 minutes).

Festivals & Events
The **Haru-no-Fujiwaru Matsuri** (Spring Fujiwara Festival) from 1 to 5 May features a costumed procession, performances of *nō*

THE LEGENDS OF TŌNO

At the beginning of the 20th century, a collection of regional folk tales was published under the title *Tōno Monogatari* (*Legends of Tōno*). They were compiled by Kunio Yanagita (1875–1962), a prominent writer and scholar regarded as the father of Japanese folklore. The collection was based on interviews with Tōno resident Kyōseki Sasaki, who was born into a peasant family and who had committed to memory over a hundred *densetsu* (local legends). What Yanagita and Sasaki unearthed immediately captured the nation's imagination, bringing into rich focus the oral storytelling traditions of a region hitherto almost completely ignored.

The cast of characters and situations are truly weird and wonderful and draw heavily on the concept of animism, a system of belief that attributes a personal spirit to everything that exists, including animals and inanimate objects. One of the more striking tales concerns a simple village girl who married her horse. Amazingly, this was against her father's wishes, so the father hung the horse from a mulberry tree and beheaded it. The girl, clutching the horse's head, then flew off to heaven where she became Oshira-sama, the fertility goddess (today, Oshira-sama dolls are still important ceremonial objects for *itako* mediums; see p483).

Elsewhere, we have shape-shifting foxes; elderly folk who are cast off into the wilderness to die; impish water spirits, called *kappa*, who sumō-wrestle passers-by to the ground and who like to pull their victim's intestines out through their anus (but who are somewhat dumb and can be fooled in the most basic of fashions); *zashiki warashi* spirits, who live in the corners of houses and play tricks on the residents; and wild men who live in the hills and eat children. Throughout all of them is a common theme: the battle with nature and the struggle to tame the elements – everyday features of rural life, of which Tōno is an exemplar.

Legends of Tōno is available, in English, for ¥2000 from the souvenir shop next to the Tōno tourist information office (see p472).

(classical Japanese dance-drama) at Chūson-ji and traditional *ennen-no-mai* (longevity dances) at Mōtsū-ji, as well as an enormous rice-cake-carrying competition in memory of the giant Benkei (see p469). A similar **Aki-no-Fujiwaru Matsuri** (Autumn Fujiwara Festival) takes place from 1 to 3 November.

Sleeping

Mōtsū-ji Youth Hostel (☎ 46-2331; 58 Osawa; dm from ¥2940) This hostel is part of the Mōtsū-ji temple grounds and is a relaxing place to stay. There's a 9pm curfew and free *zazen* (seated meditation) sessions in summer. Rates include admission to the garden.

Minshuku Yoshitsune-sō (☎ 46-4355; 10-5 Yanagino Gosho; r per person with 2 meals ¥6000) This quiet little minshuku is about 15 minutes' north of the station, around 400m from the entrance to Chūson-ji.

Shirayama Ryokan (☎ 46-2883; 139-8 Shirayama; r per person with 2 meals ¥6300) Homely and closer to the station.

Getting There & Away

From Sendai, the JR Tōhoku *shinkansen* runs to Ichinoseki (¥1790, 35 minutes), where you can either take a bus via Hiraizumi Station to Chūson-ji (¥350, 22 minutes) or a local train on the JR Tōhoku Main Line (*futsū*, ¥190, eight minutes) to Hiraizumi.

Ichinoseki is connected to Morioka by the JR Tōhoku *shinkansen* (¥3410, 45 minutes) and the JR Tōhoku Main Line (*futsū*, ¥1620, 94 minutes).

Getting Around

Frequent buses from Ichinoseki run to Hiraizumi Station and onto Chūson-ji (¥140, 10 minutes). **Bicycle rental** (per day ¥1000; ☯ 9am-4pm Apr-Oct) is available next to Hiraizumi Station.

TŌNO VALLEY 遠野
☎ 0198 / pop 20,000

Tōno is a sleepy little town set amid a dramatic valley region, surrounded by rice fields and mountains. It's an area that will appeal to those with vivid imaginations and those keen on country air. The present city was formed by the merging of eight villages and much of that rural flavour is preserved today: there are still some examples of the local architectural style of L-shaped farmhouses, known as *magariya*, where farmfolk and their prized horses lived under one roof,

NORTHERN HONSHŪ

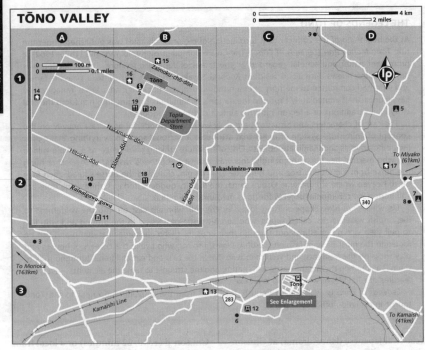

TŌNO VALLEY

albeit in different sections (unlike the fertility goddess, Osira-sama; see the boxed text, p471). There's no denying the mystique of the countryside, with its nooks and crannies, valleys and peaks. It's the ideal terrain for cheeky ghosts and spirits to dwell, so it's no surprise that Tōno is the heartland of some of Japan's most cherished folk legends, including the mischievous *kappa* water spirits, whose likenesses are found everywhere.

Information

City library (🕙 9am-5pm Tue-Sun) Free Internet access, downstairs from the Tōno Municipal Museum.

Main post office Ten minutes' walk southeast of the train station.

Tourist information office (☎ 62-1333; 🕙 8am-6pm) To the right as you exit JR Tōno Station; staff don't speak English but can supply a useful English-language brochure and a map of the three main cycling routes.

Sights

You'll need some form of transport to make the most of your stay; allow at least two days. A bicycle is a beautiful way to see the countryside, or else a JR bus tour covers the major sights. Renting a car is another option.

On the upper floors of the city library, the **Tōno Municipal Museum** (☎ 62-2340; 3-9 Higashidate chōme; admission ¥300; 🕙 9am-4.30pm Apr-Oct, 9am-4.30pm Tue-Sun Nov-Mar; closed last day of each month) has exhibits of folklore and traditional life, and some engaging audiovisual presentations of the legends of Tōno. Did you know, for example, that the people of Tōno are plagued by shape-shifting wolves? Seen from the front, it is said that they are as large as ponies, but from behind, unnaturally small.

Tōno Mukashibanashi-mura (☎ 62-7887; 2-11 Chūō-dōri; admission ¥300; ☼ 9am-4.30pm Apr-Nov, 9am-4.30pm Tue-Sun Dec-Mar, closed last day of each month) is a folk village with a restored ryokan, where Kunio Yanagita (see p471) once stayed. There's also an exhibition hall for folk art. A combined ticket with the Tōno Municipal Museum costs ¥500.

Fukusen-ji (☎ 62-3822; 7-57, Komagi, Matsuzaki; admission ¥300; ☼ 8am-5pm Apr-Oct, 9am-4pm Nov-Dec, 9am-4pm Sun Jan-Mar) is 8.5km northeast of Tōno Station. Founded in 1912, the temple's major claim to fame is the wooden Fukusen-ji Kannon statue (17m high and weighing 25 tonnes), which took 12 years to complete and is supposedly the tallest of its type in Japan. Take a bus bound for Sakanoshita and get off at Fukusen-ji (¥370, eight daily).

About 3.5km beyond Fukusen-ji, **Tōno Furusato-mura** (☎ 64-2300; 5-89-1 Kami-tsukimoushi, Tsukimoushi-chō; admission ¥500; ☼ 9am-5pm) is Tōno's largest folk village, with several different farmhouses, a water wheel and a folkcraft gallery. Buses run hourly from Tōno Station (¥490, 25 minutes).

Jōken-ji is a peaceful temple 2.5km south of Fukusen-ji, famous for the deity image **Obinzuru-sama** – some believe it will cure their illness if they rub the parts of its body corresponding to the location of their ailment.

Behind the temple is the **Kappa-buchi** pool. Legend has it that *kappa*, belying their impish nature, once put out a fire in the temple; the lion statue was erected as a gesture of thanks to honour this good deed. It is indeed a titillating place: apparently, if pregnant women worship at the shrine on the riverbank they'll produce plenty of milk, but only if they first produce a breast-shaped offering, like a cloth.

Also in this vicinity is **Denshōen** (admission ¥310; ☼ 9am-4.30pm, closed last day of each month), a small folk village featuring a hall with 1000 Oshira-sama dolls. From Tōno Station, take a direct bus to Denshōen-mae (¥300, 15 minutes), or more frequent buses bound for Sakanoshita to the Nitagai stop (¥290, 12 minutes), which is 10 minutes on foot from Denshōen.

On a wooded hillside above the **Unedori-sama shrine**, about 2.5km southwest of Tōno Station, are the **Gohyaku Rakan**, ethereal rock carvings of 500 disciples of Buddha. They were fashioned by a priest to console the spirits of those who died in a 1754 famine.

Nine kilometres west of Tōno Station is the **Chiba Family Magariya** (☎ 62-9529; admission ¥350; ☼ 8.30am-5pm, 9am-4pm Nov-Mar). This traditional L-shaped farmhouse, with the mountains as its backdrop, has been restored to evoke the traditional lifestyle of a wealthy farming family of the 18th century.

Festivals & Events

The **Tōno Matsuri** takes place on 14 September with *yabusame* (horseback-archery, in this case a 700-year-old event), traditional dances and costume parades through the city to Tonogo-hachimangu Shrine. It's a flamboyant spectacle, designed to pray for a bountiful harvest, and is deeply connected with the legends of Tōno.

Sleeping

Tōno Youth Hostel (☎ 62-8736; 13-39-5 Tsuchibuchi, Tsuchibuchi-chō; dm from ¥3200) This two-storey hostel makes a super base for exploring the valley. The manager speaks some English, is quite sociable and is well-versed in the local legends. However, he does like to get on the loudspeakers very early in the morning, so don't count on sleeping in. Bicycle rental is available (¥800 per day), there's no curfew and, thrillingly, there's an extensive manga library. From Tōno Station, take a bus bound for Sakanoshita to the Nitagai stop (¥290, 12 minutes). From there, it's a 10-minute walk; the hostel is signposted along the way.

Tōno Folkloro (☎ 62-0700; 5-7 Shinkoku-chō; r per person ¥6000) Standard business hotel, right next to the station, with Western-style rooms and breakfast included.

Minshuku Tōno (☎ 62-4396; 2-17 Zaimoku-chō; with 2 meals ¥6000) Just behind the station, this is a welcoming place where the host speaks English.

Minshuku Rindō (☎ 62-5726; 2-34 Daiku-chō; with 2 meals ¥6500) West of the station and also good value.

Minshuku Magariya (☎ 62-4564; 30-58-3 Niisato, Ayaori-chō; r per person with 2 meals from ¥11,000) About 3km southwest of the station, this is atmospheric accommodation inside a traditional farmhouse. No English is spoken.

From the station, take a bus to the *basu-sentā* (bus centre), then walk for 30 minutes on foot. Actually, you might want to catch a taxi just this once (for around ¥1000).

Eating

Taigetsu (meals from ¥500; ✆ lunch & dinner) On Eki-mae-dōri, 350m south of the train station, this one's good for coffee, *rāmen* and basic snacks.

Ume-no-ya (meals from ¥400; ✆ lunch & dinner) Across the road from Taigetsu, Ume-no-ya serves good-value set meals, as well as *rāmen* and omelettes.

Ichi-riki (☎ 62-2008; meals from ¥500; ✆ lunch & dinner) With its cosy, traditional interior, this restaurant serves terrific seafood – the delectable tempura tofu is recommended for its extraordinary lightness. There are advisory posters on the walls for those wishing to go *kappa* hunting.

Getting There & Away

The JR Tōhoku Line runs from Hiraizumi (¥820, 45 minutes) and Morioka (¥650, 40 minutes) to Hanamaki; the *shinkansen* runs from Morioka (¥840, 15 minutes) and Sendai (¥2520) to Shin-Hanamaki. On the JR Kamaishi Line, local trains connect Tōno with Shin-Hanamaki on the Tōhoku Shinkansen Line (¥740, one hour) and Hanamaki on the Tōhoku Main Line (¥820, 70 minutes). The approach into town is divine as the train winds through the valley and its mountains.

There are two afternoon buses from Morioka at 2.15pm and 3.30pm to Kamaishi that stop at Tōno's Topia department store (¥1890, two hours). In the reverse direction, buses to Morioka pass by at 7am and 10am.

Getting Around

Tōno is one place where car rental is a good idea – try **Kankō** (☎ 62-1375), inside the train

---

KENJI MIYAZAWA: A 'MAGIC LANTERN OF FONDLY REMEMBERED GREEN WIND'

Kenji Miyazawa (1896–1933) is one of Japan's best-known writers of the 20th century. Born in Morioka he lived there until his early 20s, although the town and the surrounding environment continued to influence him. Throughout Miyazawa's life, Tōhoku was very much the backwaters of Japan. Iwate-ken, in particular, was a land barely struggling to survive, as crops failed and new farming technology proved to be slow making its way north. On top of that, Miyazawa was the son of a pawnbroker and it caused him great anguish and deep shame to observe how his well-to-do family preyed on the poor by taking their property in exchange for lending them money. This experience, combined with an intense Buddhist faith, shaped his life's work.

Miyazawa developed a wondrous cosmology whereby profound empathy is felt between the animal world, the human world and the world of nature. A man is forced to hunt bears to make a living, even though he loves bears and deeply understands their ways and customs; the bears, in turn, understand and respect the bind he is in. Another man chances upon a group of deer; captivated by them, he hides in the grass to observe and before long realises he can understand the deer's 'language'. Foxes boast about their knowledge of poetry and astronomy. Stars in the sky take human form and play the flute. A cellist, rejected from an orchestra because his playing is atrocious, finds peace with the animals who visit him at night to hear him play. This communication between species has been understood as a plea for tolerance of other cultures, particularly as Miyazawa was writing during a time when Japanese society was becoming ever more closed off as the nation moved towards war.

Connections have also been made between Miyazawa's work and the legends of Tōno (p471); certainly the battle against the elements by poor people is a common thread, as is the belief in animism. But the Tōno stories are filled with casual violence and an often antagonistic relationship towards the natural world. Tōno's legends depict foxes, for example, as a constant torment to humans, whereas Miyazawa overturns the common notion of foxes as cunning and devious, and demonstrates that even the most entrenched stereotypes can be debunked – as in the scholarly fox mentioned earlier.

Ultimately, both realms are deeply infused with the rhythms and paradoxes of everyday Tōhoku life, and both are worthy additions to the library of anyone seeking to go beyond the platitudes of tourist brochures to understand what makes the region tick.

station. The **JR Bus Tour** (10.30am departure ¥5000, 5hr; noon departure ¥4000, 3½hr) departs from outside the tourist office; the earlier tour packs in more sights. Bicycle rental is available from the tourist office at ¥1000 per day, or from the youth hostel.

MORIOKA 盛岡
 019 / pop 288,000

Morioka is the capital of Iwate-ken, a lofty status that dates back to the early Edo period when it was the seat of the Nambu clan. Today, the tourism board insists on pro-

moting Morioka as the 'Castle Town of the Lord of Nambu', which is a little bit mis-leading, considering the Meiji Restoration destroyed the castle in 1868. Morioka nestles at the confluence of the Nakatsu, Kitakami and Shizukuishi Rivers, with the grand Mt Iwate volcano as its northwest backdrop, and its people are very keen to share their city's delights with outsiders. This is a trait expressed quite bizarrely in the city's *wanko-soba* culinary ritual (see p478), and more conventionally in its vibrant foreign com-munity, powered by an exchange program

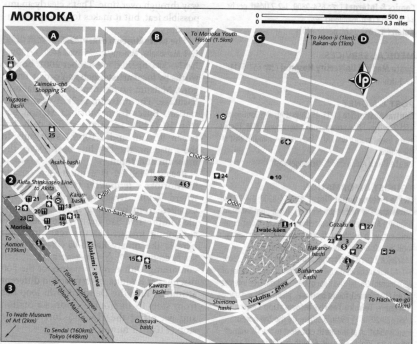

MORIOKA

INFORMATION	
Central Post Office 中央郵便局	1 C1
Comics & Internet	
コミック＆インターネットカフェ	2 B2
Iwate Bank (Ex-Head Office)	
岩手銀行 (旧本店)	3 D3
Iwate Bank 岩手銀行	4 B2
Iwate International Plaza	
岩手県立国際交流プラザ	5 B3
Iwate Medical University Hospital	6 C2
Kolon コロン	(see 13)
Morioka Tourist Information Centre	7 D3
Northern Tōhoku Information Centre	
北東北観光案内所	8 A3
Odette Plaza	(see 7)
Post Office 郵便局	9 A2

SIGHTS & ACTIVITIES	
Rock-splitting Cherry Tree 石割桜	10 C2
Sakurayama Shrine	11 C2

SLEEPING	
Hotel Metropolitan Morioka	
ホテルメトロポリタン盛岡	12 A2
Hotel Ruiz ホテルルイズ	13 A2
Morioka New City Hotel	
盛岡シティホテル	14 A2
Ryokan Kumagai 旅館熊ヶ井	15 B3
Taishōkan 大正館	16 B3

EATING	
Azumaya 東家	17 A2
Cappuccino Shiki カプチノ詩季	18 A2
Koiwai Regley 小岩井リグレ	19 A2
Pyon Pyon Sha ぴょんぴょん舎	20 A2
Seirōkaku	21 A2

DRINKING	
Brut ブリュット	22 D3
Fukakusa 深草	23 D3
Tipperary ティパレリ	24 C2

SHOPPING	
Kōgensha 光原社	25 A2
Ono Sensai-sho 小野染彩所	26 A1
Workshop Kamasada	
南部鉄器 釜定	27 D2

TRANSPORT	
Dendenmushi Bus Stop	(see 28)
JR Bus Station	28 A2
Morioka Bus Centre	
盛岡バスセンター	29 D3

OTHER	
Gen Plaza	(see 21)

with Victoria in Canada. Morioka is also a good place to make use of city facilities before venturing off the *shinkansen* line into the wilds of the far north.

Orientation

The city centre is east of the station, on the other side of the Kitakami-gawa. Ōdōri, which heads over the Kaiun-bashi up to Iwate-kōen, is the main shopping street.

Information

INTERNET ACCESS

Comics & Internet (☎ 654-9800; 3-2-2 Ōdōri; per hr ¥470; ⊙ 11am-midnight)
Kolon (☎ 652-2424; per hr ¥400)

MEDICAL SERVICES

Iwate Medical University Hospital (☎ 651-5111; 19-1 Uchi-maru)

POST & MONEY

Central post office (1-13-45 Chūō-dōri; ⊙ 9am-6pm, ATM 9am-7pm) Downtown, with international ATM. There's also a useful branch with ATM facilities five minutes east of the station.
Iwate Bank Along Ōdōri; exchanges cash.

TOURIST INFORMATION

Iwate International Plaza (☎ 654-8900; 2-4-20 Osawakawara; ⊙ 10am-9pm Mon-Fri, 10am-5pm Sat, Sun & holidays) An excellent resource for visitors and long-term residents, with helpful staff, a foreign-newspaper library, local 'what's on' information and free Internet.
Morioka Tourist Information Centre (☎ 604-3305; 1-1-10 Nakanohashi-dōri; ⊙ 9am-8pm, closed 2nd Tue of each month) On the 2nd floor of Odette Plaza. Free Internet access (30 minutes), tourist brochures, phonecards and stamps.
Northern Tōhoku Tourist Information Centre (☎ 625-2090; ⊙ 9am-5.30pm) On the 2nd floor of Morioka Station at the north exit, next to the *shinkansen* ticket gate. Highly efficient, English-speaking staff and a good supply of regional brochures.

Sights

Morioka is easily navigated on foot, but there is a tourist bus.
   Iwate-kōen (岩手公園), 20 minutes east of the station, is the park where Morioka-jō once stood. Now ruined, only the castle's moss-covered stone foundation walls remain as a testament to Edo-period life. The park has pleasing views over the city, and the grounds, with varicoloured tree foliage, are pretty. The park also contains the shrine

Sakurayama, and a totem pole presented by Morioka's sister city in British Columbia; it's a collaboration between a Native North American chief and a local woodcarver.
   The Japanese love displays of fortitude, as the many samurai legends forever enshrined in the nation's hearts and minds illustrate. This applies even if the display is exhibited by an inanimate object, like the **Rock-Splitting Cherry Tree** in front of the Morioka District Court. This 300-year-old tree, sprouting from the crack in a huge granite boulder, has the locals claiming that it's pushed its way through over time. That's clearly an impossible feat, but it makes for a very charming story.
   The **Iwate Museum of Art** (岩手県立美術館; 12-3 Matsuhaba, Motomiya; admission ¥400; ⊙ 10am-7pm Tue-Sun), opened in October 2001, houses works by local artists such as Yorozu Tetsugoro, Matsumoto Shunsuke and Funakoshi Yasutake. The museum is 2km west of the station. Buses from Morioka Station bus stop 10 (¥290, 12 minutes, five daily between 9.10am and 2.10pm) stop outside the museum; the last bus back leaves the museum at 4.38pm.
   Hōon-ji (報恩寺) is a quiet Zen temple in Morioka's *teramachi* (temple district), where Kenji Miyazawa lived after being expelled from boarding school. The temple's impressive San-mon (Main Gate) has a Kannon image, but the real attraction here is the musty **Rakan-dō** (羅漢堂; admission by donation ¥300; ⊙ 9am-4pm), a small hall containing 18th-century statues of the 500 disciples of Buddha, each posed in different attitudes. Take the Dendenmushi loop bus from stop 15 in front of Morioka Station and get off at the Honchō-dōri 1-chōme stop (¥100, 15 minutes).

Festivals & Events

The **Chagu-Chagu Umakko Matsuri**, on the second Saturday of June, features a parade of brightly decorated horses and children in traditional dress. Starting outside town, the procession passes near Iwate-kō in the afternoon (the best views are from Nakano-hashi). Iwate was historically famous for breeding horses and the festival allegedly originated when farmers took their horses to shrines to rest them after harvest and pray for their health. The name 'chagu-chagu' is said to describe the sound of the horses' bells.

Flying demon rice-paper float, Nebuta Matsuri (p481), Aomori

Gas-san (p499), Dewa Sanzan,
Yamagata-ken

Tōno Matsuri (p473), Tōno Valley, Iwate-ken

MASON FLORENCE

Haguro-san (p498), Dewa Sanzan,
Yamagata-ken

Torii at Yudono-san (p499), Dewa Sanzan,
Yamagata-ken

MASON FLORENCE

Hachiman-gū Matsuri (p477), Morioka, Iwate-ken

RICHARD I'A

During the **Hachiman-gū Matsuri** from 14 to 16 September, portable shrines and colourful floats are paraded to the rhythm of *taiko* (Japanese drums). There are also displays of horseback archery on the 15th. The parades are thoroughly engaging, and feature traditional Japanese floats pushed and wheeled through crowded streets by huffing, puffing men scantily dressed in sumō-type outfits, headed by a flying V of elegant, dancing women.

Sleeping

Morioka Youth Hostel (盛岡ユースホステル; ☎ 662-2220; 1-9-41 Takamatsu; dm from ¥2900) Along with its inconvenient location, this place is a little worse for wear and imposes a 10pm curfew. From stop 11 at Morioka Station, frequent buses depart for Matsuzono bus terminal – alight at the Takamatsu-no-ike-guchi stop (¥210, 20 minutes, last bus 10.40pm). Ask the tourist information office for an English map.

Taishōkan (☎ 622-4436; r per person from ¥3500) Ten minutes southeast of the station, this is a ramshackle but endearing option.

Ryokan Kumagai (☎ 651-3020; 3-2-5 Ōsawakawara; s/d from ¥4500/8000) The Ryokan Kumagai is an easy-going place, opposite Taishōkan. The rooms are clean and tidy.

Also recommended:

Hotel Metropolitan Morioka (☎ 625-1211; 1-44 Ekimae-dōri; s/tw from ¥8662/16,747) Upmarket hotel next to the station.

Hotel Ruiz (☎ 625-2611; 7-15 Ekimae-dōri; s/tw from ¥7507/13,860) Reliable business hotel close to the station.

Morioka New City Hotel (☎ 654-5161; 13-10 Ekimae-dōri; s/d from ¥5040/8190) Across the road from the station. More casual than other business hotels.

Eating

Famished? Let's see you eat 500 bowls of the local noodle dish, *wanko-soba*. That's the record for this unique culinary experience, which is best appreciated at **Azumaya** (☎ 622-2252; 2nd fl Miurabiru Bldg, 1-8-3 Naka-no-hashi-dōri; wanko-soba from ¥3000; ☉ 11am-8pm Wed-Sun).

Koiwai Regley (set menus from ¥900; ☉ 7am-9.30pm Mon-Sat, 9am-8pm Sun) One hundred metres east of the station, this bakery/restaurant has good-value Western-style set menus and uses ingredients from the renowned Koiwai farm outside the city.

Cappuccino Shiki (☎ 625-3608; snacks ¥420-630; ☉ 7.30am-9pm Tue-Fri, 9am-8pm Sat & Sun) An at-

mospheric old coffee shop that feels like a tavern because of its rustic, dark-wood interior. Serves tasty toasted sandwiches, good breakfast sets and heart-starting espresso.

Morioka's other speciality is *reimen*, *soba* noodles served with *kimchi* (spicy Korean pickles). **Pyon Pyon Sha** (1st fl, Jaren Jaren Bldg; reimen from ¥1500; ☉ 11am-11pm) has delicious cold *reimen* and hot *reimen* sets. **Seirōkaku** (2nd fl, Gen Plaza; reimen from ¥900; ☉ lunch & dinner) also does a mean *reimen*, as well as dishes made from the (gulp!) 1st, 2nd and 4th stomachs of cows.

Drinking

Fukakusa (☎ 622-2353; snacks ¥400-700; ☉ Mon-Sat 11am-11pm, Sun 11am-6pm) This 40-year-old bar/café, just behind the old Iwate Bank, has an unbeatable location on the banks of the Nakatsu-gawa. With its cosy wood-panelled interior, piano, warm lighting and handmade prints (depicting the 'moon that laughs over the river'), it's a romantic little hideout. When the weather is right and the river is flowing, the outside seating is simply perfect. Good snacks and charming hosts, too.

Brut (☎ 605 9006; 1F Nakanohashi-106 Bldg 1-4-22 Nakanohashi-dōri; ☉ until 11pm) This lively bar, across the road from the old Iwate Bank building, attracts an older, but still up-for-it, drinking crowd.

Tipperary (☎ 652 6070; meals ¥from 600; ☉ 5pm-3am Mon-Thu, 5pm-4am Fri, 3pm-4am Sat, 3pm-3am Sun) Common-or-garden Irish pub, with Guinness, a meat-and-potatoes menu, Gaelic memorabilia and a boisterous crowd.

Shopping

The Morioka region is famous for its *nanbu tetsubin* (cast ironware). **Workshop Kamasada** is a fine exponent of the craft, selling affordable gift items alongside tea kettles that cost as much as a small car. It's across the Nakatsu-gawa near Gozaku, a traditional merchant's area of kura (mud-walled) warehouses, coffee shops and craft studios.

The attractive Zaimoku-chō district, five minutes from the station, is home to quality craft shops for lacquerware and fabrics, including **Kōgensha** (☉ 10am-6pm, closed 15th of each month), a craft and coffee shop in a garden overlooking the river.

For hand-woven and -dyed fabrics, check out the impressive selection at **Ono Sensaisho** – the emperor himself allegedly came by to do some window shopping.

WANKO-SOBA: MORE COMPETITION THAN MEAL   *Simon Sellars*

On the face of it, Morioka's famous dish, *wanko-soba*, is unspectacular – it's just buckwheat *soba* noodles served with side dishes like raw tuna, fish flakes and shredded chicken. It's the way it's presented that's off the planet, a ritual deriving from peasant times, when the citizenry's crops were failing and they only had *soba* to serve at dinner. Considering that's all they had, Moriokans strived to make it the best *soba* and they were highly offended if guests said 'no more', even if they were full.

At Azumaya I must have been taken for an obvious mark: as soon as I showed my face five waitresses rushed over. '*Wanko-soba*! This way please,' one said, placing a smock over my head. 'Special *wanko-soba* smock!' She explained the origins of the meal and then brought out the sides. We went over the rules: she would bring out 15 bowls of *wanko-soba* at a time. As soon as I finished one, she would refill it with another. (The bowls are only small, more like large cups, and 15 equals one family-size noodle box.) She stressed that there was to be no dawdling and made it clear she would keep refilling even if I begged her to stop. The only way it could end was if I placed a lid on the bowl.

'It's only plain noodle,' she said, 'so eat some side dish with each bowl. But not too much. You must leave room for *wanko-soba*!' The first tray of 15 was brought out and I felt the eyes of the entire restaurant on me. I gobbled down one, then another. Soon all were gone. Light applause rang out. 'More!' my waitress urged me. 'Eat!' she bellowed, returning with another tray. I tucked in and applied some kind of paste from a side dish. After every few servings, I'd end up with white slop in the bottom of my bowl, which I had to constantly drain into a tub specially provided for the purpose. By the 20th bowl I was slurping like a madman under the constant pressure of my invigilator.

I tried to refocus as my waitress sweetly exhorted me to greater heights: 'Come on, one more cup. Try for me, please.' But I was stuffed. After 40 bowls, I went for the lid and tried to jam it down over my bowl; she was onto me, her lithe hand flitting under mine to slop down more *soba*. If she beat me, I had to eat it; that was the rule. I slipped into a trance: *wanko-soba…wanko-soba…must eat wanko-soba*. After five more bowls I wanted to throw up. Again I went for the lid, but my reflexes were groggy. Again she beat me to the punch. Then I saw my chance: as my tormentor was distracted by laughter from a nearby table, I slammed the lid home to freedom. And slumped backwards, exhausted.

The guy next to me was on 100, his greedy eyes turned up expectantly as the waitress refilled his bowl. He stared at her with the hard, narrow need of a mainline junky. There was absolutely no question he was out to break the record.

In the end my waitress was gracious in defeat. She signed a certificate saying how many bowls I'd had and then took my photo. I stole a glance at Mr 100-plus: his chopsticks were a blur as he shovelled the greyish *soba* into his mouth…and then suddenly, he too, jammed his lid home.

The record, by the way, is 500: that's Moriokan hospitality at it's finest.

Getting There & Away

On the JR Tōhoku Shinkansen Line, the fastest trains from Tokyo (Ueno) reach Morioka in a mere 2½ hours (¥13,440). From Morioka, the Akita Shinkansen Line runs west to Akita (¥4300, 1½ hours) via Tazawa-ko and Kakunodate, which can also be reached by infrequent local trains on the JR Tazawa-ko Line. From Morioka you can continue north to Aomori on the JR Tōhoku Main Line (*tokkyū* ¥5960, 1¾ hours).

The bus station at Morioka Station is well organised. It has abundant English signs and a directory matching buses to their relevant stops, as well as journey times and fares. Popular destinations include Iwate-san, Towada-ko and Tazawa-ko.

The easiest access to the Hachimantai area, northwest of Morioka, is also by bus, from stop 4 at Morioka Station to Hachimantai Chōjō (¥1890, two hours, four daily).

Long-distance buses leave the station for Aomori (¥3160, three hours), Hirosaki (¥2930, 2½ hours) and Sendai (¥2850, 2¾ hours). There is one night bus to Tokyo leaving at 10.40pm (¥7850, 7½ hours) and one to Yokohama (¥8950, eight hours) leaving at 10.10pm.

Getting Around

Most local buses depart from the station, although there are also some departures from the Morioka bus centre close to Iwate-kōen. The charmingly named tourist bus, **Dendenmushi** (single ride/day pass ¥100/¥300), or 'snail', makes a convenient loop around town, departing in a clockwise direction from stop 15 in front of Morioka Station (anticlockwise from stop 16) between 9am and 6pm.

IWATE-SAN 岩手山

The volcanic peak of Iwate-san (2038m) is a dominating landmark northwest of Morioka, and a popular destination for hikers. Four walking trails are open between July and October but periodically close due to volcanic activity. Check with tourist information in Morioka (p476) for the latest conditions. If you want to stay near Iwate-san, **Amihari Onsen**, at the start of one of the main trails to the summit, has numerous *minshuku*. Railway enthusiasts prefer the **Steam Locomotive Hotel** (☎ 692-4316; r per person with/without 2 meals from ¥6820/4200) at Koiwai (Japan's largest privately owned farm), where you sleep in old train compartments. From early May to early November, buses from Morioka bound for Amihari Onsen (¥1140, one hour) pass by Koiwai farm (¥720, 35 minutes). Before Amihari, there's a bus stop at Omisaka for the trailhead.

AOMORI-KEN 青森県

Aomori-ken's regional government publishes an interesting list of areas in which it is 'number one'. The prefecture's greatest hits include: the country's highest apple, rapeseed, yam and garlic production; Japan's oldest cherry trees, planted in 1882 in Hirosaki Park, and the country's oldest apple tree, 123 years old; the world's longest submarine tunnel at 54km, linking Aomori with Hokkaidō; the tastiest tap water in Japan (so they say); the country's biggest *kokeshi* dolls, made in Kuroishi – 197cm tall and weighing 130kg; the biggest crowds for a festival – the Nebuta; and Japan's oldest arched dam, the Ominato No. 1 water-source dam. The government also alleges its 'children's physical build' is Number 1, but doesn't go into detail as to what exactly that means. On top of that, the

prefecture claims Tohokū's most eerie spot, Osore-zan, Tohokū's most popular sight, Lake Towada.

AOMORI 青森
☎ 017 / pop 300,000

Aomori, Honshū's northernmost city and the prefectural capital, is an important centre for shipping and fishing, due to its position in the cradle of Aomori bay. The city was comprehensively bombed during WWII (90% was destroyed), but it has since been completely rebuilt. As a result, concrete reminders of Aomori's past are light on, although there is some interesting modern architecture in its place. Aomori is a popular place to break the journey between Tokyo and Hokkaidō, and serves as a useful transport hub for Shimokita-hantō, Towada-ko and the scenic region around Hakkōda-san. But the best reason to visit is for the Nebuta Matsuri. This raucous celebration, with its distinctive illuminated floats, is one of Japan's most memorable festivals.

Information
EMERGENCY
Main police station (☎ 723-0110; 2-15 Yasukata)

INTERNET ACCESS
Internet access (per 30min free; ⏰ 10am-9pm) On the 4th floor of the AUGA Building.

MEDICAL SERVICES
City hospital (☎ 734-2171; 1-14-20 Katsuda)

POST
Main post office East of the city centre, with a smaller branch within easy reach of the station. Both have ATM services.

TOURIST INFORMATION
Prefectural tourist information counter (☎ 734-2500; ground fl, ASPAM Bldg; ⏰ 9am-6pm)
Tourist information office (☎ 723-4670;
⏰ 8.30am-5.30pm) On the left of the station's central exit. Good English-language pamphlets and an excellent map of the city.

Sights
The astonishing, pyramid-shaped **ASPAM building** (1-1-40 Yasukata) has a top-floor viewing plaza (¥400). The view out across the bay is great but the perspective is equally as good on the lower, free floors.

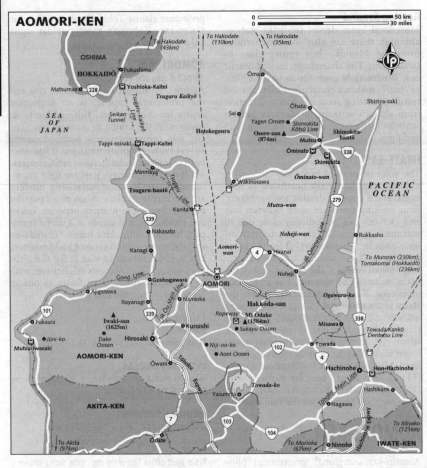

AOMORI-KEN

Nearby, **Aomori Bay Bridge** is remarkably similar to another bombed city's landmark bridge – Rotterdam's Erasmusbrug – with similar fanned struts and postmodern stylings. Climb the stairs at the Bay Bridge's station end for more top-notch views; the entire structure is a fine sight at night (as is ASPAM), when it illuminates in rotating primary colours.

Permanently moored in Aomori Bay is the ferry **Hakkoda-maru** (☎ 735-8150; admission ¥500; 9am-6pm, until 7pm for observation deck). For 25 years, it was the flagship of the famous Seikan Line that linked Honshū with Hokkaidō, before the underground tunnel rendered it obsolete. It's now a maritime museum with some interesting displays. In

summer it becomes a 'beer garden', surely the most pleasant surroundings in which to have a drink.

The **Nebuta-no-sato Museum** (ねぶたの 里; ☎ 738-1230; 1 Yaegiku, Yokouchi; admission ¥630; 9am-5.30pm) tells the story of Aomori's legendary Nebuta Matsuri, with an exhibition of the mighty illuminated floats used in the festival. Buses to the museum, 9km south of town, leave frequently from stop 9 outside the train station for the Nebuta-no-sato Iriguchi stop (¥450, 30 minutes).

Shōwa Daibutsu (☎ 726-2312; 458 Yamazaki, Kuwabara; admission ¥400; 8am-5.30pm Apr-Oct, 9am-4.30pm Nov-Mar), Japan's largest outdoor Buddha at a height of 21m and weighing 220 tonnes, is an impressive sight. The breezy temple

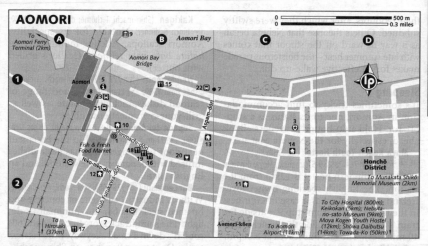

AOMORI

grounds are full of spinning pinwheels left by parents for their dead children. Buses from Aomori Station are timed so that you have about an hour to look around before catching the next bus back (¥540, 45 minutes).

The **Munakata Shikō Memorial Museum** (棟方志功記念館; ☎ 777-4567; 2-1-28 Matsubara; admission ¥300; ☯ 9.30am-4.30pm Tue-Sun Apr-Oct, 9.30am-4pm Tue-Sun Nov-Mar) houses a collection of wood-block prints, paintings and calligraphy by Munakata Shikō, an Aomori native who won international fame. The building itself is *azekura*-style, with walls of geometric wooden planks fitted together without upright supports. Buses bound for Nakatsutui leave from stop 2 outside the train station for the Munakata Shikō Kinenkan-dōri stop (¥190, 15 minutes).

The **Aomori Cultural Museum** (☎ 777-1585; 2-8-14, Hōncho; admission ¥310) has selected folk crafts, but far more rewarding displays can be found at **Keikokan** (Museum of Historical Folkcraft; ☎ 739-6422; 2071 Tamagawa Hamada Aza, Oaza; admis-

sion free; ☯ 9am-4pm Fri-Wed), a museum that explores the region's natural history as well as that of the Ainu people (p44). Buses from stops 4 or 5 outside the station run to the Kami-tamagawa stop (¥290, 25 minutes).

Festivals & Events

Even Japanese people muddle up Aomori's Nebuta and Hirosaki's Neputa (p486) festivals – not only do they sound alike but both take place at the start of August. The **Nebuta Matsuri** (2-7 Aug; www.nebuta.or.jp/english /index_e.htm) is renowned for its parades of colossal illuminated floats accompanied by thousands of rowdy, chanting dancers. The parades start at sunset and last for hours; on the final day the action starts around noon. The most dramatic account regarding the festival's origins is the tale of Sakanoue Tamuramaro, an 8th-century general who was sent by the Imperial palace to quash a rebellion by the native Ezo tribe. He's said to have used giant lanterns, along with drums and flutes, to lure the unsuspecting Ezo from their redoubts, after which they were swiftly subdued. Others theorise that Nebuta began as a way to ward off the stupor that comes with late summer heat – the boisterous parade makes for an effective wake-up call.

Sleeping

It's sometimes tricky to find accommodation in Aomori, due to its status as a stop-off for Hokkaidō-bound travellers. Book ahead, especially for the Nebuta Matsuri.

Moya Kogen Youth Hostel (雲谷高原ユースホステル; ☎ 764-2888; 9-5 Yamabuki, Moya; dm from ¥3360) This modern hostel is 12km from the station. The English-speaking owner loves Ireland and usually has a case of Guinness in the fridge. Buses from stop 9, outside the train station, stop outside the hostel (¥590, 40 minutes). The last bus leaves at 8.20pm.

Daini Ryokan (☎ 722-3037; daini@cronos.ocn.ne.jp; 1-7-8 Furukawa; r per person from ¥3000) Basic but charming, with a lovely host and spruce rooms. Facing away from Niko-niko-dōri, it's down the second street on the right.

Takko Ryokan (☎ 722-4825; Yasukata 2-chōme; r per person with/without 2 meals from ¥6500/4000) In the town centre, this is a smart option.

Aomori Plaza Hotel (☎ 775-4311; 2-4-12 Yasukata; s/tw ¥5500/10,000) Another spick-and-span business hotel, but a bit further from the station.

Aomori Grand Hotel (☎ 723-1011; 1-1-23 Shin-machi; s/d from ¥6970/13,860) Just east of the station, this hotel has rooms with sea views. Staff will exchange money after the banks close.

Hotel JAL City (☎ 732-2580; 2-4-12 Yasukata; s/tw ¥9400/12,600) Six minutes east of the station, near ASPAM, it has international-standard facilities, including a decent restaurant.

Eating & Drinking

The *tsugaru jamisen* is a version of the traditional three-stringed *shamisen* (guitar) instrument, but with a thicker neck than what's found in other regions. Practitioners are characterised by their rapid, forceful plectrum style.

Kotobukiya (☎ 722-7134; meals from ¥6000; ☺ dinner) Offers nightly dinner shows featuring *tsugaru-jamisen* music. Reservations are required and it's a 15-minute walk south of Aomori Station.

Jintako (☎ 722-7727; 1-6 Yasukata; meals from ¥5000; ☺ dinner) Another restaurant serving up *tsugaru jamisen* and local seafood.

Kakigen (Shin-machi 1-chōme; dishes from ¥1300; ☺ lunch & dinner) Notable for its speciality, Aomori scallops. Ask for mouthwatering *hotate batā yaki teishoku* (scallops grilled with butter).

Nandaimon (☎ 777-2377; Shin-machi 1-chōme; dishes from ¥580; ☺ 11am-10pm) Good range of seafood dishes, including hotate, as well as grill-your-own meat ensembles.

Supage-tei Aomori (1-8-8 Shin-machi; dishes from ¥1000; ☺ 11am-8.30pm Tue-Sun) In the basement next door to Kakigen, this has pasta dishes infused with Japanese-style seafood, and an English menu.

Bar Centaani (☎ 775-7054; Shin-machi; ☺ until late) With its industrial aesthetic of concrete and brushed steel, this bar is a minimalist's delight. The soundtrack is organic, though: '60s soul. It's down a small alleyway, which is next to the Doutour coffee shop on Shin-machi.

Getting There & Away

AIR

There are frequent flights from Aomori airport to Tokyo (¥25,800, 1¼ hours), Nagoya (¥27,800, 1½ hours), Sapporo (¥20,400, three hours), Osaka (¥31,300, 1½ hours) and an international connection to Seoul (¥51,200, three hours). Airport buses are timed for flights and depart from the front of the ASPAM building and Aomori Station (¥560, 40 minutes).

BOAT

Passenger ferries to Hakodate leave year round (¥1850, 3¾ hours), while one ferry leaves for Muroran (Hokkaidō) daily at 2.45pm. Coming back, an overnighter leaves Muroran at 11.25pm (¥3460, 6¾ hours each way).

The ferry terminal, on the western side of the city, is a 10-minute taxi ride from Aomori Station.

BUS

Between April and mid-November, JR runs five to eight buses daily from stop 8 outside the train station to Towada-ko (¥3000, three hours); the last bus leaves at 2.30pm. The bus stops at the Hakkōda ropeway (cable car; ¥1070, 50 minutes), then runs via the glorious Sukayu Onsen (p484; ¥1300, one hour) onto the Oirase Valley and the lake.

JR also operates six buses daily to both Morioka (¥3160, three hours) and Sendai

(¥5700, five hours), and one night bus to Tokyo (¥10,000, 10 hours); buses depart from the Highway Bus stop (No 10) outside the stationside tourist information office.

To visit Osore-zan (Shimokita-hantō), direct buses leave the ASPAM building at noon, 2pm and 5.20pm for Mutsu via Noheji (¥2520, 2¾ hours).

TRAIN

The JR Tsugaru Kaikyō Line runs from Aomori via the Seikan Tunnel to Hakodate on Hokkaidō (*tokkū* ¥5140, two hours). *Kaisoku* trains do the trip in 2½ hours, and on some of these services (¥3150) you take the Seikan Tunnel tour (see p518).

The JR Tōhoku Main Line runs south from Aomori to Morioka (*tokkū*, ¥5960, 2¼ hours), from where you can zip back to Tokyo in 2½ hours on the *shinkansen*. The Ōu Main Line runs via Hirosaki to Akita (¥3260, 4½ hours) where you can pick up the Akita *shinkansen*.

SHIMOKITA-HANTŌ 下北半島

☎ 0175 / pop 90,000

Sometimes called Masakari-hantō (axe peninsula) because of its shape, this isolated peninsula has long stretches of sparsely inhabited coastline and remote mountain valleys. At its western edge, **Hotokegaura** (仏ヶ浦) is a spectacular stretch of coastline dotted with 100m-tall wind-carved cliffs, which are said to resemble Buddhas. Stock up with supplies before heading to the peninsula – facilities are limited.

Mutsu むつ

This is Shimokita's main hub, from where bus services operate across the peninsula. Train connections are centred on Shimokita Station, with buses connecting to Mutsu bus terminal. North of Mutsu is Ōhata, where you can get buses to the Yagen Onsen resort. To the east is the cape, Shiriya-zaki, and to the west, Ōma, Honshū's northernmost point. At the bottom tip of the peninsula is Wakinosawa, which is popular with nature-lovers, not least for its 'snow monkeys' (Japanese macaques; see www.wakinosawa.com).

The tiny **tourist information office** (☎ 22-0909; ☯ 9am-6pm May-Oct, 9am-6pm Wed-Mon Nov-Apr) inside Masakari Plaza has few resources; comprehensive information is available in Aomori (p479).

There are numerous accommodation options clustered around the bus terminal. Next to Masakari Plaza, **Ryokan Murai** (☎ 22-4755; 9-14 Tanabu-chō, Mutsu; r with/without 2 meals from ¥6500/4500) is a safe bet. The rustic **Wakinosawa Youth Hostel** (☎ 44-2341; 41 Wakinosawasenokawame, Mutsu; dm from ¥2990) is perched on a hillside at Wakinosawa village, 15 minutes west of the ferry pier. The helpful owners drive guests to a local *onsen* (¥200) before dinner, and conduct excursions to observe 'snow monkeys'. Yagen Onsen offers upmarket accommodation, like **Hotel New Yagen** (☎ 34-3311; r from ¥10,200), with Western- or Japanese-style rooms.

Osore-zan 恐山

This barren volcanic mountain, with its **Osorezan-Bodaiji** (恐山菩提寺; admission ¥500; ☯ 6am-6pm May-Oct), is among Japan's most sacred regions. It's an eerily atmospheric place that's popular with pilgrims seeking to commune with the dead, especially parents who've lost their children. Several stone statues of the child-guardian deity, Jizō, overlook hills of craggy, sulphur-strewn rocks and hissing vapour; visitors help lost souls with their underworld penance by adding stones to the cairns. With the murky **Usuri-ko** and ravens swarming about, it's an appropriate setting for Buddhist purgatory – even the name, Osore, means fear or dread.

You can bathe on hell's doorstep at free *onsen* to the side as you approach the main hall (sex-segregated options are on the left). The two annual **Osore-zan Taisai festivals** (20–24 July & 9–11 October) attract huge crowds of visitors who come to consult blind crones. These *itako* (mediums) contact dead family members for a ¥3000 fee – it's an elaborate show, as the crones recite Buddhist sutras and rattle rosary beads to invoke the spirits.

Getting There & Away

On the JR Ōminato Line, there are two to four direct *kaisoku* trains daily from Aomori via Noheji to the terminus at Ōminato – get off one stop before at Shimokita Station (¥1890, 1½ hours) for buses to Mutsu. Buses run from the Mutsu bus terminal to Ohata (¥440, 40 minutes).

From Shimokita Station, frequent buses run to the Mutsu bus terminal (¥230, 10 minutes). Three direct buses run daily between Mutsu bus terminal and Aomori

(¥2520, 2½ hours); others run via Noheji (¥1450, 1½ hours) onto Aomori (¥1260, one hour).

From Ōma, there are two daily ferries (four in summer) to Hakodate on Hokkaidō (¥1170, 1¾ hours). The JR Tsugaru line travels from Aomori to Kanita (¥480, 43 minutes), from where two ferries run daily (three in summer) to Wakinosawa (¥1120, one hour).

Getting Around

Buses to destinations across the peninsula run from the Mutsu bus terminal. Between May and October, regular buses run from Wakinosawa to Mutsu (¥1790, 1½ hours), from where four buses leave for Osore-zan between 9am and 3.30pm (¥750, 30 minutes); the last bus back leaves Osore-zan at 4.50pm.

Nine daily buses ply the northern shore of the peninsula, passing Ōhata, Shimofuro Onsen and Ōma before terminating at Sai (¥2260, two hours). Buses for Yagen Onsen start from Ōhata (¥540, 30 minutes). Six JR buses run daily between Ominato Station (not the Mutsu bus terminal) and Wakinosawa (¥1790, 1¼ hours).

Between April and October, round-trip sightseeing boats for Hotokegaura depart Wakinosawa at 10.45am and 2.45pm (¥3800, two hours), returning from Sai (¥2170, two hours); services are often suspended in poor weather.

HAKKŌDA-SAN 八甲田山

☎ 017

Just south of Aomori, Hakkōda-san is a scenic region of peaks popular as a day trip with hikers, *onsen* enthusiasts and skiers. The Hakkōda **ropeway** (cable car; one way/return ¥1150/¥1800; ☽ 9am-4.20pm) whisks you up Tamoyachi-dake to the 1324m summit. From there you can follow a network of hiking trails. One particularly pleasant route scales the three peaks of Akakura-dake (1548m), Ido-dake (1550m) and Ōdake (1584m), and then winds its way down to Sukayu Onsen, which is about 10 minutes by bus beyond the ropeway station, in the direction of Towada-ko. This 8km hike can be done in a leisurely four hours.

Sukayu Onsen Ryokan (酸ヶ湯温泉; ☎ 738-6400; r per person with/without 2 meals from ¥15,000/10,000) is right at the end of the trail and is popular

with hikers. Alternatively you can soak in the ryokan's 1000-person **cedar bath** (¥500; ☽ 7am-7.30pm) and use the camping ground 10 minutes southeast.

JR buses leaving from stop 8 outside Aomori Station pass by the Hakkōda Ropeway-eki stop (¥1070, 50 minutes). In winter, buses terminate at the next stop, Sukayu Onsen (¥1300, one hour).

HIROSAKI 弘前

☎ 0172 / pop 176,000

Founded in the 17th century by Lord Tsugaru Tamenobu, this castle town was once one of Tōhoku's leading cultural centres. However, the Meiji Restoration combined Tsugaru's territories with those of the Nambu clan, resulting in the creation of Aomori prefecture, with the city of Aomori as its capital. Unlike Aomori, Hirosaki was spared from damage during WWII (although the castle itself had been previously destroyed by a lightning strike), and the castle grounds are well preserved, with extant keeps and towers. Hirosaki is also the site of the Neputa Matsuri – not to be confused with Aomori's Nebuta but almost as rowdy and just as popular.

Information

Hirosaki Sightseeing Information Centre (☎ 37-5501; ☽ 9am-6pm Apr-Oct, 9am-5pm Nov-Mar, later during festivals) Inside the Kankōkan (Tourism Building) on the south side of Hirosaki-kōen; has basic information.

Internet (☽ 10am-9pm; per hr ¥100) At Renaisse Avenue mall.

Main post office Has 24hr postal and ATM service available until 7pm weekdays (5pm weekends); 20 minutes' walk northwest of the station.

Tourist information office (☎ 32-0524; ☽ 8.45am-6pm Apr-Oct, 8.45am-5pm Nov-Mar) To the right as you exit Hirosaki Station; offers a basic brochure/map in English.

Sights

The **Tsugaruhan Neputa-mura** (☎ 39-1511; 61 Kamenoko-machi; admission ¥500; ☽ 9am-5pm Apr-Nov, 9am-4pm Dec-Mar) has a fine, extensive display, over two levels, of the unique fan-shaped floats that are paraded during the Neputa Matsuri. Visitors get the chance to bang the massive drums used during the parade, while wearing a Neputa smock, all to the accompaniment of a traditional flautist. Addictive fun.

Just south, the **Genbē craft shop** has fine examples of Tsugaru lacquerware, nicknamed

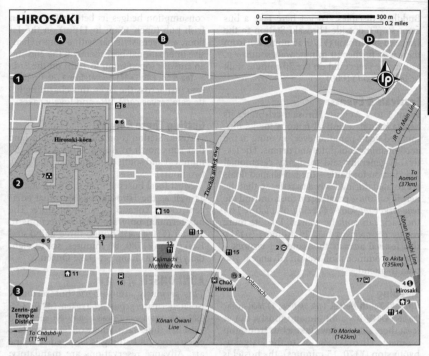

HIROSAKI

baka-nurii (fool's lacquerware), due to the tedious work involved in applying more than 40 layers of multicoloured designs to it's surface.

Hirosaki-kōen (弘前公園), the castle park, is extensive with three moats and the remains of the original castle, Hirosaki-jō, including gates and three corner keeps. It's a satisfying place for a stroll and attracts big crowds for *hanami* (cherry blossom viewing) during late April and early May. Construction of Hirosaki-jō was completed in 1611, but the castle was burnt down in 1627 after being struck by lightning. One of the corner towers was rebuilt in 1810 and now houses a small **museum** (admission ¥300; ⊙ 9am-5pm Apr-Nov) of samurai artefacts.

Fujita Kinen Tei-en (admission ¥300; ⊙ 9am-5pm Tue-Sun Apr-Nov) is a well-manicured garden outside the southwest corner of the park.

The **Zenrin-gai** (禅林街) temple district is another atmospheric spot, redolent of Old Japan. It follows the central avenue – flanked by temples – to **Chōshō-ji** (admission ¥300; ⊙ 8am-5pm Apr-Oct, 9am-4pm Nov–mid-Dec), the Tsugaru clan's family temple. After passing through the impressive gate, continue past a large 14th-century bell to the main hall, which dates from the 17th century. Turning left, a path through the trees leads to a row of mausoleums built for the early rulers of the Tsugaru clan, who dominated the region around Hirosaki during the Edo period. Also on display is a collection of 500 statues depicting

Buddha's disciples. To get here take a bus from stop 6 outside Hirosaki Station to the Daigaku-byōin stop (¥170, 15 minutes); from there it's a further 10-minute walk southwest. Otherwise you could do the 30-minute walk or take a taxi (¥1000).

Festivals & Events
From 1 to 7 August, Hirosaki celebrates its **Neputa Matsuri**, a festival famous for its illuminated floats parading every evening to the accompaniment of flutes and drums. The festival is generally said to signify ceremonial preparation for battle – the fan-shaped floats are rotated during festival parades so that the heroic *kagami-e* painting on the front and the tear-jerker *miokuri-e* ('seeing-off picture') on the back can both be viewed. Like its more rowdy counterpart held in Aomori (p481), this festival attracts thousands of visitors – book accommodation well in advance if you plan to attend.

Sleeping
Hirosaki Youth Hostel (☎ 33-7066; 11 Mori-machi; dm from ¥3045) It's a bit old and musty, but at least there's no curfew. Take a bus from stop 6 outside Hirosaki Station to the Daigaku-byōin stop (¥170, 15 minutes); the hostel is 250m west down an alleyway.

Hirosaki Grand Hotel (☎ 33-8111; 1 Ichiban-chō; s/d from ¥6000/10,050) The restaurant is a little bit grand – with ornate décor, tables and chairs – but not the rooms: they're rather bare and boring.

City Hirosaki Hotel (☎ 37-0109; 1-1-2 Ohmachi; s/tw from ¥7875/13,650) This swanky place does have grand rooms and is right next to the station. Actually, everything's grand here: the foyer, the restaurant…

Eating & Drinking
Live House Yamauta (☎ 36-1835; 1-2-7 Omachi; dinner/show per person from ¥3000; ⏰ 5pm-11pm, closed alternate Mon) A popular venue run by a family who serve local dishes and give twice-nightly performances of folk music on the *tsugaru jamisen* (p482).

Anzu (☎ 32-6684; 1-44 Oyakata-machi; set menus from ¥3000; ⏰ 5pm-11pm Mon-Sat) This is another option for the pleasing combination of traditional Japanese food and *tsugaru-jamisen* performances.

Hokusaikan (☎ 37-7741; 26-1 Dote-machi; ⏰ 11am-3pm) Over three floors, this monument to consumption hedges its bets. It features an Irish pub (open 11am to 11pm) on the 1st floor, a Cheers-style bar with a comprehensive international-beer menu on the 2nd and an *izakaya* (open noon to 1am) on the 3rd.

Tea & Co. (☎ 39-1717; sweets from ¥320; ⏰ 10am-8pm) Just across the river, this charming little café serves *caffè latte* and lovely cakes.

Getting There & Away
Hirosaki Station is on the JR Ōu Main Line that runs north to Aomori (*futsū*, ¥650, 50 minutes) and south to Akita (*tokkyū*, ¥4130, two hours).

Most local buses stop at the train station as well as the Hirosaki bus terminal adjacent to Itō Yōkadō department store. The bus terminal only services connections to Sendai (¥5090, 4½ hours, three daily) and Iwaki-san (¥1780, 80 minutes, six to eight daily), with a change at Dake Onsen.

AONI ONSEN 青荷温泉
This seriously atmospheric but seriously isolated rustic group of **ryokan** (☎ 0172-54-8588; r per person with 2 meals from ¥9700) seems to exist in a time warp, where oil lamps replace electricity and bathing is elevated to a fine art. Advance reservations are mandatory; the adjoining camping ground charges ¥1000 even if you bring your own tent. You can use just the baths for ¥500. Aoni Onsen is most accessible by car. By public transport, take the private Kounan Tetsudō Line from Hirosaki to Kuroishi (¥420, 35 minutes, four daily); Kounan buses connect with arriving passengers for Niji-no-ko (¥660, 10 minutes), from where shuttle buses run to Aoni (free, 30 minutes, four daily). This journey helps filter out the true *onsen* buffs.

IWAKI-SAN 岩木山
Soaring above Hirosaki is the sacred volcano of **Iwaki-san** (1625m), a popular peak for both pilgrims and hikers. From early April to late October, there are up to eight buses daily from the Hirosaki bus terminal to Dake Onsen (¥900, 50 minutes), where you transfer to a shuttle bus to Hachigōme (¥880, 30 minutes) at the foot of the ski lift. Open mid-April to mid-October, the lift (one way/return ¥410/750, 45 minutes) to the summit (Eighth Station) provides the easiest access, but it's also possible to hike to the top in about four hours starting from **Iwaki-jinja**.

In Hyakuzawa Onsen, **Kokumin-shukusha Iwaki-sō** (☎ 0172-83-2215; r per person with 2 meals from ¥7870) is a safe bet. From Hirosaki bus terminal stop 3, take a bus bound for Iwaki-sō and get off at the last stop (¥660, one hour).

TOWADA-KO 十和田湖

☎ 0176 / pop 6000

This 327m-deep crater lake (52km in circumference) has some impressive scenery (it's at the top of a 440m mountain), famously transparent water and superb opportunities for hiking and skiing. It's also a major tourist trap (apparently, Tōhoku's most popular sight) so it's best enjoyed as a day trip, especially as accommodation quickly books out, even in low season.

Nenokuchi, a small tourist outpost on the eastern shore of the lake, marks the entrance to the 14km **Oirase Valley Nature Trail**, a three-hour hike along the lakeshore; you might want to hike it in the early morning or late afternoon to avoid the coach parties. The path ends at Yakeyama, from where frequent buses return to Nenokuchi (¥660, 30 minutes) and Yasumiya (¥1100, one hour).

The tourist hub, Yasumiya, offers numerous boat tours of the lake, the best of which is the one-hour cruise between Yasumiya and Nenokuchi (one way ¥1320). Boats leave roughly every hour from April to early November between 8am and 4pm. You can hire mountain bikes at the dock for ¥1500 per day from April to November.

The hole-in-the-wall **tourist information centre** (☎ 75-2425; ⌚ 8am-5pm), just north of the JR bus station, stocks only Japanese-language hiking maps but can help arrange accommodation.

Sleeping

There are three camping grounds around the edge of the lake. **Towada-ko Oide Camping Ground** (☎ 75-2366; camp sites ¥300; ⌚ Apr-Oct) is about 4km west of Yasumiya. JR buses from Yasumiya to Towada-Minami pass by the Oide Kyampu-jo-mae stop (¥220).

Towada-ko Grand Hotel (十和田湖グランドホテル; ☎ 75-1111; Yasumiya-sanbashi-mae, Towada-kohan, Towada-chō, Kamikita-gun; r per person with 2 meals from ¥13,000) Offers a choice of Western- or Japanese-style rooms.

Hakubutsukan Youth Hostel (☎ 75-2002; dm from ¥4410) Rooms here are squeezed into the old wing of the Towada-ko Grand Hotel,

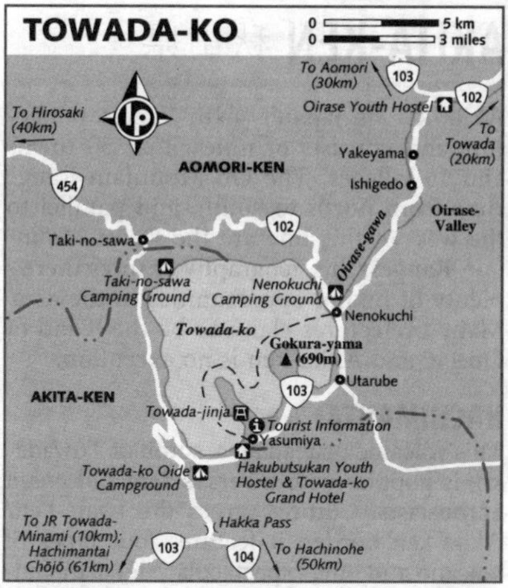

but are not available when the hotel is booked out.

Oirase Youth Hostel (おいらせユースホステル; ☎ 74-2031; 11-160 Tochikubo, Okuse; dm from ¥3940) Near the Yakeyama bus stop, this is a relaxed place with no curfew; it's quite a trek from Yasumiya, though. Buses running between Towada-ko and Aomori pass by the Yakeyama bus stop (¥1100, one hour), from where it's 200m up a small hill past the Oirase Grand Hotel car park to the hostel.

Minshuku line the track leading out of Yasumiya away from the lake. **Kokumin-shukusha Towada-ko** (国民宿舎十和田湖温泉; ☎ 75-2041; 16 Towada, Okuse-Aza; r per person ¥4350), is a few minutes northwest of the bus station, with decent rooms.

Getting There & Away

There are two bus centres in Yasumiya, one for JR buses and one for other services. Both are a couple of minutes on foot from the pier.

From April to November, JR buses run to Aomori (¥3000, three hours). There are three buses daily between April and early November to Morioka (¥2420, 2¼ hours). From late April to September, there is one bus at 8.45am to Hachimantai Chōjō, the main point of access for the Hachimantai region (¥2300, 2¼ hours).

The nearest train station is at Towada-Minami on the JR Hanawa Line, with connections to Morioka (*kaisoku*, ¥1800, 1¾ hours). Up to four connecting buses run daily 8am to 4.40pm (¥330, one hour).

AKITA-KEN 秋田県

Akita-ken is Japan's sixth-largest prefecture and consists of nine cities, 50 towns and 10 villages. The Ou Mountain Range runs from north to south, and parallel to the west of this line are the Dewa Mountain Ranges; this geography ensures there's plenty of hiking opportunities in the area. Many prefectures claim to be the 'Land of Onsen' and Akita-ken is no exception.

HACHIMANTAI 八幡平

This volcanic plateau area, south of Towadako, is popular with hikers, skiers and *onsen* enthusiasts. Cutting across the Iwate-ken/Akita-ken border, it features four types of volcano and offers spectacular views, including Iwate-san (p479). Hachimantai Chōjō, the main access point for the summit, offers gentle walks, but longer hikes are possible over a couple of days from nearby **Tōshichi Onsen**, a 2km walk downhill from the Hachimantai Chōjō car park. West of the summit, the Aspite Line Hwy, open late April to November, winds past several hot-spring resorts before joining Rte 341, which leads either south to Tazawa-ko or north towards Towada-ko.

HOT STUFF

There's an enduring myth attached to Lake Tazawa concerning a beautiful woman, Takko Hime, and her husband, Hachirōtarō. It's a very long and complex legend, and more than a little odd, but the gist of it is this: Takko Hime drank too much of the local water, believing it would make her even more beautiful. Her greed turned her into a water dragon, a metamorphosis that caused violent storms to whip up the elements, creating Lake Tazawa in the process. Meanwhile, Hachirōtarō had eaten a fish that made him very thirsty. He also drank too much water, bloated out, and became a water dragon; the fury of his transformation from man to beast created Lake Towada. Later, he fell in love with the beautiful water dragon, Takko Hime, and began to visit her regularly at Tazawa-ko. The passion of their lovemaking on the lake floor supposedly keeps Lake Tazawa from freezing over in winter.

There's a small **visitors centre** next to the car park at Hachimantai Chōjō, where you can purchase regional contour maps (Japanese only) and consult bilingual hiking sketch maps. However, the best place for English-language information on Hachimantai is Morioka's tourist office (p476).

The mountain lodge **Yuki-no-Koya** (☎ 0186-31-2118; dm from ¥4500; ◯ closed mid-Nov–Christmas & Feb-late Apr) is in a quiet riverside location at Shibari Onsen, on Rte 341, north of the turn-off for the Aspite Line Hwy to Hachimantai. Buses from Hachimantai Chōjō to Shibari Onsen (and connections to the JR Hanawa Line towards Morioka) are, at best, erratic. Do a thorough check at the visitors centre or Morioka's tourist information office before setting out.

The well-regarded **Hachimantai Youth Hostel** (八幡平ユースホステル; ☎ 0195-78-2031; 5-2 Midorigaoka, Matsuo-mura; dm from ¥3360) is 20 minutes by bus east of the summit. Get off at the Hachimantai Kankō Hoteru-mae stop (three to five buses daily, last bus 3.40pm).

Getting There & Away

Bus services to Hachimantai Chōjō run from 20 April to 31 October, with four buses departing Morioka Station daily (¥1320, two hours, hourly until noon).

Kaisoku on the JR Hanawa Line run from Morioka to Hachimantai and Kazuno-Hanawa stations (¥1910, two hours), where you can change to infrequent buses departing before noon to Hachimantai Chōjō via Shibari Onsen. Two stops further west on the Hanawa Line is Towada-Minami Station (¥2080, two hours) for access to Towada-ko. The direct bus to Towada-ko from Hachimantai Chōjō at noon is more convenient.

There are three buses daily from Hachimantai Chōjō to Tazawa Kohan (¥1880, two hours) and Tazawa-ko Station (¥1990, 2¼ hours); the last bus departs at 3.10pm.

TAZAWA-KO 田沢湖
☎ 0187 / pop 13,000

At 423m, Tazawa-ko is the deepest lake in Japan. Surrounded by wooded shores, it's a popular region for water sports, hiking around Akita Komaga-take and for the isolated Nyūtō Onsen. It's also known for the loopy legend explaining why it never freezes over in winter, and, like Towada-ko, for the clarity of its water.

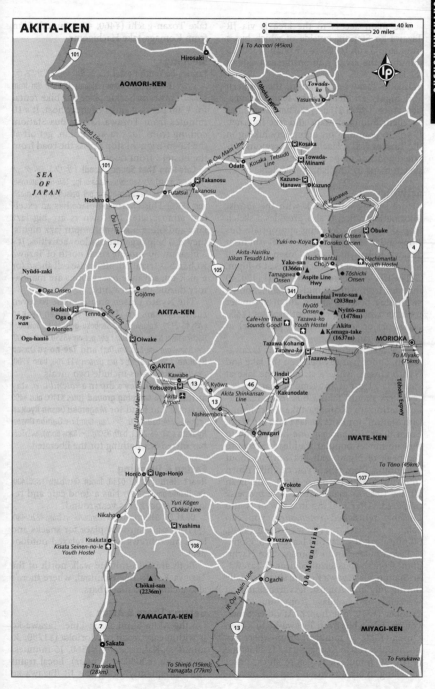

AKITA-KEN

0 — 40 km
0 — 20 miles

AOMORI-KEN

Hirosaki

To Aomori (45km)

Towada-ko

Yasumiya

Tōhoku Expwy

101

7

Kosaka

Towada-Minami

Kosaka Tetsudō Line

Ōdate

IR Ōu Main Line

Kazuno-Hanawa Kazuno

JR Hanawa Line

4

Takanosu

Takanosu

Futatsui

Noshiro

7

7

SEA OF JAPAN

101

Gonō Line

Ōu Line

Shibari Onsen
Yuki-no-Koya *Toroko Onsen*

Ōbuke

Akita-Nairiku Jūkan Tesudō Line

105

Hachimantai Chōjō

Hachimantai Youth Hostel

Nyūdō-zaki

Oga Onsen

Yake-san (1366m)

Tamagawa Onsen

Aspite Line Hwy

341

Tōshichi Onsen

Hachimantai Iwate-san (2038m)

Hadachi
Oga

Tennō

Togawan

Monzen

AKITA-KEN

Gojōme

Oga Line

Nyūtō Onsen

Cafe+Inn That
Sounds Good!

Tazawa-ko
Youth Hostel

Nyūtō-zan (1478m)

Akita Komaga-take (1637m)

Oga-hantō

Oiwake

Tazawa Kohan

Tazawa-ko

Tazawa-ko

MORIOKA

To Miyako (75km)

Tōhoku Expwy

AKITA

Kawabe

Yotsugoya

Akita
Airport

13

Kyōwa

Nishisemboku

46

Jindai

Kakunodate

Akita Shinkansen Line

13

Ōmagari

IR Ōu Main Line

IWATE-KEN

To Tōno (45km)

7

Honjō Ugo-Honjō

Yuri Kōgen
Chōkai Line

Nikaho

Yashima

Yokote

107

Yuzawa

108

Ōu Mountains

Kisakata

Kisata Seinen-no-Ie
Youth Hostel

Chōkai-san
(2236m)

YAMAGATA-KEN

Ogachi

IR Ōu Main Line

MIYAGI-KEN

7

Sakata

To Tsuruoka
(28km)

To Shinjō (15km),
Yamagata (77km)

13

To Furukawa

The main access to the area is via JR Tazawa-ko Station, outside of which buses from stop 3 run to Tazawa Kohan (¥350, 15 minutes), the area's hub on the east side of the lake.

Inside Tazawa-ko Station, the modern and highly efficient **Folake tourist information office** (☎ 43-2111; ☼ 8.30am-6.30pm) has excellent bilingual maps and free Internet. If you're planning on doing any hiking in the Tazawa-ko or Hachimantai regions, detailed contour maps in Japanese, as well as sketch maps in English, are available here.

Activities

Before setting out, check with the tourist information office; it also provides a sketch map of the area detailing appropriate bus stops and directions. Regular buses run from Tazawa Kohan to Nyūtō Onsen (¥850, 40 minutes); the last bus back leaves at 6.40pm.

The lake offers boat excursions (¥1170, 40 minutes, from April to mid-November only), swimming beaches and a 20km perimeter road for which you can rent bicycles (¥400 per hour) or scooters (¥1200 per hour) in Tazawa Kohan.

In winter, there's good skiing at Tazawa-kōgen, about halfway between the lake and Nyūtō Onsen, while a stroll by the lake at sunset is a treat at any time of year.

Hikers should take a bus from Tazawa-ko Station to Komaga-take Hachigōme (8th Station) for **Akita Komaga-take** (1637m). From there, it's an easy one-hour climb to the summit. A popular trail leads across to the peak of Nyūtō-zan (1478m) in about four hours, from where you can hike down to Nyūtō Onsen (another 5km). This is an all-day trek, so make sure you're properly prepared. After soaking in a few of Nyūtō Onsen's renowned *rotemburo*, you can catch a bus back to Tazawa Kohan (¥740, 50 minutes); the last bus leaves at 5.55pm.

Direct buses run to Komaga-take Hachigōme from the bus terminal near JR Tazawa-ko Station, via Tazawa Kohan, six times daily during July and August, less frequently on weekends and holidays from June to late October (¥810, one hour). At other times, you can take a bus from Tazawa-ko to Kōgen Onsen (¥580, 30 minutes), from where frequent buses run to Komaga-take Hachigōme (¥410, 30 minutes). If you're stuck, buses travelling to Nyūtō Onsen stop at Komaga-take Tozan-guchi (¥460, 40 minutes), 7km from Komaga-take Hachigōme.

Sleeping

Tazawa-ko Youth Hostel (田沢湖ユースホステル; ☎ 43-1281; 33-8 Kami-Ishigami, Obonai; dm from ¥2900) This ramshackle place has bike rental for ¥300 per day and a friendly host. It's 10 minutes from Tozawa Kohan Bus Station; coming from Tazawa-ko Station, get off at the Kōen-iriguchi stop across the road from the hostel's front door.

Cafe+Inn That Sounds Good! (サウンズグッド; ☎ 43-0127; sanzoku@hana.or.jp; 160-58 Katamae, Tazawako-machi, Senboku-gun; r per person with 2 meals from ¥8500) This charming place has an excellent atmosphere. The owners are big jazz fans and often host impromptu jazz nights; they also help organise outdoor activities. It's a pleasant 30-minute stroll north of Tazawa Kohan bus terminal, otherwise call ahead for a pick-up; advance reservations are mandatory during peak seasons.

The Nyūtō Onsen area is home to seven rustic ryokan. At **Tsuru-no-yu Onsen Ryokan** (☎ 46-2139; Kokuyurin 50 Senboku-gun, Akita, Towada-Hachimantai National Park; r per person ¥8550, bath ¥400; ☼ 8am-5pm Tue-Sun Apr-Oct) and **Tae-no-yu Onsen Ryokan** (☎ 46-2740; r per person ¥11,700, bath ¥700; ☼ 9am-3pm), rates include two meals.

If you just fancy a dip in a *rotemburo*, stay at the **Nyūtō camping ground** (sites ¥1100 plus ¥400 per person) and head for **Magoroku Onsen Ryokan** (☎ 46-2224; bath ¥400; ☼ 7am-6pm) or **Ganiba Onsen Ryokan** (☎ 46-2021; bath ¥500; ☼ 8am-6pm), which has mixed-sex bathing for the liberated.

Eating & Drinking

Heart Herb (☎ 43-0130; lunch sets/bath ¥880/400; ☼ 10am-9pm Apr-Nov) Has a good café and relaxing herbal baths year-round.

ORAE (37-5 Haruyama; set menus/beers from ¥820/480; ☼ 11am-9pm) A groovy place for snacks and local microbrews with its relaxed outdoor deck.

Both are a 15-minute walk north of the Tazawa Kohan bus terminal, where there's also a cluster of snack bars.

Getting There & Away

On the Akita Shinkansen Line, Tazawa-ko is within easy reach of Morioka (¥1780, 30 minutes), Kakunodate (¥1360, 15 minutes) and Akita (¥3080, one hour). Local trains run infrequently along the JR Tazawa-ko

Line to Morioka (¥740, 60 minutes) and Kakunodate (¥320, 20 minutes).

If you're heading west, it's easiest to take the bus from Tazawa Kohan via Tazawa-ko Station to Kakunodate (¥850, 45 minutes, seven daily); departures before 4.10pm continue to Akita (¥1680, 2¼ hours). From December to March, services to and from Tazawa Kohan, but not Tazawa-ko Station, are suspended.

Between 20 April and 31 October, three buses daily leave Tazawa-ko Station for Hachimantai Chōjō (¥1990, 2¼ hours); the last bus leaves at 12.40pm.

KAKUNODATE 角館
☎ 0187 / pop 15,000

In 1620 the feudal lord Ashina Yoshikatsu, founded Kakunodate as a castle town for the Satake clan. The location was considered ideal as it was relatively secure, being surrounded on three sides by mountain ranges. The castle has gone but the feudal layout is very much intact; it's as close to a samurai theme park as you might care to get in Tōhoku.

Kakunodate is known as 'Little Kyoto', and while those claims may be a little ambitious, it's still a thoughtful, immersive experience for anyone interested in old Japan. Wandering through Uchimachi, the samurai district, with its original homesteads surrounded by cherry trees and lush garden expanses, is a splendid way to pass a day – even if hundreds of other sightseers accompany you.

Information

The **tourist information office** (☎ 54-2700; ☉ 9am-6pm Apr-Oct, 9am-5pm Nov-Mar), in a small building that looks like a kura, is outside Kakunodate Station. The staff will oblige with reservations and English-language maps.

Outside the station, you can hire a **bicycle** (per hr ¥300) or a Japanese-speaking **rickshaw driver** (1-5 people ¥2000; summer only) to explain the local sights.

Free Internet access is available at the **library** (☉ 9am-7pm Tue-Sun) in the Sogō Joaho building, but beware: the staff will cut you off without warning if you go a minute over your allotted 30 minutes. Cash service is available at the post office and Akita bank.

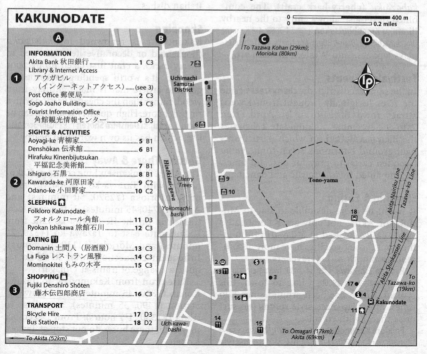

KAKUNODATE

0   400 m
0   0.2 miles

To Tazawa Kohan (29km);
Morioka (80km)

Uchimachi
Samurai
District

Hinokinai-gawa

Cherry
Trees

Yokomachi-
bashi

Tono-yama

Akita Nairiku Line

Tazawa-ko Line

Akita Shinkansen Line

To
Tazawa-ko
(19km)

Kakunodate

To Ōmagari (17km);
Akita (69km)

Uchikawa-
bashi

Uchikawabashi

To Akita (52km)

Sights

The Uchimachi samurai district is a 15-minute walk northwest from Kakunodate Station.

Ishiguro (Omotemachi; admission ¥300; 9am-5pm) was the residence of the Isihiguro family, advisers to the Satake clan; a descendant of the family still lives there, and has opened some of the rooms to the public. The house dates from 1809 and features an ornate gate, thatched roof and two entrances.

The interiors of the **Kawarada-ke** and **Odano-ke** residences can be viewed for free, while further north **Aoyagi-ke** (☎ 54-3257; Higashi Katuraku-chō 26; admission ¥500; 9am-5pm Apr-Nov, 9am-4pm Dec-Mar) is the centrepiece of the district, an agglomeration of minimuseums with folk art and Aoyagi family heirlooms. Not all of the pieces are related to feudal history – in a turn up for the books, there are also exhibits featuring old-time cameras, gramophones and classic jazz record covers.

Denshōkan (☎ 54-1700; 10-1 Omotemachi Shimocho; admission single/combined ¥300/510; 9am-4.30pm Apr-Nov, 9am-4pm Dec-Mar) is a museum that houses various exhibits and has demonstrations of *kabazaiku* (cherry-bark craft). The combined ticket also allows entry to the nearby **Hirafuku Kinenbijutsukan** (☎ 54-3888; 4-4 Kamicho Omotemachi; 9am-4.30pm Apr-Nov), which displays Japanese and Western modern art.

Festivals & Events

In the samurai district, the **cherry trees** beside the river (originally brought from Kyoto) attract crowds of visitors in late April. From 7 to 9 September Kakunodate celebrates the **Hikiyama Matsuri**, in which participants haul around enormous seven-tonne *yama* (wooden carts) to pray for peaceful times, accompanied by folk music and dancing.

Sleeping & Eating

It might be more desirable to stay in Morioka or Akita; not only are Kakunodate's sights easily covered in a day trip from either, but those two cities have more accommodation options for travellers.

Ryokan Ishikawa (☎ 54-2030; Iwamasemachi 32; r with 2 meals from ¥9000) Close to town, this ryokan, which has been around since Edo times, offers Japanese-style rooms (no surprise there) with en suite.

Folkloro Kakunodate (☎ 53-2070; Nakasuga-sawa 14; tw/q from ¥12,600/21,000) This Western-style hotel is next to Kakunodate Station; English is not spoken here and prices decrease for multiple-day stays.

Mominokitei (☎ 52-1705; mains from ¥1000; 11.30am-1.30pm & 6-9pm) Mominokitei has a lovely old trad-Japanese interior and the friendliest staff. But the menu is Italian – it's a pasta restaurant. The food is delicious but surprising, particularly the spaghetti with boiled octopus. Take the very Italian entrée of bruschetta, antipasto and garden salad: it's served up Japanese-style, arranged into minimal configurations, like sushi would be. Crisscrossed and arranged according to complementary colours, a sliver of capsicum might nestle on a bridge of finely chopped carrot, itself resting on a bed of lettuce.

La Fuga (☎ 54-2784; 34-8 Kotate; set lunches/pizzas from ¥800/1200; 11am-2pm & 5pm-8.30pm Tue-Sun) Kakunodate seems to have an Italy fetish. Like Mominokitei, this is one place worth seeking out, with its excellent pizzas and friendly owners.

Domanin (☎ 52-1703; Tamachi Bukeyashiki Hotel, 23 Shimocho Tamachi; meals from ¥2000; 11am-midnight) This funky *izakaya*-style eatery features no Italian dishes.

Shopping

Kakunodate is renowned for *kabazaiku* (household or decorative items covered in cherry bark), a craft first taken up by poor samurai. It's worth spending more on the genuine article that is made entirely from wood, rather than the cheaper version with a tin inner core. High-quality *kabazaiku* can be found at **Fujiki Denshirō Shōten** (10am-3pm Mar-Nov), which has its own workshop nearby.

Getting There & Away

The Akita Shinkansen Line connects Kakunodate with Tazawa-ko (¥1360, 15 minutes), Morioka (¥2570, 50 minutes) and Akita (¥2740, 45 minutes). Infrequent local trains run on the JR Tazawa-ko Line from Kakunodate east to Tazawa-ko (¥320, 20 minutes) and Morioka (¥1110, 1½ hours). Infrequent connections west to Akita require a change of trains at Ōmagari.

Buses run from Kakunodate to Tazawa Kohan (¥850, 45 minutes) and Tazawa-ko Station (¥490, 35 minutes), as well as to Akita (¥1330, 1½ hours). From December to March, these buses do not stop at Tazawa Kohan.

Kakunodate Bus Station is 10 minutes north of the train station.

AKITA 秋田
☎ 018 / pop 319,000

The prefectural capital is a large commercial city, handy as a base for Kakunodate and Tazawa-ko but with little in the way of sights. Still, Akita has some delicious local cuisine and stages the spectacular Kantō Matsuri, ranked among Tōhoku's top three festivals. Curiously, local tourism authorities also promote Akita's *bijin* (beautiful women) as a tourist attraction, citing the temperate climate and a diet supposedly high in malt as a contributing factor towards their distinctive fair skin. They even go so far as to claim that this quality has been 'scientifically tested and proven: Akita's women have the fairest skin in Japan'.

Information
EMERGENCY
Main police station (☎ 835-1111; 1-19 Meitoku-chō, Senshū)

INTERNET ACCESS
NTT Internet station (5th fl, Atorion Bldg; free; ⏰ 10am-4.30pm Thu-Tue)
Topico Internet (2nd fl, Topic Plaza bldg; per hr ¥400)

MEDICAL SERVICES
Red Cross Hospital (☎ 834-3361; 1-4-36 Naka-dōri)

POST
Post office (5 Hodōno Teppo-machi) Five minutes west of the train station's west exit, in the backstreets near the market.

TOURIST INFORMATION
Tourist information office (☎ 832-7941; ⏰ 9.30am-5pm) Opposite the *shinkansen* tracks on the 2nd floor of Akita Station.
Prefectural tourist information office (☎ 836-7835; ⏰ 9am-7pm Thu-Tue) Inside the Atorion Building.

Sights
The ruins of Akita's castle, Kubota-jō, are 10 minutes west of the station in **Senshū-kōen** (千秋公園). The castle dates from 1604 but, like many other feudal relics, it was destroyed by Meiji enlightenment. At the

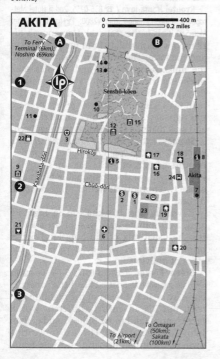

park's northern end is **Osumi-yagura**, a reconstruction of one of the castle's eight turrets, with an observation platform that delivers appealing views of the city. Near **Hachiman Akita-jinja**, the **Omonogashira-obansho** guardhouse is the only remaining original castle building, while the tiny **Satake Historical Museum** (admission ¥100; ☽ 9am-4.30pm) borders the southeast corner.

The **Masakichi Hirano Art Museum** (3-7 Senshū Meitoku; admission ¥610; ☽ 10am-5pm Tue-Sun May-Sep, 10am-4.30pm Tue-Sun Oct-Apr) is noted for its enormous painting, *Events of Akita*. Reputed to be the world's largest canvas painting, it measures 3.65m by 20.5m and depicts traditional Akita life throughout the seasons.

The **Kantō Festival Centre** (Neburi Nagashi-kan; admission ¥100; ☽ 9.30am-4.30pm, 9am-9pm during festivals), 10 minutes west of the park across the river, has exhibitions and videos of Akita's famous Kantō Matsuri and a chance for you to heft the famous kantō poles. It won't be easy: these babies are 10m long and weigh around 60kg.

Five minutes south, past Daiei department store, the **Akarengakan Museum** (☎ 864-6851; 3-3-21 Omachi; admission ¥200; ☽ 9.30am-4.30pm), in a Meiji-era, Renaissance-style, red-brick building, has wood-block prints of traditional Akita life by self-taught folk artist Katsuhira Tokushi. A combined ticket with the Kantō Festival Centre is available at either place for ¥250.

Festivals & Events

From 4 to 7 August, Akita celebrates the visually stunning **Kantō Matsuri** (Pole Lantern Festival; www.kantou.gr.jp). Starting in the evening along Kantō Ōdori, more than 160 men skilfully balance giant poles, weighing 60kg and hung with illuminated lanterns, on their heads, chins, hips and shoulders to the beat of *taiko* drumming groups. As the aim of the festival is to pray for a good harvest, the arrangement of the lanterns is designed to resemble an ear of rice. During the day, exhibitions of music and pole balancing are held in Senshū-kōen.

Sleeping

Ryokan Kohama (☎ 832-5739; 6-19-6 Naka-dōri; per person ¥5500) This well-kept ryokan is 10 minutes south of Akita Station.

Hotel Hawaii Eki-mae (☎ 833-1111; 2-2, Senshū-kubota-machi; s/tw with bath ¥6000/9000, without bath ¥4100/5500) You really shouldn't expect any

hula skirts here: it's as no frills as they come. Rooms are somewhat cramped, and the service is poor.

Ryokan Chikuba-sō (☎ 832-6446; 14-9-4 Naka-dōri; r per person with 2 meals ¥7000) Another spick-and-span choice with decent-sized rooms.

Akita View Hotel (☎ 832-1111; 6-1-2 Naka-dōri; s/tw from ¥8800/18,480) Opposite the Hotel Hawaii, this lush hotel is perhaps the swankiest in town, with its gym, pool, sauna and upmarket restaurants.

Hotel Metropolitan (☎ 832-1111; 7-2-1 Naka-dōri; s/tw from ¥10,626/16,000) Your standard business hotel, with clean rooms and all the usual features: TVs in the rooms, en suites.

Eating & Drinking

Local specialities include two types of hotpot. One is *shottsuru* – *hatahata* (local fish) with green onions and tofu. The other is the fabulous *kiritanpo*, based on rice that's kneaded and wrapped around bamboo spits, which are barbecued over a charcoal fire. The rice is then cooked in a soy-flavoured chicken broth with noodles, onions, Japanese parsley and field mushrooms.

Ryoutei Hamanoya (☎ 836-0755; 2nd fl Hotel Metropolitan bldg; kiritanpo from ¥2800; ☽ lunch & dinner Mon-Sat) This is the real deal: Hamanoya's kiritanpo is masterful, both in the preparation and the taste. The hotpot is a perfect blend, the mushrooms, onions and noodles soak the *mochi* (rice cakes) with a subtle mesh of flavours to produce a sticky rice stew. Hamanoya's kimono-clad waitresses prepare this right at your table, with a casual elegance and skill that's as seductive as the dish itself.

Suginoya (☎ 835-8903; 4-1-15 Naka-dōri; set menus from ¥1500; ☽ 10am-9pm) On the 3rd floor restaurant arcade of Akita Station's Topico Plaza, Suginoya does reasonable facsimiles of the two hotpots, as well as other regional dishes.

Kawabata-dōri is Akita's main nightlife area, a 15-minute walk west of the station. It's the usual mix of hip-hop, loud noise, bright lights and wild-eyed rebels at the gates of oblivion.

Green Pocket (☎ 863-6917; 5-1-7 Oo-machi; ☽ 7pm-midnight Mon-Sat) This little upstairs bar may be in the heart of the nightlife district, but it's an entirely different world: Jazz Central (and more Billie Holliday than John Coltrane, at that). The tuxedo-wearing owners, a cordial husband-and-wife team, work the bar and keep the old days close at hand. The bar is decked out in authentic period panelling, with an old-time piano in the corner, the aforementioned soundtrack, Vivien Leigh prints and a fabulously decadent selection of scotch whiskies and fine wines – classy. Week nights attracts a lively older crowd; weekends are quieter.

Getting There & Away

There are flights from Akita's airport south of town to Nagoya (¥24,300, 70 minutes), Osaka (¥28,300, 80 minutes), Sapporo (¥21,300, 55 minutes) and Tokyo (¥20,800, one hour). Buses run from outside JR Akita Station (¥890, 40 minutes).

The JR Akita Shinkansen Line runs via Tazawa-ko and Kakunodate to Morioka (¥4300, 1½ hours), cutting the total travel time between Akita and Tokyo to four hours (¥16,470). Painfully infrequent local trains chug along the Ōu Line to Ōmagari, where you change to the JR Tazawa-ko Line for Kakunodate (¥1280, 1½ hours) and Tazawa-ko (¥1620, 2½ hours). The JR Uetsu Line connects Akita with Niigata via Sakata and Tsuruoka (*tokkyū* ¥6510, 3¾ hours).

Ten buses run daily from Akita Station to Kakunodate (¥1330, 1½ hours) and eight daily to Tazawa-ko (¥1680, two hours). Direct night buses to Tokyo (Shinjuku) run from the Nagasakiya bus terminal via Akita Station at 9pm and 10pm (one way ¥9450, 9½ hours).

On Tuesday, Wednesday, Friday and Sunday, Shin Nihonkai morning ferries connect Akita with Niigata (¥2270, 6½ hours) and Tsuruga (¥5620, 19½ hours). On Tuesday, Thursday, Saturday and Sunday, ferries run to Tomakomai on Hokkaidō (¥3830, 11½ hours).

One bus daily at 7.25am runs to Akita's port, 8km northwest of the station (¥390, 30 minutes).

KISAKATA 象潟

☎ 0184 / pop 13,300

This was the most northerly point Bashō reached in his travels through Tōhoku. Kisakata is a small coastal town near **Chōkai-san** (2236m), Tōhoku's second-highest peak. Known as 'Dewa Fuji', Chōkai-san is an object of veneration by the same *yamabushi* (mountain priests) who worship at Dewa Sanzan (p498) in Yamagata-ken.

The **tourist information office** (☎ 43-2174; ☽ 9am-5pm), inside the station waiting room, has photocopied contour maps for hiking Chōkai-san and information on local sights, such as **Kanman-ji** (visited by Bashō) just north of the town centre.

Next door to the youth hostel is a **camping ground** (camp sites ¥500, plus per person ¥400; ☽ Jul-Sep), while nearby **Minshuku Rofusō** (☎ 43-2228; 63-3 Kanmuri Ishita; r per person with 1/2 meals ¥6610/10,500) is a simple but effective option.

Masaen (☎ 43-2467; 8-1 Hamadou Aza Kotaki Kisakata-machi; set menus ¥800; ☽ 11am-9pm Tue-Sun) is a fantastic little eatery offering up generous serves of *rāmen* and free coffee. It's 300m west of the station.

Getting There & Away

Local trains on the scenic JR Uetsu Main Line connect Kisakata with Sakata (¥650, 40 minutes) for connections to Tsuruoka (¥1120, 30 minutes). Local trains head north on the same line to Akita (¥1110, 1¼ hours).

YAMAGATA-KEN 山形県

Yamagata-ken is promoted with endearing humility: 'Admittedly, this is not the most famous place in Japan,' the prefectural guide states, 'but it is not a place you should miss'. Like Akita-ken, it claims to be Onsen Central, boasting around 100 hot springs. However, Yamagata-ken might well win the title; after all, it does have the sublime Zaō Onsen, with its atmospheric *rotemburo*, acknowledged as one of Japan's best.

TOBI-SHIMA 飛島

☎ 0234

A mere speck of an island (2.5 sq km), Tobi-shima's main attractions are rugged cliffs, sea caves, bird-watching, scuba diving and excellent fishing. You can also organise boat trips out to smaller islands.

The coastal town of Sakata is your best bet for **tourist information** (☎ 24-2454; ☽ 9am-5.30pm Apr-Oct, 9am-5pm Nov-Mar).

Rates at the island's ryokan vary seasonally from ¥7000 to ¥10,000 per person with two meals; *minshuku* cost around ¥7000 with two meals. **Sawaguchi Ryokan** (沢口旅館; ☎ 95-2246; dm from ¥2000), the island's youth hostel, is seven minutes on foot from the ferry pier; bicycle rental is available.

NORTHERN HONSHŪ

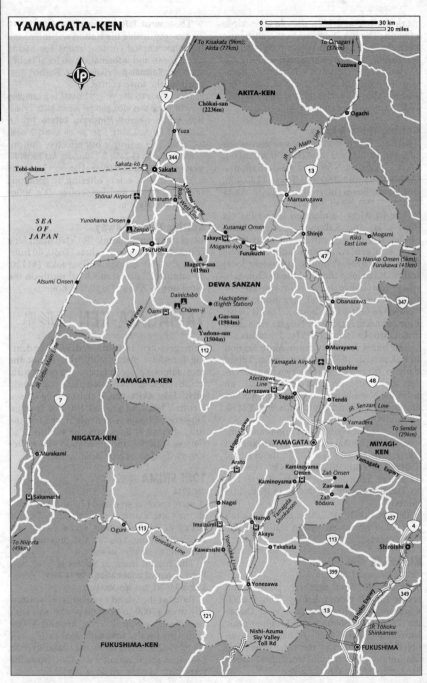

YAMAGATA-KEN

0 ——————— 30 km
0 ——————— 20 miles

To Kisakata (9km);
Akita (77km)

To Ōmagari
(37km)

Yuzawa

AKITA-KEN

7

Chōkai-san
(2236m)

Ogachi

Yuza

JR Ōu Main Line

13

344

Sakata-kō

Sakata

Tobi-shima

Shōnai Airport Amarume

Mamurogawa

SEA
OF
JAPAN

Yunohama Onsen

Zenpō-ji

Kusanagi Onsen

Takaya

Shinjō

Rikū
East Line

Mogami

Mogami-kyō Furukuchi

47

To Naruko Onsen (5km);
Furukawa (41km)

7 Tsuruoka

Haguro-san
(419m)

Atsumi Onsen

DEWA SANZAN

Dainichibō

Hachigōme
(Eighth Station)

Obanazawa

347

Ōami Chūren-ji

Gas-san
(1984m)

Yudono-san
(1504m)

112

Murayama

Yamagata Airport

Higashine

48

YAMAGATA-KEN

Aterazawa
Line

Aterazawa Sagae

Tendō

JR Senzan Line

7

Yamadera

To Sendai
(29km)

YAMAGATA

MIYAGI-
KEN

NIIGATA-KEN

Murakami

Arato

Kaminoyama
Onsen

Zaō Onsen

Kaminoyama

Zaō-san

Sakamachi

Nagai

Zaō
Bōdaira

457

4

Imaizumi Nanyō

Oguni 113

Yonesaka Line

Akayu

Shiroishi

To Niigata
(49km)

Kawanishi

Takahata

113

399

349

Yonezawa

13

121

FUKUSHIMA-KEN

Nishi-Azuma
Sky Valley
Toll Rd

FUKUSHIMA

Ferries run at least once (often twice) daily from Sakata-kō to the island (¥2040, 1½ hours); advance reservations (☎ 22-3911) are recommended in summer. To get to Sakata-kō, take the Run Run bus from Sakata to the ferry-terminal stop (¥100). The JR Uetsu Main Line runs to Sakata via Kisakata (*futsū*, ¥650, 40 minutes), Akita (¥1890, 1¾ hours), Tsuruoka (¥480, 40 minutes) and Niigata (*tokkyū*, ¥4620, 2¼ hours).

There are up to seven buses daily from Sakata to Sendai (¥2750, three hours, last bus 4.20pm) via the Tsuruoka bus terminal (¥820, 50 minutes). There is one night bus to Tokyo (Shibuya, Ikebukuro) departing Sakata at 9.30pm (¥7870, nine hours).

MOGAMI-KYŌ 最上峡

Boat tours are operated through this gorge on a section of the Mogami-gawa between Sakata and Shinjō, complete with a boatman singing a selection of local folk tunes.

From Sakata, trains on the JR Rikuu-saisen Line run to Furukuchi Station (¥740, 42 minutes); you may have to change trains en route at Amarume. From Furukuchi Station, it's eight minutes on foot to the dock. Boats depart up to nine times daily from 9am to 4.30pm during the main season from April to November (¥1970). The boat trip takes an hour to reach **Kusanagi Onsen**, where passengers are met by shuttle buses heading to Takaya Station on the JR Rikuu-saisen Line.

TSURUOKA 鶴岡

☎ 0235 / pop 100,000

In the middle of the Shōnai plain, Tsuruoka was formerly an important castle town, home to the Sakai-clan, one of the most powerful of Yamagata's feudal clans. Today, it has a few sights and is the primary access point for the nearby trio of sacred mountains, known collectively as Dewa Sanzan.

Information

Internet access (free 30min; ⌚ 10am-8pm) On the 3rd floor of the Marica Building, opposite the station.

Post office With ATM service, 300m south of the station.

Tourist information office (☎ 25-7678; ⌚ 9am-5pm) To the right as you exit JR Tsuruoka Station; can book accommodation and has lots of information about Dewa Sanzan, although little is in English.

Sights & Activities

Founded in 1950 by the former Lord Shōnai in order to develop and preserve local culture, **Chidō Museum** (致道博物館; ☎ 22-1199; 10-18 Kachu-shinmachi; admission ¥900; ⌚ 9am-4.30pm Tue-Sun) features Sakai family artefacts, a family residence, two Meiji-era buildings, a traditional storehouse and a *kabuto-zukuri* (a farmhouse with a thatched roof shaped like a samurai helmet). The museum is west of Tsuruoka-kōen, 10 minutes by bus from Tsuruoka Station. From stop 1 at the station, frequent buses bound for Yunohama Onsen pass by the Chidō Hakubutsukan-mae stop (¥200, 10 minutes).

Seven kilometres west of Tsuruoka you'll find **Zenpō-ji**, a Zen Buddhist temple with a five-tier pagoda and large gateway; it dates from the 10th century when it was dedicated to the Dragon King, guardian of the seas. Note the imposing wooden fish hanging from the ceilings and the paintings depicting fishing scenes; the latter was donated by local fishing companies hoping to gain favour from the gods of the seas.

Near the temple is a more contemporary attraction, the famous *jinmen-gyo* (human-faced carp). When viewed from above, these freaky fish actually do look to have human faces. Apparently, an urban legend spread in the '80s, claiming a dog with a human face had been seen around the country. Not only was it meant to be a fast runner, but it could talk, too. On the back of this rumour, people thronged to Zenpō-ji to see if the *jinmen-gyo* would talk to them.

From the station, take a bus bound for Yunohama Onsen to the Zenpō-ji stop (¥580, 30 minutes). If you're in the mood for surf and sand, the beach at **Yunohama Onsen** is a 10-minute bus ride away or 4km on foot.

Festivals & Events

Tsuruoka's best-known festival is the **Tenjin Matsuri** (25 May), also known as the Bakemono Matsuri (Masked Faces Festival). People used to stroll around in masks and costume for three days, serving sake and keeping an eye out for friends and acquaintances. The object is to make it through three festivals in a row without anyone recognising you, whereupon local lore states you'll have good luck for the rest of your life.

On 1 and 2 February, **nō performances** are held at night in Kurokawa village near Tsuruoka; reserve tickets well in advance via Tsuruoka tourist information.

Sleeping

Petit Hotel Tsuruoka (☎ 25-1011; 2-1 Suehiro-machi; s/tw ¥6000/11,400) This family-run business hotel, with its choice of Western or tatami rooms, is right next to the station complex. Meals are sometimes available (if you make an advance reservation) in the coffee shop downstairs.

Nara Ryokan (奈良旅館; ☎ 22-1202; r per person ¥4600) This modern ryokan is five minutes along the main street leading out from the station.

Tsuruoka Hotel (鶴岡ホテル; ☎ 22-1135; r per person with/without 2 meals ¥7000/5000) This atmospheric old place is rather far from the station. Take the Yunohama Onsen–bound bus from stop 1 at the station to the Hitoichi-dōri stop (¥100), then walk back up the street – the hotel is on the right-hand side.

Getting There & Away

From Tsuruoka Station, the JR Uetsu Main Line runs north to Sakata (*tokkyū*, ¥480, 40 minutes) for connections to Kisakata, and to Akita (*tokkyū*, ¥3510, 1½ hours); it takes a scenic route south to Niigata (*tokkyū*, ¥3820, 1¾ hours) across a backdrop of crashing waves. Taking the train to Yamagata usually requires three changes, one at the very least. Despite the extension of the Yamagata Shinkansen Line to Shinjō, it's still more convenient to take the bus.

A series of scenic local trains along the JR Rikuu-sai and Rikuu-tō lines connect Tsuruoka to Naruko Onsen (Miyagi-ken) (¥2390, two hours) via a change at Shinjō.

Night buses to Tokyo (Ikebukuro, Shibuya) depart from in front of the Tokyo Dai-ichi Hotel in Tsuruoka (¥7540, eight hours). Regular buses between Tsuruoka and Yamagata (¥2150, 1¾ hours) run via the Yudono-san Hotel (¥1330, 50 minutes), which provides access to Yudono-san. Services are often cut back during the winter months due to snowdrifts. Between July and early November, there are also up to four direct buses between Tsuruoka and Yudono-san that stop by the hotel on the way up to the Sennin-zawa trailhead (¥1480, 80 minutes).

DEWA SANZAN 出羽三山
☎ 0235

Dewa Sanzan is the collective title for three sacred peaks: Haguro-san, Gas-san and Yudono-san. The mountains have been worshipped for centuries by *yamabushi* and followers of the Shugendō sect. During the pilgrimage seasons, you can see white-clad pilgrims (equipped with wooden staff, sandals and straw hat) and the occasional *yamabushi* (equipped with conch shell, check jacket and voluminous white pantaloons) stomping along mountain trails or sitting under icy waterfalls as part of severe ascetic exercises intended to train both body and spirit.

Theoretically, if you hiked at a military pace and timed the buses perfectly, you might be able to cover all three peaks in one day. However, this would leave you no time to enjoy the scenery, and the chances of missing a key bus connection are good. If you want to tackle all three mountains it's best to devote at least two days; book accommodation and stock up on maps at the Tsuruoka tourist office (p497) before setting off.

Haguro-san 羽黒山

Because it has the easiest access, Haguro-san (414m) attracts a steady flow of tourists. At the base of the mountain is Haguro village, consisting of *shukubō* (pilgrims' lodgings) and the **Ideha Bunka Kinenkan** (い では文化記念館; admission ¥400; ☼ 8.30am-5pm Wed-Mon), a small history museum featuring films of *yamabushi* rites and festivals.

The orthodox approach to the shrine on the summit requires pilgrims to climb 2446 steps but buses also run to the top. The climb can be done in a leisurely 50 minutes and you might even be lapped by gaggles of sprightly senior citizens; don't lose heart – just take your time and enjoy the views.

From Haguro centre Bus Station, walk straight ahead through the *torii* and continue across a bridge into beautiful cryptomeria trees that form a canopy overhead. En route, you'll pass **Gojū-no-tō**, a weather-beaten five-storey pagoda dating from the 14th century. It's a stirring sight, with its aged, intricate wooden structure blending in with the trees. Then comes a very long slog up the hundreds of stone steps arranged in steep sections. Pause halfway at the **teahouse** (☼ 8.30am-5pm Apr-Nov) for refreshment and breathtaking views. If you detour to the right just past the teahouse, you'll come upon the temple ruins of **Betsu-in**, visited by Bashō during his pilgrimage here.

The scene at the top is an anticlimax. There are several shrines, often crowded with visitors except during early mornings or late afternoons, an uninspiring history museum and a row of shops and eateries. From the top you can either walk or catch a bus back down to the bottom. In summer there are two buses in the morning that go on to Gas-san.

Gas-san 月山

Accessible from June to September, Gas-san (1984m) is the highest of the three sacred peaks and attracts pilgrims to **Gassan-jinja** (admission with ritual purification ¥500; 6am-5pm), a shrine on the peak itself. To enter the shrine you need to be purified: bow your head to receive a priest's benediction, before rubbing your head and shoulders with sacred paper, which is then placed in the fountain.

The peak is usually accessed from the trailhead at Hachigōme (8th Station); the trail passes through an alpine plateau to the Kyūgōme (9th Station) in 1¾ hours and then grinds uphill for 70 minutes.

The steep descent to Yudono-san-jinja takes another 2½ hours (keep choosing the right fork). After about 45 minutes of this descent, you also have the choice of taking the trail to Ubazawa, the main ski resort on Gas-san, which has its own cable car. If you continue to Yudono-san, you'll eventually have to descend rusty ladders chained to the cliffside and carefully pick your way down through a slippery stream bed at the end of the trail.

Yudono-san 湯殿山

Accessible from June to October, the Sennin-zawa trailhead for Yudono-san (1504m) is approached via a 3km toll road from the Yudono-san Hotel. From there it's a 10-minute hike further up the mountain to **Yudonosan-jinja** (湯殿山神社; admission ¥500; 6am-5pm Apr-Nov). This sacred shrine is not a building but a large orange rock continuously lapped by water from a hot spring. It has the strictest rituals of the three, with pilgrims required to perform a bare-foot circuit of the rock, paddling through the cascading water.

Dainichibō & Chūren-ji 大日坊・注連寺

Off Rte 112 between Yudono-san and Tsuruoka, these two ordinary country temples house the exotic mummies of former priests who have become 'Buddhas in their own bodies'. The ascetic practice of self-mummification, outlawed since the 19th century, involved coming as close to death as possible through starvation, before being buried alive while meditating. The mummy at **Dainichibō** (admission ¥500; 8am-5pm) is dressed in bright orange robes and is rather ghoulish. The **Chūren-ji** (admission ¥500; 8am-5pm) mummy, also freakish, is allegedly a reformed murderer who became a powerful Buddhist priest.

Both temples are five minutes on foot from the Ōami bus stop, which is approximately halfway between Tsuruoka (¥950) and Yudono-san (¥910). Buses are spaced about two hours apart, enough time to look around.

Festivals & Events

Dewa Sanzan-jinja, on the peak of Haguro-san, is the site of several major festivals. During the **Hassaku Matsuri** (24–31 August), *yamabushi* perform ancient fire rites to pray for a bountiful harvest. During the **Shōrei-sai** festival on New Year's Eve, they perform similar rituals in competition with each other after completing 100-day-long austerities.

If just being an observer isn't enough, you can join a yamabushi training camp. On selected weekends in July and September, **Ideha Bunka Kinenkan** runs three-/eight-day courses for ¥20,000/40,000 that include fasting, mountain sprints and 4.30am wake-up calls. **Dewa Sanzan-jinja** (☎ 62-2355) runs 'real' *yamabushi* courses that are even more intensive, as well as five-day training programs for women (¥40,000) in early September. These Buddhist boot camps are not for the faint-hearted.

Sleeping & Eating

There are more than 30 *shukubō* in the Tōge district of Haguro village, charging around ¥7000 to ¥8000 per person including two meals.

Saikan (斎館; ☎ 62-2357; r per person ¥7000) This temple lodging is at the top of Haguro-san with airy rooms and spectacular views. Rates include two gourmet vegetarian meals; advance reservations are mandatory.

Sanrōjō (参籠所; ☎ 54-6131; r with 2 meals from ¥7000) This friendly place can be found beside the Sennin-zawa bus terminal. There's a very good chance that you may be expected to join in prayers.

Saikan and Sanrōjō also serve vegetarian lunches to nonguests from ¥1500; reservations are required.

Yudono-san Hotel (湯殿山ホテル; ☎ 54-6231; r per person from ¥8500) This one's a convenient base to start or finish the Yudono-san to Gas-san hike. The rooms are basic but comfortable and the rate includes a vegetarian dinner.

Getting There & Away

Buses to Haguro centre bus station depart Tsuruoka roughly every hour (¥680, 35 minutes), continuing to Haguro-sanchō (Haguro summit) less frequently between 8.30am and 4.30pm (¥990, 55 minutes).

From early July to late August, and then on weekends and holidays until late September, there are two buses from Haguro-sanchō at 10am and 11.10am, allowing pilgrims to travel towards the peak of Gas-san as far as Hachigōme (¥1240, 50 minutes). Two buses at 6am and 7am also run from Tsuruoka direct to Gas-san Hachigōme (¥1650, 1½ hours) during these times.

Buses from Tsuruoka pass by the Yudono-san Hotel en route to Yamagata (¥1750, 1¼ hours, last bus 4pm), as they do to Tsuruoka via Ōami (¥1330, 50 minutes, last bus 4.30pm).

Between June and early November, there are up to four more buses from the Sennin-zawa trailhead at Yudono-san to Tsuruoka (¥1480, 80 minutes), which also pass by the hotel and Ōami.

YAMAGATA 山形

☎ 023 / pop 250,000

Surrounded by mountains, Yamagata is the prefectural capital – a thriving industrial city with a sizable student population. Most travellers use it as a base for day trips to Yamadera, Tendō and Takahata, as well as the skiing and hiking region around Zaō Onsen.

Information

Central post office (Nanokamachi-dōri) Has ATM; a branch post office is on the 1st floor of the Kajo Central Building.

Internet access (per hr ¥400) On the 5th floor of Kajo Central, at a tiny stand adjoining the digital copy centre.

Prefectural tourism information office (☎ 630-2371; ⏱ 9.30am-8pm) On the 1st floor of the Kajo Central Building (joined to the station complex by walkways).

Tourist information office (☎ 631-7865; ⏱ 10am-6pm Mon-Fri, 10am-5pm Sat & Sun) On the 2nd floor of Yamagata Station, opposite the *shinkansen* tracks.

Hirashimizu Pottery District
平清水陶器地域

These recently revived kilns along the Hazukashii-kawa (Shy River) turn out beautiful spotted-glaze pieces, nicknamed *nashi-seiji* (peach skin), which are displayed for sale in attached workshops. The renowned **Shichiemon-gama** (七右衛門釜; ☎ 642-7777; 153 Hirachimizu; ⏱ 9am-3pm) offers instruction in pottery making at ¥1800 per 1kg of clay. To get there, buses bound for Nishi-Zaō or Geikō-dai run hourly or half-hourly from stop 5 outside Yamagata Station to the Hirashimizu stop (¥200, 15 minutes).

Festivals & Events

In early August, the **Hanagasa Matsuri** features large crowds of dancers wearing *hanagasa* (flower-laden straw hats) and singing folk songs. The lyrics are said to derive from the impromptu, often salacious tunes once improvised by construction workers to keep time to the rhythm of their labour.

The biannual **Yamagata International Documentary Film Festival** is unique: it was established in 1989 to mark the 100th anniversary of the municipalisation of Yamagata, and was the first of its kind in Asia. During the festival week in October, films from over 70 countries screen, along with retrospectives, symposiums and a Japanese panorama. All screenings have English and Japanese subtitles and most festival publications are bilingual. See www.city.yamagata.yamagata.jp/yidff/home-e.html for more information.

Sleeping & Eating

Yamashiroya Ryokan (山城屋旅館; ☎ 622-3007; r per person ¥4400) This is a simple ryokan elevated to luxury levels by the friendliness of the hosts. It's 150m north of the station's east exit, next to a fruit shop.

Green Hotel (グリーンホテル香澄町; ☎ 622-2636; 1-3-12 Kasumi-chō; Western-style r with private bath from ¥3900) Five minutes east of the station, this business hotel is marked with an English sign. Reception is on the 2nd floor.

There are plenty of places hawking marbled Yonezawa beef along Nanokamachi-dōri.

Sagorō (佐五郎; ☎ 631-3560; 6-10 1 Kasumi-chō; ⏰ 11am-9pm Mon-Sat) This is one of the best beef joints serving delicious sukiyaki (thin slices of beef) and good old steaks. Look for it on the third floor above a butcher's shop.

Sakaeya Honten (さかえや本店; ☎ 623-0766; 2-3-21 Honmachi; hiyashi rāmen ¥700; ⏰ 11.30am-8pm Thu-Tue). Try this place for *hiyashi* (chilled) *rāmen*, another Yamagata speciality. Facing east from the AZ store, take the first side street to your right.

Getting There & Away

The JR Senzan Line connects Yamagata with Yamadera and Sendai (*kaisoku*, ¥1110, one hour). The JR Ōu Main Line runs south to Yonezawa (*futsū*, ¥820, 45 minutes) and north to Ōma-gari for connections to Tazawa-ko and Akita (*kaisoku*, ¥3570, four hours).

The JR Yamagata and Tōhoku Shinkansen Lines connect Yamagata with Yonezawa (¥1860, 35 minutes), Fukushima (¥2910, 1¼ hours) and Tokyo (¥10,060, three hours).

Travellers to Tsuruoka are advised to take the bus via the Yudono-san Hotel (¥2150, 1¾ hours). Buses start from the Yama-kō Bus Station inside the Daiei department store's basement on Ekimae-dōri; most stop at Yamagata Station before leaving town. There are frequent buses from Yamagata to Zaō Onsen (¥840, 40 minutes) and five buses daily to Yamadera (¥580, 40 minutes).

Frequent highway buses run to Sendai (¥1000, one hour) and two buses run daily to Niigata (¥3500, 3¾ hours). A night bus to Tokyo (Asakusa, Ueno) departs at 9.30pm (¥6420, six hours).

TENDŌ 天童
☎ 023 / pop 63,000

Tendō makes an interesting half-day excursion from Yamagata. It produces around 90% of Japan's chess pieces annually, an exquisite art begun by poor samurai during the Edo period (their salaries were cut by the Tendō lord, who had fallen upon hard times).

The **tourist information centre** (☎ 653-1680; ⏰ 9am-5.30pm), on the 2nd floor of JR Tendō Station, has details of local attractions including the eccentric **Tendō Mingeikan** (天童民芸館; ⏰ 8am-6pm; admission ¥700), a folkcraft museum housed in a gasshō-zukuri farmhouse. The **Tendō Shōgi Museum** (天童市将棋資料館; admission ¥300; 1-1-1 Hon-chō; ⏰ 9am-5.30pm Thu-Tue) is part of JR Tendō Station and displays chess sets from Japan and abroad.

You can see chess pieces being made at the **Eishundō museum** (admission ¥500; ⏰ 9am-5pm), a 15-minute walk straight out from the station, just past the Tendō Park Hotel. Across the street, the **Hiroshige Art Museum** (広重美術館; 1-2-1 Kamatahoncho; admission ¥600; ⏰ 8.30am-6pm Wed-Mon Apr-Oct, 9am-5pm Wed-Mon Nov-Mar) displays wood-block prints by famous Edo-period master Hiroshige.

On the last weekend in April, Tendō-kōen hosts the theatrical **Ningen Shōgi**, when outdoor chess matches are played using real people as pieces. The tradition is credited to Toyotomi Hideyoshi, who once played a similar match with his son in Kyoto. If you want to become a human chess piece, visit www.ikechang.com/chess/piece-e.htm.

Tendō is six stops north of Yamagata by local train (¥230, 20 minutes) or 50 minutes by bus from Yamagata Station (¥440).

ZAŌ-SAN 蔵王山
☎ 023 / pop 18,000

The Zaō Quasi-National Park region is highly popular with skiers from December to April and hikers in summer. It's no wonder: Zaō is a delightfully atmospheric region, with simply stunning scenery. The main ski resorts are around **Zaō Onsen** and **Zaō Bōdaira**. In winter, free shuttles connect the extensive networks of ropeways and lifts; one-day passes start at ¥4600 (discounted night skiing ¥2000).

Near Zaō bus terminal, the **tourist information office** (☎ 694-9328; ⏰ 9am-5.30pm) has maps and can advise on transport and accommodation options.

In summer you can make your way up to **Okama** (御釜), a cobalt-blue, volcanic crater lake atop Zaō-san, considered by many to be the area's premier sight. Given the right weather, it is indeed beautiful and hiking around it is a joy, with Buddhist statues and monuments hidden among the greenery. The most convenient access is via Katta Chūsha-jōcar park, where the **Zaō Sky Cable** (蔵王スカイケーブル; one way/return ¥700/1200; ⏰ 8.30am-5pm) takes you to within spitting distance of the Okama overlook.

There are numerous trails around the area, including a one-hour walk over to Jizōsanchō-eki, from where you can hike

or catch the **Zaō Ropeway** (蔵王ロープウェ
イ; single/return ¥700/1200; ⏰ 8.30am-5pm) down
through Juhyō-kōgen (Ice Monster Plateau)
to Zaō Onsen. The 'monsters', best viewed
from late February to early March, are really
frozen conifers covered in snow by Siberian
winds; still, they're an arresting sight.

After a long day of hiking or skiing, you
can soak among sulphur-stained rocks at
the staggeringly atmospheric **Zaō Onsen Dai-
rotemburo** (蔵王温泉大露天風呂; admission
¥450; ⏰ 6am-sunset), where each outdoor hot-
spring pool can hold up to 200 people.

There's plenty of accommodation in the
area but advance reservations are essential if
visiting during high seasons or on weekends.

At Zaō Onsen, **Pension Boku-no-Uchi** (ペン
ション ぼくのうち; ☎ 694-9542; 904 Zaō-onsen;
r per person with 2 meals from ¥6700), next to a Lawson convenience store, is a friendly, family-
run place. The comfortable **Lodge Chitoseya**
(☎ 694-9145; r per person with/without 2 meals from
¥5800/3800) is closer to the bus station.

Buses from stop 1 outside Yamagata
Station depart frequently for Zaō Onsen
(¥840, 40 minutes). To cope with the demand during winter – when there are more
than a million visitors to the region – there
is a regular bus service direct from Tokyo.
Between late April and early November,
there are two buses daily at 9.20am and
12.50pm connecting Yamagata Station, via
Zaō Onsen, with Katta Chūsha-jō (¥1630,
1½ hours); buses in the reverse direction
leave from Katta at 12.30pm and 3.30pm.

YAMADERA 山寺
☎ 023 / pop 1600

Yamadera, also known as **Risshaku-ji** (立石
寺; ⏰ 8.30am-4.30pm), is a temple complex, a
cluster of buildings and shrines perched on
wooded slopes; it's thought that Yamadera's
rock faces are the boundary between this
world and the afterlife. Founded in 860 with a
sacred flame that was brought from Enryaku-
ji near Kyoto (supposedly the same flame is
still alight today), the complex is often besieged with tourists, so visit early morning or
late afternoon for meditative bliss.

From **Hihōkan**, the temple treasury, you
pay a ¥300 entry fee to start the steep climb
up hundreds of steps through the trees to
the Oku-no-in (Inner Sanctuary), where
trails lead off on either side to small shrines
and lookout points.

There is a small **tourist information office**
(☎ 695-2816; ⏰ 9am-5pm) near the bridge before
Risshaku-ji. Staff provide English-language
pamphlets but no English is spoken.

Five minutes from the station, **Bashō
Kinenkan** (☎ 695-2221; admission ¥400; ⏰ 9am-
4.30pm Tue-Sun) is a very quiet museum exhibiting scrolls and calligraphy related to Bashō's
famous northern journey, as well as documentary videos of the places he visited.

For clean accommodation, **Pension Yamadera** (ペンション山寺; ☎ 695-2134; r per person
with 2 meals from ¥8500) is right by the station.

The JR Senzan Line links Yamadera with
Yamagata Station (*kaisoku*, ¥230, 10 minutes) and Sendai (¥820, 50 minutes). There
are also infrequent buses from Yamagata
Station to Yamadera (¥580, 40 minutes).

TAKAHATA 高畠
☎ 0238 / pop 27,000

This is a pleasant rural place to while away
an afternoon along the **Mahoroba Cycling Road**,
passing en route ancient burial mounds,
an historical park and **Atsuku Hachiman-jinja's** eye-catching three-storey pagoda. You
can negotiate the 6km path in a three-hour
round trip and afterwards reward yourself
with a dip in the **Mahoroba Onsen** (admission
¥200; ⏰ 7am-9.40pm) inside the train station;
the station itself was built to resemble a
fairy castle in honour of local children's
author Hamada Hirosuke.

A small but friendly **tourist information
desk** (☎ 57-3844; ⏰ 9am-5pm) rents bicycles
(¥500 for three hours) and provides maps of
the cycling route, plus background on local
sights, including the **Takahata Winery**.

Takahata is on the JR Ōu Main Line, south
of Yamagata (*futsū*, ¥650, 35 minutes) and
closer to Yonezawa (¥190, 12 minutes).

YONEZAWA 米沢
☎ 0238 / pop 94,000

During the 17th century the Uesugi clan
built their castle in this town, which later
developed into a major centre for silk weaving. Today it's a quiet place but worth a
stopover – if only to sample some famous
Yonezawa beef, a result of some very controlled breeding over a period of 100 years.

You can pick up maps and information
at the **tourist information office** (☎ 24-2965;
⏰ 8am-6pm) inside the station. Rental bicycles (¥525 for two hours) are available

outside and are a good alternative to the infrequent buses that ply the main street between the station and the sights.

At the south entrance of **Matsugasaki-kōen** (松ヶ崎公園), the small **Yonezawa City Museum** (admission ¥400; ☉ 9am-5pm Tue-Sun) displays Uesugi clan artefacts. **Uesugi-jinja** (上杉神社), built on the castle ruins in 1923, is inside the park grounds with a nearby treasury, **Keishō-den**, which displays armour and works of art belonging to several generations of the Uesugi family. Just south of the shrine is **Uesugi Kinenkan** (☉ 9am-5pm Thu-Tue), a Meiji-era residence with more Uesugi relics.

To get to the park, take a bus from stop 2 from outside the station bound for Shirabu Onsen to the Uesugi-jinja-mae stop (¥190, 10 minutes).

The clan mausoleum **Uesugi-ke Gobyōsho** (admission ¥200; ☉ 9am-5pm), 1km west of the park, has several generations of the Uesugi clan entombed in gloomy individual mausoleums.

Festivals & Events

The **Uesugi Matsuri** starts off with folk singing on 29 April and mock ceremonial preparation for battle in Matsugasaki-kōen on the evening of 2 May. The real action takes place on 3 May with a re-enactment of the titanic Battle of Kawanakajima (one of the Uesugi clan's more bloody and infamous skirmishes), featuring more than 2000 participants.

Sleeping & Eating

Hotel Otowaya (ホテル音羽屋; ☎ 22-0124; r per person from ¥5000) This atmospheric, castle-like building is 100 years old; it's three minutes from the station. It was the only inn in town not to be destroyed by the Japanese military or US occupying authorities at the end of WWII, and former prime ministers, famous kabuki actors and pop stars have all stayed here.

Gourmet Kozo Mankichi (☎ 24-5455; ☉ lunch & dinner) A good bet for the famous marbled Yonezawa beef.

Getting There & Away

The JR Ōu Main Line runs north from Yonezawa to Yamagata (¥820, 45 minutes) and east to Fukushima (¥740, 45 minutes). The JR Yonesaka and Uetsu Main Lines link Yonezawa with Niigata (*kaisoku*, ¥2520, four hours) via a change at Sakamachi.

NIIGATA-KEN 新潟県

Not to be outdone by the likes of Aomori-ken, Niigata-ken's prefectural government also publishes a list of 'Number Ones', including Japan's longest river, the Shinano (367km); the country's highest Gross Rice Output (¥202.8 billion) and most popular brand of rice, Niigata Koshihikari; and Japan's largest annual shipments of cut tulip flowers (320 million), rice snacks (¥129.5 billion) and kerosene heaters (¥31.5 billion).

In 2004 the prefecture suffered a devastating earthquake in the Chuetsu region: 35 people died and 80,000 people were left homeless. The scale of the quake caught the entire nation off guard (it caused the *shinkansen's* first-ever accident when a bullet train was derailed), particularly the prefectural government, who, being in a rural area, found that resources were inadequate to cope with the number of evacuees.

NIIGATA 新潟

☎ 025 / pop 520,000

Niigata, the lively capital, is an important industrial centre, major transport hub and gateway to Sado-ga-shima. Relics of the past are in short supply, but there's a calm and spacious feel; Niigata is bisected by the Shinano-gawa, which generates a great swathe of blue sky where, in other cities, there'd be skyscrapers (people-watching is a joy along the banks). This casual air has helped create a burgeoning arts scene. If you're coming from Tokyo, say, the different pace of life here will either be a shock or a blessing.

Orientation

Higashi Ōdori is the main thoroughfare leading north from the station. Across the Bandai-bashi, Furumachi is the downtown shopping district and home to the vibrant Honchō market area.

Information

EMERGENCY

There's a police box inside the station.

INTERNET ACCESS

Banana (☉ 11am-7.50pm Mon-Fri, 10am-7.50pm Sat, 11am-7pm Sun) Thirty-minute free access inside the station's Bandai exit.

CD Garden (2nd fl, Garesson Bldg; per hr ¥200)

MEDICAL SERVICES
Niigata University Hospital (☎ 223-6161; 1-757 Asahimachi-dōri)

POST & MONEY
Central post office (2-6-26 Higashi Ōdori) ATM cash service until 11pm Monday to Friday, 7pm weekends.

TOURIST INFORMATION
Niigata International Friendship Center
(☎ 225-2727/2777; 3rd fl Miyoshi Mansion, 6-1211-5 Kamiokawamae-dōri; www.pavc.ne.jp/~nigtief/ EnglishVersion/FriendshipCenter/FriendshipCenter.htm; ⏰ 10am-6pm Thu-Tue) includes CNN broadcasts, a small library, local information and willing staff.

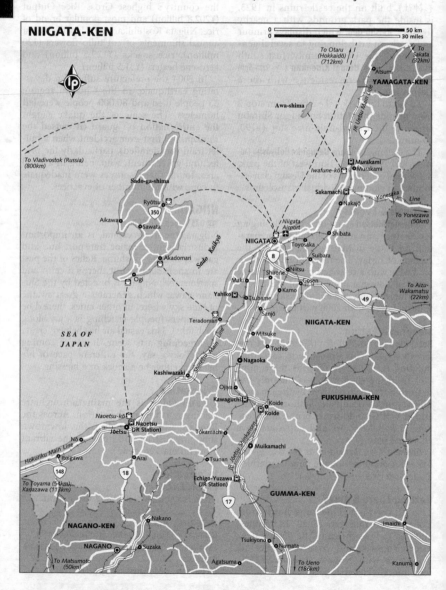

NORTHERN HONSHŪ

Tourist information centre (☎ 241-7914; ☒ 8.30am-5.30pm) To the left of Niigata Station's Bandai exit. English-speaking staff, excellent maps and brochures for both Niigata and Sado-ga-shima. Same-day accommodation bookings.

Sights

The centre is easily covered on foot, otherwise a flat rate fare of ¥180 operates on city buses.

The **Northern Culture Museum** (北方文化博物館; ☎ 222-2262; 2-562 Minamihama-dōri; admission ¥700; ☒ 8.30am-5pm Mar-Nov, 9am-4.30pm Dec-Feb) is 10km southeast of Niigata in an attractive garden complex. Situated among traditional earthen warehouses and individual tea arbours, **Sanraku-tei** is a diminutive teahouse dating from 1890; everything – even the flooring and furniture – is triangular. Buses leave roughly every hour between 10am and 4.40pm from stop 7 at the Bandai bus centre (not the train station) for the Nishi Ohata stop outside the museum (¥500, 45 minutes).

Next to the **Prefectural Government Memorial Hall** (☒ 9am-4.30pm Tue-Sun), **Hakusan-jinja** is dedicated to the local god of marriage. The grounds contain a fine lotus pond and the historic teahouse **Enkikan** (admission free, tea ¥300; ☒ 9am-5pm Tue-Sun). Take the buses from stop 8 at the station to Shiyakusho-mae (¥180, 15 minutes).

Just north of the station, the **Tsurui Museum of Art** (admission ¥500; ☒ 10am-5pm Mon-Sat) exhibits Japanese arts and local crafts.

Festivals & Events

During the **Niigata Matsuri** from 7 to 9 August, the streets are filled with afternoon parades of colourful floats and shrines. At night, thousands of folk dancers parade across the Bandai Bridge. A bumper fireworks display on the final night lights up the Shinano-gawa, as a passage of decorated boats carry the shrine of the local god of the sea.

Sleeping

Super Hotel (☎ 247-9000; 1-6-13 Akashi; r per person from ¥4800) Near the post office, this is super by name, bland by nature. Still, it's clean and comfortable, with all the usual frills: TV in rooms, en suites and so on.

Dormy Inn (☎ 247-7755; 1-6-13 Akashi; s/d from ¥5040/8295) Further down the road, this is a modern and clean business hotel with boxy, featureless rooms and its own laundry. There are a couple of cleanliness options:

pay extra for a private bathroom, or pay less and use the public bath and sauna.

Hotel Sunroute (☎ 246-6161; 1-11-25 Higashi Ōdori; s/d from ¥7700/13,200) The Sunroute is neat, white and bright, with spacious rooms and excellent amenities.

Ryokan Ueda (☎ 225-1111; 2120 Ishizuechotori-Yonnomachi; r with/without breakfast from ¥5250/4900) If you've tired of business hotels and their mass affectations, try these clean, Japanese-style lodgings just across Bandai Bridge.

Eating & Drinking

Niigata is known for the quality of its rice, seafood and sake.

Kurumiya (☎ 290-6556; 1st fl Tōkyū Inn, 1-2-4 Benten; dishes from ¥800; ☒ lunch & dinner) Right next to the train station, this place has a comprehensive selection of local sake, terribly tempting seafood set menus (including fresh sushi and zesty seafood salads) and an eclectic assortment of meat dishes, including horse and (gulp!) whale.

Kirin Bandaibashi Hall (☎ 242-2722; 2-4-28 Bandai; mains from ¥1800) This popular beer hall/restaurant, near Bandai Bridge, has a prime location overlooking Shinano-gawa. The service is attentive and the meals are quite acceptable: the Asian-fusion menu includes a very tangy, attention-grabbing Thai beef salad.

Immigrant's Cafe (☎ 242-2722; www.immigrants cafe.com; basement Niigata Central Bldg, 1-7-10 Higashi Ōdori; dishes from ¥600) Expats favour this island-themed bar/café (generally a bevy of English teachers) – more, it's suspected, for the fun atmosphere of frivolity and faux decadence than the food. Asian and Mexican mains are served and there's a happy hour from 5.30pm to 7.30pm Sunday to Thursday. Light electronic beats and a comprehensive drinks list keep everyone juiced up.

Newsflash: a team of scientists at the Niigata Prefectural Fisheries and Marine Research Institute has been developing a new form of pizza base – made from squid rather than the traditional flour. The squid are ground into paste and then mixed with water until frothy; apparently, when the stuff is cooked, it tastes a little salty and is similar to your standard pizza crust.

Unfortunately, squid-base pizza is not on the market yet so you'll have to make do with the orthodox kind at two Furumachi-based eateries: **La Barcarola** (☎ 222-9431; 7-920 Nishiborimae-dōri; pizzas from ¥1500; ☒ 10am-10pm

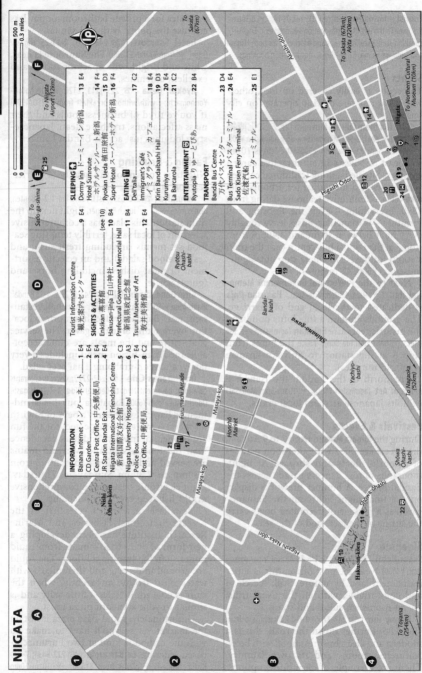

NIIGATA

INFORMATION
Banana Internet インターネット.....1 E4
CD Garden....................................2 E4
Central Post Office 中央郵便局.......3 E4
JR Station Bandai Exit.....................4 E4
Niigata International Friendship Centre
新潟国際友好会館.......................5 C3
Niigata University Hospital..............6 A3
Police Box....................................7 E4
Post Office 中郵便局.....................8 C2

Tourist Information Centre
観光案内センター.........................9 E4

SIGHTS & ACTIVITIES
Enkikan 燕喜館............................10 B4
Hakusan-jinja 白山神社..........(see 10)
Prefectural Government Memorial Hall
新潟県政記念館.........................11 B4
Tsurui Museum of Art
敦井美術館................................12 C2

SLEEPING
Dormy Inn ドーミーイン新潟.......13 E4
Hotel Sunroute.............................14 F4
Ryokan Ueda 植田旅館................15 D3
Super Hotel スーパーホテル新潟..16 F4

EATING
Dell'Italia...................................17 C2
Immigrant's Café
イミグランツ カフェ....................18 E4
Kirin Bandaibashi Hall..................19 D3
Kurumiya....................................20 E4
La Barcarola...............................21 C2

ENTERTAINMENT
Ryutopia りゅーとぴあ..................22 B4

TRANSPORT
Bandai Bus Centre
万代バスセンター.......................23 D4
Bus Terminal バスターミナル.......24 E4
Sado Kisen Ferry Terminal
佐渡汽船
フェリーターミナル....................25 E1

To Niigata
Airport (12km)

To Sakata
(67km)

To Sado-ga-shima

To Sakata (67km);
Akita (220km)

To Northern Cultural
Museum (10km)

To Nagaoka
(52km)

To Toyama
(254km)

Nishi
Ōhata-kōen

Hakusan-kōen

Furu-machi Arcade

Honchō
Market

Ryōtsu
Ōhashi-
bashi

Bandai-
bashi

Yachiyo-
bashi

Shōwa
Ōhashi-
bashi

Shimono-gawa

500 m
0.3 miles

Higashi Ōdori

Higashi Naka-dōri

Thu-Tue) and **Deli'talia** (☎ 222-3077; 2nd fl 881 Furu-machi-dōri; pizzas from ¥2000; ⏱ 11am-9pm). Both do them to perfection.

Entertainment

The city's newest attraction is **Ryutopia** (☎ 224-5611; 3-2 Ichibanbori-dōri; dance performances from ¥4000; ⏱ 9am-10pm, closed 2nd & 4th Mon of each month), a major performing arts centre with a 1900-seat concert hall, a 900-seat theatre and a 400-seat *nō* theatre. In a bold move, Ryutopia's management aims to dictate artistic terms to the Tokyo arts scene, rather than the other way around (Tokyo tends to poach Niigata's best talent). To further that, Ryutopia has initiated an innovative series of artist-in-residence programs, resulting in Japan's first professional dance company, Noism04, which has begun touring nationally and internationally.

Getting There & Away

Northeast of the city, Niigata airport has international flights to Seoul (¥48,200, 2¼ hours), Shanghai (¥79,800, three hours), Harbin (¥80,400, 2½ hours), Xian (¥112,300, 6¼ hours) and Guam (¥75,100, 3¾ hours); and domestic flights to Osaka (¥24,800, one hour), Nagoya (¥21,800, 55 minutes), Hiroshima (¥33,300, 1½ hours), Fukuoka (¥35,300, 1¾ hours) and Sapporo (¥25,300, 1¼ hours). **Kyokushin Air** (☎ 273-0312) light aeroplanes link Niigata with Ryōtsu on Sado-ga-shima (¥7350, 25 minutes). Buses run from stop 11 outside Niigata Station to the airport every half hour from 7am to 8.40pm (¥350, 25 minutes).

The JR Jōetsu Shinkansen Line runs from Niigata to Echigo-Yuzawa (¥4730, 40 minutes) and on to Tokyo (Ueno; ¥9560, two hours); change at Takisaki for the Nagano *shinkansen*. On the JR Uetsu Line, there are *tokkū* trains north from Niigata to Tsuruoka (¥3820, 1¾ hours) and Akita (¥6510, 3¾ hours).

Long-distance buses use the covered Bandai bus centre across the river from the station. Buses link Niigata with Sendai (¥4500, four hours), Yamagata (¥3500, 3¾ hours), Aizu-Wakamatsu (¥2000, 1¾ hours), Kanazawa (¥4580, five hours) and Nagano (¥3060, 3½ hours). There are also night buses to Tokyo (Ikebukuro; ¥5250, five hours) and Kyoto/Osaka (¥9450, 9½ hours). Most buses pass by Niigata Station on their way out of town.

Shin-Nihonkai (☎ 273-2171) ferries from Niigata to Otaru (Hokkaidō) are excellent value (¥5420, 18 hours, daily except Monday). Buses leave from stop 3 at Niigata Station for Rinko-nichōme. For Niigata-kō port, get off at Suehiro-bashi (¥180, 20 minutes).

From the **Sado Kisen** terminal, there are frequent ferries and hydrofoils to Ryōtsu on Sado-ga-shima (p511). Buses to the terminal (¥180, 15 minutes) leave from stop 6 at the station 45 minutes before sailing.

TO/FROM RUSSIA

Every Monday and Friday **Dalavia Far East Airways** (☎ 257-9291) flies from Niigata to Khabarovsk, Russia, for connections with the Trans-Siberian Railway. **Vladivostok Airlines** (☎ 279-5105) has flights every Thursday and Sunday to Vladivostok. For information on obtaining a Russian visa, see p744.

SADO-GA-SHIMA 佐渡島

☎ 0259 / pop 80,000

Sado-ga-shima, Japan's sixth-largest island at 855 sq km, is situated in the Sea of Japan. It's a very popular destination for its natural beauty and atmospheric hiking (the southern and northern mountain ranges are connected by a vast, fertile plain), as well as for the eccentric reminders of its rich, evocative history. In fact, Sado has a sizable robot population, employed to demonstrate the island's unique culture to tourists. In medieval times, Sado was a place of exile for intellectuals who had fallen out of favour with the government. Among those banished here were Emperor Juntoku, *nō* master Ze-Ami, and Nichiren, the founder of one of Japan's most influential Buddhist sects. When gold was discovered near Aikawa in 1601, there was a sudden influx of gold diggers, who were often vagrants press-ganged from the mainland and made to work like slaves.

Today Sado relies on its booming tourist trade, so to escape the coach parties and uncover the island's unhurried pace and natural scenery, you need to get right off the beaten track. This may well require your own transport and a minimum of two days. The best time to visit is between late April and mid-October; during winter, not only will the weather be foul, but much of the accommodation will be closed and transport will be slashed to a bare minimum.

The island is well furnished with guest-houses, youth hostels and camping, but you must book accommodation well in advance in the hectic summer months. Ask the tourist information offices for help if necessary.

At the time of writing, Sado was in the process of changing the names of some of its roads and districts. You're advised to double-check details with the latest information available from the Ryōtsu tourist information centre; they'll also mark maps with the exact location of your accommodation choices.

Ryōtsu 両津

With its grand mountain backdrop, Sado's main hub is worth a brief look-see. It's also the best place to pick up information before exploring the rest of the island. The central area is a 10-minute walk north of the ferry terminal, which is surrounded by *nō* artefacts; statues pepper the terminal and a giant mask rises above the trees.

The island's main **tourist information centre** (☎ 23-3300; ⏰ 8.30am-5pm, 8.30am-7pm Jun-Aug, closed Sat afternoon & Sun Nov-Apr) is in Ryōtsu, in the street behind the coffee and souvenir shops across from the ferry terminal. Staff speak some English and provide comprehensive maps, timetables and pamphlets for the entire island.

From bus stop 2 outside the terminal, buses (one way, including entry fee ¥800) run to **Sado nōgaku-no-sato** (☎ 23-5000; ⏰ 8.30am-5pm), a hi-tech museum of *nō* drama, with displays of masks and costumes and performances of *nō* enacted by a cast of animatronic actors.

Kunimisō (☎ 22-2316; Niibo-Shomyoji; per person ¥7000) is one of Sado's most popular *min-shuku*, due to its collection of *bunya* puppets, which the owner likes to demonstrate to guests. It's 15 minutes by bus from Ryōtsu to the Uryūya bus stop, then a long walk. Phone ahead for a pick-up.

Sado Seaside Hotel (☎ 27-7211; kkmasah@mui.bi globe.ne.jp; 80 Sumiyoshi; r per person with/without meals from ¥10,00/5500) is at Sumiyoshi Onsen, about 2km from Ryōtsu. It's cheery enough with free Internet, an *onsen* bath and an obliging free shuttle service to and from the port. Try for a room with an ocean view.

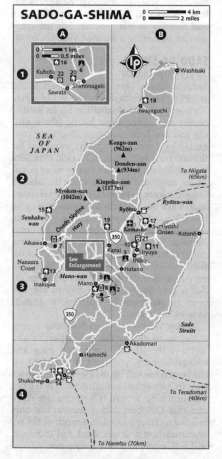

Sawata 佐和田

The town of Sawata, 15km southwest of Ryōtsu, is on the main road between Ryōtsu and Aikawa. If you get off the bus 1km east of town at Kaminagaki (¥150), you can walk for about 30 minutes into the hills to **Myōshō-ji**, a temple belonging to the Nichiren sect, with its sizable, five-storey pagoda.

Near the bus terminal in Sawata, the Silver Village resort stages **bunya puppet performances** (☎ 52-3961; Kubotahama; admission ¥350; 4 daily; ☾ Thu-Tue Apr-Nov), a traditional form of puppetry that's been a feature of Sado life for over 250 years (perhaps the island's robot fetish is a logical extension of the islanders' love affair with puppets).

From stop 1 outside the Ryōtsu ferry terminal, frequent buses run to Sawata (¥600, 45 minutes) and onto Aikawa (¥390, 20 minutes) on the Hon-sen Line.

Green Village Youth Hostel (☎ 22-2719; gvyh@e-sadonet.tv; 750-4 Niibo Uruyuya; dm from ¥3045), south of Ryōtsu, is among the island's top accommodations. There's free Internet (albeit on the slowest machine known to man), clean and spacious rooms with terrific views out to the mountains, super-relaxed hosts, sublime seafood dinners (¥1050) and bike rental (¥1000 per day). From Ryōtsu, take a bus bound for Sawata on the Minami-sen bus line and get off at the Uryūya stop (¥350, 10 minutes); walk for 10 minutes and turn left at the first bend. If you tell the driver you're going to Green Village, he'll drop you off a bit closer.

Urashima (☎ 57-3751; 978-3 Kubota; s/tw with 2 meals from ¥10,500/16,800), with its modern space-capsule design, overlooks the beach.

The **Sado Hakusan Youth Hostel** (☎ 52-4422; Yamada; dm from ¥2800) is inland in a secluded farming area; there's an *onsen* nearby that guests can use for free. Take the Hon-sen Line from Ryōtsu bound for Aikawa to Kubota (about 2km west of Sawata). From there, it's a 25-minute walk up the side street opposite the bus stop. Phone ahead for a pick-up.

Tokaen (☎ 63-2221; tokaen@on.rim.or.jp; 1636-1 Otsu; s from ¥4000) is a pleasant minshuku. The owners can help you plan all sorts of outdoor activities – hiking, fishing and so on – and they also cook up pretty good vegetarian food. Plus, there's a *shiogama-buro* (rock-salt sauna) that's certainly worth a soak. Tokaen is a bit out of the way, though. Take the Hon-sen Line to the Shinbo stop (¥400); it's about 3km to the north.

Mano 真野

This was the provincial capital and cultural centre of the island from early times until the 14th century.

Mano's **tourist information office** (☎ 55-3589; ☾ 9am-5.30pm Apr-Oct) rents bicycles (¥1100 per day) and has sketch maps of the hiking trail.

Buses between Ryōtsu and Mano on the No 2 Minami-sen Line stop in front of **Konpon-ji** (admission ¥300; ☾ 8am-5.30pm). This temple, with its thatched roof and pleasant gardens, is where Nichiren was first brought when exiled.

There are several other temples in the vicinity of Mano, many of which lie along a peaceful 7km nature trail that begins just west of Konpon-ji, near the Danpū-jōbus stop. It's a short walk from there to the **Myōsen-ji** (admission free; ☾ 8am-5pm) temple, also with a distinctive five-storey pagoda. Myōsen-ji was founded by Endo Tamemori, a samurai who became Nichiren's first disciple on Sado-ga-shima.

The trail then passes through rice fields and up old wooden steps set into the hillside to **Kokubun-ji** (国分寺), Sado-ga-shima's oldest temple (dating from 741); although sadly neglected, it's still atmospheric. Another 3km takes you past marvellous lookout points to **Mano Go-ryō**, the tomb of Emperor Juntoku. From there, it's a short walk down to **Sado Rekishi Denshōkan** (admission ¥700; ☾ 8am-5.30pm), where more tireless robots illustrate dioramas of Sado's history and festivals, as do various holograms. Next door is **Mano-gū**, a small shrine dedicated to Emperor Juntoku. It's a 15-minute walk back to the main road.

The **B&B Sado Pension** (☎ 55-3106; sadolove@e-sadonet.tv; 15 Toyota; per person with breakfast from ¥4800) is on the coast, just over a kilometre southwest of Mano on Rte 350. The rooms are comfortable and there's a new-agey café adjoining that serves wonderful vegetarian meals, like spicy beans with rice and salad. They also perform aromatherapy and the view across the bay is worthwhile, too.

Buses connect Mano with Ryōtsu (¥630, 40 minutes) and Sawata (¥260, 15 minutes) on the Minami-sen Line, and Ogi (¥830, 50 minutes) on the Ogi Line.

Ogi 小木

This drowsy port on the island's southern tip is kept in business by a ferry connection to Naoetsu. The **tourist office** (☎ 86-3233) is a few minutes' walk west of the post office (which is behind the bus terminal).

The big attraction here is a ride in a **taraibune** (tub boat; 10min ¥450; ⏰ 8am-5pm summer), a boat usually made from a barrel and rowed by women in traditional fisherfolk costumes. It looks difficult and it is – those awkward poles at the front are used to steer. You can try your hand at it in Ogi harbour.

Minshuku Sakaya (☎ 86-2535) has pared-down yet cosy rooms, and is conveniently located a few minutes' walk east of the Ogi ferry terminal. The **Ogi Sakuma-sō Youth Hostel** (☎ 86-2565; dm from ¥2888) is a 20-minute walk uphill from Ogi ferry terminal. Guests can use the nearby *onsen*.

Buses run hourly between Ogi and Sawata via Mano (¥910, 65 minutes); direct buses between Ogi and Ryōtsu (one hour 40 minutes) run only during certain festivals.

Aikawa 相川

From a tiny hamlet, Aikawa developed almost overnight into a boomtown when gold was discovered nearby in 1601; private mining continued until the end of the Edo period. The town once numbered 100,000 inhabitants, but today the population has dwindled to a few thousand and tourism is the main business. There's a small **tourist information centre** (☎ 74-3773) beside the bus terminal.

From Aikawa bus terminal, it's a 40-minute walk up a steep mountain (buses run occasionally in high season) to the bountiful **Sado Kinzan Gold Mine** (admission ¥700; ⏰ 8am-5pm Apr-Oct, 8.30am-4.30pm Nov-Mar), which produced large quantities of gold and silver until its demise in 1989. Descend into the chilly depths where you'll encounter another gang of robots who dramatise the tough existence of former miners (without complaint, too). A further 300m up the mountain is Dōyū-no-Wareto, the original opencast mine where you can still see the remains of the workings.

It takes around 30 minutes to return on foot down the mountain road to Aikawa. On the way you'll pass several temples and **Aikawa Kyōdo Hakubutsukan** (☎ 74-4313; Sakashita Machi; admission ¥300; ⏰ 8.30am-5pm Mar-Nov, 8.30am-5pm Mon-Fri, 8.30am-noon Sat Dec-Feb), a folk museum with more exhibits from the old mine.

At **Nanaura-sō** (☎ 76-2735; nanaura@jasmine.ocn.ne.jp; 1586-3 Tachibana; per person with/without 2 meals ¥7000/4700), there are several rooms with balconies overlooking the ocean and the owners

speak some English. From Aikawa, take the Nanaura-kaigan Line to the Nagatemisaki-iriguchi stop (¥330), or better still, call ahead for a pick-up. It can also be reached from Sawata, which is the southern terminus for the Nanaura-kaigan-sen Line. Note that the Hon-sen Line, which also links Sawata with Aikawa, follows a different road. Avoid it.

Aikawa bus terminal, a major transport hub for bus services on the island, has regular buses to Ryōtsu (¥780, one hour), and connections to Ogi (¥810, 1½ hours) and Sawata (¥260, 40 minutes).

Iwayaguchi 岩谷口

The scenery along the coast road further north is interesting, with its time-worn fishing villages. At Iwayaguchi, you'll find the **Sotokaifu Youth Hostel** (☎ 78-2911; info@sotokaifu.net; 131 Iwayaguchi; dm from ¥3360) in a tiny fishing hamlet – just the ticket for solitude-seekers. From late April to early August, one bus leaves Ryōtsu daily at 9.10am (¥1180, 1½ hours) and runs along the Soto-kaifu Line round the northern tip of the island to deposit you at the Iwayaguchi bus stop – in front of the hostel door. There are eight buses daily to Iwayaguchi from Aikawa on the Kaifu Line (¥1010, 70 minutes).

Senkaku-wan 尖閣湾

A 20-minute bus ride (¥280) north of Aikawa on the Kaifu Line, this bay features striking rock formations, which can be viewed on **excursions** (4 daily, 30min ¥850; ⏰ Apr-Oct) in a glass-bottom vessel.

The **Sado Belle Mer Youth Hostel** (☎ 75-2011; 369-4 Himezu; dm from ¥3200) is in the tourist area of Senkaku-wan. From Aikawa, take the Kaifu Line to the Minami-Himezu stop (¥310, 20 minutes); from there it's a five-minute walk in the direction of the shore.

Festivals & Events

One of Sado's biggest draws is the **Earth Celebration**, a three-day music, dance and arts festival usually held during the third week in August. The focal point is performances by the world-famous Kodo Drummers, who live in a small village north of Ogi, but who tour eight months a year; all members are required to adhere to strict physical, mental and spiritual training regimens. International guest performers and Japanese artists offer workshops throughout the festival. For more information contact www.kodo.or.jp. You will need to buy tickets and arrange accommodation well in advance.

Sado is also famed for its *okesa* (folk dances), *onidaiko* (demon drum dances) and *tsuburosashi* (a phallic dance with two goddesses). Other major festivals:

Aikawa Kinzan Matsuri (25–27 July) Fireworks, *okesa* and float parades.

Ogi Minato Matsuri (28–30 August) Lion dances, folk songs, tub-boat races and fireworks.

Ryotsu Tanabata Matsuri (6–8 August) Onidaiko and Sado's biggest firework display.

Sawata Shishi-ga-jō Matsuri (10–11 August) Beach volleyball and fireworks.

Getting There & Away

Kyokushin Air (☎ 23-5005) flights link Ryotsu with Niigata (one way ¥7350, return ¥11,020, 25 minutes, three to four flights daily). Buses between the airport and Ryotsu bus terminal are timed to flights (¥240, 15 minutes).

Sado Kisen passenger ferries and hydrofoils run between Niigata and Ryotsu. There are up to six regular ferries daily (one way ¥2060, two hours 20 minutes). As many as 10 jet foils daily zip across in merely an hour, but service is greatly reduced between December and February (one way ¥5960, return ¥10,730). Before embarking, you need to buy a ticket from the vending machines and to fill in a white passenger ID form.

From Naoetsu-kō, southwest of Niigata, there are ferry and hydrofoil services to Ogi, in the southwest part of Sado-ga-shima. Between April and late November, there are four or more regular ferry departures daily (2½ hours) and two hydrofoils (one hour). During the rest of the year the hydrofoil service is suspended and regular ferries run only twice daily. Fares are the same as for the Niigata–Ryotsu service. From JR Naoetsu Station, it's a 10-minute bus ride (¥160) and then a 15-minute walk to the port.

From Akadomari, on the southern edge of Sado-ga-shima, there are ferries to Teradomari, a short distance southwest of Niigata (¥1410, two hours, up to three daily, suspended mid-January to mid-February). However, Teradomari port is only convenient if you have your own transport.

Getting Around

Local buses are fine on the main routes – between Ryotsu and Aikawa, for example.

However, services to other parts of the island are often restricted to two or three a day and, in winter, services are sharply restricted.

If you plan to make extended use of local buses, there's an English-language timetable available from the ferry terminals and tourist information offices. The ¥2000 unlimited ride bus pass, also in English, is a good-value option valid for two consecutive days at weekends only (sightseeing buses excluded). Buses operate according to a 'hop-on hop-off' system: get on at the back, take a ticket and pay as you alight according to the price board above the driver.

The *teiki kankō* (sightseeing buses) have neat but hectic packaged itineraries with prices from ¥4000 to ¥8000. One useful itinerary is the Panorama Course which follows the spectacular Ōsado Skyline Hwy from Ryotsu to Aikawa – there is no local transport alternative for this route (¥3040, 2½ hours).

To explore less touristed areas, car hire is desirable. There are numerous car hire firms close to the Ryotsu terminal; rates start from ¥7000 per day to ¥9000 for 24 hours.

Otherwise, cycling is an enjoyable way to potter around off the beaten track. Bicycle rental is available in Ryotsu, Aikawa and Ogi.

ECHIGO-YUZAWA ONSEN 越後湯沢温泉
☎ 025 / pop 9000

Echigo-Yuzawa was the setting for Nobel Prize–winning writer Kawabata Yasunari's *Snow Country*, a novel about decadent *onsen* geisha. A few items in his memory are on display at the **Yukiguni-kan** (History & Folk Museum; admission ¥300; ⊙ 9am-4.30pm), 500m north of the station. Today the town is primarily a skiing and snowboarding retreat for weekending Tokyo residents. The ski season runs December to May; check www.skijapanguide .com for the latest conditions. There are opportunities for hiking in summer around **Yuzawa Kōgen**, an alpine plateau accessed via ropeway (return ¥1200) from the town.

There are two exits from the station. The east exit is the main one, with the **tourist information office** (☎ 785-5505; ⊙ 9am-5pm) to its left outside the station. To the right of the west exit, an **accommodation office** books rooms at the numerous *minshuku*, hotels and ski lodges in town. You pay them a ¥2000 deposit and they issue you with a receipt to take to your guesthouse.

Overlooking the town and its own skiing grounds, **NASPA New Ōtani Resort** (☎ 780-6111, 0120-227-021; www.naspa.co.jp/english; s/tw from ¥7300/12,000) has luxurious Western-style rooms for up to three people – good value if you share. Free shuttles run between the station and the resort and, in winter, to many major ski areas.

Asahikan (あさひ館; ☎ 787-3205; 1760 Tsuchitaru, Yuzawa-machi, Minamiuonuma-gun; r per person from ¥7000) is a friendly *minshuku* at the base of the Yuzawa Park ski area. Closer to the station, **Tatumoto** (☎ 784-2371; 317-2 Yuzawa; r per person with/without meal from ¥6000/4000) is 250m from the east. Both rates include two meals.

Echigo-Yuzawa Station is on the JR Jōetsu Shinkansen Line between Niigata (¥4730, 45 minutes) and Tokyo (Ueno) (¥6090, 1¼ hours).

Hokkaidō 北海道

HOKKAIDŌ

In a land famous for crowds, Hokkaidō remains one of the few places where roads disappear into the horizon, forests are full-sized, and mountain-range pullouts offer glimpses of grand vistas that seem more like the American West than diminutive Japan. The northernmost of the country's four main islands, Hokkaidō offers everything the outdoors has to offer: skiing, hiking, camping, motorcycling, biking, rafting, canoeing…even bird-watching. Exciting nightlife in the larger cities lets you get into as much trouble as you want, while luxurious hot springs let you ease those troubles away. While Hokkaidō comprises one-fifth of the country's land mass, only 5% of the population lives here, in part because of the Siberian cold that descends from November to March. Paradoxically, winter is still a major tourist time. People come to enjoy the skiing and snowboarding, look at the frozen northern waters of Wakkanai and Rebun, or enjoy the ice sculptures of the Yuki Matsuri.

The Ainu, Hokkaidō's indigenous culture, have shaped this island's history. Many of the names in the area, such as Sapporo and Noshappu, come from Ainu language. Though marginalised for much of the past century, the Ainu have recently won recognition as an important part of Japanese cultural heritage and are re-establishing themselves. Excellent museums can be found in Sapporo, Hakodate and Shiraoi.

Hokkaidō has four major regions: Dō-nan (southern), Dō-ō (central), Dō-hoku (northern) and Dō-tō (eastern).

HIGHLIGHTS

- Say goodbye to stress as you steam in sulphurous spas at **Noboribetsu Onsen** (p542)
- Watch cranes, deer and herons as you canoe through the wilds of **Kushiro Shitsugen National Park** (p563)
- Get a glimpse of the green flash at sunset at **Cape Sōya** (p547)
- Eat buttery, melt-in-your-mouth sea urchin in **Wakkanai** (p546)
- Look out at the mountain's majesty in **Daisetsuzan National Park** (p552)
- Have a picnic in pink beneath 10,000 blooming cherry trees in **Matsumae** (p534)
- Be mesmerised by mysterious *marimo* in **Akanko** (p562)
- Deep-sea dive among ice floes in search of Sea Angels at **Abashiri** (p557)
- Learn about the world of Hokkaidō's Ainu civilisation in **Sapporo** (p519) and **Shiraoi** (p517)
- Hike across the wildflower highlands of **Rebun-tō** (p550)

HOKKAIDŌ

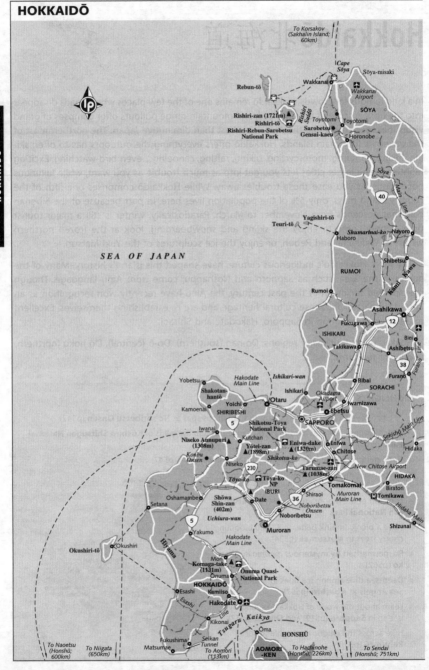

SEA OF JAPAN

To Korsakov
(Sakhalin Island;
60km)

Cape Sōya

Sōya-misaki

Wakkanai

Wakkanai
Airport

Rebun-tō

SŌYA

Rishiri-zan (1721m)
Rishiri-tō
Rishiri-Rebun-Sarobetsu
National Park

Toyotomi

Sarobetsu
Gensai-kaen

Horonobe

Rishiri Suidō

Sōya

40

Main Line

Teuri-tō

Yagishiri-tō

Shumarinai-ko Nayoro

Haboro

RUMOI

Shibetsu

Rumoi

Kami-kawa

Asahikawa

Fukagawa

12

Biei

Ashibetsu

ISHIKARI

Takikawa

Furano Line

38

Yobetsu

*Hakodate
Main Line*

Ishikari-wan

Furano

Shakotan-
hantō

Kamoenai

Yoichi

SHIRIBESHI

Otaru

Ishikari

Okadama
Airport

Iwamizawa

Bibai

SORACHI

Hidaka

Iwanai

5

*Shikotsu-Tōya
National Park*

Kutchan

SAPPORO

Ebetsu

Niseko Annupuri
(1308m)

Yōtei-zan
(1898m)

Eniwa-dake
(1320m)

Eniwa

*Konbu
Onsen*

Niseko

230

Shikotsu-ko

Chitose

Tarumae-zan
(1038m)

New Chitose Airport

Tōya-ko

Tōya-ko
NP

IBURI

HIDAKA

Oshamambe

Shōwa
Shin-zan
(402m)

Date

36

Shiraoi

Tomakomai

Biratori

Tomikawa

*Muroran
Main Line*

Setana

Uchiura-wan

*Noboribetsu
Onsen*

Noboribetsu

Hidaka Main

5

Yakumo

Muroran

Shizunai

Okushiri-tō

Okushiri

Hiyama

*Hakodate
Main Line*

Mori

Komaga-take
(1131m)

Ōnuma

Onuma Quasi-
National Park

HOKKAIDŌ

Esashi

Kamiiso

Esashi

Hakodate

Hakodate Line

Kikonai

Kaikyō

Tsugaru

Ōma

HONSHŪ

To Naoetsu
(Honshū;
600km)

To Niigata
(650km)

Fukushima

Matsumae

*Seikan
Tunnel
To Aomori
(113km)*

**AOMORI
-KEN**

To Hachinohe
(Honshū 226km)

To Sendai
(Honshū; 751km)

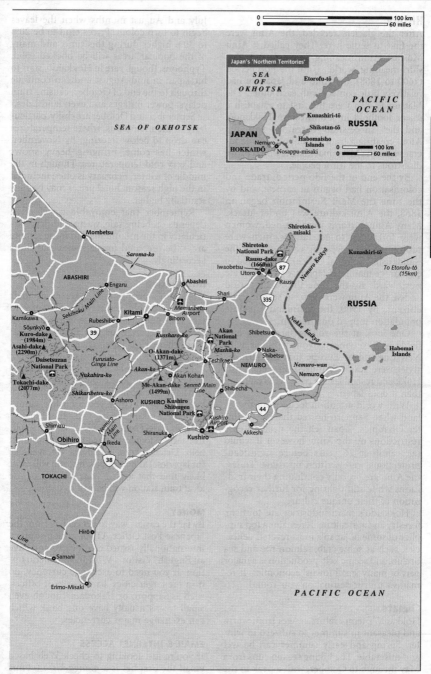

History

After the glaciers receded, the Ainu were the first to settle here. They called it Ainu Moshiri, Ainu meaning 'human', and Moshiri meaning 'world'. Until the Edo period (1600 to 1868), the Ainu and Japanese had relatively little contact with each other. The Matsumae clan were the first to establish a major foothold in southwestern Hokkaidō, and they successfully bargained with the Ainu, creating a trade monopoly. While lucrative for the Matsumae clan, it would prove disastrous to the Ainu people.

By the end of the Edo period, trade and colonisation had begun in earnest, and by the time the Meiji Restoration began in 1868, the Ainu culture was under attack. Many Ainu customs were banned, women were forbidden to get tattoos, men were prohibited from wearing earrings, and the Kaitakushi (Colonial Office) was created to encourage mainland Japanese to immigrate northward. By the time the Meiji period ended, the Ainu were de facto second-class citizens. By 1900, the mainland Japanese population topped one million.

One look at the rolling farmlands and fields will convince anyone familiar with New England or Europe that the farming styles were adopted. Indeed, in some areas Hokkaidō resembles the pastoral West more than it does Japan.

With world attention focused on the island when Sapporo hosted the 1972 Winter Olympics, Japan felt the need to ease restrictions on the Ainu; however it would take another 26 years before significant protections were written into law. Today, the Ainu are proudly continuing their traditions while still fighting for further recognition of their unique culture.

Hokkaidō's main industries are tourism, forestry and agriculture. It remains a top supplier of some of Japan's most revered delicacies, such as snow crab, salmon roe and sea urchin, and scenic kelp production is a major part of many small towns' economies. It remains a tourist destination year-round.

Climate

Hokkaidō's temperature ranges from warm and pleasant in summer to subzero in winter. Spring and early summer can be wet and miserable. The hiking season runs from May through to October, with a peak in the July and August months when the leaves begin to turn colour. Prices tend to be 20% to 30% higher during this time, and many of the popular areas will be booked solid. Typhoons, though rare in Hokkaidō, start to hit Japan in mid-August and can continue through to the end of October, causing train delays, power outages and even landslides.

September and October are chilly, particularly in the mountains, where temperatures can drop to below freezing. By November, winter has come, bringing heavy snows and very cold temperatures. Though in the middle of winter, February is often included in the high season; hotel prices may be substantially higher.

Remember that enjoyable travel often depends on being safe, warm and dry. Particularly in the mountains and more remote areas, be prepared for extremes and dress accordingly.

Information

Hokkaidō's people are as warm as their winters are cold; most will be happy to take time out of their day to help you. That said, be prepared for less English almost everywhere. (It is Japan after all: you'll find plenty of English when you return home!)

Pick up English-language brochures, maps and hotel info at many tourist offices, and if you have specific needs, a variety of bilingual booklets (¥400) cover youth hostels, camping, *onsen*, hiking, skiing and other topics.

Japan Travel Phone (☎ 0088-22-4800) is a toll-free service to questions or to get translation help. Detailed train schedules are available (in Japanese) at bookshops, but you will most likely find that asking your lodging or the local train station will be just as useful.

MONEY

By far the easiest way to get cash is from the Japanese Post Office ATMs, which support internationally-issued credit cards and have an English 'Visitor's Withdrawal' menu option. If you need to exchange currency, do it in the larger cities' banks or post offices, such as Sapporo or Hakodate, though even small towns usually have one bank which can exchange major currencies.

EMAIL & INTERNET ACCESS

If you're just looking to check Web-based email the best bet is a *manga-kissa* (comic

AINU RENAISSANCE

Although Ainu culture was once pronounced dead, the past few decades have seen people of Ainu descent assert their ethnicity both politically and culturally.

In 1899 the Hokkaidō Former Natives Protection Act formalised decades of Meiji-era discrimination against the Ainu, denying them land ownership and giving the governor of Hokkaidō sole discretion over the management of communal Ainu funds. Thus, the Ainu became dependent on the welfare of the Japanese state. Although this law had been amended over the years, many Ainu people objected to it down to its title, which used the word *kyūdo-jin* ('dirt' or 'earth' people) to describe them. It was once the standard among people of Ainu descent to hide their ethnicity out of fear of discrimination in housing, schools and employment; out of an estimated 100,000 Ainu, only 25,000 acknowledged it publicly.

But in the 1980s various Ainu groups called for the law's repeal, and in 1998 the Japanese government replaced the law with one that allocated government funds for Ainu research and the promotion of Ainu language and culture, as well as better education about Ainu traditions in public schools. The Ainu have begun to step more into the open, and travellers to Hokkaidō now have a better chance than ever of enjoying authentic Ainu festivals, cultural performances and exhibitions of traditional arts.

Most large Hokkaidō cities have some sort of Ainu museum, but the best are in the small central Hokkaidō towns of Shiraoi and Biratori.

Shiraoi's **Poroto Kotan** (ポロトコタン; ☎ 0144-82-3914; admission ¥750; 🕙 8am-5pm Apr-Oct, 8.30am-4.30pm Nov-Mar) is a lakeside village of reconstructed traditional Ainu buildings, anchored by the **Ainu Museum** (Ainu Minzoku Hakubutsukan). Museum exhibits are labelled in both Japanese and English, and in the village you may catch demonstrations of Ainu crafts and cultural performances. The museum maintains an educational website at www.ainu-museum.or.jp/english/english .html. The only drawback: access to Poroto Kotan is via a gauntlet of tourist shops.

In the village of Nibutani, in the northern part of Biratori, **Nibutani Ainu Culture Museum** (二風谷アイヌ博物館; ☎ 01457-2-2892; admission ¥400; 🕙 9am-5pm mid-Apr–mid-Nov, 9am-5pm Tue-Sun mid-Nov–mid-Apr, closed mid-Dec–mid-Jan) has arguably better collections more attractively displayed, although most exhibits are in Japanese only. Visitors could easily spend half a day watching documentary videos about Ainu folkcrafts, traditional dances, epic songs and traditional ceremonies. Other highlights include a loom for weaving traditional tree-bark cloth and some enormous canoes hewn from entire tree trunks.

Across Nibutani's main street, amid some traditional huts, the **Kayano Shigeru Ainu Memorial Museum** (萱野茂アイヌ資料館; ☎ 01457-2-3215; admission ¥400; 🕙 9am-5pm Apr-Nov, by appointment Dec-Mar) houses the private collection of Kayano Shigeru, the first person of Ainu descent to be elected to the Japanese Diet. Upstairs, the museum focuses on indigenous peoples worldwide. Signage is in Japanese only. Kayano was also the author of important books about the Ainu, including *Our Land Was a Forest: An Ainu Memoir*. Another book *Race, Resistance and the Ainu of Japan*, by Richard Siddle, is a contemporary history of the Ainu struggle for self-determination. A combined ticket for both Nibutani museums costs ¥700.

Shiraoi can be reached via several bus or train connections daily from Sapporo or Noboribetsu. Unfortunately, access to Nibutani is a trial without one's own transport – check with the museums or tourist offices for updated transit links.

Elsewhere around the island, you may catch performances of Ainu song and dance. Akan Kohan, in Akan National Park, has a theatre with daily shows, and there are occasional musical performances at Marukipune restaurant near Kawayu Onsen. Obihiro-based Kamuy-to Upopo, a group of traditional dancers, sometimes tours; officially designated as an Important Intangible Living National Treasure, the troupe is led by elder Ainu women who chant the Ainu epics from memory.

Other useful sources of information include the **Foundation for the Research and Promotion of Ainu Culture** (☎ 011-271-4171; www.frpac.or.jp) in Sapporo, the **Ainu Culture Centre** (☎ 03-3245-9831) in Tokyo and the **Ainu Association of Hokkaidō** (☎ 011-221-0462) in Sapporo.

book salon), many of which also offer Internet access. Rates are hourly and usually include free coffee, tea and other beverages. Some of the larger Internet cafés and *manga-kissa* offer showers, private rooms and discount all-night packages which rival the cheapest hotels. Those bringing a notebook computer can find wifi or LAN access in most business hotels.

National Parks

Hokkaidō boasts some of Japan's oldest and most beautiful national parks. Daisetsuzan National Park, centrally located near Asahikawa City, is a must see. This stunning expanse of mountain ranges, volcanoes, *onsen*, lakes and hiking trails is Japan's largest, covering 2309 sq km. Skiing and hiking are the main attractions, and if you want to escape off the beaten path you will need to budget a few extra days.

Akan National Park, near Kushiro, has *onsen*, volcanoes, hiking and scenery. In spring, thousands of cranes flock to Kushiro Shitsugen National Park, one of Japan's largest marshlands; deer, foxes, *shima-risu* (none other than the humble chipmunk!) and a host of birds are abundant. The northern islands of Rebun and Rishiri offer superb hiking and views of seaside cliffs, volcanic mountains and (in season) hillsides of flowers. Shiretoko National Park, in the north-

east, is as remote as it gets: two thirds of it doesn't even have roads.

Getting There & Away

Sapporo is the main hub of all Hokkaidō traffic, though Hakodate and other smaller cities also offer direct flights to many of Japan's larger cities. Be sure to check Internet deals or discount ticket agencies for substantial discounts. If you are coming from mainland Honshu, consider taking a Hokutosei Express night train to save time and the cost of a hotel stay. The *shinkansen* (bullet train) does not offer service direct to Hokkaidō; take it as far as Aomori, then take the *tokkyū* (limited express) from there. Trips from Tokyo will take about nine hours and require two train changes. A similar but much more expensive option is the Cassiopeia sleeper train (from ¥32,320).

For those without Japan Rail Passes, ferries are a low-cost alternative and cost anywhere between ¥5000 and ¥10,000. They arrive at Hakodate, Otaru, Muroran and Tomakomai; all relatively close to Sapporo. Ferries are often fancy; some include saunas and gyms. The cheap 2nd-class tickets offer sleeping on open-area mats. 2nd-class shared berths cost about ¥2000 more and may be more relaxing. Though theft is unlikely, you should take care to watch valuables.

SEIKAN TUNNEL TOUR 青函トンネルツアー

According to feng shui, the Chinese art of geomancy, Japan is shaped like a mighty dragon, with Hokkaidō as its head, Honshū as its body, and Kyūshū and Okinawa forming the tail. So practitioners of the art were not surprised at the large number of accidents and fatalities during the 17-year construction of the Seikan Tunnel (the world's longest underwater at 53.85km), which links Hokkaidō with Honshū. The tunnel, they say, cuts like a knife across the 'neck' of the dragon at Tsugaru Straits.

You can tour the tunnel at either the Yoshioka-kaitei (Hokkaidō) or Tappi-kaitei (Honshū) stations. More than 100m below sea level, you'll wind through a maze of service corridors and passageways – staff use bicycles and even cars to make their rounds. Longer tours include some of the tunnel's unique features, such as a 600m-long cable-car link to the shore of Honshū and a narrow passageway between the railway tracks that gives visitors a worm's eye view of the passing trains.

You must reserve your tunnel tour at least one day in advance from travel agencies or Japan Railways (JR) reservation centres in either Aomori (Honshū) or Hakodate (Hokkaidō). Only a few trains a day in either direction allow actual through-train/tour combinations. If you already have your train fare or a rail pass, the standard Yoshioka-kaitei or Tappi-kaitei station tour (in Japanese only) costs ¥840 extra; tours last from one to 2½ hours, depending on train schedules. For ¥2040 you can take the tour that continues from Tappi-kaitei Station, via the cable car formerly used by construction workers, up to the Seikan Tunnel Museum on dry land. Return-trip tours from Aomori (¥4320) and Hakodate (¥4040) include the museum.

FERRY TO/FROM RUSSIA

For those heading to Japan's most northern city, Wakkanai, a ferry trip to Korsakov, Russia, is an interesting option. Regular service runs from early May to mid-September; there are less frequent runs the rest of the year. Most Japanese go with a tour group, but if you plan ahead you can make the trip on your own. Visit www.embassy-avenue.jp for specific details; a Russian visa requires an invitation letter from a Sakhalin tourist agency or hotel, and you must apply at least a week in advance at a Russian consulate (the closest is in Sapporo). The **Japan Eurasia Association** (☎ 011-707-0933) can assist with arrangements for Japan residents. **Falcon Tours** (☎ 011-207-3370; www.falconjapan.co.jp in Japanese) is a good start for those interested in going with a group.

The **East Japan Sea Ferry Company** (☎ 016-223-3780, ☎ 011-518-2780 Sapporo; www.kaiferry.co.jp in Japanese) runs ships and has several office locations around Hokkaidō, including one in Sapporo. Ferries take 5½ hours and cost ¥20,000 to ¥30,000. Returns begin at ¥30,000, and if you're short on yen you can also pay in US dollars.

Getting Around

Hokkaidō is so huge that distances can be deceiving. The website www.hyperdia.com has a schedule calculator that lists up-to-date options and prices for getting around.

Sapporo has flights to all major Hokkaidō locations, but rail, car or motorcycle are preferred. Trains run frequently on the trunk lines, but reaching some locations, such as Nemuro, requires infrequent trains and pricey buses. S-kippu and R-kippu (S-tickets and R-tickets) offer substantial savings from regular fares. While there are blackout dates in the high season, the Hokkaidō Free Kippu (¥23,750) and Hokkaidō Pair Kippu (¥43,220, good when travelling with another person) offer a way to trim costs. The foreigner-only Hokkaidō Rail Pass is also available: a three-day pass costs ¥14,000.

Within cities, buses are convenient and usually cheap. Ask about a *norihōdai* (all day) pass if you're going to use them a lot; it's often a substantial discount.

If you have brought an international driver's licence (you must get it from your home country prior to arrival in Japan), renting a car or motorcycle may save time.

Local roads are often just as pretty as expressways and may yield unforeseen surprises. Rental rates vary, but expect to pay about ¥7000 per day if you walk in off the street. Going through an agency, using a combo package or getting a discount Internet deal can bring the cost down.

For fans of greener ways to get around, Hokkaidō is a good place to tour by bike. *Charida* (bicycle riders) are a common sight on major roads. Be sure to think of the weather if you're planning an extended tour, but 'rider houses' are common and cheap.

SAPPORO 札幌

☎ 011 / pop 1.85 million

Japan's fifth-largest city, Sapporo, is friendly and relaxed, with numerous parks and wide, tree-lined streets. Families play on stone sculptures, people feed pigeons and festivals happen year-round. Museums and a wonderful botanical garden make for fun-filled sightseeing. The variety of shopping arcades, restaurants and nightlife give visitors and residents plenty to do.

HISTORY

This bustling metropolis was once nothing but a quiet hunting and fishing town in the Ishikari Plain of Hokkaidō, settled by the Ainu. They were left alone until 1821, when the Tokugawa Shōgunate created an official trading post in what would eventually become Sapporo. The city was declared the capital of Hokkaidō in 1868, and its growth was carefully planned. In 1880 Japan's third major railway was constructed which linked Sapporo and the port city of Otaru.

In the 20th century Sapporo emerged as a major producer of agricultural products. Sapporo Beer, the country's first, was founded in 1876 and quickly became synonymous with the city itself. In 1972 Sapporo hosted the Winter Olympics, and it continues to attract visitors from around the world.

In addition to beer, Sapporo is also famous for its particular style of *rāmen* noodles, which rank among the best.

ORIENTATION

Sapporo, laid out in a Western-style grid pattern, is relatively easy to navigate. Blocks are labelled East, West, North and South

SAPPORO

0 ——————— 500 m
0 ——————— 0.3 miles

To Otaru (33km);
Niseko (106km)

To Sapporo City Hospital (500m)

Hokkaidō University

To Hotel Met's (300m)

To Okadama Airport (7km)

North 8

To Sapporo Beer-en (1km)

North 7

Sasshō Line

Hakodate Main Line

Some Minor Roads Not Depicted

JR Sapporo & Paseo Shopping Centre

To Asahikawa (136km)

Hakodate Main Line

Chitose Line

To Shin-Sapporo Station (10.5km); Hokkaidō Brewery (40km); New Chitose Airport (47km)

Sapporo

North 4

North 3

To Sapporo Factory (300m); Sūa (300m)

North 2

North 1

Hokudai Shokubutsuen

To South Korean Consulate

To US Consulate

To Maruyama-kōen; Hokkaidō Museum of Modern Art (300m); Sapporo Winter Sports Museum

West 14 West 13 West 12 West 11 West 10 West 9 West 8 West 7 West 6 West 5 West 4 West 3 West 2 West 1

Nishi-Juitchōme

Ōdōri-kōen

Nanboku Line

Tōhō Line

Eki-mae-dōri

Ōdōri

Ōdōri North

To Ino's Place East 1 (3.5km)

Ōdōri South

To Nishi-Juhatchōme

Tōzai Line

To Moiwa-yama Ropeway-iriguchi

M's Space Building

Tanuki-kōji Arcade

South 1

South 2

South 3

South 4

Susukino

Hōsui Susukino

South 5

South 6

To Jozankei Onsen (35km)

South 7

Love Hotel District

South 8

South 9

South 10

Nakajima-kōen

To Sapporo International Youth Hostel (1km)

Nakajima-kōen

To Hokkaidō Museum of Literature (100m); Sapporo International Youth Hostel (500m); Hokkaidō Jingu (2km); Sapporo Salmon Museum (4km); Autohouse (30km); Makomanai

To Russian Consulate (500m); Chinese Consulates (1km); Moiwa-yama Ropeway-iriguchi (1km); Sapporo Chūō Library (1.5km); Shojin Restaurant Yō (1.5km)

Toyohira-gawa

HOKKAIDŌ

INFORMATION
Australian Consulate
オーストラリア領事館 1 C3
Bon de Bon .... (see 16)
Cafe Remix 2 C3
Comic Land Sapporo 3 C3
E-comics 4 D4
JR Medical Clinic .... (see 16)
Kinokuniya Books
紀伊国屋書店 5 D3
Maruzen Books 丸善 6 C3
New Day Books
ニューデイブックス 7 C4
NTT Aurora Bell
NTTオーロラ ベル 8 C3
Ōdōri Post Office
大通り郵便局 9 C3
Post Office/ATM 10 C3
Postal Lawson 11 C3
Sapporo Chūō Tetsudō Hospital 12 C3
Sapporo Chūō Post Office
札幌中央郵便局 13 D1
Sapporo International Information
Corner 14 C2
Sapporo International Plaza i
札幌国際プラザ 15 C3
Sapporo Tourist Information Center ... 16 C2
Tokyo-Mitsubishi Bank
東京三菱銀行 17 C3
Tower Records
タワーレコード 18 C4

SIGHTS & ACTIVITIES
Ainu Association of Hokkaidō
北海道アイヌ協会 19 B3
Archives of Hokkaidō .... (see 22)
Higashi Hongan-ji 東本願寺 20 B5
Hokkaidō University Ainu Museum
北方民族資料館 21 B2
Old Hokkaidō Government Building
旧道庁 22 C2
Sapporo City Hall
札幌市役所 23 C3
Seibu Loft 西武ロフト 24 C2
Tokei-dai (Clock Tower) 時計台 25 D3
TV Tower テレビ塔 26 D3

Virgin Megastore CD & Video
バージンメガストアー 27 C4
SLEEPING
Art Hotels Sapporo
アート ホテルス札幌 28 D6
Hotel Sapporo Garden Palace
ホテル札幌ガーデンパレス 29 C3
Hotel Sunlight
ホテルサンライト 30 C3
Kapuseru Inn Sapporo 31 C4
Keiō Plaza Hotel Sapporo
京王プラザホテル札幌 32 B2
Nakamuraya Ryokan 中村屋旅館 33 B2
Sapporo Grand Hotel 34 C3
Sapporo House Youth Hostel
札幌ハウスユースホステル 35 C2
Sapporo Marks Inn
札幌マークスイン 36 C5
Sapporo Washington Hotel II 37 C2
Tōyoko Inn Sapporo Eki Kita Guchi ... 38 D1
Tōyoko Inn Sapporo Eki Minami
Guchi 39 D2
Tōyoko Inn Sapporo Hokudai-mae
東横イン札幌北大前 40 C1
Tōyoko Inn Sapporo Susukino Minami
東横イン札幌すすきの南 41 D5

EATING
Ambrosia .... (see 32)
Ebi-kani Gassen
えびかに合戦 42 C4
Ebi-kani Gassen
えびかに合戦 43 C4
Esta1 エスタ .... (see 70)
Hanamaru 44 C2
Kirin Beer-en キリンビール園 45 D6
Ni-jō Ichiba Market 二条市場 46 D4
Royal Host 47 C3
Rāmen Yokochō Alley
ラーメン横丁 48 C4
Uoisshin .... (see 59)

DRINKING
500 Bar 49 D4
Blues Alley 50 C4
Hall Stairs Espresso Bar 51 C4

ENTERTAINMENT
King Xmhu キングシェムー 52 C5
Night Stage SHU 53 C5
Precious Hall
プレシャスホール 54 B4

SHOPPING
Aurora Town Shopping Centre
オーロラタウン .... (see 8)
Bic Camera ビックカメラ .... (see 70)
Daimaru 大丸 55 C2
Marui Imai Department Store
丸井今井デパート 56 D3
Mitsukoshi Department Store
三越デパート 57 C3
Parco Department Store
パルコデパート 58 C3
Robinson's Department Store
ロビンソン札幌 59 C4
Seibu Department Store
西武デパート 60 C2
Tōkyū Department Store
東急デパート 61 D2

TRANSPORT
Chūō Bus Terminal
中央バスターミナル 62 D3
Chūō-kuyakusho-mae
中央区役所前 63 B4
Higashi Honganji-mae
東本願寺前 64 C5
Nakajima-kōen-dōri
中島公園通 65 B6
Nishi-hatchōme 西8丁目 66 B4
Nishi-jūgochōme 西15丁目 67 A4
Nishi-yonchōme 西4丁目 68 C4
Ōdōri Bus Center 69 C3
Sapporo Eki-mae Bus Terminal
札幌駅前バスターミナル 70 D2
Sosei Shōgakkō-mae
創成小学校前 71 C4
Susukino すすきの 72 C4
Yamahana-kujō 山鼻9条 73 B6

OTHER
Kaderu 2.7 Community Centre
かでる2.7 .... (see 19)

---

accordingly around a central point near the TV Tower in the city centre. For example, the famous landmark Tokei-dai (Clock Tower) is in the block of North 1, West 2 (*Kita Ichi-jo, Nishi Ni-chōme*). Streets are also named according to compass points (eg Kita 3).

Ōdōri-kōen, a narrow grass-covered section ending at the TV Tower, is a major city feature. Dividing the city north to south, it is the site of the Yuki Matsuri in February as well as other events throughout the year. Hokkaidō University is north of the JR Sapporo Station; the arboretum is a five-minute walk to the southwest. South of Ōdōri is the downtown shopping district with stores and arcades. If you are looking for a bargain, try the Tanuki-kōji or the underground plazas of Aurora Town and Pole Town. Even further south you will find Susukino, the club and entertainment district, located mainly between the South 2 and South 6 blocks. Walking from Sapporo station to Ōdōri-kōen takes about 10 minutes.

INFORMATION
Bookshops
Bookstores in Sapporo have modest English sections.

Kinokuniya (☎ 231-2131; 1-14-2 Ōdōri-nishi, Chūō-ku) Foreign books are on the 2nd floor.

Maruzen (☎ 241-7250; S1W3-8 Chūō-ku) Close to Ōdōri-kōen.

New Day (☎ 223-6819; 3F Sanyu Bldg, S2W5 Chūō-ku) A used bookshop near Tanuki-kōji. Come here for bargains.

Sapporo Chūō Library (札幌中央図書館; ☎ 512-7320; S22W13 Chūō-ku; ☺ noon-7pm Tue, 9.15am-7pm Wed-Fri, 9.15am-5.15pm Sat & Sun) Has several thousand English language titles as well as newspapers and magazines. Take the Chūō-Toshokan-mae tram stop.

Tower Records (☎ 241-3851; 7-8F Pibō Bldg, S2W4 Chūō-ku) A good resource for English CDs, DVDs, and other digital entertainment.

Internet Access
Sapporo has many Internet cafés.

Bon de Bon (☎ 213-5726; N5W2 Chūō-ku) In Paseo shopping plaza inside JR Station; deli and café. Food order required.

Cafe Remix (☎ 512-3338; B1-2 Asahikankō Bldg, S6W6 Chūō-ku; ☽ 24hr) In addition to shower and laundry facilities, this place has alcohol and even a foot *onsen*.

Comic Land Sapporo (☎ 200-3003; 2F Hinode Bldg, S1W4 Chūō-ku; per 9hr/¥2000; ☽ 24hr) Has showers and offers fixed fees as well as hourly rates. Good choice for overnights.

E-comics (☎ 221-9081; Sugai Bldg 5, S3W1 Chūō-ku; ☽ 24hr) Offers half-price to foreigners on the 23rd and 24th of each month (with membership card).

Postal Lawson Dōchō Akarengamae-ten (☎ 219-8830; N2W4-3 Chūō-ku; ☽ 24hr) Free wireless LAN for those with their own computer.

Medical Services

Dial ☎ 119 for a medical emergency. The last two hospitals listed below require that new, nonemergency patients arrive before noon.

JR Medical Plaza (JRメディカルプラザ; ☎ 209-5410; N5W2 Chūō-ku) Conveniently located on the 7th and 8th floors of the JR Tower in Sapporo Station. Open until 7pm.

Sapporo Chūō Tetsudō Hospital (札幌中央鉄道病院; ☎ 241-4971; N3E1 Chūō-ku) Closest to Sapporo Station but no emergency room.

Sapporo City Hospital (札幌市立病院; ☎ 726-2211; N11W13 1-1 Chūō-ku) Offers 24hr emergency care as well as the usual gamut of health services.

Money

Streetside ATMs do not accept non-Japanese issued cards, so the best place to get money is at the Postal ATMs; even the smaller post office branches have these now, and there is even an English 'Visitor Withdrawal' option to make getting yen even easier.

Post

Ōdōri Post Office (☎ 211-4280; 2-9 Ōdōri-nishi, Chūō-ku)

Sapporo Chūō Post Office (☎ 748-2313; N6E1-2-1 Higashi-ku) This branch is located just east of Sapporo JR Station. Take the north exit, turn right, walk towards the giant white bowling pin, and the building is right across the first major intersection. Like many larger post offices, it is open evenings and weekends and offers a variety of services. The ATMs stay open longer than the window.

Tourist Information

Several tourist offices offer excellent English brochures and the friendly staff can be relied on for more detailed help. Information can be found at www.global.city.sapporo.jp or email convention@plaza-sapporo.or.jp. A simple but useful resource can also be found at www.welcome.city.sapporo.jp/tourism/e/index.html.

Sapporo International Information Corner (☎ 213-5062; ☽ 9am-5pm summer, closed 2nd & 4th Wed autumn-spring) Inside the Sapporo JR Station's western concourse JR reservation centre.

Sapporo International Plaza (☎ 211-3678; 1F MN Bldg, N1W3 Chūō-ku; ☽ 9am-5.30pm) Has an extensive list of English resources, just opposite the Clock Tower (Tokei-dai).

Sapporo Tourist Information Center (☎ 209-5020; N5W3 Chūō-ku; ☽ daily 9am-8pm, in summer) Located on the 1st floor of Sapporo Stellar Place, inside Sapporo Station. Offers assistance with housing as well as other tourist-related info.

SIGHTS

Hokudai Shokubutsuen 北大植物園

Though damaged by a typhoon in 2004, the **Hokudai Shokubutsuen** (☎ 221-0066; N3W8 Chūō-ku; adult ¥400, in winter ¥110) is one of Sapporo's must-sees. This beautiful botanical garden and museum boasts over 4000 varieties of plants, all attractively set in a meandering 14-hectare plot. In addition to the outdoor sights, the Hokudai has two smaller museums: one of local animals (it claims to be the country's oldest, created in 1882); and another of Ainu culture and artefacts, such as tools and clothing. Across the street, the **Ainu Association of Hokkaidō** (☎ 221-0462; 7F Kaderu 2.7 Community Center, N2W7 Chūō-ku; www.ainu-assn.or.jp) has an office and a display room of robes, tools and historical information.

Clock Tower 時計台

A famous Sapporo landmark, the **Clock Tower** (Tokei-dai; ☎ 231-0838; N1W2 Chūō-ku; admission ¥200; ☽ 9am-5pm Tue-Sun) is about a 10-minute walk from the JR Sapporo Station or a three-minute walk from Ōdōri Station. Visitors can look at some clocks and get a brief history of the building, which was built in 1878 and (supposedly) has never missed tolling the hour for 120 years.

TV Tower テレビ塔

An Eiffel Tower–shaped affair at the east of Ōdōri-kōen, the **TV Tower** (☎ 241-1131; www.tv-tower.co.jp; Ōdōri-nishi 1-chōme, Chūō-ku; admission ¥700; ☽ 9.30am-9pm, 9am-10pm Jul-Aug) is 90m high. It has a 360-degree view of the city and souvenir shops below. The city hall's **viewing deck** (Kita 1-jo Nishi 2-chōme, Chūō-ku; ☽ 10am-4pm, closed in winter & during inclement weather) is free. It's just northwest of the TV Tower, on the 19th floor.

SAPPORO BEER

Let's face it: 'Sapporo' means beer. After visiting Germany (and being favourably impressed) Kihachirō Ōkura returned and selected Sapporo as the lucky place to start what would become Japan's first beer brewery, founded in 1876.

A museum and beer garden, **Sapporo Beer-En** (サッポロビール園; ☎ museum 731-4368, ☎ beer garden 0120-15-0550 ; N7E9 Higashi-ku; ⏱ 11.30am-10pm, tours 9am-3.40pm) is located in the original Sapporo Beer brewery, almost due east of Sapporo Station. Two tour options are possible: visitors on the short tour (30 minutes) get a carry-home goody bag with a can of beer per person and other miscellaneous items; those wanting to belly up to the trough should take the 50-minute option, which includes a 20-minute all-you-can-drink afterwards.

The adjoining beer garden has food, a variety of beverages and serves the local grilled lamb speciality, *jingus kān*, which has become a popular Sapporo dish.

To get here by subway take the Tōhō subway to the Higashi-Kuyakusho-mae stop and take Exit 4. Head south along Higashi-Nana-Chōme-dōri to N8E8 (about 10 minutes) and look to the left. The large brick chimney with the distinct Sapporo trademark star is unmistakable. The building itself is at N7E9. By bus, take the Chūō Bus Higashi 63 and get off at the Kitahachi Higashinana (N8E7) stop. The building will be right in front of you.

The **Sapporo Factory** (サッポロファクトリー; ☎ 207-5000; N2E4 Chūō-ku) does not, paradoxically, produce any beer. It's a shopping and food complex that is in the renovated Sapporo Beer factory building, which was used prior to the factory's relocation to the outskirts of town. There is a token self-guiding museum, but this is mainly a mall. *Jingus kān* is served here, as well as other delicacies, but there are better, less pricey places to eat in Sapporo. Expect to pay ¥700 or more for a small glass of beer. The cheapest meals begin at ¥1200 and go upwards from there.

Diehard fans will want to take the 40-minute train ride out to the current brewing and bottling facility, **Hokkaidō Brewery** (サッポロビール北海道工場; ☎ 123-32-5811; hokkaido@sapporobeer.jp; Toiso 542-1 Eniwa-shi). This mammoth production plant seems more like something out of a James Bond movie than a place where beer is made: technicians in white lab coats peer into test tubes; immaculate stainless steel tanks are covered with computerised gauges and dials; and video cameras monitor the bottles as they whiz by. The tour is self-guiding and English is minimal, but you'll be rewarded with a refreshing 20 minutes to guzzle at the end.

Take the JR Chitose line towards the airport and get off at the Sapporo Beer Teien Station. Head away from the tracks towards the giant white silos with the Sapporo logo; the entrance is a 10-minute walk away.

Hokkaidō University 北海道大学

Established in 1876, **Hokkaidō University** (www.museum.hokudai.ac.jp; N8W5 Chūō-ku; ⏱ 9.30am-4.30pm Jun-Oct, 10am-4pm Nov-May, closed Mon) is a scenic place to meander and has a number of unique buildings within its grounds. The bust of William S Clark is a landmark, as are the Poplar and Gingko Avenues. (Caution: the odoriferous gingko nuts sometimes cause an itchy rash; it's best not to handle them.) Elms and oaks are also common. Unfortunately, many of the tallest and oldest trees on campus were damaged in 2004 by a severe typhoon. The Furukawa Memorial Hall and the Seikatei are architecturally noteworthy. Several campus museums are open to the public.

Nijō Fish Market 二条市場

Nijō Fish Market (S2E1 Chūō-ku; ⏱ 7am-6pm, individual shops may close at various times) is one of Hokkaidō's best. Buy a bowl of rice and select your own sashimi toppings, gawk at the fresh delicacies (some more delicate than others!), or sit down at a shop. Get there early for the freshest selections and the most variety; things close up by 6pm, and individual restaurants have their own hours. Sea urchin and salmon roe are favourites; as is Hokkaidō's version of 'Mother and Child' (*Oyakodon*), a bowl of rice topped with salmon and roe.

Sapporo Winter Sports Museum
札幌ウィンタースポーツミュージアム

The **museum** (☎ 631-2000; 1274 Miyano-mori Chūō-ku; ⏱ 9am-6pm May-Oct, 9.30am-5pm Nov-Apr) includes the actual ski jump used in the 1972 Olympic Games, as well as a variety of other activities. Those wishing to ascend the jump can either walk or use the chairlift. Inside, a computerised ski jump simulator allows you to try your skills without risking a broken leg.

Moiwa-yama Ropeway
藻岩ロープウェイ

This **ropeway** (☎ 561-8177; ⏰ 10am-10pm Jul-Aug, 10am-9pm Sep–mid-Dec, 10am-7pm mid-Dec–Mar) offers panoramic views of Sapporo, especially at night, but don't plan on bringing your date here for a fancy meal: the food is cafeteria-style and far from romantic. You're better off eating somewhere in town. Though rare, the ropeway may be closed due to high winds. Be sure to ask for the discount coupon when you take the tram, there's a ¥200 discount if the conductor stamps your ticket.

Museums & Temples

Hokkaidō Jingu (北海道神宮; ☎ 611-0261) is near Maruyama-kōen, nestled in a forest so dense it's easy to forget that the city is just beyond the temple's grounds. Attention has been paid to labelling the natural surroundings – a large plaque lists a number of local birds and the largest trees have been hung with identification signs. To the right of the temple, near the restrooms, you'll find a small souvenir shop which serves free *ocha* (green tea) and sweets. Purchasing postcards or a confection is not required.

The **Hokkaidō Museum of Literature** (☎ 511-7655; Nakashima-kōen 1-4 Chūō-ku; admission ¥450; ⏰ Tue-Sun, closed 29 Dec-3 Jan) offers viewers the opportunity to see the private side of many of Japan's famous novelists, primarily those with a Hokkaidō connection. Letters, memorabilia, books and short films all help viewers understand why these writers have earned a place in the canon of Japanese literature. English signage is limited.

Half aquarium, half museum, the interesting **Sapporo Salmon Museum** (豊平さけ科学館; ☎ 582-7555; 2-1 Makomanai-kōen; www.sapporo-park.or.jp/sake; admission free; ⏰ 9.15am-4.45pm Tue-Sun, closed 29 Dec-3 Jan) is a tribute to one of the world's most delicious fish. It's located across the street from the Sapporo Winter Sports Museum. Over 20 different species of salmon can be seen in varying stages of development. A number of salamanders, turtles and frogs are on display as well. Great place to go with kids.

The **Hokkaidō Museum of Modern Art** (北海道近代美術館; ☎ 644-6881; N1W17 Chūō-ku; adult/student ¥450/220; ⏰ Tue-Sun, closed hols) has a nice collection of modern works by primarily Japanese artists. Special exhibitions feature a variety of foreign and native artists.

ACTIVITIES
Jozankei Onsen 定山渓温泉

The **Jozankei** area southwest of Sapporo proper has a number of famous *onsen* and hotels. The **Jozankei Grand Hotel** (定山渓グランドホテル; ☎ 598-2214) and **Jozankei Hot Spring** (定山渓温泉; ☎ 598-2012) are very popular. The area also has several 'foot *onsen*' or *'ashiyu'* where one can soak their tired feet. To get there, take the Jozankei-bound Donan or Jōtetsu Bus and get off at the Jozankei stop. It's approximately an hour from Sapporo Station.

Another *onsen* option is **Koganeyu Onsen** (小金湯温泉). It's also on the Jozankei bus route, and is known for its hot, sulphurous waters and *onsen*-steamed vegetables. Some places still have facilities where you can cook your own. Get off at the Koganeyu Onsen stop, about 55 minutes from Sapporo Station.

Winter Sports

Skiing, snowboarding and snowshoeing can all be done nearby. The closest place is Teine, 10 minutes' train ride away. Try **Teine Highland** (☎ 683-3721) or **Teine Olympia** (☎ 681-3191); find out more at www.sapporo-teine.com.

FESTIVALS & EVENTS

Yuki Matsuri (雪祭り; Snow Festival; early February) This is a major event. The ice sculptures, works of ephemeral art, depict historical figures, buildings, celebs and even pop icons like Hello Kitty or Harry Potter. View them in Ōdōri-kōen and other locations around the city, and enjoy food, concerts, karaoke and dancing. Finding reasonable accommodation can be extremely difficult, so book as far in advance as possible.

Beer Matsuri (ビール祭り; mid-July) The summer beer festival is held in Ōdōri Kōen. Sapporo, Asahi and microbrewers set up outdoor beer gardens, offering a variety of beers and other beverages as well as food and snacks.

Bon-Ōdōri (盆踊り祭り; mid-August) Families welcome back the spirits of the dead at this time. The festival provides viewers with glimpses of traditional songs, dances and summer *yukata* (light, cotton kimonos). Although there are other, more splendid summer festivals in other parts of Japan, this is the largest Hokkaidō has to offer and is well worth a look if you're in town.

SLEEPING
Budget

Sapporo International Youth Hostel (札幌国際ユースホステル; ☎ 825-3120; www.youthhostel.or.jp/kokusai/in Japanese with English reservation form;

6-5-35 Toyohira-ku; dm ¥3200, r per person ¥3800) A 10-minute subway ride, but nicer and newer than many business hotels. Located in a brand new facility just behind the Gakuenmae Station, it is immaculately clean, has inexpensive dialup Internet access, a relaxing Japanese-style bath as well as Western showers, and even those fancy wash-rinse-dry computerised toilet seats. Note: unmarried male/female couples are not allowed to share a private room.

Sapporo House Youth Hostel (☎ 726-4235; www .youthhostel.or.jp/English/menu2.htm; N6W6-3-1 Kita-ku; dm ¥2970) More conveniently located than the hostel above, this hostel is only a 10-minute walk from JR Sapporo Station, but definitely a less good deal. Older and very close to the noisy train tracks, it offers a choice of Western- and Japanese-style rooms.

Kapuseru (Capsule) Inn Sapporo (☎ 251-5571; http://capsule.cside.com; S3W3-7 Chūō-ku; ¥3200) Includes a berth with all the usual amenities, plus a sauna, large bathroom, coin laundry and even a 'book corner' with reclining chairs. A stone's throw from the Susukino Station on the Nanboku line. Take Exit 1 and go to KFC (on the corner to the right). Turn right on the side street and Kapuseru Sapporo is on the left, about halfway down. A 6am to 6pm 'rest' is also an option (¥1200).

Autohouse (オートハウス; ☎ 596-3913; dm ¥900; ☼ closed in winter) Although an hour away from Sapporo Station (by bus), this rider house – an A-frame cabin nestled in the woods – is about as cheap as it gets…it even includes a cup of instant *rāmen!* Getting there is tricky: take the Jōtetsu Bus from Sapporo Station, the Jozankei-bound No 7, and get off at Toyotaki Shōgakkō-mae Station. From there it's a 1.5km walk; ask a passerby for directions.

Ino's Place (イノーズプレイス; ☎ 832-1828; www.inos-place.com; dm from ¥3400; ☐) A bit further from Sapporo Station, it has no curfew, private rooms and friendly, English-speaking staff. Western-style facilities and Internet access (per minute ¥10) make it easy to feel at home. Take the Tōzai line to the Shiroishi stop (four past Ōdōri) and from there it's about a seven-minute walk. Free coffee and tea; breakfast is available for an additional charge.

If you're just looking for a place to crash in an emergency, many of the cyber-cafés (see p521) are open 24 hours and are often cheaper than even the cheapest of hotels. Love hotels in Susukino are a colourful (often zany!) option. Check in after 11pm for the cheapest deals.

Midrange

Tōyoko Inn Sapporo Eki Kita Guchi (☎ 728-1045; www.toyoko-inn.com/eng; N6W1-4-3 Kita-ku; s/d/tw ¥4800/6800/6800 in winter, ¥6800/8800/8800 in summer; ☒ ☒ ☐) A simple but healthy Japanese-style breakfast is served along with coffee and tea, and the lobbies have free telephones and wifi. Each room is equipped with a LAN socket as well as the usual TV, fridge and hot pot. The closest is only a two-minute walk from the North Exit of JR Sapporo Station. Rates run from ¥4800 to ¥6800 for a single depending on the time of year and season. Their English website is easy to use.

Hotel Met's (ホテルメッツ; ☎ 726-5511; www.hotelmets.co.jp/english/; N17W5-20 Kita-ku; s/tw ¥6800/10,000; ☐) One of the only places to offer reasonably priced rooms with kitchenettes and washing machines in each room. Although the website's English is hard to understand in places, reserving over the Internet saves an additional ¥1000. Take the Nanboku line north to Kita 18-Jo Station; the hotel is a minute's walk westward, across from the Hotel Sapporo-Kaikan. Offers free breakfast.

Sapporo Washington Hotel II (☎ 222-3311; www.wh-rsv.com/english/sapporo_2/; N5W6 Chūō-ku; s/d/tw ¥9770/17,850/18,950 Jun-Sep, ¥8510/13,440/14,490 May & Oct, ¥7460/12390/13440 Nov-Apr; ☒) Across from JR Sapporo Station, this business hotel offers the usual in-room amenities but no LAN. There's breakfast available for an additional ¥1000.

Nakamuraya Ryokan (☎ 241-2111; N3W7-1 Chūō-ku; r per person high season ¥7000-8000, low season ¥6000-7000) Attractive tatami rooms and delicious meals. Located directly across from the botanical garden, this is a nice place to enjoy the flavours of Hokkaidō, and large baths offer a relaxing way to soothe away the day's travel stress.

Sapporo Marks Inn (☎ 512-5001; S8W3 Chūō-ku; s/d from ¥4410/6000) Another business hotel that offers a simple breakfast and the usual 'cosy' rooms. A Marks Inn discount card allows the holder to get an additional 15% off; it costs ¥1000 and can be bought when you check in.

Hotel Sunlight Sapporo (☎ 562-3111; www.sunlight-sapporo.com; S8W3-1-4 Chūō-ku; r per person ¥5000; P) Offers a late-night (after 11pm) check-in of ¥3000, but only if there are rooms still available. Parking is ¥800 for small cars, ¥1600 for large vehicles.

Alternate Tōyoko options if the one near the station is full include:

Tōyoko Inn Hokudai-Mae (☎ 717-1045; N8W4 Chūō-ku; P ☒ ☒ ☐)

Tōyoko Inn Sapporo-eki Minami Guchi (☎ 222-1045; N3W1 Chūō-ku; P ☒ ☒ ☐)

Top End

Sapporo Grand Hotel (☎ 261-3311; www.grand1934 .com; N1W4 Chūō-ku; s/d/ste ¥18,480/27,720/69,300; ☒ ☒ ☐) Top-of-the-line hotel that won't disappoint those looking for a place to relax in style. Only a three-minute taxi ride from Sapporo Station. The lobby is gorgeous, the staff are friendly and English is spoken. Rooms are spacious. Some singles even have cushy sofas in addition to reading chairs.

Hotel Sapporo Garden Palace (☎ 261-5311; www .hotelgp-sapporo.com in Japanese; N1W6 Chūō-ku; s/d/ste low season ¥7738/17,094/28,182, high season ¥9817/20,790/34,650; P ☒ ☐) A beautiful hotel, convenient for anyone wanting to sightsee downtown or visit the Yuki Matsuri in February, and relatively affordable. The magnificent lobby and attentive staff make checking in a pleasure. Rooms are well appointed; both Japanese and Western styles are available.

Art Hotels Sapporo (☎ 511-0101; www.arthotels .co.jp/sapporo.htm in Japanese; S9W2-2-10 Chūō-ku; s/tw/ste low season ¥10,972/17,325/27,050, high season ¥15,015/23,100/27,050; ☒) If you can get someone to navigate through the Japanese website, try to do your reservation online: you'll get a buffet-style breakfast with both Japanese and Western options. The *onsen* here seems more like something out of a Roman gala, and a number of in-house restaurant options make it easy to find something you like. The less expensive rooms seem a bit small for the price; if spaciousness is important, go for the larger suites where you'll have some leg room.

Keio Plaza (☎ 271-0111; www.keioplaza-sapporo .co.jp/english/index2.html; N5W7 Chūō-ku; s/d ¥8000/14,000; P ☒ ☒) Deluxe, stylish option with a full-sized swimming pool, sauna and athletic training room. Some of the nicer rooms have a 'bath with a view' of the city. Note when you ask for a nonsmoking room: while it does have a limited number reserved for real nonsmokers, it also feels that an air-cleaner is almost the same thing.

EATING

Rāmen Yokochō (☺ 11am-3am) This famous alleyway is crammed with 16 *rāmen* noodle shops in Susukino centre. Anyone with a yen for *rāmen* shouldn't miss it, but it can be difficult to find. Take the Nanboku line to Susukino and walk south to the first crossroad. Turn left (east); Rāmen Yokochō is halfway down on the right. Note: there is now a Shin (New) Rāmen Yokochō in the same general vicinity. Either will be fine for a tasty meal, and if you can't find it just ask – it's one place people *will* know. Hours and holidays vary for different shops.

Esta (☺ 7am-9pm) A giant food court under JR Sapporo Station; one major path to the subway leads right through it. The variety, from *yakitori* (chargrilled skewers) and fish cakes to sandwiches and salads, is awe-inspiring, mouthwatering, even overwhelming. You'll know you're close when you start hearing the singsong calls of *Ikagadeshouka?* (Would you like some?) and *Irrashai!* (Welcome!). *Satsuma-age* (a sausage made with cod, often mixed with roasted vegetables) is delicious, a unique, tasty treat that's not usually found outside Kyūshū. Many of the shops offer free tastes of the daily specials; some travellers fill up on freebies in place of paying for a meal. Adjoining the food court are a supermarket, liquor store and a variety of restaurants.

Shojin Restaurant Yō (精進料理葉; ☎ 562-7020; S17W7-2-12 Chūō-ku; dishes ¥1000-3000; ☺ 11.30am-8pm Thu-Mon) Macrobiotic and vegan fare that's attractively presented and very tasty. All of the ingredients are organic and as local as possible, and the shop itself is beautifully done with brown paper lanterns, a sushi-style bar and Zen-style flower arrangements. To get there, take the Nanboku line and get off at Horohirabashi. Go left out of the station and veer right at the first traffic signal. The road curves, passing a park (on the right). Go straight through the next signal and turn left when you hit the next one (at the tram line). The restaurant is a few doors down on the right. The small sign is easy to miss.

Nijo Fish Market (S2E1 Chūō-ku; ☺ 7am-6pm) One of the best places for inexpensive sushi and sashimi, some so fresh it's still twitching. For more information see p523.

Sapporo Beer-En (☎ 731-4368; N7E9 Higashi-ku; mains from ¥1500) See Sapporo Beer (p523) for more information. Many come to try Hokkaidō speciality *jingus kān* (grilled lamb in sauce).

Kirin Beer-En (キリンビール園; ☎ 533-3000; S10W1-1-60 Chūo-ku; meals ¥2000-5500) The menu includes *jingus kān*, sushi, and (of course) beer. Set menus start at ¥1400 and go up to about ¥5000. Order the beer tower if you're in the mood to celebrate: 4L should be plenty to start off with.

Hanamaru (☎ 208-5560; 1F Yukijirushi Bldg, N3W3-1 Chūo-ku; dishes ¥600-1000) Offers inexpensive bowls of noodles and accompanying foods such as *korokke* (deep-fried potato cakes) and tempura vegetables. In Sapporo Station take the JR Minami Guchi exit and walk due south. Hanamaru is easy to miss: look for the yellow-and-orange checkered sign on the left at the end of the second block.

Royal Host (☎ 232-5250; 2F MN Bldg, N1W3 Chūo-ku; dishes ¥800-1500; ☑ 9am-midnight) Steaks, burgers, fries and the like, as well as Japanese variations; great for those who want to avoid the 'golden arches' but who still feel like beef or a burger once in a while. Many franchises of this Japan-wide chain are open 24/7; this one closes at midnight.

Uoisshin (☎ 518-7177; 2BF Robison Bldg, S4W4-1 Chūo-ku; per plate ¥200-400; ☑ 10am-10pm) Uoisshin is one of several *kaiten-zushi* shops, places where you get to watch your food chug around the room on a conveyor belt before you eat it. Pay per plate; the waitress will count them at the end.

Ebi-kani Gassen (☎ 210-0411; 12F F45 Bldg, S4W5 Chūo-ku; all-you-can-eat ¥3500-5000; ☑ 4pm-midnight) Most people come here for crab, one of Hokkaidō's best-known specialities, but the restaurant serves other items as well. Try to sit by a window if you get the chance, to enjoy the view.

Ambrosia (☎ 271-3279; N5W7 Chūo-ku; lunch from ¥2000, dinner from ¥6000) Fancy and delicious, this pricey option in the Keio Plaza Hotel offers a 22nd-floor view of the city and is a nice way to celebrate something special. Not quite the fare you'd find in France, but it's attractively served and flavourful. Ask about the nightly specials and suggested wines.

Sūa (スーア; ☎ 231-5333; N3E5-5 Chūo-ku; dishes ¥600-1000; ☑ 11.30am-8pm) Quiet, clean and delicious, this Vietnamese-café-with-a-twist offers a variety of noodle dishes, plus a host

of other Vietnam-inspired delicacies. Located right across from Sapporo Factory, it's a good alternative if you're in the mood for something light and refreshing and have had enough of *jingus kān.*

DRINKING

If you're just looking for a beer or two, an *izakaya* (Japanese pub) in the M's Space building near Tanuki-kōji might fit the bill. It's got a variety of small cafés and bars and is a good place to begin a night on the town. The places below are all within easy stumbling distance of the Susukino subway station, but there are literally hundreds of bars and clubs throughout the city.

500 Bar (Pronounced 'gohyakubaa'; ☎ 562-2556; 1F Hoshi Bldg, S4W2 Chūo-ku) Usually packed even on weekdays with a mix of foreign and local clientele. Every drink on the menu is ¥500, hence the name, and you can order food as well. This is one of the franchise's several locations in Sapporo, right across the street from the Susukino subway station's Nanboku line.

Blues Alley (☎ 231-6166; BF Miyako Bldg, S3W3 Chūo-ku) A night here can be hit or miss depending on what's happening elsewhere, but it's a good place to relax and perhaps play a game or two on the full-sized pool table. Whiskey shots start at ¥700, beers at ¥600.

Hall Stairs Espresso Bar (☎ 242-2252; S3W3 Chūo-ku; ☑ 11am-3am) Espresso with an attitude. With matte-black paint and chain link fencing, this place feels more like an avant-garde theatre production than a place to sip a cup of joe. If you're a nonsmoker, skip Hall Stairs, but if you don't mind squinting through the haze this place is about as unique as they come. Service with a snarl fits right in with the lip piercings, tattoos and day-glo hair.

ENTERTAINMENT

Susukino is the place to go for clubs and dancing. Below are just a few of the many. Cover charges vary substantially from spot to spot and night to night, depending on who's playing where and when. On a Friday or Saturday, be prepared to spend at least ¥1000 to ¥2000, which often includes a drink.

King Xmhu (☎ 531-1388; S7W4-424-10 Chūo-ku) This mammoth institution is a Susukino landmark, known for its elaborate concrete face (King Xmhu, one presumes) sculpted outside the entryway. Inside, revellers dance and drink on three floors of neon and strobe.

Precious Hall (☎ 513-2221; BF Dai 9 Green Bldg, S7W7 Chūo-ku) Right next to the Green Hotel, this place gets a decent number of folks after 10pm. Live music and shows are nightly; check www.precioushall.com for the current schedule.

Night Stage SHU (☎ 511-7111; www.nightstage-shu .com; BF S6W4 Chūo-ku; charm charge cover ¥4000) An all-male dance review that's about as extravagant as they come. Not just for the gay and lesbian crowd, SHU is 100% chorus-line-style Japanese showbiz. A dinner and show set and an all-you-can-drink (three people or more only) discount are attractive options.

GETTING THERE & AWAY
Air
Sapporo is connected by direct flights to all major cities in Japan, and many carriers also offer add-ons that allow 'direct' access (you have to change at Narita to Haneda). Look for Asia-related travel agents in your home country for round-trip packages, some of which include hotel package deals.

Sapporo's main airport is New Chitose Airport (Shin-Chitose Kūkō), about 40km south of the city. There's a smaller airport at Okadama, about 10km north of the city.

Bus
Bus services also connect Sapporo with the rest of Hokkaidō. Cheaper than trains and on some routes time-competitive as well, buses are an attractive option. Sapporo Eki-mae is the main bus station, just southeast of Sapporo Station beneath Bic Camera and Esta. The Chūō bus station (southeast of Sapporo Station) and Ōdōri bus centre are also departure spots.

Buses depart from Sapporo Eki-mae bus terminal several times a day for destinations all over Hokkaidō, including Wakkanai (¥5750, six hours), Asahikawa (¥2000, two hours), Muroran (¥2000, 2¼ hours), Noboribetsu Onsen (¥1900, 2½ hours), Tōya-ko Onsen (¥2700, 2¾ hours), and Furano (¥2100, 2½ hours).

From the Chūō bus station there are a few departures a day to Obihiro (¥3670, four hours) and Abashiri (¥6210, six hours). Buses to Hakodate depart from both the Chūō bus station and Ōdōri bus centre

(¥4680, five hours). Discounted round-trip tickets are available for most routes.

Train
Trains are an easy and inexpensive way to get to or from Sapporo. Check www.hyper dia.com for English schedules and up-to-the-minute pricing.

The Hokutosei Express, a sleeper train (¥23,520, or ¥9450 with a JR Pass), is the most convenient. It takes 16 hours and runs direct between Tokyo and Sapporo Station three times a day. The other option is to take a *shinkansen* to Morioka, then an express via Aomori (¥21,670, 10 hours). If you're heading to Osaka there's a 22½ hour sleeper train that connects the two cities; it's ¥27,130 (¥10,960 with a JR Pass).

Sapporo, a central hub, has frequent trains to almost anywhere else in Hokkaidō. If you're Hakodate-bound, a *tokkyū* (limited express) will get you there in 3½ hours (¥8080). Otaru, a popular port nearby, and Asahikawa (to the north) have frequent service. A sleeper train to Wakkanai lets people save the cost of a night at a hotel: it leaves Sapporo at 11pm and arrives (via Asahikawa) at 6am the next morning (¥15,960). Several daytime trains run that route as well.

GETTING AROUND
To/From the Airports
New Chitose Airport is accessible from Sapporo by *kaisoku* (rapid) train (¥1040, 36 minutes) or bus (¥820, 70 minutes). The airport has its own train station, car-rental counters and convenient bus services to various Hokkaidō destinations, including Shikotsu-ko, Tōya-ko Onsen, Noboribetsu Onsen and Niseko.

For Okadama airport, buses leave every 20 minutes or so from in front of the ANA ticket offices, opposite Sapporo Station (¥310, 30 minutes).

Bus & Tram
Sapporo Station is the main terminus for local buses. Late April to early November, tourist buses loop through major sights and attractions 9am to 5.30pm; a one-day pass costs ¥750, single trips are ¥200 to ¥230.

There is a single tram line that heads west from Ōdōri, turns south, then loops back to Susukino. It's convenient for a trip to Moi-wayama, and the fare is a flat ¥170.

Subway

Sapporo's three subways are efficient. Fares start at ¥200, and one-day passes cost ¥800. There are also ¥1000 day passes that include the tram and buses as well. Or get a pay-in-advance 'With You' card (¥1000 gives you ¥1100 worth of transportation), which can be used on subways, buses, trams, Jōtetsu buses and Chūō buses; unlike the one-day passes, the 'With You' card does not expire at midnight.

DŌ-NAN (SOUTHERN HOKKAIDŌ) 道南

HAKODATE 函館

☎ 0138 / pop 283,000

Hakodate is the 'gateway' to Hokkaidō, a port city on the island's southern tip, known for its seafood, scenery and history. Built on a strip of land between two harbours, Hakodate Harbor to the west and Tsugaru Channel to the east, the city resembles an hourglass: pinched in the middle and wider

at each end. Hakodate was one of the first ports opened under the Kanagawa Treaty of 1854, and as such had a small foreign community. Much of that influence can still be seen in the Motomachi district, a hillside sprinkled with historic buildings and nice views of the bay.

Spread out along the water's edge, the city is best accessed by trams: most of the sights can be walked to from stops along the way. Buses, trams and trains leave the station regularly. Head west, towards Mount Hakodate and the Motomachi district, to find most historical sites; Goryō-kaku, Japan's first Western-style fort, is to the east.

SIGHTS & ACTIVITIES	
Goryō-kaku 五稜郭	1 D2
Goryō-kaku Tower 五稜郭タワー	2 D2
Hakodate City Museum Annexe 市立函館博物館五稜郭分館	3 D2
Yachigashira Onsen 谷地頭温泉	4 B3
SLEEPING	
Hotel Oakland ホテルオークランド	5 D1
EATING	
Lucky Pierrot	6 D2
Ryountei 稜雲亭	7 D2
DRINKING	
Friday Night Club フライデイナイトクラブ	8 D2

HOKKAIDŌ

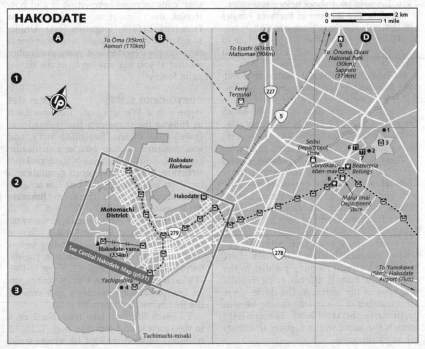

HAKODATE

0 — 2 km
0 — 1 mile

To Ōma (35km); Aomori (110km)

To Esashi (61km); Matsumae (90km)

To Onuma Quasi National Park (30km); Sapporo (319km)

Ferry Terminal

227

5

Seibu Department Store

6 • 2

1

3

Goryōkaku-kōen-mae

Beatereria Belongs

8

Hakodate Harbour

Hakodate

Motomachi District

279

Marui Imai Department Store

Hakodate-yama (334m)

See Central Hakodate Map (p531)

Yachigashira

4

278

To Yunokawa (5km); Hakodate Airport (7km)

Tachimachi-misaki

Information

The English maps and information at the **Hakodate Tourist Information Center** (☎ 23-5440; ⏰ 9am-7pm Apr-Oct, 9am-5pm Nov-Mar) inside Hakodate Station are a good starting place. The *Hakodate Guide Map* combined with street signs (many in English and Russian) should make it fairly simple to find what you're looking for.

There is also an **information desk** (☎ 27-3333; 12-18 Motomachi ⏰ 9am-5pm) in Motomachi-kōen.

Though not fancy, www.city.hakodate .hokkaido.jp has useful information as well. If museums are your thing, be sure to ask about a multiaccess pass (*kyōtsūken*) for discount entry to two, three or four museums.

Sights

MOTOMACHI DISTRICT 元町   **Map p531**
On Mount Hakodate's lower slopes, this area has many 19th-century sites and nice views of the bay – if it's not foggy.

There's a beautiful old **Russian Orthodox Church** (Greek Orthodox Church; ☎ 23-7387; 3-13 Motomachi; admission ¥200; ⏰ 10am-5pm Mon-Fri, 10am-4pm Sat, 1-4pm Sun, closed 26 Dec-Feb), restored in 1916. Remove your shoes before you enter.

Hakodate City Museum of Northern Peoples (☎ 22-4128; 21-7 Suehiromachi; admission ¥300; ⏰ 9am-7pm Apr-Oct, 9am-5pm Nov-Mar) is a good place to learn about Ainu and their culture. English signs have been added to some exhibits.

Old Public Hall of Hakodate Ward (☎ 22-1001; 11-13 Motomachi; ⏰ 9am-7pm Apr-Oct, 9am-5pm Nov-Mar) is a nice place to view the water.

English-style tea time at the **Old British Consulate** (☎ 27-8159; 33-14 Motomachi; tea ¥1000; ⏰ 9am-7pm Apr-Oct, 9am-5pm Nov-Mar) makes a relaxing afternoon that much more enjoyable.

There are a number of **Buddhist temples** here, but the **Foreigners' Cemetery** is more unusual, as it has the graves of not only well-known people of the time, but of sailors, clergy, and others as well, all of whom died far away from their homelands. Many of the graves have English, Russian, or French, and it is an interesting slice of Japan's colonial history. The walk there is a sight in itself: running parallel to the edge of the bay, it affords some beautiful views of the water. At the docks there are a number of interesting fishing vessels, particularly the **squid boats**. Lantern-light attracts the squid to the surface; few boats are as picturesque.

To get to Motomachi, take the No 5 tram from the station and get off at the Suehirō-chō stop, then walk uphill for 10 minutes. Alternatively, get off at the end of the line and walk along the waterfront first, visit the cemeteries, then stop at the buildings as you walk uphill to Suehirō-chō.

HAKODATE-YAMA 函館山   **Map p531**
This small mountain (334m) offers a great view of the city, especially at night. A **cable car** (ropeway; ☎ 23-3105; one way/return ¥640/1160; ⏰ 10am-10pm May-Oct, to 9pm Nov-Apr) whisks you to the top in a few minutes. Take tram No 2 or 5 to the Jūjigai stop (¥200) and walk uphill to the ropeway platform (seven minutes). A summit-bound bus (¥360, 30 minutes) leaves directly from the station, is cheaper and stops at several viewing places as it winds to the top. Those wanting to rough it old-style can take the hiking trail (closed from late October through to April).

A 10-minute walk from the summit is Tsutsuji-yama parking lot, a hot date spot at night, but relatively crowd-free by day. At its far end there is an overgrown path that leads to moss-covered walls and buttresses, the ruins of an old, **Hakodateyama Yōsai** (函館山要塞; forgotten fort). Unlike so many of Japan's historic sites, this one is refreshingly deserted and you can clamber around as you like among ferns the size of palm leaves.

GORYŌ-KAKU 五稜郭   **Map p529**
Japan's first Western-style fort was built in 1864 in the shape of a five-pointed star (*goryō-kaku* means 'five-sided fort'), and was designed to trap attackers in deadly crossfire. Nothing remains of the actual fort structure, but the landscaped grounds and moat are picturesque, and one can actually climb around on them. The nearby **Hakodate City Museum Annexe** (市立函館博物館五稜郭分館; ☎ 51-2548; 44-2 Goryōkakumachi; admission ¥100; ⏰ 9am-4.30pm Apr-Oct, 9am-4pm Nov-Mar) offers a taste of the fort's history, including weaponry and bloodstained uniforms (ugh!). **Goryō-kaku Tower** (五稜郭タワー; ☎ 51-4785; 43-9 Goryōkakumachi; admission ¥630; ⏰ 9am-6pm Apr-Oct, 8am-7pm Nov-Mar) provides a nice view of the fort below, but not a lot else.

To reach the fort, take tram No 2 or 5 to the Goryōkaku-kōen-mae stop (¥220, 15 minutes). From there it's a 10-minute walk.

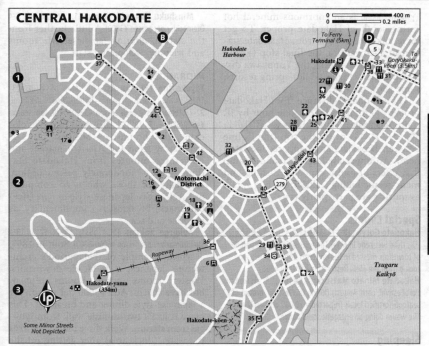

CENTRAL HAKODATE

Other Attractions

The **Asa-ichi** (morning market; Map p531; ☺ 5am-noon), located just to the right of Hakodate Station, is a great place for hungry seafood-lovers. As tightly packed as a box of ammo, freshly-caught squid glisten in ice-packed styrofoam and scarlet snow crabs wait in rows. It doesn't get any fresher than this. Most of the commerce is over by 8am,

after which the tourists come for shopping, snacks and souvenirs.

If you want to catch your own squid, the cruiser **Octopus** (Map p531; ☎ 26-4705; 24-1 Bentenmachi; ¥6000) offers two-hour expeditions. It costs extra to have them cook the unfortunate cephalopod for you.

Yachigashira Onsen (谷地頭温泉; Map p529; ☎ 22-8371; 20-7 Yachigashira; admission ¥370;

HOKKAIDŌ

☻ 6am-9.30pm) is an enormous mineral hot spring south of Hakodate proper. To get there, take tram No 2 from Hakodate station to Yachigashira, the final stop (¥220). East of the town centre, the Yunokawa district has many high-end hot-spring resorts; some allow day-use.

Though quite a distance from Hakodate proper (40 minutes by car, one hour by JR train) **Ōnuma Quasi-National Park** (大沼国定公園; ☎ 67-2170) is worth the trip (the JR line between Hakodate and Sapporo does stop here). An unusually large lake and swamp that offers beautiful canoeing, fishing and many scenic hiking trails. Bring bug spray, as tourists are particularly tasty.

Special Events

Hakodate Goryōkaku Matsuri (函館五稜郭祭り; third weekend in May) The festival features a parade of townsfolk dressed in the uniforms of the soldiers who took part in the Meiji Restoration battle of 1868.

Hakodate Minato Matsuri (函館港祭り; Hakodate Port Festival; early August) During this festival, groups of seafood-fortified locals (reportedly 10,000 of them!) move like waves doing an energetic squid dance.

Sleeping

In summer, Hakodate can be swamped with tourists en route to other parts of Hokkaidō, and accommodation can be scarce. If you have trouble booking, call the tourist information centre. Staff will know which lodgings, if any, have vacancies.

BUDGET

Hakodate Youth Guesthouse (Map p531; ☎ 26-7892; www12.ocn.ne.jp/~hakodate/; 17-6 Hōraimachi; dm Oct-Jun ¥3800, Jul-Sep ¥4500) A quick walk from Hōrai-chō tram stop, but accessible from Hakodate Station as well (after getting off the tram, walk two blocks away from the mountain and turn right; go two more blocks and you'll find it on the right, across from a big fish store and parking lot). Beds are in two- or three-person dorms. Winter hours can be irregular, so call ahead. No meals are served, but ice-cream-aholics will appreciate the free homemade ice cream.

Niceday Inn (Map p531; ☎ 22-5919; 9-11 Ōtamachi; dm ¥3000) Near the Asa-ichi morning market, this place offers bunk-style rooms and has friendly, English-speaking staff. Received enthusiastic reviews from readers.

Minshuku Kumachi (Map p531; ☎ 22-3437; 8-4 Ōtemachi; r per person ¥3800) A little further from the station, offering Japanese-style rooms and friendly, welcoming staff.

MIDRANGE

Tōyoko Inn Eki-mae Asaichi (Map p531; ☎ 23-1045; www.toyoko-inn.com/e_hotel/00063/index.html; 22-7 Ōtemachi; s/d high season ¥5800/7800, low season ¥4800/6800; P ✕ ✕ ☐) Another Tōyoko clone, this brand-new business hotel is steps away from the Asa-ichi market and only three minutes from Hakodate Station. A great, moderately priced option, especially for those who need computer or LAN access. Japanese-style *onigiri* (rice-ball snack) breakfast is complimentary, as is coffee and tea.

Auberge Kokian (Map p531; ☎ 26-5753; 13-2 Suehiromachi; r per person ¥6000-8000) Built in 1897, a typical example of that period's architecture. Japanese-style façade downstairs, Western rooms upstairs. Rooms are cosy, but have charm. Add ¥5000 per person for a Japanese-style dinner and breakfast. This place is just a two-minute walk from Jyujigai tram station. Walk three blocks towards the water (dock area) after getting off the tram; the inn is behind one of old warehouses. If it still eludes you, just ask.

TOP END

Hakodate Kokusai Hotel (Map p531; ☎ 23-5151; www.hakodate-kokusai.gp; 5-10 Ōtemachi; s/tw/d ¥11,500/23,000/30,000; P ✕ ✕ ☐) Where the Imperial household comes when they stay in Hakodate. If you're serious about staying here, find a Japanese friend to make an online reservation for you: it cuts the price of a single to only ¥6000. In-room LAN and lobby wifi make it easy for cyber-junkies to keep in touch.

Hakodate Harborview Hotel (Map p531; ☎ 22-0111; www.hvh.jp in Japanese; 14-10 Wakamachi; s/d/tr ¥10,350/15,000/24,100; P ✕ ✕ ☐) Another Hakodate option. This hotel offers a number of cheap website deals (Japanese only; prices vary), and the 10th floor is reserved entirely for nonsmokers. Several of the restaurants are Western-style, as are the bars.

Hotel Oakland (ホテルオークランド; Map p529; ☎ 43-1121; www.clever.co.jp/oakland/; 4-34-12 Shōwa; s/d ¥8400/16,800; P ✕) A snazzy place near Goryō-kaku JR Station. One of the few high-end hotels to have its own bowling alley (☎ 41-4111).

Eating & Drinking

Asa-ichi (morning market; Map p531; ☽ 5am–noon) The morning market is the place for fresh fish. Seafood *donburi* (a bowl of rice with toppings) is a local favourite. If a restaurant's more your style, see if one will whip up a Hakodate version of *oyakodon*: meaning 'mother and child *donburi*', it's usually made with chicken and egg in the rest of Japan; in Hokkaidō it's made with salmon and its roe.

Kamome Rāmen (Map p531; ☎ 22-1727; 8-2 Wakamatsumachi; rāmen ¥550-1100; ☽ 6am-3pm Apr-Oct, 6.30am-3pm Nov-Mar) Lets you top your noodles how you like it. Choose from roast pork, crab, shrimp, squid or sea urchin.

Don (Map p531; ☎ 22-7736; 17-9 Wakamatsumachi; dishes ¥450-690) A more conventional place to get *donburi* with the usual toppings: chicken and egg (*oyakodon*), tempura etc.

Jolly Jellyfish (Map p531; ☎ 23-1932; 9-6 Hōraimachi; entrees ¥580-1800; ☽ 11am-12.30am) A bar and restaurant combo at the foot of Hakodate-yama, it's popular with locals and foreigners alike. It serves a variety of food, pizza and Thai dishes. Open late enough to stop in after hitting the ropeway for a night view.

Hakodate Beer (Map p531; ☎ 23-8000; 12-12 Toyokawamachi; dishes ¥500-2500; ☽ 11am-10pm) Next to the Hakodate Kokusai Hotel, this expansive place has live music and sometimes boisterous crowds. A variety of microbrews complement a Western-style menu of pizza and items from the grill. A sample flight of four (small) glasses of different microbrews is available for ¥1200.

Nishi-Hatoba – a waterfront district with a variety of eateries in converted warehouses and English-style buildings – is a new, fairly trendy place to dine.

Ryōuntei (Map p529; 稜雲亭; ☎ 54-3221; 43-9 Goryōkakumachi; set menus ¥800-2000; ☽ 11am-10pm) Adjacent to Goryō-kaku Tower, this place has fresh seafood and a choice of counter or tatami seating. A picture menu makes ordering a straightforward affair.

Lucky Pierrot (Map p531; ☎ 55-4424; 30-14 Goryō-kakumachi; meals ¥350-800; ☽ 10am-12.30am Sun-Fri, 10am-1.30am Sat) This Hakodate-only chain has several locations. Frequented by young ladies and those craving a junk-food fix, it has a variety of burgers, fries and shakes, as well as curry and spaghetti options. The Chinese Chicken Burger is popular: teriyaki-sauce-dipped chunks of chicken served with lettuce and a bun.

Cafe Hishii (Map p531; ☎ 27-3300; www4.ocn.ne.jp/~hishii/; 9-4 Hōraimachi) Antique store, coffee shop and dessert café by day, bar by night. In an old ivy-covered *kura* (storage room) with lots of atmosphere.

Entertainment

Hakodate isn't known for its nightlife so you should be sure to ask at the tourist information booth what they suggest.

Gagyu Lounge (Map p531; ☎ 23-5151; 5-10 Ōtemachi) In the Hakodate Kokusai Hotel. Offers nice views of the harbour from its 9th-floor location, and has a sophisticated atmosphere.

Friday Night Club (Map p529; フライデイナイトクラブ; ☎ 53-5344; www.ks-pc.com/fnc/index2.html; 3F 32-35 Honchō) Local live music near the Chūō Byōin.

Getting There & Away

Nippon Airways (ANA) and Japan Airlines (JAL) connect Hakodate Airport with Nagoya, Kansai, Sendai, Niigata, Hiroshima, Fukuoka and (of course) Tokyo. All Nippon Kōkū has flights from Hakodate to Sapporo's Okadama airport (low season from ¥9000, 45 minutes).

Trains link Hakodate and Aomori via the Seikan Tunnel (*tokkyū*, ¥5340, two hours). Cheaper *kaisoku* trains make the trip in about 2½ hours for ¥3460. Some of these trains also give you the option of taking the Seikan Tunnel Tour (p518).

Hokutosei Express sleeper trains serve Tokyo's Ueno Station (¥21,000, 12 hours); there's also a sleeper service to Osaka (¥23,100, 17 hours). Either trip costs ¥9450 with a JR Pass. A combination of *tokkyū* and *shinkansen* (from Morioka) takes about seven hours to Tokyo (¥17,640).

JR's Hakodate main line runs north to Sapporo (*tokkyū* ¥8080, 3½ hours) via New Chitose Airport; S-kippu costs ¥14,160.

Buses depart from in front of Hakodate Station for Sapporo's Chūō bus station and Ōdōri bus centre (¥4680, five hours, five times daily). There are also two night buses leaving around midnight for the same locations, same price. Buses for Esashi leave six times a day (¥1830, 2¼ hours).

Ferries depart year-round for Aomori (¥1850, 3¾ hours) and Ōma on the peninsula, Shimokita-hantō (from ¥1170, 1¾ hours, two to four daily).

Getting Around

Buses to Hakodate Airport depart frequently from near Hakodate Station (¥300, 20 minutes).

A taxi from Hakodate Station to the ferry terminal costs around ¥1500. City bus No 16 runs much more frequently between the ferry terminal and the Goryō-kaku-kōen-mae tram stop, from where you can catch a tram to Hakodate Station.

Single-trip fares on trams are ¥200; buses are ¥250. One-day (¥1000) and two-day (¥1700) passes offer unlimited rides on both trams and buses, and are available at the tourist information centres or from the drivers themselves. A pass is also good for the bus to the peak of Hakodate-yama.

MATSUMAE 松前

☎ 01394

Matsumae was once the stronghold of the Matsumae clan and the centre of Japanese political power in Hokkaidō until the 19th century. Among other things, Matsumae is famous for its 10,000 *sakura* (cherry trees), which bloom towards the end of April or early May. Over 250 species can be seen, most of them in and around Matsumae-jō.

Hokkaidō's only castle, **Matsumae-jō** (松前城; ☎ 2-2216; admission ¥270; ☯ mid-Apr–Dec), and the last one to be built in Japan, was completed in 1854. The restored castle houses typical feudal relics and a small collection of Ainu items. There is a small **tourist information office** (☎ 2-3868; ☯ Apr-Oct) near the castle. Uphill is a 17th-century temple district and the burial ground of the Matsumae clan. Further along is **Matsumaehan Yashiki** (松村藩屋敷; admission ¥350; ☯ closed Nov–mid-Apr), an interesting replica of an Edo-period village built using authentic materials and construction techniques.

To reach Matsumae from Hakodate, take the JR Esashi line to Kikonai (*kaisoku* ¥810, 45 minutes), which is also on the JR Tsugaru Kaikyō line for connections with Honshū. From Kikonai Station there are direct buses to Matsumae; get off at the Matsumae-jō stop (¥1330, 90 minutes). Buses then continue to the Matsumae Station across town,

from where there are buses to Esashi between April and November (¥2720, two hours, four daily).

ESASHI 江差

☎ 01395

If Matsumae was Hokkaidō's Edo-period political centre, Esashi was the economic centre. It's still an important fishing town (herring – until the stocks were depleted in the early 20th century – and other seafood now). A number of *nishingoten* (herring barons' homes) once dominated the shoreline, and several are still quite well preserved.

Yokoyama House (横山家; ☎ 2-0018; admission ¥300) and **Nakamura House** (旧中村家住宅; ☎ 2-1617; admission ¥300) are good places to start, although there are numerous other houses to view and a trip to Esashi could easily fill the better part of an afternoon. Both are open year-round, but close on Monday during the winter. Call ahead for an appointment at Yokoyama House from November to April.

Listen to performances of Esashi Oiwake, a nationally known music style, at **Esashi Oiwake Museum** (江差追分会館; ☎ 2-0920; admission ¥500; closed Mon in winter). Shows are held at 11am, 1pm and 2.30pm.

Esashi holds an annual festival, the **Ubagami Matsuri** (姥神祭り; 9–11 August), when streets fill with more than a dozen floats in honour of Ubagami Daijingu, the oldest shrine in Hokkaidō, which was built to invoke a successful herring catch over 350 years ago. Some of the floats are antiques.

Esashi is also the most convenient gateway to Okushiri-tō, a sleepy island with small fishing villages, few foreign visitors, gorgeous coastal scenery and some tourist attractions.

Getting There & Away

There are infrequent local trains between Hakodate and Esashi (¥1790, 2½ hours). From Esashi Station, it's a 20-minute walk downhill to the tourist sites. Direct buses from Hakodate (¥1830, 2¼ hours) stop across the street from the terminal. April to November buses run between Esashi and Matsumae directly (¥2720, two hours, four daily). From Esashi ferry terminal, near the tourist sites, ferries depart twice daily for Okushiri-tō (¥2100, 2¼ hours) or once daily between January and March. From late April to October ferries also run between Okushiri-tō and Setana, further north along the western coast.

DŌ-Ō (CENTRAL HOKKAIDŌ) 道央

OTARU 小樽

☎ **0134 / pop 145,000**

Escape from Sapporo to Otaru for a weekend, a day or even an afternoon. It has a rich, interesting history as it played an important part in the herring industry, was a terminal station for Hokkaidō's first railroad and was also a literary hotspot. It remains attractive and picturesque, particularly its canal and warehouse district near the waterfront.

Information

The **tourist information office** (☎ 29-1333; 9am-6pm Apr-Sep, 9am-5pm Oct-Mar) is inside JR Otaru Station. The *Otaru Tourist Guide*, which details most of Otaru's sights, transport and hotels, is particularly useful. There is an additional information office at Unga Plaza (☎ 33-1661) near the Otaru Museum and at Asakusa-bashi (☎ 23-7740) in the canal area.

Sights & Activities

Take a romantic stroll along Otaru Canal beneath the old gas lamps or have a picnic on a sunny afternoon. Numerous old warehouses are still standing, many of them

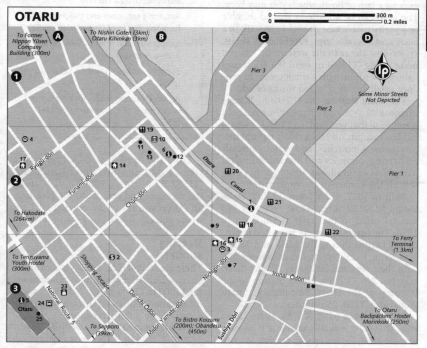

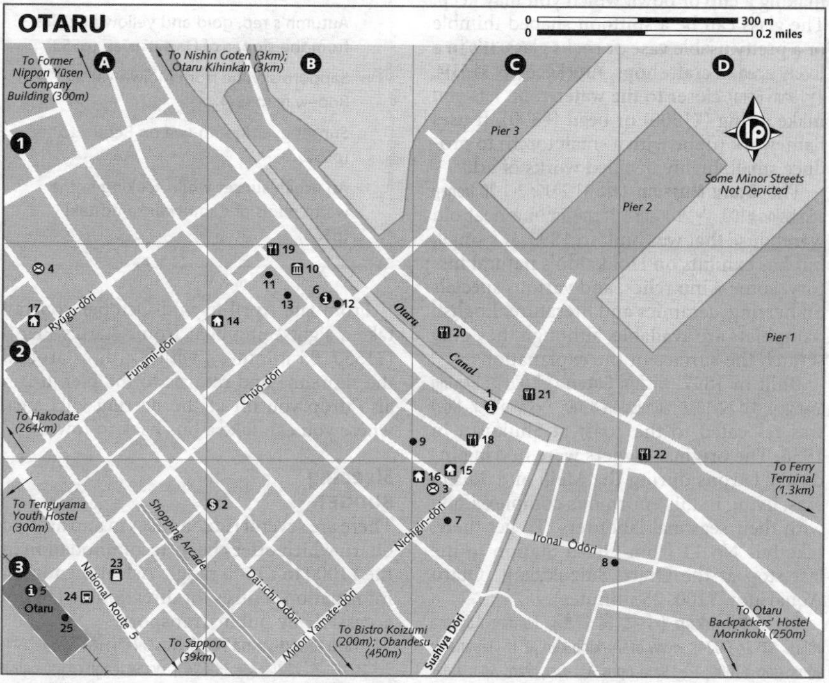
OTARU
0 300 m
0 0.2 miles
A
B
C
D
1
2
3
To Former Nippon Yūsen Company Building (300m)
To Nishin Goten (3km); Otaru Kihinkan (3km)
Pier 3
Pier 2
Pier 1
Some Minor Streets Not Depicted
Ryūgū-dōri
Funami-dōri
Chūō-dōri
Otaru Canal
To Hakodate (264km)
To Tenguyama Youth Hostel (300m)
Shopping Arcade
National Route 5
Dai-ichi Ōdōri
Midori Yamate-dōri
Nichigin-dōri
Sushiya Dōri
Ironai Ōdōri
Otaru
To Sapporo (39km)
To Bistro Koizumi (200m); Obandesu (450m)
To Ferry Terminal (1.3km)
To Otaru Backpackers' Hostel Morinkoki (250m)

INFORMATION
- Asakusa-bashi Tourist 1 C2
- Hokkaidō Bank 北海道銀行 2 B3
- Main Post Office 郵便局 3 C3
- Post Office 郵便局 4 A2
- Tourist information office 5 A3
- Unga Plaza Tourist Information Booth 運河プラザ観光案内所 6 B2

SIGHTS & ACTIVITIES
- Bank of Japan 日本銀行 7 C3
- K's Blowing ケーズ・ブローイング 8 C3
- Mitsui-Sumitomo Bank Building 三井住友銀行 9 C2
- Otaru Museum 小樽市博物館 10 B2
- Uminekoya A うみねこ屋 .... (see 11)
- Uminekoya うみねこ屋 11 B2
- Unga Plaza 運河プラザ 12 B2
- Yuzu Kōbō ゆず工房 13 B2

SLEEPING
- Ebiya Ryokan 海老屋旅館 14 B2
- Hotel 1-2-3 ホテル・ワン・ツー・スリー 15 C3
- Otaru Grand Hotel Classic 小樽グランドホテルクラシック 16 C3
- Wakaba-sō Ryokan 若葉荘旅館 17 A2

EATING
- Kita no Ice Cream Yasan 18 C2
- Mangiare Takinami マンジャーレTakinami 19 B2
- Otaru Sōko No 1 小樽倉庫 No 1 .... 20 C2
- Otaru Unga Shokudō 小樽運河食堂 21 C2
- Toppi とっぴー 22 D2

SHOPPING
- Nagasakiya Shopping Centre 長崎屋 23 A3

TRANSPORT
- Bus Station バスターミナル 24 A3
- JR Rent-a-Cycle JRレンタサイクル .... 25 A

labelled in Japanese, English and Russian. Built in the Meiji-era and Taisho-era, these structures lend themselves to picture-taking. More can be seen along Nichigin-dori, once known as the 'Wall Street of the North', including the street's namesake Bank of Japan. The **Former Nippon Yūsen Company building** (旧日本郵船ビル; ☎ 22-3316; admission ¥100; ☻ Tue-Sun) and the old **Mitsui Banking Corporation building**, which finally closed in 2002 after 123 years of operation.

Self-styled as the 'Venice of Japan', Otaru is also trying to build a name for itself as a glass-blowing town. **K's Blowing** (☎ 31-5454; www.ks-blowing.com; ¥1800-2200; ☻ 9am-5.30pm) offers short lessons (in English; 25 minutes) in making a cup or bowl, which you may keep. The glass can be a spittoon shaped thimble or a pretty usable vase or rocks glass. It's in a lively area of craft shops. **Yuzu Kōbō** (☎ 34-1314; ☻ 9am-6pm), closer to the waterfront, lets you make a ring (¥1500) or bead (¥300). It uses flamework (done with a small torch) to produce small, highly detailed works of art.

The **Otaru Museum** (☎ 33-2439; 2-1-20 Ironai; admission ¥100; ☻ 9.30am-5.30pm) is in a neat old warehouse that was built in 1893. It's small, but has exhibits on Hokkaidō's natural history, some Ainu relics, and various specials on herring, ceramics and literature. English pamphlets are available, although they only scratch the surface of the explanations.

Built in 1897, **Nishin Goten** (鰊御殿; Herring Mansion; ☎ 22-1038; admission ¥200; ☻ mid-Apr–Nov) was relocated to the coast at Shukustu in 1956. The original owners were herring industry barons during the Meiji and Taishō eras, living in this enormous complex along with their seasonal labourers. To get there, take bus No 11 from Otaru Station to the last stop at the Otaru Suizokukan (Otaru Aquarium; ¥200, 25 minutes).

Otaru Kihinkan (小樽貴賓館; Former Aoyama villa; ☎ 24-0024; www.otaru-kihinkan.jp in Japanese; admission ¥1000; ☻ 9am-6pm Apr-Oct, 9am-5pm Nov-Mar) is another herring money mansion, built by the Aoyama family in 1918. This amazing Japanese-style building has all the trimmings: an *uguisu-bari* (squeaking corridor designed to reveal intruders), a 100 tatami room, ornate woodwork and even opulent Arita porcelain pit toilets. Well worth the bus ride. To get there, take the No 11 bus (¥200) and get off at the Iwaizusan-chōme stop (20 minutes).

> **HOKKAIDŌ'S TOP 10 VIEWS**
>
> - Mashū-ko (p560) on a clear day
> - Winter drift ice in the Sea of Okhotsk (p557)
> - Whales, dolphins and porpoises during summer boat cruises from Muroran (p541)
> - Kuril seals basking below the cliffs at the cape Erimo Misaki (p568)
> - The white peaks of Tokachidake mountains rising behind the lavender fields of Furano (p552) and Biei (p553)
> - Tōya-ko's frisky young volcanoes and terrifying Usu-zan (p539)
> - Autumn's red, gold and yellow hillsides from the slopes of Daisetsuzan (p552)
> - Sapporo skyline from Moiwa-yama Ropeway (p524)
> - Sunset over Momo-iwa on Rebun-tō (p550)
> - An ocean sunset while soaking in the warm pools of Kamuiwakka-no-taki (p565)

From late April to mid-October you can take a sightseeing boat from Otaru's Pier 3 (¥1550, 85 minutes), which cruises around the shoreline and returns to the pier. It can also drop you off at the herring villa area, where you can take a bus back to town.

Sleeping
BUDGET
There are several rider houses in and around Otaru which offer cheap accommodation in the ¥1000 to ¥1500 range. Ask at the tourist information centres for directions; a few are accessible by public transport.

Otaru Tengu-yama Youth Hostel (小樽天狗山ユースホステル; ☎ 33-6944; www.tengu.co.jp/english/index.html; 2-13-1 Mogami; dm ¥3360) Two different guest houses connected to the same umbrella organisation. Close to Tengu-yama cable car and ski area. About 20 minutes by the No 3 bus to the final stop (¥200). Backtrack from the station just a little and it will be on the right, before you come to a park.

Otaru Backpackers' Hostel Morinoki (小樽バックパッカーズホステル杜の樹; ☎ 23-2175; 4-15 Aioi-chō; www.otaru-morinoki.com; dm ¥3400)

Quiet, quaint, and cosy, this place gets filled quickly so book ahead in the summer if you want to ensure a room. Just 15 minutes on foot from either Otaru or Minami Otaru JR Stations. Turn right on the main road right in front of the JR station. Follow it, and at the third traffic signal after passing under the railroad, turn left. The road eventually dead-ends at a shrine (Suitengu).The hostel is on the right of the shrine.

Wakaba-sō Ryokan (☎ 27-3111; Inaho 4-3-17; r per person with/without breakfast ¥4000/3500) On a side street west of the centre; this place is small but well-kept. Rates include a light, Japanese-style breakfast. From the JR station, turn left on the main road right in front of the station. Turn right at the second traffic light. The inn is in the third block, on the left.

MIDRANGE

Hotel 1-2-3 (say 'wan-tsū-surī'; ☎ 31-3939; www.hyper -hotel.co.jp; 1-3-1 Ironai; s/d/tr ¥4900/5900/6900) Brand new, very stylishly renovated in an old bank building. Western-style rooms have no phone, but do include a light breakfast. Turn right on the main street that runs in front of the station. Turn left at the first traffic light and walk several traffic lights and multiple blocks. The hotel is on the left side of the road across from the main post office.

Ebiya Ryokan (☎ 22-2317; 2-10-16 Ironai; r per person with breakfast ¥5800, per person with 2 meals ¥6500) In a quiet area close to the canal (take the main road from the station; turn left at the third traffic light – the inn is on the second block). The lobby needs some renovation, but the Japanese-style rooms are perfectly up to par and are handsomely decorated.

TOP END

Otaru Grand Hotel Classic (☎ 22-6500; 1-8-25 Ironai; s/d high season ¥13,500/21,000, low season ¥7500/13,000; P ✗) In another former bank, this nicely done hotel is its own slice of history. Tastefully styled Western rooms and lovely leaded glass. Behind the main post office; take the main road away from the station, turn right at the third traffic light. Go one block and the hotel is before the main post office.

Eating

The Otaru Station has the usual fare, but you're better off wandering down to the far more picturesque canal area and finding something more exciting.

Sushi-ya Dōri has numerous sushi stands, everything from the standard to the rather bizarre.

Mangiare Takinami (☎ 33-3394; 2-1-16 Ironai; set lunches ¥780-880; ✌ Thur-Tues) One block off the canal. A relaxing place with wooden rafters and nice pasta and fish sets. Paella is their speciality.

Bistro Koizumi (ビストロ小泉; ☎ 32-4965; 1-7-10 Inaho; ¥800; ✌ Thur-Tues) A hit with the younger crowd, this place specialises in Hayashi-rice, a tomato-based beef dish served on white rice. Get there early if you want some; they're often sold out.

Uminekoya (☎ 32-2914; Ironai 2-2-14; dishes ¥600-1400; ✌ 11.30am-10pm) A combo restaurant and pub, this atmospheric warehouse was built in 1906 and was the setting for several novels of Japanese literary fame. The façade, crumbling brick laced with ivy, has been featured in works by several famous writers.

Otaru Sōkō No 1 (☎ 21-2323; 5-4 Minato-machi; dishes ¥800-2000) A nice microbrewery with a selection of fresh brews on tap, plus both German and Japanese fare to complement its Bavarian décor. Potatoes and sausages are big here.

Otaru Unga Shokudō (☎ 24-8000; 6-5 Minato-machi; rāmen ¥700-1150) A food court with one section specialising in *rāmen*. Miso-vegetable is a popular option for those looking for something relatively healthy. Nearby is a beer garden with a lunch (¥1580) and dinner buffet (¥1980), both include sushi, *yakiniku*, and a variety of other delicacies.

Kita no Ice Cream Yasan (☎ 23-8983; 1-2-18 Ironai) Serves up stomach-turning flavours such as *nattō* (fermented soy beans), tofu, crab, beer…even sea urchin. About as bizarre as ice cream gets.

Toppi (☎ 27-8111; 6-4 Minato-machi; per plate ¥120-220; ✌ 11am-10pm) If you're looking for something fun, try this place. Locals say it's both cheap and delicious. It's along the canal.

Obandesu (おばんです; ☎ 25-5432; 1-10-8 Hanazono; ✌ Tue-Sun) An *izakaya* that comes highly recommended: good food, nice folks and decent prices.

Street vendors are another option. Fresh corn with a sweet teriyaki sauce is a fun snack, or if you're feeling adventurous, try *takoyaki*, little balls of grilled dough with small chunks of octopus inside.

HOKKAIDŌ

Getting There & Away

Otaru is just 30 minutes from Sapporo by *kaisoku* train or 50 minutes away by *futsū*; fares for both cost ¥620. Special airport *kaisoku* trains run via Sapporo to New Chitose Airport (¥1740, 75 minutes). Occasional local trains run south to Niseko (¥1410, two hours).

You can get frequent buses to Sapporo (¥590, one hour), and less frequent ones to Niseko (¥1330, 1¾ hours).

Ferries run daily between Otaru and Maizuru (from ¥8200, 20 hours), just north of Kyoto, and almost daily to Niigata (¥5600, 18 hours). To get to the ferry terminal, take bus No 10 from in front of the station (¥200, 10 minutes). Tourist-loop buses also stop at the port a couple of times a day.

Getting Around

The main part of town is small enough to tackle on foot. Bicycle rental is available at the station through **JR Rent-A-Cycle** (☎ 24-6300; ✦ Mar-Nov) starting at ¥800 for two hours (discounts for students and holders of certain rail passes, including JR passes).

Tourist buses loop through the city taking in most of the sights (¥200 or ¥750 for a day pass). Buses leave about every 20 minutes from Otaru Station, starting at 9am and finishing at 6.30pm.

NISEKO ニセコ

☎ 0136

One of Hokkaidō's prime ski resorts during the winter months and a hiking base during summer and autumn, Niseko sprawls between the mountain Yōtei-zan to the east and Niseko Annupuri to the west. Come here for canoeing, kayaking and river rafting in summer, and ice climbing, snowshoeing or even dogsledding in the winter. Hot springs are open year-round.

The **Niseko Outdoor Centre** (☎ 44-1133; www .noc-hokkaido.jp/nocindex_eng.html), near the Annupuri ski slope, and the **Niseko Adventure Centre** (☎ 23-2093; www.nac-web.com), in the village of Hirafu, can organise activities. Niseko Station has a **tourist information office** (☎ 44-2468), which can help plan ski weekends. Info is also available online at www .niseko.gr.jp. Depending on where you're heading, it may make more sense to travel via one of two other stations serving the area, Hirafu and Kutchan.

FIVE PLACES TO FIND GOOD POWDER

For many Japanese, Hokkaidō is synonymous with packed powder, ski lifts and soothing sore muscles in a hot bath. If you're looking to tear over moguls or telemark through snow-bound forests, these places are a good place to start. Most have winter shuttle buses direct from Sapporo.

- Niseko – Pristine ski slopes and lots of cross-country trails (left)
- Teine – Two slopes in Sapporo's backyard, just 10 minutes' train ride away (p524)
- Kamui Ski Links – In Asahikawa, some of the longest trails Hokkaidō has to offer (p543)
- Tsubetsu in Akan – Beautiful views of Kussharo-ko (p564)
- Furano – Hotel packages make this easy and convenient (p552)

Sleeping

For really cheap accommodation, check out rider houses. **Niseko Tourist Home** (ニセコツーリストホーム; ☎ 44-2517; http://homepage2 .nifty.com/niseko-th/in Japanese; dm ¥1500-¥5000; ✦ closed winter) is a perennial favourite; price includes two meals. It's 4km from JR Niseko Station.

Niseko Annupuri Youth Hostel (ニセコアンヌプリユースホステル; ☎ 58-2084; 470-4 Niseko; www.annupuri-yh.com; YHA members r per person with/without meals ¥4930/3250) A mountain lodge near the Annupuri ski ground. The owner can provide local hiking and cycling maps and plenty of recommendations. Meals are delicious, and if you phone ahead, someone can pick you up at Niseko Station.

Niseko Ambishiasu (ニセコアンビシャス; say 'ambitious'; ☎ 44-3011; http://anb.web.infoseek .co.jp/; r per person with 2 meals ¥4600) This popular place is also a Toho network member with shared Japanese-style rooms. The owners will pick you up at the station, and ski rental is also available.

Jam Garden (ジャムガーデン; ☎ 22-6676; 37-89 Kabayama, Kutchan-chō, Abuta-gun; r per person ¥5000-6000) Right near the ski lift at Hirafu, this deluxe farmhouse (it has its own Jacuzzi and sauna) has Western-style rooms and meals. If you need to be picked up from either Hirafu or Kutchan Stations, just phone ahead. It's a 15-minute taxi ride from JR Niseko Station.

Niseko Hotel Nikko Annupuri (ニセコホテル
日航アンヌプリ; ☎ 58-3311; 480-1 Niseko, Niseko-
chō; www.nikko-annupuri.co.jp; r per person with 2 meals
¥13,000) A top-of-the-line establishment near
the top of the mountain, this place boasts
splendid views of the valley and easy bus
access. Take the bus from JR Niseko Station
to Konbu Onsen, and get off at Annupri Ski
Jyo (12 minutes).

Getting There & Away

Unfortunately, in summer (the low season)
there aren't a lot of easy ways to get here
unless you want to rent a vehicle. There are
a few direct *kaisoku* trains from Sapporo
(¥2100, 2¼ hours); otherwise you'll have to
wait up to 1½ hours when changing trains
at Otaru (¥1410, two hours). Alternatively,
you could hop on a direct bus to Niseko
outside Otaru Station (¥1330, two hours).
From June to September there is a daily bus
from New Chitose Airport to the Niseko
Hotel Nikko Annupuri (¥2300, 2½ hours).

Winter is an entirely different story: there
are frequent direct buses to the area's various
ski resorts from Sapporo (¥2190, three hours)
as well as New Chitose Airport (¥2190, 3¼
hours). A discount round-trip fare is also
available from both places for ¥3660. Trains
are frequent during the ski season as well,
and all the major ski resorts have shuttles
which run to and from the stations.

SHIKOTSU-TŌYA NATIONAL PARK
支笏洞爺国立公園

☎ 0142

Part of Shikotsu-Tōya National Park (983 sq
km), Tōya-ko is a large and beautiful lake,
though its beauty is somewhat marred by
large hotels on the southern perimeter. Its
volcanoes are still making headlines: Usu-
zan erupted quite violently in 2000, sending boulders thousands of feet into the air.
Despite the volcanic interruptions, Tōya-ko
Onsen remains a popular spot for soaking,
perhaps because of its proximity to New
Chitose Airport and Sapporo. The Tōya-ko
Onsen **tourist office** (☎ 75-2446) is downhill
from the bus station.

Volcanic Sites

In 1943, after a series of earthquakes, **Shōwa-
Shin-zan** (昭和新山) emerged as an upstart
bump in some vegetable fields southeast of
Tōya-ko Onsen, it then surged upwards for

two more years to reach its present height
of 407m. At the time, Japanese officials were
keen to hush it up as they thought it was
a bad omen and might portend an inaus-
picious end to WWII. Local officials were
urged to douse the volcanic flames (they
didn't) so that Allied aircraft couldn't use
them for orientation. Shōwa-Shin-zan is
still belching sulphurous fumes, creating an
awesome spectacle for visitors and keeping
local officials nervous about its next move.

Nearby, **Usu-zan** (有珠山; 729m), a taller
and more formidable volcano, has also been
just as active, erupting violently in March
2000. The ash cloud which rained down
on Tōya-ko was 2700m high, and volcanic
bombs threatened to down news helicopters.
Visitors can wander through twisted roads
and ash-destroyed buildings, but only on
clear pathways. Usu-zan's previous eruption,
in 1977, caused far more damage: it blanketed
the area with 30cm of grainy, choking ash.

The further you walk the fewer people
you'll see, and it's possible to walk (if you're
up for it) the entire way back to Tōya, over
6km away. There's also a **ropeway** (cable car;
☎ 75-2401; return ¥1450; ☼ Jan-Nov) to the peak
of Usu-zan. It's closed in December.

Behind the tourist shops, the small **Mimatsu
Masao Memorial Museum** (☎ 75-2365; admission
¥300; ☼ 8am-5pm Apr-Dec & Feb, irregular Jan-Mar) is devoted to the local postmaster, who purchased
the volcano in 1946 (for a princely sum of
¥28,000). He spent years diagramming its
growth using an ingenious method that has
become a standard among volcanologists
today. English signage is limited.

The **Nishiyama Crater Promenade** (西山火口
散策路) is a bit like walking through an
area after a bomb blast. Steam hisses out of
fissures, azure ponds bubble from boiling
underground springs, and houses and roads
are crushed and mangled. The entryway is
about 10 minutes by bus (¥160) from Tōya-
ko Onsen; it's ¥300 to park your own vehicle
in the overly expansive parking lot.

For something sedentary, check out the
movie at the **Volcanic Science Museum** (火山
科学館; ☎ 75-4400; admission ¥600; ☼ 9am-5pm)
above the Tōya-ko Onsen bus terminal.

TŌYA-KO ONSEN 洞爺湖温泉

During summer, the town offers fireworks
displays every evening. Head to the shoreline for the best view. The 37km perimeter

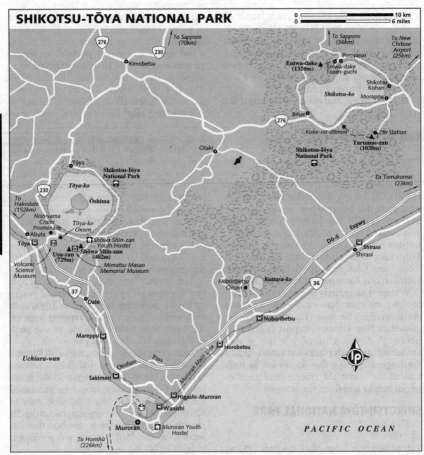

SHIKOTSU-TŌYA NATIONAL PARK

of Tōya-ko is both beautiful and daunting. You can rent a bike near the station but it's cheaper at the Shōwa-Shin-zan Youth Hostel. Cruises out to Ōshima, the island in the middle of the lake, depart every 30 minutes from 8am to 4.30pm (¥1320). An evening firework-viewing cruise (¥1500) is a little more exciting.

Sleeping

Naka-tōya Camping Ground (中洞爺キャンプ場; ☎ 66-3131; tent sites per person ¥300) On the eastern edge of the lake, several kilometres from Tōya-ko Onsen. Has its own onsen (¥370), and tents can be rented if necessary. Buses are infrequent (¥630), stopping only two or three times each day.

Shōwa-Shin-zan Youth Hostel (☎ 75-2283; 103 Soubetsu-onsen, Soubetsu-chō, Usu-gun; dm ¥3150) With comfortable shared-room accommodation, this hostel is nicely situated on the road leading up to Usu-zan. Bicycles are ¥1000 per day and offer a nice way to cover ground around town. By bus it's eight minutes from Tōya-ko Onsen; get off at the Tozan-guchi stop.

Tōya Green Hotel (洞爺グリーンホテル; ☎ 75-3030; 144-3 Toyako onsen-machi, Abiruta-machi; r per person with 2 meals ¥5300-7400) Calls itself a 'business *minshuku*' and has expansive Japanese-style rooms, full facilities (TV, minifridge, buffet breakfast/dinner, large and small public baths) and enormous meals. Quieter rooms are in the back, away from the main drag.

Hotel Grand Tōya (ホテルグランド洞爺; ☎ 75-2288; r per person with 2 meals ¥8000) Has nice lake views from every room, both Japanese and Western styles are available, with bathroom in each room.

Other resort hotels line the waterfront; rates begin around ¥12,000 per person, per night. Many of them have day-use access to their baths; rates vary from ¥500 to ¥2000. Bring your own towel to save the ¥300 rental fee.

Getting There & Away

Tokkyū, kaisoku and local trains to Hakodate (¥5340, 1½ hours) or Sapporo (¥6760, 1¾ hours) all make a brief stop at Tōya, and buses run every 30 minutes between Tōya Station and Tōya-ko Onsen (¥320, 25 minutes).

Buses are a less expensive option, running frequently between Sapporo (¥2700, 2¾ hours) or Muroran (¥1170, 1¾ hours).

From April to November there are also scenic buses which run via the Orofure pass to Noboribetsu Onsen (¥1530, 1¼ hours), and some continue onwards to New Chitose Airport (¥2140, 2½ hours).

MURORAN 室蘭

☎ 0143 / pop 100,000

This dwindling industrial city is in the process of reinventing itself. It's conveniently connected by ferry with the rest of Honshū. It's 15 minutes by bus from the pier to the **tourist office** (☎ 23-1002), which is in the oldest wooden train station in Hokkaido, built in 1912. Among other activities, there's a **whale-watching boat** (☎ 26-1822; per 3hr ¥6000) three times daily in summer that leaves from the pier. Whales, dolphins, porpoises and seals are best viewed from May to July, and tours are often booked solid weeks ahead.

While the industrialised section of the valley is definitely less than scenic, the shoreline between Wanishi (where the Muroran Youth Hostel is) and **Cape Chikyū** (地球岬) is quite stunning. A well-marked road parallels the shore and offers several spots to stop and admire the view. The observation areas at the Cape are also pretty. Cape Chikyū is known for its returning pair of *hayabusa* (peregrine falcons) and for its almost 360-degree panoramic views of the sea.

The black-sand beach behind the youth hostel is gorgeous, a perfect place for an early morning walk as you watch the sunrise. Beautiful white cliffs, giant mystic boulders and ethereal sunlight will make you feel like you've stepped inside a Wyeth painting. Surfing is a popular pastime, and hiking, skiing and snowshoeing are also available nearby.

Gourmands will appreciate Muroran's *yakitori* (grilled meat, usually chicken, on a small bamboo stick), but be warned: the preferred meat here is pork. In fact, many of the popular places don't serve chicken at all, only the skin, which is very popular. **Yakitori Fujitori** (焼き鳥ふじ鳥; ☎ 44-4986/4970; 1-36-3 Wanishichō; dishes ¥200-1000), an inconspicuous greasy spoon in the centre of town, is a favourite with locals and serves excellent *yakitori*, tofu in broth and *rāmen* that's hard to beat.

Sleeping

Muroran Youth Hostel (室蘭ユースホステル; ☎ 44-3357; www.jyh.gr.jp/muroran; dm ¥2625; **P** ☒) Institutional but clean and practical (it even has a web cam!), affording fantastic views of the bay and easy access to hiking trails along the cliff top. The beach is only 10 minutes away. From Wanishi Station, turn left and follow Rte 36 until you see Lawson on the right. Turn right and follow this road all the way until it ends after a steep hill. Look diagonally across the street to the left and you will see a small sign for the hostel. From there it's a three-minute walk to the hostel driveway.

Hotel Bayside (ホテルベイサイド; ☎ 24-8090; s/tw ¥4800/8600) Comfy and simple, this moderate hotel is just a few minutes from Muroran Station. Look for Lawson convenience store; the hotel is just a bit down the sidestreet nearby.

Camping is possible on some of the scenic pullouts along the cliffside road between Wanishi and Cape Chikyū. Several secluded areas would be easy to use, but are not officially sanctioned. Use your own judgment and caution.

Getting There & Away

Long-distance trains depart from Higashi-Muroran Station, three stops east of Muroran itself; transfer to central Muroran is included in long-distance fares. Direct *tokkyū* trains run south to Hakodate (¥6180, two hours) and north to Sapporo (¥4680, 1¼ hours).

From the bus station there are frequent departures for Sapporo (¥2000, 2¼ hours), Noboribetsu Onsen (¥710, 80 minutes) and Tōya-ko Onsen (¥1170, 1¾ hours).

Ferries at Muroran depart for Hachinohe (¥3970, eight hours) daily, and there are overnight ferries to Aomori (¥3460, seven hours) and Naoetsu (¥7030, 17 hours, three per week). The ferry terminal is about a 10-minute walk from Muroran Station. The **Higashi Nihon Ferry** (☎ 22-1668) office will have the latest details.

NOBORIBETSU ONSEN 登別温泉
☎ 0143

Nobiribetsu Onsen is the most popular *onsen* resort in Hokkaidō, boasting over 30 hotels and bath houses clustered tightly together along a narrow, winding street. The water originates from a volcanic, sulphurous 'hell' not far above. Some of the higher-end spas are as nice as Japan has to offer. There are a number of interesting hikes around the surrounding hills and sulphur vents. The **tourist association office** (☎ 84-3311; 60 Noboribetsu onsen machi; ☉ 8.30am-5pm) has English maps, hotel locations and bathing hours.

Sights & Activities
Dai-ichi Takimoto-kan (第一滝館; ☎ 84-3322; www.takimotokan.co.jp/english/; ¥2000) is the cream of the crop of the *onsen* resorts; this luxurious spa has more than 15 different kinds of baths, which range from take-your-skin-off scalding to icy cool. Several outdoor *rotemburo* (open-air baths) offer beautiful views of the valley, and there's even a swimming pool (where you will require a swimsuit). Its English website offers online booking and reservations.

Jigokudani (地獄谷; Hell Valley) is a short walk uphill, offering viewers a peek at what may await us in the afterlife: sulphurous gases, hissing vents and vividly coloured rocks. Pools of scalding water can be seen from **Ōyu-numa** (大湯沼; Boiling Water Swamp). For those of us who are far from Heaven-bound, it's good to know that Hell (if the Japanese have anything to say about it!) will surely include a lot of *onsen*.

The simple **public bath** (☎ 84-2050; 60 Noboribetsu onsen machi; ¥390; ☉ 7am-10pm), on the 1st floor of an office building next to the tourist association office (above), is relaxing,

Sleeping
Kanefuku Youth Hostel (金福ユースホステル; ☎ 84-2565; dm ¥2888) Noboribetsu Onsen's only youth hostel has received less-than-enthusiastic reviews of late. Its main attraction is price, as many of the hotel-spas are prohibitively expensive.

Ryokan Hanaya (旅館はなや; ☎ 84-2521; www .kashoutei-hanaya.co.jp; r ¥7000) A great midrange option with Japanese-style rooms, many overlooking the river. Staff are very friendly and speak some English. It also has its own hot-spring baths, private toilets and sinks.

Dai-ichi Takimoto-kan (☎ 84-3322; www.takimotokan.co.jp/english/; r from ¥11,000; P ⊠ 🖴) The *onsen* mentioned earlier also doubles as a hotel. In addition to immaculate Western- or Japanese-style rooms, meals (prices vary seasonally) are offered either buffet-style in the main dining rooms or else in-room, and they offer children's menus. Barrier-free rooms are also an option for the elderly or those with disabilities.

Getting There & Away
Noboribetsu Onsen is about 13 minutes by bus (¥330) from JR Noboribetsu Station, with local train connections to Higashi-Muroran (¥350, 20 minutes), Shiraoi (¥350, 30 minutes) and Tomakomai (¥810, 45 minutes), all of which have connections to Sapporo.

From Noboribetsu Onsen there are direct buses to Sapporo (Eki-mae terminal, ¥1900, 1½ to 2¾ hours). There are also buses to New Chitose Airport (¥1330, 65 minutes, one to three daily) and Muroran (¥710, 80 minutes). In summer (April to November) there are also scenic buses which run the length of Orofure Pass and end at Tōya-ko Onsen (¥1530, 1¼ hours).

SHIKOTSU-KO 支笏湖
☎ 0123

Part of the Shikotsu-Tōya National Park, Shikotsu-ko is a caldera lake surrounded by picturesque volcanoes. It's Japan's second-deepest lake after Tazawa-ko in Akita-ken. The area is served by Shikotsu Kohan (支笏湖畔), a tiny town consisting mainly of a bus station, **visitors centre** (☎ 25-2404; www15.ocn.ne.jp /~sikotuvc/ in Japanese; ☉ 9.30am-5.30pm summer, 9.30am-4.30pm winter, Wed-Mon), boat pier, a few souvenir shops and restaurants. Morappu (モラップ), nearby, has a few more options. Both can be enjoyed as a day trip from Muroran.

Activities

Leaving from Shikotsu Kohan's pier there are rather tame **sightseeing cruises** (☎ 25-2031; ¥960; ⏰ Apr-Nov). A nature trail runs for about an hour between the pier and Morappu. Not so tame **speedboat cruises** (☎ 0123-20-4131; per person ¥1500, min 3 people per cruise) are a faster way to take in the lake and its environs.

Cycling is a nice option if the weather is good. A full circuit of the lake is 50km, and the youth hostel rents bikes for ¥400 per hour or ¥2000 per day, with a discount for its own guests.

Fresh water scuba diving can be done through **Blue Note** (ブルーノート; ☎ 0120-43-3340; 107 Shikotsuko Onsen; www2.ocn.ne.jp/~bluenote in Japanese; ¥10,000; ⏰ year-round). Water flowers, 100m cliffs and numerous fresh-water fish are a few of the attractions.

HIKING

Mountain hikes are one of the area's most popular activities, but check at the visitors information centre, as trails are frequently closed due to bad conditions or erosion.

Eniwa-dake (恵庭岳; 1320m) lies on the northwestern side of the lake. A 3½-hour hike will bring you to a nice panoramic view.

Tarumae-zan (樽前; 1038m) is an active volcano on the southern side of the lake. Due to poisonous gas the crater itself is closed, but you can reach the rim from the seventh station in about 40 minutes. Japanese walkers all wear bear bells in this area, and you should stay on the main trails to avoid an unexpected encounter.

Koki-no-dōmon (苔の洞門; ⏰ from 9am Jun-Oct) is a spectacular mossy gorge, though recently it has been damaged by erosion. Visitors are not allowed to enter after 4pm.

Sleeping

These places are clustered in or around Shikotsu Kohan.

Shikotsu-ko Youth Hostel (支笏湖ユースホステル; ☎ 25-2311; www.youthhostel.or.jp/English/menu2 .htm; dm ¥3450) Has private family rooms as well as dorms; bike rental and a hot-spring bath (¥150) are also available. To reach the hostel head away from the visitors information centre; after about a three-minute walk, it's on the other side of a parking lot.

Log Bear (ログベアー; ☎ 25-2738; http://logbear .hoops.ne.jp; r per person ¥5000 with breakfast) An intimate, friendly log cabin right in the town centre. The owner speaks English quite fluently and makes a nice cup of coffee as well. From the visitor centre, go toward the lake and turn right at the end of the street (which is parallel to the lakeshore). Go about 300m; Log Bear is next to a bigger hotel.

Shikotsu-sō (支笏荘; ☎ 25-2718; r per person with 2 meals ¥5800) A cheerful *minshuku* right behind the bus station, primarily known for its miso, *rāmen* and trout. The owner's hobby is pressing wildflowers, from which she makes postcards, plates and other souvenirs.

Morappu Camping Ground (モラップキャンプ場; ☎ 25-2439; tent sites from ¥500; ⏰ late Apr-late Oct) In Morappu, nicely situated by the lake.

Lapland (ラップランド; ☎ 25-2239; dm with 2 meals ¥4900) In Morappu. A great little log cabin with nice views of the lake. Has carpeted Japanese-style rooms and private rooms are sometimes available (per person ¥5900). The owners will pick you up and take you back to the bus station or mountain trailheads. Buses bound for Koke-no-dōmon from Shikotsu Kohan pass Morappu (¥240, 10 minutes).

Getting There & Away

Between mid-June and mid-October there are three to four buses a day from Shikotsu Kōhan to Sapporo Station (¥1330, 80 minutes). Other buses run year round to New Chitose Airport (¥920, 55 minutes).

DŌ-HOKU (NORTHERN HOKKAIDŌ) 道北

ASAHIKAWA 旭川
☎ 0166 / pop 362,000

Asahikawa is one of the largest cities in Hokkaidō after Sapporo. It was built on a flat plain along the Ishikari River and was once one of the biggest Ainu settlements. It carries the dual honour of having the most days with snowfall, as well as the record for coldest temperature (-40°C). Though less picturesque than other Hokkaidō cities, Asahikawa is interesting both historically and as a jumping-off point to other parts of Hokkaidō: Wakkanai to the north; Daisetsuzan National Park to the southeast; and Biei and Furano due south.

In addition to its Ainu heritage, Asahikawa was also an important part of Meiji-era

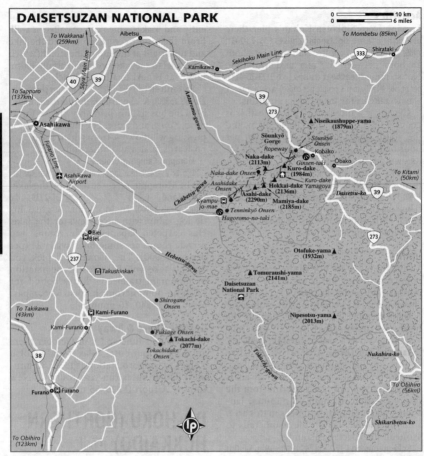

DAISETSUZAN NATIONAL PARK

settlements and has a long history of sake brewing. Among other notables, it was the location of the first ski area in Japan. It has since become one of the major industrial cities of the island, with associated urban development.

Information

Friendly, helpful assistance can be found at the **information counter** (☎ 22-6704; ⏰ 8.30am-7pm Jul-Sep, 9am-5pm Oct-Jun) inside Asahikawa Station with a number of English pamphlets and sightseeing brochures. Be sure to ask staff for the very useful bus stop map: it helps greatly in navigating to the right place on time. The staff have a wealth of information at their fingertips, quite literally, and can share tips

about the city, its sights and activities, and they may also be able to recommend places to stay. The station also has a **hotel booking desk** (☎ 22-5139) which can be relied on to find reasonable deals. If you are getting off the train, turn right once go through the ticket gate before going out of the station building. The station's post office has a postal ATM.

INTERNET ACCESS

Asahikawa has several Internet cafés, though some are far from the station.
Kissa Ton Ton (喫茶とんとん; ☎ 39-2450; Sanjōdōri 18 Hidari 10) A block to the east from Asahikawashijō Station, one JR stop from Asahikawa Station.
Terako-ya (寺子屋; ☎ 23-9789; 4F Marutoku Bldg, 9-7 Ichijō-dōri; per hr ¥500; ⏰ Mon-Sat) Closest to the

station, a few blocks' walk. When exiting the station, take the pedestrian street for two blocks. Turn right and go another block or so. It is on your right (if you get to Lawson at the corner, you've gone too far).

Sights & Activities
MUSEUMS
Asahikawa is a good spot to visit museums, many of which are quite unique and offer insights into Japanese culture and history that are difficult to find in other parts of Japan.

The **Hokkaido Folk Arts and Crafts Village** (北海道伝統美術工芸村; 2 Minamigaoka) is a collection of three museums. A free shuttle leaves from Kureyon Parking, a three-minute walk from Asahikawa Station, next to the Asahikawa Washington Hotel (Note: different from the Fujitakankō Washington Hotel, directly across from the station). Follow the plaza out to the first major intersection, then turn left. The parking lot will be on your right after the next intersection. A combined ticket (¥1400) gives entry to the following three museums. The **International Dyeing and Weaving Art Museum** (国際染織美術館; ☎ 61-6161; ¥550; Apr-Nov) is the most spectacular, displaying textiles from around the world as well as Japanese specialities, such as embroidered Ainu wood-bark cloth and a number of spectacular silk kimono. The **Yukara Ori Folk Craft Museum** (優佳良織工芸館; ☎ 62-8811; admission ¥450; 9am-5.30pm Apr-Nov, 9am-5pm Dec-Mar) has a number of examples of Ainu cloth in the interesting local weaving style. Paradoxically, the **Snow Crystal Museum** (雪の美術館; ☎ 63-2211; admission ¥650; 9am-5pm Feb & Mar, 9am-5.30pm Apr-Nov) is closed in the winter months of December and January. This museum has some dainty exhibits, a concert hall and walk-in freezers with metre-long icicles.

Kawamura Kaneto Ainu Memorial Museum (川村カ子トアイヌ記念館; ☎ 51-2461; 1 Kitamonchō; admission ¥500; 8am-6pm Jul & Aug, 9am-5pm Sep-Jun) has a ticket office that sells an English-language booklet, *Living in the Ainu Moshir*, by Kawamura Shinrit Eoripak Ainu, the present curator and museum founder's son. For more info on the founder, see right. Take the No 24 bus from the No 4 bus stop near Asahikawa Station to the Ainu Kinenkan-mae stop (¥170, 15 minutes).

BREWERIES
Several breweries located in and around Asahikawa are well worth checking out.

KANETO KAWAMURA – AINU GENIUS

While it's indisputable that Ainu culture suffered as mainland Japanese settled in Hokkaidō, a few Ainu managed to prove themselves purely on Japanese terms. Kaneto Kawamura, an Ainu chief, became a master surveyor and helped to lay the tracks for several of Hokkaidō's railways. After eye problems forced him to retire, he used his accumulated wealth to create the first Ainu museum, Kawamura Kaneto Ainu Memorial Museum. Visitors can tour the collection of Ainu and railway-related items, as well as wear Ainu clothing and take a picture for free.

Otokoyama was frequently featured in *ukiyo-e* (wood-block prints) and old literature, as the water from this area was particularly delicious. Admission is free at **Otokoyama Sake Brewery and Museum** (男山酒造; ☎ 47-7080; www.otokoyama.com; 2-7 Nagayama; 9am-5pm) and includes tasting. Take bus No 67, 68, 70, 71, 668 or 669 from the No 18 bus stop and get off at Nagayama 2-jō 6-chōme. From there it's a two-minute walk.

A 10-minute bus ride from Asahikawa Station, **Takasago Sake Brewery** (高砂酒造; ☎ 23-2251; 17 Miyashitadōri; admission free; 9am-4.30pm Mon-Fri, 9am-11.30pm Sat & Sun mid-Apr–mid-Oct, 9am-4.30pm daily mid-Oct–mid-Apr) has interesting pictures of the old buildings and brewing process, plus a large display room. From January to March they also have an *aisudōmu* (ice dome), a sake-filled igloo that you can tour. To really impress a sake-drinking friend, send them a bottle packed in Hokkaido's own snow, which they keep in a freezer year-round. Take bus No 1, 3 or 17 from the No 17 bus stop and get off at 1-jō 18-chōme.

Festivals & Events
A number of festivals are held in Asahikawa every year. Check with local tourist offices for specific dates, as many vary slightly from year to year.

Ainu Kotan Matsuri (アイヌコタン祭り; late September) Takes place on the banks of the Ishikari-gawa, south of the city. During the festival you can see traditional dances, music and *kamui-nomi* and *inau-shiki*, prayer ceremonies offered to the deities of fire, the river, *kotan* (the village), and the mountains.

HOKKAIDŌ

Yuki Matsuri (雪祭り; February) This festival is held in Asahikawa every year, and while second to the one in Sapporo (p524), it is still impressive, with ice sculptures, food and fun seasonal events.

Sleeping & Eating

Asahikawa is a large city but does not particularly cater to tourists, so the choices are limited. A large number of shops and restaurants can be found in the main plaza which runs out from Asahikawa Station.

Asahikawa Youth Hostel (旭川ユースホステル; ☎ 61-2800; 7-18 Kamii; dm ¥3360) A 15-minute bus ride from Asahikawa Station, this out-of-the-way hostel is sometimes deserted and not the best place for those looking to make new friends or enjoy the city. Take the No 444 or 550 bus from the No 11 bus stop (¥200). Has both Japanese-style and dorm-style rooms.

Tokiya Ryokan (時屋旅館; ☎ 23-2237; www .tokiya.net/tokiyaryokan2.html; Nijō-dōri 9-6; r per person with/without 2 meals ¥6300/4725) North of the station, this place is inviting and reasonably priced. Rooms with bathroom are available for a surcharge.

Tōyoko Asahikawa Ekimae (東横イン旭川駅前; ☎ 27-1045; www.toyoko-inn.com/eng/; Ichijō-dōri 9-164-1; s/d high season ¥6800/8800, low season ¥4800/6800) This chain's clean, convenient Asahikawa clone.

Asahikawa Tāminaru Hotel (旭川ターミナルホテル; ☎ 24-0111; www.asahikawa-th.com; s/d ¥6000/8400; ✉ 🖳) Just to the right of Asahikawa Station. Offers a special discount for JR Pass holders which makes even a high-season stay quite affordable.

Numerous restaurants and food stands surround the station area and the plaza beyond, near the bus stops.

Santōka (山頭火; ☎ 25-3401; Sanjō-dōri 8; dishes ¥750-1100; ✉ 11am-3pm Sun-Fri Sep-May, 11am-3pm daily Jun-Aug) The place people think of when they ask for 'Asahikawa *rāmen*. *Shio rāmen*, or noodles in a salt broth, is its speciality. Follow Midoribashi-dōri from the station out to the third major intersection (with a stoplight). Santōka is on the 1st floor of the Midoribashi building on the left corner, on Sanjō-dōri. If you reach Yonjō-dōri, a larger crossroad, you've gone one intersection too far.

Hanamaru (はなまる; ☎ 23-8704; Yonjō-dōri 8-1 dishes ¥350-1000; ✉ 9am-11pm) Three streets straight out from the station, this plaza location of the popular chain has cheap

udon noodles and accompanying foods like tempura or *korokke*. Look for the yellow-and-orange checkered sign (on the right, assuming the station's behind you).

Getting There & Around

Asahikawa is a central location so has frequent plane, train, and bus access. Flights head directly to and from Osaka, Nagoya and Tokyo. Buses between the airport and JR Asahikawa Station (¥570, 35 minutes) are timed nicely to connect with arrivals and departures.

Trains link Asahikawa with Sapporo (*tokkyū*, ¥4680, 1½ hours) to the south, Wakkanai (¥8070, four hours) to the north, Abashiri (¥7750, 3¾ hours) to the east, and to the smaller sightseeing towns of Biei (¥530, 30 minutes) and Furano (*futsū*, ¥1040, 1¼ hours).

Buses leave from 20 different stops spread out over three streets in front of the train station. If you are using Asahikawa as a springboard for a day-trip to Daisetsuzan, set your alarm early: the 9.10am bus is the only one to catch as the next one leaves at 10.45am, which by the time it arrives an hour later, does not leave much time for hiking – and don't miss the last bus back to Asahikawa at 5.05pm.

WAKKANAI 稚内
☎ 0162 / pop 42,500

Wakkanai, Japan's most northern mainland city, is closest to the island's two most northern capes, Noshappu and Sōya. Depart here for Rishiri-tō and Rebun-tō, islands off the coast, and, further off, Russia's Sakhalin Island. It's a quiet town, and Wakkanai's economy depends on kelp fishing and tourism. The views of the water and its fishing boats are very picturesque year-round, and many brave the bitter cold to see the frozen bay in the dead of winter, a majestic (but chilly!) scene. In late February, Wakkanai hosts the **Japan Cup National Dogsled Races** (全国犬ぞり稚内大会).

Information

Wakkanai station is right next to the bus terminal and only a 10-minute walk from the ferry port. Internet access is hard to come by. **Tourist information counters** (☎ 22-2384; ✉ 10am-6pm) are at Wakkanai station and the **ferry port** (✉ 7am-3.30pm Jun-Sep).

Sights & Activities

Wakkanai-kōen, atop a grassy hill a few blocks from the train station, offers a number of walking trails and the **Centennial Memorial Tower**(稚内開基百年記念塔; ☎ 24-4019; admission ¥400; Ⓨ closed winter) has 360-degree views of northern Hokkaidō. On clear days even Sakhalin Island is visible. One monument is dedicated to the 22 dogs who accompanied Japan's first South Pole expedition. The park's accessible via Japan's shortest and northernmost **ropeway** (☎ 22-0833; return ¥240), or by walking up the hill. A modest **temple** is right next to the ropeway's lower terminal.

Between Wakkanai and Cape Noshappu are interesting **kelp drying yards** (they look like gravel-covered parking lots if they're not covered with kelp) along the shoreline.

Cape Noshappu (ノシャップ岬), the second-most northern point in Japan, is a nice place for a picture or a picnic, or just to watch the water for a while. If it's clear, look for the green flash as the sun slips below the horizon; if you see it, make a wish. A pleasant walk (35 minutes) or bike ride (15 minutes) away.

Cape Sōya (宗谷岬), 30km away, is the real thing: mainland Japan's most northern point. A bus leaves four times a day (¥1350, 50 minutes). Among Cape Sōya's various monuments is one dedicated to the victims of Korean Flight 007, shot down in 1983 by a Soviet fighter jet.

Busy and bustling, **Wakkanai Onsen Dōmu** (稚内温泉童夢; ☎ 28-1160; ¥600; Ⓨ 10am-10pm, closed 1st Mon of each month) is an 18-minute bus ride from the station and offers nice views of the water, though the bath itself is more functional than luxurious.

Harp seal viewing is possible in Bakkai, where 200 harp seals arrive each year and stay from November to the end of March. Rishiri-tō makes a very scenic backdrop on a clear day. A basic viewing hut (free) provides shelter, a toilet and some information about the seals. Dress warmly as the hut is a 30-minute walk from JR Bakkai Station and temperatures can be well below freezing.

Sleeping & Eating

Wakkanai isn't much for nightlife or entertainment as most of its pleasures involve getting elsewhere, but any of the following will be good if you're going to bed down for the night. The tourist counters may have additional suggestions.

Wakkanai Moshiripa Youth Hostel (稚内モシリパユースホステル; ☎ 24-0180; 2-9-5 Chūō-ku; dm ¥3360) An eight-minute walk from Wakkanai Station and close to the ferry port. Convenient and hospitable, it is sometimes closed in the winter, so phone ahead.

Wakkanai Youth Hostel (稚内ユースホステル; ☎ 23-7162; 3-9-1 Komadori; www7.plala.or.jp/komadori-house/; dm/r ¥3300/5000) Due to its spot on top of the hill it has a beautiful, commanding view of the surrounding town and ocean. While still a youth hostel, it feels more homely – like a *minshuku* rather than an institution. The onsite coin laundry is a convenience that makes it popular with motorcyclists and bike riders. Bike rental is possible (¥1000 per day). It's a 15-minute walk from Minami-Wakkanai Station.

Rider House Midori-yu (ライダーハウス緑湯; ☎ 22-4275; 1-10-23 Midori; dm ¥1000) A good place to meet other travellers, and great if you have your own bedding. Near Minami-Wakkanai Station, and close to the *sentō* (public bath).

Saihate Ryokan (さいはて旅館; ☎ 23-3556; per person ¥4000) Simple and well maintained, but a bit noisy as it's right next to the bus and ferry terminals. Offers a choice of Japanese- and Western-style rooms.

Hotel Okabe (ホテルおかべ; ☎ 22-3411; www.virtualwakkanai.net/okabe/; per person high/low season ¥8000/6000) New and pleasant, this hotel has Western-style rooms, views of the harbour, private facilities and a luxurious Japanese bath (open 24 hours for guests). It's a 10-minute walk from the station.

ANA Hotel Wakkanai (ANAホテル稚内; ☎ 23-8111; www.ana-hotel-wakkanai.co.jp; r per person low/high season ¥7900/22,000; Ⓟ ⊠ ⊠ ⊡) Tall, sleek and stylish, this place seems a bit out of place in empty Wakkanai. Wifi is available in the lobby. Depending on the season, discounted rooms may be available. The high-season price includes two meals.

Though forests are scarce, bears are apparently not, so be sure to ask first if you plan on using the camping grounds. The camping grounds (free, there are no caretakers) are near Wakkanai-kōen on the hill behind the city. There is a toilet but no showers or other facilities – rustic is the word. It may also be possible to sneak a sleeping bag out beneath the Wakkanai Dome (a concrete half-shell beside the ferry terminal) although local officials are trying

HOKKAIDŌ

to discourage this. A well-maintained **port facility** (☎ 23-4688; ☺ 9am-5pm), 10 minutes east of the ferry dock, has showers, coin laundry, a lounge and toilets. It's a good place to freshen up if you're camping or off the overnight Sapporo–Wakkanai sleeper train.

Rāmen is good here, and several local restaurants offer handmade soba noodles (*teuchisoba*). But if you're feeling adventurous, try finding a place where you can have *unidon* (sea urchin bowl) or *ikuradon* (salmon roe bowl), fresher here than anywhere else in Hokkaidō. Fans of sea urchin will find it's more like pats of butter, smooth and sweet, not at all fishy. The *ikura* will likewise melt in your mouth.

Plan on eating earlier, as even close to the station many places are closed by 9pm. A few *izakaya* brave the lonely streets behind the shopping arcade.

Getting There & Around

Wakkanai is small enough that most of the sights can be visited by foot or bicycle, available for free through **TMO** (☎ 29-0277; ☺ Mon-Fri), a Wakkanai city tourism association. Pick one up around the corner from the TMO office in the shopping arcade or, on Saturdays, at the eyeglass shop **Megane no Nagano** (長野めがね; ☎ 22-7070; in the arcade). Hours vary. A ¥1000 deposit is required, but you get it back when the bike is returned, assuming it still has two wheels.

Considering how remote it is, Wakkanai is easy to get to. Between Wakkanai and Sapporo there is one flight daily to New Chitose Airport (50 minutes) and two to Odama (one hour); both cost ¥19,500 during peak times. Wakkanai also has direct flights to Tokyo (¥37,000, 1¾ hours) and Kansai (¥44,500, 2½ hours). Buses to Wakkanai airport (35 minutes) cost ¥590.

There are a few *tokkyū* trains that travel between Wakkanai and Asahikawa (¥8070, four hours), most continue on to Sapporo (¥10,170, six hours). R-kippu cost ¥13,000 to Sapporo and S-kippu are ¥9800 to Asahikawa. There is a sleeper service (¥15,960) that leaves Sapporo at 11pm and arrives via Asahikawa in Wakkanai at 6am, in time for an early ferry to Rishiri-tō or Rebun-tō.

There are several daily buses to Sapporo (¥5750, six hours) and a daily bus to Asahikawa (¥4350, 4¾ hours). Discounted return tickets are available for both.

BOAT

The **Higashi Nihonkai Ferry** (☎ 23-3780) leaves from Wakkanai to Rishiri-tō (¥1880, 1¾ hours) and Rebun-tō (¥2100, two hours), as well as to Russia's Sakhalin Island (¥20,000). Cars are expensive, perhaps prohibitively so, costing an additional ¥9790. Parking at Wakkanai's ferry terminal is ¥1000 per night. For details about a trip to Russia, see p519.

RISHIRI-REBUN-SAROBETSU NATIONAL PARK
利尻礼文サロベツ国立公園

Comprised mainly of two islands, Rishiri-tō and Rebun-tō, just north of Wakkanai this park offers visitors superb hikes and wildflower viewing. The park also includes Sarobetsu, a swampy area near Wakkanai on the mainland, which has beautiful flowers, mainly rhododendrons, irises and lilies, in season. The peak flower-viewing time is June and July, but all three areas have various wildflowers, some quite pretty, from May through to early September.

Rishiri-tō 利尻島
☎ 01638

A near-perfect cinder cone rising like a miniature Mt Fuji from the surrounding sea, Rishiri-zan (1721m) provides numerous hiking opportunities and stunning scenery. If you're feeling energetic and have good footwear you can hike to the summit in a day. A road encircles the island and a bus service links the small fishing villages on the way.

Oshidomari and Kutsugata are Rishiri-tō's main ports; both have ferry service and **information booths** (Oshidomari ☎ 2-2201; ☺ 8am-5.30pm May-Oct; Kutsugata ☎ 4-3622; ☺ 10am-4.30pm May-Sep) that provide maps and details about transport, sights and hiking. Staff can also help you book accommodation.

HIKING

The two most reliable trails to the summit of Rishiri-zan start at Oshidomari and Kutsugata. Either trailhead is about 3km from town. A limited bus service runs to the trailheads; otherwise you must either walk (about an hour), hitch, take a taxi or arrange a ride with your lodging (some can drop you off).

Prepare properly for a mountain hike and pay particular attention to the season.

Hiking in July will be very different from October! Aim for an early start and allow about five hours each for the ascent and descent. Late June through mid-September are best. Excellent maps and hiking details (mainly in Japanese) are available at the information booths and youth hostels.

Just past the eighth station is **Rishiri-dake Yamagoya**, an unstaffed mountain hut that perches on the edge of a precipice and provides the bare minimum for a roof over your head (no water). It is possible to spend the night here but it is bloody cold, colder still with the wind-chill factor. It's also very beautiful, especially on a crystal clear night when even Sakhalin Island is visible.

If you don't feel like heading all the way to the summit there are several other hikes that are pretty but less strenuous. One of these follows the trail from Oshidomari for an hour past the Hokuroku Camping Ground towards the summit, veering left into thick forest about 10 minutes after passing a group of A-frame chalets at the end of a paved road. In 1¾ hours, this trail leads to Hime-numa, with the option of a 30-minute side trip to Pon-yama. From Hime-numa it's 6km to Oshidomari along Rte 108.

Rishiri-Fuji Onsen (☎ 2-2388; ¥400) makes the most of its plain building with Jacuzzis, mountain-view *rotemburo*, saunas and indoor baths. The *onsen* is a 30-minute walk from Oshidomari en route to the camping ground and trailhead for Rishiri-zan. A couple of buses a day (¥150, 10 minutes) pass the *onsen* from Oshidomari.

Sleeping

Most lodgings are in Oshidomari and Kutsugata. In July and August, the high season, it's wise to book well in advance.

Rishiri-tō has five camping grounds: all are open from May to October and are free unless you wish to rent a tent or cabin.

Hokuroku Camping Ground (北麓野営場; ☎ 2-2394; cabins ¥2500) Quite popular with hikers, perhaps because it's right near the Rishiri-zan trailhead.

Rishiri-shinrin-kōen camping ground (利尻森林公園キャンプ場; ☎ 4-3551; cabins ¥2500) About 25 minutes' walk from the ferry terminal.

Kutsugata-Misaki (沓形岬キャンプ場; ☎ 4-2345) Right by the ferry terminal, this camping ground is often too windy to be particularly comfortable.

Rishiri Green Hill Youth Hostel (利尻グリーンヒルユースホステル; ☎ 2-2507; dm ¥3360; ☻ Mar-Sep) About a 25-minute walk from Oshidomari-kō port or a short bus ride (¥150) to the Gurīn-Hiru-Yūsu-Hosuteru-mae stop. Staff will be able to provide info on hiking Rishiri-zan, and you can also rent bicycles.

Pension Misaki (ペンション岬; ☎ 2-1659; r per person with 2 meals ¥7500) An informal place with nice harbour-view Japanese-style rooms and a Japanese bath.

Minshuku Kutsugata-sō (民宿沓形荘; ☎ 4-2038; r per person with 2 meals ¥7000) Right in Kutsugata, about 10 minutes' walk from the ferry pier near the town's (only!) traffic light.

Rishiri Fuji Kankō Hotel (利尻富士観光ホテル; ☎ 2-1531; per person high season ¥15,000) A popular spot for those on bus tours, this new hotel has Japanese-style rooms with private facilities as well as a public, *onsen*-fed bath. The price includes two meals.

Eating

Rishiri-tō is a great place for fresh seafood of all kinds, but *uni* (sea urchin) is mouthwatering. People have been known to travel all the way from Tokyo simply to have it here. The stall **Aji-no-Ichiba** (味の市場; ☎ 2-1105; ☻ 9am-4pm late Jun-Aug) serves seafood straight from the local fishing boats to your mouth, sometimes with no cooking inbetween. Live *uni* cost ¥500. You can find the stall from the small, nondescript building next to a warehouse; exit to the right from the Oshidomari ferry terminal.

Getting There & Around

From Rishiri-tō there are one or two flights a day to Wakkanai (¥8340, 20 minutes) and Sapporo (¥17,000, 50 minutes). The island bus runs by the airport only once a day from Oshidomari (¥310, 20 minutes) or Kutsugata-kō port (¥520, 25 minutes). A taxi costs ¥1500. For details of ferry services see Wakkanai (opposite).

Buses run in both directions around the island's perimeter, completing a circuit in about two hours (¥2200). The trip from Oshidomari to Kutsugata (¥730) takes 30 to 50 minutes, depending on whether the bus stops at the airport and/or *onsen*.

Bicycling is another great way to see the island. Rent them from the youth hostels or shops near the Oshidomari ferry terminal.

HOKKAIDŌ

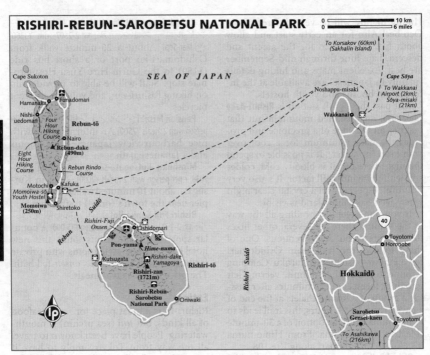

RISHIRI-REBUN-SAROBETSU NATIONAL PARK

A leisurely circuit of the island (56km) takes anywhere from five to seven hours. A 29km cycling path runs through woods and coastal plains from Oshidomari past Kutsugata.

Rebun-tō 礼文島

☎ 01638

Shaped like an arrowhead or a dead squid, Rebun Island is a naturalist's dream: fields of over 300 species of wildflower explode from May through to August; the terrain is varied and each trail is unique; and the beaches harbour all sorts of cool finds, from interesting (and edible!) marine animals to semiprecious stones. It is also a nice place to rent a scooter or motorcycle, as its one road leads past some gorgeous coastline.

The only main town is the small port of Kafuka, where the ferry arrives several times a day. From there several of the hiking trails are within walking distance, and someone at the **tourist information counter** (☎ 6-2655; ❉ 8am-5pm mid-Apr–Oct) will point out the best routes or discuss your options in detail, as well as give you maps and schedules. Assuming you start early from

Wakkanai, Rebun-tō can even be a feasible day excursion.

HIKING

Most people come to Rebun-tō to hike, whether it is the eight-hour version or some of the tamer three-hour counterparts. It's worth it to take a bus to the northern tip of the island, Cape Sukoton, and hike your way back past breathtaking cliffside vistas, fields of flowers and dwarf bamboo, thick forests, and tiny fishing villages tucked tightly into the island's many coves. It is a beautiful but isolated hike with ample opportunities to twist an ankle or worse; anyone unable to walk must be boat-rescued, so group hiking is encouraged.

A four-hour hike runs from Cape Sukoton to Nishi-uedomari, then northeast to the bus stop at Hamanaka. The common route is from north to south. Momoiwa-sō Youth Hostel and other lodgings have info about the nearby hiking options and how to get to trailheads.

Another popular hike is from Nairo, halfway down the east coast, to the top of

MINSHUKU MEALS

When you book at a remote ryokan or *minshuku* that includes one or two meals, remember that these are set courses, not pick-and-choose (especially at the small, family-run places). Be aware that this will surely include lots of seafood, shellfish, and possibly horsemeat or even whale.

If you have a particular food allergy or you simply can't stomach something for personal or religious reasons, let your host know *as soon as possible* – preferably before you book your stay, and remind them again when you arrive. Most places will try hard to accommodate you, and in most cases there is a variety of foods and several different courses; if you find a dish that you don't care for, don't complain or try to exchange it, just set it aside and focus on the others. If you're really worried, ask if a no-meal price option is possible and find a restaurant nearby.

Rebun-dake. The peak is modest by any standards (490m) but the hike is a pleasant 3½-hour return. Near the port in Kafuka there is a wildflower loop leading across a backbone of spectacular highlands to Momo-iwa (enigmatically named 'Peach Rock', as it bears far more resemblance to a breast than to its namesake fruit) and then down through flower fields and dwarf bamboo to the lighthouse at Cape Shiretoko. It's a great two-hour taste of the island's beauty for those without a lot of time.

Watch the weather carefully and plan ahead. Warm layers and raingear are recommended. Do *not*, under any circumstances, drink unpurified water, as fox faeces now contaminate the streams (foxes were introduced from Russia in the 1930s).

Sleeping & Eating

A few of the more attractive *minshuku* here no longer accept foreigners, a casualty of the food misunderstandings mentioned earlier (above), and many close on 1 September when the relatively short tourist season ends. A nice **camping ground** (☎ 7-3110; tent sites ¥300) also has cabins and bungalows.

Momoiwa-sō Youth Hostel (桃岩ユースホステル; ☎ 6-1421; dm ¥3450; ✆ Jun-Sep) Famous for hard hikes by day and camp songs and craziness until lights out at 10pm, this eclectic

youth hostel has quite a devoted following among Japanese: dedicated websites allow visitors to trade stories, some groups meet for reunions years later. Part of this may be attributed to its absolutely stunning location on Rebun's west side. It's just a few minutes' walk from several trailheads and has easy access to the rock-strewn sea. Beds are a combination of Japanese-style dorms and bunks on the 2nd floor. Staff can pick you up when the ferry docks if you call ahead: look for the flags and the enthusiastic guys yelling *okaerinasai!* (Welcome home!). If you're coming by yourself you can take a Motochi-bound bus and get off at the Yūsumae Station (15 minutes). From there it's a 17-minute walk to the hostel.

Field Inn Seikan-sō (フィールドイン星観荘; ☎ 7-2818; http://seikanso.cool.ne.jp/main/p030000.htm; dm with 2 meals ¥6000; ✆ May-Oct) More peaceful than Momoiwa-sō and also convenient for hiking. take a bus to Cape Sukoton (ask the driver to get you off at Seikan-sō). After getting off the bus, take the unpaved road to the west. Staff can pick you up at the ferry if you phone ahead.

Kāchan Yado (かあちゃん宿; ☎ 6-1406; r per person with 2 meals ¥8400) Translates to 'Mum's Place'. Warm and (according to travellers!) has nice toilets (these are in the new 'washlet' style, which allow for wash, rinse, and blow dry after the morning's business is finished). Get off the bus at the Shiretoko stop, walk five minutes along the road and the inn is on your right. Pickup at the port is also available if you call ahead.

Minshuku Shiretoko (民宿知床; ☎ 6-1335; per person with 2 meals ¥8000) Has great views of the water and the presiding Rishiri-zan beyond. To get here just get off the bus at the Shiretoko stop.

Nature Inn Hanashin (ネイチャーインはな心; ☎ 6-1648; r per person with 2 meals low/high season from ¥6800/7800) This is a popular and well-kept place. Despite the price, most rooms do not have bathroom, but it does have a new wing with a toilet and sink in each room (those rooms cost an additional ¥2000). It is a 25-minute walk from Kafuka-kō – walk toward Shimadomari and you'll find it on the left. By bus, head in the Shimadomari direction and get off at 'Youth Iriguchi'.

Hana Rebun (花礼文; ☎ 6-1177; www.hanarebun.com in Japanese; r with 2 meals ¥30,000) For honeymooners who really want to remember something special, this new, superluxury hotel offers balcony *rotemburo* in each room (a choice of porcelain or slightly pricier *hinoki* – an aromatic Japanese cypress wood often used in high-end *onsen* baths) that look out at Rishiri-tō, sunken *kotatsu* (a heated table with a cover over it to keep the legs and lower body warm) surrounded by beautiful tatami, and exquisite meals. Head right as you leave the port and Hana Rebun is about 10 minutes on the left.

Getting There & Around

From Wakkanai there are infrequent flights each day to Rebun-tō (¥9930, 20 minutes). The closest bus stop to the airport is Kūkō-shita ('Below the Airport') and you'll need to walk 15 minutes to the terminal. The ferry (two hours) leaves numerous times throughout the day.

Many lodgings will help out with rides to trailheads or the ferry port, but packing light can help make the trip more pleasant; you can leave luggage in Wakkanai's coin lockers if need be. Buses run along the island's main road from Kafuka in the south to Cape Sukuton in the north (¥1180, 70 minutes). On the way it passes the airport bus stop and Funadomari (¥900). Some routes turn here and head to Nishi-uedomari, usually four to six times a day. There are bus routes to Shiretoko (¥300, 13 minutes) and Motochi (¥440, 16 minutes) as well. Service is greatly reduced from November to April, so check the timetable at the Kafuka ferry terminal on arrival.

Bikes, scooters, motorcycles and cars can all be rented; as a last resort, hitchhiking will often get you where you need to go.

DAISETSUZAN NATIONAL PARK & ENVIRONS 大雪山国立公園

Daisetsuzan, Japan's largest national park (2309 sq km) and one of its first, consists of several stunning mountain groups, volcanoes, *onsen*, picturesque lakes and thick forests. It also includes Asahi-dake (2290m), Hokkaidō's highest peak. Those on a tight schedule should at least try to get to Asahi-dake Onsen for a quick peek, but try to give yourself two days, maybe three, if possible.

Buses come to the peak from Asahidake, Biei, Furano (all are to the west), Kamikawa (north), Kitami (east) and Obihiro (south). All have hiking information available at their

tourist information offices. There is a very detailed map of the park (in Japanese) called *Daisetsuzan Attack* (¥1200), and Lonely Planet's *Hiking in Japan* gives thorough coverage of Daisetsuzan's most spectacular hikes and how to best prepare for them.

FURANO 富良野
☎ 0167
This scenic area is famous for its lavender fields, delicious melons, excellent skiing (it is served by over a dozen resorts), and the **Heso Matsuri** (へそ祭り; Navel Festival; late July). In case you're scratching your head trying to figure out the connection between this town and belly buttons, it's because Furano is in the geographical centre of Hokkaidō: the middle.

Information

Outside Furano station there are two **information offices** (☎ 23-3388; 9am-6pm). Across the station you can rent bicycles for ¥200 per hour.

Sights & Activities

If you're not going skiing or getting behind the wheel, the **Furano Wine Factory** (ふらのワイン工場; ☎ 22-3242; 9am-4.30pm Jun-Aug, 9am-6pm Sep-May) is about 4km northwest of the station, and offers tours explaining the wine-making process. A **Grape Juice Factory** (ふらのぶどう果汁工場; ☎ 23-3033; ☾ 9am-4.30pm Jun-Sep) is nearby, about 1.5km away. Gourmands could then continue on to the **Furano Cheese Factory** (ふらのチーズ工房; ☎ 23-1156; ☾ 9am-5pm May-Oct, 9am-4pm Nov-Apr, closed 1st & 3rd Sat & Sun of each month Nov-Apr), which also includes the **Ice Milk Factory** (ふらのアイスミルク工房; ☾ 9am-5pm May-Oct). All have free admission and (excluding the Ice Milk Factory) free samples. Japanese-signage only, but it is fairly self-explanatory: just insert desired edible into your open mouth, then chew or swallow.

From June to September there are infrequent buses to most of Furano's attractions, including the famous lavender fields at **Farm Tomita** (ファーム富田; ☎ 39-3939; admission free; ☾ 9am-4.30pm Oct-late Apr, 8.30am-6pm late Apr-Sep), or the summer-only **Lavender Field station**, where a purple, lavender-flavoured, soft-serve ice-cream cone costs ¥250.

Those wanting to hit the slopes can check out **Furano Ski Jo** (富良野スキー場; ☎ 22-1111; r per person with breakfast ¥7600, standard r from ¥16,000) at the Shin Furano Prince Hotel. This is a snazzy, upscale hotel with all the fixings: numerous restaurants, a sushi bar, French, Chinese, a cafe, lounge...even its own bakery. The slopes are a mix between beginner and intermediate, with a small section devoted to advanced. Powder is good, and night skiing is available. Snowboarding is allowed on all slopes; skis, snowboards, boots, and poles can all be rented at the hotel, either as a set (¥4200) or individually (price varies). Outerwear is also available for an extra charge.

Sleeping

Minshuku, ryokan, hotels and pensions abound, but if you're planning a skiing trip it's best to book lodging through an agent, as often they have very cheap packages which include lift tickets, accommodation and sometimes train fare.

Furano Youth Hostel (ふらのユースホステル; ☎ 44-4441; www4.ocn.ne.jp/~furanoyh; dm ¥3200) Comfy and close to the station, it's in a big farmhouse with an expansive deck and their meals are made with many vegetables that they grow themselves. The hostel is also barrier free.

Rokugō Furarin Youth Hostel (らくごうふらりんユースホステル; ☎ 29-2172; www2.odn.ne.jp/rokugo-furalin/ in Japanese; dm ¥3200) This place

really feels like home. It's a nice, airy, uninstitutional place, with simple decorations that seem more like a kid's room than a hostel. Rooms have bathrooms with sinks. The breakfast is buffet style (¥600) and most ingredients are organic and locally produced. From Furano Station it's a 15-minute bus ride to the terminus at Rokugō, but you can get a free pickup at the station if you phone ahead.

Sumire Ryokan (すみれ旅館; ☎ 23-4767; per person with/without 2 meals ¥6000/4000) An informal standby, with cats and washing machines, that's only five minutes on foot from Furano Station.

Getting There & Around

Most lodgings will help you arrange transport to the ski lifts and back. You can also hoof it most of the time, as many places are close to Furano Station.

On the JR Furano line, *kaisoku* trains from Asahikawa reach Furano in 1¼ hours (¥1040), some continuing on to Obihiro (¥2420) in another two hours. Frequent local trains along this line stop at Kami-Furano (¥350, 20 minutes) and Biei (¥620, 40 minutes). Sapporo has direct *tokkyū* trains (¥4370) with S-kippu. Fairly frequent buses connect Furano with the rest of Hokkaidō as well: Asahikawa (¥860, 1½ hours) and Sapporo (¥2100, 2½ hours) are common destinations. A Lavender Express special seasonal train runs direct from Sapporo (¥4340, two hours) to Furano, daily from early June to 31 August, and on weekends and holidays from September to the end of October.

BIEI 美瑛
☎ 0166

With the dramatic Daisetsuzan mountains in the background, Biei is an artist and nature-lover's mecca. The open fields, often covered by lavender or poppies, are so different from the rest of the mainland that you'll wonder if you have left Japan and somehow ended up in rural France instead. The ubiquitous tour buses will bring you back to reality, particularly in late June and July when the flowers are at their peak. It's a fun place to visit any time of year: walking and cycling the dirt roads in summer gives way to cross-country skiing and snowshoeing in winter; and there are many coffee shops and art galleries to relax in if you want to sit down.

Information

The **tourist information building** (☎ 92-4378; www.eolas.co.jp/hokkaido/sikibiei/; ☯ 8.30am-7pm May-Oct, 8.30am-5pm Nov-Apr) is outside Biei Station. Staff here and at lodgings can supply you with cycling maps and a tourist booklet, *Hokkaidō Town of Hills Biei*, which contains an English-language map and details of local sights, outdoor activities, and even art classes if Van Gogh starts whispering in your ear. Bike rental is available at several places. Whether you walk or ride, stick to the dirt paths and roadsides: don't tramp through the farmers' fields or steal the produce that their livelihood depends upon.

Sights

There are numerous art galleries and museums in the area. One of the most famous is **Takushinkan** (拓真館; ☎ 92-3355), a lovely museum dedicated to the internationally-known photographer Shinzō Maeda (1922–98), whose stunning photographs of the Tokachi area are famous for their unusual colour and composition. The museum is a 10km-car or taxi ride from Biei in the direction of Bibaushi. The road is full of panoramic vistas of pretty hills with sunflowers, lavender, or white birches, or snow, if it's winter.

Sleeping

Most of the lodgings are set in gorgeous areas among fields or flowers, but they're not close to the station. Many will arrange to pick you up at the station if you call ahead.

Biei Potato-no-Oka Youth Hostel (美瑛ポテトの丘ユースホステル; ☎ 92-3255; www33.ocn .ne.jp/~potatovillage/; dm ¥3200) Warm and friendly English-speaking staff and comfortable bunks make this rather strangely named youth hostel a nice choice for those on a budget. Meals (extra) are also available. Star-gazing is included in their list of activities, and they also rent bikes for those looking to get away from it all.

Hoshi-no-Anne (星の庵; ☎ 92-4993; dm with 2 meals ¥5000) A Toho network member, this cosy farmhouse has Western-style accommodation amid rolling fields. Private rooms may be available in the low season; be sure to call ahead as it is sometimes closed.

Gardening House Ermitage (ガーデニングハウスエルミタージュ; ☎ 92-0991; http://lilac .hokkai.net/~erumi/ in Japanese; r per person with 2 meals ¥18,000) A comfortable place plopped in the middle of gorgeous fields. Sophisticated, and with lovely Western-style rooms, it also has delicious aromas wafting from the kitchen (all of the meals are homemade by the chef on premises). The 24-hour Jacuzzi with large picture window is a nice addition, made better by the fact that you can reserve it for private use and thus not have to share. It's a bit small, however, with only six rooms, so book ahead if you want to enjoy this upscale location.

Bibaushi Liberty Youth Hostel (美馬牛リバティユースホステル; ☎ 95-2141; www.biei.com /liberty/index-folder/liberty01.html; dm ¥3200) Visible from Bibaushi Station one stop south of Biei and accessible by foot. An attractive place near coffee shops and galleries, and in winter it offers cross-country skiing, snowshoeing and a 24-hour bath.

Getting There & Away

Biei is on the JR Furano line between Asahikawa (*futsū* ¥530, 30 minutes) and Furano (¥620, 40 minutes). From near Biei Station there are frequent buses to Asahikawa (¥570, 50 minutes).

TOKACHIDAKE, FUKIAGE & SHIROGANE ONSENS 十勝岳 吹上温泉 白金温泉

Northeast of Furano, these remote hot spring villages are less crowded than most other areas and offer good bases for hikes into Daisetsuzan National Park. You can climb the peak **Tokachi-dake** (十勝岳; 2077m) in a day; some trails extend as far as Tenninkyō Onsen or the peak Asahidake, though these require three to four days of hiking. About 3km from Tokachidake Onsen, on the road to Shorogane Onsen, Fukiage Onsen has a free, public *rotemburo* overlooking a gorge. Locals say thefts of items left in cars has occurred, so lock your doors.

Sleeping

Tokachidake Onsen has only a few places to stay. Camping is the cheapest way to go (¥350 for tent rental or ¥250 if you bring your own).

Kamihoro-sō (カミホロ荘; ☎ 0167-45-2970; r per person with 2 meals ¥9340) Large Japanese-style rooms and pleasant hot-spring baths.

Hakugin-sō (白銀荘; ☎ 0167-45-4126/3251; dm ¥2600) A dorm-style place with a nice kitchen (though no meals are served guests can cook for themselves), and beautiful baths which are open to the public for day use (¥600, 10am to 9pm). It's very close to Fukiage Onsen's public *rotemburo*.

Shirogane Onsen Shirakaba-sō (白金温泉白樺荘; ☎ 0166-94-3344; r per person ¥2550) An inexpensive option at Shirogane Onsen; rates include access to the hot-spring baths.

Hoshi-no-Akari-ya (星の灯家; ☎ 0166-94-3535; r per person with 2 meals ¥8550) New and comfortable pension with Japanese-style rooms and its own hot-spring bath.

Shirogane Onsen Hotel (白金温泉ホテル; ☎ 0166-94-3333; www7.ocn.ne.jp/~s.onsen/ in Japanese; r per person with 2 meals ¥10,000) The area's more upscale choice, with generous Japanese-style rooms and hot-spring baths that overlook a scenic gorge.

Getting There & Away

From Kami-Furano Station, it's a 45-minute bus ride to Tokachidake Onsen (¥500). Buses to Shirogane Onsen leave from Biei frequently (¥600, 30 minutes). There are also up to four buses a day direct from Asahikawa to Shirogane Onsen (¥1100, 1¼ hours).

ASAHIDAKE ONSEN 旭岳温泉
☎ 0166

This cosy, forested, hot-springs resort consists of some 10 small inns at the foot of Asahidake (2290m). At the end of the road, **Asahidake ropeway** (cable car; ☎ 68-9111; www.asahidakeropeway.com; one way/return ¥1500/2800 Jul–mid-Oct, ¥1000/1800 mid-Oct–Jun) runs to within easy hiking distance of the peak. Though Asahidake Onsen is not overdeveloped, it can become quite crowded, particularly during autumn when the leaves begin to change colour. An *onsen* map is available at the ropeway, listing the locations, prices and hours of the various baths.

Sights & Activities

Even if you're not a hiker, don't miss a chance to visit this area. It's simply spectacular, and the ropeway gives a good taste of the view. Those who enjoy hiking will love the variety of trails, many of which wind through very unique terrain that offers a mix of volcanic activity, fields, forests and foliage.

HIKING

There are dozens of hiking options in this area. The **Asahidake Visitors Centre** (☎ 97-2153; www.town.higashikawa.hokkaido.jp/vc/ in Japanese;

🕙 9am-5pm Jun-Oct, 9am-4pm Tue-Sun Nov-May) has excellent maps that the staff will mark with daily trail conditions. From June to August the flowers are at their peak; foliage turns the hills crimson and gold shortly thereafter, peaking in mid- to late September.

One popular hike follows trails from the Asahidake ropeway via several peaks to Sōunkyō Onsen. The ropeway is open from 6am to 7pm from late June to August and shorter hours for the remainder of the year.

For those without a lot of time, there is also a 1.7km loop trail that leads for about 50 minutes around the area before returning to the ropeway's upper terminal. On a clear day the views are spectacular, but even if it's cloudy or foggy, the area has an ethereal, mystical quality that is awe-inspiring, passing lakes (some of which contain the elusive Ezo-salamander), boiling pools and wildflowers. It's easy to see why this area was one of the first places to be named a national park.

There are *rotemburo* off the northern route at Nakadake Onsen; branch left at Nakadake-bunki just before ascending Nakadake. Do *not* enter Yudoku Onsen: it's poisonous. From Asahidake Onsen there's also a 5.5km trail leading through the forest in about two hours to Tenninkyō Onsen, a small hot-springs resort with a scenic gorge and the beautiful Hagoromo-no-taki (Angel's Robe Waterfall). In winter, many of the trails may be cross-country skied as well.

ONSEN

This area is famous for *onsen* for a reason, and many visitors luxuriate in the area's many baths. Most *onsen*, even at the higher-end hotels, are open for day use to the general public, but times and prices vary considerably. A useful map and guide is available from the tourist info booth at the ropeway's lower terminal. Prices range from ¥500 up to ¥1500. Bringing your own washcloth and towel can save the additional ¥200 to ¥500 rental fee.

Sleeping

If you're planning on doing lengthy day hikes, an overnight here will be much better than wasting all morning on the bus from Asahikawa.

Daisetsuzan Shirakaba-sō (大雪山白樺荘; ☎ 97-2246; http://park19.wakwak.com/~shirakaba/ in Japanese; dm ¥5190, r per person ¥7500) Both a hostel and ryokan, with separate pricing structures. Near the ropeway's lower terminal, this lodge-style place has both Japanese- and Western-style rooms and a large kitchen that one can use to cook if you prefer not to have their meals (prices do include meals). Has indoor and outdoor *onsen*.

Lodge Nutapukaushipe (☎ 97-2150; r per person with 2 meals ¥7000; ✕) One of the few non-smoking options in Japan. A cosy, log-cabin style place, it has indoor and outdoor baths with a ¥500 day-use option.

Asahidake Manseikaku Hotel Beamonte (旭岳万世閣ホテルベアモンテ; ☎ 97-2321; tw per person ¥13,275-21,150, assumes double occupancy; **P** ✕) A fancy resort hotel with giant indoor and outdoor baths, several restaurants, a well-appointed lounge, massage chairs, and nice Western- or Japanese-style rooms. Prices vary substantially depending on the season, and it can be quite full at times; calling ahead is a good plan.

Getting There & Away

For much of the year (mid-October to mid-June) the bus from Asahikawa Station to Asahidake Onsen and Tenninkyō Onsen is actually *free*. In the high season the price jumps to ¥1320, but if you spend more than ¥2000 at Asahidake Onsen (that includes lodging, a ¥2800 ropeway ticket, food…anything – just save your receipts) then you can get a coupon for a free return, available at the ropeway station's information counter. Buses from Asahikawa are infrequent and quite inconvenient for those wishing for a nice Daisetsuzan day hike: take the 9.10am bus or you'll find yourself without a lot of time. The first bus from Asahidake Onsen departs at 8.45am, the last bus is a frustratingly early 5.05pm, so keep your eye on the clock if you need to get a bus back to Asahikawa. Buses between Asahidake Onsen and Tenninkyō Onsen are always free.

SŌUNKYŌ ONSEN 層雲峡温泉
☎ 01658

Sōunkyō Onsen is a gateway for forays into the interior of the park as well as the gorge, Sōunkyō, but hikers may wish to continue to Asahidake Onsen instead of stopping here. It's mainly trails, a few seasonal attractions and some scenic views.

The **tourist information office** (☎ 5-3350; ☽ 10.30am-5pm), next to the bus station, has

several maps and English-language pamphlets. Its booking service may be useful if you arrive in high season. Just up the hill, **mountain-bike rental** is available for around ¥2000 per day. Next to the ropeway terminus, the park **visitor centre** (☎ 9-4400; http://sounkyovc.town.kamikawa.hokkaido.jp/visitor center/vc_top.html; ☽ 9am-5pm Tue-Sun) can provide information on park conditions.

After a hard day of cycling or hiking, **Kurodake-no-yu** (黒岳の湯; ☎ 5-3333; admission ¥600; ☽ 10am-6pm May-Oct, 10am-6pm Thu-Tue Nov-Apr) offers handsome hot-spring baths (including *rotemburo*), on the town's main pedestrian street. You can also soothe your aching feet in the free *ashi-no-yu* (foot bath), next to the Ginsenkaku Hotel.

Sōunkyō 層雲峡

This gorge stretches for about 8km beyond Sōunkyō Onsen and is renowned for its waterfalls – **Ryūsei-no-taki** (流星の滝; Shooting Stars Falls) and **Ginga-no-taki** (銀河の滝; Milky Way Falls) are the main ones – and for two sections of perpendicular rock columns that give an enclosed feeling – hence their names of **Ōbako** (大箱; Big Box) and **Kobako** (小箱; Little Box).

Until recently, it was possible to walk the entire 8km, but the riverside foot/bike path collapsed and may not be rebuilt. Cycling is not recommended because of hazardous tunnels. One bus runs daily to Ōbako (¥350, 35 minutes) and returns about 30 minutes later.

Hiking

The combination of a **ropeway and chairlift** (☎ 5-3031) provides fast access to **Kuro-dake** (黒岳) for hikers and sightseers. One-way/return tickets on the ropeway cost ¥900/1650 and on the chairlift ¥400/600. Hours of operation vary seasonally (8am to 7pm in July and August, closed intermittently in winter).

In fair weather, a popular hike goes to **Asahi-dake** (旭岳) from either Sōunkyō Onsen or Asahidake Onsen. You can arrange to leave your baggage at either end and pick it up later, or better yet, take advantage of the coin lockers inside Asahikawa Station before heading into the park. You could also do day hikes from the top of the Sōunkyō lift station to nearby peaks.

One bus a day leaves the trailhead for **Aka-dake** (赤岳; 2078m) at Ginsen-dai. The

Yuki Matsuri (p524), Sapporo

Assorted sashimi, Hokkaidō

Otaru Canal (p535), Otaru

MARTIN MOOS

Rebun-tō (p550), Rishiri-Rebun-Sarobetsu National Park

Ainu dance performance (p517), Shiraoi

MARTIN MOOS

Asahi-dake, Daisetsuzan National Park (p552)

JEFF CANT

bus leaves Sōunkyō Onsen at 7.35am and returns from Ginsen-dai at 2.15pm (¥800, one hour), leaving you plenty of time for your ascent and descent.

Festivals & Events

Hyōbaku Matsuri (氷爆祭り; Ice-Waterfall Festival; February & early March) The festival features ice sculptures, tunnels and domes, some lit up.

Kyōkoku Hi Matsuri (峡谷火祭り; Kyōkoku Fire Festival; last Saturday in July) This celebration is meant to purify the hot springs and appease the mountain and fire deities. Revellers perform traditional Ainu owl dances and drumming, climaxing with archers shooting flaming arrows into the gorge.

Sleeping

Sōunkyō Youth Hostel (層雲峡ユースホステル; ☎ 5-3418; www.youthhostel.or.jp/sounkyo/; dm ¥2800; ☺ Jun-Oct) Dwarfed by the Prince and Taisetsuzan hotels, this hostel is about a 10-minute walk uphill from the bus station. Mostly bunk-bed accommodation, it has information on trails in the park, organises hikes and rents out gear for braving the elements.

Minshuku Midori (民宿みどり; ☎ 5-3315; r per person with 2 meals ¥6500) On the main pedestrian street, this place is tiny and creaky. It has clean Japanese-style rooms and bathing a few doors down at Kurodake-no-yu.

Ginsenkaku (銀泉閣; ☎ 5-3003; www.ginsenkaku .com; r per person with 2 meals high/low season from ¥15,000/8000). Ginsenkaku is a professional operation across from Minshuku Midori that has some English- speaking staff, Japanese-style rooms with full facilities (ie bathroom with bath, toilet, and sink), and nice common baths, including *rotemburo*.

Getting There & Away

Buses from Sōunkyō Onsen run approximately every hour via JR Kamikawa Station to Asahikawa (¥1900, two hours) – rail pass holders can save money by transferring to the bus at Kamikawa (¥770). Up to four buses a day run direct to Kitami (¥2500, two hours), where you can transfer for connections to Bihoro (¥530, 30 minutes) or Abashiri (¥1040, one hour). From May to October, there are up to three buses a day from Bihoro to Kawayu Onsen in Akan National Park (¥2690, two to 2¾ hours).

From Sōunkyō Onsen there are two buses a day to Kushiro (¥4790, five hours) via Akan Kohan (¥3260, 3¼ hours) in Akan National Park. There are also two buses a day to Obihiro (¥2200, 2¼ hours) that follow a scenic route via Nukabira-ko.

DŌ-TŌ (EASTERN HOKKAIDŌ) 道東

ABASHIRI 網走

☎ 0152 / pop 41,500

To most Japanese, Abashiri is as synonymous with the word prison as Alcatraz is to Westerners. Mention of the prison (still in operation) once sent chills through the spines of even the most hardened criminals. Winters here are as harsh as they come. The town's economy now depends on fishing, tourism, and trade with Russia, its nearest neighbour.

The closest major city to Shiretoko, Abashiri is a good hub for hikers, but the winter ice floes, the September coral grass, its Abashiri Prison Museum (not to be confused with the prison itself) and its Northern Peoples' Museum are also worthwhile.

In the dead of winter, when up to 80% of the sea is ice-clogged, **Aurora icebreaker sightseeing boats** (流氷観光砕氷船オーロラ; ☎ 43-6000) depart four to six times a day from Abashiri port for one-hour cruises (¥3000) into the Sea of Okhotsk. In summer, the northern coastal areas are a pretty, easy walk, perfect for picture-taking, with lots of sand-dollars and other small shells.

Information

The **tourist information office** (☎ 44-5849; www2s .biglobe.ne.jp/~abashiri/e/index_e.html; ☺ 9am-5pm) outside Abashiri Station has the excellent *Okhotsk Abashiri Tourist Guide*, maps and discount coupons for several of the local attractions.

Sights & Activities

Tento-zan, the main mountain presiding over Abashiri, is steep enough that its 5km climb will leave you winded unless you're going by bus or car. At the top, however, are some excellent views, a park and several nice museums. A cycling road runs for 25km from Abashiri proper to the coral grass viewing areas and beyond, providing some beautiful views of the area's lakes, forests and pumpkin fields.

Abashiri Prison Museum (網走監獄博物館; ☎ 45-2411; www.ryuhyo.com/kangoku2; admission ¥1050) details many of the reasons why this prison was so feared. For example, inmates braved brutally cold winters with thin bedding and very little heat – one lone pipe ran the length of the corridors, providing almost no heat for those in the cells but a decent amount for the wardens. Unfortunately, the English signs here are quite difficult to understand (as is the website, although the pics are useful), making it harder to get the most from the exhibits, which are worthwhile.

Abashiri Prison (網走刑務所), across the river and still a working penitentiary, has a **gift shop and tiny museum** (☎ 43-3167; ⏰ 9am-4pm) where crafts made by inmates can be purchased. It's also possible to walk around outside the prison walls, though further entry and photographs are prohibited.

Hokkaidō Museum of Northern Peoples (北方民族博物館; ☎ 45-3888; www.ohotuku26.or.jp/hoppohm/index2.html in Japanese; admission ¥450; ⏰ Tue-Sun) is a few minutes' walk downhill from the summit of Tento-zan. It is a state-of-the-art place with numerous exhibits of Ainu culture, as well as Native American, Aleutian and other indigenous peoples. An English pamphlet and small signs help visitors make the most of their tour.

Recently renovated, the unique **Okhotsk Ryūhyō Museum** (オホーツク流氷館; Museum of Ice Floes; ☎ 43-5951; www.ryuhyokan.com/; admission ¥520; ⏰ 8am-6pm Apr-Oct, 9am-4.30pm Nov-Mar) has odd ice-related exhibits. One of the more interesting is a display relating to the tiny *kurione*, a funky relative of the sea slug that is sort of an Abashiri mascot.

Iceberg diving (☎ 61-5102; www.tar2uga.co.jp; per day, 2 dives ¥30,000; ⏰ winter) will bring you face-to-face with that odd mollusc, the *kurione*.

Stare out at the frozen landscape while grilling your preferred foods and drinking an (alcoholic) beverage of your choice in the **Ryūhyō Norokko Sightseeing Train** (流氷のろっこ観光列車; admission ¥810; ⏰ late Feb-late Mar). Steel yourself for the cold (dress warmly) and for the aroma of dried toasted *surume* (squid), as both are part and parcel of this interesting ride.

Wakka GenseiKaen (ワッカ原生花園; ⏰ May-Oct) is the biggest coastal wildflower field in Japan. The flower garden is 20km long and up to 700m wide, and boasts more than 300 species. The garden is 60 minutes' bus ride from Abashiri station; take a bus from stop No 2.

If you're looking to spend a day on the slopes, you'll find powder at **Kamui Ski Links** (カムイスキーリンクス; ☎ 72-2311; www.kamui-skilinks.com; ⏰ winter).

Festivals

Orochon-no-Hi (オロチョンの火; last Saturday in July) A fire festival derived from the shamanistic rites of the indigenous Gilyak people, who once lived in the Abashiri area.

Coral Grass Viewing (サンゴ草群落地; mid-September) Known as salt pickle or glasswort in other parts of the world, this humble marsh plant gets its 15 minutes of fame in mid-September, when it turns bright red. Busloads of tourists flock to a few boardwalk viewing spots. Nature-lovers will enjoy the bird life, as the marshes attract not only seagulls, but curlews, terns, egrets, herons and more.

Come Back Salmon Night (カムバックサーモンナイト; mid-October and mid-December, depending on the fishes' schedule) A welcome to the lake's most famous (and delicious!) fish. Each year the salmon run upstream, greeted by bright spotlights that illuminate the fish as they pass into Abashiri Lake. Nearby grilling stations serve *sanma* (a dark, oily, and delicious seasonal fish that's distantly related to mackerel, but smaller), scallops, squid and venison, often with free tastes. No salmon – the guest of honour – is served...*that* night anyway.

Sleeping

Abashiri Gensei-kaen Youth Hostel (網走原生花園ユースホステル; ☎ 46-2630; http://sapporo.cool.ne.jp/genseikaen; dm ¥3050) In the middle of a wildflower preserve, the hostel offers nice views of Shari-dake and Shiretoko-hantō. It is a good idea to call ahead as the open hours vary.

Minshuku Hokui 44 (民宿ほくい44; ☎ 44-4325; www11.plala.or.jp/hokui44/ in Japanese; dm ¥4300) This *minshuku* is a Toho network member and offers dorm-style beds. The rate includes two meals and free admission (and a ride) to the nearby *onsen* hotel. If you phone ahead, someone will pick you up at the station and save you the 20-minute walk; however, no English is spoken.

Abashiri Central Hotel (網走セントラルホテル; ☎ 44-5151; www.abashirich.com; s/d ¥7300/15,700; ⓟ ⓧ ⓓ) Another nearby option, LAN access is available in the lobby and restaurant. Rooms are equipped with fridge, PJs, slippers, and even shaving kits. Unlike some hotels, this place accepts all major credit cards.

Hotel Shinbashi (ホテル新橋; ☎ 43-4307; s/tw ¥6000/10,000) Right across from Abashiri Station, this is a classy place with both Japanese- and Western-style rooms.

Eating

There are small eateries in the side streets along the main arcade that runs the length of Abashiri, but the ones that aren't snack/whiskey bars close early. There are the usual *rāmen* shops, *izakaya* and *yakiniku* places.

Kandoū Asa-ichi fish market (感動朝市; ☎ 43-6562; ☯ 6.30am-9.30am Mon-Fri, 6.30am-10.30am Sat & Sun; mid-Jul–31 Oct) A great option for fresh fish lovers: select your own seafood and cook it on one of the open-air grills. Free shuttles leave from several major hotels; ask your lodging for details. Salmon (which can be fished right out of the river!) is superb.

Abashiri Beer Kan (網走ビール園; ☎ 45-5100; meals ¥700-2000) A microbrewery with various flavours on tap; offers mainly Western-style food, but some Japanese entrees, including a crab special, are also available.

Murakami (むらかみ; ☎ 43-1147; www.drive -net.com/murakami/in Japanese; from ¥1500) Delicious sushi in a small, Japanese-style place. The owner changes the menu daily based on what's fresh from the boat each morning. In season, *sanma*, a thin, oily fish somewhat like mackerel, is fantastic.

Getting There & Away

Memanbetsu airport links Abashiri with Sapporo, Fukuoka, Nagoya, Osaka and Tokyo. Airport buses (¥750, 30 minutes) are approximately timed to flights and run from the bus station via Abashiri Station (they're about 1km apart) to the airport.

Abashiri is the terminus for the JR Seki-hoku main line, which runs across the centre of Hokkaidō to Asahikawa (*tokkyū*, ¥7240, 3¾ hours). Local trains run along the same route and stop at Bihoro (¥530, 30 minutes) and Kitami (¥1040, 1¼ hours). From May to October there are up to three buses a day from Bihoro to Kawayu Onsen in Akan National Park (¥2690, about 2½ hours). From Kitami you can catch buses to towns near Daisetsu-zan National Park (¥2500, two hours).

Abashiri is the terminus for the JR Senmō main line, which runs east to Shiretoko-Shari Station and then south to Kushiro. One direct bus daily links Abashiri and Shari (¥1120, 65 minutes).

Direct buses from Abashiri to Sapporo (¥6210, six hours) leave from the bus terminal, a 10-minute ride east of Abashiri Station. Between June and mid-October there are three buses from Memanbetsu airport via Abashiri to Utoro in Shiretoko National Park (¥2800, 2¼ hours).

Renting a car may be the best option for those needing to make it to the remoter sections of Shiretoko-hantō or Akan. Rental agencies are located near the station, and you must have a valid international driver's licence.

A ¥900 ticket gives all-day entry on a tourist-loop bus which stops at many of the major sites, including the museums (not the coral grass), as well as the bus and train terminals. Bikes may also be rented right in front of the station, though you should make sure they inflate the tires well if you're heading up Tento-zan or out to the coral grass areas.

AKAN NATIONAL PARK 阿寒国立公園

This expansive park (905 sq km) contains volcanic peaks, large caldera lakes and thick forests. Its scenic views attract over 6.6 million visitors per year, but it is big enough that even at peak times there are ways to get away from it all, particularly if you're looking to hike or meander around the forest trails. There are numerous day-hike options and a few longer ones. Bears are a possible problem, and foxes, both common and cunning, often steal unguarded food or even sleeping bags.

The main access points are Abashiri and Bihoro to the north, and Kushiro to the south. Kawayu Onsen and Akan Kohan are its two main towns. Teshikaga (aka Mashū Onsen) is a useful transport hub.

Akan Bus Company provides tours and a running commentary (in Japanese) about the sights and attractions, stopping here and there for picture-taking at some of the most scenic viewpoints. If that's unappealing to you, rent a car and don't look back. With your own wheels you'll be free to travel anywhere, even to hop over to Shiretoko National Park.

Kawayu Onsen 川湯温泉
☎ 01548

A quiet *onsen* town, Kawayu has numerous *ashiyu* (foot *onsen*) where travellers can

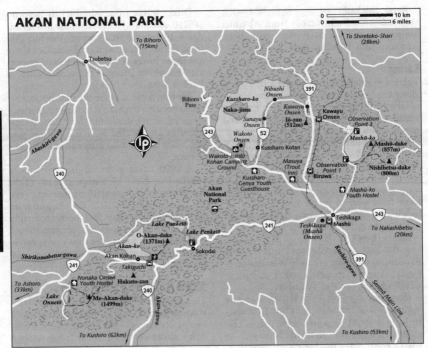

AKAN NATIONAL PARK

soak tired feet in hot water, in addition to the usual spas. Often free, they are sprinkled throughout the town and there is even one in the town's JR station.

The **tourist information office** (☎ 3-2255; ◷ 9am-6.30pm Jun-Sep, 9am-5pm Oct-May) is about 10 minutes on foot from the Kawayu bus station, and a good source of information. Pick up a copy of the English-language *Teshikaga English Guide Map*, and if you need to, ask the staff to help you book accommodation. Mashū, a little further south, is an alternate access point for the park and may actually be closer to some of the following attractions.

SIGHTS & ACTIVITIES

Koki Taiho Sumō Memorial Hall (川湯相撲記念館; ☎ 2-2924; admission ¥310) Sumo fans will enjoy this small museum, dedicated to a hometown hero.

Iō-zan (硫黄山) is a hellish mountain with steaming vents, sunshine-yellow sulphur and *onsen*-steamed eggs. You'll hear the sellers calling *Tamago! Tamago! Tamago! Tamago!* (Eggs!) even before you reach the parking lot. Though highly touted and a

sickly brownish-green, they don't taste much different from a regular kitchen-boiled egg.

The walk from Kawayu JR Station to Kawayu Onsen (4km) is very pretty and passes Iō-zan along the way (1.5km). Its birches, stunted pines and other greenery can be pretty any time of year but are particularly nice in the autumn months of August and September.

Mashū-ko (摩周湖) is considered by many to be Japan's most beautiful lake, and it once held the world record for water clarity – 35m. The island in the middle was known by the Ainu as 'Isle of the Gods', a place well worth visiting. Unfortunately, it is frequently foggy, and while still pretty it is less spectacular without the gorgeous view.

Kussharo-ko (屈斜路湖), the other major lake, is famous for its swimming, boating and volcanically-warmed sands. Naka-jima is the aptly named 'middle island' that's in the centre of the lake, which has its own version of the Loch Ness monster, named Kusshi. No one has yet claimed it to be a hoax, so if you're a Nessie fan, at least here in Hokkaidō you still have hope.

Sunayu Onsen (砂湯温泉), a stretch of hot sand along the edge of Kussharo-ko, has too many souvenir stands, paddle boats and tourist-trap kitsch to really be worth it; however, there's a totally deserted spot along the roadside where the sand is as hot or hotter: look for the inconspicuous pullout near where the sidewalk ends. It's a small circle of rocks and if you take your shoes and socks off you'll be in for a warm wade. Dig your feet down in the sand for something even hotter.

Wakoto Onsen (和琴温泉), on the southern shore, is famous for hot springs that bubble into open-air pools.

A **Museum of Ainu Folklore** (屈斜路コタンアイヌ民族資料館; ☎ 4-2128; admission ¥310; ☿ Apr-Dec) is located at **Kussharo Kotan** and displays tools and crafts.

Cycling is a good way to get around, though one should be sure to check distances carefully before a lengthy ride. Mashū-ko is a steep climb…and a quick return. Bikes can be rented at the bus station, Kawayu Onsen JR Station or at the gas station down the street (per two hours ¥600).

SLEEPING

Camping is an option, as there are seven camping grounds in the vicinity.

Wakoto-hantō Kohan Camping Ground (和琴半島湖畔キャンプ場; ☎ 4-2835; tent sites ¥400, cabins ¥4500; ☿ mid-Apr–Oct) is one of the nicest. Spartan cabins, canoes and kayaks are also available for rent, and it's accessible by bus from Mashū, Bihoro and Kawayu Onsen. This area is also accessible by train from Kushiro city, a do-able day trip.

Mashū-ko Youth Hostel (摩周湖ユースホステル; ☎ 2-3098; www.masyuko.co.jp; dm ¥3200; ☿ Jan-Nov, hrs vary Dec; 🖳 per 30min ¥100) A handsome farmhouse south of Mashū-ko. If you know you will arrive after 4pm call ahead for a lift.

Kussharo-Genya Youth Guesthouse (屈斜路原野ユースゲストハウス; ☎ 4-2609; www.gogo genya.com; dm from ¥3500; ☿ Jan-Mar, May-Oct) Fancier than the average hostel and surrounded by pretty farmland.

Minshuku Nire (民宿にれ; ☎ 3-2506; r per person with breakfast ¥4000; ☿ May-Sep) A warm and longstanding favourite, it is right in Kawayu Onsen. Toilets are Japanese-style, but it has other charms. Look for the glaring green-and-white sign for the Kōzan-sō Hotel; Nire is the smaller one on the right.

Onsen Minshuku Nibushi-no-Sato (温泉民宿にぶしの里; ☎ 3-2294; www1.ocn.ne.jp/~kussie; r per person with 2 meals ¥7500) Log-cabin feel and casual, with mountain bikes for rent and a nice indoor, lake-view hot-springs bath.

Masuya (鱒や; Trout Inn; ☎ 2-5489; dm with 2 meals ¥5500) Toho network member. The owner loves trout fishing and is happy to talk shop with fellow flycasters. Call ahead for pickup at Mashū station.

Misono Hotel (御薗ホテル; ☎ 3-2511; www.sip .or.jp/~misono/; high/low season with 2 meals ¥12,000/ 8000, without meals from ¥6800) Luxurious hot-spring baths, private facilities (bath, toilet and sink) and a choice of Western- or Japanese-style rooms. A free *ashiyu* outside marks the parking lot.

EATING

Genpei (源平; ☎ 3-3338; 1-5-30 Kawayu Onsen; dishes ¥600-1000) A clear choice in Kawayu Onsen, an atmospheric *izakaya* redolent with the aromas of *robatayaki* and *rāmen*.

Marukibune (丸木舟; ☎ 4-2644; dishes ¥400-1500; ☿ 11am-8pm) Next door to the Museum of Ainu Folklore in Kussharo Kotan. Their 'white *rāmen*' (noodles in milk broth) is unique and fun. Gourmands looking for adventure will enjoy the sashimi of *parimono* (a local river fish): so fresh that the head arrives still moving. Ainu music performances (¥3000) are given on certain Saturday nights, be sure to call for a reservation as seating is limited.

The Great Bear (グレートベア; ☎ 2-3830; breakfast ¥800, dinner ¥1000-1500) The 'de facto' hall of the Mashū-ko Youth Hostel. Serves a variety of food, including steaks and curry with rice, but make sure your dinner is ordered before 7pm.

GETTING THERE & AROUND

The JR Senmō main line runs north from Kawayu Onsen to Shiretoko-Shari (*kaisoku* ¥900, 45 minutes) and south to Kushiro (*kaisoku* ¥1790, 1½ hours) via Mashū Station. Kawayu Onsen Station is a 10-minute bus ride from the town centre (¥280) but the buses are infrequent, and while they are timed to meet most of the trains there is not much time to transfer. A soak in the *ashiyu* or a quick trip to the restroom may leave you with a long wait…or walk instead.

From Kawayu Onsen bus station there are up to three buses a day to Bihoro (¥2690, about 2½ hours). The Bihoro service runs via scenic Bihoro Pass, and some of these buses continue onward to the Memanbetsu Airport. These buses also pass Nibushi, Sunayu and Wakoto Onsen.

Between May and October a sightseeing bus service runs four times a day from Kawayu Onsen bus station via the main sights in the park to Akan Kohan (¥3250, 2¼ hours). The bus makes stops for sightseeing and picture-taking (all the major places are covered). If you're low on time and don't mind a tour then this is a nice way to see the area.

Buses between Kawayu Onsen and Mashū Station cost ¥1720. Direct buses between Mashū Station and Wakoto-hantō (¥880, 35 minutes) pass the turn-offs for the Trout Inn, Sussharo Genya Youth Guesthouse and the camping ground at Wakoto-hantō.

Between Mashū Station and Akan Kohan is a particularly scenic stretch on Rte 241, with an outstanding lookout at Sokodai that overlooks the lakes Penketō and Panketō.

Bikes can also be rented: a fun, relaxed and healthy way to get around.

Akan Kohan 阿寒湖畔
☎ 0154

Busy Akan Kohan has one of the largest Ainu *kotan* settlements in Hokkaidō and is a hot spot for anyone interested in the ancient culture. The resort area isn't scenic, but the trails are a great getaway. The **tourist information office** (☎ 67-3200; ☉ 9am-6pm) has pamphlets about the park in English, including excellent alpine trail guides with contour maps of O-Akan-dake and Me-Akan-dake.

SIGHTS & ACTIVITIES
The Ainu village is on the western side of town. At the top of the hill is the **Ainu Seikatsu Kinenkan** (アイヌ生活記念館; ☎ 67-2727; admission ¥300; ☉ 10am-10pm May-Oct), but it's so small that it will be a disappointment if you've already seen other Ainu exhibits elsewhere. **Onnechise** (オンネチセ; admission ¥1000) is next door and better value: Ainu dance performances take place six times a day in the high season (shows are at 11am, 1pm, 3pm, 8pm, 9pm and 10pm from April to October, and at least once a day the rest of the year (there are only one or two shows at night during winter). The **Akan Forest & Lake Culture Museum** (森と湖の芸術館; ☎ 67-2001; admission ¥500; ☉ 10am-5pm May-Oct) has

more Ainu exhibits, and the friendly staff are happy to explain exhibits, run the slide show and offer you a cup of coffee.

Akan-ko is famous for *marimo (Cladophora aegagropila)*, spheres of algae that are both biologically interesting (it takes as much as 200 years for them to grow to the size of a baseball) and very *kawaii* (cute). Only growing in a few places in the world, Akan *marimo* became endangered after being designated a national treasure: suddenly, everyone in Japan wanted one. The building of a power plant (which lowered the lake level several inches) did not help the plight of these green, benthic fuzzballs. The Ainu finally came to the rescue by starting the **Marimo Matsuri** (まりも祭り), held in mid-October, which returns *marimo* to Akan-ko, one by one. Their numbers are growing but they are sometimes affected by natural disasters: typhoons can push as much as 50% of them out of the lake. Luckily, locals quickly return them to the water as soon as the winds have subsided.

The **Akan Kohan Eco-Museum Center** (阿寒湖畔エコミュージアム; ☎ 67-4100; admission free; ☉ Wed-Mon) is a good way to see *marimo* up close without spending a bundle on the **boat trip** (☎ 67-2511; ¥1220). The museum has nice exhibits and a number of *marimo* in aquarium tanks. It also has hiking maps and exhibits about the local flora and fauna.

Hiking
About 6km east of Akan Kohan is **O-Akandake** (雄阿寒岳; Male Mountain; 1371m). Buses to Kushiro pass the Takiguchi trail entrance five minutes out of Akan Kohan. The ascent takes a fairly arduous 3½ hours and the descent takes about another 2½ hours. From the peak there are very fine views of the lakes Penketō and Panketō, and in summer the top is covered with alpine wildflowers. On clear days one can even see as far as Daisetsuzan National Park.

The highest mountain in the park, **Me-Akandake** (雌阿寒岳; Female Mountain; 1499m), is an active volcano and is often closed due to emissions of poisonous gas. Ask at the tourist information office about current conditions and pay careful attention to noxious effects of sulphur fumes as you hike.

Shorter, the climb to the observation platform on Hakutō-zan (650m) affords fine views of the lakes and the surrounding peaks. The trail starts at the Akan Kohan skiing ground, 2km south of town. The ascent takes about an hour, winding through birch and fir forests and past several groups of bubbling sulphur hot springs (too hot to bathe in, do not try!).

SLEEPING

There are a number of small *minshuku* in the Akan Kohan area.

Nonaka Onsen Youth Hostel (野中温泉ユースホステル; ☎ 0156-29-7454; Ashoro-chō Moashoro 159; dm ¥2700) Provides Japanese-style rooms, its own *onsen* and a base for climbing. Often booked in advance, so make reservations early.

Minshuku Kiri (民宿桐; ☎ 67-2755; www10.plala .or.jp/kiriminsyuku/in Japanese; 4-3-26 Akan Onsen; r per person with 2 meals ¥5500) Above a souvenir shop, opposite the Emerald Hotel. Famous for its hot-spring baths.

Yamaguchi (山口; ☎ 67-2555; www.tabi-hokkaido .co.jp/~yamaguchi; 5-3-2 Akan Onsen; r per person with 2 meals ¥5500) Clean and friendly with nice hot-spring baths.

New Akan Hotel Shangri-la (ニュー阿寒ホテルシャングリラ; ☎ 67-2121; www.newakanhotel .co.jp; d per person with 2 meals ¥11,700) Nice baths set this place apart, and it has both Japanese- and Western-style room options. At the same time, a fake planetarium in the lobby – though impressive – is a bit over the top.

Hotel Akanko-sō (ホテル阿寒荘; ☎ 67-2231; www.akanko.com; Akan Onsen 1-5-10) Hotel Akanko-sō is another option.

KUSHIRO SHITSUGEN NATIONAL PARK 釧路湿原国立公園

Japan's largest expanse of undeveloped marshland (269 sq km), this wetland is nearly the size of Tokyo and provides shelter for thousands of different species of wildlife. Among them is the *tanchō-zuru* (red-crested white cranes), a traditional symbol of both longevity and Japan. They're also just plain cool, and several nice viewing areas let you watch these enormous birds in relative comfort as they land, feed, tend their young or do their mating dance. The peak crane season is winter or early spring, but even in August a few stragglers may be around if you're lucky. Binoculars are a must for any serious bird-watchers. Those staying at the Kushiro Shitsugen Tōro Youth Hostel can use their spotting scope for free.

The park has a slow **scenic train** (with wood-finished cars) which runs along the eastern edge and provides good views of the marsh; the *futsū* train also follows the same tracks. Sit on the left for unhindered glimpses of the marsh.

Deer are so common in this area that the trains have a special *shika-bue* (deer whistle) to scare them off. To see wildlife, take a night train and stand in the front to look out at the tracks. You're sure to see deer, foxes are common, and other animals as well. It's an unorthodox but effective way to see wildlife, and (usually) the beasts have the sense to stay off the tracks as the train passes by.

The park is best reached by train from Kushiro, the nearest large city, about 20 minutes away. You can take either of the trains listed to **Hosooka Observatory** (細岡展望台; ☎ 40-4455; admission free; ☯ 9am-7pm summer, 9am-5pm winter) on the eastern side, or a bus (¥1320, 35 minutes) to the **Kushiro Observatory** (釧路湿原展望台; ☎ 56-2424; admission ¥360; ☯ 8.30am-6pm summer, 9am-5pm winter) on the west. The former is atop an overlook where one can appreciate the grand scale of this wetland preserve.

Sleeping & Eating

Kushiro has a number of inns, hotels, *minshuku* and ryokan. It is also the birthplace of *robatayaki* (meat or seafood slow-grilled over hot charcoal). Many Kushiro restaurants specialise in this kind of cuisine.

Kushiro Royal Hotel (釧路ロイヤルホテル; ☎ 31-2121; www.royalinn.jp; low season s/d with Internet booking ¥5000/7200; ⓟ 🗙 🖭) The rooms are what one expects in a business hotel, small but efficient, and it's (literally) a stone's throw from the station. The breakfast, served on the top floor with nice views if you can get a windowside table, is wonderful. Coffee, tea and several kinds of '100%' juice all help to make the morning feel like home. In addition, while there are Japanese-style foods (*onigiri*, *mōningu sarada* and miso soup) there is also a bread bar with a selection of rolls, breads and muffins, all of which are served warm. It's the perfect way to start a day of hard sightseeing, and a shame that other comparable business hotels haven't seen fit to follow suit.

Kushiro Shitsugen Tōro Youth Hostel (釧路湿原塘路ユースホステル; ☎ 87-2510; www.sip.or .jp/~tohro/sub1.htm in Japanese; dm ¥3150) Recently redone and very spick-and-span, this comfortable, cosy youth hostel is more like a *minshuku*, and as such is a great deal. Meals are delicious and the bunk-style rooms are big enough that you won't feel cramped. A viewing deck and excellent train station access make it even more convenient, though it can be noisy due to its proximity to the tracks.

Nagoyaka-Tei (なごやか亭; ☎ 24-2033; 15-18 Shinkawa; plates from ¥120) A conveyor-belt sushi place that's very popular. It specialises in sushi that's fancier and more eye-catching than most of the normal *nigiri*. You may have to take a taxi or rent a bike to get here, as the it's quite a way from the station.

Kawamura (川村; ☎ 22-5692; 1-12 Banchi; meals ¥1500-2500) Where salarymen come when they're tired of *izakayas* and just want good Japanese cooking. Packed after 6pm…for good reason: platters of specialities are set around the counter, easy to point at when something looks good. Sake is served the way it should be: overflowing into a *masu* (a measuring cup made of *hinoki* wood). The mackerel-in-miso is superb. From the station, turn left and look for the small alley behind the Tōkyū Inn (visible on your right). Follow the alley and turn left at the first intersection. Kawamura will be on your right, just after you turn.

Washō Market (和商市場; ☎ 22-3226; www.washoichiba.com; 25-13 Kurokane-chō; items from ¥200; ⏰ 8am-6pm Mon-Sat) Just to the right of Kushiro Station on the corner after Lawson convenience store, this impressive market features every possible seafood one can imagine, plus a food court of *bentō* boxes and other prepared dishes. It's a great place to buy a rice bowl and add your own toppings as *o-bāsan* (grandmotherly women) hand out treats for you to try.

TSUBETSU 津別

This town is quiet and peaceful in summer but gets packed with powder-hungry people in winter because it offers some of the nicest views you'll find on slopes anywhere. Tear down the slopes while overlooking Kussharo-ko, a beautiful volcanic lake with milky-blue water. Warm up in one of the many lodges, which despite the miso soup (as well as hot chocolate!) will feel to many skiers as comfy as a lodge back home.

Tsubetsu Ski Slope (津別スキー場; ⏰ 0152-76-2222; ⏰ 9am-4.30pm) has rental equipment

and a large, six-person gondola which whisks you to the top in 10 minutes.

SLEEPING & EATING
Despite the views, this is a relatively small community so there are not a lot of options. Book ahead to ensure a space.

Farmstay Tierra (☎ 01527-6-2463; r with/without 2 meals ¥5775/3675) A quaint, clean, comfortable place that is closer to a youth hostel than a hotel. There's a spacious communal dining area, and the family that runs it is very helpful and can share a lot of its knowledge about the area, including where to go for the best powder. Meals are Japanese style. In summer it offers various 'farmstay' programs for children and foreigners, so you can arrange to try your hand in the fields if you're not here when the ski slopes are open.

Hotel Forester (☎ 0152-76-3333; r from ¥10,000) A standard ski lodge close to the slopes. It offers camping out back (¥500). Soak away your soreness in the *onsen* after a long day on the slopes.

21 Century Forest Camp Spot (☎ 0152-76-2151) This is another camping option (if you're not here in winter), camping here is free, but a ¥100 donation to assist with cleaning is suggested. It's a family car–camp kind of place; don't expect a lot of communing with nature.

GETTING THERE & AWAY
There's only one bus service in the morning and one in the afternoon from Kitami (¥950, 30 minutes) and from Kushiro via Akan (¥3000, 2½ hours) by **Akan Bus** (in Kitami ☎ 0157-23-2181; ⏰ 7am-6pm). In winter check before you depart for road conditions.

SHARI 斜里
☎ 01522
Shari is the closest train stop to Shiretoko-hantō (an hour's ride away). It's small enough that unless you miss the bus you probably won't need to stay here, but the **tourist information office** (☎ 3-2424; ⏰ 10am-5pm mid-Apr–mid-Oct) near the train station can provide maps and book accommodation.

Koshimizu Gensei Kaen (小清水原生花園; ☎ 63-4187; admission free; ⏰ closed Nov-Apr) is an 8km stretch of wildflowers along the coast, only 20 minutes from Shiretoko Shari. Visit in late June to catch it at its peak: over 40 flowers simultaneously blooming.

If you need to spend the night, try:

Kurione (クリオネ; ☎ 3-1889; tent & 1 person ¥800, per additional person ¥400) A camping ground about 25 minutes' walk from the station.

Ryokan Tanakaya (旅館たなかや; ☎ 3-3165; r per person with 2 meals ¥7000) Another option.

Shari Central Hotel (斜里セントラルホテル; ☎ 3-2355; r per person ¥6300) Convenient and well-maintained.

Infrequent trains connect Shiretoko-Shari Station with Abashiri (*futsū* ¥810, 45 minutes) and Kushiro (*kaisoku* ¥2730, two hours). Shari's bus centre is to the left as you exit the station. There are between five and nine buses daily, year-round to Utoro (¥1490), but only three in summer that continue on as far as Iwaobetsu (¥1770, 70 minutes).

SHIRETOKO NATIONAL PARK
知床国立公園

The peninsula that makes up Shiretoko National Park was known in Ainu as 'the end of the world', and it's aptly named. As remote as Japan gets, this magnificent park has no paved roads within its boundaries save for a short northwest–southeast road that connects the town of Utoro (on the northwestern edge) with Rausu (on the southern side); two-thirds of the park has no roads at all. The hiking trails to Cape Shiretoko are for expert hikers only: remote and poorly maintained, they wind over slippery boulders and disappear at times on cliff sides. If the weather turns frigid or you slip and break an ankle, you'll need to hope that a passing fishing boat spots you before the bears do.

Boat rides (☎ 4-2147; ¥6000) can be an option for those who want to see Cape Shiretoko but who can't make the hike. It's an expensive 3¾-hour trip over possibly rough seas, and while the cliffs are splendid you may feel that there are better ways to make the most of your money.

The **Shiretoko Nature Center** (知床ネイチャーセンター; ☎ 4-2114; ⏰ 8am-5.40pm mid-Apr–mid-Oct, 9am-4pm mid-Oct–mid-Apr) has maps, info and a 20-minute slide show about the peninsula. So few people get here that humans haven't ruined it yet: hikers will see pristine forests, remote vistas without a sign of habitation and lots of wildlife, including bears (see p566) and foxes. The latter can be dangerous too, so don't take any chances: they're crafty little beasts, and some have been known to

steal food or sleeping bags. In addition, their faeces have contaminated the water with the parasite echinococcus, which can be deadly. Don't drink any water that hasn't been properly purified. Iwaobetsu Onsen (岩尾別温泉) and Kamuiwakka-no-taki (カムイワッカの滝), a stunning *rotemburo* waterfall, are popular destinations and are accessible by dirt roads. Swimsuits, alas, are required for modesty's sake at the waterfall.

Shiretoko Iwaobetsu Youth Hostel (知床岩尾別ユースホステル; ☎ 4-2312; www.noah.ne.jp /shiretoko-ax/; dm ¥3045; ⏰ Mar-Nov) is in Iwaobetsu, a small village within the park and is a good spot for those wanting to hike the peninsula. It offers briefings on hikes and also rents mountain bikes, but is closed much of December and April, so call ahead.

Iwaobetsu Nature Lodge (岩尾別ネイチャーロッジ; ☎ 4-2312; dm ¥3675) is another option on the premises of the youth hostel.

Kinoshita-goya (木下小屋; ☎ 4-2824; dm ¥1800; ⏰ Jun-Sep) is a mountain hut offering very basic accommodation right at the Rausu-dake trailhead. It is often booked solid, so call ahead.

SHIRETOKO-HANTŌ

0 ─── 10 km
0 ─── 6 miles

Shiretoko-misaki

SEA OF OKHOTSK

Shiretoko-hantō

Shiretoko-dake (1254m)

Rider House Kuma-no-Yado

Shiretoko National Park

Shiretoko-ōhashi
Kamuiwakka-no-taki

Shiretoko Go-ko

Iō-zan (1562m)

Shiretoko Nature Centre

Iwaobetsu Onsen

87

Shiretoko Iwaobetsu Youth Hostel

Rausu-dake (1660m)

Utoro

To Shari (35km)

Shiretoko-Tōge

Rausu-ko

Kuma-no-yu Onsen

Marumi
Rausu

335

To Shibetsu (35km);
Kushiro (130km)

Nemuro Kaikyō

Getting There & Around

From late April to October buses run three times daily from Utoro (¥1080, 50 minute) along the northern side of the peninsula, passing the nature centre, the youth hostel, Shiretoko Go-ko and Kamuiwakka-no-taki before terminating at Shiretoko-ōhashi. For the rest of the year, buses run only as far as the nature centre. From mid-June to mid-October there are also buses twice daily to Rausu via the dramatic Shiretoko-Toge pass (¥1310, 55 minutes).

During the high season (late July to mid-August) the road beyond Shiretoko Go-ko is closed to private vehicles, and visitors *must* use buses (every 20 minutes from 7am to 6.30pm) from the nature centre or youth hostel, making all stops along the way.

The one-way journey to Shiretoko-ōhashi takes 50 minutes, including breaks for gawking at deer, foxes and possibly bears. A few buses a day continue on to Utoro.

RAUSU 羅臼

☎ 01538

This fishing village once grew wealthy on the herring industry, though there's not much here now other than a few very beautiful hikes. A challenging but well-marked trailhead for Rausu-dake starts a few kilometres outside of town towards Shiretoko-Toge, near the (free) camping ground at **Kuma-no-yu Onsen** (熊の湯温泉) – yes, that's 'Bear's Boiled Water', you heard right!

Only genuinely experienced hikers should consider doing the eastern side of the peninsula out to Shiretoko-misaki (one to three days, depending on trail conditions).

Weather permitting, you could hire a local fishing boat for a ride back to the start of the trail at Rider House Kuma-no-yado at the end of Rte 87, 24km outside Rausu. Be warned: this hike is *extremely* difficult as the eroded trail sometimes crawls along steep cliffs or over slippery boulders. Bring an emergency signalling device in the event of an injury, as there will be no one except random fishing boats to assist you.

If you go, take plenty of food and water, as well as hiking boots with good ankle support, and keep an eye out for bears.

Right by the seaside, the well-regarded ryokan, **Marumi** (まるみ; ☎ 8-1313; r per person ¥8800), has Japanese rooms, lovely seafood meals, a *rotemburo* and sauna.

WARNING: BEAR ACTIVITY

The peninsula, Shiretoko-hantō, is home to around 600 brown bears, one of the largest bear populations in Japan. Park pamphlets warn visitors that once they enter Shiretoko National Park, they should assume bears can appear at any time. Favourite bear haunts include Shiretoko Go-ko (Shiretoko Five Lakes) and the falls, Kamuiwakka-no-taki.

Hikers are strongly advised not to go into the forest in the early morning or at dusk, and to avoid hiking alone. Carrying a bell or some other noise-making device is also recommended (bears don't like surprises). If you're camping, tie up your food and do not bury your rubbish. Bear activity picks up noticeably during early autumn, when the creatures are actively foraging for food ahead of their winter hibernation. Visitors should be especially cautious at this time.

Getting There & Around

From mid-June to mid-October, there are two buses a day (¥1310, 55 minutes) that run between Utoro and Rausu via Shiretoko-Toge. From Rausu, buses run four times daily (¥4740, 3½ hours) year-round to Kushiro. You may find it easiest if you rent a car in Kushiro, as it will greatly save time.

NEMURO 根室

☎ 0153 / pop 32,316

This tiny town's main attraction is its view of several islands which (though a subject of heated debate) currently belong to Russia. It's the easternmost part of Japan, so those travellers who like to collect '-mosts' should be sure to come here. That said, there's not much else to do, particularly if the weather doesn't cooperate and you end up looking at fog. The Hoppōryōdo islands are in dispute mainly because of their prime fishing grounds below the surface. English signage is limited, mainly plaques protesting the donation of these lands to Russia. Loudspeakers often blare from black trucks with *hi-no-maru* (the rising sun flags, discarded post WWII) flags on them calling for the islands' return.

Sights & Activities

A very pricey **souvenir shop**, a **museum centre** (Japanese language–only), the monuments and a few restaurants are what can be found at the tip, Cape Nosappu.

The bus passes a number of interesting **kelp-drying areas**, which are self-explanatory if kelp is being dried: it looks like black strips of twisted leather stretched in rows on the ground; otherwise, these areas look like well-maintained gravel parking lots. To the south of Nemuro there are several pretty rock formations in what is by all measures quite spectacular coastline. The **Wheel Rock** (車石) is the most famous. To get there take the (infrequent) train between Kushiro and Nemuro, getting off at the unmanned Hanasaki Station. It's a 3km-walk to Hanasaki lighthouse and the rock is nearby.

Those on the train will only get a passing glimpse of it, but the estuary between Akkeshi and the mainland is a good place to see hawks, kites, herons and even sea eagles (which are easy to mistake for hawks until the two are together and you'll realise just how darn big they are!). A car makes stopping here for a picnic or picture a possibility.

Akkeshi itself is famous for oysters, seal-watching and canoeing. Info about all three can be derived from **Akkeshi Mikaku Terminal Konkirie** (厚岸味覚ターミナルコンキリ エ; ☎ 52-4139; www.conchiglie.net; ☯ 9am-9pm Apr-Oct, 10am-9pm Nov-Mar). Reserve three days in advance for the active sports.

Getting There & Around

As with Shiretoko-hantō, renting a car for a trip to Nemuro really makes sense and will allow more freedom for those who want to explore. The bus ride from the station out to the tip is long (50 minutes) and comparatively expensive (one way/return ¥1040/1900). A discount coupon (buy it at the info centre *before* boarding the bus) knocks a few yen off the return price. It is timed to just barely meet the train, so make sure you don't dally at the station or you'll miss it.

TOKACHI 十勝

OBIHIRO 帯広

☎ 0155 / pop 172,100

This modern city is the central hub of the Tokachi plain, squeezed between the picturesque Hidaka and Daisetsuzan mountain ranges. Once an Ainu stronghold, the current city was founded in 1883 by the Banseisha, a group of 'land reclaimers' (colonial settlers) from Shizuoka prefecture.

For travellers, Obihiro is the southern back door to Daisetsuzan National Park; you may also find yourself passing through en route to Ikeda or Erimo-Misaki.

Information

Tokachi Tourist Information (☎ 23-6403; ☯ 9am-7pm) is on the 2nd floor of the Esta shopping mall at the new Obihiro Station. It can assist with various tourist-related issues. A **room-booking service** (☎ 25-1670; ☯ 11am-6pm) is on the station's ground floor.

Sleeping & Eating

Obihiro has a number of restaurants and hotels around the station. As the city is less frequently travelled, you should have an easier time booking accommodation.

Toipirka Youth Hostel (トイピルカ北帯広ユースホステル; ☎ 30-4165; http://homepage1.nifty .com/TOIPIRKA/; dm ¥3200) Attractive log house with Western-style beds and nightly teatime. It's near Tokachigawa Onsen, so you'll need to take a bus there. Staff can pick you up at the station if you phone ahead.

Hotel Musashi (ホテルムサシ; ☎ 25-1181; s/tw ¥4000/8000) A business hotel with reasonable rates.

Butadonburi (barbecued pork over rice) is an area speciality. Try getting it from the place that started it all: **Panchō** (ぱんちょう; ☎ 22-1974; dishes ¥850-1300), across from the station, and *butadonburi* is all that's on the menu. Expect long lines during peak times.

Getting There & Around

Flights connect Obihiro with Tokyo, Osaka and Nagoya. Buses from in front of Obihiro JR Station are timed to meet most flights. *Tokkyū* trains run from Obihiro to New Chitose Airport (¥6200, 1¾ hours) and Sapporo (¥6510, 2¼ hours). S-Kippu to Sapporo cost ¥11,940. The JR Nemuro main line runs east to Ikeda (*kaisoku*, ¥440, 30 minutes) and Kushiro (*tokkyū*, ¥3690, 1½ hours).

From in front of the station, buses depart for Sapporo (¥3670, 4½ hours), Kushiro (¥2240, 2½ hours) and Asahikawa (¥3150, 3¾ hours). The ones to Asahikawa go around Daisetsuzan to the north or to the west, passing either Sōunkyō Onsen or Furano/Biei, respectively. Local buses to Ikeda (¥590) take about an hour.

IKEDA 池田
☎ 01557

In the eastern Tokachi plain, Ikeda is a small farming town that became famous when the municipal government began making wine there in the 1960s. It's a nice spot for a relaxing afternoon if you're already in the area and have some time to kill. The name Tokachi in Japan is as synonymous with wine as Napa or Beaujolais is with Westerners, but oenophiles may want to decide for themselves. It may be worth a detour if you're already heading this way. Town maps are available at the **tourist information desk** (☎ 2-2024; ⏰ 10am-5pm Apr-Oct) inside the JR Ikeda Station.

Wines are made at the **Wain-jō** (ワイン城; wine castle; ☎ 2-2467; 83 Kiyomi, Ikeda-chō; admission free; ⏰ factory tours 9am-5pm) on a hillside overlooking the town; head for the Ferris wheel. A tour guides you through the production process and there's a tasting afterwards. To get here head south along the rail track from the station, you will see the hill on your left shortly afterwards.

Happiness Dairy (ハピネスデーリィ; ☎ 2-2001; 104-2 Kiyomi, Ikeda-chō; admission free; ⏰ 10am-6pm Mar-Nov, to 5pm Dec-Feb) is a pleasant walk through wheat fields. It sells ice cold gelato (¥250) or fresh cheese. From Wain-jō head east on Rte 39 about 200m, then turn left at the T-junction, head 500m north and turn right at the cross section. Go 300m, and the store is on your right.

Moon Face Gallery & Cafe (ムーンフェイス 画廊喫茶; ☎ 2-2198; 132 Kiyomi, Ikeda-chō; admission free; ⏰ 10am-6pm Wed-Mon) displays works by local artists.

Spinner's Farm (スピナーズファーム; ☎ 2-2848; www12.plala.or.jp/spinner/in Japanese; admission free; ⏰ Tue-Sun, closed 2nd Sat of each month) is an Ikeda wool-weaving workshop.

Friendly management and delicious dinners (including a glass of wine ¥1000) make **Ikeda Kita-no-kotan Youth Hostel** (池田北のコタンユースホステル; ☎ 2-3666; www11.plala .or.jp/kitanokotan/ in Japanese; dm with 2 meals ¥2900) a treat. You can rent a bike, but the hostel is within easy walking distance of the Toshibetsu Station (from the station take the main road south, turn left at the first intersection and the hostel is where the road ends), one stop west of Ikeda (¥200).

Ikeda is 30 minutes by local train from Obihiro (¥440). Frequent buses run between Ikeda and Obihiro (¥590, 55 minutes). On the privately owned Furusato-Ginga Line there are four trains daily to Kitami (¥3410, 2½ to three hours), from where you can catch buses to Sōunkyō Onsen in Daisetsuzan National Park or take the JR Sekihoku main line east to Bihoro and Abashiri.

ERIMO MISAKI 襟裳岬
☎ 01466

This remote cape, with its windswept cliffs and dramatic ocean vistas, is something of an ecological miracle. Beginning in the Meiji era, the hills surrounding this kelp-farming community were gradually deforested, so by the 1950s it was nicknamed 'Erimo Desert'. Sand blew into the ocean, destroying the kelp, and the community faced a stark choice: reforest or leave. Thanks to the locals' perseverance and a vast number of seedlings, the hills now boast a Japanese black pine forest.

At the cape are a lighthouse and a wind museum, **Kaze-no-Yakata** (風の館; ☎ 3-1133; 366-3 To-yo, Erimo-chō; admission ¥500; ⏰ 8.30am-6pm May-Sep, 9am-5pm Oct-Apr, closed Wed & Thu Dec-Feb) with weather-related films and exhibits; you can also be blasted by gale-force winds inside a man-made wind tunnel. During calm seas, Kuril seals bask on the rocks below, while nearby fishing boats harvest the kelp beds, which have finally returned. The seals are called *zenigata-azarashi*, meaning 'money shaped', because the white spots on their black bodies appear similar to old Japanese coins.

Minshuku Sentei (民宿仙庭; ☎ 3-1144; http: //city.hokkai.or.jp/~erimo123/framepage1.html in Japanese; 236-6 Erimo-misaki, Erimo-chō; dm ¥4350, r per person ¥5200) offers rustic accommodation, seafood dinners, and is a 20-minute walk from the cape. Prices include two meals.

Minshuku Misaki-sō (民宿岬荘; ☎ 3-1316; 367 Erimo-misaki, Erimo-chō; r per person with 2 meals ¥6000-8000) is another homely option nearby.

There's also a **camping ground** (☎ 4-2168; camping free; ⏰ late Apr-late Oct) on the beach at Hyakunin-hama, 8km northeast of the cape, right near the lighthouse.

Erimo Misaki is pretty darn remote and a car or motorcycle would make sense for many travellers. Those without transport will have to make do with a lone daily bus from Sapporo (¥3500, four hours) which arrives late and leaves early, or train from Tomakomai to Samani (¥3150, 3½ hours) and, after a 30-minute wait, take a bus from there (¥1370).

Shikoku 四国

In Japan's feudal past, the island of Shikoku was divided into four regions – hence the name 'shi' (four) and 'koku' (region). The provinces of Awa, Tosa, Iyo and Sanuki became the modern-day prefectures of Tokushima-ken, Kōchi-ken, Ehime-ken and Kagawa-ken. The old names are still in common use in their prefectures. Although Shikoku is Japan's fourth-largest island, it's predominantly rural and remains well off the standard tourist track for most foreigners – which makes it all the more worthwhile to go there.

The island is home to Japan's best-known pilgrimage, which is essentially the country's oldest tourist trail. Pilgrims, or *henrō* as they are known in Japanese, have been walking around the 88 Sacred Temples of Shikoku for over 1000 years. Modern *henrō*, and even foreign visitors, can hike along age-old trails in that ever-elusive search for enlightenment, or just to experience that bit of Japan that seems to have disappeared in the urban areas.

The island is rugged and mountainous. Facing the docile Inland Sea (Seto-nai-kai), Shikoku's northern coast is much more developed and industrialised; historically it was closer than the southern coast to the seats of power, easier to get to and had better weather. The island's southern coast is less developed and harder to get to; it faces the not-so-aptly-named Pacific and often bears the brunt of incoming storms and typhoons.

SHIKOKU

HIGHLIGHTS

- Search for enlightenment on the pilgrimage to the **88 Sacred Temples of Shikoku** (p574)
- Join the excitement of Tokushima's rollicking **Awa-odori festival** (p576)
- Explore the deep gorges of western Tokushima-ken's hidden **Iya Valley** (p578)
- Gaze out at the Pacific from the rocky cape at historic **Ashizuri-misaki** (p583)
- Inspect the intriguing exhibits at Uwajima's notorious **Taga-jinja** and **sex museum** (p591)
- Take a peaceful soak in the historic **Dōgo Onsen** (p595) in Matsuyama
- Climb the sacred peak of **Ishizuchi-san** (p600), the highest mountain in western Japan
- Trek up the granite steps to pay homage at **Kompira-san** (p602) in Kotohira
- Stroll through Takamatsu's exquisite gardens in **Ritsurin-kōen** (p604)
- Paddle a sea kayak through the warm waters of the **Inland Sea** (p606)

- POPULATION: 4.2 MILLION

www.lonelyplanet.com

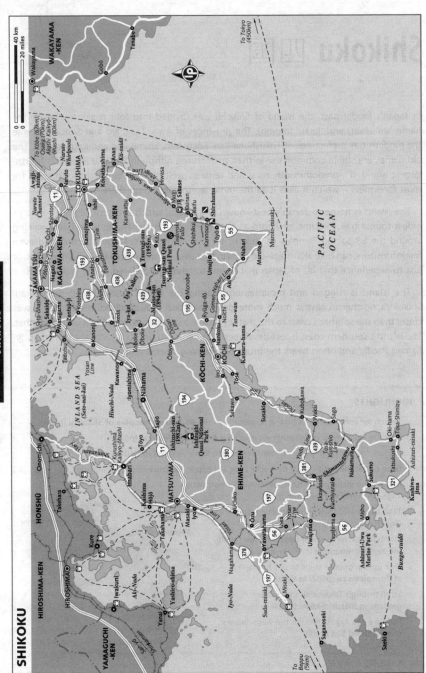

SHIKOKU

0 40 km
0 20 miles

WAKAYAMA-KEN

To Tokyo (450km)

To Kōbe (67km); Osaka (700m); Akashi Kaikyō-ōhashi (80km)

HONSHŪ

HIROSHIMA-KEN

YAMAGUCHI-KEN

INLAND SEA (Seto-nai-kai)

PACIFIC OCEAN

TOKUSHIMA-KEN

KAGAWA-KEN

KŌCHI-KEN

EHIME-KEN

Bungo-suidō

History

Despite its geographical proximity to the historical centres of power of Osaka and Kyoto, Shikoku has always been considered somewhat remote throughout Japanese history. Getting there required a boat ride – until three bridge links to Honshū were built over the last couple of decades.

Shikoku is a rugged land. In the 12th century defeated Heike warriors disappeared into the mountainous interiors to escape their Genji pursuers, and the 88 Temples pilgrims returned from Shikoku with stories of extreme hardship that had to be overcome in their search for enlightenment.

It is natural that Shikoku's northern coast is more developed. The southern coast was cut off by the island's mountainous topography, ensuring that it lagged behind the northern coast in terms of development and that the people of Kōchi were tough, hardy and independent.

The same phenomenon can be seen across the docile Inland Sea (Seto-nai-kai) in the Chūgoku region. There it is the opposite. The San-in, the less accessible northern side of Honshū, which faces the cold winter winds from the Sea of Japan, has lagged behind. The San-yō, on the sunny side of the mountains and facing the hospitable Inland Sea, developed much faster.

Climate

Shikoku has amazing variations of climate for a small island. Summer can be stiflingly hot, while in winter the higher peaks are snowcapped. Typhoons regularly pound the Pacific coast from June until October. The village of Monobe in Kōchi-ken prefecture claims to have the highest rainfall levels in Japan, while the protected northern side of the island often suffers water shortages. The landscape of Kagawa-ken is pockmarked with *tame-ike* (water-collection ponds).

Getting There & Away

Before 1986 Shikoku was considered much more remote, with access being mainly by ferry. There are now a total of three bridge systems linking Shikoku with Honshū. Heading east to west, the Akashi Kaikyō-Ōhashi is west of Kōbe and leads to Tokushima (via Awaji-shima island). The Seto-Ōhashi bridge connects Okayama to Sakaide, which is west of Takamatsu. Finally, the Kurushima Kaikyō-Ōhashi island-hops along the Shimanami Hwy (Shimanami-kaidō) from Onomichi in Hiroshima-ken prefecture to Imabari in Ehime-ken.

Air services connect major cities in Shikoku with Tokyo, Osaka and other centres on Honshū.

Numerous ferries ply the waters of the Inland Sea, linking points on Shikoku with neighbouring islands and ports on Kyūshū and the San-yō coast of Honshū.

There are frequent train services from Okayama to Shikoku via the Seto-Ōhashi, as well as direct bus services from both Osaka and Tokyo.

Getting Around

This chapter's coverage follows the same order that most of Shikoku's visitors have used to travel around the island over the past 1000 years – in a circle starting in Tokushima and moving through Kōchi, Ehime and Kagawa prefectures. Shikoku's

---

SHIKOKU ITINERARIES

If you have the time and the inclination, the best way to see and experience Shikoku is to journey around the 88 Sacred Temples (see p574). Shikoku is a very special place, but a lot of people rush through and leave without really understanding what it has to offer. This is an opportunity to immerse yourself in Japan and experience something unique – to be a 'doer' rather than a 'looker'. The pilgrimage can be hiked, biked, hitchhiked, done using public transport, a scooter, taxi or car – walking can take anywhere from 30 to 60 days. If you have a car and not much time, you can probably visit all the temples in four or five days, but that would defeat the purpose of the visit.

For those wanting a shorter visit, one popular route involves arriving in Takamatsu (p604) or Tokushima (p573), winding down through the Iya Valley (p578), heading south to Kōchi (p584), then around to the cape, Ashizuri-misaki (p589), and up the coast towards Matsuyama (p595).

88 SACRED TEMPLES OF SHIKOKU

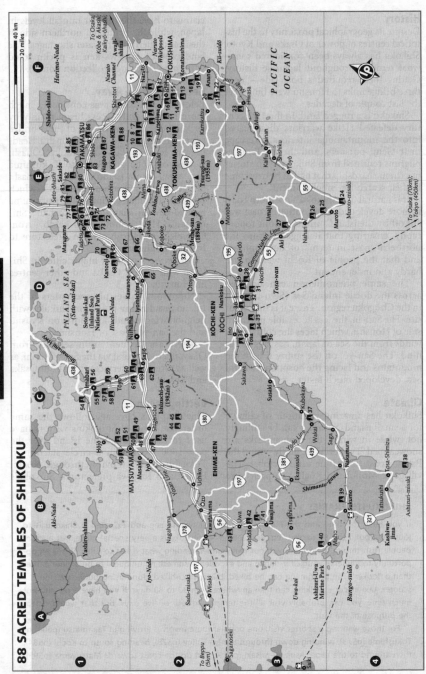

Temple 1 (Ryōzen-ji) 霊山寺 ... **1** F2	Temple 31 (Zenjibu-ji) 禅師峰寺 ... **31** D3	Temple 61 (Kōon-ji) 香園寺 ... **61** C2
Temple 2 (Gokuraku-ji) 極楽寺 ... **2** F2	Temple 32 (Chikurin-ji) 竹林寺 ... **32** D3	Temple 62 (Yokomine-ji) 横峰寺 ... **62** C2
Temple 3 (Konsen-ji) 金泉寺 ... **3** F2	Temple 33 (Sekkei-ji) 雪蹊寺 ... **33** D3	Temple 63 (Maegami-ji) 前神寺 ... **63** C2
Temple 4 (Dainichi-ji) 大日寺 ... **4** F2	Temple 34 (Tanema-ji) 種間寺 ... **34** D3	Temple 64 (Kisshō-ji) 吉祥寺 ... **64** C2
Temple 5 (Jizō-ji) 地蔵寺 ... **5** F2	Temple 35 (Kiyotaki-ji) 清滝寺 ... **35** D3	Temple 65 (Sankaku-ji) 三角寺 ... **65** D2
Temple 6 (Anraku-ji) 安楽寺 ... **6** F2	Temple 36 (Shōryū-ji) 青龍寺 ... **36** D3	Temple 66 (Unpen-ji) 雲辺寺 ... **66** D2
Temple 7 (Juraku-ji) 十楽寺 ... **7** E2	Temple 37 (Iwamoto-ji) 岩本寺 ... **37** C3	Temple 67 (Daikō-ji)
Temple 8 (Kumadani-ji) 熊谷寺 ... **8** E2	Temple 38 (Kongōfuku-ji) 金剛福寺 ... **38** B4	大興寺 (小松尾寺) ... **67** D1
Temple 9 (Hōrin-ji) 法輪寺 ... **9** F2	Temple 39 (Enkō-ji) 延光寺 ... **39** B4	Temple 68 (Jinne-in) 神恵寺 ... **68** D1
Temple 10 (Kirihata-ji) 切幡寺 ... **10** E2	Temple 40 (Kanjizai-ji) 観自在寺 ... **40** B3	Temple 69 (Kanon-ji) 観音寺 ... **69** D1
Temple 11 (Fujii-dera) 藤井寺 ... **11** F2	Temple 41 (Ryūkō-ji) 龍光寺 ... **41** B3	Temple 70 (Motoyama-ji) 本山寺 ... **70** D1
Temple 12 (Shōzan-ji) 焼山寺 ... **12** E2	Temple 42 (Butsumoku-ji) 仏木寺 ... **42** B3	Temple 71 (Iyadani-ji) 弥谷寺 ... **71** D1
Temple 13 (Dainichi-ji) 大日寺 ... **13** F2	Temple 43 (Meiseki-ji) 明石寺 ... **43** B3	Temple 72 (Mandara-ji) 曼陀羅寺 ... **72** E1
Temple 14 (Jōraku-ji) 常楽寺 ... **14** F2	Temple 44 (Taihō-ji) 大宝寺 ... **44** C2	Temple 73 (Shusshaka-ji) 出釈迦寺 ... **73** E1
Temple 15 (Kokubun-ji) 国分寺 ... **15** F2	Temple 45 (Iwaya-ji) 岩屋寺 ... **45** C2	Temple 74 (Kōyama-ji) 甲山寺 ... **74** E1
Temple 16 (Kannon-ji) 観音寺 ... **16** F2	Temple 46 (Jōruri-ji) 浄瑠璃寺 ... **46** C2	Temple 75 (Zentsū-ji) 善通寺 ... **75** E1
Temple 17 (Ido-ji) 井戸寺 ... **17** F2	Temple 47 (Yasaka-ji) 八坂寺 ... **47** C2	Temple 76 (Konzō-ji) 金倉寺 ... **76** E1
Temple 18 (Onzan-ji) 恩山寺 ... **18** F2	Temple 48 (Sairin-ji) 西林寺 ... **48** C2	Temple 77 (Dōryū-ji) 道隆寺 ... **77** E1
Temple 19 (Tatsue-ji) 立江寺 ... **19** F2	Temple 49 (Jōdo-ji) 浄土寺 ... **49** C2	Temple 78 (Gōshō-ji) 郷照寺 ... **78** E1
Temple 20 (Kakurin-ji) 鶴林寺 ... **20** F2	Temple 50 (Hanta-ji) 繁多寺 ... **50** C2	Temple 79 (Kōshō-in)
Temple 21 (Tairyō-ji) 太龍院 ... **21** F2	Temple 51 (Ishite-ji) 石手寺 ... **51** C1	高照院 (天皇寺) ... **79** E1
Temple 22 (Byōdō-ji) 平等寺 ... **22** F2	Temple 52 (Taisan-ji) 太山寺 ... **52** C1	Temple 80 (Kokubun-ji) 国分寺 ... **80** E1
Temple 23 (Yakuō-ji) 薬王寺 ... **23** F3	Temple 53 (Enmyō-ji) 円明寺 ... **53** B1	Temple 81 (Shiramine-ji) 白峰寺 ... **81** E1
Temple 24 (Hotsumisaki-ji) 最御崎寺 ... **24** E4	Temple 54 (Enmei-ji) 延命寺 ... **54** C1	Temple 82 (Negoro-ji) 根香寺 ... **82** E1
Temple 25 (Shinshō-ji) 津照寺 ... **25** E3	Temple 55 (Nankō-bō) 南光坊 ... **55** C1	Temple 83 (Ichinomiya-ji) 一宮寺 ... **83** E1
Temple 26 (Kongōchō-ji) 金剛頂寺 ... **26** E3	Temple 56 (Taisan-ji) 泰山寺 ... **56** C1	Temple 84 (Yashima-ji) 屋島寺 ... **84** E1
Temple 27 (Kōnomine-ji) 神峯寺 ... **27** E3	Temple 57 (Eifuku-ji) 栄福寺 ... **57** C1	Temple 85 (Yakuri-ji) 八栗寺 ... **85** E1
Temple 28 (Dainichi-ji) 大日寺 ... **28** D3	Temple 58 (Senyū-ji) 仙遊寺 ... **58** C1	Temple 86 (Shido-ji) 志度寺 ... **86** E1
Temple 29 (Kokubun-ji) 国分寺 ... **29** D3	Temple 59 (Kokubun-ji) 国分寺 ... **59** C1	Temple 87 (Nagao-ji) 長尾寺 ... **87** E1
Temple 30 (Zenraku-ji) 善楽寺 ... **30** D3	Temple 60 (Hōju-ji) 宝寿寺 ... **60** C2	Temple 88 (Ōkubo-ji) 大窪寺 ... **88** E1

SHIKOKU

only train connection with Honshū, however, is via the Seto-Ōhashi, so if you arrive by rail, your first prefecture will be Kagawa-ken (see p601 for details).

Over the last 1000 years, the majority of visitors to Shikoku have walked around the island. If that doesn't appeal, Shikoku is great for cycling. It is also well accessed by public transport, though to reach remote mountain areas, private transport is a boon (cars can be rented in Shikoku's major cities and airports).

TOKUSHIMA-KEN 徳島県

From the vivacious Awa-odori festival (Awa Dance Festival) and the mighty channel whirlpools of the Naruto Channel (Naruto-kaikyō), to the pristine scenery of Iya Valley and the surf beaches of the southern coast, Tokushima-ken prefecture offers an array of attractions to quench adventurous thirsts.

To pilgrims, Tokushima is known as Hosshin-no-dōjō – the place to determine to achieve enlightenment – and has the first 23 of the 88 temples. It also has Temple 66, the Umpen-ji in its far western corner. Temple 1 is the Ryōzen-ji, a 10-minute walk from Bandō station on the JR Kōtoku line north of Tokushima city. The Ryōzen-ji is number one, as through the centuries it was the first temple on Shikoku that pilgrims

reached after leaving Kōya-san mountain in Wakayama-ken. The temple has a shop where you can buy what you need for the journey, including traditional gear if you want it. There are maps and guidebooks in Japanese. It also has a **shukubō** (temple lodging; ☎ 088-689-1111; per person with meals ¥7000). Many of the temples provide accommodation for pilgrims at around that rate.

The first 10 temples are more or less on an east–west line spanning about 25km on the north side of the Yoshino-gawa river valley. They were considered a minipilgrimage in days of old, and even if you're not doing the full 88-temple pilgrimage, you can get a feel for it by visiting the first few. It's only a 15-minute walk from the Ryōzen-ji to Temple 2, the Gokuraku-ji. The walk from temples 11 to 12, in the mountains on the south side of the Yoshino-gawa valley, is infamous among *henrō* – it has the reputation of being the steepest and hardest climb on the pilgrimage, although it's possible to walk it in five hours. Temple 19, Tatsue-ji, is a barrier temple – only those who are 'pure of intention' can pass. After that, pilgrims are truly on the long road.

TOKUSHIMA 徳島
☎ 088 / pop 270,000
Tokushima is a bustling modern city known for its annual Awa-odori festival (see p576) in August, and traditional puppet theatre.

88 SACRED TEMPLES OF SHIKOKU

Henrō have been walking clockwise around Shikoku for over 1000 years, following in the footsteps of the great Buddhist saint Kōbō Daishi (774–835). Kōbō Daishi achieved enlightenment on Shikoku, the island of his birth, and by following in his path, a millennium of pilgrims have hoped to do the same.

Known as Kūkai (meaning 'the sky and the sea') during his lifetime, the great saint was awarded the title of Kōbō Daishi – *kōbō* means 'to spread widely the Buddhist teachings', and *daishi* means 'great teacher' or 'saint' – following his death. He was not the only *daishi*, but the Japanese have a saying that 'Kōbō stole the title of *daishi*', and when anyone talks of 'the *daishi*', everyone knows who is being referred to.

Kōbō Daishi founded the Shingon sect of Buddhism, the only major sect that believes enlightenment can be achieved in this lifetime. It is commonly referred to as Esoteric Buddhism. He is also credited with, among other things, putting together the first Chinese–Japanese dictionary, and creating *hiragana*, the system of syllabic writing that made it easier for Japanese to put their language into writing (see p775 for more information). Kōbō Daishi is enshrined at the Kōya-san temple complex (see p377) in Wakayama-ken prefecture on Honshū, and it is a tradition that pilgrims start and end their journey at Kōya-san, asking for Kōbō Daishi's support and blessing for their upcoming journey, and thanking him for that support and their safety on their return. Pilgrims never walk alone: Kōbō Daishi is always by their side.

For 1000 years, the pilgrimage was an arduous task – the only way to make the journey was to walk the 1400km-long track, an incredible journey. Until 1685 there was no guidebook. There were no weather forecasts, no telephones for pilgrims to use to call home if they got homesick, no paramedics to pick them up if they fell ill. Many never made it. Those who did overcame great hardships. Nowadays, for most *henrō*, hardship is not a factor. They buzz around in air-conditioned vehicles collecting the 88 temple stamps and give little thought to the past. There are still walkers, although they make up only a tiny percentage of those who make the pilgrimage. In recent years there has been a resurgence of Japanese who, disenchanted with the pace of modern life and looking for meaning and self-realisation, strike out on foot.

There is also the occasional *gaijin henrō* (foreign pilgrim). If you're interested, all the gear you need is at Temple 1, the Ryōzen-ji, just north of Tokushima city (see p573); and there's more information in each prefecture's section in this chapter. The pilgrimage is considered nonsectarian and some people out there aren't even Buddhists – just people in search of themselves. With the right attitude, the pilgrimage is as big an adventure today as it was in the past and is definitely a way to immerse yourself in Japan. Allow 30 to 60 days if walking (depending on your fitness), two weeks to a month on a bicycle, less by motorised transport. One point to remember: there are actually 89 temples. All pilgrims should travel back from Temple 88 to Temple 1 and complete the circle, for a circle is neverending, just like the search for enlightenment.

For more information pick up three English-language books: Oliver Statler's *Japanese Pilgrimage* is a classic academic work on the pilgrimage and its history; Ed Readicker-Henderson's *The Traveller's Guide to Japanese Pilgrimages* has information on each temple; and Craig McLachlan's *Tales of a Summer Henro* retells the adventures of a walking *gaijin henrō*.

Always remember the words of Kōbō Daishi – 'Do not just walk in the footsteps of the men of old, seek what they sought'.

Orientation

Tokushima is defined by two hills. Shiroyama, with the castle ruins, directly behind the train station. From in front of the station, Shinmachibashi-dōri heads southwest across the Shinmachi-gawa river to the ropeway station at the base of the other hill, Bizan. The entertainment district and main shopping arcade are west of the river, Shinmachi-gawa.

Information

There's a helpful **tourist information office** (☎ 622-8556; ⏰ 9am-8pm) in a booth outside JR Tokushima Station that has English brochures and maps, and can help with booking accommodation.

The **Tokushima Prefecture International Exchange Association** (Topia; ☎ 656-3303; www.tk2.nmt .ne.jp/~topia; ⏰ 10am-6pm) on the 6th floor of the

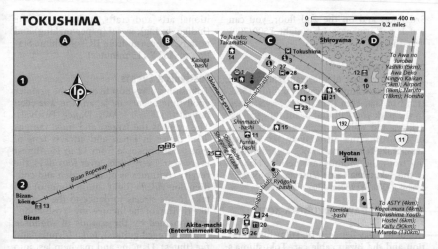

station building is also very helpful. There are English-speaking staff members, and facilities include a library, satellite TV, computers with Internet access (¥50 for 10 minutes) and an information/message board. Staff can help with finding accommodation, and you can leave your bags here during the day.

For more information, check out the useful website www.city.tokushima.tokushima.jp/english/index.html.

There are coin lockers at the station, and the ATMs at the central post office a couple of minutes' walk away (400m), accept international cards. **Kinokuniya Books** (8th fl, Sogō Department Store) outside the station has a smallish English–language books corner.

Sights & Activities
BIZAN 眉山
A broad avenue with a central parade of palm trees runs southwest from the train station to the foot of Bizan. There, from the 5th floor of the Awa Odori Kaikan building (below), a **ropeway** (cable car; ☎ 652-3617; one way/return ¥600/1000; ⏰ 9am-6.30pm, 9am-9pm Fri & Sat in summer) whizzes you to the 290m-high summit for fine views over the city and sea. You can walk down in 15 minutes.

At the top, Bizan-kōen park has a **Peace Pagoda**, erected in 1958 as a memorial to local soldiers who died in Burma (Myanmar) during WWII, and the **Wenceslão de Morães Museum** (☎ 623-5342; admission ¥200; ⏰ 9.30am-5pm, closed 2nd & 4th Wed each month). Morães, a Portuguese naval officer, lived in Japan from 1893 until his death in 1929, and produced a multivolume study of Japan.

At the foot of the ropeway, the **Awa Odori Kaikan** (☎ 611-1611; admission free; ⏰ 9am-5pm, closed 2nd & 4th Wed of month) features extensive exhibits relating to the local dance, the Awa-odori. There's a museum (admission ¥300) on the

3rd floor, and on the 2nd floor, you can watch performances (day/night ¥500/700) year-round.

CHŪŌ-KŌEN 中央公園

To the northeast of the train station, the ruins of Tokushima-jō castle, built in 1586, stand in **Chūō-kōen** (☎ 621-5295; admission free). In the park you will find beautiful gardens, bridges and walking trails, and just south of the ruins the attractively landscaped **Senshūkaku-teien** (admission ¥50), a garden dating from the Momoyama period. Nearby is the **Tokushima Castle Museum** (☎ 656-2525; admission ¥300; ☽ 9.30am-4.30pm Tue-Sun).

SHINMACHI-GAWA MIZUGIWA-KŌEN
新町川水際公園

About halfway between JR Tokushima Station and the Bizan cable car, Tokushima's main street crosses the Shinmachi-gawa. On the station side of the river, the popular **Shinmachi-gawa Mizugiwa-kōen** runs along the riverside for about 500m in both directions. There are fountains, gardens and walkways and the park is lit up in the evenings.

At Ryogoku-bashi, in the southeastern corner of the park, free 30-minute **boat rides** (☎ 655-1201; ☽ 1-4pm Sat & Sun Mar-Nov, 5-8pm daily Jul & Aug) can be taken circling Hyotan-jima, the island forming central Tokushima.

OTHER SIGHTS & ACTIVITIES

Nakasu Ichiba (☎ 652-4569; ☽ 5am-6pm Mon-Sat) started out as Tokushima's fish markets, but now has all sorts of local food products for sale. It is a lively spot with the cheapest and freshest food in town, about 1km (10 minutes' walk) southeast of JR Tokushima Station.

Near the entertainment district to the south of Ryogoku-bashi, the **dancing clock** is a curious contraption featuring figurines that perform the local Awa-odori dance; they pop out of an otherwise ordinary bus stop five times a day.

ASTY Tokushima (アスティ徳島; ☎ 624-5111; admission ¥910; ☽ 9am-5pm), southeast of the city centre, has potted highlights of regional culture (including puppet drama and pottery) under one roof. At the **Kōgei-mura** (工芸村; ☎ 624-5000; admission free; ☽ 9.30am-5pm Wed-Mon) 'arts village', which is the highlight of the complex, you can observe (and, for a nominal fee, partake in) a variety of traditional arts and crafts, including *aizome* (indigo dyeing), *washi* (paper-making) and pottery. Buses run from JR Tokushima Station to ASTY (15 minutes).

Festivals & Events

Tokushima plays host to one of the premier good-time events in Japan, the **Awa-odori festival** (阿波踊り; Awa Dance Festival). The event is the largest and most famous 'bon' dance in Japan and attracts tens of thousands of people from 12 to 15 August every year. Every night, over four days, the revelry continues as men, women and children don *yukata* (light cotton kimono) and take to the streets to dance to the samba-like rhythm of the theme song 'Yoshikono', accompanied by the sounds of *shamisen* (three-stringed guitars), *taiko* (drums) and *fue* (flutes). Dancing and mayhem last into the wee hours of the morning! Some groups delight in having gaijin join their pack; staff at Topia (see p574) can provide details. Plan early because accommodation is at a premium during the festival (1.3 million people turned up in 2004!). And if you can't be there for the real thing in August, you can always try the dance at the local hall, the Awa Odori Kaikan (see p575).

Entertainment

AWA PUPPET THEATRE 人形浄瑠璃

For hundreds of years, *bunraku* (classic puppet theatre), known in the region as *ningyō jōruri*, thrived in the farming communities in and around Tokushima as a popular form of amusement (while the wealthy were entertained by the likes of kabuki). Gradually the region's many puppet theatres dwindled and today one of the last remaining local puppet dramas can be seen at the **Awa no Jūrobei Yashiki** (阿波十郎兵衛屋敷; ☎ 665-2202; tickets ¥400; ☽ 8.30am-7pm).

This museum, to the northeast of JR Tokushima Station, is the former residence of the samurai Jūrobei, whose tragic Edo-era life story forms the material for the drama *Keisei Awa no Naruto*. A section from this puppet drama is performed by local women. Shows take place at varying times, but generally at 3pm daily. Ask at the tourist-information booth outside JR Tokushima for details – then take a bus from just outside to the Jūrobei Yashiki-mae bus stop (¥270, 15 minutes).

Next door is the **Awa Deko Ningyō Kaikan** (阿波木偶人形会館; Awa Puppet Hall; ☎ 665-5600; admission ¥400; ◷ 8.30am-5pm), with puppet displays and demonstrations of their manufacture and use.

Sleeping

BUDGET
Tokushima Youth Hostel (☎ 663-1505; dm ¥2800; P ✗) Near the sea, this hostel is about 30 minutes by bus from the centre of town. Meals are available and it has a good reputation and friendly staff, but it is rather inconveniently located.

Sakura-sō (☎ 652-9575; 1-25 Terashima-honchō-higashi; s/d 3300/6000; P ✗) This place near the station is an excellent option if you're happy with shared facilities. The Japanese-style rooms are clean and the owner is friendly. It's near the tracks though, so you're not likely to sleep late.

Tokushima Eki-mae Dai-Ichi Hotel (☎ 655-5005; 2-21 Ichiban-chō; s from ¥5000; P ✗) A modern business hotel near the station, the Dai-Ichi has semidouble beds in each of its 88 single rooms.

Tokushima Station Hotel (☎ 652-8181; 3-4 Terashima-honchō-higashi; s/d ¥5000/10,000; P ✗) Expect standard business hotel stuff at this place; it's a couple of minutes from the station.

MIDRANGE
Hayashi Bekkan (☎ 622-9191; 2-22 Nakatōri-machi; tw per person with meals ¥10,000; P ✗) Five minutes' walk south of the station, this ryokan is more upmarket.

Agnes Hotel Tokushima (☎ 626-2222; 1-28 Terashima-honchō-nishi; s/d ¥5500/12,000; P ✗) A newish Western-style hotel, the Agnes has good-sized rooms and beds, and a trendy cake and pastry shop on the 1st floor.

Tokushima Tōkyū Inn (☎ 626-0109; 1-24 Motomachi; s/d from ¥7200/12,000; P ✗) Close to the station next to Sogō department store, this is an impressive 11-storey hotel offering good views over the city.

TOP END
Hotel Clement Tokushima (☎ 656-3111; Terashima-honchō-nishi 1-chōme; s/tw ¥9860/18,700; P ✗) With 18 floors and 250 rooms as part of the major new redeveloped JR Tokushima Station complex, the Hotel Clement is the top hotel in town and has the most upmarket restaurant.

Eating
There is an expansive delicatessen area in the basement of Clement Plaza (inside JR Tokushima Station) and a variety of eateries on the 5th floor.

Sobadokoro Chikuan (☎ 656-8666; 1-20 Terashima-honchō-higashi; ◷ 10am-8.30pm) Just east of the station, this is a dinky little spot that serves up excellent local *soba* (buckwheat noodles). Try the Tokushimajō-no-soba (Tokushima Castle *soba*; ¥350), or the popular Iya-bukkake *soba* (¥700).

Shangri-La (☎ 626-0528; 1-24 Motomachi; ◷ 7am-10pm) In the Tokushima Tōkyū Inn building, this place has a popular buffet lunch (¥1000). Its excellent evening offer of *tabehōdai, nomihōdai* (eat and drink-all you can) at ¥3500/4000 for women/men is for those with a big appetite.

Ikkō (☎ 623-2311; 1-46 Nakano-chō; ◷ 5-11.30pm Mon-Sat) Opposite ACTY 21 in the entertainment district, this restaurant specialises in dishes using the region's well-known tasty chicken meat. It features trendy décor and antique furniture.

Drinking & Entertainment
There are some quality cafés and coffee houses in town. There's a variety of nightlife, especially in the entertainment area to the south of Ryogoku-bashi. A good place to start is in the ACTY 21 building, just down from the dancing clock.

Cha-Cha House Coffee (☎ 622-2907; 2-19 Yaoya-machi; ◷ 8am-10.30pm Mon-Sat) A few minutes' walk from the station, Cha-Cha has excellent coffee and cakes.

Times Café (☎ 657-7410; 1-16-4 Higashi-shinmachi; ◷ 11.30am-10pm) This is a great two-storey café in the Shinmachi shopping arcade to the west of Shinmachi-gawa.

Hung Loose (☎ 623-3255; Tōjō Bldg 2F, 20-1 Ryōgokubashi; ◷ 8pm-4am) On the opposite corner from ACTY 21, this place serves margaritas and frozen cocktails in a popular Hawaiian-style surfer bar with palm trees and deck chairs.

Swing (☎ 622-9669; Compa Bldg 3F, Akitamachi 1-chōme; ◷ 8pm-4am Mon-Sat) Just down the road, Swing is a good jazz bar with nightly live performances and a tasty food menu.

Getting There & Away
Tokushima's airport is 8km north of the city and there are direct flights to/from Tokyo

SHIKOKU

(JAS/SKY, ¥25,300, 70 minutes, six daily), Nagoya (NAL, ¥17,000, one hour, two daily) and Fukuoka (JAC, ¥21,300, 85 minutes, two daily).

Regular buses (¥430; 25 minutes) go from the airport to JR Tokushima Station.

Tokushima is one hour from Takamatsu, 2½ hours from Kōchi and 3½ hours from Matsuyama by *tokkyū* (limited express).

Overnight buses connect Tokushima with Tokyo and Nagoya, and there are plenty of buses each day to/from Osaka and Kōbe.

Ferry services are starting to dwindle, but there are still connections with Tokyo (¥8610, 18 hours), Osaka (¥4620), Kitakyūshū and various smaller ports (see Ferry Timetables, p756). **Nankai Ferry** (☎ 0120-732-156) has regular daily departures to/from Wakayama and Izumi-sano (Osaka).

Getting Around

It's easy to get around Tokushima on foot – from JR Tokushima Station to the Bizan cable-car station it's about 700m.

The bus terminal is right outside the station. Free rental **bicycles** (☎ 622-8556; ¥3000 deposit; ◷ 9am-4.30pm) are available from the underground bike-parking area to your left as you leave the station.

NORTHERN TOKUSHIMA-KEN
徳島県北部
Naruto Whirlpools 鳴門のうず潮

At the change of tide, sea water whisks through the narrow Naruto Channel with such velocity that ferocious **whirlpools** are created. Boats venture out into the channel that separates Shikoku from nearby Awaji-shima island, and travel under Naruto-Ōhashi to inspect the whirlpools close up. Brochures available at the JR Tokushima Station tourist-information booth outline tide times (ask for *naruto-no-uzu-shio*) and boat trips. The whirls occur twice a day, but at changing times. There are views over the channel from Naruto-kōen park (鳴門公園).

For a birds-eye view, you can walk the **Uzu-no-michi** (渦の道; ☎ 088-683-6262; admission ¥500; ◷ 9am-6pm Tue-Sun), a 450m-long walkway under Naruto-Ōhashi, 45m above the swirling water.

From Tokushima, take a train (see p577) to JR Naruto Station (¥330, 40 minutes) and a bus from there (¥310, 20 minutes,

infrequent) to the bridge; or take a bus directly to Naruto-kōen from Tokushima bus station (the easiest option).

Also at Naruto-kōen is the new **Ōtsuka International Museum of Art** (大塚国際美術館; ☎ 088-687-3737; admission ¥3000; ◷ 9.30am-5pm Tue-Sun), which is dedicated to the ceramic arts and has over 1000 exhibits from around the world.

WESTERN TOKUSHIMA-KEN
徳島県西部
Iya Valley 祖谷渓
☎ 0883

The remote Iya Valley, one of Japan's three 'Hidden Regions', is a welcome escape from the hustle and bustle of urban Japan. With its houses perched high on hillsides and its air of isolation, Iya has been dubbed the Tibet of Japan.

The earliest record of the valley describes a group of shamans fleeing persecution in Nara in the 9th century. Iya later became a refuge for defeated Heike warriors, fleeing the Genji clan in the 12th century civil wars. The steep mountain topography and Japan's deepest gorges have ensured that Iya remains a refuge to this day.

Along with the famed *kazura-bashi* (vine bridges) and emerald green rivers, Iya boasts some classic folk architecture, with traditional farmhouses nestled into the hills.

The Iya region is a nature and adventure-sports haven, with superb hiking around Tsurugi-san mountain, white-water rafting in the stunning Ōboke and Koboke Gorges and great – if hilly – cycling opportunities. Worn-out travellers can reward themselves at the end of the day by soaking in top-notch *onsen* (mineral hot springs) and sampling a variety of Japanese mountain cuisine such as Iya *soba*, *dengaku* (fish and vegetables roasted on skewers) and the local *iwa-dofu* (literally, 'hard tofu') noted for its firm texture.

GETTING THERE & AROUND

Most approach the Iya Valley via JR Ōboke Station. Getting around the valley, however, involves some planning, as Iya's sights are very widespread. Infrequent buses travel between Ikeda, Ōboke and Iya, but the best way to explore the region is with your own wheels. Rental cars are available in Shikoku's larger cities, and at **Ekiren** (☎ 72-0809) inside JR Awa Ikeda Station. There is a **tourist information office** (☎ 72-7620) with maps outside the station.

Ōboke & Koboke 大歩危・小歩危

South of Ikeda on Rte 32, along the scenic 8km-long stretch of the Yoshino-gawa river

between Koboke and Ōboke, rafting and kayaking trips run from April to late November. The Aussie-run **Happy Raft** (☎ 0887-75-0500; www.happyraft.com), beside JR Tosa Iwahara Station, runs reliable daily rafting trips with English-speaking guides (¥6500 for half a

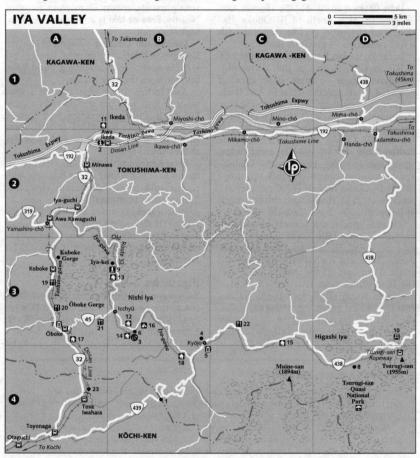

IYA VALLEY

0 — 5 km
0 — 3 miles

SHIKOKU

day), and full-day trips for ¥12,500/13,500 per weekdays/weekends. **Momiji-tei** (☎ 0883-84-1117) is a noodle shop serving great *soba* in a restored farmhouse. Thirty-minute pleasure-boat rides (¥1000 per person) leave from Restaurant Mannaka.

Lapis Ōboke (☎ 0883-84-1489; admission ¥500; ☺ 9am-5pm), 1km north of JR Ōboke Station, is a noteworthy geology museum with a fine collection of precious stones.

In Ikeda, the **Awa Ikeda Youth Hostel** (☎ 0883-72-5277; dm ¥2850) is part of the Mitsugon-ji mountain-temple complex. Book ahead if you need a pick-up/drop-off at JR Awa Ikeda Station (last pick-up 6pm). It's up a very steep mountain, so don't try to walk there. An excellent Japanese-style budget alternative near JR Ōboke Station is the riverside **Ku-Neru-Asobu** (☎ 090-9778-7133; www.k-n-a.com; Japanese-style dm ¥2000). The friendly English-speaking owners can provide pick-ups/drop-offs at JR Ōboke Station (¥200 per person). Kitchen use is ¥100, and food can be bought at Bokemart, 30m from the train station.

There is spectacular scenery in the deep canyons along old Rte 32 (Kyu-kaido). Public buses (¥880, 55 minutes, three daily) between Ikeda and Iya Valley ply this narrow route. Turn east off the main Rte 32, over the blue bridge near JR Iya-guchi Station and 8km south of JR Awa-Ikeda Station. Just beyond the intriguing **'peeing boy' statue**, the cliff-top **Iya Onsen** (☎ 0883-75-2311, www .iyaonsen.co.jp; per person with meals ¥16,000) features riverside *onsen* (¥1500 for nonguests).

Nishi Iya 西祖谷

Nishi Iya is popular for crossing the **Kazura-bashi** (¥500) vine bridge. Rivers in Shikoku's mountainous interior were once commonly spanned by these perilous catwalks, which could conveniently be cut down to prevent pursuing enemy clans from crossing. Nearby, **Biwa-no-taki** is an impressive, 50m-high waterfall.

Kazura-bashi Camping Village (☎ 090-1571-5258, tent sites ¥500 plus ¥200 per person, bungalows from ¥3100) is an excellent camping ground 500m upriver from the vine bridge.

Also in the vine bridge area are several no-frills inns with per-person rates around ¥6500, including breakfast and dinner. Consider **Shinoku Iya** (☎ 0883-87-2203), **Iya-so Minshuku** (☎ 0883-87-2242) or **Toshiko-so Minshuku** (☎ 0883-87-2842).

Hotel Kazura-bashi (☎ 0883-87-2171; r per person with meals from ¥16,000) offers Japanese-style rooms with terrific mountain views and hilltop *onsen* (nonguests ¥1000).

Worth seeking out is **Senkichi** (☎ 0883-87-2733; ☺ 10.30am-5.30pm Fri-Wed Apr-Nov), which serves home-made Iya *soba* (¥520). The stylish interior resembles a traditional Iya farmhouse.

Higashi Iya 東祖谷

To escape the throngs of Japanese tourists at the Nishi Iya Kazura-bashi (above), head 30km east to the spectacular **Oku Iya Kazura-bashi** (¥500) in Higashi Iya. Set in a pristine natural environment, the secluded

---

CHIIORI – A RURAL RETREAT

The Iya Valley is romanticised in Alex Kerr's award-winning book *Lost Japan*. In the early 1970s, Kerr bought an 18th-century thatched-roof cottage in Higashi Iya (above), which he named Chiiori (Cottage of the Flute), and has since been restoring it to its original brilliance.

Along with journalist Mason Florence, he later founded the Chiiori Project, a nonprofit organisation based in Iya. Staffed by Japanese and foreign volunteers, the project focuses on conservation of the regional culture, architecture and environment, and works to introduce sustainable, community-based tourism. The long-term goal of the project is to breathe life into the depopulated village. Scores of houses like Chiiori, with their *irori* (open-floor hearths), glistening red-pine floorboards and soaring rafters, unfortunately remain abandoned across the valley, and are waiting to be restored.

At Chiiori, visitors can learn about carpentry, organic farming and roof-thatching. Weekend events range from local craft workshops to country cooking. The rustic experience at Chiiori, however is not for everyone – there is plenty of smoke and dust and an astounding plethora of insects. In the evening, it's off to the local *onsen*. Back at Chiiori, visitors can sip sake, watch the smoke billow up into the rafters and chat until the wee hours.

To learn more about the project or arrange a visit, call ☎ 0883-88-5290 or see www.chiiori.org.

fufu-bashi (husband-and-wife vine bridges) hang side by side, high over the river gorge. Near the self-propelled, wooden cable-cart (a must-try!), there's a camping area.

Memme Juku (☎ 0883-88-2170; www.iya.jp/ta kumi) is a nature- and field-studies school led by villagers who offer courses in Iya's traditional arts, crafts and customs. For a local's perspective of Higashi Iya, log onto www.east-iya.com (in Japanese).

Up a windy road from Oku Iya Kazura-bashi, **Buke Yashiki** (☎ 0883-88-2893; admission ¥300; ☻ 9am-5pm Wed-Mon) is an enormous thatched-roof samurai house commanding spectacular views of the valley.

The interesting **Higashi Iya Folk Museum** (☎ 0883-88-2286; admission ¥400; ☻ 8.30am-5pm) is housed in the large red building in Kyōjo.

Mampu Lodge (☎ 0883-88-5001; cabins per person ¥4000; [P]) at Ryūgūgake-kōen park rents comfy forest cabins with minikitchens. **Iya-shi no Onsen-kyo** (☎ 0883-88-2975; per person with meals ¥12,000; [P] [X]) is a beautiful hotel/*onsen* complex (¥800 for nonguests) with some thatched-roof houses on the grounds and a commendable restaurant.

At **Soba Dōjō** (☎ 0883-88-2577) you can sample a bowl of Iya *soba* (¥500) and even make your own (¥2500).

Tsurugi-san 剣山

This mountain's name translates to Sword Peak, although it is gently rounded rather than sharp-edged. At 1955m, Tsurugi-san is the second-highest mountain in Shikoku and provides excellent short and long hiking opportunities, as well snowboarding in winter.

A chairlift goes midway up, from which it is a leisurely 40-minute walk to the summit, but bona fide hikers start from **Ōtsurugi-jinja**, the shrine near the car park. Information on the popular multiday hike between Tsurugi-san and Muine-san (1894m) as well as mountaintop accommodation and other detailed regional hiking information, can be found in Lonely Planet's *Hiking in Japan*.

SOUTHERN TOKUSHIMA-KEN
徳島県南部

Tokushima's spectacular southern coastline is well worth a visit. There is rugged rocky scenery, appealing beaches and decent distances between the small fishing towns.

The JR Mugi line runs down the coast as far as Kaifu, just short of the border with

Kōchi-ken prefecture. From Kaifu, the private Asa Kaigan railway runs two stops to Kannoura in Kōchi-ken. There is a train line to Nahari from Kōchi city – but there is no train around Muroto-misaki. Kannoura is at the end of the line for train travel from Tokushima. You can continue by bus or thumb to the cape at Muroto-misaki and on to Kōchi city.

Hiwasa 日和佐
☎ 0884

If you're doing the pilgrimage, you'll be visiting **Yakuō-ji** (薬王寺), Temple 23 and the last temple in Tokushima. In this fishing town, Yakuō-ji is a *yakuyoke-dera*, a temple specialising in warding off bad luck during unlucky years. Although there are a number of designated unlucky years, the unluckiest age for men is 42, while for women it is 33. The stairway up to the temple is split. The men's side has 42 steps, while the women's has 33. Pilgrims approach on the appropriate side and put a coin on each step – if you turn up at a busy time, the steps are virtually overflowing with money!

From May to late August turtles come ashore to lay their eggs on beaches in the area. The Hiwasa **Sea Turtle Museum** (日和佐 うみがめ博物館カレッタ; ☎ 77-1110; admission ¥600; ☻ 9am-5pm Tue-Sun) has all sorts of information, and turtles for up-close viewing.

Hiwasa-jō (日和佐城; ☎ 77-1370; admission ¥200; ☻ 9am-5pm Tue-Sun) is a small reconstructed castle that overlooks the town from the south and has various displays and exhibits inside.

If you have your own wheels, forget Rte 55 and take the spectacular **Minami-Awa Sun-line** (南阿波サンライン) coastal route south to Mugi. There is little traffic as the 18km road to Mugi snakes its way around the coast revealing spectacular views out to sea.

Yakuō-ji has accommodation in its **shukubō** (☎ 77-1105; per person with meals ¥7000; [P] [X]), and the **Hiwasa Youth Hostel** (日和佐 ユースホステル; ☎ 77-0755; dm ¥2750; [P] [X]), though a bit run down, is just down from the temple. Meals are available.

Mugi 牟岐
☎ 0884

The next town down the line is Mugi. It has a great **Seashell Museum** (貝の資料館モラス こむぎ; ☎ 72-2520; admission ¥300; ☻ 9am-4.30pm Tue-Sun) with over 6000 shells on display in a wooden building designed in the image of a seashell.

If you feel like a hot soak, about a 10-minute drive north of Mugi off Rte 55 is the superb **Onigaiwaya Onsen** (鬼ヶ岩屋温泉; ☎ 72-1110; admission ¥1000; ☽ 11am-8pm Tue-Sun).

Not far from JR Sabase Station, the next stop south of Mugi, is **Ozuna beach** (大砂ビーチ), popular in summer for swimming and snorkelling.

Kainan, Kaifu, Shishikui & Tōyō
海南・海部・宍喰・東洋

The next few towns are 'surf city' Japan. Kainan, Kaifu, Shishikui and Tōyō in neighbouring Kōchi-ken prefecture are where it's at in Japan for surfers. The coastline is spectacular, and there are superb beaches, colourful characters, tanned bodies and plenty of seafood. National and international surfing contests are held in the area. There is also great snorkelling and diving.

Visitors with wheels can head inland on Rte 193 from Kainan for about 25km to Shikoku's highest waterfall, the 55m-high **Todoroki Falls** (轟の滝), where there is good hiking in the surrounding area.

If you're interested in the history and culture of the region, head to **Awa-Kainan Bunka-mura** (阿波海南文化村), five minutes' drive north of JR Kainan Station. Two noteworthy buildings include the **Kainan Municipal Museum** (海南町立博物館; ☎ 0884-73-4080; admission ¥500; ☽ 9am-5pm) and the **Kainan Cultural Hall** (海南文化館; ☎ 0884-73-3100; ☽ 8.30am-5pm Tue-Sun).

A 15-minute walk east of Kaifu station is the extremely enjoyable 4km-long **Atago-yama walking trail** (愛宕山遊歩道) with great views around the coastline.

At Shishikui, take the hourly glass-bottomed boat cruise run by **Blue Marine** (ブルーマリン; ☎ 0884-76-3100; cruises per person ¥1800; ☽ 9am-4pm Wed-Mon) to see the spectacular sea life. Also check out the new **Shishikui Onsen** (宍喰温泉; admission ¥400; ☽ 11am-8pm) complex, a 10-minute walk east of Shishikui station.

For accommodation, there is the upmarket and very flash **Hotel Riviera Shishikui** (ホテルリビエラ宍喰; ☎ 0884-76-3300; per person with meals ¥13,000; Ⓟ 🐾), which is in town and not far from the station. **Kokuminshukusha Mitoko-so** (国民宿舎みとこ荘; ☎ 0884-76-3510; per person with meals ¥6400; Ⓟ 🐾) is southwest of town out on the coast. It's a government-run lodging house with great views and a big communal bath!

KŌCHI-KEN 高知県

The largest of Shikoku's four prefectures, Kōchi-ken (formerly the land of Tosa) spans the entire Pacific coastline from east of the cape at Muroto-misaki to west of Ashizuri-misaki. It is a popular domain for outdoor activities, from diving, surfing and whale-watching to canoeing, rafting and camping along Shimanto-gawa – the last undammed, naturally flowing river in Japan.

Looking at the Shikoku map (p570), this Kōchi section follows on from the Tokushima–Kōchi border and moves southwest to Muroto-misaki, westwards around Tosa-wan bay to Ashizuri-misaki, then on to the border with Ehime – the same basic route most visitors to Kōchi have taken over the last 1000 years.

EIGHT BALLS

The land of Tosa, or Kōchi as we know it now, was always considered wild and remote throughout Japanese history, cut off from the rest of Japan by a barrier of rugged mountains on one side and the not-too-aptly named Pacific Ocean on the other. The people of Tosa led tough lives, eking out an existence in a hostile environment. Consequently, the Tosa character is thought of as strong, independent and proud. While next door in Tokushima they nurtured puppet theatre, in Tosa they raised fighting dogs (see p585).

Tosa also raised strong women, who often had to fend for their children and themselves while their husbands were off fishing. The locals have a lovely word to describe a tough Kōchi woman – *hachikin*. *Hachi* means eight and *kin* means testicles, with the implication that the woman in question has 'the strength of a man with eight balls'. So if the appropriate situation arises and you want to raise a smile in Kōchi, ask a woman if she is *hachikin*, but make sure you are smiling when you ask!

SHIKOKU

To pilgrims, Kōchi-ken is known as Shūgyō-no-dōjō – the place of practice – and has a reputation as the *henrō*'s testing ground. The trip through Tosa makes up more than a third of the pilgrimage, even though there are only 16 of the 88 temples in the province.

The tough work ahead is symbolised by the fact that there's 84km between the last temple in Tokushima, the Yakuō-ji in Hiwasa, and the first in Tosa at Muroto-misaki. Kōchi's first temple, marks the spot where Kōbō Daishi achieved enlightenment at the age of 19, and holds huge significance to pilgrims. The route then follows a wide arc around Tosa-wan, visits the nine temples in and around Kōchi city, and then drops to the end of Shikoku's second great southern cape that juts out into the Pacific, Ashizuri-misaki. The distance from Temple 37 (Iwamoto-ji) in Kubokawa to Temple 38 (Kongōfuku-ji) at Ashizuri-misaki is 87km, the longest distance between temples on the pilgrimage. There are few places as remote in all Japan. Even then, there's still work to be done to get through Tosa, and the *henrō* tends to breathe a sigh of relief on moving into Ehime-ken prefecture: the hard work has been done.

TOKUSHIMA TO MUROTO-MISAKI

If you've just come down the coast from Tokushima and Hiwasa, then you're literally at the end of the line at Kannoura as you pass into Kōchi-ken prefecture. That's the end of the train line, and if you want to carry on down to Muroto-misaki you'll either have to take the bus or use your thumb. The good news is that the coast and its beaches and rocky headlands are spectacular. In particular, **Ikumi beach** is popular with surfers. Surf shops abound and national competitions are held here.

There is a host of *minshuku* (Japanese-style B&B) around, and the **White Beach Hotel** (ホワイトビーチホテル; ☎ 0887-29-3344; per person with/without meals ¥7500/6000) is right next to **Shirahama Beach** (白浜). The hotel has a **restaurant** (🕑 7am-9pm) and there's a big communal bath as well as private in-room facilities. Next door, at the beach, there is **camping** with over 50 tent sites.

Minami Kaze (みなみかぜ; ☎ 0887-29-3638; per person ¥3000), right on the beach at Ikumi, is popular with surfies. It has 10 rooms, and shared toilets and showers. Meals and draught beer are also available.

Halfway down the coast to Muroto-misaki, **whale-watching tours** (☎ 0887-27-2572; ¥5000) are available at Sakihama (佐喜浜). Call for details, as tours run irregularly.

The bus runs to/from Kannoura to Muroto-misaki (¥1480, one hour) and Kōchi city (¥2770, 2½ hours). For the last 40km to the cape, the road hugs the coast, hemmed in by mountains on one side and the sea on the other.

Muroto-misaki 室戸岬

☎ 0887

Muroto-misaki is one of Shikoku's two great capes that jut out into the Pacific. In Japanese literature, Muroto is famed as one of the wildest spots in the nation and as the doorway to the land of the dead. To pilgrims, it is the place where Kōbō Daishi achieved enlightenment, and many come to try and do the same. On a calm day, the Pacific is like a millpond; in bad weather Muroto is pounded by huge waves and buffeted by the wind. Visitors can explore Kōbō Daishi's bathing hole among the rockpools, or the cave where he meditated. A few kilometres northeast of the cape, a 5.5m-high white statue of the saint stares out to sea.

Temple 24, **Hotsumisaki-ji** (最御崎寺; also known as Higashi-dera), sits on top of the hill directly above the point. It has a **youth hostel** (☎ 23-0024; dm ¥3200) that is part of the temple complex (meals are available).

There are regular buses from Muroto to Kōchi station (¥2810, two hours 40 minutes, seven daily).

MUROTO-MISAKI TO KŌCHI

The coastline and towns between Muroto-misaki and Kōchi city have become more accessible thanks to a rare phenomenon in Japan – a new train line. The country has lost plenty of uneconomic lines since the railways were privatised in 1987, and a new line is unusual. As of 2002 the Gomen–Nahari line connects Kōchi city with Nahari, about 30km north of the cape.

Aki 安芸市

☎ 0887

Aki is a pleasant little town about 50 minutes southeast of Kōchi city by train. Bicycles are available for free at Aki station's **Jibasan-ichiba** (☎ 35-7500; 🕑 7am-8pm) and are good for touring the town's sights.

SHIKOKU

Iwasaki Yatarō, founder of the giant Mitsubishi conglomerate, was born here in 1834. You can visit his family's **thatched-roof house** (岩崎弥太郎生家; admission free; 9am-6pm), which is well preserved.

Worth a visit is the **Aki Municipal Calligraphy Art Museum** (安芸市立書道美術館; ☎ 34-1613; admission ¥300; 9am-5pm Tue-Sun), with over 1400 examples of *shodō* (Japanese calligraphy) on display.

There are also **castle ruins** and the **Aki History and Folk Museum** (安芸市立歴史民族資料館; ☎ 34-3706; admission ¥300; 9am-5pm Tue-Sun) to visit.

Ryūga-dō 龍河洞
☎ 0887

Accessible by bus from Noichi station on the new train line is the impressive limestone cave **Ryūga-dō** (☎ 53-2144; www.ryugadou.or.jp in Japanese; admission ¥1000; 8.30am-5pm). Designated as a national natural monument, the cave has characteristic stalactites and stalagmites, and traces of prehistoric habitation. About 1km of the 4km of cave is toured in the standard visit. If you're into caves and book ahead, you can do the 'adventure course' (¥3000) and don overalls for a two-hour exploration of the cave's more inner reaches.

The caves can also be reached by bus from Tosa-Yamada station (¥440, 20 minutes).

KŌCHI 高知
☎ 088 / pop 320,000

Kōchi was the castle town of what used to be Tosa province, and the small but original castle still stands. Like Kagoshima in Kyūshū and Hagi in western Honshū, this pleasant city lays claim to having played an important role in the Meiji Restoration (see p38).

Orientation

Kōchi city is 12km inland from Tosa-wan (Tosa Bay). Harimayabashi-dōri, the main street, runs on a north–south axis, with a tramline down the centre. The street crosses the main Obiyamachi shopping arcade and the other main street near **Harimaya-bashi**, a recently rebuilt replica of the original bridge. Around where the tramlines cross is the liveliest part of town.

Information

The extremely efficient **tourist information office** (☎ 882-7777; 9am-8pm) is at JR Kōchi Station. All the staff can speak English. They have English brochures and maps and can help to book accommodation; they also provides bikes for touring the town's sights (see p588).

Also well worth visiting for local information, maps and friendly advice is the **Kōchi International Association** (KIA; ☎ 875-0022; www.kochi-f.co.jp/kia; 4-1-31 Honmachi; 8.30am-5.15pm Mon-Sat, closed Sat Aug), on the south side of the castle. There is free Internet access, a library, TV and English newspapers. Check out the association's website for information and events.

There are coin lockers and a left-luggage office at the station, and a few minutes' walk west is the central post office, where ATMs accept international money cards.

Sights & Activities
KŌCHI-JŌ 高知城

Kōchi's **castle** (☎ 824-5701; admission ¥400; 9am-4.30pm) is a real survivor, not a post-war concrete reconstruction, and the lovely grounds are great for a stroll. Although a building on the site dates back to the 14th century, the present castle was built between 1601 and 1611, burnt down in 1727 and rebuilt in 1753. By this time, the peace of the Tokugawa period was well established and castles were scarcely necessary, except as a symbol of a feudal lord's power. The Kōchi lord therefore rebuilt the castle with his *kaitokukan* (living quarters) on the ground floor, with doors opening into the garden. Kōchi-jō, therefore, is not a gloomy castle, unlike those that were strongly fortified against enemy attack. The castle offers fine views over the town.

At the bottom of the castle hill is the well-preserved gateway, **Ōte-mon**.

GODAISAN-KŌEN & CHIKURIN-JI 五台山公園・竹林寺

Kōchi is a hilly city and **Godai-san**, several kilometres east of the town centre, is a large park based around a stand-alone hill. There are good views out over the city from the *tenbōdai* (viewpoint). At the top is **Chikurin-ji** (☎ 882-3085; admission to Treasure House & Gardens ¥400; 8.30am-5pm), Temple 32 on the 88 Sacred Temple Circuit, and the Godaisan-kōen gardens. The temple has a five-storey pagoda and the Treasure House has an interesting collection of statues.

SHIKOKU

On the south side of the hill are the **Kōchi Prefectural Makino Botanical Gardens** (高知県立牧野植物園; ☎ 882-2601; admission ¥500; ⊗ 9am-5pm Tue-Sun) with over 3000 different plant species.

Buses from Harimaya-bashi bus terminal run to Godaisan-kōen (¥150, 10 minutes, regularly).

KATSURA-HAMA 桂浜
Katsura-hama is a popular beach 13km south of central Kōchi at the point where Kōchi's harbour empties out into Tosa-wan. The sandy beach is appealing and there are a number of interesting attractions.

The Kōchi area is noted for its fighting dogs. These mastiff-like dogs are ranked like sumō wrestlers and even wear similar aprons. Dog-fight demonstrations are held in the **Tosa Tōken Centre** (土佐闘犬センター; ☎ 842-3315; admission ¥2000; ⊗ 8.30am-6pm) at Katsura-hama, but you may have to wait until sufficient spectators have gathered.

A five-minute walk west and up from the beach is the **Sakamoto Ryōma Memorial Museum** (高知県立坂本竜馬記念館; ☎ 841-0001; admission ¥400; ⊗ 9am-5pm), which tells the local hero's life story in miniature dioramas. Although it was the progressive samurai (warrior class) of Kagoshima and Hagi who played a major part in the dramatic events of the Meiji Restoration, the citizens of Kōchi claim it was their boy Sakamoto who brought the two sides together. His assassination in Kyoto in 1867, when he was just 32 years old, cemented his romantic albeit tragic image, and he appears – looking distinctly sour – on countless postcards and other tourist memorabilia in Kōchi. As well as the museum, there is an impressive **statue** of Sakamoto Ryōma by Katsura-hama beach.

The **Katsura-hama Aquarium** (桂浜水族館; ☎ 841-2437; admission ¥1100; ⊗ 8.30am-5.30pm) features local *akame* fished from Tosa-wan. Local kids enjoy feeding the fish and resident sea turtles.

SUNDAY MARKET 日曜市
If you're in Kōchi on a Sunday, don't miss the colourful **street market** (Ōtesuji; ⊗ 5am-6pm Sun Apr-Sep, 6am-5pm Sun Oct-Mar) along the road leading to the castle. The market, which has been going for some 300 years, has everything from fruit, vegetables and goldfish to antiques, knives and large garden stones.

Festivals
Kōchi's lively **Yosakoi-matsuri** (よさこい祭り) on 10 and 11 August complements Tokushima's Awa-odori festival (12 to 15 August; p576) perfectly. There's a night-before event on 9 August and night-after effort on the 12 August, but 10 and 11 August are the big days. Needless to say, a lot of alcohol disappears in the sweltering summer heat and a lot of fun is had by all.

Recent festivals have attracted around 20,000 dancers in around 200 teams, including one team of foreigners. If you're keen to take part, contact the Kōchi International Association (see opposite). Get things sorted out early, as accommodation is a nightmare to find on the day.

Sleeping
BUDGET
Kōchi Youth Hostel (☎ 823-0858; 4-5 Fukui-higashi-machi; dm ¥3360; ℗ ⊠) A five-minute walk from Engyoji-guchi station and two stops west of Kōchi station, this youth hostel is modern and relaxed; meals are available.

Tosa Bekkan (☎ 883-5685; 1-11-34 Sakura-chō; per person with/without meals ¥6000/4000; ℗ ⊠) The best deal near Kōchi station, this place has Japanese-style rooms and a coin laundry; it's a 10-minute walk southeast of the station.

Business Hotel Icchō (☎ 883-6000; 2-12 Aioi-chō; s ¥5000; ℗ ⊠) Also a 10-minute walk from the station, and not far from Tosa Bekkan, this business hotel has standard singles but is convenient.

Business Hotel Town (☎ 825-0055; 1-5-26 Hon-machi; s ¥5500; ℗ ⊠) Closer to the Harimaya-bashi junction action, Business Hotel Town is near the Horizume tram stop and is reasonable in terms of price. It has standard business hotel–type accommodation.

MIDRANGE
Kōchi Palace Hotel (☎ 825-0100; 1-18 Nijūdai-machi; s/d/tw ¥6200/8500/12000; ℗ ⊠) The prefecture's biggest hotel with 262 rooms, this hotel is midway between the station and Harimaya-bashi junction. Rates are reasonable for the clean and comfortable rooms. There is an excellent restaurant and bar in the hotel.

Kōchi Pacific Hotel (☎ 884-0777; 1-15 Ekimae-chō; s ¥7500; ℗ ⊠) This big modern hotel with good-sized rooms and beds is conveniently located a couple of minutes' walk south of the station.

KŌCHI

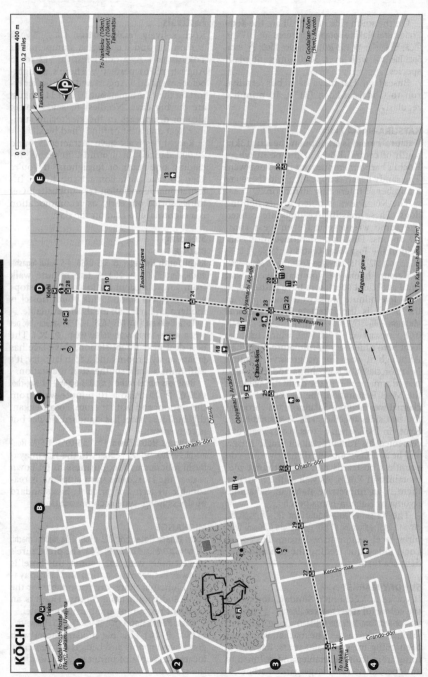

INFORMATION				EATING				TRANSPORT			
Central Post Office 中央郵便局	1	C1		Hirome Ichiba ひろめ市場	14	B3		Dentetsu taminaru-biru Mae			
Kōchi International Association				Suigeitei 酔鯨亭	15	D3		デンテツターミナルビル	20	D3	
高知国際交流センター	2	B3		Tokugetsurō 得月楼	16	D3		Grando-dōri グランドおおり	21	A4	
Tourist Information Office				Tosa-ryōri Tsukasa Kōchi-honten				Harimaya-bashi Bus Terminal			
駅観光案内所	3	D1		土佐料理司高知本店	17	D3		はりまや橋バスターミナル	22	D3	
								Harimaya-bashi はりまやばし	23	D3	
SIGHTS & ACTIVITIES				DRINKING				Hasuike-machi はすいけまち	24	D2	
Ōte-mon 追手門	4	B3		Tosa-no-izakaya Ippon-tsuri				Horizume ほりづめ	25	C3	
Harimaya-bashi	5	D3		土佐の居酒屋一本釣り	18	C2		JR Kōchi Station Bus Terminal			
Kōchi-jō 高知城	6	A3		Viva	19	C3		高知駅バスターミナル	26	D1	
								Kenchō-mae けんちょうまえ	27	A3	
SLEEPING								Kōchi-eki こうちえきまえ	28	D1	
Business Hotel Icchō								Kōchijō-mae こうちじょうまえ	29	B3	
ビジネスホテル一兆	7	D2						Saenbachō さえんばちょう	30	E3	
Business Hotel Town								Umenotsuji うめのつじ	31	D4	
ビジネスホテルタウン	8	D3						Ōhashi-dōri おおはしどおり	32	B3	
International (Kokusai) Hotel Kōchi											
国際ホテル高知	9	D3									
Kōchi Pacific Hotel											
高知パシフィックホテル	10	D1									
Kōchi Palace Hotel											
高知パレスホテル	11	D2									
Sansuien 三翠園	12	B4									
Tosa Bekkan 土佐別館	13	E2									

Kokuminshukusha Katsura-hama (国民宿舎 桂浜; ☎ 841-2201; r per person with 2 meals ¥8000; P ☒) If you're looking for a quiet place to stay, this place is a government-run hotel next to the Sakamoto Ryōma Memorial Museum, with good views and baths.

International (Kokusai) Hotel Kōchi (☎ 0120-224-111; Harimaya-bashi; s from ¥8300; P ☒) This upmarket place has good Western-style rooms, and is the place to head to if you want to be right where the action is. It is right on the Harimaya-bashi junction.

TOP END

Sansuien (☎ 822-0131; www.sansuien.co.jp in Japanese; 1-3-35 Takajō-machi; per person from ¥15,750; P ☒) South of the castle, this is a top ryokan-style place and includes some old buildings from the grounds of the Kōchi *daimyō* (regional lord under the shōgun) and an *onsen* (non-guests ¥900), which is open to the public. Rates include meals.

Eating & Drinking

Kōchi's top eating and drinking area is around the Obiyamachi shopping arcade, near the Harimaya-bashi junction, where the tramlines meet.

Tokugetsurō (☎ 882-0101; 1-17-3 Minami-har-imaya-chō; ⏾ lunch & dinner) Open since 1870, this is the place to come to if you have a fat wallet and want to try immaculately presented Tosa-ryōri (local cuisine). Don't come here if you're on a tight budget.

Suigeitei (☎ 882-6577; 1-17-25 Minami-harimaya-chō; ⏾ lunch & dinner) If you want to know what all the fuss is about concerning whale meat, head to Suigeitei. While the whale on offer probably hasn't undergone scientific experimentation, it's an opportunity to try a local delicacy.

Tosa-ryōri Tsukasa Kōchi-honten (☎ 873-4351; 1-2-15 Harimaya-chō; ⏾ lunch & dinner) Tsukasa dishes up tasty local specialities, including *katsuo tataki* (lightly cooked bonito; ¥1200).

Tosa-no-izakaya Ippon-tsuri (☎ 825-3676; 1-5-5 Obiyamachi; ⏾ 7pm-midnight) This place features excellent seafood and sake from each of the prefecture's 19 sake producers. Make sure you know how to find your way home if you intend to try all of them.

Viva (☎ 823-6362; 1-1-11 Honmachi; ⏾ 6pm-1am daily, 6pm-5am Sat) This trendy dining bar has over 100 cocktails and beer from all over the world on offer.

Hirome Ichiba (☎ 822-5287; 2-3-1 Obiyamachi; ⏾ 8am-11pm) This market boasts an interesting collection of over 60 shops, eateries and drinking establishments well worth checking out. There's something for everyone, and being right on Ōtesuji, it's a great spot during the Sunday street market (see p585).

Getting There & Away

Kōchi airport is about 10km east of the city and there are connections to Tokyo (ANA/JAS, ¥26,800, 1¼ hours, nine daily); Nagoya (JAIR, ¥22,300, one hour, three daily); Osaka (ANK, ¥15,000, 40 minutes, eight daily); Fukuoka (JAC, ¥20,300, 70 minutes, three daily); and Naha (JTA, ¥26,300, 1½ hours, three weekly). There's a regular bus service between Kōchi station and the airport (¥700, 35 minutes).

Kōchi is on the JR Dosan line, which runs from Takamatsu (*tokkyū*, or premium train; 2½ hours) on the north coast of Shikoku via Kotohira. From Kōchi, trains head westward to just beyond Kubokawa where the line splits southwest to Nakamura and west to Uwajima (three hours). From Uwajima, you can continue north to Matsuyama.

SHIKOKU

Long-distance buses run between Kōchi and the major cities. Travel between Kōchi and Matsuyama is faster by bus (¥3500, 2½ hours) than by train. To travel around the south coast, either west around Ashizuri-misaki to Uwajima or east around Muroto-misaki to Tokushima, you will have to spend some time on a bus as the train lines do not extend all the way.

Kōchi is connected by overnight ferry to Osaka (¥4500, nine hours). There are also two ferries a week to Kawasaki (¥11,420, 16 hours). See Ferry Timetables (p756) for more information.

Getting Around

Kōchi's colourful tram service (¥180 per trip) has been running since 1904. Some of the carriages have come from all over the world, including Germany, Norway and Portugal. There are two lines. The north–south line from the station intersects with the east–west tram route at the Harimaya-bashi junction. Pay when you get off. Ask for a *norikae-ken* (transfer ticket) if you have to change lines.

You can easily reach the castle on foot, though to reach the town's other attractions you'll need to take a bus. Buses make the run from Kōchi station and Harimaya-bashi bus station to Katsura-hama beach regularly (¥610, 30 minutes).

The tourist information office (p584) offers bicycles that visitors can use for free from 10am to 5pm, and overnight if they book accommodation in the city.

KŌCHI TO ASHIZURI-MISAKI

There are all sorts of interesting things going on between Kōchi and Ashizuri-misaki, particularly the closer you get to the cape. You can whale-watch, kayak and canoe on the last free-flowing river in Japan, while there's an exquisite beach at Ōki-hama and, at the cape itself, intriguing history and picturesque scenery.

Kubokawa & Around 窪川
☎ 0880

Kubokawa, one hour south of Kōchi by the fastest train, is a sleepy little town with a very pleasant **youth hostel** (☎ 22-0376; dm ¥3200) – meals available – in the **Iwamoto-ji** (岩本寺), which is also Temple 37 of the 88. The hostel is a 10-minute walk south of the station. The next temple is at the cape, 87km away, so if

you're on the pilgrimage and walking, you may want to mentally prepare yourself.

The train lines part at Kubokawa, and the JR Yodo line heads west through the mountains to Uwajima (Ehime-ken). Along the way, but still in Kōchi, is the hard-to-get-to but often-raved-about **Shimanto-gawa Youth Hostel** (四万十川ユースホステル; ☎ 54-1352; dm ¥3150; P 🌊). Get off at Ekawasaki station, and take the bus to Kuchiyanai (30 minutes). The youth hostel (meals are available) is 4.5km away across the river, but the manager will come and pick you up if you call and ask nicely. You couldn't get much more away from it all in Japan. The hostel runs canoeing trips (¥5500 per person), including all tuition and gear.

The Tosa-kuroshio line heads south to Nakamura, then west to Sukumo. There are **whale-watching trips** (¥5000, three hours) on offer in Saga (☎ 55-3131) and Ōgata (☎ 43-1058) from spring to autumn, but you might want to call ahead to see if they are running.

Nakamura 中村
☎ 0880

Nakamura is a good place to organise trips on the beautiful **Shimanto-gawa** (四万十川), proudly hailed as the last free-flowing river in Japan. Staff at the **tourist information office** (☎ 35-4171; 🕙 10am-7pm) at Nakamura station can provide information on kayaking and canoe trips, camping and outdoor activities.

Dragonfly lovers will go bananas at the **Shimanto-gawa Gakuyūkan** (四万十川学遊館; ☎ 37-4111; admission ¥840; 🕙 9am-5pm Tue-Sun) where over 3000 dragonflies from Japan and around the world are on display. There's a dragonfly park where living dragonflies cruise around, and a great display of fish from Shimanto-gawa.

Nakamura is on Shimanto-gawa, at the point where the train line continues west to Sukumo. There are no trains south of here. From Nakamura station there is a regular bus service to Ashizuri-misaki (¥1970, one hour). You can continue around the cape and on to Sukumo and Uwajima by bus or thumb.

You can also get to Kuchiyanai, close to the Shimanto-gawa Youth Hostel (see above), by bus (¥850, one hour, three daily) from here.

About 40 minutes south of Nakamura on the bus to Ashizuri-misaki is **Ōki-hama** (大

Dried starfish

Views over the Inland Sea

Torii on Ishizuchi-san (p600), Ehime-ken

Henrō on the 88 Sacred Temples of Shikoku pilgrimage (p574)

Flags flying over Yoshino-gawa (p579),
Tokushima-ken

Oku Iya Kazura-bashi (p580), Higashi Iya,
Tokushima-ken

岐浜), a 2km-long stretch of sandy white beach backed by pine trees that is likely to have you blinking in disbelief and reaching for your swimming gear. It's possible to camp here, and although local surfers don't want to advertise it, they claim that it is an excellent surfing spot.

ASHIZURI-MISAKI 足摺岬
☎ 0880

Ashizuri-misaki, like Muroto-misaki, is a wild and picturesque promontory ending at a lighthouse, and it is a popular visitors destination. Ashizuri means 'foot stamping' and the cape got its name from the story of an old monk who stamped his foot in anguish when his young disciple set off looking for the promised land of Fudaraku in a boat. Fudaraku was believed to be the blessed realm of Kannon, goddess of mercy, and many set forth from the cape in their search for paradise in this lifetime, never to be heard from again. Centuries later, Ashizuri is famous for suicides, with stories such as that of a young geisha who danced off the edge onto the beckoning rocks below.

There's a small **tourist information booth** with English maps of the area and a statue of local hero John Manjirō (see below).

The **Kongōfuku-ji** (金剛福寺; ☎ 88-0038; 7am-5.30pm) is Temple 38 of the 88, but it doesn't have Ashizuri-misaki to itself. There are hotels, ryokan, tour buses and the **Ashizuri Youth Hostel** (足摺ユースホステル; ☎ 88-0324; dm ¥2900; P ⚡), where meals are available.

A regular bus service goes to Ashizuri-misaki from Nakamura station (¥1970, one hour).

NORTHWEST TO SUKUMO & UWAJIMA
Tosa-Shimizu 土佐清水
☎ 0880

Ferries are operated by **Osaka Kōchi Tokkyū Ferry** (Osaka ☎ 06-6612-8700, Kochi 088-833-3401) to/from Osaka (¥5000, 10 hours) from Tosa-Shimizu at the northern end of the cape, via Kōchi. There are also **whale-watching tours** (☎ 84-0723) on offer for ¥5000.

From Tosa-Shimizu, the road continues around the southern coast.

Tatsukushi 竜串
☎ 0880

The scenery is particularly attractive through Tatsukushi, which means 'dragon's skewers' and got its name from spectacular rock pillars that protrude from the sea. There is a

SHIKOKU

MANJIRŌ THE HERO

Nearly every corner of Shikoku boasts a local hero, but perhaps most extraordinary of them all is Kōchi-born John Manjirō.

His real name was Nakahama Manjirō. In 1841, while helping out on a fishing boat, a violent storm swept 14-year-old Manjirō and four others onto the desolate shores of Tori-shima island, 600km off Tokyo Bay. Five months later they were rescued by a US whaler, and granted safe passage to Hawaii.

In Hawaii the ship's captain invited Manjirō to return to his home in Massachusetts, where the boy spent four years learning English, navigation and the ways of the West, before his skills took him back to sea and around the world. In 1851, 10 years after the shipwreck, Manjirō returned to Japan, where he was interrogated (Japan's National Seclusion policy forbade overseas travel; see p37 for more information), but allowed to return to Kōchi.

When Commodore Perry's 'black ships' arrived in 1853, Manjirō was summoned to Edo to advise the shōgun (military ruler of Japan). He was later the chief translator for the Harris Treaty negotiations of 1858, and subsequently published Japan's first English-language phrase book, *Shortcut to Anglo-American Conversation*. He returned to the USA in 1860 as part of a Japanese delegation, and after the Meiji Restoration in 1868 took up a post at the Kaisei School for Western Learning (which later became part of Tokyo University).

Manjirō is remembered as a man whose destiny took him from the simple life of a teenage fisherman to becoming one of Japan's first true statesmen. On the cape at Ashizuri-misaki, a large statue stands in his honour, and the museum **John Man House** (☎ 88-1136; admission ¥300; 9am-4pm Fri-Wed) is dedicated to his achievements. Manjirō's intrepid journey is recounted in Masuji Ibuse's *Castaways*.

coral museum (サンゴ博物館; ☎ 85-0231; admission ¥500; ☯ 8am-5.30pm), with a superb collection of local pink coral, and the Ashizuri Submarine Lookout (足摺海洋館; ☎ 85-0635; admission ¥700; ☯ 8am-6pm), where you can view fish from an observation room below sea level. Sightseeing boats and glass-bottom boats operate from the town.

The Ōdō Sunset Youth Hostel (大堂サンセットユースホステル; ☎ 76-0222; dm ¥2750; Ⓟ Ⓧ) is almost at the end of a 17km-long dead-end road at the end of a spiny peninsula with stunning scenery (meals are available at the hostel). The turn-off is about halfway between Tatsukushi and Sukumo. Using public transport, the hostel is best accessed by catching the bus from Sukumo to Kashiwa-jima island (¥1430, one hour), and getting off at the Shin-Kashiwa-jima Ōhashi stop. Kashiwa-jima (柏島) is a popular diving site.

Sukumo 宿毛
☎ 0880

Sukumo has a fine harbour and the Sukumo Youth Hostel (宿毛ユースホステル; ☎ 64-0233; dm ¥2900). The hostel is 20 minutes out of town, but if you call and ask nicely staff will come and get you. Meals are available.

There are several popular dive sites off islands in the area that are reached by boat from Sukumo – notably at Nishiumi and Oki-no-shima.

Sukumo is only half an hour by train from Nakamura, but the trip by bus takes much longer along the coast via the cape; travel on to Uwajima takes about two hours by bus (¥1750). From Sukumo, ferries make the three-hour crossing several times daily to Saeki on Kyūshū.

EHIME-KEN 愛媛県

Occupying the northwestern region of Shikoku, the highlights of Ehime-ken prefecture include Matsuyama-jō castle and Dōgo Onsen, the sacred peak Ishizuchi-san (1982m), and the notorious Taga-jinja (Taga Shrine) and sex museum of Uwajima.

Looking at the Shikoku map (p570), this section starts in the southwest corner of the prefecture for those who are following the circular route of the island. It then works its way north to Matsuyama, before turning east towards Kagawa-ken.

To pilgrims, Ehime-ken is known as Bodai-no-dōjō – the place of attainment of wisdom – and has the largest number (27) of pilgrimage temples. The southern part of the prefecture was always considered, like Tosa, to be wild and remote – they still have bull-fighting in Uwajima. Further north, there are two temples in the inland mountains, with the Iwaya-ji, Temple 45, well worth a visit, hanging on a cliff-side high above the valley floor. The temple oozes sacredness. As henrō approach Shikoku's largest city of Matsuyama and the eight temples in and around it, they know that the hard work of the pilgrimage has been done. There are another six temples in and around Imabari, where the Shimanami Hwy (Shimanami-kaidō) bridge system links Shikoku to Honshū. Then the trail turns east.

UWAJIMA 宇和島
☎ 0895 / pop 60,000

Uwajima is a relatively quiet and peaceful place with a small, unreconstructed castle and a notorious sex shrine! It makes a very interesting pause between Kōchi and Matsuyama.

Information

There is a tourist information office (☎ 22-3934; ☯ 8.30am-5pm Mon-Fri, 9am-5pm Sat & Sun) across the road from JR Uwajima Station that offers free Internet access (limit one hour) and the staff members are extremely helpful. They will make accommodation bookings for you and may feign surprise when you ask the way to the sex museum. The office also hires out bicycles (see p592).

There are coin lockers at the station and, for money, international ATMs at the post office.

Sights & Activities
UWAJIMA-JŌ 宇和島城

Dating from 1601, Uwajima-jō (☎ 22-2832; admission ¥200; ☯ 9am-4pm) is an interesting little three-storey structure atop an 80m-high hillock in the middle of town. This castle once stood by the sea and although land reclamation has moved the water well back, it still has good views over the town.

Inside the castle grounds are photos of its restoration and of other castles in Japan and overseas. The surrounding park, Shiroyama Kōen, is open sunrise to sunset.

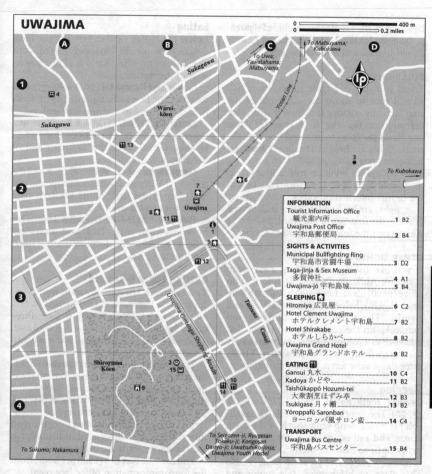

UWAJIMA

| 0 | 400 m |
| 0 | 0.2 miles |

INFORMATION
Tourist Information Office
観光案内所 **1** B2
Uwajima Post Office
宇和島郵便局 **2** B4

SIGHTS & ACTIVITIES
Municipal Bullfighting Ring
宇和島市営闘牛場 **3** D2
Taga-jinja & Sex Museum
多賀神社 **4** A1
Uwajima-jō 宇和島城 **5** B4

SLEEPING
Hiromiya 広見屋 **6** C2
Hotel Clement Uwajima
ホテルクレメント宇和島 **7** B2
Hotel Shirakabe
ホテルしらかべ **8** B2
Uwajima Grand Hotel
宇和島グランドホテル **9** B2

EATING
Gansui 丸水 **10** C4
Kadoya かどや **11** B2
Taishūkappō Hozumi-tei
大衆割烹ほずみ亭 **12** B3
Tsukigase 月ヶ瀬 **13** B2
Yōroppafū Saronban
ヨーロッパ風サロン蛮 **14** C4

TRANSPORT
Uwajima Bus Centre
宇和島バスセンター **15** B4

SHIKOKU

TAGA-JINJA & SEX MUSEUM 多賀神社

Once upon a time, many Shintō shrines had a connection to fertility rites, but this aspect was comprehensively purged when puritanism was imported from the West following the Meiji Restoration (see p37 for more information). Nevertheless, a handful of these shrines survived and Uwajima's **Taga-jinja** is one of them – it is totally dedicated to sex. There is a tree-trunk phallus and various other statues and stone carvings found around the grounds, but the three-storey **sex museum** (☎ 22-3444; www1.quolia.com /dekoboko in Japanese; admission ¥800; ⏱ 8am-5pm) is the major attraction.

Inside, the museum is packed floor to ceiling with everything from explicit Peruvian pottery to Greek vases; from the illustrated *Kama Sutra* to Tibetan Tantric sculptures; from South Pacific fertility gods to a showcase full of leather S&M gear; and from early Japanese *shunga* (explicit erotic prints) to their European Victorian equivalents, not to mention modern porn magazines.

Watching the reactions of Japanese visitors here is almost as interesting as inspecting the intriguing exhibits. Even if you're sick to death of temples and shrines, this is one to put on the 'to visit' list. For a sneak preview, check out the website.

TEMPLES & SHRINES

In the southeastern part of town, a number of less exciting old temples and a shrine can be found by the canal. They include **Seigōzen-ji**, **Ryūgesan Tōkaku-ji**, **Kongōsan Dairyū-ji**, with its old tombs, and **Uwatsuhiko-jinja**.

BULLFIGHTS

Tōgyū is a sort of bovine sumō where one animal tries to shove the other out of the ring (actually, victory is achieved when one animal forces the other to its knees, or when one forces the other to turn and flee from the ring). Fights are held at Uwajima's **municipal bullfighting ring** (admission ¥3000). You might be lucky enough to hook up with a tour group that's paid for a special performance (ask at the tourist information office; p590); otherwise, fights are held on five dates each year: 2 January, the first Sunday of April, 24 July, 14 August and the fourth Sunday of October.

OTHER SIGHTS & ACTIVITIES

If you like fishing and getting away from it all, ask Akiko in the tourist information office (p590) about her home island of **Hiburi-jima** (日振島), halfway between Shikoku and Kyūshū. There are beaches, camping and *minshuku* on the rocky isolated island that is known as a fishing mecca. Daily ferries ply the waters from Uwajima (fast ferry, ¥1990, three daily; slow ferry, ¥1360, one daily).

Sleeping

Uwajima Youth Hostel (☎ 22-7177; dm ¥3300; P 🐕) The youth hostel (meals are available) is a 2km-long walk south of the town centre and rather inconvenient. There are better options near the station.

Hiromiya (☎ 22-2162; per person ¥3000; P 🐕) This place, with Japanese-style rooms and shared facilities, is satisfactory, but since it's next to the train line, you probably won't sleep in.

Hotel Shirakabe (☎ 22-3585; www3.netwave.or.jp/~sirakabe; s/d ¥4200/6300; P 🐕 🖥 🛄) This is our top pick for those on a tight budget. Shirakabe has an English home page, offers free Internet use and is close to the station. Rooms are simple but clean.

Uwajima Grand Hotel (☎ 24-3911; s/tw ¥5500/10,500; P 🐕) Good value and convenient, this hotel is only two minutes' walk from the station. A buffet breakfast adds ¥700.

Hotel Clement Uwajima (☎ 23-6111; s/tw ¥6900/12,000; P 🐕) The top hotel in town, Hotel Clement is part of the new station building. Singles all have semidouble beds.

Eating

Kadoya (☎ 22-1543; 🕙 11am-9pm) Try the local delicacy *tai-meishi* (snapper mixed with rice; ¥1790) on offer. Kadoya is just southwest of the station.

Taishūkappō Hozumi-tei (☎ 25-6590; 🕙 lunch & dinner Mon-Sat) This restaurant dishes up fresh fish, specialising in sashimi and seafood.

Gansui (☎ 22-3636; 🕙 lunch & dinner Wed-Mon) Offering a variety of snapper dishes and alcohol, Gansui is at the southern end of the shopping arcade.

Yōroppafū Saronban (☎ 22-0594; 🕙 lunch & dinner Fri-Wed) *Yōroppafū* means European, and this place prides itself on its Western-style meals using local produce.

Tsukigase (☎ 22-4788; 🕙 lunch & dinner) Out by Warei-kōen park, Tsukigase serves excellent tempura and local seafood. Lunch sets run to ¥1500.

Getting There & Around

You can reach Uwajima by train from Matsuyama via Uchiko and Ōzu by *tokkyū* (1¼ hours, hourly). From Kōchi, it takes three hours by the fastest trains via Kubokawa. To head to Ashizuri-misaki, you'll have to resort to buses.

There is no train line along the coast heading south from Sukumo (Kōchi-ken) to Uwajima, but a bus makes the trip around the rugged coastline in under two hours (¥1750). The island-dotted coastal scenery is spectacular and rugged headlands often force the road inland. There are masses of white floats out in the sea where pearls are being grown.

You can hire bicycles (¥100 per hour) from the tourist information office (see p590).

UWAJIMA TO MATSUYAMA

The stretch of Shikoku's western coast between Uwajima and Matsuyama is rural yet peppered with interesting towns such as Ōzu, with its newly reconstructed castle, and Uchiko, with its interesting old street, Yokaichi. If you've come from points south, then from Uwajima you're back in the land of trains. There's a choice of the JR Yodo line heading back to Kubokawa and Kōchi, or the JR Yosan line heading north to Matsuyama.

Yawatahama 八幡浜
☎ 0894
Through the centuries, 88-Temple pilgrims from Kyūshū traditionally arrived in Yawa-

tahama by ferry, and for them the **Meiseki-ji**, near Uwa, was their first temple. They would start and complete their circle there.

At the port, **Dōya-ichiba** (どーや市場; ☎ 24-7147; ⏰ 7-11am Sun-Fri) is Yawatahama's fish market, with a lively set of 26 fish shops and a huge and fascinating variety of fish and other sea life up for sale. Get there early for the good stuff.

There are still ferry services from Yawatahama to Beppu (¥1770, 2½ hours) and Usuki (¥1320, 2¼ hours) on Kyūshū. Yawatahama-kō port is a five-minute bus ride (¥150) north of Yawatahama station.

Just north of Yawatahama, Sada-misaki extends about 50km towards Kyūshū, and from Misaki, near the end of the cape, car and passenger ferries (¥610 per person) make the crossing to Saganoseki (near Oita and Beppu) in just over an hour.

Ōzu 大洲
☎ 0893

On the Yosan line northeast of Yawatahama is Ōzu, where traditional **cormorant river fishing** (うかい; *ukai*) takes place on the Hiji-kawa from 1 June to 20 September. **Sightseeing boats** (やかた船, yakata-bune; ☎ 24-2029; cruises per person ¥3000; ⏰ 6.30-9pm Jun-Sep) follow the fishing boats down the river as the cormorants catch fish – a ring around the bird's neck stops it from swallowing the fish. Reservations are required.

Ōzu also boasts Japan's newest castle, **Ōzu-jō** (大洲城). The city has just completed reconstruction of its castle using original materials as much as possible. At the time of research it was not open for inspection, but the castle makes an impressive sight above the river at the southern end of town.

Ōzu Kyōdokan Youth Hostel (大洲郷土館; ☎ 24-2258; dm ¥3200; Ⓟ ✗) is in the southwest part of town near the castle. Meals are available. To reach the hostel it takes 30 minutes on foot from Ōzu station, or it's a seven-minute walk from Honmachi bus stop.

Uchiko 内子
☎ 0893

Halfway between Matsuyama and Uwajima on the JR Yosan line, the charming town of Uchiko has a photogenic street lined with traditional buildings dating from the late Edo period and early years following the Meiji Restoration. At that time, Uchiko was an important centre for the production of the vegetable wax known as *rō*, and some

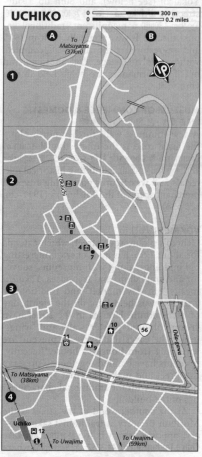

UCHIKO

INFORMATION	
Tourist Information Booth 観光案内所	1 A4

SIGHTS & ACTIVITIES	
Hon-Haga-tei 本芳我邸	2 A2
Kami-Haga-tei 上芳我邸	3 A2
Machi-ya Shiriyōkan 町家資料館	4 A3
Moribun Amazake Chaya Teahouse 森文あま酒茶屋	5 B3
Museum of Commerce and Domestic Life 商いと暮らし博物館	6 B3
Ōmori Rōsoku 大森和ろうそく屋	7 A3
Ōmura-tei 大村邸	8 A2

SLEEPING	
Matsunoya Ryokan 松乃屋旅館	9 A4
Shinmachi-sō 親町荘	10 B3

ENTERTAINMENT	
Uchiko-za 内子座	11 A3

TRANSPORT	
Retro Bus Stop	12 A4

SHIKOKU

of the houses along Yōkaichi belonged to merchants who made their fortunes from producing the wax.

Uchiko is a great day trip from Matsuyama or stopover on the way to Uwajima.

INFORMATION

There's a **tourist information booth** (☎ 43-1450; 🕑 9am-4pm Thu-Tue) on your right as you leave JR Uchiko Station. The staff are helpful and have an English brochure/map on the town, can help with accommodation bookings and have bikes for hire (see right). There are coin lockers at the station.

UCHIKO-ZA 内子座

About halfway between the station and Yōkaichi (see below), and 50m up a side-street, is **Uchiko-za** (☎ 44-2840; admission ¥300; 🕑 9am-4.30pm) a magnificent traditional ka-buki theatre. It was originally built in 1915 and was restored in the mid-1980s, complete with a revolving stage. Call ahead to find out if performances are being held during your visit.

MUSEUM OF COMMERCE & DOMESTIC LIFE 商いと暮らし博物館

A few minutes' walk further north along the main road is the interesting **Museum of Commerce & Domestic Life** (☎ 44-5220; admission ¥200; 🕑 9am-4.30pm), exhibiting historical materials and wax figures portraying a typical merchant scene of the Taishō era (1912–26; see p38).

YŌKAICHI 八日市

Uchiko's picturesque street, which extends for about 1km, has a number of interesting old buildings, along with museums, souvenir and craft shops and teahouses. *Yōkaichi* means '8th day market' and traditionally a market was held here on the eighth day of each month. Houses in the street have cream-coloured plaster walls and 'wings' under the eaves that serve to prevent fire spreading from house to house. Recently, residents have banded together to preserve the street and make sure that any renovations meet with the traditional characteristics of the buildings.

At the southern end of the street is the Moribun Brewery, a traditional sake brewery, opposite which is the **Moribun Amazake Chaya Teahouse** (☎ 44-3057; 🕑 9am-5pm), where

you can sample the local brew. A bit further up the street, **Ōmori Rosoku** (☎ 43-0385; 🕑 9am-5pm Tue-Thu & Sat & Sun) is Uchiko's sole remaining traditional candle maker. There are demonstrations of *rō* candle-making, and candles and stands are for sale.

Machi-ya Shiriyōkan (☎ 44-2111; admission free; 🕑 9am-4.30pm) is a rustic 1790s merchant house that was thoroughly restored in 1987.

As the road makes a slight bend, there come into view several well-preserved Edo-era buildings, such as **Ōmura-tei** (Ōmura residence) and **Hon-Haga-tei**, a fine example of a wealthy merchant's private home. The Hon-Haga family established the production of fine wax in Uchiko, winning awards at World Expositions in Chicago (1893) and Paris (1900). Their residence was built in 1884.

Further on is the exquisite **Kami-Haga-tei** (☎ 44-2771; admission ¥400; 🕑 9am-4.30pm), a wax merchant's house within a large complex of wax-making related buildings. Admission includes entry to the Japanese Wax Museum at the same location.

SLEEPING

While Uchiko is probably best visited on a day trip, there are a couple of traditional options should you opt to stay.

Matsunoya Ryokan (☎ 44-5000; per person with/ without meals ¥12,600/7800, 🅿 🔀) Midway between the station and Yōkaichi, on the main road, this is the place to go if you're keen to stay in a traditional Japanese ryokan.

Shinmachi-sō (☎ 44-2021; per person with/without meals ¥8400/4200, 🅿 🔀) One street back, this is another well-established ryokan.

GETTING THERE & AROUND

Uchiko can be reached by *tokkyū* from Matsuyama (¥1980, 25 minutes) and Uwajima (¥2720, 50 minutes). The tourist information office (left) offers rental bikes (¥500 for two hours, plus a ¥2000 deposit) for touring the town.

Yōkaichi is a 20-minute (1km) walk north of Uchiko station. It's a pleasant stroll, signposted in English, but you might want to consider taking the new **Retro Bus** (☎ 43-1450; tickets ¥800; 🕑 9.30am-6pm), a 1920s English bus that seats nine and shuttles back and forth from the station.

A combined ticket to Uchiko-za (left), the Museum of Commerce & Domestic Life (opposite), and Kami-Haga-tei (opposite) costs ¥700 (a ¥200 saving). The bus stop is next to the information booth.

MATSUYAMA 松山

☎ 089 / pop 478,000

Shikoku's largest city, it's a busy north-coast town and an important transport hub. Matsuyama's major attractions are its castle, Matsutyama-jō – one of the finest survivors from the feudal era – and the Dōgo Onsen area, with its magnificent old public baths. The city is well set up for foreign visitors, is easy to get around, and well worth a visit. Don't miss a soak in the Dōgo Onsen.

Orientation & Information

JR Matsuyama Station is west of the castle. The town centre is immediately south of the castle and around Matsuyama City (Shi-eki) station on the private Iyo-tetsudō line. Dōgo Onsen is east of town, while the ferry port at Takahama is north of the town centre and JR Matsuyama Station.

There is an information counter at the ferry terminal for arrivals from Hiroshima, though the main **tourist information office** (☎ 931-3914; ☺ 8.30am-8.30pm) is the JR Matsuyama Station branch. The staff are very helpful and there is a good English brochure on the city. From 4pm a staff member is on hand specifically to help visitors find accommodation.

Dōgo Onsen also has an excellent **tourist information office** (☎ 921-3708; ☺ 8am-4.45pm) near the tram terminus, at the entrance to the arcade leading to the famous public bath.

The **Ehime Prefectural International Centre** (EPIC; ☎ 943-6688; www.epic.or.jp; ☺ 8.30am-5pm Mon-Sat) has friendly advice, free Internet access, English newspapers etc. It is near tram stop T19, known as Minami-machi or Kenmin Bunkakaikan-mae. EPIC is set back off the main road and a little hard to find. Look for the big red question mark.

There is also free **Internet access** (☺ 9am-7pm) at Matsuyama City station behind the Iyo-tetsudō information booth.

Both EPIC and the information office at JR Matsuyama Station have the Seto Inland Sea Welcome Card, which can get you discounts on all sorts of things in Ehime, Hiroshima and Yamaguchi prefectures.

ATMs that accept international cards can be found at the central post office and at the

post office a couple of minutes' walk north of JR Matsuyama Station.

There are coin lockers and a left-luggage counter at JR Matsuyama, from where you can also hire bicycles (see p599).

English-language books can be found on the 4th floor of the **Kinokuniya bookshop** (☎ 932-0005; ☺ 10am-7.30pm), near Matsuyama City station.

Sights & Activities

MATSUYAMA-JŌ 松山城

Picturesquely sited atop a hill (Katsuyama) that virtually erupts in the centre of town, **Matsuyama-jō** (☎ 921-4873; admission ¥500; ☺ 9am-5pm) is one of Japan's finest original surviving castles. It only squeaks in with the 'original' label, however, as it was restored just before the end of the Edo period. In the early years of the Meiji Restoration, rebuilding feudal symbols was definitely not a high priority.

The castle was built in 1602–03 with five storeys; it burnt down and was rebuilt in 1642 with only three storeys. In 1784 it was struck by lightning and burnt down once again and, in those peaceful Edo years, it took until 1820 for a decision to be made to rebuild it and until 1854 for the reconstruction to be completed! It was completely restored between 1968 and 1986.

You don't have to climb the steep hill up to the castle; a cable car and/or chairlift (¥500 return) will whisk you up the hill.

Consider walking down the back slopes of the castle hill to stroll around the **Ninomaru Shiseki Tei-en** (☎ 921-2000; admission ¥100; ☺ 9am-5pm) gardens. From there, it's a short stroll to the **Ehime Museum of Art** (☎ 932-0010; admission ¥500; ☺ 9.40am-6pm Tue-Sun), which holds some excellent exhibitions.

SHIKI-DŌ 子規堂

Matsuyama claims to be the capital of haiku (17-syllable poems), and just south of Matsuyama City station in the temple grounds of Shoshu-ji is **Shiki-dō** (☎ 945-0400; admission ¥50; ☺ 8.30am-5pm), a replica of the humble house of the legendary haiku poet Shiki Masaoka (1867–1902).

DŌGO ONSEN 道後温泉

This popular spa centre, 2km east of the town centre, is easily reached by the regular tram service, which terminates at the start of the spa's shopping arcade. The arcade

SHIKOKU

leads to the front of Dōgo Onsen Honkan (Dōgo Spa Main Building).

A high priority for any visitor to Matsuyama should be a bath at the rambling old public bathhouse **Dōgo Onsen Honkan** (☎ 921-5141; 5-6 Dōgo-yunomachi; ☯ 6am-11pm). It's one of

those places where the correct sequence of steps can be a little confusing, but don't be put off. Pay your money outside: ¥300 for a basic bath, or ¥620 for a bath followed by tea and a snack, including a rental *yukata*. For ¥980 to ¥1240 you get the *tama-no-yu*

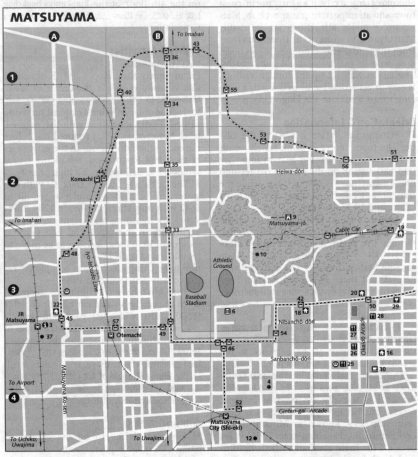

MATSUYAMA

(Bath of the Spirits), followed by tea and *dango* (a sweet dumpling), and more private resting quarters. A rental towel and soap will set you back a further ¥50.

Enter and leave your shoes in a locker. If you've paid ¥300, go to the *kami-no-yu* (Bath

of the Gods) changing room (signposted in English). There are free lockers here also.

If you've paid ¥620 or more, first go upstairs to get your *yukata*, then return to the appropriate changing room. You can leave valuables upstairs in the charge of the

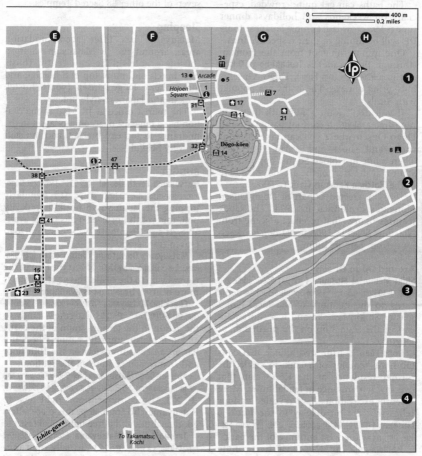

attendants who dispense the *yukata*. After your bath, those destined for upstairs can don their *yukata* and retire to the tatami mats and veranda to sip tea and gaze down on bath-hoppers clip-clopping by in *geta* (traditional wooden sandals).

The baths can get quite crowded, especially on weekends and holidays; dinner time is less crowded, as most Japanese tourists will be dining in their respective inns.

One minute on foot from the Honkan (through the arcade) is **Tsubaki-no-yu Onsen** (admission ¥300; ☺ 6am-11pm), Dōgo Onsen's hot-spring annexe. The baths are popular with locals.

If you don't want a full bath there are nine free **ashi-yu** (足湯; foot baths) around Dōgo Onsen where you can take off your socks and shoes and warm your feet. There's one in Hojoen Sq just opposite the station at the start of the arcade. Also here is the **Botchan Karakuri Clock** (坊ちゃんからくり時計), erected as part of Dōgo Onsen Honkan's centennial in 1994. The clock features figures that re-enact a scene from Natsume Soseki's 1906 novel *Botchan* each hour from 8am to 10pm.

Around Dōgo Onsen

Shiki Memorial Museum (☎ 931-5566; admission ¥300; 1-30 Dōgo-kōen; ☺ 9am-5pm Tue-Sun) is dedicated to the memory of the local haiku master Shiki Masaoka and is a short walk east of the tram stop on the north side of Dōgo-kōen.

Dōgo-kōen is a forested hillock that contains the remains of Yuzuki-jō castle, the former residence of the Kōno clan that oversaw Iyo province in feudal times. More recently excavations have revealed various relics that are on display in the **Yuzuki-jō Museum** (☎ 941-1480; admission free; ☺ 9am-5pm Tue-Sun) near the west entrance of the park.

Isaniwa-jinja (☎ 947-7447), a five-minute walk east of Dōgo Onsen Honkan, was built in 1667, and is the third-largest shrine of its kind in Japan. A national cultural treasure, the shrine was built to resemble Kyoto's Iwashimizu-Hachimangu.

Further east is the **Ishite-ji**, number 51 of the 88 Sacred Temples, which is noted for its fine Kamakura architecture. 'Ishite' means 'stone hand', from a legend about a Matsuyama lord born with a stone in his hand. The temple has a three-storey pagoda and is overlooked by a Buddha figure high up on the hill. It's said to be the second busiest of the 88 temples after the Zentsū-ji in Kagawa-ken, which was Kōbō Daishi's boyhood home. It's a 15-minute walk east of the Dōgo Onsen area to Ishite-ji. Matsuyama also has seven of the other 88 Sacred Temples.

Sleeping

Matsuyama has three accommodation areas: around the JR Matsuyama Station (business hotels); the city centre (business hotels and more top-end hotels); and atmospheric Dōgo Onsen (youth hostel, ryokan and Japanese-style hotels).

The tourist office at JR Matsuyama Station has a huge list of accommodation in the midrange to top-end bracket, and the staff are very helpful.

BUDGET

Matsuyama Youth Hostel (☎ 933-6366; 22-3 Dōgo-himezuka-otsu; dm ¥3200; P ☒ ▣) Regularly topping the Japan youth-hostel popularity poll, this youth hostel also has meals available. It's a 10-minute walk east of Dōgo Onsen tram stop.

Matsuyama Downtown Youth Hostel (☎ 986-8880; 3-8-3 Ōkaitō; dm ¥3200; ☒) At the foot of the ropeway up to the castle, this youth hostel is more central; breakfast is available.

Check Inn Matsuyama (☎ 998-7000; 2-7-3 Sanban-chō; s/d ¥4700/7200; P ☒) Extremely handy to the action in the arcades south of the castle and near Matsuyama City station, Check Inn has an *onsen*-with-a-view on the 10th floor and a convenience store on the 1st floor.

Abis Inn Dōgo Matsuyama (☎ 998-6000; www.abis.ne.jp in Japanese; 2-3-3 Katsuyama-chō; s/d ¥4980/6615; P ☒) Also convenient and right next to Katsuyama-chō tram stop, this place offers good facilities and a free light breakfast.

Terminal Hotel Matsuyama (☎ 947-5388; 9-1 Miyata-chō; s ¥5500; P ☒) Virtually right outside JR Matsuyama Station, Terminal Hotel is convenient and simple. Regular 'special rates' here are displayed on banners on the building.

MIDRANGE

Hotel Abis Matsuyama (☎ 941-9003; 4-1-8 Ichiban-chō; s ¥5250; P ☒) Just a one-minute walk from Kenchō-mae tram stop, this hotel is clean, comfy and convenient, and offers free breakfast.

Tōyoko Inn Matsuyama Ichiban-chō (☎ 941-1045; 1-10-8 Ichiban-chō; s/tw or d ¥5460/8190; P ⊗) At Katsuyama-chō tram stop, this is a good standard business hotel.

TOP END
Matsuyama Tōkyū Inn (☎ 941-0109; www.matsuyama-i.tokyuhotels.co.jp; 3-3-1 Ichiban-chō; s/tw ¥7140/17,220; P ⊗) At the northern end of the Ōkaidō shopping arcade, this hotel has excellent rooms and gourmet restaurants.

Funaya (☎ 947-0278; www.dogo-funaya.co.jp in Japanese; 1-33 Yunomachi; per person with meals ¥21,000; P ⊗) An upmarket ryokan in Dōgo Onsen, Funaya has superb bathing facilities and has been in operation since 1626. Natsume Soseki, the well-known author, was a regular here.

Eating & Drinking
The area around the Ginten-gai and Ōkaidō shopping arcades in central Matsuyama is teeming with interesting eating and drinking options.

Goshiki Sōmen Morikawa (☎ 933-3838; 5-4 San-ban-chō; ⊗ 11am-8.30pm) Matsuyama is known for its *goshiki somen*, thin noodles in five colours, and you can try them here, next to the main post office. There are plastic models in the window and an illustrated menu showing the multicoloured noodles. Japanese tourists buy sets of uncooked noodles to take home.

Kushihide Tori-ryōri-honten (☎ 921-1587; 3-2-8 Niban-chō; ⊗ 4.30-11pm) This place prides itself on its fresh and tasty free-range Ehime chicken dishes. This is the place to try *tori sashimi* (raw chicken; ¥840).

Sushitoku-honten (☎ 941-6378; 2-5-1 Ōkaidō; ⊗ 11am-11pm) On the corner of Ōkaidō and the Nibanchō-dōri arcade, you can order a top sushi lunch here for ¥660.

Izakaya Ariya (☎ 921-2501; 2-7-1 Sanban-chō; ⊗ lunch & dinner) Next to Check Inn Matsuyama hotel, this is a lively spot with Japanese, Thai and Vietnamese food on its extensive menu.

Dish & Bar After Glow (☎ 945-5453; 2-5-25 Ichiban-chō; ⊗ 5.30pm-3.30am) This place boasts excellent cuisine and presentation, as well as 200 varieties of wine from all over the world.

Olu Olu Cafe (☎ 947-0606; 2-3-5 Sanban-chō; ⊗ 11am-3am Tue-Sun) Olu Olu is an exotic place serving up island-style cocktails, meals and atmosphere.

NY Kitchen Sa Kura (☎ 948-0020; 3-7-14 Niban-chō; ⊗ 11am-midnight) With a pleasant garden setting and a healthy, varied menu, this place is worth a visit. Try the om-rice (omelette on rice; ¥820).

Dōgo Bakushukan (☎ 945-6866; 20-13 Dōgo-yu-nomachi; ⊗ 11am-10pm) Just across from the main bathhouse in Dōgo Onsen, look for the huge frosty beer on the front of the building. There is cold beer and good pub grub here for after your bath.

Getting There & Away
Matsuyama airport is on the coast west of the city and has connections with all major cities: from Tokyo (JAL/ANA, ¥27,300, 80 minutes); from Nagoya (NAL, ¥20,500, 1½ hours); from Osaka (ANA/JEX, ¥14300, 50 minutes); from Fukuoka (JAL/JAC, ¥17,800, 45 minutes); and from Sapporo, Miyazaki, Kagoshima and Naha. Buses run from JR Matsuyama Station to the airport (¥330).

The JR Yosan line connects Matsuyama with Takamatsu (¥6010, 2½ hours, hourly), and there are also services across the Seto-Ōhashi to Okayama (¥6630, 2¾ hours, hourly) on Honshū. Trains also run southwest from Matsuyama to Uwajima and then east to Kōchi (¥3500, 2½ hours), though this is a rather circuitous route – it's faster to take a bus directly to Kōchi. Direct buses also run from Osaka (¥7600, seven hours) and Tokyo (¥12,000, 12 hours).

There are frequent ferry (¥2500, 2¾ hours, 10 daily) and hydrofoil (¥5800, 1¼ hours, 10 daily) connections with Hiroshima. To get to the port, Matsuyama Kankō-kō, take the Iyo-tetsudō private train line from Matsuyama City or Ōtemachi stations to the end of the line at Takahama (¥360 from Ōtemachi). From Takahama, a connecting bus whisks you to the port.

Other boats operate to/from Matsuyama and Beppu, Kokura and Oita on Kyūshū, as well as Iwakuni, Kure, Mihara, Onomichi and Yanai on Honshū, but check with the tourist office which of the Matsuyama ports these services operate from.

Getting Around
Matsuyama has an excellent tram service costing a flat ¥150 (pay when you get off). A day ticket costs just ¥300. There's a loop line and major terminus at Dōgo Onsen and outside Matsuyama City station. The Ōkaidō

SHIKOKU

stop outside the Mitsukoshi department store is a good central stopping point. You'll find the left-luggage counter at JR Matsuyama also rents **bicycles** (☎ 943-5002; ⏰ 8.50am-6pm Mon-Sat) for ¥600 a day.

Lines 1 and 2 are loop lines, running clockwise and anticlockwise around Katsuyama (the mountain the castle is on); line 3 runs from Matsuyama City station to Dōgo Onsen; line 5 goes from JR Matsuyama Station to Dōgo Onsen; and line 6 from Kiya-chō to Dōgo Onsen.

If you're lucky with timing, you can ride the **Botchan Ressha** (坊ちゃん列車), the original small trains that were imported from Germany in 1887 and ran the lines for 67 years. They're back in use and are named after Natsume Soseki's novel *Botchan,* published in 1906. The famous author apparently enjoyed riding the trains on his way to a soak in Dōgo Onsen. The old locomotives are particularly popular with children.

NORTH & EAST OF MATSUYAMA
Kashima 鹿島
☎ 0899

Kashima is a pleasant little island popular with locals, and makes an easy day trip from Matsuyama. It's so close that you could virtually swim there, but there is a return **ferry** (☎ 93-3010; ⏰ 7am-9pm) for ¥300. The island has resident deer, an *onsen,* a nice beach, camping and *minshuku* if you plan to stay overnight. Trains from JR Matsuyama Station reach Iyo-Hōjō station in 20 minutes; from here it's a short walk to the ferry (fashioned with a plastic deer on top).

If you're looking for somewhere quiet to stay that's close to Matsuyama, there's the **Hōjō Suigun Youth Hostel** (北条水軍ユースホステル; ☎ 92-4150; dm ¥3000; P ✕) a five-minute walk from Iyo-Hōjō station. Meals are available.

Imabari 今治
☎ 0898

Imabari is an industrial port city at the southern end of the Shimanami-kaidō bridge system that island-hops to Onomichi in Hiroshima-ken prefecture.

Food freaks will enjoy the **World Food Museum** (世界食文化博物館; ☎ 24-1881; admission ¥1000; ⏰ 11am-5.30pm Mon-Fri) where there are replicas of traditional foods and meals from over 100 countries. Get off the train at Iyo-

Tomita station, one stop south of Imabari and take a taxi (10 minutes) from there.

Numerous ferry services connect Imabari with ports on Honshū, including Hiroshima, Kōbe, Mihara, Onomichi, Takehara and islands of the Inland Sea. There are also buses to Honshū.

Saijo 西条
☎ 0897

In Saijo is the **Asahi Brewery** (アサヒビール四国工場; ☎ 53-7770; ⏰ 9.30am-3pm), where visitors can tour the factory and sample freshly brewed Super Dry for free. Call ahead as reservations are required. The **Asahi beer garden** (アサヒビール園; ☎ 53-2277; ⏰ 11am-9pm) next door has all-you-can-eat barbecued mutton, and beer. There are various *tabe-nomihōdai* (all-you-can-eat, all-you-can-drink) options, ranging in price from ¥3150 to ¥3990.

Saijō matsuri (西条祭り), the annual festival held from 14 to 17 October, is a rollicking affair that attracts visitors from all over Japan. About 80 teams push and pull *danjiri* (festival floats) and carry mikoshi (portable shrines) around the town. For more information check out www.city.saijo.ehime.jp/english/index.htm.

There's a bus service that takes you to Ishizuchi-san (below); the bus leaves from JR Iyo-Saijō Station and takes you to the Nishi-no-kawa cable-car station on the northern side of the mountain.

Niihama 新居浜
☎ 0897

Niihama sits sandwiched between the Inland Sea and the mountains, and is best known for its annual **Taiko Matsuri** (新居浜太鼓祭り), a drum festival held from 16 to 18 October (complementing Saijo's festival; see above). The event involves over 200,000 people, countless drums and a lot of noise, fun and beer-drinking.

Niihama is also known for its parks, waterfalls and hiking opportunities around **Besshiyama** (別子山), and as a base for Sumitomo Corporation, which originally came to mine copper and gold out of the mountains.

Niihama station, on the JR Yosan line, is about 4km southeast of the middle of town.

Ishizuchi-san 石鎚山

At 1982m, Ishizuchi-san is the highest mountain in western Japan. It's a holy mountain and many pilgrim climbers make the hike, particularly during the July and August climbing season. In winter (late December to late March) Ishizuchi boasts a ski-field. To get to the Nishi-no-kawa cable-car station (on the northern side of the mountain) from Matsuyama, take a bus to Tsuchi-goya, southeast of the mountain, or a bus from Saijo (opposite); the bus (¥970, 55 minutes, at least four daily) leaves from JR Iyo-Saijō Station – on the Yosan line. You can climb up one way and down the other or make a complete circuit from Nishi-no-kawa to the summit, down to Tsuchi-goya and then back to Nishi-no-kawa. Allow all day and an early start for the circuit. For detailed information on hiking Ishizuchi-san mountain, snap up a copy of Lonely Planet's *Hiking in Japan*.

KAGAWA-KEN 香川県

Formerly known as Sanuki, Kagawa-ken is the smallest of Shikoku's four island regions and the second smallest of the country's 47 prefectures. Kagawa is a major arrival point on Shikoku, as the only rail link with Honshū is via the Seto-Ōhashi bridge to Okayama (see p608 and p599 for details). Highlights include the beautiful gardens of Ritsurin-kōen at Takamatsu, sea kayaking off the northeast coast, the folk village of Shikoku-mura at Yashima, and the celebrated shrine of Kompira-san at Kotohira.

This section continues the circle of Shikoku, starting in southwest Kagawa at Kanonji, then moving on to Kotohira and then Takamatsu.

To *henrō*, Kagawa-ken is known as Nehan-no-dōjō – the Place of Completion – as it has the last 22 of Kōbō Daishi's 88 sacred temples. Its hospitable weather and welcoming people have always been of great comfort to *henrō* as they complete their journey with both a sense of accomplishment and sadness that the pilgrimage and adventure are coming to an end. If you're doing it properly though, the pilgrimage is not quite over when you get to Ōkubo-ji, Temple 88 – it's still a 40km journey back to Temple 1 in Tokushima to complete the circle. The pilgrimage route follows an arc in Kagawa, starting in the southwest of the prefecture, moving up to Takamatsu in the north and finishing in the mountains in the southeast.

NORTHEAST TO TAKAMATSU

Kanonji 観音寺
☎ 0875

If you've come from Ehime-ken on the pilgrimage or on the train, the first town of consequence in Kagawa-ken is Kanonji, noted for having two of the 88 Temples in the same place: Temple 68, **Jinne-in** (神恵院), and Temple 69, **Kanon-ji** (観音寺). It's also known for **Zenigata** (銭形), a 350m circumference outline of a square-holed coin dating from the 1600s. The coin's outline and four kanji characters are formed by trenches, which it is said were dug by the local population as a warning to their feudal lord not to waste the taxes they were forced to pay him. The huge coin is beside the sea, at the foot of Kotohiki Hill in Kotohiki-kōen park, 1.5km northwest of Kanonji station.

Also in the park is a **World Coin Museum** (世界のコイン館; ☎ 23-0055; admission ¥300; ⏰ 9am-5pm Tue-Sun). There is a good swimming **beach** on the far side of the park.

Tadotsu 多度津
☎ 0877

Tadotsu is known throughout Japan as the national headquarters for the martial art of **Shorinji-kempo**. If you're extremely keen to watch training, call ☎ 33-1010 (in Japanese) and ask politely.

Tadotsu is where the rail lines split. The JR Yosan line runs around the coast between Takamatsu and Matsuyama. At Tadotsu, the JR Dosan line splits off it and runs south to Zentsū-ji (p602), Kotohira (p602), through the Iya Valley (p578) and eventually to Kōchi (p584). Most trains for the Dosan line start in Takamatsu, can be joined in Tadotsu and end their journey at Kotohira; to continue south on the line will require a change of trains there.

Tadotsu is also the spot where you will end up if you take the Inland Sea get-away-from-it-all option (see p418) and catch the ferry to Shikoku. There are also direct ferry connections with Fukuyama (¥1530, 1¾ hours, six daily) in Hiroshima-ken. The ferry terminal is about 15 minutes' walk west of the station.

Marugame 丸亀
☎ 0877

At Marugame, on the JR Yosan line and close to the southern end of Seto-Ōhashi, is

SHIKOKU

Marugame-jō (丸亀城; ☎ 24-8816; admission ¥100; ⏱ 9am-4.30pm), which dates from 1597 and has one of only 12 original wooden donjon (heavily fortified central tower) remaining of more than 5000 castles in Japan. The stepped-stone walls tower over 50m high.

In the streets just to the north of the castle, there is a weekly **market** (⏱ 7am-4pm Sun) with local produce, delicacies and arts and crafts for sale.

At the **Uchiwa-no-Minato Museum** (うちわの港ミュージアム; ☎ 24-7055; admission free; ⏱ 9.30am-5pm Tue-Sun) there are displays and craft demonstrations of traditional Japanese *uchiwa* (paper fans). Marugame is responsible for about 90% of the country's paper-fan output, making it a logical place to pick one up.

There's a **tourist information office** (☎ 22-0331; ⏱ 9.30am-6pm) at the station.

Zentsū-ji 善通寺
☎ 0877

Zentsū-ji (☎ 62-0111) is Temple 75 of the 88 Sacred Temples and holds a special significance as the boyhood home of Kōbō Daishi. It is also the largest temple – most of the other 88 could fit in its car park. The temple boasts a magnificent five-storey pagoda and giant camphor trees. To get into the Buddhist spirit, visitors can venture into the basement (admission ¥500) and traverse a 100m-long passageway in pitch darkness: by moving along with your left hand pressed to the wall (which is painted with mandalas, angels and lotus flowers) you are said to be safely following Buddha's way.

Zentsū-ji's other claim to fame is as the home of the **cube watermelon**, an ingenious square-sided Japanese modification that enables watermelons to fit into refrigerators more efficiently.

Zentsū-ji is one station north of Kotohira (see p604) on the JR Dosan line and two stations south of Tadotsu (¥200, five minutes).

KOTOHIRA 琴平
☎ 0877

The Kompira-san shrine at Kotohira is one of Shikoku's major attractions and is well known throughout Japan. If you say you've been there, everyone you meet in Japan will ask if you walked to the top – although it's not that major a mission. The official count is 1368 steps.

Orientation & Information

Kotohira is small enough to make orientation quite straightforward. Beginning a few streets southeast of the two stations, the busy shopping arcade continues until it reaches the shrine entranceway, lined with the inevitable souvenir shops. Those seeking to truly immerse themselves in the Japanese experience might like to buy a walking stick at one of the shops for the trek up to the shrine.

There is a **Tourist Information Center** (☎ 75-3500; ⏱ 9.30am-8pm) along the main road between JR Kotohira Station and Kotoden Kotohira station. Staff can provide an English-language brochure and accommodation information. They also rents bikes (¥100/500 per hour/day).

There are coin lockers at the station, and the ATMs at the post office accept international money cards.

Sights

KOMPIRA-SAN 金刀比羅宮

Kompira-san or, more formally, Kotohiragū, was originally a temple dedicated to the Guardian of Mariners but became a shrine after the Meiji Restoration. The shrine's hilltop position affords superb views over the countryside, and there are some interesting reminders of its maritime connections.

A big fuss is made about how strenuous the climb is to the top but, if you've got this far in Japan, you've probably completed a few long ascents to shrines already. If you really blanch at the thought of climbing all those steps, you can dish out ¥6500 and be carried up and down in a palanquin.

The first notable landmark on the long climb is the **Ō-mon**, a stone gateway. Just to the right, beyond the gate, is the **Hōmotsu-kan** (admission ¥500; ⏱ 8.30am-4.30pm) treasure house. Nearby you will find five traditional sweets vendors at tables shaded by large white parasols. A symbol of ancient times, these Gonin Byakushō (Five Farmers) are the descendants of the original families permitted to trade within the grounds of the shrine. Further uphill is the **Shoin** (admission ¥500; ⏱ 8.30am-4.30pm), a reception hall. Built in 1659, this National Treasure has some interesting screen paintings and a small garden.

Continuing the ascent, you eventually reach the large **Asahino Yashiro** (Shrine of the Rising Sun). The hall, built in 1837 and dedicated to the Sun Goddess Amaterasu,

KOTOHIRA

INFORMATION	
Kotohira Post Office 琴平郵便局 1 C2	
Tourist Information Office	
観光案内所 2 D1	
SIGHTS & ACTIVITIES	
Asahino Yashiro 旭社.......................................3 A3	
Ema-dō 絵馬堂...4 A3	
Gohonsha (Main Hall) 御本社.........................5 A3	
Hōmotsu-kan (Treasure House)	
宝物館 6 B3	
Kanamaru-za 金丸座.......................................7 C3	
Kinryō-no-Sato (Sake Museum)	
金陵の里 8 C2	
Marine Museum 海の科学館...........................9 C3	
Saya-bashi (Covered Bridge) 鞘橋..............10 D3	
Shoin (Reception Hall) 書院..........................11 A3	
Takadōrō (Lantern Tower) 高灯籠................12 C1	
Ō-mon 大門...13 B3	
SLEEPING	
Kotobuki Ryokan ことぶき旅館....................14 C2	
Kotohira Riverside Hotel	
琴平リバーサイドホテル................................15 C2	
Kotosankaku 琴参閣......................................16 C1	
Sakura-no-Shō 桜の抄...................................17 C3	

EATING	
Kompira Udon こんぴらうどん.....................18 C2	
Shōhachi Udon 将八うどん..........................19 C2	
Tako-zushi たこ寿司......................................20 C2	

TRANSPORT	
Bus Station バス停.......................................21 D2	

is noted for its ornate woodcarving. From here, the short final ascent, which is the most beautiful leg of the walk, brings you to the **Gohonsha** (Gohon Hall) and **Ema-dō** (Ema Pavilion); the latter is filled with maritime offerings. Exhibits range from pictures of ships and models to modern ship engines and a one-person solar sailboat hull donated to the shrine after its round-the-world navigation. The views from this level extend right down to the coast and over the Inland Sea. Incurable climbers can continue another 400-odd steps up to the **Oku-sha** (Inner Shrine).

OTHER SIGHTS

Kanamaru-za (☎ 73-3846; admission ¥300; ⏰ 9am-5pm) is Japan's oldest kabuki playhouse. It was built in 1835 and later became a cinema before being restored in 1976. Inside, you can wander backstage and see the changing rooms and old wooden bath, and admire the revolving-stage mechanism, basement trap doors and tunnel out to front-of-theatre.

There's a **Marine Museum** (☎ 73-3748; admission ¥400; ⏰ 9am-5pm) with a variety of ship models and exhibits. The **Kinryō-no-Sato** (☎ 73-

4133; admission ¥310; ⏰ 9am-4pm) sake museum is along the shrine entranceway. Sake tasting (¥100) may sap your will for the climb.

Note the curious **Takadōrō** lantern tower, beside Kotoden Kotohira station. The 27.6m-high tower was traditionally lit in times of trouble. At the southern end of the town is a wooden covered bridge, **Saya-bashi.**

Sleeping

Kotobuki Ryokan (☎ 73-3872; r per person with/without meals ¥7000/4500; **P** 🖳) Conveniently situated by the riverside, this is the top pick. Kotobuki is clean, comfortable and serves good food.

Kotohira Riverside Hotel (☎ 75-1880; s/tw ¥6500/12,000; **P** 🖳) With good views looking up at Kompira-san, this is convenient.

Kotosankaku (☎ 75-1000; r per person ¥12,000; **P** 🖳) This is an elegant, Japanese-style place that features an excellent outdoor *onsen*. With 225 rooms, it is one of Shikoku's biggest ryokan.

Sakura-no-Shō (☎ 75-3218; r per person ¥12,000-30,000; **P** 🖳) Near the bottom of the steps up to the shrine, this place is upmarket and convenient.

Eating

Many of the restaurants in Kotohira cater for day-trippers and, hence, close early.

Shōhachi Udon (☎ 75-3224; ⏲ 10am-3pm) Opposite the main post office, this is one of a couple of reasonably priced places serving udon, *katsudon* (pork cutlet served over rice) and so on.

Tako-zushi (☎ 75-2246; ⏲ 9am-5pm) Just over the bridge at the western end of the shopping arcade, this is a quaint sushi and udon shop that won't break the budget. Look for the faded big red octopus above the door (*tako* means 'octopus' in Japanese).

Up near the entrance to the shrine, many of the souvenir shops serve udon lunches.

Kompira Udon (☎ 73-5785; ⏲ 8am-5pm) Just short of the first set of steps leading up Kompira-san, at Kompira Udon you can watch the noodles being made a few minutes before you consume them.

Getting There & Away

The JR Dosan line branches off the JR Yosan line at Tadotsu and continues through Kotohira and south to Kōchi. The private Kotoden line also runs direct from Takamatsu to Kotohira (¥610, one hour). By either route, the journey takes around an hour from Takamatsu.

TAKAMATSU 高松

☎ 087 / pop 335,000

Takamatsu was founded during the rule of Toyotomi Hideyoshi (1537–98) as the castle town of the feudal lord of Kagawa. The city was virtually destroyed in WWII, but rapidly rebounded.

Despite its rail link, Takamatsu remains an important port for Inland Sea ferry services, particularly to the popular island of Shōdo-shima (see p416). There are many day-trip possibilities around the city and prefecture, including Isamu Noguchi's extraordinary sculpture garden in Murechō (p606); Marugame-jō (p602), Zentsū-ji (p602) and Kotohira (p602).

Orientation & Information

Takamatsu is surprisingly sprawling. It's a 2km-long walk to Ritsurin-kōen from JR Takamatsu Station. Chūō-dōri, the main street through Takamatsu, extends south from the port. A busy shopping arcade area extends across Chūō-dōri and then runs parallel to it to the east, passing through the entertainment district. The main shopping area is further south, near Kotoden Kawaramachi train station.

The area around the impressive JR Takamatsu Station is changing rapidly due to Sunport Takamatsu, a massive reclaimed-land project that is modernising the port. The new Takamatsu Symbol Tower dominates the skyline just north of the station.

The city is well set up to help foreign visitors. There's an excellent **tourist information office** (☎ 851-2009; ⏲ 9am-6pm) outside the station beside the bus terminal, where the helpful staff can provide useful leaflets and maps.

In the northwest corner of Chūō-kōen park is the **Kagawa International Exchange** (I-PAL Kagawa; ☎ 837-5901; www.i-pal.or.jp in Japanese; 1-11-63 Banchō; ⏲ 9am-6pm Tue-Sun). This superb resource centre has a message board, foreign books and magazines, international phone and fax access, satellite TV and free Internet access, and can even provide free legal counselling should you need it.

Visitors can pick up the free Kagawa Welcome Card at Kagawa International Exchange and the tourist information office (you'll need to show your passport). The card provides minor discounts around town, and comes with a mini-guidebook and fold-out city map.

There are coin lockers and a left-luggage office at JR Takamatsu Station, and if you're in need of money, there are international ATMs available at the central post office.

English-language books and magazines can be found on the 5th floor of **Miyawaki Shoten Bookstore** (☎ 851-3732; ⏲ 9am-10pm).

Sights & Activities

RITSURIN-KŌEN 栗林公園

Although not one of Japan's 'big three' gardens, **Ritsurin-kōen** (☎ 833-7411; admission ¥400; ⏲ sunrise-sunset) could easily be a contender. The garden, dating from the mid-1600s, winds around a series of ponds with lookouts, tearooms, bridges and islands. It took more than a century to complete. To the west, Shiun-zan mountain forms a backdrop to the garden, but to the east there is some much less impressive 'borrowed scenery' in the form of dull modern buildings. (In Japanese garden design, 'borrowed scenery' refers to a view of distant scenery that is revealed at some place along the path.)

TAKAMATSU

0 _____ 400 m
0 _____ 0.2 miles

Ferries to Tonosho
(Shodo-shima); Kôbe-Osaka;
Uno; Nao-shima; Megi-jima

INLAND SEA
(Seto-nai-kai)

Main Ferry
Terminal

To Honshū;
Sakaide (21km);
Kotohira (44km);
Matsuyama (194km)

Takamatsu

Mizuki-dōri

Kotoden
Chikkō

Tamamo-kōen

Setohashi-dōri

Kotoden
Kotoharamachi

Hyogomachi Arcade

Bijutsukan-dōri

Chūō-dōri

Maruyamamachi

Entertainment
District

To Yashima (5km);
Shikoku-mura (5km);
Mure-chō (8km)

Chūō-
kōen

Kikuchikan-dōri

Minamishinmachi

Kotoden
Kawaramachi

Kanko-dōri

To Nagao

Hachiman-dōri

Ritsurinkoen-
kitaguchi

Ritsurin-
kōen

To Takamatsu
Airport (16km);
Kotohira (30km);
Ikeda; Route 32

Kotoden
Ritsurin-kōen

To
Tokushima
(74km)

Ritsurin

SHIKOKU

In the garden, the **Sanuki Folkcraft Museum**
(讃岐民芸館; admission free; 8.45am-4.30pm) displays local crafts. The feudal-era **Kikugetsu-tei**
(菊月亭; Chrysanthemum Moon Pavilion)
teahouse, offers Japanese tea and sweets.
There are several other small teahouses
inside the park, including the lovely
thatched-roof **Higurashi-tei** (日暮亭), which
dates from 1898.

You can get there by Kotoden or JR train,
but the easiest way is by bus (¥230) from JR
Takamatsu Station.

TAKAMATSU-JŌ 高松城

There's very little left of Takamatsu-jō,
which is east of Kotoden Chikkō station.
The castle grounds today form a pleasant
park, **Tamamo-kōen** (851-1521; admission ¥200;
sunrise-sunset), yet are only one-ninth of
their original size. When the castle was built
in 1588, the moat was filled with sea water,
with the sea itself forming the fourth side.

YASHIMA 屋島

The 292m-high tabletop plateau of Yashima is 5km east of the centre of Takamatsu. It's the locale of **Yashima-ji** (屋島寺; ☎ 841-9418), number 84 of the 88 temples, and offers fine views over the surrounding countryside and the Inland Sea.

In the 12th century it was the site of titanic struggles between the Genji and Heike clans. The temple's **Treasure House** (admission ¥500; 9am-5pm) collection relates to the battle. Just behind the treasure house is the **Pond of Blood**, where victorious warriors washed the blood from their swords, staining the water red.

A **cable car** (☎ 841-1551; one way/return ¥700/1300; 7.35am-6.55pm) runs to the top of Yashima from near a smaller shrine at the bottom. At the top you can rent a bicycle (¥500) to pedal around the attractions.

If you want to stay out here, the **Yashima Royal Hotel** (屋島ロイヤルホテル; ☎ 841-1000; s/tw ¥4800/8800; P) has decent-sized rooms and beds, and is a five-minute walk from Kotoden Katamoto station (the station before Kotoden Yashima).

The best way to get to Yashima is by Kotoden train. From Kotoden Chikkō station it takes around 15 minutes (¥270) to get to Kotoden Yashima station. From here you can take the funicular railway to the top (¥700/1300 one way/return, five minutes), or hike up in about 30 minutes.

SHIKOKU-MURA 四国村

At the bottom of Yashima is this excellent **village museum** (☎ 843-3111; admission ¥800; 9am-6pm), with old buildings brought from all over Shikoku and neighbouring islands. There are explanations in English of the many buildings and their history.

The village's fine kabuki stage came from Shōdo-shima (p416), which is famed for its traditional farmers' kabuki performances. Other interesting buildings include a border guardhouse from the Tokugawa era (a time when travel was tightly restricted) and a bark-steaming hut that was used in paper-making. There's also a water-powered rice-hulling machine and a fine old stone storehouse.

Shikoku-mura is a 500m-long (seven-minute) walk north of Kotoden Yashima station.

ISAMU NOGUCHI GARDEN MUSEUM
イサムノグチ庭園美術館

Consider an excursion out to Mure-chō, east of Takamatsu, to witness the legacy of noted sculptor Isamu Noguchi (1904–88). Born in Los Angeles to a Japanese poet and an American writer, Noguchi set up a studio and residence here in 1970. Today the **complex** (☎ 870-1500; www.isamunoguchi.or.jp; admission ¥2100) is filled with hundreds of Noguchi's works and holds its own as an impressive art installation. Inspiring sculptures are on display in the beautifully restored Japanese buildings and in the surrounding landscape.

Entry is decidedly worth it, but you've got to get your act together early if you want to visit here. One-hour tours are conducted at 10am, 1pm and 3pm on Tuesday, Thursday and Saturday; visitors should fax or email ahead for reservations at least two weeks in advance (check out the website). Take the Kotoden train to Yakuri station, from

---

SEA KAYAKING ON THE INLAND SEA

For a bit of adventure, physical exertion and an enjoyable day out, you might like to try sea kayaking off the northeast coast of Kagawa-ken on the Inland Sea. **Noasobiya** (☎ 0879-26-3350; www.noasobiya.jp/noasobi/en/index.html) runs a thoroughly professional operation out of Ōchi, east of Takamatsu. Head guide Ryū holds New Zealand sea kayak–guiding qualifications and spends his off-seasons guiding in New Zealand's Abel Tasman National Park. Noasobiya ventures out to small uninhabited islands in the Inland Sea and offers half-/full-day options for ¥7000/12,000, including all gear.

The operation is run out of a large log cabin that was once used as a rest house for Emperor Hirohito, and there are cabins next door where visitors can stay (¥16,000 for up to four people). There is also a hotel nearby with a large *onsen* for an after-trip soak. Tours can be run in English, and staff will pick you up at JR Sanbonmatsu Station if you pre-request it. Depending on the weather, trips run from April to November; check out the English website for details.

where the museum is a 20-minute walk or five-minute taxi ride. It's a 10-minute taxi ride from JR Yashima Station.

MEGI-JIMA 女木島

Just offshore from Yashima is the small island of Megi-jima (pop 250), also known as Oniga-shima, or Demon Island. Several homes on the island are surrounded by ōte (high stone walls built to protect a house from waves, wind and ocean spray). It was here that Momotarō, the legendary Peach Boy (p396), met and conquered the horrible demon. You can tour the **caves** (☎ 873-0728; admission ¥500; ⏰ 8.30am-5pm) where the demon was said to have hidden, but they've been a bit ruined by the fake demons put there supposedly to make it more realistic.

Five or six boats a day run to Megi-jima from Takamatsu (¥340, 20 minutes). There are *minshuku* and camp sites on the mountainous island.

Sleeping

A useful 'accommodation desk' at the tourist information office outside JR Takamatsu Station helps visitors find suitable accommodation options.

BUDGET

Takamatsu Sakika Youth Guesthouse (☎ 822-2111; 6-9 Hyakken-machi; dm ¥3900; P 🔲) This is a good youth hostel/business hotel near Kotoden Kataharamachi Station. The hostel is run from the **New Grande Mimatsu** (☎ 823-4111; 2-3 Tōri-machi; per person with/without meals ¥8000/6000; P 🔲) ryokan about 50m northeast. Go there first or you'll never find it. The ryokan has a great *izakaya* (Japanese-style pub) attached called **Kanaya**, where youth-hostel guests can have a set-menu dinner for ¥1200 with a free beer.

Business Hotel East Park Ritsurin (☎ 861-5252; 1-14-3 Ritsurin-chō; s ¥4500; P 🔲) This is a cheapish but somewhat bland business hotel near the eastern entrance of Ritsurin-kōen.

Business Hotel Sunshine Takamatsu (☎ 837-6161; 3-17-15 Fujizuka-chō; s ¥4500; P 🔲) Also near the park, at JR Ritsurin Station, this place is reasonable, but not particularly handy.

MIDRANGE

Hotel No 1 Takamatsu (☎ 812-2222; 2-4-1 Kankō-dōri; s/tw ¥4900/7500; 🔲 P) A definite step up and convenient to Kotoden Kawaramachi

Station is this new hotel with *rotemburo* (open-air baths), sauna, room service and restaurant. This is the top pick.

Royal Park Hotel Takamatsu Annex (☎ 823-1111; 11-1 Fukuda-machi; s from ¥5280; P 🔲) Near Kotoden Kawaramachi Station and also good value, this hotel has singles with semi-double beds in each room.

Takamatsu Terminal Hotel (☎ 822-3731; 10-17 Nishinomaru-chō; s/tw ¥6100/10,000; P 🔲) If you want to be near JR Takamatsu Station, head to the Terminal Hotel, a business hotel with good facilities.

Hotel New Frontier (☎ 851-1088; 14-7 Nishinomaru-chō; s/d ¥6600/10,000; P 🔲) Also close to JR Takamatsu Station, this place has good-sized beds and a large communal bath (and each room has a private shower).

TOP END

ANA Hotel Clement Takamatsu (☎ 811-1111; 1-1 Hamano-chō; per person with breakfast ¥13,310; P 🔲) This is the best hotel in town. The 20-storey building is directly in front of you as you leave JR Takamatsu Station.

Eating & Drinking

Takamatsu has no shortage of places to eat. There are countless choices in the covered arcades and entertainment district to the west side of the tracks between Kotoden Kataharamachi and Kawaramachi Stations.

A trip to Takamatsu would not be complete without slurping back some of the region's prized *sanuki* udon noodles. Udon places are everywhere, and you'll soon be able to recognise the characters for udon (うどん).

Udonya Goemon (☎ 821-2711; 13-15 Furubaba-chō; ⏰ 6pm-3am Mon-Sat) Try this place where the *asari udon* (shellfish udon; ¥650) is superb.

Udonbō-honten (☎ 831-3204; 8-19 Kamei-chō; ⏰ 11am-9pm) Head here for a variety of tasty noodle dishes, such as Champon-udon (¥690).

There are some trendy eating and drinking spots in Kitahama Alley, at the eastern end of Takahama port.

Izara Moon (☎ 811-4531; 3-2 Kitahama-chō; ⏰ 11am-midnight Wed-Mon) In an atmospheric setting, this place serves an Oriental/European mix of dishes. Lunch of the day costs ¥800.

Cantina (☎ 811-7718; 3-2 Kitahama-chō; ⏰ 11am-12.30am Wed-Mon) This is a relaxed café by day, atmospheric dining bar in the evening.

Mikayla (☎ 811-5357; 8-40 Sunport; ☺ 11am-10pm) At the northern end of Sunport Takamatsu (north of the station), in the Takamatsu-kō Resthouse, this restaurant guarantees a harbour view and serves fresh fish straight out of the Inland Sea. There's an outdoor terrace for good days.

Ryūkyū Goten (☎ 811-0008; 4-15 Kajiya-machi; ☺ 5.30pm-1am Mon-Sat) A great place to go for excellent Okinawan fare, *awamori* (Okinawan sake) and live Okinawan music till late. It's lively and well worth a visit.

Queensberry @ café (☎ 812-0680; 1-10-4 Tokiwa-chō; ☺ 8am-midnight; 🖳) Near Kotoden Kawaramachi Station, this is a bright and cheerful café serving coffees, cocktails and meals. There's also an Internet (¥100 per hour) corner.

Mon Mon Ca Phe Vietnam (☎ 862-3492; 2-8-18 Kawaramachi; ☺ 11am-10pm Thu-Tue) Just west of the same station, this place doubles as a restaurant and a Vietnamese cooking school.

Getting There & Away

Takamatsu airport is 16km south of the city. Buses run to/from the airport and JR Takamatsu Station (¥740 one way). There are flights to all the major cities: to/from Tokyo (ANA/JAS, one hour, ¥25,300, 10 minutes, 10 daily); Fukuoka (JAC, ¥20,300, 70 minutes, one daily); and Kagoshima and Naha.

The rail line crossing the Seto-Ōhashi has brought Takamatsu much closer to the main island of Honshū. From Tokyo, you can take the *shinkansen* (bullet train) to Okayama (four hours), where you can change trains for Takamatsu (¥1470, 55 minutes). From Takamatsu, the JR Kōtoku line runs south-east to Tokushima (¥3070, one hour) and the JR Yosan line runs west to Matsuyama (¥6010, 2½ hours). There are also services between Takamatsu and Kōchi (¥5270, two hours 20 minutes). The JR Yosan line branches off at Tadotsu and becomes the Dosan line, turning southwest to Kotohira and Kōchi. The private Kotoden line also runs direct to Kotohira (¥610, one hour).

There are direct bus services that operate to/from Tokyo (¥10,000, 9½ hours), Yokohama (¥9500, 9¼ hours), Nagoya (¥7130, 7¾ hours) and Osaka.

Takamatsu has ferry services to various ports in the Inland Sea and Honshū, including Osaka (hydrofoil, ¥6100), Kōbe, Uno (in Okayama) and Shōdo-shima (regular ferry, ¥510, one hour, 15 daily; high-speed ferry, ¥1020, 35 minutes, 17 daily). The tourist information office (p604) can provide other details.

Getting Around

Takamatsu has local buses, but the major attractions are easily reached on the JR Kōtoku line or Kotoden line. The main Kotoden junction is Kotoden Kawaramachi, although the line ends at Kotoden Chikkō, near JR Takamatsu Station.

Takamatsu is flat and excellent for rental bikes. The city offers a great deal on its 'blue bicycles' (¥100 per day; photo ID required). There are four 'bicycle ports', and you can pick up at one port and drop off at another. Easiest is to pick up at **Takamatsu-shi Rental Cycles** (☎ 821-0400; ☺ 7am-10pm), underground outside JR Takamatsu Station. The other ports are at JR Ritsurin Station, Kotoden Kawaramachi Station and at Kajiyamachi.

Kyūshū 九州

Kyūshū is the third-largest and southernmost of the four major islands of Japan. Its population numbers over 15 million. During the long period of isolation from the West, the Dutch settlement at Nagasaki was Japan's only legitimate connection to the outside world, and many nearby prefectures, such as Kagoshima, secretly did trade with nearby Asian countries.

Kyūshū is the closest island to Korea and China, and it was from Kyūshū that the Yamato tribe extended its power to Honshū. Some of the earliest evidence of Japanese civilisation can still be seen at the archaeological excavations at Uenohara (p654), Kagoshima (p654), in Miyazaki, and at the many ancient stone carvings in the Usuki area (p672).

In the north, the cosmopolitan city of Fukuoka/Hakata (p612) is a major international arrival point, and the terminus for the shinkansen line from Tokyo. In the centre of the island stands the massive volcanic caldera of Aso-san, while more volcanic activity can be seen south at Sakurajima. Cities like Kumamoto and Kagoshima offer fine gardens and magnificent castles, while Beppu is one of Japan's major hot-spring centres. There are also very good hiking opportunities, particularly along the stunning Kirishima volcano chain. With volcanic ash and close proximity to Korea, it is not surprising that Kyūshū boasts numerous pottery villages in a wide range of styles, shapes, colours…and prices. Some vases made in Karatsu, no bigger than a football, sell for as much as a house.

The people of Kyūshū are reputedly hard drinkers (especially of shōchū, the preferred liquor often made from sweet potatoes) and outstandingly friendly – a visit to a local bar may provide proof of both theories, and it's often possible to drink for free much of the night in exchange for on-the-spot English practice.

KYŪSHŪ

HIGHLIGHTS

- Stare into the calm faces of 1400-year-old stone Buddhas in **Usuki** (p672)
- Clamber across twisted lava-fields beneath the active behemoth **Sakurajima** (p661)
- Take an intimate soak in a *kazoku-buro* (private family bath) in **Beppu** (p673)
- Pray to get married at the **Aoshima-jinja** (Ogre's Washboard temple; p665), in Aoshima
- Go wild until the wee hours in futuristic discos in **Fukuoka/Hakata** (p612)
- Hike among rare azaleas and absorb stunning views in **Kirishima-Yaku National Park** (p652)
- Hope that an atomic bomb, like that which hit **Nagasaki** (p627) never falls anywhere again
- Cover yourself in hot sand in **Ibusuki** (p664)
- See one of the world's largest calderas in **Aso-san** (p646)

KYŪSHŪ

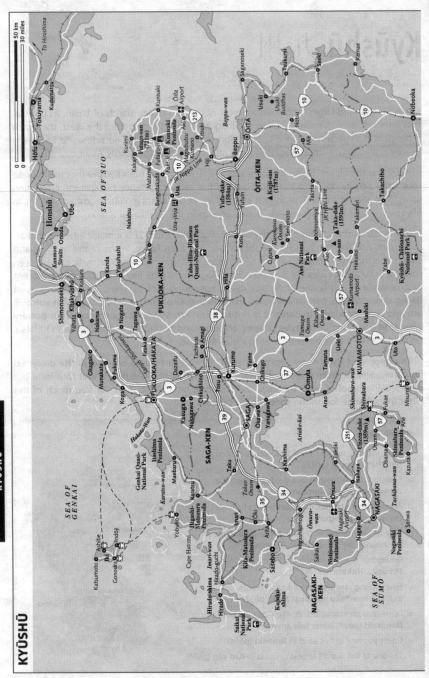

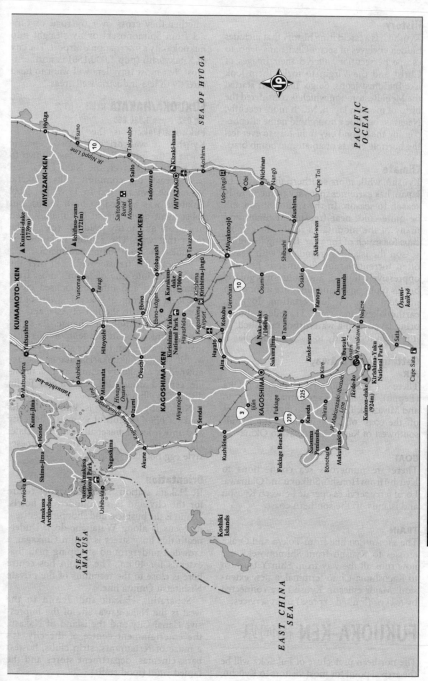

History

Kyūshū has a fascinating history that includes hidden enclaves of secret Christians, who, to escape persecution, altered their images of Christ and the Virgin to make them look like Buddhist icons. Saigo Takamori started the Meiji Restoration which is considered the birth of modern Japan. Much more recently, Nagasaki became a household name after becoming the second city in history to ever feel the horrible effects of an atomic bomb blast.

Climate

Kyūshū, while more southern than much of Japan, has extremes that vary tremendously season to season. In the winter, it can still be quite cold, near freezing at night, and many of the mountains retain their snow caps for much of the year. During the rainy season the island is inundated with heavy, often torrential rain. Summer is hot and oppressively humid, and autumn regularly brings typhoons. Landslides are a common problem due to deforestation, logging, earthquakes, and rain. Travellers should bring layers and a waterproof rain shell, as it is often too windy to use an umbrella.

Getting There & Away

AIR

There are major airports at Fukuoka, Ōita (Beppu), Nagasaki, Kagoshima, Kumamoto and Miyazaki. There are also flights to islands off the coast of Kyūshū and to the islands southwest of Kagoshima down to Okinawa.

BOAT

There are numerous sea connections to Kyūshū from Honshū, Shikoku and Okinawa. Local ferry services operate between Kyūshū and islands off the southern coast.

TRAIN

The *shinkansen* line from Tokyo and Osaka crosses to Kyūshū from Shimonoseki and now runs all the way from Shin Yatsushiro to Kagoshima-Chūō terminal, a new extension. Major cities in Kyūshū are connected by *tokkyū* (limited express) train services.

FUKUOKA-KEN 福岡県

The northern prefecture of Fukuoka will be the arrival point for most visitors to Kyūshū,

whether they cross over by road or tunnel from Shimonoseki or fly straight into Fukuoka city's international airport. The city of Kitakyūshū (pop 1,000,150) is northernmost, but most travellers will want to head directly to less-industrialised areas.

FUKUOKA/HAKATA 福岡・博多

☎ 092 / pop 1,380,800

Fukuoka/Hakata is the biggest city in Kyūshū. It was originally two separate towns – the lordly Fukuoka castle town to the west of the river, the Naka-gawa, and to the east, the common folks' Hakata. When the two merged in 1889, the label Fukuoka was applied to both towns, but subsequent development has mainly been in Hakata and many residents refer to the town that way. The airport is known as Fukuoka, the train station as Hakata.

Fukuoka has transformed itself over the last decade into one of Japan's most truly cosmopolitan and internationalised cities. The local government is keenly aware of the city's proximity to the rest of Asia, and encourages international exchange. Its sightseeing attractions are contemporary rather than traditional, but they are still very much worth seeing. Fukuoka/Hakata is also renowned as a culinary centre, and its nightlife, centred around the Nakasu and Tenjin districts, is vibrant.

Nationally the city is known for its 'Hakata *bijin*' (beautiful women), its feisty and much-loved baseball team the Daiei Hawks, and, most of all, *rāmen* (Chinese-style egg noodles in broth).

Orientation

JR Hakata station is the transport centre for the city and is surrounded by hotels. Tenjin is the business and shopping centre – its focus is along Watanabe-dōri. Underneath this busy street is Tenjin Chikagai, a crowded underground shopping mall that extends for 400m. The Tenjin bus centre here is close to the terminus of the private Nishitetsu Ōmuta line.

Separating Hakata and Tenjin to the west is the Naka-gawa, site of the impressive Canal City and the island of Nakasu, the entertainment centre of the city. It's a maze of restaurants, strip clubs, hostess bars, cinemas, department stores and the famed *yatai* (food stalls).

MAPS

The widely available *Visitors Walking Maps* for Hakata, Nakasu, Tenjin and Momochi are invaluable, as they are written in both English and kanji, and are free.

Information

BOOKSHOPS

Kinokuniya (☎ 721-7755; 6th fl, Tenjin Core, 1-11-11 Tenjin; ☯ 10am-8pm) An excellent selection of English-language books can be found here.

Maruzen (☎ 731-9000; 2nd & 3rd fl, Fukuoka Bldg, 1-11-17 Tenjin; ☯ 9.30am-8pm) Sells foreign-language titles.

INTERNET ACCESS

Fukuoka is a wired city.

Cybac Café (☎ 24-3189; www.cybac.com/infomation/tenjin/index.html in Japanese; Daimyō 1-15-1; membership fee ¥200; ☯ 24hr) Charges ¥480 for the first hour of Internet access. There's a branch near the Tenjin clubs. From 1am to 8am, unlimited Internet access with reclining chairs costs ¥1890. Local expats have been known to crash here after missing the last train home.

Kinko's (☎ 473-2677; 2-19-24 Hakata-ekimae; per 10min ¥200; ☯ 24hr) Also has other locations around the city.

Media Café (☎ 283-9393; 8th fl, Spoon Bldg, 5-1-7 Nakasu; per 30min ¥300; ☯ 24hr) Near Hakata Riverain; also offers good discount deals.

NTT (☎ 781-8888; 7th fl, Iwataya Z-side, 2-5-35 Tenjin; ☯ 10.30am-8pm Mon-Fri, 10am-8pm Sat & Sun) Free Internet browsing for 30 minutes (no email).

MEDIA

Broadcasting from Tenjin, Love 76.1FM offers programming in 10 languages. Cross 78.7FM has bilingual DJs and entertainment news.

MONEY

The best way to withdraw cash is via the many postal ATMs at post offices throughout the city. There's a **Citibank ATM** (☯ 6.30am-9.30pm) on the 1st floor of the international arrivals terminal at Fukuoka airport; **currency exchange counters** (☯ 8.30am-9pm) are upstairs. Banks around JR Hakata Station and Tenjin handle foreign exchange services.

There are international ATMs next to the post office is on the 2nd floor on Shintenchō Minami-dōri; on the basement level of Canal City; and outside the Hotel Centraza Hakata on the east side of Hakata station.

POST

The central post office, northeast of Tenjin subway station, has full services. There's another post office outside JR Hakata Station's west exit.

TOURIST INFORMATION

The **tourist information desk** (☯ 8am-8pm) in JR Hakata station has limited information and maps in English. Ask for the free 'Fukuoka Welcome Card' entitling visitors to discounts at hotels, attractions, shops and restaurants.

The Fukuoka International Association's **Rainbow Plaza** (☎ 733-2220; www.rainbowfia.or.jp; 8th fl, IMS Bldg, 1-7-11 Tenjin; ☯ 10am-8pm) in Tenjin has videos on Japan, books, magazines and a noticeboard for events, accommodation and job ads. Bilingual staff is extremely helpful.

ACROS Fukuoka (☎ 725-9100; www.acros.or.jp; 2nd fl, cultural centre, Tenjin 1-1-1; ☯ 10am-7pm, closed 2nd & 4th Mon each month), in Tenjin, has plenty of English-language information on the surrounding prefecture.

At Fukuoka airport, the **tourist information desk** (☎ 473-2518) is on the ground floor of the international terminal, beside the **reservations desk** (☎ 483-7007; ☯ 7am-9.30pm) that can arrange hotel accommodation and car rentals.

Useful local English-language publications include **Fukuoka Now** (www.fukuoka-now.com), a free monthly 'what's on' guide; *Rainbow*, the Fukuoka International Association's current events newsletter; and *Fukuoka on Foot*, which describes walking courses throughout the city.

TRAVEL AGENCIES

HIS No 1 Travel (☎ 761-9203; www.no1-travel.com; Tenjin 1-1-1; ☯ 10am-6pm Mon-Fri, 11am-4.30pm Sat) For cut-rate international air fares. Has a branch in the 3rd floor of the ACROS Fukuoka building.

Sights & Activities

CANAL CITY キャナルシティ

Rather strangely shaped, this six-building shopping mall and entertainment complex **Canal City** (☎ 282-2525; www.canalcity.co.jp) is sleek, modern, and streamlined. The central amphitheatre looks down onto an artificial canal with a fountain symphony. There are 13 cinema screens, a playhouse, two major hotels and innumerable boutiques, bars and bistros.

Canal City is 10 minutes' walk southeast of the Nakasu-Kawabata subway stop, or you can take one of many city buses to Canal City-mae.

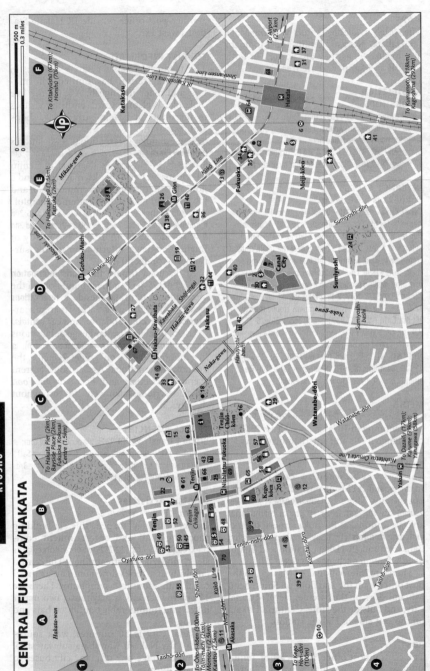

CENTRAL FUKUOKA/HAKATA

TENJIN 天神

Tenjin has historic Western-style buildings, like the 1910 **Former Prefectural Hall & Official Guest House** (☎ 751-4416; 6-29 Nishinakasu; ☻ Tue-Sun) in Tenjin Chūō-kōen. Copper-turreted **Akarenga Bunka-kan** (Akarenga Cultural Centre; admission free; ☻ 9am-9pm Tue-Sun) has simple historical exhibits and a charming coffee shop. To get there from Tenjin station, go toward Chuo post office and Daiei. At the intersection, turn right and head toward the river. Akarenga Bunka-kan is on your right just before the bridge.

FUKUOKA ASIAN ART MUSEUM
福岡アジア美術館

This modern, expansive, and well-lit **museum** (☎ 263-1100; http://faam.city.fukuoka.jp; 3-1 Shimokawabata-machi; 7th & 8th fl, Hakata Riverain; admission ¥200, special exhibitions from ¥1000; ☻ 10am-7.30pm Thu-Tue) boasts some of the finest contemporary Asian art and rotating exhibits on the 7th floor. Cutting-edge shows by artists in residence are staged in the free gallery (8th floor). The atrium coffee shop has skyline views, and you get a free postcard if you buy something (even postcards) at the museum store (7th floor).

HAKATA MACHIYA FURUSATO-KAN
博多町家ふるさと館

This folk **museum** (☎ 281-7761; www.hakatamachiya .com; 6-10 Reisen-machi; admission ¥200; ☻ 10am-5.30pm) features restored merchants' houses and displays of traditional Hakata culture. You can even hear recordings of impenetrable Hakata dialect through antique telephones, or try your hand at *Hakata-ori* (traditional weaving for kimono cloth). It's well worth a visit, despite a lack of English signage.

SHRINES & TEMPLES

Tochō-ji has impressively carved Kannon statues and upstairs, the largest wooden Buddha in Japan.

Shōfuku-ji is a Zen temple founded in 1195 by Eisai, who introduced Zen and tea to Japan. Don't confuse it with Sōfuku-ji (p631), once the temple of a feudal lord, with one gate taken from the original Fukuoka castle.

Kushida-jinja has displays of Hakata festival floats on the grounds, and a local **history museum** (☎ 291-2951; 1-41 Kamikawabata; admission ¥300; ☻ 10am-4.30pm).

Rakusuien (☎ 262-6665; 2-10-7 Sumiyoshi, Hakata; admission ¥100; ☻ Wed-Mon) is a garden and teahouse built by a Meiji-era merchant.

KYŪSHŪ

FUKUOKA-JŌ & ŌHORI-KŌEN
福岡城・大濠公園

Only the walls of Fukuoka-jō remain in what is now Maizuru-kōen, but the castle's hilltop site provides fine views of the city.

Ōhori-kōen, which is adjacent to the castle grounds, has a traditional (though recently constructed) Japanese garden, **Nihon-teien** (日本庭園; ☎ 741-8377; admission ¥240; ⏰ 9am-4.45pm Tue-Sun Sep-May, 9am-5.45pm Tue-Sun Jun-Aug).

Nearby, the **Fukuoka City Art Museum** (福岡市美術館; ☎ 714-6051; www.fukuoka-art-museum .jp; 1-6 Ōhori-kōen Chūōku; admission ¥200; ⏰ 9.30am-5pm Tue-Sun Sep-May, 9.30am-7pm Tue-Sat, 9.30am-5pm Sun Jul & Aug) has ancient pottery and Buddhist guardians on one floor, with works by Andy Warhol and Salvador Dalí upstairs. Take bus No 13 from Tenjin bus terminal, or the subway to Ōhori-kōen Station, then walk south along the pond for 10 minutes.

MOMOCHI DISTRICT 百浜
Further out in the west of the city you'll find the **Fukuoka Tower** (福岡タワー; ☎ 823-0234; www.fukuokatower.co.jp; admission ¥800; ⏰ 9.30am-10pm Apr-Sep, 9.30am-9pm Oct-Mar). The 4th floor café **Dart 234** (the tower is 234m tall) is a great place to view the city, especially at dusk. On the ground floor, there's a **traditional doll museum** (全国郷土人形ミュージアム; ☎ 823-0234; admission ¥300) for folkcraft enthusiasts.

Next to the tower is the park, **Momochi-kōen** (シーサイドももち海浜公園), and its 2.5km artificial beach, a popular spot for swimming despite occasionally murky waters. Access is by subway to Nishijin station, then walk north toward the sea for 15 minutes.

The **Fukuoka City Museum** (福岡市博物館; ☎ 845-5011; http://ikr031.i-kyushu.or.jp/english/index _e.html; 3-1-1, Momochi, Sawara-ku; admission ¥200; ⏰ 9.30am-5pm Tue-Sun) displays local history and culture that make it obvious why Kyūshū residents have such fierce pride in their island. The most precious treasure is an ancient golden snake seal with an inscription proving Japan's historic ties to China.

HAWK'S TOWN ホークスタウン
Hawk's Town (www.hawkstown.com) is something of a seafront Canal City. Set on reclaimed land near Momochi-kōen, this entertainment and shopping complex is also the location of the luxury **Sea Hawk Hotel & Resort** (シーホークホテルリゾート; opposite) and the giant **Fukuoka Dome** (福岡ドーム), home to the local

Daiei Hawks baseball team. The highlight is Sea Hawk's indoor jungle atrium, complete with waterfalls and screeching tropical bird calls. Note that anyone can ride the hotel lifts up to the 35th floor for bird's-eye views of the city – for free.

Hawk's Town is 15 minutes' walk northwest of Tōjin-machi Station. There are frequent direct buses to Fukuoka Dome from Tenjin bus station (about 15 minutes).

OFFSHORE ISLANDS
Summer sightseeing cruises depart from Bayside Place. Ferries to delightfully rural **Shikanoshima** (志賀島), where fresh seafood restaurants line the harbourside streets, depart every 40 minutes (¥650, 30 minutes). Shikanoshima also has a **fishing shrine** (志賀海神社; ☎ 603-6501) decorated with deer antlers and is famed for its *kyūdō* (Japanese archery) meets. Continuing clockwise around the island, you come to a popular **beach** about 5km from the shrine. Local buses are infrequent.

Nokonoshima, famous for its flower fields, is only about 10km in circumference. There's a swimming **beach** and **camping ground** at the northern end of the island. Ferries depart from Marinoa City outlet mall, west of the city centre near Meinohama Station (¥220, 10 minutes).

Festivals & Events
On 3 January at the shrine, **Hakozaki-gū** (箱崎宮), young men clad in loincloths raucously chase a wooden ball in the name of good fortune. The **Hakata Dontaku Matsuri** (博多どんたく祭り) on 3 and 4 May rings to the unique percussive shock of *shamoji* (wooden serving spoons for rice) being banged together like castanets, accompanied by *shamisen* (three-stringed instrument).

The city's main festival, **Hakata Yamagasa Matsuri** (博多山笠祭り), is held from 1 to 15 July. The climax starts at 4.59am on the morning of the 15th, when seven groups of men all converge at **Kushida-jinja**, just north of Canal City, and then race on a 5km-long course through the city carrying huge *mikoshi* (portable shrines). Participants supposedly follow a strict regimen beforehand, including sexual abstinence. According to legend, the festival originated after a 13th-century Buddhist priest was carried aloft, sprinkling holy water over victims of a plague.

The **Kyūshū Bashō sumō tournament** (大相撲九州場所) is held at the Fukuoka Kokusai Centre during mid-November. Limited same-day tickets (tojitsu-ken) are available starting at 8am, and people start lining up at dawn. Good luck.

Sleeping

Hakata has dozens of cut-rate business hotels around the train station. Expect a surcharge on Saturday nights.

BUDGET

Hotel Sky Court Hakata (☎ 262-4400; fax 262-8111; Gion-machi 4ban73; s from ¥4500) Offers discounts to youth hostel members. Book ahead as these discount rates have limited availability.

Sauna Wellbe (☎ 291-1009; 8-12 Gionchō 3F; capsules ¥3800) A Fukuoka capsule hotel option (for men only), offering a 24-hour bath and accompanying sauna. Breakfast (Japanese style) is included. There are several kinds of massage services available for extra charge.

Hotel Cabinas Fukuoka (☎ 436-8880; Ekimae 2-18-1; capsules ¥3800-4300) Great if you've always wanted to try a capsule hotel (for men only). Has a rooftop rotemburo (open-air bath).

Super Hotel Hakata (☎ 474-9000; 4-16-6 Hakata-ekimae; s with continental breakfast buffet ¥4800) This has impeccably clean rooms and secure 24-hour access (reception closes at 11pm).

Hotel Brave Inn Hakata (☎ 282-1111; 5-3-2 Nakasu; s ¥5000) Only charges ¥2000 for an extra person sharing a single room.

Amenity Hotel in Hakata (☎ 282-0041; 14-25 Kami-Kawabata; r from ¥4900) On the outskirts of Tenjin. They include a free light breakfast, and the rooms are basic – small but clean.

MIDRANGE

Lady's Hotel Petit Tenjin (☎ 713-2613, fax 713-4418; 1-3-1, Daimyō; capsules ¥3000-3500, s/tw from ¥5500/7000) For women only, this offers on-site spa services and a sauna. It's eight minutes' walk southwest from Tenjin station. Reception is open 24 hours.

Hakata Riverside Hotel (☎ 291-1455, 0120-20-8102; s/tw from ¥4500/8000) This hotel is in a very convenient location, right close to the night scene. It's also a family-owned business hotel, so it's small but still personal. The first floor is being remodelled as a bistro, so it should also offer excellent food as well.

Kashima Honkan (☎ 291-0746; r per person with/without 2 meals ¥9000/6000) In the Gion district just

northeast of Canal City, wholly unpretentious and built in Sukiya-zukuri style (architecture suggesting elements of the tea ceremony). Has its own enclosed garden, and is pleasantly faded – you expect a Meiji-period novelist to pop up at any moment. The meals, featuring fresh seafood, are extraordinarily good value. The owner speaks English.

Fukuoka Arty Inn (☎ 724-3511, fax 714-3200; 5-1-20 Watanabedōri; s/d ¥8085/13,652) Charmingly named and right in the centre of things, southeast of Tenjin Station. Reception staff are unerringly helpful.

JR Kyūshū Hotel (☎ 413-8787; www.jrk-hotels.com/Fukuoka/; 2-2-4 Hakataeki-higashi; s/tw from ¥7500/14,660) An oasis just a few steps from JR Hakata Station. Ask about discounts on Sunday nights and holidays.

TOP END

Hotel Twins Momochi (ホテルツインズ百浜; ☎ 852-4800, fax 845-8637; s from ¥5140, designer r from ¥12,000) In the Momochi area, refreshingly different. Spacious designer rooms have a spare, modernist feel, but also luxuries like king-sized beds. Guests share kitchenettes and coin laundry.

Sea Hawk Hotel & Resort (シーホークホテルリゾート; ☎ 844-8111; s/d from ¥9000/18,000) In Hawk's Town (opposite). The Japanese-style rooms are classier than the Western-style ones.

ANA Hotel Hakata (☎ 471-7111; www.anahotel-hakata.com; 3-3-3 Hakata-ekimae; s/d from ¥14,000/23,000) Caters to business travellers. Perks include a well-equipped business centre, a health club and swimming pool.

Grand Hyatt Fukuoka (☎ 282-1234, 0120-51-2343, http://fukuoka.grand.hyatt.com; 1-2-82 Sumiyoshi; s/d from ¥17,000/22,000, Japanese-style ste ¥70,000) A lively hotel inside Canal City. The rooftop garden is traditional, but modern hotel rooms have hi-tech amenities. There's a health club, swimming pool and spa.

Hakata Miyako Hotel (☎ 441-3111; www.miyako-hotels.ne.jp/hakata; Ekihigashi 2-1-1; s/d from ¥9000/20,000, ste from ¥46,000; P ⚇ 💻 ✕) Directly across from the station, well-appointed and very convenient for those who want to splurge. Western and Japanese rooms are available.

Eating

To the vast majority of Japanese, Hakata means rāmen. In particular it means tonkotsu-rāmen, noodles in a distinctive, whitish broth made from pork bones. The telephone book lists 401 *rāmen* shops, and there are at least twice that many *yatai* (food stalls on wheels, each with an average weight of 500kg!) that are not listed. Discovering your own *rāmen* shop is all part of the fun.

The majority of the *rāmen yatai* are on the streets around Tenjin Station, especially where Oyafuko-dōri meets Shōwa-dōri, and along the riverbanks in Nakasu and in front of Canal City. Most open as dusk approaches; bowls of noodles start at around ¥600.

Menchan (☎ 281-4018; 1st fl, 3-1 Kamikawa-bata; ⊙ 7pm-4am Mon-Sat) Across from Canal City, a friendly place that topped the honours in an online 'Rāmen Freak' questionnaire.

Uma-uma (☎ 283-1015; ⊙ 5.30pm-midnight Sun-Fri) Next to a *pachinko* (pinball game) parlour, Uma-uma took second place.

Ichiran (☎ 736-5272; 1-10-25 Tenjin, Chūō-ku; ⊙ 24hr) Has been serving noodles for 39 years. Unusually, customers eat at individual cubicles, and fill out forms requesting precisely how they want their noodles prepared. Flavour strength, fat content, noodle tenderness, quantity of 'secret sauce' and garlic content can all be regulated. Marvellously, an Englishlanguage request form is also available. Many branches of this famous noodle shop can be found around town, including at **Rāmen Stadium** (5th fl, Canal City), where noodle-lovers queue to slurp bowls of soup prepared in famous styles hailing from Hokkaidō all the way to southern Kyūshū.

Café Serena (☎ 482-1111; Hotel Nikkō Fukuoka; lunch/dinner buffet ¥1960/4000) Near Hakata Station, this has an unforgettable continental French buffet, serving succulent roast duck and tropical fruit sorbet.

Canal City also has sleek Eurasian restaurants in the section inside the Grand Hyatt Fukuoka on the 1st floor, where **CHINA** (☎ 282-1234; lunch ¥2800), a Cantonese banquet hall, offers all-you-can-eat dim sum lunch.

The IMS building in Tenjin has prime skyline views from its 12th- to 14th-floor restaurants, including **Pasta's Pietro** (☎ 733-2065; pasta plus salad bar ¥1500) and **Asahi Beer Cruiser Pier 21** (☎ 733-2037); while down in the basement **Mrs Elizabeth Muffin** (☎ 733-2083; baked goods under ¥200) sells sweet muffins with free unlimited refills on hot coffee!

Taiwan Yatai is a small but friendly place that does Taiwanese-Chinese food at very reasonable prices. It's a favourite with party-goers on Oyafuko-dōri. You'll find innovative upmarket **dining bars** a little off the beaten track in Kego. From the Kego police box, head either west on Kego Hon-dōri or north on Taishō-dōri toward Akasaka subway station, and pick one you like. Of course, if you find some other *yatai* on the way and get distracted, that's fine too.

Over in Momochi, the Sea Hawk Hotel & Resort (p617) has a diverting Chinatown complex on the 35th floor. Experience the market-like frenzy of **Bunmei Ichijōgai** (文明一条街; dishes from ¥550), in the complex, where you can kick back with dim sum or a bowl of noodles, and enjoy the sweeping views.

Drinking

Fukuoka-ites like to party, and the city is full of clubs, bars and pubs, though in recent years this is beginning to change and nights can be hit or miss. Oddly, it's Friday night that can be kind of dead, as many people still have to work six days a week. According to club owners, Thursdays and Saturdays are the busiest.

Bōkairō (望海楼; ☎ 844-8000; 35th fl, Sea Hawk Hotel & Resort; ⊙ nightly) Upscale neo-Chinese cocktail lounge with lipstick-red plush lounge seats and stellar night views. Cocktails start at ¥1000.

Off Broadway (☎ 724-5383; 2nd fl, Tenjin Centre Bldg) Quieter, this place has a *Cheers* kind of feel to it, with a long, well-appointed bar near the entrance and a bunch of tables and booths in the back.

Uprising (☎ 716-6364; 2F 1-3-4 Maizuru) Friendly bartenders, mellow music and good drinks make this place a pleasure. A bit far from Oyafuku-dōri, but worth the extra walk.

Entertainment

Nakasu Island is one of the most popular entertainment districts in Japan, but you need to go with a Japanese regular unless you're prepared to spend a fortune. Tenjin, and especially Oyafuko-dōri, are a better bet for a casual (or crazy!) night out. Generally, clubs have a weekend cover charge ¥1000 to ¥2500, usually with a free drink or two. If you show up early in the evening, the cover may be waived. 'Early' means before 11pm.

Blue Note (☎ 715-6666) A time-honoured standard for the real jazz aficionados in Fukuoka, Blue Note sometimes gets big names. Ticket prices range from ¥5500 to

¥12,000 for international acts, but prices include food and drink coupons.

Happy Cock (☎ 734-2686; 9th fl, Neo Palace Bldg; ⊗ 6pm-1am Tue-Thu & Sun, 6pm-4am Fri & Sat) Hit or miss. No cover if you come early to listen to the mix of '60s funk, '70s pop and '90s hip-hop. **Crazy Cock** (☎ 722-3006; Oyafuko-dōri; ⊗ 9pm-3am Tue-Thu, 9pm-4am Fri-Sun) is its close relative.

Dark Room (☎ 725-2989; 8th fl, Bacchus-kan; ⊗ 6pm-midnight) Offers a pool table, darts, a dance floor, and a multi-level lounge space – in short, a nice place with something for everyone. In summer, check out the outdoor patio bar on the roof, where you can snag a table, sip a drink, and look out on the city below.

Voodoo Lounge (☎ 732-4662; 3rd fl, Tenjin Centre Bldg) Funky, chilled-out bar with varied live music acts.

International Bar (☎ 714-2179; 4F Urashima Bldg, 3-1-13 Tenjin) A good place to meet a variety of folks from all over the world, with music soft enough that you can still have a good conversation.

Sam & Dave (☎ 713-2223; 3F West Side Bldg, Tenjin Nishidōri; www.samanddave.jp) The Fukuoka clone of a popular Osaka club, this place is all strobes and neon, a great place for those looking for the dance club scene.

Safari (☎ 762-6767; 2F Oyafuko Game Center, 3 chōme, Tenjin) Come here at 2am and the party's just starting; stay until it's light outside. Drinks start at around ¥500. During weekdays it's an *izakaya* (Japanese version of a pub/eatery). Cash only.

Shopping

Clay Hakata dolls (*Hakata Ningyō*) depicting women, children, samurai and geisha are a popular Fukuoka craft. Hakata obi, the silk sashes worn with a kimono, are another local product. Try the Mitsukoshi or Daimaru department stores in Tenjin (see p615).

Shopping, or at least window shopping, in Tenjin's high-rise and underground labyrinthine complexes is a popular Hakata-ite pastime. Tenjin Core, Mitsukoshi, Iwataya Z-side, Daimaru, subterranean Tenjin Chikagai and IMS building are all favourite spots. The latter gets bonus points for TVs in its lifts and a **rooftop terrace** (⊗ 11am-9pm, weather-permitting).

Getting There & Away
AIR
Fukuoka is a major international gateway with flights to and from many major cities

in Japan, Asia and even Honolulu. Domestic flights to Tokyo's Haneda airport (¥27,900, more than 50 flights daily) and Narita international airport (four flights, daily). Other domestic routes include Osaka (¥16,200) and Okinawa (Naha, ¥20,300, 1½ hours). ANA and JAL are the two most common carriers, and both have offices here.

Japan's only independent cut-price carrier, **Skymark** (☎ 736-3131, in Tokyo 03-3433-7026) has daily flights to Tokyo's Haneda airport for ¥16,000.

BOAT
Ferry services from Hakata connect to Okinawa and other islands off Kyūshū. An international high-speed hydrofoil service called Biitoru (say 'beetle') run by **JR Kyūshū** (reservations ☎ 281-2315) connects the city with Pusan in Korea (¥13,000, three hours, three daily). The **Camellia line** (☎ 262-2323) has a regular ferry service to Pusan (¥9000, 16 hours, daily).

BUS
Long-distance buses depart from the Kōtsū bus centre near JR Hakata Station and also from the Tenjin bus centre. Destinations include Tokyo (¥15,000, 14½ hours), Osaka (¥10,000, 9½ hours), Nagoya (¥10,500, 11 hours) and many other places around Kyūshū.

TRAIN
JR Hakata Station is currently the western terminus of the 1175km-long Tokyo–Osaka–Hakata *shinkansen*. There are services to/from Tokyo (¥21,720, five to six hours), Osaka (¥14,590, 2½ to three hours) and Hiroshima (¥8700, one to two hours). Prices are slightly higher for the Nozomi *shinkansen*.

JR lines also fan out from Hakata to other parts of Kyūshū. The Nippō line runs through Beppu and Miyazaki; the Kagoshima line runs through Hakata, Kumamoto and Kagoshima; and both the Nagasaki and Sasebo lines run from Hakata to Saga and Sasebo or to Nagasaki. You can also travel by subway and JR train to Karatsu and continue from there to Nagasaki by train.

Getting Around
TO/FROM THE AIRPORT
Fukuoka airport is conveniently close to the city centre. The airport has three domestic

terminals and an international terminal, all connected by a free shuttle bus.

The subway from the domestic terminals takes just five minutes to reach JR Hakata Station (¥250) and 11 minutes to Tenjin (¥250). Buses run frequently between JR Hakata Station and the international terminal.

Airport taxis cost around ¥1300/1800 to Tenjin/Hakata.

BUS

City bus services operate from the Kōtsū bus centre in Hakata and the Tenjin bus centre. Nishitetsu bus has a flat ¥100 rate for city-centre rides.

From stand E opposite JR Hakata Station, bus No 11 or 19 goes to Hakata Pier International Terminal (¥220), while bus No 47 or 48 reaches Bayside Place for ferries to islands.

SUBWAY

There are two subway lines in Fukuoka/Hakata. The Kūkō (airport) line runs from Fukuoka domestic airport terminal to Meinohama Station via Hakata, Nakasu-Kawabata and Tenjin stations. The Hakozaki line runs from Nakasu-Kawabata Station to Kaizuka. Fares around town start at ¥200; a one-day pass costs ¥600. Trains stop running around midnight.

DAZAIFU 太宰府

☎ 092 / pop 66,000

Dazaifu, once the governmental centre of Kyūshū, is an amiable enough place for a half-day visit, but the shrine and temples are the extent of the sightseeing. The **tourist information office** (☎ 925-1880; ⌚ 8.30am-5pm) at Nishitetsu-Dazaifu Station has helpful staff and an excellent English-language brochure map that details outlying ruins, temples and minor sights.

Sights

TENMAN-GŪ 天満宮

Poet and scholar Sugawara-no-Michizane was a distinguished figure in the Kyoto court until he fell foul of political intrigue and was exiled to distant Dazaifu, where he died two years later. Subsequent disasters that struck Kyoto were blamed on his unfair dismissal and he became deified as Tenman Tenjin, the god of culture and scholars. **Tenman-gū** (☎ 922-8225; www.dazaifutenmangu.or.jp; 4-7-1 Saifu), his great shrine and burial place, attracts countless visitors, among them students, who come to pray and give offerings in hopes of getting into their dream college.

The brightly painted orange shrine is entered via a picturesque arched bridge. The *honden* (main hall) was rebuilt in 1591. Behind the shrine is the **Kankō Historical Museum** (菅公歴史館; admission ¥200; ⌚ Wed-Mon) with dioramas showing events in Tenjin's life. The **treasure house** (宝物殿; admission ¥300; ⌚ 9am-4.30pm Tue-Sun) has artefacts connected with his life and the history of the shrine.

Every other month the shrine hosts an *omoshiro-ichi* (literally, 'interesting market'), a giant flea market selling everything from antique kimono to Mickey Mouse telephones. Dates vary, so check with tourist information.

KŌMYŌZEN-JI 光明禅寺

Secreted away inside this small **temple** (☎ 922-4053; admission by donation ¥200; ⌚ 9am-4.30pm) is an exquisite jewel of a Zen garden. It's a peaceful contrast to the crowds at the nearby shrine. On the southern edge of Dazaifu.

OTHER SIGHTS

The **Kyūshū Historical Museum** (九州歴史資料館; ☎ 923-0404; admission free; ⌚ 9am-4pm Tue-Sun) is not far beyond Kōmyōzen-ji (above), with items mostly from the Stone Age to the Middle Ages.

Hidden out among the rice fields, **Kaidan-in** (戒壇院) dates from 761 and was one of the most important ordination monasteries in Japan. Adjacent **Kanzeon-ji** (観世音寺; ☎ 922-1811) dates from AD 746 but only the great bell, said to be the oldest in Japan, remains from the original construction. Its **treasure hall** (宝蔵; admission ¥500; ⌚ 9am-4.30pm) has an impressive collection of statuary, most of it wood, dating from the 10th to 12th centuries. Many of the items show Indian or Tibetan influence.

Dazaifu Exhibition Hall (大宰府展示館; ☎ 922-7811; admission ¥150; ⌚ 9am-4.30pm Tue-Sun) displays finds from local archaeological excavations. Nearby are the **Tofurō ruins** (都府楼), foundations of the ancient government buildings. **Enoki-sha** (榎社) is where Sugawara-no-Michizane died. His body was transported from here to its burial place, now Tenman-gū (left), on the ox cart that appears in so many local depictions.

Eating

Ume-no-Hana (梅の花; ☎ 928-7787; meals ¥2300-6500; ◷ 11am-3.30pm & 4.30-8pm) Demurely hidden behind its own garden wall, a short curving walk east of the shrine. It's justifiably renowned for its tofu cuisine. Reservations are a good idea.

Getting There & Around

The private Nishitetsu line connects Tenjin in Fukuoka/Hakata (p619) with Dazaifu (¥390, 25 minutes), but a change of trains at Nishitetsu-Futsukaichi Station is required.

Bicycles can be rented (¥500 per day) at NishitetsuDazaifu Station.

FUTSUKAICHI ONSEN 二日市温泉

☎ 092

Fifteen minutes' walk south of JR Futsukaichi Station, this small *onsen* (mineral hot spring) town is unassuming. Its public baths are grouped together in the old main street. Favoured by traditionalists, **Gozen-yu** (御前湯; ☎ 928-1126; admission ¥200; ◷ 9am-9pm, closed 1st & 3rd Wed each month) is the most characteristic. From JR Futsukaichi Station, cross back over the tracks, then follow the road under the *torii* (gate) and across the stream.

TACHIARAI 大刀洗

☎ 0942

Even locals don't know about **Tachiarai Heiwa Kinenkan** (太刀洗平和記念館; ☎ 23-1227; admission ¥500; ◷ 9.30am-5pm), a tiny memorial museum established by ex-aviators and residents of Tachiarai, a small village set in farmland. The museum commemorates Japanese killed in WWII, including kamikaze pilots and Tachiarai locals who died when USAF B-52s bombed the area in 1945 (Tachiarai was the site of a military air base and aircraft factory). It's a strangely affecting place, with wartime memorabilia bundled together alongside speedometers from Phantom F-4s and Soviet MiG jets, and 24-year-old Toshihiro Watanabe's Zero-sen fighter, retrieved from the sea off Okinawa. Little is labelled in English.

Take the Nishitetsu private line from Fukuoka/Hakata to Ogōri by *kyūkō* (ordinary express, ¥500, 30 minutes) then change to the Amagi-tetsudō train line (¥280, 11 minutes). The museum is in front of Tachiarai station.

KURUME 久留米

☎ 0942

The town of Kurume, south of Dazaifu, is noted for its crafts, including splash-dyed indigo textiles, paper-making, lacquerware and bamboo work. Its rubber industry is responsible for *jika-tabi*, the floppy split-toed boots worn by labourers all over Japan, as well as for Bridgestone's tyres. Pottery is produced in nearby towns.

Narita-san (成田山; ☎ 21-7500; admission ¥500; ◷ 9am-5pm), a branch of the more famous temple outside Tokyo (see p198), is the town's biggest attraction, both literally and metaphorically speaking. Its 62m-high statue of the goddess of mercy, Kannon, stands beside a miniaturised replica of Borobudur. Inside the statue you can climb up past Buddhist treasures and religious dioramas right into the divine forehead.

Ishibashi Museum of Art (石橋美術館; ☎ 39-1131; www.ishibashi-museum.gr.jp; admission ¥500; ◷ Tue-Sun) An excellent private collection of Asian and Western art assembled by the founder of Bridgestone, who felt strongly that art should always be publically accessible rather than being hidden away. The museum is 1km from the Nishitetsu-Kurume station.

Going to Kurume from Fukuoka/Hakata takes 30 minutes, either on the JR Kagoshima line or the private Nishitetsu line (¥600). Local buses to Kamitsu-machi (¥210, 20 minutes), near Narita-san, depart from stand No 2 on the ground floor.

SAGA-KEN 佐賀県

KARATSU 唐津

☎ 0955 / pop 78,000

One of Japan's world-renowned pottery towns, Karatsu is a must-see for any *yaki-mono* (pottery or ceramic ware) fans. Already a well-known pottery town, Karatsu's Korean influences elevated it from useful ceramic ware to art, so much so that there is a old saying: 'Ichi-raku, ni-hagi, san-Karatsu,' awarding Karatsu the bronze medal for pottery best used in tea ceremony. Third may not sound like much until you consider that's third out of *hundreds*, not third out of three! Karatsu-made vessels are some of the finest in Japan. Not surprisingly, they are also some of the priciest: a small *sakazuki* (sake cup) can easily go for ¥20,000; a modest vase for ¥5,000,000.

KYŪSHŪ

KYŪSHŪ POTTERY TOWNS

In mountainous Kyūshū many villages had difficulty growing rice and turned towards other ways to make a living. Easy access to good clay, forests and streams made pottery-making a natural substitute, and a number of superb styles can be found here. This island's proximity to Korea made it possible for secret trade; many of the styles here have Korean origin.

Imari and Arita are the major pottery towns of Saga-ken. From the early 17th century, pottery was produced in this area using captive Korean potters, experts who were zealously guarded so that the secrets of their craft did not slip out. Pottery from this area, with its brightly coloured glazes, is still highly esteemed in Japan.

- Karatsu (p621): rough and groggy, marked by subtle earth tones, Karatsu-yaki (Karatsu pottery) is particularly prized for use in tea ceremony (Saga-ken).
- Arita (p624): a highly decorated porcelain ware, usually with squares of blue, red, green, or gold (Saga-ken).
- Imari (p624): similar to Arita, highly prized white-and-blue porcelain (Saga-ken).
- Shiro-Satsuma: the white form of Satsuma-yaki; vessels with a cracked, clear glaze and highly decorative, colourful designs (Kagoshima; p654).
- Kuro-Satsuma: Matte black, sometimes with a silvery sheen; 100 years ago this kind of pottery was used by non-noble 'commoners' (Kagoshima; p654).

Even if you're not in the market for a piece to add to your collection, meandering about the exquisite gardens and displays are a wonderful way to spend an afternoon. At JR Karatsu Station, the **tourist information office** (☎ 72-4963; ⏰ 9am-6pm) has a good English-language map booklet. Staff can book accommodation, but no English is spoken.

Sights & Activities

A modern reconstruction, **Karatsu-jō** (☎ 72-5697; admission ¥310; ⏰ 9am-4.40pm Sep-Jun, 9am-5.40pm Jul & Aug) is picturesquely perched on a hill overlooking the sea. Inside are antique ceramics, samurai armour and archaeological displays.

Karatsu-jinja (☎ 72-2264) is a scenic temple in the centre of the city, near the **Hikiyama Festival Float Exhibition Hall** (☎ 72-8278; admission ¥200), which contains the 14 floats used in the Karatsu Kunchi Matsuri (right). Designs include the Aka-jishi (Red Lion), samurai helmets, a dragon and a chicken.

Around town there are a number of **kilns and studios** where you can see local potters at work, and there are also ceramic shops along the street between Karatsu train station and the town centre. The most famous kiln-gallery is that of **Nakazato Tarōuemon** (☎ 72-8171; admission free). It's five minutes' walk southeast of Karatsu Station. Other nice galleries are nearby, and you can feel free to peep into the well-manicured gardens. Most potters feel strongly that their art is not only a work in itself, but that it is a part of the surroundings. The gallery owners try hard to display their wares as attractively as possible – and many don't allow photos to be taken because the arrangements are as much an art form as the vessels themselves. Many also offer a complimentary tea service.

Karatsu Ware Federation Exhibition Hall (☎ 73-4888; 2nd fl, Arupino Bldg) Just to the right of Karatsu Station, this hall is great for a taste of what the area's potters are producing.

A dirt cycling track cuts through the pine trees planted behind the 5km-long **Niji-no Matsubara Beach**. Each morning there is a busy *asa-ichi* (morning market) at the west end of the beach, from dawn until 9am.

Festivals & Events

In late July and early August the **doyō-yoichi** (Saturday night market) is held in the town centre with much singing and dancing. The spectacular **Karatsu Kunchi Matsuri** (唐津くんち祭り) takes place from 2–4 November. The festival is believed to have started in 1592.

Sleeping & Eating

Business Hotel SOLA (☎ 72-3003; www.hotel-sola .com in Japanese; s ¥4900) Bright, modern business hotel. The price includes a light breakfast.

Business Hotel Chitose (☎ 72-3361; s/tw ¥4700/7800) More traditional, and has very spacious rooms. It's off the end of the main shopping arcade.

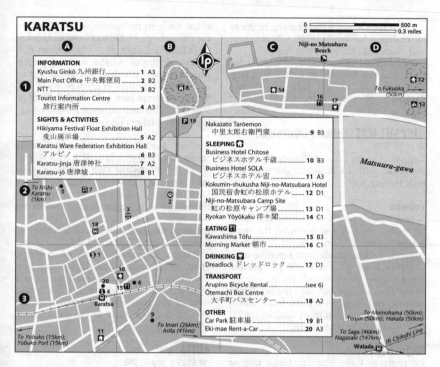

KARATSU

Ryokan Yōyōkaku (☎ 72-7181; www.yoyokaku .com; r per person from ¥15,000) A beautiful Zen-like building that harks back to earlier centuries. The owners speak English. Exquisite seafood, and a special florist does the flower arranging here. The price includes two meals.

Niji-no-Matsubara Camp Site (☎ 75-1785; tent sites per person ¥500, tent rental ¥2000; ☯ Jul & Aug) Right next to the highway, and kind of soggy.

Kokumin-shukusha Niji-no-Matsubara Hotel (☎ 73-9111, 0120-73-9100; fax 75-9991; s/tw ¥5000/ 10,000, Japanese-style r ¥14,500) Typical beach accommodation, includes in-room LAN.

Kawashima Tōfu (☎ 72-2423; www.zarudoufu.co.jp in Japanese; set meals ¥1500-2500; ☯ 8am & noon only) Only three-minutes' walk from the station, Kawashima Tōfu has been making fresh bean curd since the Edo period. Warm set-meals are served on Karatsu-yaki plates (see opposite). Zaru-dōfu, its speciality, is scooped like ice cream instead of being cut into squares. Kawashima Tōfu uses only organic, local soybeans, and its website gives details of 'the daily bean'. Only by reservation.

Mambō (☎ 75-1088; dishes ¥500-2000; ☯ lunch/ dinner) Located inside the Karatsu station

shopping arcade, this chain restaurant offers excellent tempura *teishoku* (set meal; ¥1500), great calamari, or melt-in-your-mouth squid *shūmai* (one of its specialities). Look for the blue *noren* (cloth) hanging over the entrance.

Early risers can check out the **morning market** near the water for seafood and other delicacies.

Drinking
Dreadlock (☎ 72-1207; ☯ 7pm-2am Thu-Tue) A fun reggae bar run by Karatsu's resident Rastafarian, Nishimura Eiji, and is out near the beach. The English-speaking owner has a wealth of information about diving, surfing and ceramics.

Getting There & Around
From Fukuoka/Hakata (p619), take the Kūkō subway line from Hakata or Tenjin to the end of the line, continuing on the JR Chikuhi line to reach Karatsu (¥1110, 80 minutes). Onward to Nagasaki take the JR Karatsu line to Saga (¥1080, 1¼ hour) and the JR Nagasaki line from there.

KYUSHU

From the Ōtemachi bus centre, highway buses depart for Tenjin (¥1000, 70 minutes) and Nagasaki (¥2000, two hours).

Tourists are able to borrow bicycles for free from the **Arupino** (☎ 75-5155) building. For excursions around Saga-ken, **Eki-mae Rent-a-Car** (☎ 74-6204) is located in front of Karatsu Station.

HIGASHI-MATSUURA PENINSULA
東松浦半島

Karatsu is at the base of Higashi-Matsuura Peninsula with its dramatic coastline and little fishing ports.

Yobuko 呼子

A busy fishing port with a wonderful **morning market** for fish and produce; the main action is over by 8am. A series of modern concrete ryokan (traditional Japanese inn), charging from around ¥7000 per person, line a narrow lane alongside the waterfront; rooms look straight out onto the bay. Squid sashimi and tempura are the local delicacies. Shōwa buses run from Karatsu (p623) to Yobuko (¥750, 40 minutes).

Nagoya-jō 名護屋城

En route to Cape Hatomi, buses stop at this now-ruined **castle** (admission ¥100), from which Toyotomi Hideyoshi launched his unsuccessful invasions of Korea. Look for the model of the castle in its glory days. Offers excellent views over the ruins from inside the **prefectural museum** (名護屋城博物館; ☎ 0955-82-4905; admission free; ◷ 9am-4.30pm), which holds everything from Buddhas to fishing boats. Highlights include a 14th-century scroll painting of Kannon and Toyotomi's lavishly embroidered overcoat.

IMARI 伊万里
☎ 0955 / pop 59,400

Although Imari is the name commonly associated with pottery from this area, the pottery is actually produced outside town.

Ōkawachiyama (大川内山), where 20 pottery kilns operate today, is a 20-minute bus ride from Imari (¥200). Buses are infrequent, so arrive by midday if you want to have plenty of time. The **bridge** entering Ōkawachiyama is spectacularly decorated with shards of Imari-yaki (p622) and large vases. The bus stops right near the bridge and the village is on the surrounding hillsides on both sides

of the river. At the bottom of the hill where the village begins is **Kataoka Tsurutarō Kōgeikan** (片岡鶴太郎工芸館; ☎ 22-3080; admission ¥300) gallery, dedicated to the work of potter-genius Sawada Chitōjin, whose interesting name means 'pottery-crazy person'. Uphill, **Nabeshima Hanyō-kōen** (鍋島藩窯公園; ☎ 23-3479) shows the techniques and living conditions of Feudal-era potters.

Inside a shopping arcade near the train station, **Akira Kurosawa Memorial Satellite Studio** (黒澤明記念館サテライトスタジオ; ☎ 22-9630; admission ¥500; ◷ 9am-5pm, closed 2nd & 4th Mon each month) has almost no English labelling, but die-hard fans of the legendary filmmaker will enjoy behind-the-scenes documentaries and rare outtakes from masterpieces like *Ran* (1985) and *Shichinin no Samurai* (Seven Samurai; 1954).

Karatsu is connected with Imari (*futsū*, ¥630, 50 minutes) by the JR Chikuhi line. Local buses to Ōkawachiyama depart hourly from the main bus terminal, a few blocks west of the train station, where you can also catch direct buses to Fukuoka/Hakata (¥2150, two hours).

ARITA 有田
☎ 0955 / pop 13,000

Kaolin clay was discovered here in 1615 by Ri Sampei, a naturalised Korean potter, enabling the manufacture of fine porcelain in Japan for the first time. By the mid-17th century it was being exported to Europe. The **tourist information desk** (☎ 42-4052; www.arita.or.jp/index_e.html; ◷ 9am-4.30pm) inside Arita Train Station can help orient visitors with maps and bus schedules. An annual **pottery fair** is held 29 April to 5 May.

Shops line the main street leading out from the station towards the **Kyūshū Ceramics Museum** (九州陶磁文化館; ☎ 43-3681; admission free; ◷ 9am-4.30pm Tue-Sun), well worth a visit if you want an overview of the development of ceramic arts in Kyūshū. Pottery connoisseurs are sure to find the **Imaemon Gallery** (今衛門ギャラリー; ☎ 42-5550; admission ¥300; ◷ 9am-4.30pm Mon-Sat), **Kakiemon Kiln** (柿右衛門窯; ☎ 43-2267; admission free; ◷ 9am-5pm) and **Genemon Kiln** (源衛門窯; ☎ 42-4164; admission free; ◷ 8am-5pm Mon-Sat) interesting, and there are dozens of other workshops to visit.

For the full treatment, join the Japanese package tours at **Arita Porcelain Park** (有田ポーセリンパーク; ☎ 41-0030; admission ¥500; ◷ 10am-

JUHACHIYA MATSURI   *John Ashburne*

On 18 August each year, a small roadside pit-stop of a village called Ōki in Saga-ken hosts one of Japan's most remarkable festivals – **Juhachiya Matsuri**. Almost everything about it is unique. The locals call it *'izayoi'*, and the official story is that it started life as a farmers' rain-making festival in 1576. However, even the uninitiated can see in it the origins of something far older, darker and more primitive.

The proceedings begin as night falls, with Ōki's 18-year-old males parading through the village, beating with gusto on a huge gong with metal hammers. Suspended on long bamboo poles above their heads are home-made miniflares, showering them in sulphurous sparks. Flautists and drummers add to the din and smoke – it sounds like Tom Waits's percussion section falling off a cliff. Yet this is small scale – there are only about 50 men and boys – and for that reason, it's all the more striking.

The action moves to the local temple, Ryusen-ji, where a sandy arena has been prepared. The entire village is waiting, ready to witness *Ukitate Kenka*, or the Floating-Standing Fight.

The gong is moved to one side of the ring, then all hell breaks loose. The youths rush to take possession of it. Between them and their goal, however, are the village 'elders' – blacksmiths, firemen, truck drivers, lumberjacks – none of whom look even remotely elderly. They put up a human barricade that could teach the American Football League a thing or two. Time after time the young men attack, only to be repelled or pushed face down into the sand. One youth nearly reaches the gong, only to be dealt a stabbing right-hand jab to the cheekbone by a wiry 'elder', and he's carried off to a waiting medical crew, bleeding profusely. No-one loses their temper. Finally, inevitably, the exhausted, battered youths withdraw, the gong remains in the hands of age and authority, and the temple officials rush in to set up the evening's finale, known as the *jamon*.

The *jamon* is a pyrotechnic catastrophe waiting to happen. All day, as the 18-year-olds have been psyching themselves up for the battle, their mothers, sisters and grandmothers have been hand-rolling miniature explosives and inserting them into the *jamon*, a wooden tower. At a given signal, the flame creeps slowly up the tower, the wind catches an ember, there's a glimmer of orange, and KABOOOOOOOOOOOOM!!!

And then it's over. The villagers melt away to party at home, the country darkness floods back in, and this observer is left sharing a ghostly dark station platform with an egregiously drunken civil servant who managed to get stuck here on his way back from the town office in Arita. He asks, in all innocence, 'What was all that noise?'.

5pm Mar-Nov, 10am-4pm Dec-Feb), a 10-minute bus ride from the train station, or **China on the Park** (チャイナオンザパーク; ☎ 46-3900; ☯ 9am-5pm), 5km west of town on Rte 202, where you can watch the firing process. A taxi from Arita Train Station costs ¥1000.

An Arita bus (¥150) can take you to the clay mines as well. Walk back to the station from the mines, a nice tour that will take about an hour if the many galleries don't tempt you. Along the way, note the many walls in some of the back streets: leftover pottery was often used in bricks and some of the older buildings show this quite well.

A short hop east of Arita, **Takeo Onsen** (武雄温泉) is a modern hot-springs town. The traditional baths are said to have refreshed the armies of Toyotomi Hideyoshi. Look for the lacquered Chinese-style gate, which was built without nails. **Takeo Onsen Youth Hostel** (武雄温泉ユースホステル; ☎ 0954-22-2490; fax 0954-20-1208; dm ¥2600; ☯ mid-Jun–mid-May) is an option, but the last bus to the hostel leaves Takeo Onsen Station before 6pm.

From outside JR Arita Station, private Matsuura-tetsudō trains depart for Imari (¥400, 25 minutes). JR *tokkyū* trains between Hakata (Fukuoka) and Nagasaki stop at Arita, and also Takeo Onsen. Takeo Onsen is also connected to Arita by local trains (¥270, 15 minutes). Around town, community bus routes (¥150) cover most of the outlying sights, departing hourly from Arita Station. Rental bicycles are only ¥300 per use (up to one day); ask at the train station for the closest location.

NORTHWEST ISLANDS

Five large and many smaller islands lie to the northwest of Kyūshū and are accessible from Fukuoka/Hakata, Sasebo and Nagasaki, but reaching them is not cheap. These are strictly islands for those who want to get far away from it all. Some are part of Saga-ken, but all of those below are part of Nagasaki-ken.

IKI 壱岐
☎ 09204 / pop 33,200

Attractive Iki, an island off Kyūshū's northern coast, has an area of 138 sq km and lies closer to Karatsu than Fukuoka/Hakata. As well as being home to fine beaches, it's also relatively flat and a decent place for cyclists. Toyotomi Hideyoshi fortified **Gonoura**, the busiest port and a base for exploring the island. **Ondake-jinja**, north of Ashibe, features stone statues dedicated to a half-monkey deity. These eroded figures were carved by a local lord, and were originally intended to bring health to the island's livestock. **Yunomoto Onsen** on the west coast is the island's only hot spring. Other minor sights include burial mounds, Buddhist rock carvings and historic ruins. The gorgeous little **beach** near Katsumoto on the island's north side also has a **camping ground** nearby. At the hot springs, the *kokumin-shukusha* (people's lodge) **Ikishima-sō** (壱岐島荘; ☎ 3-0124; r with 2 meals ¥6000) is good value. Cheerful **Tomita-sō** (富田荘; ☎ 7-0011; r with 2 meals ¥5000) is in Gonoura. At Gonoura ferry terminal, the **information desk** (☎ 47-3700) can help book other *minshuku* (Japanese B&B), pension and ryokan accommodation around the island.

Between April and September, jetfoils from Hakata to Gonoura or Ashibe (¥4680, 70 minutes) on Iki. Ordinary car ferry services take twice that long (¥1930). From Yobuko port near Karatsu, more frequent ferries go to Indōji (¥1310, 70 minutes). Although the port is only a five-minute ride from Yobuko town, infrequent local bus services are not timed to ferries. Express buses bound for Nagasaki sometimes meet ferries at Yobuko port.

On Iki, rental cars start at ¥3000 per three hours, costing ¥10,000 for two days. They can be rented at all of the ferry ports. Try friendly **Genkai Kotsū Rent-a-Car** (☎ 4-5658, 4-5827). Bike rental is possible from **Iki Kawabe** (☎ 44-6636; ¥1000), near the ferry terminal; for an extra ¥1000 you can have the bike dropped to you anywhere on the island.

HIRADO-SHIMA 平戸島
☎ 0950 / pop 25,000

Blessed with sunshine and verdant tea fields, Hirado-shima's proximity to the mainland makes it easy – and cheap – to access. The island has interesting historical sights, beckoning white-sand beaches, two noteworthy festivals, and a little-known collection of erotic drawings. The **tourist information booth** (☎ 0120-86-2015; ☼ 8am-5.15pm), on the waterfront by the bus terminal, has excellent English-language brochures and can book accommodation.

The island, close to Sasebo and actually joined to Kyūshū by a toll bridge (¥100) from Hirado-guchi, the nearest train station (a private line, Matsuura Tetsudō), has had an interesting European history. Portuguese ships first landed on Hirado-shima in 1549 and, a year later, St Francis Xavier visited the island (after his expulsion from Kagoshima). It was not until 1584 that the Portuguese formally established a trading post, but they were soon followed by the Dutch and the British. Relations between the British and Dutch became so acrimonious that, in 1618, the Japanese had to restore law and order on the island. In 1621, the British abandoned Hirado-shima and Japan, and turned their full attention to India.

The main town Hirado is small enough to navigate on foot. The **Matsuura Historical Museum** (松浦史料博物館; ☎ 22-2236; admission ¥500; ☼ 8am-5.30pm) is housed in the residence of the Matsuura clan, who ruled the island from the 11th to the 19th centuries. Among the esteemed treasures is **Kanun-tei**, a *chanoyu* (tea-ceremony) house for the unusual Chinshin-ryū warrior-style tea ceremony that is still practised on the island today. **Hirado Christian Museum** (平戸切支丹資料館; ☎ 28-0176; admission ¥300; ☼ 8am-5pm Jan-Nov) displays some items relating to the island's history, including a Maria-Kannon statue that the 'hidden Christians' (see p36) used in place of the Virgin Mary image.

Hirado-jō (平戸城; ☎ 22-2201; admission ¥500; ☼ 8.30am-5.30pm) presides over the town, with an enormous number of rebuilt structures. Inside you'll see traditional armour and clothing, and a few artefacts from the hid-

KYŪSHŪ

den Christian era. Not mentioned in the brochures is the more earthy **Issho-raku** (☎ 23-3434), a small private collection of erotic drawings dating back almost 400 years. Ask at the tourist information booth (opposite) to arrange a viewing. The owners of the collection don't speak English but are very friendly.

There are fine views over the islands of the Gotō-rettō from **Cape Shijiki**. About midway down the beautiful west coast of the island, **Neshiko Beach** is a lovely and long stretch of sand, while **Senri-ga-hama** is renowned for windsurfing. **Hotel Ranpu** (ホテル蘭風; ☎ 23-2111), near the beach, rents windsurfers if you're so inclined. In the northern part of the island, **Kamisuki-no-sato** has pottery workshops and kiln ruins.

Jangara Matsuri (ジャンガラ祭り), a folk festival held on 18 August, is particularly colourful. It is quite different from mainland festivals and is reminiscent of Okinawa or Korea. Arrive into Hirado by late morning, if possible, for the afternoon events. From 24 to 27 October, the **Okunchi Matsuri** (おくんち祭り) has dragon and lion dancing at Kameoka-jinja.

Over in Hirado-guchi, the closest mainland town, there's a camping ground and a beautiful **youth hostel** (たびら平戸ユースホステル; ☎ 57-1443; dm ¥3200) recently redone, with a luxurious *rotemburo* and delicious meals. The views of the water are also impressive, particularly at night when the squid boats' lights are illuminated. The kind staff will also pick you up at the station if you call ahead, and may even detour for groceries if you ask nicely.

Hirado-guchi (aka Tabira) is accessible by bus from Sasebo (¥1300, 80 minutes), and by train (¥1190, 1½ hours). Local buses cross the bridge to Hirado town (¥260, 10 minutes). Express buses run to the island from Hakata (¥2850, 3¾ hours).

GOTŌ-RETTŌ 五島列島

The two main islands in the Gotō-rettō group are **Fukue-jima** and **Nakadōri-shima**, but there are three other medium-sized islands plus over 100 small islands and islets. At one time, these islands were a refuge for Japanese Christians fleeing the Edo government's anti-Christian repression; today the main attraction is their natural beauty.

Fukue, the fishing port on the island of the same name, is the main town in the group.

The town's **Ishida-jō** was rebuilt in the 1860s. There's a street of samurai houses nearby. **Ondake**, a 40-minute walk from Fukue, is a cotyloid volcano (315m) covered by grass and an astronomical observatory. **Dozaki Tenshudō** (堂崎天主堂; ☎ 0959-73-0705; admission ¥300; ◷ 9am-4.30pm) has exhibits of artefacts from the 'hidden Christian' era, and is the oldest church in the Gotō islands. It's a 30-minute bus ride from Fukue. The island's most popular **beaches** are on the north central coast.

All Nippon Koku (ANK) has flights to Gotō-Fukue airport from Nagasaki (¥10,000) and Fukuoka/Hakata (¥15,500). Jetfoils leave Nagasaki for Fukue up to five times daily (¥6080, 1½ hours); regular ferry services depart less frequently (¥2400, 3¾ hours). Bicycles and cars can be rented on Fukue-jima.

NAGASAKI-KEN 長崎県

NAGASAKI 長崎
☎ 095 / pop 416,800

Nagasaki is a vibrant city, but its fate as the second atomic bomb target overshadows its early history of contact with the Portuguese and Dutch. Despite the tragic events of World War II, Nagasaki has a wealth of activities, interesting museums, delicious food, and scenic beauty that rivals far more visited parts of Japan. Schedule at least a few days here to take advantage of all the city has to offer.

History
Nagasaki has the most varied history of any city in Japan, much of it tied up with the dramatic events of the 'Christian Century' (see p36 for more information). The accidental arrival of an off-course Portuguese ship in 1542 signalled the start of Nagasaki's long period as Japan's principal connection with the West.

The first visitors were soon followed by the missionary St Francis Xavier in 1560 and, although their visits were brief, these Portuguese contacts were to have farreaching effects. The primitive guns introduced by the Portuguese soon revolutionised warfare in Japan, forcing the construction of new and stronger castles and bringing the anarchy and chaos of the 'Country at War' century to an end.

KYŪSHŪ

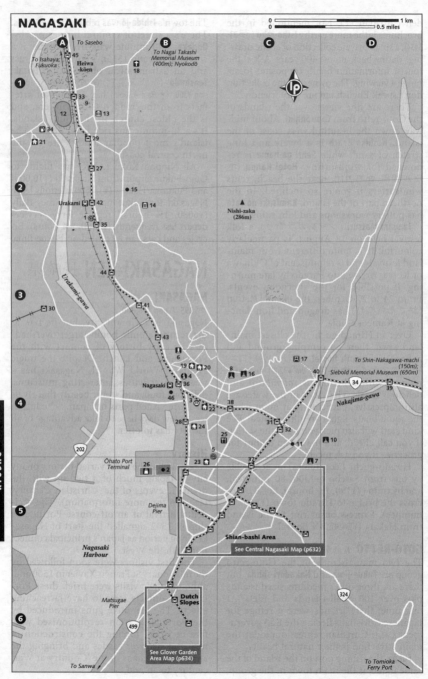

NAGASAKI

0 ————————————— 1 km
0 ————————————— 0.5 miles

To Sasebo

To Isahaya;
Fukuoka

Heiwa
-kōen

To Nagai Takashi
Memorial Museum
(400m); Nyokodō

Nishi-zaka
(286m)

Urakami-gawa

To Shin-Nakagawa-machi
(150m);
Siebold Memorial Museum
(650m)

Nagasaki

Nakajima-gawa

Ōhato Port
Terminal

Dejima
Pier

Nagasaki
Harbour

Shian-bashi Area
See Central Nagasaki Map (p632)

Matsugae
Pier

Dutch
Slopes

See Glover Garden
Area Map (p634)

To Sanwa

To Tomioka
Ferry Port

KYŪSHŪ

Among the first Japanese to be converted to Christianity by the visitors was a minor *daimyō* (regional lord), Ōmura Sumitada, in northwestern Kyūshū. Under Ōmura, Nagasaki, established in 1571, soon became the main arrival point for Portuguese trade ships. Although the Portuguese principally acted as intermediaries between China and Japan, the trade was mutually profitable, and Nagasaki quickly became a fashionable and wealthy city.

By 1587, Japanese authorities had begun to perceive the growing influence of Christianity as a threat. Jesuit missionaries were expelled and a policy of persecution was soon implemented. In 1597, 26 European and Japanese Christians were crucified in Nagasaki and in 1614 the religion was banned. Suspected Christians were rounded up, tortured and killed; the Japanese wives and children of foreigners were deported to Macau and Batavia; and the Catholic Portuguese and Spanish traders were expelled in favour of the Protestant Dutch, who were perceived as being more interested in trade and less in religion.

The Shimabara peasant uprising of 1637–38 – perceived as a Christian uprising at the time – was the final chapter in the events of the 'Christian Century'. All subsequent contact with foreigners was banned and no Japanese were allowed to travel overseas. One small loophole was the closely watched Dutch enclave on the island of Dejima near Nagasaki. Through this small outpost a trickle of Western science and culture continued to filter into Japan, and from 1720, when Dutch books were once again permitted to enter

the country, Nagasaki became an important scientific and artistic centre. When Nagasaki reopened to the West in 1859, it quickly re-established itself as a major economic force, particularly in shipbuilding, the industry that made it a target on 9 August 1945 (for details see the boxed text, p630).

Orientation

About a kilometre south of Nagasaki Station, the Hamano-machi arcade and Shian-bashi entertainment area make up Nagasaki's central city area. Nagasaki is relatively compact and it's quite feasible to walk all the way south to the Dutch slopes and Glover Garden. The atomic bomb hypocentre is in the suburb of Urakami, about 2.5km north of JR Nagasaki Station.

Information

The **tourist information office** (☎ 823-3631; ⏰ 8am-7pm) in Nagasaki Station can assist with finding accommodation, though no English is spoken.

The **Nagasaki Prefectural Tourist Federation** (Map p628; ☎ 826-9407; ⏰ 9am-5.30pm Mon-Sat Sep-May, 9am-7pm Mon-Sat Jun-Aug) has detailed information on the city and extremely helpful English-speaking staff. Cross the pedestrian walkway to enter the prefectural building on the 2nd floor.

Chikyūkan (Map p632; ☎ 822-7966; ⏰ 10am-5pm Thu-Tue), a café in the Dutch Slopes (Orandazaka) area (see p637), is aimed at long-term foreign residents and has limited information about the city and its environs. Internet access costs ¥100 per 10 minutes.

KYŪSHŪ

Most postal savings ATMs accept internationally issued cards, and there's one inside Nagasaki Station. Several branches of 18 Bank handle foreign-currency exchange.

BOOKSHOPS

Kinokuniya (Map p628; ☎ 811-4919; 4th fl, Yumesaito Bldg, 10-1 Motofune-chō) This bookshop sells CDs, software, DVDs, maps and, of course, books.

INTERNET ACCESS

Chikyū-shimin Hiroba (Map p628; ☎ 842-3783; 2nd fl, Nagasaki Brick Hall; per hr ¥100; ☯ 9am-8pm)

Cybac Café (Map p628; ☎ 818-8050; 3rd & 4th fls, Hashimoto Bldg, 2-46 Aburaya-chō; membership fee ¥200, 1st hr ¥480; ☯ 24hr)

Kinko's (Map p632; ☎ 818-2522; 1st fl, Amu Plaza; per 10min ¥200; ☯ 24hr)

Sights

URAKAMI 浦上

Urakami, the hypocentre of the atomic explosion, is today a prosperous, peaceful suburb with modern shops, restaurants, cafés and even a couple of love hotels just a few steps from the hypocentre. Nuclear ruin seems comfortably far away.

Hypocentre Park (原爆公園; Map p628) has a black, square stone column marking the exact point above which the bomb exploded.

Nearby are bomb-blasted relics, including a section of the wall of the Urakami Cathedral. The Matsuyama-machi tram stop on tram routes 1 or 3 is near the site.

The **Nagasaki Atomic Bomb Museum** (原爆資料館; Map p628; ☎ 844-1231; www1.city.nagasaki.nagasaki.jp/na-bomb/museum/; 7-8 Hirano-chō; admission ¥200, audio guide rental ¥150; ☯ 8.30am-5pm) exhibits begin with live footage of the bomb blast, then move through details of the city's destruction and loss of human life, as well as Japan's 15 years of military aggression prior to 1945. These riveting exhibitions end with an urgent report on the current status of nuclear weapons worldwide, with convincing video testimonials. A must-see, but a depressing one.

Heiwa-kōen (平和公園; Peace Park) is north of the hypocentre, and is presided over by the Nagasaki Peace Statue (Map p628). At the time of the explosion, the park was the site of the Urakami Prison and every one of the prison's 134 occupants – prisoners and warders – was killed instantly. An annual antinuclear protest is held at the park on 9 August.

Urakami Cathedral (浦上天主堂; Map p628; ☎ 844-1777; 1-79 Motoo-machi; ☯ 9am-5pm Tue-Sun), the largest church in the East, it was completed in 1914 after three decades, then flattened in

---

THE ATOMIC EXPLOSION

When the United States Air Force (USAF) B-29 bomber **Bock's Car** set off from Tinian in the Marianas on 9 August 1945 to drop the second atomic bomb on Japan, the target was Kokura on the northeastern coast of Kyūshū. Fortunately for Kokura it was a cloudy day and, despite flying over the city three times, the bomber's crew could not sight the target, so a course was set for the secondary target, Nagasaki.

The B-29 arrived over Nagasaki at 10.58am but again visibility was obscured by cloud. When a momentary gap appeared in the cloud cover, the Mitsubishi Arms Factory, not the intended Mitsubishi shipyard, was sighted and became the target. The 4.5-ton 'Fat Man' bomb had an explosive power equivalent to 21 kilotons of TNT, far more than the 13 kilotons of Hiroshima's 'Little Boy'.

The bomb actually missed its intended target and scored a near-direct hit on the largest Catholic church in Japan (Urakami Cathedral; above). The explosion took place at 11.02am, at an altitude of 500m, completely devastating the Urakami suburb of northern Nagasaki and killing 75,000 of Nagasaki's 240,000 population. Most victims were women, children and senior citizens, but those killed also included an estimated 13,000 conscripted Korean labourers and 200 allied POWs. Another 75,000 people were injured and it is estimated that as many people again have subsequently died as a result of the blast. Anybody out in the open within 2km of the hypocentre suffered severe burns from the heat of the explosion; even at 3.5km away exposed bare skin was burnt. Everything within a 1km radius of the explosion was destroyed and after the resulting fires, a third of the city was wiped out.

For details of the atomic bomb that devastated Hiroshima see p409.

three seconds in 1945. The replacement cathedral was completed in 1959.

The courage of Dr Nagai Takashi in the face of overwhelming adversity is the subject of the extraordinary **Nagai Takashi Memorial Museum** (永井隆記念館; ☎ 844-3496; 22-6 Ueno-chō; admission ¥100; ⏰ 9am-5pm). Already suffering from leukaemia, and having lost his wife during the atomic explosion, Dr Nagai devoted himself to the treatment of bomb victims until he died in 1951. Even after he became bedridden, Dr Nagai continued to write prolifically and secure donations for survivors and orphans from the international community. Make time for the short documentary videos, available in several languages.

Next door, Dr Nagai's small hut **Nyokodō** (如己堂) is preserved as a memorial. Its name echoes the sentiment 'love thy neighbour as thyself', as both the doctor and his wife were Christians.

The **'One-legged Torii'** (a *torii* is an entrance gate to a Shintō shrine; Map p628) is southeast of the hypocentre. The blast knocked down one side of the entrance arch to the Sanno-jinja, but the other leg still stands to this day.

A short walk from the *torii* is the **Nagasaki Museum of History and Folklore** (Map p628; ☎ 847-9245; 3-1 Kamizenza-machi; admission free; ⏰ 9am-4.30pm Tue-Sun), which exhibits antique household items such as fishing lures, dolls, cookware and so on, which one rarely gets to see. A 'hands on' room allows children of all ages to play around.

NAGASAKI STATION AREA

The **26 Martyrs Memorial** (Map p628) is a memorial wall with reliefs of the 26 Christians crucified in 1597, commemorating a harsh crackdown when 6 Spanish friars and 20 Japanese were killed. The youngest killed were boys aged 12 and 13. Behind the memorial is a simple **museum** (☎ 822-6000; 7-8 Nishisaka-machi; admission ¥250) with Christianity-related displays. The memorial is few minutes' walk from JR Nagaski Station on Nishi-zaka.

Although **Fukusai-ji Kannon** (Nagasaki Universal Kannon Temple; Map p628; ☎ 823-2663; 2-56 Chikugo-machi; admission ¥200; ⏰ 8am-4pm) is not on any list of architectural or cultural gems, this unique construction is interesting. The temple is in the form of a huge turtle carrying an 18m-high figure of the goddess Kannon on its back. Inside, a Foucault pendulum (a device that demonstrates the rotation of the earth on its tilted axis) hangs from near the top of the hollow statue. Only St Petersburg and Paris have larger examples.

The original temple was built in 1628 but was completely burnt by the A-bomb fire. The replacement, totally unlike the original, was built in 1976. The temple bell tolls at 11.02am daily, the exact time of the explosion (see opposite for other details of the explosion). If you're lucky, the caretaker will give you a personalised tour of the premises.

The **Shōfuku-ji** (Map p628; ☎ 823-0282; 3-77 Tamazono-machi) temple, not to be confused with Sōfuku-ji (see below), is a 10-minute walk from JR Nagasaki Station. Its gardens are particularly pleasant and contain an arched stone gate dating from 1657. The main building, of typical Chinese style, was reconstructed in 1715. The *onigawara* (ogre-covered) wall is particularly interesting, as is the book-burning kiln. There are nice views of Nagasaki port from here.

Just west is another temple, **Kanzen-ji** (Map p628), with the biggest camphor tree in Nagasaki.

SUWA-JINJA 諏訪神社

Between 7 and 9 October, this enormous **shrine** (Map p628; ☎ 824-0445; 18-15 Kaminishiyama-machi) comes to life with the dragon dance of Kunchi Matsuri (p635), Nagasaki's most important annual celebration. Inside you will find a number of cute *komainu* (prayer dogs, yes, you heard right!). Be sure to see the *kappa-komainu* (water-sprite dog, which you pray to by dribbling water on the plate on its head) and the *gan-kake komainu* (turn-table dog). The latter was used by prostitutes, who prayed that storms would arrive soon, forcing the sailors to stay at the port another day.

Suwa-jinja was originally established in 1625 and its forested hilltop setting is meditative. Tram line Nos 3, 4 and 5 run to the Suwa-jinja-mae stop.

TERAMACHI (TEMPLE ROW) 寺町

Incongruously close to the Shian-bashi entertainment area, the path between Sōfuku-ji and Kōfuku-ji (p633) is lined with a series of smaller temples.

An Ōbaku (the third-largest Zen sect after Rinzai and Sōtō) temple, and one of Nagasaki's most important, **Sōfuku-ji** (Map p632;

KYŪSHŪ

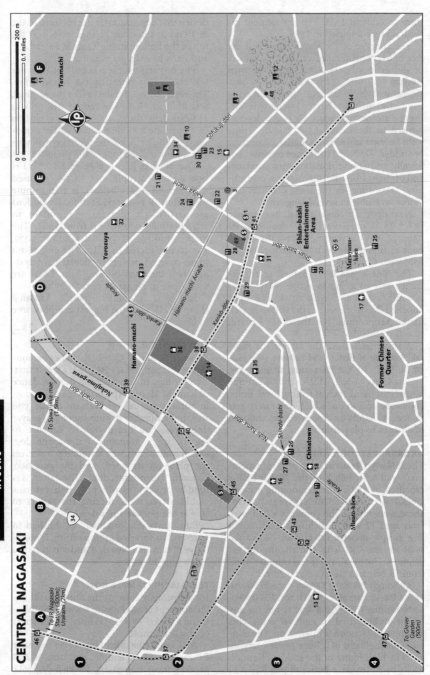

CENTRAL NAGASAKI

823-2645; 7-5 Kajiya-machi; admission ¥300; 8am-5pm) was founded in 1629 and has a Ming-style gate. Inside the temple you can admire a great bell from 1647 and a huge cauldron that was used to prepare food for victims of a famine in 1680.

Just down the road from Sōfuku-ji, steep steps lead up to **Daikō-ji** (Map p632; 822-2877; 5-74 Kajiya-machi), which has had no fires and was, unlike Urakami Cathedral, even spared from the effects of the atomic bomb. At almost the bottom of the road, turn right and take a few steps to **Hosshin-ji bell** (823-2892; 5-84 Kajiya-machi) which has the oldest temple bell in Nagasaki, cast in 1438. Then climb the stairs to the large Kuroganemochi tree at the entrance to **Daion-ji** (Map p632; 824-2367; 5-87 Kajiya-machi) and follow the path that heads to the grave of Matsudaira Zushonokami. He had been magistrate of Nagasaki for a year when, in 1808, the British warship HMS *Phaeton* sailed into Nagasaki Harbour and seized two Dutch hostages. The British and Dutch were on opposite sides in the Napoleonic War at that time. Unable to oppose the British, Zushonokami capitulated to their demands for supplies, then promptly disembowelled himself.

A short distance further on, turn down the path to **Kōtai-ji** (823-7211; 1-1 Tera-machi), the only temple in Nagasaki with active monks-in-training and a favourite with local artists; it has a notable bell dating from 1702. The final temple along the temple-row walk, **Kōfuku-ji** (Map p628; 822-1076; 4-32 Tera-machi; admission ¥200; 6am-6pm), dates from the 1620s and has always had strong Chinese connections. The temple is noted for its lawns and cycad palms and for the Chinese-influenced architecture of the main hall. Like Sōfuku-ji, it is an Ōbaku Zen temple – but this one is the oldest in Japan.

Megane-bashi めがね橋

Parallel to the temple row is the river, the Nakajima-gawa, which is crossed by a picturesque collection of stone bridges. At one time, each bridge was the distinct entranceway to a separate temple. The best-known is the double-arched **Megane-bashi** (Spectacles Bridge; Map p628), so called because if the water is at the right height, the arches and their reflection in the water come together to create a 'spectacles' effect.

SHIAN-BASHI AREA 思案橋

The Shian-bashi tram stop marks the site of the bridge over which pleasure seekers would cross into the Shian-bashi quarter. The bridge's name loosely translates to 'Bridge of Pondering': men might stop here one last time, debating whether to seek a night of pleasure or to return home. The bridge and the elegant old brothels are long gone but this is still the entertainment area of Nagasaki. During Japan's long period of isolation from the West, the Dutch – cordoned off at their Dejima trading post – were only allowed contact with Japanese trading partners and courtesans. It's said that fortunes were made as much from smuggling as from the world's oldest profession.

In between the bars, restaurants and clubs, Shian-bashi still has a few reminders of those old days. A walk south from the southern tram stop on Shian-bashi-dōri to where the first road forks leads to the **Fukusaya Castella Cake Shop** (福砂屋カステラ店;

KYŪSHŪ

Map p632; ☎ 821-2938; www.castella.co.jp; 3-1 Funadaiku-machi), which history buffs or those with an interest in Japanese sweets should check out as it's been in business since 1624. Turn left at this junction, pass the police post and you come to the driveway to Kagetsu (p637), now an elegant and expensive restaurant, but at one time an even more elegant and expensive brothel.

DEJIMA MUSEUM 出島資料館
From the mid-17th century until 1855, this small isolated conclave of Dejima was Japan's only contact with the Western world, where Dutch traded Japanese crafts for Western medicine and technology. The small **museum** (Map p632; ☎ 822-2207; www1.city.nagasaki.nagasaki.jp/dejima/main.html; 8-21 Dejima; admission ¥300; ☺ 9am-5pm) here has exhibits on the Dutch and other foreign contact with Nagasaki, and free walking tour maps of the entire site. Although the island was submerged during 19th-century land reclamation projects, the trading post, now a national historic site, has been restored.

CHINATOWN AREA 中国街
Theoretically, during Japan's long period of seclusion, Chinese traders were just as circumscribed in their movements as the Dutch, but in practice they were relatively free. Only a couple of buildings remain from the old area, but Nagasaki still has an energetic Chinese community that has had a great influence on the city's culture, festivals and cuisine.

GLOVER GARDEN AREA グラバー園周辺
Glover Garden
At the southern end of Nagasaki, some former homes of the city's pioneering Meiji period European residents have been reassembled in this hillside **garden** (Map p634; ☎ 822-8223; 8-1 Minami-yamatemachi; admission ¥600; ☺ 8am-9.30pm late Jul–mid-Oct, 8am-6pm mid-Oct–mid-Jun). The series of moving stairways up the hill, along with the goldfish ponds, fountains and squawking public announcement system, give it the air of a cultural Disneyland, but the houses are appealing, the history is interesting and the views across Nagasaki are superb.

The garden takes its name from Thomas Glover (1838–1911), whose arms-importing operations played an important part in the Meiji Restoration; he built the first train line

in Japan and he even helped establish the first modern shipyard from which Nagasaki's Mitsubishi shipyard is a direct descendant.

The best way to explore the hillside garden is to take the walkways to the top and then walk back downhill. At the top of the park is **Mitsubishi No 2 Dock building** with displays about the city's important shipyard. Going down the hill you come to **Walker House**, the **Ringer** and **Alt Houses** and finally **Glover House**. Halfway down the hill, above Glover House, is the renowned **statue** of the Japanese opera singer Miura Tamaki, which is often referred to as Madame Butterfly. You exit the garden

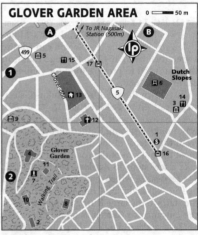

through the **Nagasaki Traditional Performing Arts Museum**, which has a display of dragons and floats used in the colourful Kunchi Matsuri.

Ōura Catholic Church 大浦天主堂

Just below Glover Garden is this attractively situated **church** (Map p634; ☎ 823-2628; www9 .ocn.ne.jp/~oura/ in Japanese; admission ¥300; ☯ 8.30am-5pm Dec-Feb, 8am-6pm Mar-Nov), built in 1864 for Nagasaki's new foreign community. Soon after its opening, a group of Japanese came to the church and announced that Christianity had been maintained among the Urakami community throughout the 250 years it had been banned in Japan. Unfortunately, despite Japan's newly opened doors to the West, Christianity was still banned for Japanese people. When this news leaked out, thousands of Urakami residents were exiled to other parts of Japan, and many of them died before Christianity was legalised in 1873. The church is dedicated to the 26 Christians crucified in 1597 (see p627 for more information).

Dutch Slopes オランダ坂

The gently inclined flagstone streets known as the Dutch Slopes (Oranda-zaka) were once lined with wooden **Dutch houses** (Map p634; ☎ 820-3386; 6-25 Higashi Yamatemachi; combined admission ¥200; ☯ 9am-5pm Tue-Sun). Several buildings have been beautifully restored and offer nice glimpses back into the past. **Maizō-shiryōkan**, has archaeological artifacts, while **Furushashin-shiryōkan**, has a collection of vintage photographs (including a rare one of the Meiji-era hero Sakamoto Ryoma). 'Oranda-zaka' comes from the name foreigners were given: Oranda-san, people from Holland.

Other Sights

Behind the jauntily coloured **Kōshi-byō**, a Confucian shrine, the **Historical Museum of China** (☎ 824-4022; 10-36 O-uramachi; admission ¥525; ☯ 8.30am-5pm) has exhibits on loan from Beijing. The original shrine dates from 1893, but was destroyed in the fires following the A-bomb explosion.

The historic **Hong Kong & Shanghai Bank Nagasaki Branch Museum** (☎ 827-8746; 4-27 Matsugaemachi; admission ¥100; ☯ 9am-5pm) is also worth a peek. It has high ceilings, burnished wood banisters, several displays, and signage in English, French, and Chinese.

SIEBOLD MEMORIAL MUSEUM シーボルト記念館

Not far from Shin-Nakagawamachi tram stop is the site of Dr Siebold's **house** (☎ 823-0707; www1.city.nagasaki.nagasaki.jp/siebold/; 2-7-40 Narutaki; admission ¥100; ☯ 9am-4.30pm Tue-Sun), an imposing Western-style structure, set in a leafy residential neighbourhood. The doctor is credited with being an important force behind the introduction of Western medicine and scientific learning to Japan between 1823 and 1829, though he was eventually expelled for trying to smuggle Japanese goods. His daughter Ine was one of Japan's first female obstetricians.

INASA-YAMA LOOKOUT 稲左山展望台

From the western side of the harbour, a **cable car** (ropeway; Map p628; ☎ 861-6321; ¥1200 return; ☯ 9am-10pm Mar-Nov, 9am-9pm Dec–Feb) ascends every 20 minutes to the top of 333m-high Inasa-yama, offering superb views over Nagasaki, particularly at night. Bus Nos 3 and 4 leave from outside JR Nagasaki Station; get off at the Ropeway-mae stop and walk up the stone steps through the grounds of Fuchi-jinja. You can also walk up to the lower ropeway entrance in 15 minutes from the Takara-machi tram stop.

Festivals & Events

Colourful **Peiron dragon boat races**, introduced by the Chinese in the mid-1600s and held to appease the god of the sea, still take place in Nagasaki Harbour in late July. On 15 August there's the beautiful **Shōrō-nagashi Matsuri**, where lantern-lit floats are carried down to the harbour in honour of one's ancestors. Hand-crafted, the boats are made from a variety of items (bamboo, wood, rice stems etc) and vary in size depending on the family or individual. Eventually they are carried out to sea and destroyed by the waves. The best viewpoint is at Ōhato (Map p632).

Kunchi Matsuri, held 7–9 October, is an energetic festival that features more Chinese dragons, this time dancing all around the city but especially at Suwa-jinja. The festival is marked by elaborate costumes, fireworks, cymbals, and giant dragon puppets on poles.

Sleeping

Nagasaki has a wide range of accommodation possibilities, from the love hotels

KYŪSHŪ

clustered around the A-bomb site to the upmarket hotels of the Glover Garden area. Central Nagasaki, the best place to be based, has a few affordable ryokan.

BUDGET

Nagasaki has a number of budget *minshuku* and ryokan, most containing basic rooms with shared bathrooms.

Nagasaki Ebisu Youth Hostel (Map p628; ☎ 824-3823; www5a.biglobe.ne.jp/~urakami; 6-10 Ebisumachi; dm with/without meals ¥4300/2800) Run by a friendly family with years of experience helping travellers. Curfew isn't until 11pm.

Fukumatsu Ryokan (Map p628; ☎ 823-3769; Daikokumachi 4-18; r ¥3500) Uphill behind Kenei bus station, this is near JR Nagasaki Station but off the main drag. It's among the cheapest in the area, but there are only a handful of rooms.

Minshuku Fumi (Map p628; ☎ 822-4962; Daikokumachi 4-9; r ¥3500) In the side street behind Kenei bus station, three minutes' walk from JR Nagasaki Station. It is small and cosy, but the place is well-accustomed to foreign guests and has an English sign at the entrance. There are only five Japanese-style rooms, however, and a very basic shared bath. No meals are served.

MIDRANGE

Miyuki-sō Business Hotel (Map p632; ☎ 821-3487; 6-46 Kajiyamachi; s ¥3500-4000, d ¥7000-7500) A five-minute walk northeast of the Shian-bashi entertainment district, has Japanese- and Western-style rooms.

Nishiki-sō (Map p632; ☎ 826-6371; 1-2-7 Nishikojima; r with bath ¥4000-4500) The pick of the pack, a delightful, creaky old building with fabulous views over Nagasaki. In Shian-bashi.

Fukumoto Ryokan (Map p632; ☎ 821-0478; 3-8 Dejimamachi; s ¥7000) Nice, friendly folks but they cater primarily to business customers as opposed to tourists. One plus is that Visa and MasterCard are accepted here. The price includes two meals.

Minshuku Tanpopo (Map p628; ☎ 861-6230; 21-7 Houeimachi; www.tanpopo-group.biz/tanpopo; s/d/tr with shared bath ¥4000/7000/9000) A Japanese Inn Group member, north of JR Nagasaki Station, near the A-bomb site. The common baths have mineral spring waters.

Tōyoko Inn Nagasaki (Map p628; ☎ 825-1045; 5-45 Gotōmachi; s/d ¥5460/7560; P ⊗ ⊑ ⊠) The Nagasaki clone of this popular business hotel

chain; offers free Japanese-style breakfast and is a five-minute walk from JR Nagasaki Station.

Shinchi Business Hotel (Map p632; ☎ 827-1123; 11-15 Shinchimachi; s/d ¥5250/8450, Japanese-style r ¥9450) Not only perfectly poised in the Chinatown shopping arcade, but also within striking distance of nightlife. This tidy hotel is a good deal.

JR Kyūshū Hotel Nagasaki (☎ 832-8000; fax 832-8001; 1-1 Onoukemachi; s/tw ¥6900/12,600) Right in the JR Nagasaki Station complex, this hotel has unusually large rooms. Check-in is from 2pm; check out by 11am.

Holiday Inn (Map p632; ☎ 828-1234, 0120-381-489; fax 828-0178; 6-24 Douzamachi; s/d from ¥9000/12,000) Near the Shian-bashi entertainment area, tastefully appointed, and good value. Caters to business travellers.

TOP END

Nagasaki Washington Hotel (Map p632; ☎ 828-1211; fax 825-8023; s/d from ¥6500/15,000) This is a rather more upmarket hotel, where the entertainment area merges into the Chinatown district.

ANA Hotel Nagasaki Glover Hill (Map p634; ☎ 818- 6601, 0120-02-9501; fax 818-6110; 1-18 Minami Yamatemachi; s/d from ¥12,000/23,000) A renovated luxury hotel with spacious rooms just below Glover Garden. Free LAN included.

Sakamoto-ya Bekkan (Map p628; ☎ 826-8211; 2-4 Kanayamachi; r per person with 2 meals from ¥16,000) An old and very well-kept ryokan, full of traditional touches.

Eating

Like Yokohama and Kōbe, Nagasaki has the reputation of being a culinary crossroads. The city's diverse influences come together in *shippoku-ryōri*, a banquet-style offering (generally you need at least four diners) that rolls together Chinese, Japanese and Portuguese influences. *Champon*, the local *rāmen* speciality (inexpensive and very popular) is made with squid, octopus, pork, *kamaboko* (white and pink fish-based patty) and vegies in a white, salt-based broth. *Sara-udon* is the stir-fried equivalent.

A good area for ferreting out restaurants is the sidestreets off the Hamano-machi arcade.

Unryūtei (Map p632; ☎ 823-5971; 3-15 Motoshikkuimachi; plate of gyoza ¥300; ⊙ 6pm-midnight) Tucked away at the end of Shian-bashi Gourmet

Street, this place only seats six and specialises in cheap and tasty gyōza (dumplings), which are excellent with beer. There's another branch nearby.

Ginrei Restaurant (Map p632; ☎ 821-2073; 2-11 Kajiya-machi; dishes from ¥800; ☾ 10.30am-9.30pm) Well-known European-style establishment (look for the ivy hanging outside), which is the oldest restaurant in Nagasaki, serving basic steaks, curries and so on since 1930. The quiet bar is intimate.

Wine Cellar Rosenthal (Map p632; ☎ 820-6218; 6-18 Kajiya-machi; mains ¥800-2500; ☾ 5pm-10pm Wed-Mon) Boasting an import list of vino to die for, this has excellently priced fresh Italian bistro dishes.

Hamakatsu Restaurant (Map p632; ☎ 826-8321; 6-50 Kajiya-machi) Banquet-style *shippoku* (range of Dutch-, Chinese-, and Japanese-influenced dishes) from around ¥3000 per person. Last order is at 8.30pm.

Hamakatsu (Map p632; ☎ 827-5783; 1-14 Kajiya-machi, Teramachi-dōri; ☾ 11am-10pm) Around the corner from Hamakatsu Restaurant and run by the same owners; it serves excellent *tonkatsu* (deep-fried breaded pork cutlets), has an illustrated menu and is far less expensive than it looks.

Kagetsu (Map p632; ☎ 822-0191; 2-1 Kajiya-machi; lunch sets from ¥5200; ☾ noon-2pm & 6-10pm Mon-Fri, 6-10pm Sat & Sun) A *shippoku* restaurant with a history that dates back to 1642. At one time it was a high-class brothel. Today it's still high class; count on ¥20,000 per person at dinner.

Harbin (Map p628; à la carte dishes ¥350-800, dinner mains ¥2000-5000) Specialises in Russian and French cuisine, worthy of connoisseurs. It's an atmospheric place, with white tablecloths, heavy cutlery and dark wood furniture. At lunch, you can select from a long menu offering a starter, main course, bread and tea or coffee (from ¥1800). Everything from smoked fish buckwheat crepes to peroshkis is delicious, but portions are small. Ask for the English-language menu.

Chikyūkan (Map p632; ☎ 822-7966; lunch ¥750; ☾ noon-2pm Thu-Tue) A casual café in the Dutch Slopes (Oranda-zaka) area serving a different international cuisine each day, prepared by foreign residents of 49 countries so far.

Shikairō (Map p634; ☎ 822-1296) An imposing Chinese-style restaurant near Glover Garden, claims to be the creator of *champon*. It has been in operation since 1899.

Beside JR Nagasaki Station, **Amu Plaza** (Map p628; 5th fl) has a surprisingly varied restaurant arcade, with meals available from ¥650. The sushi restaurant **Asajirō** (☎ 818-3356; 4th fl Amu Plaza, 1-1 Onoue-machi; dishes from ¥2500; ☾ 11am-11pm) has nice views of the harbour if you can get a seat near the window, but be careful: whale is often included in the larger platters (dark red, looks a bit like raw beef, but darker). **Dragon Deli** (ground fl, Amu Plaza) is an import grocery shop selling goodies from all across Asia and the West.

During Japan's long period of isolation from the West, Nagasaki was a conduit not only for Dutch trade and culture but also for the trade and culture of the Chinese, a history reflected in the city's restaurants. Popular Chinese restaurants cluster around the Nagasaki Washington Hotel, including: **Chūka-en** (Map p632; ☎ 822-0311; 8-4 Shinchi-machi) **Kairaku-en** (Map p632; ☎ 821-0373; 2-18 Motoshikkui-machi) Famed for its *champon*. **Kyōka-en** (Map p632; ☎ 821-1507; 9-7 Shinchi-machi)

Drinking

Nagasaki's nightlife is rather subdued for such a large city.

Moonshine (Map p632; ☎ 823-9186; Ebisu Bldg 2F 10-9 Douzamachi; dishes from ¥700) Set above a *rāmen* shop, this is a mellow, gaijin-friendly dining bar that feels somehow Dutch. Menu includes Western, Chinese, and Japanese cuisine.

Albert's Place (Map p632) Run by a former English teacher, this place is tiny but fun. Arrive later to find more of a crowd.

Entertainment

Fan Fan (Map p632; ☎ 827-3976; 5-36 Manyamachi; ☾ 7.30pm-2am) A jazz paradise with local live musicians on the first and third Saturdays of each month, and many well-known musicians come here to listen.

Ayer's Rock (Map p632; ☎ 828-0505; B1F Hananoki Bldg, 6-17 Maryamachi; cover Fri & Sat ¥1500) Alternative place with good vibes, techno DJs, bongos and beers (¥500). If you're curious about the local rave scene, ask here.

Shopping

There are displays of local crafts and products directly opposite JR Nagasaki Station on the same floor as the Nagasaki Prefectural Tourist Federation (p629). You'll also find lots of shops along the busy Hamano-machi shopping arcade.

KYŪSHŪ

Please ignore Nagasaki's tortoise-shell crafts: turtles need their shells more than humans do.

Getting There & Away

There are flights between Nagasaki and Tokyo (Haneda airport, ¥29,700), Osaka (¥19,400) and Naha (¥23,000, 1½ hours) in Okinawa, plus flights to other Kyūshū cities.

From the Kenei bus station opposite JR Nagasaki Station, buses depart for Unzen (¥1900, 1¾ hours), Sasebo (¥1450, 1½ hours), Fukuoka/Hakata (¥2900, 2¾ hours), Kumamoto (¥3790, three hours) and Beppu (¥4500, 3½ hours). Night buses for Osaka (¥11,000, 10 hours) leave from both the Kenei bus station and the highway bus station next to the Irie-machi tram stop.

JR lines from Nagasaki head for Sasebo (*kaisoku*, ¥2100, 1¾ hours) or Fukuoka/Hakata (*tokkyū*, ¥4910, two hours).

There are ferries from a few places around Nagasaki, including Ōhato terminal, south of JR Nagasaki Station.

To travel between here and the Amakusa Archipelago, take bus No 10 to Mogi port from the South Exit at Nagasaki Station (¥160, 30 minutes), then the ferry to Tomioka on Amakusa island (one way ¥1750, 40 minutes).

Getting Around

TO/FROM THE AIRPORT

Nagasaki's airport is about 40km from the city. Airport buses (¥800, 45 minutes) operate from stand No 4 of the Kenei bus station opposite JR Nagasaki Station.

BICYCLE

Bicycles can be rented (40% discount for JR Pass holders) from **JR Nagasaki Station** (☎ 826-0480) at the Eki Rent-a-Car. Some are even electric powered. Rates are reasonable (¥500/1500 per two hours/day).

BUS

A greater area is covered by buses than by trams (with buses reaching more of the sights directly) but the Japanese script on the bus service is more difficult to decipher than that on the tram service.

TRAM

The best way of getting around Nagasaki is on the easy-to-use tram service. There

are four colour-coded routes numbered 1, 3, 4 and 5 (there's no No 2). Most stops are signposted in English. It costs ¥100 to travel anywhere in town, but you can only transfer to another line at the Tsuki-machi stop unless you have a ¥500 all-day pass for unlimited travel. These passes are available from the shop beside the station information counter, from the Nagasaki Prefectural Tourist Federation (p629) across the road, or from major hotels. Most trams stop running before 11.30pm.

HUIS TEN BOSCH ハウステンボス

You'll see this 'virtual-Holland' **theme-park** (☎ 0956-27-0001; www.huistenbosch.co.jp) advertised everywhere, but most travellers could spend their time visiting real Japan…or the real Holland.

SHIMABARA PENINSULA
島原半島

A popular route between Nagasaki and Kumamoto is via this peninsula. Local bus services connect with ferries from Shimabara to the Kumamoto coast, and certain tour buses operating between Nagasaki and Kumamoto make stops around the peninsula.

It was the uprising on the Shimabara peninsula that led to the suppression of Christianity in Japan and the country's subsequent two centuries of seclusion from the West (see p36). The peasant rebels made their final valiant stand against overwhelming odds (37,000 versus 120,000) at Hara-jō, at almost the southern tip of the peninsula. The warlords even chartered a Dutch man-of-war to bombard the hapless rebels, who held out for 80 days before being slaughtered.

In June 1991, the 1500m peak of Unzendake erupted after lying dormant for 199 years. Nearby villages were evacuated and the lava flow reached the outskirts of Shimabara. The explosion left at least 40 people dead.

UNZEN 雲仙
☎ 0957

Unzen is a very active volcanic centre. Home to one of Japan's first national parks, Unzen's walks and paths are clearly signposted and it's easy to spend hours wandering around the town. Meanwhile, the friendly staff at the Shimatetsu bus station will store your luggage for ¥100 per day.

The bubbling and spurting *jigoku* (hells) currently boil nothing more sinister than the popular wayside snack of eggs, known as *onsen tamago*; a few centuries ago the same fate was reserved for Christians.

Today you can voluntarily boil yourself at any of the resort's luxury hotels, though budget travellers will likely prefer the three public baths, all within walking distance of the bus station:

Kojigoku (小地獄温泉館; ☎ 73-3273; admission ¥400; ☒ 9am-9pm)

Shin-yu (新湯温泉; ☎ 0957-73-3545; admission ¥100; ☒ 9am-11pm)

Yunosato (湯の里温泉; ☎ 73-2576; admission ¥100; ☒ 9am-10.30pm)

The ultra-modern **Unzen Spa House** (雲仙スパハウス; ☎ 73-3131; admission ¥800; ☒ 9am-6pm), opposite the post office, even has a glass-blowing workshop (lessons cost ¥2000 per 10 minutes).

From the town there are popular walks to Kinugasa, Takaiwa-san and Yadake, all situated within the Unzen-Amakusa National Park, Japan's oldest national park. The **Unzen visitors centre** (雲仙お山の情報館; ☎ 73-3636; ☒ 7am-6pm), near the Shin-yu Hotel, has excellent displays on flora and fauna and plentiful information in English, especially about hiking trails. Around town, the screeching, geyser-like **Daikyōkan Jigoku** and the 1300-year-old temple, **Manmyō-ji** (満明寺; ☎ 73-3422), are worth seeing.

Outside town, reached via Nita Pass, is **Fugen-dake** (1359m), part of the Unzen-dake range, with its popular hiking trail. The bus to Nita-tōge, the starting point for the Fugen-dake walk, operates regularly from the Unzen bus station (¥370, 25 minutes). A **cable car** (ropeway; ☎ 73-3572; return ticket ¥1220; ☒ 9am-5.30pm) whisks you almost to the 1333m-high summit of **Myōken-dake**, from where the hike to Fugen-dake via Kunimi-wakare takes just under two hours, return. The views of the lava flow from the summit are incredible. For a longer excursion, you can detour to Kunimi-dake (1347m) or walk back to Nita via the village and valley of Azami-dani in about 70 minutes. The last bus from Nita-tōge back to Unzen usually leaves around 5pm.

Sleeping

Unzen has numerous hotels, *minshuku* and ryokan (most very pricey) with nightly rates from around ¥7000, including dinner and brekkie. You can easily visit as a day-tripper, but staying overnight makes for a refreshing stop between Nagasaki (p627) and Kumamoto (p641). On Saturday nights and holidays, expect to pay a hefty surcharge.

Shirakumo-no-ike camping ground (白雲の池キャンプ場; ☎ 73-2642; tent sites from ¥300) This is a 10-minute walk downhill from the post office; tent hire is available.

Kokumin-shukusha Seiun-sō (国民宿舎青雲荘; ☎ 73-3273, fax 73-2698; r per person with 2 meals ¥7400-9400) Also quite a steep walk, this affordable option has enormous communal baths.

Ryokan Kaseya (旅館かせや; ☎ 73-3321; fax 73-3322; r per person ¥6800-9980) A smart-looking choice. On the grounds are a small garden and, naturally, a hot-springs bath.

Yumoto Hotel (湯元ホテル; ☎ 73-3259; fax 73-2126; r per person ¥10,000) A hive of activity in the town centre, has a sauna, *rotemburo* and traditional Japanese garden. Anyone can use for free its *ashiyu* (foot bath) outside the front lobby.

Unzen Kankō Hotel (雲仙観光ホテル; ☎ 73-3263, fax 73-3419; www.unzenkankohotel.com; Japanese-or Western-style s/d/tw from ¥8000/12,000/14,000) This dates back to the 1930s, when it was a summer retreat for expat gaijin. Overall its ambience is like a European mountain lodge. Meals are available at the hotel restaurant.

Getting There & Away

Direct buses between Nagasaki and Unzen take almost two hours (¥1900). Buses run more frequently from the town of Isahaya, which is 35 minutes by *kaisoku* train (¥450) from Nagasaki. From Isahaya to Unzen, buses take another 80 minutes (¥1300). Onward buses from Unzen to Shimabara (¥820, 50 minutes) stop at Shimabara's port (p641) and castle before arriving at Shimabara train station.

SHIMABARA 島原

☎ 0957 / pop 39,420

Shimabara is the ferry port to nearby Kumamoto. The **tourist information office** (☎ 62-3986) is on the 1st floor of the port terminal complex (with various shops and the bus station). Shimabara's castle, samurai street and reclining Buddha are the town's main

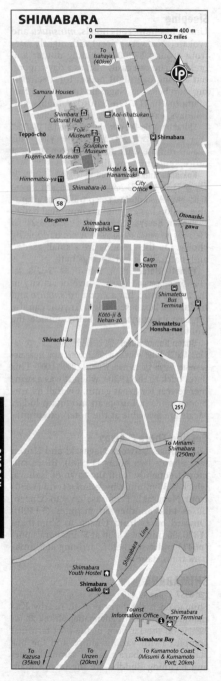

SHIMABARA

attractions. Built between 1618 and 1625, **Shimabara-jō** (☎ 62-4766; 9am-5pm) played a part in the Shimabara Rebellion and was rebuilt in 1964 during Japan's nationwide spate of castle reconstruction. Walk around its expansive grounds to see carp ponds, tangled gardens, mossy walls and picturesque pines. The **tea room**, near the exit, is built in the old style with a bark roof.

The castle itself houses a few **museums** (combined admission ¥520). The **Shimabara cultural hall** displays items relating to the Christian uprising, the **Fugen-dake museum** details Fugen-dake's pyrotechnic exploits (including the colossal explosion of 1792 in which 15,000 people died) and a third, the **Sculpture museum**, is dedicated to the artwork of Seibō Kitamura, who sculpted the Nagasaki Peace Statue. Another small **folk museum** (admission free) is stuffed with antiques from the Edo, Meiji and Shōwa periods.

In the Teppō-chō area, northwest of the castle, is a *buke-yashiki*, or collection of **samurai houses** which line a picturesque street with an unusual feature: a channel in the centre which once carried water to the households. Three of the houses are open to the public, and a free rest area serves tea and the local traditional sweet. Just south of the town centre, near the Shimatetsu bus station, are **carp streams** with lots of colourful fish and a small park. At Kōtō-ji is the rather beautiful **Nehan-zō**, or 'Nirvana Statue'. At 8.2m, it's the longest reclining **Buddha statue** in Japan.

Sleeping & Eating

Shimabara Youth Hostel (☎ 62-4451; dm ¥2750) A few minutes' walk north of Shimabara-Gaikō station, this is a hospitable hostel which happens to look like a ski chalet.

A variety of inexpensive hotels, *minshuku* and ryokan are in the castle area.

Hotel & Spa Hanamizuki (☎ 63-1000; s/tw ¥5700/9800) Newly remodelled, cosy, and has many different kinds of baths.

Shimabara's famed dishes are raw stonefish, Taira-gane crab (especially July to September), and *guzōni*, a thick soup made from seafood, vegies, and *mochi* (pounded rice). The soup's origin comes from when Amakusa Shirou and his followers took over Shimabara castle and the central government cut off their supply lines. People put anything they could find into clear broth, along with *mochi*, which takes longer to spoil.

Himematsu-ya (☎ 63-7272; meals ¥800-1800; ⊙ 10am-8pm) Serves *guzōni* as its speciality.

Aoi-rihatsukan (☎ 64-6057; snacks ¥500) A restored barbershop turned into a coffee shop, near the station.

Drinking

Shimabara Mizuyashiki (☎ 62-8555; www.mizu yashiki.com in Japanese) This is a Meiji-era private tea-house and museum which features a gorgeous Japanese garden centred around a fresh-water spring. Feel free to peek inside at the house, its collection of *manekineko* (beckoning cat designed to bring prosperity), and other interesting items. No food allowed inside.

Getting There & Around

JR trains on the Nagasaki line run to Isahaya (*kaisoku*, ¥450, 25 minutes), which then connect with the private Shimabaratetsudō line trains departing hourly to Shimabara (*futsū*, ¥1330, 1¼ hours). Shimabara Station is a few hundred metres east of the castle.

Ferries to the Kumamoto coast depart from Shimabara Port frequently between 7am and 7pm. The trip costs around ¥600, regardless of whether you take the regular car ferry or a speedboat. Most boats are bound for either Misumi or Kumamoto Port, which is a 30-minute bus ride from the city (¥500). At Misumi, you may have to wait up to an hour to catch the next slow train to Kumamoto (¥720, 50 minutes).

Local buses shuttle between Shimabara Station and the ferry terminal, which is located a short walk from Shimabara-Gaikō Station. Bikes can also be rented at the ferry terminal and at the train station.

KUMAMOTO-KEN 熊本県

KUMAMOTO 熊本

☎ 096 / pop 670,150

Kumamoto, the city that brought you *kobori* (a traditional technique for swimming upright wearing a suit of armour, often to fire arrows at an attacker) has one of Japan's finest reconstructed castles and a very fine garden. One of the most vibrant cities in southern Kyūshū, it has an active nightlife, live music, and a variety of restaurants, museums, and galleries.

Orientation & Information

The JR Kumamoto Station is some distance southwest of Kumamoto's city centre, which is where you'll find banks, hotels, restaurants, the bus centre and the entertainment area, along with the castle and other attractions.

Inside JR Kumamoto Station, the **tourist information office** (☎ 352-3743; ⊙ 9am-1pm & 2pm-5.30pm) has a helpful English-speaking assistant. South of Kumamoto-jō, **NTT Dream Plaza** (Map p644; ☎ 321-3095; 3-1 Sakuramachi; ⊙ 11am-6.30pm) offers free Internet access. **Cybac Café** (☎ 24-3189; www.cybac.com; membership fee ¥200, 1st hr ¥480; ⊙ 24hr) has a location in the city centre. **Kumamoto City International Centre** (☎ 359-2121; 4-8 Hanahatachō; ⊙ 9am-8pm Mon-Fri, 9am-7pm Sat, 9am-7pm 1st & 3rd Sun of each month) has CNN news and English-language magazines on the 2nd floor.

On the northeast side of JR Kumamoto Station is an **international ATM** (⊙ 8am-9pm Mon-Fri, 9am-7pm Sat & Sun) that accepts Visa, MasterCard and Cirrus, and a postal savings ATM. Central Higo Bank has currency-exchange facilities. Kinokuniya bookshop stocks foreign-language titles.

Sights

KUMAMOTO-JŌ 熊本城

Kumamoto's **castle** (Map p644; ☎ 352-6820; Hon-maru; admission ¥500; ⊙ 8.30am-5.30pm Apr-Oct, 8.30am-4.30pm Nov-Mar) dominates the centre of town. A modern reproduction, its sheer size and numerous exhibits make it visitworthy. A free English tour (☎ 322-5060) is available.

Built between 1601 and 1607, it was once one of the great castles of feudal Japan. Its architect, Katō Kiyomasa, was a master of castle design and some of his ingenious engineering, including slots for dropping stones and other missiles onto attackers, can be seen in the reconstruction.

Nevertheless, in 1877, during the turmoil of the Satsuma Rebellion (a postscript to the Meiji Restoration) the castle was besieged and burnt in one of the final stands made by samurai warriors against the new order. The rebel samurai held out for 50 days before finally being overcome. For more on the rebellion and its leader, Saigō Takamori, see p659.

Beyond the castle is the **Former Hosokawa Gyōbutei** (Map p642; ☎ 352-6522; 3-1 Kyō-machi;

KYŪSHŪ

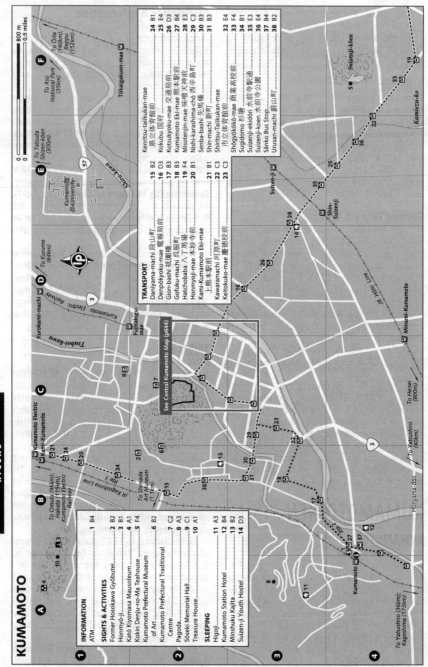

KUMAMOTO

KYŪSHŪ

INFORMATION

ATM.. 1 B4

SIGHTS & ACTIVITIES

Former Hosokawa Gyōbutei.......... 2 B2
Honmyō-ji....................................... 3 B1
Katō Kiyomasa Mausoleum............ 4 A1
Kokin Denju-no-Ma Teahouse........ 5 F4
Kumamoto Prefectural Museum
   of Art.. 6 B2
Kumamoto Prefectural Traditional
   Centre... 7 C2
Pagoda.. 8 A3
Sōseki Memorial Hall...................... 9 C1
Treasure House............................... 10 A1

SLEEPING

Higoji... 11 A3
Kumamoto Station Hotel................. 12 B4
Minshuku Kajita............................. 13 B2
Suizen-ji Youth Hostel................... 14 D3

TRANSPORT

Daniyama-machi 段山町............... 15 B2
Denpōkyoku-mae 電報局前........... 16 D3
Gion-bashi 祇園橋.......................... 17 B3
Gofuku-machi 呉服町..................... 18 B3
Hatchōbaba 八丁馬場..................... 19 F4
Honmyoji-mae 本妙寺前................ 20 B1
Kami-Kumamoto Eki-mae
   上熊本駅前................................. 21 B1
Kawaramachi 河原町...................... 22 C3
Keitokuko-mae 慶徳校前............... 23 C3

Kenritsu-taiikukan-mae
   県立体育館前............................. 24 B1
Kokubu 国府.................................... 25 E4
Kotsukyoku-mae 交通局前............. 26 D3
Kumamoto Eki-mae 熊本駅前......... 27 B4
Misotenjin-mae 味噌天神前........... 28 E3
Nishi-karashima-chō 西辛島町....... 29 C3
Senba-bashi 先馬橋........................ 30 B3
Shin-machi 新町............................. 31 B3
Shiritsu-Taiikukan-mae
   市立体育館前............................. 32 E4
Shogyōkōkō-mae 商業高校前......... 33 F4
Sugidomo 杉塘.............................. 34 B1
Suizenji-ekidōri 水前寺駅通.......... 35 E3
Suizenji-koen 水前寺公園.............. 36 E4
Sanko Bus Stop.............................. 37 B4
Urusan-machi 蔚山町..................... 38 B2

admission ¥300, combined with castle ¥640; 8.30am-5.30pm Apr-Oct, 8.30am-4.30pm Nov-Mar), a spacious samurai villa with grounds pleasant for wandering. The Hosokawa clan came into being around 1632 and held sway until the Meiji Restoration.

Closer to the main road, the **Kumamoto Prefectural Museum of Art** (Map p642; 352-2111; 2 Ninomaru; admission ¥260; 9.30am-4.30pm Tue-Sun) has ancient Buddhist sculptures and modern paintings. **Kumamoto Prefectural Traditional Crafts Centre** (324-4930; 3-35 Senjō-machi; admission ¥200; 9am-5pm Tue-Sun) has displays of local Higo inlay, Yamaga lanterns, porcelains and woodcarving.

SUIZENJI-KŌEN 水前寺公園

Southeast of the city centre, originating with a temple in 1632, this extensive strolling **garden** (383-0074; www.suizenji.or.jp/E-index.htm; 8-1 Suizenji-kōen; admission ¥400; 7.30am-6pm Mar-Nov, 8.30am-5pm Dec-Feb) imitates the 53 stations of the Tōkaidō (the old road that linked Tokyo and Kyoto), and the miniature Mt Fuji is instantly recognisable. The 400-year old **Kokin Denju-no-Ma Teahouse** (Map p642; tea & Hosokawa sweets ¥600) was where the young emperor was tutored in poetry at the Kyoto Imperial Palace (the teahouse building was moved here in 1912 and has nice views across the ornamental lake). Turn the other way and you will see less scenic souvenir stalls.

HONMYŌ-JI 本妙寺

To the northwest of the centre, on the hills sloping up from the river, is the temple and mausoleum of **Katō Kiyomasa** (Map p642), the architect of Kumamoto's great castle. A steep flight of steps leads up to the mausoleum that was designed to be at the same height as the castle's donjon (fortified central tower). There's also a **treasure house** (354-1411; 4-13-20 Hanazono; admission ¥300; 9am-4.30pm Tue-Sun).

WRITERS' HOMES

Right in the centre of town, behind the Tsuruya department store, is writer Lafcadio Hearn's **former home** (354-7842; 2-6 Ansei-machi; admission ¥200; 9am-4.30pm Tue-Sun); the writer was known to the Japanese as Koizumi Yakumo. He also had a Japanese residence in Matsue (see p439).

The former home of the Meiji-era novelist Sōseki Natsume is preserved as the **Sōseki Memorial Hall** (325-9127; 4-22 Tsubo-machi; admission ¥200; 9.30am-4.30pm Tue-Sun). Sōseki lived here as an English teacher, but only for a few years. (For more on Sōseki, see p56.)

OTHER SIGHTS

Continue north up the hill beyond the cheap ryokan and *minshuku* near JR Kumamoto Station, past the love hotels and you eventually reach the **pagoda** topping the hill. The effort of the climb is rewarded with superb views over the town.

The delightful **Shimada Art Museum** (352-4597; 4-5-28 Shimazaki; admission ¥500; 9am-5pm Thu-Tue) collects works pertaining to Miyamoto Musashi, mainly calligraphy and scrolls. The museum is within walking distance of Honmyō-ji (left).

Northeast of the town centre, **Tatsuda Shizen-kōen** (Tatsuda Nature Park; 立田自然公園; 344-6753; 4-610 Kurokami; admission ¥200; 8.30am-4.30pm) contains the 1646 Taishō-ji and a famous teahouse once used by Hosokawa lords. The grave of Hosokawa Gracia (1563–1600) is in the temple grounds. She was an early convert to Christianity but her husband arranged her death to prevent his enemies from capturing her. To get there, take a Musashigaoka-kita line bus from platform 28 at Kumamoto Kōtsū bus centre (¥190, 25 minutes).

Festivals & Events

Takigi Nō (薪能) performances at Suizenji-kōen are performed by torchlight on the first Saturday in August, sometimes in Kumamoto-jō and other places as well. A treat for anyone wanting to see this unique type of Japanese theatre.

In mid-August, the **Hi-no-kuni Matsuri** (火の国祭り; Land of Fire Festival) lights up Kumamoto with fireworks and dancing. Kumamoto-jō has its grand **autumn festival** (mid-October to early November) with *taiko* drumming and cultural events.

Sleeping

Suizen-ji Youth Hostel (Map p642; 371-9193; 1-2-20 Shiroyama; dm ¥2800) Clean but typically strict, located out toward Suizenji-kōen.

Higoji (Map p642; /fax 352-7860; r per person from ¥3000) On the hill behind the train station, this is Kumamoto's best-value traditional option. It's a small *minshuku* run by a friendly elderly gentleman. He'll pick you up from the station if you call first. English is spoken, and the night view is superb.

Minshuku Kajita (Map p642; ☎ /fax 353-1546; www4.ocn.ne.jp/~kajita; 1-2-7 Shinmachi; s/d ¥4000/7000) Rooms are Japanese-style and don't have

bathrooms. From JR Kumamoto Station, take a bus to the Shin-machi stop; from there it's a five-minute walk.

Ichibankan (Map p642; ☎ 359-6600; 1-3-9 Nihongi; s/d from ¥3500/5500) Ten minutes' walk from

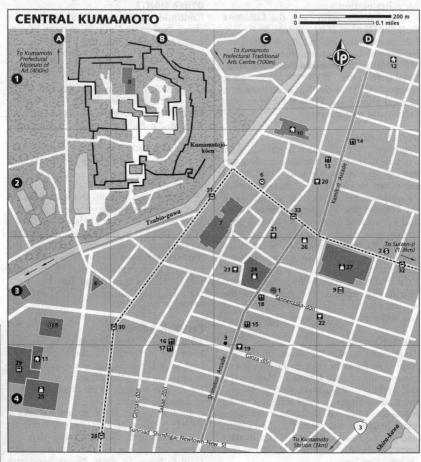

CENTRAL KUMAMOTO

To Kumamoto Prefectural Museum of Art (400m)

To Kumamoto Prefectural Traditional Arts Centre (100m)

Kumamotojō-kōen

Tsubio-gawa

To Suizen-ji (1.3km)

Sannenzaka-dōri

Ginza-dōri

Shimotōri Arcade

Kamitōri Arcade

Ginnan-dōri

Sakae-dōri

Sunroad Shinshigai-Newtown-New St

To Kumamoto Station (3km)

Shira-kawa

KYŪSHŪ

the station, just across the first small river, this place has Japanese- and Western-style rooms.

Kumamoto Station Hotel (Map p642; ☎ 325-2001; 1-3-6 Nihongi; s/d ¥6000/10,600; 💻) A standard business hotel near Ichiban-kan that offers clean, small rooms and professional staff. Not a place with much atmosphere, but certainly fine for an overnight stay. LAN access.

Kumamoto Kōtsū Center Hotel (Map p644; ☎ 326-8828; 3-10 Sakuramachi; s/d/tr from ¥5700/13,000/16,500) Above the bus terminal; reception is on the 3rd floor. While the décor is simple, this place offers slightly larger rooms than many hotels and is very convenient. It does not have the range of restaurants, but there are plenty of places outside nearby.

Maruko Hotel (Map p644; ☎ 353-1241; 11-10 Kamidōrimachi; d ¥12,000-27,000) This century-old Japanese inn is in the town centre. From JR Kumamoto Station, take a Rte 2 tram to Tetori-Honchō, then look for signs inside the covered arcade. Price includes two meals.

Kumamoto Castle Hotel (Map p642; ☎ 326-3311; fax 326-3324; 4-2 Jōtōmachi; s/tw from ¥8900/16,000, Japanese-style r ¥30,000) Overlooking the castle, this is an elegant Japanese hotel with women in kimono flitting about.

Eating

Gourmands will want to try a bite of *basashi* (raw horsemeat), *karashi-renkon* (fried lotus root with mustard) or *Higo-gyū* (Higo beef). Sometimes whale meat is also served. Most of Kumamoto's restaurants are tucked into shopping arcades, and some can be difficult to find, even for Japanese. If one person you ask doesn't know, try asking someone else.

Cafe Anding (Map p644; ☎ 352-6701; 4F 4-10 Kamidōri; dishes ¥1000) This option serves Chinese food, and is near the centre.

Chai Shop Shankar G (Map p644; ☎ 353-6189; 2nd fl Omoki Bldg, 7-1 Kamidōrimachi; meals ¥500-780; 🕙 11am-3pm & 4-11pm, closed 1st & 3rd Thu of each month) Great curry, samosas, and *chai* sets. The upstairs dining room has a reggae beat, rattan chairs and an outdoor deck. The small sign is easy to miss.

Kōran-tei (Map p644; ☎ 352-7177; 5-26 Anseimachi) Back down the Shimotori arcade, this is a Chinese restaurant with some good *teishoku* deals at lunchtime. Try the *chashūmen* (roast-pork noodle soup) for ¥650.

Harumiya (☎ 356-9652; 1st fl Ichōukaikan, 12-8 Hanahatachō; dishes ¥750) *Okonomiyaki*, a savoury

Japanese-style pancake, is a delicious alternative to *rāmen*. Kansai-style, Hiroshima-style, and even *monjayaki* (egg-and-meat based batter) is served here.

Jang Jang Go (☎ 323-1121; 12-10 Hanahatacho; 🕙 5.30pm-2am) A trendy place serving neo-Chinese cuisine in a mock Colonial–style building, down and to the right. For couples it's Kumamoto's most popular date spot. Expect to spend at least ¥2500 per person.

Dynamic Kitchen (☎ 212-5551; 1-6-27 Shimotori; multicourse dinner ¥3500-4500; 🕙 5pm-midnight) With bamboo and lanterns on the stairs, this is like walking inside a futuristic Buddhist temple. Á la carte dishes, from dim sum to Japanese seafood, are delectable.

Drinking

Kumamoto has a sprinkling of gaijin haunts if you are in need of a few drinks and some conversation.

Shark Attack (8th fl, Anty Rashon Bldg) The only bar we've come across that has sand (the stuff you usually find on beaches).

DJ's Cafè 15 (☎ 356-1687; City 9 Bldg, 1-8-26 Shimodōri) Vinyl records stacked on the walls and a retro groove.

At more traditional pubs, ask for *aka-zake*, Kumamoto's reddish sake.

Entertainment

Sharp (☎ 322-5445; 1-2-4 Shimotōri; 🕙 7.30pm-1am Sun-Thu, 7.30pm-4am Fri & Sat) A long-running place (behind Daiei) that regularly has live bands. Beers cost from ¥500.

Rock Balloon (☎ 354-6888; 4-6 Kamidōri) This is a grungy establishment – graffiti and lots of noise. Draught beers cost ¥500 and there's often no cover charge (DJ events cost ¥2000 to ¥2500 per person).

Getting There & Away

Although there are flights to Kumamoto from Tokyo, Osaka and Naha (Okinawa), most visitors come by train from elsewhere around Kyūshū. The JR Kagoshima line runs north to Hakata (*tokkyū*, ¥3430, 1½ hours) and south to Kagoshima-Chūō Station (*shinkansen*, ¥6060, 1½ hours), while the JR Hōhi line goes to Beppu (¥5330, three hours).

Highway buses depart from the Kumamoto Kōtsū bus centre for almost every major destination in Kyūshū, including Fukuoka/Hakata (¥2000, two hours).

KYŪSHŪ

See p641 for details on travel to Nagasaki via Shimabara and Unzen. Kumamoto is a popular gateway to Aso-san (right), from where you can travel across the island to Beppu (p673). The **SL Aso Boy** (☎ 096-211-2406), an old-fashioned steam train, runs between Kumamoto and Miyaji (one way ¥1880, 2¼ hours) as part of its once daily return service (limited days).

Getting Around

TO/FROM THE AIRPORT

Buses to and from the airport (¥670, 50 minutes) stop at the Kumamoto Kōtsū bus centre and JR Kumamoto Station.

BUS

One-day tram passes are valid for travel on green-coloured Shiei buses (but not any other city buses), which are handy for connecting between the tram and outlying sights, for example to Honmyō-ji and the Shimada Art Museum, or zooming between JR Kumamoto Station and the bus centre.

The Castle Loop Bus (¥130) connects the bus centre with all the sights in the castle area at least every half-hour, between 8.30am and 5pm daily. A one-day loop pass (¥300) will get you a discount at many area establishments.

TRAM

Kumamoto's tram service allows access to all the major sights. On boarding the tram, take a ticket with your starting tram stop number. When you finish your trip a display panel at the front of the tram indicates the fare for each starting point (under ¥200). A one-day pass (¥500) allows unlimited travel, and can be bought on the trams, or in front of Kumamoto Station.

Rte 2 starts near JR Kumamoto Station, runs through the town centre and out past Suizenji-kōen. Rte 3 starts to the north, near Kami-Kumamoto Station and merges with Rte 2 just before the centre. At one time several decades past, there were seven tram lines, but only the above two remain.

YAMAGA & KIKUCHI ONSEN
山鹿温泉・菊池温泉
☎ 0968
These hot-springs towns are both nice, and they're even better during the spectacular **Yamaga Chōchin Matsuri** held on 15 and 16 Au-

gust. The whole region seems to converge on Yamaga Onsen for these two nights, when the women of the town, clad in summer kimono, dance through the streets to the sound of *shamisen*, wearing lanterns on their heads. Though the sound is wholly 'Japanese', visually this is more like China or Okinawa – a reminder of Kyūshū's historical remove from 'mainland' Japan.

Outside Kikuchi Onsen, named for the lords who once ruled all of Kyūshū, **Kikuchi Gorge** (菊池渓谷; donation ¥100; ☿ mid-Apr–Nov) has walking trails and refreshingly cool waters. Back in town, the hot-springs ryokan, *minshuku* and hotels are all clustered together on a quiet maze of streets, just downhill from an impressive **statue** of a feudal lord on horseback.

Yamaga Cycling Terminal (山鹿サイクリングターミナル; ☎ 43-1136; r per person with 2 meals ¥5200), on a 35km cycling route from Kumamoto, has large communal tatami rooms and a huge bath. It's a 10-minute taxi ride from the centre of Yamaga Onsen. Don't try to walk back post-festival unless you've got infrared night vision – the terminal is set invisibly above pitch-black rice fields.

The **Kikuchi Onsen Ryokan Tourism Association** (☎ 25-2926; fax 24-4690) can book accommodation with two meals from ¥8000. **Kikuchi Kankō Hotel** (菊池観光ホテル; ☎ 25-2111, fax 24-0473; www.kkhotel.com in Japanese; d ¥14,000-22,000) has rooms with mountain views and a *rotemburo*.

Getting There & Around

From JR Kumamoto Station or the Kumamoto Kōtsū bus centre (see p645), there are frequent buses to either Yamaga Onsen (¥860, 1¼ hours) or Kikuchi Onsen (¥880, 1½ hours). Inconveniently, there are only a few bus services (¥430, 30 minutes) per day between the two onsen.

ASO-SAN AREA 阿蘇山
☎ 0967
In the centre of Kyūshū, halfway from Kumamoto to Beppu, is the gigantic Aso-san volcano caldera. There have been a series of eruptions over the past 30 million years but the explosion that formed the outer crater about 100,000 years ago must have been a big one – the crater has a 128km circumference and accommodates towns, villages and trains.

It's still the largest active caldera in the world – in 1979 an eruption of Naka-dake killed a woman on her honeymoon. The last major blast was in 1993, but the summit is regularly declared off-limits due to toxic gas emissions. Check with the tourist information office (below) for daily updates around 9am. It all depends on wind conditions – and just hope they don't change suddenly while you're at the summit.

Aso-san has literary value as well; in addition to its being used as the backdrop for a number of movies (those of Kurosawa Akira among them), it has been a key site for writers, artists and other literati to visit as well. Among them was Akiko Yosano, one of Japan's first feminists and a gifted writer, who toured this area, staying in local ryokan and writing poems as she went along.

Orientation & Information

Rtes 57, 265 and 325 make a circuit of the outer caldera, and the JR Hōhi line runs across the northern section. Daikanbō Lookout is one of the best places to see Aso from afar. Aso is the main town in the crater but there are other towns, including Takamori, on the southern side. All the roads running into the centre of the crater and to the five 'modern' peaks within the one huge, ancient outer peak are toll roads.

At JR Aso Station, there's an informative **tourist information office** (☎ 34-0751; ◷ 9am-5pm Thu-Tue) offering free hiking maps. Coin lockers are available.

Sights

ASO-GOGAKU 阿蘇五岳

The **Five Mountains of Aso** are the five smaller mountains within the outer rim. They are Eboshi-dake (1337m), Kijima-dake (1321m), Naka-dake (1506m), Neko-dake (1408m) and Taka-dake (1592m). Naka-dake is currently the active volcano in this group. Neko-dake, furthest to the east, is instantly recognisable by its craggy peak but Taka-dake, between Neko-dake and Naka-dake, is the highest.

ASO VOLCANIC MUSEUM 阿蘇火山博物館

Despite scarce English labelling, this **museum** (☎ 34-2111; www.asomuse.jp/volcano/; admission ¥840, with cable-car return ¥1480; ◷ 9am-5pm) has great live footage taken inside the active crater. An entertaining selection of big-screen videos shows various volcanoes from around the world strutting their stuff.

KUSASENRI & KOME-ZUKA 草千里・米塚

Opposite the volcanic museum is **Kusasenri** (literally, '1000km of grass'), a grassy meadow with two lakes in the flattened crater of an ancient volcano. It's a postcard-perfect picture on a clear day.

Just off the road that runs from the museum to the town of Aso is the perfectly shaped small cone of **Kome-zuka** (954m), another extinct volcano. The name means 'rice mound'.

NAKA-DAKE 中岳

Naka-dake (1506m) has been very active in recent years. The cable car to the summit was closed from August 1989 to March 1990 due to eruptions, and it had only been opened for a few weeks when the volcano erupted again in April 1990, spewing dust and ash over a large area to the north.

In 1958, when a totally unexpected eruption killed 12 onlookers, concrete 'bomb shelters' were built around the rim for sightseers to take shelter (in an emergency). Nevertheless, an eruption in 1979 killed three visitors over a kilometre from the cone, in an area that was thought to be safe. This eruption destroyed a cable car that used to run up the northeastern slope of the cone.

From the Aso Volcanic Museum (left), it's 3km up to the cable-car station. When Naka-dake is not misbehaving, the **cable car** (ropeway; ¥410; ◷ 8.30am-5pm) whisks you up to the summit in just four minutes. The walk to the top takes less than 30 minutes. The 100m-deep crater varies in width from 400m to 1100m and there's a walk around the southern edge of the crater rim. Ascending the heights early in the morning you can see a sea of clouds hovering inside the crater, with Kujū-san (1787m) on the horizon.

Activities

From the top of the cable-car run you can walk around the crater rim to the peak of Naka-dake and on to the top of Taka-dake. From there you can descend to Sensui Gorge (Sensui-kyō), which blooms with azaleas in mid-May, or to the road that runs between Taka-dake and Neko-dake. Either way will then take you to Miyaji, the next train

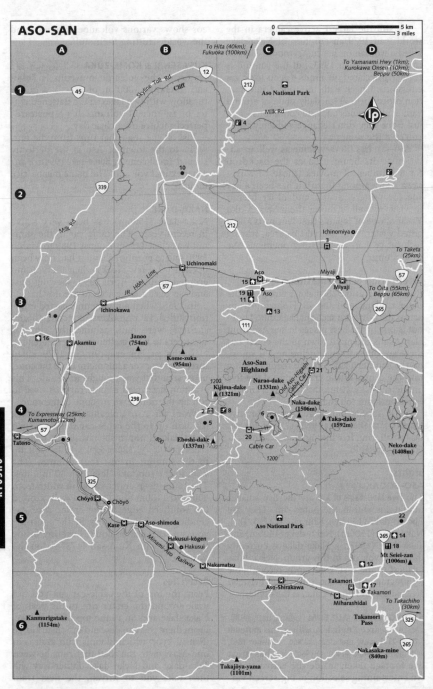

station east of Aso. The direct descent to Sensui Gorge is very steep, so it's easier to continue back from Taka-dake to the Naka-dake rim and then follow the old cable car-route down to Sensui Gorge. Allow four or five hours from the Aso-nishi cable-car station walking uphill to Sensui Gorge, then another 1½ hours for the descent.

Shorter walks include the interesting ascent of Kijima-dake from the Aso Volcanic Museum. From the top of Kijima-dake you can descend to the top of the ski lift, used for both snow skiing and summer grass skiing. You can also climb to the top of Eboshi-dake. Any of the peaks offer superb views over the whole Aso area. The outer rim of the ancient crater also has great views. Shiroyama Tembōdai, a lookout on the Yamanami Hwy as it leaves the crater, is one good point; Daikanbō Lookout, near Uchinomaki Onsen, is another.

Festivals & Events

On a Saturday in mid- to late March (dates vary), Aso-jinja (☎ 22-0064) is the scene of esoteric dances and a spectacular, highly photogenic fire festival, **hi-furi-matsuri**. The shrine is a 15-minute walk north of JR Miyaji Station, and is one of only three shrines in Japan with its original *mon* (gate). The drinking water here is supposed to be particularly delicious, and at dusk it's possible to see residents filling 20L canteens to take home with them.

Sleeping & Eating

Over 50 places to stay make finding a bed in the Aso-san area easy. They include a collection of places at Aso town, Uchinomaki Onsen and Takamori village. Most other accommodation is spread out, and sometimes difficult to get to by public transport. Bookings in advance are essential.

ASO VILLAGE

Bōchū Kyampu-jo (☎ 34-0351; tent sites per person ¥310) Reached via a path that veers off the highway below the youth hostel, this is an option for those who like it wild.

Aso Youth Hostel (☎ 34-0804; dm ¥2450) A 20-minute walk from JR Aso Station uphill toward the mountain, is this hostel. Buses up to the cable-car station stop outside the hostel.

Kokumin-shukusha Aso (☎ 34-0111; r per person with 2 meals ¥6300) Opposite JR Aso Station. Its small hot-springs bath, Yume-no-yu, is available to nonguests (admission ¥400).

Aso-no-Fumoto (☎ 32-0624; r per person with/without meals ¥6200/4200) A good *minshuku*, conveniently close to the station. The owner will pick you up.

Wild Cats Pizza (☎ 67-3307) This place is out among the noodle shops and takeaway joints on Rte 57, a 10-minute walk west.

TAKAMORI

Kumamoto YMCA Aso Camp (☎ 35-0124; dm ¥3000-3200) Has clean, modern and comfortable cabins. It's a 25-minute walk west of JR Akamizu Station, across the river.

Murataya Ryokan Youth Hostel (☎ 62-0066; dm ¥2700-2900) In Takamori town, this is quite pleasant. Book ahead in the summer months. From the train station, walk straight out past the bus terminal and post office, then turn left at the pharmacy corner and walk to the end of the block.

Bluegrass (☎ 62-3366; fax 62-3022; r per person with/without 2 meals ¥7000/4000) A rustic ranch house. Its Western-style **cookhouse** (meals from ¥1500; 🕙 11am-8pm Wed-Mon) serves steaks and BBQ cuisine.

Deer To House (meals from ¥800; 🕙 11am-8pm) A charming eatery near Takamori Station. The chef turns out hearty Western-style meals and homemade apple pie. The handwritten English menu is charmingly descriptive.

KYŪSHŪ

CRATER

Other places on the outskirts of Takamori town are farther; you'll need your own transport.

Hakuunsan-sō (白雲山荘; ☎ 35-0111; Akamizuonsen; r per person from ¥10,000) Hakuunsan-sō is a giant resort hotel in the middle of brilliant rice fields. Has a beautiful bath and rooms with balconies.

Dengaku-no-Sato (☎ 62-1899; ☺ 11am-7pm; set meals from ¥1800) At this old farmhouse restaurant, you cook your own kebab-like *dengaku* (hardened *mochi* rice dipped in miso) on individual *hibachi* (BBQ).

Kokumin-kyūkamura Minami-Aso (☎ 62-2111; r per person from ¥5500) is a national vacation village, which gets crowded in July and August. Beyond it is a *pension mura* (pension village) charging rates of around ¥8000 per person, with two meals. Try **Cream House** (☎ 62-3090) or **Flower Garden** (☎ 62-3021).

Getting There & Around

Aso is on the JR Hōhi line between Kumamoto (*tokkyū*, ¥2180, one hour, three daily) and Ōita (*tokkyū* ¥3940, two hours). From March to November the *SL Aso Boy* (¥1960, 2¼ hours) steam train makes a daily run from Kumamoto to Aso, terminating at Miyaji Station. Buses from Beppu (¥3800, 2¾ hours) may continue to the Aso-nishi cable-car station (an extra ¥1550).

To get to Takamori on the southern side of the crater, transfer from the JR Hōhi line at Tateno (¥360, 30 minutes) to the scenic Minami-Aso private line, which terminates at Takamori (¥470, 30 minutes). Buses from Takamori continue southeast to the mountain resort of Takachiho (¥1280, 70 minutes, three daily).

Buses operate approximately every 90 minutes from JR Aso Station via the youth hostel and volcano museum to Aso-nishi cable car station (¥470, 30 minutes). The first bus up leaves around 8.30am, with the last return trip down from the cable-car station around 5pm.

KUROKAWA ONSEN 黒川温泉
☎ 0967 / pop 400

A real treasure. A few dozen ryokan lie along a steep-sided valley beside the Kurokawa, some 6km west of the Yamanami Hwy. Named 'the best *onsen* village in Japan' a few years back, Kurokawa is everything a re-sort town should be without accompanying kitsch or ugliness. While it's well frequented and you certainly won't be alone, this resort still seems like it's a tiny, forgotten village which you've been lucky to stumble upon.

The enlightened Onsen Association has also made it affordable: a ticket (¥1200) from the **tourist information desk** (☎ 44-0076; ☺ 9am-6pm) and from several ryokan allows access to three baths (8.30am to 9pm) of your choice. Kurokawa is especially famous for its 23 *rotemburo*. Yamamizuki, Kurokawa-sō and the magnificent Shimmei-kan, with its cave baths and riverside *rotemburo*, are among local favourites. Most places offer *konyoku* (mixed bathing) and separate male and female baths.

Sleeping

Aso Senomoto Youth Hostel (阿蘇瀬の本ユースホステル; ☎ 44-0157; www.jyh.gr.jp/aso/next.html; dm ¥2300) One of Kyūshū's best. It has lots of information and the friendly English-speaking manager will pick you up if you call in advance. It's a good base for attacking Kujū-san, a massif of several volcanoes, including the highest peaks in Kyūshū.

The *onsen* ryokan are well worth splurging on.

Oyado Kurokawa (お宿黒川; ☎ 44-0651; www.kurokawaonsen.or.jp/kurokawa in Japanese; r per person from ¥13,000) and **Ryokan Nishimura** (旅館西村; ☎ 44-0753; www.kurokawaonsen.or.jp/nishimura/nishimu.htm in Japanese; r ¥12,000-16,000) are among the cheapest. Prices at both options include two meals.

Getting There & Away

There's a late-morning bus around 10.30am from Aso (p646) to Senomoto and Kurokawa (¥940, one hour), but the only return bus leaves the *onsen* less than two hours later. The only solution is to take a taxi out to the Yamanami Hwy (¥1000) and take a bus from the Senomoto bus stop. There's a final bus in the late afternoon to Kumamoto (one hour) around 4.15pm, and another to Beppu around 4.45pm (¥4000, three hours).

There are four buses daily to Senomoto from JR Miyaji Station (¥1150, 30 minutes).

SOUTH OF KUMAMOTO

The port of **Minamata** became infamous in the late '60s and early '70s when it was dis-

ONSEN: JAPANESE CULTURE AT ITS FINEST

So many aspects of Japanese cultural arts – tea ceremony, calligraphy, kabuki, flower-arranging – require years of intense practice, have rigid rules, and are often prohibitively expensive. It can take years of study just to understand what the masters are doing, let alone create something yourself. *Onsen*, on the other hand, are freestyle, often cheap…sometimes even free. *Onsen* come in many different shapes, sizes, and types, ranging from ice cold to skin-scaldingly hot, outdoor, indoor, mixed gender. Wilder versions include *denki-buro* (electric shocks in the water) and *suna-buro* (you get buried in hot sand). Hotel-style baths often include fancy showerheads and premium shampoos, but there's something to be said for the rough-hewn ones found beside a mountain stream. Whatever your pleasure, there's a bath out there to match.

Relaxing, healthy and sometimes breathtakingly beautiful, they're one of the few arts that can be immediately enjoyed. There's only one cardinal rule: *wash first before entering the water.*

A few decades ago it was quite common to see 'Japanese Only' signs at some baths. Foreigners, thinking of the bath like a swimming pool back home, would strip down, bypass the rinsing area, and immediately plunge right in. Much as we might make a hasty exit if someone peed in the pool, so too do avid-*onsen*-goers if they feel the water has been similarly fouled. Luckily, those stereotypes are slowly disappearing, thanks to better communication and more consideration of Japanese *onsen* culture. You're more likely now to see people coming over to chat with you than you are to see them dashing away.

You'll see Japanese breaking all of these from time to time, but some other general rules also apply:

- turn off the water when you've finished using it;
- use a washcloth to cover yourself as you walk around;
- never put the washcloth into (or worse, rinse it in) the bathwater;
- dry off thoroughly before you return to the changing room;
- for peace of mind, put valuables into a locker;
- don't use the hairdryer for anything other than hair; and
- don't forget to have a cold beer or a glass of water afterwards. Ahhhhh!

covered that the high incidence of illness and birth defects in the town were caused by mercury poisoning. A local factory had dumped waste containing high levels of mercury into the sea and this had contaminated the fish eaten by local residents. The company's ruthless efforts to suppress the story and W Eugene Smith's heart-rending documentary photos focussed worldwide attention on the town.

Further south along the coast at **Hinagu Onsen**, there are fine views out towards the Amakusa archipelago. Most of the hotsprings ryokan charge ¥9000 per person with two meals.

AMAKUSA ARCHIPELAGO 天草諸島

☎ 0969

South of the Shimabara peninsula are the islands of the Amakusa-shotō. The islands were a stronghold of Christianity during Japan's 'Christian Century' (see p36) and the grinding poverty here was a major factor in the Shimabara Rebellion of 1637–38. It's still one of the least developed regions of Japan.

Around the islands, there are opportunities for diving and dolphin-watching cruises. **Hondo** is the main town and has exhibition halls relating to the Christian era. **Amakusa Youth Hostel** (天草ユースホステル; ☎ 22-3085; dm ¥2650) is a 15-minute walk uphill from the bus terminal. Tomioka, where Nagasaki ferries berth, has castle ruins; this west-coast area is particularly interesting.

Getting to the islands usually involves a ferry from various places in Nagasaki-ken or along the Kumamoto coast. Amakusa Five Bridges link the island directly with Misumi, southwest of Kumamoto.

KYŪSHŪ

KAGOSHIMA-KEN
鹿児島県

Kyūshū's southernmost prefecture has the city of Kagoshima, overlooked by the majestic volcano of Sakurajima across the bay. To the south is the Satsuma Peninsula, while the north has Kirishima-Yaku National Park with its superb volcanoes and hiking. Here is where the Meiji Restoration began; much of the history relates to Saigō Takamori and his role in creating modern Japan (see p111). Famous also for its dialect, the prefecture's Kagoshima-ben is so difficult that it was used as code in WWII much the way Native American languages were used by the USA. The people here are friendly and warm, though it is so remote that you may have to deal with the occasional stare or even schoolchildren gawking as you pass, particularly in the small towns and villages. If you find it uncomfortable, try to keep it in perspective: you may be the only foreigner these people see for months, even years.

Atop an unimpressive bluff in Kokubu city, 40 minutes north of Kagoshima, a construction crew making a hotel foundation stumbled upon what would be identified as the oldest Jōmon-era remains ever found. Almost 10,000 years ago primitive civilisation arrived here and stayed long enough to leave relics of their passing. To date no older sites have been discovered in Japan. Needless to say, the hotel plans were scrapped and the site (post excavation) boasts a modern museum and a research centre, well worth a stop if you're heading that direction.

KIRISHIMA-YAKU NATIONAL PARK
霧島

The day walk from Ebino-kōgen (Ebino Plateau, not to be confused with the town of Ebino down on the plains) to the summits of a string of volcanoes is one of the finest volcanic hikes in Japan. Parts of the park are in Miyazaki, but much of it is in Kagoshima. It's 15km from the summit of Karakuni-dake (1700m) to the summit of Takachiho-no-mine (1574m) and there's superb scenery – if the peaks aren't being lashed by thunderstorms or shrouded in fog, which is common during the rainy season (mid-May through the end of June). Shorter

walks, such as a lake stroll on the plateau or up and down Karakuni-dake or Takachiho-no-mine, are great, too. The area is known for its spring wildflowers, hot springs and the impressive 75m waterfall, **Senriga-taki**.

Orientation & Information

The Ebino-kōgen village visitors centre and **Takachiho-gawara Visitors Centre** (☎ 0995-57-2505; ☯ 9am-5pm), at the two ends of the volcano walk, have maps and information. Ebino-kōgen has most of the hotels, restaurants and camping facilities.

The **Eco-Museum Centre** (in Miyazaki; ☎ 0984-33-3002; ☯ 9am-5pm) has displays on local wildlife and geology, plus an indoor rest area with hot drink–vending machines. Staff sell topographic hiking maps, and dispense local advice for free.

Ebino Plateau Walks

The Ebino-kōgen lake circuit is a relaxed stroll around a series of volcanic lakes – **Rokkannon Mi-ike** has the most intense colour. Across the road from the lake, Fudō-ike, at the base of Karakuni-dake, is a steaming *jigoku* (boiling mineral hot spring). The stiff climb to the 1700m summit of **Karakuni-dake** skirts the edge of the volcano's deep crater before arriving at the high point on the eastern side. The panoramic view to the south is superb, taking in the perfectly circular caldera lake of Ōnami-ike, rounded Shinmoe-dake and the perfect cone of Takachiho-no-mine. On a clear day, you can see right down to Kagoshima and the smoking cone of Sakurajima. Naka-dake is another nice half-day walk, and in May and June it offers nice views of the Miyama-Kirishima azaleas. Some areas may be closed due to poisonous gas.

Longer Walks

The view across the almost lunar landscape from any of the volcano summits is other-worldly. If you have six hours or so, you can continue from Karakuni-dake to Shishiko-dake, Shinmoe-dake, Naka-dake and Takachiho-gawara, from where you can make the ascent of Takachiho-no-mine. Close up, Takachiho is a formidable volcano with a huge, gaping crater. Legends relate that Ninigi-no-mikoto, a descendant of the sun goddess, arrived in Japan on the summit of this mountain. Some Kagoshima monks-in-training do this route daily.

JOHN ASHBURNE

Canal City (p613), Fukuoka/Hakata

View of Fugen-dake from Shimabara (p639),
Shimabara Peninsula

MARTIN MOOS

Schoolchildren, Kyūshū

JAMES MARSHALL

MARTIN MOOS

Karatsu Kunchi Matsuri (p622), Karatsu

Dainichi Buddha head (p673), Usuki

MARTIN MOOS

Takachiho-no-mine, Kirishima-Yaku National Park (p652), Kagoshima-ken

MARTIN

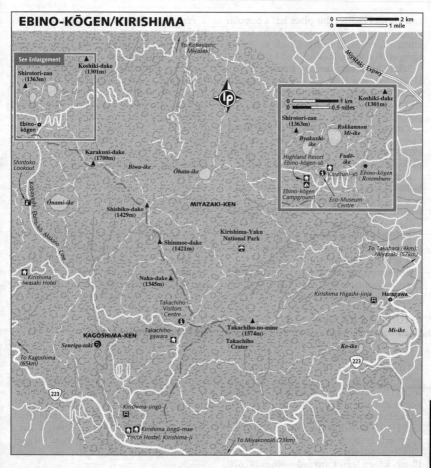

EBINO-KŌGEN/KIRISHIMA

If you miss the late afternoon bus from Takachiho-gawara to Kirishima-jingū, it's a 7km walk down to the village around the shrine.

Kirishima-jingū 霧島神宮

Bright-orange **Kirishima-jingū** (☎ 0995-57-0001) is beautifully situated, picturesque, and offers nice views of the surrounding area. Though it dates from the 6th century, the present shrine was built in 1715. It is dedicated to Ninigi-no-mikoto, who, according to the *Kojiki* (a historical book compiled in 712), made his legendary landing in Japan on the Takachiho-no-mine summit.

The shrine can be visited en route to Takachiho-gawara. It's accessible by bus

(¥240, 15 minutes) from JR Kirishima-jingū Station. The festivals of **Saitan-sai** (1 January), **Ota-ue-sai** (mid-March) and the lantern festival of **Kontō-sai** (5 August) are worth seeing. If you're a temple fan, visit Kirishima Higashi-jinja for ancient cedars and scenic views.

Sleeping & Eating

Ebino-kōgen village (on the Miyazaki side) has a reasonable choice of accommodation.

Ebino-kōgen Campground (☎ 0984-33-0800; tent sites/cabins from ¥800/1250) A 10-minute walk from the Eco-Museum Centre. Tent and blanket hire is available.

Ebino-kōgen Rotemburo (☎ 0984-33-0800; basic tatami hut per person ¥1670, futon rental ¥810) A 20-minute walk downhill from the bus terminal and visitors centre, this place has a popular series of open-air hot-spring baths (bring a torch for a night bath). Check-in is until 6pm, with reservations advised in summer.

Takachiho-gawara camping ground (☎ 0995-57-0996; tent rental ¥1100; ☀ Jul & Aug) Camping items (tent, etc) can be rented. A set up tent, blankets, and cooking utensils for five people costs ¥2760.

Karakuni-sō (☎ 0984-33-0650; fax 0984-33-4928; r per person with 2 meals ¥8600, annexe house s/d/tr ¥5000/8000/9000) This has deer lazing in the backyard and wonderful hot-spring baths.

Highland Resort Ebino-kōgen-sō (☎ 0984-33-0161; fax 0984-33-0114; r per person with 2 meals from ¥12,000) This is a surprisingly elegant *kokumin-shukusha* with *rotemburo* and sauna. Stop by its good-value restaurant, **Nokaidō** (lunch ¥600-1200).

Kirishima Jingū-mae Youth Hostel (☎ 0995-57-1188; dm ¥2500) Southeast of Kirishima-jingū, this is basic but serves its purpose.

Kirishima-ji (☎ 0995-57-0272; r per person ¥6000) A ryokan option for those needing something fancier than a hostel.

Getting There & Away
The main train junctions are JR Kobayashi Station, which is north of Ebino Plateau, and Kirishima-jinja Station to the south.

However, a direct bus to Ebino-kōgen is by far the best way to go. From Kagoshima, some Hayashida buses run direct to Ebino-kōgen starting at 10am (¥1550, 1¾ hours). Other buses terminate at the Kirishima Iwa-saki Hotel, far below the plateau. The other approach is from Miyazaki. From Miyakō City bus terminal, the first bus direct to Ebino-kōgen leaves around 8.40am (¥2620, 2¼ hours). The last afternoon buses back to Kagoshima and Miyazaki leave Ebino-kōgen at 1.30pm and 2.10pm, respectively.

KOKUBU 国分
Directly north of Sakurajima you'll find Kokubu, Kagoshima's second-largest city, which still seems like a small countryside town despite its growing population and several industries, such as Kyōcera and Sony, which have located branches nearby.

Sights
UENOHARA JŌMON ERA SITE
上の原縄文遺跡
If you have an interest in archaeology, you'll want to detour to see Uenohara. Once just

a remote make-out spot with an empty parking lot and a few lonesome vending machines, Uenohara was transformed when – in the process of laying the foundation for a planned hotel – the oldest known Jōmon-era pottery shards were uncovered, leading to entirely new views about how civilisation first came to Japan. Prior to this discovery it was thought that civilisation came from the north downward. Now it appears that the very first humans may have come from the south, via canoes or rafts, along the Ryūkyū island chain.

A beautiful, hi-tech **museum** (上野原縄文の森; ☎ 48-5701; admission ¥300; ☀ 9am-5pm, closed Mon), re-created Jōmon-era village, demonstrations, tools, and other artefacts, make this a fascinating spot. A research centre nearby employs over 200 people, making new discoveries daily. The museum does a good job of explaining the new theories and has lots of visuals, though English signs are minimal. A number of museum staff speak some English, however, so it may be possible to arrange an impromptu tour if things aren't busy.

Getting There & Around
Kokubu can be easily reached by frequent trains that run from Kagoshima (see p661). Buses from Kokubu Station (¥400, six daily) arrive at the Uenohara Jōmon Site in 24 minutes. The last bus leaves Uenohara for Kokubu Station at 5.35pm. Car rentals can be made with **Toyota Renta Lease** (Toyota Renta Riisu; ☎ 47-0600; ☀ 8am-8pm), a three minute walk from Kokubu station; turn left at the first street after the station.

KAGOSHIMA 鹿児島
☎ 099 / pop 605,300
Known as the Naples of Japan, Kagoshima is the southernmost major city in Kyūshū and a is warm, sunny and relaxed place – at least while Kagoshima's very own Vesuvius, Sakurajima, just a stone's throw across Kinkō-wan, is behaving itself. 'Dustfall' brings out the umbrellas in Kagoshima as frequently as rainfall in other parts of the world, coating cars, leaves, rooftops, and of course, any laundry left outside to dry.

History
Recent archaeological discoveries (see left) are showing that Kagoshima may actually be the birthplace of Jōmon civilisation, as its

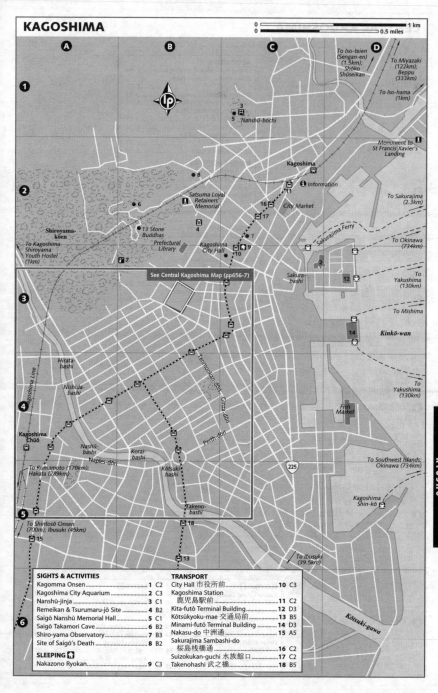

KAGOSHIMA

0 ____ 1 km
0 ____ 0.5 miles

To Iso-teien
(Sengan-en)
(1.5km);
Shōko
Shūseikan

To Miyazaki
(122km);
Beppu
(333km)

To Iso-hama
(1km)

Monument to
St Francis Xavier's
Landing

Nanshū-bochi

Kagoshima

Information

To Sakurajima
(2.3km)

City Market

Satsuma Loyal
Retainers'
Memorial

Sakurajima Ferry

To Okinawa
(734km)

Shiroyama-
kōen

13 Stone
Buddhas

To Kagoshima
Shiroyama
Youth Hostel
(1km)

Prefectural
Library

Kagoshima
City Hall

Sakura-
bashi

To
Yakushima
(130km)

See Central Kagoshima Map (pp656-7)

To Mishima

Kinkō-wan

Hirata-
bashi

Nishida-
bashi

Kagoshima Line

Temmonkan-dōri

Ginza-dōri

Perth-dōri

To
Yakushima
(130km)

Kagoshima
Chūō

Nashū-
bashi

Naples-dōri

Koral-
bashi

Kōtsuki-
bashi

Fish
Market

To Southwest Islands;
Okinawa (734km)

To Kumamoto (170km);
Hakata (289km)

225

Kagoshima
Shin-kō

Takeno-
bashi

To Shintosō Onsen
(700m); Ibusuki (45km)

To Ibusuki
(39.5km)

Kōtsuki-gawa

KYŪSHŪ

CENTRAL KAGOSHIMA

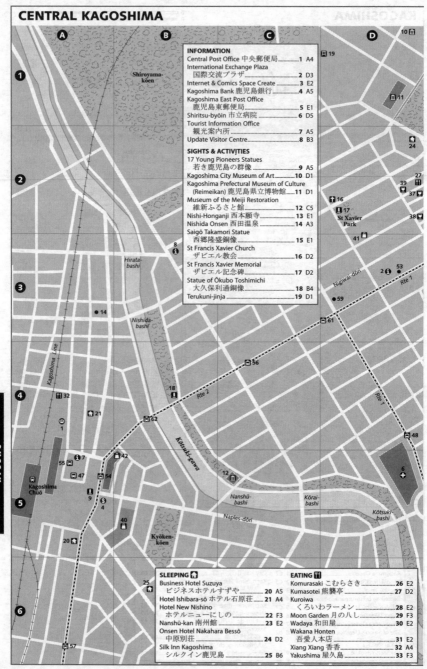

INFORMATION
Central Post Office 中央郵便局...............1 A4
International Exchange Plaza
  国際交流プラザ....................................2 D3
Internet & Comics Space Create............3 E2
Kagoshima Bank 鹿児島銀行..................4 A5
Kagoshima East Post Office
  鹿児島東郵便局....................................5 E1
Shiritsu-byōin 市立病院..........................6 D5
Tourist Information Office
  観光案内所..7 A5
Update Visitor Centre.............................8 B3

SIGHTS & ACTIVITIES
17 Young Pioneers Statues
  若き鹿児島の群像................................9 A5
Kagoshima City Museum of Art............10 D1
Kagoshima Prefectural Museum of Culture
  (Reimeikan) 鹿児島県立博物館.........11 D1
Museum of the Meiji Restoration
  維新ふるさと館..................................12 C5
Nishi-Honganji 西本願寺......................13 E1
Nishida Onsen 西田温泉......................14 A3
Saigō Takamori Statue
  西郷隆盛銅像......................................15 E1
St Francis Xavier Church
  ザビエル教会......................................16 D2
St Francis Xavier Memorial
  ザビエル記念碑..................................17 D2
Statue of Ōkubo Toshimichi
  大久保利通銅像..................................18 B4
Terukuni-jinja......................................19 D1

KYŪSHŪ

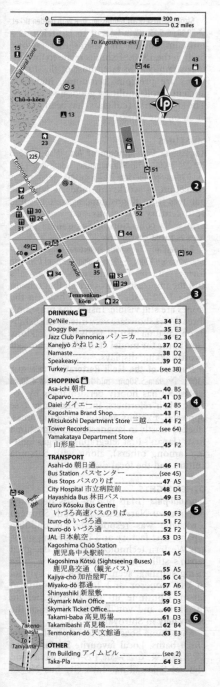

DRINKING
De'Nile	34	E3
Doggy Bar	35	E3
Jazz Club Pannonica パノニカ	36	E2
Kanejyō かねじょう	37	D2
Namaste	38	D2
Speakeasy	39	D2
Turkey	(see 38)	

SHOPPING
Asa-ichi 朝市	40	B5
Caparvo	41	D3
Daiei ダイエー	42	B5
Kagoshima Brand Shop	43	F1
Mitsukoshi Department Store 三越	44	F2
Tower Records	(see 64)	
Yamakataya Department Store 山形屋	45	F2

TRANSPORT
Asahi-dō 朝日通	46	F1
Bus Station バスセンター	(see 45)	
Bus Stops バスのりば	47	A5
City Hospital 市立病院前	48	D4
Hayashida Bus 林田バス	49	E3
Izuro Kōsoku Bus Centre いづろ高速バスのりば	50	F3
Izuro-dō いづろ通	51	F2
Izuro-dō いづろ通	52	F2
JAL 日本航空	53	D3
Kagoshima Chūō Station 鹿児島中央駅前	54	A5
Kagoshima Kōtsū (Sightseeing Buses) 鹿児島交通（観光バス）	55	A5
Kajiya-chō 加治屋町	56	C4
Miyako-dō 都通	57	A6
Shinyashiki 新屋敷	58	E5
Skymark Main Office	59	D3
Skymark Ticket Office	60	D3
Takami-baba 高見馬場	61	D3
Takamibashi 高見橋	62	B4
Tenmonkan-dō 天文館通	63	E3

OTHER
| I'm Building アイムビル | (see 2) | |
| Taka-Pla | 64 | E3 |

10,000-year-old remains are some of Japan's oldest. For much of its history, Kagoshima prefecture was dominated by one family, the Shimazu clan, who held sway for 29 generations (nearly 700 years) until the Meiji Restoration. The Kagoshima region, known as Satsuma, was always receptive to outside contact and for many years was an important centre for trade with China. St Francis Xavier first arrived here in 1549, making Kagoshima one of Japan's earliest contact points with Christianity and the West. Contact was also made with Koreans, whose pottery methods were influential in the creation of Satsuma-yaki (see p622).

The Shimazu family's interests were not confined to trade, however. In the 16th century its power extended throughout Kyūshū and it also gained control of the islands of Okinawa (p681). While many Okinawans have disliked the idea of assimilation, in recent years their resentments have shifted away from the Japanese and onto American troops, as several high-profile abuse cases have come to light in recent years.

During the 19th century, as the Tokugawa shōgunate proved its inability to respond to the challenge of the industrialised West, the Shimazu were already looking further afield. In the 1850s they established the country's first Western-style manufacturing operation. Then, in 1865, the family smuggled more than a dozen young men out of the country to study Western technology first-hand in the UK. In conjunction with the Mori clan of Hagi, the Shimazu played a leading part in the Meiji Restoration.

Orientation

Kagoshima sprawls north–south along the bayside and has two JR stations, the major one being Kagoshima-Chūō to the south. The town centre is at the point where the lively Tenmonkan-dōri shopping and entertainment arcade crosses the tram lines. Iso-teien (p658), the town's principal attraction, is north of Kagoshima Station but most other things to do are around the centre, particularly on the hillside that forms a backdrop to the city.

Information

The **tourist information office** (Map pp656-7; ☎ 253-2500; ⏰ 8.30am-7pm), located inside JR Kagoshima-Chūō Station has information

KYŪSHŪ

in English, and can help book accommodation. The quieter Kagoshima Station **branch** (☎ 222-2500; ☺ 8.30am-5pm) is also helpful. **Update Visitor Centre** (Map pp656-7; ☎ 224-8011; www.synapse.ne.jp/update; 2nd fl, Hiratabashi Bldg; ☺ 9.30am-5pm Mon-Fri, 9.30am-4pm Sat) has an excellent website.

Numerous places in the city (including the tourist information office and Update Visitor Centre) carry an excellent English guide called (not surprisingly!) *Kagoshima*. It has maps, a host of activities, model excursions broken into three-hour, half-day and whole-day parts, all with detailed maps. Some highlights include visiting local pottery kilns, silk-weaving workshops, shōchū distilleries and even a Satsuma fish-paste factory!

INTERNET ACCESS
International Exchange Plaza (Map pp656-7; ☎ 225-3279; 11th fl, I'm Bldg; free access per 30min; ☺ 9am-5.30pm Mon-Sat) In Tenmonkan; it also has magazines and books for browsing.

Internet & Comics Space Create (Map pp656-7; membership fee ¥300, per hr ¥360-480; ☺ 24hr) Has reclining chairs, unlimited soft drinks, and billiards tables.

MONEY
The postal savings ATM at the main post office near JR Kagoshima-Chūō Station accepts internationally issued cards, as do all the postal ATMs.

Sights
ISO-TEIEN (SENGAN-EN) 磯庭園
Starting in 1658, the 19th Shimazu lord laid out this beautiful bayside **garden** (☎ 274-1551; 9700-1 Yoshinochō; admission ¥1000, with guided villa tour & tea ceremony ¥1500; ☺ 8.30am-5.15pm), incorporating one of the most impressive pieces of 'borrowed scenery' to be found anywhere in Japan – the fuming peak of Sakurajima. Look for the stream where the 21st Shimazu lord once held poetry parties – the participants had to compose a poem before the next cup of sake floated down the stream to them. The villa, **Shimazu-ke**, was once the family home of the omnipotent Shimazu clan. Women in elegant kimono guide you through the villa, after which you are served traditional tea and sweets. Look for a moment at the tea bowl's pattern or shape before you take a sip, if you want to be especially polite.

Other tea shops around the garden sell *jambo* (pounded rice cakes on a stick).

Shōko Shūseikan (admission free with garden ticket; ☺ 8.30am-5.15pm), adjacent to Iso-teien, is a museum housed in Japan's first factory, built in the 1850s. Exhibits relate to the Shimazu family – in fact, most of the 10,000 items are precious heirlooms, including ancient scrolls, military goods and pottery. The art of *kiriko* (cut glass) has been revived at an on-site workshop.

MUSEUMS
Kagoshima City Museum of Art (Map pp656-7; ☎ 224-3400; 4-36 Shiroyamachō; admission ¥200; ☺ 9.30am-6pm Tue-Sun) has a small, permanent collection of works by modern Japanese painters from Kagoshima, as well as some 16th-century porcelains and wood-block prints. Its collection of Sakurajima paintings is most distinctive.

Reimeikan (Kagoshima Prefectural Museum of Culture; admission ¥300; ☺ 9am-4.30pm Tue-Sun) On the former site of Tsurumaru-jō – the walls and the impressive moat are all that remain of the 1602 castle, and bullet holes in the stones are still visible. Inside, the museum's three floors showcase very interesting exhibits on Satsuma history, festivals and folklore. Don't miss the model of the castle or ancient sword-making displays.

Museum of the Meiji Restoration (admission ¥300; ☺ 9am-5.30pm mid-Jul–Aug, 9am-4.30pm Sep–mid-Jul) has hourly performances by robotic Meiji reformers, including Saigō (see opposite). Exhibits and historical dioramas, labelled mostly in Japanese, laud Kagoshima firsts (Japan's first telegraph, first gas lighting, among others), along with Satsuma culture and the local dialect.

OTHER SIGHTS
Terukuni-jinja (Map pp656–7) is dedicated to Shimazu Nari-akira, the 28th Shimazu lord who was responsible for building Japan's first factory and introducing modern Western technology. He also designed Japan's still-controversial *hinomaru* – the rising sun flag, seen by some as a symbol of the emperor and Imperial (military) Japan. Continue up the hillside behind the shrine and you'll eventually reach the **observatory** in Shiroyama-kōen.

Kagoshima boasts no less than 50 public *onsen* baths. Local favourite **Shintosō Onsen** (新唐湊温泉; ☎ 255-4826; 1-29-1 Toso) has a good view of Sakurajima. Take city bus No 25

SAIGŌ TAKAMORI 西郷隆盛

Although the Great Saigō had played a leading part in the Meiji Restoration in 1868, in 1877 he changed his mind – possibly because he felt the curtailment of samurai power and status had gone too far – and this led to the ill-fated Satsuma or Seinan Rebellion. Kumamoto's magnificent castle was burnt down during the rebellion but when defeat became inevitable, Saigō eventually retreated to Kagoshima and committed *seppuku* (ritual suicide by disembowelment).

Despite his mixed status as both a hero and villain of the Restoration, Saigō is still a towering figure in the history of Japan. His square-headed features and bulky stature are instantly recognisable, and Kagoshima, like Ueno-kōen, Tokyo (see p111), also has a famous Saigō statue.

Reminders of Saigō Takamori's importance in Kagoshima abound, including a large statue of him near the Kagoshima City Museum of Art (opposite). The cave where he hid and the place where he eventually committed suicide are on Shiroyama. Further north are Nanshū-jinja; the **Saigō Nanshū Memorial Hall** (☎ 247-1100; 2-1 Kami Tatsuochō; admission ¥100; ☾ 9am-5pm Tue-Sun), where displays tell of the failed rebellion; and Nanshū-bochi (cemetery), which contains the graves of more than 2000 of Saigō's followers.

from JR Kagoshima-Chūō Station to Toso (15 minutes). **Nishida Onsen** (☎ 255-6354; 12-17 Takasu) is just a few minutes' walk from JR Kagoshima-Chūō.

Kagoshima City Aquarium (☎ 226-2233; 3-1 Hon Minato Shinmachi; adult/child ¥1500/750; ☾ 9am-5pm) is well done, not least the examples of local marine life, giving glimpses of spectacular diving in the Southwest Islands. **Iso-hama**, the city's popular summer beach getaway, has a cordoned off area for swimming and splashing about.

Festivals & Events

One of Kagoshima's more unusual events is the **Sogadon-no-Kasayaki** (Umbrella Burning Festival; late July). Boys burn umbrellas on the banks of Kōtsuki-gawa in honour of two brothers, who used umbrellas as torches in one of Japan's oldest revenge story. Other events include the **Isle of Fire Festival** (late July) on Sakurajima (p661) and the **Ohara Festival** (early November), featuring folk-dancing in the streets.

Sleeping

Kagoshima Shiroyama Youth Hostel (鹿児島城山 ユースホステル; ☎ 223-2648; 2-40-8 Somuta; dm ¥3100) A homey place with a kitchen and small garden. Call the English-speaking owners to ask for directions – it's hidden up in the hills, a 10-minute bus ride from JR Kagoshima-Chūō Station.

Nakazono Ryokan (Map p655; ☎ 226-5125; fax 226-5126; shindon@satsuma.ne.jp; 1-8 Yasuichō; s/d/tr ¥4000/8000/11,400) Part of the Japanese Inn Group, Nakazono is a particularly friendly

minshuku, used to dealing with the vagaries of gaijin clients. The ryokan is close to both Kagoshima Station and the Sakurajima pier, and there's a mineral-water *sentō* (public bath house) nearby. The ryokan is tucked down an alley behind a temple, near the Shiyakusho-mae (City Hall) tram stop.

Business Hotel Suzuya (☎ 258-2385; 19-15 Chūōchō; r per person ¥3500-4500) This is the cheapest place around JR Kagoshima-Chūō station. Old, but in a very nice location, this place offers basic, small rooms, tea in the rooms, and a morning coffee service.

Hotel Ishihara-sō (☎ 254-4181; 4-14 Chūōchō; s/d ¥4500/8500) Quite a step up and serves Satsuma cuisine in its restaurants.

Silk Inn Kagoshima (Map pp656-7; ☎ 258-1221; 19-30 Uenosonochō; s/d ¥5800/9500) This place has its own hot spring.

Hotel New Nishino (Map pp656-7; ☎ 224-3232; 13-24 Sennichichō; s/tw ¥5400/9600, Japanese-style r from ¥9600) Nishino reserves its 4th-floor sauna complex for men only.

Nanshū-kan (Map pp656-7; ☎ 226-8188; fax 226-9383; 19-17 Higashi-sengokuchō; s/d from ¥6000/8000) Slightly faded, but it's convenient. The water pressure in the showers is enough to knock over a horse. Ask about car-rental packages.

JR Kyūshū Hotel Kagoshima (Map pp656-7; ☎ 213-8000, fax 213-8029; kagoshima@jrk-hotels.com; 1-1-2 Take; s/tw ¥6500/12,000) An upmarket hotel attached to JR Kagoshima-Chūō Station, this has only a dozen twin rooms (as compared to over 100 singles). Check in anytime after 2pm, check out by 11am.

Onsen Hotel Nakahara Bessō (Map pp656-7; ☎ 225-2800; fax 226-3688; 15-19 Terukunichō; r per person with/without 2 meals ¥10,000/8000) Mostly Japanese-style accommodation, with its own Satsuma cuisine restaurant and a *rotemburo*. It's close to attractions and nightlife.

Eating

Side streets around JR Kagoshima-Chūō Station have an abundance of eateries.

Xiang Xiang (Map pp656-7; dishes ¥700-1100; 🕙 11am-2pm & 6pm-10pm Mon-Sat) This should be your first choice, where gracious servers in *ao dai* (traditional costume worn when serving tables) serve fresh Vietnamese fare. The owner speaks impeccable English.

Kumasotei (Map pp656-7; ☎ 222-6356; 6-10 Higashi-sengokuchō; meals from ¥1400; 🕙 11am-3pm & 5-10pm) This is a favourite for Satsuma cuisine. The ¥3000 dinner gives you a taste of all the most popular specialities.

Wakana Honten (Map pp656-7; ☎ 222-5559; 9-14 Higashi-sengokuchō; dishes around ¥700; 🕙 5.30-11.15pm) Offers a special *miso-oden* (¥650).

Moon Garden (Map pp656-7; ☎ 226-8439; 2-19 Gofukuchō; 🕙 5-11pm Mon-Fri, 5pm-1am Sat) This is a beautiful and rambunctious dining bar. Its English-language drinks menu lists regional sake and shōchū varieties.

Yakushima (Map pp656-7; ☎ 225-8366; B1F 2-23 Gofukuchō; 🕙 5-11pm Mon-Sat) A few doors north of Moon Garden (look for the jolly *o-bāsan* painted on the sign), this is a rustic place for island seafood cuisine.

There is something of a *rāmen* battle going on in the Tenmonkan area. With its stone façade and wooden horseshoe-shaped bar, **Komurasaki** (Map pp656-7; ☎ 222-5707; 11-19 Higashi-sengokuchō; 🕙 11am-9pm Fri-Wed) is good but pricey; **Kuroiwa** (Map pp656-7; ☎ 222-4808; 9-9 Higashi-sengokuchō; 🕙 10.30am-9pm) is plain but tasty; and **Wadaya** (Map pp656-7; ☎ 226-7773; 11-2 Higashi-sengokuchō; bowls ¥630-800; 🕙 11am-1.50am) is 'striking' as well as cheap, a highly recommended local favourite.

Drinking

There's a lot happening in Tenmonkan – shot bars, discos, bunny bars (where the waitresses flirt while you drink), peep shows, karaoke boxes and retro coffee shops. Most dance clubs don't get going until around 11pm.

Kanejyō (Map pp656-7; ☎ 223-0487; 2F 7-20 Higashi-sengokuchō) Asian café by day; atmospheric jazz bar by night.

Turkey (Map pp656-7; ☎ 223-5085; 9-2 Higashi-sengokuchō) A shot bar and karaoke parlour.

> ### SATSUMA RYŌRI
>
> Kagoshima's cuisine speciality is known as *Satsuma ryōri* – the food of the Satsuma region. Dishes include: *tonkotsu*, pork ribs seasoned with miso (fermented soybean paste) and black sugar, then boiled until they're at the point of falling apart; *satsuma-age*, a deep-fried fish sausage flavoured with sake; *kibinago*, a sardine-like fish that is usually prepared as *sashimi* with vinegared miso sauce; and *sakezushi*, sushi mixed with drops of sake. Legend has it that *satsuma-jiru*, miso soup with chicken, originated as a way to dispose of losers in the fiefdom's once most-popular sport, cockfighting. Kagoshima *rāmen* is also famous.
>
> *Imo-jōchū*, the Kagoshima firewater, is made from sweet potatoes, which the locals fiercely support against Ōita's *mugi-jōchū*, which is distilled from barley.

Entertainment

Jazz Bar Pannonica (Map pp656-7; ☎ 216-3430; 2F 7-12 Higashi-sengokuchō; cover ¥500-1000) This jazz bar has live vocalists.

Namaste (Map pp656-7; ☎ 227-1446; 9-2 Higashi-sengokuchō) Namaste is a basement reggae bar.

Sur Bar (☎ 222-0902; 7-20 Higashi-sengokuchō; cover ¥500) Small basement dance space suffused by white lights and incense. Look for bongos in the corner.

De'Nile (Map pp656-7; ☎ 222-4970; cover with 2 free drinks ¥1000-3000 Sat & Sun) Another subterranean dance spot with different DJs every night, located behind Taka-Pla.

Doggy Bar (Map pp656-7; ☎ 223-2452; 4th fl, 14-5 Sennichichō; cover ¥1500-3000) Hip-hop and reggae crowd, especially for live events.

Shopping

Satsuma specialities include a variation on the *ningyō* (Japanese doll), *kiriko* (cut glass) and cards printed with inks produced from Sakurajima volcanic ash. Sakurajima ash is used in the making of Sakurajima pottery, but the main ceramic wares are white and black Satsuma-yaki (see the boxed text, p622). *Imo jōchū* (sweet potato liquor) is the prefectural drink, which ranges considerably in taste and quality, some tasting like bathtub cleanser or jet fuel, others like fine cognac. You can shop for quality goods at Iso-teien and **Kagoshima Brand Shop** (Ka-

goshima-ken Bussan-kaikan; Map pp656-7; ☯ 9am-5pm)
in Tenmonkan.

Kagoshima's **asa ichi** (morning market; Map
pp656-7; ☯ 6am-noon Mon-Sat) is just south of
JR Kagoshima-Chūō Station. It's a raucous,
lively event. There's another *asa-ichi* at the
smaller Kagoshima Station.

Getting There & Away

AIR

Kagoshima's airport has international connections with Hong Kong, Shannghai, and
Seoul, as well as domestic flights to Tokyo,
Osaka and other Kyūshū destinations. Kagoshima is also the major jumping-off point
for flights to the Southwest Islands and
Okinawa.

Skymark (☎ 223-0123; 17-3 Nishi-sengokuchō) is
Japan's only cut-rate carrier, offering flights
to Tokyo (Haneda, ¥24,500). Book at the
office in Tenmonkan.

BICYCLE

Bikes can be rented reasonably (¥500/1500
per two hours/day) at JR Kagoshima-Chūō
Station and returned at a number of participating hotels. JR users get a 40% discount.
Ask at the tourist information office for details (p657).

BOAT

Ferries shuttle across the bay to Sakurajima
(¥150, 15 minutes), and from the Kita-futō
terminal further afield to Okinawa (¥14,200,
19 hours) and by jetfoil to Yakushima. Regular ferries to Yakushima depart from Mi-
nami-futō pier just 10 minutes' walk south.
For details on ferry services to Yakushima,
see p686.

From Kagoshima Shin-kō (Kagoshima
New Port), **Queen Coral Marix Line** (☎ 225-
1551) has ferries to Naha (Okinawa) via the
Amami archipelago (¥13,200, 25½ hours).

BUS

There are a few bus centres and myriad highway bus stops, mostly found around Kagoshima-Chūō station and in Tenmonkan.

Typical services include Miyazaki (¥2700,
2¾ hours), Kumamoto (¥3600, 3½ hours),
Fukuoka/Hakata (¥5300, four hours) and
Osaka (¥10,800, 12½ hours).

Hayashida buses to Ebino-kōgen (¥1550,
1¾ hours) depart from opposite Taka-Pla
department store.

TRAIN

Most trains arrive and depart from JR Kagoshima-Chūō Station, once called Nishi
Kagoshima but redone to incorporate the
shinkansen (p612). Additionally, the JR Kagoshima line heads north to Kumamoto
(*shinkansen*, ¥6060, 1½ hours) and Hakata
(Fukuoka; ¥8270, four hours). Also stopping
at Kagoshima Station, the JR Nippō line goes
to Miyazaki (*tokkyū*, ¥4690, two hours) and
Beppu (¥10,460, six hours).

Trains also run south from Kagoshima
to the popular hot-spring resort of Ibusuki
(p664) and continue partway around the
Satsuma Peninsula (¥970; 1¼ hours).

Getting Around

TO/FROM THE AIRPORT

Frequent airport buses depart from JR Kagoshima-Chūō Station, Tenmonkan and
various other stops around the city (¥1200,
one hour).

BUS

There's a comprehensive city bus network,
though trams are usually simpler.

For tourists, the City View Bus (¥180)
does a loop of all the major sights, departing every 30 minutes throughout the day,
from 9.30am to 5pm daily. A one-day pass
(¥600) is also valid on trams.

Bus tours (per person ¥4500) are organised through **tourist information office** (Map
pp656-7; ☎ 253-2500; ☯ 8.30am-7pm) inside JR
Kagoshima-Chūō Station.

CAR

Cars are available to be rented in Osumi (at
Oonejime where the ferry arrives from Ibusuki) through **Nankyu Senpaku** (☎ 0994-22-1083).

TRAM

The tram service in Kagoshima is easy to understand and operates frequently. Rte 1 starts
from Kagoshima Station, goes through the
centre and on into the suburbs. Rte 2 diverges
at Takami-baba to Kagoshima-Chūō Station
and terminates at Korimoto. Either pay the
flat fare (¥160) or buy a one-day travel pass
(¥600) from tourist information offices.

SAKURAJIMA 桜島

☎ 099
Dominating the skyline from Kagoshima is
the brooding cone of this spectacular active

KYŪSHŪ

volcano. In fact, Sakurajima is so energetic that the Japanese differentiate between its mere eruptions (since 1955 there has been an almost continuous stream of smoke and ash) and real explosions. The most violent was in 1914, when the volcano poured out over three billion tons of lava, overwhelming numerous villages and converting the island to a peninsula.

Sakurajima has three peaks, but at present only Minami-dake (1040m) is active. Although visitors are not permitted to climb the volcano, there are several good lookout points with walkways across a small corner of the immense lava flow. While some parts of Sakurajima are covered in deep volcanic ash or crumbling lava, other places have exceptionally fertile soil. Huge *daikon* (radishes) weighing up to 35kg, and tiny oranges only 3cm in diameter but ¥500 each, are locally grown.

Sights & Activities

The **Sakurajima Visitors Centre** (☎ 293-2443; ☯ 9am-5pm Tue-Sun) is located near the ferry terminal and has a variety of exhibits and videos about the volcano, its eruptions and its natural history. A working model showing the volcano's growth over the years is the visitors centre's main attraction. There's a short lava-field paved walkway nearby that leads along the coast toward a lookout.

South of the visitors centre is **Buried Karasu-jima**, where the 1914 lava flow totally engulfed the small island that had been half a kilometre offshore. On the way down the mountainside the lava swallowed three villages, destroying over 1000 homes.

Continuing anticlockwise around the island, you come to a **monument** to writer Hayashi Fumiko, whose famous poem claimed that 'though a flower's life is short, its sufferings are many.' Nearby is the hot springs at **Furusato Onsen**. Furusato Kankō hotel has a pool-sized cliffside **rotemburo** (☎ 211-3111; admission ¥1050, rental locker & towel ¥410; ☯ for hotel guests 6am-10pm, onsen-only visitors 8am-8pm, closed Mon & Thu morning). As it is also a shrine, you'll have to wear a *yukata* (cotton kimono) as you soak.

At **Kurokami Buried Torii**, only the top third of a 3m-high *torii* emerges from the volcanic ash. On the north coast you can soak

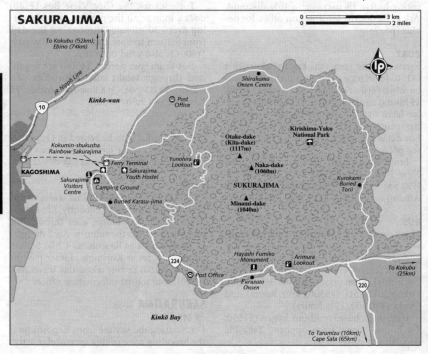

SAKURAJIMA

0 — 3 km
0 — 2 miles

To Kokubu (52km);
Ebino (74km)

JR Nippō Line

Kinkō-wan

Shirahama
Onsen Centre

Post
Office

Kirishima-Yaku
National Park

Kokumin-shukusha
Rainbow Sakurajima

Otake-dake
(Kita-dake)
(1117m) ▲

Naka-dake
(1060m) ▲

Ferry Terminal

Yunohira
Lookout

Kurokami
Buried
Torii

KAGOSHIMA

Sakurajima
Youth Hostel

SUKURAJIMA

Sakurajima
Visitors
Centre

Camping Ground

Minami-dake
(1040m) ▲

Buried Karasu-jima

Hayashi Fumiko
Monument

Arimura
Lookout

To Kokubu
(25km)

Post Office

Furusato
Onsen

Kinkō Bay

To Tarumizu (10km);
Cape Sata (65km)

in the muddy waters of **Shirahama Onsen Centre** (☎ 293-4126; admission ¥300; ☉ 10am-9pm).

Tours

Sightseeing bus tours leave from the ferry terminal (¥1700, three hours, 9.30am and 1.30pm). JR Kyūshū also runs tours of Sakurajima, leaving from JR Kagoshima-Chūō Station (see p661) at 8.45am (¥4000, 6¼ hours). While these involve listening to the guide's running discussion of sights (Japanese only), there is an English transcription book available, and the tours provide a good way to see the island if you're pressed for time.

Sleeping

There's a simple, seasonal camping ground across the road from the visitors centre.

Sakurajima Youth Hostel (☎/fax 293-2150; dm with/without 2 meals ¥3870/2650) Not new, but friendly, and only a 15-minute walk from the ferry terminal. In order to arrive before reception closes, you must catch the 8.30pm ferry from Kagoshima.

Kokumin-shukusha Rainbow Sakurajima (☎ 293-2323; r per person with 2 meals ¥8000) Also near the ferry terminal, and has an *onsen*.

Getting There & Around

A 24-hour passenger and car ferry service shuttles frequently back and forth between Kagoshima and Sakurajima (¥150, 15 minutes); pay at the Sakurajima end.

The Sakurajima ferry terminal is a short bus ride from JR Kagoshima-Chūō Station. Take the City View Bus or any bus bound for the aquarium and get off at Suizokukan-mae (¥180, half-hourly).

Getting around Sakurajima without your own transport can be difficult. Bicycles can be rented from **Sakurajima Renta Car** (☎ 293-2162; 1hr/2hr 400/600), near the ferry terminal but a complete circuit of the volcano (36km) would be quite a push, even without the climbs to the various lookouts.

Local buses operate regularly around the island until about 8pm. JR buses from the ferry terminal pass Furusato Onsen (¥290) and run up to the Arimura lookout. Otherwise, the Furusato Kankō Hotel at Furusato Onsen offers a limited free shuttle service to and from the port, departing roughly every half-hour except during lunchtime and on the mornings when the *onsen* is closed (ie Monday and Thursday mornings).

SATSUMA PENINSULA 薩摩半島

This peninsula south of Kagoshima city has fine rural scenery, a kamikaze pilots' museum, the hot-spring resort of Ibusuki (famous for its hot-sand baths), the conical peak of Kaimon-dake, and Chiran, with its well-preserved samurai street. On the other side of Kinkō-wan is Cape Sata, the southernmost point of Japan's main islands.

Using public transport around the region is time-consuming, although it is possible to make a complete loop of the peninsula by train and bus. The JR Ibusuki-Makurazaki line runs south from Kagoshima to Ibusuki then turns west to Makurazaki, from where you can eventually make your way by local bus back to Kagoshima.

Renting a car can be useful. Although there are numerous rental car places in Kagoshima City, **Eki Rent-a-Car** (12hr from ¥4720; JR Kagoshima-Chūō Station 2F tourist information booth ☎ 258-1412; ☉ 8am-8pm; Ibusuki ☎ 0993-23-3879; ☉ 8am-5pm) is one of the easiest options. The Ibuski branch is on the right side of Ibusuki JR Station when exiting it.

Daily bus tours to Ibusuki and Chiran depart from Kagoshima-Chūō Station. A daily sightseeing bus (¥4550) heads off to Chiran at 8.50am, whizzes you around the sights and then does the same thing in Ibusuki, ending the day with a soak in a hot spring.

Chiran 知覧

☎ 0993 / pop 13,900

South of Kagoshima, Chiran is a detour en route to or from Ibusuki (p664). The town has a fine collection of samurai houses and gardens, plus a fascinating memorial and museum to WWII's kamikaze pilots. Chiran was one of the major bases from which fighters left on their final missions.

All seven of the residences along Chiran's street of **samurai houses** (武家屋敷; ☎ 83-2511; admission ¥500; ☉ 9am-5pm) dating from the mid-Edo period are noted for their gardens. Look for the use of 'borrowed scenery', particularly in No 6. Water is usually symbolised by sand or gravel. Along the main road, parallel to the samurai street, is a well-stocked **carp stream**.

A modern version of the samurai is commemorated in the **Kamikaze Peace Museum** (Chiran Tokkō Heiwa-Kaikan; 知覧特攻平和会館; ☎ 83-2525; admission ¥500; ☉ 9am-4.30pm), 2km west of town, a collection of aircraft, mementos, and photos of young, fresh-faced men who were selected for the Special Attack Corps in WWII. It's difficult to see these young men as different from any other countries' soldiers: young, idealistic, doing what they were ordered to do in the hopes of defending their country. Despite the lack of English signs, it's a moving tribute.

Taki-An (高城庵) is a traditional house on the samurai street with a nice garden where you can sit on tatami mats to eat a bowl of upmarket *soba* (buckwheat noodles; ¥600) and sip Chiran's famous green tea.

Kagoshima Kōtsū buses to Chiran (¥860, 80 minutes) and Ibusuki run from JR Kagoshima-Chūō Station and the Yamakataya bus station in Tenmonkan. From Chiran, there are only a few buses per day to Ibusuki (¥900, one hour), leaving from stops along the highway.

Ibusuki 指宿

☎ 0993 / pop 30,200

At the southeastern end of the Satsuma Peninsula, 50km from Kagoshima, is the hot-spring resort of Ibusuki. It's quiet, especially in the off-season; if you're looking for nightlife be sure to head back to Kagoshima before dark. At Ibusuki Station, the **information desk** (☎ 22-2111; ⏰ 9am-6pm) has basic maps and can assist with directions.

On the beachfront is Ibusuki's *raison d'etre*, the **Tennen Sunamushi Kaikan** (天然砂蒸し会館; ☎ 35-2669; admission ¥800; ⏰ 8.30am-noon & 1-9pm). Pay at the entrance (the fee includes a *yukata* and towel), change downstairs, and wander down to the beach where the burial ladies are waiting, shovel in hand, to cover you in wonderfully hot volcanic sand. Reactions range from claustrophobic to euphoric; 15 minutes is a recommended maximum, but many stay longer. After about 30 minutes the ladies will ask if you'd like a 'warmer,' and they also gently mop your brow occasionally. Listening to the wash of the bay waves is the ultimate white noise: if you're used to the heat it's so relaxing you'll find yourself nodding off. When you're through, head back up to the bath, discard the sand-covered *yukata* and stay for as long as you like in the regular *onsen*. For hot-springs aficionados, Ibusuki's sand baths are a must.

The sand baths are a 20-minute walk or a short bus ride (¥130) southeast of Ibusuki Station.

SLEEPING & EATING

Yunosato Youth Hostel (湯の里ユースホステル; ☎ 22-5680; dm with/without 2 meals ¥4600/3000) Has its own hot spring and rents bicycles. It's 800m northeast of the station.

Tamaya Youth Hostel (圭屋ユースホステル; ☎ 22-3553; dm with/without 2 meals ¥3950/2600) Like most accommodation in Ibusuki, just a stone's throw from the sand baths.

Minshuku Marutomi (民宿丸富; ☎ 22-5579; fax 22-3993; r with 2 meals from ¥7000) A small but very popular inn, famous for its fresh seafood because the owner is a fisherman and cooks up the catch of the day.

Ryokan Ginshō (旅館吟松; ☎ 22-3231; fax 22-2219; www.ginsyou.co.jp in Japanese; r per person with 2 meals from ¥15,000) In operation for more than 50 years, with a lovely garden and nice staff out front to welcome you. Its seaside *rotemburo* has romantic lantern-lit shower stalls.

Aoba (青葉; ☎ 22-3356; dishes from ¥750; ⏰ lunch/dinner Thu-Mon) Nice Japanese food with a beautiful aquarium (for viewing, not eating!) that serves Kagoshima cuisine, *unagi-don*, tempura, and more. Very close to the station.

In summer, the **Iwasaki Hotel** (いわさきホテル; ☎ 22-2131) has a beer garden.

GETTING THERE & AWAY

Ibusuki is less than two hours from Kagoshima by bus (¥850); see p663 for details. Trains also operate from JR Kagoshima-Chūō Station (*kaisoku*, ¥970, 80 minutes).

AROUND SATSUMA PENINSULA

West of Ibusuki, **Ikeda-ko** is a beautiful volcanic caldera lake, inhabited by giant eels that can grow up to 2m long. West along the coast, you come to **Cape Nagasakibana**, from where offshore islands can be seen on a clear day. There's a **camping ground** (☎ 0993-35-0111) near the flower gardens.

Tōsenkyō-kōen Sōmen Nagashi (唐船峡公園そうめん流し; ☎ 0993-32-2143; dishes per person ¥500; ⏰ 8.30am-6pm) is only a five-minute taxi ride from JR Kaimon Station. This place is fun: *sōmen* noodles whirl around in a plexiglass table-top trough; to eat them, dip your chopsticks in for a moment and the current will do the rest – just dip them in sauce and slurp. Trout, another speciality, is tender and flavourful.

The beautifully symmetrical 922m cone of **Kaimon-dake** can be climbed in two hours from the Kaimon-dake bus stop, or also from JR Kaimon station. Start as early as possible and you'll be rewarded with views of Sakurajima, Cape Sata, and tropical islands Yakushima and Tanegashima.

At the southwestern end of the peninsula is **Makurazaki**, a busy port famous for *katsuo* (bonito) and the terminus for the train line from Kagoshima. Just beyond Makurazaki is **Bōnotsu**, a pretty little fishing village that was an unofficial trading link with the outside world via Okinawa during Japan's two centuries of seclusion. North of Bōnotsu is **Fukiage Beach**. A 15-minute walk from JR Ijūin Station, **Fukiage-hama Youth Hostel** (吹上浜ユースホステル; ☎ /fax 099-292-3455; dm ¥2750) has just a dozen beds; call in advance.

ŌSUMI PENINSULA

The southernmost point on the main islands of Japan, **Cape Sata** is on the opposite side of Kagoshima, the Ōsumi Peninsula, and is marked by the oldest lighthouse in Japan. You can reach the cape from the Kagoshima side of Kinkō-wan by taking the ferry from Yamakawa, a stop south of Ibusuki, to Nejime on the other side. However, public transport onward is nearly impossible. An 8km bicycle track leads down to the end of the cape.

If you're bent on getting here, another option is to rent a car in Kagoshima (p661) or Kokubu (p654) and drive. If you're lucky you'll see dolphins in Kinkō-wan swimming along the shore. At the cape's tip, the **Sata-Day-Go** (☎ 0994-27-3355), a glass-bottomed boat, offers views of the underwater fish and coral. Sea turtles, sharks, or dolphins may swim by. You will certainly see plenty of *fugu* (pufferfish) which are both plentiful and delicious (do *not* prepare them yourself, however, as they contain a deadly toxin which must be properly removed).

MIYAZAKI-KEN 宮崎県

Rte 222 from Miyakonojō to Obi and Nichinan on the coast is a superb road, twisting and winding over the hills along the sea. Along this rugged coastline south of Miyazaki, the usual approach is by train or bus.

AOSHIMA 青島
☎ 0985
A beach resort famed for the small island covered in betel palms, fringed by spectacu-

larly unique washboard rock formations and connected to the mainland by a thin sand causeway. Due to the prevailing warm currents, the only place you'll find warmer water in Japan is much further south in Okinawa. If you happen to be nearby when a typhoon hits, come here the day afterwards, as the heavy surf may wash up gorgeous shells which are first-come-first-served for lucky beachcombers. Also on the island, a short walk east of Aoshima station, is photogenic **Aoshima-jinja** (青島神社; Ogre's Washboard Temple; ☎ 65-1262) reputedly good for matchmaking, and the scene of two exciting **festivals**. On the second Monday in January, loincloth-wearing locals dive into the ocean, while on 17 June there's another aquatic twist when *mikoshi* are carried through the shallows to the shrine. Nearby is a **botanical garden** (青島熱帯植物園; ☎ 65-1042; admission ¥200) which boasts 64 different species of fruit trees. Wandering around the grounds and garden is free.

Aoshima is on the JR Nichinan line from Miyazaki (¥360, 30 minutes). Buses from Miyazaki Train Station stop at Aoshima (¥670, 40 minutes, hourly) en route to Udojingū (below).

UDO-JINGŪ 鵜戸神宮
If you walk through this brightly painted coastal **shrine** (☎ 0987-29-1001) to the end of the path, you'll find yourself in an open cavern overlooking some rock formations at the ocean's edge. A popular sport is to buy five *undama* (luck stones) and try to get them into a shallow depression on top of one of the turtle-shaped rocks (men, throw with your left hand; women, use your right). Succeeding at this task is supposed to make your wish come true. Wishes are usually related to marriage and childbirth, most likely because the boulders in front of the cave are said to represent Emperor Jimmu's mother's breasts!

Frequent buses from Aoshima (¥990, 40 minutes) and Miyazaki (¥1440, 90 minutes) stop on the highway, downhill from the shrine. There are few onward buses to Obi (¥820, 45 minutes). Fifteen minutes' walk from the bus stop to the shrine will take you past wonderful rock formations, more washboards, and very picturesque fishing boats.

Also on the bus route to Udo-Jingū is the **Cactus & Herb Garden** (サボテンハーブ

KYŪSHŪ

園; ☎ 0987-29-1111; admission ¥500) a botanical garden with hillsides of prickly pear and other exotic species, as well as several greenhouses with flowering tropicals, desert varieties and more. It closed in March 2005 due to a typhoon, but may be reopened by now.

OBI 飫肥

From 1587 the wealthy Ito clan ruled this town from the castle for 14 generations, surviving the 'one kingdom, one castle' ruling in 1615. The clan eventually moved out in 1869 after the Meiji Restoration ended the feudal period.

Sights & Activities

Although only the walls of the actual castle remain, the grounds of **Obi-jō** (飫肥城; ☎ 0987-25-4533; combined admission ¥600; 9.30am-4.30pm) contain a number of interesting buildings. The castle **museum** has a collection relating to the Ito clan's long rule over Obi, with everything from weapons and armour to traditional clothes and household equipment. **Matsuo-no-Maru**, the lord's private residence, has been reconstructed. When the lord visited the toilet at the far end of the house, he was accompanied by three pages – one to lead the way, one to carry water for the lord to wash his hands, and one to fan him during the summer months!

When the Obi lord was forced to abandon his castle after the Meiji Restoration, he moved down the hill to **Yōshōkan**, formerly the residence of the clan's chief retainer. It stands just outside the castle entrance and has a large garden incorporating Atago-san as 'borrowed scenery'. Beyond this house you enter the castle proper through the impressive gate, **Ōte-mon**.

Shintōku-dō, the hall adjacent to the castle, was established as a samurai school in 1831. Up the hill behind Shintōku-dō is **Tanoue Hachiman-jinja**; the shrine is shrouded by 400-year-old trees and reached by a steep flight of steps.

On the western side of the river, **Ioshi-jinja** has a pleasant garden and the Ito family mausoleum.

Getting There & Around

The JR Nichinan line connects Obi with Miyazaki (*kaisoku*, ¥910, 65 minutes) via Aoshima. From Obi Station, it's a short bus ride (¥220) or a 15-minute walk to the castle, reached by turning left outside the station. Buses from Miyazaki (¥1990, 2¼ hours, last return bus 4pm) stop along the main road below the castle entrance. Bikes can be rented (¥300 per hour) at the station or near the castle parking lot (☎ 0987-31-1134).

NICHINAN-KAIGAN & CAPE TOI 日南海岸都井岬

The beautiful 50km stretch of coast from Nichinan to Miyazaki offers stunning views, pretty little coves, interesting stretches of washboard rocks and, at holiday times, heavy traffic. Like at Cape Sata, the views over the ocean from Cape Toi are superb. On the last weekend in September, Cape Toi hosts a dramatic **fire festival**. The cape is also famed for its herds of wild horses, but don't come expecting galloping hoofbeats and unkept stallions leading a harem of mares: it's essentially a grassy park, and the horses are quite sedate, even friendly.

At the beach **Ishinami-kaigan**, during the summer only, you can stay in old farmhouse *minshuku*. The tiny island of **Kō-jima**, just off the coast, has a group of monkeys that were the focus for some interesting anthropological discoveries. There is no longer a youth hostel in this area, so you should plan on staying elsewhere in **Koigaura**, about 5km from Cape Toi or 7km from Kojima. Try **Minshuku Tanaka** (☎ 0987-76-2096; per person with 2 meals from ¥6000 yen) or **Koigaura Minshuku** (☎ 0987-76-1631; per person with 2 meals from ¥4500 yen). Koigaura is a popular surfing location and both *minshukus* offer a surfer price, which is less than what's listed here. It's worth asking even if you're not planning on surfing.

MIYAZAKI 宮崎

☎ 0985 / pop 310,800

Due to the warm offshore currents, the city of Miyazaki has a balmy climate and some of the best surfing in Japan, particularly at Kizaki-hama and other beaches further north toward Hyūga. The area around Miyazaki played an important part in early Japanese civilisation and some interesting excavations can be seen at Saitobaru (p670).

Information

At the **tourist information office** (☎ 22-6469; 9am-6.30pm) inside Miyazaki Station, some English is spoken. Make sure you pick up the excellent *Discovering Miyazaki:*

A Travel Guide or *Let's Go Miyazaki City* guidebook and pull-out map.

The **Miyazaki Prefectural International Centre** (☎ 32-8457; 6th fl, Higashi-Bekkan, Miyatashi; ☼ 8.30am-5.15pm Mon-Fri) has CNN and English-language newspapers, but no Internet access.

There's an ATM that accepts Visa, Master-Card and Cirrus in the Fresta shopping complex at Miyazaki Station. At Miyakō City bus terminal, the **postal savings ATM** (☼ 8am-9pm Mon-Fri, 10am-9pm Sat, 10am-7pm Sun) accepts internationally issued cards.

There's a 24-hour Internet café above Cafe Lanai (p670) charging ¥480 for the first hour, or ¥1900 for unlimited Internet access between midnight and 8am, including ing soft drinks.

Sights

MIYAZAKI SCIENCE CENTRE
宮崎科学技術館

A short walk from Miyazaki station, this hi-tech science **museum** (☎ 23-2700; 38-3 Miyawakichō; admission with sky show ¥730; ☼ 9am-4pm Tue-Sun), topped by a gleaming silver dome, boasts the world's largest planetarium. English-language pamphlets are available.

MIYAZAKI-JINGŪ & MUSEUM
宮崎神宮　宮崎総合博物館

Three kilometres north of the town centre, this **shrine** (☎ 27-4004; 2-4-1 Jingū) is dedicated to the Emperor Jimmu, the semimythical first emperor of Japan and founder of the Yamoto court. There are 600-year-old wisteria vines covering the thickly forested grounds.

Outside the northern end of the shrine grounds, the **Miyazaki Prefectural Museum of Nature & History** (☎ 24-2071; 2-4-4 Jingū; admission ¥300; ☼ 9am-4.30pm Tue-Sun) has kid-oriented exhibits on local history, archaeological finds, festivals and folkcrafts. Behind the museum is **Minka-en** (民家園; admission free; ☼ Tue-Sun), with its four traditional-style Kyūshū farmhouses.

The shrine is located a 15-minute walk from Miyazaki-jingū Station, one stop north of Miyazaki. Several buses from Miyazaki Station and Tachibana-dōri run directly to the shrine (¥200, 10 minutes).

HEIWADAI-KŌEN 平和台公園

The centrepiece of **Heiwadai-kōen** (Peace Park) is a 37m-high tower constructed in 1940, a time when peace in Japan was about to disappear. Standing in front of the tower and clapping your hands produces a strange echo.

Haniwa Garden, which is in the park, is dotted with reproductions of the curious clay *haniwa* (tomb guardians) that have been excavated from the Saitobaru burial mounds (p670).

Haniwa Garden is about 1.5km north of Miyazaki-jingū, but only a few buses per day go there from Miyazaki Station (¥290, 20 minutes). More frequent services depart from along Tachibana-dōri.

SEAGAIA シーガイア

About 10km north of town at Seagaia resort, **Ocean Dome** (オーシャンドーム; ☎ 21-1177; www.seagaia.co.jp/english/odr/; Hamayama Yamasakichō; adult/child ¥2000/10000; ☼ from 10am) is a relatively new attraction: a water-based theme park with a variety of razzle-dazzle attractions, such as a mock volcano and 10-minute surfing demonstrations (surfing on your own is prohibited). Swimsuits can be rented (ew!) if you haven't brought one. You'll see this place heavily advertised, but unless you're averse to spending your time on a real beach watching real surfers, Ocean Dome is a place that can safely be skipped.

Buses run to Seagaia from JR Miyazaki Station along Tachibana-dōri every 30 minutes (¥470, 25 minutes).

Festivals & Events

At Miyazaki-jingū (left) on 2 and 3 April you can witness *yabusame* (samurai-style horseback archery). The mid-April **Furusato Matsuri** has around 10,000 participants in traditional attire dancing to local folk songs on Tachibana-dōri. **Miyazaki-jingū Grand Festival** (late October) is similar with *mikoshi* (portable shrines) being carried through the streets. Miyazaki is host to Kyūshū's largest **fireworks show** in late July.

Sleeping

Most accommodation in Miyazaki fills up quickly, so book ahead.

Fujin-kaikan Youth Hostel (☎ 24-5785; 1-3-10 Asahi; dm ¥2500) A bit institutional, it's used for a variety of classes during the day and early evening, but fine overall. The 10pm curfew makes it a bad choice for those wanting to revel. It's 15 minutes' walk from Miyazaki station, and whether or not you're staying

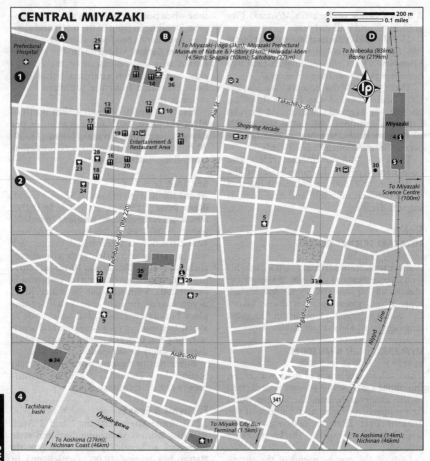

CENTRAL MIYAZAKI

two or more nights, you're required to leave the building between 10am and 3pm.

Business Family Hotel Miyako (☎ 27-9991; fax 27-0023; 13-21 Miyatachō; Japanese- or Western-style r with bath per person ¥3500) On a quiet side street midway between the station and Tachibanadōri. Reception is welcoming, but the doors are locked at midnight.

Hotel Crane (☎ 27-2111; 1-8-8 Tachibanadōri-higashi; s/tw from ¥4200/7500) This is a basic but modern business hotel. All rooms offer the hi-tech 'washlet' toilet seats. Guests can use the (men only) bath in hotel Crain-Tachibana, its sister location. The bath has big glass windows overlooking the city and offers a nice view for the uninhibited. (The windows are also probably why this is men-only.)

Hotel Crane-Tachibana (☎ 27-6868; 1-7-9 Tachibanadōri-higashi; s/d from ¥4900/7000, Japanese-style s/d ¥4760/6760) Older, but rates include breakfast.

Business Hotel Royal (☎ 25-5221; m-royal@topaz .ocn.ne.jp; 2-5-20 Segashira; s/tw from ¥4500/7000) Close to Miyazaki Station. A bit old fashioned, but after a recent remodelling all rooms have high tech toilets, mini-fridges, and free LAN access. There's up to ¥1000 off for reservations over the Net.

Hotel Kensington (☎ 20-5500; fax 32-7700; www .face.ne.jp/kensington in Japanese; 3-4-4 Tachibanadōri-higashi; s/d ¥6300/10,000) A cut above the average business hotel, this has British-style atmosphere but is nevertheless charming. Discounts are available for online bookings.

On the riverside are Miyazaki's top-end hotels. **Miyazaki Kankō Hotel** (☎ 32-5920; fax 25-8748; 1-1-1 Matsuyama; s/d from ¥7000/14,000, Japanese-style r ¥15,000-22,000) has its own hot-springs baths.

Eating

Hiya-jiru is a cold summer soup made from baked tofu, fish, miso paste and cucumbers, which you pour over a bowl of rice. Miyazaki Station is known for its *shiitake ekiben*, a boxed lunch featuring mushrooms. Be aware that many attractive-looking eateries in the entertainment district add a 'table charge' of at least a few hundred yen per person. If you're looking at the tab and scratching your head that's likely the reason.

La Dish Gourmet & Deli (11am-3am Mon-Sat, 6pm-1am Sun) An import grocery store amid the hustle of the entertainment district that sells both cold and hot deli items, plus a good selection of wines, cheeses and desserts.

Sai-en (☎ 28-5638; 2F 3-3-7 Tachibanadōri-higashi; teishoku ¥700; 11.30am-2.30pm & 5-9pm) Organic vegetarian cuisine, and there's an English-language menu. It's up on the 2nd floor, above a boutique.

Suginoko (☎ 22-5798; 2-1-4 Tachibanadōri-nishi; lunch dishes from ¥800, multicourse dinners from ¥4000) Specialises in Miyazaki cuisine, lunch by reservation only. An abbreviated menu is available in English.

Den Den Den (☎ 24-3825; 3-2-10 Tachibanadōri-nishi) A boisterous restaurant specialising in *kushiage* (deep-fried seafood on skewers).

Izakaya Seoul (☎ 29-8883; 7-26 Chūōmachi; 1st fl, Daiichi Yoshino Bldg) A bustling, no-nonsense Korean-Japanese restaurant not far away.

Restaurant Bar De-meté-r (☎ 29-0017; 3-8-18 2F Tachibanadōrinishi; dishes ¥450-1100, pizzas ¥600-1300; 6pm-late) An endless bilingual menu, draught beers, and no cover charge.

Rojak Restaurant & Bar (☎ 29-4020; 2nd fl, Daisan Miwa Bldg; dishes ¥600-1400; 6pm-midnight) Buddhas and lanterns illuminate the staircase here. The ¥200 table charge is worth it, both for Eurasian fare and sleek ambience.

APAS (☎ 31-8929; BF 3-10-36 Tachibanadōri-nishi; set meals ¥2200-3600; 11am-3pm & 5-10pm) Specialises in *Miyazaki-gyū* (Miyazaki beef), which is the real thing, and has English-speaking staff and menus.

The ground-floor café at **Hotel Kensington** (opposite) does reasonable breakfast and lunch sets (¥750). Bon Belta has an 8th-floor restaurant arcade (lunch sets under ¥1000) and a variety of takeaway is available from its basement marketplace. Don't miss the *onigiri* (rice-ball snack) counter.

Drinking

Locals claim that Miyazaki has some 3500 bars, which may be a bit of an exaggeration… or perhaps not.

Pari No Okashiyasan (☎ 29-3507; Hiroshima 1-68; 10am-8pm) French-style pastries, sweets, and coffee near the station.

Suntory Shot Bar (☎ 0985-25-4665; Chūōdōri 1-13-1F; daily) Good for a quiet, inexpensive beer, and the owner speaks some English – ask him for his 'special.'

Admiral (☎ 35-8451; Chūōdōri 8-13; cover ¥800, drinks from ¥800) Not cheap, but makes an impression: you'll notice a wall of water covering the door which stops as you approach. Inside, a wall-to-wall fishtank makes for interesting ambience.

In summer, Bon Belta department store has a rooftop **beer garden**.

Entertainment

Miyazaki certainly has a nightlife, and the establishments range from the quiet and relaxing to the wild and crazy.

Cafe Lanai (☎ 22-5727; 2-1-1 Shimizu; ☽ 5pm-10pm) Hawaiian surf-and-aloha groove that feels a lot like the Big Island. Time slows down as you enter: surfing videos play on TV, the bartenders are mellow, and folks around you take the time to chat. There's a food menu in addition to the full bar, and the place is just the right size: big enough to find a quiet corner, small enough that it still feels like home. If you're a *matcha* (powdered green tea) fan ask for Madoka's 'Jamais Vu': a sweet, green luxury that'll make you wish you could stay longer.

Octopus (☎ 27-7157; Tachibana-dōri Nishi 3-10-24; ☽ 10.30am-10pm; from ¥600) A nice coffee and lunch place with views of the square outside, famous for its omrice (omelette stuffed with ketchup-fried rice).

Beat Clap (☎ 29-7878; 10-4 Uenochō; cover ¥1000-3500) A barnlike dance club that fills to the rafters on a Saturday night. Occasionally hosts gay/straight nights as well as other themed events.

Shopping

The **Miyazaki Prefectural Products Promotion Exhibition Hall** (☎ 22-7389; 1-6 Miyatachō; ☽ 9.30am-7pm Tue-Fri, 10am-6.30pm Sat & Sun) sells hand-woven textiles, *haniwa* figures and Igo (go) chess boards.

Getting There & Away

AIR

Miyazaki is connected by air with Tokyo (¥27,900), Osaka (¥17,600) and Okinawa (¥22,500), as well as other cities around Kyūshū.

BOAT

There are ferry services linking Miyazaki with Osaka (2nd class ¥8380, 12½ hours) and Kawasaki (¥12,640, 21 hours). For reservations contact **Marine Express** (in Kyūshū ☎ 0982-55-9090, in Osaka ☎ 06-6616-4661).

BUS

Most long-distance buses originate at the Miyakō City bus terminal south of the river,

near JR Minami-Miyazaki Station, including to Kagoshima (¥4900, 2¾ hours), Ebinokōgen in Kirishima-Yaku National Park (¥2620, 2¼ hours), Kumamoto (¥4500, 3¼ hours) and Fukuoka/Hakata (¥6000, four hours).

Many buses run along Tachibana-dōri, but if you don't read Japanese you may be better off heading down to the southern bus station. There is another regional bus station opposite Miyazaki Station.

TRAIN

The JR Nippō line runs down to Kagoshima (*tokkyū*, ¥4690, two hours) and up to Beppu (*tokkyū*, ¥6270, three hours). The JR Nichinan line runs slowly along the coast south to Aoshima (¥360, 30 minutes) and Obi (¥910, 65 minutes).

Getting Around

Miyazaki's airport is connected to the city centre by bus (¥400, 30 minutes) or train (¥340, 10 minutes) from JR Miyazaki Station. Although most bus services start and finish at the Miyakō City bus terminal, many run along Tachibana-dōri in the centre. Only a few depart from outside Miyazaki Station. There are several car rental companies around Miyazaki Station and at the airport.

AROUND MIYAZAKI 宮崎周辺
Saitobaru 西都原
☎ 0983

If the *haniwa* pottery figures in Miyazaki piqued your interest in the region's archaeology, then you should head north 27km to the **Saitobaru Burial Mounds Park**, where several square kilometres of fields and forest are dotted with over 300 *kofun* (burial mounds). The mounds, dating from 300 to 600 AD, range from insignificant little bumps to hillocks large enough to appear as natural creations.

The interesting small **Saitobaru Archaeological Museum** (西都原考古博物館; ☎ 41-0041; http://saito-muse.pref.miyazaki.jp/home.html; admission free; ☽ 10am-6pm Tue-Sun) has displays of archaeological finds, including ancient swords, armour, jewellery, *haniwa* pottery figures, and much more.

The park area is always open. Buses run frequently to Saitobaru from along Tachibana-dōri in Miyazaki (left) and also from Miyakō City bus terminal (¥1040, one hour). You'll need your own transport if you

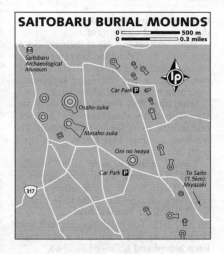

SAITOBARU BURIAL MOUNDS

want to explore the mound-dotted countryside, or you should plan to walk a lot.

Saitobaru is just outside the town of Saito, where the unique **Usudaiko** dance festival, with drummers wearing odd pole-like headgear, takes place in early September. The equally interesting **Shiromi Kagura** performances are on 14 and 15 December, part of a harvest festival which lasts from 12 to 16 December.

TAKACHIHO 高千穂
☎ 0982 / pop 15,840

The mountain resort town of Takachiho is about midway between Nobeoka on the coast and Aso-san in the centre of Kyūshū. There's a **tourist information counter** (☎ 72-4680; ⏰ 8.30am-5pm) by the tiny train station. Ask for the English-language *Guide to Takachiho*, also available from the stationmaster's office up the steps.

Sights

TAKACHIHO-KYŌ 高千穂峡
Takachiho's beautiful gorge, with its waterfalls, overhanging rocks and sheer walls, is the town's major attraction. There's a 1km-long walk alongside it, or you can view it from below in a **rowboat** (☎ 72-2457; per 30min ¥1500; ⏰ 8.30am-4.30pm Sep-Jun, 7.30am-5.30pm Jul-Aug). The gorge is about 2km from the centre. You can walk it in just over half an hour.

TAKACHIHO-JINJA 高千穂神社
Takachiho-jinja, close to the train and bus stations, is set in a grove of cryptomeria pines. From late November to February the local *iwato kagura* **dances** (☎ 73-1213; tickets ¥500) are performed for an hour each evening from 8pm (see below for details).

AMANO IWATO-JINJA 天岩戸神社
The Iwato-gawa splits **Amano Iwato-jinja** (☎ 74-8239) into two parts. The main shrine, Nishi Hongū, is on the west bank of the river while on the east bank is Higashi Hongū, at the actual cave where the sun goddess hid and was lured out by the first performance of the *iwato kagura* dance.

A beautiful short walk from the Amano Iwato-jinja beside a picture-postcard stream takes you to the **Amano Yasugawara** cave. Here, it is said, the gods conferred on how they could persuade the sun goddess to leave her hiding place and thus bring light back to the world. The shrine is 8km from Takachiho, closer to Amano Iwato-jinja Station. Buses from Miyakō bus centre bus station depart hourly (¥370).

Festivals & Events

Important *iwato kagura* festivals are held on or around 2 and 3 May, 21 to 23 September

---

TAKACHIHO LEGENDS

Ninigi-no-mikoto, a descendant of the sun goddess Amaterasu, is said to have made land fall in Japan on top of the legendary mountain Takachiho-yama in southern Kyūshū. Or at least that's what's said in most of Japan; in Takachiho the residents insist that it was in their hamlet that the sun goddess' grandson arrived.

Residents also lay claim to a few other important mythological events or tales, including Amano-Iwato, or the boulder door of heaven. Here Amaterasu hid and night fell across the world. To lure her out, another goddess performed a dance so comically lewd that the sun goddess was soon forced to emerge from hiding to find out what the merriment was about. That dance, the *iwato kagura*, is still performed in Takachiho today, characterised by masks with unusually long...noses.

TAKACHIHO

0 ——— 1 km
0 ——— 0.5 miles

To Takamori (32km);
Aso-san (43km)

Shōzanji-yama (796m)

Takachiho

To Amano
Iwato-jinja (3km);
Nishi Hongū (3km);
Amano Yasugawara (3.5km)

Takachiho-tetsudō Line

To Kunimi-ga-oka Lookout (2km)

Takachiho

Amano-
Iwato

To Kumamoto (40km)

Iwato-gawa

To Amano Iwato-
Higashi Hongū (3.5km)

Gokase-gawa

Takachiho-kyō

To Nobeoka (47km)

and 3 November at the Amano Iwato-jinja (p671). There are also all-night performances in farmhouses from the end of November to early February and a visit can be arranged by inquiring at the shrine.

Sleeping & Eating

Takachiho has three dozen hotels, ryokan, *minshuku* and pensions. Every place in town can be booked out during peak holiday periods.

Takachiho Youth Hostel (☎ /fax 72-3021; dm ¥2700) About 2km from the centre, near Amano-Iwato Station.

Kokumin Shukusha Takachiho-sō (☎ 72-3255; s from ¥12,000) This option is a five-minute walk from Takachiho-jinja. The price includes two meals.

Folkcraft Ryokan Kaminoya (☎ 72-2111; fax 72-5040; r with 2 meals from ¥10,000) Just downhill from the bus station, right in the centre of Takachiho.

Yamatoya Ryokan (☎ 72-2243; fax 72-6868; r per person with 2 meals from ¥8000) This place is easy

to recognise by the masked *iwato kagura* dancer painted on the front.

Many visitors just eat at their ryokan or *minshuku*, but Takachiho has plenty of restaurants, including a preponderance of *yakitori-ya* where you can order *kappo-zake*, local sake heated in bamboo stalks.

Young Echo (☎ 72-4948; dishes from ¥500; ⏲ 8am-11pm) This coffee shop functions like a second waiting room for the train station. The outdoor summer **beer garden** stays open until 2am.

Several *sōmen-nagashi* (thin noodles served in running water, then dipped in a soy-based broth) places offer a light, refreshing change. Try **Chiho no Ie** (千穂の家; ☎ 72-2155) or **Onoroko Chaya** (おのころ茶屋; ☎ 72-3931). You catch noodles with your chopsticks as they float by in a pipe made from halved and hollowed bamboo.

Getting There & Around

The private Takachiho-tetsudō train line runs inland from Nobeoka on the coast (¥1470, 1¼ hours).

From Miyakō bus centre, a 10-minute walk downhill from the train station, there are buses to Takamori (¥1280, 70 minutes, three daily), near Aso-san, and Kumamoto (¥2300, 2¾ hours).

Although you can walk to the gorge and Takachiho-jinja, the other sites are some distance from town and public transport is a problem. Regular tours leave from the bus station: the 'A Course' (¥1660) covers everything, while the 'B Course' (¥1150) misses Amano Iwato-jinja.

ŌITA-KEN 大分県

Ōita-ken offers Japanese *onsen* mania, Beppu and the town of Yufuin. The region also bears some traces of Japan's earliest civilisations, particularly on the Kunisaki Peninsula.

USUKI 臼杵
☎ 0972

About 5km from Usuki is a collection of some superb 10th- to 13th-century **Buddha images** (臼杵石仏; ☎ 65-3300; admission ¥530; ⏲ 8.30am-4.30pm). More than 60 images lie in a series of niches in a ravine. Some are complete statues, whereas others have only the heads remaining, but many are in won-

KYŪSHŪ

derful condition. The **Dainichi Buddha head** is the most impressive and important. Of the various other stone Buddha images at sites around Ōita-ken, the Usuki images are the most numerous and most interesting. Some of the faces are so well preserved that they almost seem alive. Serene and spectacular, a must-see well worth making a special detour for.

Usuki also has some interesting temples and well-preserved traditional houses. On the last Saturday in August, the town hosts a **fire festival**, and there are other festivities throughout the year. Ask for details at the **tourist information office** (☎ 64-7130; ☯ 8.30am-5pm). Local restaurants boast the best *fugu* in Japan; expect to pay ¥3000 to ¥5000 for dinner. Internet users can log on for free at **Sala de Usuki** (サーラデ臼杵; ☎ 64-7271), the town civic/rec centre.

The town of Usuki is about 40km southeast of Beppu. Take the JR Nippō line to Usuki Station (*futsū*, ¥1430, 85 minutes), from where it's a short bus ride to the ravine site. Bikes can be rented for free from the station (☎ 63-8955) or the town centre (☎ 64-7130), and offer a nice alternative for those who don't want to walk the few kilometres from Kami-Usuki Station.

BEPPU 別府
☎ 0977 / pop 126,500

Understanding the spa town of Beppu is in some ways to understand Japan. Quaint yet crowded, traditional and modern, Beppu remains what it always has been: a place to which people escape. For some that's hedonistic fun in the pleasure district, for others it's relaxing soaks in the hundreds of baths. Still others prefer to enjoy Beppu from the vantage point of a rooftop restaurant at a snazzy hotel. Beppu is a town that revolves around tourism and almost anything you want can be found here.

Orientation & Information

Beppu is a sprawling town and the hot-spring areas are spread out, often some distance from the town centre. The adjacent town of Ōita is virtually contiguous with Beppu, although it lacks any notable attractions. The tiny but beautiful *onsen* village Myōban (p676) is a quieter place to soak if you're so inclined.

Note: As this book went to print the Beppu Station area was undergoing a makeover and some locations may have changed. However, the **Foreign Tourist Information Office** (Map p678; ☎ 23-1119; 12-13 Ekimaemachi; ☯ 9am-5pm) has helpful English-speaking personnel who are armed with an arsenal of English-language information on Beppu and its environs. They can happily recommend accommodations, itineraries and more, and if you ask they're happy to suggest out-of-the-way places, such as real Japanese-style inns which let you bring your own foods to steam above the *onsen* vents.

Ōita International Centre (☎ 097-538-5161; 3-1-7 Nakajimanishi; ☯ 9am-5pm Mon-Fri, 9am-12.30pm Sat) is a local resource for foreigners in Ōita city. To get there walk straight out from JR Ōita Station for about 20 minutes to the Shinkawa intersection.

Back in Beppu, the Kitahama post office (Map p678) near the Cosmopia shopping centre has an ATM accepting international cards. The Ōita Bank next door handles foreign exchange services.

Sights & Activities
HOT SPRINGS

Beppu has two types of hot springs, and they pump out more than 100 million litres of hot water every day. *Jigoku* (hells) are hot springs for looking at. *Onsen* are hot springs for bathing. If you go to a high spot such as Myōban (p676) where you can look down over Beppu, you'll see the white plumes of hundreds of steam vents. Luckily it's all just water vapour, not pollution.

The Hells

Beppu's most hyped attraction is the 'hells' or *jigoku*, a collection of **hot springs** (Map p674; each hell ¥400; ☯ 8am-5pm) where the water bubbles forth from underground, often with unusual results. You can purchase a ¥2000 coupon which covers all except one (Bōzu Jigoku; p675). Unlike Unzen (p638), where you see the geothermal wonders which are natural, raw, and unadorned, these have been turned into mini-amusement parks, each with a different theme. If you're pressed for time and unsure if this is your cup of, er, *onsen* water, peek at the postcard pack in the station, which has good pictures and you'll know instantly whether these are worth your time.

The hells are in two groups – seven at Kannawa, over 4km northwest of Beppu

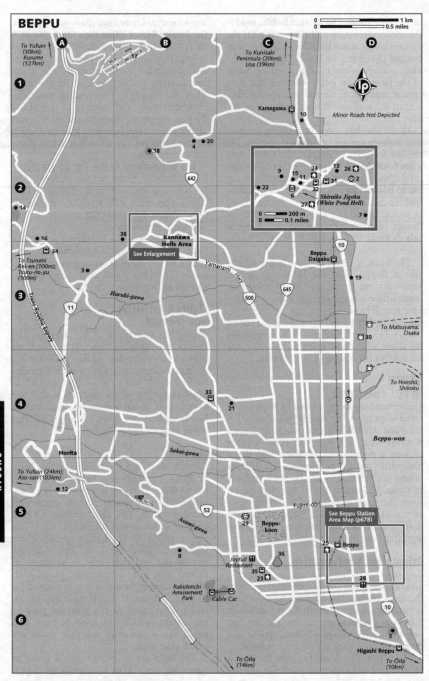

BEPPU

0 ——— 1 km
0 ——— 0.5 miles

To Yufuin (30km); Kurume (127km)

To Kunisaki Peninsula (20km); Usa (39km)

Minor Roads Not Depicted

Kamegawa

Kannawa Hells Area
See Enlargement

Shiraike Jigoku (White Pond Hell)

0 ——— 200 m
0 ——— 0.1 miles

To Tsurumi Rei-en (100m); Tsuru-no-yu (100m)

Yamanami Hwy

Haruki-gawa

Beppu Daigaku

To Matsuyama; Osaka

To Honshū; Shikoku

Trans-Kyūshū Expwy

Horita

To Yufuin (24km); Aso-san (103km)

Sakai-gawa

Beppu-wan

Fujimi-dōri

See Beppu Station Area Map (p678)

Beppu

Asami-gawa

Beppu-kōen

Joyfull Restaurant

Rakutenchi Amusement Park

Cable Car

To Ōita (14km)

Higashi Beppu

To Ōita (10km)

KYŪSHŪ

Station, and two more several kilometres away. In the Kannawa group, **Umi Jigoku** (Sea Hell), with its large expanse of steaming artificially blue water, and **Shiraike Jigoku** (White Pond Hell) may be worth a look. **Kinryū Jigoku** (Golden Dragon Hell) and **Kamado Jigoku** (Oven Hell) have dragon and demon figures overlooking the pond. Skip the **Oni-yama Jigoku** (Devil's Mountain Hell), where crocodiles are kept in miserably cramped concrete pens, and **Yama Jigoku** (Mountain Hell), where a variety of animals are kept under shamefully bad conditions.

The smaller pair has **Chi-no-ike Jigoku** (Blood Pool Hell), with its photogenically red water, and **Tatsumaki Jigoku** (Waterspout Hell), where a geyser performs regularly. The final hell, and the one not included in the group's admission ticket, is **Bōzu Jigoku** (Monk's Hell). It has a collection of hiccupping and belching hot-mud pools up the long hill from the main group of hells.

From the bus stop at JR Beppu Station, bus Nos 16 and 17 go to the main group of hells at Kannawa. There are half a dozen buses per hour but the round trip costs virtually the same as an unlimited travel day pass. The No 26 bus continues to the smaller Chi-no-ike/Tatsumaki pair and returns to the station in a loop. Bus Nos 41 and 43 go directly to Bōzu Jigoku.

Jigoku tour buses regularly depart from the JR Beppu Station (¥4500, including admission to all hells).

Onsen

The Hells, though mildly interesting, shouldn't distract you from the *real* hot springs. Scattered around the town are eight *onsen* areas. *Onsen* enthusiasts spend their time in Beppu moving from one bath to another – experts consider at least three baths a day *de rigeur*, and many Beppu visitors take up to six. Costs range from ¥60 to ¥600, though many (and two of the best) are free. Bring your own soap, washcloth, and towel, as many places don't rent them. There's an *onsen* festival during the first weekend in April. Some of the baths alternate daily between male and female so that each gender can appreciate each side.

Near JR Beppu Station, **Takegawara Onsen** (Map p678; ☎ 23-1585; 16-23 Motomachi; admission ¥100, sand bath ¥780; ◷ 6.30am-10.30pm, sand bath 8am-9.30pm) dates from the Meiji era. Its bath is very simple and *very* hot; simply scoop out water with a bucket, pour it over yourself, and jump in. It also has a relaxing sand bath where no *yukata* is necessary. You lie down in a shallow trench and are buried up to your neck in heated sand. There's a good English-language pamphlet.

North of the town, in the **Kannawa onsen area**, near the major group of hells, is the quaint **Mushi-yu steam bath** (Map p674; ☎ 67-3880; 1 Furomoto, Kannawa; admission ¥210; ◷ 6.30am-8pm). **Hyōtan Onsen** (Map p674; ☎ 66-0527; 159-2 Kannawa; admission ¥700; ◷ 8am-9pm) has a *rotemburo* and also offers sand baths (*yukata* rental ¥200). Many ryokan and *minshuku* also have public baths.

Recently rebuilt **Shibaseki onsen communal baths** (☎ 67-4100; 4 Noda; admission ¥210; ◷ 7am-8pm, closed 2nd Wed of each month) are near the smaller pair of hells. In addition to the *onsen's* communal baths, you can rent a private *kazoku-buro* (private family bath/couples bath) for ¥1310 (per hour). Also north of JR Beppu Station is the **Kamegawa onsen area**. The **Shōnin-ga-hama sand bath** (☎ 66-5737; admission ¥780; ⏰ 8.30am-6pm, Apr-Oct, 9am-5pm Nov-Mar) is 2km south of the Kamegawa *onsen* area, on the beach.

In the hills northwest of the town centre is the **Myōban onsen area** (p674). Quieter and quite hilly, you will find numerous baths as well as odd thatched-roof huts which are an Edo-era replica of the huts in which bath-salts were made. You can go inside (the salts look a bit like yellow-brown mould), wander the 'hell' outside, and even purchase salts to bring for a bath at home.

Nearby, **Onsen Hoyōland** (Map p674; ☎ 66-2221; 5-1 Myōban; admission ¥1050; ⏰ 9am-8pm) has wonderful giant mud baths, as well as mixed and open-air bathing. In the southeastern part of town, almost on the road to Ōita, is the **Hamawaki onsen area** (Map p674).

HIDDEN BATHS
Tsuru-no-yu & Hebi-no-yu
鶴の湯　蛇の湯
Beppu has a number of wonderful baths, tucked away out of the public eye. Locals built and maintain Tsuru-no-yu, a lovely free *ro-temburo* up on the edge of Ogi-yama. During July and August, a natural stream emerges to form the milky blue bath. Take a bus to Tsu-rumi Rei-en bus stop (40 minutes northwest from JR Beppu Station). Turn left by the small flower shop and hike uphill till you come to the cemetery. Walk up the small road that hugs the right side of the graveyard until the road ends. Dive into the bushes to your left, and there's the bath. Higher in the mountain greenery is another free *rotemburo*, the **Hebi-no-yu** (Snake Bath). It's impossible to describe the trail up from Tsuru-no-yu; ask another bather. The information desk ladies are also happy to make you a hand-drawn map.

Mugen-no-Sato 夢幻の里
A collection of privately available small *ro-temburo* – ideal for a romantic, secluded dip. Ask for a **kazoku-buro** (Map p674; ☎ 22-2826; 6 Hotta; admission ¥600; ⏰ 9am-9pm). Take a bus up past Suginoi Palace Hotel to Horita. Mugen-no-sato is five minutes' walk west.

Ichinoide Kaikan いちのいで会館
The owner of **Ichinoide Kaikan** (Map p674; ☎ 21-4728; 14-2 Ueharamachi) is a commercial caterer,

but he's also an *onsen* fanatic, so much so that he built three pool-sized *rotemburo* in his back yard. The view, overlooking Beppu and the bay, is the city's finest. Bathing is free when you order a set menu (*teishoku*; ¥1000), and the chefs prepare it while you swim. To get there, take a bus to Yakyū-jō-mae, walk 100m further along the main road until you reach the Joyfull 24-hour restaurant. Take the narrow road on the right of the restaurant and walk up, and up…and up, for about 30 minutes. A taxi (from the centre of town about ¥1000) might be a good investment.

OTHER SIGHTS
Given all that sybaritic bathing, **Hihōkan Sex Museum** (Map p674; ☎ 66-8790; 338-3 Shibuyu, Kan-nawa; admission ¥1000; ⏰ 9am-10pm) fits right in. Among the Kannawa hells, it hosts a bizarre collection of sex-related items ranging all the way from fine erotic *ukiyo-e* (wood-block prints) to zany porno and toys. What it lacks in focus it makes up for in breadth: genetalia-shaped sake cups, positions mod-els, and *etchi* (ribald) *ukiyo-e* are just a start. You'll proceed through a collection of rep-lica animal members, life-sized dioramas, and even an 'improve-your-technique' video room, making this one of the most surreal museums in Japan. Erotic art on display ranges from Papua New Guinean fertility figures to Tibetan Tantric figures. There's an unfortunate paucity of postcards in the gift store, but plenty of assorted toys, tools, games, and gimmicks with which to disturb the customs officials on the way home.

Near Takegawara Onsen, the **Hirano Li-brary** (Map p678; ☎ 23-4748; 11-7 Motomachi; admis-sion free; ⏰ Mon-Sun) is a private institution with historical exhibits and photographs of the Beppu area.

The hands-on **Traditional Bamboo Crafts Cen-tre** (Map p674; ☎ 23-1072; 8-3 Higashi-sōen) displays masterpieces dating from the Edo period, as well as incredible examples of what can be made with this versatile material. Seasonal hands-on demos allow you to try your own hand at making something if you're so in-clined. From Beppu Station, take Kamenoi bus No 1, 22 or 25 to Minami-baru.

The Kyoto-based **Ritsumeikan AsiaPacific University** (Map p674; ☎ 78-1114; 1-1 Jūmonjihara) has opened its landmark college in Beppu, with about half its undergraduates drawn from other parts of Asia – a unique situation in Japan. The campus overlooks the city in Jumonji-baru, a 35-minute bus trip from Beppu Station.

Sleeping

Ekimae Kōtō Onsen (Map p678; ☎ 21-0541; 13-14 Ekimae-machi; shared/private tatami r per person from ¥1500/2500) Beppu's most basic accommodation is found at a bathhouse close to the station. Shared rooms are male-only.

Beppu Youth Hostel (Map p674; ☎ 23-4116; 20-28 Nakajima; dm ¥3000) Only a 15-minute walk from JR Beppu Station, this place has a wonderful hot-springs bath and a bar upstairs, where folks tend to congregate to sip Kabosu-shōchū (the hostel owner's special) and trade *onsen* tips.

Minshuku Kokage (Map p678; ☎ 23-1753; www .tiki.ne.jp/~kokage; 8-9 Ekimae-machi; s/d/tr with bath ¥4000/7000/10,500) A member of the Japanese Inn group, just a few minutes' walk from Beppu station. There's a hot-spring bath.

Business Hotel Star (Map p678; ☎ 25-1188; 10-29 Tanoyu; s/d ¥4000/7000) Behind the train station, this has very basic rooms.

Business Hotel Kagetsu (Map p678; ☎ 24-2355; 7-22 Tanoyu; r per person ¥3500) An older *minshuku*, around the corner from the Hotel Star.

Nogami Honkan (Map p678; ☎ 22-1334; 1-12-1 Kita-hama; www008.upp.so-net.ne.jp/yuke-c/english.html; r per person with/without 2 meals ¥8000/4500; 🖳) Located near Takegawara *onsen*, this place has a *ro-temburo*. English is spoken and there's free Internet access and lobby wireless LAN.

Kamenoi Hotel (Map p678; ☎ 22-3301; www.kame noi.com; 5-17 Chūōmachi; s/d/tw from ¥5800/8800/9800) Far more comfortable than the average business hotel; has good-value restaurants, a *rotemburo* and sauna.

Takenoi Hotel (Map p678; ☎ 23-3261; fax 25-3800; 3-10-26 Kitahama; d from ¥12,500) This is a lavish, traditional-looking hotel down near Beppu Tower and the beach.

A number of *minshuku* and ryokan are around Kannawa hells area hot springs.

Rakuraku-en Ryokan (Map p674; ☎ 67-2682; 4 Miyuki; r per person with 2 meals ¥7500) Has a mixed and a women-only *rotemburo*.

Tabi no Yado Sakae-ya (Map p674; ☎ 66-6234; 2 Ide; r per person with 2 meals ¥6500) Downhill from the *jigoku*. A popular traditional *minshuku* uses the heat from the local hot spring to prepare meals.

Shiragiku Hotel (白菊ホテル; ☎ 21-2111; www.shiragiku.co.jp in Japanese; Kamitanoyu 16-36; s/d

¥17,800/35,600; Ⓟ ⚒ 🖳 ⌧) As nice as it gets, brand new, with stunning *rotemburo* which rotate daily between male and female so both genders can appreciate the different views. The lounge on the top floor shows the city lights. The price includes two meals.

Eating

Beppu is renowned for its freshwater fish, for its *fugu* (pufferfish) and for the wild vegetables grown in the mountains further inland. Also look out for *dango-jiru*, a miso soup with vegetables and dumplings. The area around Minshuku Kokage (left) also has some cheap *yakitori* restaurants.

Tomonaga Panya (友永パン屋; ☎ 23-0969; Chi-omachi 2-29; ⏰ 8.30am-5.30pm Mon-Sat) Tomonaga's hot-from-the-oven fresh rolls, breads, and pastries are a treat worth waking up early for. In business since 1917, this shop has interesting old photos on its walls and feels like yesteryear. Get there early and prepare to wait, as it closes as soon as the bread is gone…and it goes quickly. For a real treat take the bread down to the water and watch the boats as you breakfast, maybe getting a hot coffee along the way.

Fugu Matsu (Map p678; ☎ 21-1717; Kitahama 3-6-14; ⏰ 11am-9pm) This is the place to try *fugu* in style, if you're game. Expect to pay from ¥3000.

Jūtoku-ya (Map p678; ☎ 22-0521; 1932-1 Ekimae) This *izakaya* close to the station has an enormous range of dishes on its illustrated menu, all at reasonable prices.

Ureshi-ya (☎ 22-0767; 7-12 Ekimaemachi; ⏰ 5.30pm-2am Sat-Thu) A very popular *shokudō* (budget eatery) with *donburi* (dishes served over rice) and noodles for around ¥700. Fresh vegetable and meat dishes are displayed in the window.

Kuishinbō (☎ 2-1-0788; Kitahama-dōri 1-1-12; dishes from ¥600; ⏰ 5pm-midnight) A cheerful *izakaya* serving unusual tofu and *daikon* steaks, and *chawan-mushi* (savoury custard).

Drinking

Speakeasy (Map p678; ☎ 21-8116; Motomachi 12-1; ⏰ 8.30pm-3am Wed-Mon) A friendly shot bar down a back alley near Takegawara Onsen, where Beppu's cool crowd hang out. Beers and stronger stuff cost from ¥500.

Jin Robata & Beer Pub (Map p678; ☎ 21-1768; 1-15-7 Kitahama; ⏰ 5pm-11.30pm) A flashing neon fish sign directs you to this pub. Inside,

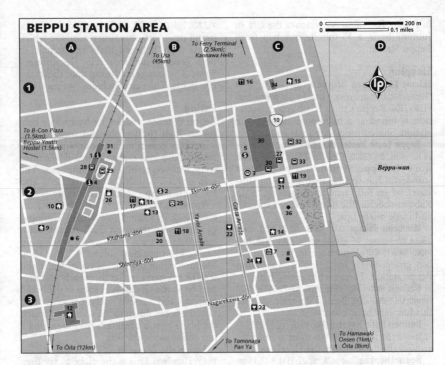

BEPPU STATION AREA

the familiar low glow of incandescent lights and rows of liquor bottles will make you feel like you've stepped back to a bar at home. Expect mostly upscale folks here early on, salarymen and office ladies, but it mixes up as the night goes on.

Beppu hides some one-of-a-kind coffee shops in the central shopping arcades.

Natsume Kissa (Map p678; ☎ 21-0988; Kitahama 1-4-23; ☷ 9.30am-9pm Thu-Tue) Makes its own mellow *onsen kōhī* (¥500), coffee made with hot-springs water.

Shingai Coffee Shop (Map p678; ☎ 24-1656; 10-2 Kusumachi) This coffee hsop displays antique maps and photographs.

Entertainment
West of the station toward Suginoi Palace the enormous **B-Con Plaza** (Map p674; ☎ 26-7111; 12-1 Yamanotechō), a convention centre marked by the 125m **Global Tower**, is the place for concerts and mega-events.

Getting There & Away
There are flights to Ōita airport from Tokyo (¥27,000), Osaka (¥16,000), Okinawa

(¥24,500) and cities around Kyūshū. It's even possible to fly direct to Seoul.

Beppu to Aso-san takes about three hours by bus and costs around ¥4000 (note the exact routing affects the price). It's another hour from Aso-san to Kumamoto.

The JR Nippō line runs from Hakata (Fukuoka) to Beppu (*tokkyū*, ¥5250, 2¼ hours) via Kitakyūshū, continuing down the coast to Miyazaki (¥6270, 3¾ hours). The JR Hōhi line connects Beppu with Kumamoto (¥5330, three hours) via Aso-san (¥3940, 1½ hours).

The **Kansai Kisen ferry service** (☎ 22-1311) does a daily run between Beppu and Osaka (¥7400, 13½ hours), stopping en route at Matsuyama (4½ hours) and Kōbe (10 hours). Late evening boats to western Honshū pass through the Inland Sea during daylight hours the next morning. For the port, take Bus No 19 from Beppu Station's west exit.

Getting Around
TO/FROM THE AIRPORT
Hovercraft (☎ 097-558-7180, 0120-81-4080) run from JR Ōita Station to Ōita airport (¥2750,

INFORMATION
Foreign Tourist Information Office
   外国人旅行者観光案内所......................**1** A2
Iyo Bank 伊予銀行..................................**2** B2
Kitahama Post Office
   別内浜郵便局..**3** C2
Tourist Information Counter
   観光案内所...**4** A2
Ōita Bank 大分銀行.................................**5** C2

SIGHTS & ACTIVITIES
Daiei ダイエー...**6** A3
Hirano Library...**7** C3
Takegawara Onsen 竹瓦温泉................**8** C3

SLEEPING
Business Hotel Kagetsu
   ビジネスホテル花月.............................**9** A2
Business Hotel Star................................**10** A2
Ekimae Kōtō Onsen
   駅前高等温泉...................................**11** B2
Kamenoi Hotel 亀の井ホテル.............**12** A3

Minshuku Kokage 民宿こかげ...........**13** B2
Nogami Honkan 野上本館.....................**14** C2
Takenoi Hotel 竹の井ホテル..............**15** C1

EATING
Fugu Matsu...**16** C1
Jūtoku-ya 十徳や...................................**17** B2
Kuishinbō くいしん坊..........................**18** B2
Royal Host...**19** C2
Ureshi-ya うれしや...............................**20** B2

DRINKING
Jin Robata & Beer Pub..........................**21** C2
Natsume Kissa なつめ喫茶..................**22** C2
Shingai Coffee Shop..............................**23** C3
Speakeasy...**24** C3

ENTERTAINMENT
Bluebird Cinema
   ブルーバードシネマ.........................**25** B2

SHOPPING
Family Mart...**26** A2

Tokiwa Department Store...................(see 35)

TRANSPORT
Airport Bus Stop 空港バス停...............**27** C2
Beppu..**28** A2
Beppu Station Bus Stop
   別府駅バス停....................................**29** A2
Bus Stop for Kannawa Onsen
   鉄輪温泉行きバス停.........................**30** C2
Car Rental Office
   駅レンタカー...................................**31** A2
Kamenoi Bus Station (Sightseeing Buses)
   亀の井バスセンター.........................**32** C2
Kitahama Bus Station (Sightseeing Buses
   & Buses to Fukuoka)
   北浜バ センター...............................**33** C2

OTHER
Beppu Tower 別府タワー.....................**34** C1
Cosmopia Shopping Centre
   コスモピア..**35** C2
JTB..**36** C2

25 minutes), located around the bay from Beppu on the Kunisaki Peninsula.

From Beppu, airport buses from Beppu stop outside the Cosmopia shopping centre (¥1450, 45 minutes, twice hourly) and sometimes also JR Beppu Station.

BUS
Of the local bus companies, **Kamenoi** (☎ 23-5170) is the largest. Most buses are numbered. An unlimited 'My Beppu Free' travel pass for Kamenoi buses comes in two varieties: the 'mini pass' (¥900), which covers all the local attractions, including the hells, and the 'wide pass' (¥1600/2400 for one/two days), which goes further afield to Yufuin. Passes are available from near the Foreign Tourist Information Office (p673) and at various lodgings around town. Buses Nos 5, 9 and 41 take you to Myoban (20 to 30 minutes).

YUFUIN 湯布院
☎ 0977 / pop 11,407
About 25km inland from Beppu (p673), beautiful and quietly rustic Yufuin has suffered in the last few years from tourist development. It's still very much worth a stop en route to Aso, but avoid weekends and holidays.

The **tourist information office** (☎ 84-2446; ⏱ 9am-7pm Sep-Jul, 9am-8pm Aug) inside the train station has information in English, including an excellent detailed map showing galleries, museums and *onsen*. Post office ATMs are the main way to get cash, and there is one next to the station.

As in Beppu, making a pilgrimage from one *onsen* to another is a popular activity in Yufuin. **Shitan-yu** (下ん湯; admission ¥200; ⏱ 10am-9pm) is a thatched bathhouse on the

northern shore of Kirin-ko, a lake fed by hot springs, so it's warm(ish) all year round. Yufuin is noted for its high-quality handicrafts. The town also has a few interesting temples and shrines; tourist information (☎ 0977-85-4464) is available.

The double-peaked **Yufu-dake** (1584m) volcano overlooks Yufuin and takes about one hour to climb. A few buses between Beppu and Yufuin stop at the trailhead, Yufudake-tozan-guchi.

Sleeping & Eating
Yufuin has many *minshuku*, ryokan and pensions; most are high class, with rates to match.

Yufuin Youth Hostel (湯布院ユースホステル; ☎ 84-3734; dm ¥3100) This is almost 2.5km northeast of the train station. A peaceful hostel set on a forested hillside with breathtaking views, but buses to the nearby Kuso-no-mori stop are infrequent.

Pension Yufuin (ペンション湯布院; ☎ 85-3311; B&B r from ¥7000) A popular 'rural Western' guesthouse fantasy with angel-pattern wallpaper and other countryside decorations, the pension is on the riverside. The owner is kind and helpful.

Makiba-no-yado (牧場の宿; ☎ 84-2138; fax 85-4045; r per person with 2 meals ¥8000-13,000) Offers accommodation in a series of thatched-roof huts around its large open-air *rotemburo*. The garden restaurant, filled with antiques, does bear and wild-boar *teishoku* (set meals; around ¥1800).

Getting There & Away
Local trains on the JR Kyūdai line connect Ōita with Yufuin (¥910, one hour). Only

KYŪSHŪ

limited express trains originate in Beppu. There is a special 'Yufuin no Mori' express train a few times daily (¥4400, 2¼ hours).

Buses depart JR Beppu Station (p678) for Yufuin every few hours (¥900). Continuing beyond Yufuin is not always easy. Buses go to Aso and Kumamoto but not year-round. There are also direct buses to Fukuoka/Hakata (¥2800).

YUFUIN TO ASO-SAN

The picturesque Yamanami Hwy extends 63km from the Aso-san region to near Yufuin; from there, the Ōita Expressway runs to Beppu on the east coast. There's a steep toll to drive along this scenic road, however, and tour buses operating between Kumamoto, Aso and Beppu also use this route. You'll cross a high plateau and pass numerous mountain peaks, including **Kujū-san** (1787m), the highest point in Kyūshū. Be sure to stop somewhere along the way for soft-serve ice cream: it's some of the best in Kyūshū.

Taketa 竹田

South of Yufuin, near the town of Taketa, are the **Oka-jō ruins**, which have a truly magnificent ridge-top position. The ruins are over 2km from JR Bungo-Taketa Station. Taketa has some interesting reminders of the Christian period, as well as some atmospheric temples and well-preserved traditional houses. **Hanamizuki Onsen** (花水月温泉; ☎ 0974-64-1126; admission ¥500; ☉ 9am-10pm) is a short walk from the station. It sells lemonade and liquor made from local citrus varieties, including *kabosu* and *yuzu*.

From Aso-san, it takes just under an hour by train on the JR Hōhi line to Bungo-Taketa (*futsū*, ¥820); from there it's just over an hour by train to Ōita (¥1250) – a little longer by bus.

KUNISAKI PENINSULA 国東半島

Immediately north of Beppu, Kunisaki-hantō bulges eastwards from the Kyūshū coast. The region is noted for its early Buddhist influence, including some rock-carved images related to more famous images at Usuki (p672).

Usa 宇佐

In the early post-WWII era, when 'Made in Japan' was no recommendation at all, it's said that companies would register

in USA so they could proclaim that their goods were 'Made in USA'! **Usa-jinja** (宇佐神社; ☎ 0978-37-0001; admission for treasure hall ¥300; ☉ Wed-Mon), the original of which dates back over 1000 years, is connected with the warrior-god Hachiman, a favourite deity of Japan's right wing. It's a 10-minute bus ride from Usa Station on the JR Nippō line from Beppu (*tokkyū*, ¥1880, 35 minutes).

Other Sights

The Kunisaki Peninsula is said to have more than half of all the stone Buddhas in Japan. The 11th-century **Fuki-ji** (富貴寺; ☎ 0978-26-3189; admission ¥200) in Bungotakada is the oldest wooden structure in Kyūshū and one of the oldest wooden temples in Japan. Ōita Kōtsū buses from Usa Station go to Fuki-ji (¥770, 30 minutes).

In the centre of the peninsula, near the summit of Futago-san (721m), is **Futago-ji** (両子寺; ☎ 0978-65-0253; admission ¥200), dedicated to Fudō-Myō-o, the ferocious, fire-enshrouded, sword-wielding deity who shows the inner power of Buddha – able to repel attacks even while appearing calm outside.

Taizō-ji (☎ 0978-26-2070; admission ¥200; 8am-5pm) is another interesting place: its set of stone stairs are famous for their unevenness, and legend says that they are so random and haphazard that the Oni (devils) must have created them in a single night.

Carved into a cliff behind Taizo-ji, 2km south of **Maki Ōdō** temple, there are two 8th-century Buddha images; a 6m-high figure of the Dainichi Buddha and an 8m figure of Fudō-Myō-o. Known as **Kumano Magaibutsu**, these are the largest Buddhist images of this type in Japan. Other stone statues, thought to be from the Heian period, can be seen in Maki Ōdō. Take the bus to Fuki-ji from Usa Station (¥1000, 70 minutes).

Getting Around

Beppu's Ōita airport is on the peninsula, about 40km from Beppu. Ōita Kōtsū buses from Usa Station do a loop around the main attractions of the peninsula; tour buses (reservations ☎ 097-534-7455) pick up and drop off at Beppu (¥5500), Ōita (¥4950), Ōita airport or Usa (pick up only). Prices include admission to all the temples...and even an *omiyage* (souvenir) to bring home. Otherwise try **Eki Rent-a-Car** (☎ 0977-24-4428) outside JR Beppu Station.

KYŪSHŪ

Okinawa & the Southwest Islands

沖縄・南西諸島

The Nansei-shotō, or Southwest Islands, is the string of islands that stretches more than 1000km from the southern tip of Kyūshū to about 110km from Taiwan. The northern half of that string is part of Kagoshima-ken, while the southern half makes up Okinawa-ken.

Japan is in the midst of an Okinawa boom, thanks in part to TV dramas such as *Chura-san*, set on Kohama-jima in the Yaeyama-shotō, which portray the islands as a relaxed, idyllic environment for a better way of life. Japanese retirees are flocking to the islands, where the cost of living is lower and their pensions go that little bit further. Younger Japanese, searching for a better lifestyle, see Okinawa as an attractive alternative. The poorest of Japan's prefectures for so long, things seem to be on the up for Okinawa.

The islands have a reputation as a tropical getaway, perfect for marine sports such as diving, snorkelling, sea kayaking, windsurfing and fishing. Many islands, such as Yakushima and Iriomote-jima, offer excellent hiking opportunities, and in the northern islands there are superb *onsen* (mineral hot springs) in natural settings in which to relax. While packaged tourism is evident, adventurous types can head off to tiny islets and discover unspoilt beauty and relative seclusion.

Despite centuries of mainland exploitation, horrific destruction during the closing months of WWII and, more recently, increasing numbers of tourists, many of the traditional ways of the islands live on – and are well worth finding.

HIGHLIGHTS

- Engage with millennia-old giant cedar trees at **Yakushima** (p684)
- Soak in hot rock pools beside the sea on tiny **Iō-jima** (p687)
- Paddle a sea kayak around the pristine waters of **Amami-Ōshima** (p688)
- Explore the wild and magnificent coastline of **Tokunoshima** (p690)
- Relax on Yurigahama, an island of sand that disappears at high tide, at **Yoron-tō** (p692)
- Enjoy the tropical hustle and bustle of Naha's **Kokusai-dōri** (p695)
- Laze in the warm waters of spectacular **Aharen Beach** (p706) on Tokashiki-jima
- Dive with the rays in **Manta Way** (p718), between Iriomote-jima and Kohama-jima
- Cycle around the 'living museum' that is **Taketomi-jima** (p717)
- Trek through the lush tropical jungle on **Iriomote-jima** (p715)

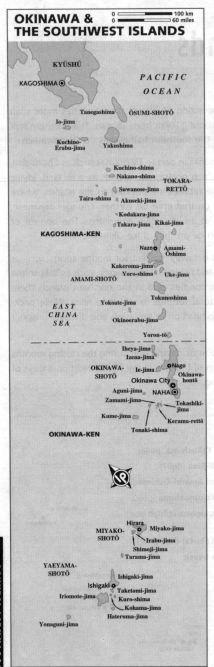

OKINAWA & THE SOUTHWEST ISLANDS

| 0 | 100 km |
| 0 | 60 miles |

KYŪSHŪ

KAGOSHIMA

PACIFIC
OCEAN

Tanegashima   ŌSUMI-SHOTŌ
Io-jima

Kuchino-
Erabu-jima   Yakushima

Kuchino-shima
Nakano-shima
Suwanose-jima   TOKARA-
RETTŌ
Taira-shima   Akuseki-jima

Kodakara-jima
Takara-jima   Kikai-jima

KAGOSHIMA-KEN

Naze   Amami-
Ōshima
Kakeroma-jima
Yoro-shima   Uke-jima

AMAMI-SHOTŌ

Yokoate-jima   Tokunoshima

EAST
CHINA
SEA   Okinoerabu-jima

Yoron-tō

Iheya-jima
Izena-jima
OKINAWA-   Nago
SHOTŌ   Ie-jima   Okinawa-
Okinawa City   hontō
Aguni-jima   NAHA
Zamami-jima   Tokashiki-
jima
Kume-jima   Kerama-rettō
Tonaki-shima

OKINAWA-KEN

Hirara
MIYAKO-   Miyako-jima
SHOTŌ   Irabu-jima
Shimoji-jima
Tarama-jima

YAEYAMA-
SHOTŌ   Ishigaki-jima
Ishigaki   Taketomi-jima
Iriomote-jima   Kuro-shima
Kohama-jima
Hateruma-jima
Yonaguni-jima

OKINAWAN ITINERARIES

For those with an adventurous spirit and a bit of time on their hands, it is possible to travel the length of the Southwest Islands by ferry between Kagoshima (on Kyūshū) and Ishigaki-jima. This is highly recommended. Ferries island-hop south from Kagoshima and north from Ishigaki-jima.

If you're tight on time, head straight to Naha on Okinawa-hontō from where you can briefly explore the main island before heading out to the *ritō* (outer islands). One popular route is to take the ferry south from Naha via Miyako-jima to the Yaeyama-shotō, where you can explore Ishigaki-jima, Iriomote-jima and other beautiful islands. From Ishigaki-jima there are regular flights back to Naha, and even to Tokyo, Osaka and Nagoya.

Alternatively, you could island-hop north from Naha, visiting Yoron-tō, Okinoerabu-jima, Tokunoshima and Amami-Ōshima on the way to Kagoshima.

Yakushima, Tanegashima and Iō-jima are accessed by ferry from, and back to, Kagoshima.

History

For centuries, the islands that we now know as Okinawa were ruled by *aji* (local chieftains) who battled for control of small fiefs and built *gusuku* (castles) of which so many ruins can be seen today. Control was splintered and the *aji* struggled among themselves for power and fame.

By the 14th century, the islands were split into three kingdoms – the Northern Kingdom (Hokuzan), the Central Kingdom (Chūzan) and the Southern Kingdom (Nanzan). In 1372 Sho Hashi, the Chūzan king, initiated tributes to the Chinese court, a practice that was quickly matched by his northern and southern rivals, creating a strong link to China that was to last for centuries.

In 1429 Sho Hashi united and gained control of the three kingdoms, establishing the Ryūkyū dynasty. Contact with China increased, and spurred by an influx of Chinese culture, Okinawan classical music and dance, literature, ceramics and other arts flourished. In this 'Golden Era', weapons were prohibited and the islands were rewarded with peace and tranquillity. Under Chinese sanction, Ryūkyū trading power reached into the far corners of Asia, bringing wealth to an archipelago poor in natural resources.

The Ryūkyū kingdom, with no weapons and little means of defence, was not prepared for war when the Shimazu clan from Satsuma (now called Kagoshima) invaded from southern Japan in 1609. The Shimazu conquered the Ryūkyūs easily, then established severe controls their over trade. While the rest of Japan closed its doors to the world until 1853, the Shimazu sustained trade with China under the guise of the Ryūkyū kingdom. The islands were controlled with an iron fist, and taxed and exploited greedily for the next 250 years.

In the 1850s the US Navy's Commodore Matthew Perry signed a treaty of friendship with the Ryūkyūs and made the islands his base when he entered into negotiations with Japan. With the restoration of the Meiji emperor and the abolition of the Japanese feudal system, the Ryūkyūs were annexed to Japan as Okinawa Prefecture in 1879. Little changed for the islanders. They were treated as foreign subjects by the Japanese government, just as they had been by the Shimazu. They were pushed to become 'real Japanese', with their language and elements of their culture forbidden. The Meiji government set up a military base, forbade the teaching of Ryūkyū history in schools, forced the locals to swear allegiance to the Meiji emperor, and made them speak Japanese.

The Okinawans paid a heavy price for their new citizenship in the closing stages of WWII, when they were trapped between the relentless US hammer and the fanatically resistant Japanese anvil. Okinawa became the only battlefield on Japanese soil, suffering through the 'typhoon of steel', the extensive pre-invasion bombardment, then three months of one of the bloodiest battles the world has ever seen. By the time the Battle of Okinawa was over, 12,500 US soldiers and an estimated quarter of a million Japanese had died. The features of hills and rivers were completely changed, villages were totally destroyed, and one out of three Okinawan civilians perished. Many locals felt betrayed that Okinawa was sacrificed to save the mainland.

For postwar history see p693. For fascinating insights into the history of Okinawa, read former governor Masahide Ota's book *Essays on Okinawa Problems*. This book details the sufferings and exploitation of the Okinawan people throughout history, from the time the Satsuma invaded, to the cultural genocide that occurred when the islands were Japanised after the Meiji Restoration; from virtual obliteration in WWII, to the collusion between the US and Tokyo to take the land and turn Okinawa into one of the most heavily armed places on earth.

Climate

The islands of the Nansei-shotō are much warmer than mainland Japan, particularly further south.

If you travel in the winter months of November to March, crowds are smaller, accommodation is less expensive and underwater visibility for divers is at its best – though ferry services are culled outside the busy summer months.

Summer can be hot and crowded, depending where you go. Typhoons, which can turn up at any time between June and October, wreak havoc with ferry schedules.

The average daily temperature in Okinawa in December is 20°C, while in July it is 31°C.

Language

The Ryūkyū islands used to have their own distinctive language, and dialects differed between the islands. This has by and large disappeared among younger people. You may run into difficulties speaking standard Japanese with one of Okinawa's remarkable number of centenarians, though.

Getting There & Away

The Nansei-shotō are becoming increasingly accessible from mainland Japan.

While Naha is the hub, with direct flights from 20 different mainland Japanese cities (p754), Amami-Ōshima, Miyako-jima and Ishigaki-jima also have daily direct flights linking them with at least Tokyo and Osaka. Other outer islands such as Yonaguni-jima, Kume-jima and Zamami-jima can be reached by air with a change of flights in Naha.

If you're heading for the northern islands, it may be best to fly into Kagoshima on Kyūshū, then change to ferries or flights to the islands. There are daily direct flights from Kagoshima to Yakushima, Tanegashima, Amami-Ōshima, Tokunoshima, Yoron-tō and Okinoerabu-jima.

Ferries from Tokyo, Nagoya, Osaka, Kobe and Kagoshima make their way with varying regularity to the Nansei-shotō. An incredible number of ferries ply the waters between the islands, so there are a lot of options to get to where you are going.

If you are arriving in Japan by air, it is worth noting that JAL and ANA both offer 'visit Japan'-type airfares for domestic flights within Japan – as long as they are bought out of Japan in conjunction with a ticket to Japan. Such tickets, if used to Okinawa, are an incredible saving from standard domestic airfares bought within Japan.

Getting Around

Countless aircraft buzz around between the islands, and almost as many ferries do the same on the water. There are ferries from Kagoshima to Naha that stop at all the major islands in between, and similarly, ferries from Naha to Ishigaki-jima.

On the islands themselves, the bigger islands have public bus routes, taxis, and rental cars, scooters and bicycles.

KAGOSHIMA-KEN

The northern half of the Nansei-shotō is administratively part of Kyūshū's southernmost prefecture of Kagoshima. Heading southwest, there are three main island groups in the chain.

Northernmost is the Ōsumi-shotō. These islands, around 100km south of the Kyūshū mainland, are accessed by ferry from, and back to, Kagoshima.

The Tokara-rettō consists of 12 small, rarely visited volcanic islands that stretch out between the Ōsumi-shotō and the Amami-shotō.

Southernmost is the Amami-shotō with its biggest island, Amami-Ōshima, being 380km south of Kyūshū. This group has bigger, more tropical islands.

ŌSUMI-SHOTŌ 大隅諸島

The northernmost island group of the Nansei-shotō is the Ōsumi-shotō. The two main islands are Yakushima, a paradise for nature-lover's, and Tanegashima, known for its surf and rocket-launch facility. Further west, tiny Iō-jima is a rarely visited gem of a volcanic island with excellent *onsen*.

Yakushima 屋久島

☎ 0997 / pop 14,000

Just 25km in diameter, Yakushima is one of Japan's most remarkable travel destinations, justifiably designated a Unesco World Heritage site (Japan's first) in 1993.

Over 75% of the island is covered with thickly forested mountains. Yakushima's towering terrain catches every inbound rain cloud, giving the island one of the wettest climates in Japan. While the high peaks are snowcapped in winter, the flat land around the coastline remains subtropical. Its beaches are favoured as nesting grounds by sea turtles. Yakushima is the furthest place north that mangroves grow in Japan. Other indigenous plants have been utilised by herbologists for centuries; in fact, the old kanji (Chinese characters) for Yakushima meant 'Medicine Island'. *Gajutsu* (a type of native ginger) is still harvested for digestive medicines.

ORIENTATION & INFORMATION

Miyanoura (宮之浦) on the northeast coast, is the main port. A road runs around the perimeter of the island, passing through the secondary port of **Anbō** (安房) on the east coast, then through the hot-springs town of **Onoaida** (尾の間) in the south. On the west coast the road narrows to just one paved lane (there's no bus service here). Watch out for monkeys and falling rocks.

Miyanoura's ferry terminal has a useful **information desk** (☎ 42-1019; ⏱ 8.30am-5pm) that can help find accommodation and sells topographic hiking maps. In Anbō there's a small **tourist office** (☎ 46-2333; ⏱ 8.30am-5pm) on the main road just north of the river.

In Miyanoura, the **Environmental and Cultural Centre** (屋久島環境文化村センター; ☎ 42-2900; admission & film ¥500; ⏱ 9am-5pm Tue-Sun, daily in summer) is at the corner of the ferry-terminal road. It has bilingual exhibits about the island's natural history and traditions. Subtitles are available upon request in several foreign languages for screenings of an inspiring 25-minute IMAX film. Staff at the centre can also recommend guided ecotour operators on the island, charging around ¥15,000 for full-day outings, which may include kayaking, snorkelling and diving.

ACTIVITIES

The island offers superb hiking through ancient forests of giant *yaku-sugi* (Cryptomeria

MASON FLORENCE

Sunayama Beach (p708), Miyako-jima, Miyako-shotō

Carved stone statue of the Iriomote *yamaneko* (p715)

MARTIN MOOS

Naze (p689), Amami Ōshima, Amami-shotō

MARTIN MOOS

Pinaisāra-no-taki (p715), Iriomote-jima, Okinawa-ken

Shurijō-kōen (p698), Naha, Okinawa-hontō

Iriomote-jima (p716), Okinawa-ken

YAKUSHIMA

0 ——— 4 km
0 ——— 2 miles

To Kagoshima (110km)

To Tanegashima

Iso-hama

Nagata Inaka-hama

Yakushima Lighthouse

Nagata

Umigame-kan

Isso Moutain Path

Environmental and Cultural Centre

Minshuku Yaedake-honkan
Miyanoura Port
Miyanoura
Seikōudoku
Lodge Yaedake-sansō
Kusugawa

Tanegashima-kaikyō

Miyanoura rindō

Miyanoura River

Nagata River

Shiratani rindō

Shiratani Unsuikyō

Kusugawa Mountain Trail

Rider House Tomarigi

Yakushima Airport

Nagata Mountain Trail

Jōmon-sugi (Giant Cedar)

Aiko-dake Mountain Trail

77

Ōko rindō

Seibu rindō

Miyanoura-dake (1935m)

Arakawa-tozanguchi

Anbō River

Hanayama Mountain Trail

Koyoji River

Kuroimi-dake (1831m)

Arakawa rindō

Ōko-no-taki

Kuromi rindō

Kigen-sugi

Yaku-sugi Land

592

Yodogawa-tozanguchi
Yodogawa Hut

Anbō rindō

Tourist Office

Anbō

Nakama River

Yudomari Mountain Trail

Onoaida Mountain Trail

Tainoko River

Anbō Port

Nakama

Yudomari rindō

Hirano

78

Yudomari Onsen

Senpiro-no-taki

Kuro-saki

Hirauchi Kaichū Onsen

Onoaida Onsen

Hara

Onoaida

Yakushima Youth Hostel

---

japonica), a local cedar species. There are plenty of options. Choose from a day-long strenuous outing to the 1935m summit of **Miyanoura-dake** (宮之浦岳; 10 hours return from Yodogawa-tozanguchi at 1370m), the highest point in southern Japan, or hike to the 2600-year-old cedar tree, **Jōmon-sugi** (縄文杉). For the latter, allow at least five hours each way from the trailhead, Arakawa-tozanguchi. You'll be hiking from 600m up to 1310m. Alternatively, plan a two- or three-day trek across several mountain peaks. For the complete scoop on the island's hikes, pick up a copy of Lonely Planet's *Hiking in Japan*.

Yaku-sugi Land (ヤクスギランド; admission ¥300; 🕙 9am-5pm) offers shorter hiking courses over wooden boardwalks, and longer treks deep into the millennia-old cedar forest. Its 80-minute hiking course passes by the 1800-year-old Buddha Cedar. The preserve is a 30-minute drive inland and up from Anbō on a rough and rugged road. It's incredibly picturesque and if you're lucky, you may see *yakuzaru,* the local species of monkey. There are two buses a day (¥720, 40 minutes from Anbō).

Onsen-lovers will be in heaven at **Hirauchi Kaichū Onsen** (平内海中温泉), a five-minute walk from the bus stop of the same name to the west of Onoaida. Outdoor baths are in the rocks by the sea and usable only when the tide is out. A tad further west, and also with its own bus stop, is **Yudomari Onsen** (湯泊温泉) also beside the sea. Neither has set costs or bathing times. **Onoaida Onsen** (尾の間温泉; ☎ 47-2872; admission ¥200; ⏰ 7am-10pm) is also superb, but inland and closer to Onoaida. It also has its own bus stop.

On the northwest coast is **Nagata Inaka-hama** (長田いなか浜), a beautiful stretch of beach where sea turtles come to lay their eggs from May to July. At Nagata, visit the **Umigame-kan** (うみがめ館; ☎ 49-6550; admission ¥200; ⏰ 9am-5pm Wed-Mon) for sea turtle displays and exhibits.

On the west coast and at the last bus stop is **Ōko-no-taki** (大川の滝), Yakushima's highest waterfall at 88m.

Native Vision (ネイティブビジョン; ☎ 42-0091; www.native-vision.com in Japanese), based in Miyanoura, runs all sorts of outdoor tours, including hiking, diving, snorkelling and canoeing.

SLEEPING & EATING

There is camping along the coast and in the highland interior, plus an established system of mountain huts along the summit trail. There are many ryokan (traditional Japanese inn), *minshuku* (Japanese-style B&B) and pensions in Miyanoura, Anbō and Onoaida. The information offices can help with bookings.

Yakushima Youth Hostel (屋久島ユースホステル; ☎ 47-3751; dm with/without meals ¥4400/2800) This is an impeccably run hostel. Bicycles can be rented for trips to nearby waterfalls and hot springs. It's a short walk from the Hirauchi Iriguchi bus stop to the west of Onoaida on the south coast.

Seikōudoku (晴耕雨読; ☎ 42-2070; r per person ¥3500) Seikōudoku is good value and has Japanese-style rooms close to the Miyanoura-Ōhashi bridge.

Minshuku Yaedake-honkan (民宿八重岳本館; ☎ 42-2552; r per person with meals ¥6000) In central Miyanoura, this is a good base.

Lodge Yaedake-sansō (ロッジ八重岳山荘; ☎ 42-1551; r per person with meals ¥7500) Run by the same people as the *minshuku* above, this lodge is great though a bit out of the way. There are Japanese-style rooms in riverside cabins, all connected by wooden walkways, and a hot-springs bath. It's inland up the Miyanoura River, but if you make a booking they'll pick you up at their town *minshuku* at 4pm.

Rider House Tomarigi (ライダーハウスとまり木; ☎ 43-5069; dm ¥2000) Rough and ready

and right by the airport on the northeast coast. You can pitch a tent here for ¥700.

GETTING THERE & AROUND

JAC (p753), part of the JAS network, flies from Kagoshima to Yakushima's airport on the northeast coast (¥11,370, 40 minutes, six daily).

Orita Kisen (☎ 099-226-0731) runs the scenic ferry route to Miyanoura (¥5000, 3¾ hours, once daily). **Toppy** (☎ 099-255-7888) speedboats from Kagoshima go to Miyanoura and Anbō (¥7000, 2½ hours, four daily). A return ticket costs ¥12,600. Keep in mind that the jet foils stop running at the slightest hint of inclement weather. Many visitors do the Kagoshima–Yakushima–Tanegashima–Kagoshima triangle by ferry, visiting both islands. There are four boats a day to Tanegashima – three fast boats (¥3200, 50 minutes) and one slow boat (¥1400, one hour 10 minutes).

Local buses travel the coastal road partway around Yakushima roughly every hour, though only a few head up into the interior. There are plenty of options for hiring cars, scooters and bicycles. A hire car is a good option on Yakushima.

Tanegashima 種子島
☎ 0997 / pop 36,000

A long narrow island standing north–south to the east of Yakushima, Tanegashima is known as the home of Japan's Space Center, and as a year-round surfing and diving mecca. It is also the spot where firearms were introduced to Japan by shipwrecked Portuguese in 1543. The local lord copied the matchlock guns and as the firearms spread throughout Japan, totally changing the balance of power among the feudal lords, they were known as *tanegashimas*.

The island's port of Nishi-no-omote is on the northwest coast. There is a helpful **information office** (観光案内所; ☎ 22-1146; ⏰ 8.30am-5.30pm) in the ferry building at the port. The airport is about halfway down the island near the west coast. Check out www.tanegashima.info for more information in Japanese.

Tanegashima's **Space Center** (宇宙センター) is on the southeastern coast of the island and is open to the public for free. There is a large parklike complex with rocket-launch facilities and a **Space Technology Museum** (宇宙科学技術館; ☎ 26-9244; ⏰ 9.30am-5.30pm Tue-Sun). The museum is closed on launch days.

The coastline in the immediate vicinity of the Space Center is the **Takesaki-kaigan** (竹崎海岸), including a beautiful stretch of white beach that is popular with surfers. The **Nagahama-kaigan** (長浜海岸) on the west coast of Tanegashima includes a 12km stretch of white sand that plays host to sea turtles laying their eggs each year from early May to early August.

The **History and Folklore Museum** (中種子町立歴史民俗資料館; ☎ 27-2233; admission ¥160; ⊗ 9am-7pm Tue-Sun), near Tanegashima's airport, has displays on the history and life of the people of the island.

A 10-minute walk from Nishi-no-omote port, **Ryokan Miharu-sō** (旅館美春荘; ☎ 22-1393; r per person with meals ¥6000; ℗ ⊠) is popular with surfers as the owners also run a surf shop. Right next to the airport in the middle of the island is **Minshuku Shirahae** (民宿白南風; ☎ 27-0379; r per person with meals ¥6000; ℗ ⊠) with Japanese-style rooms. **Umi-no-Ryokan** (うみの旅館; ☎ 26-0391; r per person with meals ¥5500; ℗ ⊠) is a good base for exploring the southern part of the island. It is a two-minute walk from Kaminaka bus stop.

JAC flies daily to Tanegashima from Kagoshima and Osaka's Itami Airport. Fast-boat services by **Kagoshima Shosen** (☎ 099-255-7888) run from Kagoshima Main Port (Kagoshima-honkō; 鹿児島本港) to Tanegashima (¥6000; 1¾ hours, four daily), and **Orita Kisen** (☎ 099-226-0731) runs a regular ferry service (¥2540, 3¾ hours, one daily).

Iō-jima 硫黄島
☎ 09913 / pop 115

A gem of an island that is rarely visited by foreigners, Iō-jima is one of three islands that make up the Mishima (三島) group. Part of the Kirishima volcanic belt, Iō-jima is a small island based around an active volcano and is well known for its wild peacocks. While there is no public transport on the island, it is relatively easy to see all the sights on foot in a day. The website www.mishimamura.jp has information in Japanese and some great photos.

The eastern end of the island is home to the often-smoking volcano **Iō-dake** (硫黄岳; 704m), while the port village is on the southwestern coast.

There are a couple of superb *onsen* on the island that are free to those willing to walk to them. On the north coast, about a 5km-long

(1½ hour) walk from the port, is **Sakamoto Onsen** (坂本温泉), a rectangular pool built into the sea. Its depth reaches 1.5m when the tide is in, but when the tide is out test the temperature with your finger because the natural flow of hot water from the spring is 50°C. On the south coast, about a one-hour walk east of the port and right below Iō-dake, is **Higashi Onsen** (東温泉). It is a big, hot rock-pool next to the pounding waves that is a must for *onsen* connoisseurs.

Iō-jima has historical links and legends associated with the 12th century struggles between the Genji and Heike clans to control Japan. At the northern tip of the island, a 2km-long walk from Sakamoto Onsen, are the remains of a Heike castle.

Right next to the port, the Iō-jima camping area is free and open year-round. You can even borrow a tent for free. Virtually at the port, **Miyukisō** (美由紀荘; ☎ 2-2116; r per person with meals ¥6000; ⊠) has a great reputation as a friendly, family-run *minshuku*. **Marine House Kujaku-no-sato** (マリンハウス孔雀の里; ☎ 2-2169; r per person with meals ¥6000; ⊠) is an ideal place to stay if you're keen to do some diving.

The only coffee shop and pub on the island is **Kameriya** (花女里家; ☎ 2-2015), which serves coffee during the day and alcohol and food at night.

Iō-jima is accessed by ferry from Kagoshima Main Port (鹿児島本港). **Mishima Soneisen** (三島村営船; ☎ 099-222-3141) runs three to four ferries a week, depending on the season, generally leaving Kagoshima at 9.30am. Ferries to Iō-jima usually go via Takeshima (¥3500, 3¼ hours).

TOKARA-RETTŌ トカラ列島
099 / pop 700

The Tokara group is made up of seven inhabited and five uninhabited islands that are strung out between Yakushima and Amami-Ōshima. In terms of travel in Japan, this is real get-away-from-it-all stuff. The total population among the seven inhabited islands is only 700. The islands are volcanic and relatively untouched, with subtropical vegetation and plentiful natural hot springs. Taking a tent, sleeping bag and supplies would be a wise move and increase flexibility. In Japanese, www.tokara.jp has pictures of each of the islands and plenty of information.

Toshima Soneibune (十島村営船; ☎ 222-2101) has a ferry that leaves Kagoshima Main Port on Mondays and Fridays and stops at each island down the chain to Takara-jima. The Monday departure continues on to Naze on Amami-Ōshima. The return trip leaves Takara-jima on Wednesdays and Sundays. It's possible to get off or on at any of the islands. Check departure dates and times before turning up as they can vary and are affected by typhoons. The islands have no airport facilities.

Travelling from the north to the south, the ferry visits Kuchinoshima (口之島), Nakanoshima (中之島), Taira-jima (平島), Suwanose-jima (諏訪之瀬島), Akuseki-jima (悪石島), Kodakara-jima (小宝島) and Takara-jima (宝島).

AMAMI-SHOTŌ 奄美諸島

The Amami-shotō is the southernmost group of islands in Kagoshima Prefecture. The main island of Amami-Ōshima is renowned as a place to enjoy outdoor pursuits such as diving, sea kayaking and hiking in a stunning natural environment. Heading south, Tokunoshima has excellent diving and a 600-year history of bullfighting, Okinoerabu-jima has intriguing coral-based land formations, and Yoron-tō is a tropical paradise from where Okinawa's main island can be seen on a good day.

Amami Park (☎ 0997-55-2333; ☼ 9am-6pm Thu-Tue), five-minutes' drive from Amami Airport on Amami-Ōshima, is the central tourism facility for the group of islands. It has information, maps and brochures on each of the islands in the Amami-shotō.

Amami-Ōshima 奄美大島

☎ 0997 / pop 72,000

Amami-Ōshima counts itself as Japan's third-largest offshore island after Okinawa's main island and Sadoshima in Niigata prefecture. The main island of the Amami group, it is 380km south-southwest of Kagoshima. It has a mild subtropical climate year-round and is home to some unusual flora and fauna, including tree ferns, mangrove forests and the Amami black rabbit. It is very popular with divers thanks to its crystal clear waters.

The island is well known in Japan for the 'Amami Rabbit Case', a dispute that divided the islanders into two factions supporting either commercial development or

---

FERRIES FROM KAGOSHIMA TO NAHA & IN-BETWEEN

Plenty of ferries ply the waters between Kagoshima city on Kyūshū and Naha, the main city in Okinawa. These ferries are in good shape and reasonable in cost. A second-class ticket admits travellers to a large tatami room that is shared with others. Tickets for a private room are more expensive.

Ōshima Unyu (Tokyo ☎ 03-5643-6170, Kagoshima 099-222-2338, Naha 098-861-1886; www.minc.ne.jp/aline in Japanese) and **Marix Line** (Tokyo ☎ 03-3274-0502, Kagoshima 099-225-1551, Naha 098-868-9098; www.marix-line .co.jp) operate to the following schedule on alternate days – ie between them, there is a daily departure in each direction. For ¥13,200 you can use either company's ferries to get between Kagoshima and Naha or vice-versa (with a seven-day time limit). You can get off and on at any of the ports listed below – make sure to tell the ship's office once on board where you want to get off. They will do the necessary paperwork.

Southbound

Day	Time	Destination
Day 1	1800	Kagoshima-shinkō
Day 2	0550	Amami-Ōshima (Naze)
Day 2	0940	Tokunoshima (Kametoku)
Day 2	1200	Okinoerabu-jima (Wadomari)
Day 2	1400	Yoron-tō
Day 2	1650	Okinawa (Motobu)
Day 2	1840	Okinawa (Naha)

Northbound

Day	Time	Destination
Day 1	0800	Okinawa (Naha)
Day 1	1010	Okinawa (Motobu)
Day 1	1300	Yoron-tō
Day 1	1510	Okinoerabu-jima (Wadomari)
Day 1	1730	Tokunoshima (Kametoku)
Day 1	2120	Amami-Ōshima (Naze)
Day 2	0830	Kagoshima-shinkō

---

nature conservation. It was the 'golf course developers' versus the 'endangered-rabbit supporters', producing intense antagonism on the island and around the country as Japanese pondered the future of their nation as a whole. The case sputtered to an inconclusive halt when a court ruled that a conservation group could not act as a plaintiff in the case on behalf of the rabbits!

The main city and port is **Naze** (名瀬), surrounded by hills and half built on reclaimed land, on the northwest coast. The airport is 55 minutes away by bus on the northeast coast. There's a **tourist information office** (☎ 63-2295) at the airport that opens for incoming flights, but nothing at the ferry terminal in Naze. Tatsuya Ryokan (right) has maps and brochures, and is the best spot for some advice should you arrive by ferry. The post office has an international ATM service, while Internet access is freely available in the lobby of the Amami Sun Plaza Hotel.

Check out www.amami.or.jp for information in Japanese about the island.

SIGHTS & ACTIVITIES

For an excellent view of Naze and its harbour head 1km south of the port to **Ogamiyama-kōen** (おがみ山公園), a park with walking trails and viewing areas.

A 10-minute walk north of the bus centre is the **Amami Habu Center** (奄美観光ハブセンター; ☎ 52-1505; admission ¥750; 8am-6pm) where you can check out the Nansei-shotō's infamous venomous snake, the habu. At 10am, 2pm and 4pm you can watch a battle between a mongoose and a habu.

At the north end of town is the **Amami Museum** (名瀬市立奄美博物館; ☎ 54-1210; admission ¥300; 9am-5pm) with displays on Amami's history, culture and environment.

Just 15 minutes west of Naze by bus is the **Ohama-Kaihin-Kōen** (大浜海浜公園), a beautiful beach park known for its white sands and stunning sunsets. The park is popular for swimming, snorkelling and sea kayaking in summer, and camping is possible here for ¥300. There is also an excellent **aquarium** (☎ 55-6000; admission ¥500; 9.30am-6pm) here.

Kankō Network Amami (観光ネットワーク奄美; ☎ 54-4991; www.amami.com in Japanese) in Naze runs nature tours year-round into the pristine **Kinsakubara** (金作原) native forest from ¥3200. It does hotel pick-ups, and are a good source of information on the island.

Island Service (アイランドサービス; ☎ 52-5346; www.synapse.ne.jp/~island-s/in Japanese) runs a guided sea-kayaking tour (¥12,000, eight hours) and mangrove canoe experience (from ¥2500, from two hours). It can also pick you up and drop you off at your accommodation.

HABU SNAKES

Any discussion of the Nansei-shotō eventually gets around to 'deadly' habu snakes. Perhaps it's a reflection of Japan's severe shortage of real dangers, but you could easily get the impression that the poor habu is the world's most dangerous snake and that there's one waiting behind every tree, shrub, bush and bar stool on the islands. They're hardly so prolific – the most likely place to see one is at a mongoose-versus-habu fight put on for tourists.

Nevertheless, they are venomous! It's not a good idea to go barefoot when stomping through the bushes. Do stomp though – the vibrations should scare any snakes away. If you do get bitten, take it seriously and seek immediate medical advice.

Native Sea Amami (ネイティブシー奄美; ☎ 62-2385; www.native-sea.com in Japanese), 40 minutes east of Naze, runs beach and boat diving trips and has excellent accommodation on site for ¥13,000 including two meals.

SLEEPING & EATING

Tatsuya Ryokan (たつや旅館; ☎ 52-0260; www.amami.com/tatsuya; r per person ¥3000; P) This is *the* place to stay in Naze. There are only five rooms though, so you better book early. There is friendly advice, maps and brochures, satellite TV in each room, plus a free light breakfast. Come out of the port, turn left, then turn right at the third traffic light and walk for 100m.

Hotel New Amami (ホテルニュー奄美; ☎ 52-2000; s/tw ¥4000/7000; P) Next door, this place can fill the void if Tatsuya is full. It's simple business hotel-type accommodation, with Internet access available.

Amami Sun Plaza Hotel (奄美サンプラザホテル; ☎ 53-5151; r per person with meals ¥10,000; P) This hotel, with Western-style rooms, is also central.

Amami Daiko (奄美太鼓; ☎ 54-3901; 5-11pm) On Rte 58 in the middle of Naze, this is the place to head for local fish dishes and black sugar *shōchu* (strong, distilled alcohol) – a wicked brew.

GETTING THERE & AROUND

Amami-Ōshima can be reached with daily direct flights from Tokyo (¥39,500, 2½ hours, one daily), Osaka (¥35,000, one hour 50 minutes, one daily) and Kagoshima (¥18,500, 55 minutes, five daily).

There are five to seven ferries from Tokyo (¥18,000, 37 hours) and Osaka (¥13,200, 28 hours) each month that carry on to Naha. Ferries also operate daily from Kagoshima and Naha (see the boxed text, p688).

Amami-Ōshima has an excellent public bus system and buses run to all corners of the main island from the bus centre in Naze. Rental cars, scooters and bicycles are readily available in Naze.

Tokunoshima 徳之島
☎ 0997 / pop 28,000

Popular with divers, Tokunoshima is the second-largest island of the Amami-shotō. It has a mild climate and spectacular natural landscapes. The coastline has some amazing rock formations, while the interior is mountainous – the highest point of Inokawa-san is 645m.

Tokunoshima's airport is on its west coast, not far from the secondary port of **Hetono** (平土野). On the island's east coast is the main port of **Kametoku-shinkō** (亀徳新港) and the main town of **Kametsu** (亀津). There is a **tourist information office** (☎ 82-0575; ⏰ 9am-6pm Mon-Sat) at the ferry building with maps and brochures. Make accommodation bookings here. There is also a small information booth at the airport. The post

office ATMs accept international money cards. Over the road, free Internet access is available in the new **public library** (☎ 82-1239; ⏰ 10am-6.30pm Tue-Fri, 9.30am-5pm Sat & Sun).

SIGHTS & ACTIVITIES
Tokunoshima has a history of **tōgyū** or **bovine sumō** (闘牛大会) dating back over 600 years. While there are 13 official fight sites on the island that hold around 20 tournaments a year, the island championships are held at **Dōmu Tōgyū-jō** (ドーム闘牛場) in the southeast of the island, not far from Kametsu. The big three events for the year are held on 3 January, 5 May and either the first or second Sunday in October. It costs ¥3000 to watch at the Dōmu, and ¥2500 at regional sites. Call the tourist office to confirm details.

The **History and Folklore Museum** (伊仙町歴史民俗資料館; ☎ 86-4183; admission free; ⏰ 9am-4.30pm Tue-Sun) is at the south end of the island and has displays on the island's culture and history.

On the northeastern coast is **Tokunoshima Fruit Garden** (徳之島フルーツガーデン; ☎ 84-9311; admission ¥410; ⏰ 9am-6pm), which has over 17,000 trees in 110 varieties. Depending on the season, they have tropical fruit such as papayas, mangos and guava for tasting.

At the northeastern tip of the island is the **Kanami Sotetsu Tunnel** (金見ソテツトンネル), an impressive 200m-long tunnel of 400-year-old cycad trees leading out to the view

---

THE OLDIES OF TOKUNOSHIMA   *Craig McLachlan*

They raise them strong on Tokunoshima. The island has had two Guinness World Record holders for the world's oldest person – and that's in the last quarter of a century. Shigechiyo Izumi (1866–1986) got the big prize in 1979 and lived a further seven years until he was 120 years, 237 days. Following on, Kamato Hongo (1887–2003) became the world's oldest person in 1999 and lived to the age of 116 years, 45 days. Mrs Hongo moved to Kagoshima at the age of 77 and lived the last 39 years of her life there.

In researching this chapter I had the pleasure of riding the public bus from Kametsu to Hetono. Apart from the driver and myself, the rest of the passengers were octogenarians. The old ladies politely answered my questions in standard Japanese before cackling between themselves in a local dialect that I found totally unintelligible. Formal bus stops seemed somewhat irrelevant as the driver dropped each of his elderly passengers virtually at their front doors, and picked up any who waved him down.

The old women were impressed when I pointed out a spot I'd visited that morning – the birthplace and practice *dōhyō* (training place) of Asashio, the 46th sumō Grand Champion or *yokozuna*, who was brought up in the tiny east coast village of Inokawa.

'I've been living here for 87 years and I didn't know we could see Asashio's practice *dōhyō*!' chortled one – in standard Japanese fortunately. 'How strange! Being informed of that by a *gaijin*!'

point at Cape Kanami. At the northwestern tip is **Mushirose** (ムシロ瀬), an amazing rippled rock formation that disappears into the sea. The **Megane-iwa** (メガネ岩), with two huge holes in the rock that look like a pair of glasses, is on the west coast.

Villa Takakura (ヴィラ高倉; ☎ 84-1185; www4.synapse.ne.jp/takakura) offers various diving trips and accommodation from ¥5500 with two meals or ¥3500 without meals. It is near Kedoku on the east coast.

SLEEPING & EATING

Cōpo Shichifukujin (コーポ七福神; ☎ 82-2618; r per person ¥3000; ⚙) A convenient, cheap place in central Kametsu. The rooms used to be apartments so have reasonable facilities.

Pension Shichifukujin (ペンシォン七福神; ☎ 82-1126; r per person with/without meals ¥5500/4000; Ⓟ ⚙) Run by the same family as above this place is great but not as convenient. Miniconcerts are held in the courtyard. Phone ahead to be picked up at the port.

Hotel Sunset Resort (ホテルサンセットリゾート; ☎ 85-2349; minshuku per person with meals ¥6300, hotel r s/tw ¥5800/9800; Ⓟ ⚙) At Yonama in the northwest corner of the island, this place has excellent views from its *rotemburo* (open-air baths). There is also a camping area at Yonama Beach.

Yagi-ryōri Hunter (山羊料理ハンター; ☎ 84-1311; ⏱ lunch & dinner Mon-Sat) Near the Megumi Shoten bus stop on the east coast, head here to try local goat meat specialities. The *yagi-yakiniku* (grilled goat meat) for ¥1200 is tasty, as is the goat sashimi for ¥600.

GETTING THERE & AROUND

There are daily flights to Tokunoshima from both Kagoshima (¥2500, one hour, two daily) and Amami-Ōshima (¥18,300, 35 minutes, two daily).

Daily ferries (see the boxed text, p688) head south to Naha and north to Amami-Ōshima.

There are bus stations at the ports of Hetono and Kametoku, and a good public bus system to all parts of the island. This is a good island to rent a car or scooter. Both are available in Kametsu.

Okinoerabu-jima 沖永良部島

☎ 0997 / pop 15,000

A raised coral island to the southwest of Tokunoshima, Okinoerabu-jima is known

for its intriguing land formations and over 300 caves. Extensive flower farming, especially of lilies, means that from March to May the island is covered in yellow and white flowers. The legendary Saigō Takamori (see the boxed text, p659) was exiled on Okinoerabu-jima for two years in 1862. He helped foster the islanders' desires to be self-sustaining, and is honoured by a statue in Wadomari's **Nanshū-jinja** (南州神社).

The airport is at the eastern tip of the island, with **Wadomari-ko** (和泊港), the main port and town, 6km away on the east coast. There is a small **tourist information booth** (☎ 92-1111; ⏱ 8.30am-5.30pm) at Wadomari port on the 2nd floor of the terminal building. A five-minute walk away in town, the post office ATMs accept international money cards, and Internet access is available at the **public library** (☎ 92-4053; per 30min ¥300; ⏱ 8.30am-5.15pm).

SIGHTS & ACTIVITIES

The **History and Folklore Museum** (和泊町歴史民俗資料館; ☎ 92-0911; admission ¥200; ⏱ 9am-4.30pm Thu-Tue) has displays on the island's history and culture, and all sorts of information on the Okinoerabu trumpet lily and lilies from all over the world.

Of the more than 300 caves on the island, **Shōryūdō** (昇竜洞; ☎ 93-4536; admission ¥1000; ⏱ 8.30am-5pm) is the most interesting and visitors can venture into 600m of its 3.3km length.

The island has many impressive geographical landforms. **Taminamisaki** (田皆崎), at the northwest tip of the island, has ancient coral that has been uplifted to form a 40m cliff. Over the years, natural erosion caused by the wind, rain and sea has made the point a rugged yet beautiful spot. On the southeast coast, **Ujijihama** (ウジジ浜) has intriguing rock formations and is popular with divers. At the island's northeast tip, not far from the airport, **Fūcha** (フーチャ) is a blowhole in the limestone rock that shoots water 10m into the air on windy days. The coastline here is spectacular.

Okinoerabu-jima claims **Japan's biggest Banyan tree** (日本一のガジュマル), a monster in the grounds of Kunigami Elementary School, in the northeast of the island.

Okierabu Dive Center (沖えらぶダイブセンター; ☎ 93-4393; www4.synapse.ne.jp/odc in Japanese) offers diving for everyone from beginners to qualified divers. Check out the website.

SLEEPING

Business Hotel Wadamari-kō (ビジネスホテル
和泊港; ☎ 92-1189; s ¥3150; P ✂) This new
place is a top deal, a few minutes' walk from
the port. It's convenient with great in-room
facilities.

Kankō Hotel Higashi (観光ホテル東; ☎ 92-
1283; r per person with meals from ¥6500; P ✂) In
the same area, this place has both Japanese-
and Western-style rooms.

GETTING THERE & AROUND

There are direct flights to Okinoerabu Airport
from Kagoshima (JAC, ¥24,950, one hour
40 minutes, three daily), Amami-Ōshima
(¥14,030, 35 minutes, one daily) and Yoron-
tō (¥7800, 25 minutes, one daily).

Ferries run daily in each direction between Amami-Ōshima and Naha, stopping
at Okinoerabu-jima on the way (see the
boxed text, p688).

The island has a good public bus system.
Just show the bus driver where you want to
go (point out the kanji in this guidebook!)
and he'll get you as close as he can. Buses
will stop if you wave them down.

Rental cars, scooters and bicycles are
available in Wadomari.

Yoron-tō 与論島 ヨロン島

☎ 0997/pop 6000

Shaped like a huge angelfish, Yoron-tō is the
southernmost island of the Amami-shotō and
of Kagoshima-ken. On a good day, Okinawa-
hontō's northernmost point of Hedo-misaki
is clearly visible 28km to the southwest.
Surrounded by a coral reef, Yoron-tō has a
reputation as a tropical paradise with white
beaches and great waters for marine sports.
Yoron-tō also sports it's own version of the
'communication drink' (see the boxed text,
p709) known as *Yoron-kempō*, which involves
imbibing copious amounts of locally made
sugar *shōchu*. Be aware that it can seriously
ruin plans for the following day.

The harbour is next to the airport on the
western tip of the island. The main town
area is **Chabana**, a couple of kilometres east.
Beside the city office in Chabana is the
useful **tourist information office** (☎ 97-5151;
🕙 8.30am-5.30pm). They have maps, an English
pamphlet and can make accommodation
bookings. Free Internet access is available at
the public library just up the road, and the
post office ATMs take international money

cards. Check out www.yoron.jp in Japanese
for more information.

SIGHTS & ACTIVITIES

Yoron-tō is a small island, it's possible to ride
around it in three or four hours on a bicycle.

The island is known for sporting and
cultural events, with one of the highlights
of the year being the **Yoron Marathon** (与論マ
ラソン) held annually on the second Sunday in March. Call the island's tourist office for details. Full marathoners go around
the island twice, while half-marathoners go
around once. There are also team events.

The **Southern Cross Center** (サザンクロスセ
ンター; ☎ 97-3396; admission ¥200; 🕙 9am-6pm),
a short walk from the Ishini (石仁) bus
stop 3km south of Chabana, is so named
as Yoron-tō is the northernmost island in
Japan from which the Southern Cross can
be seen. The centre is Yoron-tō's museum,
with displays on the history and culture of
the Amami islands. There is a 360-degree
panorama from the 5th floor. The remains
of **Yoron Castle** (与論城跡), which was half-
built by the Hokuzan king in the 15th century, can be seen next door.

Around the 15th of March, August and
October the **Yoron Jugoya-odori** (与論十五
夜踊り) is held at Kotohira Shrine by the
remains of the castle. The dance has both
Ryūkyū and Japanese influences and has
been held since 1561.

The **Yunnu Rakuen** (ユンヌ楽園; ☎ 97-2341;
admission ¥400; 🕙 9am-6pm) is a tropical botanical garden with over 300 types of plants
including hibiscus, bougainvillea, plumeria
and golden shower. It's a great place to chill
out and breathe in the tropical mood.

On the eastern side of the island, Yoron's
best beach is on the popular **Oganeku-kaigan**
(大金久海岸), where there is also a camping
area (per night ¥610). Offshore, **Yurigahama**
(百合ヶ浜) is a stunning stretch of white
sand inside the reef that disappears at high
tide. Boats putter back and forth ferrying
visitors out to it.

At the island's southeastern tip is **Yoron
Minzoku-mura** (与論民俗村; ☎ 97-2934; admission
¥400; 🕙 9am-6pm) with old thatched-roof buildings, and local arts and crafts. The owner is a
fountain of knowledge on the island.

Worth a visit is the **fishermens market**,
complete with secret bidding, each morning at 8am at the fishing port in Chabana.

SLEEPING & EATING
Minshuku Nankai-sō (民宿南海荘; ☎ 97-2145; r per person with/without meals ¥5000/3000; ℙ ☒) About 50m away from the tourist office, this place has simple Japanese-style accommodation, both convenient and clean.

Minshuku Shiomi-sō (民宿汐見荘; ☎ 97-2167; r per person with meals ¥5000; ℙ ☒) In Chabana, this *minshuku* has simple Japanese-style rooms.

Hotel Seikai-sō (ホテル青海荘; ☎ 97-2046; r per person with meals ¥6500; ℙ ☒) In a three-storey building in central Chabana, this place has both Japanese- and Western-style rooms.

Gallery Kai and Umi Café (ギャラリー海;海カフェ; ☎ 97-4621; ☽ 9am-9pm) An excellent spot, looking as though it's straight out of Yoron-tō's sister-island, Mykonos in the Greek islands, this place is great. Painted brilliant white and blue, there are homemade crafts, tasty meals and a terrace to relax on.

GETTING THERE & AROUND
Yoron-tō has direct air links with Kagoshima (JAC, ¥26,300, 1¾ hours, one daily) and Naha (RAC, ¥11,600, 35 minutes, one daily). There are also ferries (see the boxed text, p688) heading both north to Amami-Ōshima and south to Okinawa each day.

There is a good public bus system around the island. Rental cars, scooters and bicycles are readily available in Chabana. A scooter or bicycle is a great option for getting around.

OKINAWA-KEN 沖縄県

pop 1.35 million

The southern half of the Nansei-shotō is Okinawa-ken. Heading southwest, there are three main island groups in the chain.

Northernmost is the Okinawa-shotō, centred around Okinawa-hontō and the prefectural capital of Naha. The prefectural **tourist information office** (☎ 857-6884; ☽ 9am-9pm) is at Naha Airport. This office and its staff are extremely helpful. English is spoken and there are English-language brochures and maps of the islands in the Okinawa prefecture. There are accommodation lists in English, and lists of dive companies that speak English. If you're just off the plane, don't pass this by and just head into town. The Naha city tourist information office in town does not have information on the other islands, only on Naha city.

Okinawa-ken's middle group of islands is the Miyako-shotō 300km to the southwest. This group is best accessed by direct flights from the mainland, or by plane or ferry from Naha.

The southernmost island group is the Yaeyama-shotō, a further 120km southwest. The westernmost island of Yonaguni-jima is only 110km from Taiwan.

THE AMERICAN ISSUE

After the war, Okinawa had to be restored from complete destruction. While Japan recovered its sovereignty in 1953, Okinawa remained under the control of the US Military Occupation Government, which appropriated whichever land it wanted for military bases. Local protests finally forced Okinawa's return to Japan in 1972. Because of its strategic location however, collusion between Tokyo and Washington maintained a heavy US military presence in the islands, much to the displeasure of many Okinawans – especially those who had lost their land.

Okinawans found it hard to understand why, with less than 1% of Japan's landmass, they had to play host to 75% of the American military presence in Japan. The thorny issue sputtered along through the Vietnam and Cold Wars, then peaked in 1995 when three servicemen were found guilty of raping a 12-year-old Okinawan schoolgirl. In the aftermath, Governor Ōta Masahide was voted into power on a pledge to end the American military presence. Ōta's demands made little headway in Tokyo though, and in 1998 he was beaten by Inamine Keniichi, a 'pro-American base' politician who argued that the poor Okinawan economy needed the cash that the American bases brought with them. Inamine's attitude was rewarded by Tokyo when Okinawa hosted the G8 Summit in July 2000.

The issue of the American presence continues to simmer. At the time of research, Tokyo had decided that the burden of American bases should be shared more evenly around Japan, but is having problems finding prefectures and towns willing to play host.

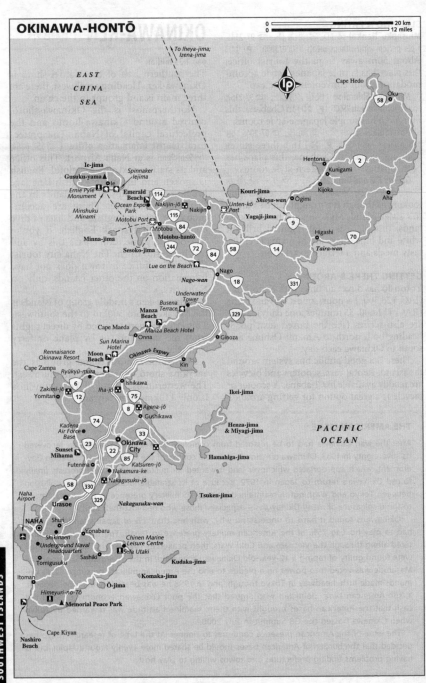

OKINAWA-HONTŌ

0 ——————— 20 km
0 ——————— 12 miles

EAST
CHINA
SEA

To Iheya-jima;
Izena-jima

Cape Hedo
Oku
58

Hentona
Kunigami
2
Kijoka
Aha

Ie-jima
Gusuku-yama ▲
Spinnaker
Iejima
Ernie Pyle
Monument
Minshuku
Minami
Emerald
Beach
114
Ocean Expo
Park
Nakijin-jō
Nakijin
115
Motobu Port
Motobu
84
Motobu-hantō
Kouri-jima
Unten-kō
Port
Shioya-wan
Ōgimi
Yagaji-jima
Higashi
70
9
Minna-jima
244
72
84
58
14
Taira-wan
Sesoko-jima
Lue on the Beach
Nago
Nago-wan
18
331
Underwater
Tower
329
Manza
Terrace
Busena
Terrace
Ginoza
Manza Beach Hotel
Cape Maeda
Sun Marina
Hotel
Onna
Kin
Rennaisance
Okinawa Resort
Moon
Beach
Okinawa Expwy
Cape Zampa
Ryūkyū-mura
Ishikawa
6
Zakimi-jō
Iha-jō
Ikei-jima
Yomitan
12
75
8
Agena-jō
Gushikawa
74
Henza-jima
& Miyagi-jima
Kadena
Air Force
Base
23
33
Hamahiga-jima
Sunset
Mihama
22
Okinawa
City
85
PACIFIC
OCEAN
Futenma
Katsuren-jō
Nakamura-ke
Nakagusuku-jō
Tsuken-jima
58
330
Naha
Airport
Urasoe
329
Nakagusuku-wan
NAHA
Shuri
Shikinaen
Yonabaru
Underground Naval
Headquarters
Chinen Marine
Leisure Centre
Sefa Utaki
Tomigusuku
Sashiki
Kudaka-jima
Itoman
Komaka-jima
Ō-jima
Himeyuri-no-Tō
Memorial Peace Park
Cape Kiyan
Nashiro
Beach

OKINAWA-HONTŌ 沖縄本島

Okinawa-hontō is the largest island in the Nansei-shotō. Its cultural differences with mainland Japan were once evident in its architecture, of which almost all traces were obliterated in WWII.

Okinawa-hontō's prefectural capital and largest city is Naha. A vibrant city, Naha is a transportation hub for the other islands in the group and for the prefecture as a whole. War memorials are clustered in the south of the island, while the central area has ruins and a few cultural attractions. If you're keen on snorkelling and diving, head straight to the Motobu Peninsula. The further north you go, the more rural things become.

Naha 那覇

☎ 098 / pop 325,000

Naha is a busy modern city that sports a new overhead monorail as its main transport link. The capital of Okinawa, it was flattened in WWII. Kokusai-dōri (International Blvd), Naha's colourful, energetic main drag, is 2km of hotels, souvenir shops, restaurants and bars. A short distance east is Shuri, the erstwhile Okinawan capital and the site of renovated ruins.

If you want to raise a smile from a local, say *nihe debīru* for 'thank you'.

INFORMATION

The city **tourist information office** (☎ 868-4887; 8.30am-8pm Mon-Fri, 10am-8pm Sat & Sun) has free maps and staff members speak some English. It's just off Kokusai-dōri on the corner with Starbucks. The **airport information desk** (☎ 857-6884; 9am-9pm) can help book accommodation and provide maps. It is the prefectural tourist office and has information on all Okinawa's islands. For information online check out the Okinawa Tourism & Convention Bureau's website www.ocvb.or.jp.

Post office ATMs accept international money cards; Naha Central Post Office is next to Tsubokawa monorail station, Tomariko Post Office is in the port building, and the Kokusai-dōri Post Office is around the corner from Makishi monorail station.

Net Café (☎ 941-2755; 2-4-14 Makishi; 9.30am-midnight) on Kokusai-dōri charges ¥300/480 for the first half hour/hour of Internet access, including free soft drinks and snacks.

There are heaps of travel agencies around Kokusai-dōri. **Nice Ticket** (☎ 866-8988; 2-16-10

Makishi; 10am-7pm Mon-Fri, 10am-5pm Sat) sells discounted airline tickets.

SIGHTS & ACTIVITIES

Central Naha 那覇中心街

The main drag, **Kokusai-dōri** (国際通り), makes a colourful walk, day or night. Turning south opposite Mitsukoshi department store leads you down **Heiwa-dōri** (平和通り) shopping arcade, which has the distinct flavour of an Asian market.

If you take the left fork at the first major junction, a short walk beyond the shopping arcade brings you to the **Tsuboya pottery area**. Over a dozen traditional potteries still operate in this compact neighbourhood, a centre of ceramic production since 1682, when Ryūkyūan kilns were consolidated here by royal decree. Most shops sell all the popular Okinawan ceramics, such as *shiisā* (lion-dog roof guardians) and containers for serving *awamori* (local firewater).

The **Tsuboya Pottery Museum** (☎ 862-3761; 1-9-32 Tsuboya; admission ¥300; 10am-6pm Tue-Sun) contains some masterpieces. You can inspect potters' wheels and appreciate *arayachi* (unglazed) and *jōyachi* (glazed) pieces.

At the eastern end of Kokusai-dōri, a few blocks past where the monorail passes overhead, a right turn takes you towards Shuri, while turning left eventually brings you to the reconstructed gates of **Sōgen-ji**. The original stone gates once led to the 16th-century temple of the Ryūkyū kings, but it was destroyed in WWII.

On the north side of Tomari port, in the fascinating **international cemetery**, is the **Commodore Perry Memorial** commemorating Perry's landing in Naha. The US naval officer subsequently used Okinawa as a base in 1853 while he forced the Tokugawa shōgunate to finally open Japanese ports to the West.

Garden fans should take a stroll through Chinese-style **Fukushū-en** (☎ 869-5384; 2-29 Kume; admission free; 9am-6pm Thu-Tue). All materials were brought from Fuzhou, Naha's sister city in China, including the pagoda that sits atop a small waterfall.

Nami-no-ue beach (9am-6pm) is a small city beach where you can relax without leaving town. It comes complete with lifeguards, jellyfish/shark nets and showers/toilets, and is below the popular **Naminoue-gu shrine** (波の上宮).

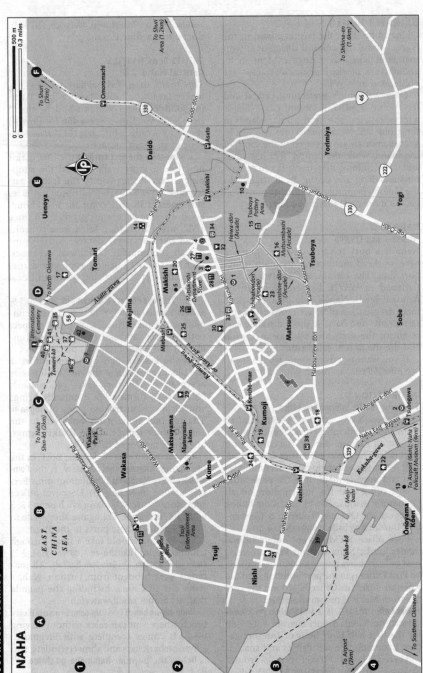

NAHA

OKINAWA & THE SOUTHWEST ISLANDS

OKINAWA: THE HOME OF KARATE

During the 'golden era' of King Sho Shin-O (1477–1526), when trade and culture flourished with China, a law was passed that banned the carrying of weapons in the Ryūkyū kingdom. A century later in 1609, when the Shimazu from Satsuma (now called Kagoshima) on Kyūshū invaded, the weaponless locals could not defend themselves against a well-armed adversary and were conquered easily. The Shimazu exploited the Ryūkyūs greedily and strictly enforced the edict of no weapons for the next 250 years. It was during this period that the *te*, or unarmed fighting techniques of the native Ryūkyūans, began to be developed and refined in secrecy.

As the Shimazu kept up trade with China under the front of the Ryūkyū kingdom, many traders and sailors from China settled in Naha, including many Chinese martial artists. Local *te* practitioners had the chance to practise with, and learn from these people. Later, Okinawans headed to China to study the Chinese fighting arts. The celebrated Higaonna Kanryō and then his successor and top student Miyagi Chōjun spent time studying in Fuzhou in southern China in the late 1800s and early 1900s.

What we now know as the martial art of karate is a mixture of traditional Okinawan *te* and techniques introduced from China. While the original characters for *karate* meant 'Chinese hand', when the martial art was introduced to mainland Japan in the 1920s, the characters 空手 meaning 'empty hand' were used.

In the years before WWII, karate gained increasing popularity on mainland Japan. After the war, occupying troops took the martial art home to America with them. Hollywood became involved and karate's popularity spread around the globe.

Traditional training continues in Okinawa. There are many styles and countless small *dōjō* (training places) around Naha. The **Okinawa Prefectural Budōkan** (Martial Arts Hall; 沖縄県立 武道館; ☎ 858-2700; ⏰ 9am-9pm) is a stunning architectural masterpiece in Onoyama Kōen in Naha. It has three floors of training rooms for all martial arts, not only karate, and welcomes visitors. It is a five-minute walk from the monorail's Tsubogawa Station.

One style that has become truly international is Okinawa Goju-Ryu. The **Okinawan International Goju-Ryu Karate Federation** (IOGKF; www.iogkf.com) has 45 member countries and is based in Naha. In July 2004 its World Budosai event attracted 750 karate practitioners from 35 countries to Naha for a week. The IOGKF is headed by Higaonna Morio Sensei, whose **Higaonna Karate Dōjō** (☎ /fax 864-1673; ⏰ 8pm-late Mon-Sat) is in the Makishi area of Naha. From the monorail's Asato Station walk south on Himeyuri-dōri. After the monorail curves away to the right you'll see a sign for the Higaonna Dōjō just before the Esso gas station on the right-hand side of the road.

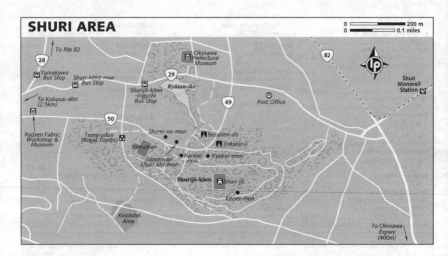

SHURI AREA

Shuri Area 首里

Prior to the Meiji Restoration, Shuri was the capital of Okinawa (that title was surrendered to Naha in 1879). Shuri's temples, shrines, tombs and castle were all destroyed in WWII, although some impressive reconstructions and repairs, with meticulous attention to detail, have been made. Take the Yui-rail monorail to its eastern terminal, Shuri Station.

The reconstructed old residence of the Okinawan royal family, **Shurijō-kōen** (首里城公園; ☎ 886-2020; www.shurijo-park.go.jp/index_e.html; admission ¥800; ☺ 9am-5.30pm Mar-Nov, 9am-5pm Dec-Feb), is well worth a visit. There is an excellent brochure in English highlighting the attractions.

The castle's walls have numerous gates, but the pick is the Chinese-influenced **Shurei-no-mon** (首里の門) which appears on Japan's ¥2000 bank note. As the ceremonial entrance to the castle, the gate was originally constructed some 500 years ago, then rebuilt after the war in 1958. It's considered to be *the* symbol of Okinawa.

The displays in the **Okinawa Prefectural Museum** (沖縄県立博物館; ☎ 884-2243; 1-1 Ōnaka-chō; admission ¥200; ☺ 9am-5pm Tue-Sun) are connected with Okinawan lifestyle, history, culture and natural environment.

Around Naha 那覇周辺

The **Shikinaen** (識名園; ☎ 855-5936; admission ¥300; ☺ 9am-5pm Thu-Tue) garden contains stone bridges, a Chinese-style viewing pavilion and a villa that belonged to the Ryūkyū royal

family. Everything had to be painstakingly rebuilt following WWII. Take bus 1 or 5 to the Shikinaen-mae stop (¥400, 20 minutes).

The **Naha Folkcraft Museum** (那覇市伝統工芸館; ☎ 858-6655; admission ¥300; ☺ 9am-5.30pm Wed-Mon) has an exquisite collection of traditional Okinawan crafts. Staff are on hand to demonstrate glass-blowing, weaving and pottery-making in the workshops. It's a three-minute walk from Akamine monorail station.

FESTIVALS & EVENTS

Naha is a festive city. Most famous are Okinawa's version of summer Obon dances, called Eisa.

Dragon-boat races are held in early May, particularly in Itoman and Naha. With Chinese origins dating back several centuries, these races – called *hari* – bless the luck and prosperity of fishing families.

In October, the **Dai-Ryōkyō Matsuri** brings together over a dozen festivals and special events celebrating Okinawan culture. The **Tsunahiki festival** takes place in Naha on the 10th, when huge teams compete in the world's biggest tug-of-war, using a gigantic 1m-thick rope weighing over 40 tons.

SLEEPING

Budget guesthouses are cheap as dirt and advertised all over the place, but many are practically falling apart. Naha's cheaper ryokan and business hotels are a definite step up, and reliably good value. The city's youth hostels are of a good standard and full of advice.

Budget

Okinawa International Youth Hostel (☎ 857-0073; 51 Ōnoyama; dm ¥3150; P ⊠) Reception stays open until 11pm at this deluxe backpacker resort with coin lockers and laundry, secure key-card entry and no curfew! It's in Ōnoyama Park, a five-minute walk from Tsubogawa or Asahibashi monorail stations.

Harumi Youth Hostel (☎ 867-3218; 2-22-10 Tomari-chō; dm ¥2950; P ⊠) A 15-minute walk north of the Kokusai-dōri, this youth hostel is near Tomari Port. This apartment-like hostel lets guests borrow bicycles for free.

Okinawa Guesthouse (☎ 090-9782-9696; 2-6-13 Nishi; dm ¥1500; ⊠) Within walking distance of Naha port, this place has plenty of alternative characters hanging out.

Shinkinichi Ryokan (☎ 869-4973; 2-12-7 Matsuo; r per person with/without bathroom ¥3600/3100; P ⊠) This is our pick. Not far off Kokusai-dōri, this is convenient, with clean and comfortable rooms (used to be an apartment building). Bigger apartments can take up to 10 guests. There's a coin washing machine and an African-themed café and pub downstairs.

Narumi Ryokan (☎ 867-2138; 2-17-46 Makishi; r per person ¥3200; P ⊠) Also convenient, Narumi is only a couple of minutes away from Kokusai-dōri and Miebashi monorail station.

Midrange

Hotel Route Inn Naha Izumizaki (☎ 860-8311; 1-19-12 Izumizaki; s/d ¥6500/12,000; P ⊠) A fairly new business hotel, this place is convenient to the bus station. Its big communal bathroom is open 24 hours.

Tōyoko Inn Naha Miebashi-eki (☎ 867-1045; 1-20-1 Makishi; s/d ¥5700/6700; P ⊠) Next to Miebashi monorail station, five minutes from Kokusai-dōri, this hotel has free Internet access.

Tōyoko Inn Naha Asahibashi-eki (☎ 951-1045; 2-1-20 Kume; s/tw ¥5800/7800; P ⊠) Good-sized Western-style rooms and convenient to Asahibashi monorail station.

Hotel Sun Okinawa (☎ 866-1111; 1-5-15 Kumoji; s/d ¥8000/12,000; P ⊠) Central and convenient, Hotel Sun is close to Kenchō-mae monorail station.

EATING & DRINKING

There is no shortage of eating, drinking and dancing establishments on and around Kokusai-dōri. It seems every little side street harbours a couple of hidden-away drinking spots.

Daitō Soba (☎ 867-3889; 1-4-59 Makishi; ☼ 11am-10pm) This is a great spot for Okinawa *soba*. It's on Midori-ga-oka Park, a block north of Kokusai-dōri.

Den (☎ 867-2016; 2-3-22 Makishi; ☼ 11am-11pm) For superb *rāmen*, head to Den, second street on the left heading east after Mitsukoshi department store. Try the *rāmen* set for ¥680.

Yakiniku Station Bambohe (☎ 861-4129; 1-3-47 Makishi; ☼ 11am-11pm) If you've got a big appetite and quantity is important, head here where an all-you-can-eat *yakiniku* meal, including dessert and soft drinks, will set you back ¥1800. If you're out before 5pm on weekdays, it's only ¥1080 per person. Beers cost ¥350.

Beer Dome (☎ 868-9838; 1-51 Matsuyama; ☼ 5pm-1am) Also tops for quantity, Beer Dome is a 500-seat beer hall that offers *tabe-hōdai* (all-you-can-eat), *nomi-hōdai* (all-you-can-drink) for ¥2625 for males and ¥2100 for females. Try not to go overboard on the *awamori* or you'll never find your way out. It's just off Rte 58 on Ichigin-dōri, 10 minutes' walk from Kokusai-dōri.

China (☎ 861-8451; 1-1-9 Makishi; ☼ 5pm-3am) A hip *izakaya* that offers a great deal, China is 100m off Kokusai-dōri on Ichigin-dōri. For the first 45 minutes, frosty beers and *awamori* cost ¥100 provided you order one food plate per person.

Paul & Mike's Place (☎ 864-0646; 3-2-2 Makishi; ☼ 5pm-2am) An excellent *gaijin* (foreigners) hangout run by Canadians this place has satellite TV, free Internet access, and two for one Tuesdays. Head here for some local advice.

Good Life Café (☎ 862-2069; 2-1-15 Matsuo; ☼ 8pm-late) This a seven-seat beauty 100m south of Kokusai-dōri on Ukijima-dōri.

Rock in Okinawa (☎ 861-6394; 3-11-2 Makishi; cover ¥500-1500; ☼ 7pm-late) With a schedule of live events and covers, this place has everything from Okinawan pop to hard rock to reggae.

Chakura (☎ 869-0283; 1-2-1 Makishi; cover ¥3000; ☼ 7pm-1am) Chakura is a celebrated 'live house' run by local music maverick Kina Shōkichi. Kina-san and his band, Champloose, perform here nightly (when not touring) starting at 8pm.

If you're on a budget, try browsing along the shopping arcade Heiwa-dōri, where you can buy anything from fresh seafood to *andagi* (Okinawan deep-fried doughnuts) to unique local citrus.

SOBA & SEAFOOD, OKINAWAN STYLE

One of the real treats of visiting the southern islands is all the fine cuisine. The exceptionally long average lifespan of the Okinawan people may in fact be attributed to their balanced diet, with an abundance of healthy *konbu* (kelp) imported from Hokkaidō.

As well as an abundance of fresh produce and seafood, prize beefsteak cows are raised in Okinawa. Pork is also widely enjoyed, particularly in *sōki soba*, bowls of hot noodles with thick slices of tender marinated pork. *Rafute* (pork stewed in ginger, brown sugar, *shōyu* and *awamori*) is a dish once served at the Ryūkyū court.

Thick Okinawan *soba* is justifiably famous, in particular the local varieties found in the Miyako and Yaeyama island groups. Another must-try Okinawan dish is *champuru*, a mixed stir-fry that can be made with a variety of ingredients such as *goya* (bitter melon), *fū* (gluten), papaya etc. For those with strong stomachs, look for stamina-inducing *hijā-jiru* (goat soup) or chewy *mimigā* (pig's ears, sliced and marinated in vinegar). Stewed pig's trotters may also take your fancy.

If you fancy spirits, *awamori*, the local firewater made from rice, has an alcohol content of 30% to 60%. A tonic version even comes with a small habu snake coiled in the bottom of the bottle.

SHOPPING

Okinawa is renowned for its colourful Ryūkyū glassware, a relatively modern folk art that originated after WWII by recycling soda pop and juice bottles used by US occupation forces.

Okinawa also has its own distinctive textiles, particularly the brightly coloured *bingata* and *ryūsen* fabrics.

Much of the Tsuboya pottery is in the form of storage vessels, but look for *shiisā*, the guardian lion-dog figures that can be seen perched on the rooftops of many traditional Okinawan buildings.

GETTING THERE & AWAY

There are direct flights to Naha's airport from 20 Japanese mainland cities (p754), and also from Seoul, Hong Kong, Shanghai and Taiwan.

Various operators have ferry services to Naha from Tokyo, Nagoya, Osaka, Kōbe, Kagoshima and other ports. The schedules are complex (and subject to weather delays), and there is a wide variety of fares. Check out **Ōshima Unyu** (☎ Tokyo 03-5643-6170, Kagoshima 099-222-2338; www.minc.ne.jp/aline in Japanese). Also, see the boxed text, p688.

Arimura Sangyō (in Japan ☎ 869-1980, in Taiwan ☎ 07-330-9811) operates a weekly ferry service between Naha and Taiwan, sometimes via Ishigaki and Miyako in Okinawa-ken. The Taiwan port alternates between Keelung and Kaohsiung. Departure from Okinawa is on Thursday or Friday; departure from

Taiwan is usually on Monday (2nd class one way US$160, 20 hours).

There are three ports in Naha, and this can be confusing. From Naha Port (Naha-kō), ferries head north to Fukuoka/Hakata and Kagoshima, while Naha New Port (Naha Shin-kō) has ferries to Nagoya, Kōbe, Osaka and Tokyo. Ferries to Miyako-jima and Ishigaki-jima may depart from either place. From Tomari Port (Tomari-kō) on Rte 58, ferries operate to a number of the smaller islands around Okinawa-hontō, including Kume-jima, Zamami-jima and Aka-jima.

GETTING AROUND

Naha's impressive new Yui-rail monorail makes things easy for getting around Naha. At one end of the line is Naha Airport, at the other, Shuri. Prices range from ¥200 to ¥290 depending on how far you go. Kenchō-mae Station is at the western end of Kokusai-dōri, while Makishi Station is at its eastern end.

Naha Port (Naha-kō) is a 10-minute walk from Asahibashi Station, while Tomari Port (Tomari-kō) is a similar distance north from Miebashi Station. Bus No 101 from Naha bus terminal heads further north to Naha New Port (Naha Shin-kō).

When riding on local town buses, simply dump ¥200 into the slot next to the driver as you enter. For longer trips, collect a ticket showing your starting point as you board and pay the appropriate fare as you disembark. Buses run from Naha to destinations all over the island.

Okinawa-hontō is a good place to get around in a rented vehicle, although traffic can be heavy. Numerous car hire agencies around Naha charge from around ¥5000 per day. Ask at hotels, guesthouses or youth hostels about hiring bicycles, scooters or motorcycles.

Southern Okinawa-hontō
沖縄本島の南部
☎ 098

The area south of Naha was the scene of some of the heaviest fighting during the closing days of the Battle of Okinawa. There are a number of reminders of those terrible days, as well as some other places of interest in this densely populated part of the island.

WAR SITES
The **Memorial Peace Park** (平和祈念公園) on the southern coast is a sobering place that should not be missed. In the park, the **Okinawa Peace Memorial Museum** (沖縄県平和祈念資料館; ☎ 997-3844; admission ¥300; ☽ 9am-4.30pm Tue-Sun) tells the gruesome story of the 90-day 'typhoon of steel' during the American invasion. The focus is on Okinawan suffering at the hands of both the Japanese military and subsequent US occupation authorities. Memorials from every prefecture in Japan dot the hillside. The **Cornerstone of Peace** (平和の礎) is inscribed with the names of everyone who died in the Battle of Okinawa, controversially listing Okinawan civilians and foreign military personnel right alongside Japanese military commanders. Take bus No 32, 33, 46 or 89 from Naha bus terminal to Itoman (¥500, one hour), from where you transfer to bus 82, which goes to Heiwa Kinen-kōen (¥400, 25 minutes).

Directly south of Naha in Kaigungo-kōen is the **Underground Naval Headquarters** (旧海軍司令部壕; ☎ 850-4055; admission ¥420; ☽ 8.30am-5pm) where 4000 men committed suicide as the battle for Okinawa drew to its prolonged and bloody conclusion. Only 250m of the tunnels are open, but you can wander through the maze of corridors, see the commander's final words on the wall of his room and inspect the holes and scars in other walls from the grenade blasts that killed many of the men. Take bus No 33, 46 or 101 from Naha bus station to the Tomigusuku-kōen-mae stop (¥230, 20 minutes). From there it's a 10-minute walk.

OTHER SIGHTS
If it is all a bit much at the Peace Park, wander a few hundred metres up Rte 331 to the **Itoman Kankō-kōen** (糸満観光農園; ☎ 997-2793; ☽ 9am-6pm) and try their Acerola, or passion fruit wine.

Further east along the coast, tiny **Ō-jima** (奥武島) is linked to the main island by bridge and is famous for its seafood. Excellent tempura is readily available and *tobi-ika* (flying squid) is the speciality in autumn. Bus 53 from Naha bus station goes direct to Ō-jima (¥600, one hour).

For centuries, **Sefa Utaki** (斎場御嶽) was the central shrine for Okinawan religious rites. An *utaki* refers to any sacred grove of trees, a reflection of Okinawans' traditional animistic beliefs. After being confirmed here, royal priestesses once went on to exercise as much secular power as the Ryūkyūan kings who were their brothers, fathers or uncles. The main altar lies past the sacred spring, inside a limestone cave with natural views out to sea and Kudaka-jima. Get off the bus at Taiku-sentā.

Further north is **Chinen Marine Leisure Centre** (知念海洋レジャーセンター; ☎ 948-3355; ☽ 9am-5.30pm) where day-trippers can hire boats to *mujin-shima* (uninhabited islands), including **Kudaka-jima** (久高島) and minute **Komaka-jima** (コマカ島), both encircled by fine beaches. Take Bus No 38 from Naha bus station (¥750, one hour).

Central Okinawa-hontō 沖縄本島の中部
Around this heavily populated stretch of Okinawa are an amazing number of artificial tourist attractions where many thousands of yen could be squandered on entry fees. The US military bases are principally in the southern part of central Okinawa-hontō, and the resorts are in the northern part.

On the east coast south of Okinawa City is **Nakagusuku-jō** (中城城跡; ☎ 895-5719; admission ¥300; ☽ 8.30am-5pm) in an enviable position overlooking the coast. These castle ruins pre-dated stone construction of this type on the mainland by at least 80 years. The castle was destroyed in 1458.

Probably the best-preserved traditional Okinawan house on the island is **Nakamura-ke** (中村家; ☎ 935-3500; admission ¥300; ☽ 9am-5.30pm). The Nakamura family's origins in the area can be traced back to the 15th century, but the foundations date only from around 1720. Notice the substantial stone pigsties, elevated storage area to deter rats and trees grown as typhoon windbreaks. It's a ten-minute walk uphill from Naka-gusuku-jō. Both are a ten-minute taxi ride from Futenma.

Okinawa City (沖縄市) is the US military centre on Okinawa-hontō, focused around Kadena Air Force Base. What was just a village before the war has mushroomed to over 120,000 people and has all the hall-marks of US influence, from pizzerias to army surplus stores.

Touristy **Ryūkyū-mura** (琉球村; ☎ 965-1234; admission ¥840; ⏰ 8.00am-5.30pm) on the west coast offers a re-creation of Okinawan farming life with folk craft demonstrations and live music and dance shows.

The Okinawan beach resort strip runs up the west coast from Cape Zampa. If the idea of staying at a major beach resort appeals, check out **Renaissance Okinawa Resort** (☎ 965-0707; www.renaissance-okinawa.com in Japanese; r per person from ¥17,000), **Manza Beach Hotel** (☎ 966-1211; www.anamanza.co.jp; r per person from ¥19,950) and **Sun Marina Hotel** (☎ 965-2222; www.sunmarina.co.jp in Japanese; r per person from ¥13,000) on the Internet. All offer superb rooms, restaurants, pools and an excellent beach.

The **Busena Terrace** (ザブセナテラス; ☎ 0980-51-1333; www.terrace.co.jp; tw from ¥33,000) looks as manicured as a golf course. This luxury hotel hosted the 2000 G8 Summit and offers water sports and an **underwater tower** (admission ¥1000; ⏰ 9am-6pm) for viewing marine life.

The city of **Nago** (名護) is about two-thirds of the way up the island. There's not a lot to appeal here, but Nago is the junction town for buses to northern Okinawa or the Motobu Peninsula. A fine old banyan tree, Himpun Gajumara, is a useful landmark in the centre of town. The small **Nago Museum** (名護博物館; ☎ 0980-53-1342; admission ¥150; ⏰ 10am-6pm Tue-Sun), south of the banyan tree, has old photographs of traditional *hejichi* (women's tattooing). Almost next door, **Orion Brewery** (オリオンビール名護工場; ☎ 0980-52-2137; ⏰ 9-11am & 1-4pm Mon-Fri) offers tours and tastings of Okinawa's local brew.

Bus No 20 from Naha runs along the west coast to Nago. It takes about one hour to get to Ryūkyū-mura, one hour and 20 minutes to get to Moon Beach, two hours to the Busena Terrace resort and 2½ hours to Nago.

Motobu-hantō 本部半島
☎ 0980

Jutting out to the northwest of Nago, hilly Motobu-hantō has some interesting spots and ferry services to nearby islands. Heading clockwise around the peninsula from Nago (Bus 65) the stretch of highway to Motobu is fairly undeveloped. **Lue on the Beach** (ルーオンザビーチ; ☎ 47-3535, fax 47-5686; s/tw/condos high season ¥7000/11,000/14,000, low season ¥5000/8000/12,000; meals under ¥1000; restaurant ⏰ 11.30am-9pm; Ⓟ ✗) is a minihotel and PADI dive shop. Its laid-back beachfront restaurant serves Okinawan seafood cuisine.

Sesoko-jima (瀬底島), connected to the peninsula by a 762m bridge south of Mo-tobu, has good beaches and camping facili-ties. The island produces tasty watermelons that are available from May in small stalls, and while Okinawa is known for its bovine sumō, Sesoko-jima has its own local goat sumō version that can be seen in May and November.

Tiny **Minna-jima** (水納島), 15 minutes from Motobu town by ferry, has fabulous beaches and diving spots, and is popular as a day trip. The **Minna Kaiun** (☎ 47-5179) ferry service (¥780, three to eight daily) pulls in right beside the beach, which has toilets, showers and stalls.

The **Ie-jima Sonei** (☎ 49-2255) ferry will take you to the popular offshore island of **Ie-jima** (伊江島) from Motobu-ko (¥580, 30 minutes), 1.5km south of Motobu town (see p688 for other details). Northwest of the peninsula, this island offers wonder-ful views from **Gusuku-yama** (城山; 172m), a 45-minute walk from the ferry. Around 10 minutes' walk west of the pier is a **monu-ment** to the US war correspondent Ernie Pyle, who was killed on the island during the early days of the Battle of Okinawa. There are plenty of places to stay including **Minshuku Minami** (民宿みなみ; ☎ 49-2910; r per person with/without meals ¥4500/3000; ✗), a short walk from the port. **Spinnaker Iejima** (スピンネーカー伊江島; ☎ 49-3012, fax 49-5918; d/tr/q ¥7000/9000/10,000; ✗) has sizeable rooms and is close to the beach. There's a camping area out on the east coast. Buses around the 8km-by-3km island are irregular, but bicycles and scooters can be rented at the pier. There are also two ferries a day from Naha's **Tomari-ko** (Asahi Kankō; ☎ 868-1174; ¥3400; 1¼hr) in summer.

A couple of kilometres north of Motobu town is **Ocean Expo Park** (海洋博記念公園; ☎ 48-3748; admission free; ⏰ 9.30am-7pm Fri-Wed Jun-Aug, 9.30am-5.30pm Fri-Wed Sep-May), the site of the 1975 International Ocean Exposition. This park boasts lovely **Emerald Beach** (エメラルド ビーチ). Most individual attractions charge entry fees and close 30 minutes earlier than the park. Worthwhile sights include the massive 10,000-ton **aquarium** (admission ¥1800); **Oceanic Culture Museum** (admission ¥170), with fascinating cultural artefacts drawn from all over Polynesia, Melanesia, Micronesia and Southeast Asia; and a **Native Okinawan Village** (admission free) of traditional houses and indigenous plants. From Nago, bus No 70 runs directly to the park (¥790, 45 minutes). Both peninsula loop lines stop outside.

Set back from the peninsula's north coast and winding over a hilltop, the 14th-century walls of **Nakijin-jō** (今帰仁城跡; ☎ 56-4400; admission ¥150; ⏰ 8.30am-5.30pm) look especially wonderful when the cherry trees bloom. The ruins were once visited by Commodore Perry, who compared its stone gate to ancient Egyptian architecture. In the past, this was the head castle of the unruly Hokuzan kings and contained shrines and sacred houses for *noro* (hereditary priestesses). From the summit of the hill, there are superb views out to sea.

Further along the coast is **Unten-kō** (運天港) from where ferries depart for Iheyajima and Izena-jima.

From Nago frequent bus services cover the peninsula, including circular routes No 66 (anticlockwise) and No 65 (clockwise).

Northern Okinawa-hontō 沖縄本島の北部
☎ 0980

The northern part of Okinawa-hontō is lightly populated and comparatively wild and rugged. Many Okinawan families escaped the obliteration in the south of the island at the end of WWII by hiding out here.

A road hugs the west coast all the way up to **Cape Hedo** (辺戸岬), which marks the northern end of Okinawa. The point is an incredibly scenic spot backed by hills, with rocks rising from the dense greenery. On a good day, Yoron-tō, the southernmost island in the Amami-shotō, is easily seen only 28km to the northeast. The elderly lady in the ramshackle *soba* shop at the point sells tasty *soba* for ¥400.

From Cape Hedo, the road continues to **Oku** (奥), the termination point for buses travelling up the west coast. Heading down the east coast, for the next 15km the road stays very close to the coastline, with more fine-looking beaches but frequent warnings of current and tide dangers. The road then turns inland, and if you're in a rental car, it seems to take forever to get back to what passes as a town. The contrast with southern Okinawa-hontō could not be more extreme.

Islands Around Okinawa-Hontō

The outer islands of the Okinawa-shotō are a completely different story from the hustle and bustle of Okinawa-hontō. Life is more relaxed, there are superb white-sand beaches, and there is more evidence of Ryūkyū culture and traditions. Tourism is still an important industry and things can get busy in summer. Kume-jima even has its own daily flight from Tokyo from June to September.

Kume-jima 久米島
☎ 098 / pop 9600

Ninety kilometres to the west of Okinawa-hontō, Kume-jima is the largest of the offshore islands. It has spectacular beaches, interesting geographical features, and is known for its excellent *awamori*. The airport is at the western extreme of the island, while the main port of Kaneshiro is on the southwest coast. For more information in Japanese check out the website www.kumejima.info

Ifu Beach (イーフビーチ) on the east coast, known for its powdery white sand, is the most popular beach. *Ifu* means 'white' in the local Kume dialect. There are plenty of places to stay on the beachfront. **Hateno-hama** (はての浜) is something special. A 20-minute boat ride from the Kumejima main island, it is a 7km-long sandbar that is surrounded by emerald green seas. The best way to get there is on an excursion. **Hatenohama Kankō Service** (☎ 090-8292-8854) runs a tour with lunch included for ¥4500. On the west coast near the airport and known for its sunsets over the East China Sea is **Shinri-hama** (シンリ浜). There is a camping area here.

On tiny Ō-jima, which is connected to Kume-jima's east coast by a causeway, is the intriguing **Tatami-ishi** (畳石), a natural formation of pentagon-shaped rocks that covers the seashore but can only be seen at low tide.

DIVING IN OKINAWA

Visitors interested in exploring Okinawa from a submarine perspective will find numerous opportunities to dive deep and get friendly with the outstanding variety of fish and coral species that inhabit the tropical Kushiro Straits. The Yaeyama island group boasts Japan's largest reef, stretching some 20km from Ishigaki-jima to Iriomote-jima, and plentiful manta rays.

Dedicated divers should start by checking out www.divejapan.com/okinawainf.htm, which has maps, photos and information on different dive spots throughout the islands. Whether you're a beginner or an old hand, wanting to dive from a boat or from the shore, chances are there's an operator to suit you. Little English is spoken at most of the dive outfits on the islands, which is something those who don't speak Japanese might want to consider.

A couple of exceptions are **Fathoms Diving** (☎ 090-8766-0868; www.fathoms.net) and **Reef Encounters** (☎ 098-968-4442; www.reefen counters.org), which are based on Okinawa-hontō and run by foreigners. Both offer classes from beginner to instructor level, rental equipment and professional guided shore and boat dives. If you're confident of your ability to go diving and speak Japanese at the same time, you'll find countless operators throughout the islands of the Nansei-shotō.

Safety Guidelines for Diving

Before embarking on a scuba diving, skin diving or snorkelling trip, carefully consider the following points to ensure a safe and enjoyable experience.

- Possess a current diving certification card from a recognised scuba diving instructional agency (if scuba diving).
- Be sure you are healthy and feel comfortable diving.
- Obtain reliable information about physical and environmental conditions at the dive site (eg from a reputable local dive operation).
- Be aware of local laws, regulations and etiquette about marine life and the environment.
- Dive only at sites within your realm of experience; if available, engage the services

of a competent, professionally trained dive instructor or dive master.

- Be aware that underwater conditions vary significantly from one region, or even site, to another. Seasonal changes can significantly alter any site and dive conditions. These differences influence the way divers dress for a dive and what diving techniques they use.
- Ask about the environmental characteristics that can affect your diving and how local-trained divers deal with these considerations.

Responsible Diving

Please consider the following tips when diving and help preserve the ecology and beauty of the reefs.

- Never use anchors on the reef, and take care not to ground boats on coral.
- Avoid touching or standing on living marine organisms or dragging equipment across the reef. Polyps can be damaged by even the gentlest contact. If you must hold on to the reef, touch only exposed rock or dead coral.
- Be conscious of your fins. Even without contact, the surge from fin strokes near the reef can damage delicate organisms. Take care not to kick up clouds of sand, which can smother organisms.
- Practise and maintain proper buoyancy control. Major damage can be done by divers descending too fast and colliding with the reef.
- Take great care in underwater caves. Spend as little time within them as possible as your air bubbles may be caught within the roof and thereby leave organisms high and dry. Take turns to inspect the interior of a small cave.
- Resist the temptation to collect or buy corals or shells or to loot marine archaeological sites (mainly shipwrecks).
- Ensure that you take home all your rubbish and any litter you may find as well. Plastics in particular are a serious threat to marine life.
- Do not feed fish.
- Minimise your disturbance of marine animals. *Never* ride on the backs of turtles.

Kumejima-no-Kumesen (久米島の久米仙; ☎ 985-2276; ☉ 10am-noon & 1-4pm) offers the opportunity to check out a real *awamori* factory that uses local spring water to manufacture its headache-inducing product. There are 50 different labels of *awamori* in the factory shop.

Ifu Beach is the place to stay. There's plenty of action along the 1.5km waterfront. The following three places are all within a couple of minutes' walk of the Ifu Beach bus stop. **Minshuku Shirahama** (民宿しらはま; ☎ 985-8336; r per person ¥3000; ✗) has shared facilities, as does **Minshuku Ei** (民宿永; ☎ 985-8142; r per person with/without meals ¥4500/3500; ✗). **Ifu Kankō Hotel** (イーフ観光ホテル; ☎ 985-7678; s/tw ¥5000/10,000; ✗) has private facilities.

JTA, part of the JAL network, has five flights a day between Naha and Kume-jima (¥9700, 30 minutes), and from June to September, a daily flight from Tokyo (¥42,900, two hours 20 minutes). **Kume Shosen** (☎ 098-868-2686) runs a daily ferry from Naha's Tomari-ko to Kume-jima's Kaneshiro-ko (¥2650, four hours).

Kume-jima has an efficient bus system. There are also taxis, rental cars, scooters and bicycles.

Kerama-rettō 慶良間列島

The Kerama Islands are 30km to 40km west of Naha. While there are many smaller islands, the big three that are easy to get to are Zamami-jima, Aka-jima and Tokashiki-jima. The islands feature beautiful beaches, clear emerald seas and excellent diving and snorkelling.

ZAMAMI-JIMA 座間味島
☎ 098 / pop 1050

Zamami-jima has a deserved reputation as an island paradise with some of the clearest waters you will ever see. There is a **tourist information office** (☎ 987-2277; ☉ 8.30am-5.30pm) at the port. More information in Japanese is available at www.vill.zamami.okinawa.jp.

Whale-watching is becoming increasingly popular between January and March, now that humpback whales have returned to these waters. Talk to the tourist information office or call the **whale-watching office** (☎ 896-4141). Tours run once or twice a day, last about two hours and cost ¥5000.

Natureland Kayaks (ネイチャーランドカヤク; ☎ 987-2187), a three-minute walk from

Zamami port, operates excellent sea kayak trips. Day trips with everything included cost ¥11,000 and half-day trips ¥7000.

The tourist office lists 24 dive operators on Zamami-jima, and many others on Okinawa-hontō that run day trips to the islands. Check out the websites in the boxed text, opposite.

Furuzamami Beach (古座間味島ビーチ), 1km east from the port, is a beauty. Boats can be hired at the port to take you out to the smaller, uninhabited islands.

Zamami-jima makes a great day trip from Naha. If you do stay, **Summer House Yūyū** (サマーハウス遊遊; ☎ 987-3055; r per person with/without meals ¥6000/3500; ✗) has both Japanese- and Western-style rooms and is a five-minute walk from the port. **Shirahama Islands Resort** (シラハマアイランズリゾート; ☎ 987-3111; r per person with meals ¥8500; ✗) is more upmarket and also near the port.

RAC, part of the JAL network, has one flight a day from Naha to the Kerama Airport (¥7140, 20 minutes), which is on Fukachi-jima, south of Aka-jima. There are boat connections to Zamami-jima from the airport. **Zamami Sonei** (☎ 098-868-4567) has two or three fast ferries a day (¥2750, 50 minutes) and one regular ferry (¥1860, 1¾ hours) from Naha's Tomari-ko.

There are no buses or taxis on Zamami-jima, though nothing is too far away. Rental cars, scooters and bicycles are available.

AKA-JIMA 阿嘉島
☎ 098 / pop 330

Only a couple of kilometres south of Zamami-jima, Aka-jima is more rugged and hosts fewer day-trippers. The two islands to the south are Keruma-jima and Fukachi-jima, and both are linked in a line to Aka-jima by causeways.

If you keep your eyes open around dusk you might spot a Kerama deer, descendants of deer that were brought by the Satsuma from Kagoshima when they conquered the Ryūkyūs in 1609. The deer are smaller and darker than their mainland cousins and have been appointed a national treasure.

Aka-jima has some good dive spots. **Pension Shiisa** (ペンションシーサー; ☎ 987-2973; r per person with meals ¥6500; ✗) is a popular dive-and-stay operation that will pick you up at the ferry terminal. The best beach is **Nishihama** (ニシハマビーチ) on the east coast, but if you're after beaches, you're better off to head to Zamami-jima.

For transport details see p705.

TOKASHIKI-JIMA 渡嘉敷島
☎ 098 / pop 750

The largest island of the Kerama-rettō, and closest to Okinawa-hontō, is Tokashiki-jima. A long, skinny, north–south standing island, Tokashiki-jima has some outstanding beaches, particularly **Tokashiku Beach** (とかしくビーチ) and **Aharen Beach** (阿波連ビーチ) on its west coast. Aharen is particularly good for snorkelling. The port of **Tokashiki** (渡嘉敷) is on the east coast, from where it is 3km by bus to Tokashiku and 5km by bus to Aharen. The island also has some superb dive sites.

Check out www.vill.tokashiki.okinawa.jp for more information on Tokashiki-jima. The photo gallery is inspiring.

For those who want to see what's under the sea without getting wet, the **Yellow Submarine** (☎ 987-2010) operates from Aharen Beach (¥2000, 40 minutes). It's not really a submarine, but has underwater viewing of the spectacular corals and fish.

Aharen is the place to stay. A few blocks back from the beach is **Minshuku Kerama-sō** (民宿けらま荘; ☎ 987-2125; r per person with/without meals ¥5500/3500; ✖), while **Pension Southern Cross** (ペンシォンサザンクロス; ☎ 987-2258; r per person with/without meals ¥6500/4000; ✖) is virtually on the beach, with the Southern Cross Marine Service attached.

Only 35 minutes from Naha by fast ferry, Tokashiki-jima makes an ideal day trip from Naha. **Tokashiki Sonei** (☎ 098-987-2537) operates two fast ferries a day (¥2210, 35 minutes) and one regular ferry (¥1470, one hour 10 minutes) from Naha's Tomari-ko.

Iheya-jima & Izena-jima 伊平島 伊是名島
☎ 0980 / pop 1600 & 1900

Usually thought of as a pair, Iheya-jima and Izena-jima are 30km offshore to the northwest of Okinawa-hontō. The northernmost islands in Okinawa Prefecture, they are accessed by ferry from Unten-ko port on the northern side of the Motobu-hantō.

Iheya-jima, to the north, is long and skinny, while Izena-jima, 5km to the south, is shaped more like a ball. The islands have good beaches and snorkelling, and plenty of places to stay.

Hillier than its southern neighbour, with five 'mountains' over 200m along its spine, Iheya-jima has some impressive natural assets. Guarding Mae-domari harbour is the landmark of **Torazu-iwa** (虎頭岩; Tiger's Head Rock), which can be climbed for some excellent views. At the northern end of the island, **Kumaya Dōkutsu** (クマヤ洞窟) is a huge natural cavern nearly 50m deep and 15m tall at its highest point. Next door is the Kumaya camping ground. A couple of kilometres south, **Nentōhiramatsu** (念頭平松) is a 300-year-old pine tree that has been trained to look like an umbrella. At the southern tip of Iheya-jima is the island's top beach, **Yonesaki Beach** (米崎ビーチ), where there is also a camping area. A 1250m bridge links Yonesaki with Noho-jima, a tiny island to the south. **Minshuku Uchima-sō** (民宿内間荘; ☎ 46-2503; r per person with/without meals ¥5000/4000; ✖) is a five-minute walk from Mae-domari port. For more information in Japanese, take a look at www.vill.iheya.okinawa.jp.

Surrounded by coral reef, Izena-jima has historical links to the Ryūkyū rulers. Check out the island's history and culture at the **Folklore Museum** (伊是名村ふれあい民俗館; ☎ 45-2165; admission ¥200; ☉ 9am-5pm Wed-Sun). One-third of the island is the **Izenayama Forest Park** (伊是名山森林公園) with a sea of Ryūkyū pines and walking trails. On the south coast, the **Futamigaura-kaigan** (二見が浦海岸) is a famous coastline with the island's most recognisable landmarks: the **Azagitara** and **Umigitara** standing rocks, which face each other, one from the land and the other from the sea. **Nakagawakan** (なか川館; ☎ 45-2100; r per person with/without meals ¥5000/3000; ✖) is five minutes' walk from Nakata port. For more information in Japanese, look up www.izena-okinawa.jp.

Iheya Sonei (☎ 0980-46-2177) operates two ferries each day to Maedomari-ko on Iheya-jima from Unten-ko port on the main island (¥2380, 1¼ hours). Similarly, **Izena Sonei** (☎ 0980-56-5084) has two ferries a day to Nakata-ko on Izena-jima from Unten-ko (¥1760, one hour). Unten-ko can be reached by bus from Nago.

MIYAKO-SHOTŌ 宮古諸島
About 300km southwest of Okinawa, directly en route to the Yaeyama-shotō, is the eight-island Miyako group, comprising Miyako-jima, Irabu-jima and Shimoji-jima a few

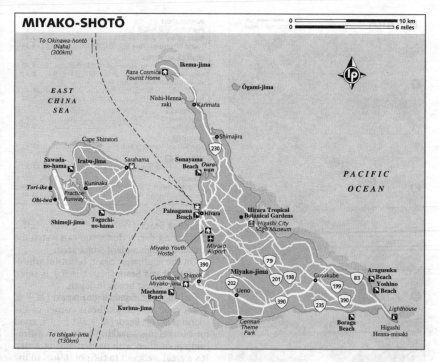

MIYAKO-SHOTŌ

kilometres to the west, plus a scattering of smaller islands.

Miyako-jima 宮古島

☎ 0980 / pop 49,000

Covered in sugar-cane plantations, Miyako-jima offers fine beaches and diving. Over 1500 triathletes flock to the island in April for the Strongman All-Japan Triathlon.

SIGHTS & ACTIVITIES
Hirara 平良

Miyako-jima's main attractions are its beaches and dive spots. The city could hardly be described as attractive, and is rather sprawling at its centre, the rough square formed by McCrum-dōri, Shimozato-dōri and Ichiba-dōri. If you think McCrum-dōri is an unusual name for a Japanese street, you're right. McCrum, the American in charge of Miyako-jima after the war, bulldozed a wide road from the port to his inland weather station. The road still bears his name.

The **tourist information office** (☎ 73-1881; ☷ 9am-6pm Mon-Sat) is helpful, if a little hard

to find, and has a useful English-language *Okinawa Miyako Islands Guide*. There's also an **airport information desk** (☎ 72-0899) that is open for all flight arrivals.

On the ground floor of the ferry terminal building, **Eco-Guide Café** (☎ 75-6050; ☷ 8.30am-5pm) offers maps of nearby islands, diving advice and Internet access. It's also possible to access the Net for free on the 2nd floor of the **public library** (cnr McCrum-dōri & Chuo-dōri). The ATMs at the **post office** (Ichiba-dōri) accept foreign money cards.

Near the waterfront is the **mausoleum** of Nakasone Tōimiyā, the 15th-century hero who not only conquered the Yaeyama-shotō, but prevented an invasion from the north. Around 500m north of town along the coast road, the **Nintōzeiseki** (人頭税石) is a 1.4m-high stone used to determine who was required to pay taxes during the heavy-handed rule of the Shimazu who invaded from southern Kyūshū in the early 1600s.

The **Hakuai (Kaiser Wilhelm) Monument** was presented as a gesture of gratitude for the rescue of the crew of a typhoon-wrecked German merchant ship in 1873. (Out on

OKINAWA & THE SOUTHWEST ISLANDS

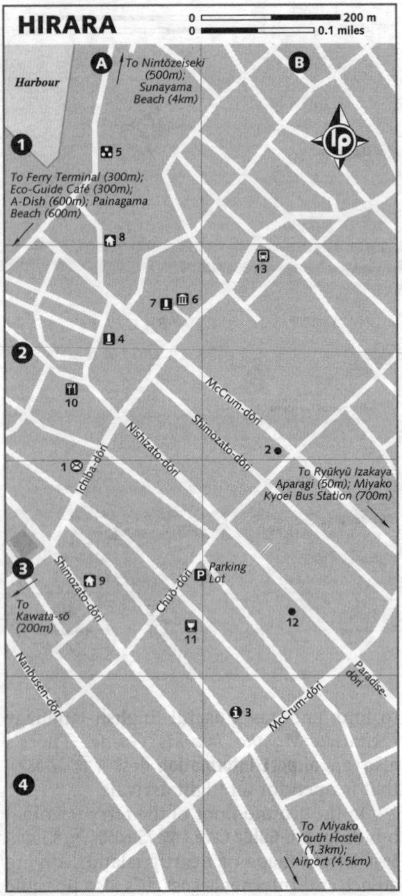

INFORMATION
Post Office 平良西郵便局 1 A3
Public Library 平良市立図書館 2 B2
Tourist Information Office 観光協会案内所 3 B4

SIGHTS & ACTIVITIES
Hakuai (Kaiser Wilhelm) Monument 博愛記念碑 4 A2
Mausoleum of Nakasone Tōimiyâ 仲宗根豊見親の墓 5 A1
Miyako Traditional Arts & Crafts Centre 宮古伝統工芸品研究センター 6 A2
Miyako-jinja 宮古神社 7 A2

SLEEPING
Hotel Kyōwa ホテル共和 8 A1
Pension Star ペンションスター 9 A3

EATING
Koja Shokudō Honten 古謝食堂本店 10 A2

DRINKING
Awamori & Music Jang Jang 泡盛&Music Jang Jang 11 A3

TRANSPORT
Tomihama Motors 富浜モータース 12 B3
Yachiyo Bus Terminal 八千代バスターミナル 13 B2

the southern coast of the island and capitalising on this historical connection is a highly kitsch German theme park.)

Miyako Traditional Arts & Crafts Centre (☎ 72-8022; admission free; 9am-6pm Mon-Sat) displays traditional crafts next to the town shrine, **Miyako-jinja**. Check out the *minsā* weaving looms on the 2nd floor.

Just a short walk south of the ferry terminal is the surprisingly attractive **Painagama Beach** (パイナガマビーチ), good for swimming. Locals often have beach parties here.

Beaches & Diving

Miyako-jima has some great beaches, surf and diving spots. North of Hirara is lovely **Sunayama Beach** (砂山ビーチ), where after clambering over a dune, you can watch the sunset through a giant stone arch.

On the southwest coast, beautiful white-sand **Maehama Beach** (前浜ビーチ) is often called the finest beach in Japan.

Just short of **Higashi Henna-misaki** (東平安名崎) cape on the southeast corner of the island is **Boraga Beach** (ボラガビーチ), good for snorkelling, kayaking and with a swimming pool filled with natural-spring water. It's a great walk out to the point. Just to the north, on the east coast, you can snorkel at **Yoshino Beach** (吉野ビーチ) and **Aragusuku Beach** (親城ビーチ).

There are also good beaches on **Ikema-jima** (池間島), off the northernmost point of Miyako-jima, and on **Kurima-jima** (来間島) to the south. Both islands are linked to the main island by a bridge. Each year the very low spring tide reveals the huge **Yaebishi reef**, north of Ikema-jima.

Miyako-jima is a wildly popular diving centre, with more than 50 dive sites and a dynamic range of underwater drop-offs and overhangs. There are plenty of dive operators on the island. Check out **Good Fellas Club** (☎ 73-5483; www.goodfellas.co.jp).

Other Sights

Six kilometres east of Hirara harbour is the worthwhile **Hirara City Sōgō Museum** (平良市総合博物館; ☎ 730567; admission ¥300; 9am-4pm Tue-Sun) with documentary videos of fast-disappearing Okinawan religious rites and traditional island festivals.

Two hundred metres north are the **Hirara Tropical Botanical Gardens** (平良市熱帯植物

園; ☎ 72-3751; admission free; ☺ 8.30am-6pm) with over 40,000 tropical trees and plants, and 1600 species. In the park grounds are the **Nangoku Art Gallery** (南国美術館) and **Miyako Triathlon Hall** (トライアスロン記念館; ☎ 75-3113; combined admission ¥600; ☺ 10am-6pm).

SLEEPING

There are camping grounds at many beaches, including Maebama, Boraga and Aragusuku. Budget guesthouses often advertise with flyers inside the ferry terminal, but you get what you pay for.

Miyako Youth Hostel (宮古島ユースホステル; ☎ 73-7700; dm ¥3000; meals available; ℙ ✗) This YH has clean air-con dorms. It's a 2km (30-minute) hike from the ferry terminal.

Kawata-sō (川田荘; ☎ 72-3368; r per person ¥3000; ℙ ✗) This place has reasonable rooms in a quiet part of town. The owners also run a great *izakaya* (Japanese pub or eatery).

Pension Star (ペンションスター; ☎ 73-1239, fax 72-9922; s/d with breakfast ¥5500/10,000; ℙ ✗) With its neon star flashing above the entertainment district, this place has a rooftop deck. Reception is on the 4th floor.

Hotel Kyōwa (ホテル共和; ☎ 73-2288; www.hotelkyowa.co.jp in Japanese; s/d/tr/q with breakfast ¥5000/9000/12,000/14,000; ℙ ✗) Convenient to the port, this hotel has good facilities and a coin laundry.

Guesthouse Miyako-jima (ゲストハウス宮古島; ☎ /fax 76-2330; yonaha233@beach.ocn.ne.jp; s ¥2500, 1 week ¥15,000; ℙ ✗) This place is close to Maehama Beach. All basic rooms have air-con and share a kitchen. Call ahead for free pick-ups from the airport or ferry terminal. Guests can borrow bicycles and 50cc motorbikes for free.

Raza Cosmica Tourist Home (ラザコスミカツーリストホーム; ☎ 75-5020; www.raza-cosmica

.com; r per person with 2 meals ¥10,000; ℙ ✗) Located on Ikema-jima, this place offers peace and quiet in truly beautiful surroundings. Run by a friendly young couple, this charmingly eclectic inn sits above a secluded little beach cove.

EATING & DRINKING

Koja Shokudō Honten (古謝食堂本店; ☎ 72-2139; ☺ 10am-10pm) Miyako-jima is known for its local *soba*. An excellent spot in central Hirara to try it is Koja, a local legend open for over 50 years.

Ryūkyū Izakeya Aparagi (琉球居酒屋あぱら樹; ☎ 73-6655; ☺ 11am-11pm) 1.5km straight inland on McCrum-dōri, Aparagi serves great local fare in a superb atmosphere.

A-Dish (☎ 72-7114; ☺ 6-12pm Tue-Sat) A short walk southwest of the ferry terminal, A-Dish offers a hip atmosphere. Its tempting pastas feature fresh local ingredients.

Awamori & Music Jang Jang (☎ 73-8668; cover ¥300; ☺ 8.30pm-2am) This lively spot offers live Okinawan folk music and wicked *awamori* in central Hirara.

GETTING THERE & AROUND

JTA, part of the JAL network, and ANK, an ANA affiliate (p753), have daily direct flights to/from Tokyo (JTA, ¥46,800, 3½ hours, one daily) and Osaka (ANK/JTA, ¥40,000, two hours, two daily), as well as flights to Naha (ANK/JTA, ¥14,500, 45 minutes, 12 daily) and Ishigaki-jima (ANK/JTA, ¥9500, 20 minutes, four daily).

There are two or three ferries a week to/from Naha (¥4250, nine hours) and to/from Ishigaki-jima (¥2070, 5½ hours). Call Arimura Sangyō (☎ 098-860-1980) or Ryūkyū Kaiun (☎ 098-868-1126). Check the latest schedules posted in the ferry terminal building.

THE 'COMMUNICATION DRINK'

The friendly people of Miyako-jima have earned a reputation for drinking, and the Izato entertainment area in the town of Hirara is said to have more bars relative to its population than any other town in Japan.

Miyako even has its unique local drinking custom, called *otori*. This group ritual involves making a speech, filling your own glass (usually with potent *awamori*, the local liquor) and then filling the glasses of all in the room. Everyone drinks up, the leader makes a short closing speech, picks the next victim and the routine starts all over again. Miyako's *otori* is so notorious that even hard-livered Okinawans from neighbouring islands are said to fear the ritual. If you happen to end up lured into an *otori* and want to sneak out before getting plastered, one local veteran boozer advises, 'Never say goodbye. Just head for the toilet and don't come back!'

Miyako-jima has a sporadic bus network. There are no buses into the centre of Hirara from the airport. Taxis cost ¥1000. Buses run from **Yachiyo bus terminal** (八千代バスターミナル) to the north of the island, including to Ikema-jima (35 minutes). Buses from **Miyako Kyōei bus station** (宮古協栄バスターミナル) head south toward Maehama and Higashi-Henna-misaki (50 minutes).

Rental cars, scooters and bicycles are readily available. **Tomihama Motors** (富浜モータース; ☎ 72-3031; ⏰ 9am-6pm) has scooters for ¥2000 a day. It's a great ride around the southern coast.

Irabu-jima & Shimoji-jima 伊良部島・下地島

Only a 10-minute ferry ride off the western coasts of Miyako-jima, Irabu-jima and Shimoji-jima, linked by six small bridges, are pleasantly rural islands with fields of sugar cane. If you fly over Shimoji-jima (between Okinawa and Ishigaki-jima), take a look down at the airport runway below. It seems longer than the island itself as it's a 'practise runway' used by airlines for touch-and-go training.

Sawada-no-hama (佐和田の浜) and **Toguchi-no-hama** (渡口の浜) are two good beaches on Irabu-jima's west coast, both with camping grounds. On Shimoji-jima's west coast, to the west of the runway, **Tōri-ike** (通り池) is linked to the sea by hidden tunnels (a great dive site!). Around 800m to the south is **Obi-iwa** (帯岩), a 13m-high rock that was thrown up from the sea floor by a tsunami after a massive earthquake in 1771.

The islands are best visited as a day trip from Hirara. **Miyako Ferry** (☎ 72-3263) and **Hayate Kaiun** (☎ 78-3337) between them operate nearly 30 speedboats a day (¥410, 10 minutes) to Irabu-jima. Rental bicycles are available once there.

YAEYAMA-SHOTŌ 八重山諸島

At the far southwestern end of the Nansei-shotō are the islands of the Yaeyama group, consisting of two main islands, Ishigaki-jima and Iriomote-jima, and a scattering of smaller isles between and beyond. The seas are renowned for their superb diving and the 19 islands for their excellent beaches. The islands are heaven for alternative life-stylers, and there are intriguing people to be met and fascinating experiences to be had.

Ishigaki-jima 石垣島
☎ 0980 / pop 45,000

Ishigaki-jima, located 410km southwest of Okinawa-hontō, is the major flight destination in the Yaeyama-shotō with direct flights from major cities on the mainland and from Naha. Boat services fan out from its harbour to the other islands. Ishigaki city is the southernmost city in Japan.

ORIENTATION & INFORMATION

The town of Ishigaki centres on its harbour. You can stroll around the rest in an hour. Parallel to the main street are two covered shopping arcades.

The **tourist information office** (☎ 82-2809; ⏰ 8.30am-5.30pm Mon-Fri), in the building next to the library, has friendly staff and an English-language brochure on the Yaeyama-shotō. If you fly in, there's a small but helpful **airport information booth** (☎ 88-0638; ⏰ 8am-8pm). For information in Japanese, check out the website www.yaeyama.or.jp

Internet access is available at **Ishigaki Net Café** (☎ 83-8684; ⏰ 12pm-3am). The ATMs at the post office (200m up the main road heading inland from the port) take international money cards.

SIGHTS & ACTIVITIES

Located near the harbour, the modest **Yaeyama Museum** (☎ 82-4712; admission ¥100; ⏰ 9am-4.30pm Tue-Sun) displays coffin palanquins, dugout canoes, island textiles and festival photographs.

Although the Nansei-shotō never really had samurai, **Miyara Dōnchi** (☎ 82-2767; admission ¥200; ⏰ 9am-5pm Wed-Mon) is essentially a samurai-style house. Worth strolling over to see, it dates from 1819 and is the only one left in the whole island chain.

Founded in 1614, the Zen temple of **Tōrin-ji** has 18th-century statues of Deva kings (said to be the guardian deities of the islands) that can be seen in the dim interiors. Immediately adjacent to the temple is **Gongen-dō**. The original shrine was built in 1614, but was destroyed by a tsunami in 1771.

About 6km northwest of the town is **Tōjin-baka** (唐人墓), a Chinese cemetery with colourful mausoleums. It commemorates those Chinese labourers who sought refuge on Ishigaki-jima after escaping from British and American taskmasters during their voyage to California.

Beaches & Diving

There are a number of beaches around the island for snorkelling and diving.

If you walk out over an expanse of coral at **Yonehara Beach** (米原ビーチ) there's good snorkelling to be found at the reef's edge. This spot is good for beginners and for underwater photography. Camping is possible at Yonehara.

Famed **Kabira-wan** (川平湾) just to the west, is a sheltered bay with fine sand; it has a cultured black-pearl industry and glass-bottomed-boat tours (¥1000, one hour) run by **Kabira Marine** (☎ 88-2335). Over the peninsula is popular white-sand **Sukuji Beach** (底地ビーチ), which extends northeast to **Kabira Ishizaki** (川平石崎). The seas off this point are known among divers for excellent manta ray spotting from spring to summer.

There are a number of dive shops on Ishigaki-jima, including **Tom Sawyer Dive Shop** (☎ 83-4677; ⏰ 8am-8pm) in Ishigaki town. Popular dive spots include the mazelike tunnels at Kabira-wan, and reefs off Yonehara Beach and Cape Hirakubo lighthouse.

Hiking

Banna-dake (バンナ岳; 230m), 4km north of Ishigaki harbour, has fine views from along its skyline approach road. To the north, **Banna-kōen** (バンナ公園; admission free), a botanical garden, has over 2500 species of tropical flora.

Omoto-dake (於茂登岳; 526m) is the highest point in Okinawa-ken, with good views from the large boulder at the top. On the slopes between Omoto-dake and Yonehara Beach are the **Yaeyama Palm Tree** (ヤエヤマヤシ) groves. The 15m- to 25m-tall palms grow wild only in the Yaeyama group and have been designated a national natural monument. There are good walks in the area.

Good hiking exists on **Nosoko-dake** (野底岳; 282m), the eroded core of a volcano, where a steep 45-minute trek takes you to the summit for excellent views, particularly of the island's northern peninsula.

Northwest of Kabira-wan, **Mae-dake** (前岳; 263m) has a moister, jungle-feel and, like Nosoko-dake, is steep at the top with great views.

SLEEPING

Ishigaki is a compact little town and there are plenty of places to stay within walking distance of the harbour. Places with shared accommodation that you may see advertised on the street are extremely basic.

Yashima Ryokan Youth Hostel (☎ 82-3157; dm ¥2600; P ✗) This is a basic youth hostel in a traditional house close to Ishigaki's town centre, a few minutes' walk north of the Yaeyama Museum.

Minshuku Tabi-no-yado (☎ 82-8038; r per person ¥2000; ✗) Near the main post office, this place is basic with shared facilities. Free coffee and bread for breakfast is included.

Rakutenya (☎ 83-8713; r per person ¥3000; P ✗) A good spot, this place has simple rooms in a rickety, old wooden house. It's the best place if you don't speak any Japanese. The friendly couple speak English and are a fantastic source of local information. Internet access is free, as are tea and coffee.

Pension Yaima-biyōri (☎ 88-5578; r per person ¥3000; ✗) This is also a good deal with big rooms and shared facilities one minute's walk from the bus terminal. A bonus of staying here is a 'free drink' coupon for Mori-no-Kokage, a superb little *izakaya* run by the owner's wife. Try learning the *sanshin*, Okinawa's version of the *shamisen* (three-stringed guitar), here.

Hyper Hotel Ishigaki-jima (☎ 82-2000; www .hyper-hotel.co.jp/ishigakijima in Japanese; s/d/tr with light breakfast ¥4900/5900/6900; P ✗) A sizeable, newish hotel, this place offers all kinds of perks, including extrawide beds, complimentary English-language maps, coin lockers and laundry.

Super Hotel Ishigaki (☎ 83-9000; www.infinix.co .jp/sh/room.html in Japanese; s with breakfast Mon-Fri ¥5800, Sat & Sun ¥4800; P ✗) Single rooms only. Both this place and the Hyper Hotel have 24-hour secure access.

EATING & DRINKING

Mori-no-Kokage (☎ 83-7933; ⏰ 5pm-midnight Mon-Sat) Our top pick, this is a superb little *izakaya* with a generous selection of Ishigaki *awamori*, local delicacies and Okinawan music. Try the *Yaeyama champon* for ¥650.

Eifuku Shokudō (☎ 82-5838; ⏰ 8.30am-11pm) Eifuku claims to serve the cheapest Yaeyama *soba* in the city (¥300). It's good – but give the goat meat *soba* a go for ¥500.

Misushi (☎ 82-3708; ⏰ 5.30-11pm) Misushi serves top sushi on an extralong counter.

Yaoya (☎ 83-0235; ⏰ 7pm-late) This is a delicious *kushi katsu* shop run by a couple from

YAEYAMA–SHOTŌ

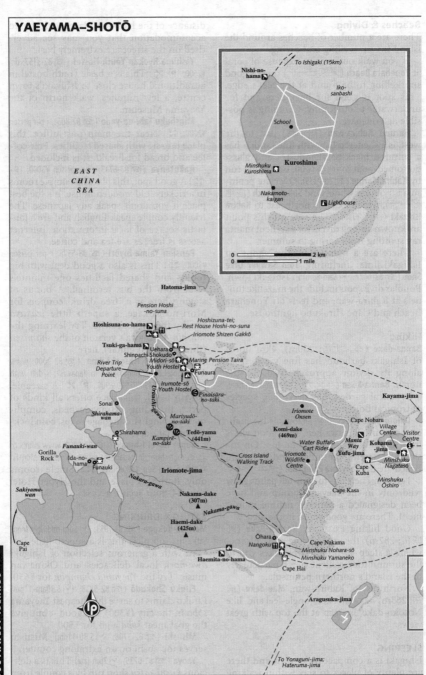

Inset map:

To Ishigaki (15km)

Nishi-no-hama

Iko-sanbashi

School

Kuroshima

Minshuku Kuroshima

Nakamoto-kaigan

Lighthouse

0   2 km
0   1 mile

Main map:

EAST
CHINA
SEA

Hatoma-jima

Pension Hoshi -no-suna

Hoshizuna-tei;
Rest House Hoshi-no-suna
Iriomote Shizen Gakkō

Hoshisuna-no-hama

Tsuki-ga-hama
Uehara
Shinpachi Shokudo
Midori-sō
Youth Hostel

River Trip
Departure
Point

Marine Pension Taira
Funaura

Irumote-sō
Youth Hostel

Pinaisāra-no-taki

Kayama-jima

Sonai
Shirahama-wan

Mariyudō-no-taki

Iriomote
Onsen

Cape Nobaru

Village Centre

Visitor Centre

Shirahama

Kampire-no-taki

Tedō-yama
(441m)

Komi-dake
(469m)

Water Buffalo
Cart Rides

Manta Way
Yufu-jima

Kohama-jima

Funauki-wan

Gorilla
Rock

Ida-no-hama
Funauki

Cross Island
Walking Track

Iriomote
Wildlife
Centre

Cape Kuba

Minshuku
Nagatasō

Iriomote-jima

Nakara-gawa

Minshuku
Ōshiro

Cape Kasa

Sakiyama-wan

Nakama-dake
(307m)

Nakama-gawa

Haemi-dake
(425m)

Cape
Pai

Ōhara
Nangoku

Cape Nakama
Minshuku Nohara-sō
Minshuku Yamaneko

Haemita-no-hama

Cape Hai

Aragusuku-jima

To Yonaguni-jima;
Hateruma-jima

Uranchi-gawa

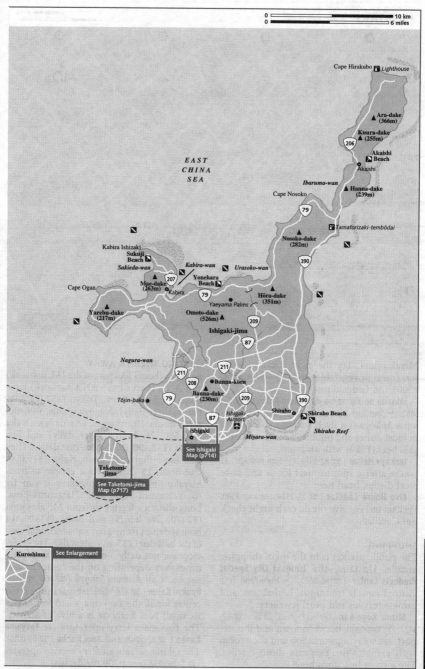

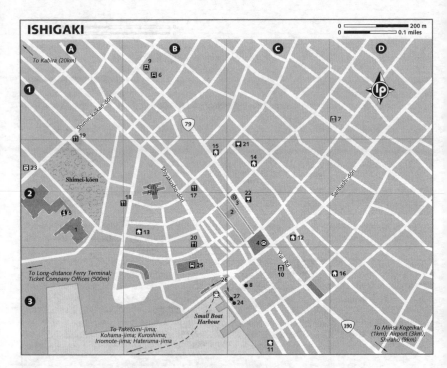

ISHIGAKI

Miyako-jima. Try the eight sticks of *yaki-tori* (meat or vegetables cooked on skewers, ¥500) and Ishigaki microbrews.

Minami-no-shima-no-daidokoro Ajikoya (☎ 88-5681; ⏳ 5pm-late) Minami-no-shima-nodaido-koro Ajikoya is a lively *izakaya* specialising in local dishes and liquors. Try the raw Ishi-gaki beef (¥980) with *awamori*.

Izakaya Haisai (☎ 82-5388; ⏳ 5pm-midnight) If you're after a spot to meet locals and taste local dishes, head here.

Live House Cadillac (☎ 83-1314; entrance ¥500; ⏳ 10pm-late) For live music each night check out Cadillac.

SHOPPING

The public market is in the main shopping arcade. Upstairs, the **Ishigaki City Special Products Centre** (☎ 88-8633; ⏳ 10am-7pm) lets visitors sample traditional herbal teas, and browse textiles and pearl jewellery.

Minsā Kōgeikan (みんさー工芸館; ☎ 82-3473; ⏳ 9am-6pm), between town and the air-port, is a weaving workshop and showroom with exhibits on Yaeyama-shotō textiles. The airport bus stops here.

GETTING THERE & AWAY

Between them JTA (part of the JAL network) and ANK (part of the ANA network) have direct flights to/from Tokyo (¥52,000, 3½ hours, three daily), Nagoya (ANK, ¥49,400, three hours 10 minutes, one daily), Osaka (¥41,500, 2¾ hours, three daily) and Fu-kuoka (¥38,400, 2¼ hours, one daily). They also have flights to/from Naha (¥19,000, one hour, 15 daily) and a couple to/from Miyako-jima. From Ishigaki you can fly to Yonaguni-jima and Hateruma-jima. Long-distance ferries to/from Miyako-jima (¥2070, five hours) and Naha (¥5900, 14 hours) depart from/arrive at a terminal west of the harbour (a 15-minute walk). These ser-vices are not daily – exact prices and travel times vary depending on the company and season. Call **Arimura Sangyō** (☎ 860-1980) or **Ryūkyū Kaiun** (☎ 868-1126). Ishigaki-jima is the centre for all the Yaeyama-shotō ferries and its small boat harbour is a hive of activity. The two main ferry operators are **Yaeyama Kankō** (☎ 82-5010) and **Anei Kankō** (☎ 83-0055). The Okinawa-Taiwan ferry service operates via Ishigaki (see p700 for details).

GETTING AROUND

The bus station is across the road from the harbour in Ishigaki town. Buses to the airport (¥200, 15 minutes) are timed to flights. Infrequent services head north to Kabira-wan (¥580, 40 minutes) and Yonehara Beach (¥720, one hour), or to Shiraho (¥350, 30 minutes) and up the east coast to the island's northern tip.

Rental cars, scooters and bicycles are readily available. It's easy to ride around the island in three or four hours on a scooter.

Iriomote-jima 西表島

☎ 0980 / pop 4500

Dense jungle blankets 90% of Iriomote-jima, an island 20km west of Ishigaki that could well qualify as Japan's last frontier. On a time line, Iriomote-jima seems decades behind the mainland and alternative lifestylers abound. The island's major attractions are beaches, rivers and waterfalls, and the Iriomote *yamaneko* (wildcat). Similar in size and appearance to a domestic cat, the wildcat is nocturnal and rarely seen. Road signs alerting drivers to its possible presence are common.

Iriomote-jima has a 58km-long perimeter road that runs about halfway around the coast. No roads run into the interior, which is virtually untouched. Boats from Ishigaki-jima either dock at Funaura or Uehara on the north coast, which are closer to the main points of interest, or at Ōhara on the southeast coast.

The majority of visitors come on day trips from Ishigaki, but Iriomote-jima offers plenty for those with a bit of time. There is no shortage of ecotour operators and options should you prefer a guided tour.

RIVER TRIPS

Iriomote's number one attraction is a trip up the **Urauchi-gawa** (浦内側), a winding brown river that's a lot like a tiny stretch of the Amazon. From where the boats stop, it's a 2km (30-minute) walk to the spectacular waterfalls, **Mariyudō-no-taki** (マリユドウの滝), and long, rapids-like **Kampirē-no-taki** (カンピレーの滝). There are some good swimming holes around the falls. **Urauchi-gawa Kankō** (浦内側観光; ☎ 85-6154; www.urauchigawa.com in Japanese) has various options including boat/falls/boat (¥1500, three hours) and boat/falls/canoe (¥8400 with guide, six hours).

From close to the Ōhara docks it is possible to take cruises (¥1260, one hour) with **Tōbu Kōtsū** (☎ 85-5304; ⏰ 8.30am-5.30pm) up Iriomote's second-largest river, the **Nakama-gawa** (仲間川), passing through mangroves and lush, jungle-like vegetation.

You can also rent canoes and kayaks near boat departure points.

HIKING

There are some great walks in Iriomote-jima's jungle-clad interior.

Pinaisāra-no-taki (ピナイサーラの滝), Okinawa's highest waterfall, on the hills behind the lagoon, are visible from boats coming into Funaura. When the tide is right, you can rent a kayak, paddle across the shallow lagoon, then follow the river up to the base of the falls. A path branches off and climbs to the top of the falls, from where there are superb views down to the coast. The walk takes less than two hours and the falls are great for a cooling dip, but get some tide advice from locals before heading out or you could find yourself wading through mud on the way back.

From Kampirē-no-taki, at the end of the Urauchi-gawa trip, you can continue on the challenging **cross-island walking track** south to Ōhara. The 18km-hike takes a full day and is particularly popular in spring, when the many trekkers manage to lay a confusing

OKINAWA & THE SOUTHWEST ISLANDS

network of false trails. All you need to know about exploring Iriomote-jima on foot is found in Lonely Planet's *Hiking in Japan*.

BEACHES & DIVING

Many of the island's scenic beaches are rocky and have shallow waters. An exception, and great for swimming, is **Tsuki-ga-hama** (月が浜; Moon Beach) shaped like a crescent moon, at the mouth of the Urauchi River on the north coast. **Hoshisuna-no-hama** (星砂の浜), around the point to the north, has star sand and good snorkelling.

From Shirahama, at the western end of the north coast road, boats to the tiny end-of-the-line settlement of **Funauki** (船浮) depart four times a day (¥410). Once there, gorgeous **Ida-no-hama** (イダの浜) beach is only 10 minutes' walk away.

If you want to have a sandy beach to yourself, head to **Haemita-no-hama** (南風見田の浜) at the extreme western end of the south coast road. On a good day, Haterumajima can be seen far to the south.

Diving around Iriomote-jima certainly isn't cheap, but there are some fine sites, like the famed Manta Way in the straits between Iriomote-jima and Kohama-jima, where you have a good chance to come across manta rays, especially in late spring and early summer.

OTHER SIGHTS & ACTIVITIES

Iriomote Onsen (西表温泉; ☎ 85-5700; admission ¥1200; ☼ 10am-10pm) on the east coast has a *rotemburo* and hot-rock sauna. Head here if outdoor activities are rained out.

Further south, carts drawn by water buffalo roll through the shallow shoreline over to **Yufu-jima** (由布島; ☎ 85-5470; including cart & park entrance ¥1300; ☼ 9am-5pm), an islet with an excellent botanical garden.

SLEEPING

Iriomote-jima has a big selection of ryokan, *minshuku* and pensions, many of which send a minibus to meet incoming boats.

Irumote-sō Youth Hostel (いるもて荘YH; ☎ 85-6255; dm ¥2800, meals available; P ✗) This youth hostel has a great hilltop location above Funaura port. Where the road uphill from the ferry port curves to the right, keep walking straight and look for the hostel signs.

Midori-sō Youth Hostel (みどり荘YH; ☎ 85-6526; dm ¥2500, meals available; P ✗) Just

south of Uehara port, this youth hostel is plain, but central.

Marine Pension Taira (マリンペンシォンたいら; ☎ 85-6505; r per person with/without meals ¥5000/3000; P ✗) This pension is family-run and friendly near the Uehara port and bus stop.

Pension Hoshi-no-Suna (ペンシォン星の砂; ☎ 85-6448; r per person with/without meals ¥5500/4000; P ✗) This place is in a great spot by the beach and bus stop of the same name at Iriomote-jima's northern tip.

Minshuku Nohara-sō (民宿のはら荘西表島; ☎ 85-5252; r per person with/without meals ¥4700/2500; P ✗) A convenient five-minute walk from Ōhara port. They serve home-grown pineapples in season.

There are camping grounds at Hoshisuna-no-hama, Haemita-no-hama and close to the ferry terminal in Funaura.

Extremely basic and cheap dormitory-style accommodation can be had at **Iriomote Shizen Gakkō** (西表自然学校; ☎ 85-6481; dm ¥1800), opposite the supermarket in Uehara, and at **Minshuku Yamaneko** (民宿やまねこ; ☎ 85-5242; dm ¥2000), a couple of minutes' walk from the port in Ōhara.

EATING

Hoshizuna-tei (ほしずな亭; ☎ 85-6640; ☼ lunch & dinner) Right on the beach at Hoshisuna-no-hama, this is a simple little place specialising in island flavours.

Rest House Hoshi-no-suna (レストハウス星の砂; ☎ 85-6448; ☼ 8.30am-8.30pm) At the same beach and with excellent terrace views, this place has refreshing fresh juices for ¥500.

Shinpachi Shokudō (新八食堂; ☎ 85-6078; ☼ lunch & dinner) In Uehara, 200m south of the port, head to Shinpachi for Okinawan food. Top seller is the *sōki soba*.

Nangoku (お食事と喫茶なんごく; ☎ 85-5253; ☼ 11am-9pm) Near Ōhara port, Nangoku also serves Okinawan fare. The *champuru* (stir-fry) for ¥650 is good, but if you feel like splashing out, go for the *inoshishi teishoku* (wild pigmeat set) for ¥1800.

GETTING THERE & AROUND

Yaeyama Kankō (☎ 82-5010) and **Anei Kankō** (☎ 83-0055) run ferries to Ōhara (¥1540, 35 minutes), Uehara (¥2000, 40 minutes) and Funaura (¥2000, 40 minutes) from Ishigaki. Exactly to where, and how many a day, depends on the season and weather.

There are hire car outlets close to each of the ports. Many *minshuku* and both youth hostels hire out bicycles, motor scooters and cars. Buses run between Ōhara and Shirahama (¥1040, 1¼ hours), at the two ends of the island's road. With plenty of alternative lifestylers and tourists in hire cars, the thumb is an effective means of transport on Iriomote-jima.

Other Islands in the Yaeyama-shotō

The Yaeyama-shotō has some excellent smaller islands, including Taketomi-jima, only 10 minutes from Ishigaki by ferry; Japan's southernmost island of Haterumajima, 63km southwest of Ishigaki; and Japan's westernmost island of Yonagunijima, 125km west of Ishigaki. Information on these and other islands can be found on http://painusima.com in Japanese.

TAKETOMI-JIMA 竹富島
☎ 0980 / pop 300

A 10-minute boat ride away from Ishigaki is the popular but relaxed little island of Taketomi-jima. It's got strong traces of Ryūkyū culture and plenty of traditional architecture. Crushed-coral roads fan out from the flower-bedecked village in the centre to various places around the island's coast. There's a small **information desk** in the port building, but for the full scoop on Taketomi-jima, head next door to the new **Yugafu-kan** (☎ 85-2488; ☼ 8am-5pm) visitor centre which has excellent displays and exhibits on this 'living museum' of an island.

In the village itself, all buildings must have traditional red *kawara* roofs and roadside walls must be made of natural materials, all asphalt roads are out, as are modern convenience stores. It's a breath of fresh air if you're sick of concrete.

One-third of the population is over 70 years old.

Sights & Activities

The ladder-like lookout, **Nagomi-no-dai** is on tiny Akayama-oka in the main village. On this otherwise pancake-flat island it offers good views over the red-tiled roofs. Look for walls of coral and rock, and angry-looking *shiisa* (mythical lion-dogs that ward off evil spirits) on the rooftops.

Nishitō Utaki is a shrine dedicated to a 16th-century ruler of the Yaeyama-shotō

who was born on Taketomi-jima. **Kihōin Shūshūkan** (☎ 85-2202; admission ¥300; ☼ 9am-5pm) is a private museum with a diverse collection of folk artefacts. **Taketomi Mingei-kan** (☎ 85-2302; admission free; ☼ 9am-5pm) is where the island's woven *minsā* belts and other textiles are produced. The *minsā* fabrics used to be woven by young women as a sign of love.

TAKETOMI–JIMA

INFORMATION	
Taketomi Post Office 竹富郵便局	**1** B2
Yugafu-kan 竹富ゆがふ館	**2** B1

SIGHTS & ACTIVITIES	
Akayama-oka 赤山の丘	**3** A2
Kihōin Shūshūkan 喜宝院蒐集館	**4** A2
Nagomi-no-dai なごみの台	(see 3)
Nishitō Utaki 西塘御嶽	**5** B2
Taketomi Mingei-kan 竹富民芸館	**6** A2

SLEEPING 🛏	
Minshuku Uchimori-sō 民宿内盛荘	**7** B2
Youth Hostel Takana ユースホステル高那	**8** B2
Ōhama-sō 大浜荘	**9** B2

EATING 🍴	
Grill Garden Taruriya グリルガーデンたるりや	**10** A2
Painu-jima ぱいぬ島	**11** A2
Sobadokoro Takenoko そば処竹の子	**12** A2

TRANSPORT	
Maruhachi Rentals 丸八レンタサイクル	**13** A2
Taketomi Port 竹富港	**14** B1
Water Buffalo Rides 水牛車乗り場	**15** A2

Most of the island is fringed with beach, but usually it is very shallow water. At **Kondoi Beach** (コンドイビーチ) on the west coast you'll find the best swimming on the island, and at the next beach south, **Gaiji-hama** (カイジ浜) the main *hoshi-suna* (star sand) hunting grounds. Although you are requested not to souvenir more than a few grains (which are actually the dried skeletons of tiny creatures), it's sold by the bucketful at local shops.

Dive boats from Ishigaki-jima often visit an **underwater hot spring** on the east coast, where there's a spouting geyser and ambient water temperature of almost 48°C 18m below the surface.

Sleeping & Eating

Many of the traditional houses around the island are Japanese-style inns. Two meals are usually included in the rates. Don't turn up on the last ferry expecting to find accommodation though. Taketomi fills up quickly. Either go on a day trip or book ahead.

Youth Hostel Takana (☎ 85-2151; per person ¥2990; ❄) Opposite the tiny post office, this youth hostel is part of Takana Ryokan. It's cheap, but no more so than *minshuku* on the island.

Ōhama-sō (☎ 85-2226; r per person with/without meals ¥5000/3000; ❄) Also beside the post office, this place is family-run. After dinner, the owner entertains on the *sanshin*.

Minshuku Uchimori-sō (☎ 85-2255; r per person with/without meals ¥5000/3000; ❄) A family-run place in a building with a traditional red roof in the same part of town.

Sobadokoro Takenoko (☎ 85-2251; ❍ lunch & dinner) This is a dinky little spot that serves excellent Yaeyama *soba* for ¥500.

Grill Garden Taruriya (☎ 85-2925; ❍ lunch & dinner) Closed when it's raining, this place dishes up good food in a garden setting.

Painu-jima (☎ 85-2505; ❍ 10am-6pm) Opposite the Mingei-kan, Painu-jima serves excellent *shima-soba* for ¥550.

Getting There & Around

Ferries run by **Yaeyama Kankō** (☎ 82-5010) and **Anei Kankō** (☎ 83-0055) from Ishigaki-jima are fast and frequent (¥580, 10 minutes).

Rental bicycles are great for exploring the crushed-coral roads. **Maruhachi Rentals** (☎ 85-2260; ❍ 8am-6pm) has bicycles for ¥300 per hour and runs a free shuttle between its shop and the port. For Japanese visitors, a popular method of touring the island is by taking a tour (¥1000, 30 minutes) in a cart drawn by **water buffalo** (☎ 85-2103; ❍ 8.30am-5pm).

HATOMA-JIMA 鳩間島
☎ 0980 / pop 50

Five kilometres directly north of Iriomotejima and clearly visible from Funaura is tiny Hatoma-jima. Only 4km around, the island has excellent beaches, snorkelling and is a great place to chill out and relax. There are good views to be had from the island's 34m high point, where there is a big white lighthouse.

Minshuku Aozorasō (民宿青空荘; ☎ 85-6558; per person with/without meals ¥5000/2500; ❄) Five minutes' walk from the port, this *minshuku* has a boat for charter fishing in summer.

Yaeyama Kankō (☎ 82-5010) has a boat to Hatoma-jima from Ishigaki on Tuesdays, Thursdays and Saturdays. The **Anei Kankō** (☎ 83-0055) ferry fills the gaps on Mondays, Wednesdays and Fridays (¥1380). Access from Iriomote-jima is by charter boat.

KOHAMA-JIMA 小浜島
☎ 0980 / pop 550

Just a few kilometres off the east coast of Iriomote-jima is Kohama-jima, famous in Japan as the location for the NHK TV drama *Chura-san*. Japanese tourists turn up in droves to visit filming locations by bicycle. There is a **tourist information centre** (☎ 85-3551; ❍ 8am-6.30pm) at the east coast port that rents bicycles, scooters and small cars.

Fifteen minutes and a bit of a climb by bicycle from the port will bring you to the island's high point of **Ufudaki** (大岳; 99m) with great views of the surrounding islands. On a good day it's even possible to see Hateruma-jima, Japan's southernmost island.

The **Yonara-suidō** (ヨナラ水道) between Kohama-jima and Iriomote-jima is a legendary spot among divers, also known as **Manta Way**. Giant manta rays and garden eels await divers who turn up during the April to June months. The diving is also superb around **Kayama-jima** (嘉弥真島) just off the Kohama-jima's northeast coast.

The small **Folklore Museum** (小浜島民俗資料館; ☎ 85-3465; admission ¥300; ❍ 9am-5pm), 15 minutes by bicycle from the port, has some intriguing masks on display.

Minshuku Nagatasō (民宿長田荘; ☎ 85-3250; per person with/without meals ¥5000/3000) is right in the middle of the island, but will do pick-ups at the port. If you really want to get away, **Minshuku Ōshiro** (民宿大城; ☎ 85-3368; per person with/without meals ¥5000/3500) is at the end of isolated **Cape Kuba**, Kohama-jima's westernmost point.

Between them, **Yaeyama Ferry** (☎ 82-5010) and **Anei Kankō** (☎ 83-0055) run 16 ferries a day to Kohama-jima from Ishigaki (¥1030, 25 minutes).

KUROSHIMA & ARAGUSUKU-JIMA
黒島・新城島
☎ 0980 / pop 225

About 25km southwest of Ishigaki and 10km southeast of Iriomote-jima is heart-shaped Kuroshima and its twin neighbours, Uechi (上地) and Shimoji (下地), which make up Aragusuku-jima. Kuroshima prospers from raising cattle, with virtually the entire island taken up with a cattle ranch. The island is renowned as the place where bulls are raised for Okinawa's bovine sumō, or *tōgyū*.

Kuroshima is flat and ideal for cycling. Bicycles are available for hire at the port at the northern tip of the island. It's 6km from there to the **lighthouse** at its southern point. 2km east of the port is the **Iko-sanbashi** (伊古桟橋), a 200m pier that sticks out into the sea and can be ridden along. The **Nakamoto-kaigan** (仲本海岸) on the west coast has excellent snorkelling.

Minshuku Kuroshima (民宿黒島; ☎ 85-4280; per person with/without meals ¥5000/3000) is two minutes' walk from the Nakamoto-kaigan. It will do pick-ups at the port. Run in conjunction with the *minshuku* is **Diving Service Kuroshima** (ダイビングサービスクロシマ; ☎ 85-4280), which operates half-day tours to Aragusuku-jima for ¥6000 that include lunch and drinks. The seas around the Aragusuku islets are known for their clear water.

Ferries run by **Yaeyama Ferry** (☎ 82-5010) and **Anei Kankō** (☎ 83-0055) make their way from Ishigaki to Kuroshima (¥1130, 25 minutes).

HATERUMA-JIMA 波照間島
☎ 0980 / pop 600

Fifty kilometres south of Iriomote-jima, and Japan's southernmost piece of inhabited real estate, is tiny Hateruma-jima. Just 15km around, Hateruma-jima has some stunning contrasts in geographical features.

A few minutes' bicycle ride west of the port on the northwest coast is **Nishihama** (ニシ浜), a perfect beach with powder snow-like sand where it is easy to while away a day in the sun. There are free public showers, toilets and a camping ground. In the opposite southeast corner of the island, directly south of the airport, is impressive **Takanasaki** (高那崎), a 1km long cliff of Ryūkyū limestone that is pounded by the Pacific Ocean. At the western end of the cliffs is a small monument marking **Japan's southernmost point** (日本最南端の碑). It's a popular spot for Japanese visitors. The island also has some excellent dive spots, especially off its eastern and western coasts.

Minshuku Minoru-sō (民宿みのる荘; ☎ 85-8438; r per person with/without meals ¥5000/2500; ✕) has simple rooms and rents bicycles, scooters and snorkelling sets. A boat for trolling fishing can also be arranged from ¥50,000. **Minshuku Kedamoto-sō** (民宿けだもと荘; ☎ 85-8249; r per person with/without meals ¥5000/2500; ✕) is also convenient and has rental bicycles for ¥200 an hour.

Ryūkyū Air Commuter (RAC), part of the JAL network, has one flight a day from Ishigaki to Hateruma-jima (¥6360, 25 minutes). Ferries run by **Anei Kankō** (☎ 83-0055) and **Hateruma Kaiun** (☎ 82-7233) each have three ferries a day to Hateruma-jima from Ishigaki (¥3000 and ¥3050, respectively, one hour). There is no public transport on the island, but rental bicycles and scooters are readily available for hire.

YONAGUNI-JIMA 与那国島
☎ 0980 / pop 1800

About 125km west of Ishigaki, and 110km east of Taiwan, is Japan's westernmost island, Yonaguni-jima. The island is renowned for its strong sake, small horses, marlin fishing and the jumbo-sized 'Yonaguni atlas moth', the largest moth in the world.

The ferry port of **Kubura** (久部良) is at the island's western extreme, with the airport between it and the main township at the port of **Sonai** (租内) on the north coast. Check out www.town.yonaguni.okinawa.jp for more information in Japanese.

Sights & Activities

Just as Hateruma-jima has a monument to mark Japan's southernmost point, Yonaguni-jima has a rock (from Taiwan!) to mark the country's **westernmost point** (日本最西端の碑) at **Irizaki** (西崎), a short walk from Kubura port. If the weather is perfect the mountains of Taiwan are visible far over the sea. Japanese visitors come to watch their country's last sunset of the day.

The seas off Irizaki are renowned for **marlin fishing** and trolling boats can often be seen from the cape. Boats in Kubura can be chartered from ¥45,000 a day. Call the **Yonaguni Fishing Co-operative** (☎ 87-2803 in Japanese) for information. The All-Japan Billfish Tournament is held here each year in June or July.

Washed by the rich Kuroshio current, the seas around Yonaguni-jima are popular with divers. Large schools of hammerhead sharks are often seen in winter. The island has a reputation of being a mysterious place. Underwater ruins resembling an ancient pyramid were discovered in the 1980s and are now a popular dive spot.

Yonaguni has an extremely rugged landscape and used to be known as *Dunan*, meaning 'hard to reach'. The coastline is marked with great rock formations, much like those on the east coast of Taiwan. The most famous of these are **Tachigami-iwa** (立神岩), literally Standing-God Rock, **Gunkan-iwa** (軍艦岩) and **Sanninu-dai** (サン二ヌ台) on the east coast. At the eastern tip of the island Yonaguni horses graze in the pastures leading out to the lighthouse at **Agarizaki** (東崎)

The giant moths called *Yonaguni-san*, with a wingspan of 25cm to 30cm, can be seen at **Ayamihabiru-kan** (アヤミハビル館; ☎ 87-2440; admission ¥500; ◷ 10am-4pm Wed-Sun) south of Sonai.

To check out the infamous local brew called Hanazake, head to one of the island's three factories in Sonai. **Irinamihira Shuzō** (☎ 87-2431; ◷ 8.30am-5.30pm), **Sakamoto Shuzō** (☎ 87-2417; ◷ 8am-5pm) and **Kokusen Awamori** (☎ 87-2315; ◷ 8am-5pm) are bunched together in Sonai and each has tasting and sales on site.

Sleeping

Hotel Minshuku Haidonan (ホテル民宿はいどなん; ☎ 87-2651; r per person with/without meals ¥4500/3000; ✸) Near the port in Kubura, this place has Western-style rooms with private facilities.

Minshuku Yoshimarusō (民宿よしまる荘; ☎ 87-2658; r per person with meals ¥6000; ✸) Also in Kubira, this *minshuku* is operated in conjunction with a dive shop.

Hotel Irifune (ホテル入船; ☎ 87-2311; r per person with meals ¥6000; ✸) Near the waterfront in Sonai, Irifune has both Japanese- and Western-style rooms. It also has its own dive shop.

Fujimi Ryokan (ふじみ旅館; ☎ 87-2143; r per person with/without meals ¥5800/3000; ✸) A block inland from Hotel Irifune is this ryokan with Japanese-style rooms.

Getting There & Around

RAC (p753), part of the JAL network, has one flight a day to Yonaguni-jima from Naha (¥27,000, 1½ hours, one hour) and two flights a day from Ishigaki (¥9500, 30 minutes, two daily).

Fukuyama Kaiun (☎ 87-2555) operates two ferries a week from Ishigaki to Kubura port (¥3460, four hours).

There are public buses and taxis found on Yonaguni-jima, as well as rental cars, scooters and bicycles.

Directory

CONTENTS

ACCOMMODATION

Japan offers a wide range of accommodation, from cheap guesthouses to first-class hotels, with almost everything in between. Although most options are more expensive than what you'd expect to pay in other Asian countries, you can still find some bargains.

Youth hostels are one of the cheapest options. The typical cost is ¥2400 to ¥3000. But staying only at youth hostels will cut you off from an essential part of the Japan experience. Try to vary your accommodation with stays at a traditional ryokan (inn),

---

PRACTICALITIES

- **Newspapers & Magazines:** There are three main English-language daily newspapers in Japan: *Asahi Shimbun/ International Herald Tribune*; *Japan Times*; and *Daily Yomiuri*. In the bigger cities, these are available at bookstores, convenience stores, train station kiosks and some hotels. In the countryside, you may not be able to find them anywhere. Foreign magazines are available in the major bookshops in the bigger cities.

- **Radio:** Recent years have seen an increase in the number of stations aimed specifically at Japan's foreign population. InterFM (76.1FM) is a favourite of Tokyo's foreign population. The Kansai equivalent of InterFM is FM Cocolo (76.5FM).

- **Electricity:** The Japanese electric current is 100V AC. Tokyo and eastern Japan are on 50Hz, and western Japan, including Nagoya, Kyoto and Osaka, is on 60Hz. Most electrical items from other parts of the world will function on Japanese current. Japanese plugs are the flat two-pin type.

- **Video Systems:** Japan uses the NTSC system.

- **Weights & Measures:** Japan uses the international metric system.

---

a *shukubō* (temple lodging) and a *minshuku* (Japanese B&B).

The best place to look for accommodation is around the main train station or bus terminal in any town. Here you'll usually find a mix of regular hotels and business hotels, with perhaps a few budget ryokan thrown in for good measure. Cheap guesthouses and youth hostels are usually some distance away from the town centre, but are almost always accessible by public transport. If you do find yourself without a place to stay and it's getting late, the best advice is to ask at the local *kōban* (police box) – they'll usually be able to point you in the right direction.

In this guide, accommodation listings have been organised by neighbourhood and price. Budget options cost ¥6000 or less; midrange rooms cost between ¥6000 and ¥15,000; and top-end rooms will cost more than ¥15,000 (per double). Listed in this section are the most common accommodation types you will encounter in this book and on your travels. A 'child', for the purposes of hotels and other accommodation options, is aged under 15.

Camping

Camping is the cheapest form of accommodation in Japan, but official camping grounds are often open only during the Japanese 'camping season' (July and August). Facilities range from bare essentials to deluxe. The JNTO (Japan National Tourist Organization) publishes *Camping in Japan*, a limited selection of camping grounds with details of prices and facilities.

In some restricted areas and national parks, wild camping is forbidden, but elsewhere foreigners have reported consistent success. Even where there is no officially designated camping ground, campers are often directed to the nearest large patch of grass. Provided you set up camp late in the afternoon and leave early, nobody seems to mind, though it is common courtesy to ask permission first (assuming you can find the person responsible). Public toilets, usually spotless, and water taps are very common, even in remote parts of Japan.

The best areas for camping are Hokkaidō, the Japan Alps, Tōhoku and Okinawa.

Cycling Terminals

Cycling terminals (*saikuringu tāminaru*) provide low-priced accommodation of the bunk-bed or tatami-mat variety and are usually found in scenic areas suited to cycling. If you don't have your own bike, you can rent one at the terminal.

Cycling terminal prices compare favourably with those of a youth hostel: at around ¥2500 per person per night or ¥4000 including two meals. For more information contact the **Bicycle Popularization Association of Japan** (www.cycle-info.bpaj.or.jp/english/begin/st.html), which produces a website that lists all the cycling terminals in Japan (be aware that some of the information may be a little dated).

Gaijin Houses

These gaijin (foreigner) houses are more an option for those planning to stay long-term in a major city, such as Tokyo or Kyoto. Some offer nightly or weekly rates, but many are geared to foreigners working in Japan, and charge by the month. If you just want a cheap place to crash and don't mind commuting into town to do your sightseeing, try ringing around the gaijin houses when you get to a major city, such as Tokyo or Kyoto.

Long-termers can expect to pay from ¥40,000 to ¥90,000 per month for a tiny private room, with no deposits or key money (a nonrefundable gift to the landlord of one or two months' rent) required.

The best ways to find a gaijin house are by word of mouth from other foreigners, looking in *Metropolis*, or going through an agency. Agencies are generally the fastest and easiest way to go, as they have extensive listings and will handle all the arrangements with the landlord. The Tokyo agency with the most listings and best rates is **Fontana** (☎ 03-3382-0151; www.fontana-apt.co.jp/; 1st fl, Asahi Mansion, 3-31-5 Chuo, Nakano-ku; ☖ 9.30am-7pm). To get there, take the Marunouchi line to Shinnakano Station (exit 3) and walk about two blocks along Oume-dōri towards Shinjuku. Also recommended is **Sakura House Management** (Map p570; ☎ 03-5330-5250; www.sakura-house .com; 2nd fl, Nishi-Shinjuku K1 Bldg, 7-2-6 Nishi-Shinjuku, Shinjuku-ku; ☖ 8.50am-5.50pm Mon-Sat) north of Shinjuku station; walk north from the west exit several blocks past the huge Ōme-kaidō intersection north of the JR station.

Guesthouses

Guesthouses are often old Japanese houses that have been converted into cheap inns, many expressly aimed at foreign travellers. Some also double as gaijin houses (above). Guesthouses are particularly common in Kyoto but you'll also find a few scattered about Tokyo and other cities. The advantage of guesthouses is that they offer youth hostel prices without the regimented routine. Of course, some guesthouses can be pretty run down, and it's well worth taking a look around before paying your money.

Hostels

For budget travellers, youth hostels are the best option, and it is quite feasible to plan an entire itinerary using them. The best source of information on youth hostels is the Japan *Youth Hostel Handbook*, which is available for ¥580 from the **Japan Youth Hostel Association** (Map pp94–5; JYHA; ☎ 03-3288-1417; www .jyh.or.jp/english; Suidobashi Nishi-guchi Kaikan, 2-20-7 Misaki-chō, Chiyoda-ku, Tokyo 101-0061). Many youth hostels in Japan sell this handbook.

The JYHA handbook is mostly in Japanese, though there is some English in the symbol key at the front and on the locater map keys. The hostels on each map are identified by name (in kanji) and given a page reference. Each hostel is accompanied by a minimap, photo, address in Japanese, fax and phone details, a row of symbols, access instructions in Japanese, open dates, number of beds and prices for beds and meals.

Another good way to find hostels is the *Youth Hostel Map of Japan*, which has one-line entries on each hostel. It's available for free from JNTO and travel information centres (TICs) in Japan.

The best way to find hostels is via the JYHA website, which has details in English on all member hostels, and allows online reservations. Youth hostels in Japan are usually comfortable, inexpensive by Japanese standards, and often good sources of information when used as a base for touring. They are also a good way to meet Japanese travellers and other foreigners. Many hostels have superb sites: some are farms, remote temples (see Shukubō; p727), outstanding private homes or elegant inns.

Some hostels, however, have a routine strongly reminiscent of school, or perhaps even prison. In the high season, you are likely to encounter waves of school children and students. Finally, if you are reliant on public transport, access to some youth hostels is complicated and time-consuming.

HOSTELS IN TOKYO

Tokyo has two standard youth hostels: Tokyo International Youth Hostel in Iidabashi; and Yoyogi Youth Hostel. The usual regulations apply – you have to be out of the building from 10am to 3pm (9am to 5pm at Yoyogi), and you have to be in by 10pm; the latter is a real drawback in a late-night city like Tokyo. There's a three-night limit to your stay and the hostels can often be fully booked during peak holiday periods. You can reserve a room in English on the YHA website (www.jyh.or.jp/english).

MEMBERSHIP & REGULATIONS

You can stay at youth hostels in Japan without being a member of either the JYHA or the International Youth Hostel Federation (IYHA). Rates are somewhat cheaper for members, however, so it pays to join if you are planning on doing a lot of hostelling. You can get a JYHA membership card if you have lived in Japan for a year, have an Alien Registration Card (see p744 for more information) and pay a ¥2500 joining fee. If you don't meet these requirements, you can purchase a one-year IYHA membership card for ¥2800. You can apply for either of these memberships at a JYHA office in Japan (visit www.jyh.or.jp /english for office locations). Of course, the easiest thing to do is join the IYHA in your own country before coming to Japan.

Youth hostel membership has a minimum age limit of four years but no maximum age – you will meet plenty of Japanese seniors, and often a few foreign ones, approaching their 70s.

Hostel charges currently average ¥3000 per night; some also add the 5% consumption tax (see p738 for more information). Private rooms are available in some hostels from ¥3500 per night. As a friendly gesture, some hostels have introduced a special reduction – sometimes as much as ¥500 per night – for foreign hostellers.

Average prices for meals are ¥500 for breakfast and ¥900 for dinner. Almost all hostels require that you use a regulation sleeping sheet, which you can rent for ¥100 if you do not have your own. Although official regulations state that you can only stay at one hostel for three consecutive nights, this is sometimes waived outside the high season.

Hostellers are expected to check in between 3pm and 8pm to 9pm. There is usually a curfew of 10pm or 11pm. Checkout is usually before 10am and dormitories are closed between 10am and 3pm. Bath time is usually between 5pm and 9pm, dinner is between 6pm and 7.30pm, and breakfast is between 7am and 8am.

RESERVATIONS

Advance reservations are essential for the New Year holiday weeks, the late April/early May Golden Week period, and for July and August (see p735 for more information). You should state the arrival date and time, number of nights' stay, number and sex of the people for whom beds are to be reserved, and which meals are required. The easiest way to reserve is via the JYHA website (www.jyh.or.jp/eng lish). Or, if you can muster enough Japanese, telephone bookings are the way to go. If you can't speak Japanese and can't get online, you can always ask a Japanese person (perhaps a fellow hosteller or a youth hostel owner) to make the call for you.

Out of season you can probably get away with booking a day or so in advance. Hostels definitely prefer you to phone, even if it's from across the street, rather than simply roll up without warning. If you arrive without warning, you shouldn't expect any meals.

Hotels

You'll find a range of standard hotels in most Japanese cities and some resort areas. These range from typical midrange hotels to first-class hotels that rank among the best in the world. Rates at standard midrange hotels average ¥9000 for a single and ¥12,000 for a double or twin. Rates at first-class hotels average ¥15,000 for a single and ¥20,000 for a double or twin.

Like business hotels, you'll often find standard hotels near the main train station in a city. You can expect someone to speak English at the front desk, so making reservations and checking in shouldn't be the hassle it can be at other types of accommodation in Japan.

If you plan to stay in standard hotels during your stay in Japan, you might save some money by getting a package deal on transport and accommodation. Check with your airline or travel agency before you arrive.

Expect to pay 10% or more as a service charge plus a 5% consumer tax.

BUSINESS HOTELS

These are economical and practical places geared to the single traveller, usually lesser-ranking business types who want to stay somewhere close to the station. Rooms are clean, Western style, just big enough for you to turn around in, and include a miniature bath/WC unit. A standard fitting for the stressed businessperson is a coin-operated TV with a porno channel. Vending machines replace room service.

ADDRESSES IN JAPAN

In Japan, finding a place from its address can be difficult, even for locals. The problem is two-fold: first, the address is usually given by an area rather than a street; and, second, the numbers are not necessarily consecutive, as prior to the mid-1950s numbers were assigned by date of construction.

In Tokyo very few streets have names – so addresses work by narrowing down the location of a building to a number within an area of a few blocks. In this guide, Tokyo addresses are organised as such: area number, block number and building number, followed by area and ward. For example, 1-11-2 Ginza, Chūō-ku.

In Kyoto, addresses are simplified. We either give the area (eg Higashiyama-ku, Nanzen-ji) or we give the street on which the place is located, followed by the nearest cross street (eg Karasuma-dōri-Imadegawa). In some cases, we also give additional information to show where the place lies in relation to the intersection of the two streets mentioned. In Kyoto, the land usually slopes gently to the south; thus, an address might indicate whether a place lies above or north of (agaru) or below or south of (sagaru or kudaru) a particular east–west road. Thus, 'Karasuma-dōri-Imadegawa' simply means the place is near the intersection of Karasuma-dōri and Imadegawa-dōri; Karasuma-dōri-Imadegawa-sagaru indicates that it's south of that intersection. An address might also indicate whether a place lies east (higashi) or west (nishi) of the north–south road.

In Sapporo, a typical address would be S17W7-2-12 Chūō-ku. The 'S17W7' is the South 17, West 7 block. The building is in the second section at number 12.

Elsewhere in this guide, addresses list area number, block number and building number, followed by area and ward. This is the more common presentation in English. For example, '1-7-2 Motomachi-dōri, Chūō-ku'. Where given, the floor number and building name are listed first.

To find an address, the usual process is to ask directions. Have your address handy. The numerous local police boxes are there largely for this purpose. Businesses often include a small map in their advertisements or on their business cards to show their location.

Cheap single rooms can sometimes be found for as low as ¥4500, though the average rate is around ¥8000. Most business hotels also have twin and double rooms; business hotels usually do not have a service charge.

CAPSULE HOTELS

One of Japan's most famous forms of accommodation is the *capseru hoteru*. As the name implies, the 'rooms' in a capsule hotel consist of banks of neat white capsules stacked in rows two or three high. The capsules themselves are around 2m by 1m by 1m – about the size of a spacious coffin. Inside is a bed, a TV, a reading light, a radio and an alarm clock. Personal belongings are kept in a locker room.

This type of hotel is common in major cities and often caters to workers who have partied too hard to make it home or have missed the last train. The majority are only for men but some also accept women; the women's quarters are usually in a separate part of the building. Most capsule hotels have the added attraction of a sauna and a large communal bath.

An average price is ¥3800 per night. You could try one as a novelty, but it's not an experience recommended to those who suffer from claustrophobia.

We've listed two capsule hotels in Tokyo that accept women; see p128 and p131. Most are open for check-in from 5pm to 10am.

LOVE HOTELS

As their name indicates, love hotels are used by Japanese couples for discreet trysts. You can use them for this purpose as well, but they're also perfectly fine, if a little twee, for overnight accommodation.

To find a love hotel on the street, just look for flamboyant façades with rococo architecture, turrets, battlements and imitation statuary. Love hotels are designed for maximum privacy: entrances and exits are kept separate; keys are provided through a small opening without contact between desk clerk and guest; and photos of the rooms are displayed to make the choice easy for the customer. There's often a discreetly curtained parking area so your car cannot be seen once inside (check out the license plate covers that are used to ensure extra anonymity).

The rooms can fulfil most fantasies, with themes ranging from harem extravaganza to Tarzan-and-Jane jungle rooms. Choices can include vibrating beds, wall-to-wall mirrors, bondage equipment and video recorders to record the experience.

During the day, you can stay for a two- or three-hour 'rest' (*kyūkei* in Japanese) for about ¥4000 (rates are for the whole room, not per person). Love hotels are of more interest to foreign visitors after 10pm, when it's possible to stay the night for about ¥6500, but you should check out early enough in the morning to avoid a return to peak-hour rates. There will usually be a sign in Japanese (occasionally in English) outside the hotel, announcing its rates. Even if you can't read Japanese, you should be able to figure out which rate applies to a 'rest' and which applies to an overnight stay.

In theory, you can cram as many people as you like into a love-hotel room; in practice you may be limited to two people and same-sex couples may be rejected outright.

Love hotels can be found in any of Tokyo's entertainment districts – particularly in Shinjuku, Shibuya, Roppongi and Ikebukuro. You can also find them along feeder roads that lead to/from most of Japan's cities, and inside some cities as well.

Kokumin-shukusha

Kokumin-shukusha (people's lodges) are government-supported institutions offering affordable accommodation in scenic areas. Private Japanese-style rooms are the norm, though some places offer Western-style rooms. Prices average ¥5500 to ¥6500 per person per night, including two meals. The best way to find *kokumin-shukusha* is to ask at local tourist offices or at *kōban*.

Long-Term Accommodation

If you intend to stay longer in Japan, a job offer that appears lucrative may seem markedly less so when you work out your rent and other living costs. Ideally, you can avoid many hassles by negotiating decent accommodation as part of your work contract.

If at all possible, you should get a Japanese friend to help you with your search and negotiations, as Japanese landlords are notoriously wary of foreign tenants and often prefer to do business with a local go-between. If you are on good terms with a Japanese friend, this person may offer to act as a *hoshō-nin* (guarantor). This represents considerable commitment and the guarantor's *hanko* (name stamp) is usually required on your rental contract.

A pitfall, often overlooked, is that you may have to lay out the equivalent of several months' rent upfront. For starters, there's the equivalent of one to two months' rent payable as *reikin* (key money). This is a non-refundable gift that goes into the pocket of the landlord. Then there's a *shikikin* (damage deposit) of one to three months' rent. This is refundable at a later date as long as both sides agree there's no damage. The *fudōsan-yasan* (real estate agent) will of course want *tesūryō* – the equivalent of one month's rent as a nonrefundable handling fee. Finally, you may have to pay *maekin*, which is equal to one month's rent in advance, and this may also be nonrefundable.

Of course, there are various ways around all these costs. If you get in with the local foreigners' scene in a particular city, you may get tipped off to open apartments and houses for which nothing more than monthly rent is required (this is particularly true outside Tokyo).

WHERE TO LOOK

There are several different methods to hunt for housing – it depends on what you want and how long you intend to stay.

Asking other foreigners at work, in schools, clubs, bars and gaijin houses (see p722) is one way of locating long-term accommodation. If you're lucky, you may find somebody leaving the country or moving on who is willing to dump their job contacts, housing and effects in one friendly package.

Notice boards are another good source of information and are often found at tourist information offices, international clubs, conversation clubs etc. Even if there's nothing on the board, ask someone in charge for a few tips.

Regional and city magazines aimed at foreigners often have classified ads offering or seeking accommodation. In Kansai you should check out *Kansai Time Out*; in Tokyo check any of the numerous English-language publications available. There are plenty of magazines all over Japan with suitable ads. The TIC or the local tourist office should know which publications are best, particularly if you decide to live somewhere more remote, such as Hokkaidō or Okinawa.

Using a real estate agent is the most expensive option, and only feasible if you intend to stay a long time and need to determine exactly the type and location of your housing. English-language magazines such as *Kansai Time Out* sometimes carry ads from estate agents specialising in accommodation for foreigners.

Minshuku

A *minshuku* is usually a family-run private lodging, rather like a Western-style B&B. *Minshuku* can be found throughout Japan and offer an experience of daily Japanese life. The average price is around ¥6000 per person, per night (with two meals). You are expected to lay out and put away your bedding, and provide your own towel. **Japan Minshuku Association** (☎ 03-3364-1855; Suegawa Bldg, 4-10-15, Takadanobaba, Shinjuku-ku, Tokyo 169-0075), has a leaflet in English describing the *minshuku* concept and providing advice on staying at one; a list of *minshuku* is also available. The **Nihon Minshuku Center** (☎ 03-5858-0103; www.koyado .net/us/make.htm; F1, Hotel Toka, 3-11-8, Hirai, Edogawa-ku, Tokyo 132-0035), can help with online bookings.

Mountain Huts

Mountain huts (*yama-goya*) are common in many of Japan's hiking and mountain-climbing areas. While you'll occasionally find free emergency shelters, most huts are privately run and charge for accommodation. These places offer bed and board (two meals) at around ¥5000 to ¥8000 per person; if you prepare your own meal that figure drops to ¥3000 to ¥5000 per person. It's best to call ahead to reserve a spot (contact numbers are available in Japanese hiking guides and maps, and in Lonely Planet's *Hiking in Japan*), but you won't be turned away if you show up without a reservation.

Pensions

Pensions are usually run by young couples offering Western-style accommodation based on the European pension concept, and many offer sports and leisure facilities. They are common in resort areas and around ski fields. Prices average ¥6000 per person per night, or ¥8500 including two meals.

Reservations & Checking In

It can be hard to find accommodation during the following holiday periods: Shōgatsu

(New Year) – 31 December to 3 January; Golden Week – 29 April to 5 May; and O-Bon – mid-August. If you plan to be in Japan during these periods, you should make reservations as far in advance as possible.

Tourist information offices at main train stations can usually help with reservations, and are often open until about 6.30pm or later. Even if you are travelling by car, the train station is a good first stop in town for information, reservations and cheap car parking.

Making phone reservations in English is usually possible in most major cities. Providing you speak clearly and simply, there will usually be someone around who can get the gist of what you want. There will also be occasions when hotel staff understand no English. If you really get stuck, try asking the desk staff at your current accommodation to phone your reservation through.

The **Welcome Inns Reservation Center** (www.itcj .or.jp/indexwel.html) is a free reservation service that represents hundreds of *minshuku*, ryokan, inns and pensions in Japan. It operates counters in the main tourist information offices in Tokyo (see p92) and Kyoto (see p276), and at the main tourist information counters in Narita and Kansai airports. You can also make reservations online through its website (which is also an excellent source of information on member hotels and inns).

A similar online service is offered by the **Japanese Inn Group** (www.jpinn.com/index.html).

The Japanese run their accommodation according to an established rhythm that favours check-ins between 5pm and 7pm and checkouts at around 10am; unannounced early- or late-comers disturb this pattern.

Rider Houses

Catering mainly to touring motorcyclists, rider houses (*raidā hausu*) provide extremely basic shared accommodation from around ¥1000 per night. Some rider houses are attached to local *rāmen* (soup with noodles and vegetables) restaurants or other eateries, and may offer discounted rates if you agree to eat there. You should bring your own sleeping bag or ask to rent bedding from the owner. For bathing facilities, you will often be directed to the local *sentō* (public bath). Although rider houses may not be the most comfortable places, they are generally safe for both sexes and are

good places to meet alternative, independent Japanese travellers, including cyclists, hitchhikers and other shoestring travellers.

There are innumerable rider houses throughout Hokkaidō, as well as a few in southern Japan, mainly Kyūshū and Okinawa. If you ask around town or at the local tourist information office for a *raidā hausu*, someone will probably point you in the right direction. Unfortunately, many rider houses are located out of town and are hard to reach on public transport. If you can read some Japanese, spiral-bound *Touring Mapple* maps, published by Shobunsha, mark almost all of the rider houses in a specific region, as well as cheap places to eat along the way. These maps are available at most Japanese bookshops.

Ryokan

For a taste of traditional Japanese life, a stay at a ryokan is mandatory. Ryokan range from ultra-exclusive establishments to reasonably priced places with a homely atmosphere. Prices start at around ¥4000 (per person, per night) for a 'no-frills' ryokan without meals (*sudomari* is the Japanese term for 'no meals'). For a classier ryokan, expect prices to start at ¥8000. Exclusive establishments – Kyoto is a prime centre for these – charge ¥25,000 and often much more.

Ryokan owners prefer to charge on a room-and-board (breakfast and dinner) basis per person. If, like many foreigners, you find yourself overwhelmed by the unusual offerings of a Japanese breakfast, it should be possible to have dinner only, but in many ryokan opting out of both meals is unacceptable. The bill is reduced by about 10% if you decline breakfast.

A service charge or consumption tax may be added to your bill in some establishments. Because this is not always the case and the amount may vary, it's best to ask when making reservations or checking in.

See Welcome Inns Reservation Center (left) and the Japanese Inn Group (left) for information about these two associations and the ryokan booking services they offer.

Shukubō

Staying in a *shukubō* (temple lodging) is one way to experience another facet of traditional Japan. Sometimes you are allocated a simple room in the temple precincts and left to your own devices. Other times, you may be asked to participate in prayers, services or *zazen* (seated) meditation. At some temples, exquisite vegetarian meals (*shōjin ryōri*) are served.

Tokyo and Kyoto TICs produce leaflets on temple lodgings in their regions. Kōya-san (p377), a renowned religious centre in the Kansai region, includes over 50 *shukubō* and is one of the best places in Japan to try this type of accommodation. The popular pilgrimage of Shikoku's 88 sacred temples also provides the opportunity to sample *shukubō* (see p574 for more information).

Over 70 youth hostels are located in temples or shrines – look for the reverse swastika symbol in the JYHA handbook. The suffixes *-ji*, *-in* or *-dera* are also clues that the hostel is a temple.

Toho

The Toho network (www.toho.net/english .html) is a diverse collection of places that has banded loosely together to offer a more flexible alternative to youth hostels. Toho network inns ascribe to a common philosophy of informal hospitality at reasonable prices. Most of the network's 90 members are in Hokkaidō, although there are a few scattered around Honshū and other islands further south. The owners may not speak much (if any) English and you should definitely phone ahead to make reservations, even if it's just from a phone box down the street. The main drawback (or attraction for some travellers) of these places is that many are difficult to reach. Many owners, however, will provide a free pick-up service from the nearest train or bus station if you make arrangements in advance.

Prices average ¥4000 per person, or ¥5000 with two meals for dormitory-style accommodation. Private rooms are sometimes available for about ¥1000 extra. A comprehensive Japanese-language Toho network guide (¥200) with detailed directions is available at bookshops in Hokkaidō or from Toho network inns. The website features a number of helpful links to individual member inn homepages.

ACTIVITIES

In addition to martial arts, which everyone naturally associates with Japan, there are a variety of activities that you can participate in while in Japan. Skiing, cycling, diving and snorkelling, hiking and mountain climbing are all popular and easy to pursue in Japan.

Cycling

Bicycle touring is fairly popular in Japan, despite the fact that most of the country is quite mountainous. See p754 for more information on cycling in Japan. See also p722 for information on places to stay.

Diving & Snorkelling

The Okinawan islands (p681) located in the far southwest of Japan and the chain of islands south of Tokyo known as Izu-shotō (Izu Seven Islands; p199) are popular among Japanese as diving destinations. Other dive sites in Japan include the waters around Tobi-shima (p495), off northern Honshū, and Ani-jima (p202) in Ogasawara-shotō.

As you would expect, diving in Japan is expensive. Typical rates are ¥12,000 per day for two boat-dives and lunch. Courses for beginners are available in places like Ishigaki-jima (p710) and Iriomote-jima (p715) in Okinawa, but starting costs are around ¥80,000. Instruction will usually be in Japanese. For these reasons, you're much better off learning to dive in a place like Thailand or Australia, if you've the choice.

Hiking & Mountain Climbing

The Japanese are keen hikers, and many national parks in Japan have hiking routes. The popular hiking areas around Tokyo are around Nikkō (p159) and Chichibu-Tama National Park (p166). In the Kansai region, Nara (p361), Shiga-ken (p331) and Kyoto-fu (p336) all have pleasant hikes.

Japan comes into its own as a hiking destination in the Japan Alps National Park, particularly in Kamikōchi (p232), the Bandai plateau (p454) in northern Honshū, and Hokkaidō's national parks (p518). In these less-populated and mountainous regions of Japan, there may be the added incentive of an *onsen* soak at the end of a long day's walk. Hikers who trek into the mountains see a side of Japan that few foreigners ever experience.

While rudimentary English-language hiking maps may be available from local tourism authorities, it's better to seek out proper Japanese maps and decipher the kanji. Shobunsha's *Yama-to-Kōgen No Chizu* series covers all of Japan's most popular hiking areas in exquisite detail. The maps are available in all major bookshops in Japan.

Serious hikers will also want to pick up a copy of Lonely Planet's *Hiking in Japan*, which covers convenient one-day hikes near major cities and extended hikes in more remote areas.

Martial Arts

Japan is renowned for its martial arts, many of which filtered through from China and were then adapted by the Japanese. During feudal times, these arts were highly valued by ruling families as a means of buttressing their power.

After WWII martial arts were perceived as contributing to the aggressive stance which had led to hostilities, and teaching them was discouraged. Within a decade, however, they had returned to favour and are now popular both in Japan and abroad.

For more information contact the TIC or the associations listed here (p743). JNTO also publishes a leaflet entitled *Traditional Sports*, which covers this subject.

Aikidō, judō, karate and kendō can be studied in Japan. Less popular disciplines, such as *kyūdō* (Japanese archery) and sumō, also attract devotees from overseas. Relevant organisations:

All-Japan Judo Federation (Zen Nihon Judo Renmei; ☎ 03-3818-4199; c/o Kodokan, 1-16-30 Kasuga, Bukyō-ku, Tokyo)

Amateur Archery Federation of Japan (☎ 03-3481-2387; www.archery.or.jp in Japanese; Kishi Memorial Hall, 4th fl, 1-1-1 Jinan, Shibuya-ku, Tokyo)

International Aikido Federation (☎ 03-3203-9236; www.aikido-international.org; 17-18 Wakamatsu-chō, Shinjuku-ku, Tokyo)

Japan Kendo Federation (☎ 03-3211-5804; www .kendo.or.jp/english-page/english-top-page.html; c/o Nippon Budokan, 2-3 Kitanomaru-kōen, Chiyoda-ku, Tokyo)

Nihon Sumō Kyōkai (☎ 03-3623-5111; www.sumo .or.jp/eng; c/o Kokugikan Sumō Hall, 1-3-28 Yokoami, Sumida-ku, Tokyo)

World Union of Karate-dō Organisation (☎ 03-3503-6640; 4th fl, Sempaku Shinkokaikan Bldg, 1-15-16 Toranomon, Minato-ku, Tokyo)

AIKIDŌ

The roots of this solely defensive art can be traced to the Minamoto clan in the 10th century, but the modern form of aikidō was started in the 1920s by Ueshiba Morihei.

Aikidō draws on many different techniques, including shintō, karate and kendō. Breathing and meditation form an integral part of aikidō training, as does the concentration on movement derived from classical Japanese dance, and the awareness of *ki* (life force or will) flowing from the fingertips.

KARATE

The martial art karate (literally meaning 'empty hands') may have originated in India, but was refined in China and travelled from there to Okinawa, where it took hold. It began in the 14th century and spread to the rest of Japan in the first half of last century. For this reason it is not considered a traditional Japanese martial art.

The emphasis is on unarmed combat, as the name of the sport implies. Blows are delivered with the fists or feet. For optimum performance, all movements require intense discipline of the mind. There are two methods of practising karate. The first is *kumite*, when two or more people spar together. The second is *kata*, when one person performs formal exercises.

KENDŌ

Meaning the 'way of the sword', kendō is the oldest of the martial arts. It was favoured by the samurai to acquire skills in swordsmanship, as well as the development of mental poise. Today it is practised with a bamboo stave and protective body armour, gauntlets and a face mask. The winner of a bout succeeds in landing blows to the face, arms, upper body or throat of an opponent.

JUDŌ

This is probably the best-known martial art; it has become a popular sport worldwide and regularly features in the Olympic Games. The origins of this art are found in jūjutsu, a means of self-defence favoured by the samurai, which was modernised in 1882 into judō (the 'gentle way') by Kano Jigoro. The basic principles and subtle skills of the art lie in defeating opponents simply by redirecting the opponents' strength against themselves.

Skiing

Skiing developed in Japan in the 1950s and there are now more than 300 ski resorts, many with high-standard runs and snowmaking equipment. The majority of resorts are concentrated on the island of Honshū, where the crowds are huge, the vertical drops rarely more than 400m and all runs start at altitudes of less than 2000m. Snow cover in southern and eastern Honshū is generally adequate, but can be sparse and icy.

Skiers on Hokkaidō, however, can look forward to powder skiing that rivals anything in the European Alps or the Rockies in the USA. Niseko (p538) and Furano (p552), two of Hokkaidō's best resorts, have excellent facilities (Niseko has 43 lifts) and neither suffers from extreme crowding.

JNTO's *Skiing in Japan* pamphlet covers 20 resorts on Honshū and Hokkaidō, and has travel information, ski season dates, accommodation details, resort facilities and costs.

Skiing is normally possible from December to April, though the season can be shorter in some of Honshū's lower-altitude resorts.

Resort accommodation ranges from hostels to expensive hotels but is heavily booked during the ski season. There are many resorts at hot springs that double as *onsen* or bathing spas. Avoid weekends and holidays, when lift lines are long and accommodation and transportation are heavily booked.

Lift passes cost ¥3000 to ¥4500 per day. Daily rental of skis, stocks and boots can cost up to ¥5000; finding larger-sized ski boots may be difficult. Equipment can be rented at resorts and some ski shops in bigger cities.

As well as downhill skiing, Japan also offers good terrain for cross-country skiing and touring, especially in the Hakodate (p529) region of Hokkaidō – a good way to escape from the crowds.

For more information on skiing in Japan, you should pick up a copy of TR Reid's *Ski Japan*. Every winter *Kansai Time Out* magazine also features articles on ski fields that are within easy reach of Kansai. For information on the Web have a look at **Snow Japan** (www.snowjapan.com).

BUSINESS HOURS

Department stores usually open at 10am and close at 6.30pm or 7pm daily (with one or two days off each month). Smaller shops are open similar hours but may close on Sunday. Large companies usually work from 9am to 5pm weekdays and some also operate on Saturday morning.

Banks are open 9am to 3pm weekdays. For information on changing money, see p738.

Restaurants are usually open from 11am to 2pm and from 6pm to 11pm, with one day off per week, usually Monday or Tuesday. Some stay open all afternoon. Cafés are usually open 11am until 11pm, with one day off per week, usually Monday or Tuesday. Bars usually open around 5pm and stay open until the wee hours.

CHILDREN

Japan is a great place to travel with kids: it's safe and clean and there's never a shortage of places to keep them amused. Look out for *Japan for Kids* by Diane Wiltshire Kanagawa and Jeane Huey Erickson, an excellent introduction to Japan's highlights from a child's perspective. In addition, Lonely Planet publishes *Travel with Children*, which gives the lowdown on getting out and about with your children.

Practicalities

Parents will find that Japan is similar to Western countries in terms of facilities and allowances made for children, with a few notable exceptions. Cots are available in most hotels and these can be booked in advance. High chairs are available in many restaurants (although this isn't an issue in the many restaurants where everyone sits on the floor). There are nappy-changing facilities in some public places, like department stores and some larger train stations; formula and nappies are widely available, even in convenience stores. Breast feeding in public is generally not done. The one major problem concerns child seats for cars and taxis: these are generally not available. Finally, child-care agencies are available in most larger cities. The only problem is the language barrier: outside of Tokyo, there are few, if any, agencies with English-speaking staff.

Sights & Activities

Tokyo has the most child-friendly attractions in Japan, including Tokyo Disneyland (p121); see p123 for more information. In Kansai, Osaka's Universal Studios Japan (p346) and Osaka Aquarium (p347) are two attractions likely to be popular with children. Another Kansai attraction that children enjoy is Nara-kōen (p364) in Nara, with its resident deer population.

Children who enjoy the beach and activities like snorkelling will really enjoy the islands of Okinawa (p681) and the Izu-shotō (p199).

CLIMATE

The combination of Japan's mountainous territory and the length of the archipelago (covering about 20° of latitude) makes for a complex climate. Most of the country is located in the northern temperate zone, which yields four distinct seasons. In addition, there are significant climatic differences between Hokkaidō in the north, which has short summers and lengthy winters with heavy snowfalls, and the southern islands, such as Okinawa in Nansei-shotō (Southwest Archipelago), which enjoy a subtropical climate.

In the winter months (December to February), cold, dry air-masses from Siberia move down over Japan, where they meet warmer, moister air-masses from the Pacific. The resulting precipitation causes huge snowfalls on the side of the country that faces the Sea of Japan. The Pacific Ocean side of Japan receives less snow but can still be very cold; Tokyo has colder average January temperatures than Reykjavík in Iceland, but snow, when it does fall on the capital, rarely lasts long.

The summer months (June to August) are dominated by warm, moist air currents from the Pacific, and produce high temperatures and humidity throughout most of Japan (with the blissful exception of Hokkaidō). In the early part of summer, usually mid-May to June, there is a rainy season lasting a few weeks that starts in the south and gradually works its way northwards. Although it can be inconvenient, this rainy season is not usually a significant barrier to travel. Further bad weather can

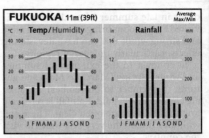

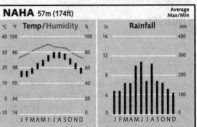

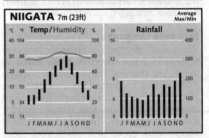

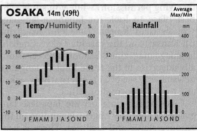

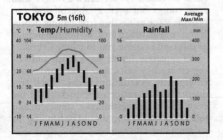

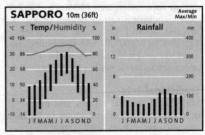

occur in late summer when the country is visited by typhoons bringing torrential rains and strong winds that can have devastating effects, particularly on coastal regions.

In contrast to the extremes of summer and winter, spring (March to May) and autumn (September to November) in Japan are comparatively mild. Rainfall is relatively low and the days are often clear. These are, without a doubt, the very best times to visit the country.

COURSES

There are courses for almost every aspect of Japanese culture. The JNTO (p744) has a wealth of printed information available. Cultural activities visas require applicants to attend 20 class-hours per week. Those wishing to work while studying need to apply for permission to do so. For more information on cultural activities visas, visit the website for **Japan Ministry of Foreign Affairs** (http://www.mofa.go.jp/j_info/visit/visa/04.html).

Japanese Language

There is no shortage of Japanese-language schools in Japan, most of them found in the bigger cities of Tokyo, Osaka, Nagoya, Kōbe and Kyoto. Some offer only part-time instruction, while others offer full-time and intensive courses and may sponsor you for a cultural activities visa, which will allow you to work up to 20 hours a week (after receiving permission) while you study. The best place to look for Japanese-language schools is in *Kansai Time Out* magazine (in Kansai) and the various Tokyo English-language magazines. Schools also occasionally advertise in the three English-language newspapers (see p721). Alternatively, ask at any tourist information office.

Costs at full-time private Japanese language schools vary hugely depending on the school's status and facilities. There is usually an application fee of ¥5000 to ¥30,000, plus an administration charge of ¥50,000 to ¥100,000 and the annual tuition fees of ¥350,000 to ¥600,000. Add accommodation and food, and it is easy to see why it may be necessary to work while you study.

Traditional Arts

Many local cultural centres and tourist offices can arrange short courses in Japanese arts, such as ceramics, *washi* (Japanese paper-

making), *aizome* (indigo dyeing), wood working, *shodō* (calligraphy), ink painting and *ikebana* (flower arranging). The best place to pursue these interests is Kyoto (p272), where the TIC (p276) or the International Community House (p276) can put you in touch with qualified teachers.

CUSTOMS

Customs allowances include the usual tobacco products plus three 760mL bottles of alcoholic beverages, 57g of perfume, and gifts and souvenirs up to a value of ¥200,000 or its equivalent. You must be over the age of 20 to qualify for these allowances. The penalties for importing drugs are very severe.

Although the Japanese are no longer censoring pubic hair in domestically produced pornography, customs officers will still confiscate any pornographic materials in which pubic hair is visible.

There are no limits on the importation of foreign or Japanese currency. The export of foreign currency is also unlimited but there is a ¥5 million export limit for Japanese currency.

Visit **Japan Customs** (www.customs.go.jp/index _e.htm) for more information on Japan's customs regulations.

DANGERS & ANNOYANCES
Beaches & Swimming

Few public beaches in Japan have lifeguards and summer weekends bring many drowning accidents. Watch for undertows or other dangers.

Earthquakes

Japan is an earthquake-prone country, although most quakes can only be detected by sensitive instruments. If you experience a strong earthquake, head for a doorway or supporting pillar. Small rooms, like a bathroom or cupboard, are often stronger than large rooms but even a table or desk can provide some protection from falling debris. If you're in an urban area, do not run outside as this could expose you to falling debris.

All Japanese hotels have maps indicating emergency exits, and local wards have emergency evacuation areas (fires frequently follow major earthquakes). In the event of a major earthquake, stay calm and follow the locals, who should be heading for a designated safe area.

In the event of a serious earthquake, the Kansai and Tokyo radio stations listed on p721 will broadcast emergency information in English and several other languages.

Fire
Although modern hotels must comply with certain safety standards, traditional Japanese buildings with their wooden construction and tightly packed surroundings can be real firetraps. Fortunately, most old buildings are low-rise, but it's still wise to check fire exits and escape routes.

Noise
In Japanese cities the assault on the auditory senses can be overwhelming, so it's no wonder so many pedestrians are plugged in to the latest musical electronic gadgetry. Pedestrian crossings are serenaded by electronic playtime music, loudspeaker systems broadcast muzak or advertisements, bus passengers are bombarded with running commentaries in Mickey Mouse tones, and accommodation may include TVs turned up full volume in dining rooms or lounges. Earplugs can help, particularly when you're trying to sleep.

Size
Even medium-sized foreigners need to mind their heads in Japanese dwellings. The Western frame may make it hard to fit into some seats and those with long legs will often find themselves wedged tight. Toilets in cramped accommodation necessitate contortions and careful aim (be warned!). Bathtubs are also sometimes on the small side and require flexibility on the part of the bather.

Theft
The low incidence of theft and crime in general in Japan is frequently commented on. Of course, theft does exist and its rarity is no reason for carelessness. It's sensible to take the normal precautions in airports and on the crowded Tokyo rail network, but there's definitely no need for paranoia.

Lost-and-found services do seem to work; if you leave something behind on a train or other mode of transport, it's always worth inquiring if it has been turned in. The Japanese word for a lost item is *wasure-mono*, and lost-and-found offices usually go by the same name. In train stations, you can also inquire at the station master's (*eki-chō*) office.

DISABLED TRAVELLERS
On the plus side, many new buildings in Japan have access ramps, traffic lights have speakers playing melodies when it is safe to cross, train platforms have raised dots and lines to provide guidance and some ticket machines in Tokyo have Braille. Some attractions also offer free entry to disabled persons and one companion. On the negative side, many of Japan's cities are still rather difficult for disabled persons to negotiate.

If you are going to travel by train and need assistance, ask one of the station workers as you enter the station. Try asking: '*karada no fujiyuū no kata no sharyō wa arimasu ka?*' (Are there train carriages for disabled travellers?).

There are carriages on most lines that have areas set aside for people in wheelchairs. Those with other physical disabilities can use the seats set near the train exits, called *yūsen-zaseki*. You will also find these seats near the front of buses; usually they're a different colour from the regular seats.

The most useful information for disabled visitors is provided by the **Japanese Red Cross Language Service Volunteers** (☎ 03-3438-1311; http://accessible.jp.org/title2-e.html; c/o Volunteers Division, Japanese Red Cross Society, 1-1-3 Shiba Daimon, Minato-ku, Tokyo 105-8521, Japan). Its website has online guides for disabled travellers to Tokyo, Kyoto and Kamakura.

For information on negotiating Japan in a wheelchair, check out the website for **Accessible Japan** (www.wakakoma.org/aj).

DISCOUNT CARDS
Hostel Cards
Youth hostel accommodation is plentiful in Japan. See p723 about obtaining a membership card.

Senior Cards
Japan is an excellent place for senior travellers. To qualify for widely available senior discounts, you have to be aged over 60 or 65, depending upon the place/company. In almost all cases a passport will be sufficient proof of age, so senior cards are rarely worth bringing.

Japanese domestic airlines (JAS, JAL and ANA) offer senior discounts of about 25% on some flights (for airline contact details see p748). JR offers a variety of discounts and special passes, including the Full Moon Green

Pass, which is good for travel in Green Car (1st class) carriages on *shinkansen* (bullet trains), regular JR trains and sleeper trains. The pass is available to couples whose combined age exceeds 88 years (passports can prove this). The pass costs ¥80,500/99,900/124,400 per couple for five/seven/12 consecutive days of travel. They are available at major JR Stations within Japan from 1 September to 31 May and they are valid for travel between 1 October and 30 June (with the exception of 21 December to 6 January, 21 March to 5 April, and 27 April to 6 May).

Discounts are also available on entry fees to many temples, museums and cinemas.

Student & Youth Cards

Japan is one of the few places left in Asia where a student card can be useful, though some places only offer discounts to high school students and younger, not to university and graduate students. Officially, you should be carrying an International Student Identity Card (ISIC) to qualify for a discount, but you will often find that any youth or student card will do the trick.

EMBASSIES & CONSULATES
Japanese Embassies & Consulates

Diplomatic representation abroad:

Australia Canberra (embassy; ☎ 02-6273 3244; www .japan.org.au; 112 Empire Circuit, Yarralumla, Canberra, ACT 2600); Brisbane (consulate; ☎ 07-3221 5188); Melbourne (consulate; ☎ 03-9639 3244); Perth (consulate; ☎ 08-9480 1800); Sydney (consulate; ☎ 02-9231 3455)

Canada Ontario (embassy; ☎ 613-241 8541; www .ca.emb-japan.go.jp; 255 Sussex Dr, Ottawa, Ontario K1N 9E6); Edmonton (consulate; ☎ 403-422 3752); Montreal (consulate; ☎ 514-866 3429); Toronto (consulate; ☎ 416-363 7038); Vancouver (consulate; ☎ 604-684 5868)

France (☎ 01 48 88 62 00; www.fr.emb-japan.go.jp; 7 Ave Hoche, 75008 Paris)

Germany (☎ 493-021 09 40; www.embjapan.de; Hiroshimastrasse 6, 10785, Berlin)

Hong Kong (consulate; ☎ 852-2522 1184; 47th fl, One Exchange Square, 8 Connaught Place, Central Hong Kong)

Ireland (☎ 01-202 8300; www.ie.emb-japan.go.jp; Nutley Bldg, Merrion Centre, Nutley Lane, Dublin 4)

Netherlands (☎ 70-346-95-44; www.nl.emb-japan .go.jp; Tobias Asserlaan 2, 2517 KC, The Hague)

New Zealand Wellington (embassy; ☎ 04-473 1540; www .nz.emb-japan.go.jp; Level 18, Majestic Centre, 100 Willis St, Wellington 1); Auckland (consulate; ☎ 09-303 4106)

South Korea (☎ 822-2170 5200; www.kr.emb-japan .go.jp; 18-11, Jhoonghak-dong, Jhongro-gu, Seoul)

UK (☎ 020-7465 6500; www.uk.emb-japan.go.jp/; 101-104 Piccadilly, London, W1V 9FN)

USA Washington DC (embassy; ☎ 202-238 6700; www .us.emb-japan.go.jp; 2520 Massachusetts Ave, NW Washington DC 20008-2869); Los Angeles (consulate; ☎ 213-617 6700); New York (consulate; ☎ 212-371 8222)

Embassies & Consulates in Japan

Diplomatic representation in Japan:

Australia Tokyo (embassy; Map pp94-5; ☎ 03-5232-4111; www.australia.or.jp/english; 2-1-14 Mita, Minato-ku, Tokyo); Fukuoka (consulate; ☎ 092-734-5055; Tsuru-takeyaki Bldg, 7F, 1-1-5 Akasaka, Chūō-ku, Fukuoka); Osaka (consulate; ☎ 06-6941-9271; 2-1-61 Shiromi, Chūō-ku, Osaka)

Canada Tokyo (embassy; ☎ 03-5412-6200; www .dfait-maeci.gc.ca/ni-ka/tokyo-en.asp; 7-3-38 Akasaka, Minato-ku, Tokyo); Fukuoka (consulate; ☎ 092-752-6055; FT Bldg, 7F, 4-8-28 Watanabe-dōri, Chuo-ku, Fukuoka); Osaka (consulate; ☎ 06-6212-4910; 2-2-3 Nishi Shinsai-bashi, Chūō-ku, Osaka)

France Tokyo (embassy; Map pp94-5; ☎ 03-5420-8800; www.ambafrance-jp.org; 4-11-44 Minami Azabu, Minato-ku, Tokyo); Osaka (consulate; ☎ 06-4790-1500; 1-2-27 Shiromi, Chūō-ku, Osaka)

Germany Tokyo (Map pp94-5; ☎ 03-5791-7700; www .tokyo.diplo.de/ja/Startseite.html; 4-5-10 Minami Azabu, Minato-ku, Tokyo); Osaka (consulate; ☎ 06-6440-5070; 1-1-88 Oyodonaka, Kita-ku, Osaka)

Ireland Tokyo (embassy; Map pp94-5; ☎ 03-3263-0695; www.embassy-avenue.jp/ireland/index_eng.html; 2-10-7 Koji-machi, Chiyoda-ku, Tokyo); Osaka (consulate; ☎ 06-6309-0055; 4-7-4 Nishinakajima, Yodogawa-ku, Osaka)

Netherlands Tokyo (embassy; Map pp106-7; ☎ 03-5401-0411; www.oranda.or.jp/index/english/index.html; 3-6-3 Shiba-kōen, Minato-ku, Tokyo); Osaka (consulate; ☎ 06-6944-7272; 2-1-61 Shiromi, Chūō-ku, Osaka)

New Zealand Tokyo (embassy; Map pp94-5; ☎ 03-3467-2271; www.nzembassy.com/home.cfm; 20-40 Kamiyama-chō, Shibuya-ku, Tokyo); Osaka (consulate; ☎ 06-6942-9016; 2-1-61 Shiromi, Chūō-ku, Osaka)

South Korea Tokyo (embassy; Map pp94-5; ☎ 03-3452-7611; www.mofat.go.kr/mission/emb/embassy_ en.mof?si_dcode=JP-JP; 1-2-5 Minami Azabu, Minato-ku, Tokyo); Fukuoka (consulate; ☎ 092-771-0461; 1-1-3 Jigyohama, Chūō-ku, Fukuoka)

UK Tokyo (embassy; Map pp94-5; ☎ 03-3265-5511; www.uknow.or.jp/index_e.htm; 1 Ichiban-chō, Chiyoda-ku, Tokyo); Osaka (consulate; ☎ 06-6120-5600; 3-5-1 Bakuromachi, Chūō-ku, Osaka)

USA Tokyo (embassy; Map pp106-7; ☎ 03-3224-5000; http://japan.usembassy.gov/t-main.html; 1-10-5 Akasaka, Minato-ku, Tokyo); Fukuoka (consulate; ☎ 092-751-9331; 2-5-26 Ohori, Chūō-ku, Fukuoka); Osaka (consulate; ☎ 06-6315-5900; 2-11-5 Nishitenma, Kita-ku, Osaka)

FESTIVALS & EVENTS

Japan has a large number of *matsuri* (festivals). Check out Japan's best *matsuri* (p22). In addition to *matsuri*, there are several important annual events, which are often Buddhist imports from China or more recent imports from the West (eg Christmas). Some of the most important annual events:

January

Shōgatsu (New Year) The celebrations from 31 December to 3 January include much eating and drinking, visits to shrines or temples and the paying of respects to relatives and business associates.

Seijin-no-hi (Coming-of-Age Day) Second Monday in January. Ceremonies are held for boys and girls who have reached the age of 20.

February–May

Setsubun (3 or 4 February) To celebrate the end of winter (last day of winter according to the lunar calendar) and drive out evil spirits, the Japanese throw beans while chanting '*fuku wa uchi oni wa soto*' ('In with good fortune, out with the devils').

Hanami (Blossom Viewing) The Japanese delight in the brief blossom-viewing season from February to April. The usual sequence is plum in February, peach in March and cherry in late March or early April.

Hina Matsuri (Doll Festival; 3 March) During this festival old dolls are displayed and young girls are presented with special dolls (*hina*) that represent ancient figures from the imperial court.

Golden Week (29 April to 5 May) Golden Week takes in Midori-no-hi (Green Day; 29 April), Kempō Kinem-bi (Constitution Day; 3 May) and Kodomo-no-hi (Children's Day; 5 May). This is definitely not a time to be on the move since transport and lodging in popular holiday areas can be booked solid.

Kodomo-no-hi (Children's Day; 5 May) This is a holiday dedicated to children, especially boys. Families fly paper streamers of carp (*koi-nobori*), which symbolise male strength.

July–August

Tanabata Matsuri (Star Festival; 7 July) The two stars Vega and Altair meet in the Milky Way on this night. According to a myth (originally Chinese), a princess and a peasant shepherd were forbidden to meet, and this was the only time in the year when the two star-crossed lovers could organise a tryst. Children copy out poems on streamers, and love poems are written on banners that are hung out on display. An especially ornate version of this festival is celebrated from 6 to 8 August in Sendai.

O-Bon (Festival of the Dead; 13 to 16 July, and mid-August) According to Buddhist tradition, this is a time when ancestors return to earth. Lanterns are lit and floated on rivers, lakes or the sea to signify the return of the departed to the underworld. Since most Japanese try to return to their native village at this time of year, this is one of the most crowded times of year to travel or look for accommodation.

November

Shichi-Go-San (Seven-Five-Three Festival; 15 November) Traditionally, this is a festival in honour of girls who are aged three and seven and boys who are aged five. Children are dressed in their finest clothes and taken to shrines or temples, where prayers are offered for good fortune.

FOOD

In the bigger cities, the restaurants that appear in the Eating sections of this guide are divided by neighbourhoods and type of cuisine (Japanese or International). Outside of the bigger cities, eating options are generally presented in one section. For more information about Japan's cuisine, see p67.

GAY & LESBIAN TRAVELLERS

With the possible exception of Thailand, Japan is Asia's most enlightened nation with regard to the sexual preferences of foreigners. Shinjuku-ni-chōme in Tokyo is an established scene where English is spoken and meeting men is fairly straight-forward. In provincial areas there may be one 'snack' bar, where you pay about ¥1,500 for the first drink, entry and the snack. Staying in hotels is simple as most have twin rooms but love hotels are less accessible; if you know someone Japanese and can overcome the language barrier, a stay in a love hotel may be possible, but some are not particularly foreigner-friendly (see p725). Gay saunas double as late-night crash spots if you, unwittingly or otherwise, miss the last train home – so ask your barman for details.

The lesbian scene is growing in Japan but is still elusive for most non-Japanese speaking foreigners. Outside of Tokyo you may find it difficult to break into the local scene unless you spend considerable time in a place or have local contacts who can show you around.

Given Japan's penchant for convenience the Internet has been a boon for the gay and lesbian scene. **Utopia Asia** (www.utopia-asia.com) and **Jguyusguy** (www.jguyusguy.org) are two of the sites most frequented by English speakers. The Utopia site has gay and lesbian information while Jguyusguy is for men. For information about gay and lesbian venues in Tokyo see p147.

There are no legal restraints to same-sex sexual activities of either gender in Japan. Public displays of affection are likely to be the only cause for concern for all visitors, gay, straight or otherwise.

HOLIDAYS

Japan has 15 national holidays. When a public holiday falls on a Sunday, the following Monday is taken as a holiday. You can expect travel and accommodation options to be fully booked during the New Year festivities (29 December to 6 January), Golden Week (29 April to 6 May) and the mid-August O-Bon festival. See p735 for more details of these festivals and events.

Japan's national holidays:

Ganjitsu (New Year's Day) 1 January
Seijin-no-hi (Coming-of-Age Day) Second Monday in January
Kenkoku Kinem-bi (National Foundation Day) 11 February
Shumbun-no-hi (Spring Equinox) 20 or 21 March
Midori-no-hi (Green Day) 29 April
Kempō Kinem-bi (Constitution Day) 3 May
Kokumin-no-Saijitsu (Adjoining Holiday Between Two Holidays) 4 May
Kodomo-no-hi (Children's Day) 5 May
Umi-no-hi (Marine Day) Third Monday in July
Keirō-no-hi (Respect-for-the-Aged Day) Third Monday in September
Shūbun-no-hi (Autumn Equinox) 23 or 24 September
Taiiku-no-hi (Health-Sports Day) Second Monday in October
Bunka-no-hi (Culture Day) 3 November
Kinrō Kansha-no-hi (Labour Thanksgiving Day) 23 November
Tennō Tanjōbi (Emperor's Birthday) 23 December

INSURANCE

A travel insurance policy to cover theft, loss and medical problems is a good idea. Some policies specifically exclude 'dangerous activities', which can include scuba diving, motorcycling and even trekking; if you plan to engage in such activities, you'll want a policy that covers them.

You may prefer a policy which pays doctors or hospitals directly rather than have you pay on the spot and claim later. If you have to claim later, make sure you keep all documentation. Some policies ask you to call (reverse-charge) a centre in your home country where an immediate assessment of your problem is made. Check that the policy covers ambulances or an emergency flight home.

Some insurance policies offer lower and higher medical-expense options; choose the

high-cost option for Japan. Be sure to bring your insurance card or other certificate of insurance to Japan; Japanese hospitals have been known to refuse treatment to foreign patients with no proof of medical insurance.

For information on car insurance, see p761. For information on health insurance, see p769.

INTERNET ACCESS

If you plan on bringing your laptop to Japan, first make sure that it is compatible with Japanese current (100V AC; 50Hz in eastern Japan and 60Hz in western Japan). Most laptops function just fine on Japanese current. Second, check to see if your plug will fit Japanese wall sockets (Japanese plugs are flat two pin, identical to most ungrounded North American plugs). Both transformers and plug adaptors are readily available in electronics districts, such as Tokyo's Akihabara (Map pp94–5), Osaka's Den Den Town (Map p339) or Kyoto's Teramachi-dōri (Map pp284–5).

Modems and phone jacks are similar to those used in the USA (RJ11 phone jacks). Conveniently, many of the grey IDD pay phones in Japan have a standard phone jack and an infrared port so that you can log on to the Internet just about anywhere in the country if your computer has an infrared port.

The major Internet service providers, such as AOL (www.aol.com) and IBM (www.ibm.com), have dial-ups in most big Japanese cities. It's best to download a list of these dial-up numbers before leaving home.

You'll find Internet cafés and other access points in most major Japanese cities. Rates vary, usually ranging from ¥200 to ¥700 per hour. As a rule, Internet connections are fast (DSL or ADSL) and reliable in Japan.

See p23 for some useful websites on Japan.

LEGAL MATTERS

Japanese police have extraordinary powers compared with their Western counterparts. For starters, Japanese police have the right to detain a suspect without charging them for up to three days, after which a prosecutor can decide to extend this period for another 20 days. Police can also choose whether to allow a suspect to phone their embassy or lawyer, though if you find yourself in police custody you should insist that you will not cooperate in any way until allowed to make such a call. Your embassy is the first place you should call if given the chance.

Police will speak almost no English; insist that an interpreter (tsuyakusha) be summoned. Police are legally bound to provide one before proceeding with any questioning. Even if you do speak Japanese, it's best to deny it and stay with your native language.

If you have a problem, call the **Japan Helpline** (☎ 0570-000-911), an emergency number that operates 24 hours a day, seven days a week.

MAPS
If you'd like to buy a map of Japan before arriving, both Nelles and Periplus produce reasonable maps of the whole country. If you want more detailed maps, it's better to buy them after you arrive in Japan.

The Japan National Tourist Organization's (JNTO) free *Tourist Map of Japan*, available at JNTO-operated tourist information centres inside the country and JNTO offices abroad, is a reasonable English-language map that is suitable for general route planning. If you'd like something a little more detailed, both Shobunsha and Kodansha (Japanese publishers) publish a series of bilingual fold-out maps (prices start at around ¥700).

The *Japan Road Atlas* (Shobunsha) is a good choice for those planning to drive around the country. Those looking for something less bulky should pick up a copy of the *Bilingual Atlas of Japan* (Kodansha). Of course, if you can read a little Japanese, you'll do much better with one of the excellent *Super Mapple* road atlases published by Shobunsha.

MONEY
The currency in Japan is the yen (¥) and banknotes and coins are easily identifiable. There are ¥1, ¥5, ¥10, ¥50, ¥100 and ¥500 coins; and ¥1000, ¥2000, ¥5000 and ¥10,000 banknotes (the ¥2000 are very rarely seen). The ¥1 coin is an aluminium lightweight coin, the ¥5 and ¥50 coins have a punched hole in the middle (the former is coloured bronze and the latter silver). Note that some vending machines do not accept older ¥500 coins (a South Korean coin of much less value was often used in its place to rip off vending machines).

> **WARNING: JAPAN IS A CASH SOCIETY!**
> Be warned that cold hard yen (¥) is the way to pay in Japan. While credit cards are becoming more common, cash is still much more widely used, and travellers cheques are rarely accepted. Do not assume that you can pay for things with a credit card; always carry sufficient cash. The only places where you can count on paying by credit card are department stores and large hotels.
>
> For those without credit cards, it would be a good idea to bring some travellers cheques as a back-up. As in most other countries, the US dollar is still the currency of choice in terms of exchanging cash and cashing travellers cheques.

The Japanese pronounce yen as 'en', with no 'y' sound. The kanji for yen is: 円.

For information on costs in Japan, see p21. For exchange rates, see the inside front cover of this guide.

ATMs
Automated teller machines are almost as common as vending machines in Japan. Unfortunately, most of these do not accept foreign-issued cards. Even if they display Visa and MasterCard logos, most accept only Japan-issued versions of these cards.

Fortunately, you will find international ATMs in bigger cities such as Tokyo, Osaka and Kyoto that do accept foreign-issued cards. Better still, the Japanese postal system has recently linked all of its ATMs to the international Cirrus and Plus cash networks (as well as some credit-card networks), making life a breeze for travellers to Japan. You'll find postal ATMs in most large post offices. Most postal ATMs are open 9am to 5pm on weekdays, 9am to noon on Saturday, and are closed on Sunday and holidays. Note that the postal ATMs are a little tricky to use: First press 'English Guidance' on the left of the screen, then press 'Other' on the screen, then choose your transaction and you're away.

Credit Cards
Except for making cash withdrawals at banks and ATMs, it is best not to rely on credit cards in Japan (for more information see above). While department stores, top-end hotels and some restaurants do

accept cards, most businesses in Japan do not. Cash-and-carry is still very much the rule. If you do decide to bring a credit card, you'll find Visa most useful, followed by MasterCard, Amex and Diners Club.

The main credit-card offices are in Tokyo:

Amex (☎ 0120-020-120; American Express Tower, 4-30-16 Ogikubo, Suginami-ku; ☼ 24hr)

MasterCard (Map p103; ☎ 03-5728-5200; Cerulean Tower, 16F, 26-1 Sakuragaoka-cho, Shibuya-ku)

Visa (Map pp106-7; ☎ 03-5251-0633, 0120-133-173; Nissho Bldg, 4F, 2-7-9 Kita-Aoyama, Minato-ku)

Exchanging Money

In theory, banks and post offices will change all major currencies. In practice, some banks refuse to exchange anything but US-dollar cash and travellers cheques. Note also that the currencies of neighbouring Taiwan (New Taiwan dollar) and Korea *(won)* are not easy to change, so you should change these into yen or US dollars before arriving in Japan.

You can change cash or travellers cheques at an Authorised Foreign Exchange Bank (signs are always displayed in English), major post offices, some large hotels and most big department stores. These are easy to find in cities, but less common elsewhere.

Note that you receive a better exchange rate when withdrawing cash from ATMs than when exchanging cash or travellers cheques in Japan; just be aware that many banks place a limit on the amount of cash you can withdraw in any one day (often around US$400).

BANK & POST OFFICE ACCOUNTS

Opening a regular bank account is difficult for foreigners on a temporary visitor visa. Most banks ask to see an Alien Registration Card (p744), and some may also require a name stamp (*hanko* or *inkan*, easily available at speciality stores in most towns). A much better option for long-term visitors or those who don't want to bother with changing money all the time is a postal savings account (*yūbin chokin*). You can open these accounts at any major post office in Japan. With a postal savings account you'll receive a cash card that enables you to withdraw funds from any post office in Japan (these are everywhere). You should be able to get things started by using the phrase: '*yūbin chokin no kōza o hirakitai desu*' ('I would like to open a post office savings account').

INTERNATIONAL TRANSFERS

In order to make an international transfer you'll have to find a Japanese bank associated with the bank transferring the money. Start by asking at the central branch of any major Japanese bank. If they don't have a relationship with your bank, they can usually refer you to a bank that does. Once you find a related bank in Japan, you'll have to give your home bank the exact details of where to send the money: the bank, branch and location. A credit-card cash advance is a worthwhile alternative.

Taxes

Japan has a 5% consumer tax. If you eat at expensive restaurants and stay in top-end accommodation, you will encounter a service charge which varies from 10% to 15%. This means it is sometimes cheaper to ask for separate bills. You can ask for separate bills by saying '*betsu-betsu ni one-gaishimasu*', before your bill is tallied.

Tipping

There is little tipping in Japan. If you want to show your gratitude to someone, give them a gift rather than a tip. If you do choose to give someone a cash gift (a maid in a ryokan, for instance), place the money in an envelope first.

PHOTOGRAPHY & VIDEO

Japan is one of the world's best places to buy film and camera equipment. You'll have no problem finding print film wherever you go, and high-quality slide film is widely available at camera shops in most cities. A 36-exposure roll of print film costs anywhere from ¥400 to ¥800. A roll of Kodachrome slide film (36-exposures) costs about ¥950 without processing; Fuji slide film, such as Velvia and Provia, is similarly priced.

Film processing is fast and economical in Japan, standards are usually high, and shops offering this service are easy to find. A 36-exposure roll of print film typically costs around ¥600 to have developed. A 36-exposure roll of slide film usually costs around ¥900 to have developed and mounted, or ¥600 to have developed only.

Digital photographers will find all manner of memory media, batteries and digital cameras widely available. Japan's photo shops also offer a wide range of services for digital photographers, like high-quality prints from digital files.

For more information on buying cameras and other photographic equipment, see p741.

Serious photographers might want to pick up a copy of Lonely Planet's *Travel Photography*.

POST

The Japanese postal system is reliable, efficient and, for regular postcards and airmail letters, not markedly more expensive than other developed countries.

Postal Rates

The airmail rate for postcards is ¥70 to any overseas destination; aerograms cost ¥90. Letters weighing less than 10g are ¥90 to other countries within Asia, ¥110 to North America, Europe or Oceania (including Australia and New Zealand) and ¥130 to Africa and South America. One peculiarity of the Japanese postal system is that you will be charged extra if your writing runs over onto the address side (the right side) of a postcard.

Sending & Receiving Mail

The symbol for post offices is a red T with a bar across the top on a white background (〒). District post offices (the main post office in a ward) are normally open from 9am to 7pm weekdays and 9am to 3pm Saturday, and are closed Sunday and public holidays. Local post offices are open 9am to 5pm weekdays, and are closed Saturday, Sunday and public holidays. Main post offices in the larger cities may have an after-hours window open 24 hours a day, seven days a week.

Mail can be sent to, from or within Japan when addressed in Roman script (*romaji*) but it should, of course, be written as clearly as possible.

Although any post office will hold mail for collection, the poste restante concept is not well known and can cause confusion in smaller places. It is probably better to have mail addressed to you at a larger central post office. Letters are usually only held for 30 days before being returned to sender. When inquiring about mail for collection ask for *kyoku dome yūbin*.

It should be addressed as follows:

Darren O'CONNELL
Poste Restante
Central Post Office
Tokyo, JAPAN

SHOPPING

Although Japan is one of the world's most expensive countries, there are some good bargains out there, and you can certainly return home with a bag full of goodies without breaking the bank. As well as all the electronic gadgetry available in Japan, there is a wide range of traditional crafts to choose from, though for good stuff you really need to spend big money. It pays to shop around if you have anything particular in mind. The big department stores, which often have the best selections of Japanese gift items, can vary enormously in their prices from one store to another. In some shops, you are paying for extras such as the high level of service (a feature of all Japanese shops anyway), location and interior décor.

Bargaining

Bargaining is largely restricted to flea markets (where anything goes) and large discount electronics shops (where a polite request will often bring the price down by around 10%).

Clothes

Japanese-made clothes and shoes are of excellent quality and needn't cost a fortune. It really is a matter of looking around and finding something that suits your budget, taste and – here's the hard part – your size! In upmarket and fashionable districts, many of the clothes shops are exclusive boutiques with exclusive prices, although there are always clusters of stores nearby that are more affordable. In less fashionable areas there are countless retail outlets for an industry providing economical, mass-produced versions of designer clothes. If you fit into the smaller sizes in your home country, you shouldn't have any problems finding clothes to fit. Shoe size can also be a problem if your feet are anything bigger than what most Westerners would consider medium-sized.

Computer Equipment

Computers, computer accessories and software are widely available. Unfortunately for the foreign traveller, most of what's out there – operating systems, keyboards and software – is in Japanese and not of any use unless you intend to work with the Japanese language. However, if you're after hardware like peripherals, chips and the like, where language isn't a factor, you will find lots to choose from, including secondhand goods at unbelievably low prices (for more information check out Osaka's Den Den Town, p351; and Tokyo's Akihabara, p151).

Electronics

Nowhere in the world will you find a better selection of electronics than in Tokyo's Akihabara district (p151) and Osaka's Den Den Town (p351). Keep in mind though that much of the electrical gadgetry on sale in Japan is designed for Japan's curious power supply (100V at 50Hz or 60Hz) and may require a transformer for use overseas. The safest bet is to go for export models – the prices may be slightly higher but, in the long run, you'll save the expense of converting the equipment to suit the conditions in your own country. Big electronics stores in Japan are about the only places where a little bargaining will bring prices down around 10% or so. Just ask politely for a discount (this word is understood in Japan) and you'll probably receive one.

Japanese Arts & Crafts

As well as all the hi-tech knick-knacks produced by the Japanese, it is also possible to go home loaded with traditional Japanese arts and crafts. Anything from carp banners to kimono can make good souvenirs for the Japanophile.

KASA (JAPANESE UMBRELLAS)

Another classic souvenir item, *kasa* (Japanese umbrellas) come in two forms: *higasa*, which are made of paper, cotton or silk and serve as a sunshade; and *bangasa*, which are made of oiled paper and keep the rain off. Again, department stores and tourist shops are your best bet for finding *kasa*.

KATANA (JAPANESE SWORDS)

A fantastic souvenir – good *katana* (Japanese swords) are going to cost more than all your other travel expenses put together! The reason for their expense is both their mystique as the symbols of samurai power, and the great care that goes into making them. Sword

shops that sell the real thing will also stock *tsuba* (sword guards), and complete sets of samurai armour. Department stores, on the other hand, stock realistic (to the untrained eye at least) imitations at affordable prices.

KIMONO & YUKATA

Kimono are most commonly worn at ceremonial occasions such as university graduations or weddings. For most non-Japanese, the cost of a kimono is prohibitively expensive. Prices start at around ¥60,000 and soar to ¥1 million or more. The best option for those interested in owning their own kimono is to head to a flea market or used-clothing shop. Used-clothing shops usually stock a variety of kimono ranging in price from ¥1500 to ¥9000, depending on quality.

For those not in the kimono league, another option might be to look for a *yukata* (the cotton bathrobes worn in ryokan and at summer festivals). They have a distinctively Japanese look and are not only affordable (from around ¥3500 up) but also highly usable. These are available from tourist shops and department stores in Japan.

KOINOBORI (CARP BANNERS)

The lovely banners that you see waving in the breeze on Kodomo-no-hi (Children's Day; 5 May) throughout Japan are called *koinobori*. The carp is much revered for its tenacity and perseverance, but you might like the banners for their simple elegance.

NINGYŌ (JAPANESE DOLLS)

Not for playing with, Japanese dolls are usually intended for display. Often quite exquisite, with coiffured hair and dressed in kimono, *ningyō* make excellent souvenirs or gifts. Also available are *gogatsu-ningyō*, dolls dressed in samurai suits used as gifts on Kodomo-no-hi (Children's Day; 5 May). The most famous dolls are made in Kyoto and are known as *kyō-ningyō*.

Ningyō can be bought in tourist shops, department stores and special doll shops. In Tokyo, Edo-dōri in Asakusa (p152) is well known for its many doll shops.

POTTERY

Numerous pottery villages still exist in Japan; many feature pottery museums and working kilns that are open to the public. Of course, it is also possible to buy examples of stoneware and porcelain. Sources of different pottery styles abound: Bizen (p397), near Okayama in western Honshū, which is famed for its Bizen-yaki pottery; and Karatsu (p621), Imari (p624) and Arita (p624) in Kyūshū (the home of Japanese pottery).

Department stores are a surprisingly good place to look for Japanese pottery, and Takashimaya (see p151 for details) often has bargain bins where you can score some real deals. For even better prices try some of Japan's flea markets.

SHIKKI (LACQUERWARE)

Another exquisite Japanese craft is *shikki* (lacquerware). The lacquerware-making process, involving as many as 15 layers of lacquer, is used to create objects as diverse as dishes and furniture. As you might expect, examples of good lacquerware cannot be had for a song, but smaller items can be bought at affordable prices from department stores. Popular, easily transportable items include bowls, trays and small boxes.

UKIYO-E (WOOD BLOCK PRINTS)

Originating in the 18th century as one of Japan's earliest manifestations of mass culture, wood block prints were used in advertising and posters. It was only later that *ukiyo-e* was considered an art form. The name (literally, 'pictures from the floating world') derives from a Buddhist term indicating the transient world of daily pleasures. *Ukiyo-e* uniquely depicts such things as street scenes, actors and courtesans.

Today, tourist shops in Japan stock modern reproductions of the work of famous *ukiyo-e* masters such as Hokusai, whose scenes of Fuji-san (Mt Fuji) are favourites. It is also possible to come across originals by lesser-known artists at prices ranging from ¥3000 to ¥40,000.

WASHI (JAPANESE PAPER)

For more than 1000 years, *washi* (Japanese paper) has been famous as the finest handmade paper in the world. Special shops stock sheets of *washi* and products made from it, such as notebooks, wallets and so on. As they're generally inexpensive and light, *washi* products make excellent gifts and souvenirs. You'll find them in the big department stores. See p326 for suggestions on places to buy *washi*.

Music

When it comes to the recording arts, Japan could teach the West a thing or two. Japanese pressings are famed for their high fidelity, and there are stores devoted to every genre and subgenre of every style of music, especially in Tokyo. Prices range from ¥1500 to ¥2300. Local pressings are more expensive than imports – but you pay for quality.

Pearls

The Japanese firm Mikimoto developed the technique of producing cultured pearls by artificially introducing an irritant into the pearl oyster. Pearls and pearl jewellery are still popular buys for foreign visitors, but it would be wise to check prices in your own country. Size, quality and colour will all have a bearing on the price.

Photographic Equipment

Tokyo is an excellent hunting ground for photographic equipment. As almost all of the big-name brands in camera equipment are locally produced, prices can be very competitive. The prices for accessories, such as motor drives and flash units, can even be compared to Singapore and Hong Kong. In addition, shopping in Japan presents the shopper with none of the rip-off risks that abound in other Asian discount capitals.

Be prepared to shop around. Tokyo's Shinjuku area is the best place for buying camera equipment, although Ginza, too, has a good selection of camera shops (see p152 for details). Secondhand camera equipment is worth checking out. In Tokyo, both Shinjuku and Ginza have a fair number of secondhand shops where camera and lens quality is usually very good and prices are around half what you would pay for new equipment. In Osaka, the area just south of Osaka station has used-camera shops as well (see p351 for more information).

Tax-Free Shopping

Shopping tax-free in Japan is not necessarily the bargain that you might expect. Although tax-free shops enable foreigners to receive an exemption from the 5% consumption tax (*shōhi-zei*) levied on most items, these still may not be the cheapest places to shop. Shops that offer this exemption usually require that you pay the consumption tax and then go to a special counter to receive a refund. You will often need to show your passport to receive this refund. Tax-free shops will usually have a sign in English that announces their tax-free status.

Toys

Tokyo has some remarkable toy shops. See p152 for more information. Elsewhere, look out for some of the traditional wooden toys produced as regional specialities – they make good souvenirs for adults and children alike.

SOLO TRAVELLERS

Japan is an excellent place for male solo travellers; it's safe, friendly and convenient. For female solo travellers, Japan can also be a good place to travel, but there are some dangers and annoyances to keep in mind (see p745).

Almost all hotels in Japan offer single rooms, and business-hotel singles can cost as little as ¥4000. Ryokan usually charge by the person, not the room, which keeps the price down for the single traveller. The only hitch is that some ryokan owners balk at renting a room to a single traveller, when they might be able to rent it to two people instead. For more on accommodation, see p727.

Many restaurants in Japan have small tables or counters which are perfect for solo travellers. *Izakaya* (Japanese-style dining pubs) are also generally welcoming to solo travellers, and you probably won't have to wait long before being offered a drink and be roped into a conversation, particularly if you sit at the counter. Finally, the 'gaijin bars' in the larger cities are generally friendly, convivial places; if you're after a travel partner or just an English-speaking conversation partner, these are good places to start.

TELEPHONE

Japanese telephone codes consist of an area code plus a local code and number. You do not dial the area code when making a call in that area. When dialling Japan from abroad, dial the country code ☎ 81, followed by the area code (drop the '0') and the number. For a list of area codes for some of Japan's major cities and emergency numbers, see the inside front cover of this guidebook. All toll-free numbers in Japan begin with the digits ☎ 0120.

Directory Assistance

For local directory assistance dial ☎ 104 (the call costs ¥100), or for assistance in English ring ☎ 0120-364-463 from 9am to 5pm weekdays. For international directory assistance dial ☎ 0057.

International Calls

The best way to make an international phone call from Japan is to use a prepaid international phone card (see below).

Paid overseas calls can be made from grey international ISDN phones. These are usually found in phone booths marked 'International & Domestic Card/Coin Phone'. Unfortunately, these are very rare; try looking in the lobbies of top-end hotels and at airports. Calls are charged by the unit, each of which is six seconds, so if you don't have much to say you could phone home for just ¥100. Reverse-charge (collect) overseas calls can be made from any pay phone.

You can save money by dialling late at night. Economy rates, with a discount of 20%, apply from 7pm to 11pm weekdays and to 11pm on weekends and holidays. From 11pm to 8am a discount rate brings the price of international calls down by 40%. Note that it is also cheaper to make domestic calls by dialling outside the standard hours.

To place an international call through the operator, dial ☎ 0051 (most international operators speak English). To make the call yourself, dial ☎ 001 010 (KDDI), ☎ 0041 010 (ITJ) or ☎ 0033 010 (NTT) – there's very little difference in their rates – then the international country code, the local code and the number.

Another option is to dial ☎ 0039 plus your country code for home country direct, which takes you straight through to a local operator in the country dialled. You can then make a reverse-charge call or a credit-card call with a telephone credit card valid in that country.

PREPAID INTERNATIONAL PHONE CARDS

Because of the lack of pay phones from which you can make international phone calls in Japan, the easiest way to make an international phone call is to buy a prepaid international phone card.

With the exception of the IC Card, which can only be used with special orange IC phones, these phone cards can be used with any regular pay phone in Japan.

Global Card These cards are only available at discount ticket shops and some guesthouses.

IC Cards These cards are sold from machines that accompany IC card phones. IC cards can only be used with IC card phones.

KDDI Superworld Card These cards can be purchased at almost any convenience store in Japan.

Local Calls

The Japanese public telephone system is very well developed. There are a great many public phones and they work almost 100% of the time.

Local calls from pay phones cost ¥10 per minute; unused ¥10 coins are returned after the call is completed but no change is given on ¥100 coins.

In general it's much easier to buy a telephone card (*terefon kādo*) when you arrive rather than worry about always having coins on hand. Phone cards are sold in ¥500 and ¥1000 denominations (the latter earns you an extra ¥50 in calls) and can be used in most green or grey pay phones. They are available from vending machines and convenience stores, come in a myriad of designs and are also a collectable item.

Mobile Phones

Several outfits specialise in short-term mobile-phone (cell) rentals for travellers and businesspeople. **Rentafone Japan** (☎ 080-3240-9183; www.rentafonejapan.com) rents phones for ¥3500 per week and offers free delivery of the phone to your accommodation. Phone charges are extra and are billed at cost.

Useful Numbers

If you're staying long-term, adjusting to life in Japan can be tough; but there are places to turn to for help. The **Foreign Residents Advisory Center** (☎ 03-5320-7744; ✆ 9.30am-noon & 1-4pm Mon-Fri) is a useful service operated by the Tokyo metropolitan government. Otherwise, try the 24-hour **Japan Helpline** (☎ 0120-461 997).

TIME

Despite the distance between Japan's east and west, the country is all on the same time: nine hours ahead of Greenwich Mean Time (GMT). Sydney and Wellington are ahead of Japan (+1 and +3 hours, respectively), and most of the world's other big cities are behind

Japan (New York -14, Los Angeles -17 and London -9).

Japan does not have daylight savings time (also known as summer time), so you must subtract one hour when calculating the time difference between Japan and a country using daylight savings time.

For more information see World Time Zones (p792).

TOILETS

In Japan you will come across Western-style toilets and Asian squat toilets. When you are compelled to squat, the correct position is facing the hood, away from the door. This is the opposite of squat toilets in most other places in Asia. Make sure the contents of your pockets don't spill out! Toilet paper isn't always provided, so carry tissues with you. You may be given small packets of tissue on the street in Japan, a common form of advertising.

In many bathrooms in Japan, separate toilet slippers are often provided just inside the toilet door. These are for use in the toilet only, so remember to change out of them when you leave.

It's quite common to see men urinating in public – the unspoken rule is that it's acceptable at night time if you happen to be drunk. Public toilets are free in Japan. The katakana script for 'toilet' is トイレ, and the kanji script is お洗い.

You'll often also see these kanji:

Female 女
Male 男

TOURIST INFORMATION

Japan's tourist information services are first-rate. You will find information offices in most cities, towns and even some small villages. They are almost always located inside or in front of the main train station in a town or city.

A note on language difficulties: English speakers are usually available at tourist information offices in larger cities. Away from the big cities, you'll find varying degrees of English-language ability. In rural areas and small towns you may find yourself relying more on one-word communication and hand signals. Nonetheless, with a little patience and a smile you will usually get the information you need from even the smallest local tourist information office.

Japan National Tourist Organization (JNTO)

The **Japan National Tourist Organization** (JNTO; www.jnto.go.jp) is the main English-language information service for foreign travellers to Japan. JNTO produces a great deal of useful literature, which is available from both its overseas offices and its Tourist Information Center in Tokyo (p92). Most publications are available in English and, in some cases, other European and Asian languages. JNTO's website is very useful in planning your journey.

Unfortunately for foreign travellers, JNTO is pulling out of the business of operating tourist information centres inside Japan. The sole remaining domestic office is the Tokyo office.

JNTO has a number of overseas offices:

Australia (☎ 02-9251 3024; Level 18, Australia Square Tower, 264 George St, Sydney, NSW 2000)

Canada (☎ 416-366 7140; 165 University Ave, Toronto, ON M5H 3B8)

France (☎ 01 42 96 20 29; 4 rue de Ventadour, 75001 Paris)

Germany (☎ 069-20353; Kaiserstrasse 11, 60311 Frankfurt am Main 1)

UK (☎ 020-7734 9638; Heathcoat House, 20 Saville Row, London W1S 3PR)

USA Los Angeles (☎ 213-623 1952; 515 South Figueroa St, Suite 1470, Los Angeles, CA 90071); New York (☎ 212-757 5640; One Rockefeller Plaza, Suite 1250, New York, NY 10020); San Francisco (☎ 415-292 5686; 1 Daniel Burnham Court, Suite 250C, San Francisco, CA 94109)

Other Information Offices

There are tourist information offices (*kankō annai-sho*; 観光案内所) in or near almost all major railway stations, but the further you venture into outlying regions, the less chance you have of finding English-speaking staff. If you want a licensed, professional tourist guide, contact the **Japan Guide Association** (☎ 03-3213-2706; www.jga21c.or.jp/f_introduction.html) in Tokyo.

VISAS

Generally, visitors who are not planning to engage in income-producing activities while in Japan are exempt from obtaining visas and will be issued a *tanki-taizai* visa (temporary visitor visa) on arrival.

Stays of up to six months are permitted for citizens of Austria, Germany, Ireland, Mexico, Switzerland and the UK. Citizens of these countries will almost always be given a 90-day temporary visitor visa upon arrival, which can usually be extended for another 90 days at immigration bureaux inside Japan (for details see below).

Citizens of the USA, Australia and New Zealand are granted 90-day temporary visitor visas, while stays of up to three months are permitted for citizens of Argentina, Belgium, Canada, Denmark, Finland, France, Iceland, Israel, Italy, the Netherlands, Norway, Singapore, Spain, Sweden and a number of other countries.

Japan requires that visitors to the country entering on a temporary visitor visa possess an ongoing air or sea ticket or evidence thereof. In practice, few travellers are asked to produce such documents, but to avoid surprises it pays to be on the safe side.

For additional information on visas and regulations, contact the nearest Japanese embassy or consulate, or visit the website of the **Japan Ministry of Foreign Affairs** (www.mofa .go.jp) where you can find out about the different types of visas available, read about working-holiday visas and find details on the Japan Exchange & Teaching (JET) program, which sponsors native English speakers to teach in the Japanese public school system.

Alien Registration Card

Anyone, and this includes tourists, who stays for more than 90 days is required to obtain an Alien Registration Card (*Gaikoku-jin Torokushō*). This card can be obtained at the municipal office of the city, town or ward in which you're living, but moving to another area requires that you re-register within 14 days.

You must carry your Alien Registration Card at all times as the police can stop you and ask to see the card. If you don't have the card, you may be taken back to the station and will have to wait there until someone fetches it for you.

Visa Extensions

With the exception of those nationals whose countries have reciprocal visa exemptions and can stay for six months, the limit for most nationalities is 90 days or three months. To extend a temporary visitor visa beyond the standard 90 days or three months, apply at the nearest immigration office (for a list of immigration

bureaux and regional offices visit www.edu
cationjapan.org/visas/immigration_offices.
html). You must provide two copies of an
Application for Extension of Stay (available
at the immigration office), a letter stating
the reasons for the extension, supporting
documentation and your passport. There
is a processing fee of ¥4000.

Many long-term visitors to Japan get
around the extension problem by briefly
leaving the country, usually going to South
Korea. Be warned, though, that immigration
officials are wise to this practice and many
'tourist visa returnees' are turned back at the
entry point.

Work Visas

It is not as easy as it once was to get a visa
to work in Japan. Ever-increasing demand
has prompted much stricter work visa requirements. Arriving in Japan and looking
for a job is quite a tough proposition these
days, though people still do it. There are
legal employment categories for foreigners that specify standards of experience and
qualifications.

Once you find an employer in Japan who
is willing to sponsor you, it is necessary
to obtain a Certificate of Eligibility from
the nearest immigration office. The same
office can then issue you your work visa,
which is valid for either one or three years.
The whole procedure usually takes two to
three months.

Working-Holiday Visas

Australians, Britons, Canadians, Germans,
New Zealanders and South Koreans between the ages of 18 and 25 (the age limit
can be pushed up to 30 in some cases) can
apply for a working-holiday visa. This visa
allows a six-month stay and two six-month
extensions. It is designed to enable young
people to travel extensively during their
stay; although employment is supposed
to be part-time or temporary, in practice
many people work full time.

A working-holiday visa is much easier to
obtain than a work visa and is popular with
Japanese employers. Single applicants must
have the equivalent of US$2000 of funds, a
married couple must have US$3000, and all
applicants must have an onward ticket from
Japan. For details, inquire at the nearest
Japanese embassy or consulate (see p734).

WOMEN TRAVELLERS

Japan is one of the world's safest countries in
which to travel – if you're a man. Japan is not
as safe for women travellers. The primary
dangers faced by women travellers to Japan
are of a sexual nature: sexual harassment,
molestation, attempted rape and rape.

Although some expats will assure you that
it's safe to walk the streets of any Japanese
city alone at night, ignore this nonsense and
follow your common sense: keep to streets
with heavier foot traffic, stay in groups etc.
Western-looking women who are alone on
foot are easy targets for verbal harassment, or
worse, by passing male pedestrians, cyclists
and motorists. Walking solo along roads in
remote rural areas (even during broad daylight), and hitchhiking are definitely advised
against. The risks simply aren't worth it.

It is the rare (or unusually lucky) woman
who stays in Japan for any length of time
without encountering some type of sexual
harassment. Jam-packed trains or buses during rush hour, or late-hour services heav-
ing with the inebriated masses, can bring
out the worst in the Japanese male. When
movement is impossible, the roving hands
of *chikan* (men who feel up women and girls
on packed trains) are sometimes at work.
A loud complaint may shame the perpetra-
tor into withdrawing his hand. Failing this,
you may be able to push your way through
to another part of even the most crowded
train, especially if other passengers realise
what is happening. Or, if possible, ride in
the women-only train carriages that have recently been introduced in Japan (see p767).

Keep your wits about you in traditional
entertainment areas, where drunken men
stumbling out of snack bars are often under
the delusion that any female passer-by will
appreciate a quick squeeze or lewd remarks.
Apparently some men find that words are
not enough to express how they feel, as
flashers and even more crude exhibition-
ists are not uncommon. These men target
women in isolated situations (say, making a
call from a phone box alone after dark) and
may publicly expose themselves or even
masturbate in front of you. They are, however, unlikely to be shamed into stopping
by merely a stern look, or even yelling. The
best thing you can do is quickly walk away.
Other Japanese men engage in the all-too-
common handshake scam, where a friendly

man pretends to want to shake your hand Western-style, then fondles your breast at the same time. When in doubt, refuse to shake hands and bow instead.

Although statistics show low rates of violent crimes against women, many Japanese women's organisations and media attribute this to under-reporting. If you or someone you know is raped and you attempt to seek help, be forewarned that police and medical personnel can be quite unhelpful, even accusatory. Insist on receiving all necessary medical care (STD tests, antibiotic booster shot and, if you choose, the morning-after pill) and, as appropriate, filing a police report.

If you do have a problem and find the local police unhelpful, you can call the **Japan Helpline** (☎ 0570-000-911), an emergency number that operates 24 hours a day, seven days a week.

Finally, an excellent resource available for any woman setting up in Japan is Caroline Pover's excellent book *Being A Broad in Japan*, which can be found in bookstores and can also be ordered from her website at www.being-a-broad.com.

WORK

Finding work in Japan is possible but it's nowhere near as easy or as lucrative as it used to be. Teaching English is still the most common job for Westerners, but bartending, hostessing, modelling and various writing/editorial jobs are also possible.

Whatever line of work you choose, it's essential to look neat and tidy for interviews – appearances are very important in Japan. You'll also need to be determined, and you should have a sizeable sum of money to carry you through while you are looking for work, and possibly to get you out of the country if you don't find any (it happens). Foreigners who have set up in Japan over the last few years maintain that a figure of around US$5000 or more is necessary to make a go of it in Japan. People do it with less, but they run the risk of ending up penniless and homeless before they find a job.

Bartending

Bartending does not qualify you for a work visa; most of the foreign bartenders in Japan are either working illegally or are on another kind of visa. Some bars in big Japanese cities hire foreign bartenders; most are strict about

visas but others don't seem to care. The best places to look are 'gaijin bars', although a few Japanese-oriented places also employ foreign bartenders for 'ambiance'. The pay is barely enough to survive on – usually about ¥1000 per hour.

English Teaching

Teaching English has always been the most popular job for native English speakers in Japan. While it's a fairly common option, competition for the good jobs is very tight since many schools have failed as a result of Japan's weakened economy. A university degree is an absolute essential as you cannot qualify for a work visa without one (be sure to bring the actual degree with you to Japan). Teaching qualifications and some teaching experience will be a huge plus when job hunting.

Consider lining up a job before arriving in Japan. Big schools, like Nova for example, now have recruitment programs in the USA and the UK. One downside to the big 'factory schools' that recruit overseas is that working conditions are often pretty dire compared with smaller schools that recruit within Japan.

Australians, New Zealanders and Canadians, who can take advantage of the Japanese working-holiday visa (p745), are in a slightly better position. Schools are happier about taking on unqualified teachers if they don't have to bother with sponsoring a teacher for a work visa.

ELT News (www.eltnews.com/home.shtml) is an excellent site with lots of information and want ads for English teachers in Japan.

GOVERNMENT SCHOOLS

The program run by **Japan Exchange & Teaching** (JET; www.jetprogramme.org) provides 2000 teaching assistant positions for foreign teachers. The job operates on a yearly contract and must be organised in your home country. The program gets very good reports from many of its teachers.

Teachers employed by the JET program are known as Assistant Language Teachers (ALTs). Although you will have to apply in your home country in order to work as an ALT with JET, it's worth bearing in mind that many local governments in Japan are also employing ALTs for their schools. Such work can sometimes be arranged within Japan.

Visit the JET website or contact the nearest Japanese embassy or consulate (p734) for more details.

INTERNATIONAL SCHOOLS

Major cities with large foreign populations, such as Tokyo and Yokohama, have a number of international schools for the children of foreign residents. Work is available for qualified, Western-trained teachers in all disciplines; the schools will usually organise your visa.

PRIVATE SCHOOLS

The classifieds section of the Monday edition of the *Japan Times* is the best place to look for teaching positions. Some larger schools rely on direct inquiries from would-be teachers.

Tokyo is the easiest place to find teaching jobs; schools across Japan advertise or recruit in the capital. Heading straight to another of Japan's major population centres (say Osaka, Fukuoka, Hiroshima or Sapporo), where there are smaller numbers of competing foreigners, is also a good bet.

Check the fine print carefully once you have an offer. Find out how many hours you will teach, whether class preparation time is paid for and whether you receive sick leave and paid holidays. Find out also how and when you will be paid and if the school will sponsor your visa. It's worth checking conditions with other foreign staff. Ask whether your school is prepared to serve as a guarantor in the event that you rent an apartment.

Hostessing

A hostess is a woman who is paid to pour drinks for and chat with (usually) male customers in a so-called 'hostess bar'. Although hostessing does involve a lot of thinly veiled sexual innuendos and the occasional furtive grab at thighs or breasts, it is not a form of prostitution. At some of the seedier places, however, there may be some pressure to perform 'extracurricular activities'.

Hostessing involves late hours, frequent pressure to drink, and exposure to astonishing amounts of cigarette smoke. Hostesses should avoid being too casual about safety precautions if seeing clients outside working hours – there have been cases of foreign hostesses being raped and murdered by clients in Japan. See p745 for more information on safety issues.

Work visas are not issued for hostesses. Rates for Western women working as hostesses typically range from ¥3000 to ¥5000 per hour (plus tips), with bonuses for bringing customers to the club. An ability to speak Japanese is an asset, but not essential – many Japanese salarymen want to practise their English.

Director Penelope Buitenhuis' *Tokyo Girls* is a fantastically illuminating documentary film about the lives of Western hostesses working in Japan.

Proofreading & Editing

There is work, particularly in the Tokyo area, for editors, proofreaders and translators (Japanese to English and vice-versa). Needless to say, it is difficult for the casual visitor to simply waltz into these jobs – you'll need to have the proper qualifications and experience. And even for proofreading and editing, some Japanese-language ability is a huge plus, if only for dealing with clients. If you think you've got what it takes, check the Monday edition of the *Japan Times* for openings.

For more information about proofreading and editing in Japan, visit the webpage for **Society of Writers, Editors and Translators** (SWET; www.swet.jp).

Transport

CONTENTS

GETTING THERE & AWAY

ENTERING THE COUNTRY

While most fly to/from Tokyo, there are several other ways of getting into and out of Japan. For a start, there are many other airports in Japan, some which make better entry points than Tokyo's somewhat inconvenient new Tokyo international airport (commonly known as Narita International Airport). It's also possible to arrive in Japan by sea from South Korea, China, Russia and Taiwan.

Passports

A passport is essential. If yours is within a few months of expiry, get a new one now – you

---

THINGS CHANGE

The information in this chapter is particularly vulnerable to change. Check directly with the airline or a travel agent to make sure you understand how a fare (and ticket you may buy) works and be aware of the security requirements for international travel. Shop carefully. The details given in this chapter should be regarded as pointers and are not a substitute for your own careful, up-to-date research.

---

will not be issued a visa if your passport is due to expire before the visa. For information on visas, see p744.

AIR

There are flights to Japan from all over the world, usually to Tokyo but also to a number of other Japanese airports. Although Tokyo may seem the obvious arrival and departure point in Japan, for many visitors this may not be the case. If you plan on exploring western Japan or the Kansai region, it might be more convenient to fly into Kansai International Airport (KIX) near Osaka.

Airports & Airlines

There are international airports on the main island of Honshū (Nagoya, Niigata, Osaka/Kansai and Tokyo Narita), Kyūshū (Fukuoka, Kagoshima, Kumamoto and Nagasaki), Okinawa (Naha) and Hokkaidō (Sapporo).

TOKYO NARITA INTERNATIONAL AIRPORT
With the exception of China Airlines, all international flights to/from Tokyo use the New Tokyo international airport, better known as **Narita International Airport** (code NRT; www.narita-airport.or.jp/airport_e). Since Narita is the most popular arrival/departure point in Japan, flights via Narita are usually cheaper than those using other airports. Of course, if you can get a cheap flight to another airport, particularly one close to your area of interest, then there's no reason not to use another airport.

OSAKA/KANSAI INTERNATIONAL AIRPORT
All of Osaka's international flights now go via the new **Kansai International Airport** (code KIX; www.kansai-airport.or.jp/english). It serves the key Kansai cities of Kyoto, Osaka and Kōbe. Airport transport to any of these cities is fast and reliable (though it can be expensive if you're going all the way to Kyoto).

NAGOYA KOMAKI INTERNATIONAL AIRPORT
Conveniently located between Tokyo and Osaka is **Nagoya Komaki International Airport** (code NGO). From Nagoya, flights connect with Australia, Canada, China, Guam, Hong Kong, Indonesia, Malaysia, New Zealand,

the Philippines, Saipan, Singapore, South Korea, Taiwan, Thailand and the USA.

FUKUOKA INTERNATIONAL AIRPORT

Fukuoka, at the northern end of Kyūshū, is the main arrival point for western Japan. **Fukuoka International Airport** (code FUK; www.fuk-ab.co.jp/english/frame_index.html), conveniently located near the city, has flights to/from Honolulu and a number of Asian destinations.

NAHA (OKINAWA) INTERNATIONAL AIRPORT

Located on Okinawa-hontō (the main island of Okinawa), Naha International Airport (code OKA) has flights to/from Hong Kong, Seoul, Shanghai and Taiwan.

NIIGATA INTERNATIONAL AIRPORT

Located north of Tokyo, Niigata International Airport (code KIJ) has flights to/from Seoul, Shanghai, Harbin, Xian, Honolulu and Guam.

OTHER AIRPORTS

On Kyūshū, Kagoshima Airport (code KOJ) has flights to/from Hong Kong, Shanghai and Seoul; Kumamoto airport has flights to/from South Korea; and Nagasaki airport has flights to/from Shanghai and Seoul.

On Hokkaidō, Sapporo Chitose International Airport (code SPK) has connections with South Korea.

AIRLINES FLYING TO & FROM JAPAN

Aeroflot (code SU; www.aeroflot.com; ☎ 03-3434-9671; hub International Airport Sheremetyevo, Moscow)

Air Canada (code AC; www.aircanada.ca/e-home.html; ☎ 03-5405-8800, 0120-048-048 toll-free; hub Lester B Pearson International Airport, Toronto)

Air China (code CA; www.china-airlines.com/en/index.htm; ☎ 03-5520-0333; hub Beijing Capital Airport, Beijing)

Air France (code AF; www.airfrance.co.jp/english/index.html; ☎ 03-3475-1511; hub Charles de Gaulle Airport, Paris)

Air India (code AI; www.airindia.com; ☎ 03-3214-1981; hub Mumbai Airport, Mumbai)

Air New Zealand (code NZ; www.airnewzealand.co.nz; ☎ 03-3287-6311, 0120 300 747 toll-free; hub Auckland International Airport, Auckland)

Air Niugini (code PX; www.airniugini.com.pg/main.htm; ☎ 03-5216-3555; hub Port Moresby Jacksons International Airport, Port Moresby)

Air Tahiti Nui (code TN; www.airtahitinui-usa.com; ☎ 03-3475-1511; hub Papeete International Airport, Papeete)

Air Pacific (code FJ; www.airpacific.com; ☎ 03-5208-5171, 0120-489311 toll-free; hub Nadi International Airport; Nadi)

Alitalia (code AZ; www.alitalia.com; ☎ 03-5166-9123; hub Malpensa Airport, Milan)

All Nippon Airways (code NH; www.anaskyweb.com; ☎ 03-5435-0333, 0120-029-333 toll-free, international; ☎ 03-3490-8800, 0120-029-222 domestic; hub Narita Airport, Tokyo)

American Airlines (code AA; www.aa.com; ☎ 03-3214-2111, 0120-000-860 toll-free; hub Dallas/Fort Worth International Airport, Dallas)

Asiana Airlines (code OZ; us.flyasiana.com; ☎ 03-3582-6600; hub Incheon International Airport, Seoul)

Austrian Airlines (code OS; www.aua.com/us/eng; ☎ 03-5222-5454; hub Vienna International Airport, Vienna)

Biman Bangladesh Airlines (code BG; www.bimanair.com; ☎ 03-3502-7922/33; hub Dhaka Zia International Airport, Dhaka)

British Airways (code BA; www.britishairways.com; ☎ 03-3593-8811, 0120-12-2881 toll-free; hub Heathrow Airport, London)

Cathay Pacific Airways (code CX; www.cathaypacific.com; ☎ 03-5159-1700; hub Hong Kong International Airport, Hong Kong)

China Eastern Airlines (code MU; www.ce-air.com/cea/en_US/homepage; ☎ 03-3506-1166; hub Shanghai Putong Airport, Shanghai)

China Southern Airlines (code CZ; www.cs-air.com/en; ☎ 03-5157-8011; hub Baiyun International Airport, Guangzhou)

Continental Airlines (code CO; www.continental.com; ☎ 03-5464-5100, 0120-242-414 toll-free; hub Houston Intercontinental Airport, Houston)

Continental Micronesia (code CS; www.continental.com; ☎ 03-5464-5050; hub Guam International Airport, Guam)

Delta Air Lines (code DL; www.delta.com; ☎ 03-3593-6666, 0120-333-742 toll-free; hub Hartsfield Atlanta International Airport, Atlanta)

Dragon Air (code KA; www.dragonair.com; ☎ 03-6202-0066; hub Hong Kong International Airport, Hong Kong)

Egypt Air (code MS; www.egyptair.com.eg; ☎ 03-3211-4521; hub Cairo International Airport, Cairo)

Finnair (code AY; www.finnair.com; ☎ 03-3222-6801, 0120-700-915 toll-free; hub Helsinki-Vantaa Airport, Helsinki)

Garuda Indonesia (code GA; www.garuda-indonesia.com; ☎ 03-3240-6161; hub Jakarta Soekarno-Hatta Airport, Jakarta)

Iberia (code IB; www.iberia.com; ☎ 03-3578-3555; hub Barcelona Airport, Barcelona)

Iran Air (code IR; www.iranairjp.com; ☎ 0476-34-8372; hub Tehran Mehrabad International Airport, Tehran)

JALWays (code JO; www.jal.co.jp/en; ☎ 03-5460-8520; hub Narita Airport, Tokyo)

Japan Airlines (code JL; www.jal.co.jp/en; ☎ 03-5460-0511, 0120-255-931 toll-free, international; ☎ 03-5460-

0522, 0120-255-971 toll-free, domestic; hub Narita Airport, Tokyo)

Japan Asia Airways (code EG; www.jal.co.jp/en; ☎ 03-5460-0533, 0120-747-801 toll-free; hub Narita Airport, Tokyo)

KLM-Royal Dutch Airlines (code KL; www.klm.com; ☎ 03-3216-0771, 0120-468-215 toll-free; hub Amsterdam Schiphol Airport, Amsterdam)

Korean Air (code KE; www.koreanair.com; ☎ 03-5443-3311; hub Incheon International Airport, Seoul)

Lufthansa Airlines (code LH; cms.lufthansa.com/fly/jp /en/index; ☎ 03-4333-7656, 0120-051-844 toll-free; hub Frankfurt Main Airport, Frankfurt)

Malaysia Airlines (code MH; hq.malaysiaairlines.com; ☎ 03-3503-5961; hub Kuala Lumpur International Airport, Kuala Lumpur)

Northwest Airlines (code NW; www.nwa.com/alliance; ☎ 03-3533-6000; hub Minneapolis-St. Paul International Airport, Minneapolis)

Pakistan International (code PK; www.piac.com.pk; ☎ 03-3216-6511; hub Karachi Quaid-e-Azam International Airport, Karachi)

Philippine Airlines (PR; www.philippineairlines.com; ☎ 03-3593-2421; hub Manila Ninoy Aquino International Airport, Manila)

Qantas (code QF; www.qantas.com; ☎ 03-3593-7000; hub Sydney Kingsford Smith Airport, Sydney)

SAS (SK; www.flysas.com; ☎ 03-5400-2331; hub Copenhagen Airport, Copenhagen)

Shanghai Airlines (code FM; www.shanghai-air.com /ywwy/home.htm; ☎ 0120-029-333 toll-free; hub Shanghai Putong Airport, Shanghai)

Singapore Airlines (code SQ; www.singaporeair.com; ☎ 03-3213-3431; hub Singapore Changi Airport, Singapore)

Sri Lankan Airlines (code UL; www.srilankan.aero; ☎ 03-3431-6611; hub Colombo Bandaranaike Airport, Colombo)

Swiss International Airlines (code LX; www.swiss.com; ☎ 03-3499-8811; hub Zurich Airport, Zurich)

Thai Airways International (code TG; www.thaiair.com; ☎ 03-3503-3311; hub Bangkok International Airport, Bangkok)

Turkish Airlines (code TK; www.turkishairlines.com; ☎ 03-5251-1551; hub Istanbul Ataturk International Airport, Istanbul)

United Airlines (code UA; www.united.com; ☎ 03-3817-4411, 0120-114-466 toll-free; hub Chicago O'Hare International Airport, Chicago)

US Airways (code US; www.usairways.com; ☎ 03-3597-9471; hub Pittsburgh International Airport, Pittsburgh)

Uzbekistan Airways (code HY; www.uzbekistanairways .nl; ☎ 03-5157-0725; hub Ulyanovsk-Vostochny International Airport, Tashkent)

VARIG-Brazilian Airlines (code RG; www.varig.com .br/english/index.htm; ☎ 0476-32-7890; hub Rio de Janeiro International Airport, Rio de Janeiro)

Vietnam Airlines (code VN; www.vietnamairlines.com; ☎ 03-3508-1481; hub Tan Son Nhut Airport, Ho Chi Minh City)

Virgin Atlantic Airways (code VS; www.virgin -atlantic.com; ☎ 03-3499-8811; hub Heathrow Airport, London)

Tickets

The price of your ticket will depend to a great extent on when you fly. High-season prices are determined by two sets of holidays and popular travel times: those in the country you're flying from and those in Japan. Generally, high season for travel between Japan and Western countries is in late December (around Christmas and the New Year period), late April to early May (around Japan's Golden Week holiday), as well as July and August. If you must fly during these periods, book well in advance.

Australia & New Zealand

Garuda, Malaysian Airlines and Cathay Pacific have some good deals for travel between Australia and Japan, but these fares often have a number of restrictions. Return fares start at around A$1200 with Garuda, which allows a stopover in Bali. Direct flights to Japan with airlines including Qantas and JAL are more expensive – expect to pay at least A$1600 for a return fare.

The best place to look for cheap fares is in the travel sections of weekend newspapers, such as the *Age* in Melbourne and the *Sydney Morning Herald*. Two well-known agencies for cheap fares are **STA Travel** (☎ 1300 733 035; www.statravel.com.au), which has offices in all major cities, and **Flight Centre** (☎ 133 133; www.flightcentre.com.au), which has dozens of offices throughout Australia.

Return fares between Auckland and Tokyo start at around NZ$1500. Airlines that fly this route include Malaysian Airlines, Thai International, Qantas and Air New Zealand. You'll save money by taking one of the Asian airlines via an Asian city rather than flying direct.

Both **Flight Centre** (☎ 0800 243 544; www.flight centre.co.nz) and **STA Travel** (☎ 0508 782 872; www .statravel.co.nz) have branches throughout New Zealand.

Canada

Return fares between Vancouver and Tokyo start at around C$900, while return fares between Toronto and Tokyo start at around C$1200. Carriers to check include JAL and ANA, and United, American, Delta and Northwest Airlines.

Travel Cuts (☎ 800-667-2887; www.travelcuts.com) is Canada's national student travel agency. For online bookings try www.expedia.ca and www.travelocity.ca.

China
There are several daily flights between Japan and Hong Kong on Cathay Pacific, as well as on JAL and ANA. In Hong Kong try **Four Seas Tours** (☎ 2200 7760; www.fourseastravel .com/english) or **STA** (☎ 2736 1618).

There are also flights between Japan and Beijing, Shanghai, Guangzhou and Dalian on all the Japanese carriers as well as on Air China, China Eastern Airways and China Southern Air.

Continental Europe
Most direct flights between Europe and Japan fly into Tokyo but there are also some flights into Kansai. Typical low-season return fares from major European cities are Frankfurt–Tokyo €500, Rome–Tokyo €700 and Paris–Tokyo €580.

Recommended travel agencies in continental Europe:

FRANCE
Anyway (☎ 0892 893 892; www.anyway.fr in French)
Lastminute (☎ 0892 705 000; www.lastminute.fr)
Nouvelles Frontières (☎ 0825 000 747; www.nouvelles -frontieres.fr in French)
OTU Voyages (www.otu.fr in French) This agency specialises in student and youth travellers.
Voyageurs du Monde (☎ 01 40 15 11 15; www.vdm .com in French)

GERMANY
Expedia (www.expedia.de in German)
Just Travel (☎ 089 747 3330; www.justtravel.de)
Lastminute (☎ 01805 284 366; www.lastminute.de)
STA Travel (☎ 01805 456 422; www.statravel.de) For travellers under the age of 26.

ITALY
CTS Viaggi (☎ 06 462 0431, www.cts.it in Italian)

SPAIN
Barcelo Viajes (☎ 902 116 226; www.barceloviajes.com in Spanish)
Nouvelles Frontières (☎ 90 217 09 79)

THE NETHERLANDS
Airfair (☎ 020 620 5121; www.airfair.nl)

South Korea
Numerous flights link Seoul and Pusan with Japan. A Seoul–Tokyo flight purchased in Seoul costs around US$180/340 one way/ return. From Tokyo, flights to Seoul are the cheapest way out of Japan. Low-season return fares start as low as ¥25,000.

In Seoul, the **Korean International Student Exchange Society** (KISES; ☎ 02-733 9494; www.kises .co.kr/in Korean; 5th fl, YMCA Bldg, Chongno 2-ga).

See p753 for information on sea-travel bargains between Korea and Japan.

Japan
In most of Japan's major cities there are travel agencies where English is spoken. For an idea of the latest prices in Tokyo check the travel ads in the various local English-language publications, and in Kansai check *Kansai Time Out*. In other parts of Japan check the *Japan Times*. For more details on travel agencies, see p92, p340 and p276.

Taiwan
Return flights from Taipei to Tokyo start at around NT10,000. Flights also operate between Kaohsiung and Osaka or Tokyo.

UK
Expect from UK£500 to UK£600 for a return ticket with a good airline via a fast route. ANA and JAL offer direct flights between London and Japan. Air France is a reliable choice for flights to Japan (usually Tokyo), but you'll have to change in Paris. For a less convenient trans-Asian route, it's about UK£350.

Recommended travel agencies:
Bridge the World (☎ 0870 444 7474; www.b-t-w.co.uk)
Flightbookers (☎ 0870 010 7000; www.ebookers.com)
Flight Centre (☎ 0870 890 8099; flightcentre.co.uk)
North-South Travel (☎ 01245 608 291; www.north southtravel.co.uk) North-South Travel donates part of its profit to projects in the developing world.
Quest Travel (☎ 0870 442 3542; www.questtravel.com)
STA Travel (☎ 0870 160 0599; www.statravel.co.uk) For travellers under the age of 26.
Trailfinders (www.trailfinders.co.uk)
Travel Bag (☎ 0870 890 1456; www.travelbag.co.uk)

USA
From New York in the low season you can find discount return fares to Japan for as

low as US$650. Some carriers to check include United Airlines, Northwest Airlines, Korean Air, Japan Airlines (JAL) and All Nippon Airways (ANA). From the US west coast, low season discount return fares start as low as US$450. High-season discount fares will just about double these figures.

The *New York Times*, the *Los Angeles Times*, the *Chicago Tribune* and the *San Francisco Examiner* all produce weekly travel sections in which you will find a good number of travel agency ads.

STA Travel (☎ 800-781-4040; www.statravel.com) is a good place to start your ticket search in the USA. San Francisco's **Avia Travel** (☎ 800-950-2842, 510-558-2150; www.aviatravel.com) is a favourite of Japan-based English teachers and can arrange tickets originating in Japan. **IACE Travel New York** (☎ 800-872-4223; www.iace-usa.com/) is a travel agency specialising in travel between the USA and Japan that can often dig up cheap fares.

The following agencies are recommended for online bookings.

- www.cheaptickets.com
- www.expedia.com
- www.itn.net
- www.lowestfare.com
- www.orbitz.com
- www.sta.com (for travellers under the age of 26)
- www.travelocity.com

Other Asian Countries

There are daily flights between Bangkok and Japan on Thai Airways International, ANA and Japan Airlines, with fares starting at about 17,000B return in the low season. From Singapore, return tickets cost about S$800; from Indonesia (Jakarta/Denpasar), a return flight costs around US$800.

From the Philippines (Manila) a return flight to Japan is around US$450 and from Malaysia (Kuala Lumpur) it's around RM2500 return. From Vietnam (Ho Chi Minh City) a return flight costs around US$650.

Other Asian countries with limited flights to Japan include India, Nepal and Myanmar (Burma).

Other Regions

There are also flights between Japan and South America (via the USA and Europe), Africa (via Europe, south Asia or southeast Asia) and the Middle East.

LAND
Trans-Siberian Railway

A little-used option of approaching or leaving Japan is the Trans-Siberian Railway. There are three Trans-Siberian Railway options, one of which is to travel on the railway to/from Vladivostok and take the ferry between Vladivostok and Fushiki in Toyama-ken. The cheaper options are the Chinese Trans-Mongolia and Russian Trans-Manchuria routes, which start/finish in China, from where there are ferry connections to/from Japan via Tientsin, Qingdao and Shanghai.

See below for information on ferry connections between Japan, Russia and China.

More detailed information is also available in a good number of publications – see Lonely Planet's *Trans-Siberian Railway: A Classic Overland Route*. Those making their way to Japan via China (or vice versa) should pick up a copy of Lonely Planet's *China* guide, which has invaluable information on travel in China as well as information on Trans-Siberian travel.

SEA
China

The **Japan China International Ferry Company** (in Japan ☎ 06-6536-6541; www.fune.co.jp/chinjif/index .html in Japanese) connects Shanghai and Osaka/Kōbe. A 2nd-class ticket costs around US$200. The journey takes around 48 hours. A similar service is provided by the **Shanghai Ferry Company** (in Japan ☎ 06-6243-6345, in China ☎ 021-6537-7999; www.shanghai-ferry.co.jp). For more information, see p352.

The **China Express Line** (in Japan ☎ 078-321-5791, in China ☎ 022-2420-5777; www.celkobe.co.jp in Japanese) operates a ferry between Kōbe and Tientsin where 1st-/2nd-class tickets cost US$260/220. The journey takes around 48 hours. For more information, see p358.

Orient Ferry Ltd (in Japan ☎ 0832-32-6615, in China ☎ 0532-389-7636; www.orientferry.co.jp in Japanese) runs between Shimonoseki and Qingdao, China, with two departures a week. The cheapest one-way tickets cost around US$180. The journey takes around 40 hours. See p427 for more details.

Russia

FKK Air Service (☎ 0766-22-2212; http://fkk-air.toyama -net.com in Japanese) operates ferries between Fushiki in Toyama-ken and Vladivostok.

One-way fares start at around US$250. The journey takes around 36 hours. The ferry operates from July until the first week of October. For more details, see p205.

An even more exotic route is the summertime route between Wakkanai (in Hokkaidō) and Korsakov (on Sahkalin Island) operated by the **East Japan Sea Ferry Company** (in Japan ☎ 0162-23-3780, in Russia ☎ 4242-42-0917; www.kaiferry.co.jp in Japanese). One-way fares start at around US$200. The journey takes around six hours. The ferry operates from mid-July to the end of September. For more details, see p519.

South Korea

South Korea is the closest country to Japan and a popular visa-renewal point. Many long-term visitors to Japan, who are teaching English or who are engaged in some other kind of work, drop over to Korea when their visa is about to expire and then come back to start a fresh stay. For this reason you can expect to have your passport rigorously inspected.

PUSAN–SHIMONOSEKI

The **Kampu Ferry Service** (in Japan ☎ 0832-24-3000, in Korea ☎ 051-464-2700; www.kampuferry.co.jp in Japanese) operates the Shimonoseki–Pusan ferry service. One-way fares range from around US$85 to US$180. The journey takes around 14 hours. See p427 for more details.

PUSAN–FUKUOKA

An international high-speed hydrofoil service known as the 'Beetle' run by **JR Kyūshū** (in Japan ☎ 092-281-2315, in Korea ☎ 051-465-6111; www.beetle.jrkyushu.co.jp/ships2e/sp2p/index.html) connects Fukuoka with Pusan in Korea (around US$130 one way, three hours). The **Camellia line** (in Japan ☎ 092-262-2323, in Korea ☎ 051-466-7799; www.camellia-line.co.jp in Japanese) also has a regular daily ferry service between Fukuoka and Pusan (around US$90, 16 hours). See p619 for more details.

Taiwan

Arimura Sangyō (in Japan ☎ 098-869-1980, in Taiwan ☎ 07-330-9811) operates a weekly ferry service between Naha (Okinawa) and Taiwan, sometimes via Ishigaki and Miyako in Okinawa-ken. The Taiwan port alternates between Keelung and Kaohsiung. Departure from Okinawa is on Thursday or Friday; de-

parture from Taiwan is usually on Monday. The journey takes about 20 hours. One-way fares cost around US$160 in second class.

GETTING AROUND

Japan is justifiably famous for its extensive, well-organised and efficient transportation network. Schedules are strictly adhered to and late or cancelled services are almost unheard of. All this convenience comes at a price, however, and you'd be well advised to look into money-saving deals whenever possible (see p764).

AIR

Air services in Japan are extensive, reliable and safe. In many cases, flying is much faster than even *shinkansen* travel and not that much more expensive. Flying is also an efficient way to travel from the main islands to the many small islands around Japan.

Airlines in Japan

Japan Air Lines (JAL; www.jal.co.jp/en) is the major international carrier and also has a domestic network linking the major cities. **All Nippon Airways** (ANA; www.ana.co.jp/eng/index.html) is the second largest international carrier and operates a more extensive domestic system. **Japan Trans Ocean Air** (JTA; www.jal.co.jp/jta/ in Japanese) is

---

BAGGAGE FORWARDING

If you have too much luggage to carry comfortably or just can't be bothered, you can do what many Japanese travellers do: send it to your next stop by *takkyūbin* (express shipping companies). Prices are surprisingly reasonable and overnight service is the norm. Perhaps the most convenient service is Yamato Takkyūbin, which operates from most convenience stores. Simply pack your luggage and bring it to the nearest convenience store; they'll help with the paperwork and arrange for pick-up. Note that you'll need the full address of your next destination in Japanese, along with the phone number of the place. Alternatively, ask the owner of your accommodation to have them come and pick it up (this is usually possible but might cost extra).

TRANSPORT

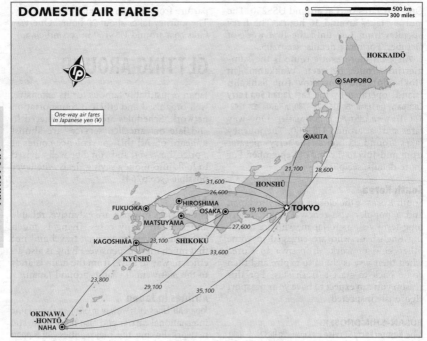

DOMESTIC AIR FARES

One-way air fares in Japanese yen (¥)

HOKKAIDŌ

SAPPORO

AKITA

21,100   28,600

HONSHŪ

31,600
26,600

FUKUOKA   HIROSHIMA
OSAKA   19,100   TOKYO
MATSUYAMA
27,600
KAGOSHIMA   23,100   SHIKOKU

33,600
KYŪSHŪ

23,800
29,100   35,100

OKINAWA
-HONTŌ
NAHA

0 ——— 500 km
0 ——— 300 miles

a smaller domestic carrier that mostly services routes in Okinawa and the Southwest Islands. In addition to these, **Skymark** (www .skymark.co.jp in Japanese) is a recent start-up airline that undercuts the prices of the more established airlines.

The Domestic Air Fares map (p754) shows some of the major connections and one-way fares. Note that return fares are usually around 10% cheaper than buying two one-way tickets. The airlines also have some weird and wonderful discounts if you know what to ask for. The most useful of these are the advance-purchase reductions: both ANA and JAL offer discounts of up to 50% if you purchase your ticket a month or more in advance, with smaller discounts for purchases made one to three weeks in advance. Seniors over 65 also qualify for discounts on most Japanese airlines, but these are sometimes only available if you fly on weekdays.

ANA also offers the Visit Japan Fare for foreign travellers. Provided you reside outside Japan, purchase your tickets outside Japan and carry a valid international ticket on any airline, you can fly up to five times

within 60 days on any ANA domestic route for only ¥12,600 per flight (a huge saving on some routes). Visit www.anaskyweb .com/us/e/travelservice/reservations/special /visit.html for more details.

BICYCLE

Exploring Japan by bicycle is perfectly feasible. The secret of enjoyable touring is to get off the busy main highways and onto the minor roads. This requires careful route planning, good maps and either some ability with kanji or the patience to decipher country road signs, where romaji is much less likely to be used. Favourite touring areas include Kyūshū, Shikoku, the Japan Alps (if you like steep hills!), Noto-hantō and Hokkaidō.

There's no point in fighting your way out of big cities by bicycle. Put your bike on the train or bus and get out to the country before you start pedalling. To take a bicycle on a train you may need to use a bicycle carrying bag, available from good bicycle shops.

See p760 for information on road maps of Japan. In addition to the maps mentioned in that section, a useful series of maps is the

TRANSPORT

CYCLING IN JAPAN *John Ashburne*

In 1899 the British adventurer John Foster Frazer, cycling across the country en route from Europe to the USA, declared Japan 'the wheelman's paradise'. Frazer may not have had to contend with the traffic on Rte 1 or the bewildering complexities of Tokyo's expressways, but his original judgment remains sound – Japan is still a great country to explore on two wheels.

Unchanged since Foster's day are the topography and the climate, both important considerations for the would-be bicycle tourer. Japan's topographic wild card is its mountains. Even the coastal roads can have their hilly moments.

The Tōkaidō coastline, stretching southwest from Tokyo through Nagoya and past Osaka, is mostly flat, but it is also polluted, congested and unrelievedly boring. Avoid Rte 1 at all costs. On the other hand, the Sea of Japan coastline – windswept, sometimes hilly but rarely congested – is a cyclist's delight. It provides the cyclist with good roads, abundant wildlife and some of the freshest seafood in Japan. Hokkaidō, Shikoku and Kyūshū offer more of the same on even quieter roads.

That said, my own favourite cycling territory is in the mountains of central Honshū – hard work but rewarded by spectacular scenery, great hot springs in which to soothe aching bones and, best of all, a glimpse of rural Japan that few city dwellers get a chance to see.

Climatic conditions require some serious consideration, particularly when planning a lengthy tour of Japan. Winter is something of a mixed bag. November and December are often sunny though cold and can be good months for touring Japan's coastal regions. In January and February, however, snowfalls, rain and cold conditions make much of Japan – particularly the Japan Alps, northern Honshū and Hokkaidō – unattractive to all but the most masochistic of cyclists. Summer, on the other hand, is swelteringly hot and humid, a good time to stick to the coast or the cooler latitudes of Hokkaidō.

The rainy season is best avoided for obvious reasons. While it generally arrives in May or June and lingers for just a few weeks, it can't always be relied on to end on time, as I discovered on one sodden trip from Niigata to Kyoto. Typhoons blow up with immense ferocity in late summer and can play havoc with a tight itinerary. This leaves spring and autumn, the best seasons to be cycling in Japan: both are blessed with cool weather and minimal rainfall.

The single biggest frustration for the cyclist in Japan is probably the lack of Romanised street names. This situation is improving gradually, but it can still be maddeningly difficult to find your way out of urban centres onto the road of your choice. (On one memorable occasion, I managed a 90-minute circumnavigation of the Kanazawa ring road that brought me back to where I'd started.) A handy way of avoiding such confusion and the frustration of inner-city traffic is to put your bike on a train. To do this, a carry bag may be required. Specialist carry bags, known in Japanese as *rinko bukuro* or *rinko baggu*, are available in bike shops, though I have made do with a blanket, two garbage bags and some sticky tape without any hassle. Strictly speaking, a ticket is required for your bike on the train (though it is rarely checked). Ask for a *temawarihin kippu* (accompanied-luggage ticket), a bargain at ¥260 and valid for any single journey. Ferries are also an opportunity to rest aching legs, and taking your bike aboard is no problem, though sometimes an extra charge will be required.

The best machine for touring Japan is a lightweight touring road machine or else a suitably equipped hybrid or cross bike. While mountain bikes are all the rage they are hardly required for Japan's well-paved roads. If you do bring a mountain bike, be sure to fit slimmer profile, preferably slick tyres, unless you're planning to spend all your time on mountain trails. Bikes with suspension forks require too much maintenance to consider as viable touring machines.

Perhaps the most important question for the cyclist looking at a holiday in Japan is costs. However you look at it, Japan is not cheap. Try to bring your own bike and accessories – even though Japan produces some of the world's best cycling equipment, prices will be cheaper at home. Camping is a good antidote to Japan's high accommodation costs, and many cyclists sustain themselves on a diet of instant noodles and sandwiches. Bear in mind, however, that after a long rainy day a comfortable inn with home cooking becomes a great temptation and it's easy to stray from a tight budget. Worst of all, if you're really pinching the pennies you'll never get into the bars, restaurants and hot springs where you can meet the Japanese at their most relaxed and welcoming. Even if you're planning to camp out and eat cheaply, it would be wise to budget ¥3600 per day.

Japan is a reasonably safe country to cycle in but, on a cautionary note, accidents happen more frequently than you might imagine. Comprehensive insurance is a must, as is a decent lightweight helmet. Also, despite Japan's reputation as a crime-free country, bicycles do get stolen and, of late, professional gangs of bike thieves have been targeting big cities, especially around train stations. I have lost no less than three expensive bikes over the last eight years. Bring a lock.

Touring Mapple (Shobunsha) series, which is aimed at motorcyclists, but is also very useful for cyclists.

For more information on cycling in Japan, you can check out the excellent **Kancycling website** (www.kancycling.com/index.html).

Hire

It is not easy to rent a touring bike for a long trip but, in many towns, you can rent bicycles to explore the town. Look for bicycle hire outlets near railway stations. Typical charges are around ¥200 per hour or ¥1000 per day. Kyoto, for example, is ideally suited to bicycle exploration and there are plenty of cheap hire shops to choose from.

Many youth hostels also have bicycles to rent – there's a symbol identifying them in the *Japan Youth Hostel Handbook*. The so-called 'cycling terminals' found in various locations around the country also rent bicycles. For more on cycling terminals, see p722.

If you already have some experience of bicycle touring you will, no doubt, have your own bicycle. Most airlines these days will accommodate bikes, sometimes as part of your baggage allowance, sometimes free.

Purchase

In Japan, prices for used bikes range from a few thousand yen for an old 'shopping bike' up to several tens of thousand yen for good mountain bikes. New bikes range anywhere from around ¥10,000 for a shopping bike to ¥100,000 for a flash mountain bike or road bike.

Touring cycles are available in Japan but prices tend to be significantly higher than you'd pay back home. If you're tall, you may not find any suitably sized bikes in stock. One solution for tall riders, or anyone who wants to save money, is to buy a used bike; in Tokyo check the English-language publications and in Kansai check *Kansai Time Out*.

BOAT

Japan is an island nation and there are a great many ferry services both between islands and between ports on the same island. Ferries can be an excellent way of getting from one place to another and seeing parts of Japan you might otherwise miss. Taking a ferry between Osaka (Honshū) and Beppu (Kyūshū), for example, is a good way of getting to Kyūshū and – if you choose the right

departure time – seeing some of the Inland Sea (Seto-nai-kai) on the way.

The routes vary widely from two-hour services between adjacent islands to 1½-day trips in what are in fact small ocean liners. The cheapest fares on the longer trips are in tatami-mat rooms where you simply unroll your futon on the floor and hope, if the ship is crowded, that your fellow passengers aren't too intent on knocking back the booze all night. In this basic class, fares are usually lower than equivalent land travel, but there are also more expensive private cabins. Bicycles can always be brought along and most ferries also carry cars and motorcycles.

Information on ferry routes, schedules and fares is found in the *JR Jikokuhyō* (p766) and on information sheets from the JNTO (p744). Some ferry services and their lowest one-way fares appear in the table (below) and major ferry companies (opposite).

FERRY TIMETABLES

Hokkaidō-Honshū	Fare	Duration
Otaru-Maizuru	¥8200	20hr
Otaru-Niigata	¥5600	18hr
Tomakomai-Nagoya	¥8700	38hr
Tomakomai-Ōarai	¥7000	19hr
Tomakomai-Sendai	¥6800	14hr

Departing from Tokyo	Fare	Duration
Kōchi (Shikoku)	¥16,310	21hr
Nachi-Katsuura (Honshū)	¥10,700	13hr
Naha (Okinawa)	¥22,000	45hr
Tokushima (Shikoku)	¥8610	18hr

Departing from Osaka/Kōbe	Fare	Duration
Beppu (Kyūshū)	¥7900	13hr
Imabari (Shikoku)	¥4600	7hr
Kōchi (Shikoku)	¥4500	9hr
Matsuyama (Shikoku)	¥5500	8hr
Naha (Okinawa)	¥17,300	30hr

Departing from Kyūshū	Fare	Duration
Hakata-Naha (Okinawa)	¥14,480	26hr
Kagoshima-Naha (Okinawa)	¥13,200	21hr

MAJOR FERRY COMPANIES

Company	Routes Served	Contact Number	Website (Language)
Shin Nihonkai Ferry	Maizuru-Otaru Tsuruga-Otaru Tsuruga-Tomakomai Niigata-Otaru	☎ 0120-4192-86	www.snf.co.jp (in Japanese)
Taiheiyō Ferry	Nagoya-Sendai Sendai-Tomakomai Nagoya-Tomakomai (via Sendai)	☎ 03-3564-4161	www.taiheiyo-ferry.co.jp (in Japanese)
Higashi Nihon Ferry	Tomakomai-Ōarai Muroran-Hachinohe Tomakomai-Hachinohe Hakodate-Aomori	☎ 03-3535-0489	www.higashinihon-ferry.co.jp (in Japanese)
Shōsen Mitsui Ferry	Tomakomai-Ōarai	☎ 0144-34-3121	www.sunflower.co.jp (in Japanese)
Ocean Tōkyū Ferry	Tokyo-Tokushima Tokyo-Kitakyūshū Tokushima- Kitakyūshū	☎ 03-5148-0109	www.otf.jp (in Japanese)
Marine Express	Kawasaki-Kōchi Kawasaki-Nachi Katsuura-Miyazaki Kawasaki-Kōchi-Hyūga Osaka-Miyazaki	☎ 03-5542-2861	www.marineexpress.co.jp (in Japanese)
Kansai Kisen	Hanshin-Beppu Hanshin-Beppu (via Matsuyama) Hanshin-Shōdo-shima (seasonal) Kokura-Matsuyama	☎ 06-6572-5181	www.kanki.co.jp (in Japanese)
Shikoku Orange Ferry	Osaka-Matsuyama	☎ 06-6612-1811	www.orange-ferry.co.jp (Japanese)
Diamond Ferry	Kōbe-Imabari Kōbe-Ōita (via Imabari) Kōbe-Ōita (via Matsuyama) Kōbe-Ōita (via Imabari & Matsuyama)	☎ 078-857-9525	www.diamond-ferry.co.jp (in Japanese)
Ōshima Unyu	Tokyo-Naha (via Shibushi) Hanshin-Naha (via Miyazaki) Kagoshima-Naha (via Amami)	☎ 03-5643-6170	www.minc.ne.jp/aline (in Japanese)
Osaka Kōchi Tokkyū Ferry	Osaka-Kōchi	☎ 06-6612-8700	www.066.upp.so-net.ne.jp/ok-ferry (in Japanese)
Ryūkyū Kaiun	Hakata-Naha Kagoshima-Naha Naha-Ishigaki	☎ 098-868-8161	www.rkkline.co.jp (in Japanese)

BUS

Japan has a comprehensive network of long-distance buses. These 'highway buses' are nowhere near as fast as the *shinkansen* but the fares are comparable with those of the *futsū* without any reservation or express surcharges. The trip between Tokyo and Sendai (Northern Honshū), for example, takes about two hours by *shinkansen*, four hours by *tokkyū* and nearly eight hours by bus. Of course, there are also many places in Japan where trains do not run and bus travel is the only public transport option.

Bookings can be made through any travel agency in Japan or at the Green Window in large JR stations. The Japan Rail Pass is valid on some highway buses, but in most cases the *shinkansen* would be far preferable (it's much faster and more comfortable). Note, however, that the storage racks on most buses are generally too small for large backpacks, but you can usually stow them in the luggage compartment underneath the bus.

Costs

Some typical long-distance fares and travel times out of Tokyo include:

Destination	Fare	Duration
Aomori	¥10,000	10 hrs
Hakata	¥15,000	14½ hrs
Hiroshima	¥11,600	11 hrs
Kyoto	¥8180	8 hrs
Nagoya	¥6420	7 hrs
Niigata	¥5250	5 hrs
Osaka	¥8610	8 hrs
Sendai	¥6210	7½ hrs

Night Services

Night buses are a good option for those on a tight budget without a Japan Rail Pass. They are relatively cheap, spacious (allowing room to stretch out and get some sleep) and they also save on a night's accommodation. They typically leave at around 10pm or 11pm and arrive the following day at around 6am or 7am.

CAR & MOTORCYCLE

Driving in Japan is quite feasible, even for the just mildly adventurous. The major roads are signposted in English; road rules are generally adhered to and driving is safer than in other Asian countries; and gas, while expensive, is not prohibitively so. Indeed, in some areas of the country it can prove much more convenient than other forms of travel and, between a group of people, it can also prove quite economical.

Automobile Associations

If you're a member of an automobile association in your home country, you're eligible for reciprocal rights at the **Japan Automobile Federation** (JAF; ☎ 03-3578-4910; www.jaf.or.jp/e/index_e.htm; Jidōsha Kaikan 14F, 1-1-30 Shiba-daimon, Minato-ku, Tokyo 105-0012). Its office is near Onarimon Station on the Tōei Mita line. JAF publishes a variety of publications, and will make up strip maps for its members.

Driving Licence

Travellers from most nations are able to drive in Japan with an International Driving Permit backed up by their own regular licence. The international permit is issued by your national automobile association and costs around US$5 in most countries. Make sure it's endorsed for cars and motorcycles if you're licensed for both.

Travellers from Switzerland, France and Germany (and others whose countries are not signatories to the Geneva Convention of 1949 concerning international driver's licences) are not allowed to drive in Japan on a regular international licence. Rather, travellers from these countries must have their own licence backed by an authorised translation of the same licence. These translations can be made by their country's embassy or consulate in Japan or by the Japan Automobile Federation (above). If you are unsure which category your country falls into, contact the nearest JNTO office (p744).

Foreign licences and International Driving Permits are only valid in Japan for six months. If you are staying longer, you will have to get a Japanese licence from the local department of motor vehicles. To do this, you will need to provide your own licence, passport photos, Alien Registration Card, the fee, and also take a simple eyesight test.

Expressways

The expressway system will get you from one end of the country to another but it is not particularly extensive. Also, since all the expressways charge tolls, it is uniformly expensive – about ¥27 per kilometre. Tokyo

TRANSPORT

ROAD DISTANCES (KM)

	Aomori	Fukuoka	Fukushima	Hiroshima	Kagoshima	Kanazawa	Kitakyūshū	Kōbe	Kōchi	Kyoto	Maebashi	Matsue	Matsuyama	Mito	Miyazaki	Morioka	Nagano	Nagasaki	Nagoya	Niigata	Osaka	Sapporo	Sendai	Shizuoka	Tokushima	Tokyo	Tottori	Toyama	Urawa	Yokohama
Aomori	⋮																													
Fukuoka	1746	⋮																												
Fukushima	481	1495	⋮																											
Hiroshima	1463	283	1212	⋮																										
Kagoshima	2067	321	1816	604	⋮																									
Kanazawa	798	948	552	665	1269	⋮																								
Kitakyūshū	1679	67	1428	216	388	881	⋮																							
Kōbe	1151	595	900	312	916	353	528	⋮																						
Kōchi	1436	618	1185	335	939	638	551	285	⋮																					
Kyoto	1066	680	815	397	1001	268	613	85	370	⋮																				
Maebashi	714	1211	285	928	1532	392	1144	616	901	531	⋮																			
Matsue	1380	409	1134	185	730	582	342	313	439	343	874	⋮																		
Matsuyama	1449	631	1198	348	952	651	564	298	121	383	914	452	⋮																	
Mito	658	1328	223	1045	1649	539	1261	733	1018	147	991	682	1031	⋮																
Miyazaki	2019	407	1768	556	142	1221	340	868	891	953	1484	682	904	1601	⋮															
Morioka	213	1654	268	1381	1985	801	1597	1069	1354	891	716	1298	1439	317	1937	⋮														
Nagano	695	1084	414	801	1405	263	1017	489	774	404	129	747	984	445	1367	613	⋮													
Nagasaki	1920	174	1669	457	314	1122	241	755	610	512	1719	769	792	1838	805	1357	276	⋮												
Nagoya	957	822	673	539	1143	272	895	227	670	142	525	368	316	827	908	436	238	1478	⋮											
Niigata	481	1265	235	982	1586	317	1198	670	955	585	233	899	968	354	1538	399	214	1439	358	⋮										
Osaka	1117	866	629	346	950	281	1081	34	319	51	582	347	332	699	902	1035	455	803	193	636	⋮									
Sapporo	283	2029	764	1746	2350	1081	1962	1434	1719	1349	997	1663	1732	941	2302	496	978	2203	1240	803	1357	⋮								
Sendai	398	1578	83	1295	1899	635	1511	983	1268	898	368	1217	1281	260	1851	185	497	1752	756	318	941	1400	⋮							
Shizuoka	967	1009	486	726	1330	459	942	414	699	329	316	672	712	319	1282	754	277	1183	187	491	380	949	681	⋮						
Tokushima	1245	994	557	274	878	447	490	94	224	179	710	378	238	827	830	1163	583	731	321	764	128	1528	1077	569	⋮					
Tokyo	771	1205	290	922	1526	492	895	525	610	486	120	868	747	127	1478	525	229	1379	353	358	558	1090	353	187	764	⋮				
Tottori	1253	536	1007	309	857	455	469	186	312	216	864	127	325	716	325	1286	474	620	358	252	220	1536	710	358	220	545	⋮			
Toyama	733	1013	487	730	1334	65	946	418	635	920	333	327	647	893	1404	249	252	710	358	204	544	1090	570	436	545	427	520	⋮		
Urawa	757	1230	276	947	1551	492	1163	635	920	550	95	832	872	159	1442	408	328	1404	359	160	601	1040	221	512	729	36	766	463	⋮	
Yokohama	807	1169	326	886	1490	528	1102	574	859	489	156	550	920	160	1536	409	347	1343	265	594	540	1090	668	160	705	25	705	402	61	⋮

to Kyoto, for example, will cost about ¥9000 in tolls. The speed limit on expressways is 80km/h but seems to be uniformly ignored. At a steady 100km/h, you will still find as many cars overtaking you as you overtake, some of them going very fast indeed.

There are good rest stops and service centres at regular intervals. A prepaid highway card, available from tollbooths or at the service areas, saves you having to carry so much cash and gives you a 4% to 8% discount in the larger card denominations. You can also pay tolls with most major credit cards, although some toll-booth operators seem unaware of this. Exits are usually fairly well-signposted in romaji but make sure you know the name of your exit as it may not necessarily be the same as the city you're heading towards.

Fuel & Spare Parts

You'll find *gasoreen sutando* (petrol stations) in almost every town in Japan and in service stations along the country's expressways. The cost of petrol ranges from ¥95 to ¥140 per litre.

Spare parts are widely available in Japan for Japanese cars. For foreign cars, you may have to place a special order with a garage or parts store.

Insurance

When you own a car, it is necessary to get compulsory third-party insurance (*jidosha songai baishō sekinin hoken*). This is paid when your car undergoes the compulsory inspection (*shaken*). It is also recommended that you get comprehensive vehicle insurance (*jidosha hoken*) to cover any expenses that aren't covered by the compulsory third-party insurance.

Motorcycles

For citizens of most countries, your overseas licence and an International Driving Permit are all you need to ride a motorcycle in Japan (see p758 for details on which nationalities require different documentation). Crash helmets are compulsory and you should also ensure your riding gear is adequate to cope with the weather, particularly rain. For much of the year the climate is ideal for motorcycle touring, but when it rains it really rains.

Touring equipment – panniers, carrier racks, straps and the like – is readily available

from dealers. Remember to pack clothing in plastic bags to ensure it stays dry, even if you don't. An adequate supply of tools and a puncture repair kit can prove invaluable.

Riding in Japan is no more dangerous than anywhere else in the world, which is to say it is not very safe and great care should be taken at all times. Japan has the full range of motorcycle hazards from single-minded taxi drivers to unexpected changes in road surface, heedless car-door openers to runaway dogs.

Maps & Navigation

Get yourself a copy of the *Japan Road Atlas* (Shobunsha, ¥2890). It's all in romaji with enough names in kanji to make navigation possible even off the major roads. If you're really intent on making your way through the back blocks, a Japanese map will prove useful even if your knowledge of kanji is nil. The best Japanese road atlases by far are the *Super Mapple* series (Shobunsha), which are available in bookshops and some convenience stores.

These days, there is a great deal of signposting in romaji so getting around isn't all that difficult. Road route numbers also help; for example, if you know you want to follow Route 9 until you get to Route 36 the frequent roadside numbers make navigation child's play. If you are attempting tricky navigation, use your maps imaginatively – watch out for the railway line, the rivers, the landmarks. They're all useful ways of locating yourself when you can't read the signs. A compass will also come in handy when navigating.

Parking

In most big cities, free curbside parking spots are almost nonexistent, while in rural areas you'll be able to park your car just about wherever you want to. If you do have the nerve to drive into a big Japanese city, you'll find that you usually have to pay ¥200 per hour for metred street parking, or anywhere from ¥300 to ¥600 per hour for a spot in a multistorey car park. You'll find car parks around most department stores and near some train stations. Fortunately, most hotels have free parking for guests, as do some restaurants and almost all department stores (you'll have to get a stamp inside the store to show that you've actually been shopping there).

Hire

Car hire offices cluster around train stations and the best way to use hire cars in Japan is to take a train for the long-distance part of your trip, then hire a car when you get to the area you want to explore. For example, the northern San-in coast of Western Honshū is a good place to drive – but don't drive there from Tokyo. Take the train to Kyoto and hire a car from there.

Japanese car hire companies are set up for this type of operation and offer lots of short-term rates – such as for people who just want a car for half a day. However, they're not much good at one-way rentals; you'll usually have to pay a repositioning charge and if the car has to be brought back from another island, the cost can be very high indeed. Typical one-way charges within the island of Honshū are ¥6000 for 100km and ¥2400 for each additional 50km. It makes a lot of sense to make your trip a loop one and return the car to the original hiring office. Two of the main Japanese car hire companies and their Tokyo phone numbers:

Hertz (☎ 0120-489-882)
Toyota Rent-a-Lease (☎ 0070-8000-10000)

Typical hire rates for a small car are ¥6500 to ¥9000 for the first day and ¥4500 to ¥7000 per day thereafter. Move up a bracket and you're looking at ¥9000 to ¥13,500 for the first day and ¥7000 to ¥9000 thereafter. On top of the hire charge, there's a ¥1000 per day insurance cost.

Many hire places offer unlimited kilometres but check before heading out. It's also good to check prices at local hire car places. These places can usually match the rates of the big chains and are a good choice when you just want to hire for three or six hours to get around an island or obscure peninsula.

It's also worth bearing in mind that car hire costs go up during high seasons – 28 April to 6 May, 20 July to 31 August, and 28 December to 5 January. The increase can make quite a difference to costs. A car that costs ¥8800 a day will usually go up to ¥9700 during any of the peak times.

Communication can be a major problem when hiring a car. Some of the offices will have a rent-a-car phrasebook, with questions you might need to ask in English. Otherwise, just speak as slowly as possible and hope for the best.

MOTORCYCLE HIRE & PURCHASE

Hiring a motorcycle for long-distance touring is not as easy as hiring a car, although small scooters are available in many places for local sightseeing.

If you enjoy motorcycles and you're staying long enough to make buying and selling a motorcycle worthwhile, then this can be a great way of getting around the country. A motorcycle provides the advantages of your own transport without the automotive drawback of finding a place to park. Nor do you suffer so badly from the congested traffic.

Although Japan is famed for its large-capacity road burners, most bikes on the road are 400cc or less. This is because a special licence is required to ride a bike larger than 400cc and few Japanese and even fewer foreigners pass the test necessary to get this licence.

The 400cc machines are the most popular large motorcycles in Japan but, for general touring, a 250cc machine is probably the best bet. Apart from being large enough for a compact country like Japan, machines up to 250cc are also exempt from the expensive *shaken* (inspections).

Smaller machines (those below 125cc) are banned from expressways and are generally less suitable for long-distance touring but people have ridden from one end of Japan to another on little 50cc 'step-thrus'. An advantage of these bikes is that you can ride them with just a regular driving licence, and you won't need to get a motorcycle licence.

Buying a new machine is no problem, though you will find a better choice of large capacity machines in the big cities. Used motorcycles are often not much cheaper than new ones and, unless you buy from another foreigner, you will face the usual language problems in finding and buying one.

The best place to look for motorcycles in Japan is the Korin-chō motorcycle neighbourhood in Tokyo's Ueno district. There are over 20 motorcycle shops in the area and some employ foreign salespeople who speak both Japanese and English. For used bikes in Kansai check *Kansai Time Out, Kansai Flea Market*, or the message board in the Kyoto International Community House.

Road Rules

Driving in Japan is on the left. There are no real problems with driving in Japan. There are no unusual rules or interpretations of them and most signposts follow international conventions. JAF (p758) has a *Rules of the Road* book available in English and five other languages for ¥1000.

HITCHING

Hitching is never entirely safe in any country in the world, and we don't recommend it. Travellers who decide to hitch should understand that they are taking a small but potentially serious risk. In particular, Japan is a very dangerous place for solitary female hitchhikers; there have been countless cases of solitary female hitchers being attacked, molested and raped. People who do choose to hitch will be safer if they travel in pairs and let someone know where they are planning to go.

Provided you understand the risks and take appropriate precautions, Japan can be an excellent country for hitchhiking. Many hitchhikers have tales of extraordinary kindness from motorists who have picked them up.

The rules for hitchhiking are similar to anywhere else in the world. Dress neatly and look for a good place to hitch – expressway onramps and expressway service areas are probably your best bet.

Truck drivers are particularly good for long-distance travel as they often head out on the expressways at night. If a driver is exiting before your intended destination, try to get dropped off at one of the expressway service areas. The *Service Area Parking Area* (SAPA) guide maps are excellent for hitchers. They're available free from expressway service areas and show full details of each interchange (IC) and rest stop. These are important orientation points if you have a limited knowledge of Japanese.

For more on hitching in Japan pick up a copy of the excellent *Hitchhiker's Guide to Japan* by Will Ferguson. In addition to lots of general advice, this book details suggested routes and places to stay on the road. All in all, it's just about invaluable for anyone contemplating a long hitch around Japan.

LOCAL TRANSPORT

All the major cities offer a wide variety of public transport. In many cities you can get day passes for unlimited travel on bus, tram or subway systems. Such passes are usually called an *ichi-nichi-jōsha-ken*. If you're staying for an extended period in one city, commuter passes are available for regular travel.

Bus

Almost every Japanese city has an extensive bus service but it's usually the most difficult public transport system for foreign travellers to use. The destination names are almost always written in kanji and often there are no numbers to identify which bus you want.

Fares are either paid to the driver on entering or as you leave the bus and usually operate on one of two systems. In Tokyo and some other cities, there's a flat fare irrespective of distance. In the other system, you take a ticket as you board which indicates the zone number at your starting point. When you get off, an electric sign at the front of the bus indicates the fare charged at that point for each starting zone number. You simply pay the driver the fare that matches your zone number. There is often a change machine near the front of the bus that can change ¥100 and ¥500 coins and ¥1000 notes.

In many tourist towns there are also *teiki kankō basu* (tour buses), often run from the main railway station. Tours are usually conducted in Japanese but English-language tours are available in popular areas like Kyoto and Tokyo. In places where the attractions are widespread or hard to reach by public transport, tours can be a good bet.

Taxi

Taxis are convenient but expensive and are found in even quite small towns; the train station is the best place to look. Fares are fairly uniform throughout the country – flagfall (posted on the taxi windows) is ¥600 to ¥660 for the first 2km, after which it's around ¥100 for each 350m (approximately). There's also a time charge if the speed drops below 10km/h. During the day, it's almost impossible to tell if a moving taxi is occupied (just wave at it and it will stop if it's free); at night, vacant taxis are distinguishable by an illuminated light on the roof – an occupied taxi will have its light turned off.

Don't whistle for a taxi, a simple wave should bring one politely to a halt. Don't open the door when it stops, the driver does that with a remote release. The driver will also shut the door when you leave the taxi.

Drivers are normally as polite as anybody else in Japan but, like the majority of Japanese, they are not linguists. If you can't tell the driver where you want to go, it's useful to have the name written down in Japanese. At hotel front desks there will usually be business cards complete with name and location, which can be used for just this purpose. Of course, Japanese script is provided on map keys in this guidebook, too.

Taxi drivers have just as much trouble finding Japanese addresses as anyone else. Just because you've gone round the block five times does not mean your driver has no idea. Asking directions and stopping at police boxes for help in finding the address is standard practice.

Tipping is not necessary. A 20% surcharge is added after 11pm or for taxis summoned by radio. There may also be an added charge if you summon the taxi by phone or reserve the taxi.

Train & Subway

Several cities, especially Osaka and Tokyo, have mass transit rail systems comprising a loop line around the city centre and radial lines into the central stations and the subway system. Subway systems operate in Fukuoka, Kōbe, Kyoto, Nagoya, Osaka, Sapporo, Sendai, Tokyo and Yokohama. They are usually the fastest and most convenient way to get around the city.

For subways and local trains you'll most likely have to buy your ticket from a machine. They're pretty easy to understand even if you can't read kanji as there is a diagram explaining the routes; from this you can find out what your fare should be. If you can't work the fare out, a solution is to buy a ticket for the lowest fare. When you finish your trip, go to the fare adjustment machine (seisan-ki) or counter before you reach the exit gate and pay the excess. JR train stations and most subway stations not only have their names posted above the platform in kanji and romaji but also the names of the preceding and following stations.

Tram

Many cities have tram lines – particularly Nagasaki, Kumamoto and Kagoshima in Kyūshū, Kōchi and Matsuyama in Shikoku, and Hakodate in Hokkaidō. These are excellent ways of getting around as they combine many of the advantages of bus travel (eg good views) with those of subways (it's easy to work out where you're going). Fares work on similar systems to bus travel and there are also unlimited-travel day tickets available.

TRAIN

Japanese rail services are among the best in the world: they are fast, frequent, clean and comfortable. The services range from small local lines to the shinkansen super-expresses or 'bullet trains' which have become a symbol of modern Japan.

The 'national' railway is **Japan Railways** (JR; www.japanrail.com/) which is actually a number of separate private rail systems which provide one linked service. The JR system covers the country from one end to the other and also provides local services around major cities like Tokyo and Osaka. There is more than 20,000km of railway line and about 20,000 services daily. JR operates the shinkansen network throughout Japan. Shinkansen lines are totally separate from the regular railways and, in some places, the shinkansen stations are a fair distance from the main JR station (as is the case in Osaka). JR also operates buses and ferries, and ticketing can combine more than one form of transport.

Classes

All JR trains, including the shinkansen, have regular and Green Car carriages. The seating is slightly more spacious in Green Car carriages, but most people will find the regular carriages perfectly acceptable.

The slowest trains stopping at all stations are called futsū or kaku-eki-teisha. A step up from this is the kyūkō (ordinary express), which stops at only a limited number of stations. A variation on the kyūkō trains is the kaisoku (rapid) service. Finally, the fastest regular (non-shinkansen) trains are the tokkyū services, which are sometimes known as shin-kaisoku.

Train Types

shinkansen	新幹線	bullet train
tokkyū	特急	limited express
shin-kaisoku	新快速	JR special rapid train
kyūkō	急行	express
kaisoku	快速	JR rapid or express
futsū	普通	local
kaku-eki-teisha	各駅停車	local

TRANSPORT

Other Useful Words

jiyū-seki	自由席	unreserved seat
shitei-seki	指定席	reserved seat
green-sha	グリーン車	1st-class car
Ōfuku	往復	round trip
katamichi	片道	one way
kin'en-sha	禁煙車	nonsmoking car
kitsuen-sha	喫煙車	smoking car

Costs

JR fares are calculated on the basis of *futsū-unchin* (basic fare), *tokkyū-ryōkin* (an express surcharge levied only on express services) and *shinkansen-ryōkin* (a special charge for *shinkansen* services); see below for more info. The following are some typical fares from Tokyo or Ueno, not including the new Nozomi super express (prices given for *shinkansen* are the total price of the ticket):

Destination	Basic Fare	Shinkansen
Fukushima	¥4620	¥8700
Hakata	¥13,440	¥21,720
Hiroshima	¥11,340	¥18,050
Kyoto	¥7980	¥13,220
Morioka	¥8190	¥13,840
Nagoya	¥6090	¥10,580
Niigata	¥5460	¥10,270
Okayama	¥10,190	¥16,360
Osaka	¥8510	¥13,750
Sendai	¥5780	¥10,590
Shimonoseki	¥12,810	¥20,570

SURCHARGES

Various surcharges may be added to the basic fare. These include reserved seat, Green Car, express service and *shinkansen* surcharges. You may also have to pay a surcharge for special trains to resort areas or for a seat in an observation car. The express surcharges (but not the *shinkansen* super-express surcharge) can be paid to the train conductor on board the train.

Further surcharges apply for overnight sleepers, and these vary with the berth type, from ¥5250 for a regular three-tier bunk, ¥6300 to ¥10,500 for various types of two-tier bunks, and up to ¥13,350 to ¥17,180 for a standard or 'royal' compartment. Note that there are no sleepers on the *shinkansen* services as none of these run overnight. Japan Rail Pass users must still pay the sleeper surcharge (for more on the Japan Rail Pass,

see below). Sleeper services mainly operate on trains from Tokyo or Osaka to destinations in Western Honshū and Kyūshū.

The Nozomi super express has higher surcharges than other *shinkansen* services and cannot be used with a Japan Rail Pass. As a guideline, the Nozomi surcharge for Tokyo–Kyoto is ¥6210 as opposed to ¥5240 by other *shinkansen*; for Tokyo–Hakata ¥10,120 as opposed to ¥8280 by other *shinkansen*.

TRAVEL SEASONS

Some of the fare surcharges are slightly higher (5% to 10%) during peak travel seasons. This applies mainly to reserved seat tickets. High season dates are 21 March to 5 April, 28 April to 6 May, 21 July to 31 August, and 25 December to 10 January.

Passes & Discount Tickets

If you plan to do any extended travel in Japan, a Japan Rail Pass is almost essential. Not only will it save you lots of money, it will also spare you the hassle of buying tickets each time you want to board a train.

In addition to the Japan Rail Pass, there are various discount tickets and special fares available. The most basic is the return fare discount: if you buy a return ticket for a trip which is more than 600km each way, you qualify for a 10% discount on the return leg.

JAPAN RAIL PASS

One of Japan's few real travel bargains is the Japan Rail Pass. It is available to foreign tourists and Japanese overseas residents (but not foreign residents of Japan). The pass lets you use any JR service for seven days for ¥28,300, 14 days for ¥45,100 or 21 days for ¥57,700. Green Car passes are ¥37,800, ¥61,200 and ¥79,600, respectively. The pass cannot be used for the new super express Nozomi *shinkansen* service, but is OK for everything else (including other *shinkansen* services).

The only surcharge levied on the Japan Rail Pass is for overnight sleepers. Since a one-way reserved seat Tokyo–Kyoto *shinkansen* ticket costs ¥13,220, you only have to travel Tokyo–Kyoto–Tokyo to make a seven-day pass come close to paying off. Note that the pass is valid only on JR services; you will still have to pay for private train services.

In order to get a pass, you must first purchase an 'exchange order' outside of Japan at JAL and ANA offices and major travel agen-

TRANSPORT

cies. Once you arrive in Japan, you must bring this exchange order to a JR Travel Service Centre (these can be found in most major JR stations and at Narita and Kansai airports). When you validate your pass, you'll have to show your passport. The pass can only be used by those with a temporary visitor visa, which means it cannot be used by foreign residents of Japan (those on any visa other than the temporary visitor visa).

The clock starts to tick on the pass as soon as you validate your pass. So don't validate it if you're just going into Tokyo or Kyoto and intend to hang around for a few days.

For more details on the pass and overseas purchase locations, visit the JR website's **Japan Rail Pass section** (www.japanrailpass.net/eng /en01.html).

JR EAST PASS

This is a great deal for those who only want to travel in eastern Japan. The passes are good on all JR lines in eastern Japan (including Tōhoku, Yamagata, Akita, Jōetsu and Nagano *shinkansen*, but not including the Tōkaidō *shinkansen*). This includes the area around Tokyo and everything north of Tokyo to the tip of Honshū, but doesn't include Hokkaidō.

Prices for five-day passes are ¥20,000/ 16,000/10,000 for adults over 26/ youths 12 to 25/children aged six to 11. Ten-day passes are ¥32,000/25,000/16,000 for the same age groups. Four-day 'flexible' passes are also available which allow travel on any four consecutive or non-consecutive days within any one-month period. These cost ¥20,000/16,000/10,000 for the same age groups. Green Car passes are available for higher prices.

As with the Japan Rail Pass, this can only be purchased outside Japan (in the same locations as the Japan Rail Pass) and can only be used by those with temporary visitor visas (you'll need to show your passport). See the preceding Japan Rail Pass section for more details on purchase places and validation procedures.

For more information on the JR East Pass, visit the website's **JR East Pass section** (www.jreast .co.jp/e/eastpass/top.html).

JR WEST SAN-YŌ AREA PASS

Similar to the JR East Pass, this pass allows unlimited travel on the San-yō *shinkansen* line (including the Nozomi super express) between Osaka and Hakata, as well as local trains running between the same cities. A four-day pass costs ¥20,000 and an eight-day pass costs ¥30,000 (children's passes are half-price). These can be purchased both inside Japan (at major train stations, travel agencies and Kansai airport) and outside Japan (same locations as the Japan Rail Pass) but can only be used by those with a temporary visitor visa. The pass also entitles you to discounts on hiring cars at station rent-a-car offices. For more information on this pass, see the JR West website's **San-yo Area Pass section** (www .westjr.co.jp/english/english/travel/con05/sanyo.html).

JR WEST KANSAI AREA PASS

A great deal for those who only want to explore the Kansai area, this pass covers unlimited travel on JR lines between most major Kansai cities, such as Himeji, Kōbe, Osaka, Kyoto and Nara. It also covers JR trains to/from Kansai airport but does not cover any *shinkansen* lines. One-, two-, three- and four-day passes cost ¥2000/4000/5000/6000, respectively (children's passes are half-price). These can be purchased at the same places as the San-yō area rail pass (both inside and outside Japan) and also entitle you to discounts on station hire car offices. Like the San-yō Area Pass, this pass can only be used by those with a temporary visitor visa. For more information on this pass, see the JR West website's **Kansai Area Pass section** (www .westjr.co.jp/english/english/travel/con04/kansai.html).

JR KYŪSHŪ RAIL PASS

This pass is valid on all JR lines in Kyūshū with the exception of the *shinkansen* line. A five-day pass (the only option) costs ¥16,000 (child passes are half-price). It can be purchased both inside Japan, at Joyroad Travel Agencies in major train stations in Kyūshū, and outside Japan, at the same locations as the Japan Rail Pass (see opposite for purchase details) and can only be used by those on a temporary visitor visa. If you purchase an exchange order overseas, you can pick up your pass at major train stations in Kyūshū. For more information, visit the website of **JR Kyūshū** (www.jrkyushu.co.jp/english/kyushu_railpass.html).

SEISHUN JŪHACHI KIPPU

If you don't have a Japan Rail Pass, one of the best deals going is a five-day Seishun

TRANSPORT

Jūhachi Kippu (literally a 'Youth 18 Ticket'). Despite its name, it can be used by anyone of any age. Basically, for ¥11,500 you get five one-day tickets valid for travel anywhere in Japan on JR lines. The only catches are that you can't travel on *tokkyū* or *shinkansen* trains and each ticket must be used within 24 hours. However, even if you only have to make a return trip, say, between Tokyo and Kyoto, you'll be saving a lot of money. Seishun Jūhachi Kippu can be purchased at most JR stations in Japan.

The tickets are intended to be used during Japanese university holidays. There are three periods of sales and validity: spring – which is from 20 February to 31 March and valid for use between 1 March and 10 April; summer – from 1 July to 31 August and valid for use between 20 July and 10 September; winter – from 1 December to 10 January and valid for use between 10 December and 20 January. Note that these periods are subject to change. For more information, ask at any JR ticket window.

If you don't want to buy the whole book of five tickets, you can sometimes purchase separate tickets at the discount ticket shops around train stations (right).

For more on the Seishun Jūhachi Kippu, see the JR East website's **Seishun Jūhachi Kippu section** (www.jreast.co.jp/e/pass/seishun18.html).

KANSAI THRU PASS
See p273 for details on this excellent pass, which allows unlimited travel on all non-JR private train lines and most bus lines in Kansai.

SHŪYŪ-KEN & FURII KIPPU
There are a number of excursion tickets, known as *shūyū-ken* or *furii kippu* (*furii* is Japanese for 'free'). These tickets include the return fare to your destination and give you unlimited JR local travel within the destination area. There are *shūyū-ken* available to travel from Tokyo to Hokkaidō and then around Hokkaidō for up to seven days. A Kyūshū or Shikoku *shūyū-ken* gets you to and from either island and gives you four or five days of travel around them. You can even go to Kyūshū one way by rail and one way by ferry. These tickets are available at major JR stations in Japan. For more information on these and other special ticket deals, see the JR East website's 'Useful

Tickets and Rail Passes for Visitors to East Japan' section (www.jreast.co.jp/e/pass/index.html).

Discount ticket shops are known as *kakuyasu-kippu-uriba* in Japanese. These stores deal in discounted tickets for trains, buses, domestic plane flights, ferries, and a host of other things like cut-rate stamps and phone cards. You can typically save between 5% and 10% on *shinkansen* tickets. Discount ticket agencies are found around train stations in medium and large cities. The best way to find one is to ask at the *kōban* (police box) outside the station.

Schedules & Information
The most complete timetables can be found in the JR *Jikokuhyō* (book of timetables; available at all Japanese bookstores; written in Japanese). The Japan National Tourist Organization (JNTO), however, produces a handy English-language Railway Timetable booklet which explains a great deal about the services in Japan and gives timetables for the *shinkansen* services, JR *tokkyū* (limited express services) and major private lines. If your visit to Japan is a short one and you will not be straying far from the major tourist destinations, this booklet may well be all you need.

Major train stations all have information counters, and you can usually get your point across in simplified English.

If you need to know anything about JR, such as schedules, fares, fastest routes, lost baggage, discounts on rail travel, hotels and car hire, call the **JR East-Infoline** (☎ 03-3423-0111; www.jreast.co.jp/e/info/index.html; ☽ 10am-6pm, closed during the year-end/new year period). Information is available in English, Korean and Chinese. More information can be found on the website.

Services
SHINKANSEN
The fastest and best-known train services in Japan are the *shinkansen* (bullet trains). The *shinkansen* reach speeds of up to 300km/h and some experimental models have gone significantly faster. In addition to being incredibly fast, *shinkansen* are also incredibly safe: in more than 30 years of operation, there has never been a fatality.

The service efficiency starts even before you board the train. Your ticket indicates your carriage and seat number, and platform signs indicate where you should stand for that carriage entrance. The train pulls in precisely to the scheduled minute and, sure enough, the carriage door you want is right beside where you're standing.

On most *shinkansen* routes, there are two or three types of services: faster express services stopping at a limited number of stations and slower local services stopping at all *shinkansen* stations. There is no difference in fare with the exception of the super-express Nozomi service on the Tōkaidō/San-yō *shinkansen* line. There are, however, regular and Green Car (1st class) carriages.

There are a limited number of *kin'en-sha* (nonsmoking carriages); request one when booking or ask on the platform for the *kin'en-sha-jiyū-seki* (unreserved nonsmoking cars). Unreserved carriages are available on all but the super-express Nozomi service, but at peak holiday periods they can be very crowded and you may have to stand for the entire trip.

For prices on specific *shinkansen* routes, see p764. For information on *shinkansen* routes, see the *shinkansen* lines map (below).

PRIVATE RAILWAYS

The private train lines usually operate short routes, often no more than 100km in length. Local commuter services are often on private train lines. Unlike JR stations, the private-line stations do not usually form the central focus of a town.

WOMEN-ONLY CARS

Several train companies in Japan have recently introduced women-only cars to protect female passengers from *chikan* (men who feel up women and girls on packed trains). These cars are usually available during rush-hour periods on weekdays on busy urban lines. There are signs (usually pink in colour) on the platform indicating where to board these cars, and the cars themselves are usually labelled in both Japanese and English (again, these are often marked in pink).

OTHER TRAIN SERVICES

In addition to the *shinkansen* routes that run most of the length of Honshū and down into Kyūshū, a network of JR lines, supplemented by a scattering of shorter private

TRANSPORT

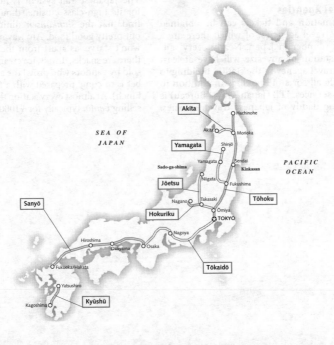

lines, cover much of the rest of Japan. Although these services are efficient, they are nowhere near as fast as the *shinkansen*, and typically take about twice as long.

Reservations

Tickets for most journeys can be bought from vending machines or ticket counters/ reservation offices. For reservations of complicated tickets, larger train stations have *midori-no-madoguchi* (green counters) – look for the counter with the green band across the glass. Major travel agencies in Japan also sell reserved-seat tickets, and you can buy *shinkansen* tickets through JAL offices overseas if you will be flying JAL to Japan.

On *futsū* services, there are no reserved seats. On the faster *tokkyū* and *shinkansen* services you can choose to travel reserved or unreserved. However, if you travel unreserved, there's always the risk of not getting a seat and having to stand, possibly for the entire trip. This is a particular danger at weekends, peak travel seasons and on holidays. Reserved-seat tickets can be bought any time from a month in advance to the day of departure.

Travel Agencies

Information and tickets can be obtained from travel agencies, of which there are a great number in Japan. Nearly every railway station of any size will have at least one travel agency in the station building to handle all sorts of bookings in addition to train services. JTB (Japan Travel Bureau) is the big daddy of Japanese travel agencies.

However, for most train tickets and long-distance bus reservations, you don't need a travel agency – just go to the ticket counters or *midori-no-madoguchi* (green counters) of any major train station.

Train Stations

Train stations in Japan are usually very well equipped. The main station is often literally the town centre and, in many cases, is part of a large shopping centre with a wide variety of restaurants, bars, fast-food outlets and other facilities.

LEFT LUGGAGE

Only major stations have left-luggage facilities, however there are almost always coin-operated storage lockers costing ¥100 to ¥500 per day, depending on their size. The lockers work until midnight (not for 24 hours) so, after that time, you have to insert more money before your key will work. If your bag is simply too large to fit in the locker, ask someone 'tenimotsu azukai wa doko desu ka' ('Where is the left-luggage office?').

MEALS

The Japanese rail system is not renowned for its high-class cuisine, though you may find that the *shinkansen* dining cars turn out pretty good food. Anyway, you certainly won't starve, as apart from the dining cars, there are snacks, drinks, ice creams and meals sold by vendors who prowl the aisles. A good bet is to come prepared with a *bentō* (boxed lunch). At almost every station there is a shop selling *bentō*, typically for ¥1000 or less.

Health Dr Trish Batchelor

CONTENTS

Japan is a wealthy industrialised country with a high standard of medical care. The level of care in rural areas, however, is not usually up to the same high standards as in the major cities. Food and water sanitation is generally good, though there is some risk of disease transmission through eating certain raw or undercooked foods. There is a low risk of catching an insect-borne disease such as Japanese encephalitis, Lyme disease and tick-borne encephalitis in specific areas at certain times of the year. Medical care is expensive, so ensure you have adequate travel insurance.

BEFORE YOU GO

Prevention is the key to staying healthy while abroad. A little planning before departure, particularly for pre-existing illnesses, will save trouble later. See your dentist before a long trip, carry a spare pair of contact lenses and glasses, and take your optical prescription with you. Bring medications in their original, clearly labelled containers. A signed and dated letter from your physician describing your medical conditions and medications, including generic names, is also a good idea. If carrying syringes or needles, be sure to have a physician's letter documenting their medical necessity. If you have a heart condition bring a copy of a recent electrocardiogram (ECG/EKG). If you take any regular medication bring extra supplies in case of loss or theft – it may be difficult to get exactly the same medications in Japan. In particular it can be difficult to get oral contraceptives.

Although medical care in most of Japan is quite reasonable, it is still wise to carry a basic medical kit suitable for treating minor ailments. Recommended items include simple painkillers, antiseptic and dressings for minor wounds, insect repellent, sunscreen, antihistamine tablets and adequate supplies of your personal medications.

INSURANCE

Even if you are fit and healthy, don't travel without specific travel health insurance – accidents can happen. If your health insurance does not cover you for medical expenses while abroad, get supplemental insurance. Find out in advance if your insurance plan will make payments directly to providers or reimburse you later for overseas health expenditures. Take a higher medical expense option as health costs in Japan are high. If you are seeing a doctor as an outpatient in Japan you will usually be expected to pay up front. If you're admitted to hospital, your insurance company may be able to pay the hospital directly; however, this is much easier if the company actually has an office in Japan.

RECOMMENDED VACCINATIONS

No vaccinations are required for Japan. However, you should be aware that Japan scrupulously checks visitors who arrive from countries where there is a risk of yellow fever and other similar diseases.

The World Health Organization (WHO) recommends that all travellers be covered for diphtheria, tetanus, measles, mumps and rubella, regardless of their destination. Since most vaccines don't produce immunity until at least two weeks after they're given, visit a physician at least six weeks before departure. Specialised travel medicine clinics are your best source of information as they will be able to give you personalised information for you

HEALTH

and your trip. The doctors will take into account factors like your medical history, past vaccination history, the length of your trip, time of year you are travelling, and any activities you may be undertaking, as any of these factors can alter general recommendations. Ensure you receive an International Certificate of Vaccination (the yellow booklet), which lists the vaccines you have received.

Adult diphtheria/tetanus (ADT) – a booster is recommended if it is more than 10 years since your last shot. Side effects include a sore arm and fever.

Measles/Mumps/Rubella (MMR) – two doses of MMR are recommended unless you have had the diseases. Many adults under the age of 35 require a booster. Occasionally a rash and flu-like illness can occur about a week after vaccination.

Varicella (Chickenpox) – if you have not had chickenpox you should discuss this vaccine with your doctor. Chickenpox can be a serious disease in adults with complications such as pneumonia and encephalitis. As an adult you require two shots, six weeks apart (usually given after a blood test to prove you have no immunity).

Under certain circumstances, or for those at special risk, the following vaccinations are recommended. These should be discussed with a doctor specialised in travel medicine.

Hepatitis A – the risk in Japan is low but travellers spending extensive amounts of time in rural areas may consider vaccination. One injection gives almost 100% protection for six to 12 months; after a booster at least 20 years' protection is provided. This vaccine is commonly combined with the hepatitis B vaccine in the form of 'Twinrix'.

Hepatitis B – for those staying long term or who may be exposed to body fluids by sexual contact, acupuncture, dental work etc, or for health care workers. Three shots are required, given over six months (a rapid schedule is also available).

Influenza – if you are over 50 years of age or have a chronic medical condition such as diabetes, lung disease or heart disease you should have a flu shot annually. Side effects include a mild fever and sore arm.

Japanese B encephalitis – there is no risk in Tokyo, but there is risk in rural areas of all islands. The risk is highest in the western part of the country from July to October. Three shots are given over the course of a month, with a booster after two years. Rarely, allergic reactions can occur, so the course is best completed 10 days prior to travel.

Pneumonia (Pneumococcal) – this vaccine is recommended to travellers over the age of 65 or with chronic lung or heart disease.

Tick-borne encephalitis – this is present only in the wooded areas of Hokkaido and is transmitted from April to October. This vaccine is readily available in Europe but can be difficult or impossible to find elsewhere.

INTERNET RESOURCES

There is a wealth of travel health advice on the Internet. For further information, the Lonely Planet website, at www.lonelyplanet .com, is a good place to start. WHO publishes a superb book called *International Travel and Health*, which is revised annually and is available free online at www.who.int/ith/. Other websites of general interest are MD Travel Health at www.mdtravelhealth.com, which provides complete travel health recommendations for every country; the Centers for Disease Control and Prevention has a good site at www.cdc.gov; and Fit for Travel at www.fitfortravel.scot.nhs.uk has up-to-date information about outbreaks and is very user-friendly.

It's also a good idea to consult your government's travel health website before departure, if one is available.

Australia (www.dfat.gov.au/travel/)
Canada (www.travelhealth.gc.ca)
New Zealand (www.moh.govt.nz)
UK (www.dh.gov.uk)
USA (www.cdc.gov/travel/)

FURTHER READING

For those spending an extended period of time in Japan the best book is the *Japan Health Handbook* by Meredith Maruyama, Louise Picon Shimizu and Nancy Smith Tsurumaki. It gives an excellent overview of the Japanese medical system for expats. Lonely Planet's *Healthy Travel Asia & India* is a useful pocket-sized guide to travel health. *Travel with Children* from Lonely Planet is useful if you are taking children with you. Other recommended general travel health references are *Traveller's Health* by Dr Richard Dawood and *Travelling Well* by Dr Deborah Mills – check out the website www.travellingwell.com.au for other trips.

IN TRANSIT

DEEP VEIN THROMBOSIS (DVT)

Blood clots may form in the legs during plane flights, chiefly because of prolonged immobility. The longer the flight, the greater the risk. The chief symptom of DVT is swelling or pain of the foot, ankle or calf, usually but not always on just one side. If a blood clot travels to the lungs it may cause chest pain and breathing difficulties.

Travellers with any of these symptoms should immediately seek medical attention.

To prevent the development of DVT on long flights you should walk about the cabin, contract the leg muscles while sitting, drink plenty of fluids and avoid alcohol. If you have previously had DVT speak with your doctor about preventive medications (usually given in the form of an injection just prior to travel).

JET LAG & MOTION SICKNESS

To avoid jet lag (common when crossing more than five time zones) try drinking plenty of nonalcoholic fluids and eating light meals. Upon arrival, get exposure to natural sunlight and readjust your schedule (for meals, sleep and so on) as soon as possible.

Antihistamines such as dimenhydrinate (Dramamine), prochlorperazine (Phenergan) and meclizine (Antivert, Bonine) are usually the first choice for treating motion sickness. The main side effect of these medications is drowsiness. A herbal alternative is ginger.

IN JAPAN

AVAILABILITY & COST OF HEALTH CARE

Medical care in Japan is significantly better in the major cities compared to rural areas. Outside urban areas it may be difficult to access English-speaking doctors, so try to take a Japanese speaker with you to any medical facility. Japan has a national health insurance system, but this is only available to foreigners if they have long-term visas in Japan. Be aware that medical facilities will require full payment at the time of treatment or proof that your travel insurance will pay for any treatment that you receive. Insurance companies in the West are comfortable with the facilities in Japan's major urban centres, but have found variable standards of care in the country areas.

JNTO-operated tourist offices (p744) have lists of English-speaking doctors and dentists, and hospitals where English is spoken. You can also contact your insurance company or embassy to find out where the nearest English-speaking facility is.

Dental services are widespread and of good standard; however, they are very expensive so make sure you have a check-up before you leave home.

Drugs that require a prescription in the West also generally require one in Japan. Ensure you bring adequate supplies of your own medications from home.

There are certain medications that are illegal to bring into Japan, including some commonly used cough and cold medications such as pseudoephedrine (found in Actifed, Sudafed etc) and codeine. Some prescription medications not allowed into Japan include narcotics, psychotropic drugs, stimulants and codeine. If you need to take more than a one-month supply of any other prescription drug, you should check with your local Japanese embassy as you may need permission. Ensure you have a letter from your doctor outlining your medical condition and the need for any prescription medication.

Pregnant women should receive specialised advice before travelling. Some vaccines are definitely not recommended, others are only prescribed after an individual risk/benefit analysis. The ideal time to travel is during the second trimester (between 15 and 28 weeks), when the risk of pregnancy-related problems are at their lowest and pregnant women generally feel at their best. During the first trimester there is a risk of miscarriage and in the third trimester problems such as premature labour and high blood pressure are possible. Always travel with a companion, have a list of quality medical facilities available at your destination and ensure you continue your standard antenatal care while you travel. Avoid travel to rural areas with poor transport and medical facilities. Most importantly, ensure your travel insurance covers you for pregnancy-related problems, including premature labour. There have recently been reports of hepatitis E in Japan, contracted from undercooked pork liver, boar and deer meat.

Supplies of sanitary products are readily available in Japan. It can be very difficult to get the oral contraceptive pill so ensure you bring adequate supplies of your own pill from home.

Japan is a safe country to travel with children. Ensure they are up to date with their basic vaccinations prior to travel.

INFECTIOUS DISEASES
AIDS & STDs

AIDS and STDs can be avoided completely only by abstaining from sexual contact with

HEALTH

new partners. Condom use in Japanese society is low. HIV is still relatively uncommon in Japan, but the incidence is slowly increasing. In the year 2000, 78% of new cases were contracted via sexual contact. Condoms can help prevent some sexually transmitted infections, but not all. If you have had sexual contact with a new partner while travelling, or have any symptoms such as a rash, pain or discharge, see a doctor for a full STD check-up.

Hepatitis B

Hepatitis B is a virus spread via body fluids, eg through sexual contact, unclean medical facilities or shared needles. People who carry the virus are often unaware they are carriers. In the short term hepatitis B can cause the typical symptoms of hepatitis – jaundice, tiredness and nausea – but in the long term it can lead to cancer of the liver and cirrhosis. Vaccination against hepatitis B is now part of most countries' routine childhood vaccination schedule and should be considered by anyone travelling for a long period of time or who may have contact with body fluids.

Hepatitis E

Hepatitis E is a virus spread via contaminated food and water. There have been a number of cases reported from Japan, linked to eating boar and deer meat, and most recently, undercooked pork liver. The disease causes jaundice (yellow skin and eyes), tiredness and nausea. There is no specific treatment and those infected usually recover after four to six weeks. However, it can be a disaster in pregnant women, with a death rate of both mother and baby of up to 30% in the third trimester. Pregnant women should be particularly careful to avoid eating any undercooked foods. There is no vaccine yet available to prevent hepatitis E.

Influenza

Influenza is generally transmitted between November and April. Symptoms include high fever, muscle aches, runny nose, cough and sore throat. It can be a very severe illness in those aged over 65 or with underlying medical conditions such as heart disease or diabetes. Vaccination is recommended for these high-risk travellers or for anyone who wishes to reduce their risk of catching the illness. There is no specific treatment for 'the flu', just rest and paracetamol.

Japanese B Encephalitis

Japanese B encephalitis is a viral disease transmitted by mosquitoes. It is a rare disease in travellers and the vaccine is part of the routine childhood vaccination schedule in Japan. Risk exists in rural areas of all islands, but is highest in the western part of the country. In western Japan the risk season is from July to October. On Ryuku Island (Okinawa) the risk season runs from April to December. Vaccination is recommended for travellers spending more than a month in rural areas during the transmission season. Other precautions include general insect avoidance measures such as using repellents and sleeping under nets if not in screened rooms. Although this is a rare disease, it is very serious – there is no specific treatment and a third of people infected will die and a third will suffer permanent brain damage.

Lyme Disease

Lyme disease is spread via ticks and is present in the summer months in wooded areas. Symptoms include an early rash and general viral symptoms, followed weeks to months later by joint, heart or neurological problems. The disease is treated with the antibiotic doxycycline. Prevent Lyme disease by using general insect avoidance measures and checking yourself for ticks after walking in forested areas.

Tick-Borne Encephalitis

Tick-borne encephalitis occurs on the northern island of Hokkaidō only, and, as its name suggests, is a virus transmitted by ticks. The illness starts with general flu-like symptoms, which last a few days and then subside. After a period of remission (about one week) the second phase of the illness occurs with symptoms such as headache, fever and stiff neck (meningitis), or drowsiness, confusion and other neurological signs such as paralysis (encephalitis). There is no specific treatment, and about 10% to 20% of those who progress to the second phase of illness will have permanent neurological problems. You can prevent this disease by using insect avoidance measures and checking yourself for ticks after walking in forested areas. A vaccine is available in Europe but is very difficult if not impossible to find elsewhere. Two doses are given four to 12 weeks apart with a third shot after nine to 12 months. Boosters are required every three years to maintain immunity.

TRAVELLER'S DIARRHOEA

There is a low risk of traveller's diarrhoea in Japan, only 10% to 20% of travellers will experience some stomach upset. If you develop diarrhoea, be sure to drink plenty of fluids, preferably an oral rehydration solution (eg Dioralyte). A few loose stools don't require treatment, but if you start having more than four or five stools a day you should start taking an antibiotic (such as norfloxacin, ciprofloxacin or azithromycin) and an anti-diarrhoeal agent (such as loperamide). If diarrhoea is bloody, persists for more than 72 hours, is accompanied by fever, shaking, chills or severe abdominal pain, or doesn't respond quickly to your antibiotic, you should seek medical attention.

ENVIRONMENTAL HAZARDS
Air Pollution

Air pollution can be a problem in major centres such as Tokyo if you have an underlying lung condition. If you have a pre-existing lung condition speak with your doctor to ensure you have adequate medications to treat an exacerbation.

Altitude Sickness

Altitude sickness could develop in some people when climbing Mt Fuji (for more information, see p171) or some of the higher Japanese alps. Altitude sickness is best avoided by slowly acclimatising to higher altitudes. If this is impossible, the medication Diamox can be a helpful preventative if taken on a doctor's recommendation. The symptoms of altitude sickness include headache, nausea and exhaustion and the best treatment is descending to a lower altitude. We recommend that you familiarise yourself with the condition and how to prevent it before setting out on any climb over 2000m. Rick Curtis's *Outdoor Action Guide to High Altitude: Acclimatization and Illness* (www .princeton.edu/~oa/safety/altitude.html) provides a comprehensive overview.

Hypothermia

Hypothermia is possible if walking or climbing in the alps. It is surprisingly easy to progress from very cold to dangerously cold due to a combination of wind, wet clothing, fatigue and hunger, even if the air temperature is above freezing. It is best to dress in layers; silk, wool and some of the new artificial fibres are all good insulating materials. A hat is important, as a lot of heat is lost through the head. A strong, waterproof outer layer (and a space blanket for emergencies) is essential. Carry basic supplies, including food containing simple sugars to generate heat quickly and fluid to drink. Symptoms of hypothermia are exhaustion, numb skin (particularly the toes and fingers), shivering, slurred speech, irrational or violent behaviour, lethargy, stumbling, dizzy spells, muscle cramps and violent bursts of energy. Irrationality may take the form of sufferers claiming they are warm and trying to take off their clothes. To treat mild hypothermia, first get the person out of the wind and/or rain, remove their clothing if it's wet and replace it with dry, warm clothing. Give them hot liquids – not alcohol – and some high-calorie, easily digestible food. The early recognition and treatment of mild hypothermia is the only way to prevent severe hypothermia, which is a critical condition.

Insect Bites & Stings

Insect bites and stings are not a common problem in Japan. You should, however, follow general insect avoidance measures if you are hiking in the woods or are in rural areas during the summer months. These include using an insect repellant containing 20% to 30% DEET (diethyl-M-toluamide), covering up with light-coloured clothing and checking yourself for ticks after being in the forest. When removing ticks ensure you also remove their heads. Some people have an allergic reaction to ticks so it is a good idea to carry an antihistamine with you.

Water

The water is generally safe to drink in Japan.

TRADITIONAL MEDICINE

The two most well known forms of traditional Japanese medicine are shiatsu and *reiki*.

Shiatsu is a type of massage that emerged in Japan out of traditional Chinese medicine. It is a form of manual therapy incorporating gentle manipulations and stretches derived from physiotherapy and chiropractic, combined with pressure techniques exerted through the fingers or thumbs. The

HEALTH

philosophy underlying shiatsu is similar to many traditional Asian medical systems and involves the body's vital energy *(ki)* flowing through the body in a series of channels known as meridians. If the *ki* is blocked from flowing freely, illness can occur. The technique is used to improve the flow of *ki*. Shiatsu was officially recognised by the Japanese government as a therapy in its own right in the mid-1900s.

Reiki claims to heal by charging this same life force with positive energy, thus allowing the *ki* to flow in a natural, healthy manner. In a standard treatment, *reiki* energy flows from the practitioner's hands into the client. The practitioner places their hands on or near the clients' body in a series of positions that are held for three to 10 minutes. People become practitioners after receiving an 'attunement' from a *reiki* master.

If you decide to have any traditional medical treatments make sure you tell your practitioner if you are taking any Western medicines.

Language

CONTENTS

Japanese is the language spoken across all of Japan. While the standard language, or *hyōjungo*, is understood by almost all Japanese, regardless of their level of education, many Japanese speak strong local dialects (known as *ben*, as in the famous dialect of Kansai, *Kansai-ben*). These dialects, particularly in rural areas, can be quite difficult to understand, even for Japanese from other parts of the country. Luckily, you can always get your point across in *hyōjungo*.

In this language guide you'll find a selection of useful Japanese words and phrases. For information on food and dining, including words and phrases that will help in deciphering menus and ordering food in Japanese, see p85. For information on language courses available in Japan, see p732.

GRAMMAR

To English speakers, Japanese language patterns often seem to be back to front and lacking in essential information. For example, where an English speaker would say 'I'm going to the shop' a Japanese speaker would say 'shop to going', omitting the subject pronoun (I) altogether and putting the verb at the end of the sentence. To make

---

TRYING ENGLISH IN JAPAN

Visitors to Japan should be warned that many Japanese do not speak or understand much English. Although English is a required subject in both junior high school and high school, and many students go on to study more of it in university, several factors conspire to prevent many Japanese from acquiring usable English. These include the nature of the English educational system, which uses outdated methods like translation; the extreme difference between English and Japanese pronunciation and grammar; and the typical reticence of the Japanese, who may be shy to speak a language that they haven't mastered.

There are several ways to facilitate communication with Japanese who may not have a mastery of spoken English:

- Always start with a smile to create a sense of ease.
- Speak very slowly and clearly.
- When asking for information, choose people of university age or thereabouts, as these people are most likely to speak some English. Also, Japanese women tend to speak and understand English much better than Japanese men.
- If necessary, write down your question; Japanese are often able to understand written English even when they can't understand spoken English.
- Use the sample phrases in this chapter and, if necessary, point to the Japanese phrase in question.

---

matters worse, many moods which are indicated at the beginning of a sentence in English occur at the end of a sentence in Japanese, as in the Japanese sentence 'Japan to going if' – 'if you're going to Japan'.

Fortunately for visitors to Japan, it's not all bad news. In fact, with a little effort, getting together a repertoire of travellers' phrases should be no trouble – the only problem will be understanding the replies you get.

WRITTEN JAPANESE

Japanese has one of the most complex writing systems in the world, which uses three different scripts – four if you include the increasingly used Roman script romaji. The most difficult of the three, for foreigners and Japanese alike, is kanji, the ideographic script developed by the Chinese. Not only do you have to learn a couple of thousand of them, but unlike Chinese many Japanese kanji have wildly variant pronunciations depending on context.

Due to the differences between Chinese and Japanese grammar, kanji had to be supplemented with a 'syllabary' (an alphabet of syllables), known as hiragana. And there is yet another syllabary that is used largely for representing foreign loan words such as *terebi* (TV) and *biiru* (beer); this script is known as katakana. If you're serious about learning to read Japanese you'll have to set aside several years.

If you're thinking of tackling the Japanese writing system before you go or while you're in Japan, your best bet would be to start with hiragana or katakana. Both these syllabaries have 48 characters each, and can be learned within a week, although it'll take at least a month to consolidate them. Once in the country, you can practise your katakana on restaurant menus, where such things as *kōhii* (coffee) and *kēiki* (cake) are frequently found. Practise your hiragana on train journeys, as station names are usually indicated in hiragana (in addition to English and kanji). If you fancy continuing on to learn the kanji, be warned that it'll take quite a few years.

ROMANISATION

The romaji used in this book follows the Hepburn system of romanisation. In addition, common Japanese nouns like *ji* or *tera* (temple) and *jinja* or *jingū* (shrine) are written without an English translation.

Silent Letters

Hepburn romaji is a direct system of Romanisation that doesn't fully reflect all elements of spoken Japanese. The most obvious of these is the tendency in everyday speech to omit the vowel 'u' in many instances. In this language guide, and in Useful Words & Phrases on p85, these silent letters have been retained to provide accuracy in the written Romanisations, but they have been enclosed in square brackets to aid accurate pronunciation.

LANGUAGE BOOKS

Lonely Planet's *Japanese Phrasebook* gives you a comprehensive mix of practical and social words and phrases that should cover almost any situation confronting the traveller to Japan.

If you'd like to delve deeper into the intricacies of the language, we recommend *Japanese for Busy People* for beginners, *Introduction to Intermediate Japanese* (Mizutani Nobuko) for intermediate students, and *Kanji in Context* (Nishiguchi Koichi and Kono Tamaki) for more advanced students. One of the best guides to the written language, for both study and reference, is *Kanji & Kana* (Wolfgang Hadamizky and Mark Spahn).

PRONUNCIATION

Unlike other languages in the region with complicated tonal systems (eg Chinese, Vietnamese and Thai), Japanese pronunciation is fairly easy to master.

The following examples reflect British pronunciation:

a	as in 'father'
e	as in 'get'
i	as in 'macaroni'
o	as in 'bone'
u	as in 'flu'

Vowels appearing in this book with a macron (or bar) over them (**ā, ē, ō, ū**) are pronounced in the same way as standard vowels except that the sound is held twice as long. You need to take care with this as vowel length can change the meaning of a word, eg *yuki* means 'snow', while *yūki* means 'bravery'.

Consonants are generally pronounced as in English, with the following exceptions:

f	this sound is produced by pursing the lips and blowing lightly
g	as in 'get' at the start of word; and nasalised as the 'ng' in 'sing' in the middle of a word
r	more like an 'l' than an 'r'

ACCOMMODATION

I'm looking for a ...
... o sagashite imas[u]
...を探しています。

  camping ground
  kyampu-jō   キャンプ場
  family-style inn
  minshiku   民宿
  guesthouse
  gesuto hausu   ゲストハウス
  hotel
  hoteru   ホテル
  inn
  ryokan   旅館
  Japanese-style inn
  ryokan   旅館
  youth hostel
  yūsu hosuteru   ユースホステル

Do you have any vacancies?
aki-beya wa arimas[u] ka?
空き部屋はありますか?
I don't have a reservation.
yoyaku wa shiteimasen
予約はしていません。

single room
  shinguru rūmu   シングルルーム
double room
  daburu rūmu   ダブルルーム
twin room
  tsuin rūmu   ツインルーム
Japanese-style room
  washitsu   和室
Western-style room
  yōshitsu   洋室
Japanese-style bath
  o-furo   お風呂
room with a (Western-style) bath
  basu tsuki no heya   バス付きの部屋

How much is it (per night/per person)?
(ippaku/hitori) ikura des[u] ka?
(一泊/一人)いくらですか?
Does it include breakfast/a meal?
chōshoku/shokuji wa tsuite imas[u] ka?
(朝食/食事)は付いていますか?
I'm going to stay for one night/two nights.
hito-ban/futa-ban tomarimas[u]
(一晩/二晩)泊まります。
Can I leave my luggage here?
nimotsu o azukatte itadakemasen ka?
荷物を預かっていただけませんか?

CONVERSATION & ESSENTIALS

The all-purpose title *san* is used after a name as an honorific and is the equivalent of Mr, Miss, Mrs and Ms.

Good morning.
ohayō gozaimas[u]
おはようございます。
Good afternoon.
konnichiwa
こんにちは。
Good evening.
kombanwa
こんばんは。
Goodbye.
sayōnara
さようなら。
See you later.
dewa mata
ではまた
Please/Go ahead. (when offering)
dōzo
どうぞ。
Please. (when asking)
onegai shimas[u]
お願いします。
Thanks. (informal)
dōmo
どうも。
Thank you.
dōmo arigatō
どうもありがとう。
Thank you very much.
dōmo arigatō gozaimas[u]
どうもありがとうございます。
Thanks for having me. (when leaving)
o-sewa ni narimash[i]ta
お世話になりました。
You're welcome.
dō itashimashite
どういたしまして。
No, thank you.
iie, kekkō des[u]
いいえ,けっこうです。
Excuse me/Pardon.
sumimasen
すみません。
Excuse me. (when entering a room)
o-jama shimas[u]/shitsurei shimas[u]
おじゃまします。/失礼します。
I'm sorry.
gomen nasai
ごめんなさい。

What's your name?
o-namae wa nan des[u] ka?
お名前は何ですか？

My name is ...
watashi wa ... des[u]
私は．．．です。

This is Mr/Mrs/Ms (Smith).
kochira wa (Sumisu) san des[u]
こちらは（スミス）さんです。

Pleased to meet you.
dōzo yorosh[i]ku
どうぞよろしく。

Where are you from?
dochira no kata des[u] ka?
どちらのかたですか？

How are you?
o-genki des[u] ka?
お元気ですか？

Fine.
genki des[u]
元気です。

Is it OK to take a photo?
shashin o totte mo ii des[u] ka?
写真を撮ってもいいですか？

Cheers!
kampai!
乾杯！

Yes.
hai
はい。

No.
iie
いいえ。

No. (for indicating disagreement)
chigaimas[u]
違います。

No. (for indicating disagreement; less emphatic)
chotto chigaimas[u]
ちょっと違います。

OK.
daijōbu (des[u])/ōke
だいじょうぶ（です）。／オーケー。

Requests
Please give me this/that.
kore/sore o kudasai
（これ/それ）をください。

Please give me a (cup of tea).
(o-cha) o kudasai
（お茶）をください。

Please wait (a while).
(shōshō) o-machi kudasai
（少々）お待ちください。

SIGNS	
Information	
annaijo	案内所
Open	
eigyōchū	営業中
Closed	
junbichū	準備中
Entrance	
iriguchi	入口
Exit	
deguchi	出口
Toilets	
o-tearai/toire	お手洗い／トイレ
Male	
otoko	男
Female	
onna	女

Please show me the (ticket).
(kippu) o misete kudasai
（切符）を見せてください。

DIRECTIONS
Where is the ...?
... wa doko des[u] ka?
．．．はどこですか？

How far is it to walk?
aruite dono kurai kakarimas[u] ka?
歩いてどのくらいかかりますか？

How do I get to ...?
... e wa dono yō ni ikeba ii des[u] ka?
．．．へはどのように行けばいいですか？

Where is this address please?
kono jūsho wa doko des[u] ka?
この住所はどこですか？

Could you write down the address for me?
jūsho o kaite itadakemasen ka?
住所を書いていただけませんか？

Go straight ahead.
massugu itte
まっすぐ行って。

Turn left/right.
hidari/migi e magatte
（左/右）へ曲がって。

near/far
chikai/tōi
近い/遠い

HEALTH
I need a doctor.
isha ga hitsuyō des[u]
医者が必要です。

How do you feel?
kibun wa ikaga des[u] ka?
気分はいかがですか？

I'm ill.
kibun ga warui des[u]
気分が悪いです。

It hurts here.
koko ga itai des[u]
ここが痛いです。

I have diarrhoea.
geri o shite imas[u]
下痢をしています。

I have a toothache.
ha ga itamimas[u]
歯が痛みます。

I'm ...
watashi wa ...   私は...
  diabetic
  tōnyōbyō des[u]   糖尿病です。
  epileptic
  tenkan des[u]   てんかんです。
  asthmatic
  zensoku des[u]   喘息です。

I'm allergic to antibiotics.
kōsei-busshitsu ni areruii ga arimas[u]
抗生物質にアレルギーがあります。

I'm allergic to penicillin.
penishirin ni areruii ga arimas[u]
ペニシリン）にアレルギーがあります。

antiseptic
shōdokuyaku   消毒薬
aspirin
asupirin   アスピリン
condoms
kondōmu   コンドーム
contraceptive
hinin yō piru   避妊用ピル
dentist
ha-isha   歯医者
doctor
isha   医者
hospital
byōin   病院
medicine
kusuri   薬
pharmacy
yakkyoku   薬局
tampons
tampon   タンポン
(a) cold
kaze   風邪

EMERGENCIES

Help!
tas[u]kete!
助けて！

Call a doctor!
isha o yonde kudasai!
医者を呼んでください！

Call the police!
keisatsu o yonde kudasai!
警察を呼んでください！

I'm lost.
michi ni mayoi mash[i]ta
道に迷いました。

Go away!
hanarero!
離れろ！

---

diarrhoea
geri   下痢
fever
hatsunetsu   発熱
migraine
henzutsū   偏頭痛

LANGUAGE DIFFICULTIES

Do you speak English?
eigo ga hanasemas[u] ka?
英語が話せますか？

Does anyone speak English?
donata ka eigo o hanasemas[u] ka?
どなたか英語を話せますか？

Do you understand English/Japanese?
ei-go/nihon-go wa wakarimas[u] ka?
（英語／日本語）はわかりますか？

I don't understand.
wakarimasen
わかりません。

I can't speak Japanese.
nihongo wa dekimasen
日本語はできません。

How do you say ... in Japanese?
nihongo de ... wa nan to iimas[u] ka?
日本語で...は何といいますか？

What does ... mean?
... wa donna imi des[u] ka?
...はどんな意味ですか？

What is this called?
kore wa nan to iimas[u] ka?
これは何といいますか？

Please write in Japanese/English.
nihongo/eigo de kaite kudasai
（日本語／英語）で書いてください。

LANGUAGE

Please speak more slowly.
mō chotto yukkuri itte kudasai
もうちょっとゆっくり言ってください。

Please say it again more slowly.
mō ichidō, yukkuri itte kudasai
もう一度，ゆっくり言ってください。

NUMBERS

0	zero/rei	ゼロ/零
1	ichi	一
2	ni	二
3	san	三
4	yon/shi	四
5	go	五
6	roku	六
7	nana/shichi	七
8	hachi	八
9	kyū/ku	九
10	jū	十
11	jūichi	十一
12	jūni	十二
13	jūsan	十三
14	jūyon/jūshi	十四
20	nijū	二十
21	nijūichi	二十一
30	sanjū	三十
100	hyaku	百
200	nihyaku	二百
1000	sen	千
5000	gosen	五千
10,000	ichiman	一万
20,000	niman	二万
100,000	jūman	十万
one million	hyakuman	百万

QUESTION WORDS

What?
nani? なに?

When?
itsu? いつ?

Where?
doko? どこ?

Who?
dare? だれ?

SHOPPING & SERVICES

bank
ginkō 銀行

embassy
taishi-kan 大使館

post office
yūbin kyoku 郵便局

market
ichiba 市場

a public telephone
kōshū denwa 公衆電話

toilet
o-tearai/toire お手洗い/トイレ

the tourist office
kankō annaijo 観光案内所

What time does it open/close?
nanji ni akimas[u]/shimarimas[u] ka?
何時に（開きます/閉まります）か?

I'd like to buy ...
... o kaitai des[u]
．．．を買いたいです。

How much is it?
ikura des[u] ka?
いくらですか?

I'm just looking.
miteiru dake des[u]
見ているだけです。

It's cheap.
yasui des[u]
安いです。

It's too expensive.
taka-sugi mas[u]
高すぎます。

I'll take this one.
kore o kudasai
これをください。

Can I have a receipt?
ryōshūsho o itadakemasen ka?
領収書をいただけませんか?

big
ōkii 大きい

small
chiisai 小さい

shop
mise 店

supermarket
sūpā スーパー

bookshop
hon ya 本屋

camera shop
shashin ya 写真屋

department store
depāto デパート

TIME & DAYS

What time is it?
ima nan-ji des[u] ka? 今何時ですか?

today
kyō 今日

GLOSSARY OF USEFUL TERMS

Geography

-dake/-take	岳	peak
-dani/-tani	谷	valley
-gawa/-kawa	川	river
-hama	浜	beach
-hantō	半島	peninsula
-jima/-shima	島	island
-kaikyō	海峡	channel/-strait
-ko	湖	lake
-kō	港	port
-kōen	公園	park
-kōgen	高原	plateau
kokutei kōen	国定公園	quasi-national park
kokuritsu kōen	国立公園	national park
-kyō	峡	gorge
-minato	港	harbour
-misaki	岬	cape
... no-yu	...の湯	hot spring
-oka	丘	hill
onsen	温泉	hot spring
-san/-zan	山	mountain
-shima/-jima	島	island
shokubutsu-en	植物園	botanic garden
-shotō	諸島	archipelago
-take/-dake	岳	peak
-taki	滝	waterfall
-tani/-dani	谷	valley
-tō	島	island
-wan	湾	bay
-yama	山	mountain

-yu	湯	hot spring
-zaki/-misaki	岬	cape
-zan/-san	山	mountain

Regions

-shi	市	city
-chō	町	neighbourhood/village/s
-mura	村	village
-ken	県	prefecture
-gun	郡	county
-ku	区	ward

Sights

-dera/-tera	寺	temple
-dō	堂	temple/hall of a temple
-en	園	garden
-in	院	temple/hall of a temple
-gū	宮	shrine
-ji	寺	temple
-jō	城	castle
-kōen	公園	park
-mon	門	gate
shokubutsu-en	植物園	botanical garden
-hori/-bori	堀	moat
-jingū	神宮	shrine
-jinja	神社	shrine
-taisha	大社	shrine
-teien	庭園	garden
-tera/-dera	寺	temple
-torii	鳥居	shrine gate

tomorrow
ash[i]ta 明日
yesterday
kinō きのう
morning/afternoon
asa/hiru 朝/昼

Monday
getsuyōbi 月曜日
Tuesday
kayōbi 火曜日
Wednesday
suiyōbi 水曜日
Thursday
mokuyōbi 木曜日
Friday
kinyōbi 金曜日
Saturday
doyōbi 土曜日
Sunday
nichiyōbi 日曜日

TRANSPORT
What time does the next ... leave?
tsugi no ... wa nanji ni demas[u] ka?
次の...は何時に出ますか?
What time does the next ... arrive?
tsugi no ... wa nanji ni tsukimas[u] ka?
次の...は何時に着きますか?
boat
bōto/fune ボート/船
bus (city)
shibas[u] 市バス
bus (intercity)
chōkyoribas[u] 長距離バス
tram
romen densha 路面電車
train
densha 電車
bus stop
basutei バス停
station
eki 駅

subway (train)
  chikatetsu   地下鉄
ticket
  kippu   切符
ticket office
  kippu uriba   切符売り場
timetable
  jikokuhyō   時刻表
taxi
  takushi   タクシー
left-luggage office
  nimotsu azukarijo 荷物預かり所
one way
  katamichi   片道
return
  ōfuku   往復
non-smoking seat
  kin'en seki   禁煙席

How much is the fare to ...?
  ... made ikura des[u] ka?
  . . .までいくらですか?
Does this (train, bus, etc) go to ...?
  kore wa ... e ikimas[u] ka?
  これは. . .へ行きますか?
Please tell me when we get to ...
  ... ni tsuitara oshiete kudasai
  . . .に着いたら教えてください。
I'd like to hire a ...
  ... o karitai no des[u] ka.
  . . .を借りたいのですが。
I'd like to go to ...
  ... ni ikitai desu
  . . .に行きたいです。
Please stop here.
  koko de tomete kudasai
  ここで停めてください。

Glossary

ageya – magnificent banquet halls where artists, writers and statesmen gathered in a 'floating world' ambience of conversation, art and fornication

aimai – ambiguous and unclear

Ainu – indigenous people of Hokkaidō and parts of northern Honshū

aka-chōchin – red lantern; a working man's pub marked by red lanterns outside

akirame – to relinquish; resignation

ama – women divers

Amaterasu – sun goddess and link to the imperial throne

ama-zake – sweet sake served at winter festivals

ANA – All Nippon Airlines

ANK – All Nippon Koku

annai-sho – information office

arubaito – from the German *arbeit*, meaning 'to work', adapted into Japanese to refer to part-time work; often contracted to *baito*

asa-ichi – morning market

Aum Shinrikyō – the cult responsible for the 1995 sarin gas attacks on Tokyo's subway

awamori – local alcohol of Okinawa

ayu – sweetfish caught during *ukai* (cormorant fishing)

baito – a part-time job (from *arbeit*, the German word meaning 'to work')

bangasa – rain umbrella made from oiled paper

banzai – 'hurrah' or 'hurray'; in the West this exclamation is, for the most part, associated with WWII, although its more modern usage is quite peaceful; literally '10,000 years'

bashō – *sumō* wrestling tournament

basho-gara – fitting to the particular conditions or circumstances; literally 'the character of a place'

bentō – boxed lunch, usually of rice, with a main dish and pickles or salad

bonsai – the art of growing miniature trees by careful pruning of branches and roots

boso-zoku – 'hot-car' or motorcycle gangs, usually noisy but harmless

bottle-keep – system whereby you buy a whole bottle of liquor in a bar, which is kept for you to drink on subsequent visits

bugaku – dance pieces played by court orchestras in ancient Japan

buke yashiki – *samurai* residence

bunraku – classical puppet theatre using huge puppets to portray dramas similar to *kabuki*

burakumin – traditionally outcasts associated with lowly occupations such as leather work; literally 'village people'

bushidō – a set of values followed by the *samurai*; literally 'the way of the warrior'

butsudan – Buddhist altar in Japanese homes

champuru – stir-fry with mixed ingredients such as *goya* and *fū*

chanelah – fashionable young woman with a predilection for name brands, in particular Chanel products

chaniwa – tea garden

chanoyu – tea ceremony

charm – small dish of peanuts or other snack food served with a drink at a bar – it's often not requested but is still added to your bill

chikan – men who feel up women and girls on packed trains

chimpira – *yakuza* understudy; usually used pejoratively of a male with *yakuza* aspirations

chizu – map

chō – city area (for large cities) between a *ku* and *chōme* in size; also a street

chōchin – paper lantern

chōme – city area of a few blocks

chōnan – oldest son

chu – loyalty

daibutsu – Great Buddha

daifuku – sticky rice cakes filled with red bean paste and eaten on festive occasions; literally 'great happiness'

daimyō – regional lords under the *shōgun*

daira – plain

danchi – public apartments

dantai – a group of people

danjiri – festival floats

dengaku – fish and vegetables roasted on skewers

donko – name for local trains in country areas

eboshi – black, triangular *samurai* hat

eki – train station

ekiben – *bentō* lunch box bought at a train station

ema – small votive plaques hung in shrine precincts as petitions for assistance from the resident deities

engawa – traditional veranda of a Japanese house overlooking the garden

enka – often described as the Japanese equivalent of country and western music, these are folk ballads about love and human suffering that are popular among the older generation

enryō – individual restraint and reserve

ero-guro – erotic and grotesque *manga*

fu – urban prefecture

fū – gluten

fude – brush used for calligraphy
fugu – poisonous blowfish or pufferfish
fundoshi – loincloth or breechcloth; a traditional male garment consisting of a wide belt and a cloth drawn over the genitals and between the buttocks. Usually seen only at festivals or on *sumō* wrestlers.
furigana – Japanese script used to aid pronunciation of *kanji*
furii-kippu – one-day open ticket
fusuma – sliding screen
futon – traditional quilt-like mattress that is rolled up and stowed away during the day
futsū – a local train; literally 'ordinary'

gagaku – music of the imperial court
gaijin – foreigners; literally 'outside people'
gaijin house – cheap accommodation for long-term foreign residents
gajutsu – native ginger
gaman – to endure
gasoreen sutando – petrol stations
gasshō-zukuri – an architectural style; literally 'hands in prayer'
gei-no-kai – the 'world of art and talent'; usually refers to TV
geisha – woman versed in arts and dramas who entertains guests; not a prostitute
gekijō – theatre
genkan – foyer area where shoes are removed or replaced when entering or leaving a building
geta – traditional wooden sandals
giri – social obligations
giri-ninjō – combination of social obligations and personal values; the two are often in conflict
go – board game; players alternately place white and black counters down, with the object to surround the opponent and make further moves impossible; probably originated in China, where it's known as *weiqi*
goya – bitter melon

habu – a venomous snake found in Okinawa
hachimaki – headband worn as a symbol of resolve; *kamikaze* pilots wore them in WWII, students wear them to exams
haiku – 17-syllable poems
hanami – blossom viewing (usually cherry blossoms)
haniwa – earthenware figures found in Kōfun-period tombs
hanko – stamp or seal used to authenticate any document; in Japan your *hanko* carries much more weight than your signature
hantō – peninsula
hara – marshlands
hara-kiri – belly cutting; common name for *seppuku* or ritual suicide
hara-kyū – acupuncture
hari – dragon-boat races

hashi – chopsticks
heiwa – peace
henrō – pilgrims on the Shikoku 88 Temple Circuit
higasa – sunshade umbrella
higawari ranchi – daily lunch special
Hikari – express *shinkansen*
hiragana – phonetic syllabary used to write Japanese words
hondō – main route
honsen – main rail line

ichi-go – square wooden sake 'cups' holding 180mL
ichi-nichi-jōsha-ken – day passes for unlimited travel on bus, tram or subway systems
IDC – International Digital Communications
ijime – bullying or teasing; a problem in Japanese schools
ike-ike onna – young Japanese woman who favours dyed brown hair, a boutique suntan and bright lipstick; literally 'go-go girl'
ikebana – art of flower arrangement
imobō – a dish consisting of a local type of sweet potato and dried fish
irezumi – a tattoo or the art of tattooing
irori – hearth or fireplace
itadakimasu – an expression used before meals; literally 'I will receive'
ITJ – International Telecom Japan
ittaikan – feeling of unity, of being one type
izakaya – Japanese version of a pub; beer and sake and lots of snacks available in a rustic, boisterous setting

JAC – Japan Air Commuter
JAF – Japan Automobile Federation
JAL – Japan Airlines
JAS – Japan Air System
jiage-ya – specialists used by developers to persuade recalcitrant landowners to sell up
jigoku – boiling mineral hot springs, which are definitely not for bathing in; literally 'hells'
jika-tabi – split-toe boots traditionally worn by Japanese carpenters and builders
jikokuhyō – timetable or book of timetables
jinja – shrine
jitensha – bicycle
jizō – small stone statues of the Buddhist protector of travellers and children
JNTO – Japan National Tourist Organization
JR – Japan Railways
JTB – Japan Travel Bureau
jujitsu – martial art from which judō was derived
juku – after-school 'cram' schools
JYHA – Japan Youth Hostel Association

kabuki – a form of Japanese theatre based on popular legends, which is characterised by elaborate costumes, stylised acting and the use of male actors for all roles

kaikan – hotel-style accommodation sponsored by government; literally 'meeting hall'

kaiseki – Japanese cuisine which obeys very strict rules of etiquette for every detail of the meal, including the setting

kaisha – a company, firm

kaisoku – rapid train

kaisū-ken – a book of tickets

kaiten-zushi – sushi served at a conveyor-belt restaurant (also the name of such a restaurant)

kakizome – New Year's resolutions

kami – Shintō gods; spirits of natural phenomena

kani-ryori – mainly steamed crab

kamidana – Shintō altar in Japanese homes

kamikaze – typhoon that sunk Kublai Khan's 13th-century invasion fleet and the name adopted by suicide pilots in the waning days of WWII; literally 'divine wind'

kampai – 'Cheers!'

kampō – Chinese herbal medicines that were dominant in Japan until the 19th century, when Western pharmaceuticals were introduced

kana – the two phonetic syllabaries, *hiragana* and *katakana*

kanji – Chinese ideographic script used for writing Japanese; literally 'Chinese script'

Kannon – Buddhist goddess of mercy (Sanskrit: Avalokiteshvara)

kannushi – chief priest of a Shintō shrine

karakasa – oiled paper umbrella

karakuri – mechanical puppets

karaoke – bars where you sing along with taped music; literally 'empty orchestra'

kasa – umbrella

kashiwa-mochi – pounded glutinous rice with a sweet filling, wrapped in an aromatic oak leaf

katakana – phonetic syllabary used to write foreign words

katamichi – one-way ticket

katana – Japanese sword

katsuo-bushi – thin flakes of *katsuo* (bonito) fish often used as a flavouring for broth or as a condiment

KDD – Kokusai Denshin Denwa (International Telephone & Telegraph)

keigo – honorific language used to show respect to elders or those of high rank

keiretsu – business cartels

ken – prefecture

kendō – oldest martial art; literally 'the way of the sword'

ki – life force, will

kimono – brightly coloured, robe-like traditional outer garment

kin'en-sha – nonsmoking carriage

kissaten – coffee shop

kōban – police box

kōgen – general area, plain

koi – carp; considered to be a brave, tenacious and vigorous fish. Many towns have carp ponds or channels teeming with colourful ornamental *nishiki-goi* (ornamental carp).

koinobori – carp banners and windsocks; the colourful fish pennants that are flown in honour of sons whom it is hoped will inherit a carp's virtues. These wave over countless homes in Japan in late April and early May for Boys' Day, the final holiday of Golden Week. These days, Boys' Day has become Children's Day and the windsocks don't necessarily simply fly in honour of the household's sons.

kokki – Japanese national flag

kokuritsu kōen – national park

kūkō – airport

kokumin-shukusha – peoples' lodges; an inexpensive form of accommodation

kokutetsu – Japanese word for Japan Railways (JR)

Komeitō – Clean Government Party; third-largest political party

kotatsu – heated table with a quilt or cover over it to keep the legs and lower body warm

koto – 13-stringed instrument that is played flat on the floor

ku – ward

kuidaore – eat until you drop (Kansai)

kura – mud-walled storehouses

kyakuma – drawing room of a home, where guests are met

kyōiku mama – a woman who pushes her kids through the Japanese education system; literally 'education mother'

kyūkō – ordinary express train (faster than a *futsū*, only stopping at certain stations)

live house – nightclub or bar where live music is performed

machi – city area (for large cities) between a *ku* and *chōme* in size; also street or area

machiya – traditional Japanese townhouse

maiko – apprentice *geisha*

mama-san – woman who manages a bar or club

maneki-neko – beckoning cat figure frequently seen in restaurants and bars; it's supposed to attract customers and trade

manga – Japanese comics

matcha – powdered green tea

matsuri – festival

meinichi – the 'deathday' or anniversary of someone's death

meishi – business card

mentsu – face

miai-kekkon – arranged marriage

mibun – social rank

miko – shrine maidens

mikoshi – portable shrines carried during festivals

minshuku – the Japanese equivalent of a B&B; family-run budget accommodation

miso-shiru – bean-paste soup

MITI – Ministry of International Trade & Industry

mitsubachi – accommodation for motorcycle tourers

mizu-shōbai – entertainment, bars, prostitution etc

mochi – pounded rice made into cakes and eaten at festive occasions

mōfu – blanket

morning service – *mōningu sābisu*; a light breakfast served until 10am in many *kissaten*

mura – village

nagashi-somen – flowing noodles

nengajō – New Year cards

N'EX – Narita Express

NHK – Nihon Hōsō Kyōkai (Japan Broadcasting Corporation)

Nihon – Japanese word for Japan; literally 'source of the sun'

nihonga – term for Japanese-style painting

ningyō – Japanese doll

ninja – practitioners of *ninjutsu*

ninjutsu – 'the art of stealth'

Nippon – see *Nihon*

nō – classical Japanese drama performed on a bare stage

noren – cloth hung as a sunshade, typically carrying the name of the shop or premises; indicates that a restaurant is open for business

norikae – to change buses or trains; make a connection

norikae-ken – transfer ticket (trams and buses)

NTT – Nippon Telegraph & Telephone Corporation

o- – prefix used to show respect to anything it is applied to; see *san*

obanzai-ryōri – home-style cooking

o-bāsan – grandmotherly type; an old woman

obi – sash or belt worn with a *kimono*

o-cha – tea

ofuku – return ticket

o-furo – traditional Japanese bath

o-jōsan – young college-age woman of conservative taste and aspirations

okashi-ya – sweet shops

okiya – *geisha* quarters

okonomiyaki – cabbage pancakes

OL – 'office lady'; female employee of a large firm; usually a clerical worker – pronounced 'ō-eru'

o-miai – arranged marriage

o-miyage – souvenir

on – favour

onnagata – male actor playing a woman's role (usually in *kabuki*)

onsen – mineral hot-spring spa area, usually with accommodation

origami – art of paper folding

o-shibori – hot towels provided in restaurants

o-tsumami – bar snacks or *charms*

oyaki – wheat buns filled with pickles, squash, radish and red-bean paste

pachinko – vertical pinball game which is a Japanese craze (estimated to take in over ¥6 trillion a year) and a major source of tax evasion, *yakuza* funds etc

puripeido kādo – 'prepaid card'; a sort of reverse credit card: you buy a magnetically coded card for a given amount and it can be used for certain purchases until spent. The prepaid phonecards are the most widespread but there are many others such as Prepaid Highway Cards for use on toll roads.

raidā hausu – basic shared accommodation/houses, catering mainly to those touring on motorcycles

rakugo – Japanese raconteurs, stand-up comics

reien – cemetery

reimen – *soba* noodles served with *kimchi* (spicy Korean pickles)

reisen – cold mineral spring

Rinzai – school of Zen Buddhism which places an emphasis on *kōan* (riddles)

robatayaki – *yakitori-ya* with a deliberately rustic, friendly, homy atmosphere; see also *izakaya*

romaji – Japanese roman script

rō – vegetable wax

rōnin – students who must resit university entrance exams; literally 'masterless *samurai*'

ropeway – Japanese word for a cable car or tramway

rotemburo – open-air or outdoor baths

ryokan – traditional Japanese inn

ryōri – cuisine

sadō – tea ceremony; literally 'way of tea'

saisen-bako – offering box at Shintō shrines

sakazuki – sake cups

sakoku – Japan's period of national seclusion prior to the Meiji Restoration

sakura – cherry blossoms

salaryman – standard male employee of a large firm

sama – even more respectful suffix than *san*; used in instances such as *o-kyaku-sama* – the 'honoured guest'

samurai – warrior class

san – suffix which shows respect to the person it is applied to; see also *o-*, the equivalent honorific. Both can occasionally be used together as *o-kyaku-san*, where *kyaku* is the word for guest or customer.

sansai – mountain vegetables

san-sō – mountain cottage

satori – Zen concept of enlightenment

seku-hara – sexual harassment

sembei – flavoured rice crackers often sold in tourist areas

sempai – one's elder or senior at school or work

sensei – generally translates as 'teacher' but has wider reference

sentō – public baths

seppuku – ritual suicide by disembowelment

setto – set meal

seza – a kneeling position

shamisen – a three-stringed traditional Japanese instrument that resembles a banjo

shi – city (to distinguish cities with prefectures of the same name eg Kyoto-shi)

shiken-jigoku – the enormously important and stressful entrance exams to various levels of the Japanese education system; literally 'examination hell'

shikki – lacquerware

shinkansen – ultra fast 'bullet' trains; literally 'new trunk line', since new train lines were laid for the high speed trains

Shintō – the indigenous religion of Japan

shirabyōshi – traditional dancer

shitamachi – traditionally the low-lying, less affluent parts of Tokyo

shōchū – strong distilled alcohol often made from potatoes; sometimes wheat, or rice is used

shodō – Japanese calligraphy; literally the 'way of writing'

shōgi – a version of chess in which each player has 20 pieces and the object is to capture the opponent's king

shōgun – former military ruler of Japan

shōgunate – military government

shogekijō – small theatre

shōji – sliding rice-paper screens

shōjin ryōri – vegetarian meals (especially at temple lodgings)

Shugendō – offbeat Buddhist school, which incorporates ancient Shamanistic rites, Shintō beliefs and ascetic Buddhist traditions

shūji – a lesser form of *shodō*; literally 'the practice of letters'

shukubō – temple lodgings

shunga – explicit erotic prints; literally 'spring pictures', the season of spring being a popular Chinese and Japanese euphemism for sexuality

shuntō – spring labour offensive; an annual 'strike'

shūyū-ken – excursion train ticket

soapland – Japanese euphemism for bathhouses that offer sexual services

soba – buckwheat noodles

soroban – abacus

Sōtō – a school of Zen Buddhism which places emphasis on *zazen*

sukebe – lewd in thought and deed; can be a compliment in the right context (eg among male drinking partners), but generally shouldn't be used lightly; the English equivalent would be 'sleaze bag'

sukiyaki – thin slices of beef cooked in sake, soy and vinegar broth

sumi-e – black-ink brush paintings

sumō – Japanese wrestling

tabi – split-toed Japanese socks used when wearing *geta*

tadaima – a traditional greeting called out upon returning home; literally 'now' or 'present'

taiko – drum

tako – kite

tanin – outsider, stranger, someone not connected with the current situation

tanka – poems of 31 syllables; see *waka*

tanuki – racoon or dog-like folklore character frequently represented in ceramic figures

tarento – 'talent'; generally refers to musical performers

tatami – tightly woven floor matting on which shoes are never worn. Traditionally, room size is defined by the number of tatami mats.

tatemae – 'face'; how you act in public, your public position

TCAT – Tokyo City Air Terminal

teiki-ken – discount commuter passes

teishoku – set meal

tekitō – suitable or appropriate

tennō – heavenly king, the emperor

TIC – Tourist Information Center

to – metropolis, eg Tokyo-to

tosu – toilet

tokkuri – sake flask

tokkyū – limited express; faster than an ordinary express (*kyūkō*) train

tokonoma – alcove in a house in which flowers may be displayed or a scroll hung

torii – entrance gate to a Shintō shrine

tsukiai – after-work socialising among salarymen

tsunami – huge tidal waves caused by an earthquake

tsuru – cranes; a symbol of longevity often reproduced in *origami* and represented in traditional gardens

uchi –has meanings relating to 'belonging' and 'being part of'; literally 'one's own house'

uchiwa – paper fan

udon – thick white noodles

ukai – fishing using trained cormorants

ukiyo-e – wood-block prints; literally 'pictures of the floating world'

umeboshi – pickled plums thought to aid digestion; often served with rice in *bentō* sets

wa – harmony, team spirit; also the old *kanji* used to denote Japan, and still used in Chinese and Japanese as a prefix to indicate things of Japanese origin; see *wafuku*

wabi – enjoyment of peace and tranquillity

wafuku – Japanese-style clothing

waka – 31-syllable poem; see *tanka*

wanko – lacquerware bowls

waribashi – disposable wooden chopsticks

warikan – custom of sharing the bill (among good friends)

wasabi – Japanese horseradish

washi – Japanese handmade paper

yabusame – horseback archery

yakimono – pottery or ceramic ware

yakitori – charcoal-broiled chicken and other meats or vegetables, cooked on skewers

yakitori-ya – restaurant specialising in *yakitori*

yakuza – Japanese mafia

yamabushi – mountain priests (Shugendō Buddhism practitioners)

yama-goya – mountain huts

yamato – a term of much debated origins that refers to the Japanese world

yamato damashii – Japanese spirit, a term with parallels to the German Volksgeist; it was harnessed by the militarist government of the 1930s and 1940s and was identified with unquestioning loyalty to the emperor

yamato-e – traditional Japanese painting

yanqui – tastelessly dressed male, with dyed hair and a cellular phone

yatai – festival floats/hawker stalls

YCAT – Yokohama City Air Terminal

yōfuku – Western-style clothing

yukar – epic poems

yukata – light cotton summer *kimono*, worn for lounging or casual use; standard issue when staying at a *ryokan*

zabuton – small cushions for sitting on (used in *tatami* rooms)

zaibatsu – industrial conglomerates; the term arose prior to WWII but the Japanese economy is still dominated by huge firms like Mitsui, Marubeni and Mitsubishi, which are involved in many different industries

zazen – seated meditation emphasised in the Sōtō school of Zen Buddhism

Zen – introduced to Japan in the 12th century from China, this offshoot of Buddhism emphasises a direct, intuitive approach to enlightenment rather than rational analysis

Behind the Scenes

THIS BOOK

This 9th edition of *Japan* was written by a team of authors led by Chris Rowthorn. Kara Knafelc wrote The Culture chapter. Chris Rowthorn wrote all the other front chapters, all of the back chapters, and the Kansai chapter. Ray Bartlett (Hokkaidō and Kyūshū), Justin Ellis (Western Honshū), Craig McLachlan (Shikoku and Okinawa & the Southwest Islands), Regis St Louis (Around Tokyo and Central Honshū), Simon Sellars (Northern Honshū) and Wendy Yanagihara (Tokyo) contributed tirelessly to this edition. Chris Rowthorn coordinated the 7th and 8th editions.

THANKS from the Authors

Chris Rowthorn I would like to thank the following people: Toshiko Doi for everything; the tireless Keiko Hagiwara for her fantastic input; Anthony and Denise Weersing for their excellent restaurant picks, among many other things; Paul Carty for great restaurant info and much besides; Divyam for providing the perfect retreat; Masako Nakamura and Matsumiya-san for their great restaurant picks; Shaheed Rupani for his brilliant Kyoto nightlife picks; KS and HS for their great input, computer assistance and Kyoto information; Kishimoto Yorihiku for his great Osaka restaurant picks and a fantastic sushi dinner; and all the readers of Lonely Planet books on Japan who sent in letters and emails with information about Japan – your input really helps and I've tried to use as much of it as possible!

Ray Bartlett So many thanks: to friends, family, Mom, Dad – for putting up with me. To Kana, the Ijichis, the Shiojiris – for putting me up. To Rebecca, Chris (and all the LP staff!), for expert hand-holding as I learned the ropes. To Usui-sensei for all those ghastly vocab quizzes and such demure, graceful cracking of the grammar whip. To all the kind people of Hokkaidō and Kyūshū: station attendants, policemen, students, bartenders, *genki* hostel friends…I hope you treat each reader of this book as wonderfully as you've treated me. いい旅を。 Lastly, enormous thanks to my tush-saving, dog-sitting, partner-in-crimeing, fault-tolerating, fact-checker extraordinaire…without whom none of this would have happened. Robert Frost said it better than I ever can: 'Two roads diverged in a yellow wood, and sorry I could not travel both and be one traveler…' You know the rest. I never knew 10 years' meandering of this less-travelled path could pass so quickly. Thank you so much. I dedicate my two sections to the late William H Avery, PhD (1913–2004), rocket scientist and alternative energy pioneer. Kind, creative, brilliant, and generous, you led a charmed life, and in all capacities – as mentor, grandfather, and inspiration – are deeply missed.

Justin Ellis Gorgeous Dejan gets most of the credit for this work. Time, support, patience. Thank you. Maki Numata for prompt responses to impatient inquiries and Masami Ito for her long-distance research skills. Matsumoto Miki for her generous

THE LONELY PLANET STORY

The story begins with a classic travel adventure: Tony and Maureen Wheeler's 1972 journey across Europe and Asia to Australia. There was no useful information about the overland trail then, so Tony and Maureen published the first Lonely Planet guidebook to meet a growing need.

From a kitchen table, Lonely Planet has grown to become the largest independent travel publisher in the world, with offices in Melbourne (Australia), Oakland (USA) and London (UK). Today Lonely Planet guidebooks cover the globe. There is an ever-growing list of books and information in a variety of media. Some things haven't changed. The main aim is still to make it possible for adventurous travellers to get out there – to explore and better understand the world.

At Lonely Planet we believe travellers can make a positive contribution to the countries they visit – if they respect their host communities and spend their money wisely. Every year 5% of company profit is donated to charities around the world.

cunning, Arabella Lee's motivational skills and Kylie Budge's quiet apartment. Chris Rowthorn for his advice and patience, all at Nakazonoso and the British Council Kyoto and every tourist information office in Western Honshū. And finally the readers. Thank you.

Craig McLachlan Most importantly, I must thank my living kanji dictionary and exceptionally beautiful wife, Yuriko, for all her help on this book. Cheers also to our boys, Riki and Ben, for putting up with a somewhat distracted father for weeks on end; to my parents-in-law for reminding me of meal-times; and to the guys at Wilderness Adventures in Queenstown for keeping things going while I was away. Chris is a great coordinating author and the LP team in Melbourne was excellent. A hearty thanks to those readers who sent in letters re the last *Japan* guide, and to all those who helped while I was out on the road. And yes, I did beat Typhoon 23 back to Osaka!

Regis St Louis Many thanks to the JNTO offices in New York and Tokyo. *Arigatō gozaimasu* to friends in Takayama, Kioka, Dawn, Hirose and Masa, as well as the lovely people in Nagoya, Robin, Makoto, Ishitatsu and Mars. Thanks also to the travellers on the road who helped along the way, particularly the Australian Fuji climbers, the Japanese girls at Monkey Park, Kim in Matsumoto and the expats in Kanazawa. *Arigatō* to Ohwaki-san for the sashimi feast in Hachijō-jima and the help with the bicycle, and thanks to Hiro in New York for the language help. Many TIC offices were particularly kind and helpful: Kanazawa, Takayama, Fuji-Yoshida, Nagano, Nagoya and others. Thanks also to my family and to Cassandra, for making it all worthwhile.

Simon Sellars I'd like to especially thank Kumi Kawamura and Beatka Provis for their invaluable translation expertise and general advice. To Anna Hyde, Ben Woud, Melanie Chilianis, Anita Dahinden, Hiromi Ohashi, Hidei and Miki-chan in Japan – you made my stay an absolute pleasure. Shout-outs, no less, to Daniel New, Shell Farley and Rachel Thorpe, you kept me sane back home. At Lonely Planet, many thanks to Rebecca Chau, Kate Cody, Mick Day, Hunor Csutoros, Csanad Csutoros, Sam Benson, Gina Tsarouhas, Jack Gavran, Chizuru Inoue and Chris Rowthorn for smoothing out the creases. Extra-special thanks to Yukari Yamaguchi and the Japan Travel Bureau in Melbourne for last-minute translation assistance.

Wendy Yanagihara A thousand thank yous to my mother, Michiko Yanagihara, for not only starting me down the road to everywhere, but for inspiring me with her admirable strength and sense of humour. Thanks also to my family in Japan, who converged on Ginza for a last-minute reunion dinner during a downtown deluge. I am also grateful to Anazawa Kenichi, Kisaburo Minato and Aaron Held for their insights and for the illuminating conversations, and to the countless Tokyoites who unwittingly acted as expert informants on my undercover assignment. To Sarah, Lana, Anja and Enrique, thank you for perspective and playtime in Tokyo.

CREDITS
Commissioning Editor: Rebecca Chau
Coordinating Editor: Gina Tsarouhas
Coordinating Cartographer: Jakov Gavran
Coordinating Layout Designer: Adam Bextream
Managing Cartographer: Corie Waddell
Assisting Editors & Proofers: Holly Alexander, David Andrew, Sarah Bailey, Yvonne Byron, Adrienne Costanzo, Charlotte Harrison, Sarah Hassall, Trent Holden, Katie Lynch, Kim Noble and Suzannah Shwer
Assisting Cartographers: Hunor Csutoros, Jovan Djukanovic, James Ellis, Owen Eszeki, Tadhgh Knaggs, Jacqueline Nguyen and Amanda Sierp
Assisting Layout Designers: Kaitlin Beckett, Indra Kilfoyle and Jacqui Saunders
Cover Designer: Yukiyoshi Kamimura
Colour Designer: Laura Jane
Project Manager: Chris Love

Thanks to Yvonne Bischofberger, Darren O'Connell, Sally Darmody, Martin Heng, Rachel Imeson, Rebecca Lalor, Adriana Mammarella and Eri Tomida.

ACKNOWLEDGMENTS
Globe on back cover © Mountain High Maps 1993 Digital Wisdom, Inc.
Osaka Subway System Map © Osaka Municipal Transportation Bureau 2004
Tokyo Metro Map © Tokyo Metro 2002

THANKS from Lonely Planet
Many thanks to the hundreds of travellers who used the last edition and wrote to us with helpful hints, useful advice and interesting anecdotes:
A Kyle Acierno, Zara Acosta, Melissa Addy, Karsten Albers, Riccardo Albertini, Katja Alcock, Ahmed Ali, Craig Allatt, James Allen, Mark Anastein, Trygve Anderson, Trevor Armstrong, Warren Askew, John Atchison, Andrew Atkins **B** Alex Baar, Sophia Ballanger, Kevin Bao, Michael G Bare, Miren Bari, Angelika Barthel, Peter Barthel, Chris Batchelor, Claire Bates, Linley & Dennis Batterham, Darren Bauer, Patty Beauchamp, Walter Bertschinger, Simone Bianchi,

Mike Bigler, Maria Birch, G D Bowen, Jac Boyle, Patrick Boyle, Andy Bracher, Keir Brady, David Brander, John Bravo, Gabrielle Brick, Euan Brown, Thomas Browne, Mary Bryant, Christopher Buchanan, Adrian Buergler, Attila Bujdosó, Alex Burr, Tim Burress, Mary Beth Bursey, Janet Busk, Rod Byatt **C** Richard A Calhoun, Pierre-Luigi Camedda, Sarah Cameron, Martin Caminada, Eddy Campos, Lauren Campy, Amy Cannan, Tyrone N Castelanelli, A A Castilla, Tyi Cedars, Sam Chappell, Lisa Chew, Norbert Christlieb, John Clark, Susan Clark, Angela Cleary, David Clinch, Sean Conry, Brian Cook, Connie Cook, J Cordes, Erin Corry, Jason Cotter, Angela Coutts, Nancy Cox, Dan Coy, Michael Crompton, Michael Czechowicz **D** Thomas Danielsen, Yvonne Davich, Lynsey Davies, Alard de Boer, Smadar De Lange, Sam De Vriendt, Susan Depeters, Jo Devine, Alexandra Dimos, Francesco Diodato, Robert Donnelly, Daniel Dourneau, Karsten Dressbach, Katherine Dube, Dave Duckett, Derek Dunbar, Rachael Dunlop, Fleur-Eve Durin **E** Christine Easdown, Rachelle Eerhart, Karl Emerson, Marianne Erikson, Jeffrey C Esser, Megan Esson **F** Walter Falk, Scott Feldstein, Fred Fels, Daniel Ferguson, Nils Ferry, Adrian Fischer, Moshe Fishelevich, Tim Fletcher, Signe Foersom, Diodato Francesco, Sven Friedel, Steven Fripp, Kevin Friskel, Eriko Fujimura, Cecilia Fujishima, Taku Fujiyama **G** Roey Gafter, Helene Gagnon, Ruth Gamble, Sue Gardiner, Aleksandr Gekht, Stephen Gibbons, Christina & Scott Gifford, Hana Gilbert, Denis Giraud, Stephen Glade, Gary Glassman, Darran Gold, Tony Gordon, Chelsea Green, Alison Greene, Roger Grevis-James, Michael Griffiths, John Grummitt, Aurelie Guillet **H** Mike Hainke, Peter G Halverson, Catherine Hancorne, John Hanson, Wesley J Hayter, Joeren Haytorian, Felicity Heffernan, N Heins, Lyn Henderson, Peter Hill, Ha Hoang, Kelli Holm, Robert Horan, Benjamin Houssa, Rachel Howden, Nicola Howells, Heather Howes, David Hunter, Alice Hutchings, Nichola Hutchinson, Youngdeok Hwang **I** Tsuyodino Inohara, Danielle Irving **J** Jeff Jared, Lachlan Jarvis, Jakob Jensen, Eva Jespersen, Susanne Jordan, Marc Jurriens **K** Tye Kadota, Marcus Karia, Jenny Karlsson, Kikuo Kataoka, Fernando Kawai, Fergus Keane, Megan Kelly, Louise Kiely, Ash Kinghorn, Eva Kisgyorgy, Tibor Kiss, Anne-Marie Kleijberg, Martin Koch, Yoko Komukai, Robin Kortright, Franz Krause, Nicole Kresgi, Tobias Kroke, Amylouise Kruger, Danai Kuangparichat, Meghan Kushnir, Craig Kuykendall, Judy Kwan **L** Igor Lackovic, Sally Laird, Robert Lange, Alasha Lantinga, Melissa Lau, Adam Lawrenson, Maria Leah, C Lee, Mary Lettnaba, Bethe Lewis, Diana Litz, David Livingstone Gangarapu, Geraldine Lopez, John & Jill Lorriman, Chris Louie, Alan Lovett **M** Estelle Ma, Saiko Maeda, Diana Maestre, Rob Mallett, William Marshall, Philip Marston, Claude Martin, Stephanie Marton, Annerose Matsushita, Alex McCallum, Shane McCarthy, Janet McDermott, Victoria E McGraw, Prue McKay, Paul McLennan, Berthold Melcher, Jordan Menzies, Martin Merris, Sam Meyer, Scott Meyer, Brian Micek, Lisa Miebach, Shannon Miller, Michael Moloney, John Mosley, Liz Mossington, Shannon Munro **N** Samantha Nelson, Chris Newlands, T Phong Nguyen, Elke Niblock, Tod Niblock, Andrea Nicholas, Bittner Norbert, Maria Nordmark, Gavin Norman, Michael Nyongha, Ryan Nystuen, Lizette **O** Oberholster, Masha Obolensky, John O'Doherty, Sara Olvebo, Koyo Onda, Cheryl Owen **P** Natacha Pacoud, Marc Pageau, David Palmer, Joanne Pantelidis, Michael Parkes, Keith Parkinson, Cheryl & Kai Parsons-Galka, Brendan Paull, Andreas Pawelec, Natee Pechsuttitanasan, Efrat Peleg, Darlene Pepi, Helmut Pfeifle, Emile Phaneuf, Helia Phoenix, David Pile, Mike Plumb, Kerstin Pohle, Gregor Prahl **Q** Peter Quarry **R** Alexander

Radon, Lawrence Redfern, Chris Reeves, Lane Rettig, Lewis Revill, Jim Richards, Josephine Richardson, Sarah Riches, Michaela Rizler, Dale Rizzuto, Neil Robb, Rosemary Robenn, Catherine Rose, Cerise Roth-Vinson, Daniel Ryntjes **S** Martin Sackett, Ben Salzberg, Koji Sambonsugi, Karen Sandness, Louisa Sanfey, Felis Sarcepuedes, Lowell Sayers, Wendy Schaffer, Alden Schaub, Daniel Scherk, Ed Schlenk, Brittney Schoonebeek, Jan Schutte, Edwin Schuurman, John Schwenninger, Richard Secare, Greg Seiffert, Mihael Sellars, Anne Sey, Shahid Shaikh, Joshua Sharkey, Carly Sheehan, Michael Sheehan, Faye Shelton, Ayumi Shibata, Francis Shillitoe, L Siffredi, Ellen Simon, Frei Simon, Justin Sinodinos, Alexander Skrabal, Adam Smith, Keith Smith, Charles Son, Leeyong Soo, Amanda Spielman, Aden Steinke, Conny Stvckli, Kristy Surak, Kelly Sutton, Maartje Swart, Beata Switek, Andra Sydorko-Flock **T** Heinz Tagman, Kiminori Takahata, Hiroshi Takemoto, Hajime Tanaka, Hallvard Tangeraas, Ryan Tannenbaum, Veronika Tarasova, Francois Tardif, Caroline Tasker, Jeanette A Taudin Chabot, Ryan Taylor, Dave Tell, Chi-Hong Teo, Amar Thakkar, Alain Thierion, Philipp Tillmann, Joan Torres, Nicholas Tripodi, Ian Turner **U** Bill Underwood, François Uzan **V** Laurens Van Der Plaat, Hans Van Der Veen, Erwin Van Engelen, Elizabeth Vaughan, Liz Vaughan, Alexander T Vella, Lluis Vinagre Solans, Georgie Viney, Niels Viveen, Christoffer Von Sabsay, Jon Vooght **W** Caroline Wagner, Suzy Rakoczi Wagner, Chris Walker, Jennifer Walker, Par Wallin, Mary Walsh, Raymond Wan, Ryan Wardman, David W Warren, Satoshi Watanabe, Jacqui Webber, Susanna Weber, Rose Weingarten, Jonas Wernli, Jayne West, Simon White, Stefani Whitehead, Julien Wilk, Vikki Williams, Iain Willis, TT Winant, Andrew Wolstenholme, Stevey Wong, Kim Woodruff, Dave & Hannah Wright **Y** A Yama, Barry Yau, Jim Yu, Al & Chris Yuen, Kuramasu Yutaka **Z** Edme Zalinski and Beat Zurfluh.

SEND US YOUR FEEDBACK

We love to hear from travellers – your comments keep us on our toes and help make our books better. Our well-travelled team reads every word on what you loved or loathed about this book. Although we cannot reply individually to postal submissions, we always guarantee that your feedback goes straight to the appropriate authors, in time for the next edition. Each person who sends us information is thanked in the next edition – and the most useful submissions are rewarded with a free book.

To send us your updates – and find out about Lonely Planet events, newsletters and travel news – visit our award-winning website: **www.lonelyplanet.com/feedback**.

Note: We may edit, reproduce and incorporate your comments in Lonely Planet products such as guidebooks, websites and digital products, so let us know if you don't want your comments reproduced or your name acknowledged. For a copy of our privacy policy visit www.lonelyplanet.com/privacy.

Index

INDEX

INDEX

000 Map pages
000 Location of colour photographs

INDEX

000 Map pages
000 Location of colour photographs

MAP LEGEND

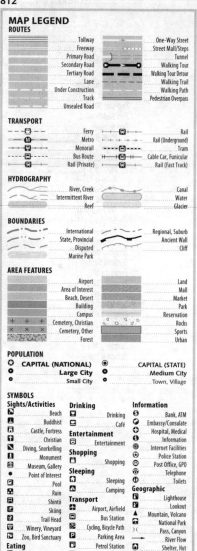

ROUTES

Tollway	One-Way Street
Freeway	Street Mall/Steps
Primary Road	Tunnel
Secondary Road	Walking Tour
Tertiary Road	Walking Tour Detour
Lane	Walking Trail
Under Construction	Walking Path
Track	Pedestrian Overpass
Unsealed Road	

TRANSPORT

Ferry	Rail
Metro	Rail (Underground)
Monorail	Tram
Bus Route	Cable Car, Funicular
Rail (Private)	Rail (Fast Track)

HYDROGRAPHY

River, Creek	Canal
Intermittent River	Water
Reef	Glacier

BOUNDARIES

International	Regional, Suburb
State, Provincial	Ancient Wall
Disputed	Cliff
Marine Park	

AREA FEATURES

Airport	Land
Area of Interest	Mall
Beach, Desert	Market
Building	Park
Campus	Reservation
Cemetery, Christian	Rocks
Cemetery, Other	Sports
Forest	Urban

POPULATION

◎ **CAPITAL (NATIONAL)**	◉ CAPITAL (STATE)
● **Large City**	● **Medium City**
● Small City	○ Town, Village

SYMBOLS

Sights/Activities
- Beach
- Buddhist
- Castle, Fortress
- Christian
- Diving, Snorkelling
- Monument
- Museum, Gallery
- Point of Interest
- Pool
- Ruin
- Shintō
- Skiing
- Trail Head
- Winery, Vineyard
- Zoo, Bird Sanctuary

Eating
- Eating

Drinking
- Drinking
- Café

Entertainment
- Entertainment

Shopping
- Shopping

Sleeping
- Sleeping
- Camping

Transport
- Airport, Airfield
- Bus Station
- Cycling, Bicycle Path
- Parking Area
- Petrol Station
- Taxi Rank

Information
- Bank, ATM
- Embassy/Consulate
- Hospital, Medical
- Information
- Internet Facilities
- Police Station
- Post Office, GPO
- Telephone
- Toilets

Geographic
- Lighthouse
- Lookout
- Mountain, Volcano
- National Park
- Pass, Canyon
- River Flow
- Shelter, Hut
- Waterfall

LONELY PLANET OFFICES

Australia
Head Office
Locked Bag 1, Footscray, Victoria 3011
☎ 03 8379 8000, fax 03 8379 8111
talk2us@lonelyplanet.com.au

USA
150 Linden St, Oakland, CA 94607
☎ 510 893 8555, toll free 800 275 8555
fax 510 893 8572, info@lonelyplanet.com

UK
72–82 Rosebery Ave,
Clerkenwell, London EC1R 4RW
☎ 020 7841 9000, fax 020 7841 9001
go@lonelyplanet.co.uk

Published by Lonely Planet Publications Pty Ltd
ABN 36 005 607 983

© Lonely Planet 2005

© photographers as indicated 2005

Cover photographs by Lonely Planet Images: Detail of geisha's kimono and shoes, Kyoto, Frank Carter (front); Mt Fuji, capped in snow, and the upper levels of a temple, Chūbu, Adina Tovy Amsel (back). Many of the images in this guide are available for licensing from Lonely Planet Images: www.lonelyplanetimages.com

Printed through The Bookmaker International Ltd
Printed in Hong Kong